William Cullen Bryant

Edgar A. Poe

Walt Whitman

J. R. Lowell

Henry W. Longfellow

Oliver Wendell Holmes

R. Waldo Emerson

Sidney Lanier

John G. Whittier

TABLE OF CONTENTS[1]

[1] The poems of each author are arranged in chronological order. Exact dates will be found at the end of each poem.

BIOGRAPHICAL SKETCHES

LIST OF REFERENCES

INDEXES

THE CHIEF AMERICAN POETS

WILLIAM CULLEN BRYANT

[The poems from Bryant are printed by the kind permission of Messrs. D. Appleton & Co., the authorized publishers of his works.]

THANATOPSIS [1]

To him who in the love of Nature holds
Communion with her visible forms, she
   speaks
A various language; for his gayer hours
She has a voice of gladness, and a smile
And eloquence of beauty, and she glides
Into his darker musings, with a mild
And healing sympathy, that steals away
Their sharpness, ere he is aware. When
   thoughts
Of the last bitter hour come like a blight
Over thy spirit, and sad images   10
Of the stern agony, and shroud, and pall,
And breathless darkness, and the narrow
   house,
Make thee to shudder, and grow sick at
   heart; —
Go forth, under the open sky, and list

[1] This, the first great poem written in America, was published in the *North American Review* for September, 1817, vol. v, pp. 338–340. Bryant's father had found it, together with the 'Fragment,' later known as 'Inscription for the Entrance to a Wood,' among other papers in a desk; and had immediately taken it to Boston and shown it to his friend Willard Phillips, one of the editors of the *North American Review.* When Phillips read the poem to his fellow editors, one of them, Richard H. Dana, exclaimed, 'Ah, Phillips, you have been imposed upon; no one on this side of the Atlantic is capable of writing such verses;' and though soon persuaded that the verses really were by an American, the editors still believed that 'Thanatopsis' must have been written by the young poet's father. Phillips says in a letter to Bryant, December, 1817: 'Your "Fragment" was exceedingly liked here. . . . All the best judges say that it and your father's "Thanatopsis" are the very best poetry that has been published in this country.'

As originally printed in the *North American Review*, the poem began with what is now line 17,

   — Yet a few days,

and ended with lines 65 and 66,

               shall come,
   And make their bed with thee.

It was preceded by four stanzas of four lines each, which did not properly belong to the poem, but had been found with it. The beginning and ending of the poem as it now stands were first given in the volume of poems published by Bryant in 1821.

See Mr. Godwin's account of the origin of the poem, in his *Life of Bryant*, vol. i, pp. 97–101; and of its first publication, pp. 148–155.

To Nature's teachings, while from all
   around —
Earth and her waters, and the depths of
   air —
Comes a still voice — Yet a few days, and
   thee
The all-beholding sun shall see no more
In all his course; nor yet in the cold
   ground,
Where thy pale form was laid, with many
   tears,   20
Nor in the embrace of ocean, shall exist
Thy image. Earth, that nourished thee,
   shall claim
Thy growth, to be resolved to earth again,
And, lost each human trace, surrendering up
Thine individual being, shalt thou go
To mix forever with the elements,
To be a brother to the insensible rock
And to the sluggish clod, which the rude
   swain
Turns with his share, and treads upon. The
   oak
Shall send his roots abroad, and pierce thy
   mould.   30

Yet not to thine eternal resting-place
Shalt thou retire alone, nor couldst thou
   wish
Couch more magnificent. Thou shalt lie
   down
With patriarchs of the infant world — with
   kings,
The powerful of the earth — the wise, the
   good,
Fair forms, and hoary seers of ages past,
All in one mighty sepulchre. The hills
Rock-ribbed and ancient as the sun, — the
   vales
Stretching in pensive quietness between;
The venerable woods — rivers that move   40
In majesty, and the complaining brooks
That make the meadows green; and, poured
   round all,
Old Ocean's gray and melancholy waste, —

Are but the solemn decorations all
Of the great tomb of man. The golden
 sun,
The planets, all the infinite host of heaven,
Are shining on the sad abodes of death,
Through the still lapse of ages. All that
 tread
The globe are but a handful to the tribes
That slumber in its bosom. — Take the
 wings   50
Of morning, pierce the Barcan wilderness,
Or lose thyself in the continuous woods
Where rolls the Oregon, and hears no
 sound,
Save his own dashings — yet the dead are
 there:
And millions in those solitudes, since first
The flight of years began, have laid them
 down
In their last sleep — the dead reign there
 alone.
So shalt thou rest, and what if thou with-
 draw
In silence from the living, and no friend
Take note of thy departure? All that
 breathe   60
Will share thy destiny. The gay will
 laugh
When thou art gone, the solemn brood of
 care
Plod on, and each one as before will chase
His favorite phantom; yet all these shall
 leave
Their mirth and their employments, and
 shall come
And make their bed with thee. As the long
 train
Of ages glide away, the sons of men,
The youth in life's green spring, and he who
 goes
In the full strength of years, matron and
 maid,
The speechless babe, and the gray-headed
 man —   70
Shall one by one be gathered to thy side,
By those, who in their turn shall follow
 them.

 So live, that when thy summons comes
  to join
The innumerable caravan, which moves
To that mysterious realm, where each shall
 take
His chamber in the silent halls of death,
Thou go not, like the quarry-slave at night,

Scourged to his dungeon, but, sustained and
 soothed
By an unfaltering trust, approach thy
 grave,
Like one who wraps the drapery of his
 couch   80
About him, and lies down to pleasant
 dreams.

1811?   1817.[1]

THE YELLOW VIOLET

WHEN beechen buds begin to swell,
 And woods the blue-bird's warble know,
The yellow violet's modest bell
  Peeps from the last year's leaves be-
   low.

Ere russet fields their green resume,
 Sweet flower, I love, in forest bare,
To meet thee, when thy faint perfume
  Alone is in the virgin air.

Of all her train, the hands of Spring
 First plant thee in the watery mould, 10
And I have seen thee blossoming
  Beside the snow-bank's edges cold.

Thy parent sun, who bade thee view
 Pale skies, and chilling moisture sip,
Has bathed thee in his own bright hue,
  And streaked with jet thy glowing lip.

Yet slight thy form, and low thy seat,
 And earthward bent thy gentle eye,
Unapt the passing view to meet,
  When loftier flowers are flaunting nigh. 20

Oft, in the sunless April day,
 Thy early smile has stayed my walk;
But midst the gorgeous blooms of May,
 I passed thee on thy humble stalk.

[1] Figures at the left, in italics, give the date of writing; those at the right, in roman, the date of publication. For Bryant's poems the dates are taken from
Godwin's standard edition of the Poetical Works.
 Mr. Godwin states in his note to 'Thanatopsis' that
the poem was written in the summer of 1811, which
would make Bryant only sixteen years old at the time
not seventeen, as Mr. Godwin himself elsewhere says
Bryant's own account of the matter is given in a lette
of 1855, which Mr. Godwin quotes: ' I cannot give
you any information of the occasion which suggested
to my mind the idea of my poem " Thanatopsis." It was
written when I was seventeen or eighteen years old — I
have not now at hand the memorandums [*sic*] which
would enable me to be precise — and I believe it was
composed in my solitary rambles in the woods.'

So they, who climb to wealth, forget
   The friends in darker fortunes tried.
I copied them — but I regret
   That I should ape the ways of pride.

And when again the genial hour
   Awakes the painted tribes of light, 30
I 'll not o'erlook the modest flower
   That made the woods of April bright.
1814.   *1821.*

INSCRIPTION FOR THE ENTRANCE TO A WOOD

STRANGER, if thou hast learned a truth
   which needs
No school of long experience, that the world
Is full of guilt and misery, and hast seen
Enough of all its sorrows, crimes, and cares,
To tire thee of it, enter this wild wood
And view the haunts of Nature. The calm
   shade
Shall bring a kindred calm, and the sweet
   breeze
That makes the green leaves dance, shall
   waft a balm
To thy sick heart. Thou wilt find nothing
   here
Of all that pained thee in the haunts of
   men,   10
And made thee loathe thy life. The primal
   curse
Fell, it is true, upon the unsinning earth,
But not in vengeance. God hath yoked to
   guilt
Her pale tormentor, misery. Hence, these
   shades
Are still the abodes of gladness; the thick
   roof
Of green and stirring branches is alive
And musical with birds, that sing and sport
In wantonness of spirit; while below
The squirrel, with raised paws and form
   erect,
Chirps merrily. Throngs of insects in the
   shade   20
Try their thin wings and dance in the warm
   beam
That waked them into life. Even the green
   trees
Partake the deep contentment; as they bend
To the soft winds, the sun from the blue
   sky
Looks in and sheds a blessing on the scene.

Scarce less the cleft-born wild-flower seems
   to enjoy
Existence, than the wingèd plunderer
That sucks its sweets. The mossy rocks
   themselves,
And the old and ponderous trunks of prostrate trees
That lead from knoll to knoll a causey
   rude   30
Or bridge the sunken brook, and their dark
   roots,
With all their earth upon them, twisting
   high,
Breathe fixed tranquillity. The rivulet
Sends forth glad sounds, and tripping o'er
   its bed
Of pebbly sands, or leaping down the rocks,
Seems, with continuous laughter, to rejoice
In its own being. Softly tread the marge,
Lest from her midway perch thou scare the
   wren
That dips her bill in water.[1] The cool wind,
That stirs the stream in play, shall come to
   thee,   40
Like one that loves thee nor will let thee
   pass
Ungreeted, and shall give its light embrace.
1815.   *1817.*

TO A WATERFOWL [2]

WHITHER, midst falling dew,
While glow the heavens with the last steps
   of day,
Far, through their rosy depths, dost thou
   pursue
   Thy solitary way?

Vainly the fowler's eye
Might mark thy distant flight to do thee
   wrong,
As, darkly seen against the crimson sky,
   Thy figure floats along.

Seek'st thou the plashy brink
Of weedy lake, or marge of river wide, 10

[1] The poem, as first published in the *North American Review* for September, 1817, under the title 'A Fragment,' ended at this point. The last lines were added in the first edition of the *Poems*, in 1821.

[2] On the origin of this poem, see Godwin's *Life of Bryant*, vol. i, pp. 143, 144. Hartley Coleridge once called it 'the best short poem in the English language;' and Matthew Arnold was inclined to agree with his judgment. See an account of the incident in Bigelow's *Life of Bryant*, note to pp. 42, 43.

Or where the rocking billows rise and sink
  On the chafed ocean-side ?

There is a Power whose care
Teaches thy way along that pathless coast —
The desert and illimitable air —
  Lone wandering, but not lost.

All day thy wings have fanned,
At that far height, the cold, thin atmos-
    phere,
Yet stoop not, weary, to the welcome land,
  Though the dark night is near.   20

And soon that toil shall end;
Soon shalt thou find a summer home, and
    rest,
And scream among thy fellows; reeds shall
    bend,
  Soon, o'er thy sheltered nest.

Thou 'rt gone, the abyss of heaven
Hath swallowed up thy form; yet, on my
    heart
Deeply has sunk the lesson thou hast given,
  And shall not soon depart.

He who, from zone to zone,
Guides through the boundless sky thy cer-
    tain flight,   30
In the long way that I must tread alone,
  Will lead my steps aright.

1815.   *1818.*

GREEN RIVER [1]

WHEN breezes are soft and skies are fair,
I steal an hour from study and care,
And hie me away to the woodland scene,
Where wanders the stream with waters of
    green,
As if the bright fringe of herbs on its
    brink
Had given their stain to the waves they
    drink;
And they, whose meadows it murmurs
    through,
Have named the stream from its own fair
    hue.

Yet pure its waters — its shallows are
    bright   9
With colored pebbles and sparkles of light,

[1] This was Bryant's favorite among his early poems.

And clear the depths where its eddies play
And dimples deepen and whirl away,
And the plane-tree's speckled arms o'er-
    shoot
The swifter current that mines its root,
Through whose shifting leaves, as you walk
    the hill,
The quivering glimmer of sun and rill
With a sudden flash on the eye is thrown,
Like the ray that streams from the dia-
    mond-stone.
Oh, loveliest there the spring days come,
With blossoms, and birds, and wild-bees'
    hum;   20
The flowers of summer are fairest there,
And freshest the breath of the summer
    air;
And sweetest the golden autumn day
In silence and sunshine glides away.

Yet, fair as thou art, thou shunnest to
    glide,
Beautiful stream ! by the village side;
But windest away from haunts of men,
To quiet valley and shaded glen;
And forest, and meadow, and slope of hill,
Around thee, are lonely, lovely, and still; 30
Lonely — save when, by thy rippling tides,
From thicket to thicket the angler glides,
Or the simpler comes, with basket and
    book,
For herbs of power on thy banks to look;
Or haply, some idle dreamer, like me,
To wander, and muse, and gaze on thee,
Still — save the chirp of birds that feed
On the river cherry and seedy reed,
And thy own wild music gushing out
With mellow murmur of fairy shout,   40
From dawn to the blush of another day,
Like traveller singing along his way.

That fairy music I never hear,
Nor gaze on those waters so green and
    clear,
And mark them winding away from sight,
Darkened with shade or flashing with light,
While o'er them the vine to its thicket
    clings,
And the zephyr stoops to freshen his wings,
But I wish that fate had left me free
To wander these quiet haunts with thee, 50
Till the eating cares of earth should de-
    part,
And the peace of the scene pass into my
    heart:

And I envy thy stream, as it glides along
Through its beautiful banks in a trance of
    song.

Though forced to drudge for the dregs
    of men,
And scrawl strange words with the bar-
    barous pen,
And mingle among the jostling crowd,
Where the sons of strife are subtle and
    loud —
I often come to this quiet place,
To breathe the airs that ruffle thy face, 60
And gaze upon thee in silent dream,
For in thy lonely and lovely stream
An image of that calm life appears
That won my heart in my greener years.
1819.   *1820.*

A WINTER PIECE

THE time has been that these wild soli-
    tudes,
Yet beautiful as wild, were trod by me
Oftener than now; and when the ills of life
Had chafed my spirit — when the unsteady
    pulse
Beat with strange flutterings — I would
    wander forth
And seek the woods. The sunshine on my
    path
Was to me as a friend. The swelling hills,
The quiet dells retiring far between,
With gentle invitation to explore
Their windings, were a calm society   10
That talked with me and soothed me. Then
    the chant
Of birds, and chime of brooks, and soft
    caress
Of the fresh sylvan air, made me forget
The thoughts that broke my peace, and I
    began
To gather simples by the fountain's brink,
And lose myself in day-dreams. While I
    stood
In Nature's loneliness, I was with one
With whom I early grew familiar, one
Who never had a frown for me, whose
    voice
Never rebuked me for the hours I stole   20
From cares I loved not, but of which the
    world
Deems highest, to converse with her. When
    shrieked

The bleak November winds, and smote the
    woods,
And the brown fields were herbless, and
    the shades,
That met above the merry rivulet,
Were spoiled, I sought, I loved them still;
    they seemed
Like old companions in adversity.
Still there was beauty in my walks; the
    brook,
Bordered with sparkling frost-work, was
    as gay
As with its fringe of summer flowers.
    Afar,   30
The village with its spires, the path of
    streams
And dim receding valleys, hid before
By interposing trees, lay visible
Through the bare grove, and my familiar
    haunts
Seemed new to me. Nor was I slow to
    come
Among them, when the clouds, from their
    still skirts,
Had shaken down on earth the feathery
    snow,
And all was white. The pure keen air
    abroad,
Albeit it breathed no scent of herb, nor
    heard
Love-call of bird nor merry hum of bee, 40
Was not the air of death. Bright mosses
    crept
Over the spotted trunks, and the close buds,
That lay along the boughs, instinct with
    life,
Patient, and waiting the soft breath of
    Spring,
Feared not the piercing spirit of the North.
The snow-bird twittered on the beechen
    bough,
And 'neath the hemlock, whose thick
    branches bent
Beneath its bright cold burden, and kept
    dry
A circle, on the earth, of withered leaves,
The partridge found a shelter. Through
    the snow   50
The rabbit sprang away. The lighter track
Of fox, and the raccoon's broad path, were
    there,
Crossing each other. From his hollow
    tree
The squirrel was abroad, gathering the
    nuts

Just fallen, that asked the winter cold and
    sway
Of winter blast, to shake them from their
    hold.

But Winter has yet brighter scenes — he
        boasts
Splendors beyond what gorgeous Summer
        knows;
Or Autumn with his many fruits, and woods
All flushed with many hues. Come when
        the rains   60
Have glazed the snow and clothed the trees
    with ice,
While the slant sun of February pours
Into the bowers a flood of light.   Approach !
The incrusted surface shall upbear thy steps,
And the broad arching portals of the grove
Welcome thy entering.   Look ! the massy
        trunks
Are cased in the pure crystal; each light
        spray,
Nodding and tinkling in the breath of
        heaven,
Is studded with its trembling water-drops,
That glimmer with an amethystine light.
But round the parent-stem the long low
        boughs   71
Bend, in a glittering ring, and arbors hide
The glassy floor.   Oh ! you might deem
        the spot
The spacious cavern of some virgin mine,
Deep in the womb of earth — where the
        gems grow,
And diamonds put forth radiant rods and
        bud
With amethyst and topaz — and the place
Lit up, most royally, with the pure beam
That dwells in them. Or haply the vast hall
Of fairy palace, that outlasts the night, 80
And fades not in the glory of the sun; —
Where crystal columns send forth slender
        shafts
And crossing arches; and fantastic aisles
Wind from the sight in brightness, and are
        lost
Among the crowded pillars.   Raise thine
        eye;
Thou seest no cavern roof, no palace vault;
There the blue sky and the white drifting
        cloud
Look in.   Again the wildered fancy dreams
Of spouting fountains, frozen as they rose,
And fixed, with all their branching jets, in
        air,   90

And all their sluices sealed. All, all is light;
Light without shade. But all shall pass
        away
With the next sun.   From numberless vast
        trunks
Loosened, the crashing ice shall make a
        sound
Like the far roar of rivers, and the eve
Shall close o'er the brown woods as it was
        wont.

And it is pleasant, when the noisy streams
Are just set free, and milder suns melt off
The plashy snow, save only the firm drift
In the deep glen or the close shade of
        pines —   100
'T is pleasant to behold the wreaths of
        smoke
Roll up among the maples of the hill,
Where the shrill sound of youthful voices
        wakes
The shriller echo, as the clear pure lymph,
That from the wounded trees, in twinkling
        drops,
Falls, mid the golden brightness of the morn,
Is gathered in with brimming pails, and
        oft,
Wielded by sturdy hands, the stroke of
        axe
Makes the woods ring. Along the quiet
        air,
Come and float calmly off the soft light
        clouds,   110
Such as you see in summer, and the winds
Scarce stir the branches. Lodged in sunny
        cleft,
Where the cold breezes come not, blooms
        alone
The little wind-flower, whose just opened
        eye
Is blue as the spring heaven it gazes at —
Startling the loiterer in the naked groves
With unexpected beauty, for the time
Of blossoms and green leaves is yet afar.
And ere it comes, the encountering winds
        shall oft
Muster their wrath again, and rapid clouds
Shade heaven, and bounding on the frozen
        earth   121
Shall fall their volleyed stores, rounded like
        hail
And white like snow, and the loud North
        again
Shall buffet the vexed forest in his rage.
1820.   1821

HYMN TO DEATH

Oh! could I hope the wise and pure in
    heart
Might hear my song without a frown, nor
    deem
My voice unworthy of the theme it tries, —
I would take up the hymn to Death, and
    say
To the grim power, The world hath slan-
    dered thee
And mocked thee.   On thy dim and shad-
    owy brow
They place an iron crown, and call thee king
Of terrors, and the spoiler of the world,
Deadly assassin, that strik'st down the fair,
The loved, the good — that breathest on the
    lights   10
Of virtue set along the vale of life,
And they go out in darkness.   I am come,
Not with reproaches, not with cries and
    prayers,
Such as have stormed thy stern, insensible
    ear
From the beginning; I am come to speak
Thy praises.   True it is, that I have wept
Thy conquests, and may weep them yet
    again,
And thou from some I love wilt take a life
Dear to me as my own.   Yet while the spell
Is on my spirit, and I talk with thee   20
In sight of all thy trophies, face to face,
Meet is it that my voice should utter forth
Thy nobler triumphs; I will teach the world
To thank thee.   Who are thine accusers ?
    — Who ?
The living ! — they who never felt thy
    power,
And know thee not.   The curses of the
    wretch
Whose crimes are ripe, his sufferings when
    thy hand
Is on him, and the hour he dreads is come,
Are writ among thy praises.   But the good —
Does he whom thy kind hand dismissed to
    peace,   30
Upbraid the gentle violence that took off
His fetters, and unbarred his prison-cell ?

Raise then the hymn to Death.   Deliv-
    erer !
God hath anointed thee to free the op-
    pressed
And crush the oppressor.   When the armed
    chief,

The conqueror of nations, walks the world,
And it is changed beneath his feet, and all
Its kingdoms melt into one mighty realm —
Thou, while his head is loftiest and his heart
Blasphemes, imagining his own right hand 40
Almighty, thou dost set thy sudden grasp
Upon him, and the links of that strong chain
Which bound mankind are crumbled; thou
    dost break
Sceptre and crown, and beat his throne to
    dust.
Then the earth shouts with gladness, and
    her tribes
Gather within their ancient bounds again.
Else had the mighty of the olden time,
Nimrod, Sesostris, or the youth who feigned
His birth from Libyan Ammon, smitten yet
The nations with a rod of iron, and driven
Their chariot o'er our necks.   Thou dost
    avenge,   51
In thy good time, the wrongs of those who
    know
No other friend.   Nor dost thou interpose
Only to lay the sufferer asleep,
Where he who made him wretched troubles
    not
His rest — thou dost strike down his tyrant
    too.
Oh, there is joy when hands that held the
    scourge
Drop lifeless, and the pitiless heart is cold.
Thou too dost purge from earth its horrible
And old idolatries; — from the proud fanes
Each to his grave their priests go out, till
    none   61
Is left to teach their worship; then the fires
Of sacrifice are chilled, and the green moss
O'ercreeps their altars; the fallen images
Cumber the weedy courts, and for loud
    hymns,
Chanted by kneeling multitudes, the wind
Shrieks in the solitary aisles.   When he
Who gives his life to guilt, and laughs at all
The laws that God or man has made, and
    round
Hedges his seat with power, and shines in
    wealth, —   70
Lifts up his atheist front to scoff at Hea-
    ven,
And celebrates his shame in open day,
Thou, in the pride of all his crimes, cutt'st
    off
The horrible example.   Touched by thine,
The extortioner's hard hand foregoes the
    gold

Wrung from the o'er-worn poor. The per-
    jurer,
Whose tongue was lithe, e'en now, and vol-
    uble
Against his neighbor's life, and he who
    laughed
And leaped for joy to see a spotless fame
Blasted before his own foul calumnies,   80
Are smit with deadly silence. He, who
    sold
His conscience to preserve a worthless life,
Even while he hugs himself on his escape,
Trembles, as, doubly terrible, at length,
Thy steps o'ertake him, and there is no time
For parley, nor will bribes unclench thy
    grasp.
Oft, too, dost thou reform thy victim, long
Ere his last hour. And when the reveller,
Mad in the chase of pleasure, stretches on,
And strains each nerve, and clears the path
    of life   90
Like wind, thou point'st him to the dread-
    ful goal,
And shak'st thy hour-glass in his reeling
    eye,
And check'st him in mid course. Thy
    skeleton hand
Shows to the faint of spirit the right path,
And he is warned, and fears to step aside.
Thou sett'st between the ruffian and his
    crime
Thy ghastly countenance, and his slack
    hand
Drops the drawn knife. But, oh, most
    fearfully
Dost thou show forth Heaven's justice,
    when thy shafts
Drink up the ebbing spirit — then the hard
Of heart and violent of hand restores   101
The treasure to the friendless wretch he
    wronged.
Then from the writhing bosom thou dost
    pluck
The guilty secret; lips, for ages sealed,
Are faithless to their dreadful trust at
    length,
And give it up; the felon's latest breath
Absolves the innocent man who bears his
    crime;
The slanderer, horror-smitten, and in tears,
Recalls the deadly obloquy he forged
To work his brother's ruin. Thou dost
    make   110
Thy penitent victim utter to the air
The dark conspiracy that strikes at life,

And aims to whelm the laws; ere yet the
    hour
Is come, and the dread sign of murder
    given.

Thus, from the first of time, hast thou
    been found
On virtue's side; the wicked, but for thee,
Had been too strong for the good; the great
    of earth
Had crushed the weak for ever. Schooled
    in guile
For ages, while each passing year had
    brought   119
Its baneful lesson, they had filled the world
With their abominations; while its tribes,
Trodden to earth, imbruted, and despoiled,
Had knelt to them in worship; sacrifice
Had smoked on many an altar, temple-
    roofs
Had echoed with the blasphemous prayer
    and hymn:
But thou, the great reformer of the world,
Tak'st off the sons of violence and fraud
In their green pupilage, their lore half
    learned —
Ere guilt had quite o'errun the simple
    heart
God gave them at their birth, and blotted
    out   130
His image. Thou dost mark them flushed
    with hope,
As on the threshold of their vast designs
Doubtful and loose they stand, and strik'st
    them down.[1]

.   .   .   .

    Alas ! I little thought that the stern
    power,
Whose fearful praise I sang, would try me
    thus
Before the strain was ended. It must
    cease —
For he is in his grave who taught my youth
The art of verse, and in the bud of life
Offered me to the Muses. Oh, cut off   139
Untimely ! when thy reason in its strength,
Ripened by years of toil and studious search,
And watch of Nature's silent lessons, taught
Thy hand to practise best the lenient art
To which thou gavest thy laborious days,
And, last, thy life. And, therefore, when
    the earth

[1] The poem was at first left unfinished, at this point.
Its concluding lines were added after the death of
Bryant's father, in 1820, at the age of fifty-three.

Received thee, tears were in unyielding
    eyes
And on hard cheeks, and they who deemed
    thy skill
Delayed their death-hour, shuddered and
    turned pale
When thou wert gone. This faltering
    verse, which thou
Shalt not, as wont, o'erlook, is all I have
To offer at thy grave — this — and the
    hope   151
To copy thy example, and to leave
A name of which the wretched shall not
    think
As of an enemy's, whom they forgive
As all forgive the dead. Rest, therefore,
    thou
Whose early guidance trained my infant
    steps —
Rest, in the bosom of God, till the brief
    sleep
Of death is over, and a happier life
Shall dawn to waken thine insensible dust.

Now thou art not — and yet the men
    whose guilt   160
Has wearied Heaven for vengeance — he
    who bears
False witness — he who takes the orphan's
    bread,
And robs the widow — he who spreads
    abroad
Polluted hands in mockery of prayer,
Are left to cumber earth. Shuddering I
    look
On what is written, yet I blot not out
The desultory numbers; let them stand,
The record of an idle revery.

1820.   *1825.*

'O FAIREST OF THE RURAL MAIDS'[1]

O FAIREST of the rural maids!
Thy birth was in the forest shades;
Green boughs, and glimpses of the sky,
Were all that met thine infant eye.

Thy sports, thy wanderings, when a child,
Were ever in the sylvan wild;
And all the beauty of the place
Is in thy heart and on thy face.

[1] ' O Fairest of the Rural Maids ' will strike every poet as the truest *poem* written by Bryant. (POE.)

The twilight of the trees and rocks
Is in the light shade of thy locks;
Thy step is as the wind, that weaves
Its playful way among the leaves.

Thine eyes are springs, in whose serene
And silent waters heaven is seen;
Their lashes are the herbs that look
On their young figures in the brook.

The forest depths, by foot unpressed,
Are not more sinless than thy breast;
The holy peace, that fills the air
Of those calm solitudes, is there.

1820.   *1832.*

MONUMENT MOUNTAIN [2]

THOU who wouldst see the lovely and the
    wild
Mingled in harmony on Nature's face,
Ascend our rocky mountains. Let thy foot
Fail not with weariness, for on their tops
The beauty and the majesty of earth,
Spread wide beneath, shall make thee to
    forget
The steep and toilsome way. There, as
    thou stand'st,
The haunts of men below thee, and around
The mountain-summits, thy expanding
    heart   9
Shall feel a kindred with that loftier world
To which thou art translated, and partake
The enlargement of thy vision. Thou shalt
    look

[2] The mountain called by this name is a remarkable precipice in Great Barrington, overlooking the rich and picturesque valley of the Housatonic, in the western part of Massachusetts. At the southern extremity is, or was a few years since, a conical pile of small stones, erected, according to the tradition of the surrounding country, by the Indians, in memory of a woman of the Stockbridge tribe who killed herself by leaping from the edge of the precipice. Until within a few years past, small parties of that tribe used to arrive from their settlement in the western part of the State of New York, on visits to Stockbridge, the place of their nativity and former residence. A young woman belonging to one of these parties related, to a friend of the author, the story on which the poem of 'Monument Mountain' is founded. An Indian girl had formed an attachment for her cousin, which, according to the customs of the tribe, was unlawful. She was, in consequence, seized with a deep melancholy, and resolved to destroy herself. In company with a female friend, she repaired to the mountain, decked out for the occasion in all her ornaments, and, after passing the day on the summit in singing with her companion the traditional songs of her nation, she threw herself headlong from the rock and was killed. (BRYANT.)

Upon the green and rolling forest-tops,
And down into the secrets of the glens,
And streams that with their bordering
thickets strive
To hide their windings. Thou shalt gaze,
at once,
Here on white villages, and tilth, and herds,
And swarming roads, and there on soli-
tudes
That only hear the torrent, and the wind,
And eagle's shriek. There is a precipice 20
That seems a fragment of some mighty
wall,
Built by the hand that fashioned the old
world,
To separate its nations, and thrown down
When the flood drowned them. To the
north, a path
Conducts you up the narrow battlement.
Steep is the western side, shaggy and
wild
With mossy trees, and pinnacles of flint,
And many a hanging crag. But, to the
east,
Sheer to the vale go down the bare old
cliffs —
Huge pillars, that in middle heaven up-
bear
30
Their weather-beaten capitals, here dark
With moss, the growth of centuries, and
there
Of chalky whiteness where the thunder-
bolt
Has splintered them. It is a fearful thing
To stand upon the beetling verge, and see
Where storm and lightning, from that huge
gray wall,
Have tumbled down vast blocks, and at
the base
Dashed them in fragments, and to lay thine
ear
Over the dizzy depth, and hear the sound
Of winds, that struggle with the woods be-
low,
40
Come up like ocean murmurs. But the
scene
Is lovely round; a beautiful river there
Wanders amid the fresh and fertile meads,
The paradise he made unto himself,
Mining the soil for ages. On each side
The fields swell upward to the hills; be-
yond,
Above the hills, in the blue distance, rise
The mountain-columns with which earth
props heaven.

There is a tale about these reverend
rocks,
A sad tradition of unhappy love, 50
And sorrows borne and ended, long ago,
When over these fair vales the savage
sought
His game in the thick woods. There was
a maid,
The fairest of the Indian maids, bright-
eyed,
With wealth of raven tresses, a light form,
And a gay heart. About her cabin-door
The wide old woods resounded with her
song
And fairy laughter all the summer day.
She loved her cousin; such a love was
deemed,
By the morality of those stern tribes, 60
Incestuous, and she struggled hard and
long
Against her love, and reasoned with her
heart,
As simple Indian maiden might. In vain.
Then her eye lost its lustre, and her step
Its lightness, and the gray-haired men that
passed
Her dwelling, wondered that they heard no
more
The accustomed song and laugh of her,
whose looks
Were like the cheerful smile of Spring,
they said,
Upon the Winter of their age. She went
To weep where no eye saw, and was not
found
70
Where all the merry girls were met to
dance,
And all the hunters of the tribe were out;
Nor when they gathered from the rustling
husk
The shining ear; nor when, by the river's
side,
They pulled the grape and startled the
wild shades
With sounds of mirth. The keen-eyed
Indian dames
Would whisper to each other, as they saw
Her wasting form, and say, *The girl will
die.*

One day into the bosom of a friend,
A playmate of her young and innocent
years
80
She poured her griefs. 'Thou know'st, and
thou alone,'

She said, ' for I have told thee, all my love,
And guilt, and sorrow. I am sick of life.
All night I weep in darkness, and the morn
Glares on me, as upon a thing accursed,
That has no business on the earth. I hate
The pastimes and the pleasant toils that
    once
I loved; the cheerful voices of my friends
Sound in my ear like mockings, and, at
    night,
In dreams, my mother, from the land of
    souls,   90
Calls me and chides me. All that look on
    me
Do seem to know my shame; I cannot bear
Their eyes; I cannot from my heart root
    out
The love that wrings it so, and I must die.'

It was a summer morning, and they
    went
To this old precipice. About the cliffs
Lay garlands, ears of maize, and shaggy
    skins
Of wolf and bear, the offerings of the tribe
Here made to the Great Spirit, for they
    deemed,
Like worshippers of the elder time, that
    God   100
Doth walk on the high places and affect
The earth-o'erlooking mountains. She had
    on
The ornaments with which her father lovèd
To deck the beauty of his bright-eyed girl,
And bade her wear when stranger warriors
    came
To be his guests. Here the friends sat
    them down,
And sang, all day, old songs of love and
    death,
And decked the poor wan victim's hair with
    flowers,
And prayed that safe and swift might be
    her way
To the calm world of sunshine, where no
    grief   110
Makes the heart heavy and the eyelids red.
Beautiful lay the region of her tribe
Below her — waters resting in the embrace
Of the wide forest, and maize-planted
    glades
Opening amid the leafy wilderness.
She gazed upon it long, and at the sight
Of her own village peeping through the
    trees,

And her own dwelling, and the cabin roof
Of him she loved with an unlawful love,
And came to die for, a warm gush of tears
Ran from her eyes. But when the sun
    grew low   121
And the hill shadows long, she threw herself
From the steep rock and perished. There
    was scooped,
Upon the mountain's southern slope, a
    grave;
And there they laid her, in the very garb
With which the maiden decked herself for
    death,
With the same withering wild-flowers in
    her hair,
And o'er the mould that covered her, the
    tribe
Built up a simple monument, a cone
Of small loose stones. Thenceforward all
    who passed,   130
Hunter, and dame, and virgin, laid a stone
In silence on the pile. It stands there yet.
And Indians from the distant West, who
    come
To visit where their fathers' bones are laid,
Yet tell the sorrowful tale, and to this day
The mountain where the hapless maiden
    died
Is called the Mountain of the Monument.
1824.   1824.

AUTUMN WOODS

ERE, in the northern gale,
The summer tresses of the trees are gone,
The woods of Autumn, all around our vale,
    Have put their glory on.

The mountains that infold,
In their wide sweep, the colored landscape
    round,
Seem groups of giant kings, in purple and
    gold,
    That guard the enchanted ground.

I roam the woods that crown
The uplands, where the mingled splendors
    glow,   10
Where the gay company of trees look down
    On the green fields below.

My steps are not alone
In these bright walks; the sweet south
    west, at play,

Flies, rustling, where the painted leaves
are strown
Along the winding way.

And far in heaven, the while,
The sun, that sends that gale to wander
here,
Pours out on the fair earth his quiet
smile —
The sweetest of the year.　　　20

Where now the solemn shade,
Verdure and gloom where many branches
meet;
So grateful, when the noon of summer
made
The valleys sick with heat?

Let in through all the trees
Come the strange rays; the forest depths
are bright;
Their sunny colored foliage, in the breeze,
Twinkles, like beams of light.

The rivulet, late unseen,
Where bickering through the shrubs its
waters run,　　　30
Shines with the image of its golden
screen,
And glimmerings of the sun.

But 'neath yon crimson tree,
Lover to listening maid might breathe his
flame,
Nor mark, within its roseate canopy,
Her blush of maiden shame.

Oh, Autumn! why so soon
Depart the hues that make thy forests
glad,
Thy gentle wind and thy fair sunny noon,
And leave thee wild and sad!　　　40

Ah! 't were a lot too blest
Forever in thy colored shades to stray;
Amid the kisses of the soft southwest
To roam and dream for aye;

And leave the vain low strife
That makes men mad — the tug for wealth
and power —
The passions and the cares that wither
life,
And waste its little hour.

1824.　　　　　　　　　　1824.

A FOREST HYMN [1]

THE groves were God's first temples.
Ere man learned
To hew the shaft, and lay the architrave,
And spread the roof above them — ere he
framed
The lofty vault, to gather and roll back
The sound of anthems; in the darkling
wood,
Amid the cool and silence, he knelt down,
And offered to the Mightiest solemn thanks
And supplication. For his simple heart
Might not resist the sacred influences
Which, from the stilly twilight of the
place,　　　10
And from the gray old trunks that high in
heaven
Mingled their mossy boughs, and from the
sound
Of the invisible breath that swayed at once
All their green tops, stole over him, and
bowed
His spirit with the thought of boundless
power
And inaccessible majesty. Ah, why
Should we, in the world's riper years, neg-
lect
God's ancient sanctuaries, and adore
Only among the crowd, and under roofs
That our frail hands have raised? Let me,
at least,　　　20
Here, in the shadow of this aged wood,
Offer one hymn — thrice happy, if it find
Acceptance in his ear.

　　　　　　　　　　Father, thy hand
Hath reared these venerable columns, Thou
Didst weave this verdant roof. Thou didst
look down
Upon the naked earth, and, forthwith, rose
All these fair ranks of trees. They, in thy
sun,
Budded, and shook their green leaves in
thy breeze,
And shot toward heaven. The century-
living crow,
Whose birth was in their tops, grew old
and died　　　30
Among their branches, till, at last, they
stood,
As now they stand, massy, and tall, and
dark,
Fit shrine for humble worshipper to hold

[1] See Godwin's *Life of Bryant*, vol. i, p. 214.

Communion with his Maker. These dim
vaults,
These winding aisles, of human pomp or
pride
Report not. No fantastic carvings show
The boast of our vain race to change the
form
Of thy fair works. But Thou art here —
Thou fill'st
The solitude. Thou art in the soft winds
That run along the summit of these trees
In music; Thou art in the cooler breath 41
That from the inmost darkness of the place
Comes, scarcely felt; the barky trunks, the
ground,
The fresh moist ground, are all instinct with
Thee.
Here is continual worship; — Nature, here,
In the tranquillity that Thou dost love,
Enjoys thy presence. Noiselessly, around,
From perch to perch, the solitary bird
Passes; and yon clear spring, that, midst its
herbs,
Wells softly forth and wandering steeps the
roots   50
Of half the mighty forest, tells no tale
Of all the good it does. Thou hast not left
Thyself without a witness, in the shades,
Of thy perfections. Grandeur, strength, and
grace
Are here to speak of Thee. This mighty
oak —
By whose immovable stem I stand and seem
Almost annihilated — not a prince,
In all that proud old world beyond the
deep,
E'er wore his crown as loftily as he
Wears the green coronal of leaves with
which   60
Thy hand has graced him. Nestled at his
root
Is beauty, such as blooms not in the glare
Of the broad sun. That delicate forest
flower,
With scented breath and look so like a
smile,
Seems, as it issues from the shapeless mould,
An emanation of the indwelling Life,
A visible token of the upholding Love,
That are the soul of this great universe.

My heart is awed within me when I
think
Of the great miracle that still goes on, 70
In silence, round me — the perpetual work

Of thy creation, finished, yet renewed
Forever. Written on thy works I read
The lesson of thy own eternity.
Lo ! all grow old and die — but see again,
How on the faltering footsteps of decay
Youth presses — ever gay and beautiful
youth
In all its beautiful forms. These lofty
trees
Wave not less proudly that their ancestors
Moulder beneath them. Oh, there is not
lost   80
One of earth's charms: upon her bosom
yet,
After the flight of untold centuries,
The freshness of her far beginning lies
And yet shall lie. Life mocks the idle
hate
Of his arch-enemy Death — yea, seats him·
self
Upon the tyrant's throne — the sepulchre,
And of the triumphs of his ghastly foe
Makes his own nourishment. For he came
forth
From thine own bosom, and shall have no
end.

There have been holy men who hid
themselves   90
Deep in the woody wilderness, and gave
Their lives to thought and prayer, till they
outlived
The generation born with them, nor seemed
Less aged than the hoary trees and rocks
Around them; — and there have been holy
men
Who deemed it were not well to pass life
thus.
But let me often to these solitudes
Retire, and in thy presence reassure
My feeble virtue. Here its enemies,
The passions, at thy plainer footsteps shrink
And tremble and are still. O God ! when
Thou   101
Dost scare the world with tempests, set on
fire
The heavens with falling thunderbolts, or
fill,
With all the waters of the firmament,
The swift dark whirlwind that uproots the
woods
And drowns the villages; when, at thy call,
Uprises the great deep and throws himself
Upon the continent, and overwhelms
Its cities — who forgets not, at the sight

Of these tremendous tokens of thy power,
His pride, and lays his strifes and follies
    by ?   111
Oh, from these sterner aspects of thy face
Spare me and mine, nor let us need the
    wrath
Of the mad unchained elements to teach
Who rules them. Be it ours to meditate,
In these calm shades, thy milder majesty,
And to the beautiful order of thy works
Learn to conform the order of our lives.[1]
1825.   1825.

JUNE [2]

I GAZED upon the glorious sky
    And the green mountains round,
And thought that when I came to lie
    At rest within the ground,
'T were pleasant, that in flowery June,
When brooks send up a cheerful tune,
    And groves a joyous sound,
The sexton's hand, my grave to make,
The rich, green mountain-turf should break.

A cell within the frozen mould,   10
    A coffin borne through sleet,
And icy clods above it rolled,
    While fierce the tempests beat —
Away ! — I will not think of these —
Blue be the sky and soft the breeze,
    Earth green beneath the feet,
And be the damp mould gently pressed
Into my narrow place of rest.

There through the long, long summer
    hours,
    The golden light should lie,   20
And thick young herbs and groups of flow-
    ers
    Stand in their beauty by.

[1] These are lines ' of whose great rhythmical beauty it is scarcely possible to speak too highly.' (POE.)

[2] Among the minor poems of Bryant, none has so much impressed me as the one which he entitles ' June.' The rhythmical flow, here, is even voluptuous — nothing could be more melodious. The poem has always affected me in a remarkable manner. The intense melancholy which seems to well up, perforce, to the surface of all the poet's cheerful sayings about his grave, we find thrilling us to the soul — while there is the truest poetic elevation in the thrill. The impression left is one of a pleasurable sadness. And if, in the remaining compositions which I shall introduce to you, there be more or less of a similar tone always apparent, let me remind you that (how or why we know not) this certain taint of sadness is inseparably connected with all the higher manifestations of true Beauty. (POE.)

The oriole should build and tell
His love-tale close beside my cell;
    The idle butterfly
Should rest him there, and there be heard
The housewife bee and humming-bird.

And what if cheerful shouts at noon
    Come, from the village sent,
Or songs of maids, beneath the moon   30
    With fairy laughter blent ?
And what if, in the evening light,
Betrothèd lovers walk in sight
    Of my low monument ?
I would the lovely scene around
Might know no sadder sight nor sound.

I know that I no more should see
    The season's glorious show,
Nor would its brightness shine for me,
    Nor its wild music flow;   40
But if, around my place of sleep,
The friends I love should come to weep,
    They might not haste to go.
Soft airs, and song, and light, and bloom
Should keep them lingering by my tomb.

These to their softened hearts should bear
    The thought of what has been,
And speak of one who cannot share
    The gladness of the scene;
Whose part, in all the pomp that fills   50
The circuit of the summer hills,
    Is that his grave is green;
And deeply would their hearts rejoice
To hear again his living voice.[3]
1825.   1826.

OCTOBER

AY, thou art welcome, heaven's delicious
    breath !
When woods begin to wear the crimson leaf,
And suns grow meek, and the meek suns
    grow brief,
And the year smiles as it draws near its
    death.
Wind of the sunny south ! oh, still delay
In the gay woods and in the golden air,
Like to a good old age released from care,
Journeying, in long serenity, away.
In such a bright, late quiet, would that I

[3] Bryant died in the month of June (1878), and was buried in the beautiful village cemetery at Roslyn, Long Island.

Might wear out life like thee, 'mid bowers
    and brooks,
And, dearer yet, the sunshine of kind looks,
And music of kind voices ever nigh;
And when my last sand twinkled in the
    glass,
Pass silently from men, as thou dost pass.
1826.   1826.

THE PAST [1]

THOU unrelenting Past!
Strong are the barriers round thy dark
    domain,
    And fetters, sure and fast,
Hold all that enter thy unbreathing reign.

    Far in thy realm withdrawn,
Old empires sit in sullenness and gloom,
    And glorious ages gone
Lie deep within the shadow of thy womb.

    Childhood, with all its mirth,
Youth, Manhood, Age that draws us to the
    ground,   10
    And last, Man's Life on earth,
Glide to thy dim dominions, and are bound.

    Thou hast my better years;
Thou hast my earlier friends, the good, the
    kind,
    Yielded to thee with tears —
The venerable form, the exalted mind.

    My spirit yearns to bring
The lost ones back — yearns with desire
    intense,
    And struggles hard to wring
Thy bolts apart, and pluck thy captives
    thence.   20

    In vain; thy gates deny
All passage save to those who hence de-
    part;
    Nor to the streaming eye
Thou giv'st them back — nor to the broken
    heart.

    In thy abysses hide
Beauty and excellence unknown; to thee

    Earth's wonder and her pride
Are gathered, as the waters to the sea;

    Labors of good to man,
Unpublished charity, unbroken faith,   30
    Love, that midst grief began,
And grew with years, and faltered not in
    death.

    Full many a mighty name
Lurks in thy depths, unuttered, unrevered;
    With thee are silent fame,
Forgotten arts, and wisdom disappeared.

    Thine for a space are they —
Yet shalt thou yield thy treasures up at last:
    Thy gates shall yet give way,
Thy bolts shall fall, inexorable Past!   40

    All that of good and fair
Has gone into thy womb from earliest time,
    Shall then come forth to wear
The glory and the beauty of its prime.

    They have not perished — no!
Kind words, remembered voices once so
    sweet,
    Smiles, radiant long ago,
And features, the great soul's apparent seat.

    All shall come back; each tie
Of pure affection shall be knit again;   50
    Alone shall Evil die,
And Sorrow dwell a prisoner in thy reign.

    And then shall I behold
Him, by whose kind paternal side I sprung,
    And her, who, still and cold,
Fills the next grave — the beautiful and
    young.
1828.   1829.

THE EVENING WIND [2]

SPIRIT that breathest through my lattice,
    thou
That cool'st the twilight of the sultry day,
Gratefully flows thy freshness round my
    brow;
    Thou hast been out upon the deep at
    play,

---

[1] According to Godwin, Bryant considered this his
best poem, setting it above 'Thanatopsis.'
    The last stanza alludes to his father, and to a sister
who died in her twenty-second year. See Godwin's *Life*,
vol. i, p. 192.

[2] This poem, by its imaginative treatment of nature,
and by its artistic completeness, aroused Poe's great
admiration. He speaks of the last lines in the third
stanza as 'breathing all the spirit of Shelley.'

Riding all day the wild blue waves till now,
　　Roughening their crests, and scattering
　　　high their spray,
And swelling the white sail.   I welcome
　　thee
To the scorched land, thou wanderer of the
　　sea!

Nor I alone; a thousand bosoms round
　　Inhale thee in the fulness of delight;   10
And languid forms rise up, and pulses
　　bound
　　Livelier, at coming of the wind of night;
And, languishing to hear thy grateful
　　sound,
　　Lies the vast inland stretched beyond the
　　　sight.
Go forth into the gathering shade; go
　　forth,
God's blessing breathed upon the fainting
　　earth !

Go, rock the little wood-bird in his nest,
　　Curl the still waters, bright with stars,
　　　and rouse
The wide old wood from his majestic rest,
　　Summoning from the innumerable
　　　boughs   20
The strange, deep harmonies that haunt
　　his breast:
　　Pleasant shall be thy way where meekly
　　　bows
The shutting flower, and darkling waters
　　pass,
And where the o'ershadowing branches
　　sweep the grass.

The faint old man shall lean his silver head
　　To feel thee; thou shalt kiss the child
　　　asleep,
And dry the moistened curls that over-
　　spread
　　His temples, while his breathing grows
　　　more deep;
And they who stand about the sick man's
　　bed,
　　Shall joy to listen to thy distant sweep, 30
And softly part his curtains to allow
Thy visit, grateful to his burning brow.

Go — but the circle of eternal change,
　　Which is the life of Nature, shall re-
　　　store,
With sounds and scents from all thy mighty
　　range,

Thee to thy birthplace of the deep once
　　more;
Sweet odors in the sea-air, sweet and
　　strange,
　　Shall tell the home-sick mariner of the
　　shore;
And, listening to thy murmur, he shall
　　deem
He hears the rustling leaf and running
　　stream.   40
1829.   1830.

TO THE FRINGED GENTIAN [1]

THOU blossom bright with autumn dew,
And colored with the heaven's own blue,
That openest when the quiet light
Succeeds the keen and frosty night,

Thou comest not when violets lean
O'er wandering brooks and springs un-
　　seen,
Or columbines, in purple dressed,
Nod o'er the ground-bird's hidden nest.

Thou waitest late and com'st alone,
When woods are bare and birds are
　　flown,
And frosts and shortening days portend
The aged year is near his end.

Then doth thy sweet and quiet eye
Look through its fringes to the sky,
Blue — blue — as if that sky let fall
A flower from its cerulean wall.

I would that thus, when I shall see
The hour of death draw near to me,
Hope, blossoming within my heart,
May look to heaven as I depart.
1829.   1832.

[1] Compare with this poem Wordsworth's 'To the Small Celandine,' and others.
　　Notice that Bryant addresses his verses to a distinctively American flower; as later he chooses an American bird, the bobolink, for the subject of a poem which is to be contrasted with Wordsworth's 'To the Skylark,' 'To the Green Linnet,' etc.   Bryant gives the reason for this choice in a letter to his brother John, February 19, 1832: 'I saw some lines by you to the skylark.   Did you ever see such a bird?   Let me counsel you to draw your images, in describing Nature, from what you observe around you, unless you are professedly composing a description of some foreign country, when, of course, you will learn what you can from books.   The skylark is an English bird, and an American who has never visited Europe has no right to be in raptures about it.'

HYMN OF THE CITY

Not in the solitude
Alone may man commune with Heaven, or
    see,
    Only in savage wood
And sunny vale, the present Deity;
    Or only hear his voice
Where the winds whisper and the waves re-
    joice.

Even here do I behold
Thy steps, Almighty! — here, amidst the
    crowd
    Through the great city rolled,
With everlasting murmur deep and loud —
    Choking the ways that wind   11
'Mongst the proud piles, the work of hu-
    man kind.

Thy golden sunshine comes
From the round heaven, and on their
    dwellings lies
    And lights their inner homes;
For them Thou fill'st with air the unbounded
    skies,
    And givest them the stores
Of ocean, and the harvests of its shores.

Thy Spirit is around,
Quickening the restless mass that sweeps
    along;   20
    And this eternal sound —
Voices and footfalls of the numberless
    throng —
    Like the resounding sea,
Or like the rainy tempest, speaks of Thee.

And when the hour of rest
Comes, like a calm upon the mid-sea
    brine,
    Hushing its billowy breast —
The quiet of that moment too is thine;
    It breathes of Him who keeps
The vast and helpless city while it sleeps.   30

1830?   1830.

SONG OF MARION'S MEN [1]

Our band is few but true and tried,
    Our leader frank and bold;

The British soldier trembles [2]
    When Marion's name is told.
Our fortress is the good greenwood,
    Our tent the cypress-tree;
We know the forest round us,
    As seamen know the sea.
We know its walls of thorny vines,
    Its glades of reedy grass,   10
Its safe and silent islands
    Within the dark morass.

Woe to the English soldiery
    That little dread us near!
On them shall light at midnight
    A strange and sudden fear:
When, waking to their tents on fire,
    They grasp their arms in vain,
And they who stand to face us
    Are beat to earth again;   20
And they who fly in terror deem
    A mighty host behind,
And hear the tramp of thousands
    Upon the hollow wind.

Then sweet the hour that brings release
    From danger and from toil:
We talk the battle over,
    And share the battle's spoil.
The woodland rings with laugh and shout,
    As if a hunt were up,   30
And woodland flowers are gathered
    To crown the soldier's cup.
With merry songs we mock the wind
    That in the pine-top grieves,
And slumber long and sweetly
    On beds of oaken leaves.

Well knows the fair and friendly moon
    The band that Marion leads —
The glitter of their rifles,
    The scampering of their steeds.   40

and successful warfare which he kept up at the head
of a few daring followers, that they sent an officer to
remonstrate with him for not coming into the open
field and fighting 'like a gentleman and a Christian.'
(Bryant.)

On the occasion of a reception given to Bryant in
Charleston, South Carolina, in 1873. one of the speakers said that the 'Song of Marion's Men' had been
sung in many a Southern bivouac, and warmed the
soldier's heart at many a Confederate camp-fire.' See
Godwin's *Life of Bryant*, vol. ii, pp. 330, 331.

[2] In the edition of Bryant's poems published in England in 1832, and edited by Washington Irving, this
line was changed to

    The foeman trembles in his camp.

Considerable discussion over this change arose later in
America, of which a full account can be found in Bigelow's *Life of Bryant*, pp. 129–139.

[1] The exploits of General Francis Marion, the famous
partisan warrior of South Carolina, form an interesting
chapter in the annals of the American Revolution.
The British troops were so harassed by the irregular

'T is life to guide the fiery barb
  Across the moonlight plain;
'T is life to feel the night-wind
  That lifts the tossing mane.
A moment in the British camp —
  A moment — and away
Back to the pathless forest,
  Before the peep of day.

Grave men there are by broad Santee,
  Grave men with hoary hairs;   50
Their hearts are all with Marion,
  For Marion are their prayers.
And lovely ladies greet our band
  With kindliest welcoming,
With smiles like those of summer,
  And tears like those of spring.
For them we wear these trusty arms,
  And lay them down no more
Till we have driven the Briton,
  Forever, from our shore.   60
1831.   1831.

THE PRAIRIES [1]

THESE are the gardens of the Desert,
  these
The unshorn fields, boundless and beautiful,
For which the speech of England has no
  name —
The Prairies. I behold them for the first,
And my heart swells, while the dilated
  sight
Takes in the encircling vastness. Lo ! they
  stretch,
In airy undulations, far away,
As if the ocean, in his gentlest swell,
Stood still, with all his rounded billows
  fixed,

[1] See the account of Bryant's first visit to the West,
in Godwin's *Life*, vol. i, pp. 282–286. Especially significant is a passage from Bryant's letter to Richard H.
Dana : ' I have seen the great West, where I ate corn
and hominy, slept in log houses, with twenty men,
women, and children in the same room. . . . At Jackson-
ville, where my two brothers live, I got on a horse, and
travelled about a hundred miles to the northward over
the immense prairies, with scattered settlements, on
the edges of the groves. These prairies, of a soft, fertile garden soil, and a smooth undulating surface, on
which you may put a horse to full speed, covered with
high, thinly growing grass, full of weeds and gaudy
flowers, and destitute of bushes or trees, perpetually
brought to my mind the idea of their having been once
cultivated. They looked to me like the fields of a race
which had passed away, whose enclosures and habitations had decayed, but on whose vast and rich plains,
smoothed and levelled by tillage, the forest had not yet
encroached.'

And motionless forever. — Motionless ? —
No — they are all unchained again. The
  clouds   11
Sweep over with their shadows, and, be-
  neath,
The surface rolls and fluctuates to the eye;
Dark hollows seem to glide along and chase
The sunny ridges. Breezes of the South!
Who toss the golden and the flame-like
  flowers,
And pass the prairie-hawk that, poised on
  high,
Flaps his broad wings, yet moves not[c] —
  ye have played
Among the palms of Mexico and vines
Of Texas, and have crisped the limpid
  brooks   20
That from the fountains of Sonora glide
Into the calm Pacific — have ye fanned
A nobler or a lovelier scene than this ?
Man hath no power in all this glorious
  work:
The hand that built the firmament hath
  heaved
And smoothed these verdant swells, and
  sown their slopes
With herbage, planted them with island
  groves,
And hedged them round with forests. Fit-
  ting floor
For this magnificent temple of the sky —
With flowers whose glory and whose mul-
  titude   30
Rival the constellations ! The great hea-
  vens
Seem to stoop down upon the scene in
  love, —
A nearer vault, and of a tenderer blue,
Than that which bends above our eastern
  hills.

As o'er the verdant waste I guide my
  steed,
Among the high rank grass that sweeps his
  sides
The hollow beating of his footstep seems
A sacrilegious sound. I think of those
Upon whose rest he tramples. Are they
  here —
The dead of other days ? — and did the
  dust   40
Of these fair solitudes once stir with life

[2] I have seen the prairie-hawk balancing himself in
the air for hours together, apparently over the same
spot ; probably watching his prey. (BRYANT.)

And burn with passion? Let the mighty mounds
That overlook the rivers, or that rise
In the dim forest crowded with old oaks,
Answer. A race, that long has passed away,
Built them; — a disciplined and populous race
Heaped, with long toil, the earth, while yet the Greek
Was hewing the Pentelicus to forms
Of symmetry, and rearing on its rock
The glittering Parthenon. These ample fields 50
Nourished their harvests, here their herds were fed,
When haply by their stalls the bison lowed,
And bowed his manèd shoulder to the yoke.
All day this desert murmured with their toils,
Till twilight blushed, and lovers walked, and wooed
In a forgotten language, and old tunes,
From instruments of unremembered form,
Gave the soft winds a voice. The red man came —
The roaming hunter tribes, warlike and fierce,
And the mound-builders vanished from the earth. 60
The solitude of centuries untold
Has settled where they dwelt. The prairie-wolf
Hunts in their meadows, and his fresh-dug den
Yawns by my path. The gopher mines the ground
Where stood their swarming cities. All is gone ;
All — save the piles of earth that hold their bones,
The platforms where they worshipped unknown gods,
The barriers which they builded from the soil
To keep the foe at bay — till o'er the walls
The wild beleaguerers broke, and, one by one, 70
The strongholds of the plain were forced, and heaped
With corpses. The brown vultures of the wood
Flocked to those vast uncovered sepulchres,
And sat unscared and silent at their feast.
Haply some solitary fugitive,

Lurking in marsh and forest, till the sense
Of desolation and of fear became
Bitterer than death, yielded himself to die.
Man's better nature triumphed then. Kind words
Welcomed and soothed him; the rude conquerors 80
Seated the captive with their chiefs; he chose
A bride among their maidens, and at length
Seemed to forget — yet ne'er forgot — the wife
Of his first love, and her sweet little ones,
Butchered, amid their shrieks, with all his race.

Thus change the forms of being. Thus arise
Races of living things, glorious in strength,
And perish, as the quickening breath of God
Fills them, or is withdrawn. The red man, too,
Has left the blooming wilds he ranged so long, 90
And, nearer to the Rocky Mountains, sought
A wilder hunting-ground. The beaver builds
No longer by these streams, but far away,
On waters whose blue surface ne'er gave back
The white man's face — among Missouri's springs,
And pools whose issues swell the Oregon —
He rears his little Venice. In these plains
The bison feeds no more. Twice twenty leagues
Beyond remotest smoke of hunter's camp,
Roams the majestic brute, in herds that shake 100
The earth with thundering steps — yet here I meet
His ancient footprints stamped beside the pool.

Still this great solitude is quick with life.
Myriads of insects, gaudy as the flowers
They flutter over, gentle quadrupeds,
And birds, that scarce have learned the fear of man,
Are here, and sliding reptiles of the ground,
Startlingly beautiful. The graceful deer
Bounds to the wood at my approach. The bee,
A more adventurous colonist than man. 110

With whom he came across the eastern
    deep,
Fills the savannas with his murmurings,
And hides his sweets, as in the golden age,
Within the hollow oak. I listen long
To his domestic hum, and think I hear
The sound of that advancing multitude
Which soon shall fill these deserts. From
    the ground
Comes up the laugh of children, the soft
    voice
Of maidens, and the sweet and solemn
    hymn
Of Sabbath worshippers. The low of herds
Blends with the rustling of the heavy
    grain   121
Over the dark brown furrows. All at once
A fresher wind sweeps by, and breaks my
    dream,
And I am in the wilderness alone.
1832.   1833.

THE BATTLE-FIELD

ONCE this soft turf, this rivulet's sands,
    Were trampled by a hurrying crowd,
And fiery hearts and armèd hands
    Encountered in the battle-cloud.

Ah ! never shall the land forget
    How gushed the life-blood of her brave —
Gushed, warm with hope and courage yet,
    Upon the soil they fought to save.

Now all is calm, and fresh, and still;
    Alone the chirp of flitting bird,   10
And talk of children on the hill,
    And bell of wandering kine, are heard.

No solemn host goes trailing by
    The black-mouthed gun and staggering
        wain;
Men start not at the battle-cry,
    Oh, be it never heard again !

Soon rested those who fought; but thou
    Who minglest in the harder strife
For truths which men receive not now,
    Thy warfare only ends with life.   20

A friendless warfare ! lingering long
    Through weary day and weary year,
A wild and many-weaponed throng
    Hang on thy front, and flank, and rear.

Yet nerve thy spirit to the proof,
    And blench not at thy chosen lot.
The timid good may stand aloof,
    The sage may frown — yet faint thou
        not.

Nor heed the shaft too surely cast,
    The foul and hissing bolt of scorn;   20
For with thy side shall dwell, at last,
    The victory of endurance born.

Truth, crushed to earth, shall rise again,
    Th' eternal years of God are hers;
But Error, wounded, writhes in pain,
    And dies among his worshippers.

Yea, though thou lie upon the dust,
    When they who helped thee flee in fear,
Die full of hope and manly trust,
    Like those who fell in battle here.   40

Another hand thy sword shall wield,
    Another hand the standard wave,
Till from the trumpet's mouth is pealed
    The blast of triumph o'er thy grave.
1837.   1837

THE ANTIQUITY OF FREEDOM

HERE are old trees, tall oaks, and gnarlèd
    pines,
That stream with gray-green mosses; here
    the ground
Was never trenched by spade, and flowers
    spring up
Unsown, and die ungathered. It is sweet
To linger here, among the flitting birds
And leaping squirrels, wandering brooks,
    and winds
That shake the leaves, and scatter, as they
    pass,
A fragrance from the cedars, thickly set
With pale-blue berries. In these peaceful
    shades —
Peaceful, unpruned, immeasurably old — 10
My thoughts go up the long dim path of
    years,
Back to the earliest days of liberty.

O FREEDOM ! thou art not, as poets
    dream,
A fair young girl, with light and delicate
    limbs,
And wavy tresses gushing from the cap

With which the Roman master crowned
  his slave
When he took off the gyves. A bearded
  man,
Armed to the teeth, art thou; one mailèd
  hand
Grasps the broad shield, and one the sword;
  thy brow,
Glorious in beauty though it be, is scarred
With tokens of old wars; thy massive
  limbs   21
Are strong with struggling. Power at thee
  has launched
His bolts, and with his lightnings smitten
  thee;
They could not quench the life thou hast
  from heaven;
Merciless Power has dug thy dungeon
  deep,
And his swart armorers, by a thousand
  fires,
Have forged thy chain; yet, while he deems
  thee bound,
The links are shivered, and the prison-walls
Fall outward; terribly thou springest forth,
As springs the flame above a burning pile,
And shoutest to the nations, who return   31
Thy shoutings, while the pale oppressor
  flies.

    Thy birthright was not given by human
      hands:
Thou wert twin-born with man. In plea-
  sant fields,
While yet our race was few, thou sat'st
  with him,
To tend the quiet flock and watch the stars,
And teach the reed to utter simple airs.
Thou by his side, amid the tangled wood,
Didst war upon the panther and the wolf,
His only foes; and thou with him didst
  draw   40
The earliest furrow on the mountain-side,
Soft with the deluge. Tyranny himself,
Thy enemy, although of reverend look,
Hoary with many years, and far obeyed,
Is later born than thou; and as he meets
The grave defiance of thine elder eye,
The usurper trembles in his fastnesses.

    Thou shalt wax stronger with the lapse
      of years,
But he shall fade into a feebler age —
Feebler, yet subtler. He shall weave his
  snares,   50

And spring them on thy careless steps, and
  clap
His withered hands, and from their ambush
  call
His hordes to fall upon thee. He shall
  send
Quaint maskers, wearing fair and gallant
  forms
To catch thy gaze, and uttering graceful
  words
To charm thy ear; while his sly imps, by
  stealth,
Twine round thee threads of steel, light
  thread on thread,
That grow to fetters; or bind down thy
  arms
With chains concealed in chaplets. Oh!
  not yet
Mayst thou unbrace thy corslet, nor lay
  by   . 60
Thy sword; nor yet, O Freedom! close thy
  lids
In slumber; for thine enemy never sleeps,
And thou must watch and combat till the
  day
Of the new earth and heaven. But wouldst
  thou rest
Awhile from tumult and the frauds of
  men,
These old and friendly solitudes invite
Thy visit. They, while yet the forest-trees
Were young upon the unviolated earth,
And yet the moss-stains on the rock were
  new,
Beheld thy glorious childhood, and re-
  joiced.   70
1842.   1842.

          'O MOTHER OF A MIGHTY
                    RACE'

O MOTHER of a mighty race,
Yet lovely in thy youthful grace!
The elder dames, thy haughty peers,
Admire and hate thy blooming years.
      With words of shame
And taunts of scorn they join thy name.

For on thy cheeks the glow is spread
That tints thy morning hills with red;
Thy step — the wild-deer's rustling feet
Within thy woods are not more fleet;   10
      Thy hopeful eye
Is bright as thine own sunny sky.

Ay, let them rail — those haughty ones,
While safe thou dwellest with thy sons.
They do not know how loved thou art,
How many a fond and fearless heart
          Would rise to throw
Its life between thee and the foe.

They know not, in their hate and pride,
What virtues with thy children bide;   20
How true, how good, thy graceful maids
Make bright, like flowers, the valley-shades;
          What generous men
Spring, like thine oaks, by hill and glen; —

What cordial welcomes greet the guest
By thy lone rivers of the West;
How faith is kept, and truth revered,
And man is loved, and God is feared,
          In woodland homes,
And where the ocean border foams.   30

There's freedom at thy gates and rest
For Earth's down-trodden and opprest,
A shelter for the hunted head,
For the starved laborer toil and bread.
          Power, at thy bounds,
Stops and calls back his baffled hounds.

O fair young mother! on thy brow
Shall sit a nobler grace than now.
Deep in the brightness of the skies
The thronging years in glory rise,   40
          And, as they fleet,
Drop strength and riches at thy feet.

Thine eye, with every coming hour,
Shall brighten, and thy form shall tower;
And when thy sisters, elder born,
Would brand thy name with words of
          scorn,
          Before thine eye,
Upon their lips the taunt shall die.
1846.   1847.

THE PLANTING OF THE APPLE-TREE

Come, let us plant the apple-tree.
Cleave the tough greensward with the
          spade;
Wide let its hollow bed be made;
There gently lay the roots, and there
Sift the dark mould with kindly care,
          And press it o'er them tenderly,

As, round the sleeping infant's feet,
We softly fold the cradle-sheet;
          So plant we the apple-tree.

What plant we in this apple-tree?   10
Buds, which the breath of summer days
Shall lengthen into leafy sprays;
Boughs where the thrush, with crimson
          breast,
Shall haunt and sing and hide her nest;
We plant, upon the sunny lea,
A shadow for the noontide hour,
A shelter from the summer shower,
          When we plant the apple-tree.

What plant we in this apple-tree?
Sweets for a hundred flowery springs   20
To load the May-wind's restless wings,
When, from the orchard-row, he pours
Its fragrance through our open doors;
          A world of blossoms for the bee,
Flowers for the sick girl's silent room,
For the glad infant sprigs of bloom,
          We plant with the apple-tree.

What plant we in this apple-tree?
Fruits that shall swell in sunny June,
And redden in the August noon,   30
And drop, when gentle airs come by,
That fan the blue September sky,
          While children come, with cries of
          glee,
And seek them where the fragrant grass
Betrays their bed to those who pass,
          At the foot of the apple-tree.

And when, above this apple-tree,
The winter stars are quivering bright,
And winds go howling through the night,
Girls, whose young eyes o'erflow with mirth,
Shall peel its fruit by cottage-hearth,   41
          And guests in prouder homes shall see,
Heaped with the grape of Cintra's vine
And golden orange of the line,
          The fruit of the apple-tree.

The fruitage of this apple-tree
Winds and our flag of stripe and star
Shall bear to coasts that lie afar,
Where men shall wonder at the view,
And ask in what fair groves they grew;   50
          And sojourners beyond the sea
Shall think of childhood's careless day,
And long, long hours of summer play,
          In the shade of the apple-tree.

Each year shall give this apple-tree
A broader flush of roseate bloom,
A deeper maze of verdurous gloom,
And loosen, when the frost-clouds lower,
The crisp brown leaves in thicker shower.
  The years shall come and pass, but we
Shall hear no longer, where we lie,   61
The summer's songs, the autumn's sigh,
  In the boughs of the apple-tree.

And time shall waste this apple-tree.
Oh, when its aged branches throw
Thin shadows on the ground below,
Shall fraud and force and iron will
Oppress the weak and helpless still ?
What shall the tasks of mercy be,
Amid the toils, the strifes, the tears   70
Of those who live when length of years
Is wasting this little apple-tree ?

' Who planted this old apple-tree ? '
The children of that distant day
Thus to some aged man shall say;
And, gazing on its mossy stem,   .
The gray-haired man shall answer them:
' A poet of the land was he,
Born in the rude but good old times;
'T is said he made some quaint old rhymes,
  On planting the apple-tree.' [1]   81

1849.   *1864.*

ROBERT OF LINCOLN

MERRILY swinging on brier and weed,
  Near to the nest of his little dame,
Over the mountain-side or mead,
  Robert of Lincoln is telling his name·
    Bob-o'-link, bob-o'-link,
    Spink, spank, spink;
Snug and safe is that nest of ours,
Hidden among the summer flowers.
    Chee, chee, chee.

[1] Compare a letter of Bryant's written November 17, 1846 (Godwin's *Life of Bryant*, vol. ii, pp. 27, 28): ' I have been, and am, at my place on Long Island, planting and transplanting trees, in the mist ; sixty or seventy ; some for shade ; most for fruit. Hereafter, men, whose existence is at present merely possible, will gather pears from the trees which I have set in the ground, and wonder what old *covey* — for in those days the slang terms of the present time, by the ordinary process of change in languages, will have become classical — what old *covey* of past ages planted them ? Or they will walk in the shade of the mulberry, apricot, and cherry trees that I have set in a row beside a green lane, and think, if they think at all about the matter — for who can tell what the great-grandchildren of ours will think about — that they sprang up of themselves by the way.'

Robert of Lincoln is gayly drest,   10
  Wearing a bright black wedding-coat;
White are his shoulders and white his crest.
  Hear him call in his merry note:
    Bob-o'-link, bob-o'-link,
    Spink, spank, spink;
Look, what a nice new coat is mine,
Sure there was never a bird so fine.
    Chee, chee, chee.

Robert of Lincoln's Quaker wife,
  Pretty and quiet, with plain **brown**
    wings,   20
Passing at home a patient life,
  Broods in the grass while her **husband**
    sings:
    Bob-o'-link, bob-o'-link,
    Spink, spank, spink;
Brood, kind creature; you need not **fear**
Thieves and robbers while I am here.
    Chee, chee, chee.

Modest and shy as a nun is she;
  One weak chirp is her only note.
Braggart and prince of braggarts is he,   30
  Pouring boasts from his little throat:
    Bob-o'-link, bob-o'-link,
    Spink, spank, spink;
Never was I afraid of man;
Catch me, cowardly knaves, if you can !
    Chee, chee, chee.

Six white eggs on a bed of hay,
  Flecked with purple, a pretty sight !
There as the mother sits all day,
  Robert is singing with all his might: 40
    Bob-o'-link, bob-o'-link,
    Spink, spank, spink;
Nice good wife, that never goes out,
Keeping house while I frolic about.
    Chee, chee, chee.

Soon as the little ones chip the shell,
  Six wide mouths are open for food;
Robert of Lincoln bestirs him well,
  Gathering seeds for the hungry **brood**.
    Bob-o'-link, bob-o'-link,   50
    Spink, spank, spink;
This new life is likely to be
Hard for a gay young fellow like me.
    Chee, chee, chee.

Robert of Lincoln at length is made
  Sober with work, and silent with **care;**
Off is his holiday garment laid,

Half forgotten that merry air:
    Bob-o'-link, bob-o'-link,
    Spink, spank, spink;   60
Nobody knows but my mate and I
Where our nest and our nestlings lie.
    Chee, chee, chee.

Summer wanes; the children are grown;
    Fun and frolic no more he knows;
Robert of Lincoln 's a humdrum crone;
Off he flies, and we sing as he goes:
    Bob-o'-link, bob-o'-link,
    Spink, spank, spink;
When you can pipe that merry old strain, 70
Robert of Lincoln, come back again.
    Chee, chee, chee.
1855.   1855.

OUR COUNTRY'S CALL

LAY down the axe; fling by the spade;
    Leave in its track the toiling plough;
The rifle and the bayonet-blade
    For arms like yours were fitter now;
And let the hands that ply the pen
    Quit the light task, and learn to wield
The horseman's crooked brand, and rein
    The charger on the battle-field.

Our country calls; away ! away !
    To where the blood-stream blots the
      green.   10
Strike to defend the gentlest sway
    That Time in all his course has seen.
See, from a thousand coverts — see,
    Spring the armed foes that haunt her
      track;
They rush to smite her down, and we
    Must beat the banded traitors back.

Ho ! sturdy as the oaks ye cleave,
    And moved as soon to fear and flight,
Men of the glade and forest ! leave
    Your woodcraft for the field of fight. 20
The arms that wield the axe must pour
    An iron tempest on the foe;
His serried ranks shall reel before
    The arm that lays the panther low.

And ye who breast the mountain-storm
    By grassy steep or highland lake,
Come, for the land ye love, to form
    A bulwark that no foe can break.
Stand, like your own gray cliffs that mock

The whirlwind, stand in her defence: 30
The blast as soon shall move the rock
    As rushing squadrons bear ye thence.

And ye whose homes are by her grand
    Swift rivers, rising far away,
Come from the depth of her green land,
    As mighty in your march as they;
As terrible as when the rains
    Have swelled them over bank and bourne,
With sudden floods to drown the plains
    And sweep along the woods uptorn. 40

And ye who throng, beside the deep,
    Her ports and hamlets of the strand,
In number like the waves that leap
    On his long-murmuring marge of sand —
Come like that deep, when, o'er his brim,
    He rises, all his floods to pour,
And flings the proudest barks that swim,
    A helpless wreck, against the shore !

Few, few were they whose swords of old
    Won the fair land in which we dwell; 50
But we are many, we who hold
    The grim resolve to guard it well.
Strike, for that broad and goodly land,
    Blow after blow, till men shall see
That Might and Right move hand in hand,
    And glorious must their triumph be !
September, 1861.   1861

THE LITTLE PEOPLE OF THE SNOW

   Alice. One of your old-world stories,
    Uncle John,
Such as you tell us by the winter fire,
Till we all wonder it is grown so late.
   Uncle John. The story of the witch that
    ground to death
Two children in her mill, or will you have
The tale of Goody Cutpurse ?
   Alice.   Nay, now, nay;
Those stories are too childish, Uncle John,
Too childish even for little Willy here,
And I am older, two good years, than he;
No, let us have a tale of elves that ride, 10
By night, with jingling reins, or gnomes of
    the mine,
Or water-fairies, such as you know how
To spin, till Willy's eyes forget to wink,
And good Aunt Mary, busy as she is,
Lays down her knitting.

Uncle John.   Listen to me, then.
'T was in the olden time, long, long ago,
And long before the great oak at our door
Was yet an acorn, on a mountain's side
Lived, with his wife, a cottager. They dwelt
Beside a glen and near a dashing brook, 20
A pleasant spot in spring, where first the
    wren
Was heard to chatter, and, among the grass,
Flowers opened earliest; but when winter
    came,
That little brook was fringed with other
    flowers, —
White flowers, with crystal leaf and stem,
    that grew
In clear November nights. And, later still,
That mountain-glen was filled with drifted
    snows
From side to side, that one might walk
    across;
While, many a fathom deep, below, the
    brook
Sang to itself, and leaped and trotted on 30
Unfrozen, o'er its pebbles, toward the vale.
    Alice. A mountain-side, you said; the
        Alps, perhaps,
Or our own Alleghanies.
    Uncle John.   Not so fast,
My young geographer, for then the Alps,
With their broad pastures, haply were un-
    trod
Of herdsman's foot, and never human voice
Had sounded in the woods that overhang
Our Alleghanies' streams. I think it was
Upon the slopes of the great Caucasus,
Or where the rivulets of Ararat   40
Seek the Armenian vales. That mountain
    rose
So high, that, on its top, the winter snow
Was never melted, and the cottagers
Among the summer blossoms, far below,
Saw its white peaks in August from their
    door.
One little maiden, in that cottage-home,
Dwelt with her parents, light of heart and
    limb,
Bright, restless, thoughtless, flitting here
    and there,
Like sunshine on the uneasy ocean-waves,
And sometimes she forgot what she was bid,
As Alice does.
    Alice.   Or Willy, quite as oft.   51
    Uncle John. But you are older, Alice, two
        good years,
And should be wiser. Eva was the name

Of this young maiden, now twelve summers
    old.
    Now you must know that, in those early
        times,
When autumn days grew pale, there came
    a troop
Of childlike forms from that cold mountain-
    top;
With trailing garments through the air they
    came,
Or walked the ground with girded loins,
    and threw
Spangles of silvery frost upon the grass, 60
And edged the brooks with glistening para-
    pets,
And built it crystal bridges, touched the
    pool,
And turned its face to glass, or, rising
    thence,
They shook from their full laps the soft,
    light snow,
And buried the great earth, as autumn
    winds
Bury the forest-floor in heaps of leaves.
    A beautiful race were they, with baby
        brows,
And fair, bright locks, and voices like the
    sound
Of steps on the crisp snow, in which they
    talked
With man, as friend with friend. A merry
    sight   70
It was, when, crowding round the traveller,
They smote him with their heaviest snow-
    flakes, flung
Needles of frost in handfuls at his cheeks,
And, of the light wreaths of his smoking
    breath,
Wove a white fringe for his brown beard,
    and laughed
Their slender laugh to see him wink and
    grin
And make grim faces as he floundered on.
    But, when the spring came on, what ter-
        ror reigned
Among these Little People of the Snow !
To them the sun's warm beams were shafts
    of fire,   80
And the soft south-wind was the wind of
    death.
Away they flew, all with a pretty scowl
Upon their childish faces, to the north,
Or scampered upward to the mountain's
    top,
And there defied their enemy, the Spring;

Skipping and dancing on the frozen peaks,
And moulding little snow-balls in their
    palms,
And rolling them, to crush her flowers be-
    low,   88
Down the steep snow-fields.
    Alice.   That, too, must have been
A merry sight to look at.
    Uncle John.   You are right,
But I must speak of graver matters now.
    Midwinter was the time, and Eva stood,
Within the cottage, all prepared to dare
The outer cold, with ample furry robe
Close-belted round her waist, and boots of
    fur,
And a broad kerchief, which her mother's
    hand
Had closely drawn about her ruddy cheek.
'Now, stay not long abroad,' said the
    good dame,
'For sharp is the outer air, and, mark me
    well,
Go not upon the snow beyond the spot   100
Where the great linden bounds the neigh-
    boring field.'
    The little maiden promised, and went
    forth,
And climbed the rounded snow-swells firm
    with frost
Beneath her feet, and slid, with balancing
    arms
Into the hollows. Once, as up a drift
She slowly rose, before her, in the way,
She saw a little creature, lily-cheeked,
With flowing flaxen locks, and faint blue
    eyes,
That gleamed like ice, and robe that only
    seemed
Of a more shadowy whiteness than her
    cheek.   110
On a smooth bank she sat.
    Alice.   She must have been
One of your Little People of the Snow.
    Uncle John. She was so, and, as Eva
    now drew near,
The tiny creature bounded from her seat;
'And come,' she said, 'my pretty friend;
    to-day
We will be playmates. I have watched
    thee long,
And seen how well thou lov'st to walk these
    drifts,
And scoop their fair sides into little cells,
And carve them with quaint figures, huge-
    limbed men,   119

Lions, and griffins. We will have, to-day,
A merry ramble over these bright fields,
And thou shalt see what thou hast never
    seen.'
On went the pair, until they reached the
    bound
Where the great linden stood, set deep in
    snow,
Up to the lower branches. 'Here we
    stop,'
Said Eva, 'for my mother has my word
That I will go no farther than this tree.'
Then the snow-maiden laughed: 'And
    what is this?
This fear of the pure snow, the innocent
    snow,
That never harmed aught living? Thou
    mayst roam   130
For leagues beyond this garden, and return
In safety; here the grim wolf never prowls,
And here the eagle of our mountain-crags
Preys not in winter. I will show the
    way,
And bring thee safely home. Thy mother,
    sure,
Counselled thee thus because thou hadst no
    guide.'
    By such smooth words was Eva won to
    break
Her promise, and went on with her new
    friend,
Over the glistening snow and down a bank
Where a white shelf, wrought by the eddy-
    ing wind,   140
Like to a billow's crest in the great sea,
Curtained an opening. 'Look, we enter
    here.'
And straight, beneath the fair o'erhanging
    fold,
Entered the little pair that hill of snow,
Walking along a passage with white walls,
And a white vault above where snow-stars
    shed
A wintry twilight. Eva moved in awe,
And held her peace, but the snow-maiden
    smiled,
And talked and tripped along, as down the
    way,
Deeper they went into that mountainous
    drift.   150
    And now the white walls widened, and
    the vault
Swelled upward, like some vast cathedral-
    dome,
Such as the Florentine, who bore the name

Of heaven's most potent angel, reared
　　long since,
Or the unknown builder of that wondrous
　　fane,
The glory of Burgos. Here a garden lay,
In which the Little People of the Snow
Were wont to take their pastime when
　　their tasks
Upon the mountain's side and in the clouds
Were ended. Here they taught the silent
　　frost　　　　　　　　　　　　160
To mock, in stem and spray, and leaf and
　　flower,
The growths of summer. Here the palm
　　upreared
Its white columnar trunk and spotless
　　sheaf
Of plume-like leaves; here cedars, huge as
　　those
Of Lebanon, stretched far their level
　　boughs,
Yet pale and shadowless; the sturdy oak
Stood, with its huge gnarled roots of seem-
　　ing strength,
Fast anchored in the glistening bank; light
　　sprays
Of myrtle, roses in their bud and bloom,
Drooped by the winding walks; yet all
　　seemed wrought　　　　　　　170
Of stainless alabaster; up the trees
Ran the lithe jessamine, with stalk and
　　leaf
Colorless as her flowers. 'Go softly on,'
Said the snow-maiden; 'touch not, with
　　thy hand,
The frail creation round thee, and beware
To sweep it with thy skirts. Now look
　　above.
How sumptuously these bowers are lighted
　　up
With shifting gleams that softly come and
　　go !
These are the northern lights, such as thou
　　seest
In the midwinter nights, cold, wandering
　　flames,　　　　　　　　　180
That float with our processions, through
　　the air;
And here, within our winter palaces,
Mimic the glorious daybreak.' Then she
　　told
How, when the wind, in the long winter
　　nights,
Swept the light snows into the hollow dell,
She and her comrades guided to its place

Each wandering flake, and piled them
　　quaintly up,
In shapely colonnade and glistening arch,
With shadowy aisles between, or bade them
　　grow,　　　　　　　　　189
Beneath their little hands, to bowery walks
In gardens such as these, and, o'er them all,
Built the broad roof. 'But thou hast yet
　　to see
A fairer sight,' she said, and led the way
To where a window of pellucid ice
Stood in the wall of snow, beside their
　　path.
'Look, but thou mayst not enter.' Eva
　　looked,
And lo ! a glorious hall, from whose high
　　vault
Stripes of soft light, ruddy and delicate
　　green,
And tender blue, flowed downward to the
　　floor
And far around, as if the aërial hosts,　200
That march on high by night, with beamy
　　spears,
And streaming banners, to that place had
　　brought
Their radiant flags to grace a festival.
　　And in that hall a joyous multitude
Of those by whom its glistening walls were
　　reared,
Whirled in a merry dance to silvery sounds,
That rang from cymbals of transparent ice,
And ice-cups, quivering to the skilful touch
Of little fingers. Round and round they
　　flew,
As when, in spring, about a chimney-top,
A cloud of twittering swallows, just re-
　　turned,　　　　　　　　　211
Wheel round and round, and turn and wheel
　　again,
Unwinding their swift track. So rapidly
Flowed the meandering stream of that fair
　　dance,
Beneath that dome of light. Bright eyes
　　that looked
From under lily-brows, and gauzy scarfs
Sparkling like snow-wreaths in the early
　　sun,
Shot by the window in their mazy whirl.
And there stood Eva, wondering at the
　　sight
Of those bright revellers and that graceful
　　sweep　　　　　　　　　220
Of motion as they passed her; — long she
　　gazed,

And listened long to the sweet sounds that
    thrilled
The frosty air, till now the encroaching
    cold
Recalled her to herself. 'Too long, too
    long
I linger here,' she said, and then she sprang
Into the path, and with a hurried step
Followed it upward. Ever by her side
Her little guide kept pace. As on they
    went,
Eva bemoaned her fault: 'What must they
    think —   229
The dear ones in the cottage, while so long,
Hour after hour, I stay without? I know
That they will seek me far and near, and
    weep
To find me not. How could I, wickedly,
Neglect the charge they gave me?' As
    she spoke,
The hot tears started to her eyes; she knelt
In the mid-path. 'Father! forgive this
    sin;
Forgive myself I cannot' — thus she
    prayed,
And rose and hastened onward. When, at
    last,
They reached the outer air, the clear north
    breathed
A bitter cold, from which she shrank with
    dread,   240
But the snow-maiden bounded as she felt
The cutting blast, and uttered shouts of
    joy,
And skipped, with boundless glee, from
    drift to drift,
And danced round Eva, as she labored up
The mounds of snow. 'Ah me! I feel my
    eyes
Grow heavy,' Eva said; 'they swim with
    sleep;
I cannot walk for utter weariness,
And I must rest a moment on this bank,
But let it not be long.' As thus she spoke,
In half-formed words, she sank on the
    smooth snow,   250
With closing lids. Her guide composed
    the robe
About her limbs, and said: 'A pleasant spot
Is this to slumber in; on such a couch
Oft have I slept away the winter night,
And had the sweetest dreams.' So Eva
    slept,
But slept in death; for when the power of
    frost

Locks up the motions of the living frame,
The victim passes to the realm of Death
Through the dim porch of Sleep. The little
    guide,
Watching beside her, saw the hues of life
Fade from the fair smooth brow and
    rounded cheek,   261
As fades the crimson from a morning
    cloud,
Till they were white as marble, and the
    breath
Had ceased to come and go, yet knew she
    not
At first that this was death. But when she
    marked
How deep the paleness was, how motionless
That once lithe form, a fear came over her.
She strove to wake the sleeper, plucked her
    robe,
And shouted in her ear, but all in vain;
The life had passed away from those young
    limbs.   270
Then the snow-maiden raised a wailing
    cry,
Such as the dweller in some lonely wild,
Sleepless through all the long December
    night,
Hears when the mournful East begins to
    blow.
    But suddenly was heard the sound of
    steps,
Grating on the crisp snow; the cottagers
Were seeking Eva; from afar they saw
The twain, and hurried toward them. As
    they came
With gentle chidings ready on their lips,
And marked that deathlike sleep, and heard
    the tale   280
Of the snow-maiden, mortal anguish fell
Upon their hearts, and bitter words of grief
And blame were uttered: 'Cruel, cruel
    one,
To tempt our daughter thus, and cruel we,
Who suffered her to wander forth alone
In this fierce cold!' They lifted the dear
    child,
And bore her home and chafed her tender
    limbs,
And strove, by all the simple arts they
    knew,
To make the chilled blood move, and win
    the breath
Back to her bosom; fruitlessly they strove,
The little maid was dead. In blank de-
    spair   291

They stood, and gazed at her who never
      more
Should look on them. 'Why die we not
      with her?'
They said; 'Without her, life is bitterness.'
   Now came the funeral-day; the simple
      folk
Of all that pastoral region gathered round
To share the sorrow of the cottagers.
They carved a way into the mound of snow
To the glen's side, and dug a little grave
In the smooth slope, and, following the bier,
In long procession from the silent door, 301
Chanted a sad and solemn melody:
   'Lay her away to rest within the ground.
Yea, lay her down whose pure and innocent
      life
Was spotless as these snows; for she was
      reared
In love, and passed in love life's pleasant
      spring,
And all that now our tenderest love can
      do
Is to give burial to her lifeless limbs.'
   They paused.   A thousand slender voices
      round,   309
Like echoes softly flung from rock and hill,
Took up the strain, and all the hollow air
Seemed mourning for the dead; for, on
      that day,
The Little People of the Snow had come,
From mountain-peak, and cloud, and icy
      hall,
To Eva's burial. As the murmur died,
The funeral-train renewed the solemn chant:
   'Thou, Lord, hast taken her to be with
      Eve,
Whose gentle name was given her. Even
      so,
For so thy wisdom saw that it was best
For her and us. We bring our bleeding
      hearts,   320
And ask the touch of healing from thy
      hand,
As, with submissive tears, we render back
The lovely and beloved to Him who gave.'
   They ceased. Again the plaintive mur-
      mur rose.
From shadowy skirts of low-hung cloud it
      came,
And wide white fields, and fir-trees capped
      with snow,
Shivering to the sad sounds. They sank
      away
To silence in the dim-seen distant woods.

The little grave was closed; the funeral-
      train
Departed; winter wore away; the Spring
Steeped, with her quickening rains, the
      violet-tufts,   331
By fond hands planted where the maiden
      slept.
But, after Eva's burial, never more
The Little People of the Snow were seen
By human eye, nor ever human ear
Heard from their lips articulate speech
      again;
For a decree went forth to cut them off,
Forever, from communion with mankind.
The winter-clouds, along the mountainside,
Rolled downward toward the vale, but no
      fair form   340
Leaned from their folds, and, in the icy
      glens,
And aged woods, under snow-loaded pines,
Where once they made their haunt, was
      emptiness.
   But ever, when the wintry days drew
      near,
Around that little grave, in the long night,
Frost-wreaths were laid and tufts of silvery
      rime
In shape like blades and blossoms of the
      field
As one would scatter flowers upon a bier.
1863.   *1864.*

THE POET

THOU who wouldst wear the name
   Of poet 'mid thy brethren of mankind,
And clothe in words of flame
      Thoughts that shall live within the gen-
         eral mind!
Deem not the framing of a deathless lay
The pastime of a drowsy summer day.

But gather all thy powers,
   And wreak them on the verse that thou
         dost weave,
And in thy lonely hours,
      At silent morning or at wakeful eve, 10
While the warm current tingles through
         thy veins
Set forth the burning words in fluent
         strains.

No smooth array of phrase,
      Artfully sought and ordered though it be,

Which the cold rhymer lays
  Upon his page with languid industry,
Can wake the listless pulse to livelier
    speed,
Or fill with sudden tears the eyes that
    read.

The secret wouldst thou know
  To touch the heart or fire the blood at
    will ?   20
Let thine own eyes o'erflow;
  Let thy lips quiver with the passionate
    thrill;
Seize the great thought, ere yet its power
    be past,
And bind, in words, the fleet emotion fast.

Then, should thy verse appear
  Halting and harsh, and all unaptly
    wrought,
Touch the crude line with fear,
  Save in the moment of impassioned
    thought;
Then summon back the original glow, and
    mend
The strain with rapture that with fire was
    penned.   30

Yet let no empty gust
  Of passion find an utterance in thy lay,
A blast that whirls the dust
  Along the howling street and dies away;
But feelings of calm power and mighty
    sweep,
Like currents journeying through the wind-
    less deep.

Seek'st thou, in living lays,
  To limn the beauty of the earth and
    sky ?
Before thine inner gaze
  Let all that beauty in clear vision lie; 40
Look on it with exceeding love, and write
The words inspired by wonder and de-
    light.

Of tempests wouldst thou sing,
  Or tell of battles — make thyself a part
Of the great tumult; cling
  To the tossed wreck with terror in thy
    heart;
Scale, with the assaulting host, the ram-
    part's height,
And strike and struggle in the thickest
    fight.

So shalt thou frame a lay
  That haply may endure from age to age,
And they who read shall say: 51
  'What witchery hangs upon this poet's
    page !
What art is his the written spells to find
That sway from mood to mood the willing
    mind !'
1863.   **1864.**

MY AUTUMN WALK

On woodlands ruddy with autumn
  The amber sunshine lies;
I look on the beauty round me,
  And tears come into my eyes.

For the wind that sweeps the meadows
  Blows out of the far Southwest,
Where our gallant men are fighting,
  And the gallant dead are at rest.

The golden-rod is leaning,
  And the purple aster waves 10
In a breeze from the land of battles,
  A breath from the land of graves.

Full fast the leaves are dropping
  Before that wandering breath;
As fast, on the field of battle,
  Our brethren fall in death.

Beautiful over my pathway
  The forest spoils are shed;
They are spotting the grassy hillocks
  With purple and gold and red. 20

Beautiful is the death-sleep
  Of those who bravely fight
In their country's holy quarrel,
  And perish for the Right.

But who shall comfort the living,
  The light of whose homes is gone:
The bride that, early widowed,
  Lives broken-hearted on;

The matron whose sons are lying
  In graves on a distant shore; 30
The maiden, whose promised husband
  Comes back from the war no more ?

I look on the peaceful dwellings
  Whose windows glimmer in sight,

With croft and garden and orchard,
  That bask in the mellow light;

And I know that, when our couriers
  With news of victory come,
They will bring a bitter message
  Of hopeless grief to some.   40

Again I turn to the woodlands,
  And shudder as I see
The mock-grape's blood-red banner
  Hung out on the cedar-tree;

And I think of days of slaughter,
  And the night-sky red with flames,
On the Chattahoochee's meadows,
  And the wasted banks of the James.

Oh, for the fresh spring-season,
  When the groves are in their prime; 50
And far away in the future
  Is the frosty autumn-time !

Oh, for that better season,
  When the pride of the foe shall yield,
And the hosts of God and Freedom
  March back from the well-won field;

And the matron shall clasp her first-
    born
  With tears of joy and pride;
And the scarred and war-worn lover
  Shall claim his promised bride !   60

The leaves are swept from the branches;
  But the living buds are there,
With folded flower and foliage,
  To sprout in a kinder air.
October, 1864.   *January, 1865.*

THE DEATH OF LINCOLN [1]

OH, slow to smite and swift to spare,
  Gentle and merciful and just !
Who, in the fear of God, didst bear
  The sword of power, a nation's trust !

In sorrow by thy bier we stand,
  Amid the awe that hushes all,
And speak the anguish of a land
  That shook with horror at thy fall.

[1] Bryant wrote this poem for the day when Lincoln's body was carried in funeral procession through the streets of New York city.

Thy task is done; the bond are free:
  We bear thee to an honored grave,
Whose proudest monument shall be
  The broken fetters of the slave.

Pure was thy life; its bloody close
  Hath placed thee with the sons of light,
Among the noble host of those
  Who perished in the cause of Right.
April, 1865.   *January, 1866*

A LIFETIME

I SIT in the early twilight,
  And, through the gathering shade,
I look on the fields around me
  Where yet a child I played.

And I peer into the shadows,
  Till they seem to pass away,
And the fields and their tiny brooklet
  Lie clear in the light of day.

A delicate child and slender,
  With locks of light-brown hair,   10
From knoll to knoll is leaping
  In the breezy summer air.

He stoops to gather blossoms
  Where the running waters shine;
And I look on him with wonder,
  His eyes are so like mine.

I look till the fields and brooklet
  Swim like a vision by,
And a room in a lowly dwelling
  Lies clear before my eye.   20

There stand, in the clean-swept fireplace,
  Fresh boughs from the wood in bloom
And the birch-tree's fragrant branches
  Perfume the humble room.

And there the child is standing
  By a stately lady's knee,
And reading of ancient peoples
  And realms beyond the sea:

Of the cruel King of Egypt
  Who made God's people slaves,   30
And perished, with all his army,
  Drowned in the Red Sea waves;

Of Deborah who mustered
  Her brethren long oppressed,

And routed the heathen army,
    And gave her people rest;

And the sadder, gentler story
    How Christ, the crucified,
With a prayer for those who slew Him,
    Forgave them as He died.   40

I look again, and there rises
    A forest wide and wild,
And in it the boy is wandering,
    No longer a little child.

He murmurs his own rude verses
    As he roams the woods alone;
And again I gaze with wonder,
    His eyes are so like my own.

I see him next in his chamber,
    Where he sits him down to write   50
The rhymes he framed in his ramble,
    And he cons them with delight.

A kindly figure enters,
    A man of middle age,
And points to a line just written,
    And 't is blotted from the page.

And next, in a hall of justice,
    Scarce grown to manly years,
'Mid the hoary-headed wranglers
    The slender youth appears.   60

With a beating heart he rises,
    And with a burning cheek,
And the judges kindly listen
    To hear the young man speak.

Another change, and I see him
    Approach his dwelling-place,
Where a fair-haired woman meets him,
    With a smile on her young face —

A smile that spreads a sunshine
    On lip and cheek and brow;   70
So sweet a smile there is not
    In all the wide earth now.

She leads by the hand their first-born,
    A fair-haired little one,
And their eyes as they meet him sparkle
    Like brooks in the morning sun.

Another change, and I see him
    Where the city's ceaseless coil

Sends up a mighty murmur
    From a thousand modes of toil.   80

And there, 'mid the clash of presses,
    He plies the rapid pen
In the battles of opinion,
    That divide the sons of men.

I look, and the clashing presses
    And the town are seen no more,
But there is the poet wandering
    A strange and foreign shore.

He has crossed the mighty ocean
    To realms that lie afar,   90
In the region of ancient story,
    Beneath the morning star.

And now he stands in wonder
    On an icy Alpine height;
Now pitches his tent in the desert
    Where the jackal yells at night;

Now, far on the North Sea islands,
    Sees day on the midnight sky,
Now gathers the fair strange fruitage
    Where the isles of the Southland lie.

I see him again at his dwelling,   101
    Where, over the little lake,
The rose-trees droop in their beauty
    To meet the image they make.

Though years have whitened his temples,
    His eyes have the first look still,
Save a shade of settled sadness,
    A forecast of coming ill.

For in that pleasant dwelling,
    On the rack of ceaseless pain,   110
Lies she who smiled so sweetly,
    And prays for ease in vain.

And I know that his heart is breaking,
    When, over those dear eyes,
The darkness slowly gathers,
    And the loved and loving dies.

A grave is scooped on the hillside
    Where often, at eve or morn,
He lays the blooms of the garden —
    He, and his youngest born.   120

And well I know that a brightness
    From his life has passed away,

And a smile from the green earth's beauty,
  And a glory from the day.

But I behold, above him,
  In the far blue deeps of air,
Dim battlements shining faintly,
  And a throng of faces there;

See over crystal barrier
  The airy figures bend,   130
Like those who are watching and waiting
  The coming of a friend.

And one there is among them,
  With a star upon her brow,
In her life a lovely woman,
  A sinless seraph now.

I know the sweet calm features;
  The peerless smile I know,
And I stretch my arms with transport
  From where I stand below.   140

And the quick tears drown my eyelids,
  But the airy figures fade,
And the shining battlements darken
  And blend with the evening shade.

I am gazing into the twilight
  Where the dim-seen meadows lie,
And the wind of night is swaying
  The trees with a heavy sigh.

1876.   1876.

THE FLOOD OF YEARS

A MIGHTY Hand, from an exhaustless Urn,
Pours forth the never - ending Flood of
    Years,
Among the nations. How the rushing waves
Bear all before them! On their foremost
    edge,
And there alone, is Life. The Present there
Tosses and foams, and fills the air with
    roar
Of mingled noises. There are they who toil,
And they who strive, and they who feast,
    and they
Who hurry to and fro. The sturdy swain —
Woodman and delver with the spade — is
    there,   10
And busy artisan beside his bench,
And pallid student with his written roll.
A moment on the mounting billow seen,

The flood sweeps over them and they are
    gone.
There groups of revellers whose brows are
    twined
With roses, ride the topmost swell awhile,
And as they raise their flowing cups and
    touch
The clinking brim to brim, are whirled be-
    neath
The waves and disappear. I hear the jar
Of beaten drums, and thunders that break
    forth   20
From cannon, where the advancing billow
    sends
Up to the sight long files of armèd men,
That hurry to the charge through flame and
    smoke.
The torrent bears them under, whelmed and
    hid
Slayer and slain, in heaps of bloody foam.
Down go the steed and rider, the plumed
    chief
Sinks with his followers; the head that
    wears
The imperial diadem goes down beside
The felon's with cropped ear and branded
    cheek.
A funeral-train — the torrent sweeps away
Bearers and bier and mourners. By the
    bed   31
Of one who dies men gather sorrowing,
And women weep aloud; the flood rolls
    on;
The wail is stifled and the sobbing group
Borne under. Hark to that shrill, sudden
    shout,
The cry of an applauding multitude,
Swayed by some loud-voiced orator who
    wields
The living mass as if he were its soul!
The waters choke the shout and all is still.
Lo! next a kneeling crowd, and one who
    spreads   40
The hands in prayer — the engulfing wave
    o'ertakes
And swallows them and him. A sculptor
    wields
The chisel, and the stricken marble grows
To beauty; at his easel, eager-eyed,
A painter stands, and sunshine at his touch
Gathers upon his canvas, and life glows;
A poet, as he paces to and fro,
Murmurs his sounding lines. Awhile they
    ride
The advancing billow, till its tossing crest

Strikes them and flings them under, while
their tasks   50
Are yet unfinished. See a mother smile
On her young babe that smiles to her again;
The torrent wrests it from her arms; she
shrieks
And weeps, and midst her tears is carried
down.
A beam like that of moonlight turns the
spray
To glistening pearls; two lovers, hand in
hand,
Rise on the billowy swell and fondly look
Into each other's eyes. The rushing flood
Flings them apart: the youth goes down;
the maid
With hands outstretched in vain, and
streaming eyes,   60
Waits for the next high wave to follow
him.
An aged man succeeds; his bending form
Sinks slowly. Mingling with the sullen
stream
Gleam the white locks, and then are seen
no more.
    Lo ! wider grows the stream — a sea-like
flood
Saps earth's walled cities; massive palaces
Crumble before it; fortresses and towers
Dissolve in the swift waters; populous
realms
Swept by the torrent see their ancient
tribes
Engulfed and lost; their very languages 70
Stifled, and never to be uttered more.
    I pause and turn my eyes, and looking
back
Where that tumultuous flood has been, I
see
The silent ocean of the Past, a waste
Of waters weltering over graves, its shores
Strewn with the wreck of fleets where
mast and hull
Drop away piecemeal; battlemented walls
Frown idly, green with moss, and temples
stand
Unroofed, forsaken by the worshipper.
There lie memorial stones, whence time
has gnawed   80
The graven legends, thrones of kings o'er-
turned,
The broken altars of forgotten gods,
Foundations of old cities and long streets
Where never fall of human foot is heard,
On all the desolate pavement. I behold

Dim glimmerings of lost jewels, far within
The sleeping waters, diamond, sardonyx,
Ruby and topaz, pearl and chrysolite,
Once glittering at the banquet on fair
brows
That long ago were dust, and all around 90
Strewn on the surface of that silent sea
Are withering bridal wreaths, and glossy
locks
Shorn from dear brows, by loving hands,
and scrolls
O'erwritten, haply with fond words of love
And vows of friendship, and fair pages
flung
Fresh from the printer's engine. There
they lie
A moment, and then sink away from sight.
    I look, and the quick tears are in my
eyes,
For I behold in every one of these
A blighted hope, a separate history   100
Of human sorrows, telling of dear ties
Suddenly broken, dreams of happiness
Dissolved in air, and happy days too brief
That sorrowfully ended, and I think
How painfully must the poor heart have
beat
In bosoms without number, as the blow
Was struck that slew their hope and broke
their peace.
    Sadly I turn and look before, where yet
The Flood must pass, and I behold a mist
Where swarm dissolving forms, the brood
of Hope,   110
Divinely fair, that rest on banks of flowers,
Or wander among rainbows, fading soon
And reappearing, haply giving place
To forms of grisly aspect such as Fear
Shapes from the idle air — where serpents
lift
The head to strike, and skeletons stretch
forth
The bony arm in menace. Further on
A belt of darkness seems to bar the way,
Long, low, and distant, where the Life to
come
Touches the Life that is. The Flood of
Years   120
Rolls toward it near and nearer. It must
pass
That dismal barrier. What is there be-
yond ?
Hear what the wise and good have said.
Beyond
That belt of darkness, still the Years roll on

More gently, but with not less mighty
    sweep.
They gather up again and softly bear
All the sweet lives that late were over-
    whelmed
And lost to sight, all that in them was good,
Noble, and truly great, and worthy of
    love —   129
The lives of infants and ingenuous youths,
Sages and saintly women who have made
Their households happy; all are raised and
    borne
By that great current in its onward sweep,
Wandering and rippling with caressing
    waves
Around green islands with the breath
Of flowers that never wither. So they pass
From stage to stage along the shining
    course
Of that bright river, broadening like a sea
As its smooth eddies curl along their way.

They bring old friends together; hands are
    clasped   140
In joy unspeakable; the mother's arms
Again are folded round the child she loved
And lost. Old sorrows are forgotten now,
Or but remembered to make sweet the
    hour
That overpays them; wounded hearts that
    bled
Or broke are healed forever. In the room
Of this grief-shadowed present, there shall
    be
A Present in whose reign no grief shall
    gnaw
The heart, and never shall a tender tie
Be broken; in whose reign the eternal
    Change   150
That waits on growth and action shall pro-
    ceed
With everlasting Concord hand in hand.
1876.   1876.

EDGAR ALLAN POE

TAMERLANE [1]

KIND solace in a dying hour ! [2]
  Such, father, is not (now) my theme — [3]
I will not madly deem that power

[1] 'Tamerlane,' which first appeared in 1827 in *Tamerlane and Other Poems*, was entirely re-written for Poe's volume of 1829, *Al Aaraaf, Tamerlane, and Minor Poems*. The text of the poem as here given is practically that of 1829. It follows the edition of 1845 (as given in the Virginia and Stedman-Woodberry editions of Poe's works), but the differences of this edition from that of 1829 are confined (with one exception) to matters of punctuation and typography. The edition of 1831 offers somewhat greater variations, all of which are carefully recorded in the notes of both the Virginia and the Stedman-Woodberry editions. The version of 1827 is given complete in the notes to both these editions, and may also be found in Mr. R. H. Shepherd's complete reprint of the 1827 volume (London, 1884).

The subject of the poem, not very clear at first reading, is the evil triumph of ambition over love, illustrated in the career of the Mogul emperor Tamerlane, who, according to the story as conceived by Poe, was born a shepherd, left his mountain home and his early love for the conquest of the eastern world, and returned only to find that his love had died of his neglect.

The well-worn device of a death-bed narrative to the conventional friar is lamely excused by Poe in his first note to the 1827 edition : 'How I shall account for giving him "a friar" as a death-bed confessor, — I cannot exactly determine. He wanted some one to listen to his tale — and why not a friar ? It does not pass the bounds of possibility, — quite sufficient for my purpose, — and I have at least good authority on my side for such innovations.'

[2] The beginning of the poem is somewhat clearer in the 1827 version : —

    I have sent for thee, holy friar ;
    But 't was not with the drunken hope,
    Which is but agony of desire
    To shun the fate, with which to cope
    Is more than crime may dare to dream,
    That I have call'd thee at this hour :
    Such, father, is not my theme —
    Nor am I mad, to deem that power
    Of earth may shrive me of the sin
    Unearthly pride hath revell'd in —
    I would not call thee fool, old man,
    But hope is not a gift of thine ;
    If I *can* hope (O God ! I can)
    It falls from an eternal shrine.

    The gay wall of this gaudy tower
    Grows dim around me — death is near.
    I had not thought, until this hour
    When passing from the earth, that ear
    Of any, were it not the shade
    Of one whom in life I made
    All mystery but a simple name,
    Might know the secret of a spirit
    Bow'd down in sorrow, and in shame. —

[3] Poe's own somewhat peculiar punctuation is followed throughout, as given in the Virginia edition of Poe's Works. Faithfulness to this punctuation, about which Poe was particular, makes the Virginia edition, in text, superior to all others.

Of Earth may shrive me of the sin
  Unearthly pride hath revell'd in —
I have no time to dote or dream:
You call it hope — that fire of fire!
It is but agony of desire:
If I *can* hope — O God! I can —
  Its fount is holier — more divine —   10
I would not call thee fool, old man,
  But such is not a gift of thine.

Know thou the secret of a spirit
  Bow'd from its wild pride into shame.
O yearning heart! I did inherit
  Thy withering portion with the fame,
The searing glory which hath shone
Amid the Jewels of my throne,
Halo of Hell ! and with a pain
Not Hell shall make me fear again —   20
O craving heart, for the lost flowers
And sunshine of my summer hours!
The undying voice of that dead time,
With its interminable chime,
Rings, in the spirit of a spell,
Upon thy emptiness — a knell.

I have not always been as now:
The fever'd diadem on my brow
  I claim'd and won usurpingly——
Hath not the same fierce heirdom given   30
  Rome to the Cæsar — this to me ?
    The heritage of a kingly mind,
And a proud spirit which hath striven
    Triumphantly with human kind.

On mountain soil I first drew life:
  The mists of the Taglay have shed [4]
  Nightly their dews upon my head,
And, I believe, the wingèd strife
And tumult of the headlong air
Have nestled in my very hair.   40

So late from Heaven — that dew — it fell
  ('Mid dreams of an unholy night)
Upon me with the touch of Hell,

[4] The mountains of Belur Taglay are a branch of the Imaus, in the southern part of Independent Tartary. They are celebrated for the singular wildness and beauty of their valleys. (POE, 1827.)

While the red flashing of the light
From clouds that hung, like banners, o'er,
  Appeared to my half-closing eye
  The pageantry of monarchy,
And the deep trumpet-thunder's roar
Came hurriedly upon me, telling
  Of human battle, where my voice,   50
My own voice, silly child! — was swel-
    ling
  (O! how my spirit would rejoice,
And leap within me at the cry)
  The battle-cry of Victory!

The rain came down upon my head
  Unshelter'd — and the heavy wind
Rendered me mad and deaf and blind.
It was but man, I thought, who shed
  Laurels upon me: and the rush —
The torrent of the chilly air   60
Gurgled within my ear the crash
Of empires — with the captive's prayer—
The hum of suitors — and the tone
Of flattery 'round a sovereign's throne.

My passions, from that hapless hour,
  Usurp'd a tyranny which men
Have deem'd, since I have reach'd to power,
  My innate nature — be it so :
But, father, there liv'd one who, then,
Then — in my boyhood — when their fire 70
  Burn'd with a still intenser glow
(For passion must, with youth, expire)
  E'en *then* who knew this iron heart
In woman's weakness had a part.

I have no words — alas ! — to tell
  The loveliness of loving well !
Nor would I now attempt to trace
  The more than beauty of a face
Whose lineaments upon my mind,
Are —— shadows on th' unstable wind: 80
Thus I remember having dwelt
  Some page of early lore upon,
With loitering eye, till I have felt
  The letters — with their meaning — melt
  To fantasies — with none.

O, she was worthy of all love !
  Love — as in infancy was mine —
'T was such as angel minds above
  Might envy; her young heart the shrine
On which my every hope and thought   90
  Were incense — then a goodly gift,
  For they were childish and upright —
Pure —— as her young example taught:

Why did I leave it, and, adrift,
  Trust to the fire within, for light ?

We grew in age — and love —— together —
  Roaming the forest, and the wild ;
My breast her shield in wintry weather —
  And, when the friendly sunshine smil'd,
And she would mark the opening skies, 100
I saw no Heaven — but in her eyes.

Young Love's first lesson is — the heart:
  For 'mid that sunshine, and those smiles,
When, from our little cares apart,
  And laughing at her girlish wiles,
I'd throw me on her throbbing breast,
  And pour my spirit out in tears —
There was no need to speak the rest —
  No need to quiet any fears
Of her — who ask'd no reason why,   110
But turn'd on me her quiet eye !

Yet *more* than worthy of the love
My spirit struggled with, and strove,
When, on the mountain peak, alone,
  Ambition lent it a new tone —
I had no being — but in thee :
  The world, and all it did contain
In the earth — the air — the sea —
  Its joy — its little lot of pain
That was new pleasure —— the ideal,   120
  Dim, vanities of dreams by night —
And dimmer nothings which were real —
  (Shadows — and a more shadowy light !)
Parted upon their misty wings,
    And, so, confusedly, became
    Thine image and — a name — a name!
Two separate — yet most intimate things.

I was ambitious — have you known
    The passion, father ? You have not :
A cottager, I mark'd a throne   130
Of half the world as all my own,
    And murmur'd at such lowly lot —
But, just like any other dream,
    Upon the vapor of the dew
My own had past, did not the beam
    Of beauty which did while it thro'
The minute — the hour — the day — op-
    press
My mind with double loveliness.[1]

[1] The last two paragraphs, twenty-seven lines in all,
should be compared with the corresponding paragraphs (numbered vii and viii) in the version of 1827,
which contain seventy-one lines, in order to appreciate
the greater condensation and strength of the 1829 version. The advance which Poe made between these two

We walk'd together on the crown
Of a high mountain which look'd down   140
Afar from its proud natural towers
  Of rock and forest, on the hills —
The dwindled hills ! begirt with bowers
And shouting with a thousand rills.

I spoke to her of power and pride,
  But mystically — in such guise
That she might deem it nought beside
  The moment's converse ; in her eyes
I read, perhaps too carelessly —
  A mingled feeling with my own —   150
The flush on her bright cheek, to me
  Seem'd to become a queenly throne
Too well that I should let it be
  Light in the wilderness alone.

I wrapp'd myself in grandeur then
  And donn'd a visionary crown ——
    Yet it was not that Fantasy
    Had thrown her mantle over me —
But that, among the rabble — men,
    Lion ambition is chain'd down —   160
And crouches to a keeper's hand —
Not so in deserts where the grand —
The wild — the terrible conspire
With their own breath to fan his fire.[1]

Look 'round thee now on Samarcand ![2] —
  Is she not queen of Earth ? her pride
Above all cities ? in her hand
  Their destinies ? in all beside
Of glory which the world hath known
Stands she not nobly and alone ?   170
Falling — her veriest stepping-stone
Shall form the pedestal of a throne —
And who her sovereign ? Timour[3] — he
  Whom the astonished people saw
Striding o'er empires haughtily
  A diadem'd outlaw !

O, human love ! thou spirit given,
On Earth, of all we hope in Heaven !
Which fall'st into the soul like rain
Upon the Siroc-wither'd plain,   180

And, failing in thy power to bless,
But leav'st the heart a wilderness !
Idea ! which bindest life around
With music of so strange a sound
And beauty of so wild a birth —
Farewell ! for I have won the Earth.

When Hope, the eagle that tower'd, could
    see
  No cliff beyond him in the sky,
His pinions were bent droopingly —
And homeward turn'd his soften'd eye.[4]   190
'T was sunset: when the sun will part
There comes a sullenness of heart
To him who still would look upon
The glory of the summer sun.
That soul will hate the ev'ning mist
So often lovely, and will list
To the sound of the coming darkness
    (known
To those whose spirits harken) as one
Who, in a dream of night, *would* fly
But *cannot* from a danger nigh.   200

What tho' the moon — the white moon
Shed all the splendor of her noon,
Her smile is chilly — and *her* beam,
In that time of dreariness, will seem
(So like you gather in your breath)
A portrait taken after death.

And boyhood is a summer sun
Whose waning is the dreariest one —
For all we live to know is known
And all we seek to keep hath flown —   210
Let life, then, as the day-flower, fall
With the noon-day beauty — which is all.

I reach'd my home — my home no more —
  For all had flown who made it so.
I pass'd from out its mossy door,
  And, tho' my tread was soft and low,
A voice came from the threshold stone
Of one whom I had earlier known —
  O, I defy thee, Hell, to show
On beds of fire that burn below,   220
An humbler heart — a deeper woe.

versions, the way in which he 'found himself,' is
strikingly illustrated by the characteristic suggestiveness, beauty, and perhaps vagueness of expression in
these two paragraphs as they now stand.
  [1] These ten lines have taken the place of ninety-
three lines (sections xi-xiv) in the 1827 edition.
  [2] I believe it was after the battle of Angora that
Tamerlane made Samarcand his residence. It became
for a time the seat of learning and the arts. (Poe, 1827.)
  [3] He was called Timur Bek as well as Tamerlane.
(Poe, 1827.)

[4] At this point the story is given more clearly in the
version of 1827 : —

  My eyes were still on pomp and power,
  My wilder'd heart was far away
  In the valleys of the wild Taglay,
  In mine own Ada's matted bower.
  I dwelt not long in Samarcand
  Ere, in a peasant's lowly guise,
  I sought my long-abandon'd land ;
  By sunset did its mountains rise
  In dusky grandeur to my eyes.

Father, I firmly do believe — [1]
  I *know* — for Death who comes for me
  From regions of the blest afar,
Where there is nothing to deceive,
  Hath left his iron gate ajar,
  And rays of truth you cannot see
  Are flashing thro' Eternity ——
I do believe that Eblis hath
  A snare in every human path —   230
Else how, when in the holy grove
I wandered of the idol, Love,
Who daily scents his snowy wings
With incense of burnt offerings
From the most unpolluted things,
Whose pleasant bowers are yet so riven
Above with trellic'd rays from Heaven
No mote may shun — no tiniest fly —
The light'ning of his eagle eye —
How was it that Ambition crept,   240
  Unseen, amid the revels there,
Till growing bold, he laughed and leapt
  In the tangles of Love's very hair ?

1821?–1829. [2]   1827, 1829.

TO —— ——

I saw thee on thy bridal day —
  When a burning blush came o'er thee,
Though happiness around thee lay,
  The world all love before thee :

And in thine eye a kindling light
  (Whatever it might be)
Was all on Earth my aching sight
  Of Loveliness could see.

That blush, perhaps, was maiden shame —
  As such it well may pass —

[1] This last paragraph of the poem was added in the edition of 1829.

[2] In his preface to the original edition of *Tamerlane*, Poe says : ' The greater part of the poems which compose this little volume were written in the year 1821–1822, when the author had not completed his fourteenth year.' This statement is not to be trusted implicitly. But even if we assign the composition of these poems to the latest possible date, 1826–1827, the early development of their author seems hardly the less remarkable ; for he would then be only seventeen or eighteen years old. Keats was almost twenty-two at the time when his first volume was published. ' Both in promise and in actual performance,' says Mr. Shepherd in his preface to the 1884 reprint of *Tamerlane and Other Poems* (quoted by Mr. Harrison), ' it may claim to rank as the most remarkable production that any English-speaking or English-writing poet of this century has published in his teens.' Poe was only eighteen years old when the volume was published, and it is interesting to note that the printer and publisher of the book, Calvin Thomas of Boston, was then only nineteen years old.

Though its glow hath raised a fiercer flame
  In the breast of him, alas !

Who saw thee on that bridal day,
  When that deep blush *would* come o'er
    thee,
Though happiness around thee lay,
  The world all love before thee.
1826.   1827.

SONG FROM AL AARAAF [3]

'Neath blue-bell or streamer —
  Or tufted wild spray
That keeps, from the dreamer,
  The moonbeam away —
Bright beings ! that ponder,
  With half closing eyes,
On the stars which your wonder
  Hath drawn from the skies,
'Till they glance thro' the shade, and
  Come down to your brow   10
Like —— eyes of the maiden
  Who calls on you now —
Arise ! from your dreaming
  In violet bowers,
To duty beseeming
  These star-litten hours —
And shake from your tresses
  Encumber'd with dew
The breath of those kisses
  That cumber them too —   20

[3] This song was introduced in the second part of ' Al Aaraaf ' as being sung to summon the spirit of music, or better the spirit of universal harmony. One of the most beautiful of Poe's tales, called ' Ligeia,' is an even finer embodiment of this conception.

Mr. Thomas Wentworth Higginson gives in his *Short Studies of American Authors* some vivid reminiscences of the evening when Poe read ' Al Aaraaf ' to an audience in Boston. The story is told in more condensed form in Higginson and Boynton's *Reader's History of American Literature*, page 214 : ' The verses had long since been printed in his youthful volume . . . and they produced no very distinct impression on the audience until Poe began to read the maiden's song in the second part. Already his tones had been softening to a finer melody than at first, and when he came to the verses, —

Ligeia ! Ligeia !
My beautiful one !

his voice seemed attenuated to the faintest golden thread ; the audience became hushed, and, as it were, breathless ; there seemed no life in the hall but his ; and every syllable was accentuated with such delicacy, and sustained with such sweetness, as I never heard equaled by other lips. When the lyric ended, it was like the ceasing of the gypsy's chant in Browning's '' Flight of the Duchess ; '' and I remember nothing more, except that in walking back to Cambridge my comrades and I felt that we had been under the spell of some wizard. Indeed, I feel much the same in the retrospect, to this day.'

(O ! how, without you, Love !
    Could angels be blest ?)
Those kisses of true love
    That lull'd ye to rest !
Up ! — shake from your wing
    Each hindering thing:
The dew of the night —
    It would weigh down your flight;
And true love caresses —
    O ! leave them apart !   30
They are light on the tresses,
    But lead on the heart.

Ligeia! Ligeia!
    My beautiful one !
Whose harshest idea.
    Will to melody run,
O! is it thy will
    On the breezes to toss ?
Or, capriciously still,
    Like the lone Albatross,   40
Incumbent on night
    (As she on the air)
To keep watch with delight
    On the harmony there ?

Ligeia ! wherever
    Thy image may be,
No magic shall sever
    Thy music from thee.
Thou hast bound many eyes
    In a dreamy sleep —   50
But the strains still arise
    Which *thy* vigilance keep —
The sound of the rain
    Which leaps down to the flower,
And dances again
    In the rhythm of the shower —
The murmur that springs
    From the growing of grass
Are the music of things —
    But are modell'd, alas ! —   60
Away, then my dearest,
    O ! hie thee away
To springs thàt lie clearest
    Beneath the moon-ray —
To lone lake that smiles,
    In its dream of deep rest,
At the many star-isles
    That enjewel its breast —
Where wild flowers, creeping,
    Have mingled their shade,   70
On its margin is sleeping
    Full many a maid —
Some have left the cool glade, and

Have slept with the bee —
Arouse them my maiden,
    On moorland and lea —
Go ! breathe on their slumber,
    All softly in ear,
The musical number
    They slumber'd to hear —   80
For what can awaken
    An angel so soon
Whose sleep hath been taken
    Beneath the cold moon,
As the spell which no slumber
    Of witchery may test,
The rhythmical number
    Which lull'd him to rest ?

1829 ?   1829.

ROMANCE

ROMANCE, who loves to nod and sing,
With drowsy head and folded wing,
Among the green leaves as they shake
Far down within some shadowy lake,
To me a painted paroquet
Hath been — a most familiar bird —
Taught me my alphabet to say —
To lisp my very earliest word
While in the wild wood I did lie,
A child — with a most knowing eye.

Of late, eternal Condor years
So shake the very Heaven on high
With tumult as they thunder by,
I have no time for idle cares
Through gazing on the unquiet sky.
And when an hour with calmer wings
Its down upon my spirit flings —
That little time with lyre and rhyme
To while away — forbidden things !
My heart would feel to be a crime
Unless it trembled with the strings.

                                            1829.

SONNET — TO SCIENCE

SCIENCE ! true daughter of Old Time thou
    art !
Who alterest all things with thy peering
    eyes.
Why preyest thou thus upon the poet's
    heart,
Vulture, whose wings are dull realities ?
How should he love thee ? or how deem
    thee wise,

Who wouldst not leave him in his wandering
To seek for treasure in the jewelled skies,
Albeit he soared with an undaunted wing ?
Hast thou not dragged Diana from her car ?
And driven the Hamadryad from the wood
To seek a shelter in some happier star ?
Hast thou not torn the Naiad from her flood,
The Elfin from the green grass, and from me
The summer dream beneath the tamarind
    tree ?

1829.

TO ——

The bowers whereat, in dreams, I see
  The wantonest singing birds,
Are lips — and all thy melody
  Of lip-begotten words —

Thine eyes, in Heaven of heart enshrined
  Then desolately fall,
O God ! on my funereal mind
  Like starlight on a pall —

Thy heart — *thy* heart ! — I wake and sigh,
  And sleep to dream till day
Of the truth that gold can never buy —
  Of the baubles that it may.

1829.

TO ——

I heed not that my earthly lot
  Hath little of Earth in it,
That years of love have been forgot
  In the hatred of a minute :
I mourn not that the desolate
  Are happier, sweet, than I,
But that you sorrow for my fate
  Who am a passer-by.

1829.

A DREAM WITHIN A DREAM

Take this kiss upon the brow !
And, in parting from you now,
Thus much let me avow —
You are not wrong, who deem
That my days have been a dream;
Yet if hope has flown away
In a night, or in a day,
In a vision, or in none,
Is it therefore the less *gone* ?
All that we see or seem
Is but a dream within a dream.

I stand amid the roar
Of a surf-tormented shore,
And I hold within my hand
Grains of the golden sand —
How few! yet how they creep
Through my fingers to the deep,
While I weep — while I weep !
O God ! can I not grasp
Them with a tighter clasp ?
O God ! can I not save
One from the pitiless wave ?
Is *all* that we see or seem
But a dream within a dream ?

1829, 1849.[1]

TO HELEN

Helen, thy beauty is to me
  Like those Nicéan barks of yore,
That gently, o'er a perfumed sea,
  The weary, way-worn wanderer bore
    To his own native shore.

On desperate seas long wont to roam,
  Thy hyacinth hair, thy classic face,
Thy Naiad airs have brought me home
  To the glory that was Greece,
  And the grandeur that was Rome.

Lo! in yon brilliant window-niche
  How statue-like I see thee stand,
The agate lamp within thy hand!
  Ah, Psyche, from the regions which
  Are Holy-Land!

1831.

ISRAFEL[2]

In Heaven a spirit doth dwell
  ' Whose heart-strings are a lute;'
None sing so wildly well

---

[1] This poem suffered more changes than any other of Poe's. The germ of it is perhaps to be found in ' Imitation,' in the 1827 volume ; but no phrase of that poem is identical with any phrase of this. ' To ——,' in the volume of 1829, contains one line taken from ' Imitation.' Part of ' To —— ——' was used as a last paragraph of ' Tamerlane ' in the edition of 1831; and the whole was later revised and considerably shortened, and was published by Griswold in 1849 with its present title.

[2] And the angel Israfel, whose heart-strings are a lute, and who has the sweetest voice of all God's creatures. — Koran. (Poe's note, 1845.)

Poe alone is responsible for the words ' Whose heart-strings are a lute.' The rest of the phrase had been quoted by Thomas Moore, in his ' Lalla Rookh,' from Sale's ' Preliminary Discourse ' to the *Koran*. Poe, as Professor Woodberry has pointed out, took the phrase from Moore.

As the angel Israfel,
And the giddy stars (so legends tell)
Ceasing their hymns, attend the spell
　Of his voice, all mute.

Tottering above
　In her highest noon,
　The enamored moon   10
Blushes with love,
　While, to listen, the red levin
　(With the rapid Pleiads, even,
　Which were seven,)
　Pauses in Heaven.

And they say (the starry choir
　And the other listening things)
That Israfeli's fire
Is owing to that lyre
　By which he sits and sings —   20
The trembling living wire
Of those unusual strings.

But the skies that angel trod,
　Where deep thoughts are a duty —
Where Love 's a grown-up God —
　Where the Houri glances are
Imbued with all the beauty
　Which we worship in a star.

Therefore, thou art not wrong,
　Israfeli, who despisest   30
An unimpassioned song ;
To thee the laurels belong,
　Best bard, because the wisest!
Merrily live, and long!

The ecstasies above
　With thy burning measures suit —
Thy grief, thy joy, thy hate, thy love,
　With the fervor of thy lute —
　Well may the stars be mute!

Yes, Heaven is thine; but this   40
　Is a world of sweets and sours;
　Our flowers are merely — flowers,
And the shadow of thy perfect bliss
　Is the sunshine of ours.

If I could dwell
Where Israfel
　Hath dwelt, and he where I,
He might not sing so wildly well
　A mortal melody,   49
While a bolder note than this might swell
　From my lyre within the sky.

　　　　　　　　　　　　　　　　1831.

THE CITY IN THE SEA

Lo! Death has reared himself a throne
In a strange city lying alone
Far down within the dim West,
Where the good and the bad and the worst
　　and the best
Have gone to their eternal rest.
There shrines and palaces and towers
(Time-eaten towers that tremble not!)
Resemble nothing that is ours.
Around, by lifting winds forgot,
Resignedly beneath the sky   10
The melancholy waters lie.

No rays from the holy heaven come down
On the long night-time of that town;
But light from out the lurid sea
Streams up the turrets silently —
Gleams up the pinnacles far and free —
Up domes — up spires — up kingly halls —
Up fanes — up Babylon-like walls —
Up shadowy long-forgotten bowers
Of sculptured ivy and stone flowers —   20
Up many and many a marvellous shrine
Whose wreathèd friezes intertwine
The viol, the violet, and the vine.
Resignedly beneath the sky
The melancholy waters lie.
So blend the turrets and shadows there
That all seem pendulous in air,
While from a proud tower in the town
Death looks gigantically down.

There open fanes and gaping graves   30
Yawn level with the luminous waves
But not the riches there that lie
In each idol's diamond eye —
Not the gayly-jewelled dead
Tempt the waters from their bed;
For no ripples curl, alas!
Along that wilderness of glass —
No swellings tell that winds may be
Upon some far-off happier sea —
No heavings hint that winds have been   40
On seas less hideously serene.

But lo, a stir is in the air!
The wave — there is a movement there!
As if the towers had thrust aside,
In slightly sinking, the dull tide —.
As if their tops had feebly given
A void within the filmy Heaven.
The waves have now a redder glow —
The hours are breathing faint and low —

And when, amid no earthly moans,   50
Down, down that town shall settle hence,
Hell, rising from a thousand thrones,
Shall do it reverence.

                          1831, 1845.

THE SLEEPER [1]

At midnight, in the month of June,
I stand beneath the mystic moon.
An opiate vapor, dewy, dim,
Exhales from out her golden rim,
And, softly dripping, drop by drop,
Upon the quiet mountain top,
Steals drowsily and musically
Into the universal valley.
The rosemary nods upon the grave;
The lily lolls upon the wave;   10
Wrapping the fog about its breast,
The ruin moulders into rest;
Looking like Lethe, see ! the lake
A conscious slumber seems to take,
And would not, for the world, awake.
All Beauty sleeps ! — and lo ! where lies
Irene, with her Destinies!

Oh, lady bright ! can it be right —
This window open to the night ?
The wanton airs, from the tree-top,   20
Laughingly through the lattice drop —
The bodiless airs, a wizard rout,
Flit through thy chamber in and out,
And wave the curtain canopy
So fitfully — so fearfully —
Above the closed and fringèd lid
'Neath which thy slumb'ring soul lies hid,
That, o'er the floor and down the wall,
Like ghosts the shadows rise and fall !
Oh, lady dear, hast thou no fear ?   30
Why and what art thou dreaming here ?
Sure thou art come o'er far-off seas,
A wonder to these garden trees !
Strange is thy pallor ! strange thy dress !
Strange, above all, thy length of tress,
And this all solemn silentness !

The lady sleeps ! Oh, may her sleep,
Which is enduring, so be deep !

[1] Poe says in a letter, probably of 1845 : ' Your appreciation of " The Sleeper " delights me. In the higher qualities of poetry it is better than " The Raven ; " but there is not one man in a million who could be brought to agree with me in this opinion. " The Raven " of course, is far the better as a work of art ; but in the true basis of all art, " The Sleeper " is the superior. I wrote the latter when quite a boy '

Heaven have her in its sacred keep !
This chamber changed for one more holy,
This bed for one more melancholy,   41
I pray to God that she may lie
Forever with unopened eye,
While the pale sheeted ghosts go by !

My love, she sleeps ! Oh, may her sleep,
As it is lasting, so be deep !
Soft may the worms about her creep !
Far in the forest, dim and old,
For her may some tall vault unfold —
Some vault that oft hath flung its black   50
And wingèd panels fluttering back,
Triumphant, o'er the crested palls,
Of her grand family funerals —
Some sepulchre, remote, alone,
Against whose portal she hath thrown,
In childhood, many an idle stone —
Some tomb from out whose sounding door
She ne'er shall force an echo more,
Thrilling to think, poor child of sin !
It was the dead who groaned within.   60

                          1831.

LENORE [2]

Ah, broken is the golden bowl ! the spirit
    flown forever!

[2] The first and third stanzas are supposed to be spoken by the ' wretches,' relatives or false friends of Lenore ; the second and fourth stanzas by Guy De Vere, her lover.

In this one case, perhaps, Poe's latest version is not so good as an earlier one. The form of Lenore published in 1843 is given below for comparison.

Ah, broken is the golden bowl!
        The spirit flown forever!
Let the bell toll ! — A saintly soul
    Glides down the Stygian river !
And let the burial rite be read —
    The funeral song be sung —
A dirge for the most lovely dead
    That ever died so young !
        And, Guy De Vere,
        Hast *thou* no tear ?
            Weep now or nevermore !
    See, on yon drear
    And rigid bier,
        Low lies thy love Lenore !

' Yon heir, whose cheeks of pallid hue
    With tears are streaming wet,
Sees only, through
Their crocodile dew,
    A vacant coronet —
        False friends ! ye loved her for her wealth
        And hated her for her pride,
    And, when she fell in feeble health,
    Ye blessed her — that she died.
How *shall* the ritual, then, be read ?
    The requiem *how* be sung
For her most wrong'd of all the dead
    That ever died so young ?'

Peccavimus!
But rave not thus !
    And let the solemn song
Go up to God so mournfully that *she* may feel no wrong
    The sweet Lenore
    Hath ' gone before '

Let the bell toll! — a saintly soul floats on
  the Stygian river;
And, Guy De Vere, hast *thou* no tear ? —
  weep now or never more !
See! on yon drear and rigid bier low lies
  thy love, Lenore !
Come ! let the burial rite be read — the
  funeral song be sung ! —
An anthem for the queenliest dead that
  ever died so young —
A dirge for her the doubly dead in that she
  died so young.

'Wretches! ye loved her for her wealth
  and hated her for her pride,
'And when she fell in feeble health, ye
  blessed her — that she died !
'How *shall* the ritual, then, be read ? —
  the requiem how be sung
'By you — by yours, the evil eye, — by
  yours, the slanderous tongue

> With young hope at her side,
>   And thou art wild
>   For the dear child
> That should have been thy bride —
>   For her, the fair
>   And debonair,
> That now so lowly lies —
>   The life still there
>   Upon her hair,
> The death upon her eyes.
>
> 'Avaunt ! — to-night
> My heart is light —
>   No dirge will I upraise,
> But waft the angel on her flight
> With a Pæan of old days !
>   Let no bell toll !
>   Lest her sweet soul,
>   Amid its hallow'd mirth,
>   Should catch the note
>   As it doth float
> Up from the damnèd earth —
>   To friends above, from fiends below,
>   Th' indignant ghost is riven —
>   From grief and moan
>   To a gold throne
>   Beside the King of Heaven !'

It seems probable that Poe was influenced by the success of 'The Raven' to rearrange 'Lenore' in somewhat similar lines of even length.

In the text above I have given the last stanza of the
poem as it stands in the Lorimer Graham copy — a
copy of the edition of 1845, corrected by Poe's own
hand. In the edition of 1845, uncorrected, the stanza
reads as follows : —

'Avaunt ! — avaunt ! from fiends below, the indignant ghost
  is riven —
'From Hell unto a high estate far up within the Heaven —
'From grief and groan, to a golden throne, beside the King
  of Heaven.'
Let no bell toll then ! — lest her soul, amid its hallowed mirth,
Should catch the note as it doth float up from the damnèd
  Earth ! —
And I . — to-night my heart is light ! No dirge will I up-
  raise,
But waft the angel on her flight with a Pæan of old days !

It is interesting to note that in this case, and perhaps
in this case only, Poe, after changing considerably a
passage of his work, later returned to a previous version. The arrangement of ideas in his *corrected* copy of
this fourth stanza is much closer to the 1843 version
than to that of 1845.

'That did to death the innocence that died,
  and died so young ?'

Peccavimus ; but rave not thus ! and let a
  Sabbath song
Go up to God so solemnly the dead may
  feel no wrong!
The sweet Lenore hath 'gone before,' with
  Hope, that flew beside,
Leaving thee wild for the dear child that
  should have been thy bride —
For her, the fair and *debonair,* that now so
  lowly lies,
The life upon her yellow hair but not within
  her eyes —
The life still there, upon her hair — the
  death upon her eyes.

'Avaunt ! to-night my heart is light. No
  dirge will I upraise.
'But waft the angel on her flight with a
  pæan of old days !
'Let *no* bell toll ! — lest her sweet soul,
  amid its hallowed mirth,
'Should catch the note, as it doth float up
  from the damnèd Earth.
'To friends above, from fiends below, the
  indignant ghost is riven —
'From Hell unto a high estate far up
  within the Heaven —
'From grief and groan, to a golden throne,
  beside the King of Heaven.'

                              1831, 1843, 1845.

THE VALLEY OF UNREST

Once it smiled a silent dell
Where the people did not dwell;
They had gone unto the wars,
Trusting to the mild-eyed stars,
Nightly, from their azure towers,
To keep watch above the flowers,
In the midst of which all day
The red sun-light lazily lay.
Now each visiter shall confess
The sad valley's restlessness.
Nothing there is motionless —
Nothing save the airs that brood
Over the magic solitude.
Ah, by no wind are stirred those trees
That palpitate like the chill seas
Around the misty Hebrides !
Ah, by no wind those clouds are driven
That rustle through the unquiet Heaven

Uneasily, from morn till even,
Over the violets there that lie
In myriad types of the human eye —
Over the lilies there that wave
And weep above a nameless grave !
They wave : — from out their fragrant tops
Eternal dews come down in drops.
They weep : — from off their delicate stems
Perennial tears descend in gems.

1831, 1845.

THE COLISEUM [1]

TYPE of the antique Rome ! Rich reliquary
Of lofty contemplation left to Time
By buried centuries of pomp and power !
At length — at length — after so many
days
Of weary pilgrimage and burning thirst,
(Thirst for the springs of lore that in thee
lie,)
I kneel, an altered and an humble man,
Amid thy shadows, and so drink within
My very soul thy grandeur, gloom, and
glory !   9

Vastness ! and Age ! and Memories of Eld !
Silence ! and Desolation ! and dim Night !
I feel ye now — I feel ye in your strength —
O spells more sure than e'er Judæan king
Taught in the gardens of Gethsemane !
O charms more potent than the rapt
Chaldee
Ever drew down from out the quiet stars !

Here, where a hero fell, a column falls !
Here, where the mimic eagle glared in gold,
A midnight vigil holds the swarthy bat !
Here, where the dames of Rome their
gilded hair   20
Waved to the wind, now wave the reed and
thistle !
Here, where on golden throne the monarch
lolled,
Glides, spectre-like, unto his marble home,
Lit by the wan light of the hornèd moon,
The swift and silent lizard of the stones !

But stay ! these walls — these ivy-clad
arcades —
These mouldering plinths — these sad and
blackened shafts —

These vague entablatures — this crumbling
frieze —
These shattered cornices — this wreck —
this ruin —
These stones — alas ! these gray stones —
are they all —   30
All of the famed, and the colossal left
By the corrosive Hours to Fate and me ?

' Not all ' — the Echoes answer me — ' not
all !
Prophetic sounds and loud, arise forever
From us, and from all Ruin, unto the
wise,
As melody from Memnon to the Sun.
We rule the hearts of mightiest men — we
rule
With a despotic sway all giant minds.
We are not impotent — we pallid stones.
Not all our power is gone — not all our
fame —   40
Not all the magic of our high renown —
Not all the wonder that encircles us —
Not all the mysteries that in us lie —
Not all the memories that hang upon
And cling around about us as a garment,
Clothing us in a robe of more than glory.'

1833.

HYMN

AT morn — at noon — at twilight dim —
Maria ! thou hast heard my hymn !
In joy and woe — in good and ill —
Mother of God, be with me still !
When the Hours flew brightly by,
And not a cloud obscured the sky,
My soul, lest it should truant be,
Thy grace did guide to thine and thee·
Now, when storms of Fate o'ercast
Darkly my Present and my Past,
Let my Future radiant shine
With sweet hopes of thee and thine !

1835.

TO ONE IN PARADISE [2]

THOU wast all that to me, love,
For which my soul did pine —
A green isle in the sea, love,
A fountain and a shrine,

---

[1] Compare the descriptions of the Coliseum by
Byron (*Manfred*, act. iii, scene iv, *Childe Harold*,
canto iv, stanzas 114 and following), by Chateaubriand
(*Itinéraire de Paris à Jérusalem*), etc.

[2] Originally in the tale, ' The Visionary ' (now called
' The Assignation '). There, and in most later versions,
the first line reads, —

Thou wast that all to me, love . . ·

All wreathed with fairy fruits and flowers,
  And all the flowers were mine.

Ah, dream too bright to last !
  Ah, starry Hope ! that didst arise
But to be overcast !
  A voice from out the Future cries,
' On ! on ! ' — but o'er the Past
  (Dim gulf !) my spirit hovering lies
Mute, motionless, aghast !

For, alas! alas! with me
  The light of Life is o'er !
  ' No more — no more — no more — '
(Such language holds the solemn sea
  To the sands upon the shore)
Shall bloom the thunder-blasted tree,
  Or the stricken eagle soar !

And all my days are trances,
  And all my nightly dreams
Are where thy gray eye glances,
  And where thy footstep gleams —
In what ethereal dances,
  By what eternal streams.

                                1834, 1835.

TO F—— [1]

BELOVED ! amid the earnest woes
  That crowd around my earthly path —
(Drear path, alas ! where grows
Not even one lonely rose) —
  My soul at least a solace hath
In dreams of thee, and therein knows
An Eden of bland repose.

And thus thy memory is to me
  Like some enchanted far-off isle
In some tumultuous sea —
Some ocean throbbing far and free
  With storms — but where meanwhile
Serenest skies continually
  Just o'er that one bright island smile.

                                    1835.

TO F——S S. O——D [2]

THOU wouldst be loved ? — then let thy
    heart
  From its present pathway part not !

---

[1] The title was in 1835 ' To Mary,' in 1842 ' To One
Departed,' and in 1845 ' To F——.'
[2] Addressed in 1845, with some changes from the
version of 1835 to Frances Sargent Osgood. See the
biographies.

Being everything which now thou art,
  Be nothing which thou art not.
So with the world thy gentle ways,
  Thy grace, thy more than beauty,
Shall be an endless theme of praise,
  And love — a simple duty.

                                1835, 1845.

SONNET TO ZANTE

FAIR isle, that from the fairest of all
    flowers,
  Thy gentlest of all gentle names dost
    take ! [3]
How many memories of what radiant hours
  At sight of thee and thine at once awake !
How many scenes of what departed bliss !
  How many thoughts of what entombèd
    hopes !
How many visions of a maiden that is
  No more — no more upon thy verdant
    slopes !
No more ! alas, that magical sad sound
  Transforming all ! Thy charms shall
    please *no more —*
Thy memory *no more !* Accursèd ground
  Henceforth I hold thy flower-enamelled
    shore,
O hyacinthine isle ! O purple Zante !
' Isola d'oro ! Fior di Levante ! '

                                    1837.

THE HAUNTED PALACE [4]

IN the greenest of our valleys
  By good angels tenanted,
Once a fair and stately palace —
  Radiant palace — reared its head.
In the monarch Thought's dominion —
  It stood there !
Never seraph spread a pinion
  Over fabric half so fair !

---

[3] Je souscris à ses noms d'Isola d'oro, de Fior di
Levante. Ce nom de fleur me rappelle qu' l'hyacinthe
était originaire de l'île de Zante, et que cette île reçut
son nom de la plante qu'elle avait portée. (CHA-
TEAUBRIAND, *Itinéraire de Paris à Jérusalem.*)
[4] This poem is a part of Poe's tale of the ' Fall of
the House of Usher,' which should be read entire.
Lowell calls it ' one of the most beautiful of his
poems,' and goes on : ' It loses greatly by being taken
out of its rich and appropriate setting . . . We know
no modern poet who might not have been justly proud
of it. . . . Was ever the wreck and desolation of a noble
mind so musically sung ? ' ' By the " Haunted Palace " I mean to imply a mind haunted by phantoms — a
disordered brain,' says Poe himself, in a letter in
which he also accuses Longfellow of plagiarizing from
this poem in the ' Beleaguered City.'

Banners yellow, glorious, golden,
  On its roof did float and flow,   10
(This — all this — was in the olden
  Time long ago,)
And every gentle air that dallied,
  In that sweet day,
Along the ramparts plumed and pallid,
  A wingèd odor went away.

Wanderers in that happy valley,
  Through two luminous windows, saw
Spirits moving musically,
  To a lute's well-tunèd law,   20
Round about a throne where, sitting,
  (Porphyrogene !)
In state his glory well befitting,
  The ruler of the realm was seen.

And all with pearl and ruby glowing
  Was the fair palace door,
Through which came flowing, flowing,
    flowing
  And sparkling evermore,
A troop of Echoes, whose sweet duty
  Was but to sing,   30
In voices of surpassing beauty,
  The wit and wisdom of their king.

But evil things, in robes of sorrow,
  Assailed the monarch's high estate.
(Ah, let us mourn ! — for never morrow
  Shall dawn upon him desolate !)
And round about his home the glory
  That blushed and bloomed,
Is but a dim-remembered story
  Of the old time entombed.   40

And travellers, now, within that valley,
  Through the red-litten windows see
Vast forms, that move fantastically
  To a discordant melody ;
While, like a ghastly rapid river,
  Through the pale door
A hideous throng rush out forever
  And laugh — but smile no more.

              1839.

SONNET — SILENCE

There are some qualities — some incorpo-
  rate things,
That have a double life, which thus is made
A type of that twin entity which springs
From matter and light, evinced in solid and
  shade.

There is a two-fold *Silence* — sea and
  shore —
Body and soul. One dwells in lonely places,
Newly with grass o'ergrown ; some solemn
  graces,
Some human memories and tearful lore,
Render him terrorless : his name 's 'No
  More.'
He is the corporate Silence : dread him
  not !
No power hath he of evil in himself ;
But should some urgent fate (untimely
  lot !)
Bring thee to meet his shadow (nameless
  elf,
That haunteth the lone regions where hath
  trod
No foot of man,) commend thyself to God !
              1840.

THE CONQUEROR WORM

Lo ! 't is a gala night
  Within the lonesome latter years !
An angel throng, bewinged, bedight
  In veils, and drowned in tears,
Sit in a theatre, to see
  A play of hopes and fears,
While the orchestra breathes fitfully
  The music of the spheres.

Mimes, in the form of God on high,
  Mutter and mumble low,   10
And hither and thither fly —
  Mere puppets they, who come and go
At bidding of vast formless things
  That shift the scenery to and fro,
Flapping from out their Condor wings
  Invisible Woe !

That motley drama — oh, be sure
  It shall not be forgot !
With its Phantom chased for evermore,
  By a crowd that seize it not,   20
Through a circle that ever returneth in
  To the self-same spot,
And much of Madness, and more of Sin,
  And Horror the soul of the plot.

But see, amid the mimic rout
  A crawling shape intrude !
A blood-red thing that writhes from out
  The scenic solitude !
It writhes ! — it writhes ! — with mortal
  pangs

The mimes become its food,   30
And seraphs sob at vermin fangs
    In human gore imbued.

Out — out are the lights — out all !
    And, over each quivering form,
The curtain, a funeral pall,
    Comes down with the rush of a storm,
While the angels, all pallid and wan,
    Uprising, unveiling, affirm
That the play is the tragedy, 'Man,'   40
    And its hero the Conqueror Worm.
                                    1843.

DREAM-LAND

By a route obscure and lonely,
Haunted by ill angels only,
Where an Eidolon, named NIGHT,
On a black throne reigns upright,
I have reached these lands but newly
From an ultimate dim Thule —
From a wild weird clime that lieth, sub-
        lime,
    Out of SPACE — out of TIME.

Bottomless vales and boundless floods,
And chasms, and caves and Titan woods,
With forms that no man can discover   11
For the tears that drip all over;
Mountains toppling evermore
Into seas without a shore;
Seas that restlessly aspire,
Surging, unto skies of fire;
Lakes that endlessly outspread
Their lone waters — lone and dead, —
Their still waters — still and chilly
With the snows of the lolling lily.   20

By the lakes that thus outspread
Their lone waters, lone and dead, —
Their sad waters, sad and chilly
With the snows of the lolling lily, —
By the mountains — near the river
Murmuring lowly, murmuring ever, —
By the gray woods, — by the swamp
Where the toad and the newt encamp, —
By the dismal tarns and pools
    Where dwell the Ghouls, —   30
By each spot the most unholy —
In each nook most melancholy, —
There the traveller meets, aghast,
Sheeted Memories of the Past —
Shrouded forms that start and sigh
As they pass the wanderer by —

White-robed forms of friends long given,
In agony, to the Earth — and Heaven.

For the heart whose woes are legion
'T is a peaceful, soothing region —   40
For the spirit that walks in shadow
'T is — oh 't is an Eldorado !
But the traveller, travelling through it,
May not — dare not openly view it;
Never its mysteries are exposed
To the weak human eye unclosed;
So wills its King, who hath forbid
The uplifting of the fringèd lid;
And thus the sad Soul that here passes
Beholds it but through darkened glasses.

By a route obscure and lonely,   51
Haunted by ill angels only,
Where an Eidolon, named NIGHT,
On a black throne reigns upright,
I have wandered home but newly
From this ultimate dim Thule.
                                    1844.

THE RAVEN [1]

ONCE upon a midnight dreary, while I pon-
        dered, weak and weary,
Over many a quaint and curious volume of
        forgotten lore —

[1] In connection with the 'Raven' Poe's 'Philosophy of Composition' must be read. See also: Ingram (John H.), *The Raven*, London, 1885. Benton
(Joel), *In the Poe Circle*. Kent (Charles W.), 'Poe
and Chivers' (in the Virginia Edition of Poe's *Works*,
vol. vii, pp. 266–288). Woodberry (G. E.), 'The Poe-
Chivers Papers' (in the *Century*, January and February, 1903). Newcomer (A. G.), 'The Poe-Chivers Tradition re-examined' (in the *Sewanee Review*, January,
1904.) Stedman (E. C.), *The Raven*, illustrated by
Doré, with comment by E. C. Stedman.
    Whether or not Poe in the 'Raven' owed anything
to Chivers, he unquestionably, as Mr. Stedman has
pointed out, owed less to Chivers than to Mrs. Browning. With the beginning of Poe's third stanza,
'And the silken, sad, uncertain rustling of each purple
    curtain,'
compare Mrs. Browning's fourth stanza in the 'Conclusion' of *Lady Geraldine's Courtship*,
'With a murmurous stir uncertain, in the air the purple
    curtain
Swelleth in and swelleth out around her motionless pale
    brows,
While the gliding of the river sends a rippling noise for ever
Through the open casement whitened by the moonlight's
    slant repose.'
    Here, if we use the method adopted by Poe in his
arraignment of Longfellow and his attack on Longfellow's defenders, where he insists that rhythm, metre,
and stanza must form an essential part of any comparison, and that the probability of imitation is in direct
ratio to the brevity of the passages compared as well as
to the number of coincidences, it would be easy to show
that Poe has followed, or as he would say plagiarized

While I nodded, nearly napping, suddenly
there came a tapping,
As of some one gently rapping, rapping at
my chamber door.

from, Mrs. Browning. The rhythm is the same, trochaic; the metre is the same, octameter; the first four lines of the stanza which Poe uses throughout the 'Raven' are exactly identical with Mrs. Browning's stanza, the first and third lines having internal feminine rhyme at the fourth foot, and the second and fourth having single masculine rhymes. The only difference is that Poe has added another internal rhyme in the fourth line. He has then added a fifth line (always in part a repetition of the fourth and ending with the same word or words), and the refrain. Again to adopt Poe's method of comparison, one might note that in the first line of Poe's third stanza and of Mrs. Browning's fourth, the same word, 'curtain' occupies the same, and the most prominent, place, that it is matched in each case with the same rhyme-word, 'uncertain,' that the curtain is in each case a purple curtain, and in each case a vaguely waving curtain, and that in each case it produces a murmuring or rustling sound — and finally, that all these coincidences occur within the compass of one line, and are as numerous and peculiar as those which Poe insists upon, in what he calls the brief compass of eight or sixteen lines, in his article against Longfellow and Aldrich (see the *Longfellow War* in the Virginia Edition of Poe's *Works*, vol. xii, pp. 41–106, especially pp. 76–82). Other minute resemblances might be pointed out, such as the mention in both poems of the lattice-window; but this would be less profitable than to recognize the essential originality of Poe's conception and expression. He was a frank admirer of Mrs. Browning's poetry, and dedicated his chief volume, the *Raven and Other Poems*, to her: ' To the Noblest of her Sex — to the Author of "The Drama of Exile " — to Miss Elizabeth Barrett of England — I dedicate this volume, with the most enthusiastic admiration and with the most sincere esteem.' It is to be noted also that Mrs. Browning was more fond than any other English poet of the refrain. On Poe's use of the refrain, and also of the repetend, on which point he may be best compared with Coleridge, see C. A. Smith's *Repetition and Parallelism in English Verse*, J. P. Fruit's *The Mind and Art of Poe's Poetry*, etc.

However much of the 'Raven' may have been suggested by Poe's predecessors, it suggested even more to his followers. The most important instance of this (not forgetting his influence on Baudelaire and Mallarmé) is perhaps to be found in its having suggested to Rossetti ' The Blessed Damozel.' See W. M. Rossetti's *Dante Gabriel Rossetti: His Family Letters, etc.*, 1895, vol. i, p. 107 : ' " The Blessed Damozel " was written with a view to its insertion in a manuscript family magazine, of brief vitality. In 1881 Rossetti gave Mr. Caine an account of its origin, as deriving from his perusal and admiration of Edgar Poe's " Raven." " I saw " (this is Mr. Caine's version of Rossetti's statement) " that Poe had done the utmost it was possible to do with the grief of the lover on earth, and I determined to reverse the condition, and give utterance to the yearning of the loved one in heaven." Along with " The Raven " and other poems by Poe, " Ulalume," " For Annie," " The Haunted Palace," and many another were a deep well of delight to Rossetti in all these years. He once wrote a parody of " Ulalume." I do not rightly remember it, nor has it left a vestige behind.'

On the time and place of composition of the ' Raven,' see the long note in the Stedman-Woodberry edition of the *Poems*, pages 156–9, and the authorities there cited ; the last pages of chapter ix in Harrison's *Life of Poe;* and Ingram's *The Raven*, referred to above.

' 'T is some visiter,' I muttered, 'tapping
at my chamber door —
Only this and nothing more.'

Ah, distinctly I remember it was in the
bleak December;
And each separate dying ember wrought
its ghost upon the floor.
Eagerly I wished the morrow; — vainly I
had sought to borrow
From my books surcease of sorrow — sorrow for the lost Lenore —   10
For the rare and radiant maiden whom the
angels name Lenore —
Nameless *here* for evermore.

And the silken, sad, uncertain rustling of
each purple curtain
Thrilled me — filled me with fantastic terrors never felt before;
So that now, to still the beating of my heart,
I stood repeating
' 'T is some visiter entreating entrance at
my chamber door —
Some late visiter entreating entrance at my
chamber door; —
This it is and nothing more.'

Presently my soul grew stronger; hesitating then no longer,
' Sir,' said I, ' or Madam, truly your forgiveness I implore;   20
But the fact is I was napping, and so gently
you came rapping,
And so faintly you came tapping, tapping at
my chamber door,
That I scarce was sure I heard you ' — here
I opened wide the door;
Darkness there and nothing more.

Deep into that darkness peering, long I
stood there wondering, fearing,
Doubting, dreaming dreams no mortal ever
dared to dream before;
But the silence was unbroken, and the stillness gave no token,
And the only word there spoken was the
whispered word, ' Lenore ! '
This I whispered, and an echo murmured
back the word ' Lenore ! '
Merely this and nothing more.   30

Back into the chamber turning, all my soul
within me burning,
Soon again I heard a tapping somewhat
louder than before.

'Surely,' said I, 'surely that is something
    at my window lattice;
Let me see, then, what thereat is, and this
    mystery explore —
Let my heart be still a moment and this
    mystery explore; —
    'T is the wind and nothing more ! '

Open here I flung the shutter, when, with
    many a flirt and flutter
In there stepped a stately Raven of the
    saintly days of yore.
Not the least obeisance made he; not a min-
    ute stopped or stayed he ;
But, with mien of lord or lady, perched
    above my chamber door —   40
Perched upon a bust of Pallas just above
    my chamber door —
    Perched, and sat, and nothing more.

Then this ebony bird beguiling my sad fancy
    into smiling,
By the grave and stern decorum of the
    countenance it wore,
'Though thy crest be shorn and shaven,
    thou,' I said, 'art sure no craven,
Ghastly grim and ancient Raven wandering
    from the Nightly shore —
Tell me what thy lordly name is on the
    Night's Plutonian shore !'
    Quoth the Raven, 'Nevermore.'

Much I marvelled this ungainly fowl to
    hear discourse so plainly,
Though its answer little meaning — little
    relevancy bore;   50
For we cannot help agreeing that no living
    human being
Ever yet was blessed with seeing bird above
    his chamber door —
Bird or beast upon the sculptured bust above
    his chamber door,
    With such name as ' Nevermore.'

But the Raven, sitting lonely on the placid
    bust, spoke only
That one word, as if his soul in that one
    word he did outpour.
Nothing farther then he uttered — not a
    feather then he fluttered —
Till I scarcely more than muttered ' Other
    friends have flown before —
On the morrow he will leave me, as my
    hopes have flown before.'
    Then the bird said ' Nevermore.'   60

Startled at the stillness broken by reply so
    aptly spoken,
' Doubtless,' said I, ' what it utters is its
    only stock and store
Caught from some unhappy master whom
    unmerciful Disaster
Followed fast and followed faster till his
    songs one burden bore —
Till the dirges of his Hope that melancholy
    burden bore
    Of " Never — nevermore." '

But the Raven still beguiling all my fancy
    into smiling,
Straight I wheeled a cushioned seat in front
    of bird, and bust and door;
Then, upon the velvet sinking, I betook
    myself to linking
Fancy unto fancy, thinking what this omi-
    nous bird of yore —   70
What this grim, ungainly, ghastly, gaunt,
    and ominous bird of yore
    Meant in croaking ' Nevermore.'

This I sat engaged in guessing, but no syl-
    lable expressing
To the fowl whose fiery eyes now burned
    into my bosom's core;
This and more I sat divining, with my head
    at ease reclining
On the cushion's velvet lining that the lamp-
    light gloated o'er,
But whose velvet violet lining with the
    lamp-light gloating o'er,
    She shall press, ah, nevermore !

Then, methought, the air grew denser, per-
    fumed from an unseen censer
Swung by Seraphim whose foot-falls tinkled
    on the tufted floor.   80
' Wretch,' I cried, ' thy God hath lent
    thee — by these angels he hath sent
    thee
Respite — respite and nepenthe from thy
    memories of Lenore;
Quaff, oh quaff this kind nepenthe and for-
    get this lost Lenore ! '
    Quoth the Raven ' Nevermore.'

' Prophet ! ' said I, ' thing of evil ! prophet
    still, if bird or devil ! —
Whether Tempter sent, or whether tempest
    tossed thee here ashore,
Desolate yet all undaunted, on this desert
    land enchanted —

On this home by Horror haunted — tell me
    truly, I implore —
Is there — *is* there balm in Gilead ? — tell
    me — tell me, I implore ! '
    Quoth the Raven ' Nevermore. '   90

' Prophet ! ' said I, ' thing of evil ! —
    prophet still, if bird or devil !
By that Heaven that bends above us — by
    that God we both adore —
Tell this soul with sorrow laden if, within
    the distant Aidenn,
It shall clasp a sainted maiden whom the
    angels name Lenore —
Clasp a rare and radiant maiden whom the
    angels name Lenore. '
    Quoth the Raven ' Nevermore. '

' Be that word our sign of parting, bird or
    fiend ! ' I shrieked, upstarting —
' Get thee back into the tempest and the
    Night's Plutonian shore !
Leave no black plume as a token of that lie
    thy soul hath spoken !
Leave my loneliness unbroken ! — quit the
    bust above my door !   100
Take thy beak from out my heart, and
    take thy form from off my door ! '
    Quoth the Raven ' Nevermore. '

And the Raven, never flitting, still is sitting,
    still is sitting
On the pallid bust of Pallas just above my
    chamber door;
And his eyes have all the seeming of a de-
    mon's that is dreaming,
And the lamp-light o'er him streaming
    throws his shadow on the floor;
And my soul from out that shadow that lies
    floating on the floor
    Shall be lifted — nevermore ! [1]

1842–44 ?   1845.

EULALIE — A SONG

I DWELT alone
  In a world of moan,
And my soul was a stagnant tide,
Till the fair and gentle Eulalie became my
    blushing bride —
Till the yellow-haired young Eulalie be-
    came my smiling bride.

[1] In the concluding stanza . . . I convert him [the raven] into an allegorical emblem or personification of Mournful Remembrance, out of the Shadow of which the poet is ' lifted nevermore.' (POE, *Works*, vol. xii, p. 75.)

  Ah, less — less bright
  The stars of the night
Than the eyes of the radiant girl !
  And never a flake
  That the vapor can make
With the moon-tints of purple and
    pearl,
Can vie with the modest Eulalie's most un-
    regarded curl —
Can compare with the bright-eyed Eulalie's
    most humble and careless curl.

  Now Doubt — now Pain
  Come never again,
For her soul gives me sigh for sigh,
  And all day long
  Shines, bright and strong,
Astarte within the sky,
While ever to her dear Eulalie upturns her
    matron eye —
While ever to her young Eulalie upturns
    her violet eye.

    1845.

ULALUME [2]

THE skies they were ashen and sober ;
  The leaves they were crisped and sere —
  The leaves they were withering and sere;
It was night in the lonesome October
  Of my most immemorial year ;
It was hard by the dim lake of Auber,
  In the misty mid region of Weir —
It was down by the dank tarn of Auber,
  In the ghoul-haunted woodland of Weir.

Here once, through an alley Titanic,   10
  Of cypress, I roamed with my Soul —
  Of cypress, with Psyche, my Soul.
These were days when my heart was vol-
    canic
  As the scoriac rivers that roll —
  As the lavas that restlessly roll
Their sulphurous currents down Yaanek
  In the ultimate climes of the pole —
That groan as they roll down Mount Yaanek
  In the realms of the boreal pole.

Our talk had been serious and sober,   20
  But our thoughts they were palsied and
    sere —
  Our memories were treacherous and
    sere —

[2] Poe's child-wife Virginia died in January of 1847, and this poem was published in December. See the biographical sketch.

For we knew not the month was October,
  And we marked not the night of the
     year —
  (Ah, night of all nights in the year !)
We noted not the dim lake of Auber —
  (Though once we had journeyed down
     here) —
Remembered not the dank tarn of Auber,
  Nor the ghoul-haunted woodland of Weir.

And now, as the night was senescent   30
  And star-dials pointed to morn —
  As the star-dials hinted of morn —
At the end of our path a liquescent
  And nebulous lustre was born,
Out of which a miraculous crescent
  Arose with a duplicate horn —
Astarte's bediamonded crescent
  Distinct with its duplicate horn.

And I said — ' She is warmer than Dian :
  She rolls through an ether of sighs —   40
  She revels in a region of sighs :
She has seen that the tears are not dry on
  These cheeks, where the worm never
     dies
And has come past the stars of the Lion
  To point us the path to the skies —
  To the Lethean peace of the skies —
Come up, in despite of the Lion,
  To shine on us with her bright eyes —
Come up through the lair of the Lion,
  With love in her luminous eyes.'   50

But Psyche, uplifting her finger,
  Said — ' Sadly this star I mistrust —
  Her pallor I strangely mistrust : —
Oh, hasten ! — oh, let us not linger !
  Oh, fly ! — let us fly ! — for we must.'
In terror she spoke, letting sink her
  Wings until they trailed in the dust —
In agony sobbed, letting sink her
  Plumes till they trailed in the dust —
  Till they sorrowfully trailed in the
    dust.   60

I replied — ' This is nothing but dreaming :
  Let us on by this tremulous light !
  Let us bathe in this crystalline light !
Its Sibyllic splendor is beaming
  With Hope and in Beauty to-night : —
  See ! — it flickers up the sky through
    the night !
Ah, we safely may trust to its gleaming,
  And be sure it will lead us aright —

We safely may trust to a gleaming
  That cannot but guide us aright,   70
  Since it flickers up to Heaven through
    the night.'

Thus I pacified Psyche and kissed her,
  And tempted her out of her gloom —
  And conquered her scruples and gloom ;
And we passed to the end of the vista,
  But were stopped by the door of a tomb —
  By the door of a legended tomb ;
And I said — ' What is written, sweet
    sister,
  On the door of this legended tomb ? '
  She replied — ' Ulalume — Ulalume —
  'T is the vault of thy lost Ulalume ! '   81

Then my heart it grew ashen and sober
  As the leaves that were crisped and
    sere —
  As the leaves that were withering and
    sere,
And I cried — ' It was surely October
  On *this* very night of last year
  That I journeyed — I journeyed down
    here —
  That I brought a dread burden down
    here —
  On this night of all nights in the year,
  Ah, what demon has tempted me here ? 90
Well I know, now, this dim lake of Auber —
  This misty mid region of Weir —
Well I know, now, this dank tarn of Auber,
  This ghoul-haunted woodland of Weir.'

                   1847.

TO HELEN [1]

I saw thee once — once only — years ago:
I must not say *how* many — but *not* many.
It was a July midnight; and from out
A full-orbed moon, that, like thine own
    soul, soaring,
Sought a precipitate pathway up through
    heaven,

[1] The occasion of Poe's first sight of Mrs. Whitman
is romantically described as follows : —
' Poe caught a glimpse of a white figure wandering
in a moonlit garden in Providence, on his way from
Boston, when he visited that city to deliver a poem
before the Lyceum there. Restless, near midnight, he
wandered from his hotel near where she lived, until he
saw her walking in a garden. He related the incident
afterwards in one of his most exquisite poems, worthy
of himself, of her, and of the most exalted passion.'
(Harrison's *Life of Poe*, p. 284.) See also Mrs. Whitman's *Poems*, and Woodberry's *Life of Poe*, pp. 308-
325.

There fell a silvery-silken veil of light,
With quietude and sultriness and slumber,
Upon the upturn'd faces of a thousand
Roses that grew in an enchanted garden,
Where no wind dared to stir, unless on tip-
    toe —   10
Fell on the upturn'd faces of these roses
That gave out, in return for the love-light,
Their odorous souls in an ecstatic death —
Fell on the upturn'd faces of these roses
That smiled and died in this parterre, en-
    chanted
By thee, and by the poetry of thy presence.

Clad all in white, upon a violet bank
I saw thee half reclining; while the moon
Fell on the upturn'd faces of the roses,
And on thine own, upturn'd — alas, in sor-
    row!   20

Was it not Fate, that, on this July mid-
    night —
Was it not Fate, (whose name is also Sor-
    row),
That bade me pause before that garden-
    gate,
To breathe the incense of those slumbering
    roses ?
No footstep stirred: the hated world all
    slept,
Save only thee and me. (Oh, heaven ! —
    oh, God !
How my heart beats in coupling those two
    words !)
Save only thee and me. I paused — I
    looked —
And in an instant all things disappeared.
(Ah, bear in mind this garden was en-
    chanted !)   30
The pearly lustre of the moon went out:
The mossy banks and the meandering paths,
The happy flowers and the repining trees,
Were seen no more: the very roses' odors
Died in the arms of the adoring airs.
All — all expired save thee — save less
    than thou:
Save only the divine light in thine eyes —
Save but the soul in thine uplifted eyes.
I saw but them — they were the world to
    me.
I saw but them — saw only them for
    hours —   40
Saw only them until the moon went down.
What wild heart-histories seemed to lie en-
    written

Upon those crystalline, celestial spheres !
How dark a woe ! yet how sublime a hope !
How silently serene a sea of pride !
How daring an ambition ! yet how deep —
How fathomless a capacity for love !

But now, at length, dear Dian sank from
    sight,
Into a western couch of thunder-cloud;
And thou, a ghost, amid the entombing
    trees   50
Didst glide away. *Only thine eyes remained.*
  They *would not* go — they never yet have
    gone.
Lighting my lonely pathway home that
    night,
They have not left me (as my hopes have)
    since.
They follow me — they lead me through
    the years
They are my ministers — yet I their slave.
Their office is to illumine and enkindle —
My duty, *to be saved* by their bright light,
And purified in their electric fire,
And sanctified in their elysian fire.   60
They fill my soul with Beauty (which is
    Hope),
And are far up in Heaven — the stars I
    kneel to
In the sad, silent watches of my night;
While even in the meridian glare of day
I see them still — two sweetly scintillant
Venuses, unextinguished by the sun !
1848.   1848.

THE BELLS [1]

I

HEAR the sledges with the bells —
    Silver bells !
What a world of merriment their melody
    foretells !

[1] It was shortly after this, during the summer, that
Poe wrote the first rough draft of ' The Bells,' at Mrs.
Shew's residence. ' One day he came in,' she records,
' and said, " Marie Louise, I have to write a poem ; I
have no feeling, no sentiment, no inspiration."' His
hostess persuaded him to have some tea. It was served
in the conservatory, the windows of which were open,
and admitted the sound of neighboring church bells.
Mrs. Shew said, playfully, ' Here is paper;' but the
poet, declining it, declared, ' I so dislike the noise of
bells to-night, I cannot write. I have no subject
— I am exhausted.' The lady then took up the pen,
and, pretending to mimic his style, wrote, ' The Bells,
by E. A. Poe; ' and then in pure sportiveness, ' The
Bells, the little silver Bells,' Poe finishing off the stanza.
She then suggested for the next verse, ' The heavy iron

How they tinkle, tinkle, tinkle,
　　In the icy air of night !
While the stars that oversprinkle
All the heavens, seem to twinkle
　　With a crystalline delight;
　　Keeping time, time, time,
　　In a sort of Runic rhyme,　　10
To the tintinnabulation that so musically
　　wells
From the bells, bells, bells, bells,
　　　Bells, bells, bells —
From the jingling and the tinkling of the
　bells.

II

Hear the mellow wedding bells —
　　　Golden bells !
What a world of happiness their harmony
　foretells !
Through the balmy air of night
How they ring out their delight ! —
　　From the molten-golden notes,　　20
　　　And all in tune,
　　What a liquid ditty floats
To the turtle-dove that listens, while she
　gloats

Bells;' and this Poe also expanded into a stanza. He
next copied out the complete poem, and headed it, ' By
Mrs. M. L. Shew,' remarking that it was her poem, as
she had suggested and composed so much of it. (IN-
GRAM, *Life of Poe*.)

Such was the beginning of the poem ; its development is described by the editor of *Sartain's Union
Magazine*, a month after it was first published : 'This
poem came into our possession about a year since. It
then consisted of *eighteen lines !* They were as follows :

　　　THE BELLS — A SONG

　　The bells! — hear the bells !
　　The merry wedding-bells !
　　The little silver bells !
How fairy-like a melody there swells
　　From the silver tinkling cells
　　Of the bells, bells, bells !
　　　Of the bells !

　　The bells ! — ah, the bells !
　　The heavy iron bells !
　　Hear the tolling of the bells !
　　　Hear the knells !
How horrible a monody there floats
　　From their throats —
　　From their deep-toned throats !
How I shudder at the notes
　　From the melancholy throats
　　Of the bells, bells, bells !
　　　Of the bells !

' About six months after this we received the poem
enlarged and altered nearly to its present size and
form ; and about three months since, the author sent
another alteration and enlargement, in which condition
the poem was left at the time of his death.' '

Professor Woodberry suggests that Poe probably had
the idea of his poem in mind for some time before Mrs.
Shew induced him to begin writing it, and remarks on
' his frequent reference to the magical sound of bells
throughout his literary life.' (*Life of Poe*, pp. 302–304.)
He also quotes a striking parallel passage from Chateaubriand's *Génie du Christianisme*.

　　　On the moon !
　Oh, from out the sounding cells,
What a gush of euphony voluminously
　wells !
　　How it swells !
　　How it dwells
　On the Future ! — how it tells
　Of the rapture that impels　　30
To the swinging and the ringing
　Of the bells, bells, bells —
　Of the bells, bells, bells, bells,
　　Bells, bells, bells —
To the rhyming and the chiming of the
　bells !

III

Hear the loud alarum bells —
　　　Brazen bells !
What a tale of terror, now their turbulency
　tells !
　In the startled ear of night
How they scream out their affright ! 40
　Too much horrified to speak,
　They can only shriek, shriek,
　　　Out of tune,
In a clamorous appealing to the mercy of
　the fire,
In a mad expostulation with the deaf and
　frantic fire,
　Leaping higher, higher, higher,
　　With a desperate desire,
　And a resolute endeavor
　Now — now to sit, or never,
By the side of the pale-faced moon. 50
　Oh, the bells, bells, bells !
　　What a tale their terror tells
　　　Of Despair !
How they clang, and clash, and roar !
　What a horror they outpour
On the bosom of the palpitating air !
　Yet the ear, it fully knows,
　　By the twanging,
　　And the clanging,
How the danger ebbs and flows ; 60
　Yet the ear distinctly tells,
　　In the jangling,
　　And the wrangling,
How the danger sinks and swells,
By the sinking or the swelling in the anger
　of the bells —
　　Of the bells —
　Of the bells, bells, bells, bells,
　　Bells, bells, bells —
In the clamor and the clanging of the
　bells !

IV

Hear the tolling of the bells —   70
    Iron bells!
What a world of solemn thought their
        monody compels!
    In the silence of the night,
    How we shiver with affright
At the melancholy menace of their tone!
    For every sound that floats
    From the rust within their throats
        Is a groan.
    And the people — ah, the people —
    They that dwell up in the steeple,   80
        All alone,
    And who, tolling, tolling, tolling,
        In that muffled monotone,
    Feel a glory in so rolling
        On the human heart a stone —
    They are neither man nor woman —
    They are neither brute nor human —
        They are Ghouls: —
    And their king it is who tolls: —
    And he rolls, rolls, rolls,   90
        Rolls
    A pæan from the bells !
    And his merry bosom swells
        With the pæan of the bells !
    And he dances, and he yells;
        Keeping time, time, time,
        In a sort of Runic rhyme,
    To the pæan of the bells: —
        Of the bells:
    Keeping time, time, time   100
        In a sort of Runic rhyme,
    To the throbbing of the bells —
    Of the bells, bells, bells —
        To the sobbing of the bells: —
    Keeping time, time, time,
        As he knells, knells, knells,
    In a happy Runic rhyme,
    To the rolling of the bells —
    Of the bells, bells, bells :—
        To the tolling of the bells —   110
    Of the bells, bells, bells, bells,
        Bells, bells, bells —
To the moaning and the groaning of the
        bells.

1848–49   1849.

TO MY MOTHER [1]

BECAUSE I feel that, in the Heavens above,
The angels, whispering to one another,

Can find, among their burning terms of
        love,
None so devotional as that of 'Mother,'
Therefore by that dear name I long have
        called you —
You who are more than mother unto me,
And fill my heart of hearts, where Death
        installed you,
In setting my Virginia's spirit free.
My mother — my own mother, who died
        early,
Was but the mother of myself; but you
Are mother to the one I loved so dearly,
And thus are dearer than the mother I
        knew
By that infinity with which my wife
Was dearer to my soul than its soul-life.

                                    1849.

FOR ANNIE [2]

THANK Heaven ! the crisis —
    The danger is past,
And the lingering illness
    Is over at last —
And the fever called ' Living '
    Is conquered at last.

Sadly, I know
    I am shorn of my strength,
And no muscle I move
    As I lie at full length —   10
But no matter ! — I feel
    I am better at length.

And I rest so composedly
    Now, in my bed,
That any beholder
    Might fancy me dead —
Might start at beholding me,
    Thinking me dead.

The moaning and groaning,
    The sighing and sobbing,   20
Are quieted now,
    With that horrible throbbing
At heart: — ah that horrible,
    Horrible throbbing !

The sickness — the nausea —
  The pitiless pain —
Have ceased with the fever
  That maddened my brain —
With the fever called 'Living'
  That burned in my brain.   30

And oh ! of all tortures
  That torture the worst
Has abated — the terrible
  Torture of thirst
For the napthaline river
  Of Passion accurst : —
I have drank of a water
  That quenches all thirst: —

Of a water that flows,
  With a lullaby sound,   40
From a spring but a very few
  Feet under ground —
From a cavern not very far
  Down under ground.

And ah ! let it never
  Be foolishly said
That my room it is gloomy
  And narrow my bed;
For a man never slept
  In a different bed —   50
And, to sleep, you must slumber
  In just such a bed.

My tantalized spirit
  Here blandly reposes,
Forgetting, or never
  Regretting, its roses —
Its old agitations
  Of myrtles and roses:

For now, while so quietly
  Lying, it fancies   60
A holier odor
  About it, of pansies —
A rosemary odor,
  Commingled with pansies —
With rue and the beautiful
  Puritan pansies.

And so it lies happily,
  Bathing in many
A dream of the truth
  And the beauty of Annie —   70
Drowned in a bath
  Of the tresses of Annie.

She tenderly kissed me,
  She fondly caressed,
And then I fell gently
  To sleep on her breast —
Deeply to sleep
  From the heaven of her breast.

When the light was extinguished,
  She covered me warm,   80
And she prayed to the angels
  To keep me from harm —
To the queen of the angels
  To shield me from harm.

And I lie so composedly,
  Now, in my bed,
(Knowing her love)
  That you fancy me dead —
And I rest so contentedly,
  Now, in my bed,   90
(With her love at my breast)
  That you fancy me dead —
That you shudder to look at me,
  Thinking me dead: —

But my heart it is brighter
  Than all of the many
Stars of the sky,
  For it sparkles with Annie —
It glows with the light
  Of the love of my Annie —   100
With the thought of the light
  Of the eyes of my Annie.

                              1849.

ANNABEL LEE

IT was many and many a year ago,
  In a kingdom by the sea
That a maiden there lived whom you may
    know
  By the name of ANNABEL LEE;
And this maiden she lived with no other
    thought
  Than to love and be loved by me.

I was a child and *she* was a child,
  In this kingdom by the sea,
But we loved with a love that was more
    than love —
  I and my ANNABEL LEE —   10
With a love that the wingèd seraphs of
    heaven
  Coveted her and me.

And this was the reason that, long ago,
  In this kingdom by the sea,
A wind blew out of a cloud, chilling
  My beautiful ANNABEL LEE;
So that her high-born kinsmen came
  And bore her away from me,
To shut her up in a sepulchre
  In this kingdom by the sea.   20

The angels, not half so happy in heaven,
  Went envying her and me —
Yes! — that was the reason (as all men
    know,
  In this kingdom by the sea)
That the wind came out of the cloud by
    night,
  Chilling and killing my ANNABEL LEE.

But our love it was stronger by far than
    the love
  Of those who were older than we —
  Of many far wiser than we —
And neither the angels in heaven above, 30
  Nor the demons down under the sea,
Can ever dissever my soul from the soul
  Of the beautiful ANNABEL LEE :

For the moon never beams, without bring-
    ing me dreams
  Of the beautiful ANNABEL LEE,
And the stars never rise, but I feel the
    bright eyes
  Of the beautiful ANNABEL LEE :
And so, all the night-tide, I lie down by
    the side

Of my darling — my darling — my life and
    my bride,
  In the sepulchre there by the sea —   40
  In her tomb by the sounding sea.
1849.   1849.

ELDORADO

GAILY bedight,
  A gallant knight,
In sunshine and in shadow,
  Had journeyed long,
  Singing a song,
In search of Eldorado.

But he grew old —
  This knight so bold —
And o'er his heart a shadow
  Fell as he found
  No spot of ground
That looked like Eldorado.

And, as his strength
  Failed him at length,
He met a pilgrim shadow —
  ' Shadow,' said he,
  ' Where can it be —
This land of Eldorado ? '

' Over the Mountains
  Of the Moon,
Down the Valley of the Shadow,
  Ride, boldly ride,'
  The shade replied, —
' If you seek for Eldorado.'

1850.

RALPH WALDO EMERSON

GOOD-BYE [1]

GOOD-BYE, proud world! I 'm going home:
Thou art not my friend, and I 'm not thine.
Long through the weary crowds I roam;
A river-ark on the ocean brine,
Long I 've been tossed like the driven foam;
But now, proud world! I 'm going home.

Good-bye to Flattery's fawning face;
To Grandeur with his wise grimace;
To upstart Wealth's averted eye;
To supple Office, low and high;   10
To crowded halls, to court and street;
To frozen hearts and hasting feet;
To those who go, and those who come;
Good-bye, proud world! I 'm going home.

I am going to my own hearth-stone,
Bosomed in yon green hills alone, —
A secret nook in a pleasant land,
Whose groves the frolic fairies planned;
Where arches green, the livelong day,
Echo the blackbird's roundelay,   20
And vulgar feet have never trod
A spot that is sacred to thought and God.

O, when I am safe in my sylvan home,
I tread on the pride of Greece and Rome;
And when I am stretched beneath the pines,
Where the evening star so holy shines,
I laugh at the lore and the pride of man,
At the sophist schools and the learned clan;
For what are they all, in their high conceit,
When man in the bush with God may meet?
1823.   1839.

[1] In sending these verses to Rev. James Freeman Clarke, in 1839, Emerson said: 'They were written sixteen years ago, when I kept school in Boston, and lived in a corner of Roxbury called Canterbury. They have a slight misanthropy, a shade deeper than belongs to me. . . .'
   This 'corner of Roxbury' is now a part of Franklin Park. It is called 'Schoolmaster's Hill,' and one of its rocks bears the inscription: 'Near this rock, A. D. 1823-1825, was the house of Schoolmaster Ralph Waldo Emerson. Here some of his earlier poems were written; among them that from which the following lines are taken. . . .' There follows the last stanza of this poem.

THOUGHT

I AM not poor, but I am proud,
   Of one inalienable right,
Above the envy of the crowd, —
   Thought's holy light.

Better it is than gems or gold,
   And oh! it cannot die,
But thought will glow when the sun
      grows cold,
   And mix with Deity.
1823.   1904.

THE RIVER [2]

AND I behold once more
My old familiar haunts; here the blue river,
The same blue wonder that my infant eye
Admired, sage doubting whence the travel-
      ler came, —
Whence brought his sunny bubbles ere he
      washed
The fragrant flag-roots in my father's fields,
And where thereafter in the world he went.
Look, here he is, unaltered, save that now
He hath broke his banks and flooded all
      the vales   10
With his redundant waves.
Here is the rock where, yet a simple child,
I caught with bended pin my earliest fish,
Much triumphing, — and these the fields
Over whose flowers I chased the butterfly,
A blooming hunter of a fairy fine.
And hark! where overhead the ancient
      crows
Hold their sour conversation in the sky: —
These are the same, but I am not the same,
But wiser than I was, and wise enough   19
Not to regret the changes, tho' they cost
Me many a sigh. Oh, call not nature dumb;

[2] This poem should be compared with Wordsworth's 'Lines left upon a Seat in a Yew-tree,' both because the two poems are similar in thought and mood, and because each marks the same point of development in its author's thought and powers of expression. This was written when Emerson was twenty-four years old, and Wordsworth's when he was twenty-five.

These trees and stones are audible to me,
These idle flowers, that tremble in the wind,
I understand their faery syllables,
And all their sad significance. The wind,
That rustles down the well-known forest
    road —
It hath a sound more eloquent than speech.
The stream, the trees, the grass, the sighing
    wind,
All of them utter sounds of 'monishment
And grave parental love.   30
They are not of our race, they seem to say,
And yet have knowledge of our moral
    race,
And somewhat of majestic sympathy,
Something of pity for the puny clay,
That holds and boasts the immeasurable
    mind.
I feel as I were welcome to these trees
After long months of weary wandering,
Acknowledged by their hospitable boughs;
They know me as their son, for side by
    side,
They were coeval with my ancestors,   40
Adorned with them my country's primitive
    times,
And soon may give my dust their funeral
    shade.

1827.   1904.

LINES TO ELLEN

TELL me, maiden, dost thou use
Thyself thro' Nature to diffuse ?
All the angles of the coast
Were tenanted by thy sweet ghost,
Bore thy colors every flower,
Thine each leaf and berry bore;
All wore thy badges and thy favors
In their scent or in their savors,
Every moth with painted wing,
Every bird in carolling,
The wood-boughs with thy manners waved,
The rocks uphold thy name engraved,
The sod throbbed friendly to my feet,
And the sweet air with thee was sweet.
The saffron cloud that floated warm
Studied thy motion, took thy form,
And in his airy road benign
Recalled thy skill in bold design,
Or seemed to use his privilege
To gaze o'er the horizon's edge,
To search where now thy beauty glowed,
Or made what other purlieus proud.
1829.   1904.

TO ELLEN AT THE SOUTH

THE green grass is bowing,
    The morning wind is in it;
'T is a tune worth thy knowing,
    Though it change every minute.

'T is a tune of the Spring;
    Every year plays it over
To the robin on the wing,
    And to the pausing lover.

O'er ten thousand, thousand acres,
    Goes light the nimble zephyr;   10
The Flowers — tiny sect of Shakers —
    Worship him ever.

Hark to the winning sound !
    They summon thee, dearest, —
Saying, ' We have dressed for thee the
    ground,
    Nor yet thou appearest.

' O hasten; 't is our time,
    Ere yet the red Summer
Scorch our delicate prime,
    Loved of bee, — the tawny hummer. 20

' O pride of thy race !
    Sad, in sooth, it were to ours,
If our brief tribe miss thy face,
    We poor New England flowers.

' Fairest, choose the fairest members
    Of our lithe society;
June's glories and September's
    Show our love and piety.

' Thou shalt command us all, —
    April's cowslip, summer's clover,
To the gentian in the fall,   30
    Blue-eyed pet of blue-eyed lover.

' O come, then, quickly come !
    We are budding, we are blowing;
And the wind that we perfume
    Sings a tune that 's worth the knowing.'
1829.   1843.

TO ELLEN

AND Ellen, when the graybeard years
    Have brought us to life's evening hour,
And all the crowded Past appears
    A tiny scene of sun and shower,

Then, if I read the page aright
  Where Hope, the soothsayer, reads our
      lot,
Thyself shalt own the page was bright,
  Well that we loved, woe had we not,

When Mirth is dumb and Flattery's fled,
  And mute thy music's dearest tone,
When all but Love itself is dead
  And all but deathless Reason gone.
1829.   1904.

THINE EYES STILL SHINED

THINE eyes still shined for me, though far
  I lonely roved the land or sea:
As I behold yon evening star,
  Which yet beholds not me.

This morn I climbed the misty hill
  And roamed the pastures through;
How danced thy form before my path
  Amidst the deep-eyed dew !

When the redbird spread his sable wing,
  And showed his side of flame;
When the rosebud ripened to the rose,
  In both I read thy name.
1829 or 1830.   1846.[1]

WRITTEN IN NAPLES [2]

WE are what we are made; each following
    day
Is the Creator of our human mould

[1] The first collected edition of Emerson's *Poems*, which bears the date 1847, and is listed under that year in the bibliographies, actually appeared in 1846.

[2] Remember the Sunday morning in Naples when I said, 'This moment is the truest vision, the best spectacle I have seen amid all the wonders; and this moment, this very moment, I might have had in my own closet in Boston.' (EMERSON's *Journal*, 1834.)

Compare the essay on 'Self-Reliance : ' —

'Our first journeys discover to us the indifference of places. At home I dream that at Naples, at Rome, I can be intoxicated with beauty and lose my sadness. I pack my trunk, embrace my friends, embark on the sea and at last wake up in Naples, and there beside me is the stern fact, the sad self, unrelenting, identical, that I fled from. I seek the Vatican and the palaces. I affect to be intoxicated with sights and suggestions, but I am not intoxicated. My giant goes with me wherever I go.'

Compare also 'The Day's Ration,' and Whittier's 'The Last Walk in Autumn.'

(The illustrative passages from Emerson's *Journal* given in these notes, and many of the parallel passages from Emerson's essays, are quoted by Mr. E. W. Emerson in his exceedingly valuable notes to the 'Centenary Edition' of the *Poems*, or in his *Emerson in Concord*.)

Not less than was the first; the all-wise God
Gilds a few points in every several life,
And as each flower upon the fresh hillside
And every colored petal of each flower,
Is sketched and dyed, each with a new design,
Its spot of purple, and its streak of brown,
So each man's life shall have its proper
    lights,
And a few joys, a few peculiar charms,
For him round-in the melancholy hours
And reconcile him to the common days.
Not many men see beauty in the fogs
Of close low pine-woods in a river town;
Yet unto me not morn's magnificence,
Nor the red rainbow of a summer eve,
Nor Rome, nor joyful Paris, nor the halls
Of rich men blazing hospitable light,
Nor wit, nor eloquence, — no, nor even the
    song
Of any woman that is now alive, —
Hath such a soul, such divine influence,
Such resurrection of the happy past,
As is to me when I behold the morn
Ope in such low moist roadside, and beneath
Peep the blue violets out of the black
    loam,
Pathetic silent poets that sing to me
Thine elegy, sweet singer, sainted wife.[3]
1833.   1883.

WRITTEN AT ROME [4]

ALONE in Rome. Why, Rome is lonely
    too; —
Besides, you need not be alone; the soul
Shall have society of its own rank.
Be great, be true, and all the Scipios,
The Catos, the wise patriots of Rome,
Shall flock to you and tarry by your side,
And comfort you with their high company.
Virtue alone is sweet society,
It keeps the key to all heroic hearts,
And opens you a welcome in them all.
You must be like them if you desire them,
Scorn trifles and embrace a better aim
Than wine or sleep or praise;
Hunt knowledge as the lover wooes a maid,

[3] Emerson's first wife, the 'Ellen' of the previous poems, died of consumption after they had been married only a year and a half.

[4] Don't you see you are the Universe to yourself ? You carry your fortunes in your own hand. Change of place won't mend the matter. You will weave the same web at Pernambuco as at Boston, if you have only learned how to make *one* texture. (*Journal*, Divinity Hall, Cambridge, November, 1827.)

And ever in the strife of your own thoughts
Obey the nobler impulse; that is Rome:
That shall command a senate to your side;
For there is no might in the universe
That can contend with love. It reigns for-
    ever.
Wait then, sad friend, wait in majestic peace
The hour of heaven. Generously trust
Thy fortune's web to the beneficent hand
That until now has put his world in fee
To thee. He watches for thee still. His
    love
Broods over thee, and as God lives in heaven,
However long thou walkest solitary,
The hour of heaven shall come, the man ap-
    pear.
1833.   1883.

WEBSTER[1]

ILL fits the abstemious Muse a crown to
    weave
For living brows; ill fits them to receive:
And yet, if virtue abrogate the law,
One portrait — fact or fancy — we may
    draw;
A form which Nature cast in the heroic
    mould
Of them who rescued liberty of old;
He, when the rising storm of party roared,
Brought his great forehead to the council
    board,
There, while hot heads perplexed with fears
    the state,
Calm as the morn the manly patriot sate;
Seemed, when at last his clarion accents
    broke,
As if the conscience of the country spoke.
Not on its base Monadnoc surer stood,
Than he to common sense and common
    good:
No mimic; from his breast his counsel
    drew,
Believed the eloquent was aye the true;

---

[1] The only passage from the Phi Beta Kappa poem
of 1834 which has been preserved in Emerson's Works.
After Webster's death he wrote (1854), with uninten-
tional injustice, —

    Why did all manly gifts in Webster fail ?
    He wrote on Nature's grandest brow, *For Sale.*

Compare Whittier's arraignment of Webster in 'Ichabod,' and his partial retractation in 'The Lost Occasion.' Most of the New England abolitionists, many
of whom, so long as the party of slavery was in power,
were quite willing to disrupt the Union rather than to
submit to its pro-slavery laws, could never forgive or
at all understand Webster's position in setting the
Union above all else, even abolition.

He bridged the gulf from th' alway good
    and wise
To that within the vision of small eyes.
Self-centred; when he launched the genuine
    word
It shook or captivated all who heard,
Ran from his mouth to mountains and the
    sea,
And burned in noble hearts proverb and
    prophecy.
1834.   1883.

THE RHODORA:

ON BEING ASKED, WHENCE IS THE
FLOWER?

IN May, when sea-winds pierced our soli-
    tudes,
I found the fresh Rhodora in the woods,
Spreading its leafless blooms in a damp
    nook,
To please the desert and the sluggish brook.
The purple petals, fallen in the pool,
Made the black water with their beauty
    gay;
Here might the redbird come his plumes
    to cool,
And court the flower that cheapens his ar-
    ray.
Rhodora ! if the sages ask thee why
This charm is wasted on the earth and sky,
Tell them, dear, that if eyes were made for
    seeing,
Then Beauty is its own excuse for being:[2]
Why thou wert there, O rival of the rose !
I never thought to ask, I never knew:
But, in my simple ignorance, suppose
The self-same Power that brought me there
    brought you.
1834.   1839.

EACH AND ALL

LITTLE thinks, in the field, yon red-cloaked
    clown
Of thee from the hill-top looking down;
The heifer that lows in the upland farm,

---

[2] Compare the chapter on Beauty, in Emerson's
'Nature:' 'This element [Beauty] I call an ultimate
end. No reason can be asked or given why the soul
seeks beauty. Beauty, in its largest and profoundest
sense, is one expression for the universe. . . . The
ancient Greeks called the world κόσμος, Beauty.'
Compare also the 'Michael Angelo:' 'Beauty cannot be defined. Like Truth, it is an ultimate aim of
the human being.'

Far-heard, lows not thine ear to charm;
The sexton, tolling his bell at noon,
Deems not that great Napoleon
Stops his horse, and lists with delight,
Whilst his files sweep round yon Alpine
        height; [1]
Nor knowest thou what argument
Thy life to thy neighbor's creed has lent. 10
All are needed by each one;
Nothing is fair or good alone.
I thought the sparrow's note from heaven,
Singing at dawn on the alder bough;
I brought him home, in his nest, at even;
He sings the song, but it cheers not now,
For I did not bring home the river and sky; —
He sang to my ear, — they sang to my
        eye.
The delicate shells lay on the shore;
The bubbles of the latest wave   20
Fresh pearls to their enamel gave,
And the bellowing of the savage sea
Greeted their safe escape to me.
I wiped away the weeds and foam,
I fetched my sea-born treasures home;
But the poor, unsightly, noisome things
Had left their beauty on the shore
With the sun and the sand and the wild up-
        roar.[2]
The lover watched his graceful maid,
As 'mid the virgin train she strayed,   30
Nor knew her beauty's best attire
Was woven still by the snow-white choir.
At last she came to his hermitage,
Like the bird from the woodlands to the
        cage; —
The gay enchantment was undone,
A gentle wife, but fairy none.
Then I said, 'I covet truth;
Beauty is unripe childhood's cheat;
I leave it behind with the games of
        youth: ' —
As I spoke, beneath my feet   40
The ground-pine curled its pretty wreath,
Running over the club-moss burrs;

[1] Buonaparte was sensible to the music of bells.
Hearing the bell of a parish church, he would pause,
and his voice faltered as he said, 'Ah! that reminds
me of the first years I spent at Brienne; I was then
happy.' (*Journal*, 1844.)
[2] I remember when I was a boy going upon the beach
and being charmed with the colors and forms of the
shells. I picked up many and put them in my pocket.
When I got home I could find nothing that I gathered
— nothing but some dry, ugly mussel and snail shells.
Thence I learned that Composition was more important
than the beauty of individual forms to Effect. On the
shore they lay wet and social, by the sea and under the
sky. (*Journal*, May 16, 1834.)

I inhaled the violet's breath;
Around me stood the oaks and firs;
Pine-cones and acorns lay on the ground;
Over me soared the eternal sky,
Full of light and of deity;
Again I saw, again I heard,
The rolling river, the morning bird; —
Beauty through my senses stole;   50
I yielded myself to the perfect whole.
1834 ?   1839.

THE APOLOGY[3]

THINK me not unkind and rude
    That I walk alone in grove and glen;
I go to the god of the wood
    To fetch his word to men.

Tax not my sloth that I
    Fold my arms beside the brook;
Each cloud that floated in the sky
    Writes a letter in my book.

Chide me not, laborious band,
    For the idle flowers I brought;
Every aster in my hand
    Goes home loaded with a thought.

There was never mystery
    But 't is figured in the flowers;
Was never secret history
    But birds tell it in the bowers.

One harvest from thy field
    Homeward brought the oxen strong;
A second crop thine acres yield,
    Which I gather in a song.[4]
1834 ?   1846.

[3] Compare Wordsworth's 'Expostulation and Reply,' and 'The Tables Turned.'
Compare also a passage in Emerson's description of
Thoreau, as reported by Charles J. Woodbury: —
    'Men of note would come to talk with him.
    ' "I don't know," he would say ; "perhaps a minute
would be enough for both of us."
    ' "But I come to walk with you when you take your
exercise."
    ' "Ah, walking — that is my holy time." ' (WOOD-
BURY's *Talks with Emerson*, p. 80.)
[4] Compare the beautiful lines in Emerson's poem,
'The Dirge,' 1838 : —

        Knows he who tills this lonely field
          To reap its scanty corn,
        What mystic fruit his acres yield
          At midnight and at morn ?

        In the long sunny afternoon
          The plain was full of ghosts ;
        I wandered up, I wandered down,
          Beset by pensive hosts.

CONCORD HYMN [1]

SUNG AT THE COMPLETION OF THE BAT-
TLE MONUMENT, JULY 4, 1837

By the rude bridge that arched the flood,
  Their flag to April's breeze unfurled,
Here once the embattled farmers stood
  And fired the shot heard round the world.

The foe long since in silence slept;
  Alike the conqueror silent sleeps;
And Time the ruined bridge has swept
  Down the dark stream which seaward
    creeps.

On this green bank, by this soft stream,
  We set to-day a votive stone;
That memory may their deed redeem,
  When, like our sires, our sons are gone.

Spirit, that made those heroes dare
  To die, and leave their children free,
Bid Time and Nature gently spare
  The shaft we raise to them and thee.
1837.   1837.

THE HUMBLE-BEE [2]

  Burly, dozing humble-bee,
  Where thou art is clime for me.
  Let them sail for Porto Rique,
  Far-off heats through seas to seek;
  I will follow thee alone,
  Thou animated torrid-zone!

Zigzag steerer, desert cheerer,
Let me chase thy waving lines;
Keep me nearer, me thy hearer,
Singing over shrubs and vines.   10

Insect lover of the sun,
Joy of thy dominion!
Sailor of the atmosphere;
Swimmer through the waves of air;
Voyager of light and noon;
Epicurean of June;
Wait, I prithee, till I come
Within earshot of thy hum, —
All without is martyrdom.

When the south wind, in May days,   20
With a net of shining haze
Silvers the horizon wall,
And with softness touching all,
Tints the human countenance
With a color of romance,
And infusing subtle heats,
Turns the sod to violets,
Thou, in sunny solitudes,
Rover of the underwoods,
The green silence dost displace   30
With thy mellow, breezy bass.

Hot midsummer's petted crone,
Sweet to me thy drowsy tone
Tells of countless sunny hours,
Long days, and solid banks of flowers;
Of gulfs of sweetness without bound
In Indian wildernesses found;
Of Syrian peace, immortal leisure,
Firmest cheer, and bird-like pleasure.

Aught unsavory or unclean   40
Hath my insect never seen;
But violets and bilberry bells,
Maple-sap and daffodels,
Grass with green flag half-mast high,
Succory to match the sky,
Columbine with horn of honey,
Scented fern, and agrimony,
Clover, catchfly, adder's-tongue
And brier-roses, dwelt among;
All beside was unknown waste,   50
All was picture as he passed.

Wiser far than human seer,
Yellow-breeched philosopher!
Seeing only what is fair,
Sipping only what is sweet,
Thou dost mock at fate and care,

---

[1] Compare Emerson's 'Historical Discourse at Concord, September 12, 1835,' and his 'Address at the Hundredth Anniversary of the Concord Fight,' especially a passage in the first of these addresses, describing the battle and its motives: ' These poor farmers who came up, that day, to defend their native soil, acted from the simplest instincts. They did not know it was a deed of fame they were doing,' etc.

The first quatrain of the poem is now inscribed on the Battle Monument at Concord.

Emerson's grandfather, William Emerson, was minister at Concord in 1775; in his pulpit he strongly advocated resistance to the British, and when the day of the fight came, he was among the ' embattled farmers.' The fight took place near his own house, later known as ' The old Manse,' and the home successively of Emerson and of Hawthorne. (See Bartlett's *Concord, Historic and Literary.*) 'Let us stand our ground,' he said to the minutemen; ' if we die, let us die here.'

[2] Containing much of the quintessence of poetry. (Longfellow.)

Yesterday in the woods I followed the fine humble-bee with rhymes and fancies fine. . . . The humble-bee and pine-warbler seem to me the proper objects of attention in these disastrous times. (*Journal*, 1837.)

Leave the chaff, and take the wheat.
When the fierce northwestern blast
Cools sea and land so far and fast,
Thou already slumberest deep;   60
Woe and want thou canst outsleep;
Want and woe, which torture us,
Thy sleep makes ridiculous.

1837 ?   1839.

URIEL [1]

It fell in the ancient periods
    Which the brooding soul surveys,
Or ever the wild Time coined itself
    Into calendar months and days.

This was the lapse of Uriel
    Which in Paradise befell.
Once, among the Pleiads walking,
Seyd overheard the young gods talking;
And the treason, too long pent,
To his ears was evident.   10
The young deities discussed
Laws of form, and metre just,
Orb, quintessence, and sunbeams,
What subsisteth and what seems.
One, with low tones that decide,
And doubt and reverend use defied,
With a look that solved the sphere,
And stirred the devils everywhere,
Gave his sentiment divine
Against the being of a line.   20
' Line in nature is not found;
Unit and universe are round;
In vain produced, all rays return;
Evil will bless, and ice will burn.'
As Uriel spoke with piercing eye,
A shudder ran around the sky;
The stern old war-gods shook their heads,
The seraphs frowned from myrtle-beds;

[1] From its strange presentation in a celestial parable of the story of a crisis in its author's life, this poem demands especial comment. In his essay on 'Circles' — which sheds light upon it — Emerson said, 'Beware when the great God lets loose a thinker on this planet.'
The earnest young men on the eve of entering the ministry asked him to speak to them. After serious thought he went to Cambridge (July 15, 1838) to give them the good and emancipating words which had been given to him in solitude, well aware, however, that he must shock or pain the older clergy who were present. The poem, when read with the history of the Divinity School Address, and its consequences, in mind, is seen to be an account of that event generalized and sublimed, — the announcement of an advance in truth, won not without pain and struggle, to hearers not yet ready, resulting in banishment to the prophet; yet the spoken word sticks like a barbed arrow, or works like a leaven. (E. W. EMERSON.)

Seemed to the holy festival
The rash word boded ill to all;   30
The balance-beam of Fate was bent;
The bounds of good and ill were rent;
Strong Hades could not keep his own,
But all slid to confusion.

A sad self-knowledge, withering, fell
On the beauty of Uriel;
In heaven once eminent, the god
Withdrew, that hour, into his cloud;
Whether doomed to long gyration
In the sea of generation,   40
Or by knowledge grown too bright
To hit the nerve of feebler sight.
Straightway, a forgetting wind
Stole over the celestial kind,
And their lips the secret kept,
If in ashes the fire-seed slept.
But now and then, truth-speaking things
Shamed the angels' veiling wings;
And, shrilling from the solar course,
Or from fruit of chemic force,   50
Procession of a soul in matter,
Or the speeding change of water,
Or out of the good of evil born,
Came Uriel's voice of cherub scorn,
And a blush tinged the upper sky,
And the gods shook, they knew not why.

1838.   1846.

THE PROBLEM [2]

I like a church; I like a cowl;
I love a prophet of the soul;
And on my heart monastic aisles
Fall like sweet strains, or pensive smiles;
Yet not for all his faith can see
Would I that cowlèd churchman be.

Why should the vest on him allure,
Which I could not on me endure ?

Not from a vain or shallow thought [3]
His awful Jove young Phidias brought;
Never from lips of cunning fell   11
The thrilling Delphic oracle;

[2] It is very grateful to my feelings to go into a Roman Cathedral, yet I look as my countrymen do at the Roman priesthood. It is very grateful to me to go into an English Church and hear the liturgy read, yet nothing would induce me to be the English priest. (*Journal*, August 28, 1838.)

[3] Compare the essay on 'Compensation:' 'This voice of fable has in it something divine. It came from thought above the will of the writer. . . . Phidias it is not,' etc.

Out from the heart of nature rolled
The burdens of the Bible old;
The litanies of nations came,
Like the volcano's tongue of flame,
Up from the burning core below, —
The canticles of love and woe:
The hand that rounded Peter's dome [1]
And groined the aisles of Christian Rome
Wrought in a sad sincerity: [2]   21
Himself from God he could not free; [3]
He builded better than he knew; — [4]
The conscious stone to beauty grew.
Know'st thou what wove yon woodbird's
        nest
Of leaves, and feathers from her breast ?
Or how the fish outbuilt her shell,
Painting with morn her annual cell ?
Or how the sacred pine-tree adds
To her old leaves new myriads ?   30
Such and so grew these holy piles,
Whilst love and terror laid the tiles.
Earth proudly wears the Parthenon,
As the best gem upon her zone,
And Morning opes with haste her lids
To gaze upon the Pyramids ;
O'er England's abbeys bends the sky,
As on its friends, with kindred eye ;
For out of Thought's interior sphere
These wonders rose to upper air ; [5]   40
And Nature gladly gave them place,
Adopted them into her race,
And granted them an equal date
With Andes and with Ararat. [6]

These temples grew as grows the grass;
Art might obey, but not surpass.
The passive Master lent his hand
To the vast soul that o'er him planned; [7]
And the same power that reared the
        shrine
Bestrode the tribes that knelt within.   50
Ever the fiery Pentecost
Girds with one flame the countless host,
Trances the heart through chanting choirs,
And through the priest the mind in-
        spires.
The word unto the prophet spoken
Was writ on tables yet unbroken;
The word by seers or sibyls told,
In groves of oak, or fanes of gold,
Still floats upon the morning wind,
Still whispers to the willing mind.   60
One accent of the Holy Ghost
The heedless world hath never lost.
I know what say the fathers wise,
The Book itself before me lies,
Old *Chrysostom*, best Augustine,
And he who blent both in his line,
The younger *Golden Lips* or mines,
Taylor, the Shakspeare of divines.
His words are music in my ear,
I see his cowlèd portrait dear;   70
And yet, for all his faith could see,
I would not the good bishop be.
1839.   1840.

WRITTEN IN A VOLUME OF GOETHE [8]

Six thankful weeks, — and let it be
A meter of prosperity, —
In my coat I bore this book,
And seldom therein could I look,
For I had too much to think,
Heaven and earth to eat and drink.
Is he hapless who can spare
In his plenty things so rare ?
1840 ?   1883.

---

[1] See Emerson's essay on 'Michael Angelo ;' and the quotation from his 'Poetry and Imagination,' in note 7 in the next column.

[2] Compare Emerson's essay on 'Art :' 'The Iliad of Homer, the songs of David, the odes of Pindar, the tragedies of Æschylus, the Doric temples, the Gothic cathedrals, the plays of Shakespeare, all and each were made not for sport, but in grave earnest, in tears and smiles of suffering and loving men.'

[3] Compare the essay on 'Art :' 'The Gothic cathedrals were built when the builder and the priest and the people were overpowered by their faith. Love and fear laid every stone.' Compare also line 32 of the poem : —

Whilst love and terror laid the tiles.

[4] Compare the essay on 'Art :' ' Our arts are happy hits. We are like the musician on the lake, whose melody is sweeter than he knows.'

[5] It is in the soul that architecture exists, and Santa Croce and the Duomo are poor, far-behind imitations. (*Journal*, Florence, 1833.)

[6] Compare the essay on 'Art :' ' And so every genuine work of art has as much reason for being as the earth and the sun. . . . We feel in seeing a noble building which rhymes well, as we do in hearing a perfect song, that it is spiritually organic ; that it had a necessity in nature for being ; was one of the possible forms in the Divine mind, and is now only discovered and executed by the artist, not arbitrarily composed by him.'

[7] Compare Emerson's essay on 'Poetry and Imagination,' in *Letters and Social Aims :* ' Michael Angelo is largely filled with the Creator that made and makes men. How much of the original craft remains in him, and he a mortal man . . . . He knows that he did not make his thought, — no, his thought made him, and made the sun and stars.'

[8] Emerson wrote to Carlyle, in April, 1840 : ' You asked me if I read German. . . . I have contrived to read almost every volume of Goethe, and I have fifty-five, but I have read nothing else — but I have not now looked even into Goethe, for a long time.'

WOODNOTES

I

1

WHEN the pine tosses its cones
To the song of its waterfall tones,
Who speeds to the woodland walks?
To birds and trees who talks?
Cæsar of his leafy Rome,
There the poet is at home.
He goes to the river-side, —
Not hook nor line hath he;
He stands in the meadows wide, —
Nor gun nor scythe to see.   10
Sure some god his eye enchants:
What he knows nobody wants.
In the wood he travels glad,
Without better fortune had,
Melancholy without bad.
Knowledge this man prizes best
Seems fantastic to the rest:
Pondering shadows, colors, clouds,
Grass-buds and caterpillar-shrouds,
Boughs on which the wild bees settle,   20
Tints that spot the violet's petal,
Why Nature loves the number five,
And why the star-form she repeats: [1]
Lover of all things alive,
Wonderer at all he meets,
Wonderer chiefly at himself,
Who can tell him what he is?
Or how meet in human elf
Coming and past eternities?

2

And such I knew, a forest seer,   30
A minstrel of the natural year,
Foreteller of the vernal ides,
Wise harbinger of spheres and tides,
A lover true, who knew by heart
Each joy the mountain dales impart;
It seemed that Nature could not raise
A plant in any secret place,
In quaking bog, on snowy hill,
Beneath the grass that shades the rill,
Under the snow, between the rocks,   40
In damp fields known to bird and fox,
But he would come in the very hour
It opened in its virgin bower,

As if a sunbeam showed the place,
And tell its long-descended race.
It seemed as if the breezes brought him,
It seemed as if the sparrows taught him;
As if by secret sight he knew
Where, in far fields, the orchis grew.
Many haps fall in the field   50
Seldom seen by wishful eyes,
But all her shows did Nature yield,
To please and win this pilgrim wise.
He saw the partridge drum in the woods; [2]
He heard the woodcock's evening hymn;
He found the tawny thrushes' broods;
And the shy hawk did wait for him; [3]
What others did at distance hear,
And guessed within the thicket's gloom,
Was shown to this philosopher,   60
And at his bidding seemed to come. [4]

3

In unploughed Maine he sought the lum-
    berers' gang
Where from a hundred lakes young rivers
    sprang;
He trode the unplanted forest floor, whereon
The all-seeing sun for ages hath not shone;
Where feeds the moose, and walks the surly
    bear,
And up the tall mast runs the woodpecker.
He saw beneath dim aisles, in odorous beds,
The slight Linnæa hang its twin-born heads,
And blessed the monument of the man of
    flowers,   70
Which breathes his sweet fame through the
    northern bowers.
He heard, when in the grove, at intervals,
With sudden roar the aged pine-tree falls,—
One crash, the death-hymn of the perfect
    tree,
Declares the close of its green century.

---

[1] Trifles move us more than laws. Why am I more curious to know the reason why the star-form is so oft repeated in botany, or why the number five is such a favorite with Nature, than to understand the circulation of the sap and the formation of bud? (*Journal*, 1835.)

[2] Compare Emerson's 'Thoreau:' 'His powers of observation seemed to indicate additional senses. He saw as with microscope, heard as with ear-trumpet, and his memory was a photographic register of all he saw and heard. And yet none knew better than he that it is not the fact that imprints but the impression or effect of the fact on your mind. Every fact lay in glory in his mind, a type of the order and beauty of the whole.'

[3] Compare the 'Thoreau' again: 'He knew how to sit immovable, a part of the rock he rested on, until the bird, the reptile, the fish, which had retired from him, should come back and resume its habits,—nay, moved by curiosity, should come to him and watch him.'

[4] The passages about the forest seer fit Thoreau so well that the general belief that Mr. Emerson had him in mind may be accepted, but one member of the family recalls his saying that a part of this picture was drawn before he knew Thoreau's gifts and experiences. (E. W. EMERSON, in the *Centenary Edition*.)

Low lies the plant to whose creation went
Sweet influence from every element;
Whose living towers the years conspired to
    build,
Whose giddy top the morning loved to gild.
Through these green tents, by eldest Nature
    dressed,   80
He roamed, content alike with man and
    beast.
Where darkness found him he lay glad at
    night;
There the red morning touched him with its
    light.
Three moons his great heart him a hermit
    made,
So long he roved at will the boundless shade.
The timid it concerns to ask their way,
And fear what foe in caves and swamps can
    stray,
To make no step until the event is known,
And ills to come as evils past bemoan.
Not so the wise ; no coward watch he
    keeps   90
To spy what danger on his pathway creeps;
Go where he will, the wise man is at home,[1]
His hearth the earth, — his hall the azure
    dome;
Where his clear spirit leads him, there's
    his road
By God's own light illumined and fore-
    showed.

4

'T was one of the charmèd days
When the genius of God doth flow;
The wind may alter twenty ways,
A tempest cannot blow;
It may blow north, it still is warm;   100
Or south, it still is clear;
Or east, it smells like a clover-farm;
Or west, no thunder fear.
The musing peasant, lowly great,
Beside the forest water sate;
The rope-like pine-roots crosswise grown
Composed the network of his throne;
The wide lake, edged with sand and grass,
Was burnished to a floor of glass,
Painted with shadows green and proud   110
Of the tree and of the cloud.
He was the heart of all the scene;
On him the sun looked more serene;
To hill and cloud his face was known, —
It seemed the likeness of their own;
They knew by secret sympathy

[1] Cf. the note on 'Written in Naples,' p. 60.

The public child of earth and sky.
'You ask,' he said, 'what guide
Me through trackless thickets led,
Through thick-stemmed woodlands rough
    and wide.   120
I found the water's bed.
The watercourses were my guide;
I travelled grateful by their side,
Or through their channel dry;
They led me through the thicket damp,
Through brake and fern, the beavers' camp,
Through beds of granite cut my road,
And their resistless friendship showed.
The falling waters led me,
The foodful waters fed me,   130
And brought me to the lowest land,
Unerring to the ocean sand.
The moss upon the forest bark
Was pole-star when the night was dark;
The purple berries in the wood
Supplied me necessary food;
For Nature ever faithful is
To such as trust her faithfulness.
When the forest shall mislead me,
When the night and morning lie,   140
When sea and land refuse to feed me,
'T will be time enough to die;
Then will yet my mother yield
A pillow in her greenest field,
Nor the June flowers scorn to cover
The clay of their departed lover.'

                1840.

WOODNOTES[2]

II

As sunbeams stream through liberal space
And nothing jostle or displace,
So waved the pine-tree through my thought
And fanned the dreams it never brought.

'Whether is better, the gift or the donor?
Come to me,'

[2] The stately white pine of New England was Emerson's favorite tree. . . . This poem records the actual fact ; nearly every day, summer or winter, when at home, he went to listen to its song. The pine grove by Walden, still standing, though injured by time and fire, was one of his most valued possessions. He questioned whether he should not name his book *Forest Essays*, for, he said, 'I have scarce a day-dream on which the breath of the pines has not blown and their shadow waved.' The great pine on the ridge over Sleepy Hollow was chosen by him as his monument. When a youth, in Newton, he had written, 'Here sit Mother and I under the pine-trees, still almost as we shall lie by and by under them.' — (E. W. EMERSON, in the *Centenary Edition*.)

Quoth the pine-tree,
' I am the giver of honor.
My garden is the cloven rock,
And my manure the snow;   10
And drifting sand-heaps feed my stock,
In summer's scorching glow.
He is great who can live by me:
The rough and bearded forester
Is better than the lord;
God fills the scrip and canister,
Sin piles the loaded board.
The lord is the peasant that was,
The peasant the lord that shall be;
The lord is hay, the peasant grass,   20
One dry, and one the living tree.
Who liveth by the ragged pine
Foundeth a heroic line;
Who liveth in the palace hall
Waneth fast and spendeth all.[1]
He goes to my savage haunts,
With his chariot and his care;
My twilight realm he disenchants,
And finds his prison there.

What prizes the town and the tower ? 30
Only what the pine-tree yields;
Sinew that subdued the fields;
The wild-eyed boy, who in the woods
Chants his hymn to hills and floods,
Whom the city's poisoning spleen
Made not pale, or fat, or lean;
Whom the rain and the wind purgeth,
Whom the dawn and the day-star urgeth,
In whose cheek the rose-leaf blusheth,
In whose feet the lion rusheth   40
Iron arms, and iron mould,
That know not fear, fatigue, or cold.
I give my rafters to his boat,
My billets to his boiler's throat,
And I will swim the ancient sea
To float my child to victory,
And grant to dwellers with the pine
Dominion o'er the palm and vine.
Who leaves the pine-tree, leaves his friend,
Unnerves his strength, invites his end. 50
Cut a bough from my parent stem,
And dip it in thy porcelain vase;
A little while each russet gem
Will swell and rise with wonted grace;
But when it seeks enlarged supplies,
The orphan of the forest dies.

[1] Compare the essay on 'Manners:' 'The city
would have died out, rotted and exploded, long ago,
but that it was reinforced from the fields. It is only
country which came to town day before yesterday that
is city and court to-day.'

Whoso walks in solitude
And inhabiteth the wood,
Choosing light, wave, rock and bird,
Before the money-loving herd,   60
Into that forester shall pass,
From these companions, power and grace.
Clean shall he be, without, within,
From the old adhering sin,
All ill dissolving in the light
Of his triumphant piercing sight:
Not vain, sour, nor frivolous;
Not mad, athirst, nor garrulous;
Grave, chaste, contented, though retired,
And of all other men desired.   70
On him the light of star and moon
Shall fall with purer radiance down;
All constellations of the sky
Shed their virtue through his eye.
Him Nature giveth for defence
His formidable innocence;
The mountain sap, the shells, the sea,
All spheres, all stones, his helpers be;
He shall meet the speeding year,
Without wailing, without fear;   80
He shall be happy in his love,
Like to like shall joyful prove;
He shall be happy whilst he wooes,
Muse-born, a daughter of the Muse.
But if with gold she bind her hair,
And deck her breast with diamond,
Take off thine eyes, thy heart forbear,
Though thou lie alone on the ground.

' Heed the old oracles,
Ponder my spells;   90
Song wakes in my pinnacles
When the wind swells.
Soundeth the prophetic wind,
The shadows shake on the rock behind,
And the countless leaves of the pine are
          strings
Tuned to the lay the wood-god sings.
          Hearken ! Hearken !
If thou wouldst know the mystic song
Chanted when the sphere was young.
Aloft, abroad, the pæan swells;   100
O wise man ! hear'st thou half it tells ?
O wise man ! hear'st thou the least part ?
'T is the chronicle of art.
To the open ear it sings
Sweet the genesis of things,
Of tendency through endless ages,[2]

[2] These lines are a sort of poetic 'Doctrine of Evolution.' Compare the 1849 motto of Emerson's 'Nature' (p. 87). It is interesting to remember Tyndall's

Of star-dust, and star-pilgrimages,
Of rounded worlds, of space and time,
Of the old flood's subsiding slime,
Of chemic matter, force and form,   110
Of poles and powers, cold, wet, and warm:
The rushing metamorphosis
Dissolving all that fixture is,
Melts things that be to things that seem,
And solid nature to a dream.
O, listen to the undersong,
The ever old, the ever young;
And, far within those cadent pauses,
The chorus of the ancient Causes !
Delights the dreadful Destiny   120
To fling his voice into the tree,
And shock thy weak ear with a note
Breathed from the everlasting throat.
In music he repeats the pang
Whence the fair flock of Nature sprang.
O mortal ! thy ears are stones;
These echoes are laden with tones
Which only the pure can hear;
Thou canst not catch what they recite
Of Fate and Will, of Want and Right,   130
Of man to come, of human life,
Of Death and Fortune, Growth and Strife.'

Once again the pine-tree sung : —
'Speak not thy speech my boughs among :
Put off thy years, wash in the breeze ;
My hours are peaceful centuries.
Talk no more with feeble tongue;
No more the fool of space and time,
Come weave with mine a nobler rhyme.
Only thy Americans   140
Can read thy line, can meet thy glance,
But the runes that I rehearse
Understands the universe;
The least breath my boughs which tossed
Brings again the Pentecost;
To every soul resounding clear
In a voice of solemn cheer, —
" Am I not thine ? Are not these thine ? "
And they reply, " Forever mine ! "
My branches speak Italian,   150
English, German, Basque, Castilian,
Mountain speech to Highlanders,
Ocean tongues to islanders,
To Fin and Lap and swart Malay,
To each his bosom-secret say.

' Come learn with me the fatal song
Which knits the world in music strong,

saying: ' Whatever I have done the world owes to Emerson.'

Come lift thine eyes to lofty rhymes,
Of things with things, of times with times,
Primal chimes of sun and shade,   160
Of sound and echo, man and maid,
The land reflected in the flood,
Body with shadow still pursued.
For Nature beats in perfect tune,
And rounds with rhyme her every rune,
Whether she work in land or sea,
Or hide underground her alchemy.
Thou canst not wave thy staff in air,
Or dip thy paddle in the lake,
But it carves the bow of beauty there,   170
And the ripples in rhymes the oar forsake.[1]
The wood is wiser far than thou;
The wood and wave each other know
Not unrelated, unaffied,
But to each thought and thing allied,
Is perfect Nature's every part,
Rooted in the mighty Heart.
But thou, poor child ! unbound, unrhymed,
Whence camest thou, misplaced, mistimed,
Whence, O thou orphan and defrauded ?   180
Is thy land peeled, thy realm marauded ?
Who thee divorced, deceived and left ?
Thee of thy faith who hath bereft,
And torn the ensigns from thy brow,
And sunk the immortal eye so low ?
Thy cheek too white, thy form too slender,
Thy gait too slow, thy habits tender
For royal man; — they thee confess
An exile from the wilderness, —
The hills where health with health agrees,
And the wise soul expels disease.   191
Hark ! in thy ear I will tell the sign
By which thy hurt thou may'st divine.
When thou shalt climb the mountain cliff,
Or see the wide shore from thy skiff,
To thee the horizon shall express
But emptiness on emptiness;
There lives no man of Nature's worth
In the circle of the earth;
And to thine eye the vast skies fall,   200
Dire and satirical,

[1] ' As for beauty, I need not look beyond an oar's length for my fill of it.' I do not know whether he [William Ellery Channing] used the expression with design or no, but my eye rested on the charming play of light on the water which he was striking with his paddle. I fancied I had never seen such color, such transparency, such eddies ; it was the hue of Rhine wines, it was jasper and verd-antique, topaz and chalcedony, it was gold and green and chestnut and hazel in bewitching succession and relief, without cloud or confusion. (*Journal*, 1846.)

Compare also the paragraph in Emerson's ' Nature' beginning : ' It seems as if the day was not wholly profane in which we have given heed to some natural object.'

On clucking hens and prating fools,
On thieves, on drudges and on dolls.
And thou shalt say to the Most High,
"Godhead ! all this astronomy,
And fate and practice and invention,
Strong art and beautiful pretension,
This radiant pomp of sun and star,
Throes that were, and worlds that are,
Behold ! were in vain and in vain; —   210
It cannot be, — I will look again.[1]
Surely now will the curtain rise,
And earth's fit tenant me surprise; —
But the curtain doth *not* rise,
And Nature has miscarried wholly
Into failure, into folly."

' Alas ! thine is the bankruptcy,
Blessed Nature so to see.
Come, lay thee in my soothing shade,
And heal the hurts which sin has made.   220
I see thee in the crowd alone;
I will be thy companion.
Quit thy friends as the dead in doom,
And build to them a final tomb;
Let the starred shade that nightly falls
Still celebrate their funerals,
And the bell of beetle and of bee
Knell their melodious memory.
Behind thee leave thy merchandise,
Thy churches and thy charities;   230
And leave thy peacock wit behind;
Enough for thee the primal mind
That flows in streams, that breathes in wind:
Leave all thy pedant lore apart;
God hid the whole world in thy heart.
Love shuns the sage, the child it crowns,
Gives all to them who all renounce.
The rain comes when the wind calls;
The river knows the way to the sea;
Without a pilot it runs and falls,   240
Blessing all lands with its charity;
The sea tosses and foams to find
Its way up to the cloud and wind;
The shadow sits close to the flying ball;
The date fails not on the palm-tree tall;
And thou, — go burn thy wormy pages, —
Shalt outsee seers, and outwit sages.
Oft didst thou thread the woods in vain
To find what bird had piped the strain: —

[1] What has the imagination created to compare with the science of Astronomy ? What is there in *Paradise Lost* to elevate and astonish like Herschel or Somerville ? The contrast between the magnitude and duration of the things, and the animalcule observer ! . . . I hope the time will come when there will be a telescope in every street. (*Journal*, May, 1832.)

Seek not, and the little eremite   250
Flies gayly forth and sings in sight.

' Hearken once more !
I will tell thee the mundane lore.
Older am I than thy numbers wot,
Change I may, but I pass not.
Hitherto all things fast abide,
And anchored in the tempest ride,
Trenchant time behoves to hurry
All to yean and all to bury:
All the forms are fugitive,   260
But the substances survive.
Ever fresh the broad creation,
A divine improvisation,
From the heart of God proceeds,
A single will, a million deeds.
Once slept the world an egg of stone,
And pulse, and sound, and light was none;
And God said, "Throb !" and there was
        motion
And the vast mass became vast ocean.
Onward and on, the eternal Pan,   270
Who layeth the world's incessant plan,
Halteth never in one shape,
But forever doth escape,
Like wave or flame, into new forms
Of gem, and air, of plants, and worms.
I, that to-day am a pine,
Yesterday was a bundle of grass.
He is free and libertine,
Pouring of his power the wine
To every age, to every race;   280
Unto every race and age
He emptieth the beverage;
Unto each, and unto all,
Maker and original.
The world is the ring of his spells,
And the play of his miracles.
As he giveth to all to drink,
Thus or thus they are and think.
With one drop sheds form and feature;
With the next a special nature;   290
The third adds heat's indulgent spark;
The fourth gives light which eats the dark;
Into the fifth himself he flings,
And conscious Law is King of kings.
As the bee through the garden ranges,
From world to world the godhead changes;
As the sheep go feeding in the waste,
From form to form He maketh haste;
This vault which glows immense with light
Is the inn where he lodges for a night.   300
What recks such Traveller if the bowers
Which bloom and fade like meadow flowers

A bunch of fragrant lilies be,
Or the stars of eternity?
Alike to him the better, the worse, —
The glowing angel, the outcast corse.
Thou metest him by centuries,
And lo! he passes like the breeze;
Thou seek'st in globe and galaxy,
He hides in pure transparency; 310
Thou askest in fountains and in fires,
He is the essence that inquires.
He is the axis of the star;
He is the sparkle of the spar;
He is the heart of every creature;
He is the meaning of each feature;
And his mind is the sky,
Than all it holds more deep, more high.'
1841.

THE SPHINX[1]

THE Sphinx is drowsy,
    Her wings are furled:
Her ear is heavy,
    She broods on the world.
'Who 'll tell me my secret,
    The ages have kept? —
I awaited the seer
    While they slumbered and slept: —

'The fate of the man-child,
    The meaning of man; 10
Known fruit of the unknown;
    Dædalian plan;
Out of sleeping a waking,
    Out of waking a sleep;
Life death overtaking;
    Deep underneath deep?

'Erect as a sunbeam,
    Upspringeth the palm;
The elephant browses,
    Undaunted and calm; 20
In beautiful motion
    The thrush plies his wings;
Kind leaves of his covert,
    Your silence he sings.

'The waves, unashamèd,
    In difference sweet,
Play glad with the breezes,
    Old playfellows meet;
The journeying atoms,
    Primordial wholes, 30
Firmly draw, firmly drive,
    By their animate poles.

'Sea, earth, air, sound, silence,
    Plant, quadruped, bird,
By one music enchanted,
    One deity stirred, —
Each the other adorning,
    Accompany still;
Night veileth the morning,
    The vapor the hill. 40

'The babe by its mother
    Lies bathèd in joy;
Glide its hours uncounted, —
    The sun is its toy;
Shines the peace of all being,
    Without cloud, in its eyes;
And the sum of the world
    In soft miniature lies.

'But man crouches and blushes,
    Absconds and conceals; 50
He creepeth and peepeth,
    He palters and steals;
Infirm, melancholy,
    Jealous glancing around,
An oaf, an accomplice,
    He poisons the ground.[2]

'Out spoke the great mother,
    Beholding his fear; —
At the sound of her accents
    Cold shuddered the sphere: — 60
"Who has drugged my boy's cup?
    Who has mixed my boy's bread?
Who, with sadness and madness,
    Has turned my child's head?"'

I heard a poet answer
    Aloud and cheerfully,
'Say on, sweet Sphinx! thy dirges

---

[1] Mr. Emerson wrote in his note-book in 1859: 'I have often been asked the meaning of the "Sphinx." It is this: The perception of identity unites all things and explains one by another, and the most rare and strange is equally facile as the most common. But if the mind live only in particulars, and see only differences (wanting the power to see the whole — all in each), then the world addresses to this mind a question it cannot answer, and each new fact tears it in pieces and it is vanquished by the distracting variety.' (*Centenary Edition*.)

[2] Compare Emerson's essay on 'Self-Reliance:' 'Let a man then know his worth, and keep things under his feet. Let him not peep or steal, or skulk up and down with the air of a charity-boy, a bastard, or an interloper in the world which exists for him. . . Man is timid and apologetic; he is no longer upright; he dares not say "I think," "I am," but quotes some saint or sage. He is ashamed before the blade of grass or the blowing rose.'

Are pleasant songs to me.
Deep love lieth under
   These pictures of time;   70
They fade in the light of
   Their meaning sublime.

'The fiend that man harries
   Is love of the Best;
Yawns the pit of the Dragon,
   Lit by rays from the Blest.
The Lethe of Nature
   Can't trance him again,
Whose soul sees the perfect,
   Which his eyes seek in vain.   80

'To vision profounder,
   Man's spirit must dive;
His aye-rolling orb
   At no goal will arrive;
The heavens that now draw him
   With sweetness untold,
Once found, — for new heavens
   He spurneth the old.[1]

'Pride ruined the angels,
   Their shame them restores;   90
Lurks the joy that is sweetest
   In stings of remorse.
Have I a lover
   Who is noble and free ? —
I would he were nobler
   Than to love me.

'Eterne alternation
   Now follows, now flies;
And under pain, pleasure,—
   Under pleasure, pain lies.   100
Love works at the centre,
   Heart-heaving alway;
Forth speed the strong pulses
   To the borders of day.

'Dull Sphinx, Jove keep thy five wits;
   Thy sight is growing blear;
Rue, myrrh and cummin for the Sphinx,
   Her muddy eyes to clear!'
The old Sphinx bit her thick lip,—
   Said, 'Who taught thee me to name ? 110
I am thy spirit, yoke-fellow;
   Of thine eye I am eyebeam.

[1] Compare Emerson's address on 'The American Scholar,' the paragraph beginning : 'First one, then another, we drain all cisterns, and waxing greater by all these supplies, we crave a better and more abundant food.'

'Thou art the unanswered question;
   Couldst see thy proper eye,
Alway it asketh, asketh;
   And each answer is a lie.
So take thy quest through nature,
   It through thousand natures ply;
Ask on, thou clothed eternity;
   Time is the false reply.'   120

Uprose the merry Sphinx,
   And crouched no more in stone;
She melted into purple cloud,
   She silvered in the moon;
She spired into a yellow flame;
   She flowered in blossoms red;
She flowed into a foaming wave:
   She stood Monadnoc's head.

Thorough a thousand voices
   Spoke the universal dame;   130
'Who telleth one of my meanings
   Is master of all I am.'

                      1841.

THE SNOW-STORM

ANNOUNCED by all the trumpets of the sky,
Arrives the snow, and, driving o'er the
   fields,
Seems nowhere to alight : the whited air
Hides hills and woods, the river, and the
   heaven,
And veils the farm-house at the garden's
   end.
The sled and traveller stopped, the courier's
   feet
Delayed, all friends shut out, the house-
   mates sit
Around the radiant fireplace, enclosed
In a tumultuous privacy of storm.

Come see the north wind's masonry.
Out of an unseen quarry evermore
Furnished with tile, the fierce artificer
Curves his white bastions with projected
   roof
Round every windward stake, or tree, or
   door.
Speeding, the myriad-handed, his wild work
So fanciful, so savage, nought cares he
For number or proportion. Mockingly,
On coop or kennel he hangs Parian wreaths;
A swan-like form invests the hidden thorn;
Fills up the farmer's lane from wall to
   wall,

Maugre the farmer's sighs; and at the gate
A tapering turret overtops the work.
And when his hours are numbered, and the
world
Is all his own, retiring, as he were not,
Leaves, when the sun appears, astonished
Art
To mimic in slow structures, stone by stone,
Built in an age, the mad wind's night-
work,
The frolic architecture of the snow.

1841.

FABLE

THE mountain and the squirrel
Had a quarrel,
And the former called the latter ' Little
Prig;'
Bun replied,
' You are doubtless very big;
But all sorts of things and weather
Must be taken in together,
To make up a year
And a sphere.
And I think it no disgrace
To occupy my place.
If I'm not so large as you,
You are not so small as I,
And not half so spry.
I'll not deny you make
A very pretty squirrel track;
Talents differ; all is well and wisely put;
If I cannot carry forests on my back,
Neither can you crack a nut.'
1840?   1846.

THE INFORMING SPIRIT [1]

I

THERE is no great and no small
To the Soul that maketh all:
And where it cometh, all things are;
And it cometh everywhere.

II

I am owner of the sphere,
Of the seven stars and the solar year,
Of Cæsar's hand, and Plato's brain,
Of Lord Christ's heart, and Shakspeare's
strain.

1841.

[1] First printed, without title, as motto to the essay
on ' History.'

FRIENDSHIP [2]

A RUDDY drop of manly blood
The surging sea outweighs,
The world uncertain comes and goes;
The lover rooted stays.
I fancied he was fled, —
And, after many a year,
Glowed unexhausted kindliness,
Like daily sunrise there.
My careful heart was free again,
O friend, my bosom said,
Through thee alone the sky is arched,
Through thee the rose is red;
All things through thee take nobler form,
And look beyond the earth,
The mill-round of our fate appears
A sun-path in thy worth.
Me too thy nobleness has taught
To master my despair;
The fountains of my hidden life
Are through thy friendship fair.

1841.

FORBEARANCE

HAST thou named all the birds without a
gun ?
Loved the wood-rose, and left it on its
stalk ?
At rich men's tables eaten bread and pulse ?
Unarmed, faced danger with a heart of
trust ?
And loved so well a high behavior,
In man or maid, that thou from speech re-
frained,
Nobility more nobly to repay ?
O, be my friend, and teach me to be
thine !

1842.

HOLIDAYS

FROM fall to spring, the russet acorn,
Fruit beloved of maid and boy,
Lent itself beneath the forest,
To be the children's toy.

Pluck it now ! In vain, — thou canst not;
Its root has pierced yon shady mound;
Toy no longer — it has duties;
It is anchored in the ground.

[2] First printed as motto to the essay on ' Friendship.'

Year by year the rose-lipped maiden,
　Playfellow of young and old,
Was frolic sunshine, dear to all men,
　More dear to one than mines of gold.

Whither went the lovely hoyden ?
　Disappeared in blessed wife;
Servant to a wooden cradle,
　Living in a baby's life.

Still thou playest; — short vacation
　Fate grants each to stand aside;
Now must thou be man and artist, —
　'T is the turning of the tide.

1842.

SAADI[1]

TREES in groves,
Kine in droves,
In ocean sport the scaly herds,
Wedge-like cleave the air the birds,
To northern lakes fly wind-borne ducks,
Browse the mountain sheep in flocks,
Men consort in camp and town,
But the poet dwells alone.

God, who gave to him the lyre,
Of all mortals the desire,　　　　10
For all breathing men's behoof,
Straitly charged him, ' Sit aloof;'
Annexed a warning, poets say,
To the bright premium, —
Ever, when twain together play,
Shall the harp be dumb.

Many may come,
But one shall sing;
Two touch the string,
The harp is dumb.　　　　20
Though there come a million,
Wise Saadi dwells alone.

Yet Saadi loved the race of men, —
No churl, immured in cave or den;
In bower and hall
He wants them all,
Nor can dispense

[1] It does not appear in what year Mr. Emerson first
read in translation the poems of Saadi, but although in
later years he seems to have been strangely stimulated
by Hafiz, whom he names ' the prince of Persian poets,'
yet Saadi was his first love ; indeed, he adopted his
name, in its various modifications, for the ideal poet,
and under it describes his own longings and his most
intimate experiences. (E. W. EMERSON.)

With Persia for his audience;
They must give ear,
Grow red with joy and white with fear;
But he has no companion;　　　　31
Come ten, or come a million,
Good Saadi dwells alone.

Be thou ware where Saadi dwells;
Wisdom of the gods is he, —
Entertain it reverently.
Gladly round that golden lamp
Sylvan deities encamp,
And simple maids and noble youth
Are welcome to the man of truth.　　　40
Most welcome they who need him most,
They feed the spring which they exhaust;
For greater need
Draws better deed:
But, critic, spare thy vanity,
Nor show thy pompous parts,
To vex with odious subtlety
The cheerer of men's hearts.

Sad-eyed Fakirs swiftly say
Endless dirges to decay,　　　　50
Never in the blaze of light
Lose the shudder of midnight;
Pale at overflowing noon
Hear wolves barking at the moon;
In the bower of dalliance sweet
Hear the far Avenger's feet:
And shake before those awful Powers,
Who in their pride forgive not ours.
Thus the sad-eyed Fakirs preach:
' Bard, when thee would Allah teach,　　60
And lift thee to his holy mount,
He sends thee from his bitter fount
Wormwood, — saying, "Go thy ways;
Drink not the Malaga of praise,
But do the deed thy fellows hate,
And compromise thy peaceful state ;
Smite the white breasts which thee fed,
Stuff sharp thorns beneath the head
Of them thou shouldst have comforted;
For out of woe and out of crime　　　70
Draws the heart a lore sublime." '
And yet it seemeth not to me
That the high gods love tragedy;
For Saadi sat in the sun,
And thanks was his contrition;
For haircloth and for bloody whips,
Had active hands and smiling lips;
And yet his runes he rightly read,
And to his folk his message sped.
Sunshine in his heart transferred　　80

Lighted each transparent word,
And well could honoring Persia learn
What Saadi wished to say;
For Saadi's nightly stars did burn
Brighter than Jami's day.

Whispered the Muse in Saadi's cot:
' O gentle Saadi, listen not,
Tempted by thy praise of wit,
Or by thirst and appetite
For the talents not thine own,   90
To sons of contradiction.
Never, son of eastern morning,
Follow falsehood, follow scorning.
Denounce who will, who will deny,
And pile the hills to scale the sky;
Let theist, atheist, pantheist,
Define and wrangle how they list,
Fierce conserver, fierce destroyer, —
But thou, joy-giver and enjoyer,
Unknowing war, unknowing crime,   100
Gentle Saadi, mind thy rhyme;
Heed not what the brawlers say,
Heed thou only Saadi's lay.[1]

' Let the great world bustle on
With war and trade, with camp and town;
A thousand men shall dig and eat;
At forge and furnace thousands sweat;
And thousands sail the purple sea,
And give or take the stroke of war,
Or crowd the market and bazaar;   110
Oft shall war end, and peace return,
And cities rise where cities burn,
Ere one man my hill shall climb,
Who can turn the golden rhyme.
Let them manage how they may,
Heed thou only Saadi's lay.
Seek the living among the dead, —
Man in man is imprisonèd;
Barefooted Dervish is not poor,
If fate unlock his bosom's door,   120
So that what his eye hath seen
His tongue can paint as bright, as keen;
And what his tender heart hath felt

With equal fire thy heart shalt melt.
For, whom the Muses smile upon,
And touch with soft persuasion,
His words like a storm-wind can bring
Terror and beauty on their wing;
In his every syllable
Lurketh Nature veritable;   130
And though he speak in midnight dark, —
In heaven no star, on earth no spark, —
Yet before the listener's eye
Swims the world in ecstasy,
The forest waves, the morning breaks,
The pastures sleep, ripple the lakes,
Leaves twinkle, flowers like persons be,
And life pulsates in rock or tree.
Saadi, so far thy words shall reach:
Suns rise and set in Saadi's speech ! ' 140

And thus to Saadi said the Muse:
' Eat thou the bread which men refuse;
Flee from the goods which from thee flee;
Seek nothing, — Fortune seeketh thee.
Nor mount, nor dive; all good things keep
The midway of the eternal deep.
Wish not to fill the isles with eyes
To fetch the birds of paradise:
On thine orchard's edge belong
All the brags of plume and song;   150
Wise Ali's sunbright sayings pass
For proverbs in the market-place;
Through mountains bored by regal art,
Toil whistles as he drives his cart.
Nor scour the seas, nor sift mankind,
A poet or a friend to find:
Behold, he watches at the door !
Behold his shadow on the floor !
Open innumerable doors
The heaven where unveiled Allah pours   160
The flood of truth, the flood of good,
The Seraph's and the Cherub's food.
Those doors are men: the Pariah hind
Admits thee to the perfect Mind.
Seek not beyond thy cottage wall
Redeemers that can yield thee all:
While thou sittest at thy door
On the desert's yellow floor,
Listening to the gray-haired crones,
Foolish gossips, ancient drones,   170
Saadi, see ! they rise in stature
To the height of mighty Nature,
And the secret stands revealed
Fraudulent Time in vain concealed, —
That blessed gods in servile masks
Plied for thee thy household tasks.'

1842.

---

[1] Compare the essay on 'Experience': 'So many things are unsettled . . . the debate goes forward . . . much is to say on both sides . . . Right to hold land, right of property, is disputed . . . Dig away in your garden, and spend your earnings as a waif or a god-send, to all serene and beautiful purposes. Life itself is a bubble and a scepticism and a sleep within a sleep. Grant it, and as much more as they will, — but thou, God's darling, heed thy private dream; thou wilt not be missed in the scorning and scepticism; there are enough of them; stay thou in thy closet and toil . . .'

ODE TO BEAUTY

WHO gave thee, O Beauty,
The keys of this breast, —
Too credulous lover
Of blest and unblest?
Say, when in lapsed ages
Thee knew I of old?
Or what was the service
For which I was sold?
When first my eyes saw thee,
I found me thy thrall,   10
By magical drawings,
Sweet tyrant of all!
I drank at thy fountain
False waters of thirst;
Thou intimate stranger,
Thou latest and first!
Thy dangerous glances
Make women of men;
New-born, we are melting
Into nature again.   20

Lavish, lavish promiser,
Nigh persuading gods to err!
Guest of million painted forms,
Which in turn thy glory warms!
The frailest leaf, the mossy bark,
The acorn's cup, the raindrop's arc,
The swinging spider's silver line,
The ruby of the drop of wine,
The shining pebble of the pond,
Thou inscribest with a bond,   30
In thy momentary play,
Would bankrupt nature to repay.

Ah, what avails it
To hide or to shun
Whom the Infinite One
Hath granted his throne?
The heaven high over
Is the deep's lover;
The sun and sea,
Informed by thee,   40
Before me run
And draw me on,
Yet fly me still,
As Fate refuses
To me the heart Fate for me chooses.
Is it that my opulent soul
Was mingled from the generous whole;
Sea-valleys and the deep of skies
Furnished several supplies;
And the sands whereof I'm made   50

Draw me to them, self-betrayed?
I turn the proud portfolio
Which holds the grand designs
Of Salvator, of Guercino,
And Piranesi's lines.
I hear the lofty pæans
Of the masters of the shell,
Who heard the starry music
And recount the numbers well;
Olympian bards who sung   60
Divine Ideas below,
Which always find us young
And always keep us so.
Oft, in streets or humblest places,
I detect far-wandered graces,
Which, from Eden wide astray,
In lowly homes have lost their way.

Thee gliding through the sea of form,[1]
Like the lightning through the storm,
Somewhat not to be possessed,   70
Somewhat not to be caressed,
No feet so fleet could ever find,
No perfect form could ever bind.
Thou eternal fugitive,
Hovering over all that live,
Quick and skilful to inspire
Sweet, extravagant desire,
Starry space and lily-bell
Filling with thy roseate smell,
Wilt not give the lips to taste   80
Of the nectar which thou hast.

All that's good and great with thee
Works in close conspiracy;
Thou hast bribed the dark and lonely
To report thy features only,
And the cold and purple morning
Itself with thoughts of thee adorning;
The leafy dell, the city mart,
Equal trophies of thine art;
E'en the flowing azure air   90
Thou hast touched for my despair;
And, if I languish into dreams,
Again I meet the ardent beams.
Queen of things! I dare not die
In Being's deeps past ear and eye;
Lest there I find the same deceiver
And be the sport of Fate forever.
Dread Power, but dear! if God thou be,
Unmake me quite, or give thyself to me!
                1843.

[1] Compare Emerson's 'Nature:' 'Nature is a sea of forms. . . . What is common to them all, — that perfectness and harmony, — is Beauty.'

NATURE[1]

THE rounded world is fair to see,
Nine times folded in mystery:
Though baffled seers cannot impart
The secret of its laboring heart,
Throb thine with Nature's throbbing breast,
And all is clear from east to west.
Spirit that lurks each form within
Beckons to spirit of its kin;
Self-kindled every atom glows
And hints the future which it owes.

1844.

EXPERIENCE

THE lords of life, the lords of life, —
I saw them pass
In their own guise,
Like and unlike,
Portly and grim, —
Use and Surprise,
Surface and Dream,
Succession swift and spectral Wrong,
Temperament without a tongue,
And the inventor of the game
Omnipresent without name; —
Some to see, some to be guessed,
They marched from east to west:
Little man, least of all,
Among the legs of his guardians tall,
Walked about with puzzled look.
Him by the hand dear Nature took,
Dearest Nature, strong and kind,
Whispered, ' Darling, never mind !
To-morrow they will wear another face,
The founder thou; these are thy race !'

1844.

THRENODY[2]

THE South-wind brings
Life, sunshine and desire,
And on every mount and meadow
Breathes aromatic fire;

But over the dead he has no power,
The lost, the lost, he cannot restore;
And, looking over the hills, I mourn
The darling who shall not return.

I see my empty house,
I see my trees repair their boughs;   10
And he, the wondrous child,
Whose silver warble wild
Outvalued every pulsing sound
Within the air's cerulean round, —
The hyacinthine boy, for whom
Morn well might break and April bloom,
The gracious boy, who did adorn
The world whereinto he was born,
And by his countenance repay
The favor of the loving Day, —   20
Has disappeared from the Day's eye;
Far and wide she cannot find him;
My hopes pursue, they cannot bind him.
Returned this day, the South-wind searches,
And finds young pines and budding birches;
But finds not the budding man;
Nature, who lost, cannot remake him;
Fate let him fall, Fate can't retake him;
Nature, Fate, men, him seek in vain.

And whither now, my truant wise and
     sweet,   30
O, whither tend thy feet ?
I had the right, few days ago,
Thy steps to watch, thy place to know:
How have I forfeited the right ?
Hast thou forgot me in a new delight ?
I hearken for thy household cheer,
O eloquent child !
Whose voice, an equal messenger,
Conveyed thy meaning mild.
What though the pains and joys   40
Whereof it spoke were toys
Fitting his age and ken,
Yet fairest dames and bearded men,
Who heard the sweet request,
So gentle, wise and grave,
Bended with joy to his behest
And let the world's affairs go by,

[1] This and the following poem were first used as mottoes for the essays ' Nature ' and ' Experience.'

[2] Emerson wrote to Carlyle, February 28, 1842 : ' My dear friend, you should have had this letter and these messages by the last steamer ; but when it sailed, my son, a perfect little boy of five years and three months, had ended his earthly life. You can never sympathize with me ; you can never know how much of me such a young child can take away. A few weeks ago I accounted myself a very rich man, and now the poorest of all. What would it avail to tell you anecdotes of a sweet and wonderful boy, such as we solace and sadden ourselves with at home every morning and evening ? From a perfect health and as happy a life and as happy influences as ever child enjoyed, he was hurried out of my arms in three short days.' (Carlyle-Emerson Correspondence, vol. i, pp. 389, 390.)

In his Journal, January 30, he wrote : ' This boy, in whose remembrance I have both slept and awaked so oft, decorated for me the morning star and the evening cloud, — how much more all the particulars of daily economy. . . . A boy of early wisdom, of a grave and even majestic deportment, of a perfect gentleness. . . .'

See also Cabot's Life of Emerson, vol. ii, pp. 481–489.

A while to share his cordial game,
Or mend his wicker wagon-frame,
Still plotting how their hungry ear   50
That winsome voice again might hear;
For his lips could well pronounce
Words that were persuasions.

Gentlest guardians marked serene
His early hope, his liberal mien;
Took counsel from his guiding eyes
To make this wisdom earthly wise.
Ah, vainly do these eyes recall
The school-march, each day's festival,
When every morn my bosom glowed   60
To watch the convoy on the road;
The babe in willow wagon closed,
With rolling eyes and face composed;
With children forward and behind,
Like Cupids studiously inclined;
And he the chieftain paced beside,
The centre of the troop allied,
With sunny face of sweet repose,
To guard the babe from fancied foes.
The little captain innocent   70
Took the eye with him as he went;
Each village senior paused to scan
And speak the lovely caravan.
From the window I look out
To mark thy beautiful parade,
Stately marching in cap and coat
To some tune by fairies played; —
A music heard by thee alone
To works as noble led thee on.

Now Love and Pride, alas! in vain,   80
Up and down their glances strain.
The painted sled stands where it stood;
The kennel by the corded wood;
His gathered sticks to stanch the wall
Of the snow-tower, when snow should fall;
The ominous hole he dug in the sand,
And childhood's castles built or planned;
His daily haunts I well discern, —
The poultry-yard, the shed, the barn, —
And every inch of garden ground   90
Paced by the blessed feet around,
From the roadside to the brook
Whereinto he loved to look.
Step the meek fowls where erst they
        ranged;
The wintry garden lies unchanged;
The brook into the stream runs on;
But the deep-eyed boy is gone.[1]

On that shaded day,
Dark with more clouds than tempests are,
When thou didst yield thy innocent
        breath   100
In birdlike heavings unto death,
Night came, and Nature had not thee;
I said, 'We are mates in misery.'
The morrow dawned with needless glow;
Each snowbird chirped, each fowl must
        crow;
Each tramper started; but the feet
Of the most beautiful and sweet
Of human youth had left the hill
And garden, — they were bound and still.
There 's not a sparrow or a wren,   110
There 's not a blade of autumn grain,
Which the four seasons do not tend
And tides of life and increase lend;
And every chick of every bird,
And weed and rock-moss is preferred.
O ostrich-like forgetfulness!
O loss of larger in the less!
Was there no star that could be sent,
No watcher in the firmament,
No angel from the countless host   120
That loiters round the crystal coast,
Could stoop to heal that only child,
Nature's sweet marvel undefiled,
And keep the blossom of the earth,
Which all her harvests were not worth?
Not mine, — I never called thee mine,
But Nature's heir, — if I repine,
And seeing rashly torn and moved
Not what I made, but what I loved,
Grow early old with grief that thou   130
Must to the wastes of Nature go, —
'T is because a general hope
Was quenched, and all must doubt and
        grope.
For flattering planets seemed to say
This child should ills of ages stay,
By wondrous tongue, and guided pen,
Bring the flown Muses back to men.
Perchance not he but Nature ailed,
The world and not the infant failed.
It was not ripe yet to sustain   140
A genius of so fine a strain,
Who gazed upon the sun and moon
As if he came unto his own,
And, pregnant with his grander thought,
Brought the old order into doubt.
His beauty once their beauty tried;
They could not feed him, and he died,

[1] The chrysalis which he brought in with care and tenderness and gave to his mother to keep is still alive, and he, most beautiful of the children of men, is not here. (*Journal*, 1842.)

And wandered backward as in scorn,
To wait an æon to be born.
Ill day which made this beauty waste,   150
Plight broken, this high face defaced !
Some went and came about the dead;
And some in books of solace read;
Some to their friends the tidings say;
Some went to write, some went to pray;
One tarried here, there hurried one;
But their heart abode with none.
Covetous death bereaved us all,
To aggrandize one funeral.
The eager fate which carried thee   160
Took the largest part of me:
For this losing is true dying;
This is lordly man's down-lying,
This his slow but sure reclining,
Star by star his world resigning.

O child of paradise,
Boy who made dear his father's home,
In whose deep eyes
Men read the welfare of the times to come,
I am too much bereft.   170
The world dishonored thou hast left.
O truth's and nature's costly lie !
O trusted broken prophecy !
O richest fortune sourly crossed !
Born for the future, to the future lost !

The deep Heart answered, ' Weepest thou ?
Worthier cause for passion wild
If I had not taken the child.
And deemest thou as those who pore,
With aged eyes, short way before, —   180
Think'st Beauty vanished from the coast
Of matter, and thy darling lost ?
Taught he not thee — the man of eld,
Whose eyes within his eyes beheld
Heaven's numerous hierarchy span
The mystic gulf from God to man ?
To be alone wilt thou begin
When worlds of lovers hem thee in ?
To-morrow, when the masks shall fall
That dizen Nature's carnival,   190
The pure shall see by their own will,
Which overflowing Love shall fill,
'T is not within the force of fate
The fate-conjoined to separate.
But thou, my votary, weepest thou ?
I gave thee sight — where is it now ?
I taught thy heart beyond the reach
Of ritual, bible, or of speech;
Wrote in thy mind's transparent table,
As far as the incommunicable;   200

Taught thee each private sign to raise
Lit by the supersolar blaze.
Past utterance, and past belief,
And past the blasphemy of grief,
The mysteries of Nature's heart;
And though no Muse can these impart,
Throb thine with Nature's throbbing breast,
And all is clear from east to west.

' I came to thee as to a friend;
Dearest, to thee I did not send   210
Tutors, but a joyful eye,
Innocence that matched the sky,
Lovely locks, a form of wonder,
Laughter rich as woodland thunder,
That thou might'st entertain apart
The richest flowering of all art:
And, as the great all-loving Day
Through smallest chambers takes its way,
That thou might'st break thy daily bread
With prophet, savior and head;   220
That thou might'st cherish for thine own
The riches of sweet Mary's Son,
Boy-Rabbi, Israel's paragon.
And thoughtest thou such guest
Would in thy hall take up his rest ?
Would rushing life forget her laws,
Fate's glowing revolution pause ?
High omens ask diviner guess;
Not to be conned to tediousness.
And know my higher gifts unbind   230
The zone that girds the incarnate mind.
When the scanty shores are full
With Thought's perilous, whirling pool;
When frail Nature can no more,
Then the Spirit strikes the hour :
My servant Death, with solving rite,
Pours finite into infinite.
Wilt thou freeze love's tidal flow,
Whose streams through Nature circling go ?
Nail the wild star to its track   240
On the half-climbed zodiac ?
Light is light which radiates,
Blood is blood which circulates,
Life is life which generates,
And many-seeming life is one, — .
Wilt thou transfix and make it none ?
Its onward force too starkly pent
In figure, bone and lineament ?
Wilt thou, uncalled, interrogate,
Talker ! the unreplying Fate ?   250
Nor see the genius of the whole
Ascendant in the private soul,
Beckon it when to go and come,
Self-announced its hour of doom ?

Fair the soul's recess and shrine,
Magic-built to last a season;
Masterpiece of love benign,
Fairer that expansive reason
Whose omen 't is, and sign.
Wilt thou not ope thy heart to know   260
What rainbows teach, and sunsets show ?
Verdict which accumulates
From lengthening scroll of human fates,
Voice of earth to earth returned,
Prayers of saints that inly burned, —
Saying, *What is excellent,*
As God lives, is permanent ;
Hearts are dust, hearts' loves remain ;
Heart's love will meet thee again.
Revere the Maker; fetch thine eye   270
Up to his style, and manners of the sky.
Not of adamant and gold
Built he heaven stark and cold;
No, but a nest of bending reeds,
Flowering grass and scented weeds;
Or like a traveller's fleeing tent,
Or bow above the tempest bent ;
Built of tears and sacred flames,
And virtue reaching to its aims ;
Built of furtherance and pursuing,   280
Not of spent deeds, but of doing.
Silent rushes the swift Lord
Through ruined systems still restored,
Broadsowing, bleak and void to bless,
Plants with worlds the wilderness;
Waters with tears of ancient sorrow
Apples of Eden ripe to-morrow.
House and tenant go to ground,
Lost in God, in Godhead found.'

                                1846.

TO J. W.[1]

SET not thy foot on graves;
Hear what wine and roses say ;
The mountain chase, the summer waves,
The crowded town, thy feet may well de-
    lay.

Set not thy foot on graves;
Nor seek to unwind the shroud
Which charitable Time
And Nature have allowed
To wrap the errors of a sage sublime.

Set not thy foot on graves;
Care not to strip the dead

[1] To John Weiss, who had written a severe judgment
of Coleridge.

Of his sad ornament,
His myrrh, and wine, and rings,

His sheet of lead,
And trophies burièd:
Go, get them where he earned them
        when alive;
As resolutely dig or dive.

Life is too short to waste
In critic peep or cynic bark,
Quarrel or reprimand:
'T will soon be dark;
Up! mind thine own aim, and
God speed the mark !

                                1846.

ODE[2]

INSCRIBED TO W. H. CHANNING

THOUGH loath to grieve
The evil time's sole patriot,
I cannot leave
My honeyed thought
For the priest's cant,
Or statesman's rant.

If I refuse
My study for their politique,
Which at the best is trick,
The angry Muse   10
Puts confusion in my brain.

But who is he that prates
Of the culture of mankind,
Of better arts and life?
Go, blindworm, go,
Behold the famous States
Harrying Mexico
With rifle and with knife !

[2] The circumstance which gave rise to this poem,
though not known, can easily be inferred. Rev. William
Henry Channing, nephew of the great Unitarian divine,
a man most tender in his sympathies, with an apostle's
zeal for right, had, no doubt, been urging his friend to
join the brave band of men who were dedicating their
lives to the destruction of human slavery in the United
States. To these men Mr. Emerson gave honor and
sympathy and active aid by word and presence on important occasions. He showed his colors from the first,
and spoke fearlessly on the subject in his lectures, but
his method was the reverse of theirs, affirmative not
negative ; he knew his office and followed his genius.
He said, ' I have quite other slaves to free than those negroes, to wit, imprisoned spirits, imprisoned thoughts.'
(E. W. EMERSON.)

Or who, with accent bolder,
Dare praise the freedom-loving mountain-
eer ? 20
I found by thee, O rushing Contoocook !
And in thy valleys, Agiochook !
The jackals of the negro-holder.

The God who made New Hampshire
Taunted the lofty land
With little men; —
Small bat and wren
House in the oak: —
If earth-fire cleave
The upheaved land, and bury the folk, 30
The southern crocodile would grieve.
Virtue palters ; Right is hence;
Freedom praised, but hid;
Funeral eloquence
Rattles the coffin-lid.

What boots thy zeal,
O glowing friend,
That would indignant rend
The northland from the south ?
Wherefore ? to what good end ? 40
Boston Bay and Bunker Hill
Would serve things still; —
Things are of the snake.[1]

The horseman serves the horse,
The neatherd serves the neat,
The merchant serves the purse,
The eater serves his meat;
'T is the day of the chattel,
Web to weave, and corn to grind;
Things are in the saddle, 50
And ride mankind.

There are two laws discrete,
Not reconciled, —
Law for man, and law for thing;
The last builds town and fleet,
But it runs wild,
And doth the man unking.

'T is fit the forest fall,
The steep be graded,
The mountain tunnelled, 60
The sand shaded,
The orchard planted,
The glebe tilled,

[1] Compare the essay on 'Self-Reliance:' 'Let a
man then know his worth, and keep things under his
feet.'

The prairie granted,
The steamer built.

Let man serve law for man;
Live for friendship, live for love,
For truth's and harmony's behoof;
The state may follow how it can,
As Olympus follows Jove. 70

    Yet do not I implore
The wrinkled shopman to my sounding
woods,
Nor bid the unwilling senator
Ask votes of thrushes in the solitudes.
Every one to his chosen work; —
Foolish hands may mix and mar;
Wise and sure the issues are.
Round they roll till dark is light,
Sex to sex, and even to odd; —
The over-god 8c
Who marries Right to Might,
Who peoples, unpeoples, —
He who exterminates
Races by stronger races,
Black by white faces, —
Knows to bring honey
Out of the lion;
Grafts gentlest scion
On pirate and Turk.
The Cossack eats Poland, 9c
Like stolen fruit ;
Her last noble is ruined,
Her last poet mute :
Straight, into double band
The victors divide;
Half for freedom strike and stand; —
The astonished Muse finds thousands at her
side.

1846.

MERLIN

THY trivial harp will never please
Or fill my craving ear;
Its chords should ring as blows the breeze,
Free, peremptory, clear.
No jingling serenader's art,
Nor tinkle of piano strings,
Can make the wild blood start
In its mystic springs.
The kingly bard
Must smite the chords rudely and hard, 1c
As with hammer or with mace;
That they may render back
Artful thunder, which conveys

Secrets of the solar track,
Sparks of the supersolar blaze.
Merlin's blows are strokes of fate,
Chiming with the forest tone,
When boughs buffet boughs in the wood;
Chiming with the gasp and moan
Of the ice-imprisoned flood;   20
With the pulse of manly hearts;
With the voice of orators;
With the din of city arts;
With the cannonade of wars;
With the marches of the brave;
And prayers of might from martyrs' cave.

Great is the art,
Great be the manners, of the bard.
He shall not his brain encumber
With the coil of rhythm and number;   30
But, leaving rule and pale forethought,
He shall aye climb
For his rhyme.
'Pass in, pass in,' the angels say,
'In to the upper doors,
Nor count compartments of the floors,
But mount to paradise
By the stairway of surprise.'

Blameless master of the games,
King of sport that never shames,   40
He shall daily joy dispense
Hid in song's sweet influence.
Forms more cheerly live and go,
What time the subtle mind
Sings aloud the tune whereto
Their pulses beat,
And march their feet,
And their members are combined.

By Sybarites beguiled,
He shall no task decline.   50
Merlin's mighty line
Extremes of nature reconciled, —
Bereaved a tyrant of his will,
And made the lion mild.
Songs can the tempest still,
Scattered on the stormy air,
Mould the year to fair increase,
And bring in poetic peace.

He shall not seek to weave,
In weak, unhappy times,   60
Efficacious rhymes;
Wait his returning strength.
Bird that from nadir's floor
To the zenith's top can soar, —

The soaring orbit of the muse exceeds that
    journey's length.
Nor profane affect to hit
Or compass that, by meddling wit,
Which only the propitious mind
Publishes when 't is inclined.
There are open hours   70
When the God's will sallies free,
And the dull idiot might see
The flowing fortunes of a thousand years;—
Sudden, at unawares,
Self-moved, fly-to the doors,
Nor sword of angels could reveal
What they conceal.
1845–46.   1846.

THE WORLD–SOUL

THANKS to the morning light,
    Thanks to the foaming sea,
To the uplands of New Hampshire,
    To the green-haired forest free;
Thanks to each man of courage,
    To the maids of holy mind,
To the boy with his games undaunted
    Who never looks behind.

Cities of proud hotels,
    Houses of rich and great,   10
Vice nestles in your chambers,
    Beneath your roofs of slate.
It cannot conquer folly, —
    Time-and-space-conquering steam,—
And the light-outspeeding telegraph
    Bears nothing on its beam.

The politics are base;
    The letters do not cheer;
And 't is far in the deeps of history,
    The voice that speaketh clear.   20
Trade and the streets ensnare us,
    Our bodies are weak and worn;
We plot and corrupt each other,
    And we despoil the unborn.

Yet there in the parlor sits
    Some figure of noble guise, —
Our angel, in a stranger's form,
    Or woman's pleading eyes;
Or only a flashing sunbeam
    In at the window-pane;   30
Or Music pours on mortals
    Its beautiful disdain.

The inevitable morning
  Finds them who in cellars be;
And be sure the all-loving Nature
  Will smile in a factory.
Yon ridge of purple landscape,
  Yon sky between the walls,
Hold all the hidden wonders
  In scanty intervals.   40

Alas ! the Sprite that haunts us
  Deceives our rash desire;
It whispers of the glorious gods,
  And leaves us in the mire.
We cannot learn the cipher
  That 's writ upon our cell;
Stars taunt us by a mystery
  Which we could never spell.

If but one hero knew it,
  The world would blush in flame;   50
The sage, till he hit the secret,
  Would hang his head for shame.
Our brothers have not read it,
  Not one has found the key;
And henceforth we are comforted, —
  We are but such as they.[1]

Still, still the secret presses;
  The nearing clouds draw down;
The crimson morning flames into
  The fopperies of the town.   60
Within, without the idle earth,
  Stars weave eternal rings;
The sun himself shines heartily,
  And shares the joy he brings.

And what if Trade sow cities
  Like shells along the shore,
And thatch with towns the prairie broad
  With railways ironed o'er ? —
They are but sailing foam-bells
  Along Thought's causing stream,   70
And take their shape and sun-color
  From him that sends the dream.

For Destiny never swerves
  Nor yields to men the helm;
He shoots his thought, by hidden nerves,
  Throughout the solid realm.
The patient Dæmon sits,
  With roses and a shroud ;

[1] There is something — our brothers over the sea
do not know it or own it — . . . which is setting them
all aside, and the whole world also, and planting itself
forever and ever. (*Journal*, 1851.)

He has his way, and deals his gifts, —
  But ours is not allowed.   80

He is no churl nor trifler,
  And his viceroy is none, —
Love-without-weakness, —
  Of Genius sire and son.
And his will is not thwarted;
  The seeds of land and sea
Are the atoms of his body bright,
  And his behest obey.

He serveth the servant,
  The brave he loves amain;   90
He kills the cripple and the sick,
  And straight begins again;
For gods delight in gods,
  And thrust the weak aside;
To him who scorns their charities
  Their arms fly open wide.

When the old world is sterile
  And the ages are effete,
He will from wrecks and sediment
  The fairer world complete.   100
He forbids to despair;
  His cheeks mantle with mirth;
And the unimagined good of men
  Is yeaning at the birth.

Spring still makes spring in the mind
  When sixty years are told;
Love wakes anew this throbbing heart,
  And we are never old;
Over the winter glaciers
  I see the summer glow,   110
And through the wild-piled snow-drift
  The warm rosebuds below.

                                   1846.

HAMATREYA

BULKELEY, Hunt, Willard, Hosmer, Meri-
  am, Flint [2]
Possessed the land which rendered to their
  toil
Hay, corn, roots, hemp, flax, apples, wool
  and wood.
Each of these landlords walked amidst his
  farm,
Saying, ' 'T is mine, my children's and my
  name's.
How sweet the west wind sounds in my
  own trees!

[2] All names of early settlers in the town of Concord.

How graceful climb those shadows on my
    hill !
I fancy these pure waters and the flags
Know me, as does my dog: we sympathize;
And, I affirm, my actions smack of the
    soil.'   10

Where are these men ?   Asleep beneath
    their grounds:
And strangers, fond as they, their furrows
    plough.
Earth laughs in flowers, to see her boastful
    boys
Earth-proud, proud of the earth which is
    not theirs;
Who steer the plough, but cannot steer
    their feet
Clear of the grave.
They added ridge to valley, brook to pond,
And sighed for all that bounded their do-
    main;
' This suits me for a pasture; that 's my
    park;
We must have clay, lime, gravel, granite-
    ledge,   20
And misty lowland, where to go for peat.
The land is well, — lies fairly to the south.
'T is good, when you have crossed the sea
    and back,
To find the sitfast acres where you left
    them.'
Ah ! the hot owner sees not Death, who
    adds
Him to his land, a lump of mould the more.
Hear what the Earth says: —

EARTH–SONG

' Mine and yours;
Mine, not yours.
Earth endures;   30
Stars abide —
Shine down in the old sea;
Old are the shores;
But where are old men ?
I who have seen much,
Such have I never seen.

' The lawyer's deed
Ran sure,
In tail,
To them, and to their heirs   40
Who shall succeed,
Without fail,
Forevermore.

' Here is the land,
Shaggy with wood,
With its old valley,
Mound and flood.
But the heritors ? —
Fled like the flood's foam.
The lawyer, and the laws,   50
And the kingdom,
Clean swept herefrom.

' They called me theirs,
Who so controlled me;
Yet every one
Wished to stay, and is gone,
How am I theirs,
If they cannot hold me,
But I hold them ? '

When I heard the Earth-song   60
I was no longer brave;
My avarice cooled
Like lust in the chill of the grave.

                                        1846.

FORERUNNERS [1]

Long I followed happy guides,
I could never reach their sides;
Their step is forth, and, ere the day
Breaks up their leaguer, and away.
Keen my sense, my heart was young,
Right good-will my sinews strung,
But no speed of mine avails
To hunt upon their shining trails.
On and away, their hasting feet
Make the morning proud and sweet;   10
Flowers they strew, — I catch the scent;
Or tone of silver instrument
Leaves on the wind melodious trace;
Yet I could never see their face.
On eastern hills I see their smokes,
Mixed with mist by distant lochs.
I met many travellers
Who the road had surely kept;
They saw not my fine revellers, —   19
These had crossed them while they slept.
Some had heard their fair report,
In the country or the court.
Fleetest couriers alive
Never yet could once arrive,

[1] Compare Lowell's ' Envoi, To the Muse,' and Whittier's ' The Vanishers ; ' and also, in Emerson's essay
on ' Nature ' (*Essays, Second Series*), the third paragraph from the end, beginning ' Quite analogous to the
deceits in life.'

As they went or they returned,
At the house where these sojourned.
Sometimes their strong speed they slacken,
Though they are not overtaken;
In sleep their jubilant troop is near, —
I tuneful voices overhear;   30
It may be in wood or waste, —
At unawares 't is come and past.
Their near camp my spirit knows
By signs gracious as rainbows.
I thenceforward and long after
Listen for their harp-like laughter,
And carry in my heart, for days,
Peace that hallows rudest ways.

                                1846.

GIVE ALL TO LOVE

GIVE all to love;
Obey thy heart;
Friends, kindred, days,
Estate, good-fame,
Plans, credit and the Muse, —
Nothing refuse.

' T is a brave master;
Let it have scope :
Follow it utterly,
Hope beyond hope :   10
High and more high
It dives into noon,
With wing unspent,
Untold intent;
But it is a god,
Knows its own path
And the outlets of the sky.

It was never for the mean;
It requireth courage stout.
Souls above doubt,   20
Valor unbending,
It will reward, —
They shall return
More than they were,
And ever ascending.

Leave all for love;
Yet, hear me, yet,
One word more thy heart behoved,
One pulse more of firm endeavor, —
Keep thee to-day,   30
To-morrow, forever,
Free as an Arab
Of thy beloved.

Cling with life to the maid;
But when the surprise,
First vague shadow of surmise
Flits across her bosom young,
Of a joy apart from thee,
Free be she, fancy-free;
Nor thou detain her vesture's hem,   40
Nor the palest rose she flung
From her summer diadem.

Though thou loved her as thyself,
As a self of purer clay,
Though her parting dims the day,
Stealing grace from all alive;
Heartily know,
When half-gods go,
The gods arrive.

                                1846.

THE DAY'S RATION [1]

WHEN I was born,
From all the seas of strength Fate filled a
    chalice,
Saying, 'This be thy portion, child; this
    chalice,
Less than a lily's, thou shalt daily draw
From my great arteries, — nor less, nor
    more.'
All substances the cunning chemist Time
Melts down into that liquor of my life, —
Friends, foes, joys, fortunes, beauty and
    disgust.
And whether I am angry or content,
Indebted or insulted, loved or hurt,   10
All he distils into sidereal wine
And brims my little cup; heedless, alas !
Of all he sheds how little it will hold,
How much runs over on the desert sands.
If a new Muse draw me with splendid ray,
And I uplift myself into its heaven,
The needs of the first sight absorb my
    blood,
And all the following hours of the day
Drag a ridiculous age.
To-day, when friends approach, and every
    hour   20
Brings book, or starbright scroll of genius,
The little cup will hold not a bead more,
And all the costly liquor runs to waste;

[1] Compare the essay on ' Montaigne,' in *Representative Men:* ' To each man is administered a single drop,
a bead of dew of vital power, *per day*, — a cup as large
as space, and one drop of the water of life in it.' See
the whole passage.

Nor gives the jealous lord one diamond
　　drop
So to be husbanded for poorer days.
Why need I volumes, if one word suffice ?
Why need I galleries, when a pupil's
　　draught
After the master's sketch fills and o'erfills
My apprehension ? Why seek Italy,
Who cannot circumnavigate the sea　　30
Of thoughts and things at home, but still
　　adjourn
The nearest matters for a thousand days ? [1]

1846.

MEROPS

WHAT care I, so they stand the same, —
　　Things of the heavenly mind, —
How long the power to give them name
　　Tarries yet behind ?

Thus far to-day your favors reach,
　　O fair, appeasing presences !
Ye taught my lips a single speech,
　　And a thousand silences.

Space grants beyond his fated road
　　No inch to the god of day;
And copious language still bestowed
　　One word, no more, to say.

1846.

MUSKETAQUID

BECAUSE I was content with these poor
　　fields,
Low, open meads, slender and sluggish
　　streams,
And found a home in haunts which others
　　scorned,
The partial wood-gods overpaid my love,
And granted me the freedom of their
　　state,
And in their secret senate have prevailed
With the dear, dangerous lords that rule
　　our life,[2]
Made moon and planets parties to their
　　bond,
And through my rock-like, solitary wont
Shot million rays of thought and tender-
　　ness.　　10

---

[1] See the poems 'Written at Rome' and 'Written in Naples,' with the notes on them ; and compare also Whittier's 'To ——,' and 'The Last Walk in Autumn.'
[2] Compare the poem 'Experience.'

For me, in showers, in sweeping showers,
　　the Spring
Visits the valley; — break away the
　　clouds, —
I bathe in the morn's soft and silvered air,
And loiter willing by yon loitering stream.
Sparrows far off, and nearer, April's bird,
Blue-coated, — flying before from tree to
　　tree,
Courageous sing a delicate overture
To lead the tardy concert of the year.
Onward and nearer rides the sun of May;
And wide around, the marriage of the
　　plants　　20
Is sweetly solemnized. Then flows amain
The surge of summer's beauty; dell and
　　crag,
Hollow and lake, hillside and pine arcade,
Are touched with genius. Yonder ragged
　　cliff
Has thousand faces in a thousand hours.

Beneath low hills, in the broad interval
Through which at will our Indian rivulet
Winds mindful still of sannup and of
　　squaw,
Whose pipe and arrow oft the plough un-
　　buries,
Here in pine houses built of new-fallen
　　trees,　　30
Supplanters of the tribe, the farmers dwell.
Traveller, to thee, perchance, a tedious
　　road,
Or, it may be, a picture; to these men,
The landscape is an armory of powers,
Which, one by one, they know to draw and
　　use.
They harness beast, bird, insect, to their
　　work;
They prove the virtues of each bed of
　　rock,
And, like the chemist 'mid his loaded jars,
Draw from each stratum its adapted use
To drug their crops or weapon their arts
　　withal.　　40
They turn the frost upon their chemic heap,
They set the wind to winnow pulse and
　　grain,
They thank the spring-flood for its fertile
　　slime,
And, on cheap summit-levels of the snow,
Slide with the sledge to inaccessible woods
O'er meadows bottomless. So, year by
　　year,
They fight the elements with elements

(That one would say, meadow and forest
    walked,
Transmuted in these men to rule their like),
And by the order in the field disclose   50
The order regnant in the yeoman's brain.

What these strong masters wrote at large
    in miles,
I followed in small copy in my acre;
For there 's no rood has not a star above it; [1]
The cordial quality of pear or plum
Ascends as gladly in a single tree
As in broad orchards resonant with bees;
And every atom poises for itself,
And for the whole.   The gentle deities
Showed me the lore of colors and of sounds,
The innumerable tenements of beauty,   61
The miracle of generative force,
Far-reaching concords of astronomy
Felt in the plants and in the punctual birds;
Better, the linked purpose of the whole,
And, chiefest prize, found I true liberty
In the glad home plain-dealing Nature gave.
The polite found me impolite; the great
Would mortify me, but in vain; for still
I am a willow of the wilderness,   70
Loving the wind that bent me. All my hurts
My garden spade can heal. A woodland
    walk,
A quest of river-grapes, a mocking thrush,
A wild-rose, or rock-loving columbine,
Salve my worst wounds.
For thus the wood-gods murmured in my
    ear:
' Dost love our manners ? Canst thou silent
    lie ?
Canst thou, thy pride forgot, like Nature
    pass
Into the winter night's extinguished mood ?
Canst thou shine now, then darkle,   80
And being latent, feel thyself no less ?
As, when the all-worshipped moon attracts
    the eye,
The river, hill, stems, foliage are obscure,
Yet envies none, none are unenviable.'
                      1846.

NATURE

A SUBTLE chain of countless rings
The next unto the farthest brings;

[1] Over every chimney is a star: in every field is an oaken garland or a wreath of parsley, laurel or wheat-ears. Nature waits to decorate every child. (*Journal*, 1840.)

The eye reads omens where it goes,
And speaks all languages the rose;
And, striving to be man, the worm
Mounts through all the spires of form.[2]
                      1849.

DAYS [3]

DAUGHTERS of Time, the hypocritic Days,
Muffled and dumb like barefoot dervishes,
And marching single in an endless file,
Bring diadems and fagots in their hands.
To each they offer gifts after his will,
Bread, kingdoms, stars, and sky that holds
    them all.
I, in my pleached garden, watched the pomp,
Forgot my morning wishes, hastily
Took a few herbs and apples, and the Day
Turned and departed silent. I, too late,
Under her solemn fillet saw the scorn.
1851 ?   1857.

TWO RIVERS [4]

THY summer voice, Musketaquit,
Repeats the music of the rain;

[2] Prefixed to Emerson's ' Nature,' in the second edition (1849), ten years before the publication of Darwin's *Origin of Species.*

[3] Compare Emerson's expression in prose of the same idea in his ' Works and Days ' : ' The days are ever divine, as to the first Aryans. They come and go like muffled and veiled figures, sent from a distant friendly party ; but they say nothing, and if we do not use the gifts they bring, they carry them as silently away.' See Holmes's comparison of this passage with the poem, as typical of the essential differences between prose and poetry, in his *Life of Emerson*, pp. 310-314.

Lowell calls this poem ' as limpid and complete as a Greek epigram.' (*Life of Lowell*, vol. i, p. 414.)

[4] The *Journal* of 1856 shows the ' Two Rivers,' perhaps the most musical of his poems, as the thought first came to him by the river-bank and was then brought into form.

' Thy voice is sweet, Musketaquid, and repeats the music of the rain, but sweeter is the silent stream which flows even through thee, as thou through the land.

' Thou art shut in thy banks, but the stream I love flows in thy water, and flows through rocks and through the air and through rays of light as well, and through darkness, and through men and women.

' I hear and see the inundation and the eternal spending of the stream in winter and in summer, in men and animals, in passion and thought. Happy are they who can hear it.'

    ' I see thy brimming, eddying stream
      And thy enchantment.
    For thou changest every rock in thy bed
      Into a gem,
      All is opal and agate,
      And at will thou pavest with diamonds;
    Take them away from the stream
      And they are poor, shreds and flints.
    So is it with me to-day.'

(E. W. EMERSON, *Emerson in Concord*, pp. 232-233)

But sweeter rivers pulsing flit
Through thee, as thou through Concord
   Plain.

Thou in thy narrow banks art pent:
The stream I love unbounded goes
Through flood and sea and firmament;
Through light, through life, it forward flows.

I see the inundation sweet,
I hear the spending of the stream
Through years, through men, through Na-
   ture fleet,
Through love and thought, through power
   and dream.

Musketaquit, a goblin strong,
Of shard and flint makes jewels gay;
They lose their grief who hear his song,
And where he winds is the day of day.

So forth and brighter fares my stream, —
Who drink it shall not thirst again;
No darkness stains its equal gleam
And ages drop in it like rain.
1856–57.   1858.

BRAHMA [1]

IF the red slayer think he slays,
  Or if the slain think he is slain,
They know not well the subtle ways
  I keep, and pass, and turn again.

[1] This simple and condensed figurative statement of one of the commonplaces of any idealistic philosophy, whether Hindu, Platonist, Berkeleian, or Hegelian, greatly astonished the matter-of-fact Americans of 1857, and aroused more ridicule and parody than any other of Emerson's poems. J. T. Trowbridge describes its effect as follows: 'It was more talked about and puzzled over and parodied than any other poem of sixteen lines published within my recollection. "What does it mean?" was the question readers everywhere asked; and if one had the reputation of seeing a little way into the Concord philosophy, he was liable at any time to be stopped on the street by some perplexed inquirer, who would draw him into the nearest doorway, produce a crumpled newspaper clipping from the recesses of a waistcoat pocket, and, with knitted brows, exclaim, "Here! you think you understand Emerson; now tell me what all this is about, — *If the red slayer think he slays*," and so forth.' (Quoted in Scudder's *Life of Lowell*, vol. i, p. 415.)

Somewhat wiser was the little school-girl in the story vouched for by Mr. E. W. Emerson. 'She ' was bidden by her teacher to learn some verses of Emerson. Next day she recited "Brahma." The astonished teacher asked why she chose that poem. The child answered that she tried several, but could n't understand them at all, so learned this one, "for it was so easy. *It just means 'God everywhere.*' "'

Lowell wrote to Emerson after the poem had appeared in the first number of the *Atlantic Monthly*, of which

Far or forgot to me is near;
  Shadow and sunlight are the same;
The vanished gods to me appear;
  And one to me are shame and fame.

They reckon ill who leave me out;
  When me they fly, I am the wings;
I am the doubter and the doubt,
  And I the hymn the Brahmin sings.

The strong gods pine for my abode,
  And pine in vain the sacred Seven;
But thou, meek lover of the good!
  Find me, and turn thy back on heaven.
                        1857.

ODE

SUNG IN THE TOWN HALL, CONCORD,
JULY 4, 1857

O TENDERLY the haughty day
  Fills his blue urn with fire;
One morn is in the mighty heaven,
  And one in our desire.

The cannon booms from town to town,
  Our pulses beat not less,
The joy-bells chime their tidings down,
  Which children's voices bless.

For He that flung the broad blue fold
  O'er-mantling land and sea,
One third part of the sky unrolled
  For the banner of the free.

The men are ripe of Saxon kind
  To build an equal state, —
To take the statute from the mind
  And make of duty fate.

Lowell was editor : 'You have seen, no doubt, how the Philistines have been parodying your "Brahma," and showing how they still believe in their special god Baal, and are unable to arrive at a conception of an omnipresent Deity. . . . Let me thank you in especial for one line in "Brahma," which abides with me as an intimate —

   'When me they fly, I am the wings.

You have crammed meaning there with an hydraulic press.' It is this condensation of meaning which makes the great effectiveness of the poem, and also its difficulty, if difficulty there be.

The direct source of this particular expression of Emerson's idealism seems to be Krishna's song in the Bhagavat-Gita, which in Edwin Arnold's translation is as follows : —

He who shall say, 'Lo! I have slain a man,'
He who shall think, 'Lo! I am slain!' those both
Know naught! Life cannot slay. Life is not slain!

United States ! the ages plead, —
  Present and Past in under-song, —
Go put your creed into your deed,
  Nor speak with double tongue.   20

For sea and land don't understand,
  Nor skies without a frown
See rights for which the one hand fights
  By the other cloven down.

Be just at home; then write your scroll
  Of honor o'er the sea,
And bid the broad Atlantic roll,
  A ferry of the free.

And henceforth there shall be no chain,
  Save underneath the sea   30
The wires shall murmur through the main
  Sweet songs of liberty.

The conscious stars accord above,
  The waters wild below,
And under, through the cable wove,
  Her fiery errands go.

For He that worketh high and wise,
  Nor pauses in his plan,
Will take the sun out of the skies
  Ere freedom out of man.   40

1857.   1857.

SEASHORE[1]

I HEARD or seemed to hear the chiding Sea
Say, Pilgrim, why so late and slow to come ?

[1] In July, 1857, Mr. Emerson, induced by Dr. Bartol, took his family to spend two weeks at Pigeon Cove, on Cape Ann. The day after our return to Concord, he came into our mother's room, where we were all sitting, with his journal in his hand, and said, 'I came in yesterday from walking on the rocks and wrote down what the sea had said to me ; and to-day, when I open my book, I find it all reads as blank verse, with scarcely a change.'

Here is the passage from that journal, as he read it to us : July 23. 'Returned from Pigeon Cove, where we have made acquaintance with the sea, for seven days. 'T is a noble, friendly power, and seemed to say to me, Why so late and slow to come to me ? Am I not here always, thy proper summer home ? Is not my voice thy needful music ; my breath thy healthful climate in the heats ; my touch thy cure ? Was ever building like my terraces ? Was ever couch so magnificent as mine? Lie down on my warm ledges and learn that a very little hut is all you need. I have made this architecture superfluous, and it is paltry beside mine. Here are twenty Romes and Ninevehs and Karnacs in ruins together, obelisk and pyramid and Giant's Causeway ; here they all are prostrate or half piled. And behold the sea, the opaline, plentiful and strong, yet beautiful as the rose or the rainbow, full of food, nourisher of men, purger of the world, creating a sweet climate and in its

Am I not always here, thy summer home ?
Is not my voice thy music, morn and eve ?
My breath thy healthful climate in the heats,
My touch thy antidote, my bay thy bath ?
Was ever building like my terraces ?
Was ever couch magnificent as mine ?
Lie on the warm rock-ledges, and there learn
A little hut suffices like a town.   10
I make your sculptured architecture vain,
Vain beside mine. I drive my wedges home,
And carve the coastwise mountain into caves.
Lo ! here is Rome and Nineveh and Thebes,
Karnak and Pyramid and Giant's Stairs
Half piled or prostrate; and my newest
    slab
Older than all thy race.

          Behold the Sea,
The opaline, the plentiful and strong,
Yet beautiful as is the rose in June,
Fresh as the trickling rainbow of July;   20
Sea full of food, the nourisher of kinds,
Purger of earth, and medicine of men;
Creating a sweet climate by my breath,
Washing out harms and griefs from mem-
    ory,
And, in my mathematic ebb and flow,
Giving a hint of that which changes not.
Rich are the sea-gods: — who gives gifts
    but they ?
They grope the sea for pearls, but more
    than pearls:
They pluck Force thence, and give it to the
    wise.
For every wave is wealth to Dædalus,   30
Wealth to the cunning artist who can work
This matchless strength. Where shall he
    find, O waves !
A load your Atlas shoulders cannot lift ?

I with my hammer pounding evermore
The rocky coast, smite Andes into dust,
Strewing my bed, and, in another age,
Rebuild a continent of better men.
Then I unbar the doors: my paths lead out
The exodus of nations: I disperse
Men to all shores that front the hoary main.

I too have arts and sorceries;   41
Illusion dwells forever with the wave.
I know what spells are laid. Leave me to
    deal

unchangeable ebb and flow, and in its beauty at a few furlongs, giving a hint of that which changes not, and is perfect.' (E. W. EMERSON, in the *Centenary Edition*.)

With credulous and imaginative man;
For, though he scoop my water in his palm,
A few rods off he deems it gems and clouds.
Planting strange fruits and sunshine on the
        shore,
I make some coast alluring, some lone isle,
To distant men, who must go there, or die.
1857.   *1867.*

WALDEINSAMKEIT

I DO not count the hours I spend
In wandering by the sea;
The forest is my loyal friend,
Like God it useth me.

In plains that room for shadows make
Of skirting hills to lie,
Bound in by streams which give and take
Their colors from the sky;

Or on the mountain-crest sublime,
Or down the oaken glade,   10
O what have I to do with time?
For this the day was made.

Cities of mortals woe-begone
Fantastic care derides,
But in the serious landscape lone
Stern benefit abides.

Sheen will tarnish, honey cloy,
And merry is only a mask of sad,
But, sober on a fund of joy,
The woods at heart are glad.   20

There the great Planter plants
Of fruitful worlds the grain,
And with a million spells enchants
The souls that walk in pain.

Still on the seeds of all he made
The rose of beauty burns;
Through times that wear and forms that
        fade,
Immortal youth returns.

The black ducks mounting from the lake,
The pigeon in the pines,   30
The bittern's boom, a desert make
Which no false art refines.

Down in yon watery nook,
Where bearded mists divide,

The gray old gods whom Chaos knew,
The sires of Nature, hide.

Aloft, in secret veins of air,
Blows the sweet breath of song,
O, few to scale those uplands dare,
Though they to all belong!   40

See thou bring not to field or stone
The fancies found in books;
Leave authors' eyes, and fetch your own,
To brave the landscape's looks.

Oblivion here thy wisdom is,
Thy thrift, the sleep of cares;
For a proud idleness like this
Crowns all thy mean affairs.
1857.   *1858.*

FRAGMENTS ON NATURE AND LIFE

NATURE

DAILY the bending skies solicit man,
The seasons chariot him from this exile,
The rainbow hours bedeck his glowing
        wheels,
The storm-winds urge the heavy weeks
        along,
Suns haste to set, that so remoter lights
Beckon the wanderer to his vaster home.

FOR Nature, true and like in every place,
Will hint her secret in a garden patch,
Or in lone corners of a doleful heath,
As in the Andes watched by fleets at sea,
Or the sky-piercing horns of Himmaleh;
And, when I would recall the scenes I
        dreamed
On Adirondac steeps, I know
Small need have I of Turner or Daguerre,
Assured to find the token once again
In silver lakes that unexhausted gleam
And peaceful woods beside my cottage door.

BUT never yet the man was found
Who could the mystery expound,
Though Adam, born when oaks were
        young,
Endured, the Bible says, as long;

But when at last the patriarch died
The Gordian noose was still untied.
He left, though goodly centuries old,
Meek Nature's secret still untold.

ATOM from atom yawns as far
As moon from earth, or star from star.

TEACH me your mood, O patient stars !
  Who climb each night the ancient sky,
Leaving on space no shade, no scars,
  No trace of age, no fear to die.

THE sun athwart the cloud thought it no
    sin
To use my land to put his rainbows in.

DAY by day for her darlings to her much
    she added more;
In her hundred-gated Thebes every cham-
    ber was a door,
A door to something grander, — loftier
    walls, and vaster floor.

SHE paints with white and red the moors
To draw the nations out of doors.

NIGHT IN JUNE

I LEFT my dreary page and sallied forth,
Received the fair inscriptions of the night;
The moon was making amber of the world,
Glittered with silver every cottage pane,
The trees were rich, yet ominous with
    gloom.
              The meadows broad
From ferns and grapes and from the folded
    flowers
Sent a nocturnal fragrance; harlot flies
Flashed their small fires in air, or held their
    court
In fairy groves of herds-grass.

BUT Nature whistled with all her winds,
Did as she pleased and went her way.

LIFE

A TRAIN of gay and clouded days
Dappled with joy and grief and praise,
Beauty to fire us, saints to save,
Escort us to a little grave.

No fate, save by the victim's fault, is low,
For God hath writ all dooms magnificent,
So guilt not traverses his tender will.

THIS shining moment is an edifice
Which the Omnipotent cannot rebuild.

ROOMY Eternity
Casts her schemes rarely,
And an æon allows
For each quality and part
Of the multitudinous
And many-chambered heart.

BE of good cheer, brave spirit; steadfastly
Serve that low whisper thou hast served;
    for know,
God hath a select family of sons
Now scattered wide thro' earth, and each
    alone,
Who are thy spiritual kindred, and each one
By constant service to that inward law,
Is weaving the sublime proportions
Of a true monarch's soul. Beauty and
    strength,
The riches of a spotless memory,
The eloquence of truth, the wisdom got
By searching of a clear and loving eye
That seeth as God seeth, — these are their
    gifts ;
And Time, who keeps God's word, brings
    on the day
To seal the marriage of these minds with
    thine,
Thine everlasting lovers.   Ye shall be
The salt of all the elements, world of the
    world.

LOVE
Asks nought his brother cannot give;
Asks nothing, but does all receive.
Love calls not to his aid events;

He to his wants can well suffice:
Asks not of others soft consents,
Nor kind occasion without eyes;
Nor plots to ope or bolt a gate,
Nor heeds Condition's iron walls, —
Where he goes, goes before him Fate;
Whom he uniteth, God installs;
Instant and perfect his access
To the dear object of his thought,
Though foes and land and seas between
Himself and his love intervene.

TELL men what they knew before;
Paint the prospect from their door.

HIM strong Genius urged to roam,
Stronger Custom brought him home.

THAT each should in his house abide,
Therefore was the world so wide.[1]

YES, sometimes to the sorrow-stricken
Shall his own sorrow seem impertinent,
A thing that takes no more root in the world
Than doth the traveller's shadow on the
        rock.

REX

THE bard and mystic held me for their own,
I filled the dream of sad, poetic maids,
I took the friendly noble by the hand,
I was the trustee of the hand-cart man,
The brother of the fisher, porter, swain,
And these from the crowd's edge well
        pleased beheld
The service done to me as done to them.

SHUN passion, fold the hands of thrift,
    Sit still, and Truth is near :
Suddenly it will uplift
    Your eyelids to the sphere :

[1] A common thought with Emerson (see 'Written in Naples,' 'Written at Rome,' 'The Day's Ration,' and the essay 'Self-Reliance'), but, as here expressed, evidently meant for a direct answer to the last words of Goethe's *Wilhelm Meister*, so often quoted by Carlyle : —

> To give space for wandering is it
> That the world was made so wide.

Wait a little, you shall see
The portraiture of things to be.

OH, what is Heaven but the fellowship
Of minds that each can stand against the
        world
By its own meek and incorruptible will ?

ON bravely through the sunshine and the
        showers!
Time hath his work to do and we have ours.
1830–60.   1883.

FRAGMENTS ON THE POET AND THE POETIC GIFT

THE gods talk in the breath of the woods,
They talk in the shaken pine,
And fill the long reach of the old seashore
With dialogue divine;
And the poet who overhears
Some random word they say
Is the fated man of men
Whom the ages must obey.

THE sun set, but set not his hope : —
Stars rose, his faith was earlier up :
Fixed on the enormous galaxy,
Deeper and older seemed his eye,
And matched his sufferance sublime
The taciturnity of Time.[2]
He spoke, and words more soft than rain
Brought the Age of Gold again:
His action won such reverence sweet
As hid all measure of the feat.

THE Dervish whined to Said,
'Thou didst not tarry while I prayed.
Beware the fire that Eblis burned.'
But Saadi coldly thus returned,
'Once with manlike love and fear
I gave thee for an hour my ear,
I kept the sun and stars at bay,
And love, for words thy tongue could say.
I cannot sell my heaven again
For all that rattles in thy brain.'

[2] The first six lines were originally written as part of 'The Poet,' but were first printed, with the four following, as motto to the essay on 'Character'.

THE free winds told him what they knew,
Discoursed of fortune as they blew;
Omens and signs that filled the air
To him authentic witness bare;
The birds brought auguries on their wings,
And carolled undeceiving things
Him to beckon, him to warn;
Well might then the poet scorn
To learn of scribe or courier
Things writ in vaster character;
And on his mind at dawn of day
Soft shadows of the evening lay.

PALE genius roves alone,
No scout can track his way,
None credits him till he have shown
His diamonds to the day.

Not his the feaster's wine,
Nor land, nor gold, nor power,
By want and pain God screeneth him
Till his elected hour.

Go, speed the stars of Thought
On to their shining goals: —
The sower scatters broad his seed,
The wheat thou strew'st be souls.

FOR thought, and not praise;
Thought is the wages
For which I sell days,
Will gladly sell ages
And willing grow old
Deaf, and dumb, and blind, and cold,
Melting matter into dreams,
Panoramas which I saw
And whatever glows or seems
Into substance, into Law.

A DULL uncertain brain,
But gifted yet to know
That God has cherubim who go
Singing an immortal strain,
Immortal here below.
I know the mighty bards,
I listen when they sing,
And now I know
The secret store
Which these explore
When they with torch of genius pierce
The tenfold clouds that cover

The riches of the universe
From God's adoring lover.
And if to me it is not given
To fetch one ingot thence
Of the unfading gold of Heaven
His merchants may dispense,
Yet well I know the royal mine,
And know the sparkle of its ore,
Know Heaven's truth from lies that
shine —
Explored they teach us to explore.

FOR Fancy's gift
Can mountains lift;
The Muse can knit
What is past, what is done,
With the web that 's just begun;
Making free with time and size,
Dwindles here, there magnifies,
Swells a rain-drop to a tun;
So to repeat
No word or feat
Crowds in a day the sum of ages,
And blushing Love outwits the sages.

TRY the might the Muse affords
And the balm of thoughtful words;
Bring music to the desolate;
Hang roses on the stony fate.

AND as the light divides the dark
Through with living swords,
So shalt thou pierce the distant age
With adamantine words.

I FRAMED his tongue to music,
I armed his hand with skill,
I moulded his face to beauty
And his heart the throne of Will.

THAT book is good
Which puts me in a working mood.[1]
Unless to Thought is added Will,
Apollo is an imbecile.

[1] Compare the essay 'Inspiration: ' 'Every book is good to read which sets the reader in a working mood.' . . . 'Fact-books, if the facts be well and thoroughly told, are much more nearly allied to poetry than many books that are written in rhyme.'

What parts, what gems, what colors shine, —
Ah, but I miss the grand design.

FOR what need I of book or priest,
Or sibyl from the mummied East,
When every star is Bethlehem star ?
I count as many as there are
Cinquefoils or violets in the grass,
So many saints and saviors,
So many high behaviors
Salute the bard who is alive
And only sees what he doth give.

COIN the day-dawn into lines
In which its proper splendor shines;
Coin the moonlight into verse
Which all its marvel shall rehearse,

.   .   .   .

Chasing with words fast-flowing things;
    nor try
To plant thy shrivelled pedantry
On the shoulders of the sky.

HIS instant thought a poet spoke,
And filled the age his fame;
An inch of ground the lightning strook
But lit the sky with flame.[1]

1840–1860.   1883.

QUATRAINS AND TRANSLA-
TIONS

POET

EVER the Poet *from* the land
Steers his bark and trims his sail;
Right out to sea his courses stand,
New worlds to find in pinnace frail.

POET

To clothe the fiery thought
In simple words succeeds,
For still the craft of genius is
To mask a king in weeds.[2]

[1] Compáre Emerson's ' Address at the Hundredth Anniversary of the Concord Fight : ' ' The thunderbolt falls on an inch of ground, but the light of it fills the horizon.'

[2] Compare the essay on ' Beauty,' in *The Conduct of Life* : ' This art of omission is a chief secret of power, _____ it is a proof of high culture to say the ____ the simplest way.'

BOTANIST

Go thou to thy learned task,
I stay with the flowers of Spring:
Do thou of the Ages ask
What me the Hours will bring.

GARDENER

TRUE Brahmin, in the morning meadows
    wet,
Expound the Vedas of the violet,
Or, hid in vines, peeping through many a
    loop,
See the plum redden, and the beurré stoop.[3]

NORTHMAN

THE gale that wrecked you on the sand,
It helped my rowers to row;
The storm is my best galley hand
And drives me where I go.

FROM ALCUIN

THE sea is the road of the bold,
Frontier of the wheat-sown plains,
The pit wherein the streams are rolled
And fountain of the rains.

EXCELSIOR

OVER his head were the maple buds,
And over the tree was the moon,
And over the moon were the starry studs
That drop from the angels' shoon.

(*May 1, 1838.*)

BORROWING

(FROM THE FRENCH)

SOME of your hurts you have cured,
And the sharpest you still have survived,
But what torments of grief you endured
From evils which never arrived !

NATURE

BOON Nature yields each day a brag which
    we now first behold,
And trains us on to slight the new, as if it
    were the old:

[3] Go to the forest, if God has made thee a poet, and make thy life clean and fragrant as thy office.

True Brahmin, in the morning meadows wet.
Expound the Vedas in the violet.

Thy love must be thy art. . . . Nature also must teach thee rhetoric. She can teach thee not only to speak truth, but to speak it truly. (*Journal*, July, 1840.)

But blest is he, who, playing deep, yet haply
    asks not why,
Too busied with the crowded hour to fear
    to live or die.

NATURE IN LEASTS

As sings the pine-tree in the wind,
So sings in the wind a sprig of the pine;
Her strength and soul has laughing France
Shed in each drop of wine.

CLIMACTERIC

I AM not wiser for my age,
    Nor skilful by my grief;
Life loiters at the book's first page, —
    Ah! could we turn the leaf.

HERI, CRAS, HODIE

SHINES the last age, the next with hope is
    seen,
To-day slinks poorly off unmarked between:
Future or Past no richer secret folds,
O friendless Present! than thy bosom holds.

SACRIFICE

THOUGH love repine, and reason chafe,
    There came a voice without reply, —
' 'T is man's perdition to be safe,
    When for the truth he ought to die.' [1]

CASELLA [2]

TEST of the poet is knowledge of love,
For Eros is older than Saturn or Jove;
Never was poet, of late or of yore,
Who was not tremulous with love-lore.

[1] This quatrain was chosen by James Russell Lowell to be inscribed on the simple monument at Soldiers' Field in Cambridge, which was given as an athletic ground by Col. Henry Lee Higginson, in memory of his classmates and friends, Charles Russell Lowell, James Jackson Lowell, Robert Gould Shaw, James Savage, Jr., Edward Barry Dalton, and Stephen George Perkins, who died in the war or soon after.

Compare Emerson's two addresses referred to in the note on ' Voluntaries.' The best commentary, however, is Colonel Higginson's story of the lives and deaths of his comrades, in his addresses on the presentation of Soldiers' Field, 1890, and on Robert Gould Shaw, 1897 (*Four Addresses*, Boston, 1902.)

[2] A famous singer of Florence. Dante tells of meeting him (*Purgatory*, Canto II, lines 76–133) and begging him to sing: 'If a new law take not from thee memory or practice of the song of love which was wont to quiet all my longings, may it please thee therewith somewhat to comfort my soul.' (Norton's Translation.) Casella then sings Dante's *Amor che nella mente mi ragiona* ('Love, that within my mind discourses with me'), ' so sweetly, that the sweetness still within me sounds. My Master, and I, and the folk who were with

SHAKSPEARE

I SEE all human wits
Are measured but a few;
Unmeasured still my Shakspeare sits.
Lone as the blessed Jew.

HAFIZ

HER passions the shy violet
From Hafiz never hides;
Love-longings of the raptured bird
The bird to him confides.

ΑΔΑΚΡΥΝ ΝΕΜΟΝΤΑΙ ΑΙΩΝΑ

' A NEW commandment,' said the smiling
    Muse,
' I give my darling son, Thou shalt not
    preach '; —
Luther, Fox, Behmen, Swedenborg, grew
    pale,
And, on the instant, rosier clouds upbore
Hafiz and Shakspeare with their shining
    choirs.

FRIENDSHIP

THOU foolish Hafiz! Say, do churls
Know the worth of Oman's pearls ?
Give the gem which dims the moon
To the noblest, or to none.

ON prince or bride no diamond stone
Half so gracious ever shone,
As the light of enterprise
Beaming from a young man's eyes.

UNBAR the door, since thou the Opener art,
Show me the forward way, since thou art
    guide,
I put no faith in pilot or in chart,
Since they are transient, and thou dost
    abide.

IF Thought unlock her mysteries,
    If Friendship on me smile,
I walk in marble galleries,
    I talk with kings the while.

1850–60 ?   1883.

him, appeared so content as if naught else could touch the mind of any.'

Milton speaks of Casella in his ' Sonnet to Mr. Henry Lawes : '—

Dante shall give Fame leave to set thee higher
Than his Casella, whom he wooed to sing,
Met in the milder shades of Purgatory.

THE BOHEMIAN HYMN [1]

IN many forms we try
To utter God's infinity,
But the boundless hath no form,
And the Universal Friend
Doth as far transcend
An angel as a worm.

The great Idea baffles wit
Language falters under it,
It leaves the learned in the lurch;
Nor art, nor power, nor toil can find
The measure of the eternal Mind,
Nor hymn, nor prayer, nor church.

                                                        1883.

PAN

O WHAT are heroes, prophets, men,
But pipes through which the breath of Pan
        doth blow
A momentary music. Being's tide
Swells hitherward, and myriads of forms
Live, robed with beauty, painted by the
        sun;
Their dust, pervaded by the nerves of God,
Throbs with an overmastering energy
Knowing and doing. Ebbs the tide, they
        lie
White hollow shells upon the desert shore,
But not the less the eternal wave rolls on
To animate new millions, and exhale
Races and planets, its enchanted foam. [2]

                                                        1883.

THE ENCHANTER

IN the deep heart of man a poet dwells
Who all the day of life his summer story
        tells;
Scatters on every eye dust of his spells,
Scent, form and color; to the flowers and
        shells
Wins the believing child with wondrous
        tales;
Touches a cheek with colors of romance,
And crowds a history into a glance;

Gives beauty to the lake and fountain,
Spies oversea the fires of the mountain;
When thrushes ope their throat, 't is he
        that sings,
And he that paints the oriole's fiery wings.
The little Shakspeare in the maiden's
        heart
Makes Romeo of a plough-boy on his cart;
Opens the eye to Virtue's starlike meed
And gives persuasion to a gentle deed.

                                                        1883.

EROS

THEY put their finger on their lip,
    The Powers above:
    The seas their islands clip,
    The moons in ocean dip,
They love, but name not love.

                                                        1883.

MUSIC [3]

LET me go where'er I will,
I hear a sky-born music still:
It sounds from all things old,
It sounds from all things young,
From all that's fair, from all that's foul,
Peals out a cheerful song.

It is not only in the rose,
It is not only in the bird,
Not only where the rainbow glows,
Nor in the song of woman heard,
But in the darkest, meanest things
There alway, alway something sings.

'T is not in the high stars alone,
Nor in the cup of budding flowers,
Nor in the redbreast's mellow tone,
Nor in the bow that smiles in showers,
But in the mud and scum of things
There alway, alway something sings.

                                                        1883.

THE TITMOUSE [4]

YOU shall not be overbold
When you deal with arctic cold,

---

[1] Compare the essay on 'Plato:' 'Plato apprehended the cardinal facts. He could prostrate himself on the earth and cover his eyes whilst he adored that which cannot be numbered, or gauged, or known, or named . . . He even stood ready, as in the Parmenides, to demonstrate . . . that this Being exceeded the limits of intellect. No man ever more fully acknowledged the Ineffable.'

[2] Compare Bryant's 'Flood of Years.'

[3] In 1883 this poem was printed among the 'Fragments on Nature and Life,' in an Appendix. It first appears as a separate poem, with title, in the *Centenary Edition* of 1904.

[4] The snow still lies even with the tops of the walls across the Walden road, and, this afternoon, I waded through the woods to my grove. A chickadee came out to greet me, flew about within reach of my hands.

As late I found my lukewarm blood
Chilled wading in the snow-choked wood.
How should I fight ? my foeman fine
Has million arms to one of mine:
East, west, for aid I looked in vain,
East, west, north, south, are his domain.
Miles off, three dangerous miles, is home;
Must borrow his winds who there would
    come.   10
Up and away for life ! be fleet ! —
The frost-king ties my fumbling feet,
Sings in my ears, my hands are stones,
Curdles the blood to the marble bones,
Tugs at the heart-strings, numbs the sense,
And hems in life with narrowing fence.
Well, in this broad bed lie and sleep, —
The punctual stars will vigil keep, —
Embalmed by purifying cold;
The winds shall sing their dead-march old, 20
The snow is no ignoble shroud,
The moon thy mourner, and the cloud.

Softly, — but this way fate was pointing,
'T was coming fast to such anointing,
When piped a tiny voice hard by,
Gay and polite, a cheerful cry,
Chic-chic-a-dee-dee! saucy note
Out of sound heart and merry throat,
As if it said, 'Good day, good sir !
Fine afternoon, old passenger !   30
Happy to meet you in these places,
Where January brings few faces.'

This poet, though he live apart,
Moved by his hospitable heart,
Sped, when I passed his sylvan fort,
To do the honors of his court,
As fits a feathered lord of land;
Flew near, with soft wing grazed my
    hand,

perched on the nearest bough, flew down into the snow,
rested there two seconds, then up again just over my
head, and busied himself on the dead bark. I whistled to him through my teeth, and (I think, in response) he began at once to whistle. I promised him
crumbs, and must not go again to these woods without
them. I suppose the best food to carry would be the
meat of shagbarks or Castile nuts. Thoreau tells me
that they are very sociable with wood-choppers, and
will take crumbs from their hands. (*Journal*, March
3, 1862.)

Compare Holmes's characteristic comment on this
poem, in his *Pages from an Old Volume of Life :* 'The
moral of the poem is as heroic as the verse is exquisite ;
but we must not forget the non-conducting quality of
fur and feathers, and remember, if we are at all delicate, to go

    Wrapped in our virtue, *and* a good surtout,

by way of additional security.'

Hopped on the bough, then, darting low,
Prints his small impress on the snow,   40
Shows feats of his gymnastic play,
Head downward, clinging to the spray.

Here was this atom in full breath,
Hurling defiance at vast death;
This scrap of valor just for play
Fronts the north-wind in waistcoat gray,
As if to shame my weak behavior;
I greeted loud my little savior,
'You pet ! what dost here ? and what for ?
In these woods, thy small Labrador,   50
At this pinch, wee San Salvador !
What fire burns in that little chest
So frolic, stout and self-possest ?
Henceforth I wear no stripe but thine;
Ashes and jet all hues outshine.
Why are not diamonds black and gray,
To ape thy dare-devil array ?
And I affirm, the spacious North
Exists to draw thy virtue forth.
I think no virtue goes with size;   60
The reason of all cowardice
Is, that men are overgrown,
And, to be valiant, must come down
To the titmouse dimension.'

'T is good will makes intelligence,
And I began to catch the sense
Of my bird's song: 'Live out of doors
In the great woods, on prairie floors.
I dine in the sun; when he sinks in the sea,
I too have a hole in a hollow tree;   70
And I like less when Summer beats
With stifling beams on these retreats,
Than noontide twilights which snow makes
With tempest of the blinding flakes.
For well the soul, if stout within,
Can arm impregnably the skin;
And polar frost my frame defied,
Made of the air that blows outside.'

With glad remembrance of my debt,
I homeward turn; farewell, my pet !   80
When here again thy pilgrim comes,
He shall bring store of seeds and crumbs.
Doubt not, so long as earth has bread,
Thou first and foremost shalt be fed;
The Providence that is most large
Takes hearts like thine in special charge,
Helps who for their own need are strong,
And the sky doats on cheerful song.
Henceforth I prize thy wiry chant
O'er all that mass and minster vaunt;   90

For men mis-hear thy call in Spring,
As 't would accost some frivolous wing,
Crying out of the hazel copse, *Phe-be!*
And, in winter, *Chic-a-dee-dee!*
I think old Cæsar must have heard
In northern Gaul my dauntless bird,
And, echoed in some frosty wold,
Borrowed thy battle-numbers bold.
And I will write our annals new,
And thank thee for a better clew,   100
I, who dreamed not when I came here
To find the antidote of fear,
Now hear thee say in Roman key,
Pæan! Veni, vidi, vici.

1862.   1862.

BOSTON HYMN

READ IN MUSIC HALL, JANUARY 1, 1863 [1]

THE word of the Lord by night
To the watching Pilgrims came,
As they sat by the seaside,
And filled their hearts with flame.

God said, I am tired of kings,
I suffer them no more;
Up to my ear the morning brings
The outrage of the poor.

Think ye I made this ball
A field of havoc and war,   10
Where tyrants great and tyrants small
Might harry the weak and poor?

My angel, — his name is Freedom, —
Choose him to be your king;
He shall cut pathways east and west
And fend you with his wing.

Lo! I uncover the land
Which I hid of old time in the West,
As the sculptor uncovers the statue
When he has wrought his best;   20

I show Columbia, of the rocks
Which dip their foot in the seas
And soar to the air-borne flocks
Of clouds and the boreal fleece.

I will divide my goods;
Call in the wretch and slave:

[1] The day when the Emancipation Proclamation went into effect. The Proclamation was issued on September 22, 1862.

None shall rule but the humble,
And none but Toil shall have.

I will have never a noble,
No lineage counted great;   30
Fishers and choppers and ploughmen
Shall constitute a state.

Go, cut down trees in the forest
And trim the straightest boughs;
Cut down trees in the forest
And build me a wooden house.

Call the people together,
The young men and the sires,
The digger in the harvest-field,
Hireling and him that hires;   40

And here in a pine state-house
They shall choose men to rule
In every needful faculty,
In church and state and school.

Lo, now! if these poor men
Can govern the land and sea
And make just laws below the sun,
As planets faithful be.

And ye shall succor men;
'T is nobleness to serve;   50
Help them who cannot help again:
Beware from right to swerve.

I break your bonds and masterships,
And I unchain the slave:
Free be his heart and hand henceforth
As wind and wandering wave.

I cause from every creature
His proper good to flow:
As much as he is and doeth,
So much he shall bestow.   60

But, laying hands on another
To coin his labor and sweat,
He goes in pawn to his victim
For eternal years in debt.

To-day unbind the captive,
So only are ye unbound;
Lift up a people from the dust,
Trump of their rescue, sound!

Pay ransom to the owner
And fill the bag to the brim.   70

Who is the owner ?   The slave is owner,
And ever was. Pay him.

O North ! give him beauty for rags,
And honor, O South ! for his shame;
Nevada ! coin thy golden crags
With Freedom's image and name.

Up ! and the dusky race
That sat in darkness long, —
Be swift their feet as antelopes,
And as behemoth strong.   80

Come, East and West and North,
By races, as snow-flakes,
And carry my purpose forth,
Which neither halts nor shakes.

My will fulfilled shall be,
For, in daylight or in dark,
My thunderbolt has eyes to see
His way home to the mark.

1862.   1863.

VOLUNTARIES

I

Low and mournful be the strain,
Haughty thought be far from me;
Tones of penitence and pain,
Moanings of the tropic sea;
Low and tender in the cell
Where a captive sits in chains,
Crooning ditties treasured well
From his Afric's torrid plains.
Sole estate his sire bequeathed, —
Hapless sire to hapless son, —   10
Was the wailing song he breathed,
And his chain when life was done.

What his fault, or what his crime ?
Or what ill planet crossed his prime ?
Heart too soft and will too weak
To front the fate that crouches near, —
Dove beneath the vulture's beak ; —
Will song dissuade the thirsty spear ?
Dragged from his mother's arms and
            breast,
Displaced, disfurnished here,   20
His wistful toil to do his best
Chilled by a ribald jeer.

Great men in the Senate sate,
Sage and hero, side by side,
Building for their sons the State,
Which they shall rule with pride.
They forbore to break the chain
Which bound the dusky tribe,
Checked by the owners' fierce disdain,
Lured by ' Union ' as the bribe.   30
Destiny sat by, and said,
' Pang for pang your seed shall pay,
Hide in false peace your coward head,
I bring round the harvest day.'

II

FREEDOM all winged expands,
Nor perches in a narrow place;
Her broad van seeks unplanted lands;
She loves a poor and virtuous race.
Clinging to a colder zone
Whose dark sky sheds the snowflake
                       down,   40
The snowflake is her banner's star,
Her stripes the boreal streamers are.
Long she loved the Northman well;
Now the iron age is done,
She will not refuse to dwell
With the offspring of the Sun;
Foundling of the desert far,
Where palms plume, siroccos blaze,
He roves unhurt the burning ways
In climates of the summer star.   50
He has avenues to God
Hid from men of Northern brain,
Far beholding, without cloud,
What these with slowest steps attain.
If once the generous chief arrive
To lead him willing to be led,
For freedom he will strike and strive,
And drain his heart till he be dead.

III

IN an age of fops and toys,
Wanting wisdom, void of right,   60
Who shall nerve heroic boys
To hazard all in Freedom's fight, —
Break sharply off their jolly games,
Forsake their comrades gay
And quit proud homes and youthful dames
For famine, toil and fray ?
Yet on the nimble air benign
Speed nimbler messages,
That waft the breath of grace divine
To hearts in sloth and ease.   70
So nigh is grandeur to our dust,
So near is God to man,

When Duty whispers low, *Thou must*,
The youth replies, *I can*.[1]

IV

OH, well for the fortunate soul
Which Music's wings infold,
Stealing away the memory
Of sorrows new and old !
Yet happier he whose inward sight,
Stayed on his subtile thought,   80
Shuts his sense on toys of time,
To vacant bosoms brought.
But best befriended of the God
He who, in evil times,
Warned by an inward voice,
Heeds not the darkness and the dread,
Biding by his rule and choice,
Feeling only the fiery thread
Leading over heroic ground,
Walled with mortal terror round,   90
To the aim which him allures,
And the sweet heaven his deed secures.
Peril around, all else appalling,
Cannon in front and leaden rain
Him duty through the clarion calling
To the van called not in vain.

Stainless soldier on the walls,
Knowing this, — and knows no more, —
Whoever fights, whoever falls,
Justice conquers evermore,   100
Justice after as before, —
And he who battles on her side,
God, though he were ten times slain,
Crowns him victor glorified,
Victor over death and pain.

V

BLOOMS the laurel which belongs
To the valiant chief who fights;
I see the wreath, I hear the songs
Lauding the Eternal Rights,
Victors over daily wrongs :   110
Awful victors, they misguide
Whom they will destroy,
And their coming triumph hide
In our downfall, or our joy:

They reach no term, they never sleep,
In equal strength through space abide;
Though, feigning dwarfs, they crouch and
    creep,
The strong they slay, the swift outstride :
Fate's grass grows rank in valley clods,
And rankly on the castled steep, —   120
Speak it firmly, these are gods,
All are ghosts beside.

                                       1863.

MY GARDEN [2]

IF I could put my woods in song
And tell what 's there enjoyed,
All men would to my gardens throng,
And leave the cities void.

In my plot no tulips blow, —
Snow-loving pines and oaks instead;
And rank the savage maples grow
From Spring's faint flush to Autumn red.

My garden is a forest ledge
Which older forests bound;   10
The banks slope down to the blue lake-
    edge,
Then plunge to depths profound.

Here once the Deluge ploughed,
Laid the terraces, one by one;
Ebbing later whence it flowed,
They bleach and dry in the sun.

The sowers make haste to depart, —
The wind and the birds which sowed it;
Not for fame, nor by rules of art,
Planted these, and tempests flowed it.   20

Waters that wash my garden-side
Play not in Nature's lawful web,
They heed not moon or solar tide, —
Five years elapse from flood to ebb.

Hither hasted, in old time, Jove,
And every god, — none did refuse;
And be sure at last came Love,
And after Love, the Muse.

---

[1] These lines, a moment after they were written, seemed as if they had been carved on marble for a thousand years. (HOLMES, *Life of Emerson*.)
Compare Emerson's ' Address at the Dedication of the Soldiers' Monument in Concord,' especially the paragraph beginning : ' All sorts of men went to the war ; ' and his ' Harvard Commemoration Speech, July 21, 1865.'

[2] Emerson wrote to Carlyle, May 14, 1846: ' I, too, have a new plaything, the best I ever had, — a wood-lot. Last fall I bought a piece of more than forty acres, on the border of a little lake half a mile wide and more, called Walden Pond ; — a place to which my feet have for years been accustomed to bring me once or twice a week at all seasons.' See the whole letter, in the *Carlyle-Emerson Correspondence*, vol. ii, pp. 123-125.

Keen ears can catch a syllable,
As if one spake to another,   30
In the hemlocks tall, untamable,
And what the whispering grasses smother.

Æolian harps in the pine
Ring with the song of the Fates;
Infant Bacchus in the vine, —
Far distant yet his chorus waits.

Canst thou copy in verse one chime
Of the wood-bell's peal and cry,
Write in a book the morning's prime,
Or match with words that tender sky ?   40

Wonderful verse of the gods,
Of one import, of varied tone;
They chant the bliss of their abodes
To man imprisoned in his own.

Ever the words of the gods resound;
But the porches of man's ear
Seldom in this low life's round
Are unsealed, that he may hear.

Wandering voices in the air
And murmurs in the wold   50
Speak what I cannot declare,
Yet cannot all withhold.

When the shadow fell on the lake,
The whirlwind in ripples wrote
Air-bells of fortune that shine and break,
And omens above thought.

But the meanings cleave to the lake,
Cannot be carried in book or urn;
Go thy ways now, come later back,
On waves and hedges still they burn.   60

These the fates of men forecast,
Of better men than live to-day;
If who can read them comes at last
He will spell in the sculpture, 'Stay.'

                                              1866.

TERMINUS [1]

It is time to be old,
To take in sail: —

[1] In the last days of the year 1866, when I was returning from a long stay in the Western States, I met
my father in New York just starting for his usual win-

The god of bounds,
Who sets to seas a shore,
Came to me in his fatal rounds,
And said : 'No more !
No farther shoot
Thy broad ambitious branches, and thy root.
Fancy departs: no more invent;
Contract thy firmament   10
To compass of a tent.
There 's not enough for this and that,
Make thy option which of two;
Economize the failing river,
Not the less revere the Giver,
Leave the many and hold the few.
Timely wise accept the terms,
Soften the fall with wary foot;
A little while
Still plan and smile,   20
And, — fault of novel germs, —
Mature the unfallen fruit.
Curse, if thou wilt, thy sires,
Bad husbands of their fires,
Who, when they gave thee breath,
Failed to bequeath
The needful sinew stark as once,
The Baresark marrow to thy bones,
But left a legacy of ebbing veins,
Inconstant heat and nerveless reins, —   30
Amid the Muses, left thee deaf and dumb,
Amid the gladiators, halt and numb.'

As the bird trims her to the gale,
I trim myself to the storm of time,
I man the rudder, reef the sail,
Obey the voice at eve obeyed at prime:
'Lowly faithful, banish fear,
Right onward drive unharmed;
The port, well worth the cruise, is near,
And every wave is charmed.'   40
1867.

ter lecturing trip, in those days extending beyond the
Mississippi. We spent the night together at the St.
Denis Hotel, and as we sat by the fire, he read me two
or three of his poems for the new May-Day volume,
among them 'Terminus.' It almost startled me. No
thought of his ageing had ever come to me, and there
he sat, with no apparent abatement of bodily vigor, and
young in spirit, recognizing with serene acquiescence
his failing forces; I think he smiled as he read. He
recognized, as none of us did, that his working days
were nearly done. They lasted about five years longer,
although he lived, in comfortable health, yet ten years
beyond those of his activity. Almost at the time when
he wrote 'Terminus' he wrote in his journal : —
  'Within I do not find wrinkles and used heart, but
unspent youth.' (E. W. EMERSON, in the *Centenary
Edition.*)

HENRY WADSWORTH LONGFELLOW

THE SPIRIT OF POETRY

THERE is a quiet spirit in these woods,
That dwells where'er the gentle south-wind
  blows;
Where, underneath the white-thorn in the
  glade,
The wild flowers bloom, or, kissing the soft
  air,
The leaves above their sunny palms out-
  spread.
With what a tender and impassioned voice
It fills the nice and delicate ear of thought,
When the fast ushering star of morning
  comes
O'er-riding the gray hills with golden
  scarf;
Or when the cowled and dusky-sandalled
  Eve,   10
In mourning weeds, from out the western
  gate,
Departs with silent pace ! That spirit
  moves
In the green valley, where the silver brook,
From its full laver, pours the white cas-
  cade;
And, babbling low amid the tangled woods,
Slips down through moss-grown stones with
  endless laughter.
And frequent, on the everlasting hills,
Its feet go forth, when it doth wrap itself
In all the dark embroidery of the storm,
And shouts the stern, strong wind. And
  here, amid   20
The silent majesty of these deep woods,
Its presence shall uplift thy thoughts from
  earth,
As to the sunshine and the pure, bright
  air
Their tops the green trees lift. Hence
  gifted bards
Have ever loved the calm and quiet shades.
For them there was an eloquent voice in
  all
The sylvan pomp of woods, the golden
  sun,
The flowers, the leaves, the river on its
  way,

Blue skies, and silver clouds, and gentle
  winds,
The swelling upland, where the sidelong
  sun   30
Aslant the wooded slope, at evening, goes,
Groves, through whose broken roof the sky
  looks in,
Mountain, and shattered cliff, and sunny
  vale,
The distant lake, fountains, and mighty
  trees,
In many a lazy syllable, repeating
Their old poetic legends to the wind.

  And this is the sweet spirit, that doth fill
The world; and, in these wayward days of
  youth,
My busy fancy oft embodies it,
As a bright image of the light and beauty 40
That dwell in nature; of the heavenly
  forms
We worship in our dreams, and the soft
  hues
That stain the wild bird's wing, and flush
  the clouds
When the sun sets. Within her tender
  eye
The heaven of April, with its changing
  light,
And when it wears the blue of May, is
  hung,
And on her lip the rich, red rose. Her
  hair
Is like the summer tresses of the trees,
When twilight makes them brown, and on
  her cheek
Blushes the richness of an autumn sky,   50
With ever-shifting beauty. Then her
  breath,
It is so like the gentle air of Spring,
As, from the morning's dewy flowers, it
  comes
Full of their fragrance, that it is a joy
To have it round us, and her silver voice
Is the rich music of a summer bird,
Heard in the still night, with its passionate
  cadence.

1825.   1827.

BURIAL OF THE MINNISINK [1]

On sunny slope and beechen swell,
The shadowed light of evening fell;
And, where the maple's leaf was brown,
With soft and silent lapse came down
The glory that the wood receives,
At sunset, in its golden leaves.

Far upward in the mellow light
Rose the blue hills. One cloud of white,
Around a far uplifted cone,
In the warm blush of evening shone;   10
An image of the silver lakes,
By which the Indian's soul awakes.

But soon a funeral hymn was heard
Where the soft breath of evening stirred
The tall, gray forest; and a band
Of stern in heart, and strong in hand,
Came winding down beside the wave,
To lay the red chief in his grave.

They sang, that by his native bowers
He stood, in the last moon of flowers,   20
And thirty snows had not yet shed
Their glory on the warrior's head;
But, as the summer fruit decays,
So died he in those naked days.

A dark cloak of the roebuck's skin
Covered the warrior, and within
Its heavy folds the weapons, made
For the hard toils of war, were laid;
The cuirass, woven of plaited reeds,
And the broad belt of shells and beads.   30

Before, a dark-haired virgin train
Chanted the death dirge of the slain;
Behind, the long procession came
Of hoary men and chiefs of fame,
With heavy hearts, and eyes of grief,
Leading the war-horse of their chief.

Stripped of his proud and martial dress,
Uncurbed, unreined, and riderless,

With darting eye, and nostril spread,
And heavy and impatient tread,   40
He came; and oft that eye so proud
Asked for his rider in the crowd.

They buried the dark chief; they freed
Beside the grave his battle steed;
And swift an arrow cleaved its way
To his stern heart! One piercing neigh
Arose, and, on the dead man's plain,
The rider grasps his steed again.
1825.   *1826.*

THE RETURN OF SPRING

FROM CHARLES D'ORLÉANS [2]

Now Time throws off his cloak again
Of ermined frost, and wind, and rain,
And clothes him in the embroidery
Of glittering sun and clear blue sky.
With beast and bird the forest rings,
Each in his jargon cries or sings;
And Time throws off his cloak again
Of ermined frost, and wind, and rain.

River, and fount, and tinkling brook
Wear in their dainty livery
Drops of silver jewelry;
In new-made suit they merry look;
And Time throws off his cloak again
Of ermined frost, and wind, and rain.
1830.   *1831.*

[1] This poem, written when Longfellow was eighteen years old, is interesting as an early example of that love for Indian subjects which later produced 'Hiawatha.' It should be compared with Whittier's early poems on Indian subjects, 'Pentucket,' 'The Funeral Tree of the Sokokis,' 'Mary Garvin,' 'Mogg Megone,' etc; with Lowell's 'Chippewa Legend;' and with Bryant's 'The Indian Girl's Lament,' 'Monument Mountain,' etc.

[2] Longfellow's work as a translator extended from almost the beginning to the end of his poetical career, included versions from the French, Spanish, Italian, Portuguese, Latin, German, Danish, and Anglo-Saxon, and culminated in his rendering of Dante's *Divine Comedy*. This work unquestionably played an important part in his development, increasing the range and suppleness of his powers, and keeping the poet alive in him during the long period when he was completely absorbed by teaching, lecturing, prose writing, the composition and editing of text-books, and foreign travel. For twelve or thirteen years, between his early poems and the new beginning of his poetical work in the 'Psalm of Life,' he wrote practically nothing in verse except translations.
Toward the end of his life (in a letter of March 7, 1879) he said of translation: 'And what a difficult work! There is evidently a great and strange fascination in translating. It seizes people with irresistible power, and whirls them away till they are beside themselves. It is like a ghost beckoning one to follow.' (*Life*, vol. iii, p. 298.) (In all notes on Longfellow's poems, the 'Life' referred to is Samuel Longfellow's *Life of Henry Wadsworth Longfellow*, 3 volumes, 1887.)

ART AND NATURE

FROM FRANCISCO DE MEDRANO

THE works of human artifice soon tire
The curious eye; the fountain's sparkling
    rill,
And gardens, when adorned by human
    skill,
Reproach the feeble hand, the vain desire.
But oh ! the free and wild magnificence
Of Nature, in her lavish hours, doth steal,
In admiration silent and intense,
The soul of him who hath a soul to feel.
The river moving on its ceaseless way,
The verdant reach of meadows fair and
    green,
And the blue hills, that bound the sylvan
    scene,
These speak of grandeur, that defies
    decay, —
Proclaim the Eternal Architect on high,
Who stamps on all his works his own
    eternity.
1832.   1832.

A PSALM OF LIFE[1]

WHAT THE HEART OF THE YOUNG MAN SAID TO THE PSALMIST

TELL me not, in mournful numbers,
    Life is but an empty dream ! —
For the soul is dead that slumbers,
    And things are not what they seem.

[1] This poem has been called 'the very heart-beat of the American conscience.' When it was first published, anonymously, in the *Knickerbocker* magazine for October, 1838, it at once attracted attention. Whittier wrote of it in the *Freeman :* ' We know not who the author may be, but he or she is no common man or woman. These nine simple verses are worth more than all the dreams of Shelley, and Keats, and Wordsworth. They are alive and vigorous with the spirit of the day in which we live, — the moral steam enginery of an age of action.' (Quoted by Professor Carpenter in his *Life of Whittier.*)
    The writing of the ' Psalm ' is recorded in Longfellow's *Journal* under the date of July 26, 1838. He afterwards said of it, ' I kept it some time in manuscript, unwilling to show it to any one, it being a voice from my inmost heart at a time when I was rallying from depression.' (*Life of Longfellow*, vol. i, p. 301.) In other passages of his *Journal* he speaks of writing ' another psalm,' ' a psalm of death,' etc. The ' psalmist ' to whom the young man speaks, is therefore the poet himself. ' It was the young man's better heart answering and refuting his own mood of despondency.' (*Life*, vol. i, pp. 283–284.) See further the *Life of Longfellow*, vol. i, pp. 281–284 ; and vol. ii, pp. 186, 283. The poem has been translated into many languages, including Chinese and Sanscrit. (*Life*, vol. i, p. 376 ; vol. iii, pp. 43, 64.)

Life is real ! Life is earnest !
    And the grave is not its goal;
Dust thou art, to dust returnest,
    Was not spoken of the soul.

Not enjoyment, and not sorrow,
    Is our destined end or way;   10
But to act, that each to-morrow
    Find us farther than to-day.

Art is long, and Time is fleeting,
    And our hearts, though stout and brave,
Still, like muffled drums, are beating
    Funeral marches to the grave.

In the world's broad field of battle,
    In the bivouac of Life,
Be not like dumb, driven cattle !
    Be a hero in the strife !   20

Trust no Future, howe'er pleasant !
    Let the dead Past bury its dead !
Act, — act in the living Present !
    Heart within, and God o'erhead !

Lives of great men all remind us
    We can make our lives sublime,
And, departing, leave behind us
    Footprints on the sands of time;

Footprints, that perhaps another,
    Sailing o'er life's solemn main,   30
A forlorn and shipwrecked brother,
    Seeing, shall take heart again.

Let us, then, be up and doing,
    With a heart for any fate;
Still achieving, still pursuing,
    Learn to labor and to wait.
1838.   1838.

THE LIGHT OF STARS[2]

THE night is come, but not too soon;
    And sinking silently,
All silently, the little moon
    Drops down behind the sky.

[2] 'This poem was written on a beautiful summer night. The moon, a little strip of silver, was just setting behind the grove at Mount Auburn, and the planet Mars blazing in the southeast. There was a singular light in the sky.' (H. W. L.) It was published in the same number of the *Knickerbocker* as the last, where it was headed *A Second Psalm of Life.* (*Cambridge Edition* of Longfellow's *Poetical Works.*)

There is no light in earth or heaven
    But the cold light of stars;
And the first watch of night is given
    To the red planet Mars.

Is it the tender star of love ?
    The star of love and dreams ?   10
Oh no ! from that blue tent above
    A hero's armor gleams.

And earnest thoughts within me rise,
    When I behold afar,
Suspended in the evening skies,
    The shield of that red star.

O star of strength ! I see thee stand
    And smile upon my pain;
Thou beckonest with thy mailed hand,
    And I am strong again.   20

Within my breast there is no light
    But the cold light of stars;
I give the first watch of the night
    To the red planet Mars.

The star of the unconquered will,
    He rises in my breast,
Serene, and resolute, and still,
    And calm, and self-possessed.

And thou, too, whosoe'er thou art,
    That readest this brief psalm,   30
As one by one thy hopes depart,
    Be resolute and calm.

Oh, fear not in a world like this,
    And thou shalt know erelong,
Know how sublime a thing it is
    To suffer and be strong.

1838.   1838.

HYMN TO THE NIGHT [1]

'Ασπασίη, τρίλλιστος

I HEARD the trailing garments of the Night
    Sweep through her marble halls !
I saw her sable skirts all fringed with
            light
    From the celestial walls !

[1] ' No poem ever opened with a beauty more august,'
says Poe in his early review of the *Voices of the Night*
(February, 1840). See his further criticism of the poem,
line by line, in the *Virginia Edition* of his *Works*, vol.
x, pp. 72-76.

I felt her presence, by its spell of might,
    Stoop o'er me from above;
The calm, majestic presence of the Night,
    As of the one I love.

I heard the sounds of sorrow and delight,
    The manifold, soft chimes,
That fill the haunted chambers of the
            Night,
    Like some old poet's rhymes.

From the cool cisterns of the midnight
            air
    My spirit drank repose;
The fountain of perpetual peace flows
            there, —
    From those deep cisterns flows.

O holy Night ! from thee I learn to bear
    What man has borne before !
Thou layest thy finger on the lips of Care,
    And they complain no more.

Peace ! Peace ! Orestes-like I breathe this
            prayer !
    Descend with broad-winged flight,
The welcome, the thrice-prayed for, the
            most fair,
    The best-beloved Night !

1839.   1839.

FOOTSTEPS OF ANGELS [2]

WHEN the hours of Day are numbered,
    And the voices of the Night
Wake the better soul, that slumbered,
    To a holy, calm delight;

Ere the evening lamps are lighted,
    And, like phantoms grim and tall,
Shadows from the fitful firelight
    Dance upon the parlor wall;

[2] A slightly different version of the first, second,
third, sixth, seventh and eighth stanzas, with the title
' Evening Shadows,' is to be found in Longfellow's
Journal under the date of February 27, 1838. (*Life*, vol.
i, pp. 287-288). The poem was finished March 26, 1839
(*Life*, vol. i, pp. 327-328). The fourth stanza alludes
to his brother-in-law and closest friend, George W.
Pierce, of whose death he had heard in Germany on
Christmas Eve of 1835, and of whom he wrote nearly
twenty years later : ' I have never ceased to feel that
in his death something was taken from my own life
which could never be restored. I have constantly in
my memory his beautiful and manly character, frank,
generous, impetuous, gentle.' The sixth and following
stanzas allude to Mrs. Longfellow, who died at Rotter-
dam, November 29, 1835.

Then the forms of the departed
  Enter at the open door;   10
The beloved, the true-hearted,
  Come to visit me once more;

He, the young and strong, who cherished
  Noble longings for the strife,
By the roadside fell and perished,
  Weary with the march of life!

They, the holy ones and weakly,
  Who the cross of suffering bore,
Folded their pale hands so meekly,
  Spake with us on earth no more!   20

And with them the Being Beauteous,
  Who unto my youth was given,
More than all things else to love me,
  And is now a saint in heaven.

With a slow and noiseless footstep
  Comes that messenger divine,
Takes the vacant chair beside me,
  Lays her gentle hand in mine.

And she sits and gazes at me
  With those deep and tender eyes,   30
Like the stars, so still and saint-like,
  Looking downward from the skies.

Uttered not, yet comprehended,
  Is the spirit's voiceless prayer,
Soft rebukes, in blessings ended,
  Breathing from her lips of air.

Oh, though oft depressed and lonely,
  All my fears are laid aside,
If I but remember only
  Such as these have lived and died!   40
1838, 1839.   1839.

THE BELEAGUERED CITY

I HAVE read, in some old, marvellous
      tale,[1]
  Some legend strange and vague,

[1] During his visit to his friend Ward, in New York, in August, strolling into the library one day after breakfast, he took carelessly from the shelf a volume of Scott's *Border Minstrelsy*, and opened at one of the notes, containing the tradition about the city of Prague upon which this poem is founded : 'Similar to this was the *Nacht Lager*, or midnight camp, which seemed nightly to beleaguer the walls of Prague, but which disappeared upon the recitation of certain magical words.' (*Life*, vol. i, p. 344, note.)

That a midnight host of spectres pale
  Beleaguered the walls of Prague.

Beside the Moldau's rushing stream,
  With the wan moon overhead,
There stood, as in an awful dream,
  The army of the dead.

White as a sea-fog, landward bound,
  The spectral camp was seen,   10
And, with a sorrowful, deep sound,
  The river flowed between.

No other voice nor sound was there,
  No drum, nor sentry's pace;
The mist-like banners clasped the air
  As clouds with clouds embrace.

But when the old cathedral bell
  Proclaimed the morning prayer,
The white pavilions rose and fell
  On the alarmèd air.   20

Down the broad valley fast and far
  The troubled army fled;
Up rose the glorious morning star,
  The ghastly host was dead.

I have read, in the marvellous heart of man,
  That strange and mystic scroll,
That an army of phantoms vast and wan
  Beleaguer the human soul.

Encamped beside Life's rushing stream,
  In Fancy's misty light,   30
Gigantic shapes and shadows gleam
  Portentous through the night.

Upon its midnight battle-ground
  The spectral camp is seen,
And, with a sorrowful, deep sound,
  Flows the River of Life between.

No other voice nor sound is there,
  In the army of the grave;
No other challenge breaks the air,
  But the rushing of Life's wave.   40

And when the solemn and deep church-bell
  Entreats the soul to pray,
The midnight phantoms feel the spell,
  The shadows sweep away.

Down the broad Vale of Tears afar
  The spectral camp is fled;

Faith shineth as a morning star,
Our ghastly fears are dead.

1839.   1839.

THE WRECK OF THE HESPERUS [1]

IT was the schooner Hesperus,
That sailed the wintry sea;
And the skipper had taken his little daugh-
ter,
To bear him company.

Blue were her eyes as the fairy-flax,
Her cheeks like the dawn of day,
And her bosom white as the hawthorn
buds,
That ope in the month of May.

The skipper he stood beside the helm,
His pipe was in his mouth,   10
And he watched how the veering flaw did
blow
The smoke now West, now South.

Then up and spake an old Sailòr,
Had sailed to the Spanish Main,
'I pray thee, put into yonder port,
For I fear a hurricane.

'Last night, the moon had a golden ring,
And to-night no moon we see !'
The skipper, he blew a whiff from his
pipe,
And a scornful laugh laughed he.   20

Colder and louder blew the wind,
A gale from the Northeast,
The snow fell hissing in the brine,
And the billows frothed like yeast.

---

[1] Longfellow wrote in his *Journal* on December 17,
1839: ' News of shipwrecks horrible on the coast.
Twenty bodies washed ashore near Gloucester, one
lashed to a piece of the wreck. There is a reef called
Norman's Woe where many of these took place; among
others the schooner Hesperus. Also the Sea-flower on
Black Rock. I must write a ballad upon this.'
   The ballad was actually written twelve days later, on
the night of December 29: ' I wrote last evening a notice of Allston's poems. After which I sat till twelve
o'clock by my fire, smoking, when suddenly it came into
my mind to write the " Ballad of the Schooner Hesperus ; " which I accordingly did. Then I went to bed,
but could not sleep. New thoughts were running in
my mind, and I got up to add them to the ballad. It
was three by the clock. I then went to bed and fell
asleep. I feel pleased with the ballad. It hardly cost
me an effort. It did not come into my mind by lines
but by stanzas.' (*Journal*, December 30.)

Down came the storm, and smote amain
The vessel in its strength;
She shuddered and paused, like a frighted
steed,
Then leaped her cable's length.

' Come hither ! come hither ! my little
daughtèr,
And do not tremble so;   30
For I can weather the roughest gale
That ever wind did blow.'

He wrapped her warm in his seaman's coat
Against the stinging blast;
He cut a rope from a broken spar,
And bound her to the mast.

' O father ! I hear the church-bells ring,
Oh say, what may it be ?'
' 'T is a fog-bell on a rock-bound coast ! ' —
And he steered for the open sea.   40

' O father ! I hear the sound of guns,
Oh say, what may it be ?'
' Some ship in distress, that cannot live
In such an angry sea !'

' O father ! I see a gleaming light,
Oh say, what may it be ?'
But the father answered never a word,
A frozen corpse was he.

Lashed to the helm, all stiff and stark,
With his face turned to the skies,   50
The lantern gleamed through the gleaming
snow
On his fixed and glassy eyes.

Then the maiden clasped her hands and
prayed
That savèd she might be;
And she thought of Christ, who stilled the
wave,
On the Lake of Galilee.

And fast through the midnight dark and
drear,
Through the whistling sleet and snow,
Like a sheeted ghost, the vessel swept
Tow'rds the reef of Norman's Woe.   60

And ever the fitful gusts between
A sound came from the land;
It was the sound of the trampling surf
On the rocks and the hard sea-sand.

The breakers were right beneath her bows,
  She drifted a dreary wreck,
And a whooping billow swept the crew
  Like icicles from her deck.

She struck where the white and fleecy waves
  Looked soft as carded wool,   70
But the cruel rocks, they gored her side
  Like the horns of an angry bull.

Her rattling shrouds, all sheathed in ice,
  With the masts went by the board;
Like a vessel of glass, she stove and sank,
  Ho! ho! the breakers roared!

At daybreak, on the bleak sea-beach,
  A fisherman stood aghast,
To see the form of a maiden fair,
  Lashed close to a drifting mast.   80

The salt sea was frozen on her breast,
  The salt tears in her eyes;
And he saw her hair, like the brown sea-
    weed,
  On the billows fall and rise.

Such was the wreck of the Hesperus,
  In the midnight and the snow!
Christ save us all from a death like this,
  On the reef of Norman's Woe!
1839.   1840.

THE VILLAGE BLACKSMITH [1]

Under a spreading chestnut-tree
  The village smithy stands;
The smith, a mighty man is he,
  With large and sinewy hands;
And the muscles of his brawny arms
  Are strong as iron bands.

His hair is crisp, and black, and long,
  His face is like the tan;
His brow is wet with honest sweat,
  He earns whate'er he can,   10
And looks the whole world in the face,
  For he owes not any man.

[1] Longfellow at first called 'The Village Blacksmith' a 'new Psalm of Life, but later it was included
among the *Ballads*. See the *Life*, vol. i, pp. 345, 374
and note.
Iu 1876 the 'spreading chestnut-tree' was cut down
to give room for the widening of Brattle Street, and
from its wood was made the armchair presented to
Longfellow by the schoolchildren of Cambridge. See
p. 255.

Week in, week out, from morn till night,
  You can hear his bellows blow;
You can hear him swing his heavy sledge,
  With measured beat and slow,
Like a sexton ringing the village bell,
  When the evening sun is low.

And children coming home from school
  Look in at the open door;   20
They love to see the flaming forge,
  And hear the bellows roar,
And catch the burning sparks that fly
  Like chaff from a threshing-floor.

He goes on Sunday to the church,
  And sits among his boys;
He hears the parson pray and preach,
  He hears his daughter's voice,
Singing in the village choir,
  And it makes his heart rejoice.   30

It sounds to him like her mother's voice,
  Singing in Paradise!
He needs must think of her once more
  How in the grave she lies;
And with his hard, rough hand he wipes
  A tear out of his eyes.

Toiling, — rejoicing, — sorrowing,
  Onward through life he goes;
Each morning sees some task begin,
  Each evening sees it close;   40
Something attempted, something done,
  Has earned a night's repose.

Thanks, thanks to thee, my worthy
    friend,
  For the lesson thou hast taught!
Thus at the flaming forge of life
  Our fortunes must be wrought;
Thus on its sounding anvil shaped
  Each burning deed and thought.
1839.   1840.

THE SKELETON IN ARMOR [2]

Speak! speak! thou fearful guest!
  Who, with thy hollow breast
  Still in rude armor drest,
    Comest to daunt me!

[2] Longfellow wrote in his Journal on May 3, 1838:
'I have been looking at the old Northern Sagas, and

Wrapt not in Eastern balms,
But with thy fleshless palms
Stretched, as if asking alms,
    Why dost thou haunt me ?

Then, from those cavernous eyes
Pale flashes seemed to rise,   10
As when the Northern skies
    Gleam in December;

thinking of a series of ballads or a romantic poem on the
deeds of the first bold viking who crossed to this western world, with storm-spirits and devil-machinery under
water. New England ballads I have long thought of.
This seems to be an introduction. I will dream more of
this.'

A few months later, returning to Cambridge from
Newport, where he had doubtless seen the 'Round
Tower,' he passed through Fall River just after the
skeleton in armor had been unearthed. These two
things fitted in with his previous conception, and on
May 24, 1839, he speaks of his 'plan for a heroic poem
on the Discovery of America by the Northmen, in which
the Round Tower at Newport and the Skeleton in Armor
have a part to play.' In a letter to his father, of December 13, 1840, after the ballad was written, he speaks
of having himself seen the skeleton: 'I suppose it to
be the remains of one of the old Northern sea rovers
who came to this country in the tenth century. Of
course I make the tradition myself.'

For a full account of the finding of the skeleton, see
the *American Monthly Magazine* of January, 1836, from
which the following description is taken : —

'In digging down a hill near the village, a large mass
of earth slid off, leaving in the bank and partially
uncovered a human skull, which on examination was
found to belong to a body buried in a sitting posture;
the head being about one foot below what had been for
many years the surface of the ground. The surrounding earth was carefully removed, and the body found
to be enveloped in a covering of coarse bark of a dark
color. Within this envelope were found the remains of
another of coarse cloth, made of fine bark, and about
the texture of a Manilla coffee bag. On the breast was
a plate of brass, thirteen inches long, six broad at the
upper end, and five in the lower. This plate appears to
have been cast, and is from one eighth to three thirty-
seconds of an inch in thickness. It is so much corroded
that whether or not anything was engraved upon it has
not yet been ascertained. It is oval in form, the edges
being irregular, apparently made so by corrosion.
Below the breastplate, and entirely encircling the body,
was a belt composed of brass tubes, each four and a
half inches in length, and three sixteenths of an inch in
diameter, arranged longitudinally and close together,
the length of the tube being the width of the belt. The
tubes are of thin brass, cast upon hollow reeds, and
were fastened together by pieces of sinew. Near the
right knee was a quiver of arrows. The arrows are of
brass, thin, flat, and triangular in shape, with a round
hole cut through near the base. The shaft was fastened
to the head by inserting the latter in an opening at the
end of the wood and then tying with a sinew through
the round hole, a mode of constructing the weapon
never practised by the Indians, not even with their
arrows of thin shell. Parts of the shaft still remain on
some of them. When first discovered, the arrows were
in a sort of quiver of bark, which fell to pieces when
exposed to the air.'

Poe calls 'The Skeleton in Armor' 'a pure and
perfect thesis artistically treated.' See his review of
Longfellow's *Ballads and Other Poems*, April, 1842, in
the *Virginia Edition* of his *Works*, vol. xi.

And, like the water's flow
Under December's snow,
Came a dull voice of woe
    From the heart's chamber.

' I was a Viking old !
My deeds, though manifold,
No Skald in song has told,
    No Saga taught thee !   20
Take heed, that in thy verse
Thou dost the tale rehearse,
Else dread a dead man's curse ;
    For this I sought thee.

' Far in the Northern Land,
By the wild Baltic's strand,
I, with my childish hand,
    Tamed the gerfalcon;
And, with my skates fast-bound,
Skimmed the half-frozen Sound,   30
That the poor whimpering hound
    Trembled to walk on.

' Oft to his frozen lair
Tracked I the grisly bear,
While from my path the hare
    Fled like a shadow;
Oft through the forest dark
Followed the were-wolf's bark,
Until the soaring lark
    Sang from the meadow.   40

' But when I older grew,
Joining a corsair's crew,
O'er the dark sea I flew
    With the marauders.
Wild was the life we led;
Many the souls that sped,
Many the hearts that bled,
    By our stern orders.

' Many a wassail-bout
Wore the long Winter out;   50
Often our midnight shout
    Set the cocks crowing,
As we the Berserk's tale
Measured in cups of ale,
Draining the oaken pail,
    Filled to o'erflowing.

' Once as I told in glee
Tales of the stormy sea,
Soft eyes did gaze on me,
    Burning yet tender;   60

And as the white stars shine
On the dark Norway pine,
On that dark heart of mine
   Fell their soft splendor.

'I wooed the blue-eyed maid,
Yielding, yet half afraid,
And in the forest's shade
   Our vows were plighted.
Under its loosened vest
Fluttered her little breast,   70
Like birds within their nest
   By the hawk frighted.

'Bright in her father's hall
Shields gleamed upon the wall,
Loud sang the minstrels all,
   Chanting his glory;
When of old Hildebrand
I asked his daughter's hand,
Mute did the minstrels stand
   To hear my story.   80

'While the brown ale he quaffed,
Loud then the champion laughed,
And as the wind-gusts waft
   The sea-foam brightly,
So the loud laugh of scorn,
Out of those lips unshorn,
From the deep drinking-horn
   Blew the foam lightly.

'She was a Prince's child,
I but a Viking wild,
And though she blushed and smiled,   90
   I was discarded!
Should not the dove so white
Follow the sea-mew's flight,
Why did they leave that night
   Her nest unguarded?

'Scarce had I put to sea,
Bearing the maid with me,
Fairest of all was she
   Among the Norsemen!   100
When on the white sea-strand,
Waving his armed hand,
Saw we old Hildebrand,
   With twenty horsemen.

'Then launched they to the blast,
Bent like a reed each mast,
Yet we were gaining fast,
   When the wind failed us;

And with a sudden flaw
Came round the gusty Skaw,   110
So that our foe we saw
   Laugh as he hailed us.

'And as to catch the gale
Round veered the flapping sail,
"Death!" was the helmsman's hail,
   "Death without quarter!"
Mid-ships with iron keel
Struck we her ribs of steel;
Down her black hulk did reel
   Through the black water!   120

'As with his wings aslant,
Sails the fierce cormorant,
Seeking some rocky haunt,
   With his prey laden, —
So toward the open main,
Beating to sea again,
Through the wild hurricane,
   Bore I the maiden.

'Three weeks we westward bore,
And when the storm was o'er,   130
Cloud-like we saw the shore
   Stretching to leeward;
There for my lady's bower
Built I the lofty tower,
Which, to this very hour,
   Stands looking seaward.

'There lived we many years;
Time dried the maiden's tears;
She had forgot her fears,
   She was a mother;   140
Death closed her mild blue eyes,
Under that tower she lies; [1]
Ne'er shall the sun arise
   On such another!

'Still grew my bosom then,
Still as a stagnant fen!
Hateful to me were men,
   The sunlight hateful!
In the vast forest here,
Clad in my warlike gear,   150
Fell I upon my spear,
   Oh, death was grateful!

[1] The 'Round Tower' at Newport, sometimes called the Old Mill, is of a style of architecture belonging to the eleventh century, and is thought by some to have been built by the Northmen. This is exceedingly doubtful, however.

'Thus, seamed with many scars,
Bursting these prison bars,
Up to its native stars
    My soul ascended!
There from the flowing bowl
Deep drinks the warrior's soul,
Skoal! to the Northland! *skoal!*'[1]
    Thus the tale ended.   160

1840.   1841.

SERENADE

FROM 'THE SPANISH STUDENT'

STARS of the summer night!
    Far in yon azure deeps,
Hide, hide your golden light!
        She sleeps!
My lady sleeps!
        Sleeps!

Moon of the summer night!
    Far down yon western steeps,
Sink, sink in silver light!
        She sleeps!
My lady sleeps!
        Sleeps!

Wind of the summer night!
    Where yonder woodbine creeps,
Fold, fold thy pinions light!
        She sleeps!
My lady sleeps!
        Sleeps!

Dreams of the summer night!
    Tell her, her lover keeps
Watch! while in slumbers light
        She sleeps!
My lady sleeps!
        Sleeps!

1840.   1842.

ENDYMION

THE rising moon has hid the stars;
Her level rays, like golden bars,
    Lie on the landscape green,
    With shadows brown between.

And silver white the river gleams,
As if Diana, in her dreams
    Had dropt her silver bow
    Upon the meadows low.

On such a tranquil night as this,
She woke Endymion with a kiss,   10
    When, sleeping in the grove,
    He dreamed not of her love.

Like Dian's kiss, unasked, unsought,
Love gives itself, but is not bought;
    Nor voice, nor sound betrays
    Its deep, impassioned gaze.

It comes, — the beautiful, the free,
The crown of all humanity, —
    In silence and alone
    To seek the elected one.   20

It lifts the boughs, whose shadows deep
Are Life's oblivion, the soul's sleep,
    And kisses the closed eyes
    Of him who slumbering lies.

O weary hearts! O slumbering eyes!
O drooping souls, whose destinies
    Are fraught with fear and pain,
    Ye shall be loved again!

No one is so accursed by fate,
No one so utterly desolate,   30
    But some heart, though unknown,
    Responds unto his own.

Responds, — as if with unseen wings,
An angel touched its quivering strings;
    And whispers, in its song,
    'Where hast thou stayed so long?'
1841.   1841.

THE RAINY DAY

THE day is cold, and dark, and dreary;
It rains, and the wind is never weary;
The vine still clings to the mouldering
        wall,
But at every gust the dead leaves fall,
    And the day is dark and dreary.

My life is cold, and dark, and dreary;
It rains, and the wind is never weary;
My thoughts still cling to the mouldering
        Past.

[1] In Scandinavia, this is the customary salutation
when drinking a health. I have slightly changed the
orthography of the word [*skaal*] in order to preserve
the correct pronunciation. (LONGFELLOW.)

But the hopes of youth fall thick in the
     blast,
     And the days are dark and dreary.

Be still, sad heart! and cease repining;
Behind the clouds is the sun still shin-
     ing;
Thy fate is the common fate of all,
Into each life some rain must fall,
     Some days must be dark and dreary.
1841.   1841.

MAIDENHOOD [1]

MAIDEN! with the meek, brown eyes,
In whose orbs a shadow lies
Like the dusk in evening skies!

Thou whose locks outshine the sun,
Golden tresses, wreathed in one,
As the braided streamlets run!

Standing, with reluctant feet,
Where the brook and river meet,
Womanhood and childhood fleet!

Gazing, with a timid glance,   10
On the brooklet's swift advance,
On the river's broad expanse!

Deep and still, that gliding stream
Beautiful to thee must seem,
As the river of a dream.

Then why pause with indecision,
When bright angels in thy vision
Beckon thee to fields Elysian?

Seest thou shadows sailing by,
As the dove, with startled eye,   20
Sees the falcon's shadow fly?

Hearest thou voices on the shore,
That our ears perceive no more,
Deafened by the cataract's roar?

Oh, thou child of many prayers!
Life hath quicksands, — Life hath snares!
Care and age come unawares!

[1] Longfellow wrote to his father on December 18,
1841: 'The *Ballads and Other Poems* will be published
to-morrow. . . . I think the last two pieces ["Maidenhood" and "Excelsior"] the best, — perhaps as good
as anything I have written.' (*Life,* vol. i, p. 109.)

Like the swell of some sweet tune,
Morning rises into noon,
May glides onward into June.   30

Childhood is the bough, where slumbered
Birds and blossoms many-numbered; —
Age, that bough with snows encumbered.

Gather, then, each flower that grows,
When the young heart overflows,
To embalm that tent of snows.

Bear a lily in thy hand;
Gates of brass cannot withstand
One touch of that magic wand.

Bear through sorrow, wrong, and ruth, 40
In thy heart the dew of youth,
On thy lips the smile of truth.

Oh, that dew, like balm, shall steal
Into wounds that cannot heal,
Even as sleep our eyes doth seal;

And that smile, like sunshine, dart
Into many a sunless heart,
For a smile of God thou art.
1841.   1841.

EXCELSIOR [2]

THE shades of night were falling fast,
As through an Alpine village passed

[2] 'Excelsior' was inspired by the motto on the shield
of New York State, which Longfellow happened to see
copied as the heading of a newspaper. The significance
of the poem is well expressed by Poe at the end of his
review of Longfellow's *Ballads and Other Poems,* in a
passage beginning, 'It depicts the *earnest upward impulse of the soul,* — an impulse not to be subdued even
in death.' Longfellow himself has described his purpose fully in a letter to C. K. Tuckerman: —
    'I have had the pleasure of receiving your note in re-
gard to the poem "Excelsior," and very willingly give
you my intention in writing it. This was no more than
to display, in a series of pictures, the life of a man of
genius, resisting all temptations, laying aside all fears,
heedless of all warnings, and pressing right on to
accomplish his purpose. His motto is *Excelsior,*
"higher." He passes through the Alpine village —
through the rough, cold paths of the world — where the
peasants cannot understand him, and where the watch-
word is an "unknown tongue." He disregards the happiness of domestic peace and sees the glaciers — his fate —
before him. He disregards the warning of the old man's
wisdom and the fascinations of woman's love. He answers to all, "Higher yet!" The monks of St. Bernard
are the representatives of religious forms and ceremonies, and with their oft-repeated prayer mingles the
sound of his voice, telling them there is something
higher than forms and ceremonies. Filled with these
aspirations, he perishes; without having reached the

A youth, who bore, 'mid snow and ice,
A banner with the strange device,
        Excelsior !

His brow was sad; his eye beneath,
Flashed like a falchion from its sheath,
And like a silver clarion rung
The accents of that unknown tongue,
        Excelsior!

In happy homes he saw the light
Of household fires gleam warm and bright;
Above, the spectral glaciers shone,
And from his lips escaped a groan,
        Excelsior !

' Try not the Pass ! ' the old man said;
' Dark lowers the tempest overhead,
The roaring torrent is deep and wide ! '
And loud that clarion voice replied,
        Excelsior !

' Oh stay,' the maiden said, ' and rest
Thy weary head upon this breast ! '
A tear stood in his bright blue eye,
But still he answered, with a sigh,
        Excelsior !

' Beware the pine-tree's withered branch !
Beware the awful avalanche ! '
This was the peasant's last Good-night,
A voice replied, far up the height,
        Excelsior !

At break of day, as heavenward
The pious monks of Saint Bernard
Uttered the oft-repeated prayer,
A voice cried through the startled air,
        Excelsior !

A traveller, by the faithful hound,
Half-buried in the snow was found,
Still grasping in his hand of ice
That banner with the strange device,
        Excelsior !

There in the twilight cold and gray,
Lifeless, but beautiful, he lay,

And from the sky, serene and far,
A voice fell, like a falling star,
        Excelsior !
1841.   **1841.**

MEZZO CAMMIN [1]

HALF of my life is gone, and I have let
The years slip from me and have not ful-
        filled
The aspiration of my youth, to build
Some tower of song with lofty parapet.
Not indolence, nor pleasure, nor the fret
Of restless passions that would not be
        stilled,
But sorrow, and a care that almost killed,
Kept me from what I may accomplish yet;
Though, half-way up the hill, I see the Past
Lying beneath me with its sounds and
        sights, —
A city in the twilight dim and vast,
With smoking roofs, soft bells, and gleam-
        ing lights, —
And hear above me on the autumnal blast
The cataract of Death far thundering from
        the heights.
1842.   **1886.**

THE SLAVE'S DREAM [2]

BESIDE the ungathered rice he lay,
        His sickle in his hand;
His breast was bare, his matted hair
        Was buried in the sand.
Again, in the mist and shadow of sleep,
        He saw his Native Land.

Wide through the landscape of his dreams
        The lordly Niger flowed;

perfection he longed for ; and the voice heard in the
air is the promise of immortality and progress ever upward.'
        The manuscript of the poem, containing many altera-
tions, is kept on exhibition in the Art Room of the
Harvard University Library. It is written on the back
of a letter from Charles-Sumner, and dated ' September
28, 1841. Half-past three o'clock, morning.' See H. E.
Scudder's *Men and Letters*, pp. 137-146 : ' The Shaping
of Excelsior.'

[1] Longfellow's health was so seriously impaired by
his close work as teacher, lecturer, editor, and author,
that in the spring of 1842 he took six months' leave of
absence, and spent most of the time at the 'water-
cure' of Marienberg. While there he wrote no verse
except this sonnet, dated August 25, just before leaving for England on his way home. It was first published in the *Life*.
[2] Longfellow wrote all his *Poems on Slavery* during
his voyage home in 1842, and they were published
in a small volume of thirty-one pages in December of
that year. The intense sincerity of Whittier's poems
against slavery is lacking in Longfellow's sentimental
and ' romantic' treatment of the subject ; but it
meant much for him to take the side which he did, so
early as 1842. See the *Life*, vol. i, pp. 443-453, vol. ii.
pp. 7-10, 20-21 ; and T. W. Higginson's *Life of Longfellow*, pp. 163-167. Compare the notes on Lowell's
' Stanzas on Freedom ' and on Whittier's ' To William
Lloyd Garrison.'

Beneath the palm-trees on the plain
  Once more a king he strode;   10
And heard the tinkling caravans
  Descend the mountain road.

He saw once more his dark-eyed queen
  Among her children stand;
They clasped his neck, they kissed his
    cheeks,
  They held him by the hand ! —
A tear burst from the sleeper's lids
  And fell into the sand.

And then at furious speed he rode
  Along the Niger's bank;   20
His bridle-reins were golden chains,
  And, with a martial clank,
At each leap he could feel his scabbard of
    steel
  Smiting his stallion's flank.

Before him, like a blood-red flag,
  The bright flamingoes flew;
From morn till night he followed their
    flight,
  O'er plains where the tamarind grew,
Till he saw the roofs of Caffre huts,
  And the ocean rose to view.   30

At night he heard the lion roar,
  And the hyena scream,
And the river-horse, as he crushed the
    reeds
  Beside some hidden stream;
And it passed, like a glorious roll of
    drums,
  Through the triumph of his dream.

The forests, with their myriad tongues,
  Shouted of liberty;
And the Blast of the Desert cried aloud,
  With a voice so wild and free,   40
That he started in his sleep and smiled
  At their tempestuous glee.

He did not feel the driver's whip,
  Nor the burning heat of day;
For Death had illumined the Land of
    Sleep,
  And his lifeless body lay
A worn-out fetter, that the soul
  Had broken and thrown away !

1842.   1842.

THE ARSENAL AT SPRING-FIELD [1]

THIS is the Arsenal. From floor to ceil-
    ing,
  Like a huge organ, rise the burnished
    arms;
But from their silent pipes no anthem peal-
    ing
  Startles the villages with strange alarms.

Ah ! what a sound will rise, how wild and
    dreary,
  When the death-angel touches those
    swift keys !
What loud lament and dismal Miserere
  Will mingle with their awful sympho-
    nies !

I hear even now the infinite fierce cho-
    rus,
  The cries of agony, the endless groan, 10
Which, through the ages that have gone
    before us,
  In long reverberations reach our own.

On helm and harness rings the Saxon ham-
    mer,
  Through Cimbric forest roars the Norse-
    man's song,
And loud, amid the universal clamor,
  O'er distant deserts sounds the Tartar
    gong.

I hear the Florentine, who from his pal-
    ace
  Wheels out his battle-bell with dreadful
    din,
And Aztec priests upon their teocallis
  Beat the wild war-drums made of ser-
    pent's skin;   20

[1] Longfellow was married to Frances Appleton in 1843. On their wedding journey Mr. and Mrs. Longfellow visited the Arsenal at Springfield, in company with Charles Sumner. This visit, and the origin of the poem, are described in the *Life:* 'While Mr. Sumner was endeavoring to impress upon the attendant that the money expended upon these weapons of war would have been much better spent upon a great library, Mrs. Longfellow pleased her husband by remarking how like an organ looked the ranged and shining gun-barrels which covered the walls from floor to ceiling, and suggesting what mournful music Death would bring from them. "We grew quite warlike against war," she wrote, "and I urged H. to write a peace poem." From this hint came "The Arsenal at Springfield," written some months later.' (Vol. ii, pp. 2, 3.) See also Lowell's *Letters,* vol. i, p. 97, letter of Aug. 13, 1845.

The tumult of each sacked and burning
village;
The shout that every prayer for mercy
drowns;
The soldiers' revels in the midst of pil-
lage;
The wail of famine in beleaguered
towns;

The bursting shell, the gateway wrenched
asunder,
The rattling musketry, the clashing
blade;
And ever and anon, in tones of thunder
The diapason of the cannonade.

Is it, O man, with such discordant noises,
With such accursed instruments as
these,   30
Thou drownest Nature's sweet and kindly
voices,
And jarrest the celestial harmonies ?

Were half the power that fills the world
with terror,
Were half the wealth bestowed on
camps and courts,
Given to redeem the human mind from
error,
There were no need of arsenals or forts:

The warrior's name would be a name ab-
horrèd !
And every nation, that should lift again
Its hand against a brother, on its fore-
head
Would wear forevermore the curse of
Cain !   40

Down the dark future, through long gener-
ations,
The echoing sounds grow fainter and
then cease;
And like a bell, with solemn, sweet vibra-
tions,
I hear once more the voice of Christ say,
' Peace ! '

Peace ! and no longer from its brazen por-
tals
, The blast of War's great organ shakes
the skies !
But beautiful as songs of the immortals,
The holy melodies of love arise.

1844.   1844.

THE DAY IS DONE [1]

The day is done, and the darkness
Falls from the wings of Night,
As a feather is wafted downward
From an eagle in his flight.

I see the lights of the village
Gleam through the rain and the mist,
And a feeling of sadness comes o'er me
That my soul cannot resist:

A feeling of sadness and longing,
That is not akin to pain,   10
And resembles sorrow only
As the mist resembles the rain.

Come, read to me some poem,
Some simple and heartfelt lay,
That shall soothe this restless feeling,
And banish the thoughts of day.

Not from the grand old masters,
Not from the bards sublime,
Whose distant footsteps echo
Through the corridors of Time.   20

For, like strains of martial music,
Their mighty thoughts suggest
Life's endless toil and endeavor;
And to-night I long for rest.

Read from some humbler poet,
Whose songs gushed from his heart,
As showers from the clouds of summer,
Or tears from the eyelids start;

Who, through long days of labor,
And nights devoid of ease,   30
Still heard in his soul the music
Of wonderful melodies.

Such songs have power to quiet
The restless pulse of care,
And come like the benediction
That follows after prayer.

Then read from the treasured volume
The poem of thy choice,
And lend to the rhyme of the poet
The beauty of thy voice.   40

[1] Originally written as the proem to a volume of selections from minor poets, called *The Waif*, and edited
by Longfellow.

And the night shall be filled with music,
  And the cares, that infest the day,
Shall fold their tents, like the Arabs,
  And as silently steal away.
1844.   1844.

SEAWEED

WHEN descends on the Atlantic
  The gigantic
Storm-wind of the equinox,
Landward in his wrath he scourges
  The toiling surges,
Laden with seaweed from the rocks:

From Bermuda's reefs; from edges
  Of sunken ledges,
In some far-off, bright Azore;
From Bahama, and the dashing,   10
  Silver-flashing
Surges of San Salvador;

From the tumbling surf, that buries
  The Orkneyan skerries,
Answering the hoarse Hebrides;
And from wrecks of ships, and drifting
  Spars, uplifting
On the desolate, rainy seas; —

Ever drifting, drifting, drifting
  On the shifting   20
Currents of the restless main;
Till in sheltered coves, and reaches
  Of sandy beaches,
All have found repose again.

So when storms of wild emotion
  Strike the ocean
Of the poet's soul, erelong
From each cave and rocky fastness,
  In its vastness,
Floats some fragment of a song: 30

From the far-off isles enchanted,
  Heaven has planted
With the golden fruit of Truth ;
From the flashing surf, whose vision
  Gleams Elysian
In the tropic clime of Youth;

From the strong Will, and the Endeavor
  That forever
Wrestle with the tides of Fate;

From the wreck of Hopes far-scattered,
  Tempest-shattered,   41
Floating waste and desolate; —

Ever drifting, drifting, drifting
  On the shifting
Currents of the restless heart;
Till at length in books recorded,
  They, like hoarded
Household words, no more depart.
1844.   1845.

NUREMBERG[1]

IN the valley of the Pegnitz, where across
  broad meadow-lands
Rise the blue Franconian mountains, Nuremberg, the ancient, stands.

Quaint old town of toil and traffic, quaint
  old town of art and song,
Memories haunt thy pointed gables, like
  the rooks that round them throng:

Memories of the Middle Ages, when the
  emperors, rough and bold,
Had their dwelling in thy castle, time-
  defying, centuries old;

And thy brave and thrifty burghers boasted,
  in their uncouth rhyme,
That their great imperial city stretched its
  hand through every clime.[2]

In the court-yard of the castle, bound with
  many an iron band,
Stands the mighty linden planted by Queen
  Cunigunde's hand;   10

[1] This poem is typical of the impressions which Long-fellow received from travel in Europe, as expressed in the *Belfry of Bruges* volume and elsewhere. The prose material of the poem is to be found in a letter of September 24, 1842, to the German poet Freiligrath: —
  'Without any doubt, I am in the ancient city of Nürnberg. I arrived last night at ten o'clock, and took my first view by moonlight, strolling alone through the broad, silent streets, and listening to the musical bells that ever and anon gave a hint that it was bed-time.
  'To-day has been a busy, exciting day. I have seen the best works of Albrecht Dürer, Peter Vischer, and other worthies of Nürnberg. I have seen Dürer's house and his grave ; also those of Hans Sachs. The old shoe-maker's house is now an ale-house. His portrait is on the sign of the door, with this inscription : ' *Gasthaus zum Hans Sachs.*' . . .
[2] An old popular proverb of the town runs thus : —
    Nürnbergs Hand
    Geht durch alle Land.
    Nuremberg's hand
    Goes through every land. (LONGFELLOW.)

On the square the oriel window, where in
  old heroic days
Sat the poet Melchior singing Kaiser Maximilian's praise.[1]

Everywhere I see around me rise the wondrous world of Art:
Fountains wrought with richest sculpture
  standing in the common mart;

And above cathedral doorways saints and
  bishops carved in stone,
By a former age commissioned as apostles
  to our own.

In the church of sainted Sebald sleeps enshrined his holy dust,[2]
And in bronze the Twelve Apostles guard
  from age to age their trust;

In the church of sainted Lawrence stands a
  pix of sculpture rare,[3]
Like the foamy sheaf of fountains, rising
  through the painted air.   20

Here, when Art was still religion, with a
  simple, reverent heart,
Lived and labored Albrecht Dürer, the
  Evangelist of Art;

Hence in silence and in sorrow, toiling still
  with busy hand,
Like an emigrant he wandered, seeking for
  the Better Land.

Emigravit is the inscription on the tomb-
  stone where he lies;
Dead he is not, but departed, — for the
  artist never dies.

Fairer seems the ancient city, and the sunshine seems more fair,
That he once has trod its pavement, that
  he once has breathed its air !

Through these streets so broad and stately,
  these obscure and dismal lanes,
Walked of yore the Mastersingers, chanting rude poetic strains.   30

From remote and sunless suburbs came
  they to the friendly guild,
Building nests in Fame's great temple, as
  in spouts the swallows build.

As the weaver plied the shuttle, wove he
  too the mystic rhyme,
And the smith his iron measures hammered
  to the anvil's chime;

Thanking God, whose boundless wisdom
  makes the flowers of poesy bloom
In the forge's dust and cinders, in the tissues of the loom.

Here Hans Sachs, the cobbler-poet, laureate
  of the gentle craft,
Wisest of the Twelve Wise Masters, in
  huge folios sang and laughed.[4]

But his house is now an ale-house, with a
  nicely sanded floor,
And a garland in the window, and his face
  above the door;   40

Painted by some humble artist, as in Adam
  Puschman's song,[5]
As the old man gray and dove-like, with
  his great beard white and long.

And at night the swart mechanic comes to
  drown his cark and care,
Quaffing ale from pewter tankards, in the
  master's antique chair.

---

[1] Melchior Pfinzing was one of the most celebrated German poets of the sixteenth century. The hero of his *Teuerdank* was the reigning Emperor, Maximilian; and the poem was to the Germans of that day what the *Orlando Furioso* was to the Italians. (LONGFELLOW.)

[2] The tomb of Saint Sebald, in the church which bears his name, is one of the richest works of art in Nuremberg. It is of bronze, and was cast by Peter Vischer and his sons, who labored upon it thirteen years. It is adorned with nearly one hundred figures, among which those of the Twelve Apostles are conspicuous for size and beauty. (LONGFELLOW.)

[3] This pix, or tabernacle for the vessels of the sacrament, is by the hand of Adam Kraft. It is an exquisite piece of sculpture in white stone, and rises to the height of sixty-four feet. It stands in the choir, whose richly painted windows cover it with varied colors. (LONGFELLOW.)

[4] The Twelve Wise Masters was the title of the original corporation of the Mastersingers. Hans Sachs, the cobbler of Nuremberg, though not one of the original Twelve, was the most renowned of the Mastersingers, as well as the most voluminous. He flourished in the sixteenth century; and left behind him thirty-four folio volumes of manuscript, containing two hundred and eight plays, one thousand and seven hundred comic tales, and between four and five thousand lyric poems. (LONGFELLOW.)

[5] Adam Puschman, in his poem on the death of Hans Sachs, describes him as he appeared in a vision:—

> An old man,
> Gray and white, and dove-like,
> Who had, in sooth, a great beard,
> And read in a fair, great book,
> Beautiful with golden clasps.
>
> (LONGFELLOW.)

Vanished is the ancient splendor, and before my dreamy eye
Wave these mingled shapes and figures,
   like a faded tapestry.

Not thy Councils, not thy Kaisers, win for
   thee the world's regard;
But thy painter, Albrecht Dürer, and Hans
   Sachs thy cobbler bard.

Thus, O Nuremberg, a wanderer from a
   region far away,
As he paced thy streets and court-yards,
   sang in thought his careless lay: 50

Gathering from the pavement's crevice, as
   a floweret of the soil,
The nobility of labor, — the long pedigree
   of toil.

1844.   1844.

THE BELFRY OF BRUGES

CARILLON

In the ancient town of Bruges,
In the quaint old Flemish city,
As the evening shades descended,
Low and loud and sweetly blended,
Low at times and loud at times,
And changing like a poet's rhymes,
Rang the beautiful wild chimes
From the Belfry in the market
Of the ancient town of Bruges.

Then, with deep sonorous clangor 10
Calmly answering their sweet anger,
When the wrangling bells had ended,
Slowly struck the clock eleven,
And, from out the silent heaven,
Silence on the town descended.
Silence, silence everywhere,
On the earth and in the air,
Save that footsteps here and there
Of some burgher home returning,
By the street lamps faintly burning, 20
For a moment woke the echoes
Of the ancient town of Bruges.

But amid my broken slumbers
Still I heard those magic numbers,
As they loud proclaimed the flight
And stolen marches of the night;
Till their chimes in sweet collision
Mingled with each wandering vision,
Mingled with the fortune-telling
Gypsy-bands of dreams and fancies, 30
Which amid the waste expanses
Of the silent land of trances
Have their solitary dwelling;
All else seemed asleep in Bruges,
In the quaint old Flemish city.

And I thought how like these chimes
Are the poet's airy rhymes,
All his rhymes and roundelays,
His conceits, and songs, and ditties,
From the belfry of his brain, 40
Scattered downward, though in vain,
On the roofs and stones of cities!
For by night the drowsy ear
Under its curtains cannot hear,
And by day men go their ways,
Hearing the music as they pass,
But deeming it no more, alas!
Than the hollow sound of brass.
Yet perchance a sleepless wight,
Lodging at some humble inn 50
In the narrow lanes of life,
When the dusk and hush of night
Shut out the incessant din
Of daylight and its toil and strife,
May listen with a calm delight
To the poet's melodies,
Till he hears, or dreams he hears,
Intermingled with the song,
Thoughts that he has cherished long;
Hears amid the chime and singing 60
The bells of his own village ringing,
And wakes, and finds his slumberous eyes
Wet with most delicious tears.

Thus dreamed I, as by night I lay
In Bruges, at the Fleur-de-Blé,
Listening with a wild delight
To the chimes that, through the night,
Rang their changes from the Belfry
Of that quaint old Flemish city.

1845.   1845.[1]

DANTE

Tuscan, that wanderest through the realms
   of gloom,
With thoughtful pace, and sad, majestic
   eyes,

---

[1] The *Belfry of Bruges* volume bears the date 1846,
and is listed as of that year in the bibliographies of
Longfellow and in at least two books on the first editions of American authors; but it was actually published on December 23, 1845.

Stern thoughts and awful from thy soul
    arise,
Like Farinata from his fiery tomb.
Thy sacred song is like the trump of
    doom;
Yet in thy heart what human sympathies,
What soft compassion glows; as in the
    skies
The tender stars their clouded lamps re-
    lume!
Methinks I see thee stand with pallid
    cheeks
By Fra Hilario in his diocese,
As up the convent-walls, in golden streaks,
The ascending sunbeams mark the day's
    decrease;
And, as he asks what there the stranger
    seeks,
Thy voice along the cloister whispers
    'Peace!'

1843?   1845.

THE BRIDGE [1]

I STOOD on the bridge at midnight,
    As the clocks were striking the hour,
And the moon rose o'er the city,
    Behind the dark church-tower.

I saw her bright reflection
    In the waters under me,
Like a golden goblet falling
    And sinking into the sea. [2]

And far in the hazy distance
    Of that lovely night in June,   10
The blaze of the flaming furnace
    Gleamed redder than the moon.

Among the long, black rafters
    The wavering shadows lay,
And the current that came from the ocean
    Seemed to lift and bear them away;

---

[1] Called 'The Bridge over the Charles,' in Longfellow's *Journal*, Oct. 9, 1845. In an earlier passage
of his *Journal*, March 15, 1838, he speaks of his delight in walking to and from Boston, and says: 'I
always stop on the bridge; tide-waters are beautiful.
From the ocean up into the land they go, like messengers, to ask why the tribute has not been paid.
The brooks and rivers answer that there has been
little harvest of snow and rain this year.' *Life*, vol. i,
p. 289.

[2] An excellent example of the 'literary' character of
Longfellow's inspiration. This is evidently a reminiscence of the German ballads, not of anything seen or
conceived by the poet himself.

As, sweeping and eddying through them,
    Rose the belated tide,
And, streaming into the moonlight,
    The seaweed floated wide.   20

And like those waters rushing
    Among the wooden piers,
A flood of thoughts came o'er me
    That filled my eyes with tears.

How often, oh how often,
    In the days that had gone by,
I had stood on that bridge at midnight
    And gazed on that wave and sky!

How often, oh how often,
    I had wished that the ebbing tide   30
Would bear me away on its bosom
    O'er the ocean wild and wide!

For my heart was hot and restless,
    And my life was full of care,
And the burden laid upon me
    Seemed greater than I could bear.

But now it has fallen from me,
    It is buried in the sea;
And only the sorrow of others
    Throws its shadow over me.   40

Yet whenever I cross the river
    On its bridge with wooden piers,
Like the odor of brine from the ocean
    Comes the thought of other years.

And I think how many thousands
    Of care-encumbered men,
Each bearing his burden of sorrow,
    Have crossed the bridge since then.

I see the long procession
    Still passing to and fro,   50
The young heart hot and restless,
    And the old subdued and slow!

And forever and forever,
    As long as the river flows,
As long as the heart has passions,
    As long as life has woes;

The moon and its broken reflection
    And its shadows shall appear,
As the symbol of love in heaven,
    And its wavering image here.   60

1845.   1845.

THE OLD CLOCK ON THE STAIRS[1]

SOMEWHAT back from the village street
Stands the old-fashioned country-seat.
Across its antique portico
Tall poplar-trees their shadows throw;
And from its station in the hall
An ancient timepiece says to all, —
      ' Forever — never !
      Never — forever ! '

Half-way up the stairs it stands,
And points and beckons with its hands   10
From its case of massive oak,
Like a monk, who, under his cloak,
Crosses himself, and sighs, alas !
With sorrowful voice to all who pass, —
      ' Forever — never !
      Never — forever ! '

By day its voice is low and light;
But in the silent dead of night,
Distinct as a passing footstep's fall,
It echoes along the vacant hall,   20
Along the ceiling, along the floor,
And seems to say, at each chamber-door, —
      ' Forever — never !
      Never — forever ! '

Through days of sorrow and of mirth,
Through days of death and days of birth,
Through every swift vicissitude
Of changeful time, unchanged it has stood,
And as if, like God, it all things saw,
It calmly repeats those words of awe, —   30
      ' Forever — never !
      Never — forever ! '

In that mansion used to be
Free-hearted Hospitality;
His great fires up the chimney roared;

[1] Longfellow wrote in his *Journal* under the date of November 12, 1845 : ' Began a poem on a clock, with the words " Forever, never," as the burden ; suggested by the words of Bridaine, the old French missionary, who said of eternity, *C'est une pendule dont le balancier dit et redit sans cesse ces deux mots seulement dans le silence des tombeaux, — Toujours, jamais ! Jamais, toujours ! Et pendant ces effrayables révolutions, un réprouvé s'écrie, " Quelle heure est-il ? " et la voix d'un autre misérable lui répond, " L'Eternité." '
The ' old-fashioned country-seat,' where the clock stood, is in Pittsfield, Mass.   Mr. and Mrs. Longfellow visited it on their wedding journey in 1843. (*Life*, vol. ii, pp. 2, 24, 25.)   The house belonged to relatives of Mrs. Longfellow, and when it was sold in 1853, the ' old clock ' was alone reserved by the family. (*Life*, vol. ii, p. 259.)

The stranger feasted at his board;
But, like the skeleton at the feast,
That warning timepiece never ceased, —
      ' Forever — never !
      Never — forever ! '   40

There groups of merry children played,
There youths and maidens dreaming
      strayed;
O precious hours !   O golden prime.
And affluence of love and time !
Even as a miser counts his gold,
Those hours the ancient timepiece told, —
      ' Forever — never !
      Never — forever ! '

From that chamber, clothed in white,
The bride came forth on her wedding
      night;   50
There, in that silent room below,
The dead lay in his shroud of snow;
And in the hush that followed the prayer,
Was heard the old clock on the stair, —
      ' Forever — never !
      Never — forever ! '

All are scattered now and fled,
Some are married, some are dead;
And when I ask, with throbs of pain,
' Ah ! when shall they all meet again ? '
As in the days long since gone by,   61
The ancient timepiece makes reply, —
      ' Forever — never !
      Never — forever ! '

Never here, forever there,
Where all parting, pain, and care,
And death, and time shall disappear, —
Forever there, but never here !
The horologe of Eternity
Sayeth this incessantly, —   70
      ' Forever — never !
      Never — forever ! '

1845.   1845.

THE ARROW AND THE SONG

I SHOT an arrow into the air,
It fell to earth, I knew not where;
For, so swiftly it flew, the sight
Could not follow it in its flight.

I breathed a song into the air,
It fell to earth, I knew not where;

For who has sight so keen and strong,
That it can follow the flight of song?

Long, long afterward, in an oak
I found the arrow, still unbroke;
And the song, from beginning to end,
I found again in the heart of a friend.

1845.   1845.

CURFEW [1]

I

SOLEMNLY, mournfully,
    Dealing its dole,
The Curfew Bell
    Is beginning to toll.

Cover the embers,
    And put out the light;
Toil comes with the morning,
    And rest with the night.

Dark grow the windows,
    And quenched is the fire;
Sound fades into silence, —
    All footsteps retire.

No voice in the chambers,
    No sound in the hall!
Sleep and oblivion
    Reign over all!

II

The book is completed,
    And closed, like the day;
And the hand that has written it
    Lays it away.

Dim grow its fancies;
    Forgotten they lie;
Like coals in the ashes,
    They darken and die.

Song sinks into silence,
    The story is told,
The windows are darkened,
    The hearth-stone is cold.

Darker and darker
    The black shadows fall;
Sleep and oblivion
    Reign over all.

1845.   1845.

EVANGELINE [2]

A TALE OF ACADIE

THIS is the forest primeval. The murmur-
    ing pines and the hemlocks,
Bearded with moss, and in garments green,
    indistinct in the twilight,

Stand like Druids of eld, with voices sad
    and prophetic,
Stand like harpers hoar, with beards that
    rest on their bosoms.

[1] The concluding poem in the *Belfry of Bruges* volume.

[2] The origin of 'Evangeline' is described as follows in the *Life of Longfellow* : ' Mr. Hawthorne came one day to dine at Craigie House, bringing with him his friend Mr. H. L. Conolly, who had been the rector of a church in South Boston. At dinner Conolly said that he had been trying in vain to interest Hawthorne to write a story upon an incident which had been related to him by a parishioner of his, Mrs. Haliburton. It was the story of a young Acadian maiden, who at the dispersion of her people by the English troops had been separated from her betrothed lover; they sought each other for years in their exile; and at last they met in a hospital where the lover lay dying. Mr. Longfellow was touched by the story, especially by the constancy of its heroine, and said to his friend, " If you really do not want this incident for a tale, let me have it for a poem ; " and Hawthorne consented.' (*Life*, vol. ii, pp. 70-71.)

The account given by Hawthorne is substantially the same, but contains a somewhat fuller outline of the story : ' H. L. C. heard from a French Canadian a story of a young couple in Acadie. On their marriage-day all the men of the Province were summoned to assemble in the church to hear a proclamation. When assembled, they were all seized and shipped off to be distributed through New England, — among them the new bridegroom. His bride set off in search of him — wandered about New England all her lifetime, and at last, when she was old, she found her bridegroom on his deathbed. The shock was so great that it killed her likewise.' (*American Notebooks*, vol. i, p. 203.)

Another American poet, Whittier, had also thought of writing on the expulsion of the Acadians : ' Before Longfellow considered the matter of writing " Evangeline," Whittier had made a study of the history of the banishment of the Acadians, and had intended to write upon it, but he put it off until he found that Hawthorne was thinking about it, and had suggested it to Longfellow. After the appearance of " Evangeline," Mr. Whittier was glad of his delay, for he said : " Longfellow was just the one to write it. If I had attempted it I should have spoiled the artistic effect of the poem by my indignation at the treatment of the exiles by the Colonial Government." ' (Pickard's *Life of Whittier*, vol. i, p. 342). See also Whittier's poem, ' Marguerite,' and the note on it.

Whittier welcomed the 'Evangeline' heartily when it appeared, in a review beginning ' Eureka ! Here, then,

Loud from its rocky caverns, the deep-
voiced neighboring ocean
Speaks, and in accents disconsolate answers
the wail of the forest.

This is the forest primeval ; but where
are the hearts that beneath it
Leaped like the roe, when he hears in the
woodland the voice of the huntsman?

we have it at last, — an American poem, with the lack
of which British reviewers have so long reproached us.'
(*Prose Works*, vol. iii, p. 365.)

The historical basis which Longfellow used for his
poem was somewhat scanty : ' For the history of the
dispersion of the Acadians the poet read such books as
were attainable ; Haliburton, for instance, with his
quotations from the Abbé Raynal. . . . Later investi-
gations and more recent publications have shown that
the deportation had more justification than had been
supposed; that some, at least, of the Acadians, so far
from being innocent sufferers, had been troublesome
subjects of Great Britain, — fomenting insubordination
and giving help to the enemy. But if the expatriation
was necessary, it was none the less cruel, and involved
in suffering many who were innocent of wrong.' (*Life
of Longfellow*, vol. ii, p. 71.)

The exact title of Haliburton's book spoken of above
is *An Historical and Statistical Account of Nova Scotia*.
See also, on the poem, its subject, and its historical basis:
Life, vol. ii, pp. 26–140.

Hannay (James), *The History of Acadie.*

Journal of Colonel John Winslow, in the *Report and
Collections of the Nova Scotia Historical Society*, iii,
71–196.

Gayarré, *The History of Louisiana*.

Anderson (William James), ' *Evangeline* ' and ' *The
Archives of Nova Scotia ;* ' or, *the Poetry and Prose of
History*. Quebec, 1870.

Porter (Noah), *Evangeline, the place, the story, and
the poem*. New York, 1882.

Sayler (H. L.) *The Real Evangeline*. In the *Bookman*, vol. xviii, p. 12 ; September, 1903.

Whittier : *Prose Works*, vol. iii, pp. 365–373.

Chasles (Philarète), *Etudes sur la Littérature et les
Mœurs des Anglo-américains au XIXᵐᵉ Siècle*, 1851.

Longfellow himself never visited either Nova Scotia
or the Mississippi. He actually seems to have got some
of his conceptions from a diorama of the Mississippi exhibited in Boston, which he eagerly went to see while
writing the poem ! (*Life*, vol. ii, pp. 67–68.) He also, as
seems to be probable from letters recently published in
the New York *Times* (February and March, 1905) wrote
to Mr. Edouard Simon of St. Martinsville, a former
student at the Harvard law school, with whom he had
discussed the expulsion of the Acadians from Nova
Scotia and their settlement in Louisiana, and obtained
from him a description of the country along the Mississippi where they settled.

It may also be suggested that he probably obtained
some inspiration, and perhaps a great deal, from Chateaubriand's descriptions of America, especially of the
primeval forests and the country along the Ohio and
Mississippi rivers, in his *Atala*, *René*, and *Voyages*.
Longfellow was reading Chateaubriand, and with enthusiasm, just at the time when he began to write
' Evangeline.' (*Life*, vol. ii, p. 27.)

The metre of ' Evangeline ' has been much discussed.
See the *Life of Longfellow*, vol. ii, pp. 26, 36, 66, 76,
107, etc. ; Stedman's *Poets of America*, pp. 195–200 ;
Scudder's *Life of Lowell*, vol. ii, p. 75, and Lowell's
' Fable for Critics ' ; Holmes's verdict, quoted in the
Life of Longfellow, vol. iii, pp. 339–340 ; and Matthew
Arnold's essays *On Translating Homer*.

Where is the thatch-roofed village, the
home of Acadian farmers, —
Men whose lives glided on like rivers that
water the woodlands,
Darkened by shadows of earth, but reflecting an image of heaven ?
Waste are those pleasant farms, and the
farmers forever departed !
Scattered like dust and leaves, when the
mighty blasts of October
Seize them, and whirl them aloft, and
sprinkle them far o'er the ocean.
Naught but tradition remains of the beautiful village of Grand-Pré.

Ye who believe in affection that hopes,
and endures, and is patient,
Ye who believe in the beauty and strength
of woman's devotion,
List to the mournful tradition, still sung by
the pines of the forest;
List to a Tale of Love in Acadie, home of
the happy.

PART THE FIRST

I

In the Acadian land, on the shores of the
Basin of Minas,
Distant, secluded, still, the little village of
Grand Pré
Lay in the fruitful valley. Vast meadows
stretched to the eastward,
Giving the village its name, and pasture to
flocks without number.
Dikes, that the hands of the farmers had
raised with labor incessant,
Shut out the turbulent tides; but at stated
seasons the flood-gates
Opened, and welcomed the sea to wander
at will o'er the meadows.
West and south there were fields of flax,
and orchards and cornfields
Spreading afar and unfenced o'er the plain;
and away to the northward
Blomidon rose, and the forests old, and
aloft on the mountains   10
Sea-fogs pitched their tents, and mists from
the mighty Atlantic
Looked on the happy valley, but ne'er from
their station descended.
There, in the midst of its farms, reposed
the Acadian village.

Strongly built were the houses, with frames of oak and of hemlock,
Such as the peasants of Normandy built in the reign of the Henries.
Thatched were the roofs, with dormer-windows ; and gables projecting
Over the basement below protected and shaded the doorway.
There in the tranquil evenings of summer, when brightly the sunset
Lighted the village street, and gilded the vanes on the chimneys,
Matrons and maidens sat in snow-white caps and in kirtles   20
Scarlet and blue and green, with distaffs spinning the golden
Flax for the gossiping looms, whose noisy shuttles within doors
Mingled their sounds with the whir of the wheels and the songs of the maidens.
Solemnly down the street came the parish priest, and the children
Paused in their play to kiss the hand he extended to bless them.
Reverend walked he among them; and up rose matrons and maidens,
Hailing his slow approach with words of affectionate welcome.
Then came the laborers home from the field, and serenely the sun sank
Down to his rest, and twilight prevailed. Anon from the belfry
Softly the Angelus sounded, and over the roofs of the village   30
Columns of pale blue smoke, like clouds of incense ascending,
Rose from a hundred hearths, the homes of peace and contentment.
Thus dwelt together in love these simple Acadian farmers, —
Dwelt in the love of God and of man. Alike were they free from
Fear, that reigns with the tyrant, and envy, the vice of republics.
Neither locks had they to their doors, nor bars to their windows;
But their dwellings were open as day and the hearts of the owners;
There the richest was poor, and the poorest lived in abundance.

Somewhat apart from the village, and nearer the Basin of Minas,
Benedict Bellefontaine, the wealthiest farmer of Grand-Pré,   40

Dwelt on his goodly acres; and with him, directing his household,
Gentle Evangeline lived, his child, and the pride of the village.
Stalwart and stately in form was the man of seventy winters;
Hearty and hale was he, an oak that is covered with snow-flakes;
White as the snow were his locks, and his cheeks as brown as the oak-leaves.
Fair was she to behold, that maiden of seventeen summers.
Black were her eyes as the berry that grows on the thorn by the wayside,
Black, yet how softly they gleamed beneath the brown shade of her tresses !
Sweet was her breath as the breath of kine that feed in the meadows.
When in the harvest heat she bore to the reapers at noontide   50
Flagons of home-brewed ale, ah ! fair in sooth was the maiden.
Fairer was she when, on Sunday morn, while the bell from its turret
Sprinkled with holy sounds the air, as the priest with his hyssop
Sprinkles the congregation, and scatters blessings upon them,
Down the long street she passed, with her chaplet of beads and her missal,
Wearing her Norman cap, and her kirtle of blue, and the ear-rings,
Brought in the olden time from France, and since, as an heirloom,
Handed down from mother to child, through long generations.
But a celestial brightness — a more ethereal beauty —
Shone on her face and encircled her form, when, after confession,   60
Homeward serenely she walked with God's benediction upon her.
When she had passed, it seemed like the ceasing of exquisite music.

Firmly builded with rafters of oak, the house of the farmer
Stood on the side of a hill commanding the sea; and a shady
Sycamore grew by the door, with a woodbine wreathing around it.
Rudely carved was the porch, with seats beneath; and a footpath
Led through an orchard wide, and disappeared in the meadow

Under the sycamore-tree were hives over-
    hung by a penthouse,
Such as the traveller sees in regions remote
    by the roadside,
Built o'er a box for the poor, or the blessed
    image of Mary.   70
Farther down, on the slope of the hill, was
    the well with its moss-grown
Bucket, fastened with iron, and near it a
    trough for the horses.
Shielding the house from storms, on the
    north, were the barns and the farm-
    yard.
There stood the broad-wheeled wains and
    the antique ploughs and the har-
    rows;
There were the folds for the sheep; and
    there, in his feathered seraglio,
Strutted the lordly turkey, and crowed the
    cock, with the selfsame
Voice that in ages of old had startled the
    penitent Peter.
Bursting with hay were the barns, them-
    selves a village. In each one
Far o'er the gable projected a roof of
    thatch; and a staircase,
Under the sheltering eaves, led up to the
    odorous corn-loft.   80
There too the dove-cot stood, with its meek
    and innocent inmates
Murmuring ever of love; while above in
    the variant breezes
Numberless noisy weathercocks rattled and
    sang of mutation.

    Thus, at peace with God and the world,
    the farmer of Grand-Pré
Lived on his sunny farm, and Evangeline
    governed his household.
Many a youth, as he knelt in church and
    opened his missal,
Fixed his eyes upon her as the saint of his
    deepest devotion;
Happy was he who might touch her hand
    or the hem of her garment!
Many a suitor came to her door, by the
    darkness befriended,
And, as he knocked and waited to hear the
    sound of her footsteps,   90
Knew not which beat the louder, his heart
    or the knocker of iron;
Or at the joyous feast of the Patron Saint
    of the village,
Bolder grew, and pressed her hand in the
    dance as he whispered

Hurried words of love, that seemed a part
    of the music.
But, among all who came, young Gabriel
    only was welcome;
Gabriel Lajeunesse, the son of Basil the
    blacksmith,
Who was a mighty man in the village, and
    honored of all men;
For, since the birth of time, throughout all
    ages and nations,
Has the craft of the smith been held in re-
    pute by the people.
Basil was Benedict's friend. Their children
    from earliest childhood   100
Grew up together as brother and sister; and
    Father Felician,
Priest and pedagogue both in the village,
    had taught them their letters
Out of the selfsame book, with the hymns
    of the church and the plain-song.
But when the hymn was sung, and the daily
    lesson completed,
Swiftly they hurried away to the forge of
    Basil the blacksmith.
There at the door they stood, with wonder-
    ing eyes to behold him
Take in his leathern lap the hoof of the horse
    as a plaything,
Nailing the shoe in its place; while near him
    the tire of the cart-wheel
Lay like a fiery snake, coiled round in a cir-
    cle of cinders.
Oft on autumnal eves, when without in the
    gathering darkness   110
Bursting with light seemed the smithy,
    through every cranny and crev-
    ice,
Warm by the forge within they watched
    the laboring bellows,
And as its panting ceased, and the sparks
    expired in the ashes,
Merrily laughed, and said they were nuns
    going into the chapel.
Oft on sledges in winter, as swift as the
    swoop of the eagle,
Down the hillside bounding, they glided
    away o'er the meadow.
Oft in the barns they climbed to the popu-
    lous nests on the rafters,
Seeking with eager eyes that wondrous
    stone, which the swallow
Brings from the shore of the sea to restore
    the sight of its fledglings;
Lucky was he who found that stone in the
    nest of the swallow!   120

Thus passed a few swift years, and they no
    longer were children.
He was a valiant youth, and his face, like
    the face of the morning,
Gladdened the earth with its light, and
    ripened thought into action.
She was a woman now, with the heart and
    hopes of a woman.
' Sunshine of Saint Eulalie ' was she called;
    for that was the sunshine
Which, as the farmers believed, would load
    their orchards with apples; [1]
She, too, would bring to her husband's house
    delight and abundance,
Filling it with love and the ruddy faces of
    children.

II

Now had the season returned, when the
    nights grow colder and longer,
And the retreating sun the sign of the Scor-
    pion enters.   130
Birds of passage sailed through the leaden
    air, from the ice-bound,
Desolate northern bays to the shores of trop-
    ical islands.
Harvests were gathered in; and wild with
    the winds of September
Wrestled the trees of the forest, as Jacob
    of old with the angel.
All the signs foretold a winter long and in-
    clement.
Bees, with prophetic instinct of want, had
    hoarded their honey
Till the hives overflowed; and the Indian
    hunters asserted
Cold would the winter be, for thick was the
    fur of the foxes.
Such was the advent of autumn. Then fol-
    lowed that beautiful season,
Called by the pious Acadian peasants the
    Summer of All-Saints !   140
Filled was the air with a dreamy and magi-
    cal light; and the landscape
Lay as if new-created in all the freshness of
    childhood.
Peace seemed to reign upon earth, and the
    restless heart of the ocean
Was for a moment consoled. All sounds
    were in harmony blended.
Voices of children at play, the crowing of
    cocks in the farm-yards,

[1] From the old Norman-French proverb : —

    Si le soleil rit le jour Sainte-Eulalie
    Il y aura pommes et cidre à folie.

Whir of wings in the drowsy air, and the
    cooing of pigeons,
All were subdued and low as the murmurs
    of love, and the great sun
Looked with the eye of love through the
    golden vapors around him;
While arrayed in its robes of russet and
    scarlet and yellow,
Bright with the sheen of the dew, each
    glittering tree of the forest   150
Flashed like the plane-tree the Persian
    adorned with mantles and jew-
    els.[2]

Now recommenced the reign of rest and
    affection and stillness.
Day with its burden and heat had departed,
    and twilight descending
Brought back the evening star to the sky,
    and the herds to the homestead.
Pawing the ground they came, and resting
    their necks on each other,
And with their nostrils distended inhaling
    the freshness of evening.
Foremost, bearing the bell, Evangeline's
    beautiful heifer,
Proud of her snow-white hide, and the rib-
    bon that waved from her collar,
Quietly paced and slow, as if conscious of
    human affection.
Then came the shepherd back with his
    bleating flocks from the seaside.   160
Where was their favorite pasture. Behind
    them followed the watch-dog,
Patient, full of importance, and grand in the
    pride of his instinct,
Walking from side to side with a lordly air,
    and superbly
Waving his bushy tail, and urging forward
    the stragglers;
Regent of flocks was he when the shepherd
    slept; their protector,
When from the forest at night, through the
    starry silence the wolves howled.
Late, with the rising moon, returned the
    wains from the marshes,
Laden with briny hay, that filled the air
    with its odor.
Cheerily neighed the steeds, with dew on
    their manes and their fetlocks,
While aloft on their shoulders the wooden
    and ponderous saddles,   170
Painted with brilliant dyes, and adorned
    with tassels of crimson,

[2] See Evelyn's *Silva*, ii, 53. (LONGFELLOW.)

Nodded in bright array, like hollyhocks
    heavy with blossoms.
Patiently stood the cows meanwhile, and
    yielded their udders
Unto the milkmaid's hand; whilst loud and
    in regular cadence
Into the sounding pails the foaming stream-
    lets descended.
Lowing of cattle and peals of laughter were
    heard in the farm-yard,
Echoed back by the barns. Anon they
    sank into stillness;
Heavily closed, with a jarring sound, the
    valves of the barn-doors,
Rattled the wooden bars, and all for a sea-
    son was silent.

In-doors, warm by the wide-mouthed
    fireplace, idly the farmer   180
Sat in his elbow-chair and watched how the
    flames and the smoke-wreaths
Struggled together like foes in a burning
    city. Behind him,
Nodding and mocking along the wall, with
    gestures fantastic,
Darted his own huge shadow, and vanished
    away into darkness.
Faces, clumsily carved in oak, on the back
    of his arm-chair
Laughed in the flickering light; and the
    pewter plates on the dresser
Caught and reflected the flame, as shields
    of armies the sunshine.
Fragments of song the old man sang, and
    carols of Christmas,
Such as at home, in the olden time, his
    fathers before him
Sang in their Norman orchards and bright
    Burgundian vineyards.   190
Close at her father's side was the gentle
    Evangeline seated,
Spinning flax for the loom, that stood in
    the corner behind her.
Silent awhile were its treadles, at rest was
    its diligent shuttle,
While the monotonous drone of the wheel,
    like the drone of a bagpipe,
Followed the old man's song and united the
    fragments together.
As in a church, when the chant of the choir
    at intervals ceases,
Footfalls are heard in the aisles, or words
    of the priest at the altar,
So, in each pause of the song, with mea-
    sured motion the clock clicked.

Thus as they sat, there were footsteps
    heard, and, suddenly lifted,
Sounded the wooden latch, and the door
    swung back on its hinges.   200
Benedict knew by the hob-nailed shoes it
    was Basil the blacksmith,
And by her beating heart Evangeline knew
    who was with him.
'Welcome!' the farmer exclaimed, as their
    footsteps paused on the thres-
    hold,
'Welcome, Basil, my friend! Come, take
    thy place on the settle
Close by the chimney-side, which is always
    empty without thee;
Take from the shelf overhead thy pipe and
    the box of tobacco;
Never so much thyself art thou as when
    through the curling
Smoke of the pipe or the forge thy friendly
    and jovial face gleams
Round and red as the harvest moon through
    the mist of the marshes.'
Then, with a smile of content, thus an-
    swered Basil the blacksmith,   210
Taking with easy air the accustomed seat
    by the fireside : —
'Benedict Bellefontaine, thou hast ever thy
    jest and thy ballad!
Ever in cheerfullest mood art thou, when
    others are filled with
Gloomy forebodings of ill, and see only ruin
    before them.
Happy art thou, as if every day thou hadst
    picked up a horseshoe.'
Pausing a moment, to take the pipe that
    Evangeline brought him,
And with a coal from the embers had
    lighted, he slowly continued : —
'Four days now are passed since the Eng-
    lish ships at their anchors
Ride in the Gaspereau's mouth, with their
    cannon pointed against us.
What their design may be is unknown; but
    all are commanded   220
On the morrow to meet in the church,
    where his Majesty's mandate
Will be proclaimed as law in the land.
    Alas! in the mean time
Many surmises of evil alarm the hearts of
    the people.'
Then made answer the farmer : 'Perhaps
    some friendlier purpose
Brings these ships to our shores. Perhaps
    the harvests in England

By untimely rains or untimelier heat have
  been blighted,
And from our bursting barns they would
  feed their cattle and children.'
' Not so thinketh the folk in the village,'
  said, warmly, the blacksmith,
Shaking his head, as in doubt; then, heaving a sigh, he continued : —
' Louisburg is not forgotten, nor Beau Sé-
  jour, nor Port Royal.   230
Many already have fled to the forest, and
  lurk on its outskirts,
Waiting with anxious hearts the dubious
  fate of to-morrow.
Arms have been taken from us, and warlike weapons of all kinds;
Nothing is left but the blacksmith's sledge
  and the scythe of the mower.'
Then with a pleasant smile made answer the
  jovial farmer : —
' Safer are we unarmed, in the midst of our
  flocks and our cornfields,
Safer within these peaceful dikes, besieged
  by the ocean,
Than our fathers in forts, besieged by the
  enemy's cannon.
Fear no evil, my friend, and to-night may
  no shadow of sorrow
Fall on this house and earth; for this is the
  night of the contract.   240
Built are the house and the barn. The
  merry lads of the village
Strongly have built them and well; and,
  breaking the glebe round about them,
Filled the barn with hay, and the house
  with food for a twelvemonth.
René Leblanc will be here anon, with his
  papers and inkhorn.
Shall we not then be glad, and rejoice in the
  joy of our children ? '
As apart by the window she stood, with her
  hand in her lover's,
Blushing Evangeline heard the words that
  her father had spoken,
And, as they died on his lips, the worthy
  notary entered.

III

Bent like a laboring oar, that toils in the
  surf of the ocean,
Bent, but not broken, by age was the form
  of the notary public;   250
Shocks of yellow hair, like the silken floss
  of the maize, hung

Over his shoulders; his forehead was high;
  and glasses with horn bows
Sat astride on his nose, with a look of wisdom supernal.
Father of twenty children was he, and more
  than a hundred
Children's children rode on his knee, and
  heard his great watch tick.
Four long years in the times of the war had
  he languished a captive,
Suffering much in an old French fort as the
  friend of the English.
Now, though warier grown, without all
  guile or suspicion,
Ripe in wisdom was he, but patient, and
  simple, and childlike.
He was beloved by all, and most of all by
  the children;   260
For he told them tales of the Loup-garou
  in the forest,
And of the goblin that came in the night to
  water the horses,
And of the white Létiche, the ghost of a
  child who unchristened
Died, and was doomed to haunt unseen the
  chambers of children;
And how on Christmas eve the oxen talked
  in the stable,
And how the fever was cured by a spider
  shut up in a nutshell,
And of the marvellous powers of four-
  leaved clover and horseshoes,
With whatsoever else was writ in the lore
  of the village.
Then up rose from his seat by the fireside
  Basil the blacksmith,
Knocked from his pipe the ashes, and slowly
  extending his right hand,   270
' Father Leblanc,' he exclaimed, ' thou
  hast heard the talk in the vil-
  lage,
And, perchance, canst tell us some news of
  these ships and their errand.'
Then with modest demeanor made answer
  the notary public, —
' Gossip enough have I heard, in sooth, yet
  am never the wiser;
And what their errand may be I know not
  better than others.
Yet am I not of those who imagine some
  evil intention
Brings them here, for we are at peace; and
  why then molest us ? '
' God's name ! ' shouted the hasty and
  somewhat irascible blacksmith;

'Must we in all things look for the how,
    and the why, and the where-
    fore ?
Daily injustice is done, and might is the
    right of the strongest ! '   280
But without heeding his warmth, continued
    the notary public, —
' Man is unjust, but God is just; and finally
    justice
Triumphs; and well I remember a story,
    that often consoled me,
When as a captive I lay in the old French
    fort at Port Royal.'
This was the old man's favorite tale, and
    he loved to repeat it
When his neighbors complained that any
    injustice was done them.
' Once in an ancient city, whose name I no
    longer remember,
Raised aloft on a column, a brazen statue
    of Justice
Stood in the public square, upholding the
    scales in its left hand,
And in its right a sword, as an emblem that
    justice presided   290
Over the laws of the land, and the hearts
    and homes of the people.
Even the birds had built their nests in the
    scales of the balance,
Having no fear of the sword that flashed in
    the sunshine above them.
But in the course of time the laws of the
    land were corrupted;
Might took the place of right, and the weak
    were oppressed, and the mighty
Ruled with an iron rod.   Then it chanced
    in a nobleman's palace
That a necklace of pearls was lost, and ere-
    long a suspicion
Fell on an orphan girl who lived as a maid
    in the household.
She, after form of trial condemned to die
    on the scaffold,
Patiently met her doom at the foot of the
    statue of Justice.   300
As to her Father in heaven her innocent
    spirit ascended,
Lo ! o'er the city a tempest rose; and the
    bolts of the thunder
Smote the statue of bronze, and hurled in
    wrath from its left hand
Down on the pavement below the clattering
    scales of the balance,
And in the hollow thereof was found the
    nest of a magpie,

Into whose clay-built walls the necklace of
    pearls was inwoven.'
Silenced, but not convinced, when the story
    was ended, the blacksmith
Stood like a man who fain would speak,
    but findeth no language;
All his thoughts were congealed into lines
    on his face, as the vapors
Freeze in fantastic shapes on the window-
    panes in the winter.   310

    Then Evangeline lighted the brazen lamp
    on the table,
Filled, till it overflowed, the pewter tankard
    with home-brewed
Nut-brown ale, that was famed for its
    strength in the village of Grand-
    Pré;
While from his pocket the notary drew his
    papers and inkhorn,
Wrote with a steady hand the date and the
    age of the parties,
Naming the dower of the bride in flocks of
    sheep and in cattle.
Orderly all things proceeded, and duly and
    well were completed,
And the great seal of the law was set like
    a sun on the margin.
Then from his leathern pouch the farmer
    threw on the table
Three times the old man's fee in solid
    pieces of silver;   320
And the notary rising, and blessing the
    bride and the bridegroom,
Lifted aloft the tankard of ale and drank
    to their welfare.
Wiping the foam from his lip, he solemnly
    bowed and departed,
While in silence the others sat and mused
    by the fireside,
Till Evangeline brought the draught-board
    out of its corner.
Soon was the game begun.   In friendly
    contention the old men
Laughed at each lucky hit, or unsuccessful
    manœuvre,
Laughed when a man was crowned, or a
    breach was made in the king-
    row.
Meanwhile apart, in the twilight gloom of
    a window's embrasure,
Sat the lovers, and whispered together, be-
    holding the moon rise   330
Over the pallid sea, and the silvery mists
    of the meadows.

Silently one by one, in the infinite meadows
of heaven,
Blossomed the lovely stars, the forget-me-
nots of the angels.

Thus was the evening passed.   Anon the
bell from the belfry
Rang out the hour of nine, the village cur-
few, and straightway
Rose the guests and departed; and silence
reigned in the household.
Many a farewell word and sweet good-
night on the door-step
Lingered long in Evangeline's heart, and
filled it with gladness.
Carefully then were covered the embers
that glowed on the hearth-stone,
And on the oaken stairs resounded the
tread of the farmer.   340
Soon with a soundless step the foot of
Evangeline followed.
Up the staircase moved a luminous space
in the darkness,
Lighted less by the lamp than the shining
face of the maiden.
Silent she passed the hall, and entered the
door of her chamber.
Simple that chamber was, with its curtains
of white, and its clothes-press
Ample and high, on whose spacious shelves
were carefully folded
Linen and woollen stuffs, by the hand of
Evangeline woven.
This was the precious dower she would
bring to her husband in mar-
riage,
Better than flocks and herds, being proofs
of her skill as a housewife.
Soon she extinguished her lamp, for the
mellow and radiant moonlight   350
Streamed through the windows, and lighted
the room, till the heart of the
maiden
Swelled and obeyed its power, like the
tremulous tides of the ocean.
Ah ! she was fair, exceeding fair to behold,
as she stood with
Naked snow-white feet on the gleaming
floor of her chamber !
Little she dreamed that below, among the
trees of the orchard,
Waited her lover and watched for the
gleam of her lamp and her shadow.
Yet were her thoughts of him, and at times
a feeling of sadness

Passed o'er her soul, as the sailing shade of
clouds in the moonlight
Flitted across the floor and darkened the
room for a moment.
And, as she gazed from the window, she
saw serenely the moon pass   360
Forth from the folds of a cloud, and one
star follow her footsteps,
As out of Abraham's tent young Ishmael
wandered with Hagar !

IV

Pleasantly rose next morn the sun on the
village of Grand Pré.
Pleasantly gleamed in the soft, sweet air
the Basin of Minas,
Where the ships, with their wavering sha-
dows, were riding at anchor.
Life had long been astir in the village, and
clamorous labor
Knocked with its hundred hands at the
golden gates of the morning.
Now from the country around, from the
farms and neighboring hamlets,
Came in their holiday dresses the blithe
Acadian peasants.
Many a glad good-morrow and jocund
laugh from the young folk   370
Made the bright air brighter, as up from
the numerous meadows,
Where no path could be seen but the track
of wheels in the greensward,
Group after group appeared, and joined, or
passed on the highway.
Long ere noon, in the village all sounds of
labor were silenced.
Thronged were the streets with people; and
noisy groups at the house-doors
Sat in the cheerful sun, and rejoiced and
gossipped together.
Every house was an inn, where all were
welcomed and feasted;
For with this simple people, who lived like
brothers together,
All things were held in common, and what
one had was another's.
Yet under Benedict's roof hospitality seemed
more abundant: 380
For Evangeline stood among the guests of
her father;
Bright was her face with smiles, and words
of welcome and gladness
Fell from her beautiful lips, and blessed
the cup as she gave it.

Under the open sky, in the odorous air of
the orchard,
Stript of its golden fruit, was spread the
feast of betrothal.
There in the shade of the porch were the
priest and the notary seated;
There good Benedict sat, and sturdy Basil
the blacksmith.
Not far withdrawn from these, by the
cider-press and the beehives,
Michael the fiddler was placed, with the
gayest of hearts and of waistcoats.
Shadow and light from the leaves alter-
nately played on his snow-white   390
Hair, as it waved in the wind; and the jolly
face of the fiddler
Glowed like a living coal when the ashes
are blown from the embers.
Gayly the old man sang to the vibrant
sound of his fiddle,
Tous les Bourgeois de Chartres, and *Le
Carillon de Dunquerque,*
And anon with his wooden shoes beat time
to the music.
Merrily, merrily whirled the wheels of the
dizzying dances
Under the orchard-trees and down the path
to the meadows;
Old folk and young together, and children
mingled among them.
Fairest of all the maids was Evangeline,
Benedict's daughter !
Noblest of all the youths was Gabriel, son
of the blacksmith !   400

So passed the morning away. And lo !
with a summons sonorous
Sounded the bell from its tower, and over
the meadows a drum beat.
Thronged erelong was the church with men.
Without, in the churchyard,
Waited the women. They stood by the
graves, and hung on the headstones
Garlands of autumn-leaves and evergreens
fresh from the forest.
Then came the guard from the ships, and
marching proudly among them
Entered the sacred portal. With loud and
dissonant clangor
Echoed the sound of their brazen drums
from ceiling and casement, —
Echoed a moment only, and slowly the
ponderous portal
Closed, and in silence the crowd awaited
the will of the soldiers,   410

Then uprose their commander, and spake
from the steps of the altar,
Holding aloft in his hands, with its seals,
the royal commission.
'You are convened this day,' he said, ' by
his Majesty's orders.
Clement and kind has he been; but how
you have answered his kindness,
Let your own, hearts reply ! To my natural make and my temper
Painful the task is I do, which to you I
know must be grievous.
Yet must I bow and obey, and deliver the
will of our monarch;
Namely, that all your lands, and dwellings,
and cattle of all kinds
Forfeited be to the crown; and that you
yourselves from this province
Be transported to other lands. God grant
you may dwell there   420
Ever as faithful subjects, a happy and
peaceable people !
Prisoners now I declare you; for such is
his Majesty's pleasure ! '
As, when the air is serene in sultry solstice
of summer,
Suddenly gathers a storm, and the deadly
sling of the hailstones
Beats down the farmer's corn in the field
and shatters his windows,
Hiding the sun, and strewing the ground
with thatch from the house-roofs,
Bellowing fly the herds, and seek to break
their enclosures;
So on the hearts of the people descended the
words of the speaker.
Silent a moment they stood in speechless
wonder, and·then rose
Louder and ever louder a wail of sorrow
and anger,   430
And, by one impulse moved, they madly
rushed to the door-way.
Vain was the hope of escape; and cries and
fierce imprecations
Rang through the house of prayer; and
high o'er the heads of the others
Rose, with his arms uplifted, the figure of
Basil the blacksmith,
As, on a stormy sea, a spar is tossed by the
billows.
Flushed was his face and distorted with
passion; and wildly he shouted, —
'Down with the tyrants of England !
we never have sworn them allegiance !

Death to these foreign soldiers, who seize
    on our homes and our harvests !'
More he fain would have said, but the
    merciless hand of a soldier
Smote him upon the mouth, and dragged
    him down to the pavement.   440

In the midst of the strife and tumult of
    angry contention,
Lo! the door of the chancel opened, and
    Father Felician
Entered, with serious mien, and ascended
    the steps of the altar.
Raising his reverend hand, with a gesture
    he awed into silence
All that clamorous throng; and thus he
    spake to his people;
Deep were his tones and solemn; in accents
    measured and mournful
Spake he, as, after the tocsin's alarum, dis-
    tinctly the clock strikes.
'What is this that ye do, my chil-
    dren? what madness has seized
    you?
Forty years of my life have I labored
    among you, and taught you,
Not in word alone, but in deed, to love one
    another !   450
Is this the fruit of my toils, of my vigils
    and prayers and privations?
Have you so soon forgotten all lessons of
    love and forgiveness?
This is the house of the Prince of Peace,
    and would you profane it
Thus with violent deeds and hearts over-
    flowing with hatred?
Lo! where the crucified Christ from his
    cross is gazing upon you!
See! in those sorrowful eyes what meek-
    ness and holy compassion!
Hark! how those lips still repeat the
    prayer, " O Father, forgive them ! "
Let us repeat that prayer in the hour when
    the wicked assail us,
Let us repeat it now, and say, " O Father,
    forgive them ! " '
Few were his words of rebuke, but deep in
    the hearts of his people   460
Sank they, and sobs of contrition succeeded
    the passionate outbreak,
While they repeated his prayer, and said,
    ' O Father, forgive them ! '

Then came the evening service. The
    tapers gleamed from the altar.

Fervent and deep was the voice of the
    priest, and the people responded,
Not with their lips alone, but their hearts;
    and the Ave Maria
Sang they, and fell on their knees, and
    their souls, with devotion trans-
    lated,
Rose on the ardor of prayer, like Elijah
    ascending to heaven.

Meanwhile had spread in the village the
    tidings of ill, and on all sides
Wandered, wailing, from house to house
    the women and children.
Long at her father's door Evangeline stood,
    with her right hand   470
Shielding her eyes from the level rays of
    the sun, that, descending,
Lighted the village street with mysterious
    splendor, and roofed each
Peasant's cottage with golden thatch, and
    emblazoned its windows.
Long within had been spread the snow-
    white cloth on the table;
There stood the wheaten loaf, and the
    honey fragrant with wild-flow-
    ers;
There stood the tankard of ale, and the
    cheese fresh brought from the dairy,
And, at the head of the board, the great
    arm-chair of the farmer.
Thus did Evangeline wait at her father's
    door, as the sunset
Threw the long shadows of trees o'er the
    broad ambrosial meadows.
Ah! on her spirit within a deeper shadow
    had fallen,   480
And from the fields of her soul a fragrance
    celestial ascended, —
Charity, meekness, love, and hope, and for-
    giveness, and patience !
Then, all-forgetful of self, she wandered
    into the village,
Cheering with looks and words the mourn-
    ful hearts of the women,
As o'er the darkening fields with lingering
    steps they departed,
Urged by their household cares, and the
    weary feet of their children.
Down sank the great red sun, and in golden,
    glimmering vapors
Veiled the light of his face, like the Prophet
    descending from Sinai.
Sweetly over the village the bell of the
    Angelus sounded.

Meanwhile, amid the gloom, by the church Evangeline lingered.   490
All was silent within; and in vain at the door and the windows
Stood she, and listened and looked, till, overcome by emotion,
'Gabriel!' cried she aloud with tremulous voice; but no answer
Came from the graves of the dead, nor the gloomier grave of the living.
Slowly at length she returned to the tenantless house of her father.
Smouldered the fire on the hearth, on the board was the supper untasted,
Empty and drear was each room, and haunted with phantoms of terror.
Sadly echoed her step on the stair and the floor of her chamber.
In the dead of the night she heard the disconsolate rain fall
Loud on the withered leaves of the sycamore-tree by the window.   500
Keenly the lightning flashed; and the voice of the echoing thunder
Told her that God was in heaven, and governed the world He created!
Then she remembered the tale she had heard of the justice of Heaven;
Soothed was her troubled soul, and she peacefully slumbered till morning.

V

Four times the sun had risen and set; and now on the fifth day
Cheerily called the cock to the sleeping maids of the farm-house.
Soon o'er the yellow fields, in silent and mournful procession,
Came from the neighboring hamlets and farms the Acadian women,
Driving in ponderous wains their household goods to the sea-shore,
Pausing and looking back to gaze once more on their dwellings,   510
Ere they were shut from sight by the winding road and the woodland.
Close at their sides their children ran, and urged on the oxen,
While in their little hands they clasped some fragments of playthings.

Thus to the Gaspereau's mouth they hurried; and there on the sea-beach

Piled in confusion lay the household goods of the peasants.
All day long between the shore and the ships did the boats ply;
All day long the wains came laboring down from the village.
Late in the afternoon, when the sun was near to his setting,
Echoed far o'er the fields came the roll of drums from the churchyard.
Thither the women and children thronged. On a sudden the church-doors   520
Opened, and forth came the guard, and marching in gloomy procession
Followed the long-imprisoned, but patient, Acadian farmers.
Even as pilgrims, who journey afar from their homes and their country,
Sing as they go, and in singing forget they are weary and wayworn,
So with songs on their lips the Acadian peasants descended
Down from the church to the shore, amid their wives and their daughters.
Foremost the young men came; and, raising together their voices,
Sang with tremulous lips a chant of the Catholic Missions: —
'Sacred heart of the Saviour! O inexhaustible fountain!
Fill our hearts this day with strength and submission and patience!'   530
Then the old men, as they marched, and the women that stood by the wayside
Joined in the sacred psalm, and the birds in the sunshine above them
Mingled their notes therewith, like voices of spirits departed.

Half-way down to the shore Evangeline waited in silence,
Not overcome with grief, but strong in the hour of affliction, —
Calmly and sadly she waited, until the procession approached her,
And she beheld the face of Gabriel pale with emotion.
Tears then filled her eyes, and, eagerly running to meet him,
Clasped she his hands, and laid her head on his shoulder, and whispered, —
'Gabriel! be of good cheer! for if we love one another   540
Nothing, in truth, can harm us, whatever mischances may happen!'

Smiling she spake these words; then suddenly paused, for her father
Saw she slowly advancing. Alas! how changed was his aspect!
Gone was the glow from his cheek, and the fire from his eye, and his footstep
Heavier seemed with the weight of the heavy heart in his bosom.
But with a smile and a sigh, she clasped his neck and embraced him,
Speaking words of endearment where words of comfort availed not.
Thus to the Gaspereau's mouth moved on that mournful procession.

There disorder prevailed, and the tumult and stir of embarking.
Busily plied the freighted boats; and in the confusion   550
Wives were torn from their husbands, and mothers, too late, saw their children
Left on the land, extending their arms, with wildest entreaties.
So unto separate ships were Basil and Gabriel carried,
While in despair on the shore Evangeline stood with her father.
Half the task was not done when the sun went down, and the twilight
Deepened and darkened around; and in haste the refluent ocean
Fled away from the shore, and left the line of the sand-beach
Covered with waifs of the tide, with kelp and the slippery sea-weed.
Farther back in the midst of the household goods and the wagons,
Like to a gypsy camp, or a leaguer after a battle,   560
All escape cut off by the sea, and the sentinels near them,
Lay encamped for the night the houseless Acadian farmers.
Back to its nethermost caves retreated the bellowing ocean,
Dragging adown the beach the rattling pebbles, and leaving
Inland and far up the shore the stranded boats of the sailors.
Then, as the night descended, the herds returned from their pastures;
Sweet was the moist still air with the odor of milk from their udders;
Lowing they waited, and long, at the well-known bars of the farm-yard, —

Waited and looked in vain for the voice and the hand of the milk-maid.
Silence reigned in the streets; from the church no Angelus sounded,   570
Rose no smoke from the roofs, and gleamed no lights from the windows.

But on the shores meanwhile the evening fires had been kindled,
Built of the drift-wood thrown on the sands from wrecks in the tempest.
Round them shapes of gloom and sorrowful faces were gathered,
Voices of women were heard, and of men, and the crying of children.
Onward from fire to fire, as from hearth to hearth in his parish,
Wandered the faithful priest, consoling and blessing and cheering,
Like unto shipwrecked Paul on Melita's desolate sea-shore.
Thus he approached the place where Evangeline sat with her father,
And in the flickering light beheld the face of the old man,   580
Haggard and hollow and wan, and without either thought or emotion,
E'en as the face of a clock from which the hands have been taken.
Vainly Evangeline strove with words and caresses to cheer him,
Vainly offered him food; yet he moved not, he looked not, he spake not,
But, with a vacant stare, ever gazed at the flickering fire-light.
' Benedicite! ' murmured the priest, in tones of compassion.
More he fain would have said, but his heart was full, and his accents
Faltered and paused on his lips, as the feet of a child on a threshold,
Hushed by the scene he beholds, and the awful presence of sorrow.
Silently, therefore, he laid his hand on the head of the maiden,   590
Raising his tearful eyes to the silent stars that above them
Moved on their way, unperturbed by the wrongs and sorrows of mortals.
Then sat he down at her side, and they wept together in silence.

Suddenly rose from the south a light, as in autumn the blood-red

Moon climbs the crystal walls of heaven,
    and o'er the horizon
Titan-like stretches its hundred hands upon
    the mountain and meadow,
Seizing the rocks and the rivers and piling
    huge shadows together.
Broader and ever broader it gleamed on
    the roofs of the village,
Gleamed on the sky and sea, and the ships
    that lay in the roadstead.
Columns of shining smoke uprose, and
    flashes of flame were   600
Thrust through their folds and withdrawn,
    like the quivering hands of a mar-
    tyr.
Then as the wind seized the gleeds and the
    burning thatch, and, uplifting,
Whirled them aloft through the air, at
    once from a hundred house-tops
Started the sheeted smoke with flashes of
    flame intermingled.

These things beheld in dismay the crowd
    on the shore and on shipboard.
Speechless at first they stood, then cried
    aloud in their anguish,
' We shall behold no more our homes in
    the village of Grand-Pré ! '
Loud on a sudden the cocks began to crow
    in the farm-yards,
Thinking the day had dawned; and anon
    the lowing of cattle
Came on the evening breeze, by the bark-
    ing of dogs interrupted.   610
Then rose a sound of dread, such as startles
    the sleeping encampments
Far in the western prairies or forests that
    skirt the Nebraska,
When the wild horses affrighted sweep
    by with the speed of the whirl-
    wind,
Or the loud bellowing herds of buffaloes
    rush to the river.
Such was the sound that arose on the night,
    as the herds and the horses
Broke through their folds and fences, and
    madly rushed o'er the meadows.

Overwhelmed with the sight, yet speech-
    less, the priest and the maiden
Gazed on the scene of terror that reddened
    and widened before them:
And as they turned at length to speak to
    their silent companion,

Lo ! from his seat he had fallen, and
    stretched abroad on the sea-shore
Motionless lay his form, from which the
    soul had departed.   621
Slowly the priest uplifted the lifeless head,
    and the maiden
Knelt at her father's side, and wailed aloud
    in her terror.
Then in a swoon she sank, and lay with her
    head on his bosom.
Through the long night she lay in deep, ob-
    livious slumber;
And when she awoke from the trance, she
    beheld a multitude near her.
Faces of friends she beheld, that were
    mournfully gazing upon her,
Pallid, with tearful eyes, and looks of sad-
    dest compassion.
Still the blaze of the burning village illu-
    mined the landscape,
Reddened the sky overhead, and gleamed
    on the faces around her,   630
And like the day of doom it seemed to her
    wavering senses.
Then a familiar voice she heard, as it said
    to the people, —
' Let us bury him here by the sea. When
    a happier season
Brings us again to our homes from the un-
    known land of our exile,
Then shall his sacred dust be piously laid
    in the churchyard.'
Such were the words of the priest. And
    there in haste by the sea-side,
Having the glare of the burning village for
    funeral torches,
But without bell or book, they buried the
    farmer of Grand-Pré.
And as the voice of the priest repeated the
    service of sorrow,
Lo ! with a mournful sound, like the voice
    of a vast congregation,   640
Solemnly answered the sea, and mingled its
    roar with the dirges.
'T was the returning tide, that afar from
    the waste of the ocean,
With the first dawn of the day, came heav-
    ing and hurrying landward.
Then recommenced once more the stir and
    noise of embarking;
And with the ebb of the tide the ships
    sailed out of the harbor,
Leaving behind them the dead on the shore,
    and the village in ruins.

PART THE SECOND

I

MANY a weary year had passed since the
burning of Grand-Pré,
When on the falling tide the freighted ves-
sels departed,
Bearing a nation, with all its household
gods, into exile,
Exile without an end, and without an ex-
ample in story.
Far asunder, on separate coasts, the Aca-
dians landed;
Scattered were they, like flakes of snow,
when the wind from the northeast
Strikes aslant through the fogs that darken
the Banks of Newfoundland.
Friendless, homeless, hopeless, they wan-
dered from city to city,
From the cold lakes of the North to sultry
Southern savannas, —
From the bleak shores of the sea to the
lands where the Father of Waters 10
Seizes the hills in his hands, and drags them
down to the ocean,
Deep in their sands to bury the scattered
bones of the mammoth.
Friends they sought and homes; and many,
despairing, heart-broken,
Asked of the earth but a grave, and no
longer a friend nor a fireside.
Written their history stands on tablets of
stone in the churchyards.
Long among them was seen a maiden who
waited and wandered,
Lowly and meek in spirit, and patiently
suffering all things.
Fair was she and young: but, alas! before
her extended,
Dreary and vast and silent, the desert of
life, with its pathway
Marked by the graves of those who had
sorrowed and suffered before her, 20
Passions long extinguished, and hopes long
dead and abandoned,
As the emigrant's way o'er the Western
desert is marked by
Camp-fires long consumed, and bones that
bleach in the sunshine.
Something there was in her life incomplete,
imperfect, unfinished;
As if a morning of June, with all its music
and sunshine,
Suddenly paused in the sky, and, fading,
slowly descended

Into the east again, from whence it late had
arisen.
Sometimes she lingered in towns, till, urged
by the fever within her,
Urged by a restless longing, the hunger and
thirst of the spirit,
She would commence again her endless
search and endeavor; 30
Sometimes in churchyards strayed, and
gazed on the crosses and tombstones,
Sat by some nameless grave, and thought
that perhaps in its bosom
He was already at rest, and she longed to
slumber beside him.
Sometimes a rumor, a hearsay, an inarticulate whisper,
Came with its airy hand to point and beckon
her forward.
Sometimes she spake with those who had
seen her beloved and known him,
But it was long ago, in some far-off place or
forgotten.
'Gabriel Lajeunesse!' they said; 'Oh yes!
we have seen him.
He was with Basil the blacksmith, and both
have gone to the prairies;
Coureurs-des-Bois are they, and famous
hunters and trappers.'   40
'Gabriel Lajeunesse!' said others; 'Oh yes!
we have seen him.
He is a Voyageur in the lowlands of Louisi-
ana.'
Then would they say, 'Dear child! why
dream and wait for him longer?
Are there not other youths as fair as Ga-
briel? others
Who have hearts as tender and true, and
spirits as loyal?
Here is Baptiste Leblanc, the notary's son,
who has loved thee
Many a tedious year; come, give him thy
hand and be happy!
Thou art too fair to be left to braid St.
Catherine's tresses.'[1]
Then would Evangeline answer, serenely
but sadly, 'I cannot!
Whither my heart has gone, there follows
my hand, and not elsewhere.   50
For when the heart goes before, like a lamp,
and illumines the pathway,
Many things are made clear, that else lie
hidden in darkness.'

[1] There is a common expression in French, '*coiffer
Sainte Catherine*,' meaning to be an old maid.

Thereupon the priest, her friend and father-
   confessor,
Said, with a smile, 'O daughter! thy God
   thus speaketh within thee!
Talk not of wasted affection, affection never
   was wasted;
If it enrich not the heart of another, its
   waters, returning
Back to their springs, like the rain, shall fill
   them full of refreshment;
That which the fountain sends forth returns
   again to the fountain.
Patience; accomplish thy labor; accomplish
   thy work of affection!
Sorrow and silence are strong, and patient
   endurance is godlike.   60
Therefore accomplish thy labor of love, till
   the heart is made godlike,
Purified, strengthened, perfected, and rendered more worthy of heaven!'
Cheered by the good man's words, Evangeline labored and waited.
Still in her heart she heard the funeral dirge
   of the ocean,
But with its sound there was mingled
   a voice that whispered, 'Despair
   not!'
Thus did that poor soul wander in want and
   cheerless discomfort,
Bleeding, barefooted, over the shards and
   thorns of existence.
Let me essay, O Muse! to follow the wanderer's footsteps; —
Not through each devious path, each changeful year of existence,
But as a traveller follows a streamlet's
   course through the valley: 70
Far from its margin at times, and seeing the
   gleam of its water
Here and there, in some open space, and at
   intervals only;
Then drawing nearer its banks, through
   sylvan glooms that conceal it,
Though he behold it not, he can hear its
   continuous murmur;
Happy, at length, if he find the spot where
   it reaches an outlet.

II

It was the month of May. Far down the
   Beautiful River,
Past the Ohio shore and past the mouth of
   the Wabash,
Into the golden stream of the broad and
   swift Mississippi,

Floated a cumbrous boat, that was rowed
   by Acadian boatmen.
It was a band of exiles: a raft, as it were,
   from the shipwrecked   80
Nation, scattered along the coast, now
   floating together,
Bound by the bonds of a common belief
   and a common misfortune;
Men and women and children, who, guided
   by hope or by hearsay,
Sought for their kith and their kin among
   the few-acred farmers
On the Acadian coast, and the prairies of
   fair Opelousas.
With them Evangeline went, and her guide,
   the Father Felician.
Onward o'er sunken sands, through a wilderness sombre with forests,
Day after day they glided adown the turbulent river;
Night after night, by their blazing fires,
   encamped on its borders.
Now through rushing chutes, among green
   islands, where plumelike   90
Cotton-trees nodded their shadowy crests,
   they swept with the current,
Then emerged into broad lagoons, where
   silvery sand-bars
Lay in the stream, and along the wimpling
   waves of their margin,
Shining with snow - white plumes, large
   flocks of pelicans waded.
Level the landscape grew, and along the
   shores of the river,
Shaded by china-trees, in the midst of luxuriant gardens,
Stood the houses of planters, with negro-
   cabins and dove-cots.
They were approaching the region where
   reigns perpetual summer,
Where through the Golden Coast, and
   groves of orange and citron,
Sweeps with majestic curve the river away
   to the eastward.   100
They, too, swerved from their course; and
   entering the Bayou of Plaque-
   mine,
Soon were lost in a maze of sluggish and
   devious waters,
Which, like a network of steel, extended in
   every direction.
Over their heads the towering and tene-
   brous boughs of the cypress
Met in a dusky arch, and trailing mosses in
   mid-air

Waved like banners that hang on the walls
of ancient cathedrals.
Deathlike the silence seemed, and unbroken, save by the herons
Home to their roosts in the cedar-trees returning at sunset,
Or by the owl, as he greeted the moon with
demoniac laughter.
Lovely the moonlight was as it glanced and
gleamed on the water,   110
Gleamed on the columns of cypress and
cedar sustaining the arches,
Down through whose broken vaults it fell
as through chinks in a ruin.
Dreamlike, and indistinct, and strange were
all things around them;
And o'er their spirits there came a feeling
of wonder and sadness, —
Strange forebodings of ill, unseen and that
cannot be compassed.
As, at the tramp of a horse's hoof on the
turf of the prairies,
Far in advance are closed the leaves of the
shrinking mimosa,
So, at the hoof-beats of fate, with sad forebodings of evil,
Shrinks and closes the heart, ere the stroke
of doom has attained it.
But Evangeline's heart was sustained by a
vision, that faintly   120
Floated before her eyes, and beckoned her
on through the moonlight.
It was the thought of her brain that assumed the shape of a phantom.
Through those shadowy aisles had Gabriel
wandered before her,
And every stroke of the oar now brought
him nearer and nearer.

Then in his place, at the prow of the
boat, rose one of the oarsmen,
And, as a signal sound, if others like them
peradventure
Sailed on those gloomy and midnight
streams, blew a blast on his bugle.
Wild through the dark colonnades and corridors leafy the blast rang,
Breaking the seal of silence, and giving
tongues to the forest.
Soundless above them the banners of moss
just stirred to the music.   130
Multitudinous echoes awoke and died in
the distance,
Over the watery floor, and beneath the re-
verberant branches;

But not a voice replied; no answer came
from the darkness;
And, when the echoes had ceased, like a
sense of pain was the silence.
Then Evangeline slept; but the boatmen
rowed through the midnight,
Silent at times, then singing familiar Canadian boat-songs,
Such as they sang of old on their own Acadian rivers,
While through the night were heard the
mysterious sounds of the desert,
Far off, — indistinct, — as of wave or wind
in the forest,
Mixed with the whoop of the crane and
the roar of the grim alligator.   140

Thus ere another noon they emerged
from the shades; and before them
Lay, in the golden sun, the lakes of the
Atchafalaya.
Water-lilies in myriads rocked on the slight
undulations
Made by the passing oars, and, resplendent
in beauty, the lotus
Lifted her golden crown above the heads
of the boatmen.
Faint was the air with the odorous breath
of magnolia blossoms,
And with the heat of noon; and numberless
sylvan islands,
Fragrant and thickly embowered with blos-
soming hedges of roses,
Near to whose shores they glided along,
invited to slumber.
Soon by the fairest of these their weary
oars were suspended.   150
Under the boughs of Wachita willows, that
grew by the margin,
Safely their boat was moored; and scattered about on the greensward,
Tired with their midnight toil, the weary
travellers slumbered.
Over them vast and high extended the cope
of a cedar.
Swinging from its great arms, the trumpet-
flower and the grapevine
Hung their ladder of ropes aloft like the
ladder of Jacob,
On whose pendulous stairs the angels ascending, descending,
Were the swift humming-birds, that flitted
from blossom to blossom.
Such was the vision Evangeline saw as she
slumbered beneath it.

Filled was her heart with love, and the
   dawn of an opening heaven   160
Lighted her soul in sleep with the glory of
   regions celestial.

   Nearer, and ever nearer, among the
   numberless islands,
Darted a light, swift boat, that sped away
   o'er the water,
Urged on its course by the sinewy arms of
   hunters and trappers.
Northward its prow was turned, to the land
   of the bison and beaver.
At the helm sat a youth, with countenance
   thoughtful and careworn.
Dark and neglected locks overshadowed his
   brow, and a sadness
Somewhat beyond his years on his face was
   legibly written.
Gabriel was it, who, weary with waiting,
   unhappy and restless,
Sought in the Western wilds oblivion of
   self and of sorrow.   170
Swiftly they glided along, close under the
   lee of the island,
But by the opposite bank, and behind a
   screen of palmettos,
So that they saw not the boat, where it lay
   concealed in the willows;
All undisturbed by the dash of their oars,
   and unseen, were the sleepers.
Angel of God was there none to awaken the
   slumbering maiden.
Swiftly they glided away, like the shade of
   a cloud on the prairie.
After the sound of their oars on the tholes
   had died in the distance,
As from a magic trance the sleepers awoke,
   and the maiden
Said with a sigh to the friendly priest, 'O
   Father Felician !
Something says in my heart that near me
   Gabriel wanders.   180
Is it a foolish dream, an idle and vague
   superstition ?
Or has an angel passed, and revealed the
   truth to my spirit ?'
Then, with a blush, she added, 'Alas for
   my credulous fancy !
Unto ears like thine such words as these
   have no meaning.'
But made answer the reverend man, and he
   smiled as he answered, —
'Daughter, thy words are not idle; nor are
   they to me without meaning.

Feeling is deep and still; and the word that
   floats on the surface
Is as the tossing buoy, that betrays where
   the anchor is hidden.
Therefore trust to thy heart, and to what
   the world calls illusions.
Gabriel truly is near thee; for not far away
   to the southward,   190
On the banks of the Têche, are the towns
   of St. Maur and St. Martin.
There the long-wandering bride shall be
   given again to her bridegroom,
There the long-absent pastor regain his
   flock and his sheepfold.
Beautiful is the land, with its prairies and
   forests of fruit-trees;
Under the feet a garden of flowers, and the
   bluest of heavens
Bending above, and resting its dome on the
   walls of the forest.
They who dwell there have named it the
   Eden of Louisiana ! '

   With these words of cheer they arose and
   continued their journey.
Softly the evening came. The sun from
   the western horizon
Like a magician extended his golden wand
   o'er the landscape;   200
Twinkling vapors arose; and sky and water
   and forest
Seemed all on fire at the touch, and melted
   and mingled together.
Hanging between two skies, a cloud with
   edges of silver,
Floated the boat, with its dripping oars, on
   the motionless water.
Filled was Evangeline's heart with inexpressible sweetness.
Touched by the magic spell, the sacred
   fountains of feeling
Glowed with the light of love, as the skies
   and waters around her.
Then from a neighboring thicket the mocking-bird, wildest of singers,
Swinging aloft on a willow spray that hung
   o'er the water,
Shook from his little throat such floods of
   delirious music,   210
That the whole air and the woods and the
   waves seemed silent to listen.
Plaintive at first were the tones and sad:
   then soaring to madness
Seemed they to follow or guide the revel
   of frenzied Bacchantes.

Single notes were then heard, in sorrowful,
    low lamentation;
Till, having gathered them all, he flung
    them abroad in derision,
As when, after a storm, a gust of wind
    through the tree-tops
Shakes down the rattling rain in a crystal
    shower on the branches.
With such a prelude as this, and hearts
    that throbbed with emotion,
Slowly they entered the Têche, where it
    flows through the green Opelou-
    sas,
And, through the amber air, above the
    crest of the woodland,   220
Saw the column of smoke that arose from
    a neighboring dwelling; —
Sounds of a horn they heard, and the dis-
    tant lowing of cattle.

III

Near to the bank of the river, o'ershad-
    owed by oaks, from whose branches
Garlands of Spanish moss and of mystic
    mistletoe flaunted,
Such as the Druids cut down with golden
    hatchets at Yule-tide,
Stood, secluded and still, the house of the
    herdsman. A garden
Girded it round about with a belt of luxuri-
    ant blossoms,
Filling the air with fragrance. The house
    itself was of timbers
Hewn from the cypress-tree, and carefully
    fitted together.
Large and low was the roof; and on slender
    columns supported,   230
Rose-wreathed, vine-encircled, a broad and
    spacious veranda,
Haunt of the humming-bird and the bee,
    extended around it.
At each end of the house, amid the flowers
    of the garden,
Stationed the dove-cots were, as love's per-
    petual symbol,
Scenes of endless wooing, and endless con-
    tentions of rivals.
Silence reigned o'er the place. The line of
    shadow and sunshine
Ran near the tops of the trees; but the
    house itself was in shadow,
And from its chimney-top, ascending and
    slowly expanding
Into the evening air, a thin blue column of
    smoke rose.

In the rear of the house, from the garden
    gate, ran a pathway   240
Through the great groves of oak to the
    skirts of the limitless prairie,
Into whose sea of flowers the sun was
    slowly descending.
Full in his track of light, like ships with
    shadowy canvas
Hanging loose from their spars in a motion-
    less calm in the tropics,
Stood a cluster of trees, with tangled cord-
    age of grape-vines.

Just where the woodlands met the flow-
    ery surf of the prairie,
Mounted upon his horse, with Spanish sad-
    dle and stirrups,
Sat a herdsman, arrayed in gaiters and
    doublet of deerskin.
Broad and brown was the face that from
    under the Spanish sombrero
Gazed on the peaceful scene, with the
    lordly look of its master.   250
Round about him were numberless herds
    of kine, that were grazing
Quietly in the meadows, and breathing the
    vapory freshness
That uprose from the river, and spread
    itself over the landscape.
Slowly lifting the horn that hung at his side,
    and expanding
Fully his broad, deep chest, he blew a blast,
    that resounded
Wildly and sweet and far, through the still
    damp air of the evening.
Suddenly out of the grass the long white
    horns of the cattle
Rose like flakes of foam on the adverse
    currents of ocean.
Silent a moment they gazed, then bellow-
    ing rushed o'er the prairie,
And the whole mass became a cloud, a
    shade in the distance.   260
Then, as the herdsman turned to the house,
    through the gate of the garden
Saw he the forms of the priest and the
    maiden advancing to meet him.
Suddenly down from his horse he sprang in
    amazement, and forward
Rushed with extended arms and exclama-
    tions of wonder;
When they beheld his face, they recognized
    Basil the blacksmith.
Hearty his welcome was, as he led his
    guests to the garden.

There in an arbor of roses with endless
    question and answer
Gave they vent to their hearts, and renewed
    their friendly embraces,
Laughing and weeping by turns, or sitting
    silent and thoughtful.
Thoughtful, for Gabriel came not; and now
    dark doubts and misgivings   270
Stole o'er the maiden's heart; and Basil,
    somewhat embarrassed,
Broke the silence and said, 'If you came
    by the Atchafalaya,
How have you nowhere encountered my
    Gabriel's boat on the bayous?'
Over Evangeline's face at the words of
    Basil a shade passed.
Tears came into her eyes, and she said,
    with a tremulous accent,
'Gone? is Gabriel gone?' and, conceal-
    ing her face on his shoulder,
All her o'erburdened heart gave way, and
    she wept and lamented.
Then the good Basil said, — and his voice
    grew blithe as he said it, —
'Be of good cheer, my child ; it is only to-
    day he departed.
Foolish boy! he has left me alone with my
    herds and my horses.   280
Moody and restless grown, and tried and
    troubled, his spirit
Could no longer endure the calm of this
    quiet existence,
Thinking ever of thee, uncertain and sor-
    rowful ever,
Ever silent, or speaking only of thee and
    his troubles,
He at length had become so tedious to men
    and to maidens,
Tedious even to me, that at length I be-
    thought me, and sent him
Unto the town of Adayes to trade for mules
    with the Spaniards.
Thence he will follow the Indian trails to
    the Ozark Mountains,
Hunting for furs in the forests, on rivers
    trapping the beaver.
Therefore be of good cheer; we will fol-
    low the fugitive lover;   290
He is not far on his way, and the
    Fates and the streams are against
    him.
Up and away to-morrow, and through the
    red dew of the morning
We will follow him fast, and bring him
    back to his prison.'

Then glad voices were heard, and up
    from the banks of the river,
Borne aloft on his comrades' arms, came
    Michael the fiddler.
Long under Basil's roof had he lived like a
    god on Olympus,
Having no other care than dispensing
    music to mortals.
Far renowned was he for his silver locks
    and his fiddle.
'Long live Michael,' they cried, 'our brave
    Acadian minstrel!'
As they bore him aloft in triumphal pro-
    cession; and straightway   300
Father Felician advanced with Evangeline,
    greeting the old man
Kindly and oft, and recalling the past,
    while Basil, enraptured,
Hailed with hilarious joy his old compan-
    ions and gossips,
Laughing loud and long, and embracing
    mothers and daughters.
Much they marvelled to see the wealth of
    the ci-devant blacksmith,
All his domains and his herds, and his pa-
    triarchal demeanor,
Much they marvelled to hear his tales of
    the soil and the climate,
And of the prairies, whose numberless
    herds were his who would take them;
Each one thought in his heart, that he, too,
    would go and do likewise.
Thus they ascended the steps, and crossing
    the breezy veranda,   310
Entered the hall of the house, where al-
    ready the supper of Basil
Waited his late return; and they rested
    and feasted together.

Over the joyous feast the sudden dark-
    ness descended.
All was silent without, and, illuming the
    landscape with silver,
Fair rose the dewy moon and the myriad
    stars; but within doors,
Brighter than these, shone the faces of
    friends in the glimmering lamplight.
Then from his station aloft, at the head of
    the table, the herdsman
Poured forth his heart and his wine to-
    gether in endless profusion.
Lighting his pipe, that was filled with sweet
    Natchitoches tobacco,
Thus he spake to his guests, who listened,
    and smiled as they listened:—   320

'Welcome once more, my friends, who long
    have been friendless and homeless,
Welcome once more to a home, that is
    better perchance than the old one !
Here no hungry winter congeals our blood
    like the rivers;
Here no stony ground provokes the wrath
    of the farmer.
Smoothly the ploughshare runs through the
    soil, as a keel through the water.
All the year round the orange-groves are
    in blossom; and grass grows
More in a single night than a whole Cana-
    dian summer.
Here, too, numberless herds run wild and
    unclaimed in the prairies;
Here, too, lands may be had for the asking,
    and forests of timber
With a few blows of the axe are hewn and
    framed into houses.   330
After your houses are built, and your fields
    are yellow with harvests,
No King George of England shall drive
    you away from your homesteads,
Burning your dwellings and barns, and
    stealing your farms and your cat-
    tle.'
Speaking these words, he blew a wrathful
    cloud from his nostrils,
While his huge, brown hand came thunder-
    ing down on the table,
So that the guests all started; and Father
    Felician, astounded,
Suddenly paused, with a pinch of snuff
    half-way to his nostrils.
But the brave Basil resumed, and his
    words were milder and gayer: —
'Only beware of the fever, my friends,
    beware of the fever !
For it is not like that of our cold Acadian
    climate,   340
Cured by wearing a spider hung round
    one's neck in a nutshell ! '
Then there were voices heard at the door,
    and footsteps approaching
Sounded upon the stairs and the floor of
    the breezy veranda.
It was the neighboring Creoles and small
    Acadian planters,
Who had been summoned all to the house
    of Basil the Herdsman.
Merry the meeting was of ancient com-
    rades and neighbors:
Friend clasped friend in his arms; and they
    who before were as strangers,

Meeting in exile, became straightway as
    friends to each other,
Drawn by the gentle bond of a common
    country together.
But in the neighboring hall a strain of mu-
    sic, proceeding   350
From the accordant strings of Michael's
    melodious fiddle,
Broke up all further speech. Away, like
    children delighted,
All things forgotten beside, they gave them-
    selves to the maddening
Whirl of the giddy dance, as it swept and
    swayed to the music,
Dreamlike, with beaming eyes and the rush
    of fluttering garments.

Meanwhile, apart, at the head of the
    hall, the priest and the herdsman
Sat, conversing together of past and present
    and future;
While Evangeline stood like one entranced,
    for within her
Olden memories rose, and loud in the midst
    of the music
Heard she the sound of the sea, and an ir-
    repressible sadness   360
Came o'er her heart, and unseen she stole
    forth into the garden.
Beautiful was the night. Behind the black
    wall of the forest,
Tipping its summit with silver, arose the
    moon. On the river
Fell here and there through the branches a
    tremulous gleam of the moonlight,
Like the sweet thoughts of love on a dark-
    ened and devious spirit.
Nearer and round about her, the manifold
    flowers of the garden
Poured out their souls in odors, that were
    their prayers and confessions
Unto the night, as it went its way, like a
    silent Carthusian.
Fuller of fragrance than they, and as heavy
    with shadows and night-dews,
Hung the heart of the maiden. The calm
    and the magical moonlight   370
Seemed to inundate her soul with indefin-
    able longings,
As, through the garden-gate, and beneath
    the shade of the oak-trees,
Passed she along the path to the edge of
    the measureless prairie.
Silent it lay, with a silvery haze upon it,
    and fire-flies

Gleamed and floated away in mingled and
   infinite numbers.
Over her head the stars, the thoughts of
   God in the heavens,
Shone on the eyes of man, who had ceased
   to marvel and worship,
Save when a blazing comet was seen on the
   walls of that temple,
As if a hand had appeared and written
   upon them, 'Upharsin.'
And the soul of the maiden, between the
   stars and the fire-flies,   380
Wandered alone, and she cried, 'O Ga-
   briel! O my beloved!
Art thou so near unto me, and yet I cannot
   behold thee?
Art thou so near unto me, and yet thy voice
   does not reach me?
Ah! how often thy feet have trod this path
   to the prairie!
Ah! how often thine eyes have looked on
   the woodlands around me!
Ah! how often beneath this oak, returning
   from labor,
Thou hast lain down to rest, and to dream
   of me in thy slumbers!
When shall these eyes behold, these arms
   be folded about thee?'
Loud and sudden and near the notes of a
   whippoorwill sounded
Like a flute in the woods; and anon, through
   the neighboring thickets,   390
Farther and farther away it floated and
   dropped into silence.
'Patience!' whispered the oaks from oracular caverns of darkness:
And, from the moonlit meadow, a sigh responded, 'To-morrow!'

Bright rose the sun next day; and all the
   flowers of the garden
Bathed his shining feet with their tears,
   and anointed his tresses
With the delicious balm that they bore in
   their vases of crystal.
'Farewell!' said the priest, as he stood at
   the shadowy threshold;
'See that you bring us the Prodigal Son
   from his fasting and famine,
And, too, the Foolish Virgin, who slept when
   the bridegroom was coming.'
'Farewell!' answered the maiden, and,
   smiling, with Basil descended   400
Down to the river's brink, where the boatmen already were waiting.

Thus beginning their journey with morn-
   ing, and sunshine, and gladness,
Swiftly they followed the flight of him who
   was speeding before them,
Blown by the blast of fate like a dead leaf
   over the desert.
Not that day, nor the next, nor yet the day
   that succeeded,
Found they the trace of his course, in lake
   or forest or river,
Nor, after many days, had they found him;
   but vague and uncertain
Rumors alone were their guides through a
   wild and desolate country;
Till, at the little inn of the Spanish town of
   Adayes,
Weary and worn, they alighted, and learned
   from the garrulous landlord,   410
That on the day before, with horses and
   guides and companions,
Gabriel left the village, and took the road
   of the prairies.

IV

Far in the West there lies a desert land,
   where the mountains
Lift, through perpetual snows, their lofty
   and luminous summits.
Down from their jagged, deep ravines,
   where the gorge, like a gate-
   way,
Opens a passage rude to the wheels of the
   emigrant's wagon,
Westward the Oregon flows and the Walle-
   way and Owyhee.
Eastward, with devious course, among the
   Wind-river Mountains,
Through the Sweet-water Valley precipitate leaps the Nebraska;
And to the south, from Fontaine-qui-bout
   and the Spanish sierras,   420
Fretted with sands and rocks, and swept by
   the wind of the desert,
Numberless torrents, with ceaseless sound,
   descend to the ocean,
Like the great chords of a harp, in loud and
   solemn vibrations.
Spreading between these streams are the
   wondrous, beautiful prairies;
Billowy bays of grass ever rolling in shadow
   and sunshine,
Bright with luxuriant clusters of roses and
   purple amorphas.
Over them wandered the buffalo herds, and
   the elk and the roebuck;

Over them wandered the wolves, and herds
    of riderless horses;
Fires that blast and blight, and winds that
    are weary with travel;
Over them wander the scattered tribes of
    Ishmael's children,   430
Staining the desert with blood; and above
    their terrible war-trails
Circles and sails aloft, on pinions majestic,
    the vulture,
Like the implacable soul of a chieftain
    slaughtered in battle,
By invisible stairs ascending and scaling
    the heavens.
Here and there rise smokes from the
    camps of these savage maraud-
    ers;
Here and there rise groves from the mar-
    gins of swift-running rivers;
And the grim, taciturn bear, the anchorite
    monk of the desert,
Climbs down their dark ravines to dig for
    roots by the brook-side,
And over all is the sky, the clear and crys-
    talline heaven,
Like the protecting hand of God inverted
    above them.   440

Into this wonderful land, at the base of
    the Ozark Mountains,
Gabriel far had entered, with hunters and
    trappers behind him.
Day after day, with their Indian guides, the
    maiden and Basil
Followed his flying steps, and thought each
    day to o'ertake him.
Sometimes they saw, or thought they saw,
    the smoke of his camp-fire
Rise in the morning air from the distant
    plain; but at nightfall,
When they had reached the place they
    found only embers and ashes.
And, though their hearts were sad at times
    and their bodies were weary,
Hope still guided them on, as the magic
    Fata Morgana
Showed them her lakes of light, that re-
    treated and vanished before them. 450

Once, as they sat by their evening fire,
    there silently entered
Into their little camp an Indian woman,
    whose features
Wore deep traces of sorrow, and patience
    as great as her sorrow.

She was a Shawnee woman returning home
    to her people,
From the far-off hunting-grounds of the
    cruel Camanches,
Where her Canadian husband, a Coureur-
    des-Bois, had been murdered.
Touched were their hearts at her story,
    and warmest and friendliest wel-
    come
Gave they, with words of cheer, and she sat
    and feasted among them
On the buffalo-meat and the venison cooked
    on the embers.
But when their meal was done, and Basil
    and all his companions,   460
Worn with the long day's march and the
    chase of the deer and the bison,
Stretched themselves on the ground, and
    slept where the quivering fire-light
Flashed on their swarthy cheeks, and their
    forms wrapped up in their blankets,
Then at the door of Evangeline's tent she
    sat and repeated
Slowly, with soft, low voice, and the charm
    of her Indian accent,
All the tale of her love, with its pleasures,
    and pains, and reverses.
Much Evangeline wept at the tale, and to
    know that another
Hapless heart like her own had loved and
    had been disappointed.
Moved to the depths of her soul by pity
    and woman's compassion,
Yet in her sorrow pleased that one who
    had suffered was near her,   470
She in turn related her love and all its dis-
    asters.
Mute with wonder the Shawnee sat, and
    when she had ended
Still was mute; but at length, as if a mys-
    terious horror
Passed through her brain, she spake, and
    repeated the tale of the Mowis;
Mowis, the bridegroom of snow, who won
    and wedded a maiden,
But, when the morning came, arose and
    passed from the wigwam,
Fading and melting away and dissolving
    into the sunshine,
Till she beheld him no more, though she
    followed far into the forest.
Then, in those sweet, low tones, that seemed
    like a weird incantation,
Told she the tale of the fair Lilinau, who
    was wooed by a phantom,   480

That through the pines o'er her father's
    lodge, in the hush of the twilight,
Breathed like the evening wind, and whis-
    pered love to the maiden,
Till she followed his green and waving
    plume through the forest,
And nevermore returned, nor was seen
    again by her people.
Silent with wonder and strange surprise,
    Evangeline listened
To the soft flow of her magical words, till
    the region around her
Seemed like enchanted ground, and her
    swarthy guest the enchantress.
Slowly over the tops of the Ozark Moun-
    tains the moon rose,
Lighting the little tent, and with a myste-
    rious splendor
Touching the sombre leaves, and embracing
    and filling the woodland.   490
With a delicious sound the brook rushed
    by, and the branches
Swayed and sighed overhead in scarcely
    audible whispers.
Filled with the thoughts of love was Evan-
    geline's heart, but a secret,
Subtile sense crept in of pain and indefinite
    terror,
As the cold, poisonous snake creeps into the
    nest of the swallow.
It was no earthly fear. A breath from the
    region of spirits
Seemed to float in the air of night; and she
    felt for a moment
That, like the Indian maid, she, too, was
    pursuing a phantom.
With this thought she slept, and the fear
    and the phantom had vanished.

Early upon the morrow the march was
    resumed; and the Shawnee   500
Said, as they journeyed along, 'On the
    western slope of these mountains
Dwells in his little village the Black Robe
    chief of the Mission.
Much he teaches the people, and tells them
    of Mary and Jesus.
Loud laugh their hearts with joy, and weep
    with pain, as they hear him.'
Then, with a sudden and secret emotion,
    Evangeline answered,
'Let us go to the Mission, for there good
    tidings await us!'
Thither they turned their steeds; and be-
    hind a spur of the mountains,

Just as the sun went down, they heard a
    murmur of voices,
And in a meadow green and broad, by the
    bank of a river,
Saw the tents of the Christians, the tents
    of the Jesuit Mission.   510
Under a towering oak, that stood in the
    midst of the village,
Knelt the Black Robe chief with his chil-
    dren. A crucifix fastened
High on the trunk of the tree, and over-
    shadowed by grapevines,
Looked with its agonized face on the multi-
    tude kneeling beneath it.
This was their rural chapel. Aloft, through
    the intricate arches
Of its aerial roof, arose the chant of their
    vespers,
Mingling its notes with the soft susurrus
    and sighs of the branches.
Silent, with heads uncovered, the travellers,
    nearer approaching,
Knelt on the swarded floor, and joined in
    the evening devotions.
But when the service was done, and the
    benediction had fallen   520
Forth from the hands of the priest, like
    seed from the hands of the sower,
Slowly the reverend man advanced to the
    strangers, and bade them
Welcome; and when they replied, he smiled
    with benignant expression,
Hearing the homelike sounds of his mother-
    tongue in the forest,
And, with words of kindness, conducted
    them into his wigwam.
There upon mats and skins they reposed,
    and on cakes of the maize-ear
Feasted, and slaked their thirst from the
    water-gourd of the teacher.
Soon was their story told; and the priest
    with solemnity answered: —
'Not six suns have risen and set since
    Gabriel, seated
On this mat by my side, where now the
    maiden reposes,   530
Told me this same sad tale; then arose and
    continued his journey!'
Soft was the voice of the priest, and he
    spake with an accent of kind-
    ness;
But on Evangeline's heart fell his words as
    in winter the snow-flakes
Fall into some lone nest from which the
    birds have departed.

'Far to the north he has gone,' continued
   the priest; 'but in autumn,
When the chase is done, will return again
   to the Mission.'
Then Evangeline said, and her voice was
   meek and submissive,
'Let me remain with thee, for my soul is
   sad and afflicted.'
So seemed it wise and well unto all; and
   betimes on the morrow,
Mounting his Mexican steed, with his Indian guides and companions,   540
Homeward Basil returned, and Evangeline
   stayed at the Mission.

Slowly, slowly, slowly the days succeeded
   each other, —
Days and weeks and months; and the fields
   of maize that were springing
Green from the ground when a stranger
   she came, now waving above
   her,
Lifted their slender shafts, with leaves in-
   terlacing, and forming
Cloisters for mendicant crows and granaries
   pillaged by squirrels.
Then in the golden weather the maize was
   husked, and the maidens
Blushed at each blood-red ear, for that be-
   tokened a lover,
But at the crooked laughed, and called it a
   thief in the corn-field.
Even the blood-red ear to Evangeline
   brought not her lover.   550
'Patience!' the priest would say; 'have
   faith, and thy prayer will be answered!
Look at this vigorous plant that lifts its
   head from the meadow,
See how its leaves are turned to the north,
   as true as the magnet;
This is the compass-flower, that the finger
   of God has planted
Here in the houseless wild, to direct the
   traveller's journey
Over the sea-like, pathless, limitless waste
   of the desert.
Such in the soul of man is faith. The blossoms of passion,
Gay and luxuriant flowers, are brighter and
   fuller of fragrance,
But they beguile us, and lead us astray, and
   their odor is deadly.
Only this humble plant can guide us here,
   and hereafter   560

Crown us with asphodel flowers, that are
   wet with the dews of nepenthe.'

So came the autumn, and passed, and the
   winter, — yet Gabriel came not;
Blossomed the opening spring, and the notes
   of the robin and bluebird
Sounded sweet upon wold and in wood, yet
   Gabriel came not.
But on the breath of the summer winds a
   rumor was wafted
Sweeter than song of bird, or hue or odor
   of blossom.
Far to the north and east, it said, in the
   Michigan forests,
Gabriel had his lodge by the banks of the
   Saginaw River.
And, with returning guides, that sought the
   lakes of St. Lawrence,
Saying a sad farewell, Evangeline went
   from the Mission.   570
When over weary ways, by long and peril-
   ous marches,
She had attained at length the depths of
   the Michigan forests,
Found she the hunter's lodge deserted and
   fallen to ruin!

Thus did the long sad years glide on,
   and in seasons and places
Divers and distant far was seen the wan-
   dering maiden; —
Now in the Tents of Grace of the meek
   Moravian Missions,
Now in the noisy camps and the battle-fields
   of the army,
Now in secluded hamlets, in towns and
   populous cities.
Like a phantom she came, and passed away
   unremembered.
Fair was she and young, when in hope began the long journey;   580
Faded was she and old, when in disappointment it ended.
Each succeeding year stole something away
   from her beauty,
Leaving behind it, broader and deeper, the
   gloom and the shadow.
Then there appeared and spread faint
   streaks of gray o'er her forehead,
Dawn of another life, that broke o'er her
   earthly horizon,
As in the eastern sky the first faint streaks
   of the morning.

V [1]

In that delightful land which is washed by
the Delaware waters,
Guarding in sylvan shades the name of
Penn the apostle,
Stands on the banks of its beautiful stream
the city he founded.
There all the air is balm, and the peach is
the emblem of beauty,   590
And the streets still reëcho the names of
the trees of the forest,
As if they fain would appease the Dryads
whose haunts they molested.
There from the troubled sea had Evange-
line landed, an exile,
Finding among the children of Penn a home
and a country.
There old René Leblanc had died; and
when he departed,
Saw at his side only one of all his hundred
descendants.
Something at least there was in the friendly
streets of the city,
Something that spake to her heart, and
made her no longer a stranger;
And her ear was pleased with the Thee and
Thou of the Quakers,
For it recalled the past, the old Acadian
country,   600
Where all men were equal, and all were
brothers and sisters.
So, when the fruitless search, the disappointed endeavor,
Ended, to recommence no more upon earth,
uncomplaining,
Thither, as leaves to the light, were
turned her thoughts and her footsteps.
As from the mountain's top the rainy mists
of the morning
Roll away, and afar we behold the land-
scape below us,

[1] I fear that I cannot establish by any historic
proof the identity of the old building you speak of in
your kind letter, with that in which Evangeline found
Gabriel. A great many years ago, strolling through
the streets of Philadelphia, I passed an old almshouse
within high brick walls, and with trees growing in its
enclosure. The quiet and seclusion of the place . . .
impressed me deeply. This was long before the poem
was written and before I had heard the tradition on
which it was founded. But remembering the place, I
chose it for the final scene. (LONGFELLOW, in a letter to Miss E. S. Phelps, March 12, 1876; *Life*, vol. iii,
pp. 259, 260.)
This visit to Philadelphia was made fifty years before, in 1826, when Longfellow was waiting at New
York for the ship which was to take him on his first
trip to Europe.

Sun-illumined, with shining rivers and cities
and hamlets,
So fell the mists from her mind, and she
saw the world far below her,
Dark no longer, but all illumined with love;
and the pathway
Which she had climbed so far, lying smooth
and fair in the distance.   610
Gabriel was not forgotten. Within her
heart was his image,
Clothed in the beauty of love and youth, as
last she beheld him,
Only more beautiful made by his death-like
silence and absence.
Into her thoughts of him time entered not,
for it was not.
Over him years had no power; he was not
changed, but transfigured;
He had become to her heart as one who is
dead, and not absent;
Patience and abnegation of self, and devo-
tion to others,
This was the lesson a life of trial and sor-
row had taught her.
So was her love diffused, but, like to some
odorous spices,
Suffered no waste nor loss, though filling
the air with aroma.   620
Other hope had she none, nor wish in life,
but to follow
Meekly, with reverent steps, the sacred
feet of her Saviour.
Thus many years she lived as a Sister of
Mercy; frequenting
Lonely and wretched roofs in the crowded
lanes of the city,
Where distress and want concealed them-
selves from the sunlight,
Where disease and sorrow in garrets lan-
guished neglected.
Night after night, when the world was
asleep, as the watchman repeated
Loud, through the gusty streets, that all
was well in the city,
High at some lonely window he saw the
light of her taper.
Day after day, in the gray of the dawn, as
slow through the suburbs   630
Plodded the German farmer, with flowers
and fruits for the market,
Met he that meek, pale face, returning home
from its watchings.

Then it came to pass that a pestilence
fell on the city,

Presaged by wondrous signs, and mostly by
   flocks of wild pigeons,
Darkening the sun in their flight, with
   naught in their craws but an acorn.
And, as the tides of the sea arise in the
   month of September,
Flooding some silver stream, till it spreads
   to a lake in the meadow,
So death flooded life, and, o'erflowing its
   natural margin,
Spread to a brackish lake, the silver stream
   of existence.
Wealth had no power to bribe, nor beauty
   to charm, the oppressor;   640
But all perished alike beneath the scourge
   of his anger; —
Only, alas! the poor, who had neither
   friends nor attendants,
Crept away to die in the almshouse, home
   of the homeless.
Then in the suburbs it stood, in the midst
   of meadows and woodlands; —
Now the city surrounds it; but still, with
   its gateway and wicket
Meek, in the midst of splendor, its humble
   walls seemed to echo
Softly the words of the Lord: 'The poor
   ye always have with you.'
Thither, by night and by day, came the
   Sister of Mercy. The dying
Looked up into her face, and thought, in-
   deed, to behold there
Gleams of celestial light encircle her fore-
   head with splendor,   650
Such as the artist paints o'er the brows of
   saints and apostles,
Or such as hangs by night o'er a city seen
   at a distance.
Unto their eyes it seemed the lamps of the
   city celestial,
Into whose shining gates erelong their
   spirits would enter.

Thus, on a Sabbath morn, through the
   streets, deserted and silent,
Wending her quiet way, she entered the
   door of the almshouse.
Sweet on the summer air was the odor of
   flowers in the garden;
And she paused on her way to gather the
   fairest among them,
That the dying once more might rejoice in
   their fragrance and beauty.
Then, as she mounted the stairs to the corridors, cooled by the east-wind, 660

Distant and soft on her ear fell the
   chimes from the belfry of Christ
   Church,
While, intermingled with these, across the
   meadows were wafted
Sounds of psalms, that were sung by the
   Swedes in their church at Wicaco.
Soft as descending wings fell the calm of
   the hour on her spirit:
Something within her said, 'At length thy
   trials are ended;'
And, with light in her looks, she entered
   the chambers of sickness.
Noiselessly moved about the assiduous,
   careful attendants,
Moistening the feverish lip, and the aching
   brow, and in silence
Closing the sightless eyes of the dead, and
   concealing their faces,
Where on their pallets they lay, like drifts
   of snow by the roadside.   670
Many a languid head, upraised as Evange-
   line entered,
Turned on its pillow of pain to gaze while
   she passed, for her presence
Fell on their hearts like a ray of the sun
   on the walls of a prison.
And, as she looked around, she saw how
   Death, the consoler,
Laying his hand upon many a heart, had
   healed it forever.
Many familiar forms had disappeared in
   the night time;
Vacant their places were, or filled already
   by strangers.

Suddenly, as if arrested by fear or a
   feeling of wonder,
Still she stood, with her colorless lips
   apart, while a shudder
Ran through her frame, and, forgotten,
   the flowerets dropped from her fingers,   680
And from her eyes and cheeks the light and
   bloom of the morning.
Then there escaped from her lips a cry of
   such terrible anguish,
That the dying heard it, and started up
   from their pillows.
On the pallet before her was stretched the
   form of an old man.
Long, and thin, and gray were the locks
   that shaded his temples;
But, as he lay in the morning light, his
   face for a moment

Seemed to assume once more the forms of
its earlier manhood;
So are wont to be changed the faces of
those who are dying.
Hot and red on his lips still burned the
flush of the fever,
As if life, like the Hebrew, with blood had
besprinkled its portals,   690
That the Angel of Death might see the
sign, and pass over.
Motionless, senseless, dying, he lay, and
his spirit exhausted
. Seemed to be sinking down through infinite
depths in the darkness,
Darkness of slumber and death, forever
sinking and sinking.
Then through those realms of shade, in
multiplied reverberations,
Heard he that cry of pain, and through
the hush that succeeded
Whispered a gentle voice, in accents tender
and saint-like,
'Gabriel! O my beloved!' and died away
into silence.
Then he beheld, in a dream, once more
the home of his childhood;
Green Acadian meadows, with sylvan rivers
among them,   700
Village, and mountain, and woodlands; and,
walking under their shadow,
As in the days of her youth, Evangeline
rose in his vision.
Tears came into his eyes; and as slowly he
lifted his eyelids,
Vanished the vision away, but Evangeline
knelt by his bedside.
Vainly he strove to whisper her name, for
the accents unuttered
Died on his lips, and their motion revealed
what his tongue would have spoken.
Vainly he strove to rise; and Evangeline,
kneeling beside him,
Kissed his dying lips, and laid his head on
her bosom.
Sweet was the light of his eyes; but it suddenly sank into darkness,
As when a lamp is blown out by a gust of
wind at a casement.   710

All was ended now, the hope, and the
fear, and the sorrow,
All the aching of heart, the restless, unsat-
isfied longing,
All the dull, deep pain, and constant an-
guish of patience!
And, as she pressed once more the lifeless
head to her bosom,
Meekly she bowed her own, and murmured,
'Father, I thank thee!'

Still stands the forest primeval; but far
away from its shadow,
Side by side, in their nameless graves, the
lovers are sleeping.
Under the humble walls of the little Catholic churchyard,
In the heart of the city, they lie, unknown
and unnoticed.
Daily the tides of life go ebbing and flowing beside them,   720
Thousands of throbbing hearts, where
theirs are at rest and forever,
Thousands of aching brains, where theirs
no longer are busy,
Thousands of toiling hands, where theirs
have ceased from their labors,
Thousands of weary feet, where theirs have
completed their journey!

Still stands the forest primeval; but under the shade of its branches
Dwells another race, with other customs
and language.
Only along the shore of the mournful and
misty Atlantic
Linger a few Acadian peasants, whose fathers from exile
Wandered back to their native land to die
in its bosom.
In the fisherman's cot the wheel and the
loom are still busy;   730
Maidens still wear their Norman caps and
their kirtles of homespun,
And by the evening fire repeat Evangeline's
story,
While from its rocky caverns the deep-
voiced, neighboring ocean
Speaks, and in accents disconsolate answers
the wail of the forest.

1845–47.   1847.

WANDERER'S NIGHT–SONGS

(WANDRERS NACHTLIED AND EIN GLEICHES)

FROM GOETHE

I

Thou that from the heavens art,
Every pain and sorrow stillest,
And the doubly wretched heart
Doubly with refreshment fillest,
I am weary with contending !
Why this rapture and unrest ?
Peace descending
Come, ah, come into my breast !

II

O'er all the hill-tops
Is quiet now,
In all the tree-tops
Hearest thou
Hardly a breath;
The birds are asleep in the trees:
Wait; soon like these
Thou too shalt rest.

1845, 1870.   1870.

THE BUILDERS

All are architects of Fate,
    Working in these walls of Time;
Some with massive deeds and great,
    Some with ornaments of rhyme.

Nothing useless is, or low;
    Each thing in its place is best;
And what seems but idle show
    Strengthens and supports the rest.

For the structure that we raise,
    Time is with materials filled;   10
Our to-days and yesterdays
    Are the blocks with which we build.

Truly shape and fashion these;
    Leave no yawning gaps between;
Think not, because no man sees,
    Such things will remain unseen.

In the elder days of Art,
    Builders wrought with greatest care
Each minute and unseen part;
    For the Gods see everywhere.   20

Let us do our work as well,
    Both the unseen and the seen;
Make the house, where Gods may dwell,
    Beautiful, entire, and clean.

Else our lives are incomplete,
    Standing in these walls of Time,
Broken stairways, where the feet
    Stumble as they seek to climb.

Build to-day, then, strong and sure,
    With a firm and ample base;   30
And ascending and secure
    Shall to-morrow find its place.

Thus alone can we attain
    To those turrets, where the eye
Sees the world as one vast plain,
    And one boundless reach of sky.
1846.   1849.

RESIGNATION [1]

There is no flock, however watched and
        tended,
    But one dead lamb is there !
There is no fireside, howsoe'er defended,
    But has one vacant chair !

The air is full of farewells to the dying,
    And mournings for the dead;
The heart of Rachel, for her children cry-
        ing,
    Will not be comforted !

Let us be patient ! These severe afflictions
    Not from the ground arise,[2]   10
But oftentimes celestial benedictions
    Assume this dark disguise.

We see but dimly through the mists and
        vapors;
    Amid these earthly damps
What seem to us but sad, funereal tapers
    May be heaven's distant lamps.

---

[1] See the *Life of Longfellow*, vol. ii, pp. 129–131, on the death of Fanny Longfellow and her burial, September 11 and 12, 1848; and the entry in Longfellow's *Journal* a month later, November 12 : ' An inappeasable longing to see her comes over me at times, which I can hardly control.'
See also the letter from Edward Everett, *Life*, vol. ii, p. 165.
[2] ' Although affliction cometh not forth of the dust, neither doth trouble spring out of the ground.' Job v, 6. (Quoted by Longfellow.)

There is no Death ! What seems so is tran-
      sition;
  This life of mortal breath
Is but a suburb of the life elysian,
  Whose portal we call Death.   20

She is not dead, — the child of our affec-
      tion, —
  But gone unto that school
Where she no longer needs our poor protec-
      tion,
  And Christ himself doth rule.

In that great cloister's stillness and seclu-
      sion,
  By guardian angels led,
Safe from temptation, safe from sin's pollu-
      tion,
  She lives whom we call dead.

Day after day we think what she is doing
  In those bright realms of air;   30
Year after year, her tender steps pursuing,
  Behold her grown more fair.

Thus do we walk with her, and keep un-
      broken
  The bond which nature gives,
Thinking that our remembrance, though
      unspoken,
  May reach her where she lives.

Not as a child shall we again behold her;
  For when with raptures wild
In our embraces we again enfold her,
  She will not be a child;   40

But a fair maiden, in her Father's mansion,
  Clothed with celestial grace;
And beautiful with all the soul's expansion
  Shall we behold her face.

And though at times impetuous with emo-
      tion
  And anguish long suppressed,
The swelling heart heaves moaning like the
      ocean,
  That cannot be at rest, —

We will be patient, and assuage the feel-
      ing
  We may not wholly stay;   50
By silence sanctifying, not concealing,
  The grief that must have way.
1848.   *1849.*

CHILDREN [1]

Come to me, O ye children !
  For I hear you at your play,
And the questions that perplexed me
  Have vanished quite away.

Ye open the eastern windows,
  That look towards the sun,
Where thoughts are singing swallows
  And the brooks of morning run.

In your hearts are the birds and the sun-
      shine,
  In your thoughts the brooklet's flow, 10
But in mine is the wind of Autumn
  And the first fall of the snow.

Ah ! what would the world be to us
  If the children were no more ?
We should dread the desert behind us
  Worse than the dark before.

What the leaves are to the forest,
  With light and air for food,
Ere their sweet and tender juices
  Have been hardened into wood, —   20

That to the world are children;
  Through them it feels the glow
Of a brighter and sunnier climate
  Than reaches the trunks below.

Come to me, O ye children !
  And whisper in my ear
What the birds and the winds are singing
  In your sunny atmosphere.

For what are all our contrivings,
  And the wisdom of our books,   30
When compared with your caresses,
  And the gladness of your looks ?

Ye are better than all the ballads
  That ever were sung or said;
For ye are living poems,
  And all the rest are dead.
1849.   (1858.)

GASPAR BECERRA

By his evening fire the artist
  Pondered o'er his secret shame;

[1] See note on 'The Children's Hour ;' and the *Life
of Longfellow*, vol. ii, pp. 188, 189, 376, 390-393.

Baffled, weary, and disheartened,
  Still he mused, and dreamed of fame.

'T was an image of the Virgin
  That had tasked his utmost skill;
But, alas ! his fair ideal
  Vanished and escaped him still.

From a distant Eastern island
  Had the precious wood been brought;
Day and night the anxious master
  At his toil untiring wrought;

Till, discouraged and desponding,
  Sat he now in shadows deep,
And the day's humiliation
  Found oblivion in sleep.

Then a voice cried, 'Rise, O master !
  From the burning brand of oak
Shape the thought that stirs within thee !' —
  And the startled artist woke, —

Woke, and from the smoking embers
  Seized and quenched the glowing wood;
And therefrom he carved an image,
  And he saw that it was good.

O thou sculptor, painter, poet !
  Take this lesson to thy heart:
That is best which lieth nearest;
  Shape from that thy work of art.

1849.   1849.

THE BUILDING OF THE SHIP

'Build me straight, O worthy Master !
  Stanch and strong, a goodly vessel,
That shall laugh at all disaster,
  And with wave and whirlwind wrestle !'

The merchant's word
Delighted the Master heard;
For his heart was in his work, and the heart
Giveth grace unto every Art.
A quiet smile played round his lips,
As the eddies and dimples of the tide   10
Play round the bows of ships
That steadily at anchor ride.
And with a voice that was full of glee,
He answered, 'Erelong we will launch
A vessel as goodly, and strong, and stanch,
As ever weathered a wintry sea !'
And first with nicest skill and art,

Perfect and finished in every part,
A little model the Master wrought,
Which should be to the larger plan   20
What the child is to the man,
Its counterpart in miniature;
That with a hand more swift and sure
The greater labor might be brought
To answer to his inward thought.
And as he labored, his mind ran o'er
The various ships that were built of yore,
And above them all, and strangest of all
Towered the Great Harry,[1] crank and tall,
Whose picture was hanging on the wall,   30
With bows and stern raised high in air,
And balconies hanging here and there,
And signal lanterns and flags afloat,
And eight round towers, like those that
    frown
From some old castle, looking down
Upon the drawbridge and the moat.
And he said with a smile, 'Our ship, I wis,
Shall be of another form than this !'
It was of another form, indeed;
Built for freight, and yet for speed,   40
A beautiful and gallant craft;
Broad in the beam, that the stress of the
    blast,
Pressing down upon sail and mast,
Might not the sharp bows overwhelm;
Broad in the beam, but sloping aft
With graceful curve and slow degrees,
That she might be docile to the helm,
And that the currents of parted seas,
Closing behind, with mighty force,
Might aid and not impede her course.   50

In the ship-yard stood the Master,
With the model of the vessel,
That should laugh at all disaster,
And with wave and whirlwind wrestle !

Covering many a rood of ground,
Lay the timber piled around;
Timber of chestnut, and elm, and oak,
And scattered here and there, with these,
The knarred and crooked cedar knees;
Brought from regions far away,   60
From Pascagoula's sunny bay,
And the banks of the roaring Roanoke !
Ah ! what a wondrous thing it is
To note how many wheels of toil

---

[1] There was an English warship of this name under Henry VII, and another, which Longfellow here describes, under Henry VIII. See note in the *Riverside Literature Series.*

One thought, one word, can set in motion !
There 's not a ship that sails the ocean,
But every climate, every soil,
Must bring its tribute, great or small,
And help to build the wooden wall !

The sun was rising o'er the sea,   70
And long the level shadows lay,
As if they, too, the beams would be
Of some great, airy argosy,
Framed and launched in a single day.
That silent architect, the sun,
Had hewn and laid them every one,
Ere the work of man was yet begun.
Beside the Master, when he spoke,
A youth, against an anchor leaning,
Listened, to catch his slightest meaning, 80
Only the long waves, as they broke
In ripples on the pebbly beach,
Interrupted the old man's speech.

Beautiful they were, in sooth,
The old man and the fiery youth !
The old man, in whose busy brain
Many a ship that sailed the main
Was modelled o'er and o'er again;
The fiery youth, who was to be
The heir of his dexterity,   90
The heir of his house, and his daughter's
    hand,
When he had built and launched from land
What the elder head had planned.

' Thus,' said he, ' will we build this ship !
Lay square the blocks upon the slip,
And follow well this plan of mine.
Choose the timbers with greatest care;
Of all that is unsound beware;
For only what is sound and strong
To this vessel shall belong.   100
Cedar of Maine and Georgia pine
Here together shall combine.
A goodly frame, and a goodly fame,
And the UNION be her name !
For the day that gives her to the sea
Shall give my daughter unto thee ! '

The Master's word
Enraptured the young man heard;
And as he turned his face aside,
With a look of joy and a thrill of pride 110
Standing before
Her father's door,
He saw the form of his promised bride.
The sun shone on her golden hair,

And her cheek was glowing fresh and fair,
With the breath of morn and the soft sea air.
Like a beauteous barge was she,
Still at rest on the sandy beach,
Just beyond the billow's reach;
But he   120
Was the restless, seething, stormy sea !
Ah, how skilful grows the hand
That obeyeth Love's command !
It is the heart, and not the brain,
That to the highest doth attain,
And he who followeth Love's behest
Far excelleth all the rest !

Thus with the rising of the sun
Was the noble task begun,
And soon throughout the ship-yard's
    bounds   130
Were heard the intermingled sounds
Of axes and of mallets, plied
With vigorous arms on every side;
Plied so deftly and so well,
That, ere the shadows of evening fell,
The keel of oak for a noble ship,
Scarfed and bolted, straight and strong,
Was lying ready, and stretched along
The blocks, well placed upon the slip.
Happy, thrice happy, every one   140
Who sees his labor well begun,
And not perplexed and multiplied,
By idly waiting for time and tide !

And when the hot, long day was o'er,
The young man at the Master's door
Sat with the maiden calm and still,
And within the porch, a little more
Removed beyond the evening chill,
The father sat, and told them tales
Of wrecks in the great September gales, 150
Of pirates coasting the Spanish Main,
And ships that never came back again,
The chance and change of a sailor's life,
Want and plenty, rest and strife,
His roving fancy, like the wind,
That nothing can stay and nothing can
    bind,
And the magic charm of foreign lands,
With shadows of palms, and shining sands,
Where the tumbling surf,
O'er the coral reefs of Madagascar,   160
Washes the feet of the swarthy Lascar,
As he lies alone and asleep on the turf.
And the trembling maiden held her breath
At the tales of that awful, pitiless sea,
With all its terror and mystery,

The dim, dark sea, so like unto Death,
That divides and yet unites mankind !
And whenever the old man paused, a gleam
From the bowl of his pipe would awhile
    illume
The silent group in the twilight gloom, 170
And thoughtful faces, as in a dream;
And for a moment one might mark
What had been hidden by the dark,
That the head of the maiden lay at rest,
Tenderly, on the young man's breast !

Day by day the vessel grew,
With timbers fashioned strong and true,
Stemson and keelson and sternson-knee,
Till, framed with perfect symmetry,
A skeleton ship rose up to view ! 180
And around the bows and along the side
The heavy hammers and mallets plied,
Till after many a week, at length,
Wonderful for form and strength,
Sublime in its enormous bulk,
Loomed aloft the shadowy hulk !
And around it columns of smoke, upwreath-
    ing,
Rose from the boiling, bubbling, seething
Caldron, that glowed,
And overflowed 190
With the black tar, heated for the sheath-
    ing.
And amid the clamors
Of clattering hammers,
He who listened heard now and then
The song of the Master and his men: —

'Build me straight, O worthy Master,
  Stanch and strong, a goodly vessel,
That shall laugh at all disaster,
    And with wave and whirlwind wrestle !'

With oaken brace and copper band, 200
Lay the rudder on the sand,
That, like a thought, should have control
Over the movement of the whole;
And near it the anchor, whose giant hand
Would reach down and grapple with the
    land,
And immovable and fast
Hold the great ship against the bellowing
    blast !
And at the bows an image stood,[1]

[1] Compare the story by Hawthorne, 'Drowne's Wooden Image,' in *Mosses from an old Manse;* and the entry in Longfellow's *Journal*, March 14, 1856. (*Life*, vol. ii, p. 307.)

By a cunning artist carved in wood,
With robes of white, that far behind 210
Seemed to be fluttering in the wind.
It was not shaped in a classic mould,
Not like a Nymph or Goddess of old,
Or Naiad rising from the water,
But modelled from the Master's daughter !
On many a dreary and misty night,
'T will be seen by the rays of the signal
    light,
Speeding along through the rain and the
    dark,
Like a ghost in its snow-white sark,
The pilot of some phantom bark, 220
Guiding the vessel, in its flight,
By a path none other knows aright !

Behold, at last,
Each tall and tapering mast
Is swung into its place;
Shrouds and stays
Holding it firm and fast ![2]

Long ago,
In the deer-haunted forests of Maine,
When upon mountain and plain 230
Lay the snow,
They fell, — those lordly pines !
Those grand, majestic pines!
'Mid shouts and cheers
The jaded steers,
Panting beneath the goad,
Dragged down the weary, winding road
Those captive kings so straight and tall,
To be shorn of their streaming hair,
And naked and bare, 240
To feel the stress and the strain
Of the wind and the reeling main,
Whose roar
Would remind them forevermore
Of their native forests they should not see
    again.

[2] I wish to anticipate a criticism on this passage, by stating that sometimes, though not usually, vessels are launched fully sparred and rigged. I have availed my-self of the exception as better suited to my purposes than the general rule ; but the reader will see that it is neither a blunder nor a poetic license. On this subject a friend in Portland, Maine, writes me thus : 'In this State, and also, I am told, in New York, ships are sometimes rigged upon the stocks, in order to save time, or to make a show. There was a fine large ship launched last summer at Ellsworth, fully sparred and rigged. Some years ago a ship was launched here, with her rigging, spars, sails, and cargo aboard. She sailed the next day and — was never heard of again ! I hope this will not be the fate of your poem !' (LONGFEL-LOW.)

And everywhere
The slender, graceful spars
Poise aloft in the air,
And at the mast-head,
White, blue, and red,   250
A flag unrolls the stripes and stars.
Ah ! when the wanderer, lonely, friendless,
In foreign harbors shall behold
That flag unrolled,
'T will be as a friendly hand
Stretched out from his native land,
Filling his heart with memories sweet and
        endless !

All is finished ! and at length
Has come the bridal day
Of beauty and of strength.   260
To-day the vessel shall be launched !
With fleecy clouds the sky is blanched,
And o'er the bay,
Slowly, in all his splendors dight,
The great sun rises to behold the sight.
The ocean old,
Centuries old,
Strong as youth, and as uncontrolled,
Paces restless to and fro,
Up and down the sands of gold.   270
His beating heart is not at rest;
And far and wide,
With ceaseless flow,
His beard of snow
Heaves with the heaving of his breast.
He waits impatient for his bride.
There she stands,
With her foot upon the sands,
Decked with flags and streamers gay,
In honor of her marriage day,   280
Her snow-white signals fluttering, blend-
        ing,
Round her like a veil descending,
Ready to be
The bride of the gray old sea.

On the deck another bride
Is standing by her lover's side.
Shadows from the flags and shrouds,
Like the shadows cast by clouds,
Broken by many a sudden fleck,
Fall around them on the deck.   290

The prayer is said,
The service read,
The joyous bridegroom bows his head;
And in tears the good old Master
Shakes the brown hand of his son,

Kisses his daughter's glowing cheek
In silence, for he cannot speak,
And ever faster
Down his own the tears begin to run.
The worthy pastor —   300
The shepherd of that wandering flock,
That has the ocean for its wold,
That has the vessel for its fold,
Leaping ever from rock to rock —
Spake, with accents mild and clear,
Words of warning, words of cheer,
But tedious to the bridegroom's ear.
He knew the chart
Of the sailor's heart,
All its pleasures and its griefs,   310
All its shallows and rocky reefs,
All those secret currents, that flow
With such resistless undertow,
And lift and drift, with terrible force,
The will from its moorings and its course.
Therefore he spake, and thus said he: —
' Like unto ships far off at sea,
Outward or homeward bound, are we.
Before, behind, and all around,
Floats and swings the horizon's bound,   320
Seems at its distant rim to rise
And climb the crystal wall of the skies,
And then again to turn and sink,
As if we could slide from its outer brink.
Ah ! it is not the sea,
It is not the sea that sinks and shelves,
But ourselves
That rock and rise
With endless and uneasy motion,
Now touching the very skies,   330
Now sinking into the depths of ocean.
Ah ! if our souls but poise and swing
Like the compass in its brazen ring,
Ever level and ever true
To the toil and the task we have to do,
We shall sail securely, and safely reach
The Fortunate Isles, on whose shining beach
The sights we see, and the sounds we
        hear,
Will be those of joy and not of fear !'

Then the Master,   340
With a gesture of command,
Waved his hand;
And at the word,
Loud and sudden there was heard,
All around them and below,
The sound of hammers, blow on blow,
Knocking away the shores and spurs.
And see ! she stirs !

She starts, — she moves, — she seems to feel
The thrill of life along her keel,   350
And, spurning with her foot the ground,
With one exulting, joyous bound,
She leaps into the ocean's arms !

And lo ! from the assembled crowd
There rose a shout, prolonged and loud,
That to the ocean seemed to say,
'Take her, O bridegroom, old and gray,
Take her to thy protecting arms,
With all her youth and all her charms!'

How beautiful she is ! How fair   360
She lies within those arms, that press
Her form with many a soft caress
Of tenderness and watchful care !
Sail forth into the sea, O ship !
Through wind and wave, right onward steer !
The moistened eye, the trembling lip,
Are not the signs of doubt or fear.

Sail forth into the sea of life,
O gentle, loving, trusting wife,
And safe from all adversity   370
Upon the bosom of that sea
Thy comings and thy goings be !
For gentleness and love and trust
Prevail o'er angry wave and gust;
And in the wreck of noble lives
Something immortal still survives !

Thou, too, sail on, O Ship of State !
Sail on, O UNION, strong and great !
Humanity with all its fears,
With all the hopes of future years,   380
Is hanging breathless on thy fate !
We know what Master laid thy keel,
What Workmen wrought thy ribs of steel,
Who made each mast, and sail, and rope,
What anvils rang, what hammers beat,
In what a forge and what a heat
Were shaped the anchors of thy hope !
Fear not each sudden sound and shock,
'T is of the wave and not the rock;
'T is but the flapping of the sail,   390
And not a rent made by the gale !
In spite of rock and tempest's roar,
In spite of false lights on the shore,
Sail on, nor fear to breast the sea !
Our hearts, our hopes, are all with thee,
Our hearts, our hopes, our prayers, our tears,

Our faith triumphant o'er our fears,
Are all with thee, — are all with thee ![1]
1849.   1849.[2]

THE LADDER OF SAINT AUGUSTINE

SAINT AUGUSTINE ! well hast thou said,[3]
   That of our vices we can frame
A ladder, if we will but tread
   Beneath our feet each deed of shame !

All common things, each day's events,
   That with the hour begin and end,
Our pleasures and our discontents,
   Are rounds by which we may ascend.

The low desire, the base design,
   That makes another's virtues less;   10
The revel of the ruddy wine,
   And all occasions of excess;

The longing for ignoble things;
   The strife for triumph more than truth;
The hardening of the heart, that brings
   Irreverence for the dreams of youth;

All thoughts of ill; all evil deeds,
   That have their root in thoughts of ill;
Whatever hinders or impedes
   The action of the nobler will; —   20

[1] These lines, written twelve years before the beginning of the Civil War (and substituted for a weaker ending with which Longfellow was dissatisfied — see the *Life*, vol. iii, pp. 363, 443-4), seemed word by word to fit the circumstances and feelings of the nation in that great struggle, and during its progress roused thousands of audiences to passionate enthusiasm. Lincoln's feeling for them typifies that of the whole people. Mr. Noah Brooks in his paper on *Lincoln's Imagination* (*Scribner's Monthly*, August, 1879), mentions that he found the President one day attracted by these stanzas, quoted in a political speech. 'Knowing the whole poem,' he adds, 'as one of my early exercises in recitation, I began, at his request, with the description of the launch of the ship, and repeated it to the end. As he listened to the last lines, his eyes filled with tears, and his cheeks were wet. He did not speak for some minutes, but finally said, with simplicity : " It is a wonderful gift to be able to stir men like that." ' (Quoted in the *Cambridge Edition* of Longfellow.) The first public reading of the poem, by Fanny Kemble, is described in Longfellow's *Journal*, February 12, 1850. *Life*, vol. ii, p. 172.

[2] *The Seaside and the Fireside*, in which 'The Building of the Ship' holds the first place, is dated 1850; but the book was actually published late in 1849.

[3] The words of St. Augustine are, 'De vitiis nostris scalam nobis facimus, si vitia ipsa calcamus.' — Sermon III. *De Ascensione*. (LONGFELLOW.)

All these must first be trampled down
  Beneath our feet, if we would gain
In the bright fields of fair renown
  The right of eminent domain.

We have not wings, we cannot soar;
  But we have feet to scale and climb
By slow degrees, by more and more,
  The cloudy summits of our time.

The mighty pyramids of stone
  That wedge-like cleave the desert airs,   30
When nearer seen, and better known,
  Are but gigantic flights of stairs.

The distant mountains, that uprear
  Their solid bastions to the skies,
Are crossed by pathways, that appear
  As we to higher levels rise.

The heights by great men reached and
      kept
  Were not attained by sudden flight,
But they, while their companions slept,
  Were toiling upward in the night.   40

Standing on what too long we bore
  With shoulders bent and downcast eyes,
We may discern — unseen before —
  A path to higher destinies,

Nor deem the irrevocable Past
  As wholly wasted, wholly vain,
If, rising on its wrecks, at last
  To something nobler we attain.[1]
1850.   (1858.)

DAYLIGHT AND MOONLIGHT

In broad daylight, and at noon,
Yesterday I saw the moon
Sailing high, but faint and white,
As a schoolboy's paper kite.

In broad daylight, yesterday,
I read a Poet's mystic lay;
And it seemed to me at most
As a phantom, or a ghost.

But at length the feverish day
Like a passion died away,

---

[1] Compare Tennyson ('In Memoriam'): —
      'Men may rise on stepping-stones
      Of their dead selves to higher things.'

And the night, serene and still,
Fell on village, vale, and hill.

Then the moon, in all her pride,
Like a spirit glorified,
Filled and overflowed the night
With revelations of her light.

And the Poet's song again
Passed like music through my brain;
Night interpreted to me
All its grace and mystery.
1852.   (1858.)

THE WARDEN OF THE CINQUE PORTS [2]

A mist was driving down the British Chan-
      nel,
  The day was just begun,
And through the window-panes, on floor
      and panel,
  Streamed the red autumn sun.

It glanced on flowing flag and rippling
      pennon,
  And the white sails of ships;
And, from the frowning rampart, the black
      cannon
  Hailed it with feverish lips.

Sandwich and Romney, Hastings, Hithe,
      and Dover
  Were all alert that day,   10
To see the French war-steamers speeding
      over,
  When the fog cleared away.

Sullen and silent, and like couchant
      lions,
  Their cannon, through the night,
Holding their breath, had watched, in grim
      defiance,
  The sea-coast opposite.

And now they roared at drum-beat from
      their stations
  On every citadel;
Each answering each, with morning saluta-
      tions,
  That all was well.   20

---

[2] The Duke of Wellington, who died September 13, 1852.

And down the coast, all taking up the
burden,
Replied the distant forts,
As if to summon from his sleep the Warden
And Lord of the Cinque Ports.

Him shall no sunshine from the fields of
azure,
No drum-beat from the wall,
No morning gun from the black fort's em-
brasure,
Awaken with its call!

No more, surveying with an eye impartial
The long line of the coast,   30
Shall the gaunt figure of the old Field
Marshal
Be seen upon his post!

For in the night, unseen, a single warrior,
In sombre harness mailed,
Dreaded of man, and surnamed the De-
stroyer,
The rampart wall had scaled.

He passed into the chamber of the sleeper,
The dark and silent room,
And as he entered, darker grew, and deeper,
The silence and the gloom.   40

He did not pause to parley or dissemble,
But smote the Warden hoar;
Ah! what a blow! that made all England
tremble
And groan from shore to shore.

Meanwhile, without, the surly cannon
waited,
The sun rose bright o'erhead;
Nothing in Nature's aspect intimated
That a great man was dead.

1852.   (1858.)

THE TWO ANGELS [1]

Two angels, one of Life and one of Death,
Passed o'er our village as the morning
broke;

[1] In a letter of April 25, 1855, Longfellow speaks of
this poem as 'written on the birth of my younger
daughter, and the death of the young and beautiful wife
of my neighbor and friend, the poet Lowell. It will
serve as an answer to one of your questions about life
and its many mysteries. To these dark problems there
is no other solution possible, except the one word *Providence.*' (*Life*, vol. ii, p. 285.)

The dawn was on their faces, and beneath,
The sombre houses hearsed with plumes
of smoke.

Their attitude and aspect were the same,
Alike their features and their robes of
white;
But one was crowned with amaranth, as
with flame,
And one with asphodels, like flakes of
light.

I saw them pause on their celestial way;
Then said I, with deep fear and doubt
oppressed,   10
'Beat not so loud, my heart, lest thou betray
The place where thy beloved are at
rest!'

And he who wore the crown of asphodels,
Descending, at my door began to knock,
And my soul sank within me, as in wells
The waters sink before an earthquake's
shock.

I recognized the nameless agony,
The terror and the tremor and the
pain,
That oft before had filled or haunted
me,
And now returned with threefold strength
again.   20

The door I opened to my heavenly guest,
And listened, for I thought I heard God's
voice;
And, knowing whatsoe'er He sent was
best,
Dared neither to lament nor to rejoice.

Then with a smile, that filled the house
with light,
'My errand is not Death, but Life,' he
said;
And ere I answered, passing out of sight,
On his celestial embassy he sped.

'T was at thy door, O friend! and not at
mine,   29
The angel with the amaranthine wreath,
Pausing, descended, and with voice divine
Whispered a word that had a sound like
Death.

Then fell upon the house a sudden gloom,
  A shadow on those features fair and
      thin;
And softly, from that hushed and darkened
      room,
  Two angels issued, where but one went
      in.

All is of God !   If He but wave his hand,
  The mists collect, the rain falls thick and
      loud,

Till, with a smile of light on sea and land,
  Lo ! He looks back from the departing
      cloud.   40

Angels of Life and Death alike are his;
  Without his leave they pass no threshold
      o'er;
Who,. then, would wish or dare, believing
      this,
  Against his messengers to shut the door ?
  1853.   (1858.)

THE SONG OF HIAWATHA [1]

INTRODUCTION [2]

SHOULD you ask me, whence these stories ?
Whence these legends and traditions,
With the odors of the forest,
With the dew and damp of meadows,
With the curling smoke of wigwams,

With the rushing of great rivers,
With their frequent repetitions,
And their wild reverberations,
As of thunder in the mountains ?
  I should answer, I should tell you,   10
' From the forests and the prairies,
From the great lakes of the Northland,
From the land of the Ojibways,
From the land of the Dacotahs,
From the mountains, moors, and fenlands
Where the heron, the Shuh-shuh-gah,
Feeds among the reeds and rushes.

[1] Those to whom ' Hiawatha' is familiar from their childhood, but who feel it to be hardly fit food for mature intellects, and those who are wearied by its repetitions, its simplicity, and the monotony of its rhythm, should reread at least the Introduction, and Cantos iii (Hiawatha's Childhood), vii (His Sailing), x (His Wooing), xx (The Famine), and xxii (Hiawatha's Departure). The whole poem, however, without omissions, is necessary to any real knowledge of Longfellow's work or of American poetry. The simplicity of his own character enabled him to reproduce the effects of primitive poetry and legend better than other modern poets have done, and to create what is at least our nearest approach to an American epic. It is greatly superior to all other attempts at epic treatment of the Indian legends. Bayard Taylor said of it : ' It will be parodied, perhaps ridiculed, in many quarters, but it will live after the Indian race has vanished from our Continent, and there will be no parodies then.' Emerson called it ' sweet and wholesome as maize.'

Longfellow wrote ' Hiawatha ' with more enthusiasm than any other of his poems. Cf. the Journal, October 19, 1854 : '"Hiawatha" occupies and delights me. Have I no misgivings about it ? Yes, sometimes. Then the theme seizes me and hurries me away, and they vanish.' (Life, vol. ii, p. 277.) ' The hero,' he wrote to Freiligrath (who afterward translated "Hiawatha" into German), ' is a kind of American Prometheus.' From the first he felt sure of his subject and his metre : ' I have at length hit upon a plan for a poem on the American Indians, which seems to me the right one, and the only. It is to weave together their beautiful traditions into a whole. I have hit upon a measure, too, which I think the right and only one for such a theme.' (Journal, June 22, 1854.)

The metre was avowedly taken from that of the Finnish epic Kalevala, which he had read with Freiligrath twelve years before. See Freiligrath's letter in the London Athenæum, December 22, 1855.

On the sources from which Longfellow drew his material, see his own notes given below.

Further, on ' Hiawatha,' see : —

Life, vol. ii, pp. 272-311.

Longfellow (Alice M.), A Visit to Hiawatha's People.

Schoolcraft (Henry R.), The Myth of Hiawatha and other Oral Legends, Mythologic and Allegoric, of the North American Indians.

Broili (Otto), Die Hauptquellen Longfellows Song of Hiawatha. Wurzburg, 1898.

Lang (Andrew), Letters on Literature.

Cracroft, Essays, vol. ii (on the translation of parts of ' Hiawatha ' into Latin, for school use, by F. W. Newman).

Hale (E. E.), in the North American Review, January, 1856.

Chasles (Philarète), in the Journal des Débats, April 20, 1856.

Montégut (Émile), in the Revue des Deux Mondes, June, 1857.

Hale (Henry), ' Hiawatha played by real Indians,' in the Critic, July, 1905.

[2] This Indian Edda — if I may so call it — is founded on a tradition, prevalent among the North American Indians, of a personage of miraculous birth, who was sent among them to clear their rivers, forests, and fishing-grounds, and to teach them the arts of peace. He was known among different tribes by the several names of Michabou, Chiabo, Manabozo, Tarenya-wagon and Hiawatha. Mr. Schoolcraft gives an account of him in his Algic Researches, vol. i, p. 134, and in his History, Condition, and Prospects of the Indian Tribes of the United States, part iii, p. 314, may be found the Iroquois form of the tradition, derived from the verbal narrations of an Onondaga chief.

Into this old tradition I have woven other curious Indian legends, drawn chiefly from the various and valuable writings of Mr. Schoolcraft, to whom the literary world is greatly indebted for his indefatigable zeal in rescuing from oblivion so much of the legendary lore of the Indians.

The scene of the poem is among the Ojibways on the southern shore of Lake Superior, in the region between the Pictured Rocks and the Grand Sable. (LONGFELLOW.)

I repeat them as I heard them
From the lips of Nawadaha,
The musician, the sweet singer.'   20
  Should you ask where Nawadaha
Found these songs so wild and wayward,
Found these legends and traditions,
I should answer, I should tell you,
' In the bird's-nests of the forest,
In the lodges of the beaver,
In the hoof-prints of the bison,
In the eyry of the eagle !
  ' All the wild-fowl sang them to him,
In the moorlands and the fen-lands,   30
In the melancholy marshes;
Chetowaik, the plover, sang them,
Mahng, the loon, the wild-goose, Wawa,
The blue heron, the Shuh-shuh-gah,
And the grouse, the Mushkodasa ! '
  If still further you should ask me,
Saying, ' Who was Nawadaha ?
Tell us of this Nawadaha,'
I should answer your inquiries
Straightway in such words as follow.   40
  ' In the vale of Tawasentha,[1]
In the green and silent valley,
By the pleasant water-courses,
Dwelt the singer Nawadaha.
Round about the Indian village
Spread the meadows and the corn-fields,
And beyond them stood the forest,
Stood the groves of singing pine-trees,
Green in Summer, white in Winter,
Ever sighing, ever singing.   50
  ' And the pleasant water-courses,
You could trace them through the valley,
By the rushing in the Spring-time,
By the alders in the Summer,
By the white fog in the Autumn,
By the black line in the Winter;
And beside them dwelt the singer,
In the vale of Tawasentha,
In the green and silent valley.
  ' There he sang of Hiawatha,   60
Sang the Song of Hiawatha,
Sang his wondrous birth and being,
How he prayed and how he fasted,
How he lived, and toiled, and suffered,
That the tribes of men might prosper,
That he might advance his people ! '
  Ye who love the haunts of Nature,
Love the sunshine of the meadow,
Love the shadow of the forest,
Love the wind among the branches,   70

[1] This valley, now called Norman's Kill, is in Albany County, New York. (LONGFELLOW.)

And the rain-shower and the snow-storm,
And the rushing of great rivers
Through their palisades of pine-trees,
And the thunder in the mountains,
Whose innumerable echoes
Flap like eagles in their eyries; —
Listen to these wild traditions,
To this Song of Hiawatha !
  Ye who love a nation's legends,
Love the ballads of a people,   80
That like voices from afar off
Call to us to pause and listen,
Speak in tones so plain and childlike,
Scarcely can the ear distinguish
Whether they are sung or spoken; —
Listen to this Indian Legend,
To this Song of Hiawatha !
  Ye whose hearts are fresh and simple,
Who have faith in God and Nature,
Who believe that in all ages   90
Every human heart is human,
That in even savage bosoms
There are longings, yearnings, strivings
For the good they comprehend not,
That the feeble hands and helpless,
Groping blindly in the darkness,
Touch God's right hand in that darkness
And are lifted up and strengthened; —
Listen to this simple story,
To this Song of Hiawatha !   100
  Ye, who sometimes, in your rambles
Through the green lanes of the country,
Where the tangled barberry-bushes
Hang their tufts of crimson berries
Over stone walls gray with mosses,
Pause by some neglected graveyard,
For a while to muse, and ponder
On a half-effaced inscription,
Written with little skill of song-craft,
Homely phrases, but each letter   110
Full of hope and yet of heart-break,
Full of all the tender pathos
Of the Here and the Hereafter; —
Stay and read this rude inscription,
Read this Song of Hiawatha !

I

THE PEACE-PIPE [2]

ON the Mountains of the Prairie,
On the great Red Pipe-stone Quarry,

[2] Mr. Catlin, in his *Letters and Notes on the Manners, Customs, and Condition of the North American Indians*, vol. ii, p. 160, gives an interesting account of the

Gitche Manito, the mighty,
He the Master of Life, descending,
On the red crags of the quarry
Stood erect, and called the nations,
Called the tribes of men together.

From his footprints flowed a river,
Leaped into the light of morning,
O'er the precipice plunging downward   10
Gleamed like Ishkoodah, the comet.
And the Spirit, stooping earthward,
With his finger on the meadow
Traced a winding pathway for it,
Saying to it, ' Run in this way ! '

From the red stone of the quarry
With his hand he broke a fragment,
Moulded it into a pipe-head,
Shaped and fashioned it with figures;
From the margin of the river   20
Took a long reed for a pipe-stem,
With its dark green leaves upon it;
Filled the pipe with bark of willow,
With the bark of the red willow;
Breathed upon the neighboring forest,
Made its great boughs chafe together,
Till in flame they burst and kindled;
And erect upon the mountains,
Gitche Manito, the mighty,
Smoked the calumet, the Peace-Pipe,   30
As a signal to the nations.

And the smoke rose slowly, slowly,
Through the tranquil air of morning,
First a single line of darkness,
Then a denser, bluer vapor,

Côteau des Prairies, and the Red Pipestone Quarry.
He says : —
' Here (according to their traditions) happened the
mysterious birth of the red pipe, which has blown its
fumes of peace and war to the remotest corners of the
continent ; which has visited every warrior, and passed
through its reddened stem the irrevocable oath of war
and desolation. And here, also, the peace-breathing
calumet was born, and fringed with the eagle's quills,
which has shed its thrilling fumes over the land, and
soothed the fury of the relentless savage.
' The Great Spirit at an ancient period here called the
Indian nations together, and, standing on the precipice
of the red pipe-stone rock, broke from its wall a piece,
and made a huge pipe by turning it in his hand, which
he smoked over them, and to the North, the South, the
East, and the West, and told them that this stone was
red, — that it was their flesh, — that they must use it for
their pipes of peace, — that it belonged to them all, and
that the war-club and scalping-knife must not be raised
on its ground. At the last whiff of his pipe his head
went into a great cloud, and the whole surface of the
rock for several miles was melted and glazed ; two great
ovens were opened beneath, and two women (guardian
spirits of the place) entered them in a blaze of fire ; and
they are heard there yet (Tso-mec-cos-tee and Tso-me-
cos-te-won-dee), answering to the invocations of the
high-priests or medicine-men, who consult them when
they are visitors to this sacred place.' (LONGFELLOW.)

Then a snow-white cloud unfolding,
Like the tree-tops of the forest,
Ever rising, rising, rising,
Till it touched the top of heaven,
Till it broke against the heaven,   40
And rolled outward all around it.

From the Vale of Tawasentha,
From the Valley of Wyoming,
From the groves of Tuscaloosa,
From the far-off Rocky Mountains,
From the Northern lakes and rivers
All the tribes beheld the signal,
Saw the distant smoke ascending,
The Pukwana of the Peace-Pipe.

And the Prophets of the nations   50
Said: ' Behold it, the Pukwana !
By this signal from afar off,
Bending like a wand of willow,
Waving like a hand that beckons,
Gitche Manito, the mighty,
Calls the tribes of men together,
Calls the warriors to his council ! '

Down the rivers, o'er the prairies,
Came the warriors of the nations,
Came the Delawares and Mohawks,   60
Came the Choctaws and Camanches,
Came the Shoshonies and Blackfeet,
Came the Pawnees and Omahas,
Came the Mandans and Dacotahs,
Came the Hurons and Ojibways,
All the warriors drawn together
By the signal of the Peace-Pipe,
To the Mountains of the Prairie,
To the great Red Pipe-stone Quarry.

And they stood there on the meadow,   70
With their weapons and their war-gear,
Painted like the leaves of Autumn,
Painted like the sky of morning,
Wildly glaring at each other;
In their faces stern defiance,
In their hearts the feuds of ages,
The hereditary hatred,
The ancestral thirst of vengeance.

Gitche Manito, the mighty,
The creator of the nations,   80
Looked upon them with compassion,
With paternal love and pity;
Looked upon their wrath and wrangling
But as quarrels among children,
But as feuds and fights of children !

Over them he stretched his right hand,
To subdue their stubborn natures,
To allay their thirst and fever,
By the shadow of his right hand;
Spake to them with voice majestic   90

As the sound of far-off waters,
Falling into deep abysses,
Warning, chiding, spake in this wise: —
  'O my children ! my poor children !
Listen to the words of wisdom,
Listen to the words of warning,
From the lips of the Great Spirit,
From the Master of Life, who made you !
  'I have given you lands to hunt in,
I have given you streams to fish in,   100
I have given you bear and bison,
I have given you roe and reindeer,
I have given you brant and beaver,
Filled the marshes full of wild-fowl,
Filled the rivers full of fishes;
Why then are you not contented ?
Why then will you hunt each other ?
  'I am weary of your quarrels,
Weary of your wars and bloodshed,
Weary of your prayers for vengeance,   110
Of your wranglings and dissensions;
All your strength is in your union,
All your danger is in discord;
Therefore be at peace henceforward,
And as brothers live together.
  'I will send a Prophet to you,
A Deliverer of the nations,
Who shall guide you and shall teach you,
Who shall toil and suffer with you.
If you listen to his counsels,   120
You will multiply and prosper;
If his warnings pass unheeded,
You will fade away and perish !
  'Bathe now in the stream before you,
Wash the war-paint from your faces,
Wash the blood-stains from your fingers,
Bury your war-clubs and your weapons,
Break the red stone from this quarry,
Mould and make it into Peace-Pipes,
Take the reeds that grow beside you,   130
Deck them with your brightest feathers,
Smoke the calumet together,
And as brothers live henceforward !'
  Then upon the ground the warriors
Threw their cloaks and shirts of deer-skin,
Threw their weapons and their war-gear,
Leaped into the rushing river,
Washed the war-paint from their faces.
Clear above them flowed the water,
Clear and limpid from the footprints   140
Of the Master of Life descending;
Dark below them flowed the water,
Soiled and stained with streaks of crimson,
As if blood were mingled with it !
  From the river came the warriors,

Clean and washed from all their war-paint;
On the banks their clubs they buried,
Buried all their warlike weapons.
Gitche Manito, the mighty,
The Great Spirit, the creator,   150
Smiled upon his helpless children !
  And in silence all the warriors
Broke the red stone of the quarry,
Smoothed and formed it into Peace-Pipes,
Broke the long reeds by the river,
Decked them with their brightest feathers,
And departed each one homeward,
While the Master of Life, ascending,
Through the opening of cloud-curtains,
Through the doorways of the heaven,   160
Vanished from before their faces,
In the smoke that rolled around him,
The Pukwana of the Peace-Pipe !

II

THE FOUR WINDS

'HONOR be to Mudjekeewis !'
Cried the warriors, cried the old men,
When he came in triumph homeward
With the sacred Belt of Wampum,
From the regions of the North-Wind,
From the kingdom of Wabasso,
From the land of the White Rabbit.
  He had stolen the Belt of Wampum
From the neck of Mishe-Mokwa,
From the Great Bear of the mountains,   10
From the terror of the nations,
As he lay asleep and cumbrous
On the summit of the mountains,
Like a rock with mosses on it,
Spotted brown and gray with mosses.
  Silently he stole upon him
Till the red nails of the monster
Almost touched him, almost scared him,
Till the hot breath of his nostrils
Warmed the hands of Mudjekeewis,   20
As he drew the Belt of Wampum
Over the round ears, that heard not,
Over the small eyes, that saw not,
Over the long nose and nostrils,
The black muffle of the nostrils,
Out of which the heavy breathing
Warmed the hands of Mudjekeewis.
  Then he swung aloft his war-club,
Shouted loud and long his war-cry,
Smote the mighty Mishe-Mokwa   30
In the middle of the forehead,
Right between the eyes he smote him.

With the heavy blow bewildered,
Rose the Great Bear of the mountains;
But his knees beneath him trembled.
And he whimpered like a woman,
As he reeled and staggered forward,
As he sat upon his haunches;
And the mighty Mudjekeewis,
Standing fearlessly before him,   40
Taunted him in loud derision,
Spake disdainfully in this wise: —
'Hark you, Bear! you are a coward;[1]
And no Brave, as you pretended;
Else you would not cry and whimper
Like a miserable woman!
Bear! you know our tribes are hostile,
Long have been at war together;
Now you find that we are strongest,
You go sneaking in the forest,   50
You go hiding in the mountains!
Had you conquered me in battle
Not a groan would I have uttered;
But you, Bear! sit here and whimper,
And disgrace your tribe by crying,
Like a wretched Shaugodaya,
Like a cowardly old woman!'
Then again he raised his war-club,
Smote again the Mishe-Mokwa
In the middle of his forehead,   60
Broke his skull, as ice is broken
When one goes to fish in winter.
Thus was slain the Mishe-Mokwa,
He the Great Bear of the mountains,
He the terror of the nations.
'Honor be to Mudjekeewis!'
With a shout exclaimed the people,
'Honor be to Mudjekeewis!
Henceforth he shall be the West-Wind,
And hereafter and forever   70
Shall he hold supreme dominion
Over all the winds of heaven.
Call him no more Mudjekeewis,
Call him Kabeyun, the West-Wind!'
Thus was Mudjekeewis chosen
Father of the Winds of Heaven.
For himself he kept the West-Wind,
Gave the others to his children;

[1] This anecdote is from Heckewelder. In his account of the Indian Nations, he describes an Indian hunter as addressing a bear in nearly these words. 'I was present,' he says, 'at the delivery of this curious invective; when the hunter had despatched the bear, I asked him how he thought that poor animal could understand what he said to it. "Oh," said he in answer, "the bear understood me very well; did you not observe how *ashamed* he looked while I was upbraiding him?"' — *Transactions of the American Philosophical Society*, vol. i. p. 240. (LONGFELLOW.)

Unto Wabun gave the East-Wind,
Gave the South to Shawondasee,   80
And the North-Wind, wild and cruel,
To the fierce Kabibonokka.
Young and beautiful was Wabun;
He it was who brought the morning,
He it was whose silver arrows
Chased the dark o'er hill and valley;
He it was whose cheeks were painted
With the brightest streaks of crimson,
And whose voice awoke the village,
Called the deer and called the hunter.   90
Lonely in the sky was Wabun;
Though the birds sang gayly to him,
Though the wild-flowers of the meadow
Filled the air with odors for him;
Though the forests and the rivers
Sang and shouted at his coming,
Still his heart was sad within him,
For he was alone in heaven.
But one morning, gazing earthward,
While the village still was sleeping,   100
And the fog lay on the river,
Like a ghost, that goes at sunrise,
He beheld a maiden walking
All alone upon a meadow,
Gathering water-flags and rushes
By a river in the meadow.
Every morning, gazing earthward,
Still the first thing he beheld there
Was her blue eyes looking at him,
Two blue lakes among the rushes.   110
And he loved the lonely maiden,
Who thus waited for his coming;
For they both were solitary,
She on earth and he in heaven.
And he wooed her with caresses,
Wooed her with his smile of sunshine,
With his flattering words he wooed her,
With his sighing and his singing,
Gentlest whispers in the branches,
Softest music, sweetest odors,   120
Till he drew her to his bosom,
Folded in his robes of crimson,
Till into a star he changed her,
Trembling still upon his bosom;
And forever in the heavens
They are seen together walking,
Wabun and the Wabun-Annung,
Wabun and the Star of Morning.
But the fierce Kabibonokka
Had his dwelling among icebergs,   130
In the everlasting snow-drifts,
In the kingdom of Wabasso,
In the land of the White Rabbit.

He it was whose hand in Autumn
Painted all the trees with scarlet,
Stained the leaves with red and yellow;
He it was who sent the snow-flakes,
Sifting, hissing through the forest,
Froze the ponds, the lakes, the rivers,
Drove the loon and sea-gull southward,   140
Drove the cormorant and curlew
To their nests of sedge and sea-tang
In the realms of Shawondasee.

Once the fierce Kabibonokka
Issued from his lodge of snow-drifts,
From his home among the icebergs,
And his hair, with snow besprinkled,
Streamed behind him like a river,
Like a black and wintry river,
As he howled and hurried southward,   150
Over frozen lakes and moorlands.

There among the reeds and rushes
Found he Shingebis, the diver,
Trailing strings of fish behind him,
O'er the frozen fens and moorlands,
Lingering still among the moorlands,
Though his tribe had long departed
To the land of Shawondasee.

Cried the fierce Kabibonokka,
'Who is this that dares to brave me ?   160
Dares to stay in my dominions,
When the Wawa has departed,
When the wild-goose has gone southward,
And the heron, the Shuh-shuh-gah,
Long ago departed southward ?
I will go into his wigwam,
I will put his smouldering fire out !'

And at night Kabibonokka
To the lodge came wild and wailing,
Heaped the snow in drifts about it,   170
Shouted down into the smoke-flue,
Shook the lodge-poles in his fury,
Flapped the curtain of the door-way.
Shingebis, the diver, feared not,
Shingebis, the diver, cared not;
Four great logs had he for firewood,
One for each moon of the winter,
And for food the fishes served him.
By his blazing fire he sat there,
Warm and merry, eating, laughing,   180
Singing, 'O Kabibonokka,
You are but my fellow-mortal !'

Then Kabibonokka entered,
And though Shingebis, the diver,
Felt his presence by the coldness,
Felt his icy breath upon him,
Still he did not cease his singing,
Still he did not leave his laughing,

Only turned the log a little,
Only made the fire burn brighter,   190
Made the sparks fly up the smoke-flue.

From Kabibonokka's forehead,
From his snow-besprinkled tresses,
Drops of sweat fell fast and heavy,
Making dints upon the ashes,
As along the eaves of lodges,
As from drooping boughs of hemlock,
Drips the melting snow in spring-time,
Making hollows in the snow-drifts.

Till at last he rose defeated,   200
Could not bear the heat and laughter,
Could not bear the merry singing,
But rushed headlong through the door-way,
Stamped upon the crusted snow-drifts,
Stamped upon the lakes and rivers,
Made the snow upon them harder,
Made the ice upon them thicker,
Challenged Shingebis, the diver,
To come forth and wrestle with him,
To come forth and wrestle naked   210
On the frozen fens and moorlands.

Forth went Shingebis, the diver,
Wrestled all night with the North-Wind,
Wrestled naked on the moorlands
With the fierce Kabibonokka,
Till his panting breath grew fainter,
Till his frozen grasp grew feebler,
Till he reeled and staggered backward,
And retreated, baffled, beaten,
To the kingdom of Wabasso,   220
To the land of the White Rabbit,
Hearing still the gusty laughter,
Hearing Shingebis, the diver,
Singing, 'O Kabibonokka,
You are but my fellow-mortal !'

Shawondasee, fat and lazy,
Had his dwelling far to southward,
In the drowsy, dreamy sunshine,
In the never-ending Summer.
He it was who sent the wood-birds,   230
Sent the robin, the Opechee,
Sent the bluebird, the Owaissa,
Sent the Shawshaw, sent the swallow,
Sent the wild-goose, Wawa, northward,
Sent the melons and tobacco,
And the grapes in purple clusters.

From his pipe the smoke ascending
Filled the sky with haze and vapor,
Filled the air with dreamy softness,
Gave a twinkle to the water,   240
Touched the rugged hills with smooth-
    ness,
Brought the tender Indian Summer

To the melancholy north-land,
In the dreary Moon of Snow-shoes.
  Listless, careless Shawondasee!
In his life he had one shadow,
In his heart one sorrow had he.
Once, as he was gazing northward,
Far away upon a prairie
He beheld a maiden standing,   250
Saw a tall and slender maiden
All alone upon a prairie;
Brightest green were all her garments,
And her hair was like the sunshine.
  Day by day he gazed upon her,
Day by day he sighed with passion,
Day by day his heart within him
Grew more hot with love and longing
For the maid with yellow tresses.
But he was too fat and lazy   260
To bestir himself and woo her.
Yes, too indolent and easy
To pursue her and persuade her;
So he only gazed upon her,
Only sat and sighed with passion
For the maiden of the prairie.
  Till one morning, looking northward,
He beheld her yellow tresses
Changed and covered o'er with white-
    ness,
Covered as with whitest snow-flakes. 270
'Ah! my brother from the North-land,
From the kingdom of Wabasso,
From the land of the White Rabbit!
You have stolen the maiden from me,
You have laid your hand upon her,
You have wooed and won my maiden,
With your stories of the North-land!'
  Thus the wretched Shawondasee
Breathed into the air his sorrow;
And the South-Wind o'er the prairie   280
Wandered warm with sighs of passion,
With the sighs of Shawondasee,
Till the air seemed full of snow-flakes,
Full of thistle-down the prairie,
And the maid with hair like sunshine
Vanished from his sight forever;
Never more did Shawondasee
See the maid with yellow tresses!
  Poor, deluded Shawondasee!
'T was no woman that you gazed at,   290
'T was no maiden that you sighed for,
'T was the prairie dandelion
That through all the dreamy Summer
You had gazed at with such longing,
You had sighed for with such passion,
And had puffed away forever,

Blown into the air with sighing.
Ah! deluded Shawondasee!
  Thus the Four Winds were divided;
Thus the sons of Mudjekeewis   300
Had their stations in the heavens,
At the corners of the heavens,
For himself the West-Wind only
Kept the mighty Mudjekeewis.

III

HIAWATHA'S CHILDHOOD

DOWNWARD through the evening twilight,
In the days that are forgotten,
In the unremembered ages,
From the full moon fell Nokomis,
Fell the beautiful Nokomis,
She a wife, but not a mother.
  She was sporting with her women,
Swinging in a swing of grape-vines,
When her rival the rejected,
Full of jealousy and hatred,   10
Cut the leafy swing asunder,
Cut in twain the twisted grape-vines,
And Nokomis fell affrighted
Downward through the evening twilight,
On the Muskoday, the meadow,
On the prairie full of blossoms.
'See! a star falls!' said the people;
'From the sky a star is falling!'
  There among the ferns and mosses,
There among the prairie lilies,   20
On the Muskoday, the meadow,
In the moonlight and the starlight,
Fair Nokomis bore a daughter.
And she called her name Wenonah,
As the first-born of her daughters.
And the daughter of Nokomis
Grew up like the prairie lilies,
Grew a tall and slender maiden,
With the beauty of the moonlight,
With the beauty of the starlight.   30
  And Nokomis warned her often,
Saying oft, and oft repeating,
'Oh, beware of Mudjekeewis,
Of the West-Wind, Mudjekeewis;
Listen not to what he tells you;
Lie not down upon the meadow,
Stoop not down among the lilies,
Lest the West-Wind come and harm you!'
  But she heeded not the warning,
Heeded not those words of wisdom,   40
And the West-Wind came at evening,

Walking lightly o'er the prairie,
Whispering to the leaves and blossoms,
Bending low the flowers and grasses,
Found the beautiful Wenonah,
Lying there among the lilies,
Wooed her with his words of sweetness,
Wooed her with his soft caresses,
Till she bore a son in sorrow,
Bore a son of love and sorrow.   50

Thus was born my Hiawatha,
Thus was born the child of wonder;
But the daughter of Nokomis,
Hiawatha's gentle mother,
In her anguish died deserted
By the West-Wind, false and faithless,
By the heartless Mudjekeewis.

For her daughter long and loudly
Wailed and wept the sad Nokomis;
'Oh that I were dead!' she murmured,   60
'Oh that I were dead, as thou art!
No more work, and no more weeping,
Wahonowin! Wahonowin!'

By the shores of Gitche Gumee,
By the shining Big-Sea-Water,
Stood the wigwam of Nokomis,
Daughter of the Moon, Nokomis.
Dark behind it rose the forest,
Rose the black and gloomy pine-trees,
Rose the firs with cones upon them;   70
Bright before it beat the water,
Beat the clear and sunny water,
Beat the shining Big-Sea-Water.

There the wrinkled old Nokomis
Nursed the little Hiawatha,
Rocked him in his linden cradle,
Bedded soft in moss and rushes,
Safely bound with reindeer sinews;
Stilled his fretful wail by saying,
'Hush! the Naked Bear will hear thee!' 80
Lulled him into slumber, singing,
'Ewa-yea! my little owlet!
Who is this, that lights the wigwam?
With his great eyes lights the wigwam?
Ewa-yea! my little owlet!'

Many things Nokomis taught him
Of the stars that shine in heaven;
Showed him Ishkoodah, the comet,
Ishkoodah, with fiery tresses;
Showed the Death-Dance of the spirits, 90
Warriors with their plumes and war-
    clubs,
Flaring far away to northward
In the frosty nights of Winter;
Showed the broad white road in heaven,
Pathway of the ghosts, the shadows,

Running straight across the heavens,
Crowded with the ghosts, the shadows.

At the door on summer evenings
Sat the little Hiawatha;
Heard the whispering of the pine-trees,
Heard the lapping of the waters,   101
Sounds of music, words of wonder;
'Minne-wawa!' said the pine-trees,
'Mudway-aushka!' said the water.

Saw the fire-fly, Wah-wah-taysee,
Flitting through the dusk of evening,
With the twinkle of its candle
Lighting up the brakes and bushes,
And he sang the song of children,
Sang the song Nokomis taught him: 110
'Wah-wah-taysee, little fire-fly,
Little, flitting, white-fire insect,
Little, dancing, white-fire creature,
Light me with your little candle,
Ere upon my bed I lay me,
Ere in sleep I close my eyelids!'

Saw the moon rise from the water
Rippling, rounding from the water,
Saw the flecks and shadows on it,
Whispered, 'What is that, Nokomis?'   120
And the good Nokomis answered:
'Once a warrior, very angry,
Seized his grandmother, and threw her
Up into the sky at midnight;
Right against the moon he threw her;
'T is her body that you see there.'

Saw the rainbow in the heaven,
In the eastern sky, the rainbow,
Whispered, 'What is that, Nokomis?'
And the good Nokomis answered: 130
''T is the heaven of flowers you see there;
All the wild-flowers of the forest,
All the lilies of the prairie,
When on earth they fade and perish,
Blossom in that heaven above us.'

When he heard the owls at midnight,
Hooting, laughing in the forest,
'What is that?' he cried in terror,
'What is that,' he said, 'Nokomis?'
And the good Nokomis answered: 140
'That is but the owl and owlet,
Talking in their native language,
Talking, scolding at each other.'

Then the little Hiawatha
Learned of every bird its language,
Learned their names and all their secrets,
How they built their nests in Summer,
Where they hid themselves in Winter,
Talked with them whene'er he met them,
Called them 'Hiawatha's Chickens.'   150

Of all beasts he learned the language,
Learned their names and all their secrets,
How the beavers built their lodges,
Where the squirrels hid their acorns,
How the reindeer ran so swiftly,
Why the rabbit was so timid,
Talked with them whene'er he met them,
Called them 'Hiawatha's Brothers.'

Then Iagoo, the great boaster,
He the marvellous story-teller,   160
He the traveller and the talker,
He the friend of old Nokomis,
Made a bow for Hiawatha;
From a branch of ash he made it,
From an oak-bough made the arrows,
Tipped with flint, and winged with feathers,
And the cord he made of deer-skin.

Then he said to Hiawatha:
'Go, my son, into the forest,
Where the red deer herd together,   170
Kill for us a famous roebuck,
Kill for us a deer with antlers ! '

Forth into the forest straightway
All alone walked Hiawatha
Proudly, with his bow and arrows;
And the birds sang round him, o'er him,
' Do not shoot us, Hiawatha ! '
Sang the robin, the Opechee,
Sang the bluebird, the Owaissa,
' Do not shoot us, Hiawatha ! '   180

Up the oak-tree, close beside him,
Sprang the squirrel, Adjidaumo,
In and out among the branches,
Coughed and chattered from the oak-tree,
Laughed, and said between his laughing,
' Do not shoot me, Hiawatha ! '

And the rabbit from his pathway
Leaped aside, and at a distance
Sat erect upon his haunches,
Half in fear and half in frolic,   190
Saying to the little hunter,
' Do not shoot me, Hiawatha ! '

But he heeded not, nor heard them,
For his thoughts were with the red deer;
On their tracks his eyes were fastened,
Leading downward to the river,
To the ford across the river,
And as one in slumber walked he.

Hidden in the alder-bushes,
There he waited till the deer came,   200
Till he saw two antlers lifted,
Saw two eyes look from the thicket,
Saw two nostrils point to windward,
And a deer came down the pathway,
Flecked with leafy light and shadow.

And his heart within him fluttered,
Trembled like the leaves above him,
Like the birch-leaf palpitated,
As the deer came down the pathway.

Then, upon one knee uprising,   210
Hiawatha aimed an arrow;
Scarce a twig moved with his motion,
Scarce a leaf was stirred or rustled,
But the wary roebuck started,
Stamped with all his hoofs together,
Listened with one foot uplifted,
Leaped as if to meet the arrow;
Ah ! the singing, fatal arrow,
Like a wasp it buzzed and stung him !

Dead he lay there in the forest,   220
By the ford across the river;
Beat his timid heart no longer,
But the heart of Hiawatha
Throbbed and shouted and exulted,
As he bore the red deer homeward,
And Iagoo and Nokomis
Hailed his coming with applauses.

From the red deer's hide Nokomis
Made a cloak for Hiawatha,
From the red deer's flesh Nokomis   230
Made a banquet to his honor.
All the village came and feasted,
All the guests praised Hiawatha,
Called him Strong-Heart, Soan-ge-taha !
Called him Loon-Heart, Mahn-go-taysee !

IV

HIAWATHA AND MUDJEKEEWIS

OUT of childhood into manhood
Now had grown my Hiawatha,
Skilled in all the craft of hunters,
Learned in all the lore of old men,
In all youthful sports and pastimes,
In all manly arts and labors.

Swift of foot was Hiawatha;
He could shoot an arrow from him,
And run forward with such fleetness,
That the arrow fell behind him !   10
Strong of arm was Hiawatha,
He could shoot ten arrows upward,
Shoot them with such strength and swift-
        ness,
That the tenth had left the bow-string
Ere the first to earth had fallen !

He had mittens, Minjekahwun,
Magic mittens made of deer-skin;
When upon his hands he wore them,

He could smite the rocks asunder,
He could grind them into powder.   20
He had moccasins enchanted,
Magic moccasins of deer-skin;
When he bound them round his ankles,
When upon his feet he tied them,
At each stride a mile he measured !
   Much he questioned old Nokomis
Of his father Mudjekeewis;
Learned from her the fatal secret
Of the beauty of his mother,
Of the falsehood of his father;   30
And his heart was hot within him,
Like a living coal his heart was.
   Then he said to old Nokomis,
' I will go to Mudjekeewis,
See how fares it with my father,
At the doorways of the West-Wind,
At the portals of the Sunset ! '
   From his lodge went Hiawatha,
Dressed for travel, armed for hunting;
Dressed in deer-skin shirt and leggings, 40
Richly wrought with quills and wampum;
On his head his eagle-feathers,
Round his waist his belt of wampum,
In his hand his bow of ash-wood,
Strung with sinews of the reindeer;
In his quiver oaken arrows,
Tipped with jasper, winged with feathers;
With his mittens, Minjekahwun,
With his moccasins enchanted.
   Warning said the old Nokomis,   50
' Go not forth, O Hiawatha !
To the kingdom of the West-Wind,
To the realms of Mudjekeewis,
Lest he harm you with his magic,
Lest he kill you with his cunning ! '
   But the fearless Hiawatha
Heeded not her woman's warning;
Forth he strode into the forest,
At each stride a mile he measured;
Lurid seemed the sky above him,   60
Lurid seemed the earth beneath him,
Hot and close the air around him,
Filled with smoke and fiery vapors,
As of burning woods and prairies,
For his heart was hot within him,
Like a living coal his heart was.
   So he journeyed westward, westward,
Left the fleetest deer behind him,
Left the antelope and bison;
Crossed the rushing Esconaba,   70
Crossed the mighty Mississippi,
Passed the Mountains of the Prairie,
Passed the land of Crows and Foxes,

Passed the dwellings of the Blackfeet,
Came unto the Rocky Mountains,
To the kingdom of the West-Wind,
Where upon the gusty summits
Sat the ancient Mudjekeewis,
Ruler of the winds of heaven.
   Filled with awe was Hiawatha   80
At the aspect of his father.
On the air about him wildly
Tossed and streamed his cloudy tresses,
Gleamed like drifting snow his tresses,
Glared like Ishkoodah, the comet,
Like the star with fiery tresses.
   Filled with joy was Mudjekeewis
When he looked on Hiawatha,
Saw his youth rise up before him
In the face of Hiawatha,   90
Saw the beauty of Wenonah
From the grave rise up before him.
   ' Welcome ! ' said he, ' Hiawatha,
To the kingdom of the West-Wind !
Long have I been waiting for you !
Youth is lovely, age is lonely,
Youth is fiery, age is frosty;
You bring back the days departed,
You bring back my youth of passion,
And the beautiful Wenonah ! '   100
   Many days they talked together,
Questioned, listened, waited, answered;
Much the mighty Mudjekeewis
Boasted of his ancient prowess,
Of his perilous adventures,
His indomitable courage,
His invulnerable body.
   Patiently sat Hiawatha,
Listening to his father's boasting;
With a smile he sat and listened,   110
Uttered neither threat nor menace,
Neither word nor look betrayed him,
But his heart was hot within him,
Like a living coal his heart was.
   Then he said, ' O Mudjekeewis,
Is there nothing that can harm you ?
Nothing that you are afraid of ? '
And the mighty Mudjekeewis,
Grand and gracious in his boasting,
Answered, saying, ' There is nothing,   120
Nothing but the black rock yonder,
Nothing but the fatal Wawbeek ! '
   And he looked at Hiawatha
With a wise look and benignant,
With a countenance paternal,
Looked with pride upon the beauty
Of his tall and graceful figure,
Saying, ' O my Hiawatha !

Is there anything can harm you?
Anything you are afraid of?'   130
    But the wary Hiawatha
Paused awhile, as if uncertain,
Held his peace, as if resolving,
And then answered, 'There is nothing,
Nothing but the bulrush yonder,
Nothing but the great Apukwa!
    And as Mudjekeewis, rising,
Stretched his hand to pluck the bul-
        rush,
Hiawatha cried in terror,
Cried in well-dissembled terror,   140
'Kago! kago! do not touch it!'
'Ah, kaween!' said Mudjekeewis,
'No indeed, I will not touch it!'
    Then they talked of other matters;
First of Hiawatha's brothers,
First of Wabun, of the East-Wind,
Of the South-Wind, Shawondasee,
Of the North, Kabibonokka;
Then of Hiawatha's mother,
Of the beautiful Wenonah,   150
Of her birth upon the meadow,
Of her death, as old Nokomis
Had remembered and related.
    And he cried, 'O Mudjekeewis,
It was you who killed Wenonah,
Took her young life and her beauty,
Broke the Lily of the Prairie,
Trampled it beneath your footsteps;
You confess it! you confess it!'
And the mighty Mudjekeewis   160
Tossed upon the wind his tresses,
Bowed his hoary head in anguish,
With a silent nod assented.
    Then up started Hiawatha,
And with threatening look and gesture
Laid his hand upon the black rock,
On the fatal Wawbeek laid it,
With his mittens, Minjekahwun,
Rent the jutting crag asunder,
Smote and crushed it into fragments,   170
Hurled them madly at his father,
The remorseful Mudjekeewis,
For his heart was hot within him,
Like a living coal his heart was.
    But the ruler of the West-Wind
Blew the fragments backward from him,
With the breathing of his nostrils,
With the tempest of his anger,
Blew them back at his assailant;
Seized the bulrush, the Apukwa,   180
Dragged it with its roots and fibres
From the margin of the meadow,

From its ooze the giant bulrush;
Long and loud laughed Hiawatha!
    Then began the deadly conflict,
Hand to hand among the mountains;
From his eyry screamed the eagle,
The Keneu, the great war-eagle,
Sat upon the crags around them,
Wheeling flapped his wings above them.   190
    Like a tall tree in the tempest
Bent and lashed the giant bulrush;
And in masses huge and heavy
Crashing fell the fatal Wawbeek;
Till the earth shook with the tumult
And confusion of the battle,
And the air was full of shoutings,
And the thunder of the mountains,
Starting, answered, 'Baim-wawa!'
    Back retreated Mudjekeewis,   200
Rushing westward o'er the mountains,
Stumbling westward down the mountains,
Three whole days retreated fighting,
Still pursued by Hiawatha
To the doorways of the West-Wind,
To the portals of the Sunset,
To the earth's remotest border,
Where into the empty spaces
Sinks the sun, as a flamingo
Drops into her nest at nightfall   210
In the melancholy marshes.
    'Hold!' at length cried Mudjekeewis,
'Hold, my son, my Hiawatha!
'T is impossible to kill me,
For you cannot kill the immortal.
I have put you to this trial,
But to know and prove your courage;
Now receive the prize of valor!
    'Go back to your home and people,
Live among them, toil among them,   220
Cleanse the earth from all that harms it,
Clear the fishing-grounds and rivers,
Slay all monsters and magicians,
All the Wendigoes, the giants,
All the serpents, the Kenabeeks,
As I slew the Mishe-Mokwa,
Slew the Great Bear of the mountains.
    'And at last when Death draws near you,
When the awful eyes of Pauguk
Glare upon you in the darkness,   230
I will share my kingdom with you,
Ruler shall you be thenceforward
Of the Northwest-Wind, Keewaydin,
Of the home-wind, the Keewaydin.'
    Thus was fought that famous battle
In the dreadful days of Shah-shah,
In the days long since departed,

In the kingdom of the West-Wind.
Still the hunter sees its traces
Scattered far o'er hill and valley;   240
Sees the giant bulrush growing
By the ponds and water-courses,
Sees the masses of the Wawbeek
Lying still in every valley.

Homeward now went Hiawatha;
Pleasant was the landscape round him,
Pleasant was the air above him,
For the bitterness of anger
Had departed wholly from him,
From his brain the thought of vengeance,   250
From his heart the burning fever.

Only once his pace he slackened,
Only once he paused or halted,
Paused to purchase heads of arrows
Of the ancient Arrow-maker,
In the land of the Dacotahs,
Where the Falls of Minnehaha
Flash and gleam among the oak-trees,
Laugh and leap into the valley.[1]

There the ancient Arrow-maker   260
Made his arrow-heads of sandstone,
Arrow-heads of chalcedony,
Arrow-heads of flint and jasper,
Smoothed and sharpened at the edges,
Hard and polished, keen and costly.

With him dwelt his dark-eyed daughter
Wayward as the Minnehaha,
With her moods of shade and sunshine,
Eyes that smiled and frowned alternate,
Feet as rapid as the river,   270
Tresses flowing like the water,
And as musical a laughter:
And he named her from the river,
From the water-fall he named her,
Minnehaha, Laughing Water.

Was it then for heads of arrows,
Arrow-heads of chalcedony,
Arrow-heads of flint and jasper,
That my Hiawatha halted
In the land of the Dacotahs?   280

Was it not to see the maiden,
See the face of Laughing Water
Peeping from behind the curtain,
Hear the rustling of her garments
From behind the waving curtain,

As one sees the Minnehaha
Gleaming, glancing through the branches,
As one hears the Laughing Water
From behind its screen of branches?

Who shall say what thoughts and visions
Fill the fiery brains of young men?   290
Who shall say what dreams of beauty
Filled the heart of Hiawatha?
All he told to old Nokomis,
When he reached the lodge at sunset,
Was the meeting with his father,
Was his fight with Mudjekeewis;
Not a word he said of arrows,
Not a word of Laughing Water.

V

HIAWATHA'S FASTING[2]

You shall hear how Hiawatha
Prayed and fasted in the forest,
Not for greater skill in hunting,
Not for greater craft in fishing,
Not for triumphs in the battle,
And renown among the warriors,
But for profit of the people,
For advantage of the nations.

First he built a lodge for fasting,
Built a wigwam in the forest,   10
By the shining Big-Sea-Water,
In the blithe and pleasant Spring-time,
In the Moon of Leaves he built it,
And, with dreams and visions many,
Seven whole days and nights he fasted.

On the first day of his fasting
Through the leafy woods he wandered;
Saw the deer start from the thicket,
Saw the rabbit in his burrow,
Heard the pheasant, Bena, drumming,   20
Heard the squirrel, Adjidaumo,
Rattling in his hoard of acorns,
Saw the pigeon, the Omeme,
Building nests among the pine-trees,
And in flocks the wild-goose, Wawa,
Flying to the fen-lands northward,
Whirring, wailing far above him.
'Master of Life!' he cried, desponding,
'Must our lives depend on these things?'

On the next day of his fasting   30
By the river's brink he wandered,
Through the Muskoday, the meadow,
Saw the wild rice, Mahnomonee,
Saw the blueberry, Meenahga,
And the strawberry, Odahmin,

[1] 'The scenery about Fort Snelling is rich in beauty. The Falls of St. Anthony are familiar to travellers, and to readers of Indian sketches. Between the fort and these falls are the "Little Falls," forty feet in height, on a stream that empties into the Mississippi. The Indians called them Mine-hah-hah, or "laughing waters."'— Mrs. Eastman's *Dacotah, or Legends of the Sioux*, Introd. p. ii. (LONGFELLOW.)

[2] See Longfellow's note on section xiii, p. 188.

And the gooseberry, Shahbomin,
And the grape-vine, the Bemahgut,
Trailing o'er the alder-branches,
Filling all the air with fragrance !
' Master of Life !' he cried, desponding,   40
' Must our lives depend on these things ? '
    On the third day of his fasting
By the lake he sat and pondered,
By the still, transparent water;
Saw the sturgeon, Nahma, leaping,
Scattering drops like beads of wampum,
Saw the yellow perch, the Sahwa,
Like a sunbeam in the water,
Saw the pike, the Maskenozha,
And the herring, Okahahwis,   50
And the Shawgashee, the craw-fish !
' Master of Life !' he cried, desponding,
' Must our lives depend on these things ? '
    On the fourth day of his fasting
In his lodge he lay exhausted;
From his couch of leaves and branches
Gazing with half-open eyelids,
Full of shadowy dreams and visions,
On the dizzy, swimming landscape,
On the gleaming of the water,   60
On the splendor of the sunset.
    And he saw a youth approaching,
Dressed in garments green and yellow,
Coming through the purple twilight,
Through the splendor of the sunset;
Plumes of green bent o'er his forehead,
And his hair was soft and golden.
    Standing at the open doorway,
Long he looked at Hiawatha,
Looked with pity and compassion   70
On his wasted form and features,
And, in accents like the sighing
Of the South-Wind in the tree-tops,
Said he, ' O my Hiawatha !
All your prayers are heard in heaven,
For you pray not like the others;
Not for greater skill in hunting,
Not for greater craft in fishing,
Not for triumph in the battle,
Nor renown among the warriors,   80
But for profit of the people,
For advantage of the nations.
    ' From the Master of Life descending,
I, the friend of man, Mondamin,
Come to warn you and instruct you,
How by struggle and by labor
You shall gain what you have prayed for.
Rise up from your bed of branches,
Rise, O youth, and wrestle with me !'
    Faint with famine, Hiawatha   90

Started from his bed of branches,
From the twilight of his wigwam
Forth into the flush of sunset
Came, and wrestled with Mondamin;
At his touch he felt new courage
Throbbing in his brain and bosom,
Felt new life and hope and vigor
Run through every nerve and fibre.
    So they wrestled there together
In the glory of the sunset,   100
And the more they strove and struggled,
Stronger still grew Hiawatha;
Till the darkness fell around them,
And the heron, the Shuh-shuh-gah,
From her nest among the pine-trees,
Gave a cry of lamentation,
Gave a scream of pain and famine.
    ' 'T is enough !' then said Mondamin,
Smiling upon Hiawatha,
' But to-morrow, when the sun sets,   110
I will come again to try you.'
And he vanished, and was seen not;
Whether sinking as the rain sinks,
Whether rising as the mists rise,
Hiawatha saw not, knew not,
Only saw that he had vanished,
Leaving him alone and fainting,
With the misty lake below him,
And the reeling stars above him.
    On the morrow and the next day,   120
When the sun through heaven descending,
Like a red and burning cinder
From the hearth of the Great Spirit,
Fell into the western waters,
Came Mondamin for the trial,
For the strife with Hiawatha;
Came as silent as the dew comes,
From the empty air appearing,
Into empty air returning,
Taking shape when earth it touches,   130
But invisible to all men
In its coming and its going.
    Thrice they wrestled there together
In the glory of the sunset,
Till the darkness fell around them,
Till the heron, the Shuh-shuh-gah,
From her nest among the pine-trees,
Uttered her loud cry of famine,
And Mondamin paused to listen.
    Tall and beautiful he stood there,   40
In his garments green and yellow;
To and fro his plumes above him
Waved and nodded with his breathing,
And the sweat of the encounter
Stood like drops of dew upon him.

And he cried, ' O Hiawatha !
Bravely have you wrestled with me,
Thrice have wrestled stoutly with me,
And the Master of Life, who sees us,
He will give to you the triumph ! '   150
   Then he smiled, and said : ' To-morrow
Is the last day of your conflict,
Is the last day of your fasting.
You will conquer and o'ercome me;
Make a bed for me to lie in,
Where the rain may fall upon me,
Where the sun may come and warm me;
Strip these garments, green and yellow,
Strip this nodding plumage from me,
Lay me in the earth, and make it   160
Soft and loose and light above me.
   ' Let no hand disturb my slumber,
Let no weed nor worm molest me,
Let not Kahgahgee, the raven,
Come to haunt me and molest me,
Only come yourself to watch me,
Till I wake, and start, and quicken,
Till I leap into the sunshine.'
   And thus saying, he departed;
Peacefully slept Hiawatha,   170
But he heard the Wawonaissa,
Heard the whippoorwill complaining,
Perched upon his lonely wigwam;
Heard the rushing Sebowisha,
Heard the rivulet rippling near him,
Talking to the darksome forest;
Heard the sighing of the branches,
As they lifted and subsided
At the passing of the night-wind,
Heard them, as one hears in slumber   180
Far-off murmurs, dreamy whispers:
Peacefully slept Hiawatha.
   On the morrow came Nokomis,
On the seventh day of his fasting,
Came with food for Hiawatha,
Came imploring and bewailing,
Lest his hunger should o'ercome him,
Lest his fasting should be fatal.
   But he tasted not, and touched not,
Only said to her, ' Nokomis,   190
Wait until the sun is setting,
Till the darkness falls around us,
Till the heron, the Shuh-shuh-gah,
Crying from the desolate marshes,
Tells us that the day is ended.'
   Homeward weeping went Nokomis,
Sorrowing for her Hiawatha,
Fearing lest his strength should fail him,
Lest his fasting should be fatal.
He meanwhile sat weary waiting   200

For the coming of Mondamin,
Till the shadows, pointing eastward,
Lengthened over field and forest,
Till the sun dropped from the heaven,
Floating on the waters westward,
As a red leaf in the Autumn
Falls and floats upon the water,
Falls and sinks into its bosom.
   And behold ! the young Mondamin,
With his soft and shining tresses,   210
With his garments green and yellow,
With his long and glossy plumage,
Stood and beckoned at the doorway.
And as one in slumber walking,
Pale and haggard, but undaunted,
From the wigwam Hiawatha
Came and wrestled with Mondamin.
   Round about him spun the landscape,
Sky and forest reeled together,
And his strong heart leaped within him,   220
As the sturgeon leaps and struggles
In a net to break its meshes.
Like a ring of fire around him
Blazed and flared the red horizon,
And a hundred suns seemed looking
At the combat of the wrestlers.
   Suddenly upon the greensward
All alone stood Hiawatha,
Panting with his wild exertion,
Palpitating with the struggle;   230
And before him breathless, lifeless,
Lay the youth, with hair dishevelled,
Plumage torn, and garments tattered,
Dead he lay there in the sunset.
   And victorious Hiawatha
Made the grave as he commanded,
Stripped the garments from Mondamin,
Stripped his tattered plumage from him,
Laid him in the earth, and made it
Soft and loose and light above him;   240
And the heron, the Shuh-shuh-gah,
From the melancholy moorlands,
Gave a cry of lamentation,
Gave a cry of pain and anguish !
   Homeward then went Hiawatha
To the lodge of old Nokomis,
And the seven days of his fasting
Were accomplished and completed.
But the place was not forgotten
Where he wrestled with Mondamin;   250
Nor forgotten nor neglected
Was the grave where lay Mondamin,
Sleeping in the rain and sunshine,
Where his scattered plumes and garments
Faded in the rain and sunshine.

Day by day did Hiawatha
Go to wait and watch beside it;
Kept the dark mould soft above it,
Kept it clean from weeds and insects,
Drove away, with scoffs and shoutings,   260
Kahgahgee, the king of ravens.
    Till at length a small green feather
From the earth shot slowly upward,
Then another and another,
And before the Summer ended
Stood the maize in all its beauty,
With its shining robes about it,
And its long, soft, yellow tresses;
And in rapture Hiawatha
Cried aloud, 'It is Mondamin!   270
Yes, the friend of man, Mondamin!'
    Then he called to old Nokomis
And Iagoo, the great boaster,
Showed them where the maize was grow-
    ing,
Told them of his wondrous vision,
Of his wrestling and his triumph,
Of this new gift to the nations,
Which should be their food forever.
    And still later, when the Autumn
Changed the long, green leaves to yellow,   280
And the soft and juicy kernels
Grew like wampum hard and yellow,
Then the ripened ears he gathered,
Stripped the withered husks from off
    them,
As he once had stripped the wrestler,
Gave the first Feast of Mondamin,
And made known unto the people
This new gift of the Great Spirit.

VI

HIAWATHA'S FRIENDS

Two good friends had Hiawatha,
Singled out from all the others,
Bound to him in closest union,
And to whom he gave the right hand
Of his heart, in joy and sorrow;
Chibiabos, the musician,
And the very strong man, Kwasind.
    Straight between them ran the pathway,
Never grew the grass upon it;
Singing birds, that utter falsehoods,   10
Story-tellers, mischief-makers,
Found no eager ear to listen,
Could not breed ill-will between them,
For they kept each other's counsel,

Spake with naked hearts together,
Pondering much and much contriving
How the tribes of men might prosper.
    Most beloved by Hiawatha
Was the gentle Chibiabos,
He the best of all musicians,   20
He the sweetest of all singers.
Beautiful and childlike was he,
Brave as man is, soft as woman,
Pliant as a wand of willow,
Stately as a deer with antlers.
    When he sang, the village listened;
All the warriors gathered round him,
All the women came to hear him;
Now he stirred their souls to passion,
Now he melted them to pity.   30
    From the hollow reeds he fashioned
Flutes so musical and mellow,
That the brook, the Sebowisha,
Ceased to murmur in the woodland,
That the wood-birds ceased from singing,
And the squirrel, Adjidaumo,
Ceased his chatter in the oak-tree,
And the rabbit, the Wabasso,
Sat upright to look and listen.
    Yes, the brook, the Sebowisha,   40
Pausing, said, 'O Chibiabos,
Teach my waves to flow in music,
Softly as your words in singing!'
    Yes, the bluebird, the Owaissa,
Envious, said, 'O Chibiabos,
Teach me tones as wild and wayward,
Teach me songs as full of frenzy!'
    Yes, the robin, the Opechee,
Joyous, said, 'O Chibiabos,
Teach me tones as sweet and tender,   50
Teach me songs as full of gladness!'
    And the whippoorwill, Wawonaissa,
Sobbing, said, 'O Chibiabos,
Teach me tones as melancholy,
Teach me songs as full of sadness!'
    All the many sounds of nature
Borrowed sweetness from his singing;
All the hearts of men were softened
By the pathos of his music;
For he sang of peace and freedom,   60
Sang of beauty, love, and longing;
Sang of death, and life undying
In the Islands of the Blessed,
In the kingdom of Ponemah,
In the land of the Hereafter.
    Very dear to Hiawatha
Was the gentle Chibiabos,
He the best of all musicians,
He the sweetest of all singers;

For his gentleness he loved him,   70
And the magic of his singing.
    Dear, too, unto Hiawatha
Was the very strong man, Kwasind,
He the strongest of all mortals,
He the mightiest among many;
For his very strength he loved him,
For his strength allied to goodness.
    Idle in his youth was Kwasind,
Very listless, dull, and dreamy,
Never played with other children,   80
Never fished and never hunted,
Not like other children was he;
But they saw that much he fasted,
Much his Manito entreated,
Much besought his Guardian Spirit.
    'Lazy Kwasind!' said his mother,
'In my work you never help me!
In the Summer you are roaming
Idly in the fields and forests;
In the Winter you are cowering   90
O'er the firebrands in the wigwam!
In the coldest days of Winter
I must break the ice for fishing;
With my nets you never help me!
At the door my nets are hanging,
Dripping, freezing with the water;
Go and wring them, Yenadizze!
Go and dry them in the sunshine!'
    Slowly, from the ashes, Kwasind
Rose, but made no angry answer;   100
From the lodge went forth in silence,
Took the nets, that hung together,
Dripping, freezing at the doorway;
Like a wisp of straw he wrung them,
Like a wisp of straw he broke them,
Could not wring them without breaking,
Such the strength was in his fingers.
    'Lazy Kwasind!' said his father,
'In the hunt you never help me;
Every bow you touch is broken,   110
Snapped asunder every arrow;
Yet come with me to the forest,
You shall bring the hunting home-
    ward.'
    Down a narrow pass they wandered,
Where a brooklet led them onward,
Where the trail of deer and bison
Marked the soft mud on the margin,
Till they found all further passage
Shut against them, barred securely
By the trunks of trees uprooted,   120
Lying lengthwise, lying crosswise,
And forbidding further passage.
    'We must go back,' said the old man,

'O'er these logs we cannot clamber;
Not a woodchuck could get through them,
Not a squirrel clamber o'er them!'
And straightway his pipe he lighted,
And sat down to smoke and ponder.
But before his pipe was finished,
Lo! the path was cleared before him;   130
All the trunks had Kwasind lifted,
To the right hand, to the left hand,
Shot the pine-trees swift as arrows,
Hurled the cedars light as lances.
    'Lazy Kwasind!' said the young men,
As they sported in the meadow:
'Why stand idly looking at us,
Leaning on the rock behind you?
Come and wrestle with the others,
Let us pitch the quoit together!'   140
    Lazy Kwasind made no answer,
To their challenge made no answer,
Only rose, and slowly turning,
Seized the huge rock in his fingers,
Tore it from its deep foundation,
Poised it in the air a moment,
Pitched it sheer into the river,
Sheer into the swift Pauwating,
Where it still is seen in Summer.
    Once as down that foaming river,   150
Down the rapids of Pauwating,
Kwasind sailed with his companions,
In the stream he saw a beaver,
Saw Ahmeek, the King of Beavers,
Struggling with the rushing currents,
Rising, sinking in the water.
    Without speaking, without pausing,
Kwasind leaped into the river,
Plunged beneath the bubbling surface,
Through the whirlpools chased the beaver,
Followed him among the islands,   161
Stayed so long beneath the water,
That his terrified companions
Cried, 'Alas! good-by to Kwasind!
We shall never more see Kwasind!'
But he reappeared triumphant,
And upon his shining shoulders
Brought the beaver, dead and drip-
    ping,
Brought the King of all the Beavers.
    And these two, as I have told you,   170
Were the friends of Hiawatha,
Chibiabos, the musician,
And the very strong man, Kwasind.
Long they lived in peace together,
Spake with naked hearts together,
Pondering much and much contriving
How the tribes of men might prosper.

VII

HIAWATHA'S SAILING

'Give me of your bark, O Birch-tree!
Of your yellow bark, O Birch-tree!
Growing by the rushing river,
Tall and stately in the valley!
I a light canoe will build me,
Build a swift Cheemaun for sailing,
That shall float upon the river,
Like a yellow leaf in Autumn,
Like a yellow water-lily!
 'Lay aside your cloak, O Birch-tree! 10
Lay aside your white-skin wrapper,
For the Summer-time is coming,
And the sun is warm in heaven,
And you need no white-skin wrapper!'
 Thus aloud cried Hiawatha
In the solitary forest,
By the rushing Taquamenaw,
When the birds were singing gayly,
In the Moon of Leaves were singing,
And the sun, from sleep awaking, 20
Started up and said, 'Behold me!
Gheezis, the great Sun, behold me!'
 And the tree with all its branches
Rustled in the breeze of morning,
Saying, with a sigh of patience,
'Take my cloak, O Hiawatha!'
 With his knife the tree he girdled
Just beneath its lowest branches,
Just above the roots, he cut it,
Till the sap came oozing outward; 30
Down the trunk, from top to bottom,
Sheer he cleft the bark asunder,
With a wooden wedge he raised it,
Stripped it from the trunk unbroken.
 'Give me of your boughs, O Cedar!
Of your strong and pliant branches,
My canoe to make more steady,
Make more strong and firm beneath me!'
 Through the summit of the Cedar
Went a sound, a cry of horror, 40
Went a murmur of resistance;
But it whispered, bending downward,
'Take my boughs, O Hiawatha!'
 Down he hewed the boughs of cedar,
Shaped them straightway to a frame-work,
Like two bows he formed and shaped them,
Like two bended bows together.
 'Give me of your roots, O Tamarack!
Of your fibrous roots, O Larch-tree!
My canoe to bind together, 50
So to bind the ends together

That the water may not enter,
That the river may not wet me!'
 And the Larch, with all its fibres,
Shivered in the air of morning,
Touched his forehead with its tassels,
Said, with one long sigh of sorrow,
'Take them all, O Hiawatha!'
 From the earth he tore the fibres,
Tore the tough roots of the Larch-tree, 60
Closely sewed the bark together,
Bound it closely to the frame-work.
 'Give me of your balm, O Fir-tree!
Of your balsam and your resin,
So to close the seams together
That the water may not enter,
That the river may not wet me!'
 And the Fir-tree, tall and sombre,
Sobbed through all its robes of darkness,
Rattled like a shore with pebbles, 70
Answered wailing, answered weeping,
'Take my balm, O Hiawatha!'
 And he took the tears of balsam,
Took the resin of the Fir-tree,
Smeared therewith each seam and fissure,
Made each crevice safe from water.
 'Give me of your quills, O Hedgehog!
All your quills, O Kagh, the Hedgehog!
I will make a necklace of them,
Make a girdle for my beauty, 80
And two stars to deck her bosom!'
 From a hollow tree the Hedgehog
With his sleepy eyes looked at him,
Shot his shining quills, like arrows,
Saying with a drowsy murmur,
Through the tangle of his whiskers,
'Take my quills, O Hiawatha!'
 From the ground the quills he gathered,
All the little shining arrows,
Stained them red and blue and yellow, 90
With the juice of roots and berries;
Into his canoe he wrought them,
Round its waist a shining girdle,
Round its bows a gleaming necklace,
On its breast two stars resplendent.
 Thus the Birch Canoe was builded
In the valley, by the river,
In the bosom of the forest;
And the forest's life was in it,
All its mystery and its magic, 100
All the lightness of the birch-tree,
All the toughness of the cedar,
All the larch's supple sinews;
And it floated on the river
Like a yellow leaf in Autumn,
Like a yellow water-lily.

Paddles none had Hiawatha,
Paddles none he had or needed,
For his thoughts as paddles served him,
And his wishes served to guide him;   110
Swift or slow at will he glided,
Veered to right or left at pleasure.

  Then he called aloud to Kwasind,
To his friend, the strong man, Kwasind,
Saying, ' Help me clear this river
Of its sunken logs and sand-bars.'

  Straight into the river Kwasind
Plunged as if he were an otter,
Dived as if he were a beaver,
Stood up to his waist in water,   120
To his arm-pits in the river,
Swam and shouted in the river,
Tugged at sunken logs and branches,
With his hands he scooped the sand-bars,
With his feet the ooze and tangle.

  And thus sailed my Hiawatha
Down the rushing Taquamenaw,
Sailed through all its bends and windings,
Sailed through all its deeps and shallows,
While his friend, the strong man, Kwa-
      sind,   130
Swam the deeps, the shallows waded.

  Up and down the river went they,
In and out among its islands,
Cleared its bed of root and sand-bar,
Dragged the dead trees from its channel,
Made its passage safe and certain,
Made a pathway for the people,
From its springs among the mountains,
To the waters of Pauwating,
To the bay of Taquamenaw.   140

VIII

HIAWATHA'S FISHING

FORTH upon the Gitche Gumee,
On the shining Big-Sea-Water,
With his fishing-line of cedar,
Of the twisted bark of cedar,
Forth to catch the sturgeon Nahma,
Mishe-Nahma, King of Fishes,
In his birch canoe exulting
All alone went Hiawatha.

  Through the clear, transparent water
He could see the fishes swimming   10
Far down in the depths below him;
See the yellow perch, the Sahwa,
Like a sunbeam in the water,
See the Shawgashee, the craw-fish,

Like a spider on the bottom,
On the white and sandy bottom.

  At the stern sat Hiawatha,
With his fishing-line of cedar;
In his plumes the breeze of morning
Played as in the hemlock branches;   20
On the bows, with tail erected,
Sat the squirrel, Adjidaumo;
In his fur the breeze of morning
Played as in the prairie grasses.

  On the white sand of the bottom
Lay the monster Mishe-Nahma,
Lay the sturgeon, King of Fishes;
Through his gills he breathed the water,
With his fins he fanned and winnowed,
With his tail he swept the sand-floor.   30

  There he lay in all his armor;
On each side a shield to guard him,
Plates of bone upon his forehead,
Down his sides and back and shoulders
Plates of bone with spines projecting!
Painted was he with his war-paints,
Stripes of yellow, red, and azure,
Spots of brown and spots of sable;
And he lay there on the bottom,
Fanning with his fins of purple,   40
As above him Hiawatha
In his birch canoe came sailing,
With his fishing-line of cedar.

  ' Take my bait,' cried Hiawatha,
Down into the depths beneath him,
' Take my bait, O Sturgeon, Nahma!
Come up from below the water,
Let us see which is the stronger!'
And he dropped his line of cedar
Through the clear, transparent water,   50
Waited vainly for an answer,
Long sat waiting for an answer,
And repeating loud and louder,
' Take my bait, O King of Fishes!'

  Quiet lay the sturgeon, Nahma,
Fanning slowly in the water,
Looking up at Hiawatha,
Listening to his call and clamor,
His unnecessary tumult,
Till he wearied of the shouting;   60
And he said to the Kenozha,
To the pike, the Maskenozha,
' Take the bait of this rude fellow,
Break the line of Hiawatha!'

  In his fingers Hiawatha
Felt the loose line jerk and tighten;
As he drew it in, it tugged so
That the birch canoe stood endwise,
Like a birch log in the water.

With the squirrel, Adjidaumo,   70
Perched and frisking on the summit.
    Full of scorn was Hiawatha
When he saw the fish rise upward,
Saw the pike, the Maskenozha,
Coming nearer, nearer to him,
And he shouted through the water,
'Esa! esa! shame upon you!
You are but the pike, Kenozha,
You are not the fish I wanted,
You are not the King of Fishes!'   80
    Reeling downward to the bottom
Sank the pike in great confusion,
And the mighty sturgeon, Nahma,
Said to Ugudwash, the sun-fish,
To the bream, with scales of crimson,
'Take the bait of this great boaster,
Break the line of Hiawatha!'
    Slowly upward, wavering, gleaming,
Rose the Ugudwash, the sun-fish,
Seized the line of Hiawatha,   90
Swung with all his weight upon it,
Made a whirlpool in the water,
Whirled the birch canoe in circles,
Round and round in gurgling eddies,
Till the circles in the water
Reached the far-off sandy beaches,
Till the water-flags and rushes
Nodded on the distant margins.
    But when Hiawatha saw him
Slowly rising through the water,   100
Lifting up his disk refulgent,
Loud he shouted in derision,
'Esa! esa! shame upon you!
You are Ugudwash, the sun-fish,
You are not the fish I wanted,
You are not the King of Fishes!'
    Slowly downward, wavering, gleaming,
Sank the Ugudwash, the sun-fish,
And again the sturgeon, Nahma,
Heard the shout of Hiawatha,   110
Heard his challenge of defiance,
The unnecessary tumult,
Ringing far across the water.
    From the white sand of the bottom
Up he rose with angry gesture,
Quivering in each nerve and fibre,
Clashing all his plates of armor,
Gleaming bright with all his war-paint;
In his wrath he darted upward,
Flashing leaped into the sunshine,   120
Opened his great jaws, and swallowed
Both canoe and Hiawatha.
    Down into that darksome cavern
Plunged the headlong Hiawatha,

As a log on some black river
Shoots and plunges down the rapids,
Found himself in utter darkness,
Groped about in helpless wonder,
Till he felt a great heart beating,
Throbbing in that utter darkness.   130
    And he smote it in his anger,
With his fist, the heart of Nahma,
Felt the mighty King of Fishes
Shudder through each nerve and fibre,
Heard the water gurgle round him
As he leaped and staggered through it,
Sick at heart, and faint and weary.
    Crosswise then did Hiawatha
Drag his birch-canoe for safety,
Lest from out the jaws of Nahma,   140
In the turmoil and confusion,
Forth he might be hurled and perish.
And the squirrel, Adjidaumo,
Frisked and chattered very gayly,
Toiled and tugged with Hiawatha
Till the labor was completed.
    Then said Hiawatha to him,
'O my little friend, the squirrel,
Bravely have you toiled to help me ;
Take the thanks of Hiawatha,   150
And the name which now he gives you;
For hereafter and forever
Boys shall call you Adjidaumo,
Tail-in-air the boys shall call you !'
    And again the sturgeon, Nahma,
Gasped and quivered in the water,
Then was still, and drifted landward
Till he grated on the pebbles,
Till the listening Hiawatha
Heard him grate upon the margin,   160
Felt him strand upon the pebbles,
Knew that Nahma, King of Fishes,
Lay there dead upon the margin.
    Then he heard a clang and flapping,
As of many wings assembling,
Heard a screaming and confusion,
As of birds of prey contending,
Saw a gleam of light above him,
Shining through the ribs of Nahma,
Saw the glittering eyes of sea-gulls,   170
Of Kayoshk, the sea-gulls, peering,
Gazing at him through the opening,
Heard them saying to each other,
''T is our brother, Hiawatha !'
    And he shouted from below them,
Cried exulting from the caverns:
'O ye sea-gulls ! O my brothers !
I have slain the sturgeon, Nahma;
Make the rifts a little larger,

With your claws the openings widen,   180
Set me free from this dark prison,
And henceforward and forever
Men shall speak of your achievements,
Calling you Kayoshk, the sea-gulls,
Yes, Kayoshk, the Noble Scratchers !'
        And the wild and clamorous sea-gulls
Toiled with beak and claws together,
Made the rifts and openings wider
In the mighty ribs of Nahma,
And from peril and from prison,   190
From the body of the sturgeon,
From the peril of the water,
They released my Hiawatha.
        He was standing near his wigwam,
On the margin of the water,
And he called to old Nokomis,
Called and beckoned to Nokomis,
Pointed to the sturgeon, Nahma,
Lying lifeless on the pebbles,
With the sea-gulls feeding on him.   200
' I have slain the Mishe-Nahma,
Slain the King of Fishes !' said he;
' Look ! the sea-gulls feed upon him,
Yes, my friends Kayoshk, the sea-gulls;
Drive them not away, Nokomis,
They have saved me from great peril
In the body of the sturgeon,
Wait until their meal is ended,
Till their craws are full with feasting,
Till they homeward fly, at sunset,   210
To their nests among the marshes;
Then bring all your pots and kettles,
And make oil for us in Winter.'
        And she waited till the sun set,
Till the pallid moon, the Night-sun,
Rose above the tranquil water,
Till Kayoshk, the sated sea-gulls,
From their banquet rose with clamor,
And across the fiery sunset
Winged their way to far-off islands,   220
To their nests among the rushes.
        To his sleep went Hiawatha,
And Nokomis to her labor,
Toiling patient in the moonlight,
Till the sun and moon changed places,
Till the sky was red with sunrise,
And Kayoshk, the hungry sea-gulls,
Came back from the reedy islands,
Clamorous for their morning banquet.
Three whole days and nights alternate   230
Old Nokomis and the sea-gulls
Stripped the oily flesh of Nahma,
Till the waves washed through the rib-
        bones,

Till the sea-gulls came no longer,
And upon the sands lay nothing
But the skeleton of Nahma.

IX

HIAWATHA AND THE PEARL-FEATHER

On the shores of Gitche Gumee,
Of the shining Big-Sea-Water,
Stood Nokomis, the old woman,
Pointing with her finger westward,
O'er the water pointing westward,
To the purple clouds of sunset.
        Fiercely the red sun descending
Burned his way along the heavens,
Set the sky on fire behind him,
As war-parties, when retreating,   10
Burn the prairies on their war-trail;
And the moon, the Night-sun, eastward,
Suddenly starting from his ambush,
Followed fast those bloody footprints,
Followed in that fiery war-trail,
With its glare upon his features.
        And Nokomis, the old woman,
Pointing with her finger westward,
Spake these words to Hiawatha:
' Yonder dwells the great Pearl-Feather,   20
Megissogwon, the Magician,
Manito of Wealth and Wampum,
Guarded by his fiery serpents,
Guarded by the black pitch-water.
You can see his fiery serpents,
The Kenabeek, the great serpents,
Coiling, playing in the water;
You can see the black pitch-water
Stretching far away beyond them,
To the purple clouds of sunset !   30
        ' He it was who slew my father,
By his wicked wiles and cunning,
When he from the moon descended,
When he came on earth to seek me.
He, the mightiest of Magicians,
Sends the fever from the marshes,
Sends the pestilential vapors,
Sends the poisonous exhalations,
Sends the white fog from the fen-lands,
Sends disease and death among us !   40
        ' Take your bow, O Hiawatha,
Take your arrows, jasper-headed,
Take your war-club, Puggawaugun,
And your mittens, Minjekahwun,
And your birch-canoe for sailing,
And the oil of Mishe-Nahma,
So to smear its sides, that swiftly

You may pass the black pitch-water;
Slay this merciless magician,
Save the people from the fever   50
That he breathes across the fen-lands,
And avenge my father's murder!'
  Straightway then my Hiawatha
Armed himself with all his war-gear,
Launched his birch-canoe for sailing;
With his palm its sides he patted,
Said with glee, 'Cheemaun, my darling,
O my Birch-canoe! leap forward,
Where you see the fiery serpents,
Where you see the black pitch-water!'   60
  Forward leaped Cheemaun exulting,
And the noble Hiawatha
Sang his war-song wild and woful,
And above him the war-eagle,
The Keneu, the great war-eagle,
Master of all fowls with feathers,
Screamed and hurtled through the heavens.
  Soon he reached the fiery serpents,
The Kenabeek, the great serpents,
Lying huge upon the water,   70
Sparkling, rippling in the water,
Lying coiled across the passage,
With their blazing crests uplifted,
Breathing fiery fogs and vapors,
So that none could pass beyond them.
  But the fearless Hiawatha
Cried aloud, and spake in this wise,
'Let me pass my way, Kenabeek,
Let me go upon my journey!'
And they answered, hissing fiercely,   80
With their fiery breath made answer:
'Back, go back! O Shaugodaya!
Back to old Nokomis, Faint-heart!'
  Then the angry Hiawatha
Raised his mighty bow of ash-tree,
Seized his arrows, jasper-headed,
Shot them fast among the serpents;
Every twanging of the bow-string
Was a war-cry and a death-cry,
Every whizzing of an arrow   90
Was a death-song of Kenabeek.
  Weltering in the bloody water,
Dead lay all the fiery serpents,
And among them Hiawatha
Harmless sailed, and cried exulting:
'Onward, O Cheemaun, my darling!
Onward to the black pitch-water!'
  Then he took the oil of Nahma,
And the bows and sides anointed,
Smeared them well with oil, that swiftly
He might pass the black pitch-water.   101
  All night long he sailed upon it,

Sailed upon that sluggish water,
Covered with its mould of ages,
Black with rotting water-rushes,
Rank with flags and leaves of lilies,
Stagnant, lifeless, dreary, dismal,
Lighted by the shimmering moonlight,
And by will-o'-the-wisps illumined,
Fires by ghosts of dead men kindled,   110
In their weary night-encampments.
  All the air was white with moonlight,
All the water black with shadow,
And around him the Suggema,
The mosquito, sang his war-song,
And the fire-flies, Wah-wah-taysee,
Waved their torches to mislead him;
And the bull-frog, the Dahinda,
Thrust his head into the moonlight,
Fixed his yellow eyes upon him,   120
Sobbed and sank beneath the surface;
And anon a thousand whistles,
Answered over all the fen-lands,
And the heron, the Shuh-shuh-gah,
Far off on the reedy margin,
Heralded the hero's coming.
  Westward thus fared Hiawatha,
Toward the realm of Megissogwon,
Toward the land of the Pearl-Feather,
Till the level moon stared at him,   130
In his face stared pale and haggard,
Till the sun was hot behind him,
Till it burned upon his shoulders,
And before him on the upland
He could see the Shining Wigwam
Of the Manito of Wampum,
Of the mightiest of Magicians.
  Then once more Cheemaun he patted,
To his birch-canoe said, 'Onward!'
And it stirred in all its fibres,   140
And with one great bound of triumph
Leaped across the water-lilies,
Leaped through tangled flags and rushes,
And upon the beach beyond them
Dry-shod landed Hiawatha.
  Straight he took his bow of ash-tree,
On the sand one end he rested,
With his knee he pressed the middle,
Stretched the faithful bow-string tighter,
Took an arrow, jasper-headed,   150
Shot it at the Shining Wigwam,
Sent it singing as a herald,
As a bearer of his message,
Of his challenge loud and lofty:
'Come forth from your lodge, Pearl-Fea-
          ther!
Hiawatha waits your coming!'

Straightway from the Shining Wigwam
Came the mighty Megissogwon,
Tall of stature, broad of shoulder,
Dark and terrible in aspect,   160
Clad from head to foot in wampum,
Armed with all his warlike weapons,
Painted like the sky of morning,
Streaked with crimson, blue, and yel-
    low,
Crested with great eagle-feathers,
Streaming upward, streaming outward.
' Well I know you, Hiawatha ! '
Cried he in a voice of thunder,
In a tone of loud derision.
' Hasten back, O Shaugodaya !   170
Hasten back among the women,
Back to old Nokomis, Faint-heart !
I will slay you as you stand there,
As of old I slew her father ! '
    But my Hiawatha answered,
Nothing daunted, fearing nothing:
' Big words do not smite like war-clubs,
Boastful breath is not a bow-string,
Taunts are not so sharp as arrows,
Deeds are better things than words are, 180
Actions mightier than boastings ! '
    Then began the greatest battle
That the sun had ever looked on,
That the war-birds ever witnessed.
All a summer's day it lasted,
From the sunrise to the sunset;
For the shafts of Hiawatha
Harmless hit the shirt of wampum,
Harmless fell the blows he dealt it
With his mittens, Minjekahwun,   190
Harmless fell the heavy war-club;
It could dash the rocks asunder,
But it could not break the meshes
Of that magic shirt of wampum.
    Till at sunset Hiawatha,
Leaning on his bow of ash-tree,
Wounded, weary, and desponding,
With his mighty war-club broken,
With his mittens torn and tattered,
And three useless arrows only,   200
Paused to rest beneath a pine-tree,
From whose branches trailed the mosses,
And whose trunk was coated over
With the Dead-man's Moccasin-leather,
With the fungus white and yellow.
    Suddenly from the boughs above him
Sang the Mama, the woodpecker:
' Aim your arrows, Hiawatha,
At the head of Megissogwon,
Strike the tuft of hair upon it,   210

At their roots the long black tresses;
There alone can he be wounded ! '
    Winged with feathers, tipped with jasper,
Swift flew Hiawatha's arrow,
Just as Megissogwon, stooping,
Raised a heavy stone to throw it.
Full upon the crown it struck him,
At the roots of his long tresses,
And he reeled and staggered forward,
Plunging like a wounded bison,   220
Yes, like Pezhekee, the bison,
When the snow is on the prairie.
    Swifter flew the second arrow,
In the pathway of the other,
Piercing deeper than the other,
Wounding sorer than the other;
And the knees of Megissogwon
Shook like windy reeds beneath him,
Bent and trembled like the rushes.
    But the third and latest arrow   230
Swiftest flew, and wounded sorest,
And the mighty Megissogwon
Saw the fiery eyes of Pauguk,
Saw the eyes of Death glare at him,
Heard his voice call in the darkness;
At the feet of Hiawatha
Lifeless lay the great Pearl-Feather,
Lay the mightiest of Magicians.
    Then the grateful Hiawatha
Called the Mama, the woodpecker,   240
From his perch among the branches
Of the melancholy pine-tree,
And, in honor of his service,
Stained with blood the tuft of feathers
On the little head of Mama;
Even to this day he wears it,
Wears the tuft of crimson feathers,
As a symbol of his service.
    Then he stripped the shirt of wampum
From the back of Megissogwon,   250
As a trophy of the battle,
As a signal of his conquest.
On the shore he left the body,
Half on land and half in water,
In the sand his feet were buried,
And his face was in the water.
And above him, wheeled and clamored
The Keneu, the great war-eagle,
Sailing round in narrower circles,
Hovering nearer, nearer, nearer.   260
    From the wigwam Hiawatha
Bore the wealth of Megissogwon,
All his wealth of skins and wampum,
Furs of bison and of beaver,
Furs of sable and of ermine.

Wampum belts and strings and pouches,
Quivers wrought with beads of wampum,
Filled with arrows, silver-headed.
   Homeward then he sailed exulting,   269
Homeward through the black pitch-water,
Homeward through the weltering serpents
With the trophies of the battle,
With a shout and song of triumph.
   On the shore stood old Nokomis,
On the shore stood Chibiabos,
And the very strong man, Kwasind,
Waiting for the hero's coming,
Listening to his songs of triumph.
And the people of the village
Welcomed him with songs and dances,   280
Made a joyous feast, and shouted:
' Honor be to Hiawatha !
He has slain the great Pearl-Feather,
Slain the mightiest of Magicians,
Him, who sent the fiery fever,
Sent the white fog from the fen-lands,
Sent disease and death among us ! '
   Ever dear to Hiawatha
Was the memory of Mama !
And in token of his friendship,   290
As a mark of his remembrance,
He adorned and decked his pipe-stem
With the crimson tuft of feathers,
With the blood-red crest of Mama.
But the wealth of Megissogwon,
All the trophies of the battle,
He divided with his people,
Shared it equally among them.

                    X

              HIAWATHA'S WOOING

' As unto the bow the cord is,
So unto the man is woman;
Though she bends him, she obeys him,
Though she draws him, yet she follows;
Useless each without the other ! '
   Thus the youthful Hiawatha
Said within himself and pondered,
Much perplexed by various feelings,
Listless, longing, hoping, fearing,
Dreaming still of Minnehaha,   10
Of the lovely Laughing Water,
In the land of the Dacotahs.
   ' Wed a maiden of your people,'
Warning said the old Nokomis;
' Go not eastward, go not westward,
For a stranger, whom we know not !

Like a fire upon the hearth-stone
Is a neighbor's homely daughter,
Like the starlight or the moonlight
Is the handsomest of strangers ! '   20
   Thus dissuading spake Nokomis,
And my Hiawatha answered
Only this: ' Dear old Nokomis,
Very pleasant is the firelight,
But I like the starlight better,
Better do I like the moonlight : '
   Gravely then said old Nokomis:
' Bring not here an idle maiden,
Bring not here a useless woman,
Hands unskilful, feet unwilling;   30
Bring a wife with nimble fingers,
Heart and hand that move together,
Feet that run on willing errands ! '
   Smiling answered Hiawatha:
' In the land of the Dacotahs
Lives the Arrow-maker's daughter,
Minnehaha, Laughing Water,
Handsomest of all the women.
I will bring her to your wigwam,
She shall run upon your errands,   40
Be your starlight, moonlight, firelight,
Be the sunlight of my people ! '
   Still dissuading said Nokomis:
' Bring not to my lodge a stranger
From the land of the Dacotahs !
Very fierce are the Dacotahs,
Often is there war between us,
There are feuds yet unforgotten,
Wounds that ache and still may open ! '
   Laughing answered Hiawatha: 50
' For that reason, if no other,
Would I wed the fair Dacotah,
That our tribes might be united,
That old feuds might be forgotten,
And old wounds be healed forever ! '
   Thus departed Hiawatha
To the land of the Dacotahs,
To the land of handsome women;
Striding over moor and meadow,
Through interminable forests,   60
Through uninterrupted silence.
   With his moccasins of magic,
At each stride a mile he measured;
Yet the way seemed long before him,
And his heart outran his footsteps;
And he journeyed without resting,
Till he heard the cataract's laughter,
Heard the Falls of Minnehaha
Calling to him through the silence.
' Pleasant is the sound ! ' he murmured,   70
' Pleasant is the voice that calls me ! '

On the outskirts of the forests,
'Twixt the shadow and the sunshine,
Herds of fallow deer were feeding,
But they saw not Hiawatha;
To his bow he whispered, ' Fail not ! '
To his arrow whispered, ' Swerve not ! '
Sent it singing on its errand,
To the red heart of the roebuck;
Threw the deer across his shoulder,   80
And sped forward without pausing.

At the doorway of his wigwam
Sat the ancient Arrow-maker,
In the land of the Dacotahs,
Making arrow-heads of jasper,
Arrow-heads of chalcedony.
At his side, in all her beauty,
Sat the lovely Minnehaha,
Sat his daughter, Laughing Water,
Plaiting mats of flags and rushes;   90
Of the past the old man's thoughts were,
And the maiden's of the future.

He was thinking, as he sat there,
Of the days when with such arrows
He had struck the deer and bison,
On the Muskoday, the meadow;
Shot the wild goose, flying southward,
On the wing, the clamorous Wawa;
Thinking of the great war-parties,
How they came to buy his arrows,   100
Could not fight without his arrows.
Ah, no more such noble warriors
Could be found on earth as they were !
Now the men were all like women,
Only used their tongues for weapons !

She was thinking of a hunter,
From another tribe and country,
Young and tall and very handsome,
Who one morning, in the Spring-time,
Came to buy her father's arrows,   110
Sat and rested in the wigwam,
Lingered long about the doorway,
Looking back as he departed.
She had heard her father praise him,
Praise his courage and his wisdom;
Would he come again for arrows
To the Falls of Minnehaha ?
On the mat her hands lay idle,
And her eyes were very dreamy.

Through their thoughts they heard a foot-
   step,   120
Heard a rustling in the branches,
And with glowing cheek and forehead,
With the deer upon his shoulders,
Suddenly from out the woodlands
Hiawatha stood before them.

Straight the ancient Arrow-maker
Looked up gravely from his labor,
Laid aside the unfinished arrow,
Bade him enter at the doorway,
Saying, as he rose to meet him,   130
' Hiawatha, you are welcome ! '
   At the feet of Laughing Water
Hiawatha laid his burden,
Threw the red deer from his shoulders;
And the maiden looked up at him,
Looked up from her mat of rushes,
Said with gentle look and accent,
' You are welcome, Hiawatha ! '
   Very spacious was the wigwam,
Made of deer-skins dressed and whitened,   140
With the Gods of the Dacotahs
Drawn and painted on its curtains,
And so tall the doorway, hardly
Hiawatha stooped to enter,
Hardly touched his eagle-feathers
As he entered at the doorway.

Then uprose the Laughing Water,
From the ground fair Minnehaha,
Laid aside her mat unfinished,
Brought forth food and set before them,   150
Water brought them from the brooklet,
Gave them food in earthen vessels,
Gave them drink in bowls of bass-wood,
Listened while the guest was speaking,
Listened while her father answered,
But not once her lips she opened,
Not a single word she uttered.

Yes, as in a dream she listened
To the words of Hiawatha,
As he talked of old Nokomis,   160
Who had nursed him in his childhood,
As he told of his companions,
Chibiabos, the musician,
And the very strong man, Kwasind,
And of happiness and plenty
In the land of the Ojibways,
In the pleasant land and peaceful.

' After many years of warfare,
Many years of strife and bloodshed,
There is peace between the Ojibways   170
And the tribe of the Dacotahs.'
Thus continued Hiawatha,
And then added, speaking slowly,
' That this peace may last forever,
And our hands be clasped more closely,
And our hearts be more united,
Give me as my wife this maiden,
Minnehaha, Laughing Water,
Loveliest of Dacotah Women ! '
   And the ancient Arrow-maker   180

Paused a moment ere he answered,
Smoked a little while in silence,
Looked at Hiawatha proudly,
Fondly looked at Laughing Water,
And made answer very gravely:
' Yes, if Minnehaha wishes;
Let your heart speak, Minnehaha ! '
    And the lovely Laughing Water
Seemed more lovely as she stood there,
Neither willing nor reluctant,   190
As she went to Hiawatha,
Softly took the seat beside him,
While she said, and blushed to say it,
' I will follow you, my husband ! '
    This was Hiawatha's wooing !
Thus it was he won the daughter
Of the ancient Arrow-maker,
In the land of the Dacotahs !
    From the wigwam he departed,
Leading with him Laughing Water;   200
Hand in hand they went together,
Through the woodland and the meadow,
Left the old man standing lonely
At the doorway of his wigwam,
Heard the Falls of Minnehaha
Calling to them from the distance,
Crying to them from afar off,
' Fare thee well, O Minnehaha ! '
    And the ancient Arrow-maker
Turned again unto his labor,   210
Sat down by his sunny doorway,
Murmuring to himself, and saying:
' Thus it is our daughters leave us,
Those we love, and those who love us !
Just when they have learned to help us,
When we are old and lean upon them,
Comes a youth with flaunting feathers,
With his flute of reeds, a stranger
Wanders piping through the village,
Beckons to the fairest maiden,   220
And she follows where he leads her,
Leaving all things for the stranger ! '
    Pleasant was the journey homeward,
Through interminable forests,
Over meadow, over mountain,
Over river, hill, and hollow.
Short it seemed to Hiawatha,
Though they journeyed very slowly,
Though his pace he checked and slackened
To the steps of Laughing Water.   230
    Over wide and rushing rivers
In his arms he bore the maiden;
Light he thought her as a feather,
As the plume upon his head-gear;
Cleared the tangled pathway for her,

Bent aside the swaying branches,
Made at night a lodge of branches,
And a bed with boughs of hemlock,
And a fire before the doorway
With the dry cones of the pine-tree.   240
    All the travelling winds went with them,
O'er the meadows, through the forest;
All the stars of night looked at them,
Watched with sleepless eyes their slumber;
From his ambush in the oak-tree
Peeped the squirrel, Adjidaumo,
Watched with eager eyes the lovers;
And the rabbit, the Wabasso,
Scampered from the path before them,
Peering, peeping from his burrow,   250
Sat erect upon his haunches,
Watched with curious eyes the lovers.
    Pleasant was the journey homeward !
All the birds sang loud and sweetly
Songs of happiness and heart's-ease;
Sang the bluebird, the Owaissa,
' Happy are you, Hiawatha,
Having such a wife to love you ! '
Sang the robin, the Opechee,
' Happy are you, Laughing Water,   260
Having such a noble husband ! '
    From the sky the sun benignant
Looked upon them through the branches,
Saying to them, ' O my children,
Love is sunshine, hate is shadow,
Life is checkered shade and sunshine,
Rule by love, O Hiawatha ! '
    From the sky the moon looked at them,
Filled the lodge with mystic splendors,
Whispered to them, ' O my children,   270
Day is restless, night is quiet,
Man imperious, woman feeble;
Half is mine, although I follow;
Rule by patience, Laughing Water ! '
    Thus it was they journeyed homeward;
Thus it was that Hiawatha
To the lodge of old Nokomis
Brought the moonlight, starlight, firelight,
Brought the sunshine of his people,
Minnehaha, Laughing Water,   280
Handsomest of all the women
In the land of the Dacotahs,
In the land of handsome women.

XI

HIAWATHA'S WEDDING-FEAST

You shall hear how Pau-Puk-Keewis,
How the handsome Yenadizze

Danced at Hiawatha's wedding;
How the gentle Chibiabos,
He the sweetest of musicians,
Sang his songs of love and longing;
How Iagoo, the great boaster,
He the marvellous story-teller,
Told his tales of strange adventure,
That the feast might be more joyous,   10
That the time might pass more gayly,
And the guests be more contented.
   Sumptuous was the feast Nokomis
Made at Hiawatha's wedding;
All the bowls were made of bass-wood,
White and polished very smoothly,
All the spoons of horn of bison,
Black and polished very smoothly.
   She had sent through all the village
Messengers with wands of willow,   20
As a sign of invitation,
As a token of the feasting;
And the wedding guests assembled,
Clad in all their richest raiment,
Robes of fur and belts of wampum,
Splendid with their paint and plumage,
Beautiful with beads and tassels.
   First they ate the sturgeon, Nahma,
And the pike, the Maskenozha,
Caught and cooked by old Nokomis;   30
Then on pemican they feasted,
Pemican and buffalo marrow,
Haunch of deer and hump of bison,
Yellow cakes of the Mondamin,
And the wild rice of the river.
   But the gracious Hiawatha,
And the lovely Laughing Water,
And the careful old Nokomis,
Tasted not the food before them,
Only waited on the others,   40
Only served their guests in silence.
   And when all the guests had finished,
Old Nokomis, brisk and busy,
From an ample pouch of otter,
Filled the red-stone pipes for smoking
With tobacco from the South-land,
Mixed with bark of the red willow,
And with herbs and leaves of fragrance.
   Then she said, 'O Pau-Puk-Keewis,
Dance for us your merry dances,   50
Dance the Beggar's Dance to please us,
That the feast may be more joyous,
That the time may pass more gayly,
And our guests be more contented!'
   Then the handsome Pau-Puk-Keewis,
He the idle Yenadizze,
He the merry mischief-maker,

Whom the people called the Storm-Fool,
Rose among the guests assembled.
   Skilled was he in sports and pastimes,   60
In the merry dance of snow-shoes,
In the play of quoits and ball-play ;
Skilled was he in games of hazard,
In all games of skill and hazard,
Pugasaing, the Bowl and Counters,
Kuntassoo, the Game of Plum-stones.
Though the warriors called him Faint-
      Heart,
Called him coward, Shaugodaya,
Idler, gambler, Yenadizze,
Little heeded he their jesting,   70
Little cared he for their insults,
For the women and the maidens
Loved the handsome Pau-Puk-Keewis.
   He was dressed in shirt of doeskin,
White and soft, and fringed with ermine,
All inwrought with beads of wampum ;
He was dressed in deer-skin leggings,
Fringed with hedgehog quills and ermine,
And in moccasins of buck-skin,   79
Thick with quills and beads embroidered.
On his head were plumes of swan's down,
On his heels were tails of foxes,
In one hand a fan of feathers,
And a pipe was in the other.
   Barred with streaks of red and yellow,
Streaks of blue and bright vermilion,
Shone the face of Pau-Puk-Keewis.
From his forehead fell his tresses,
Smooth, and parted like a woman's,
Shining bright with oil, and plaited,   90
Hung with braids of scented grasses,
As among the guests assembled,
To the sound of flutes and singing,
To the sound of drums and voices,
Rose the handsome Pau-Puk-Keewis,
And began his mystic dances.
   First he danced a solemn measure,
Very slow in step and gesture,
In and out among the pine-trees,
Through the shadows and the sunshine,   100
Treading softly like a panther.
Then more swiftly and still swifter,
Whirling, spinning round in circles,
Leaping o'er the guests assembled,
Eddying round and round the wigwam,
Till the leaves went whirling with him,
Till the dust and wind together
Swept in eddies round about him.
   Then along the sandy margin
Of the lake, the Big-Sea-Water,   110
On he sped with frenzied gestures,

Stamped upon the sand, and tossed it
Wildly in the air around him;
Till the wind became a whirlwind,
Till the sand was blown and sifted
Like great snowdrifts o'er the landscape,
Heaping all the shores with Sand Dunes,
Sand Hills of the Nagow Wudjoo ! [1]
    Thus the merry Pau-Puk-Keewis
Danced his Beggar's Dance to please
    them,   120
And, returning, sat down laughing
There among the guests assembled,
Sat and fanned himself serenely
With his fan of turkey-feathers.
    Then they said to Chibiabos,
To the friend of Hiawatha,
To the sweetest of all singers,
To the best of all musicians,
' Sing to us, O Chibiabos !
Songs of love and songs of longing,   130
That the feast may be more joyous,
That the time may pass more gayly,
And our guests be more contented ! '
    And the gentle Chibiabos
Sang in accents sweet and tender,
Sang in tones of deep emotion,
Songs of love and songs of longing;
Looking still at Hiawatha,
Looking at fair Laughing Water,
Sang he softly, sang in this wise: 140
    ' Onaway ! Awake, beloved !
Thou the wild-flower of the forest !
Thou the wild-bird of the prairie !
Thou with eyes so soft and fawn-like !
    ' If thou only lookest at me,
I am happy, I am happy,
As the lilies of the prairie,
When they feel the dew upon them !
    ' Sweet thy breath is as the fragrance
Of the wild-flowers in the morning,   150
As their fragrance is at evening,
In the Moon when leaves are falling.
    ' Does not all the blood within me
Leap to meet thee, leap to meet thee,
As the springs to meet the sunshine,
In the Moon when nights are brightest ?
    ' Onaway ! my heart sings to thee,
Sings with joy when thou art near me,
As the sighing, singing branches
In the pleasant Moon of Strawberries !   160
    ' When thou art not pleased, beloved,

Then my heart is sad and darkened,
As the shining river darkens
When the clouds drop shadows on it !
    ' When thou smilest, my beloved,
Then my troubled heart is brightened,
As in sunshine gleam the ripples
That the cold wind makes in rivers.
    ' Smiles the earth, and smile the waters,
Smile the cloudless skies above us,   170
But I lose the way of smiling
When thou art no longer near me !
    ' I myself, myself ! behold me !
Blood of my beating heart, behold me !
Oh awake, awake, beloved !
Onaway ! awake, beloved ! ' [2]
    Thus the gentle Chibiabos
Sang his song of love and longing;
And Iagoo, the great boaster,
He the marvellous story-teller,   180
He the friend of old Nokomis,
Jealous of the sweet musician,
Jealous of the applause they gave him,
Saw in all the eyes around him,
Saw in all their looks and gestures,
That the wedding guests assembled
Longed to hear his pleasant stories,
His immeasurable falsehoods.
    Very boastful was Iagoo;
Never heard he an adventure   190
But himself had met a greater;
Never any deed of daring
But himself had done a bolder;
Never any marvellous story
But himself could tell a stranger.
    Would you listen to his boasting,
Would you only give him credence,
No one ever shot an arrow
Half so far and high as he had;
Ever caught so many fishes,   200
Ever killed so many reindeer,
Ever trapped so many beaver !
    None could run so fast as he could,
None could dive so deep as he could,
None could swim so far as he could,
None had made so many journeys,
None had seen so many wonders,
As this wonderful Iagoo,
As this marvellous story-teller !
    Thus his name became a by-word   210
And a jest among the people;
And whene'er a boastful hunter
Praised his own address too highly,
Or a warrior, home returning,

---

[1] A description of the *Grand Sable*, or great sand-dunes of Lake Superior, is given in Foster and Whitney's *Report on the Geology of the Lake Superior Land District*, part ii, p. 131. (LONGFELLOW.)

[2] The original of this song may be found in *Littell's Living Age*, vol. xxxv, p. 45. (LONGFELLOW.)

Talked too much of his achievements,
All his hearers cried ' Iagoo !
Here 's Iagoo come among us ! '
    He it was who carved the cradle
Of the little Hiawatha,
Carved its framework out of linden,   220
Bound it strong with reindeer sinews ;
He it was who taught him later
How to make his bows and arrows,
How to make the bows of ash-tree,
And the arrows of the oak-tree.
So among the guests assembled
At my Hiawatha's wedding
Sat Iagoo, old and ugly,
Sat the marvellous story-teller.
    And they said, ' O good Iagoo,   230
Tell us now a tale of wonder,
Tell us of some strange adventure,
That the feast may be more joyous,
That the time may pass more gayly,
And our guests be more contented ! '
    And Iagoo answered straightway,
' You shall hear a tale of wonder,
You shall hear the strange adventures
Of Osseo, the Magician,
From the Evening Star descended.'   240

XII

THE SON OF THE EVENING STAR

CAN it be the sun descending
O'er the level plain of water?
Or the Red Swan floating, flying,
Wounded by the magic arrow,
Staining all the waves with crimson,
With the crimson of its life-blood,
Filling all the air with splendor,
With the splendor of its plumage ?
    Yes; it is the sun descending,
Sinking down into the water;   10
All the sky is stained with purple,
All the water flushed with crimson !
No; it is the Red Swan floating,
Diving down beneath the water;
To the sky its wings are lifted,
With its blood the waves are reddened !
    Over it the Star of Evening
Melts and trembles through the purple,
Hangs suspended in the twilight.
No; it is a bead of wampum   20
On the robes of the Great Spirit
As he passes through the twilight,
Walks in silence through the heavens.

    This with joy beheld Iagoo
And he said in haste: ' Behold it !
See the sacred Star of Evening !
You shall hear a tale of wonder,
Hear the story of Osseo,
Son of the Evening Star, Osseo !
    ' Once, in days no more remembered,   30
Ages nearer the beginning,
When the heavens were closer to us,
And the Gods were more familiar,
In the North-land lived a hunter,
With ten young and comely daughters,
Tall and lithe as wands of willow;
Only Oweenee, the youngest,
She the wilful and the wayward,
She the silent, dreamy maiden,
Was the fairest of the sisters.   40
    ' All these women married warriors,
Married brave and haughty husbands;
Only Oweenee, the youngest,
Laughed and flouted all her lovers,
All her young and handsome suitors,
And then married old Osseo,
Old Osseo, poor and ugly,
Broken with age and weak with coughing,
Always coughing like a squirrel.
    ' Ah, but beautiful within him   50
Was the spirit of Osseo,
From the Evening Star descended,
Star of Evening, Star of Woman,
Star of tenderness and passion !
All its fire was in his bosom,
All its beauty in his spirit,
All its mystery in his being,
All its splendor in his language !
    ' And her lovers, the rejected,
Handsome men with belts of wampum,   60
Handsome men with paint and feathers,
Pointed at her in derision,
Followed her with jest and laughter.
But she said : " I care not for you,
Care not for your belts of wampum,
Care not for your paint and feathers,
Care not for your jests and laughter;
I am happy with Osseo ! "
    ' Once to some great feast invited,
Through the damp and dusk of evening,   70
Walked together the ten sisters,
Walked together with their husbands;
Slowly followed old Osseo,
With fair Oweenee beside him;
All the others chatted gayly,
These two only walked in silence.
    ' At the western sky Osseo
Gazed intent, as if imploring,

Often stopped and gazed imploring
At the trembling Star of Evening,   80
At the tender Star of Woman;
And they heard him murmur softly,
"*Ah, showain nemeshin, Nosa!*
Pity, pity me, my father!"
"Listen!" said the eldest sister,
"He is praying to his father!
What a pity that the old man
Does not stumble in the pathway,
Does not break his neck by falling!"
And they laughed till all the forest   90
Rang with their unseemly laughter.
  'On their pathway through the woodlands
Lay an oak, by storms uprooted,
Lay the great trunk of an oak-tree,
Buried half in leaves and mosses,
Mouldering, crumbling, huge and hollow.
And Osseo, when he saw it,
Gave a shout, a cry of anguish,
Leaped into its yawning cavern,
At one end went in an old man,   100
Wasted, wrinkled, old, and ugly;
From the other came a young man,
Tall and straight and strong and handsome.
  'Thus Osseo was transfigured,
Thus restored to youth and beauty;
But, alas for good Osseo,
And for Oweenee, the faithful!
Strangely, too, was she transfigured.
Changed into a weak old woman,
With a staff she tottered onward,   110
Wasted, wrinkled, old, and ugly!
And the sisters and their husbands
Laughed until the echoing forest
Rang with their unseemly laughter.
  'But Osseo turned not from her,
Walked with slower step beside her,
Took her hand, as brown and withered
As an oak-leaf is in Winter,
Called her sweetheart, Nenemoosha,
Soothed her with soft words of kindness,   120
Till they reached the lodge of feasting,
Till they sat down in the wigwam,
Sacred to the Star of Evening,
To the tender Star of Woman.
  'Wrapt in visions, lost in dreaming,
At the banquet sat Osseo;
All were merry, all were happy,
All were joyous but Osseo.
Neither food nor drink he tasted,
Neither did he speak nor listen,   130
But as one bewildered sat he,
Looking dreamily and sadly,

First at Oweenee, then upward
At the gleaming sky above them.
  'Then a voice was heard, a whisper,
Coming from the starry distance,
Coming from the empty vastness,
Low, and musical, and tender;
And the voice said: "O Osseo!
O my son, my best beloved!   140
Broken are the spells that bound you,
All the charms of the magicians,
All the magic powers of evil;
Come to me; ascend, Osseo!
  '"Taste the food that stands before you:
It is blessed and enchanted,
It has magic virtues in it,
It will change you to a spirit.
All your bowls and all your kettles
Shall be wood and clay no longer;   150
But the bowls be changed to wampum,
And the kettles shall be silver;
They shall shine like shells of scarlet,
Like the fire shall gleam and glimmer.
  '"And the women shall no longer
Bear the dreary doom of labor,
But be changed to birds, and glisten
With the beauty of the starlight,
Painted with the dusky splendors
Of the skies and clouds of evening!"   160
  'What Osseo heard as whispers,
What as words he comprehended,
Was but music to the others,
Music as of birds afar off,
Of the whippoorwill afar off,
Of the lonely Wawonaissa
Singing in the darksome forest.
  'Then the lodge began to tremble,
Straight began to shake and tremble,
And they felt it rising, rising,   170
Slowly through the air ascending,
From the darkness of the tree-tops
Forth into the dewy starlight,
Till it passed the topmost branches;
And behold! the wooden dishes
All were changed to shells of scarlet!
And behold! the earthen kettles
All were changed to bowls of silver!
And the roof-poles of the wigwam
Were as glittering rods of silver,   180
And the roof of bark upon them
As the shining shards of beetles.
  'Then Osseo gazed around him,
And he saw the nine fair sisters,
All the sisters and their husbands,
Changed to birds of various plumage.
Some were jays and some were magpies,

Others thrushes, others blackbirds;
And they hopped, and sang, and twittered,
Perked and fluttered all their feathers,   190
Strutted in their shining plumage,
And their tails like fans unfolded.
'Only Oweenee, the youngest,
Was not changed, but sat in silence,
Wasted, wrinkled, old, and ugly,
Looking sadly at the others;
Till Osseo, gazing upward,
Gave another cry of anguish,
Such a cry as he had uttered
By the oak-tree in the forest.   200
'Then returned her youth and beauty,
And her soiled and tattered garments
Were transformed to robes of ermine,
And her staff became a feather,
Yes, a shining silver feather !
'And again the wigwam trembled,
Swayed and rushed through airy currents,
Through transparent cloud and vapor,
And amid celestial splendors
On the Evening Star alighted,   210
As a snow-flake falls on snow-flake,
As a leaf drops on a river,
As the thistle-down on water.
'Forth with cheerful words of welcome
Came the father of Osseo,
He with radiant locks of silver,
He with eyes serene and tender.
And he said : " My son, Osseo,
Hang the cage of birds you bring there,
Hang the cage with rods of silver,   220
And the birds with glistening feathers,
At the doorway of my wigwam."
'At the door he hung the bird-cage,
And they entered in and gladly
Listened to Osseo's father,
Ruler of the Star of Evening,
As he said : " O my Osseo !
I have had compassion on you,
Given you back your youth and beauty,
Into birds of various plumage   230
Changed your sisters and their husbands;
Changed them thus because they mocked
          you
In the figure of the old man,
In that aspect sad and wrinkled,
Could not see your heart of passion,
Could not see your youth immortal;
Only Oweenee, the faithful,
Saw your naked heart and loved you.
'" In the lodge that glimmers yonder,
In the little star that twinkles   240
Through the vapors, on the left hand,

Lives the envious Evil Spirit,
The Wabeno, the magician,
Who transformed you to an old man.
Take heed lest his beams fall on you,
For the rays he darts around him
Are the power of his enchantment,
Are the arrows that he uses."
'Many years, in peace and quiet,
On the peaceful Star of Evening   250
Dwelt Osseo with his father;
Many years, in song and flutter,
At the doorway of the wigwam,
Hung the cage with rods of silver,
And fair Oweenee, the faithful,
Bore a son unto Osseo,
With the beauty of his mother,
With the courage of his father.
'And the boy grew up and prospered,
And Osseo, to delight him,   260
Made him little bows and arrows,
Opened the great cage of silver,
And let loose his aunts and uncles,
All those birds with glossy feathers,
For his little son to shoot at.
'Round and round they wheeled and
          darted,
Filled the Evening Star with music,
With their songs of joy and freedom;
Filled the Evening Star with splendor,
With the fluttering of their plumage;   270
Till the boy, the little hunter,
Bent his bow and shot an arrow,
Shot a swift and fatal arrow,
And a bird, with shining feathers,
At his feet fell wounded sorely.
'But, O wondrous transformation !
'T was no bird he saw before him,
'T was a beautiful young woman,
With the arrow in her bosom !
'When her blood fell on the planet,   280
On the sacred Star of Evening,
Broken was the spell of magic,
Powerless was the strange enchantment,
And the youth, the fearless bowman,
Suddenly felt himself descending,
Held by unseen hands, but sinking
Downward through the empty spaces,
Downward through the clouds and vapors,
Till he rested on an island,
On an island, green and grassy,   290
Yonder in the Big-Sea-Water.
'After him he saw descending
All the birds with shining feathers,
Fluttering, falling, wafted downward,
Like the painted leaves of Autumn;

And the lodge with poles of silver,
With its roof like wings of beetles,
Like the shining shards of beetles,
By the winds of heaven uplifted,
Slowly sank upon the island,   300
Bringing back the good Osseo,
Bringing Oweenee, the faithful.
  'Then the birds, again transfigured,
Reassumed the shape of mortals,
Took their shape, but not their stature;
They remained as Little People,
Like the pygmies, the Puk-Wudjies,
And on pleasant nights of summer,
When the Evening Star was shining,
Hand in hand they danced together   310
On the island's craggy headlands,
On the sand-beach low and level.
  'Still their glittering lodge is seen there,
On the tranquil Summer evenings,
And upon the shore the fisher
Sometimes hears their happy voices,
Sees them dancing in the starlight!'
  When the story was completed,
When the wondrous tale was ended,
Looking round upon his listeners,   320
Solemnly Iagoo added:
'There are great men, I have known
      such,
Whom their people understand not,
Whom they even make a jest of,
Scoff and jeer at in derision.
From the story of Osseo
Let us learn the fate of jesters!'
  All the wedding guests delighted
Listened to the marvellous story,
Listened laughing and applauding,   330
And they whispered to each other:
'Does he mean himself, I wonder?
And are we the aunts and uncles?'
  Then again sang Chibiabos,
Sang a song of love and longing,
In those accents sweet and tender,
In those tones of pensive sadness,
Sang a maiden's lamentation
For her lover, her Algonquin.
  'When I think of my beloved,   340
Ah me! think of my beloved,
When my heart is thinking of him,
O my sweetheart, my Algonquin!
  'Ah me! when I parted from him,
Round my neck he hung the wampum,
As a pledge, the snow-white wampum,
O my sweetheart, my Algonquin!
  'I will go with you, he whispered,
Ah me! to your native country;

Let me go with you, he whispered,   350
O my sweetheart, my Algonquin!
  'Far away, away, I answered,
Very far away, I answered,
Ah me! is my native country,
O my sweetheart, my Algonquin!
  'When I looked back to behold him,
Where we parted, to behold him,
After me he still was gazing,
O my sweetheart, my Algonquin!
  'By the tree he still was standing,   360
By the fallen tree was standing,
That had dropped into the water,
O my sweetheart, my Algonquin!
  'When I think of my beloved,
Ah me! think of my beloved,
When my heart is thinking of him,
O my sweetheart, my Algonquin!'[1]
  Such was Hiawatha's Wedding,
Such the dance of Pau-Puk-Keewis,
Such the story of Iagoo,   370
Such the songs of Chibiabos;
Thus the wedding banquet ended,
And the wedding guests departed,
Leaving Hiawatha happy
With the night and Minnehaha.

XIII

BLESSING THE CORNFIELDS [2]

SING, O Song of Hiawatha,
Of the happy days that followed,

[1] The original of this song may be found in *Oneóta*,
p. 15. (LONGFELLOW.)

[2] The Indians hold the maize, or Indian corn, in
great veneration. 'They esteem it so important and
divine a grain,' says Schoolcraft, 'that their story-tellers invented various tales, in which this idea is sym-
bolized under the form of a special gift from the Great
Spirit. The Odjibwa-Algonquins, who call it Mon-da-
min, that is, this Spirit's grain or berry, have a pretty
story of the kind, in which the stalk in full tassel is
represented as descending from the sky, under the
guise of a handsome youth, in answer to the prayers of
a young man at his fast of virility, or coming to manhood.
  'It is well known that corn-planting and corn-gather-
ing, at least among all the still *uncolonized* tribes, are
left entirely to the females and children, and a few
superannuated old men. It is not generally known,
perhaps, that this labor is not compulsory, and that it
is assumed by the females as a just equivalent, in their
view, for the onerous and continuous labor of the other
sex, in providing meats, and skins for clothing, by the
chase, and in defending their villages against their
enemies, and keeping intruders off their territories.
A good Indian housewife deems this a part of her prerogative, and prides herself to have a store of corn to
exercise her hospitality, or duly honor her husband's
hospitality in the entertainment of the lodge guests.'
— *Oneóta*, p. 82. (LONGFELLOW.)

In the land of the Ojibways,
In the pleasant land and peaceful !
Sing the mysteries of Mondamin,
Sing the Blessing of the Cornfields !
  Buried was the bloody hatchet,
Buried was the dreadful war-club,
Buried were all warlike weapons,
And the war-cry was forgotten.   10
There was peace among the nations;
Unmolested roved the hunters,
Built the birch canoe for sailing,
Caught the fish in lake and river,
Shot the deer and trapped the beaver;
Unmolested worked the women,
Made their sugar from the maple,
Gathered wild rice in the meadows,
Dressed the skins of deer and beaver.
  All around the happy village   20
Stood the maize-fields, green and shining,
Waved the green plumes of Mondamin,
Waved his soft and sunny tresses,
Filling all the land with plenty.
'T was the women who in spring-time
Planted the broad fields and fruitful,
Buried in the earth Mondamin;
'T was the women who in Autumn
Stripped the yellow husks of harvest,
Stripped the garments from Mondamin,   30
Even as Hiawatha taught them.
  Once, when all the maize was planted,
Hiawatha, wise and thoughtful,
Spake and said to Minnehaha,
To his wife, the Laughing Water:
'You shall bless to-night the cornfields
Draw a magic circle round them,
To protect them from destruction,
Blast of mildew, blight of insect,
Wagemin, the thief of cornfields,   40
Paimosaid, who steals the maize-ear !
  'In the night, when all is silence,
In the night, when all is darkness,
When the Spirit of Sleep, Nepahwin,
Shuts the doors of all the wigwams,
So that not an ear can hear you,
So that not an eye can see you,
Rise up from your bed in silence,
Lay aside your garments wholly,
Walk around the fields you planted,   50
Round the borders of the cornfields,
Covered by your tresses only,
Robed with darkness as a garment.
  'Thus the fields shall be more fruitful,
And the passing of your footsteps
Draw a magic circle round them,
So that neither blight nor mildew,

Neither burrowing worm nor insect,
Shall pass o'er the magic circle;
Not the dragon-fly, Kwo-ne-she,   60
Nor the spider, Subbekashe,
Nor the grasshopper, Pah-puk-keena,
Nor the mighty caterpillar,
Way-muk-kwana, with the bear-skin,
King of all the caterpillars !' [1]
  On the tree-tops near the cornfields
Sat the hungry crows and ravens,
Kahgahgee, the King of Ravens,
With his band of black marauders.
And they laughed at Hiawatha,   70
Till the tree-tops shook with laughter,
With their melancholy laughter,
At the words of Hiawatha.
'Hear him !' said they; 'hear the Wise
      Man,
Hear the plots of Hiawatha !'
  When the noiseless night descended
Broad and dark o'er field and forest,
When the mournful Wawonaissa
Sorrowing sang among the hemlocks,
And the Spirit of Sleep, Nepahwin,   80
Shut the doors of all the wigwams,
From her bed rose Laughing Water,
Laid aside her garments wholly,
And with darkness clothed and guarded,
Unashamed and unaffrighted,
Walked securely round the cornfields,
Drew the sacred, magic circle
Of her footprints round the cornfields.
  No one but the Midnight only
Saw her beauty in the darkness,   90
No one but the Wawonaissa
Heard the panting of her bosom;
Guskewau, the darkness, wrapped her
Closely in his sacred mantle,
So that none might see her beauty,
So that none might boast, 'I saw her !'
  On the morrow, as the day dawned,
Kahgahgee, the King of Ravens,
Gathered all his black marauders,

[1] 'A singular proof of this belief, in both sexes, of
the mysterious influence of the steps of a woman on the
vegetable and insect creation, is found in an ancient
custom, which was related to me, respecting corn-
planting. It was the practice of the hunter's wife, when
the field of corn had been planted, to choose the first
dark or overclouded evening to perform a secret circuit, *sans habillement,* around the field. For this purpose she slipped out of the lodge in the evening, unob-
served, to some obscure nook, where she completely
disrobed. Then, taking her matchecota, or principal
garment, in one hand, she dragged it around the field.
This was thought to insure a prolific crop, and to prevent the assaults of insects and worms upon the grain.
It was supposed they could not creep over the charmed
line.' — *Oneóta,* p. 83. (LONGFELLOW.)

Crows and blackbirds, jays and ravens,   100
Clamorous on the dusky tree-tops,
And descended, fast and fearless,
On the fields of Hiawatha,
On the grave of the Mondamin.
  'We will drag Mondamin,' said they,
'From the grave where he is buried,
Spite of all the magic circles
Laughing Water draws around it,
Spite of all the sacred footprints
Minnehaha stamps upon it !'   110
  But the wary Hiawatha,
Ever thoughtful, careful, watchful,
Had o'erheard the scornful laughter
When they mocked him from the tree-tops.
'Kaw !' he said, 'my friends the ravens !
Kahgahgee, my King of Ravens !
I will teach you all a lesson
That shall not be soon forgotten !'
  He had risen before the daybreak,
He had spread o'er all the cornfields   120
Snares to catch the black marauders,
And was lying now in ambush
In the neighboring grove of pine-trees,
Waiting for the crows and blackbirds,
Waiting for the jays and ravens.
  Soon they came with caw and clamor,
Rush of wings and cry of voices,
To their work of devastation,
Settling down upon the cornfields,
Delving deep with beak and talon,   130
For the body of Mondamin.
And with all their craft and cunning,
All their skill in wiles of warfare,
They perceived no danger near them,
Till their claws became entangled,
Till they found themselves imprisoned
In the snares of Hiawatha.
  From his place of ambush came he,
Striding terrible among them,
And so awful was his aspect   140
That the bravest quailed with terror.
Without mercy he destroyed them
Right and left, by tens and twenties,
And their wretched, lifeless bodies
Hung aloft on poles for scarecrows
Round the consecrated cornfields,
As a signal of his vengeance,
As a warning to marauders.
  Only Kahgahgee, the leader,
Kahgahgee, the King of Ravens,   150
He alone was spared among them
As a hostage for his people.
With his prisoner-string he bound him,
Led him captive to his wigwam,

Tied him fast with cords of elm-bark
To the ridge-pole of his wigwam.
  'Kahgahgee, my raven !' said he,
'You the leader of the robbers,
You the plotter of this mischief,
The contriver of this outrage,   160
I will keep you, I will hold you,
As a hostage for your people,
As a pledge of good behavior !'
And he left him, grim and sulky,
Sitting in the morning sunshine
On the summit of the wigwam,
Croaking fiercely his displeasure,
Flapping his great sable pinions,
Vainly struggling for his freedom,
Vainly calling on his people !   170
  Summer passed, and Shawondasee
Breathed his sighs o'er all the landscape,
From the South-land sent his ardors,
Wafted kisses warm and tender;
And the maize-field grew and ripened,
Till it stood in all the splendor
Of its garments green and yellow,
Of its tassels and its plumage,
And the maize-ears full and shining
Gleamed from bursting sheaths of verdure.
  Then Nokomis, the old woman,   181
Spake, and said to Minnehaha:
''T is the Moon when leaves are falling;
All the wild rice has been gathered,
And the maize is ripe and ready;
Let us gather in the harvest,
Let us wrestle with Mondamin,
Strip him of his plumes and tassels,
Of his garments green and yellow!'
  And the merry Laughing Water   190
Went rejoicing from the wigwam,
With Nokomis, old and wrinkled,
And they called the women round them,
Called the young men and the maidens,
To the harvest of the cornfields,
To the husking of the maize-ear.
  On the border of the forest,
Underneath the fragrant pine-trees,
Sat the old men and the warriors
Smoking in the pleasant shadow.   200
In uninterrupted silence
Looked they at the gamesome labor
Of the young men and the women;
Listened to their noisy talking,
To their laughter and their singing,
Heard them chattering like the magpies,
Heard them laughing like the blue-jays,
Heard them singing like the robins.
  And whene'er some lucky maiden

Found a red ear in the husking,   210
Found a maize-ear red as blood is,
'Nushka!' cried they all together,
'Nushka! you shall have a sweetheart,
You shall have a handsome husband!'
'Ugh!' the old men all responded
From their seats beneath the pine-trees.

And whene'er a youth or maiden
Found a crooked ear in husking,
Found a maize-ear in the husking
Blighted, mildewed, or misshapen,   220
Then they laughed and sang together,
Crept and limped about the cornfields,
Mimicked in their gait and gestures
Some old man, bent almost double,
Singing singly or together:
'Wagemin, the thief of cornfields!
Paimosaid, who steals the maize-ear!'[1]

Till the cornfields rang with laughter,
Till from Hiawatha's wigwam
Kahgahgee, the King of Ravens,   230
Screamed and quivered in his anger,
And from all the neighboring tree-tops
Cawed and croaked the black marauders.
'Ugh!' the old men all responded,
From their seats beneath the pine-trees!

XIV

PICTURE-WRITING

In those days said Hiawatha,
'Lo! how all things fade and perish!
From the memory of the old men

---

[1] 'If one of the young female huskers finds a *red* ear of corn, it is typical of a brave admirer, and is regarded as a fitting present to some young warrior. But if the ear be *crooked*, and tapering to a point, no matter what color, the whole circle is set in a roar, and *wa-ge-min* is the word shouted aloud. It is the symbol of a thief in the cornfield. It is considered as the image of an old man stooping as he enters the lot. Had the chisel of Praxiteles been employed to produce this image, it could not more vividly bring to the minds of the merry group the idea of a pilferer of their favorite mondámin. . . .

'The literal meaning of the term is, a mass, or crooked ear of grain; but the ear of corn so called is a conventional type of a little old man pilfering ears of corn in a cornfield. It is in this manner that a single word or term, in these curious languages, becomes the fruitful parent of many ideas. And we can thus perceive why it is that the word *wagemin* is alone competent to excite merriment in the husking circle.

'This term is taken as a basis of the cereal chorus, or corn song, as sung by the Northern Algonquin tribes. It is coupled with the phrase *Paimosaid*, — a permutative form of the Indian substantive, made from the verb *pim-o-sa*, to walk. Its literal meaning is, *he who walks*, or *the walker;* but the ideas conveyed by it are, he who walks by night to pilfer corn. It offers, therefore, a kind of parallelism in expression to the preceding term.' — *Oneóta,* p. 254. (Longfellow.)

Pass away the great traditions,
The achievements of the warriors,
The adventures of the hunters,
All the wisdom of the Medas,
All the craft of the Wabenos,
All the marvellous dreams and visions
Of the Jossakeeds, the Prophets!   10
'Great men die and are forgotten,
Wise men speak; their words of wisdom
Perish in the ears that hear them,
Do not reach the generations
That, as yet unborn, are waiting
In the great, mysterious darkness
Of the speechless days that shall be!
'On the grave-posts of our fathers
Are no signs, no figures painted;
Who are in those graves we know not,   20
Only know they are our fathers.
Of what kith they are and kindred,
From what old, ancestral Totem,
Be it Eagle, Bear, or Beaver,
They descended, this we know not,
Only know they are our fathers.
'Face to face we speak together,
But we cannot speak when absent,
Cannot send our voices from us
To the friends that dwell afar off;   30
Cannot send a secret message,
But the bearer learns our secret,
May pervert it, may betray it,
May reveal it unto others.'
Thus said Hiawatha, walking
In the solitary forest,
Pondering, musing in the forest,
On the welfare of his people.

From his pouch he took his colors,
Took his paints of different colors,   40
On the smooth bark of a birch-tree
Painted many shapes and figures,
Wonderful and mystic figures,
And each figure had a meaning,
Each some word or thought suggested.
Gitche Manito the Mighty,
He, the Master of Life, was painted
As an egg, with points projecting
To the four winds of the heavens.
Everywhere is the Great Spirit,   50
Was the meaning of this symbol.
Mitche Manito the Mighty,
He the dreadful Spirit of Evil,
As a serpent was depicted,
As Kenabeek, the great serpent.
Very crafty, very cunning,
Is the creeping Spirit of Evil,
Was the meaning of this symbol.

Life and Death he drew as circles,
Life was white, but Death was dark-
   ened;   60
Sun and moon and stars he painted,
Man and beast, and fish and reptile,
Forests, mountains, lakes, and rivers.
  For the earth he drew a straight line,
For the sky a bow above it;
White the space between for daytime,
Filled with little stars for night-time;
On the left a point for sunrise,
On the right a point for sunset,
On the top a point for noontide,   70
And for rain and cloudy weather
Waving lines descending from it.
  Footprints pointing towards a wigwam
Were a sign of invitation,
Were a sign of guests assembling;
Bloody hands with palms uplifted
Were a symbol of destruction,
Were a hostile sign and symbol.
  All these things did Hiawatha
Show unto his wondering people,   80
And interpreted their meaning,
And he said: 'Behold, your grave-posts
Have no mark, no sign, nor symbol,
Go and paint them all with figures;
Each one with its household symbol,
With its own ancestral Totem;
So that those who follow after
May distinguish them and know them.
  And they painted on the grave-posts
On the graves yet unforgotten,   90
Each his own ancestral Totem,
Each the symbol of his household;
Figures of the Bear and Reindeer,
Of the Turtle, Crane, and Beaver,
Each inverted as a token
That the owner was departed,
That the chief who bore the symbol
Lay beneath in dust and ashes.
  And the Jossakeeds, the Prophets,
The Wabenos, the Magicians,   100
And the Medicine-men, the Medas,
Painted upon bark and deer-skin
Figures for the songs they chanted,
For each song a separate symbol,
Figures mystical and awful,
Figures strange and brightly colored;
And each figure had its meaning,
Each some magic song suggested.
  The Great Spirit, the Creator,
Flashing light through all the heaven;   110
The Great Serpent, the Kenabeek,
With his bloody crest erected,

Creeping, looking into heaven;
In the sky the sun, that listens,
And the moon eclipsed and dying;
Owl and eagle, crane and hen-hawk,
And the cormorant, bird of magic;
Headless men, that walk the heavens,
Bodies lying pierced with arrows,
Bloody hands of death uplifted,   120
Flags on graves, and great war-captains
Grasping both the earth and heaven!
  Such as these the shapes they painted
On the birch-bark and the deer-skin;
Songs of war and songs of hunting,
Songs of medicine and of magic,
All were written in these figures,
For each figure had its meaning,
Each its separate song recorded.
  Nor forgotten was the Love-Song,   130
The most subtle of all medicines,
The most potent spell of magic,
Dangerous more than war or hunting!
Thus the Love-Song was recorded,
Symbol and interpretation.
  First a human figure standing,
Painted in the brightest scarlet;
'T is the lover, the musician,
And the meaning is, 'My painting
Makes me powerful over others.'   140
  Then the figure seated, singing,
Playing on a drum of magic,
And the interpretation, 'Listen!
'T is my voice you hear, my singing!'
  Then the same red figure seated
In the shelter of a wigwam,
And the meaning of the symbol,
'I will come and sit beside you
In the mystery of my passion!'
  Then two figures, man and woman,   150
Standing hand in hand together
With their hands so clasped together
That they seemed in one united,
And the words thus represented
Are, 'I see your heart within you,
And your cheeks are red with blushes!'
  Next the maiden on an island,
In the centre of an island;
And the song this shape suggested
Was, 'Though you were at a distance,   160
Were upon some far-off island,
Such the spell I cast upon you,
Such the magic power of passion,
I could straightway draw you to me!'
  Then the figure of the maiden
Sleeping, and the lover near her,
Whispering to her in her slumbers,

Saying, 'Though you were far from me
In the land of Sleep and Silence,
Still the voice of love would reach you!'   170
And the last of all the figures
Was a heart within a circle,
Drawn within a magic circle;
And the image had this meaning:
'Naked lies your heart before me,
To your naked heart I whisper!'
    Thus it was that Hiawatha,
In his wisdom, taught the people
All the mysteries of painting,
All the art of Picture-Writing,   180
On the smooth bark of the birch-tree,
On the white skin of the reindeer,
On the grave-posts of the village.

XV

HIAWATHA'S LAMENTATION

IN those days the Evil Spirits,
All the Manitos of mischief,
Fearing Hiawatha's wisdom,
And his love for Chibiabos,
Jealous of their faithful friendship,
And their noble words and actions,
Made at length a league against them,
To molest them and destroy them.
    Hiawatha, wise and wary,
Often said to Chibiabos,   10
'O my brother! do not leave me,
Lest the Evil Spirits harm you!'
Chibiabos, young and heedless,
Laughing shook his coal-black tresses,
Answered ever sweet and childlike,
'Do not fear for me, O brother!
Harm and evil come not near me!'
    Once when Peboan, the Winter,
Roofed with ice the Big-Sea-Water,
When the snow-flakes, whirling downward,
Hissed among the withered oak-leaves,   21
Changed the pine-trees into wigwams,
Covered all the earth with silence, —
Armed with arrows, shod with snow-shoes,
Heeding not his brother's warning,
Fearing not the Evil Spirits,
Forth to hunt the deer with antlers
All alone went Chibiabos.
    Right across the Big-Sea-Water
Sprang with speed the deer before him.   30
With the wind and snow he followed,
O'er the treacherous ice he followed,
Wild with all the fierce commotion
And the rapture of the hunting.

    But beneath, the Evil Spirits
Lay in ambush, waiting for him,
Broke the treacherous ice beneath him,
Dragged him downward to the bottom,
Buried in the sand his body.
Unktahee, the god of water,   40
He the god of the Dacotahs,
Drowned him in the deep abysses
Of the lake of Gitche Gumee.
    From the headlands Hiawatha
Sent forth such a wail of anguish,
Such a fearful lamentation,
That the bison paused to listen,
And the wolves howled from the prairies,
And the thunder in the distance
Starting answered, 'Baim-wawa!'   50
    Then his face with black he painted,
With his robe his head he covered,
In his wigwam sat lamenting,
Seven long weeks he sat lamenting,
Uttering still this moan of sorrow: —
    'He is dead, the sweet musician!
He the sweetest of all singers!
He has gone from us forever,
He has moved a little nearer
To the Master of all music,   60
To the Master of all singing!
O my brother, Chibiabos!'
    And the melancholy fir-trees
Waved their dark green fans above him,
Waved their purple cones above him,
Sighing with him to console him,
Mingling with his lamentation
Their complaining, their lamenting.
    Came the Spring, and all the forest
Looked in vain for Chibiabos;   70
Sighed the rivulet, Sebowisha,
Sighed the rushes in the meadow.
    From the tree-tops sang the bluebird,
Sang the bluebird, the Owaissa,
'Chibiabos! Chibiabos!
He is dead, the sweet musician!'
    From the wigwam sang the robin,
Sang the robin, the Opechee,
'Chibiabos! Chibiabos!
He is dead, the sweetest singer!'   80
    And at night through all the forest
Went the whippoorwill complaining,
Wailing went the Wawonaissa,
'Chibiabos! Chibiabos!
He is dead, the sweet musician!
He the sweetest of all singers!'
    Then the Medicine-men, the Medas,
The magicians, the Wabenos,
And the Jossakeeds, the Prophets,

Came to visit Hiawatha;   90
Built a Sacred Lodge beside him,
To appease him, to console him,
Walked in silent, grave procession,
Bearing each a pouch of healing,
Skin of beaver, lynx, or otter,
Filled with magic roots and simples,
Filled with very potent medicines.

When he heard their steps approaching,
Hiawatha ceased lamenting,
Called no more on Chibiabos;   100
Naught he questioned, naught he answered,
But his mournful head uncovered,
From his face the mourning colors
Washed he slowly and in silence,
Slowly and in silence followed
Onward to the Sacred Wigwam.

There a magic drink they gave him,
Made of Nahma-wusk, the spearmint,
And Wabeno-wusk, the yarrow,
Roots of power, and herbs of healing;   110
Beat their drums, and shook their rattles;
Chanted singly and in chorus,
Mystic songs like these, they chanted.
' I myself, myself ! behold me !
'T is the great Gray Eagle talking;
Come, ye white crows, come and hear him!
The loud-speaking thunder helps me;
All the unseen spirits help me;
I can hear their voices calling,
All around the sky I hear them !   120
I can blow you strong, my brother,
I can heal you, Hiawatha ! '
' Hi-au-ha ! ' replied the chorus,
' Way-ha-way ! ' the mystic chorus.
' Friends of mine are all the serpents !
Hear me shake my skin of hen-hawk !
Mahng, the white loon, I can kill him;
I can shoot your heart and kill it !
I can blow you strong, my brother,
I can heal you, Hiawatha ! '   130
' Hi-au-ha ! ' replied the chorus.
' Way-ha-way ! ' the mystic chorus.
' I myself, myself ! the prophet !
When I speak the wigwam trembles,
Shakes the Sacred Lodge with terror,
Hands unseen begin to shake it !
When I walk, the sky I tread on
Bends and makes a noise beneath me !
I can blow you strong, my brother!
Rise and speak, O Hiawatha ! '   140
' Hi-au-ha ! ' replied the chorus,
' Way-ha-way ! ' the mystic chorus.
Then they shook their medicine-pouches
O'er the head of Hiawatha,

Danced their medicine-dance around him;
And upstarting wild and haggard,
Like a man from dreams awakened,
He was healed of all his madness.
As the clouds are swept from heaven,
Straightway from his brain departed   150
All his moody melancholy;
As the ice is swept from rivers,
Straightway from his heart departed
All his sorrow and affliction.

Then they summoned Chibiabos
From his grave beneath the waters,
From the sands of Gitche Gumee
Summoned Hiawatha's brother.
And so mighty was the magic
Of that cry and invocation,   160
That he heard it as he lay there
Underneath the Big-Sea-Water;
From the sand he rose and listened,
Heard the music and the singing,
Came, obedient to the summons,
To the doorway of the wigwam,
But to enter they forbade him.

Through a chink a coal they gave him,
Through the door a burning fire-brand;
Ruler in the Land of Spirits,   17
Ruler o'er the dead, they made him,
Telling him a fire to kindle
For all those that died thereafter,
Camp-fires for their night encampments
On their solitary journey
To the kingdom of Ponemah,
To the land of the Hereafter.

From the village of his childhood,
From the homes of those who knew him,
Passing silent through the forest,   180
Like a smoke-wreath wafted sideways,
Slowly vanished Chibiabos !
Where he passed, the branches moved not
Where he trod, the grasses bent not,
And the fallen leaves of last year
Made no sound beneath his footsteps.

Four whole days he journeyed onward
Down the pathway of the dead men;
On the dead-man's strawberry feasted,
Crossed the melancholy river,   19
On the swinging log he crossed it,
Came unto the Lake of Silver,
In the Stone Canoe was carried
To the Islands of the Blessed,
To the land of ghosts and shadows.

On that journey, moving slowly,
Many weary spirits saw he,
Panting under heavy burdens,
Laden with war-clubs, bows and arrows,

Robes of fur, and pots and kettles,   200
And with food that friends had given
For that solitary journey.
  'Ay! why do the living,' said they,
'Lay such heavy burdens on us!
Better were it to go naked,
Better were it to go fasting,
Than to bear such heavy burdens
On our long and weary journey!'
  Forth then issued Hiawatha,
Wandered eastward, wandered westward,
Teaching men the use of simples   211
And the antidotes for poisons,
And the cure of all diseases.
Thus was first made known to mortals
All the mystery of Medamin,
All the sacred art of healing.

XVI

PAU–PUK–KEEWIS

YOU shall hear how Pau-Puk-Keewis,
He, the handsome Yenadizze,
Whom the people called the Storm-Fool,
Vexed the village with disturbance;
You shall hear of all his mischief,
And his flight from Hiawatha,
And his wondrous transmigrations,
And the end of his adventures.
  On the shores of Gitche Gumee,
On the dunes of Nagow Wudjoo,   10
By the shining Big-Sea-Water
Stood the lodge of Pau-Puk-Keewis.
It was he who in his frenzy
Whirled these drifting sands together,
On the dunes of Nagow Wudjoo,
When, among the guests assembled,
He so merrily and madly
Danced at Hiawatha's wedding,
Danced the Beggar's Dance to please them.
  Now, in search of new adventures,   20
From his lodge went Pau-Puk-Keewis,
Came with speed into the village,
Found the young men all assembled
In the lodge of old Iagoo,
Listening to his monstrous stories,
To his wonderful adventures.
  He was telling them the story
Of Ojeeg, the Summer-Maker,
How he made a hole in heaven,
How he climbed up into heaven,   30
And let out the summer-weather,
The perpetual, pleasant Summer;

How the Otter first essayed it;
How the Beaver, Lynx, and Badger
Tried in turn the great achievement,
From the summit of the mountain
Smote their fists against the heavens,
Smote against the sky their foreheads,
Cracked the sky, but could not break it;
How the Wolverine, uprising,   40
Made him ready for the encounter,
Bent his knees down, like a squirrel,
Drew his arms back, like a cricket.
  'Once he leaped,' said old Iagoo,
'Once he leaped, and lo! above him
Bent the sky, as ice in rivers
When the waters rise beneath it;
Twice he leaped, and lo! above him
Cracked the sky, as ice in rivers
When the freshet is at highest!   50
Thrice he leaped, and lo! above him
Broke the shattered sky asunder,
And he disappeared within it,
And Ojeeg, the Fisher Weasel,
With a bound went in behind him!'
  'Hark you!' shouted Pau-Puk-Keewis
As he entered at the doorway;
'I am tired of all this talking,
Tired of old Iagoo's stories,
Tired of Hiawatha's wisdom.   60
Here is something to amuse you,
Better than this endless talking.'
  Then from out his pouch of wolf-skin
Forth he drew, with solemn manner,
All the game of Bowl and Counters,[1]
Pugasaing, with thirteen pieces.
White on one side were they painted,
And vermilion on the other;
Two Kenabeeks or great serpents,
Two Ininewug or wedge-men,   70
One great war-club, Pugamaugun,
And one slender fish, the Keego,
Four round pieces, Ozawabeeks,
And three Sheshebwug or ducklings.
All were made of bone and painted,
All except the Ozawabeeks;
These were brass, on one side burnished,
And were black upon the other.
  In a wooden bowl he placed them,
Shook and jostled them together,   80
Threw them on the ground before him,
Thus exclaiming and explaining:

---

[1] This Game of the Bowl is the principal game of hazard among the Northern tribes of Indians. Mr. Schoolcraft gives a particular account of it in *Oneóta*, p. 85. . . . See also his *History, Conditions, and Prospects of the Indian Tribes*, part ii, p. 72. (LONGFELLOW.)

'Red side up are all the pieces,
And one great Kenabeek standing
On the bright side of a brass piece,
On a burnished Ozawabeek;
Thirteen tens and eight are counted.'
  Then again he shook the pieces,
Shook and jostled them together,
Threw them on the ground before him, 90
Still exclaiming and explaining:
'White are both the great Kenabeeks,
White the Ininewug, the wedge-men,
Red are all the other pieces;
Five tens and an eight are counted.'
  Thus he taught the game of hazard,
Thus he displayed it and explained it,
Running through its various chances,
Various changes, various meanings:
Twenty curious eyes stared at him, 100
Full of eagerness stared at him.
  'Many games,' said old Iagoo,
'Many games of skill and hazard
Have I seen in different nations,
Have I played in different countries.
He who plays with old Iagoo
Must have very nimble fingers;
Though you think yourself so skilful,
I can beat you, Pau-Puk-Keewis,
I can even give you lessons 110
In your game of Bowl and Counters!'
  So they sat and played together,
All the old men and the young men,
Played for dresses, weapons, wampum,
Played till midnight, played till morn-
    ing,
Played until the Yenadizze,
Till the cunning Pau-Puk-Keewis,
Of their treasures had despoiled them,
Of the best of all their dresses,
Shirts of deer-skin, robes of ermine, 120
Belts of wampum, crests of feathers,
Warlike weapons, pipes and pouches.
Twenty eyes glared wildly at him,
Like the eyes of wolves glared at him.
  Said the lucky Pau-Puk-Keewis:
'In my wigwam I am lonely,
In my wanderings and adventures
I have need of a companion,
Fain would have a Meshinauwa,
An attendant and pipe-bearer. 130
I will venture all these winnings,
All these garments heaped about me,
All this wampum, all these feathers,
On a single throw will venture
All against the young man yonder!'
'T was a youth of sixteen summers,

'T was a nephew of Iagoo;
Face-in-a-Mist, the people called him.
  As the fire burns in a pipe-head
Dusky red beneath the ashes, 140
So beneath his shaggy eyebrows
Glowed the eyes of old Iagoo.
'Ugh!' he answered very fiercely;
'Ugh!' they answered all and each one.
  Seized the wooden bowl the old man,
Closely in his bony fingers
Clutched the fatal bowl, Onagon,
Shook it fiercely and with fury,
Made the pieces ring together
As he threw them down before him. 150
  Red were both the great Kenabeeks,
Red the Ininewug, the wedge-men,
Red the Sheshebwug, the ducklings,
Black the four brass Ozawabeeks,
White alone the fish, the Keego;
Only five the pieces counted!
  Then the smiling Pau-Puk-Keewis
Shook the bowl and threw the pieces;
Lightly in the air he tossed them,
And they fell about him scattered; 160
Dark and bright the Ozawabeeks,
Red and white the other pieces,
And upright among the others
One Ininewug was standing,
Even as crafty Pau-Puk-Keewis
Stood alone among the players,
Saying, 'Five tens! mine the game is!'
  Twenty eyes glared at him fiercely,
Like the eyes of wolves glared at him,
As he turned and left the wigwam, 170
Followed by his Meshinauwa,
By the nephew of Iagoo,
By the tall and graceful stripling,
Bearing in his arms the winnings,
Shirts of deer-skin, robes of ermine,
Belts of wampum, pipes and weapons.
  'Carry them,' said Pau-Puk-Keewis,
Pointing with his fan of feathers,
'To my wigwam far to eastward,
On the dunes of Nagow Wudjoo!' 180
  Hot and red with smoke and gambling
Were the eyes of Pau-Puk-Keewis
As he came forth to the freshness
Of the pleasant Summer morning.
All the birds were singing gayly,
All the streamlets flowing swiftly,
And the heart of Pau-Puk-Keewis
Sang with pleasure as the birds sing,
Beat with triumph like the streamlets,
As he wandered through the village, 190
In the early gray of morning,

With his fan of turkey-feathers,
With his plumes and tufts of swan's down,
Till he reached the farthest wigwam,
Reached the lodge of Hiawatha.

Silent was it and deserted;
No one met him at the doorway,
No one came to bid him welcome;
But the birds were singing round it,
In and out and round the doorway,   200
Hopping, singing, fluttering, feeding,
And aloft upon the ridge-pole
Kahgahgee, the King of Ravens,
Sat with fiery eyes, and, screaming,
Flapped his wings at Pau-Puk-Keewis.

'All are gone! the lodge is empty!'
Thus it was spake Pau-Puk-Keewis,
In his heart resolving mischief; —
'Gone is wary Hiawatha,
Gone the silly Laughing Water,   210
Gone Nokomis, the old woman,
And the lodge is left unguarded!'

By the neck he seized the raven,
Whirled it round him like a rattle,
Like a medicine-pouch he shook it,
Strangled Kahgahgee, the raven,
From the ridge-pole of the wigwam
Left its lifeless body hanging,
As an insult to its master,
As a taunt to Hiawatha.   220

With a stealthy step he entered,
Round the lodge in wild disorder
Threw the household things about him,
Piled together in confusion
Bowls of wood and earthen kettles,
Robes of buffalo and beaver,
Skins of otter, lynx, and ermine,
As an insult to Nokomis,
As a taunt to Minnehaha.

Then departed Pau-Puk-Keewis,   230
Whistling, singing through the forest,
Whistling gayly to the squirrels,
Who from hollow boughs above him
Dropped their acorn-shells upon him,
Singing gayly to the wood birds,
Who from out the leafy darkness
Answered with a song as merry.

Then he climbed the rocky headlands,
Looking o'er the Gitche Gumee,
Perched himself upon their summit,   240
Waiting full of mirth and mischief
The return of Hiawatha.

Stretched upon his back he lay there;
Far below him plashed the waters,
Plashed and washed the dreamy waters;
Far above him swam the heavens,

Swam the dizzy, dreamy heavens;
Round him hovered, fluttered, rustled
Hiawatha's mountain chickens,
Flock-wise swept and wheeled about him,
Almost brushed him with their pinions.   251

And he killed them as he lay there,
Slaughtered them by tens and twenties,
Threw their bodies down the headland,
Threw them on the beach below him,
Till at length Kayoshk, the sea-gull,
Perched upon a crag above them,
Shouted: 'It is Pau-Puk-Keewis!
He is slaying us by hundreds!
Send a message to our brother,   260
Tidings send to Hiawatha!'

XVII

THE HUNTING OF PAU-PUK-KEEWIS

FULL of wrath was Hiawatha
When he came into the village,
Found the people in confusion,
Heard of all the misdemeanors,
All the malice and the mischief,
Of the cunning Pau-Puk-Keewis.

Hard his breath came through his nostrils,
Through his teeth he buzzed and muttered
Words of anger and resentment,
Hot and humming, like a hornet.   10
'I will slay this Pau-Puk-Keewis,
Slay this mischief-maker!' said he.
'Not so long and wide the world is,
Not so rude and rough the way is,
That my wrath shall not attain him,
That my vengeance shall not reach him!'

Then in swift pursuit departed
Hiawatha and the hunters
On the trail of Pau-Puk-Keewis,
Through the forest, where he passed it,
To the headlands where he rested;
But they found not Pau-Puk-Keewis,
Only in the trampled grasses,
In the whortleberry-bushes,
Found the couch where he had rested,
Found the impress of his body.

From the lowlands far beneath them,
From the Muskoday, the meadow,
Pau-Puk-Keewis, turning backward,
Made a gesture of defiance,   30
Made a gesture of derision;
And aloud cried Hiawatha,
From the summit of the mountains:

'Not so long and wide the world is,
Not so rude and rough the way is,
But my wrath shall overtake you,
And my vengeance shall attain you!'
Over rock and over river,
Thorough bush, and brake, and forest,
Ran the cunning Pau-Puk-Keewis;   40
Like an antelope he bounded,
Till he came unto a streamlet
In the middle of the forest,
To a streamlet still and tranquil,
That had overflowed its margin,
To a dam made by the beavers,
To a pond of quiet water,
Where knee-deep the trees were standing,
Where the water-lilies floated,
Where the rushes waved and whispered.   50
On the dam stood Pau-Puk-Keewis,
On the dam of trunks and branches,
Through whose chinks the water spouted,
O'er whose summit floved the streamlet.
From the bottom rose the beaver,
Looked with two great eyes of wonder,
Eyes that seemed to ask a question,
At the stranger, Pau-Puk-Keewis.
On the dam stood Pau-Puk-Keewis,
O'er his ankles flowed the streamlet,   60
Flowed the bright and silvery water,
And he spake unto the beaver,
With a smile he spake in this wise:
'O my friend Ahmeek, the beaver,
Cool and pleasant is the water;
Let me dive into the water,
Let me rest there in your lodges;
Change me, too, into a beaver!'
Cautiously replied the beaver,
With reserve he thus made answer: 70
'Let me first consult the others,
Let me ask the other beavers.'
Down he sank into the water,
Heavily sank he, as a stone sinks,
Down among the leaves and branches,
Brown and matted at the bottom.
On the dam stood Pau-Puk-Keewis,
O'er his ankles flowed the streamlet,
Spouted through the chinks below him,
Dashed upon the stones beneath him,   80
Spread serene and calm before him,
And the sunshine and the shadows
Fell in flecks and gleams upon him,
Fell in little shining patches,
Through the waving, rustling branches.
From the bottom rose the beavers,
Silently above the surface
Rose one head and then another,

Till the pond seemed full of beavers,
Full of black and shining faces.   90
To the beavers Pau-Puk-Keewis
Spake entreating, said in this wise:
'Very pleasant is your dwelling,
O my friends! and safe from danger;
Can you not, with all your cunning,
All your wisdom and contrivance,
Change me, too, into a beaver?'
'Yes!' replied Ahmeek, the beaver,
He the King of all the beavers,
'Let yourself slide down among us,   100
Down into the tranquil water.'
Down into the pond among them
Silently sank Pau-Puk-Keewis;
Black became his shirt of deer-skin,
Black his moccasins and leggings,
In a broad black tail behind him
Spread his fox-tails and his fringes;
He was changed into a beaver.
'Make me large,' said Pau-Puk-Keewis,
'Make me large and make me larger,   110
Larger than the other beavers.'
'Yes,' the beaver chief responded,
'When our lodge below you enter,
In our wigwam we will make you
Ten times larger than the others.'
Thus into the clear, brown water
Silently sank Pau-Puk-Keewis:
Found the bottom covered over
With the trunks of trees and branches,
Hoards of food against the winter,   120
Piles and heaps against the famine;
Found the lodge with arching doorway,
Leading into spacious chambers.
Here they made him large and larger,
Made him largest of the beavers,
Ten times larger than the others.
'You shall be our ruler,' said they;
'Chief and King of all the beavers.'
But not long had Pau-Puk-Keewis
Sat in state among the beavers,   130
When there came a voice of warning
From the watchman at his station
In the water-flags and lilies,
Saying, 'Here is Hiawatha!
Hiawatha with his hunters!'
Then they heard a cry above them,
Heard a shouting and a tramping,
Heard a crashing and a rushing,
And the water round and o'er them
Sank and sucked away in eddies,   140
And they knew their dam was broken.
On the lodge's roof the hunters
Leaped, and broke it all asunder;

Streamed the sunshine through the crevice,
Sprang the beavers through the doorway,
Hid themselves in deeper water,
In the channel of the streamlet;
But the mighty Pau-Puk-Keewis
Could not pass beneath the doorway;
He was puffed with pride and feeding, 150
He was swollen like a bladder.

Through the roof looked Hiawatha,
Cried aloud, 'O Pau-Puk-Keewis !
Vain are all your craft and cunning,
Vain your manifold disguises !
Well I know you, Pau-Puk-Keewis !'
With their clubs they beat and bruised
    him,
Beat to death poor Pau-Puk-Keewis,
Pounded him as maize is pounded,
Till his skull was crushed to pieces. 160

Six tall hunters, lithe and limber,
Bore him home on poles and branches,
Bore the body of the beaver;
But the ghost, the Jeebi in him,
Thought and felt as Pau-Puk-Keewis,
Still lived on as Pau-Puk-Keewis.

And it fluttered, strove, and struggled,
Waving hither, waving thither,
As the curtains of a wigwam
Struggle with their thongs of deer-skin, 170
When the wintry wind is blowing;
Till it drew itself together,
Till it rose up from the body,
Till it took the form and features
Of the cunning Pau-Puk-Keewis
Vanishing into the forest.

But the wary Hiawatha
Saw the figure ere it vanished,
Saw the form of Pau-Puk-Keewis
Glide into the soft blue shadow 180
Of the pine-trees of the forest;
Toward the squares of white beyond it,
Toward an opening in the forest,
Like a wind it rushed and panted,
Bending all the boughs before it,
And behind it, as the rain comes,
Came the steps of Hiawatha.

To a lake with many islands
Came the breathless Pau-Puk-Keewis,
Where among the water-lilies 190
Pishnekuh, the brant, were sailing;
Through the tufts of rushes floating,
Steering through the reedy islands,
Now their broad black beaks they lifted,
Now they plunged beneath the water,
Now they darkened in the shadow,
Now they brightened in the sunshine.

'Pishnekuh !' cried Pau-Puk-Keewis,
'Pishnekuh ! my brothers !' said he,
'Change me to a brant with plumage, 200
With a shining neck and feathers,
Make me large, and make me larger,
Ten times larger than the others.'

Straightway to a brant they changed him,
With two huge and dusky pinions,
With a bosom smooth and rounded,
With a bill like two great paddles,
Made him larger than the others,
Ten times larger than the largest,
Just as, shouting from the forest, 210
On the shore stood Hiawatha.

Up they rose with cry and clamor,
With a whir and beat of pinions,
Rose up from the reedy islands,
From the water-flags and lilies.
And they said to Pau-Puk-Keewis:
'In your flying, look not downward,
Take good heed and look not downward,
Lest some strange mischance should hap-
    pen,
Lest some great mishap befall you !' 220

Fast and far they fled to northward,
Fast and far through mist and sunshine,
Fed among the moors and fen-lands,
Slept among the reeds and rushes.

On the morrow as they journeyed,
Buoyed and lifted by the South-wind,
Wafted onward by the South-wind,
Blowing fresh and strong behind them,
Rose a sound of human voices,
Rose a clamor from beneath them, 230
From the lodges of a village,
From the people miles beneath them.

For the people of the village
Saw the flock of brant with wonder,
Saw the wings of Pau-Puk-Keewis
Flapping far up in the ether,
Broader than two doorway curtains.
Pau-Puk-Keewis heard the shouting,
Knew the voice of Hiawatha,
Knew the outcry of Iagoo, 240
And, forgetful of the warning,
Drew his neck in, and looked downward,
And the wind that blew behind him
Caught his mighty fan of feathers,
Sent him wheeling, whirling downward !
All in vain did Pau-Puk-Keewis
Struggle to regain his balance !
Whirling round and round and downward,
He beheld in turn the village
And in turn the flock above him, 250
Saw the village coming nearer,

And the flock receding farther,
Heard the voices growing louder,
Heard the shouting and the laughter;
Saw no more the flocks above him,
Only saw the earth beneath him;
Dead out of the empty heaven,
Dead among the shouting people,
With a heavy sound and sullen,
Fell the brant with broken pinions.   260

But his soul, his ghost, his shadow,
Still survived as Pau-Puk-Keewis,
Took again the form and features
Of the handsome Yenadizze,
And again went rushing onward,
Followed fast by Hiawatha,
Crying: 'Not so wide the world is,
Not so long and rough the way is,
But my wrath shall overtake you,
But my vengeance shall attain you!'   270

And so near he came, so near him,
That his hand was stretched to seize him,
His right hand to seize and hold him,
When the cunning Pau-Puk-Keewis
Whirled and spun about in circles,
Fanned the air into a whirlwind,
Danced the dust and leaves about him,
And amid the whirling eddies
Sprang into a hollow oak-tree,
Changed himself into a serpent,   280
Gliding out through root and rubbish.

With his right hand Hiawatha
Smote amain the hollow oak-tree,
Rent it into shreds and splinters,
Left it lying there in fragments.
But in vain; for Pau-Puk-Keewis,
Once again in human figure,
Full in sight ran on before him,
Sped away in gust and whirlwind,
On the shores of Gitche Gumee,   290
Westward by the Big-Sea-Water,
Came unto the rocky headlands,
To the Pictured Rocks of sandstone,
Looking over lake and landscape.

And the Old Man of the Mountain,
He the Manito of Mountains,
Opened wide his rocky doorways,
Opened wide his deep abysses,
Giving Pau-Puk-Keewis shelter
In his caverns dark and dreary,   300
Bidding Pau-Puk-Keewis welcome
To his gloomy lodge of sandstone.

There without stood Hiawatha,
Found the doorways closed against him,
With his mittens, Minjekahwun,
Smote great caverns in the sandstone,

Cried aloud in tones of thunder,
'Open! I am Hiawatha!'
But the Old Man of the Mountain
Opened not, and made no answer   310
From the silent crags of sandstone,
From the gloomy rock abysses.

Then he raised his hands to heaven,
Called imploring on the tempest,
Called Waywassimo, the lightning,
And the thunder, Annemeekee;
And they came with night and darkness,
Sweeping down the Big-Sea-Water
From the distant Thunder Mountains;
And the trembling Pau-Puk-Keewis   320
Heard the footsteps of the thunder,
Saw the red eyes of the lightning,
Was afraid, and crouched and trembled.

Then Waywassimo, the lightning,
Smote the doorways of the caverns,
With his war-club smote the doorways,
Smote the jutting crags of sandstone,
And the thunder, Annemeekee,
Shouted down into the caverns,
Saying, 'Where is Pau-Puk-Keewis!'   330
And the crags fell, and beneath them
Dead among the rocky ruins
Lay the cunning Pau-Puk-Keewis,
Lay the handsome Yenadizze,
Slain in his own human figure.

Ended were his wild adventures,
Ended were his tricks and gambols,
Ended all his craft and cunning,
Ended all his mischief-making,
All his gambling and his dancing,   340
All his wooing of the maidens.

Then the noble Hiawatha
Took his soul, his ghost, his shadow,
Spake and said: 'O Pau-Puk-Keewis,
Never more in human figure
Shall you search for new adventures;
Never more with jest and laughter
Dance the dust and leaves in whirlwinds;
But above there in the heavens
You shall soar and sail in circles;   350
I will change you to an eagle,
To Keneu, the great war-eagle,
Chief of all the fowls with feathers,
Chief of Hiawatha's chickens.'

And the name of Pau-Puk-Keewis
Lingers still among the people,
Lingers still among the singers,
And among the story-tellers;
And in Winter, when the snow-flakes
Whirl in eddies round the lodges,   360
When the wind in gusty tumult

O'er the smoke-flue pipes and whistles,
'There,' they cry, 'comes Pau-Puk-Kee-
      wis;
He is dancing through the village,
He is gathering in his harvest!'

XVIII

THE DEATH OF KWASIND

FAR and wide among the nations
Spread the name and fame of Kwasind;
No man dared to strive with Kwasind,
No man could compete with Kwasind.
But the mischievous Puk-Wudjies,
They the envious Little People,
They the fairies and the pygmies,
Plotted and conspired against him.
  ' If this hateful Kwasind,' said they,
' If this great, outrageous fellow   10
Goes on thus a little longer,
Tearing everything he touches,
Rending everything to pieces,
Filling all the world with wonder,
What becomes of the Puk-Wudjies ?
Who will care for the Puk-Wudjies ?
He will tread us down like mushrooms,
Drive us all into the water,
Give our bodies to be eaten
By the wicked Nee-ba-naw-baigs,   20
By the Spirits of the water !'
  So the angry Little People
All conspired against the Strong Man,
All conspired to murder Kwasind,
Yes, to rid the world of Kwasind,
The audacious, overbearing,
Heartless, haughty, dangerous Kwasind !
  Now this wondrous strength of Kwasind
In his crown alone was seated;
In his crown too was his weakness;   30
There alone could he be wounded,
Nowhere else could weapon pierce him,
Nowhere else could weapon harm him.
  Even there the only weapon
That could wound him, that could slay him,
Was the seed-cone of the pine-tree,
Was the blue cone of the fir-tree.
This was Kwasind's fatal secret,
Known to no man among mortals;
But the cunning Little People,   40
The Puk-Wudjies, knew the secret,
Knew the only way to kill him.
  So they gathered cones together,
Gathered seed-cones of the pine-tree,
Gathered blue cones of the fir-tree,
In the woods by Taquamenaw,
Brought them to the river's margin,
Heaped them in great piles together,
Where the red rocks from the margin
Jutting overhang the river.   50
There they lay in wait for Kwasind,
The malicious Little People.
  'T was an afternoon in Summer;
Very hot and still the air was,
Very smooth the gliding river,
Motionless the sleeping shadows:
Insects glistened in the sunshine,
Insects skated on the water,
Filled the drowsy air with buzzing,
With a far resounding war-cry.   60
  Down the river came the Strong Man,
In his birch canoe came Kwasind,
Floating slowly down the current
Of the sluggish Taquamenaw,
Very languid with the weather,
Very sleepy with the silence.
  From the overhanging branches,
From the tassels of the birch-trees,
Soft the Spirit of Sleep descended;
By his airy hosts surrounded,   70
His invisible attendants,
Came the Spirit of Sleep, Nepahwin;
Like a burnished Dush-kwo-ne-she,
Like a dragon-fly, he hovered
O'er the drowsy head of Kwasind.
  To his ear there came a murmur
As of waves upon a sea-shore,
As of far-off tumbling waters,
As of winds among the pine-trees;
And he felt upon his forehead   80
Blows of little airy war-clubs,
Wielded by the slumbrous legions
Of the Spirit of Sleep, Nepahwin,
As of some one breathing on him.
  At the first blow of their war-clubs,
Fell a drowsiness on Kwasind;
At the second blow they smote him,
Motionless his paddle rested;
At the third, before his vision
Reeled the landscape into darkness,   90
Very sound asleep was Kwasind.
  So he floated down the river,
Like a blind man seated upright,
Floated down the Taquamenaw,
Underneath the trembling birch-trees,
Underneath the wooded headlands,
Underneath the war encampment
Of the pygmies, the Puk-Wudjies.
  There they stood, all armed and waiting,

Hurled the pine-cones down upon him, 100
Struck him on his brawny shoulders,
On his crown defenceless struck him.
' Death to Kwasind ! ' was the sudden
War-cry of the Little People.

And he sideways swayed and tumbled,
Sideways fell into the river,
Plunged beneath the sluggish water
Headlong, as an otter plunges;
And the birch canoe, abandoned,
Drifted empty down the river, 110
Bottom upward swerved and drifted:
Nothing more was seen of Kwasind.

But the memory of the Strong Man
Lingered long among the people,
And whenever through the forest
Raged and roared the wintry tempest,
And the branches, tossed and troubled,
Creaked and groaned and split asunder,
' Kwasind !' cried they; ' that is Kwasind !
He is gathering in his fire-wood ! ' 120

XIX

THE GHOSTS

NEVER stoops the soaring vulture
On his quarry in the desert,
On the sick or wounded bison,
But another vulture, watching
From his high aerial look-out,
Sees the downward plunge, and follows;
And a third pursues the second,
Coming from the invisible ether,
First a speck, and then a vulture,
Till the air is dark with pinions. 10

So disasters come not singly;
But as if they watched and waited,
Scanning one another's motions,
When the first descends, the others
Follow, follow, gathering flock-wise
Round their victim, sick and wounded,
First a shadow, then a sorrow,
Till the air is dark with anguish.

Now, o'er all the dreary North-land,
Mighty Peboan, the Winter, 20
Breathing on the lakes and rivers,
Into stone had changed their waters.
From his hair he shook the snow-flakes,
Till the plains were strewn with whiteness,
One uninterrupted level,
As if, stooping, the Creator
With his hand had smoothed them over.

Through the forest, wide and wailing,

Roamed the hunter on his snow-shoes;
In the village worked the women, 30
Pounded maize, or dressed the deer-skin;
And the young men played together
On the ice the noisy ball-play,
On the plain the dance of snow-shoes.

One dark evening, after sundown,
In her wigwam Laughing Water
Sat with old Nokomis, waiting
For the steps of Hiawatha
Homeward from the hunt returning.

On their faces gleamed the firelight, 40
Painting them with streaks of crimson,
In the eyes of old Nokomis
Glimmered like the watery moonlight,
In the eyes of Laughing Water
Glistened like the sun in water;
And behind them crouched their shadows
In the corners of the wigwam,
And the smoke in wreaths above them
Climbed and crowded through the smoke-
flue.

Then the curtain of the doorway 50
From without was slowly lifted;
Brighter glowed the fire a moment,
And a moment swerved the smoke-wreath
As two women entered softly,
Passed the doorway uninvited,
Without word of salutation,
Without sign of recognition,
Sat down in the farthest corner,
Crouching low among the shadows.

From their aspect and their garments, 60
Strangers seemed they in the village;
Very pale and haggard were they,
As they sat there sad and silent,
Trembling, cowering with the shadows.

Was it the wind above the smoke-flue,
Muttering down into the wigwam ?
Was it the owl, the Koko-koho,
Hooting from the dismal forest ?
Sure a voice said in the silence:
' These are corpses clad in garments, 7c
These are ghosts that come to haunt you,
From the kingdom of Ponemah,
From the land of the Hereafter ! '

Homeward now came Hiawatha
From his hunting in the forest,
With the snow upon his tresses,
And the red deer on his shoulders.
At the feet of Laughing Water
Down he threw his lifeless burden;
Nobler, handsomer she thought him, 80
Than when first he came to woo her,
First threw down the deer before her.

As a token of his wishes,
As a promise of the future.
   Then he turned and saw the strangers,
Cowering, crouching with the shadows;
Said within himself, 'Who are they ?
What strange guests has Minnehaha ?'
But he questioned not the strangers,
Only spake to bid them welcome   90
To his lodge, his food, his fireside.
   When the evening meal was ready,
And the deer had been divided,
Both the pallid guests, the strangers,
Springing from among the shadows,
Seized upon the choicest portions,
Seized the white fat of the roebuck,
Set apart for Laughing Water,
For the wife of Hiawatha,
Without asking, without thanking,   100
Eagerly devoured the morsels,
Flitted back among the shadows
In the corner of the wigwam.
   Not a word spake Hiawatha,
Not a motion made Nokomis,
Not a gesture Laughing Water;
Not a change came o'er their features;
Only Minnehaha softly
Whispered, saying, 'They are famished;
Let them do what best delights them;   110
Let them eat, for they are famished.'
   Many a daylight dawned and darkened,
Many a night shook off the daylight
As the pine shakes off the snow-flakes
From the midnight of its branches;
Day by day the guests unmoving
Sat there silent in the wigwam;
But by night, in storm or starlight,
Forth they went into the forest,
Bringing fire-wood to the wigwam,   120
Bringing pine-cones for the burning,
Always sad and always silent.
   And whenever Hiawatha
Came from fishing or from hunting,
When the evening meal was ready,
And the food had been divided,
Gliding from their darksome corner,
Came the pallid guests, the strangers,
Seized upon the choicest portions
Set aside for Laughing Water,   130
And without rebuke or question
Flitted back among the shadows.
   Never once had Hiawatha
By a word or look reproved them;
Never once had old Nokomis
Made a gesture of impatience;
Never once had Laughing Water

Shown resentment at the outrage.
All had they endured in silence,
That the rights of guest and stranger,   140
That the virtue of free-giving,
By a look might not be lessened,
By a word might not be broken.
   Once at midnight Hiawatha,
Ever wakeful, ever watchful,
In the wigwam, dimly lighted
By the brands that still were burning,
By the glimmering, flickering firelight,
Heard a sighing, oft repeated,
Heard a sobbing, as of sorrow.   150
   From his couch rose Hiawatha,
From his shaggy hides of bison,
Pushed aside the deer-skin curtain,
Saw the pallid guests, the shadows,
Sitting upright on their couches,
Weeping in the silent midnight.
   And he said: 'O guests ! why is it
That your hearts are so afflicted,
That you sob so in the midnight ?
Has perchance the old Nokomis, .   160
Has my wife, my Minnehaha,
Wronged or grieved you by unkindness,
Failed in hospitable duties ?'
   Then the shadows ceased from weeping,
Ceased from sobbing and lamenting,
And they said, with gentle voices:
'We are ghosts of the departed,
Souls of those who once were with you.
From the realms of Chibiabos
Hither have we come to try you,   170
Hither have we come to warn you.
   'Cries of grief and lamentation
Reach us in the Blessed Islands;
Cries of anguish from the living,
Calling back their friends departed,
Sadden us with useless sorrow.
Therefore have we come to try you;
No one knows us, no one heeds us.
We are but a burden to you,
And we see that the departed   180
Have no place among the living.
   'Think of this, O Hiawatha !
Speak of it to all the people,
That henceforward and forever
They no more with lamentations
Sadden the souls of the departed
In the Islands of the Blessed.
   'Do not lay such heavy burdens
In the graves of those you bury,
Not such weight of furs and wampum,   190
Not such weight of pots and kettles,
For the spirits faint beneath them.

Only give them food to carry,
Only give them fire to light them.
 'Four days is the spirit's journey
To the land of ghosts and shadows,
Four its lonely night encampments;
Four times must their fires be lighted.
Therefore, when the dead are buried,
Let a fire, as night approaches,   200
Four times on the grave be kindled,
That the soul upon its journey
May not lack the cheerful firelight,
May not grope about in darkness.
 'Farewell, noble Hiawatha!
We have put you to the trial,
To the proof have put your patience,
By the insult of our presence,
By the outrage of our actions.
We have found you great and noble.   210
Fail not in the greater trial,
Faint not in the harder struggle.'
 When they ceased, a sudden darkness
Fell and filled the silent wigwam.
Hiawatha heard a rustle
As of garments trailing by him,
Heard the curtain of the doorway
Lifted by a hand he saw not,
Felt the cold breath of the night air,
For a moment saw the starlight;   220
But he saw the ghosts no longer,
Saw no more the wandering spirits
From the kingdom of Ponemah,
From the land of the Hereafter.

XX

THE FAMINE

OH, the long and dreary Winter!
Oh, the cold and cruel Winter!
Ever thicker, thicker, thicker
Froze the ice on lake and river,
Ever deeper, deeper, deeper
Fell the snow o'er all the landscape,
Fell the covering snow, and drifted
Through the forest, round the village.
 Hardly from his buried wigwam
Could the hunter force a passage;   10
With his mittens and his snow-shoes
Vainly walked he through the forest,
Sought for bird or beast and found none,
Saw no track of deer or rabbit,
In the snow beheld no footprints,
In the ghastly, gleaming forest

Fell, and could not rise from weakness,
Perished there from cold and hunger.
 Oh the famine and the fever!
Oh the wasting of the famine!   20
Oh the blasting of the fever!
Oh the wailing of the children!
Oh the anguish of the women!
 All the earth was sick and famished;
Hungry was the air around them,
Hungry was the sky above them,
And the hungry stars in heaven
Like the eyes of wolves glared at them!
 Into Hiawatha's wigwam
Came two other guests, as silent   30
As the ghosts were, and as gloomy,
Waited not to be invited,
Did not parley at the doorway,
Sat there without word of welcome
In the seat of Laughing Water;
Looked with haggard eyes and hollow
At the face of Laughing Water.
 And the foremost said: 'Behold me!
I am Famine, Bukadawin!'
And the other said: 'Behold me!   40
I am Fever, Ahkosewin!'
 And the lovely Minnehaha
Shuddered as they looked upon her,
Shuddered at the words they uttered,
Lay down on her bed in silence,
Hid her face, but made no answer;
Lay there trembling, freezing, burning
At the looks they cast upon her,
At the fearful words they uttered.
 Forth into the empty forest   50
Rushed the maddened Hiawatha;
In his heart was deadly sorrow,
In his face a stony firmness;
On his brow the sweat of anguish
Started, but it froze and fell not.
 Wrapped in furs and armed for hunting,
With his mighty bow of ash-tree,
With his quiver full of arrows,
With his mittens, Minjekahwun,
Into the vast and vacant forest   60
On his snow-shoes strode he forward.
 'Gitche Manito, the Mighty!'
Cried he with his face uplifted
In that bitter hour of anguish,
'Give your children food, O father!
Give us food, or we must perish!
Give me food for Minnehaha,
For my dying Minnehaha!'
 Through the far-resounding forest,
Through the forest vast and vacant   70

Rang that cry of desolation,
But there came no other answer
Than the echo of his crying,
Than the echo of the woodlands,
'Minnehaha ! Minnehaha !'
    All day long roved Hiawatha
In that melancholy forest,
Through the shadow of whose thickets,
In the pleasant days of Summer,
Of that ne'er forgotten Summer,   80
He had brought his young wife home-
        ward
From the land of the Dacotahs;
When the birds sang in the thickets,
And the streamlets laughed and glistened,
And the air was full of fragrance,
And the lovely Laughing Water
Said with voice that did not tremble,
'I will follow you, my husband !'
    In the wigwam with Nokomis,
With those gloomy guests that watched
        her,   90
With the Famine and the Fever,
She was lying, the Beloved,
She, the dying Minnehaha.
    'Hark !' she said; 'I hear a rushing,
Hear a roaring and a rushing,
Hear the Falls of Minnehaha
Calling to me from a distance !'
'No, my child !' said old Nokomis,
''T is the night-wind in the pine-trees !'
    'Look !' she said; 'I see my father   100
Standing lonely at his doorway,
Beckoning to me from his wigwam
In the land of the Dacotahs !'
'No, my child !' said old Nokomis,
''T is the smoke, that waves and beckons !'
    'Ah !' said she, 'the eyes of Pauguk
Glare upon me in the darkness,
I can feel his icy fingers
Clasping mine amid the darkness !
Hiawatha ! Hiawatha !'   110
    And the desolate Hiawatha,
Far away amid the forest,
Miles away among the mountains,
Heard that sudden cry of anguish,
Heard the voice of Minnehaha
Calling to him in the darkness,
'Hiawatha ! Hiawatha !'
    Over snow-fields waste and pathless,
Under snow-encumbered branches,
Homeward hurried Hiawatha,   120
Empty-handed, heavy-hearted,
Heard Nokomis moaning, wailing:
'Wahonowin ! Wahonowin !

Would that I had perished for you,
Would that I were dead as you are !
Wahonowin ! Wahonowin !'
    And he rushed into the wigwam,
Saw the old Nokomis slowly
Rocking to and fro and moaning,
Saw his lovely Minnehaha   130
Lying dead and cold before him,
And his bursting heart within him
Uttered such a cry of anguish,
That the forest moaned and shuddered,
That the very stars in heaven
Shook and trembled with his anguish.
    Then he sat down, still and speech-
        less,
On the bed of Minnehaha,
At the feet of Laughing Water,
At those willing feet, that never   140
More would lightly run to meet him,
Never more would lightly follow.
    With both hands his face he covered,
Seven long days and nights he sat there,
As if in a swoon he sat there,
Speechless, motionless, unconscious
Of the daylight or the darkness.
    Then they buried Minnehaha;
In the snow a grave they made her,
In the forest deep and darksome,   150
Underneath the moaning hemlocks;
Clothed her in her richest garments,
Wrapped her in her robes of ermine,
Covered her with snow, like ermine;
Thus they buried Minnehaha.
    And at night a fire was lighted,
On her grave four times was kindled,
For her soul upon its journey
To the Islands of the Blessed.
From his doorway Hiawatha   160
Saw it burning in the forest,
Lighting up the gloomy hemlocks;
From his sleepless bed uprising,
From the bed of Minnehaha,
Stood and watched it at the doorway,
That it might not be extinguished,
Might not leave her in the darkness.
'Farewell !' said he, 'Minnehaha !
Farewell, O my Laughing Water !
All my heart is buried with you,   170
All my thoughts go onward with you !
Come not back again to labor,
Come not back again to suffer,
Where the Famine and the Fever
Wear the heart and waste the body.
Soon my task will be completed,
Soon your footsteps I shall follow

To the Islands of the Blessed,
To the Kingdom of Ponemah,
To the Land of the Hereafter!'   180

XXI

THE WHITE MAN'S FOOT

In his lodge beside a river,
Close beside a frozen river,
Sat an old man, sad and lonely.
White his hair was as a snow-drift;
Dull and low his fire was burning,
And the old man shook and trembled,
Folded in his Waubewyon,
In his tattered white-skin-wrapper,
Hearing nothing but the tempest
As it roared along the forest,   10
Seeing nothing but the snow-storm,
As it whirled and hissed and drifted.
    All the coals were white with ashes,
And the fire was slowly dying,
As a young man, walking lightly,
At the open doorway entered.
Red with blood of youth his cheeks were,
Soft his eyes, as stars in Spring-time,
Bound his forehead was with grasses;
Bound and plumed with scented grasses, 20
On his lips a smile of beauty,
Filling all the lodge with sunshine,
In his hand a bunch of blossoms
Filling all the lodge with sweetness.
    'Ah, my son!' exclaimed the old man,
'Happy are my eyes to see you.
Sit here on the mat beside me,
Sit here by the dying embers,
Let us pass the night together,
Tell me of your strange adventures,   30
Of the lands where you have travelled;
I will tell you of my prowess,
Of my many deeds of wonder.'
    From his pouch he drew his peace-pipe,
Very old and strangely fashioned;
Made of red stone was the pipe-head,
And the stem a reed with feathers;
Filled the pipe with bark of willow,
Placed a burning coal upon it,
Gave it to his guest, the stranger,   40
And began to speak in this wise:
'When I blow my breath about me,
When I breathe upon the landscape,
Motionless are all the rivers,
Hard as stone becomes the water!'
    And the young man answered, smiling:

'When I blow my breath about me,
When I breathe upon the landscape,
Flowers spring up o'er all the meadows,
Singing, onward rush the rivers!'   50
    'When I shake my hoary tresses,'
Said the old man darkly frowning,
'All the land with snow is covered;
All the leaves from all the branches
Fall and fade and die and wither,
For I breathe, and lo! they are not.
From the waters and the marshes
Rise the wild goose and the heron,
Fly away to distant regions,
For I speak, and lo! they are not.   60
And where'er my footsteps wander,
All the wild beasts of the forest
Hide themselves in holes and caverns,
And the earth becomes as flintstone!'
    'When I shake my flowing ringlets,'
Said the young man, softly laughing,
'Showers of rain fall warm and welcome,
Plants lift up their heads rejoicing,
Back into their lakes and marshes
Come the wild goose and the heron,   70
Homeward shoots the arrowy swallow,
Sing the bluebird and the robin,
And where'er my footsteps wander,
All the meadows wave with blossoms,
All the woodlands ring with music,
All the trees are dark with foliage!'
    While they spake, the night departed:
From the distant realms of Wabun,
From his shining lodge of silver,
Like a warrior robed and painted,   80
Came the sun, and said, 'Behold me
Gheezis, the great sun, behold me!'
    Then the old man's tongue was speechless
And the air grew warm and pleasant,
And upon the wigwam sweetly
Sang the bluebird and the robin,
And the stream began to murmur,
And a scent of growing grasses
Through the lodge was gently wafted.
    And Segwun, the youthful stranger,   90
More distinctly in the daylight
Saw the icy face before him;
It was Peboan, the Winter!
    From his eyes the tears were flowing,
As from melting lakes the streamlets,
And his body shrunk and dwindled
As the shouting sun ascended,
Till into the air it faded,
Till into the ground it vanished,
And the young man saw before him,   100
On the hearth-stone of the wigwam,

Where the fire had smoked and smouldered,
Saw the earliest flower of Spring-time,
Saw the Beauty of the Spring-time,
Saw the Miskodeed in blossom.

Thus it was that in the North-land
After that unheard-of coldness,
That intolerable Winter,
Came the Spring with all its splendor,
All its birds and all its blossoms,   110
All its flowers and leaves and grasses.

Sailing on the wind to northward,
Flying in great flocks, like arrows,
Like huge arrows shot through heaven,
Passed the swan, the Mahnahbezee,
Speaking almost as a man speaks;
And in long lines waving, bending
Like a bow-string snapped asunder,
Came the white goose, Waw-be-wawa;
And in pairs, or singly flying,   120
Mahng the loon, with clangorous pinions,
The blue heron, the Shuh-shuh-gah,
And the grouse, the Mushkodasa.

In the thickets and the meadows
Piped the bluebird, the Owaissa,
On the summit of the lodges
Sang the robin, the Opechee,
In the covert of the pine-trees
Cooed the pigeon, the Omemee;
And the sorrowing Hiawatha,   130
Speechless in his infinite sorrow,
Heard their voices calling to him,
Went forth from his gloomy doorway,
Stood and gazed into the heaven,
Gazed upon the earth and waters.

From his wanderings far to eastward,
From the regions of the morning,
From the shining land of Wabun,
Homeward now returned Iagoo,
The great traveller, the great boaster,   140
Full of new and strange adventures,
Marvels many and many wonders.

And the people of the village
Listened to him as he told them
Of his marvellous adventures,
Laughing answered him in this wise:
'Ugh! it is indeed Iagoo!
No one else beholds such wonders!'

He had seen, he said, a water
Bigger than the Big-Sea-Water,   150
Broader than the Gitche Gumee,
Bitter so that none could drink it!
At each other looked the warriors,
Looked the women at each other,
Smiled, and said, 'It cannot be so!
Kaw!' they said, 'it cannot be so!'

'O'er it,' said he, 'o'er this water
Came a great canoe with pinions,
A canoe with wings came flying,
Bigger than a grove of pine-trees,   160
Taller than the tallest tree-tops!'
And the old men and the women
Looked and tittered at each other;
'Kaw!' they said, 'we don't believe it!'

From its mouth, he said, to greet him,
Came Waywassimo, the lightning,
Came the thunder, Annemeekee!
And the warriors and the women
Laughed aloud at poor Iagoo;
'Kaw!' they said, 'what tales you tell
        us!'   170
'In it,' said he, 'came a people,
In the great canoe with pinions
Came, he said, a hundred warriors;
Painted white were all their faces
And with hair their chins were covered!'
And the warriors and the women
Laughed and shouted in derision,
Like the ravens on the tree-tops,
Like the crows upon the hemlocks.
'Kaw!' they said, 'what lies you tell
        us!   180
Do not think that we believe them!'

Only Hiawatha laughed not,
But he gravely spake and answered
To their jeering and their jesting:
'True is all Iagoo tells us;
I have seen it in a vision,
Seen the great canoe with pinions,
Seen the people with white faces,
Seen the coming of this bearded
People of the wooden vessel   190
From the regions of the morning,
From the shining lands of Wabun.

'Gitche Manito, the Mighty,
The Great Spirit, the Creator,
Sends them hither on his errand,
Sends them to us with his message.
Wheresoe'er they move, before them
Swarms the stinging fly, the Ahmo,
Swarms the bee, the honey-maker;
Wheresoe'er they tread, beneath them   200
Springs a flower unknown among us,
Springs the White-man's Foot in blossom.

'Let us welcome, then, the strangers,
Hail them as our friends and brothers,
And the heart's right hand of friendship
Give them when they come to see us.
Gitche Manito, the Mighty,
Said this to me in my vision.
'I beheld, too, in that vision

All the secrets of the future, 210
Of the distant days that shall be.
I beheld the westward marches
Of the unknown, crowded nations.
All the land was full of people,
Restless, struggling, toiling, striving,
Speaking many tongues, yet feeling
But one heart-beat in their bosoms.
In the woodlands rang their axes,
Smoked their towns in all the valleys,
Over all the lakes and rivers 220
Rushed their great canoes of thunder.
  'Then a darker, drearier vision
Passed before me, vague and cloud-like;
I beheld our nation scattered,
All forgetful of my counsels,
Weakened, warring with each other:
Saw the remnants of our people
Sweeping westward, wild and woful,
Like the cloud-rack of a tempest,
Like the withered leaves of Autumn!' 230

XXII

HIAWATHA'S DEPARTURE

By the shore of Gitche Gumee,
By the shining Big-Sea-Water,
At the doorway of his wigwam,
In the pleasant summer morning,
Hiawatha stood and waited.
All the air was full of freshness,
All the earth was bright and joyous,
And before him, through the sunshine,
Westward toward the neighboring forest
Passed in golden swarms the Ahmo, 10
Passed the bees, the honey-makers,
Burning, singing in the sunshine.
  Bright above him shone the heavens,
Level spread the lake before him;
From its bosom leaped the sturgeon,
Sparkling, flashing in the sunshine;
On its margin the great forest
Stood reflected in the water,
Every tree-top had its shadow,
Motionless beneath the water. 20
  From the brow of Hiawatha
Gone was every trace of sorrow,
As the fog from off the water,
As the mist from off the meadow.
With a smile of joy and triumph,
With a look of exultation,
As of one who in a vision
Sees what is to be, but is not,
Stood and waited Hiawatha.

Toward the sun his hands were lifted,[1] 30
Both the palms spread out against it,
And between the parted fingers
Fell the sunshine on his features,
Flecked with light his naked shoulders,
As it falls and flecks an oak-tree
Through the rifted leaves and branches.
  O'er the water floating, flying,
Something in the hazy distance,
Something in the mists of morning,
Loomed and lifted from the water, 40
Now seemed floating, now seemed flying,
Coming nearer, nearer, nearer.
Was it Shingebis the diver?
Or the pelican, the Shada?
Or the heron, the Shuh-shuh-gah?
Or the white goose, Waw-be-wawa,
With the water dripping, flashing,
From its glossy neck and feathers?
  It was neither goose nor diver,
Neither pelican nor heron, 50
O'er the water floating, flying,
Through the shining mist of morning,
But a birch canoe with paddles,
Rising, sinking on the water,
Dripping, flashing in the sunshine;
And within it came a people
From the distant land of Wabun,
From the farthest realms of morning
Came the Black-Robe chief, the Prophet,
He the Priest of Prayer, the Pale-face, 60
With his guides and his companions.
  And the noble Hiawatha,
With his hands aloft extended,
Held aloft in sign of welcome,
Waited, full of exultation,
Till the birch canoe with paddles
Grated on the shining pebbles,
Stranded on the sandy margin,
Till the Black-Robe chief, the Pale-face,
With the cross upon his bosom, 70
Landed on the sandy margin.
  Then the joyous Hiawatha
Cried aloud and spake in this wise:
'Beautiful is the sun, O strangers,
When you come so far to see us!
All our town in peace awaits you,
All our doors stand open for you;
You shall enter all our wigwams,
For the heart's right hand we give you.
  'Never bloomed the earth so gayly, 80
Never shone the sun so brightly,

---

[1] In this manner, and with such salutations, was Father Marquette received by the Illinois. See his *Voyages et Découvertes*, section v. (LONGFELLOW.)

As to-day they shine and blossom
When you come so far to see us!
Never was our lake so tranquil,
Nor so free from rocks and sand-bars;
For your birch canoe in passing
Has removed both rock and sand-bar.

'Never before had our tobacco
Such a sweet and pleasant flavor,
Never the broad leaves of our cornfields 90
Were so beautiful to look on,
As they seem to us this morning,
When you come so far to see us!'
    And the Black-Robe chief made an-
        swer,
Stammered in his speech a little,
Speaking words yet unfamiliar:
'Peace be with you, Hiawatha,
Peace be with you and your people,
Peace of prayer, and peace of pardon,
Peace of Christ, and joy of Mary!'   100
    Then the generous Hiawatha
Led the strangers to his wigwam,
Seated them on skins of bison,
Seated them on skins of ermine,
And the careful old Nokomis
Brought them food in bowls of basswood,
Water brought in birchen dippers,
And the calumet, the peace-pipe,
Filled and lighted for their smoking.
    All the old men of the village,   110
All the warriors of the nation,
All the Jossakeeds, the Prophets,
The magicians, the Wabenos,
And the Medicine-men, the Medas,
Came to bid the strangers welcome;
'It is well,' they said, 'O brothers,
That you come so far to see us!'
    In a circle round the doorway,
With their pipes they sat in silence,
Waiting to behold the strangers,   120
Waiting to receive their message;
Till the Black-Robe chief, the Pale-face,
From the wigwam came to greet them,
Stammering in his speech a little,
Speaking words yet unfamiliar;
'It is well,' they said, 'O brother,
That you come so far to see us!'
    Then the Black-Robe chief, the Prophet,
Told his message to the people,
Told the purport of his mission,   130
Told them of the Virgin Mary,
And her blessed Son, the Saviour,
How in distant lands and ages
He had lived on earth as we do;
How he fasted, prayed, and labored;

How the Jews, the tribe accursed,
Mocked him, scourged him, crucified him;
How he rose from where they laid him,
Walked again with his disciples,
And ascended into heaven.   140
    And the chiefs made answer, saying:
'We have listened to your message,
We have heard your words of wisdom,
We will think on what you tell us.
It is well for us, O brothers,
That you come so far to see us!'
    Then they rose up and departed
Each one homeward to his wigwam,
To the young men and the women
Told the story of the strangers   150
Whom the Master of Life had sent
        them
From the shining land of Wabun.
    Heavy with the heat and silence
Grew the afternoon of summer;
With a drowsy sound the forest
Whispered round the sultry wigwam,
With a sound of sleep the water
Rippled on the beach below it;
From the cornfields shrill and ceaseless
Sang the grasshopper, Pah-puk-keena;   160
And the guests of Hiawatha,
Weary with the heat of Summer,
Slumbered in the sultry wigwam.
    Slowly o'er the simmering landscape
Fell the evening's dusk and coolness,
And the long and level sunbeams
Shot their spears into the forest,
Breaking through its shields of shadow,
Rushed into each secret ambush,
Searched each thicket, dingle, hollow;   170
Still the guests of Hiawatha
Slumbered in the silent wigwam.
    From his place rose Hiawatha,
Bade farewell to old Nokomis,
Spake in whispers, spake in this wise,
Did not wake the guests, that slum-
        bered:
'I am going, O Nokomis,
On a long and distant journey,
To the portals of the Sunset,
To the regions of the home-wind,   180
Of the Northwest-Wind, Keewaydin.
But these guests I leave behind me,
In your watch and ward I leave them;
See that never harm comes near them,
See that never fear molests them,
Never danger nor suspicion,
Never want of food or shelter,
In the lodge of Hiawatha!'

Forth into the village went he,
Bade farewell to all the warriors, 190
Bade farewell to all the young men,
Spake persuading, spake in this wise:
'I am going, O my people,
On a long and distant journey;
Many moons and many winters
Will have come, and will have vanished.
Ere I come again to see you.
But my guests I leave behind me;
Listen to their words of wisdom,
Listen to the truth they tell you, 200
For the Master of Life has sent them
From the land of light and morning!'
On the shore stood Hiawatha,
Turned and waved his hand at parting;
On the clear and luminous water
Launched his birch canoe for sailing,
From the pebbles of the margin
Shoved it forth into the water;
Whispered to it, 'Westward! westward!'
And with speed it darted forward. 210
And the evening sun descending
Set the clouds on fire with redness,
Burned the broad sky, like a prairie,
Left upon the level water
One long track and trail of splendor,
Down whose stream, as down a river,
Westward, westward, Hiawatha
Sailed into the fiery sunset,
Sailed into the purple vapors,
Sailed into the dusk of evening. 220
And the people from the margin
Watched him floating, rising, sinking,
Till the birch canoe seemed lifted
High into that sea of splendor,
Till it sank into the vapors
Like the new moon slowly, slowly
Sinking in the purple distance.
And they said, 'Farewell forever!'
Said, 'Farewell, O Hiawatha!'
And the forests, dark and lonely, 230
Moved through all their depths of darkness,
Sighed, 'Farewell, O Hiawatha!'
And the waves upon the margin
Rising, rippling on the pebbles,
Sobbed, 'Farewell, O Hiawatha!'
And the heron, the Shuh-shuh-gah,
From her haunts among the fen-lands,
Screamed, 'Farewell, O Hiawatha!'
Thus departed Hiawatha,
Hiawatha the Beloved, 240
In the glory of the sunset,
In the purple mists of evening,
To the regions of the home-wind,
Of the Northwest-Wind, Keewaydin,
To the Islands of the Blessed,
To the Kingdom of Ponemah,
To the Land of the Hereafter!

June 25, 1854–Mar. 21, 1855. Nov. 1855.

MY LOST YOUTH

OFTEN I think of the beautiful town [1]
  That is seated by the sea;
Often in thought go up and down
The pleasant streets of that dear old town,
  And my youth comes back to me.
    And a verse of a Lapland song
    Is haunting my memory still:
'A boy's will is the wind's will,
And the thoughts of youth are long, long
    thoughts.'

I can see the shadowy lines of its trees, 10
  And catch, in sudden gleams,
The sheen of the far-surrounding seas,
And islands that were the Hesperides
  Of all my boyish dreams.
    And the burden of that old song,
    It murmurs and whispers still:
'A boy's will is the wind's will,
And the thoughts of youth are long, long
    thoughts.'

I remember the black wharves and the
    slips,
  And the sea-tides tossing free; 20
And the Spanish sailors with bearded lips,
And the beauty and mystery of the ships,
  And the magic of the sea.
    And the voice of that wayward song
    Is singing and saying still:
'A boy's will is the wind's will,
And the thoughts of youth are long, long
    thoughts.'

[1] From Longfellow's *Journal:* March 29, 1855 — At
night as I lie in bed, a poem comes into my mind, —
a memory of Portland, — my native town, the city by
the sea.
        Siede la terra dove nato fui
        Sulla marina.
    March 30 — Wrote the poem; and am rather pleased
with it, and with the bringing in of the two lines of the
old Lapland song,
    A boy's will is the wind's will,
And the thoughts of youth are long, long thoughts.
                    (*Life*, vol. ii., p. 284.)

I remember the bulwarks by the shore,
  And the fort upon the hill;
The sunrise gun, with its hollow roar,   30
The drum-beat repeated o'er and o'er,
  And the bugle wild and shrill.
    And the music of that old song
    Throbs in my memory still:
  'A boy's will is the wind's will,
And the thoughts of youth are long, long
    thoughts.'

I remember the sea-fight far away,[1]
  How it thundered o'er the tide!
And the dead captains, as they lay
In their graves, o'erlooking the tranquil bay
  Where they in battle died.   41
    And the sound of that mournful song
    Goes through me with a thrill:
  'A boy's will is the wind's will,
And the thoughts of youth are long, long
    thoughts.'

I can see the breezy dome of groves,
  The shadows of Deering's Woods;
And the friendships old and the early loves
Come back with a Sabbath sound, as of
    doves
  In quiet neighborhoods.   50
    And the verse of that sweet old song,
    It flutters and murmurs still:
  'A boy's will is the wind's will,
And the thoughts of youth are long, long
    thoughts.'

I remember the gleams and glooms that dart
  Across the school-boy's brain;
The song and the silence in the heart,
That in part are prophecies, and in part
  Are longings wild and vain.
    And the voice of that fitful song   60
    Sings on, and is never still:
  'A boy's will is the wind's will,
And the thoughts of youth are long, long
    thoughts.'

There are things of which I may not speak;
  There are dreams that cannot die;

There are thoughts that make the strong
    heart weak,
And bring a pallor into the cheek,
  And a mist before the eye.
    And the words of that fatal song
    Come over me like a chill: 70
  'A boy's will is the wind's will,
And the thoughts of youth are long, long
    thoughts.'

Strange to me now are the forms I meet
  When I visit the dear old town;
But the native air is pure and sweet,
And the trees that o'ershadow each well-
    known street,
  As they balance up and down,
    Are singing the beautiful song,
    Are sighing and whispering still:
  'A boy's will is the wind's will,   80
And the thoughts of youth are long, long
    thoughts.'

And Deering's Woods are fresh and fair,[2]
  And with joy that is almost pain
My heart goes back to wander there,
And among the dreams of the days that were,
  I find my lost youth again.
    And the strange and beautiful song,
    The groves are repeating it still:
  'A boy's will is the wind's will,
And the thoughts of youth are long, long
    thoughts.'   90
1855   (1858.)

THE FIFTIETH BIRTHDAY OF AGASSIZ [3]

MAY 28, 1857

It was fifty years ago
  In the pleasant month of May,
In the beautiful Pays de Vaud,
  A child in its cradle lay.

And Nature, the old nurse, took
  The child upon her knee,
Saying: 'Here is a story-book
  Thy Father has written for thee.'

---

[1] This was the engagement between the Enterprise and Boxer off the harbor of Portland, in which both captains were slain. They were buried side by side in the cemetery on Mountjoy. (LONGFELLOW.)
The fight took place in 1813. The Enterprise was an American brig, the Boxer, an English one. The fight, which could be seen from the shore, lasted for three quarters of an hour, when the Enterprise came into the harbor, bringing her captive with her. (*Cambridge Edition.*)

[2] See the *Life*, vol. i, p. 25.

[3] A dinner was given to Agassiz on his fiftieth birthday, at which Longfellow presided, and poems were read by Longfellow, Holmes, and Lowell.
See Longfellow's 'Noel,' and 'Three Friends of Mine,' Lowell's 'Agassiz,' Whittier's 'The Prayer of Agassiz,' Holmes's 'A Farewell to Agassiz' and 'At the Saturday Club,' and T. W. Parsons's Sonnet, 'Agassiz.'

'Come, wander with me,' she said,
  'Into regions yet untrod;   10
And read what is still unread
  In the manuscripts of God.'

And he wandered away and away
  With Nature, the dear old nurse,
Who sang to him night and day
  The rhymes of the universe.

And whenever the way seemed long,
  Or his heart began to fail,
She would sing a more wonderful song,
  Or tell a more marvellous tale.   20

So she keeps him still a child,
  And will not let him go,
Though at times his heart beats wild
  For the beautiful Pays de Vaud;

Though at times he hears in his dreams
  The Ranz des Vaches of old,
And the rush of mountain streams
  From glaciers clear and cold;

And the mother at home says, 'Hark!
  For his voice I listen and yearn;   30
It is growing late and dark,
  And my boy does not return!'
'857.   (1858.)

DAYBREAK

A WIND came up out of the sea,
And said, 'O mists, make room for me.'

It hailed the ships, and cried, 'Sail on,
Ye mariners, the night is gone.'

And hurried landward far away,
Crying, 'Awake! it is the day.'

It said unto the forest, 'Shout!
Hang all your leafy banners out!'

It touched the wood-bird's folded wing,
And said, 'O bird, awake and sing.'   10

And o'er the farms, 'O chanticleer,
Your clarion blow; the day is near.'

It whispered to the fields of corn,
'Bow down, and hail the coming morn.'

It shouted through the belfry-tower,
'Awake, O bell! proclaim the hour.'

It crossed the churchyard with a sigh,
And said, 'Not yet! in quiet lie.'
1857.   (1858.)

SANTA FILOMENA [1]

WHENE'ER a noble deed is wrought,
Whene'er is spoken a noble thought,
  Our hearts, in glad surprise,
  To higher levels rise.

The tidal wave of deeper souls
Into our inmost being rolls,
  And lifts us unawares
  Out of all meaner cares.

Honor to those whose words or deeds
Thus help us in our daily needs,   10
  And by their overflow
  Raise us from what is low!

Thus thought I, as by night I read
Of the great army of the dead,
  The trenches cold and damp,
  The starved and frozen camp, —

The wounded from the battle-plain,
In dreary hospitals of pain,
  The cheerless corridors,
  The cold and stony floors.   20

Lo! in that house of misery
A lady with a lamp I see
  Pass through the glimmering gloom,
  And flit from room to room.

And slow, as in a dream of bliss,
The speechless sufferer turns to kiss
  Her shadow, as it falls
  Upon the darkening walls.

As if a door in heaven should be
Opened and then closed suddenly,   30
  The vision came and went,
  The light shone and was spent.

On England's annals, through the long
Hereafter of her speech and song,
  That light its rays shall cast
  From portals of the past.

[1] For the legend, see Mrs. Jameson's *Legendary Art*
(ii, 298). The modern application you will not miss.
In Italian, one may say *Filomela* or *Filomena*. (LONG-
FELLOW.)
  The 'modern application' is to Florence Nightin-
gale.

A Lady with a Lamp shall stand
In the great history of the land,
   A noble type of good,   40
   Heroic womanhood.

1857.

Nor even shall be wanting here
The palm, the lily, and the spear,
The symbols that of yore
Saint Filomena bore.

1857.

THE COURTSHIP OF MILES STANDISH [1]

I

MILES STANDISH

In the Old Colony days, in Plymouth the
   land of the Pilgrims,
To and fro in a room of his simple and
   primitive dwelling,
Clad in doublet and hose, and boots of Cor-
   dovan leather,
Strode, with a martial air, Miles Standish
   the Puritan Captain.
Buried in thought he seemed, with his
   hands behind him, and pausing
Ever and anon to behold his glittering
   weapons of warfare,
Hanging in shining array along the walls
   of the chamber, —
Cutlass and corselet of steel, and his trusty
   sword of Damascus,
Curved at the point and inscribed with its
   mystical Arabic sentence,
While underneath, in a corner, were fowl-
   ing-piece, musket, and matchlock. 10
Short of stature he was, but strongly built
   and athletic,
Broad in the shoulders, deep-chested, with
   muscles and sinews of iron;
Brown as a nut was his face, but his russet
   beard was already
Flaked with patches of snow, as hedges
   sometimes in November.
Near him was seated John Alden, his friend
   and household companion,
Writing with diligent speed at a table of
   pine by the window;
Fair-haired, azure-eyed, with delicate Saxon
   complexion,
Having the dew of his youth, and the
   beauty thereof, as the captives

Whom Saint Gregory saw, and exclaimed,
   'Not Angles, but Angels.'
Youngest of all was he of the men who
   came in the Mayflower. 20

Suddenly breaking the silence, the dili-
   gent scribe interrupting,
Spake, in the pride of his heart, Miles
   Standish the Captain of Plymouth.
'Look at these arms,' he said, 'the war-
   like weapons that hang here
Burnished and bright and clean, as if for
   parade or inspection !
This is the sword of Damascus I fought
   with in Flanders ; this breastplate,
Well I remember the day ! once saved my
   life in a skirmish;
Here in front you can see the very dint of
   the bullet
Fired point-blank at my heart by a Spanish
   arcabucero.
Had it not been of sheer steel, the forgot-
   ten bones of Miles Standish
Would at this moment be mould, in their
   grave in the Flemish morasses.' 30
Thereupon answered John Alden, but
   looked not up from his writing:
'Truly the breath of the Lord hath slackened the speed of the bullet;
He in his mercy preserved you, to be our
   shield and our weapon !'
Still the Captain continued, unheeding the
   words of the stripling:
'See, how bright they are burnished, as if
   in an arsenal hanging;
That is because I have done it myself, and
   not left it to others.
Serve yourself, would you be well served,
   is an excellent adage;
So I take care of my arms, as you of your
   pens and your inkhorn.
Then, too, there are my soldiers, my great,
   invincible army,
Twelve men, all equipped, having each his
   rest and his matchlock, 40

[1] Priscilla's reply to John Alden was a well-known
tradition before Longfellow took up the story. Longfellow himself, and also the poet Bryant, were descendants of John and Priscilla Alden. For the details of
colonial life, Longfellow followed especially Elliott's
History of New England, which he read in 1857. (*Life*,
vol. ii, pp. 328-329.)

Eighteen shillings a month, together with
    diet and pillage,
And, like Cæsar, I know the name of each
    of my soldiers ! '
This he said with a smile, that danced in
    his eyes, as the sunbeams
Dance on the waves of the sea, and vanish
    again in a moment.
Alden laughed as he wrote, and still the
    Captain continued:
' Look ! you can see from this window my
    brazen howitzer planted
High on the roof of the church, a preacher
    who speaks to the purpose,
Steady, straightforward, and strong, with
    irresistible logic,
Orthodox, flashing conviction right into the
    hearts of the heathen.
Now we are ready, I think, for any assault
    of the Indians;   50
Let them come, if they like, and the sooner
    they try it the better, —
Let them come, if they like, be it sagamore,
    sachem, or pow-wow,
Aspinet, Samoset, Corbitant, Squanto, or
    Tokamahamon ! '

Long at the window he stood, and wist-
    fully gazed on the landscape,
Washed with a cold gray mist, the vapory
    breath of the east-wind,
Forest and meadow and hill, and the steel-
    blue rim of the ocean,
Lying silent and sad, in the afternoon shad-
    ows and sunshine.
Over his countenance flitted a shadow like
    those on the landscape,
Gloom intermingled with light ; and his
    voice was subdued with emotion,
Tenderness, pity, regret, as after a pause
    he proceeded :   60
' Yonder there, on the hill by the sea, lies
    buried Rose Standish;
Beautiful rose of love, that bloomed for me
    by the wayside !
She was the first to die of all who came in
    the Mayflower !
Green above her is growing the field of
    wheat we have sown there,
Better to hide from the Indian scouts the
    graves of our people,
Lest they should count them and see how
    many already have perished ! '
Sadly his face he averted, and strode up
    and down, and was thoughtful.

Fixed to the opposite wall was a shelf of
    books, and among them
Prominent three, distinguished alike for
    bulk and for binding;
Bariffe's Artillery Guide, and the Com-
    mentaries of Cæsar   70
Out of the Latin translated by Arthur
    Goldinge of London,
And, as if guarded by these, between them
    was standing the Bible.
Musing a momont before them, Miles
    Standish paused, as if doubtful
Which of the three he should choose for
    his consolation and comfort,
Whether the wars of the Hebrews, the fa-
    mous campaigns of the Romans,
Or the Artillery practice, designed for bel-
    ligerent Christians.
Finally down from its shelf he dragged the
    ponderous Roman,
Seated himself at the window, and opened
    the book, and in silence
Turned o'er the well-worn leaves, where
    thumb-marks thick on the margin,
Like the trample of feet, proclaimed the
    battle was hottest.   80
Nothing was heard in the room but the
    hurrying pen of the stripling,
Busily writing epistles important, to go by
    the Mayflower,
Ready to sail on the morrow, or next day
    at latest, God willing !
Homeward bound with the tidings of all
    that terrible winter,
Letters written by Alden, and full of the
    name of Priscilla !
Full of the name and the fame of the Pu-
    ritan maiden Priscilla !

II

LOVE AND FRIENDSHIP

Nothing was heard in the room but the
    hurrying pen of the stripling,
Or an occasional sigh from the laboring
    heart of the Captain,
Reading the marvellous words and achieve-
    ments of Julius Cæsar.
After a while he exclaimed, as he smote
    with his hand, palm downwards,
Heavily on the page : ' A wonderful man
    was this Cæsar !
You are a writer, and I am a fighter, but
    here is a fellow

Who could both write and fight, and in
    both was equally skilful! '
Straightway answered and spake John
    Alden, the comely, the youthful :
' Yes, he was equally skilled, as you say,
    with his pen and his weapons.
Somewhere have I read, but where I for-
    get, he could dictate   10
Seven letters at once, at the same time
    writing his memoirs.'
' Truly,' continued the Captain, not heed-
    ing or hearing the other,
' Truly a wonderful man was Caius Julius
    Cæsar !
Better be first, he said, in a little Iberian
    village,
Than be second in Rome, and I think he was
    right when he said it.
Twice was he married before he was twenty,
    and many times after ;
Battles five hundred he fought, and a thou-
    sand cities he conquered ;
He, too, fought in Flanders, as he himself
    has recorded ;
Finally he was stabbed by his friend, the
    orator Brutus !
Now, do you know what he did on a certain
    occasion in Flanders,   20
When the rear-guard of his army retreated,
    the front giving way too,
And the immortal Twelfth Legion was
    crowded so closely together
There was no room for their swords ? Why,
    he seized a shield from a soldier,
Put himself straight at the head of his
    troops, and commanded the captains,
Calling on each by his name, to order for-
    ward the ensigns ;
Then to widen the ranks, and give more
    room for their weapons ;
So he won the day, the battle of something-
    or-other.
That 's what I always say ; if you wish a
    thing to be well done,
You must do it yourself, you must not leave
    it to others ! '

All was silent again; the Captain con-
    tinued his reading,   30
Nothing was heard in the room but the
    hurrying pen of the stripling
Writing epistles important to go next day
    by the Mayflower,
Filled with the name and the fame of the
    Puritan maiden Priscilla;

Every sentence began or closed with the
    name of Priscilla,
Till the treacherous pen, to which he con-
    fided the secret,
Strove to betray it by singing and shouting
    the name of Priscilla!
Finally closing his book, with a bang of the
    ponderous cover,
Sudden and loud as the sound of a soldier
    grounding his musket,
Thus to the young man spake Miles Stan-
    dish the Captain of Plymouth:
' When you have finished your work, I
    have something important to tell
    you.   40
Be not however in haste; I can wait; I shall
    not be impatient! '
Straightway Alden replied, as he folded the
    last of his letters,
Pushing his papers aside, and giving respect-
    ful attention:
' Speak; for whenever you speak, I am al-
    ways ready to listen,
Always ready to hear whatever pertains to
    Miles Standish.'
Thereupon answered the Captain, embar-
    rassed, and culling his phrases:
' 'T is not good for a man to be alone, say
    the Scriptures.
This I have said before, and again and again
    I repeat it;
Every hour in the day, I think it, and feel
    it, and say it.
Since Rose Standish died, my life has been
    weary and dreary;   50
Sick at heart have I been, beyond the heal-
    ing of friendship;
Oft in my lonely hours have I thought of
    the maiden Priscilla.
She is alone in the world; her father and
    mother and brother
Died in the winter together; I saw her
    going and coming,
Now to the grave of the dead, and now to
    the bed of the dying,
Patient, courageous, and strong, and said to
    myself, that if ever
There were angels on earth, as there are
    angels in heaven,
Two have I seen and known; and the angel
    whose name is Priscilla
Holds in my desolate life the place which
    the other abandoned.
Long have I cherished the thought, but
    never have dared to reveal it,   60

Being a coward in this, though valiant
  enough for the most part.
Go to the damsel Priscilla, the loveliest
  maiden of Plymouth,
Say that a blunt old Captain, a man not of
  words but of actions,
Offers his hand and his heart, the hand and
  heart of a soldier.
Not in these words, you know, but this in
  short is my meaning;
I am a maker of war, and not a maker of
  phrases.
You, who are bred as a scholar, can say it in
  elegant language,
Such as you read in your books of the plead-
  ings and wooings of lovers,
Such as you think best adapted to win the
  heart of a maiden.'

When he had spoken, John Alden, the
  fair-haired, taciturn stripling,   70
All aghast at his words, surprised, embarrassed, bewildered,
Trying to mask his dismay by treating the
  subject with lightness,
Trying to smile, and yet feeling his heart
  stand still in his bosom,
Just as a timepiece stops in a house that is
  stricken by lightning,
Thus made answer and spake, or rather
  stammered than answered:
'Such a message as that, I am sure I should
  mangle and mar it;
If you would have it well done, — I am only
  repeating your maxim, —
You must do it yourself, you must not leave
  it to others !'
But with the air of a man whom nothing can
  turn from his purpose,
Gravely shaking his head, made answer the
  Captain of Plymouth :   80
'Truly the maxim is good, and I do not
  mean to gainsay it;
But we must use it discreetly, and not waste
  powder for nothing.
Now, as I said before, I was never a maker
  of phrases.
I can march up to a fortress and summon
  the place to surrender,
But march up to a woman with such a pro-
  posal, I dare not.
I 'm not afraid of bullets, nor shot from the
  mouth of a cannon,
But of a thundering "No!" point-blank
  from the mouth of a woman,

That I confess I 'm afraid of, nor am I
  ashamed to confess it !
So you must grant my request, for you are
  an elegant scholar,
Having the graces of speech, and skill in the
  turning of phrases.'   90
Taking the hand of his friend, who still was
  reluctant and doubtful,
Holding it long in his own, and pressing it
  kindly, he added:
'Though I have spoken thus lightly, yet
  deep is the feeling that prompts me;
Surely you cannot refuse what I ask in the
  name of our friendship !'
Then made answer John Alden: 'The name
  of friendship is sacred;
What you demand in that name, I have not
  the power to deny you !'
So the strong will prevailed, subduing and
  moulding the gentler,
Friendship prevailed over love, and Alden
  went on his errand.

III

THE LOVER'S ERRAND

So the strong will prevailed, and Alden
  went on his errand,
Out of the street of the village, and into the
  paths of the forest,
Into the tranquil woods, where bluebirds
  and robins were building
Towns in the populous trees, with hanging
  gardens of verdure,
Peaceful, aerial cities of joy and affection
  and freedom.
All around him was calm, but within him
  commotion and conflict,
Love contending with friendship, and self
  with each generous impulse.
To and fro in his breast his thoughts were
  heaving and dashing,
As in a foundering ship, with every roll of
  the vessel,
Washes the bitter sea, the merciless surge
  of the ocean !   10
'Must I relinquish it all,' he cried with a
  wild lamentation, —
'Must I relinquish it all, the joy, the hope,
  the illusion ?
Was it for this I have loved, and waited,
  and worshipped in silence ?
Was it for this I have followed the flying
  feet and the shadow

Over the wintry sea, to the desolate shores
    of New England ?
Truly the heart is deceitful, and out of its
    depths of corruption
Rise, like an exhalation, the misty phantoms
    of passion;
Angels of light they seem, but are only de-
    lusions of Satan.
All is clear to me now; I feel it, I see it
    distinctly!
This is the hand of the Lord; it is laid upon
    me in anger,   20
For I have followed too much the heart's
    desires and devices,
Worshipping Astaroth blindly, and impious
    idols of Baal.
This is the cross I must bear; the sin and
    the swift retribution.'

    So through the Plymouth woods John
    Alden went on his errand;
Crossing the brook at the ford, where it
    brawled over pebble and shallow,
Gathering still, as he went, the May-flowers
    blooming around him,
Fragrant, filling the air with a strange and
    wonderful sweetness,
Children lost in the woods, and covered
    with leaves in their slumber.
'Puritan flowers,' he said, 'and the type of
    Puritan maidens,
Modest and simple and sweet, the very
    type of Priscilla !   30
So I will take them to her; to Priscilla the
    Mayflower of Plymouth,
Modest and simple and sweet, as a parting
    gift will I take them;
Breathing their silent farewells, as they
    fade and wither and perish,
Soon to be thrown away as is the heart of
    the giver.'
So through the Plymouth woods John
    Alden went on his errand;
Came to an open space, and saw the disk of
    the ocean,
Sailless, sombre and cold with the comfort-
    less breath of the east wind;
Saw the new-built house, and people at
    work in a meadow;
Heard, as he drew near the door, the mu-
    sical voice of Priscilla
Singing the hundredth Psalm, the grand old
    Puritan anthem,   40
Music that Luther sang to the sacred words
    of the Psalmist,

Full of the breath of the Lord, consoling
    and comforting many.
Then, as he opened the door, he beheld the
    form of the maiden
Seated beside her wheel, and the carded
    wool like a snow-drift
Piled at her knee, her white hands feeding
    the ravenous spindle,
While with her foot on the treadle she
    guided the wheel in its motion.
Open wide on her lap lay the well-worn
    psalm-book of Ainsworth,
Printed in Amsterdam, the words and the
    music together,
Rough-hewn, angular notes, like stones in
    the wall of a churchyard,
Darkened and overhung by the running
    vine of the verses.   50
Such was the book from whose pages she
    sang the old Puritan anthem,
She, the Puritan girl, in the solitude of the
    forest,
Making the humble house and the modest
    apparel of homespun
Beautiful with her beauty, and rich with
    the wealth of her being !
Over him rushed, like a wind that is keen
    and cold and relentless,
Thoughts of what might have been, and the
    weight and woe of his errand;
All the dreams that had faded, and all the
    hopes that had vanished,
All his life henceforth a dreary and tenant-
    less mansion,
Haunted by vain regrets, and pallid, sorrow-
    ful faces.
Still he said to himself, and almost fiercely
    he said it,   60
'Let not him that putteth his hand to the
    plough look backwards;
Though the ploughshare cut through the
    flowers of life to its fountains,
Though it pass o'er the graves of the dead
    and the hearths of the living,
It is the will of the Lord; and his mercy
    endureth forever !'

    So he entered the house: and the hum of
    the wheel and the singing
Suddenly ceased; for Priscilla, aroused by
    his step on the threshold,
Rose as he entered, and gave him her hand,
    in signal of welcome,
Saying, 'I knew it was you, when I heard
    your step in the passage;

For I was thinking of you, as I sat there
    singing and spinning.'
Awkward and dumb with delight, that a
    thought of him had been mingled 70
Thus in the sacred psalm, that came from
    the heart of the maiden,
Silent before her he stood, and gave her
    the flowers for an answer,
Finding no words for his thought. He re-
    membered that day in the winter,
After the first great snow, when he broke
    a path from the village,
Reeling and plunging along through the
    drifts that encumbered the doorway,
Stamping the snow from his feet as he en-
    tered the house, and Priscilla
Laughed at his snowy locks, and gave him
    a seat by the fireside,
Grateful and pleased to know he had
    thought of her in the snow-storm.
Had he but spoken then ! perhaps not in
    vain had he spoken;
Now it was all too late; the golden mo-
    ment had vanished !   80
So he stood there abashed, and gave her
    the flowers for an answer.

Then they sat down and talked of the
    birds and the beautiful spring-time,
Talked of their friends at home, and the
    Mayflower that sailed on the morrow.
'I have been thinking all day,' said gently
    the Puritan maiden,
'Dreaming all night, and thinking all day,
    of the hedge-rows of England, —
They are in blossom now, and the country
    is all like a garden:
Thinking of lanes and fields, and the song
    of the lark and the linnet,
Seeing the village street, and familiar faces
    of neighbors
Going about as of old, and stopping to gos-
    sip together,
And, at the end of the street, the village
    church, with the ivy   90
Climbing the old gray tower, and the quiet
    graves in the churchyard.
Kind are the people I live with, and dear
    to me my religion;
Still my heart is so sad, that I wish myself
    back in Old England.
You will say it is wrong, but I cannot help
    it : I almost
Wish myself back in Old England, I feel
    so lonely and wretched.'

Thereupon answered the youth: ' Indeed
    I do not condemn you;
Stouter hearts than a woman's have quailed
    in this terrible winter.
Yours is tender and trusting, and needs a
    stronger to lean on;
So I have come to you now, with an offer
    and proffer of marriage
Made by a good man and true, Miles Stan-
    dish the Captain of Plymouth ! ' 100

Thus he delivered his message, the dex-
    terous writer of letters, —
Did not embellish the theme, nor array it
    in beautiful phrases,
But came straight to the point, and blurted
    it out like a school-boy;
Even the Captain himself could hardly
    have said it more bluntly.
Mute with amazement and sorrow, Priscilla
    the Puritan maiden
Looked into Alden's face, her eyes dilated
    with wonder,
Feeling his words like a blow, that stunned
    her and rendered her speech-
    less;
Till at length she exclaimed, interrupting
    the ominous silence:
'If the great Captain of Plymouth is so
    very eager to wed me,
Why does he not come himself, and take
    the trouble to woo me ?   110
If I am not worth the wooing, I surely am
    not worth the winning ! '
Then John Alden began explaining and
    smoothing the matter,
Making it worse as he went, by saying the
    Captain was busy, —
Had no time for such things — such things !
    the words grating harshly
Fell on the ear of Priscilla; and swift as a
    flash she made answer:
'Has he no time for such things, as you
    call it, before he is married,
Would he be likely to find it, or make it,
    after the wedding ?
That is the way with you men; you don't
    understand us, you cannot.
When you have made up your minds,
    after thinking of this one and that
    one,
Choosing, selecting, rejecting, comparing
    one with another,   120
Then you make known your desire, with
    abrupt and sudden avowal,

And are offended and hurt, and indignant
  perhaps, that a woman
Does not respond at once to a love that she
  never suspected,
Does not attain at a bound the height to
  which you have been climbing.
This is not right nor just: for surely a
  woman's affection
Is not a thing to be asked for, and had for
  only the asking.
When one is truly in love, one not only
  says it, but shows it.
Had he but waited awhile, had he only
  showed that he loved me,
Even this Captain of yours — who knows ?
  — at last might have won me,
Old and rough as he is; but now it never
  can happen.'   130

Still John Alden went on, unheeding the
  words of Priscilla,
Urging the suit of his friend, explaining,
  persuading, expanding;
Spoke of his courage and skill, and of all
  his battles in Flanders,
How with the people of God he had chosen
  to suffer affliction;
How, in return for his zeal, they had made
  him Captain of Plymouth;
He was a gentleman born, could trace his
  pedigree plainly
Back to Hugh Standish of Duxbury Hall,
  in Lancashire, England,
Who was the son of Ralph, and the grandson of Thurston de Standish;
Heir unto vast estates, of which he was
  basely defrauded,
Still bore the family arms, and had for his
  crest a cock argent,   140
Combed and wattled gules, and all the rest
  of the blazon.
He was a man of honor, of noble and generous nature;
Though he was rough, he was kindly; she
  knew how during the winter
He had attended the sick, with a hand as
  gentle as woman's;
Somewhat hasty and hot, he could not deny
  it, and headstrong,
Stern as a soldier might be, but hearty, and
  placable always,
Not to be laughed at and scorned, because
  he was little of stature;
For he was great of heart, magnanimous,
  courtly, courageous;

Any woman in Plymouth, nay, any woman
  in England,
Might be happy and proud to be called the
  wife of Miles Standish !   150

But as he warmed and glowed, in his
  simple and eloquent language,
Quite forgetful of self, and full of the praise
  of his rival,
Archly the maiden smiled, and, with eyes
  overrunning with laughter,
Said, in a tremulous voice, ' Why don't you
  speak for yourself, John ? '

IV

JOHN ALDEN

INTO the open air John Alden, perplexed
  and bewildered,
Rushed like a man insane, and wandered
  alone by the sea-side;
Paced up and down the sands, and bared his
  head to the east-wind,
Cooling his heated brow, and the fire and
  fever within him.
Slowly as out of the heavens, with apocalyp-
  tical splendors,
Sank the City of God, in the vision of John
  the Apostle,
So, with its cloudy walls of chrysolite, jasper, and sapphire,
Sank the broad red sun, and over its turrets
  uplifted
Glimmered the golden reed of the angel
  who measured the city.

' Welcome, O wind of the East ! ' he exclaimed in his wild exultation,   10
' Welcome, O wind of the East, from the
  caves of the misty Atlantic !
Blowing o'er fields of dulse, and measureless meadows of sea-grass,
Blowing o'er rocky wastes, and the grottoes
  and gardens of ocean !
Lay thy cold, moist hand on my burning
  forehead, and wrap me
Close in thy garments of mist, to allay the
  fever within me ! '

Like an awakened conscience, the sea was
  moaning and tossing,
Beating remorseful and loud the mutable
  sands of the sea-shore.

Fierce in his soul was the struggle and tu-
    mult of passions contending;
Love triumphant and crowned, and friend-
    ship wounded and bleeding,
Passionate cries of desire, and importunate
    pleadings of duty !   20
' Is it my fault,' he said, ' that the maiden
    has chosen between us ?
Is it my fault that he failed, — my fault
    that I am the victor ? '
Then within him there thundered a voice,
    like the voice of the Prophet:
' It hath displeased the Lord ! ' — and he
    thought of David's transgression,
Bathsheba's beautiful face, and his friend
    in the front of the battle !
Shame and confusion of guilt, and abase-
    ment and self-condemnation,
Overwhelmed him at once; and he cried
    in the deepest contrition:
' It hath displeased the Lord! It is the
    temptation of Satan! '

Then, uplifting his head, he looked at the
    sea, and beheld there
Dimly the shadowy form of the Mayflower
    riding at anchor,   30
Rocked on the rising tide, and ready to sail
    on the morrow;
Heard the voices of men through the mist,
    the rattle of cordage
Thrown on the deck, the shouts of the mate,
    and the sailors' ' Ay, ay, Sir ! '
Clear and distinct, but not loud, in the drip-
    ping air of the twilight.
Still for a moment he stood, and listened,
    and stared at the vessel,
Then went hurriedly on, as one who, seeing
    a phantom,
Stops, then quickens his pace, and follows
    the beckoning shadow.
' Yes, it is plain to me now,' he murmured;
    ' the hand of the Lord is
Leading me out of the land of darkness,
    the bondage of error,
Through the sea, that shall lift the walls of
    its waters around me,   40
Hiding me, cutting me off, from the cruel
    thoughts that pursue me.
Back will I go o'er the ocean, this dreary
    land will abandon,
Her whom I may not love, and him whom
    my heart has offended.
Better to be in my grave in the green old
    churchyard in England,

Close by my mother's side, and among the
    dust of my kindred;
Better be dead and forgotten, than living
    in shame and dishonor;
Sacred and safe and unseen, in the dark of
    the narrow chamber
With me my secret shall lie, like a buried
    jewel that glimmers
Bright on the hand that is dust, in the
    chambers of silence and dark-
    ness, —
Yes, as the marriage ring of the great es-
    pousal hereafter ! '   50

Thus as he spake, he turned, in the
    strength of his strong resolution,
Leaving behind him the shore, and hurried
    along in the twilight,
Through the congenial gloom of the forest
    silent and sombre,
Till he beheld the lights in the seven houses
    of Plymouth,
Shining like seven stars in the dusk and
    mist of the evening.
Soon he entered his door, and found the re-
    doubtable Captain
Sitting alone, and absorbed in the martial
    pages of Cæsar,
Fighting some great campaign in Hainault
    or Brabant or Flanders.
' Long have you been on your errand,' he
    said with a cheery demeanor,
Even as one who is waiting an answer, and
    fears not the issue.   60
' Not far off is the house, although the
    woods are between us;
But you have lingered so long, that while
    you were going and coming
I have fought ten battles and sacked and
    demolished a city.
Come, sit down, and in order relate to me
    all that has happened.'

Then John Alden spake, and related the
    wondrous adventure,
From beginning to end, minutely, just as it
    happened;
How he had seen Priscilla, and how he had
    sped in his courtship,
Only smoothing a little, and softening down
    her refusal.
But when he came at length to the words
    Priscilla had spoken,
Words so tender and cruel: ' Why don't
    you speak for yourself, John ? '   70

Up leaped the Captain of Plymouth, and
    stamped on the floor, till his armor
Clanged on the wall, where it hung, with a
    sound of sinister omen.
All his pent-up wrath burst forth in a sud-
    den explosion,
E'en as a hand-grenade, that scatters de-
    struction around it.
Wildly he shouted, and loud: ' John Alden!
    you have betrayed me!
Me, Miles Standish, your friend! have
    supplanted, defrauded, betrayed me!
One of my ancestors ran his sword through
    the heart of Wat Tyler;
Who shall prevent me from running my
    own through the heart of a traitor ?
Yours is the greater treason, for yours is a
    treason to friendship !
You, who lived under my roof, whom I
    ' cherished and loved as a brother; 80
You, who have fed at my board, and drunk
    at my cup, to whose keeping
I have intrusted my honor, my thoughts the
    most sacred and secret, —
You too, Brutus ! ah woe to the name of
    friendship hereafter !
Brutus was Cæsar's friend, and you were
    mine, but henceforward
Let there be nothing between us save war,
    and implacable hatred ! '

So spake the Captain of Plymouth, and
    strode about in the chamber,
Chafing and choking with rage; like cords
    were the veins on his temples.
But in the midst of his anger a man ap-
    peared at the doorway,
Bringing in uttermost haste a message of
    urgent importance,
Rumors of danger and war and hostile in-
    cursions of Indians !   90
Straightway the Captain paused, and, with-
    out further question or parley,
Took from the nail on the wall his sword
    with its scabbard of iron,
Buckled the belt round his waist, and,
    frowning fiercely, departed.
Alden was left alone. He heard the clank
    of the scabbard
Growing fainter and fainter, and dying
    away in the distance.
Then he arose from his seat, and looked
    forth into the darkness,
Felt the cool air blow on his cheek that
    was hot with the insult,

Lifted his eyes to the heavens, and, folding
    his hands as in childhood,
Prayed in the silence of night to the Father
    who seeth in secret.

Meanwhile the choleric Captain strode
    wrathful away to the council, 100
Found it already assembled, impatiently
    waiting his coming;
Men in the middle of life, austere and grave
    in deportment,
Only one of them old, the hill that was
    nearest to heaven,
Covered with snow, but erect, the excellent
    Elder of Plymouth.
God had sifted three kingdoms to find the
    wheat for his planting,
Then had sifted the wheat, as the living
    seed of a nation;
So say the chronicles old, and such is the
    faith of the people !
Near them was standing an Indian, in atti-
    tude stern and defiant,
Naked down to the waist, and grim and
    ferocious in aspect;
While on the table before them was lying
    unopened a Bible, 110
Ponderous, bound in leather, brass-studded,
    printed in Holland,
And beside it outstretched the skin of a
    rattlesnake glittered,
Filled, like a quiver, with arrows; a signal
    and challenge of warfare,
Brought by the Indian, and speaking with
    arrowy tongues of defiance.
This Miles Standish beheld, as he entered,
    and heard them debating
What were an answer befitting the hostile
    message and menace,
Talking of this and of that, contriving, sug-
    gesting, objecting;
One voice only for peace, and that the
    voice of the Elder,
Judging it wise and well that some at least
    were converted,
Rather than any were slain, for this was
    but Christian behavior ! 120
Then out spake Miles Standish, the stal-
    wart Captain of Plymouth,
Muttering deep in his throat, for his voice
    was husky with anger,
' What ! do you mean to make war with
    milk and the water of roses ?
Is it to shoot red squirrels you have your
    howitzer planted

There on the roof of the church, or is it to
    shoot red devils ?
Truly the only tongue that is understood
    by a savage
Must be the tongue of fire that speaks from
    the mouth of the cannon ! '
Thereupon answered and said the excellent
    Elder of Plymouth,
Somewhat amazed and alarmed at this ir-
    reverent language;
' Not so thought St. Paul, nor yet the other
    Apostles;   130
Not from the cannon's mouth were the
    tongues of fire they spake with ! '
But unhceded fell this mild rebuke on the
    Captain,
Who had advanced to the table, and thus
    continued discoursing:
' Leave this matter to me, for to me by
    right it pertaineth.
War is a terrible trade; but in the cause
    that is righteous,
Sweet is the smell of powder; and thus I
    answer the challenge ! '

Then from the rattlesnake's skin, with a
    sudden, contemptuous gesture,
Jerking the Indian arrows, he filled it with
    powder and bullets
Full to the very jaws, and handed it back to
    the savage,
Saying, in thundering tones: ' Here, take
    it ! this is your answer ! '   140
Silently out of the room then glided the
    glistening savage,
Bearing the serpent's skin, and seeming
    himself like a serpent,
Winding his sinuous way in the dark to the
    depths of the forest.

V

THE SAILING OF THE MAYFLOWER

JUST in the gray of the dawn, as the mists
    uprose from the meadows,
There was a stir and a sound in the slum-
    bering village of Plymouth;
Clanging and clicking of arms, and the order
    imperative, ' Forward ! '
Given in tone suppressed, a tramp of feet,
    and then silence.
Figures ten, in the mist, marched slowly out
    of the village.

Standish the stalwart it was, with eight of
    his valorous army,
Led by their Indian guide, by Hobomok,
    friend of the white men,
Northward marching to quell the sudden
    revolt of the savage.
Giants they seemed in the mist, or the
    mighty men of King David;
Giants in heart they were, who believed in
    God and the Bible, —   10
Ay, who believed in the smiting of Midian-
    ites and Philistines.
Over them gleamed far off the crimson
    banners of morning;
Under them loud on the sands, the serried
    billows, advancing,
Fired along the line, and in regular order
    retreated.

Many a mile had they marched, when at
    length the village of Plymouth
Woke from its sleep, and arose, intent on
    its manifold labors.
Sweet was the air and soft; and slowly the
    smoke from the chimneys
Rose over roofs of thatch, and pointed
    steadily eastward;
Men came forth from the doors, and paused
    and talked of the weather,
Said that the wind had changed, and was
    blowing fair for the Mayflower;   20
Talked of their Captain's departure, and
    all the dangers that menaced,
He being gone, the town, and what should
    be done in his absence.
Merrily sang the birds, and the tender voices
    of women
Consecrated with hymns the common cares
    of the household.
Out of the sea rose the sun, and the billows
    rejoiced at his coming;
Beautiful were his feet on the purple tops
    of the mountains;
Beautiful on the sails of the Mayflower rid-
    ing at anchor,
Battered and blackened and worn by all
    the storms of the winter.
Loosely against her masts was hanging and
    flapping her canvas,
Rent by so many gales, and patched by the
    hands of the sailors.   30
Suddenly from her side, as the sun rose over
    the ocean,
Darted a puff of smoke, and floated sea-
    ward; anon rang

Loud over field and forest the cannon's
     roar, and the echoes
Heard and repeated the sound, the signal-
     gun of departure !
Ah ! but with louder echoes replied the
     hearts of the people !
Meekly, in voices subdued, the chapter was
     read from the Bible,
Meekly the prayer was begun, but ended in
     fervent entreaty !
Then from their houses in haste came forth
     the Pilgrims of Plymouth,
Men and women and children, all hurrying
     down to the sea-shore,
Eager, with tearful eyes, to say farewell to
     the Mayflower,   40
Homeward bound o'er the sea, and leaving
     them here in the desert.

Foremost among them was Alden. All
     night he had lain without slumber,
Turning and tossing about in the heat and
     unrest of his fever.
He had beheld Miles Standish, who came
     back late from the council,
Stalking into the room, and heard him mut-
     ter and murmur;
Sometimes it seemed a prayer, and some-
     times it sounded like swearing.
Once he had come to the bed, and stood
     there a moment in silence;
Then he had turned away, and said: ' I will
     not awake him;
Let him sleep on, it is best; for what is the
     use of more talking ! '
Then he extinguished the light, and threw
     himself down on his pallet,   50
Dressed as he was, and ready to start at
     the break of the morning, —
Covered himself with the cloak he had worn
     in his campaigns in Flanders, —
Slept as a soldier sleeps in his bivouac,
     ready for action.
But with the dawn he arose; in the twilight
     Alden beheld him
Put on his corselet of steel, and all the rest
     of his armor,
Buckle about his waist his trusty blade of
     Damascus,
Take from the corner his musket, and so
     stride out of the chamber.
Often the heart of the youth had burned
     and yearned to embrace him,
Often his lips had essayed to speak, im-
     ploring for pardon;

All the old friendship came back, with its
     tender and grateful emotions;   60
But his pride overmastered the nobler na-
     ture within him, —
Pride, and the sense of his wrong, and the
     burning fire of the insult.
So he beheld his friend departing in anger,
     but spake not,
Saw him go forth to danger, perhaps to
     death, and he spake not !
Then he arose from his bed, and heard
     what the people were saying,
Joined in the talk at the door, with Stephen
     and Richard and Gilbert,
Joined in the morning prayer, and in the
     reading of Scripture,
And, with the others, in haste went hurry-
     ing down to the sea-shore,
Down to the Plymouth Rock, that had been
     to their feet as a doorstep
Into a world unknown, — the corner-stone
     of a nation !   70

There with his boat was the Master, al-
     ready a little impatient
Lest he should lose the tide, or the wind
     might shift to the eastward,
Square-built, hearty, and strong, with an
     odor of ocean about him,
Speaking with this one and that, and cram-
     ming letters and parcels
Into his pockets capacious, and messages
     mingled together
Into his narrow brain, till at last he was
     wholly bewildered.
Nearer the boat stood Alden, with one foot
     placed on the gunwale,
One still firm on the rock, and talking at
     times with the sailors,
Seated erect on the thwarts, all ready and
     eager for starting.
He too was eager to go, and thus put an
     end to his anguish,   80
Thinking to fly from despair, that swifter
     than keel is or canvas,
Thinking to drown in the sea the ghost
     that would rise and pursue him.
But as he gazed on the crowd, he beheld
     the form of Priscilla
Standing dejected among them, unconscious
     of all that was passing.
Fixed were her eyes upon his, as if she di-
     vined his intention,
Fixed with a look so sad, so reproachful,
     imploring, and patient,

That with a sudden revulsion his heart re-
  coiled from its purpose,
As from the verge of a crag, where one
  step more is destruction.
Strange is the heart of man, with its quick,
  mysterious instincts !
Strange is the life of man, and fatal or
  fated are moments,   90
Whereupon turn, as on hinges, the gates of
  the wall adamantine !
'Here I remain !' he exclaimed, as he
  looked at the heavens above him,
Thanking the Lord whose breath had scattered the mist and the madness,
Wherein, blind and lost, to death he was
  staggering headlong.
'Yonder snow-white cloud, that floats in
  the ether above me,
Seems like a hand that is pointing and beck-
  oning over the ocean.
There is another hand, that is not so spec-
  tral and ghost-like,
Holding me, drawing me back, and clasping mine for protection.
Float, O hand of cloud, and vanish away in
  the ether !
Roll thyself up like a fist, to threaten and
  daunt me; I heed not   100
Either your warning or menace, or any
  omen of evil !
There is no land so sacred, no air so pure
  and so wholesome,
As is the air she breathes, and the soil that
  is pressed by her footsteps.
Here for her sake will I stay, and like an
  invisible presence
Hover around her forever, protecting, sup-
  porting her weakness ; .
Yes ! as my foot was the first that stepped
  on this rock at the landing,
So, with the blessing of God, shall it be the
  last at the leaving !'

Meanwhile the Master alert, but with dignified air and important,
Scanning with watchful eye the tide and
  the wind and the weather,
Walked about on the sands, and the people
  crowded around him   110
Saying a few last words, and enforcing his
  careful remembrance.
Then, taking each by the hand, as if he
  were grasping a tiller,
Into the boat he sprang, and in haste
  shoved off to his vessel,

Glad in his heart to get rid of all this worry
  and flurry,
Glad to be gone from a land of sand and
  sickness and sorrow,
Short allowance of victual, and plenty of
  nothing but Gospel !
Lost in the sound of the oars was the last
  farewell of the pilgrims.
O strong hearts and true ! not one went
  back in the Mayflower !
No, not one looked back, who had set his
  hand to this ploughing !

Soon were heard on board the shouts
  and songs of the sailors   120
Heaving the windlass round, and hoisting
  the ponderous anchor.
Then the yards were braced, and all sails
  set to the west-wind,
Blowing steady and strong; and the Mayflower sailed from the harbor,
Rounded the point of the Gurnet, and leaving far to the southward
Island and cape of sand, and the Field of
    .   the First Encounter,
Took the wind on her quarter, and stood
  for the open Atlantic,
Borne on the send of the sea, and the swelling hearts of the Pilgrims.

Long in silence they watched the receding sail of the vessel,
Much endeared to them all, as something
  living and human;
Then, as if filled with the spirit, and wrapt
  in a vision prophetic,   130
Baring his hoary head, the excellent Elder
  of Plymouth
Said, 'Let us pray !' and they prayed, and
  thanked the Lord and took courage.
Mournfully sobbed the waves at the base
  of the rock, and above them
Bowed and whispered the wheat on the
  hill of death, and their kindred
Seemed to awake in their graves, and to
  join in the prayer that they uttered.
Sun-illumined and white, on the eastern
  verge of the ocean
Gleamed the departing sail, like a marble
  slab in a graveyard;
Buried beneath it lay forever all hope of
  escaping.
Lo ! as they turned to depart, they saw the
  form of an Indian,

Watching them from the hill; but while
    they spake with each other,   140
Pointing with outstretched hands, and say-
    ing, ' Look ! ' he had vanished.
So they returned to their homes; but Alden
    lingered a little,
Musing alone on the shore, and watching
    the wash of the billows
Round the base of the rock, and the sparkle
    and flash of the sunshine,
Like the spirit of God, moving visibly over
    the waters.

VI

PRISCILLA

THUS for a while he stood, and mused by
    the shore of the ocean,
Thinking of many things, and most of all
    of Priscilla;
And as if thought had the power to draw
    to itself, like the loadstone,
Whatsoever it touches, by subtile laws of
    its nature,
Lo! as he turned to depart, Priscilla was
    standing beside him.

' Are you so much offended, you will not
    speak to me ? ' said she.
' Am I so much to blame, that yesterday,
    when you were pleading
Warmly the cause of another, my heart,
    impulsive and wayward,
Pleaded your own, and spake out, forgetful
    perhaps of decorum ?
Certainly you can forgive me for speaking
    so frankly, for saying   10
What I ought not to have said, yet now I
    can never unsay it;
For there are moments in life, when the
    heart is so full of emotion,
That if by chance it be shaken, or into its
    depths like a pebble
Drops some careless word, it overflows, and
    its secret,
Spilt on the ground like water, can never
    be gathered together.
Yesterday I was shocked, when I heard
    you speak of Miles Standish,
Praising his virtues, transforming his very
    defects into virtues,
Praising his courage and strength, and even
    his fighting in Flanders,

As if by fighting alone you could win the
    heart of a woman,
Quite overlooking yourself and the rest, in
    exalting your hero.   20
Therefore I spake as I did, by an irre-
    sistible impulse.
You will forgive me, I hope, for the sake
    of the friendship between us,
Which is too true and too sacred to be so
    easily broken!'
Thereupon answered John Alden, the
    scholar, the friend of Miles Stand-
    ish:
' I was not angry with you, with myself
    alone I was angry,
Seeing how badly I managed the matter I
    had in my keeping.'
' No! ' interrupted the maiden, with answer
    prompt and decisive;
' No; you were angry with me, for speak-
    ing so frankly and freely.
It was wrong, I acknowledge; for it is the
    fate of a woman
Long to be patient and silent, to wait like
    a ghost that is speechless,   30
Till some questioning voice dissolves the
    spell of its silence.
Hence is the inner life of so many suffering
    women
Sunless and silent and deep, like subter-
    ranean rivers
Running through caverns of darkness, un-
    heard, unseen, and unfruitful,
Chafing their channels of stone, with end-
    less and profitless murmurs.'
Thereupon answered John Alden, the young
    man, the lover of women:
' Heaven forbid it, Priscilla; and truly they
    seem to me always
More like the beautiful rivers that watered
    the garden of Eden,
More like the river Euphrates, through
    deserts of Havilah flowing,
Filling the land with delight, and memories
    sweet of the garden!'   40
' Ah, by these words, I can see,' again in-
    terrupted the maiden,
' How very little you prize me, or care for
    what I am saying.
When from the depths of my heart, in pain
    and with secret misgiving,
Frankly I speak to you, asking for sympa-
    thy only and kindness,
Straightway you take up my words, that
    are plain and direct and in earnest,

Turn them away from their meaning, and
    answer with flattering phrases.
This is not right, is not just, is not true to
    the best that is in you;
For I know and esteem you, and feel that
    your nature is noble,
Lifting mine up to a higher, a more ethereal
    level.
Therefore I value your friendship, and feel
    it perhaps the more keenly   50
If you say aught that implies I am only as
    one among many,
If you make use of those common and com-
    plimentary phrases
Most men think so fine, in dealing and
    speaking with women,
But which women reject as insipid, if not
    as insulting.'

    Mute and amazed was Alden; and lis-
        tened and looked at Priscilla,
Thinking he never had seen her more fair,
    more divine in her beauty.
He who but yesterday pleaded so glibly the
    cause of another,
Stood there embarrassed and silent, and
    seeking in vain for an answer.
So the maiden went on, and little divined
    or imagined
What was at work in his heart, that made
    him so awkward and speechless.   60
' Let us, then, be what we are, and speak
    what we think, and in all things
Keep ourselves loyal to truth, and the sa-
    cred professions of friendship.
It is no secret I tell you, nor am I ashamed
    to declare it:
I have liked to be with you, to see you, to
    speak with you always.
So I was hurt at your words, and a little
    affronted to hear you
Urge me to marry your friend, though he
    were the Captain Miles Standish.
For I must tell you the truth: much more
    to me is your friendship
Than all the love he could give, were he
    twice the hero you think him.'
Then she extended her hand, and Alden,
    who eagerly grasped it,
Felt all the wounds in his heart, that were
    aching and bleeding so sorely,   70
Healed by the touch of that hand, and he
    said, with a voice full of feeling:
' Yes, we must ever be friends; and of all
    who offer you friendship

Let me be ever the first, the truest, the
    nearest and dearest !'

    Casting a farewell look at the glimmer-
        ing sail of the Mayflower,
Distant, but still in sight, and sinking be-
    low the horizon,
Homeward together they walked, with a
    strange, indefinite feeling,
That all the rest had departed and left
    them alone in the desert.
But, as they went through the fields in
    the blessing and smile of the sun-
    shine,
Lighter grew their hearts, and Priscilla
    said very archly:
' Now that our terrible Captain has gone
    in pursuit of the Indians,   80
Where he is happier far than he would be
    commanding a household,
You may speak boldly, and tell me of all
    that happened between you,
When you returned last night, and said
    how ungrateful you found me.'
Thereupon answered John Alden, and told
    her the whole of the story, —
Told her his own despair, and the direful
    wrath of Miles Standish.
Whereat the maiden smiled, and said be-
    tween laughing and earnest,
' He is a little chimney, and heated hot in
    a moment !'
But as he gently rebuked her, and told her
    how he had suffered, —
How he had even determined to sail that
    day in the Mayflower,
And had remained for her sake, on hearing
    the dangers that threatened, — 90
All her manner was changed, and she said
    with a faltering accent,
' Truly I thank you for this : how good
    you have been to me always !'

    Thus, as a pilgrim devout, who toward
        Jerusalem journeys,
Taking three steps in advance, and one
    reluctantly backward,
Urged by importunate zeal, and withheld
    by pangs of contrition;
Slowly but steadily onward, receding yet
    ever advancing,
Journeyed this Puritan youth to the Holy
    Land of his longings,
Urged by the fervor of love, and withheld
    by remorseful misgivings.

VII

THE MARCH OF MILES STANDISH

MEANWHILE the stalwart Miles Standish
        was marching steadily northward,
Winding through forest and swamp, and
        along the trend of the sea-shore,
All day long, with hardly a halt, the fire of
        nis anger
Burning and crackling within, and the sul-
        phurous odor of powder
Seeming more sweet to his nostrils than all
        the scents of the forest.
Silent and moody he went, and much he
        revolved his discomfort;
He who was used to success, and to easy
        victories always,
Thus to be flouted, rejected, and laughed
        to scorn by a maiden,
Thus to be mocked and betrayed by the
        friend whom most he had trusted !
Ah ! 't was too much to be borne, and he
        fretted and chafed in his armor !   10

' I alone am to blame,' he muttered,
        ' for mine was the folly.
What has a rough old soldier, grown grim
        and gray in the harness,
Used to the camp and its ways, to do with
        the wooing of maidens ?
'T was but a dream, — let it pass, — let it
        vanish like so many others !
What I thought was a flower, is only a
        weed, and is worthless;
Out of my heart will I pluck it, and throw
        it away, and henceforward
Be but a fighter of battles, a lover and
        wooer of dangers ! '
Thus he revolved in his mind his sorry de-
        feat and discomfort,
While he was marching by day or lying at
        night in the forest,
Looking up at the trees, and the constella-
        tions beyond them.   20

After a three days' march he came to an
        Indian encampment
Pitched on the edge of a meadow, between
        the sea and the forest;
Women at work by the tents, and warriors,
        horrid with war-paint,
Seated about a fire, and smoking and talk-
        ing together;
Who, when they saw from afar the sudden
        approach of the white men,

Saw the flash of the sun on breastplate and
        sabre and musket,
Straightway leaped to their feet, and two,
        from among them advancing,
Came to parley with Standish, and offer him
        furs as a present;
Friendship was in their looks, but in their
        hearts there was hatred.
Braves of the tribe were these, and brothers,
        gigantic in stature,   30
Huge as Goliath of Gath, or the terrible
        Og, king of Bashan;
One was Pecksuot named, and the other
        was called Wattawamat.
Round their necks were suspended their
        knives in scabbards of wampum,
Two-edged, trenchant knives, with points as
        sharp as a needle.
Other arms had they none, for they were
        cunning and crafty.
' Welcome, English ! ' they said, — these
        words they had learned from the
        traders
Touching at times on the coast, to barter
        and chaffer for peltries.
Then in their native tongue they began to
        parley with Standish,
Through his guide and interpreter, Hobo-
        mok, friend of the white man,
Begging for blankets and knives, but mostly
        for muskets and powder,   40
Kept by the white man, they said, con-
        cealed, with the plague, in his cellars,
Ready to be let loose, and destroy his
        brother the red man !
But when Standish refused, and said he
        would give them the Bible,
Suddenly changing their tone, they began
        to boast and to bluster.
Then Wattawamat advanced with a stride
        in front of the other,
And, with a lofty demeanor, thus vaunt-
        ingly spake to the Captain:
' Now Wattawamat can see, by the fiery
        eyes of the Captain,
Angry is he in his heart; but the heart of
        the brave Wattawamat
Is not afraid at the sight. He was not
        born of a woman,
But on a mountain at night, from an oak-
        tree riven by lightning,   50
Forth he sprang at a bound, with all his
        weapons about him,
Shouting, " Who is there here to fight with
        the brave Wattawamat ? " '

Then he unsheathed his knife, and, whet-
    ting the blade on his left hand,
Held it aloft and displayed a woman's face
    on the handle;
Saying, with bitter expression and look of
    sinister meaning:
'I have another at home, with the face of
    a man on the handle;
By and by they shall marry; and there
    will be plenty of children!'

Then stood Pecksuot forth, self-vaunting,
    insulting Miles Standish :
While with his fingers he patted the knife
    that hung at his bosom,
Drawing it half from its sheath, and plung-
    ing it back, as he muttered,   60
'By and by it shall see; it shall eat; ah, ha!
    but shall speak not!
This is the mighty Captain the white men
    have sent to destroy us!
He is a little man; let him go and work
    with the women!'

Meanwhile Standish had noted the faces
    and figures of Indians
Peeping and creeping about from bush to
    tree in the forest,
Feigning to look for game, with arrows set
    on their bow-strings,
Drawing about him still closer and closer
    the net of their ambush.
But undaunted he stood, and dissembled
    and treated them smoothly;
So the old chronicles say, that were writ in
    the days of the fathers.
But when he heard their defiance, the boast,
    the taunt, and the insult,   70
All the hot blood of his race, of Sir Hugh
    and of Thurston de Standish,
Boiled and beat in his heart, and swelled in
    the veins of his temples.
Headlong he leaped on the boaster, and,
    snatching his knife from its scab-
    bard,
Plunged it into his heart, and, reeling back-
    ward, the savage
Fell with his face to the sky, and a fiend-
    like fierceness upon it.
Straight there arose from the forest the
    awful sound of the war-whoop.
And, like a flurry of snow on the whistling
    wind of December,
Swift and sudden and keen came a flight of
    feathery arrows.

Then came a cloud of smoke, and out of the
    cloud came the lightning,
Out of the lightning thunder; and death un-
    seen ran before it.   80
Frightened the savages fled for shelter in
    swamp and in thicket,
Hotly pursued and beset; but their sachem,
    the brave Wattawamat,
Fled not; he was dead. Unswerving and
    swift had a bullet
Passed through his brain, and he fell with
    both hands clutching the greensward,
Seeming in death to hold back from his foe
    the land of his fathers.

There on the flowers of the meadow the
    warriors lay, and above them,
Silent, with folded arms, stood Hobomok,
    friend of the white man.
Smiling at length he exclaimed to the stal-
    wart Captain of Plymouth: —
'Pecksuot bragged very loud, of his cour-
    age, his strength, and his stature, —
Mocked the great Captain, and called him
    a little man; but I see now   90
Big enough have you been to lay him
    speechless before you!'

Thus the first battle was fought and won
    by the stalwart Miles Standish.
When the tidings thereof were brought to
    the village of Plymouth,
And as a trophy of war the head of the
    brave Wattawamat
Scowled from the roof of the fort, which at
    once was a church and a fortress,
All who beheld it rejoiced, and praised the
    Lord, and took courage.
Only Priscilla averted her face from this
    spectre of terror,
Thanking God in her heart that she had not
    married Miles Standish;
Shrinking, fearing almost, lest, coming
    home from his battles,
He should lay claim to her hand, as the
    prize and reward of his valor.   100

VIII

THE SPINNING-WHEEL

MONTH after month passed away, and in
    autumn the ships of the merchants
Came with kindred and friends, with cattle
    and corn for the Pilgrims.

All in the village was peace; the men were
    intent on their labors,
Busy with hewing and building, with gar-
    den-plot and with merestead,
Busy with breaking the glebe, and mowing
    the grass in the meadows,
Searching the sea for its fish, and hunting
    the deer in the forest.
All in the village was peace; but at times
    the rumor of warfare
Filled the air with alarm, and the appre-
    hension of danger.
Bravely the stalwart Standish was scouring
    the land with his forces,
Waxing valiant in fight and defeating the
    alien armies,
Till his name had become a sound of fear
    to the nations.
Anger was still in his heart, but at times
    the remorse and contrition
Which in all noble natures succeed the pas-
    sionate outbreak,
Came like a rising tide, that encounters the
    rush of a river,
Staying its current awhile, but making it
    bitter and brackish.

Meanwhile Alden at home had built him
    a new habitation,
Solid, substantial, of timber rough - hewn
    from the firs of the forest.
Wooden-barred was the door, and the roof
    was covered with rushes;
Latticed the windows were, and the win-
    dow-panes were of paper,
Oiled to admit the light, while wind and
    rain were excluded.   20
There too he dug a well, and around it
    planted an orchard:
Still may be seen to this day some trace of
    the well and the orchard.
Close to the house was the stall, where, safe
    and secure from annoyance,
Raghorn, the snow-white bull, that had
    fallen to Alden's allotment
In the division of cattle, might ruminate in
    the night-time
Over the pastures he cropped, made fra-
    grant by sweet pennyroyal.

Oft when his labor was finished, with
    eager feet would the dreamer
Follow the pathway that ran through
    the woods to the house of Pris-
    cilla,

Led by illusions romantic and subtile
    deceptions of fancy,
Pleasure disguised as duty, and love in the
    semblance of friendship.   30
Ever of her he thought, when he fashioned
    the walls of his dwelling;
Ever of her he thought, when he delved
    in the soil of his garden;
Ever of her he thought, when he read in
    his Bible on Sunday
Praise of the virtuous woman, as she is
    described in the Proverbs, —
How the heart of her husband doth safely
    trust in her always,
How all the days of her life she will do him
    good, and not evil,
How she seeketh the wool and the flax and
    worketh with gladness,
How she layeth her hand to the spindle and
    holdeth the distaff,
How she is not afraid of the snow for her-
    self or her household,
Knowing her household are clothed with
    the scarlet cloth of her weaving ! 40

So as she sat at her wheel one afternoon
    in the Autumn,
Alden, who opposite sat, and was watching
    her dexterous fingers,
As if the thread she was spinning were that
    of his life and his fortune,
After a pause in their talk, thus spake to
    the sound of the spindle.
'Truly, Priscilla,' he said, 'when I see
    you spinning and spinning,
Never idle a moment, but thrifty and
    thoughtful of others,
Suddenly you are transformed, are visibly
    changed in a moment;
You are no longer Priscilla, but Bertha
    the Beautiful Spinner.'
Here the light foot on the treadle grew
    swifter and swifter; the spindle
Uttered an angry snarl, and the thread
    snapped short in her fingers;   50
While the impetuous speaker, not heeding
    the mischief, continued:
'You are the beautiful Bertha, the spinner,
    the queen of Helvetia;
She whose story I read at a stall in the
    streets of Southampton,
Who, as she rode on her palfrey, o'er
    valley and meadow and mountain,
Ever was spinning her thread from a distaff
    fixed to her saddle.

She was so thrifty and good, that her name
    passed into a proverb.
So shall it be with your own, when the
    spinning-wheel shall no longer
Hum in the house of the farmer, and fill
    its chambers with music.
Then shall the mothers, reproving, relate
    how it was in their childhood,
Praising the good old times, and the days
    of Priscilla the spinner!'   60
Straight uprose from her wheel the beau-
    tiful Puritan maiden,
Pleased with the praise of her thrift from
    him whose praise was the sweetest,
Drew from the reel on the table a snowy
    skein of her spinning,
Thus making answer, meanwhile, to the
    flattering phrases of Alden;
'Come, you must not be idle; if I am a
    pattern for housewives,
Show yourself equally worthy of being the
    model of husbands.
Hold this skein on your hands, while I wind
    it, ready for knitting;
Then who knows but hereafter, when fash-
    ions have changed and the manners,
Fathers may talk to their sons of the good
    old times of John Alden!'
Thus, with a jest and a laugh, the skein on
    his hands she adjusted,   70
He, sitting awkwardly there, with his arms
    extended before him,
She, standing graceful, erect, and winding
    the thread from his fingers,
Sometimes chiding a little his clumsy man-
    ner of holding,
Sometimes touching his hands, as she dis-
    entangled expertly
Twist or knot in the yarn, unawares — for
    how could she help it? —
Sending electrical thrills through every
    nerve in his body.

Lo! in the midst of this scene, a breath-
    less messenger entered,
Bringing in hurry and heat the terrible
    news from the village.
Yes; Miles Standish was dead! — an Indian
    had brought them the tidings, —
Slain by a poisoned arrow, shot down in the
    front of the battle,   80
Into an ambush beguiled, cut off with the
    whole of his forces;
All the town would be burned, and all the
    people be murdered!

Such were the tidings of evil that burst on
    the hearts of the hearers.
Silent and statue-like stood Priscilla, her
    face looking backward
Still at the face of the speaker, her arms
    uplifted in horror;
But John Alden, upstarting, as if the barb
    of the arrow
Piercing the heart of his friend had struck
    his own, and had sundered
Once and forever the bonds that held him
    bound as a captive,
Wild with excess of sensation, the awful
    delight of his freedom,
Mingled with pain and regret, unconscious
    of what he was doing,   90
Clasped, almost with a groan, the motion-
    less form of Priscilla,
Pressing her close to his heart, as forever
    his own, and exclaiming:
'Those whom the Lord hath united, let no
    man put them asunder!'

Even as rivulets twain, from distant and
    separate sources,
Seeing each other afar, as they leap from
    the rocks, and pursuing
Each one its devious path, but drawing
    nearer and nearer,
Rush together at last, at their trysting-place
    in the forest;
So these lives that had run thus far in sep-
    arate channels,
Coming in sight of each other, then swerv-
    ing and flowing asunder,
Parted by barriers strong, but drawing
    nearer and nearer,   100
Rushed together at last, and one was lost
    in the other.

IX

THE WEDDING-DAY

FORTH from the curtain of clouds, from the
    tent of purple and scarlet,
Issued the sun, the great High-Priest, in
    his garments resplendent,
Holiness unto the Lord, in letters of light,
    on his forehead,
Round the hem of his robe the golden bells
    and pomegranates.
Blessing the world he came, and the bars
    of vapor beneath him

Gleamed like a grate of brass, and the sea
    at his feet was a laver !

  This was the wedding morn of Priscilla
    the Puritan maiden.
Friends were assembled together; the Elder
    and Magistrate also
Graced the scene with their presence, and
    stood like the Law and the Gospel,
One with the sanction of earth and one with
    the blessing of heaven.   10
Simple and brief was the wedding, as that
    of Ruth and of Boaz.
Softly the youth and the maiden repeated
    the words of betrothal,
Taking each other for husband and wife in
    the Magistrate's presence,
After the Puritan way, and the laudable
    custom of Holland.
Fervently then, and devoutly, the excellent
    Elder of Plymouth
Prayed for the hearth and the home, that
    were founded that day in affec-
    tion,
Speaking of life and of death, and implor-
    ing Divine benedictions.

  Lo ! when the service was ended, a form
    appeared on the threshold,
Clad in armor of steel, a sombre and sor-
    rowful figure !
Why does the bridegroom start and stare
    at the strange apparition ?   20
Why does the bride turn pale, and hide her
    face on his shoulder ?
Is it a phantom of air, — a bodiless, spec-
    tral illusion ?
Is it a ghost from the grave, that has come
    to forbid the betrothal ?
Long had it stood there unseen, a guest un-
    invited, unwelcomed;
Over its clouded eyes there had passed at
    times an expression
Softening the gloom and revealing the warm
    heart hidden beneath them,
As when across the sky the driving rack of
    the rain-cloud
Grows for a moment thin, and betrays the
    sun by its brightness.
Once it had lifted its hand, and moved its
    lips, but was silent,
As if an iron will had mastered the fleeting
    intention.   30
But when were ended the troth and the
    prayer and the last benediction,

Into the room it strode, and the people be-
    held with amazement
Bodily there in his armor Miles Standish,
    the Captain of Plymouth !
Grasping the bridegroom's hand, he said
    with emotion, ' Forgive me !
I have been angry and hurt, — too long have
    I cherished the feeling;
I have been cruel and hard, but now, thank
    God ! it is ended.
Mine is the same hot blood that leaped in
    the veins of Hugh Standish,
Sensitive, swift to resent, but as swift in
    atoning for error.
Never so much as now was Miles Standish
    the friend of John Alden.'
Thereupon answered the bridegroom: ' Let
    all be forgotten between us, —   40
All save the dear old friendship, and that
    shall grow older and dearer ! '
Then the Captain advanced, and, bowing,
    saluted Priscilla,
Gravely, and after the manner of old-fash-
    ioned gentry in England,
Something of camp and of court, of town
    and of country, commingled,
Wishing her joy of her wedding, and loudly
    lauding her husband.
Then he said with a smile: ' I should have
    remembered the adage, —
If you would be well served, you must serve
    yourself; and moreover,
No man can gather cherries in Kent at the
    season of Christmas ! '

  Great was the people's amazement, and
    greater yet their rejoicing,
Thus to behold once more the sunburnt face
    of their Captain,   50
Whom they had mourned as dead; and they
    gathered and crowded about him,
Eager to see him and hear him, forgetful
    of bride and of bridegroom,
Questioning, answering, laughing, and each
    interrupting the other,
Till the good Captain declared, being quite
    overpowered and bewildered,
He had rather by far break into an Indian
    encampment,
Than come again to a wedding to which he
    had not been invited.

  Meanwhile the bridegroom went forth
    and stood with the bride at the door-
    way,

Breathing the perfumed air of that warm
    and beautiful morning.
Touched with autumnal tints, but lonely
    and sad in the sunshine,
Lay extended before them the land of toil
    and privation;   60
There were the graves of the dead, and the
    barren waste of the sea-shore,
There the familiar fields, the groves of
    pine, and the meadows;
But to their eyes transfigured, it seemed
    as the Garden of Eden,
Filled with the presence of God, whose
    voice was the sound of the ocean.

Soon was their vision disturbed by the
    noise and stir of departure,
Friends coming forth from the house, and
    impatient of longer delaying,
Each with his plan for the day, and the
    work that was left uncompleted.
Then from a stall near at hand, amid ex-
    clamations of wonder,
Alden the thoughtful, the careful, so happy,
    so proud of Priscilla,
Brought out his snow-white bull, obeying
    the hand of its master,   70
Led by a cord that was tied to an iron ring
    in its nostrils,
Covered with crimson cloth, and a cushion
    placed for a saddle.
She should not walk, he said, through
    the dust and heat of the noon-
    day;
Nay, she should ride like a queen, not plod
    along like a peasant.
Somewhat alarmed at first, but reassured
    by the others,

Placing her hand on the cushion, her foot
    in the hand of her husband,
Gayly, with joyous laugh, Priscilla mounted
    her palfrey.
'Nothing is wanting now,' he said with a
    smile, 'but the distaff;
Then you would be in truth my queen, my
    beautiful Bertha!'

Onward the bridal procession now moved
    to their new habitation,   80
Happy husband and wife, and friends con-
    versing together.
Pleasantly murmured the brook, as they
    crossed the ford in the forest,
Pleased with the image that passed, like a
    dream of love, through its bosom,
Tremulous, floating in air, o'er the depths
    of the azure abysses.
Down through the golden leaves the sun
    was pouring his splendors,
Gleaming on purple grapes, that, from
    branches above them suspended,
Mingled their odorous breath with the
    balm of the pine and the fir-tree,
Wild and sweet as the clusters that grew
    in the valley of Eshcol.
Like a picture it seemed of the primitive,
    pastoral ages,
Fresh with the youth of the world, and re-
    calling Rebecca and Isaac,   90
Old and yet ever new, and simple and
    beautiful always,
Love immortal and young in the endless
    succession of lovers.
So through the Plymouth woods passed on-
    ward the bridal procession.

1857–58.   1858.

THE CHILDREN'S HOUR [1]

BETWEEN the dark and the daylight,
    When the night is beginning to lower,

Comes a pause in the day's occupations,
    That is known as the Children's Hour.

[1] The ideal commentary on this poem is found in a
letter of Longfellow's 'To Emily A——,' August 18,
1859 :
    'Your letter followed me down here by the seaside,
where I am passing the summer with my three little
girls. The oldest is about your age; but as little girls'
ages keep changing every year, I can never remember
exactly how old she is, and have to ask her mamma,
who has a better memory than I have. Her name is
Alice; I never forget that. She is a nice girl, and
loves poetry almost as much as you do.
    'The second is Edith, with blue eyes and beautiful

golden locks which I sometimes call her "nankeen
hair" to make her laugh. She is a very busy little
woman, and wears gray boots.
    'The youngest is Allegra; which, you know, means
merry; and she is the merriest little thing you ever
saw, — always singing and laughing all over the
house. . . .
    'I do not say anything about the two boys. They
are such noisy fellows it is of no use to talk about
them.' (*Life*, vol. ii. pp. 392–93.)
    Longfellow and Victor Hugo may perhaps be called
the two greatest poets of childhood, and Victor Hugo's
letters to his own children are strikingly like the one
just quoted.

I hear in the chamber above me
  The patter of little feet,
The sound of a door that is opened,
  And voices soft and sweet.

From my study I see in the lamplight,
  Descending the broad hall stair,   10
Grave Alice, and laughing Allegra,
  And Edith with golden hair.

A whisper, and then a silence:
  Yet I know by their merry eyes
They are plotting and planning together
  To take me by surprise.

A sudden rush from the stairway,
  A sudden raid from the hall !
By three doors left unguarded
  They enter my castle wall !   20

They climb up into my turret
  O'er the arms and back of my chair;
If I try to escape, they surround me;
  They seem to be everywhere.

They almost devour me with kisses,
  Their arms about me entwine,
Till I think of the Bishop of Bingen
  In his Mouse-Tower on the Rhine !

Do you think, O blue-eyed banditti,
  Because you have scaled the wall,   30
Such an old mustache as I am
  Is not a match for you all !

I have you fast in my fortress,
  And will not let you depart,
But put you down into the dungeon
  In the round-tower of my heart.

And there will I keep you forever,
  Yes, forever and a day,
Till the walls shall crumble to ruin,
  And moulder in dust away !   40

1859.   *1860.*

PAUL REVERE'S RIDE[1]

LISTEN, my children, and you shall hear
Of the midnight ride of Paul Revere,

[1] It is possible that Mr. Longfellow derived the story from Paul Revere's account of the incident in a letter to Dr. Jeremy Belknap, printed in Mass. Hist. Coll. V. Mr. Frothingham, in his *Siege of Boston*, pp. 57–59, gives the story mainly according to a memorandum of Richard Devens, Revere's friend and associate. The publication of Mr. Longfellow's poem called out a protracted discussion both as to the church from which

On the eighteenth of April, in Seventy-five;
Hardly a man is now alive
Who remembers that famous day and year.
He said to his friend, ' If the British march
By land or sea from the town to-night,
Hang a lantern aloft in the belfry arch
Of the North Church tower as a signal
  light, —
One, if by land, and two, if by sea;   10
And I on the opposite shore will be,
Ready to ride and spread the alarm
Through every Middlesex village and farm,
For the country folk to be up and to arm.'

Then he said, ' Good-night !' and with
  muffled oar
Silently rowed to the Charlestown shore,
Just as the moon rose over the bay,
Where swinging wide at her moorings lay
The Somerset, British man-of-war;
A phantom ship, with each mast and spar 20
Across the moon like a prison bar,
And a huge black hulk, that was magnified
By its own reflection in the tide.

Meanwhile, his friend, through alley and
  street,
Wanders and watches with eager ears,
Till in the silence around him he hears
The muster of men at the barrack door,
The sound of arms, and the tramp of feet,
And the measured tread of the grenadiers,
Marching down to their boats on the shore. 30

the signals were hung, and as to the friend who hung the lanterns. The subject is discussed and authorities cited in *Memorial History of Boston*, iii, 101. (*Cambridge Edition*, p. 668.)

'Paul Revere's Ride' is the first story in the *Tales of a Wayside Inn*, a series of tales in verse set in a frame-work something like that of Chaucer's *Canterbury Tales*, and supposed to be told by a group of friends gathered at the Red-Horse Inn at Sudbury, about twenty miles from Cambridge. The story of Paul Revere is told by the landlord, whose portrait is thus drawn in the ' Prelude : ' —

> But first the Landlord will I trace ;
> Grave in his aspect and attire ;
> A man of ancient pedigree,
> A Justice of the Peace was he,
> Known in all Sudbury as ' The Squire.'
> Proud was he of his name and race,
> Of old Sir William and Sir Hugh,
> And in the parlor, full in view,
> His coat-of-arms, well framed and glazed,
> Upon the wall in colors blazed ;
> He heareth gules upon his shield,
> A chevron argent in the field,
> With three wolf's-heads, and for the crest
> A wyvern part-per-pale addressed
> Upon a helmet barred ; below
> The scroll reads, ' By the name of Howe.'
> And over this, no longer bright,
> Though glimmering with a latent light,
> Was hung the sword his grandsire bore
> In the rebellious days of yore,
> Down there in Concord in the fight.

Then he climbed the tower of the Old North
     Church,
By the wooden stairs, with stealthy tread,
To the belfry-chamber overhead,
And startled the pigeons from their perch
On the sombre rafters, that round him
     made
Masses and moving shapes of shade, —
By the trembling ladder, steep and tall,
To the highest window in the wall,
Where he paused to listen and look down
A moment on the roofs of the town,   40
And the moonlight flowing over all.

Beneath, in the churchyard, lay the dead,
In their night-encampment on the hill,
Wrapped in silence so deep and still
That he could hear, like a sentinel's tread,
The watchful night-wind, as it went
Creeping along from tent to tent,
And seeming to whisper, ' All is well ! '
A moment only he feels the spell
Of the place and the hour, and the secret
     dread   50
Of the lonely belfry and the dead;
For suddenly all his thoughts are bent
On a shadowy something far away,
Where the river widens to meet the bay, —
A line of black that bends and floats
On the rising tide, like a bridge of boats.

Meanwhile, impatient to mount and ride,
Booted and spurred, with a heavy stride
On the opposite shore walked Paul Revere.
Now he patted his horse's side,   60
Now gazed at the landscape far and near,
Then, impetuous, stamped the earth,
And turned and tightened his saddle-girth;
But mostly he watched with eager search
The belfry-tower of the Old North Church,
As it rose above the graves on the hill,
Lonely and spectral and sombre and still.
And lo ! as he looks, on the belfry's height
A glimmer, and then a gleam of light !
He springs to the saddle, the bridle he
     turns,   70
But lingers and gazes, till full on his sight
A second lamp in the belfry burns !

A hurry of hoofs in a village street,
A shape in the moonlight, a bulk in the dark,
And beneath, from the pebbles, in passing,
     a spark
Struck out by a steed flying fearless and
     fleet;

That was all ! And yet, through the gloom
     and the light,
The fate of a nation was riding that night;
And the spark struck out by that steed, in
     his flight,
Kindled the land into flame with its heat. 80

He has left the village and mounted the
     steep,
And beneath him, tranquil and broad and
     deep,
Is the Mystic, meeting the ocean tides;
And under the alders that skirt its edge,
Now soft on the sand, now loud on the
     ledge,
Is heard the tramp of his steed as he rides.

It was twelve by the village clock,
When he crossed the bridge into Medford
     town.
He heard the crowing of the cock,
And the barking of the farmer's dog,   90
And felt the damp of the river fog,
That rises after the sun goes down.

It was one by the village clock,
When he galloped into Lexington.
He saw the gilded weathercock
Swim in the moonlight as he passed,
And the meeting-house windows, blank and
     bare,
Gaze at him with a spectral glare,
As if they already stood aghast
At the bloody work they would look
     upon.   100

It was two by the village clock,
When he came to the bridge in Concord
     town.
He heard the bleating of the flock,
And the twitter of birds among the trees,
And felt the breath of the morning breeze
Blowing over the meadows brown.
And one was safe and asleep in his bed
Who at the bridge would be first to fall,
Who that day would be lying dead,
Pierced by a British musket-ball.   110

You know the rest. In the books you have
     read,
How the British Regulars fired and fled, —
How the farmers gave them ball for ball,
From behind each fence and farm-yard wall,
Chasing the red-coats down the lane,
Then crossing the fields to emerge again

Under the trees at the turn of the road,
And only pausing to fire and load.

So through the night rode Paul Revere;
And so through the night went his cry of
    alarm   120
To every Middlesex village and farm, —
A cry of defiance and not of fear,
A voice in the darkness, a knock at the door,
And a word that shall echo forevermore !
For, borne on the night-wind of the Past,
Through all our history, to the last,
In the hour of darkness and peril and need,
The people will waken and listen to hear
The hurrying hoof-beats of that steed,
And the midnight message of Paul
    Revere.   130
1860.   1860.

THE CUMBERLAND

At anchor in Hampton Roads we lay,
  On board of the Cumberland, sloop-of-
    war;
And at times from the fortress across the
    bay
  The alarum of drums swept past,
  Or a bugle blast
From the camp on the shore.

Then far away to the south uprose
  A little feather of snow-white smoke,
And we knew that the iron ship of our foes
  Was steadily steering its course   10
  To try the force
Of our ribs of oak.

Down upon us heavily runs,
  Silent and sullen, the floating fort;
Then comes a puff of smoke from her guns,
  And leaps the terrible death,
  With fiery breath,
From each open port.

We are not idle, but send her straight
  Defiance back in a full broadside !   20
As hail rebounds from a roof of slate,
  Rebounds our heavier hail
  From each iron scale
Of the monster's hide.

'Strike your flag !' the rebel cries,
  In his arrogant old plantation strain.
'Never !' our gallant Morris replies;

'It is better to sink than to yield !'
  And the whole air pealed
With the cheers of our men.   30

Then, like a kraken huge and black,
  She crushed our ribs in her iron grasp !
Down went the Cumberland all a wrack,
  With a sudden shudder of death,
  And the cannon's breath
For her dying gasp.

Next morn, as the sun rose over the bay,
  Still floated our flag at the mainmast head.
Lord, how beautiful was thy day !
  Every waft of the air   40
  Was a whisper of prayer,
Or a dirge for the dead.

Ho ! brave hearts that went down in the
    seas !
Ye are at peace in the troubled stream;
Ho ! brave land ! with hearts like these,
  Thy flag, that is rent in twain,
  Shall be one again,
And without a seam !
1862.   1862.

THE BIRDS OF KILLINGWORTH [1]

It was the season, when through all the
    land
  The merle and mavis build, and building
    sing
Those lovely lyrics, written by his hand,
  Whom Saxon Cædmon calls the Blithe-
    heart King;
When on the boughs the purple buds ex-
    pand,

[1] The last story in *Tales of a Wayside Inn, First Series*, and the only one of those 'tales' which was almost wholly original with Longfellow. There is a slight foundation for it, in the history of the town of Killingworth in Connecticut. The *Cambridge Edition* of Longfellow quotes a letter of Mr. Henry Hull, who, writing from personal recollection, says : —

'The men of the northern part of the town did yearly in the spring choose two leaders, and then the two sides were formed : the side that got beaten should pay the bills. Their special game was the hawk, the owl, the crow, the blackbird, and any other bird supposed to be mischievous to the corn. Some years each side would bring them in by the bushel. This was followed up for only a few years, for the birds began to grow scarce.'

In this poem, for once, Longfellow enters a field peculiarly belonging to Lowell : the half-humorous treatment of New England country life.

Emerson considered it the best of the *Tales*, and called it (perhaps with a little exaggeration !), 'Serene happy, and immortal as Chaucer.'

The banners of the vanguard of the
    Spring,
And rivulets, rejoicing, rush and leap,
And wave their fluttering signals from the
    steep.

The robin and the bluebird, piping loud,
    Filled all the blossoming orchards with
        their glee;   10
The sparrows chirped as if they still were
        proud
    Their race in Holy Writ should men-
        tioned be;
And hungry crows, assembled in a crowd,
    Clamored their piteous prayer incessantly,
Knowing who hears the ravens cry, and
        said:
'Give us, O Lord, this day, our daily
        bread!'

Across the Sound the birds of passage
        sailed,
    Speaking some unknown language strange
        and sweet
Of tropic isle remote, and passing hailed
    The village with the cheers of all their
        fleet;   20
Or quarrelling together, laughed and railed
    Like foreign sailors, landed in the street
Of seaport town, and with outlandish noise
Of oaths and gibberish frightening girls and
        boys.

Thus came the jocund Spring in Killing-
        worth,
    In fabulous days, some hundred years
        ago;
And thrifty farmers, as they tilled the
        earth,
    Heard with alarm the cawing of the crow,
That mingled with the universal mirth,
    Cassandra-like, prognosticating woe;   30
They shook their heads, and doomed with
        dreadful words
To swift destruction the whole race of
        birds.

And a town-meeting was convened straight-
        way
    To set a price upon the guilty heads
Of these marauders, who, in lieu of pay,
    Levied black-mail upon the garden beds
And cornfields, and beheld without dismay
    The awful scarecrow, with his fluttering
        shreds;

The skeleton that waited at their feast,
Whereby their sinful pleasure was in-
        creased.   40

Then from his house, a temple painted
        white,
    With fluted columns, and a roof of red,
The Squire came forth, august and splen-
        did sight!
    Slowly descending, with majestic tread,
Three flights of steps, nor looking left nor
        right,
    Down the long street he walked, as one
        who said,
'A town that boasts inhabitants like me
Can have no lack of good society!'

The Parson, too, appeared, a man austere,
    The instinct of whose nature was to kill; 50
The wrath of God he preached from year
        to year,
    And read, with fervor, Edwards on the
        Will;
His favorite pastime was to slay the deer
    In summer on some Adirondac hill;
E'en now, while walking down the rural
        lane,
He lopped the wayside lilies with his cane.

From the Academy, whose belfry crowned
    The hill of Science with its vane of brass,
Came the Preceptor, gazing idly round,
    Now at the clouds, and now at the green
        grass,   60
And all absorbed in reveries profound
    Of fair Almira in the upper class,
Who was, as in a sonnet he had said,
As pure as water, and as good as bread.

And next the Deacon issued from his door,
    In his voluminous neck-cloth, white as
        snow;
A suit of sable bombazine he wore;
    His form was ponderous, and his step
        was slow;
There never was so wise a man before;
    He seemed the incarnate 'Well, I told
        you so!'   70
And to perpetuate his great renown
There was a street named after him in
        town.

These came together in the new town-hall,
    With sundry farmers from the region
        round.

The Squire presided, dignified and tall,
  His air impressive and his reasoning
    sound;
Ill fared it with the birds, both great and
    small;
  Hardly a friend in all that crowd they
    found,
But enemies enough, who every one
Charged them with all the crimes beneath
    the sun.   80

When they had ended, from his place apart
  Rose the Preceptor, to redress the
    wrong,
And, trembling like a steed before the
    start,
  Looked round bewildered on the expect-
    ant throng;
Then thought of fair Almira, and took
    heart
  To speak out what was in him, clear and
    strong,
Alike regardless of their smile or frown,
And quite determined not to be laughed
    down.

' Plato, anticipating the Reviewers,
  From his Republic banished without pity
The Poets; in this little town of yours,   91
  You put to death, by means of a Com-
    mittee,
The ballad-singers and the Troubadours,
  The street-musicians of the heavenly
    city,
The birds, who make sweet music for us
    all
In our dark hours, as David did for Saul.

' The thrush that carols at the dawn of
    day
  From the green steeples of the piny
    wood;
The oriole in the elm; the noisy jay,
  Jargoning like a foreigner at his food;
The bluebird balanced on some topmost
    spray,   101
  Flooding with melody the neighborhood;
Linnet and meadow-lark, and all the throng
That dwell in nests, and have the gift of
    song.

' You slay them all ! and wherefore ? for
    the gain
  Of a scant handful more or less of
    wheat,

Or rye, or barley, or some other grain,
  Scratched up at random by industrious
    feet,
Searching for worm or weevil after rain!
  Or a few cherries, that are not so sweet
As are the songs these uninvited guests   111
  Sing at their feast with comfortable
    breasts.

' Do you ne'er think what wondrous beings
    these ?
  Do you ne'er think who made them, and
    who taught
The dialect they speak, where melodies
  Alone are the interpreters of thought ?
Whose household words are songs in many
    keys,
  Sweeter than instrument of man e'er
    caught !
Whose habitations in the tree-tops even
Are half-way houses on the road to
    heaven!   120

' Think, every morning when the sun peeps
    through
  The dim, leaf-latticed windows of the
    grove,
How jubilant the happy birds renew
  Their old, melodious madrigals of love !
And when you think of this, remember too
  'T is always morning somewhere, and
    above
The awakening continents, from shore to
    shore,
Somewhere the birds are singing evermore.

' Think of your woods and orchards with-
    out birds !
  Of empty nests that cling to boughs and
    beams   130
As in an idiot's brain remembered words
  Hang empty 'mid the cobwebs of his
    dreams !
Will bleat of flocks or bellowing of herds
  Make up for the lost music, when your
    teams
Drag home the stingy harvest, and no
    more
The feathered gleaners follow to your
    door ?

' What ! would you rather see the inces-
    sant stir
  Of insects in the windrows of the hay,
And hear the locust and the grasshopper

Their melancholy hurdy-gurdies play ?₁₄₀
Is this more pleasant to you than the whir
  Of meadow-lark, and her sweet rounde-
    lay,
Or twitter of little field-fares, as you take
Your nooning in the shade of bush and
    brake ?

'You call them thieves and pillagers; but
    know,
  They are the wingèd wardens of your
    farms,
Who from the cornfields drive the insidi-
    ous foe,
  And from your harvests keep a hundred
    harms;
Even the blackest of them all, the crow,
  Renders good service as your man-at-
    arms,   ₁₅₀
Crushing the beetle in his coat of mail,
And crying havoc on the slug and snail.

' How can I teach your children gentleness,
  And mercy to the weak, and reverence
For Life, which, in its weakness or excess,
  Is still a gleam of God's omnipotence,
Or Death, which, seeming darkness, is no
    less
  The selfsame light, although averted
    hence,
When by your laws, your actions, and
    your speech,   ₁₅₉
You contradict the very things I teach ? '

With this he closed; and through the au-
    dience went
  A murmur, like the rustle of dead
    leaves;
The farmers laughed and nodded, and some
    bent
  Their yellow heads together like their
    sheaves;
Men have no faith in fine-spun sentiment
  Who put their trust in bullocks and in
    beeves.
The birds were doomed; and, as the record
    shows,
A bounty offered for the heads of crows.

There was another audience out of reach,
  Who had no voice nor vote in making
    laws,   ₁₇₀
But in the papers read his little speech,
  And crowned his modest temples with
    applause ;

They made him conscious, each one more
    than each,
  He still was victor, vanquished in their
    cause.
Sweetest of all the applause he won from
    thee,
O fair Almira at the Academy !

And so the dreadful massacre began;
  O'er fields and orchards, and o'er wood-
    land crests,
The ceaseless fusillade of terror ran.
  Dead fell the birds, with blood-stains on
    their breasts,   ₁₈₀
Or wounded crept away from sight of man,
  While the young died of famine in their
    nests;
A slaughter to be told in groans, not words,
The very St. Bartholomew of Birds !

The summer came, and all the birds were
    dead;
  The days were like hot coals; the very
    ground
Was burned to ashes; in the orchards fed
  Myriads of caterpillars, and around
The cultivated fields and garden beds
  Hosts of devouring insects crawled, and
    found   ₁₉₀
No foe to check their march, till they had
    made
The land a desert without leaf or shade.

Devoured by worms, like Herod, was the
    town,
  Because, like Herod, it had ruthlessly
Slaughtered the Innocents. From the trees
    spun down
  The canker-worms upon the passers-by,
Upon each woman's bonnet, shawl, and
    gown,
  Who shook them off with just a little
    cry;
They were the terror of each favorite
    walk,
The endless theme of all the village talk. ₂₀₀

The farmers grew impatient, but a few
  Confessed their error, and would not
    complain,
For after all, the best thing one can do
  When it is raining, is to let it rain.
Then they repealed the law, although they
    knew
  It would not call the dead to life again;

As school-boys, finding their mistake too
    late,
Draw a wet sponge across the accusing
    slate.

That year in Killingworth the Autumn
    came
    Without the light of his majestic look, 210
The wonder of the falling tongues of flame,
    The illumined pages of his Doom's-Day
    book.
A few lost leaves blushed crimson with
    their shame,
    And drowned themselves despairing in
    the brook,
While the wild wind went moaning every-
    where,
Lamenting the dead children of the air !

But the next spring a stranger sight was
    seen,
    A sight that never yet by bard was
    sung,
As great a wonder as it would have been
    If some dumb animal had found a
    tongue !   220
A wagon, overarched with evergreen,
    Upon whose boughs were wicker cages
    hung,
All full of singing birds, came down the
    street,
Filling the air with music wild and sweet.

From all the country round these birds
    were brought,
    By order of the town, with anxious quest,
And, loosened from their wicker prisons,
    sought
    In woods and fields the places they loved
    best,
Singing loud canticles, which many thought
    Were satires to the authorities ad-
    dressed,   230
While others, listening in green lanes,
    averred
Such lovely music never had been heard !

But blither still and louder carolled they
    Upon the morrow, for they seemed to
    know
It was the fair Almira's wedding-day,
    And everywhere, around, above, below,
When the Preceptor bore his bride away,
    Their songs burst forth in joyous over-
    flow,

And a new heaven bent over a new earth
Amid the sunny farms of Killingworth. 240
1863.   1863.

WEARINESS

O LITTLE feet ! that such long years
Must wander on through hopes and fears,
    Must ache and bleed beneath your load;
I, nearer to the wayside inn
Where toil shall cease and rest begin,
    Am weary, thinking of your road !

O little hands ! that, weak or strong,
Have still to serve or rule so long,
    Have still so long to give or ask;
I, who so much with book and pen
Have toiled among my fellow-men,
    Am weary, thinking of your task.

O little hearts ! that throb and beat
With such impatient, feverish heat,
    Such limitless and strong desires;
Mine, that so long has glowed and burned,
With passions into ashes turned,
    Now covers and conceals its fires.

O little souls ! as pure and white
And crystalline as rays of light
    Direct from heaven, their source divine,
Refracted through the mist of years,
How red my setting sun appears,
    How lurid looks this soul of mine !
1863 ?   1863

HAWTHORNE[1]

How beautiful it was, that one bright day
In the long week of rain !
Though all its splendor could not chase
    away
    The omnipresent pain.

The lovely town was white with apple
    blooms,
    And the great elms o'erhead
Dark shadows wove on their aerial looms
    Shot through with golden thread.

[1] Hawthorne and Longfellow were friends for many
years. This poem records the impressions and feelings
of the day of Hawthorne's burial, May 23, 1864 : ' It
was a lovely day ; the village all sunshine and blossoms
and the song of birds. You cannot imagine anything at
once more sad and beautiful. He is buried on a hill-top
under the pines.' (See the *Life*, vol. iii, pp. 36, 38, 39 ;
and Mrs. Hawthorne's letter to Longfellow, pp. 40-42.)

Across the meadows, by the gray old manse,
  The historic river flowed :
I was as one who wanders in a trance,
  Unconscious of his road.

The faces of familiar friends seemed
    strange;
  Their voices I could hear,
And yet the words they uttered seemed to
    change
  Their meaning to my ear.

For the one face I looked for was not there,
  The one low voice was mute;
Only an unseen presence filled the air,
  And baffled my pursuit.

Now I look back, and meadow, manse, and
    stream
  Dimly my thought defines;
I only see — a dream within a dream —
  The hill-top hearsed with pines.

I only hear above his place of rest
  Their tender undertone,
The infinite longings of a troubled breast,
  The voice so like his own.

There in seclusion and remote from men
  The wizard hand lies cold,
Which at its topmost speed let fall the pen,
  And left the tale half told.

Ah ! who shall lift that wand of magic
    power,
  And the lost clew regain ?
The unfinished window in Aladdin's tower
  Unfinished must remain !
1864.   1864.

DIVINA COMMEDIA[1]

I

OFT have I seen at some cathedral door
A laborer, pausing in the dust and heat,

---

[1] The poet's life and work were interrupted by the tragic death, through fire, of Mrs. Longfellow. What he felt most deeply, he never expressed, and this burden of sorrow is scarcely alluded to in his poetry, except in the first of these sonnets, and in ' The Cross of Snow,' written eighteen years later, and not published till after his death. Unable to write, and unable to live without writing, he took refuge in the work of translating Dante's *Divine Comedy,* which he had begun in 1843, taken up again in 1853, and now continued and completed, finishing the long task in 1867. From 1861 to 1869 he wrote hardly anything else, except some

Lay down his burden, and with reverent
    feet
Enter, and cross himself, and on the floor
Kneel to repeat his paternoster o'er;
Far off the noises of the world retreat;
The loud vociferations of the street
Become an undistinguishable roar.
So, as I enter here from day to day,
And leave my burden at this minster gate,
Kneeling in prayer, and not ashamed to
    pray,
The tumult of the time disconsolate
To inarticulate murmurs dies away,
While the eternal ages watch and wait.
1864.   1864.

II

How strange the sculptures that adorn these
    towers !
This crowd of statues, in whose folded
    sleeves
Birds build their nests; while canopied with
    leaves
Parvis and portal bloom like trellised bow-
    ers,
And the vast minster seems a cross of flow-
    ers !
But fiends and dragons on the gargoyled
    eaves
Watch the dead Christ between the living
    thieves,
And, underneath, the traitor Judas lowers !
Ah ! from what agonies of heart and brain,
What exultations trampling on despair,
What tenderness, what tears, what hate of
    wrong,
What passionate outcry of a soul in pain,
Uprose this poem of the earth and air,
This mediæval miracle of song !
1864.   1866.

III

I enter, and I see thee in the gloom
Of the long aisles, O poet saturnine !

---

fragments needed to complete the first part of *Tales of a Wayside Inn.*

During the same years Robert Browning was trying to benumb the intensity of his own sorrow through absorption in the *Ring and the Book;* and Bryant, after the loss of a wife whom he had worshipped, yet whom he scarcely alludes to in his verse (see ' O Fairest of the Rural Maids,' ' The Future Life,' and ' A Lifetime '), took for his task the translation of Homer.

Longfellow's *Journal,* and his letters to Sumner, show also how deeply he felt the life-and-death crisis through which his country was passing in the same years, and to which, also, his verse hardly alludes except for the first of these sonnets.

And strive to make my steps keep pace
    with thine.
The air is filled with some unknown per-
    fume;
The congregation of the dead make room
For thee to pass; the votive tapers shine;
Like rooks that haunt Ravenna's groves of
    pine
The hovering echoes fly from tomb to tomb.
From the confessionals I hear arise
Rehearsals of forgotten tragedies,
And lamentations from the crypts below;
And then a voice celestial that begins
With the pathetic words, ' Although your
    sins
As scarlet be,' and ends with ' as the snow.'
1865.   1866.

IV

With snow-white veil and garments as of
    flame,
She stands before thee, who so long ago
Filled thy young heart with passion and the
    woe
From which thy song and all its splendors
    came;
And while with stern rebuke she speaks thy
    name,
The ice about thy heart melts as the snow
On mountain heights, and in swift overflow
Comes gushing from thy lips in sobs of
    shame.
Thou makest full confession; and a gleam,
As of the dawn on some dark forest cast,
Seems on thy lifted forehead to increase;
Lethe and Eunoë — the remembered dream
And the forgotten sorrow — bring at last
That perfect pardon which is perfect peace.
1867.   1867.

V

I lift mine eyes, and all the windows blaze
With forms of Saints and holy men who
    died,
Here martyred and hereafter glorified;
And the great Rose upon its leaves dis-
    plays
Christ's Triumph, and the angelic rounde-
    lays,
With splendor upon splendor multiplied;
And Beatrice again at Dante's side
No more rebukes, but smiles her words of
    praise.
And then the organ sounds, and unseen
    choirs

Sing the old Latin hymns of peace and love
And benedictions of the Holy Ghost;
And the melodious bells among the spires
O'er all the house-tops and through heaven
    above
Proclaim the elevation of the Host !
1866.   1866.

VI

O star of morning and of liberty !
O bringer of the light, whose splendor
    shines
Above the darkness of the Apennines,
Forerunner of the day that is to be !
The voices of the city and the sea,
The voices of the mountains and the pines,
Repeat thy song, till the familiar lines
Are footpaths for the thought of Italy !
Thy flame is blown abroad from all the
    heights,
Through all the nations, and a sound is
    heard,
As of a mighty wind, and men devout,
Strangers of Rome, and the new proselytes,
In their own language hear the wondrous
    word,
And many are amazed and many doubt.
1866.   1866.

KILLED AT THE FORD [1]

He is dead, the beautiful youth,
The heart of honor, the tongue of truth,
He, the life and light of us all,
Whose voice was blithe as a bugle-call,
Whom all eyes followed with one consent,
The cheer of whose laugh, and whose plea-
    sant word,
Hushed all murmurs of discontent.

Only last night, as we rode along,
Down the dark of the mountain gap,
To visit the picket-guard at the ford,   10
Little dreaming of any mishap,
He was humming the words of some old
    song:

[1] The poem you speak of was not a record of any
one event which came to my knowledge, but of many
which came to my imagination. It is an attempt to express something of the inexpressible sympathy which
I feel for the death of the young men in the war, which
makes my heart bleed whenever I think of it. (Longfellow, in a letter of March 23, 1866.)

Longfellow's oldest son, Charles, was a lieutenant of
cavalry in the Army of the Potomac before he was
twenty years old. Toward the end of 1863 he was seriously wounded, but recovered. (*Life*, vol. iii, pp. 21,
24–27.)

'Two red roses he had on his cap
And another he bore at the point of his
    sword.'

Sudden and swift a whistling ball
Came out of a wood, and the voice was
    still;
Something I heard in the darkness fall,
And for a moment my blood grew chill;
I spake in a whisper, as he who speaks
In a room where some one is lying dead; 20
But he made no answer to what I said.

We lifted him up to his saddle again,
And through the mire and the mist and
    the rain
Carried him back to the silent camp,
And laid him as if asleep on his bed;
And I saw by the light of the surgeon's
    lamp
Two white roses upon his cheeks,
And one, just over his heart, blood-red!

And I saw in a vision how far and fleet
That fatal bullet went speeding forth,   30
Till it reached a town in the distant North,
Till it reached a house in a sunny street,
Till it reached a heart that ceased to beat
Without a murmur, without a cry;
And a bell was tolled, in that far-off town,
For one who had passed from cross to
    crown,
And the neighbors wondered that she should
    die.
1866.   1866.

GIOTTO'S TOWER

How many lives, made beautiful and sweet
By self-devotion and by self-restraint,
Whose pleasure is to run without complaint
On unknown errands of the Paraclete,
Wanting the reverence of unshodden feet,
Fail of the nimbus which the artists paint
Around the shining forehead of the saint,
And are in their completeness incomplete !
In the old Tuscan town stands Giotto's
    tower,
The lily of Florence blossoming in stone, —
A vision, a delight, and a desire, —
The builder's perfect and centennial flower,
That in the night of ages bloomed alone,
But wanting still the glory of the spire.
1866.   1866.

FINALE OF CHRISTUS

SAINT JOHN

SAINT JOHN *wandering over the face of the
    Earth.*

SAINT JOHN:

THE Ages come and go,
The Centuries pass as Years;
My hair is white as the snow,
My feet are weary and slow,
The earth is wet with my tears !
The kingdoms crumble, and fall
Apart, like a ruined wall,
Or a bank that is undermined
By a river's ceaseless flow,
And leave no trace behind !   10
The world itself is old;
The portals of Time unfold
On hinges of iron, that grate
And groan with the rust and the weight
Like the hinges of a gate
That hath fallen to decay;
But the evil doth not cease;
There is war instead of peace,
Instead of Love there is hate;
And still I must wander and wait,   20
Still I must watch and pray,
Not forgetting in whose sight,
A thousand years in their flight
Are as a single day.

The life of man is a gleam
Of light, that comes and goes
Like the course of the Holy Stream,
The cityless river, that flows
From fountains no one knows,
Through the Lake of Galilee,   30
Through forests and level lands,
Over rocks, and shallows, and sands
Of a wilderness wild and vast,
Till it findeth its rest at last
In the desolate Dead Sea !
But alas ! alas for me
Nor yet this rest shall be !

What, then ! doth Charity fail ?
Is Faith of no avail ?
Is Hope blown out like a light   40
By a gust of wind in the night ?
The clashing of creeds, and the strife
Of the many beliefs, that in vain
Perplex man's heart and brain,
Are naught but the rustle of leaves,

When the breath of God upheaves
The boughs of the Tree of Life,
And they subside again !
And I remember still
The words, and from whom they came,   51
Not he that repeateth the name,
But he that doeth the will !

And Him evermore I behold
Walking in Galilee,
Through the cornfield's waving gold,
In hamlet, in wood, and in wold,
By the shores of the Beautiful Sea.
He toucheth the sightless eyes;
Before Him the demons flee;
To the dead He sayeth: Arise !   60
To the living: Follow me !
And that voice still soundeth on
From the centuries that are gone,
To the centuries that shall be !

From all vain pomps and shows,
From the pride that overflows,
And the false conceits of men;
From all the narrow rules
And subtleties of Schools,
And the craft of tongue and pen;   70
Bewildered in its search,
Bewildered with the cry:
Lo, here ! lo, there, the Church !
Poor, sad Humanity
Through all the dust and heat
Turns back with bleeding feet,
By the weary road it came,
Unto the simple thought
By the great Master taught,
And that remaineth still: 80
Not he that repeateth the name,
But he that doeth the will !

1871.   *1872.*

THE HANGING OF THE CRANE [1]

I

THE lights are out, and gone are all the
          guests
That thronging came with merriment and
          jests

[1] ' One morning in the spring of 1867,' writes Mr.
T. B. Aldrich, ' Mr. Longfellow came to the little home
in Pinckney Street [Boston], where we had set up house-
keeping in the light of our honeymoon. As we lingered
a moment at the dining-room door, Mr. Longfellow
turning to me said, " Ah, Mr. Aldrich, your small round
table will not always be closed. By and by you will
find new young faces clustering about it ; as years go

To celebrate the Hanging of the Crane
In the new house, — into the night are
          gone;
But still the fire upon the hearth burns on,
          And I alone remain.

O fortunate, O happy day,
When a new household finds its place
Among the myriad homes of earth,
Like a new star just sprung to birth,   10
And rolled on its harmonious way
Into the boundless realms of space !

So said the guests in speech and song,
As in the chimney, burning bright,
We hung the iron crane to-night,
And merry was the feast and long.

II

And now I sit and muse on what may be,
And in my vision see, or seem to see,
          Through floating vapors interfused with
               light,
Shapes indeterminate, that gleam and
          fade,   20
As shadows passing into deeper shade
          Sink and elude the sight.

For two alone, there in the hall,
Is spread the table round and small;
Upon the polished silver shine
The evening lamps, but, more divine,
The light of love shines over all;
Of love, that says not mine and thine,
But ours, for ours is thine and mine.

They want no guests, to come between   30
Their tender glances like a screen,
 ·   And tell them tales of land and sea,

on, leaf after leaf will be added until the time comes
when the young guests will take flight, one by one, to
build nests of their own elsewhere. Gradually the long
table will shrink to a circle again, leaving two old people sitting there alone together. This is the story of
life, the sweet and pathetic poem of the fireside. Make
an idyl of it. I give the idea to you." Several months
afterward, I received a note from Mr. Longfellow in
which he expressed a desire to use this *motif* in case I
had done nothing in the matter. The theme was one
peculiarly adapted to his sympathetic handling, and out
of it grew *The Hanging of the Crane.*' Just when the
poem was written does not appear, but its first publication was in the *New York Ledger*, March 28, 1874. Mr.
Longfellow's old friend, Mr. Samuel Ward, had heard
the poem, and offered to secure it for Mr. Robert Bonner, the proprietor of the *Ledger*, ' touched ' as he wrote
to Mr. Longfellow, ' by your kindness to poor ——,
and haunted by the idea of increasing handsomely
your noble charity fund.' Mr. Bonner paid the poet
the sum of three thousand dollars for this poem. (*Cambridge Edition.*)

And whatsoever may betide
The great, forgotten world outside;
They want no guests; they needs must be
Each other's own best company.

III

The picture fades; as at a village fair
A showman's views, dissolving into air,
　Again appear transfigured on the screen,
So in my fancy this; and now once more,　40
In part transfigured, through the open door
　Appears the selfsame scene.

Seated, I see the two again,
But not alone; they entertain
A little angel unaware,
With face as round as is the moon,
A royal guest with flaxen hair,
Who, throned upon his lofty chair,
Drums on the table with his spoon,
Then drops it careless on the floor,　50
To grasp at things unseen before.

Are these celestial manners? these
The ways that win, the arts that please?
Ah yes; consider well the guest,
And whatsoe'er he does seems best;
He ruleth by the right divine
Of helplessness, so lately born
In purple chambers of the morn,
As sovereign over thee and thine.
He speaketh not; and yet there lies　60
A conversation in his eyes;
The golden silence of the Greek,
The gravest wisdom of the wise,
Not spoken in language, but in looks
More legible than printed books,
As if he could but would not speak.
And now, O monarch absolute,
Thy power is put to proof; for, lo!
Resistless, fathomless, and slow,
The nurse comes rustling like the sea,　70
And pushes back thy chair and thee,
And so good night to King Canute.

IV

As one who walking in a forest sees
A lovely landscape through the parted
　　trees,
　Then sees it not, for boughs that inter-
　　vene;
Or as we see the moon sometimes revealed
Through drifting clouds, and then again
　　concealed,
　So I behold the scene.

There are two guests at table now;
The king, deposed and older grown,　80
No longer occupies the throne, —
The crown is on his sister's brow;
A Princess from the Fairy Isles,
The very pattern girl of girls,
All covered and embowered in curls,
Rose-tinted from the Isle of Flowers,
And sailing with soft, silken sails
From far-off Dreamland into ours.
Above their bowls with rims of blue
Four azure eyes of deeper hue　90
Are looking, dreamy with delight;
Limpid as planets that emerge
Above the ocean's rounded verge,
Soft-shining through the summer night.
Steadfast thy gaze, yet nothing see
Beyond the horizon of their bowls;
Nor care they for the world that rolls
With all its freight of troubled souls
Into the days that are to be.

V

Again the tossing boughs shut out the
　　scene,　100
Again the drifting vapors intervene,
　And the moon's pallid disk is hidden quite;
And now I see the table wider grown,
As round a pebble into water thrown
　　Dilates a ring of light.

I see the table wider grown,
I see it garlanded with guests,
As if fair Ariadne's Crown
Out of the sky had fallen down;
Maidens within whose tender breasts　110
A thousand restless hopes and fears,
Forth reaching to the coming years,
Flutter awhile, then quiet lie,
Like timid birds that fain would fly,
But do not dare to leave their nests; —
And youths, who in their strength elate
Challenge the van and front of fate,
Eager as champions to be
In the divine knight-errantry
Of youth, that travels sea and land　120
Seeking adventures, or pursues,
Through cities, and through solitudes
Frequented by the lyric Muse,
The phantom with the beckoning hand,
That still allures and still eludes.
O sweet illusions of the brain!
O sudden thrills of fire and frost!
The world is bright while ye remain,
And dark and dead when ye are lost!

VI

The meadow-brook, that seemeth to stand
    still,   130
Quickens its current as it nears the mill;
    And so the stream of Time that linger-
        eth
In level places, and so dull appears,
Runs with a swifter current as it nears
    The gloomy mills of Death.

And now, like the magician's scroll,
That in the owner's keeping shrinks
With every wish he speaks or thinks,
Till the last wish consumes the whole,
The table dwindles, and again   140
I see the two alone remain.
The crown of stars is broken in parts;
Its jewels, brighter than the day,
Have one by one been stolen away
To shine in other homes and hearts.
One is a wanderer now afar
In Ceylon or in Zanzibar,
Or sunny regions of Cathay;
And one is in the boisterous camp
'Mid clink of arms and horses' tramp, 150
And battle's terrible array.
I see the patient mother read,
With aching heart, of wrecks that float
Disabled on those seas remote,
Or of some great heroic deed
On battle-fields, where thousands bleed
To lift one hero into fame.
Anxious she bends her graceful head
Above these chronicles of pain,
And trembles with a secret dread   160
Lest there among the drowned or slain
She find the one beloved name.

VII

After a day of cloud and wind and rain
Sometimes the setting sun breaks out again,
    And, touching all the darksome woods
        with light,
Smiles on the fields, until they laugh and
    sing,
Then like a ruby from the horizon's ring
    Drops down into the night.

What see I now? The night is fair,
The storm of grief, the clouds of care,   170
The wind, the rain, have passed away;
The lamps are lit, the fires burn bright,
The house is full of life and light;
It is the Golden Wedding day.
The guests come thronging in once more,

Quick footsteps sound along the floor,
The trooping children crowd the stair,
And in and out and everywhere
Flashes along the corridor
The sunshine of their golden hair.   180
On the round table in the hall
Another Ariadne's Crown
Out of the sky hath fallen down;
More than one Monarch of the Moon
Is drumming with his silver spoon;
The light of love shines over all.

O fortunate, O happy day!
The people sing, the people say.
The ancient bridegroom and the bride,
Smiling contented and serene   190
Upon the blithe, bewildering scene,
Behold, well pleased, on every side
Their forms and features multiplied,
As the reflection of a light
Between two burnished mirrors gleams,
Or lamps upon a bridge at night
Stretch on and on before the sight,
Till the long vista endless seems.
1873.   *1874.*

CHAUCER

An old man in a lodge within a park;
The chamber walls depicted all around
With portraitures of huntsman, hawk, and
    hound,
And the hurt deer. He listeneth to the lark,
Whose song comes with the sunshine
    through the dark
Of painted glass in leaden lattice bound;
He listeneth and he laugheth at the sound,
Then writeth in a book like any clerk.
He is the poet of the dawn, who wrote
The Canterbury Tales, and his old age
Made beautiful with song; and as I read
I hear the crowing cock, I hear the note
Of lark and linnet, and from every page
Rise odors of ploughed field or flowery
    mead.
1873.   (1875.)

SHAKESPEARE

A vision as of crowded city streets,
With human life in endless overflow;
Thunder of thoroughfares; trumpets that
    blow

To battle; clamor, in obscure retreats,
Of sailors landed from their anchored fleets;
Tolling of bells in turrets, and below
Voices of children, and bright flowers that
throw
O'er garden walls their intermingled
sweets!
This vision comes to me when I unfold
The volume of the Poet paramount,
Whom all the Muses loved, not one
alone; —
Into his hands they put the lyre of gold,
And, crowned with sacred laurel at their
fount,
Placed him as Musagetes on their throne.
1873. (1875.)

MILTON

I PACE the sounding sea-beach and behold
How the voluminous billows roll and run,
Upheaving and subsiding, while the sun
Shines through their sheeted emerald far
unrolled,
And the ninth wave, slow gathering fold by
fold
All its loose-flowing garments into one,
Plunges upon the shore, and floods the dun
Pale reach of sands, and changes them to
gold.
So in majestic cadence rise and fall
The mighty undulations of thy song,
O sightless bard, England's Mæonides!
And ever and anon, high over all
Uplifted, a ninth wave superb and strong,
Floods all the soul with its melodious seas.
1873. (1875.)

KEATS

THE young Endymion sleeps Endymion's
sleep;
The shepherd-boy whose tale was left half
told!
The solemn grove uplifts its shield of gold
To the red rising moon, and loud and deep
The nightingale is singing from the steep;
It is midsummer, but the air is cold;
Can it be death? Alas, beside the fold
A shepherd's pipe lies shattered near his
sheep.
Lo! in the moonlight gleams a marble
white,

On which I read: 'Here lieth one whose
name
Was writ in water.' [1] And was this the meed
Of his sweet singing? Rather let me write:
'The smoking flax before it burst to flame
Was quenched by death, and broken the
bruised reed.'
1873. (1875.)

THE SOUND OF THE SEA

THE sea awoke at midnight from its sleep,
And round the pebbly beaches far and wide
I heard the first wave of the rising tide
Rush onward with uninterrupted sweep;
A voice out of the silence of the deep,
A sound mysteriously multiplied
As of a cataract from the mountain's side,
Or roar of winds upon a wooded steep.
So comes to us at times, from the unknown
And inaccessible solitudes of being,
The rushing of the sea-tides of the soul;
And inspirations, that we deem our own,
Are some divine foreshadowing and foresee-
ing
Of things beyond our reason or control.
1874. (1875.)

THREE FRIENDS OF MINE

I

WHEN I remember them, those friends of
mine,
Who are no longer here, the noble three,
Who half my life were more than friends to
me,
And whose discourse was like a generous
wine,
I most of all remember the divine
Something, that shone in them, and made us
see
The archetypal man, and what might be
The amplitude of Nature's first design.
In vain I stretch my hands to clasp their
hands;
I cannot find them. Nothing now is left 10

---

[1] Keats' epitaph upon himself, inscribed on the simple
stone that stands at the head of his grave beside the
walls of Rome. Of the many poets' protests against
its cutting pathos, perhaps the best is this, by J. E.
Spingarn: —

  The Star of Fame shines down upon the river,
    And answering, the stream of Life repeats:
  'Upon *our* waters shall be writ forever
    The name of Keats!'

But a majestic memory. They mean-
 while
Wander together in Elysian lands,
Perchance remembering me, who am bereft
Of their dear presence, and, remembering,
 smile.

II [1]

In Attica thy birthplace should have been,
On the Ionian Isles, or where the seas
Encircle in their arms the Cyclades,
So wholly Greek wast thou in thy serene
And childlike joy of life, O Philhellene !
Around thee would have swarmed the Attic
 bees;   20
Homer had been thy friend, or Socrates,
And Plato welcomed thee to his demesne.
For thee old legends breathed historic
 breath;
Thou sawest Poseidon in the purple sea,
And in the sunset Jason's fleece of gold !
Oh, what hadst thou to do with cruel Death,
Who wast so full of life, or Death with
 thee,
That thou shouldst die before thou hadst
 grown old !

III [2]

I stand again on the familiar shore,
And hear the waves of the distracted sea
Piteously calling and lamenting thee, 31
And waiting restless at thy cottage door.
The rocks, the sea-weed on the ocean
 floor,
The willows in the meadow, and the free
Wild winds of the Atlantic welcome me;
Then why shouldst thou be dead, and come
 no more ?
Ah, why shouldst thou be dead, when com-
 mon men
Are busy with their trivial affairs,
Having and holding ? Why, when thou
 hadst read
Nature's mysterious manuscript, and then 40
Wast ready to reveal the truth it bears,
Why art thou silent ? Why shouldst thou
 be dead ?

IV [3]

River, that stealest with such silent pace
Around the City of the Dead,[4] where lies
A friend who bore thy name, and whom
 these eyes
Shall see no more in his accustomed
 place,
Linger and fold him in thy soft embrace,
And say good night, for now the western
 skies
Are red with sunset, and gray mists arise
Like damps that gather on a dead man's
 face.   50
Good night ! good night ! as we so oft have
 said
Beneath this roof at midnight, in the days
That are no more, and shall no more re-
 turn.
Thou hast but taken thy lamp and gone to
 bed;
I stay a little longer, as one stays
To cover up the embers that still burn.

V

The doors are all wide open; at the gate
The blossomed lilacs counterfeit a blaze,
And seem to warm the air; a dreamy
 haze
Hangs o'er the Brighton meadows like a
 fate,   60
And on their margin, with sea-tides elate,
The flooded Charles, as in the happier
 days,
Writes the last letter of his name, and
 stays
His restless steps, as if compelled to wait.
I also wait; but they will come no more,
Those friends of mine, whose presence sat-
 isfied
The thirst and hunger of my heart. Ah
 me !
They have forgotten the pathway to my
 door !
Something is gone from nature since they
 died,
And summer is not summer, nor can be. 70
1874.   (1875.)

[1] C. C. Felton, for many years professor of Greek at Harvard, and president of the University from 1860 till his death in 1862. See the *Life of Longfellow*, in many passages, but especially vol. iii, pp. 4, 7, 9.

[2] Agassiz was a constant companion of Longfellow's. See note on p. 211, and many passages in the *Life*.

[3] Charles Sumner was lecturer in the Harvard Law School when Longfellow first came to Cambridge, in 1836, and from that time until his death, in 1874, was one of Longfellow's closest friends.

[4] The River Charles, whose windings 'write the last letter of his name,' flows near the Cemetery of Mount Auburn. There Sumner is buried, on the hillside near-est the river. Longfellow himself and Agassiz, Lowell, Holmes, Pierpont, Willis, and Parsons, and the histo-rians Prescott, Motley, and Parkman now lie buried there also.

MORITURI SALUTAMUS [1]

POEM FOR THE FIFTIETH ANNIVERSARY
OF THE CLASS OF 1825 IN BOWDOIN
COLLEGE

Tempora labuntur, tacitisque senescimus annis,
  Et fugiunt freno non remorante dies.
              OVID, *Fastorum*, Lib. vi.

'O CÆSAR, we who are about to die
Salute you!' was the gladiators' cry
In the arena, standing face to face
With death and with the Roman populace.

O ye familiar scenes, — ye groves of pine,
That once were mine and are no longer
    mine, —
Thou river, widening through the meadows
    green
To the vast sea, so near and yet unseen, —
Ye halls, in whose seclusion and repose
Phantoms of fame, like exhalations, rose 10
And vanished, — we who are about to die,
Salute you; earth and air and sea and sky,
And the Imperial Sun that scatters down
His sovereign splendors upon grove and
    town.

Ye do not answer us! ye do not hear!
We are forgotten; and in your austere
And calm indifference, ye little care
Whether we come or go, or whence or
    where.
What passing generations fill these halls,
What passing voices echo from these walls,

Ye heed not; we are only as the blast, 21
A moment heard, and then forever past.

Not so the teachers who in earlier days
Led our bewildered feet through learning's
    maze;
They answer us — alas! what have I said?
What greetings come there from the voice-
    less dead?
What salutation, welcome, or reply?
What pressure from the hands that lifeless
    lie?
They are no longer here; they all are
    gone
Into the land of shadows, — all save one. 30
Honor and reverence, and the good repute
That follows faithful service as its fruit,
Be unto him, whom living we salute.

The great Italian poet, when he made
His dreadful journey to the realms of
    shade,
Met there the old instructor of his youth,
And cried in tones of pity and of ruth:
'Oh, never from the memory of my heart
Your dear, paternal image shall depart,
Who while on earth, ere yet by death sur-
    prised,   40
Taught me how mortals are immortalized;
How grateful am I for that patient care
All my life long my language shall de-
    clare.' [2]

To-day we make the poet's words our own,
And utter them in plaintive undertone;
Nor to the living only be they said,
But to the other living called the dead,
Whose dear, paternal images appear
Not wrapped in gloom, but robed in sun-
    shine here;
Whose simple lives, complete and without
    flaw,   50
Were part and parcel of great Nature's
    law;
Who said not to their Lord, as if afraid,
'Here is thy talent in a napkin laid,'
But labored in their sphere, as men who
    live
In the delight that work alone can give.
Peace be to them; eternal peace and rest,
And the fulfilment of the great behest:
'Ye have been faithful over a few things,
Over ten cities shall ye reign as kings.'

And ye who fill the places we once filled, 60
And follow in the furrows that we tilled,
Young men, whose generous hearts are
      beating high,
We who are old, and are about to die,
Salute you; hail you; take your hands in
      ours,
And crown you with our welcome as with
      flowers!

How beautiful is youth! how bright it
      gleams
With its illusions, aspirations, dreams!
Book of Beginnings, Story without End,
Each maid a heroine, and each man a
      friend!
Aladdin's Lamp, and Fortunatus' Purse, 70
That holds the treasures of the universe!
All possibilities are in its hands,
No danger daunts it, and no foe withstands;
In its sublime audacity of faith,
'Be thou removed!' it to the mountain
      saith,
And with ambitious feet, secure and proud,
Ascends the ladder leaning on the cloud!

As ancient Priam at the Scæan gate
Sat on the walls of Troy in regal state
With the old men, too old and weak to
      fight,   80
Chirping like grasshoppers in their delight
To see the embattled hosts, with spear and
      shield,
Of Trojans and Achaians in the field;
So from the snowy summits of our years
We see you in the plain, as each appears,
And question of you; asking, 'Who is he
That towers above the others? Which
      may be
Atreides, Menelaus, Odysseus,
Ajax the great, or bold Idomeneus?'

Let him not boast who puts his armor on 90
As he who puts it off, the battle done.
Study yourselves; and most of all note
      well
Wherein kind Nature meant you to excel.
Not every blossom ripens into fruit;
Minerva, the inventress of the flute,
Flung it aside, when she her face sur-
      veyed
Distorted in a fountain as she played;
The unlucky Marsyas found it, and his
      fate
Was one to make the bravest hesitate.

Write on your doors the saying wise and
      old,   100
'Be bold! be bold!' and everywhere, 'Be
      bold;
Be not too bold!' Yet better the excess
Than the defect; better the more than less;
Better like Hector in the field to die,
Than like a perfumed Paris turn and fly.

And now, my classmates; ye remaining few
That number not the half of those we knew,
Ye, against whose familiar names not yet
The fatal asterisk of death is set,
Ye I salute! The horologe of Time   110
Strikes the half-century with a solemn
      chime,
And summons us together once again,
The joy of meeting not unmixed with pain.

Where are the others? Voices from the
      deep
Caverns of darkness answer me: 'They
      sleep!'
I name no names; instinctively I feel
Each at some well-remembered grave will
      kneel,
And from the inscription wipe the weeds
      and moss,
For every heart best knoweth its own loss.
I see their scattered gravestones gleaming
      white   120
Through the pale dusk of the impending
      night;
O'er all alike the impartial sunset throws
Its golden lilies mingled with the rose;
We give to each a tender thought, and pass
Out of the graveyards with their tangled
      grass,
Unto these scenes frequented by our feet
When we were young, and life was fresh
      and sweet.

What shall I say to you? What can I say
Better than silence is? When I survey
This throng of faces turned to meet my
      own,   130
Friendly and fair, and yet to me unknown,
Transformed the very landscape seems to
      be;
It is the same, yet not the same to me.
So many memories crowd upon my brain,
So many ghosts are in the wooded plain,
I fain would steal away, with noiseless
      tread,
As from a house where some one lieth dead

I cannot go; — I pause; — I hesitate;
My feet reluctant linger at the gate;
As one who struggles in a troubled dream 140
To speak and cannot, to myself I seem.

Vanish the dream ! Vanish the idle fears !
Vanish the rolling mists of fifty years !
Whatever time or space may intervene,
I will not be a stranger in this scene.
Here every doubt, all indecision, ends;
Hail, my companions, comrades, classmates,
    friends !

Ah me ! the fifty years since last we met
Seem to me fifty folios bound and set
By Time, the great transcriber, on his
    shelves,   150
Wherein are written the histories of our-
    selves.
What tragedies, what comedies, are there;
What joy and grief, what rapture and de-
    spair !
What chronicles of triumph and defeat,
Of struggle, and temptations, and retreat !
What records of regrets, and doubts, and
    fears !
What pages blotted, blistered by our tears !
What lovely landscapes on the margin
    shine,
What sweet, angelic faces, what divine
And holy images of love and trust,   160
Undimmed by age, unsoiled by damp or
    dust !

Whose hand shall dare to open and explore
These volumes, closed and clasped forever-
    more ?
Not mine. With reverential feet I pass;
I hear a voice that cries, ' Alas ! alas !
Whatever hath been written shall remain,
Nor be erased nor written o'er again;
The unwritten only still belongs to thee:
Take heed, and ponder well what that shall
    be.'

As children frightened by a thunder-cloud
Are reassured if some one reads aloud 171
A tale of wonder,with enchantment fraught,
Or wild adventure, that diverts their
    thought,
Let me endeavor with a tale to chase
The gathering shadows of the time and
    place,
And banish what we all too deeply feel
Wholly to say, or wholly to conceal.

In mediæval Rome, I know not where,
There stood an image with its arm in air,
And on its lifted finger, shining clear,   18c
A golden ring with the device, ' Strike
    here ! '
Greatly the people wondered, though none
    guessed
The meaning that these words but half ex-
    pressed,
Until a learned clerk who at noonday
With downcast eyes was passing on his
    way,
Paused, and observed the spot, and marked
    it well,
Whereon the shadow of the finger fell;
And, coming back at midnight, delved, and
    found
A secret stairway leading underground.
Down this he passed into a spacious hall, 190
Lit by a flaming jewel on the wall;
And opposite, in threatening attitude,
With bow and shaft a brazen statue stood.
Upon its forehead, like a coronet,
Were these mysterious words of menace
    set:
' That which I am, I am; my fatal aim
None can escape, not even yon luminous
    flame ! '

Midway the hall was a fair table placed,
With cloth of gold, and golden cups en-
    chased
With rubies, and the plates and knives
    were gold,   200
And gold the bread and viands manifold.
Around it, silent, motionless, and sad,
Were seated gallant knights in armor clad,
And ladies beautiful with plume and zone,
But they were stone, their hearts within
    were stone;
And the vast hall was filled in every part
With silent crowds, stony in face and heart.

Long at the scene, bewildered and amazed,
The trembling clerk in speechless wonder
    gazed;
Then from the table, by his greed made
    bold,   210
He seized a goblet and a knife of gold,
And suddenly from their seats the guests
    upsprang,
The vaulted ceiling with loud clamors
    rang,
The archer sped his arrow, at their call,
Shattering the lambent jewel on the wall,

And all was dark around and overhead; —
Stark on the floor the luckless clerk lay
   dead !

The writer of this legend then records
Its ghostly application in these words:
The image is the Adversary old,   220
Whose beckoning finger points to realms of
   gold;
Our lusts and passions are the downward
   stair
That leads the soul from a diviner air;
The archer, Death; the flaming jewel,
   Life;
Terrestrial goods, the goblet and the knife;
The knights and ladies, all whose flesh and
   bone
By avarice have been hardened into stone;
The clerk, the scholar whom the love of
   pelf
Tempts from his books and from his nobler
   self.

The scholar and the world ! The endless
   strife,   230
The discord in the harmonies of life !
The love of learning, the sequestered nooks,
And all the sweet serenity of books;
The market-place, the eager love of gain,
Whose aim is vanity, and whose end is
   pain !

But why, you ask me, should this tale be
   told
To men grown old, or who are growing old ?
It is too late ! Ah, nothing is too late
Till the tired heart shall cease to palpitate.
Cato learned Greek at eighty; Sophocles 240
Wrote his grand Œdipus, and Simonides
Bore off the prize of verse from his com-
   peers,
When each had numbered more than four-
   score years,
And Theophrastus, at fourscore and ten,
Had but begun his ' Characters of Men.'
Chaucer, at Woodstock with the nightin-
   gales,
At sixty wrote the Canterbury Tales;
Goethe at Weimar, toiling to the last,
Completed Faust when eighty years were
   past.
These are indeed exceptions; but they
   show   250
How far the gulf-stream of our youth may
   flow

Into the arctic regions of our lives,
Where little else than life itself survives.

As the barometer foretells the storm
While still the skies are clear, the weather
   warm,
So something in us, as old age draws near,
Betrays the pressure of the atmosphere.
The nimble mercury, ere we are aware,
Descends the elastic ladder of the air;
The telltale blood in artery and vein   260
Sinks from its higher levels in the brain;
Whatever poet, orator, or sage
May say of it, old age is still old age.
It is the waning, not the crescent moon;
The dusk of evening, not the blaze of
   noon;
It is not strength, but weakness; not de-
   sire,
But its surcease; not the fierce heat of fire,
The burning and consuming element,
But that of ashes and of embers spent,
In which some living sparks we still dis-
   cern,   270
Enough to warm, but not enough to burn.

What then ? Shall we sit idly down and
   say
The night hath come ; it is no longer day ?
The night hath not yet come; we are not
   quite
Cut off from labor by the failing light;
Something remains for us to do or dare;
Even the oldest tree some fruit may bear;
Not Œdipus Coloneus, or Greek Ode,
Or tales of pilgrims that one morning rode
Out of the gateway of the Tabard Inn, 280
But other something, would we but begin;
For age is opportunity no less
Than youth itself, though in another dress,
And as the evening twilight fades away
The sky is filled with stars, invisible by day.
1874.   *1875.*

THE HERONS OF ELMWOOD [1]

WARM and still is the summer night,
  As here by the river's brink I wander;
White overhead are the stars, and white
    The glimmering lamps on the hillside
    yonder.

[1] ' Elmwood ' was the home of James Russell Lowell,
in Cambridge, about a half mile distant from the Long
fellow home.

Silent are all the sounds of day;
  Nothing I hear but the chirp of crickets,
And the cry of the herons winging their
      way
  O'er the poet's house in the Elmwood
      thickets.

Call to him, herons, as slowly you pass
  To your roosts in the haunts of the exiled
      thrushes,   10
Sing him the song of the green morass,
  And the tides that water the weeds and
      rushes.

Sing him the mystical Song of the Hern,
  And the secret that baffles our utmost
      seeking;
For only a sound of lament we discern,
  And cannot interpret the words you are
      speaking.

Sing of the air, and the wild delight
  Of wings that uplift and winds that up-
      hold you,
The joy of freedom, the rapture of flight
  Through the drift of the floating mists
      that infold you;   20

Of the landscape lying so far below,
  With its towns and rivers and desert
      places;
And the splendor of light above, and the
      glow
  Of the limitless, blue, ethereal spaces.

Ask him if songs of the Troubadours,
  Or of Minnesingers in old black-letter,
Sound in his ears more sweet than yours,
  And if yours are not sweeter and wilder
      and better.

Sing to him, say to him, here at his gate,
  Where the boughs of the stately elms are
      meeting,   30
Some one hath lingered to meditate,
  And send him unseen this friendly greet-
      ing;

That many another hath done the same,
  Though not by a sound was the silence
      broken;
The surest pledge of a deathless name
  Is the silent homage of thoughts un-
      spoken.
1876.   1877.

IN THE CHURCHYARD AT TARRYTOWN [1]

HERE lies the gentle humorist, who died
In the bright Indian Summer of his fame!
A simple stone, with but a date and name,
Marks his secluded resting-place beside
The river that he loved and glorified.
Here in the autumn of his days he came,
But the dry leaves of life were all aflame
With tints that brightened and were multi-
    plied.
How sweet a life was his; how sweet a death!
Living, to wing with mirth the weary hours,
Or with romantic tales the heart to cheer;
Dying, to leave a memory like the breath
Of summers full of sunshine and of showers,
A grief and gladness in the atmosphere.
1876.   1877.

THE POETS

O YE dead Poets, who are living still
Immortal in your verse, though life be fled,
And ye, O living Poets, who are dead
Though ye are living, if neglect can kill,
Tell me if in the darkest hours of ill,
With drops of anguish falling fast and
    red
From the sharp crown of thorns upon your
    head,
Ye were not glad your errand to fulfil?
Yes; for the gift and ministry of Song
Have something in them so divinely sweet,
It can assuage the bitterness of wrong;
Not in the clamor of the crowded street,
Not in the shouts and plaudits of the throng,
But in ourselves, are triumph and defeat.
1876.   (1878.)

NATURE

As a fond mother, when the day is o'er,
Leads by the hand her little child to bed,
Half willing, half reluctant to be led,
And leave his broken playthings on the
    floor,
Still gazing at them through the open door,
Nor wholly reassured and comforted
By promises of others in their stead,

[1] The burial-place of Washington Irving. On Longfellow's great admiration for Irving, see the *Life*, vol
i, p. 12.

Which, though more splendid, may not
  please him more;
So Nature deals with us, and takes away
Our playthings one by one, and by the hand
Leads us to rest so gently, that we go
Scarce knowing if we wish to go or stay,
Being too full of sleep to understand
How far the unknown transcends the what
  we know.[1]

1876.   1877.

VENICE

WHITE swan of cities, slumbering in thy
  nest
So wonderfully built among the reeds
Of the lagoon, that fences thee and feeds,
As sayeth thy old historian and thy guest !
White water-lily, cradled and caressed
By ocean streams, and from the silt and
  weeds
Lifting thy golden filaments and seeds,
Thy sun-illumined spires, thy crown and
  crest !
White phantom city, whose untrodden
  streets
Are rivers, and whose pavements are the
  shifting
Shadows of palaces and strips of sky;
I wait to see thee vanish like the fleets
Seen in mirage, or towers of cloud uplifting
In air their unsubstantial masonry.

1876.   1877.

VICTOR AND VANQUISHED

AS one who long hath fled with panting
  breath
Before his foe, bleeding and near to fall,
I turn and set my back against the wall,
And look thee in the face, triumphant
  Death.
I call for aid, and no one answereth;
I am alone with thee, who conquerest all;

Yet me thy threatening form doth not
  appall,
For thou art but a phantom and a wraith.
Wounded and weak, sword broken at the
  hilt,
With armor shattered, and without a shield,
I stand unmoved; do with me what thou
  wilt;
I can resist no more, but will not yield.
This is no tournament where cowards tilt;
The vanquished here is victor of the field.

1876.   (1882.)

THE THREE SILENCES OF MOLINOS

TO JOHN GREENLEAF WHITTIER [2]

THREE Silences there are: the first of
  speech,
The second of desire, the third of thought;
This is the lore a Spanish monk, distraught
With dreams and visions, was the first to
  teach.
These Silences, commingling each with
  each,
Made up the perfect Silence that he sought
And prayed for, and wherein at times he
  caught
Mysterious sounds from realms beyond our
  reach.
O thou, whose daily life anticipates
The life to come, and in whose thought and
  word
The spiritual world preponderates,
Hermit of Amesbury ! thou too hast heard
Voices and melodies from beyond the gates,
And speakest only when thy soul is stirred !

1877.   (1878.)

WAPENTAKE [3]

TO ALFRED TENNYSON

POET ! I come to touch thy lance with mine;
Not as a knight, who on the listed field

---

[1] Foremost among American sonneteers stands
Longfellow, the only member of the supreme group
who uses this form with ease and dignity. Some score
of examples — including the beautiful ' Divina Commedia ' series — might be selected from his works and
compared with twenty by any modern English poet,
save Wordsworth, nor lose thereby for nobility of sentiment and graciousness of diction. Wordsworth himself
might have been proud to include ' Nature,' for instance, among his finest sonnets. (WILLIAM SHARP,
American Sonnets.)

[2] Written for Whittier's seventieth birthday.
[3] When any came to take the government of the
Hundred or Wapentake in a day and place appointed,
as they were accustomed to meete, all the better sort
met him with lances, and he alighting from his horse,
all rise up to him, and he setting or holding his lance
upright, all the rest come with their lances, according
to the auncient custome in confirming league and pub-
like peace and obedience, and touch his lance or weapon, and thereof called Wapentake, for the Saxon or

Of tourney touched his adversary's shield
In token of defiance, but in sign
Of homage to the mastery, which is thine,
In English song; nor will I keep con-
    cealed,
And voiceless as a rivulet frost-congealed,
My admiration for thy verse divine.
Not of the howling dervishes of song,
Who craze the brain with their delirious
    dance,
Art thou, O sweet historian of the heart!
Therefore to thee the laurel-leaves be-
    long,
To thee our love and our allegiance,
For thy allegiance to the poet's art.

1877.   1877.

A BALLAD OF THE FRENCH FLEET [1]

OCTOBER, 1746

Mr. Thomas Prince *loquitur.*

A FLEET with flags arrayed
    Sailed from the port of Brest,
And the Admiral's ship displayed
    The signal: 'Steer southwest.'
For this Admiral D'Anville
    Had sworn by cross and crown
To ravage with fire and steel
    Our helpless Boston Town.

old English *wapun* is weapon, and *tac, tactus,* a touching, thereby this meeting called Wapentake, or touching of weapon, because that by that signe and ceremo-
nie of touching weapon or the lance, they were sworne
and confederate. — Master Lamberd in *Minshew.*
(LONGFELLOW.)

[1] After the capture of Louisburg in 1745 by the Massachusetts colonists, the French in revenge sent a large
fleet against Boston the next year; but it was so disabled by storms that it had to put back.

Mr Thomas Prince was the pastor of the Old South
Meeting-house.

In 1877, when the Old South was in danger of
being destroyed, Rev. Edward Everett Hale wrote to
Longfellow: 'You told me that if the spirit moved,
you would try to sing us a song for the Old South
Meeting-house. I have found such a charming story
that I think it will really tempt you. I want at least
to tell it to you. . . . The whole story of the fleet is
in Hutchinson's *Massachusetts,* ii. 384, 385. The story
of Prince and the prayer is in a tract in the College
Library, which I will gladly send you, or Mr. Sibley
will. I should think that the assembly in the meeting-
house in the gale, and then the terror of the fleet when
the gale struck them, would make a ballad — if the
spirit moved!'

Compare Whittier's 'In the Old South' and 'The
Landmarks,' and Holmes's 'An Appeal for the Old
South.'

There were rumors in the street,
    In the houses there was fear   10
Of the coming of the fleet,
    And the danger hovering near.
And while from mouth to mouth
    Spread the tidings of dismay,
I stood in the Old South,
    Saying humbly: 'Let us pray!

'O Lord! we would not advise;
    But if in thy Providence
A tempest should arise
    To drive the French Fleet hence,   20
And scatter it far and wide,
    Or sink it in the sea,
We should be satisfied,
    And thine the glory be.'

This was the prayer I made,
    For my soul was all on flame,
And even as I prayed
    The answering tempest came;
It came with a mighty power,
    Shaking the windows and walls,   30
And tolling the bell in the tower,
    As it tolls at funerals.

The lightning suddenly
    Unsheathed its flaming sword,
And I cried: 'Stand still, and see
    The salvation of the Lord!'
The heavens were black with cloud,
    The sea was white with hail,
And ever more fierce and loud
    Blew the October gale.   40

The fleet it overtook,
    And the broad sails in the van
Like the tents of Cushan shook,
    Or the curtains of Midian.
Down on the reeling decks
    Crashed the o'erwhelming seas;
Ah, never were there wrecks
    So pitiful as these!

Like a potter's vessel broke
    The great ships of the line;   50
They were carried away as a smoke,
    Or sank like lead in the brine.
O Lord! before thy path
    They vanished and ceased to be,
When thou didst walk in wrath
    With thine horses through the sea!

1877.   1877.

SONG

STAY, stay at home, my heart, and rest;
Home-keeping hearts are happiest,
For those that wander they know not
    where
Are full of trouble and full of care;
    To stay at home is best.

Weary and homesick and distressed,
They wander east, they wander west,
And are baffled and beaten and blown
    about
By the winds of the wilderness of doubt:
    To stay at home is best.

Then stay at home, my heart, and rest;
The bird is safest in its nest;
O'er all that flutter their wings and fly
A hawk is hovering in the sky;
    To stay at home is best.

1877.   *1878.*

FROM MY ARM-CHAIR

TO THE CHILDREN OF CAMBRIDGE

WHO PRESENTED TO ME, ON MY SEVENTY-
SECOND BIRTHDAY, FEBRUARY 27, 1879, THIS
CHAIR MADE FROM THE WOOD OF THE VIL-
LAGE BLACKSMITH'S CHESTNUT TREE.[1]

AM I a king, that I should call my own
    This splendid ebon throne?
Or by what reason, or what right divine,
    Can I proclaim it mine?

Only, perhaps, by right divine of song
    It may to me belong;
Only because the spreading chestnut tree
    Of old was sung by me.

Well I remember it in all its prime,
    When in the summer-time   10
The affluent foliage of its branches made
    A cavern of cool shade.

There, by the blacksmith's forge, beside
    the street,
    Its blossoms white and sweet

---

[1] For an account of the chair, with its inscriptions,
see the *Life*, vol. iii, pp. 446–448. Longfellow gave
orders that every child who wished to see the chair
and sit in it should be allowed to do so; and had a
large number of copies of this poem printed, one of
which was given to each child who wished it.

Enticed the bees, until it seemed alive,
    And murmured like a hive.

And when the winds of autumn, with a
    shout,
    Tossed its great arms about,
The shining chestnuts, bursting from the
    sheath,
    Dropped to the ground beneath.   20

And now some fragments of its branches
    bare,
    Shaped as a stately chair,
Have by my hearthstone found a home at
    last,
    And whisper of the past.

The Danish king could not in all his
    pride
    Repel the ocean tide,
But, seated in this chair, I can in rhyme
    Roll back the tide of Time.

I see again, as one in vision sees,
    The blossoms and the bees,   30
And hear the children's voices shout and
    call,
    And the brown chestnuts fall.

I see the smithy with its fires aglow,
    I hear the bellows blow,
And the shrill hammers on the anvil beat
    The iron white with heat!

And thus, dear children, have ye made for
    me
    This day a jubilee,
And to my more than threescore years and
    ten
    Brought back my youth again.   40

The heart hath its own memory, like the
    mind,
    And in it are enshrined
The precious keepsakes, into which is
    wrought
    The giver's loving thought.

Only your love and your remembrance
    could
    Give life to this dead wood,
And make these branches, leafless now so
    long,
    Blossom again in song.

1879.   *1879*

ROBERT BURNS [1]

I SEE amid the fields of Ayr
A ploughman, who, in foul and fair,
   Sings at his task
So clear, we know not if it is
The laverock's song we hear, or his,
   Nor care to ask.

For him the ploughing of those fields
A more ethereal harvest yields
   Than sheaves of grain;
Songs flush with purple bloom the rye,   10
The plover's call, the curlew's cry,
   Sing in his brain.

Touched by his hand, the wayside weed
Becomes a flower; the lowliest reed
   Beside the stream
Is clothed with beauty; gorse and grass
And heather, where his footsteps pass,
   The brighter seem.

He sings of love, whose flame illumes
The darkness of lone cottage rooms;   20
   He feels the force,
The treacherous undertow and stress
Of wayward passions, and no less
   The keen remorse.

At moments, wrestling with his fate,
His voice is harsh, but not with hate;
   The brush-wood, hung
Above the tavern door, lets fall
Its bitter leaf, its drop of gall
   Upon his tongue.   30

But still the music of his song
Rises o'er all, elate and strong;
   Its master-chords
Are Manhood, Freedom, Brotherhood,
Its discords but an interlude
   Between the words.

And then to die so young and leave
Unfinished what he might achieve!
   Yet better sure
Is this, than wandering up and down,   40
An old man in a country town,
   Infirm and poor.

For now he haunts his native land
As an immortal youth; his hand

Guides every plough;
He sits beside each ingle-nook,
His voice is in each rushing brook,
   Each rustling bough.

His presence haunts this room to-night,
A form of mingled mist and light   50
   From that far coast.
Welcome beneath this roof of mine!
Welcome! this vacant chair is thine,
   Dear guest and ghost!

1879.   1880.

THE TIDE RISES, THE TIDE FALLS

THE tide rises, the tide falls,
The twilight darkens, the curlew calls;
Along the sea-sands damp and brown
The traveller hastens toward the town,
   And the tide rises, the tide falls.

Darkness settles on roofs and walls,
But the sea, the sea in the darkness calls;
The little waves, with their soft, white
   hands,
Efface the footprints in the sands,
   And the tide rises, the tide falls.

The morning breaks; the steeds in their
   stalls
Stamp and neigh, as the hostler calls;
The day returns, but nevermore
Returns the traveller to the shore,
   And the tide rises, the tide falls.

1879.   (1880.)

JUGURTHA

How cold are thy baths, Apollo!
   Cried the African monarch, the splendid,
As down to his death in the hollow
   Dark dungeons of Rome he descended,
   Uncrowned, unthroned, unattended;
How cold are thy baths, Apollo!

How cold are thy baths, Apollo!
   Cried the Poet, unknown, unbefriended,
As the vision, that lured him to follow,
   With the mist and the darkness blended,
   And the dream of his life was ended;
How cold are thy baths, Apollo!

1879.   (1880.)

---

[1] Compare the poems on Burns by Whittier, Lowell ('At the Burns Centennial,' and 'Incident in a Railroad Car'), Holmes, Wordsworth, etc.

THE CROSS OF SNOW [1]

IN the long, sleepless watches of the night,
A gentle face — the face of one long dead —
Looks at me from the wall, where round
  its head
The night-lamp casts a halo of pale light.
Here in this room she died; and soul more
  white
Never through martyrdom of fire was led
To its repose; nor can in books be read
The legend of a life more benedight.
There is a mountain in the distant West,
That, sun-defying, in its deep ravines
Displays a cross of snow upon its side.
Such is the cross I wear upon my breast
These eighteen years, through all the chang-
  ing scenes
And seasons, changeless since the day she
  died.

1879.   1886.

NIGHT

INTO the darkness and hush of night
Slowly the landscape sinks, and fades away,
And with it fade the phantoms of the day,
The ghosts of men and things, that haunt
  the light.
The crowd, the clamor, the pursuit, the
  flight,
The unprofitable splendor and display,
The agitations, and the cares that prey
Upon our hearts, all vanish out of sight.
The better life begins; the world no more
Molests us; all its records we erase
From the dull commonplace book of our
  lives,
That like a palimpsest is written o'er
With trivial incidents of time and place,
And lo ! the ideal, hidden beneath, revives.

1879.   (1880.)

L'ENVOI

THE POET AND HIS SONGS

As the birds come in the spring,
  We know not from where;
As the stars come at evening
  · From depths of the air;

As the rain comes from the cloud,
  And the brook from the ground;

[1] See the note on ' Divina Commedia,' p. 240.

As suddenly, low or loud,
  Out of silence a sound;

As the grape comes to the vine,
  The fruit to the tree;
As the wind comes to the pine,
  And the tide to the sea;

As come the white sails of ships
  O'er the ocean's verge;
As comes the smile to the lips,
  The foam to the surge;

So come to the Poet his songs,
  All hitherward blown
From the misty realm, that belongs
  To the vast Unknown.

His, and not his, are the lays
  He sings; and their fame
Is his, and not his; and the praise
  And the pride of a name.

For voices pursue him by day,
  And haunt him by night,
And he listens, and needs must obey,
  When the Angel says, ' Write ! '

1880.   1880.

POSSIBILITIES [2]

WHERE are the Poets, unto whom belong
The Olympian heights; whose singing
  shafts were sent
Straight to the mark, and not from bows
  half bent,
But with the utmost tension of the thong ?
Where are the stately argosies of song,
Whose rushing keels made music as they
  went
Sailing in search of some new continent,
With all sail set, and steady winds and
  strong ?
Perhaps there lives some dreamy boy, un-
  taught
In schools, some graduate of the field or
  street,
Who shall become a master of the art,
An admiral sailing the high seas of thought,
Fearless and first, and steering with his
  fleet
For lands not yet laid down in any chart.

1882.   1882.

[2] This is the last, but two, of Longfellow's poems.

THE BELLS OF SAN BLAS[1]

WHAT say the Bells of San Blas
To the ships that southward pass
   From the harbor of Mazatlan ?
To them it is nothing more
Than the sound of surf on the shore, —
   Nothing more to master or man.

But to me, a dreamer of dreams,
To whom what is and what seems
   Are often one and the same, —
The Bells of San Blas to me   10
Have a strange, wild melody,
   And are something more than a name.

For bells are the voice of the church;
They have tones that touch and search
   The hearts of young and old;
One sound to all, yet each
Lends a meaning to their speech,
   And the meaning is manifold.

They are a voice of the Past,
Of an age that is fading fast,   20
   Of a power austere and grand;
When the flag of Spain unfurled
Its folds o'er this western world,
   And the priest was lord of the land.

The chapel that once looked down
On the little seaport town
   Has crumbled into the dust;
And on oaken beams below
The bells swing to and fro,
   And are green with mould and rust. 30

' Is, then, the old faith dead,'
They say, ' and in its stead

   Is some new faith proclaimed,
That we are forced to remain
Naked to sun and rain,
   Unsheltered and ashamed ?

' Once in our tower aloof
We rang over wall and roof
   Our warnings and our complaints;
And round about us there   40
The white doves filled the air,
   Like the white souls of the saints.

' The saints !   Ah, have they grown
Forgetful of their own ?
   Are they asleep, or dead,
That open to the sky
Their ruined Missions lie,
   No longer tenanted ?

' Oh, bring us back once more
The vanished days of yore,
   When the world with faith was filled; 50
Bring back the fervid zeal,
The hearts of fire and steel,
   The hands that believe and build.

' Then from our tower again
We will send over land and main
   Our voices of command,
Like exiled kings who return
To their thrones, and the people learn
   That the Priest is lord of the land !' 60

O Bells of San Blas, in vain
Ye call back the Past again !
   The Past is deaf to your prayer;
Out of the shadows of night
The world rolls into light;
   It is daybreak everywhere.[2]

1882.   1882.

[1] Longfellow's last poem, written (except the concluding stanza) on March 12, 1882. The subject was suggested by a few lines of an article on Mexico, in *Harper's Magazine* for March, telling of the destroyed convent of San Blas (on the Pacific Coast) and its bells.

[2] These were Longfellow's last verses. He added the concluding stanza of the poem, written in a firm hand, and dated, only nine days before his death.

JOHN GREENLEAF WHITTIER

THE VAUDOIS TEACHER [1]

'O LADY fair, these silks of mine are beautiful and rare, —
The richest web of the Indian loom, which
 beauty's queen might wear;
And my pearls are pure as thy own fair neck,
 with whose radiant light they vie;
I have brought them with me a weary way,
 — will my gentle lady buy ? '

The lady smiled on the worn old man
 through the dark and clustering
 curls
Which veiled her brow, as she bent to view
 his silks and glittering pearls;
And she placed their price in the old man's
 hand and lightly turned away,
But she paused at the wanderer's earnest
 call, — ' My gentle lady, stay !

'O lady fair, I have yet a gem which a
 purer lustre flings,
Than the diamond flash of the jewelled
 crown on the lofty brow of kings;
A wonderful pearl of exceeding price,
 whose virtue shall not decay,
Whose light shall be as a spell to thee and
 a blessing on thy way ! '

The lady glanced at the mirroring steel
 where her form of grace was seen,
Where her eye shone clear, and her dark
 locks waved their clasping pearls
 between;
' Bring forth thy pearl of exceeding worth,
 thou traveller gray and old,
And name the price of thy precious gem,
 and my page shall count thy gold.'

The cloud went off from the pilgrim's
 brow, as a small and meagre book,
Unchased with gold or gem of cost, from
 his folding robe he took !
' Here, lady fair, is the pearl of price, may
 it prove as such to thee !
Nay, keep thy gold — I ask it not, for the
 word of God is free ! '

The hoary traveller went his way, but the
 gift he left behind
Hath had its pure and perfect work on that
 highborn maiden's mind,
And she hath turned from the pride of sin
 to the lowliness of truth,
And given her human heart to God in its
 beautiful hour of youth !

And she hath left the gray old halls, where
 an evil faith had power,
The courtly knights of her father's train,
 and the maidens of her bower;
And she hath gone to the Vaudois vales by
 lordly feet untrod,
Where the poor and needy of earth are
 rich in the perfect love of God !

1830.

[1] This poem was suggested by the account given of the manner in which the Waldenses disseminated their principles among the Catholic gentry. They gained access to the house through their occupation as pedlers of silks, jewels, and trinkets. 'Having disposed of some of their goods,' it is said by a writer who quotes the inquisitor Rainerus Sacco, 'they cautiously intimated that they had commodities far more valuable than these, inestimable jewels, which they would show if they could be protected from the clergy. They would then give their purchasers a Bible or Testament, and thereby many were deluded into heresy.' (WHITTIER.)

The poem was early translated into French and Italian, and became a favorite among all the Waldenses, who however did not know of its American origin. When the Waldensian synod learned of this, in 1875, they instructed their Moderator to send Whittier a letter of thanks and appreciation. This letter, which Whittier greatly prized, began : —

'Dear and Honored Brother, — I have recently learned by a letter from my friend, J. C. Fletcher, now residing in Naples, that you are the author of the charming little poem, "The Vaudois Colporteur," which was translated several years ago in French by Professor de Felicé, of Montauban, and of which there is also an excellent Italian translation, made by M. Giovanni Nicolini, Professor of our College at Torré Pellicé. There is not a single Vaudois who has received any education who cannot repeat from memory "The Vaudois Colporteur " in French or in Italian.'

See the whole letter, in Pickard's *Life of Whittier*, vol. ii, pp. 607–608. Whittier's reply (given in the *Life*, pp. 608–609) was translated into Italian and circulated throughout Italy.

TO WILLIAM LLOYD GARRISON [1]

CHAMPION of those who groan beneath
    Oppression's iron hand:
In view of penury, hate, and death,
    I see thee fearless stand.
Still bearing up thy lofty brow,
    In the steadfast strength of truth,
In manhood sealing well the vow
    And promise of thy youth.

Go on, for thou hast chosen well;
    On in the strength of God!   10
Long as one human heart shall swell
    Beneath the tyrant's rod.
Speak in a slumbering nation's ear,

As thou hast ever spoken,
Until the dead in sin shall hear,
    The fetter's link be broken!

I love thee with a brother's love,
    I feel my pulses thrill,
To mark thy spirit soar above
    The cloud of human ill.   20
My heart hath leaped to answer thine,
    And echo back thy words,
As leaps the warrior's at the shine
    And flash of kindred swords!

They tell me thou art rash and vain,
    A searcher after fame;
That thou art striving but to gain
    A long-enduring name;
That thou hast nerved the Afric's hand
    And steeled the Afric's heart,   30
To shake aloft his vengeful brand,
    And rend his chain apart.

Have I not known thee well, and read
    Thy mighty purpose long?
And watched the trials which have made
    Thy human spirit strong?
And shall the slanderer's demon breath
    Avail with one like me,
To dim the sunshine of my faith
    And earnest trust in thee?   40

Go on, the dagger's point may glare
    Amid thy pathway's gloom;
The fate which sternly threatens there
    Is glorious martyrdom!
Then onward with a martyr's zeal;
    And wait thy sure reward
When man to man no more shall kneel,
    And God alone be Lord!

1831.

RANDOLPH OF ROANOKE [2]

O MOTHER EARTH! upon thy lap
    Thy weary ones receiving,
And o'er them, silent as a dream,
    Thy grassy mantle weaving,

[1] The earliest poem in this division [the Anti-Slavery Poems] was my youthful tribute to the great reformer when, himself a young man, he was sounding his trumpet in Essex County. (WHITTIER.)
On Whittier's early relations with Garrison, see Pickard's *Life of Whittier*, pp. 50–52. See also the article on Garrison in Whittier's *Prose Works*, iii, 189–192.
Whittier's anti-slavery poems must necessarily occupy a large place in any selection at all representative of his work. For more than thirty years they formed the chief part of his poetical production. Even to-day no one can fail to recognize the intense sincerity and strength of such poems as 'Expostulation,' 'Massachusetts to Virginia,' 'Ichabod,' 'The Rendition,' etc. On his rôle in the anti-slavery movement, and the sacrifices which he made to it, see especially Professor Carpenter's *Whittier*, chapters iv and v. See also the notes on 'Ichabod' and on Lowell's 'Stanzas on Freedom,' and the passage on Whittier in Lowell's 'Fable for Critics.'
After the war Whittier was one of the most earnest workers against sectional prejudice in the North. It was largely through his efforts that the vote of censure against Sumner, who wished Civil War names expunged from army flags, was repealed. But he would never consent that the anti-slavery poems should be omitted from any edition of his works. His attitude is well shown by a passage in Pickard's *Life of Whittier*, with its significant quotation from one of his letters: —
'Some other American poets, even those who had written bravely against the system of slavery, consented to leave out of their collected works such poems as would be offensive to their Southern readers. Whittier never made this concession . . . and issued no edition of his works that did not present him as an uncompromising foe of slavery. But it was easy to see that his enmity to the institution did not extend to individuals. All his life he numbered among his personal friends not only apologists for slavery, but slaveholders themselves. In replying to the charge of a Southern paper that he was an enemy of the South, he once wrote to a friend: "I was never an enemy to the South or the holders of slaves. I inherited from my Quaker ancestry hatred of slavery, but not of slaveholders. To every call of suffering or distress in the South I have promptly responded to the extent of my ability. I was one of the very first to recognize the rare gift of the Carolinian poet Timrod, and I was the intimate friend of the lamented Paul H. Hayne, though both wrote fiery lyrics against the North."'
This poem was read at the Convention in Philadelphia which founded the American Anti-Slavery Society, in December, 1833. Whittier was a delegate from Massachusetts. 'I set a higher value on my name as appended to the Anti-Slavery Declaration of 1833,' he said in later life, 'than on the title-page of any book.'

[2] In an article published in the *Essex Gazette*, in July, 1833, less than a month after Randolph's death, Whittier says: 'The late noble example of the eloquent statesman of Roanoke, the manumission of his slaves, speaks volumes to his political friends. In the last hour of his existence, when his soul was struggling from its broken tenement, his latest effort was the confirmation of this generous act of a former period. Light rest the turf upon him, beneath his patrimonial oaks! The prayers of many hearts made happy by his benevolence shall linger over his grave, and bless it.' The poem was

Fold softly in thy long embrace
  That heart so worn and broken,
And cool its pulse of fire beneath
  Thy shadows old and oaken.

Shut out from him the bitter word
  And serpent hiss of scorning ;   10
Nor let the storms of yesterday
  Disturb his quiet morning.
Breathe over him forgetfulness
  Of all save deeds of kindness,
And, save to smiles of grateful eyes,
  Press down his lids in blindness.

There, where with living ear and eye
  He heard Potomac's flowing,
And, through his tall ancestral trees,
  Saw autumn's sunset glowing,   20
He sleeps, still looking to the west,
  Beneath the dark wood shadow,
As if he still would see the sun
  Sink down on wave and meadow.

Bard, Sage, and Tribune ! in himself
  All moods of mind contrasting, —
The tenderest wail of human woe,
  The scorn like lightning blasting;
The pathos which from rival eyes
  Unwilling tears could summon,   30
The stinging taunt, the fiery burst
  Of hatred scarcely human !

Mirth, sparkling like a diamond shower,
  From lips of life-long sadness;
Clear picturings of majestic thought
  Upon a ground of madness;
And over all Romance and Song
  A classic beauty throwing,
And laurelled Clio at his side
  Her storied pages showing.   40

All parties feared him: each in turn
  Beheld its schemes disjointed,
As right or left his fatal glance
  And spectral finger pointed.
Sworn foe of Cant, he smote it down
  With trenchant wit unsparing,
And, mocking, rent with ruthless hand
  The robe Pretence was wearing.

Too honest or too proud to feign
  A love he never cherished,   50

probably written, according to Mr. Pickard, at the same
time as the article. It was printed in the first number
of the *National Era* issued after Whittier became corresponding editor, in January, 1847.

Beyond Virginia's border line
  His patriotism perished.
While others hailed in distant skies
  Our eagle's dusky pinion,
He only saw the mountain bird
  Stoop o'er his Old Dominion !

Still through each change of fortune
        strange,
  Racked nerve, and brain all burning,
His loving faith in Mother-land
  Knew never shade of turning ;   60
By Britain's lakes, by Neva's tide,
  Whatever sky was o'er him,
He heard her rivers' rushing sound,
  Her blue peaks rose before him.

He held his slaves, yet made withal
  No false and vain pretences,
Nor paid a lying priest to seek
  For Scriptural defences.
His harshest words of proud rebuke,
  His bitterest taunt and scorning,   70
Fell fire-like on the Northern brow
  That bent to him in fawning.

He held his slaves; yet kept the while
  His reverence for the Human;
In the dark vassals of his will
  He saw but Man and Woman !
No hunter of God's outraged poor
  His Roanoke valley entered;
No trader in the souls of men
  Across his threshold ventured.   80

And when the old and wearied man
  Lay down for his last sleeping,
And at his side, a slave no more,
  His brother-man stood weeping,
His latest thought, his latest breath,
  To Freedom's duty giving,
With failing tongue and trembling hand
  The dying blest the living.

Oh, never bore his ancient State
  A truer son or braver !   90
None trampling with a calmer scorn
  On foreign hate or favor.
He knew her faults, yet never stooped
  His proud and manly feeling
To poor excuses of the wrong
  Or meanness of concealing.

But none beheld with clearer eye
  The plague-spot o'er her spreading,

None heard more sure the steps of Doom
  Along her future treading.   100
For her as for himself he spake,
  When, his gaunt frame upbracing,
He traced with dying hand ' Remorse ! '
  And perished in the tracing.

As from the grave where Henry sleeps,
  From Vernon's weeping willow,
And from the grassy pall which hides
  The Sage of Monticello,
So from the leaf-strewn burial-stone
  Of Randolph's lowly dwelling,   110
Virginia! o'er thy land of slaves
  A warning voice is swelling !

And hark ! from thy deserted fields
  Are sadder warnings spoken,
From quenched hearths, where thy exiled
    sons
  Their household gods have broken.
The curse is on thee, — wolves for men,
  And briers for corn-sheaves giving !
Oh, more than all thy dead renown
  Were now one hero living !   120
1833?   1847.

EXPOSTULATION [1]

Our fellow-countrymen in chains !
  Slaves, in a land of light and law !
Slaves, crouching on the very plains
  Where rolled the storm of Freedom's war!
A groan from Eutaw's haunted wood,
A wail where Camden's martyrs fell,

[1] Dr. Charles Follen, a German patriot, who had
come to America for the freedom which was denied
him in his native land, allied himself with the abolitionists, and at a convention of delegates from all the
anti-slavery organizations in New England, held at
Boston in May, 1834, was chairman of a committee to
prepare an address to the people of New England.
Toward the close of the address occurred the passage
which suggested these lines : —
  ' The despotism which our fathers could not bear in
their native country is expiring, and the sword of justice in her reformed hands has applied its exterminat-
ing edge to slavery. Shall the United States — the free
United States, which could not bear the bonds of a
king — cradle the bondage which a king is abolishing ?
Shall a Republic be less free than a Monarchy ? Shall
we, in the vigor and buoyancy of our manhood, be less
energetic in righteousness than a kingdom in its age ? '
(Whittier.)
  The original title of the poem was simply ' Stanzas,'
and later it was called ' Follen.' Garrison said of it
when it first appeared : —
  ' Our gifted Brother Whittier has again seized the
great trumpet of Liberty, and blown a blast that shall
ring from Maine to the Rocky Mountains.'
  The poem became popular throughout the North and
West, and was for many years a favorite at declamation
contests and anti-slavery meetings.

By every shrine of patriot blood,
  From Moultrie's wall and Jasper's well!

By storied hill and hallowed grot,
  By mossy wood and marshy glen,   10
Whence rang of old the rifle-shot,
  And hurrying shout of Marion's men !
The groan of breaking hearts is there,
  The falling lash, the fetter's clank !
Slaves, slaves are breathing in that air
  Which old De Kalb and Sumter drank !

What ho ! our countrymen in chains !
  The whip on woman's shrinking flesh !
Our soil yet reddening with the stains
  Caught from her scourging, warm and
    fresh !   20
What ! mothers from their children riven !
  What ! God's own image bought and sold !
Americans to market driven,
  And bartered as the brute for gold !

Speak ! shall their agony of prayer
  Come thrilling to our hearts in vain ?
To us whose fathers scorned to bear
  The paltry menace of a chain;
To us, whose boast is loud and long
  Of holy Liberty and Light ;   30
Say, shall these writhing slaves of Wrong
  Plead vainly for their plundered Right ?

What ! shall we send, with lavish breath,
  Our sympathies across the wave,
Where Manhood, on the field of death,
  Strikes for his freedom or a grave ?
Shall prayers go up, and hymns be sung
  For Greece, the Moslem fetter spurning,
And millions hail with pen and tongue
  Our light on all her altars burning ?   40

Shall Belgium feel, and gallant France,
  By Vendome's pile and Schoenbrun's wall,
And Poland, gasping on her lance,
  The impulse of our cheering call ?
And shall the slave, beneath our eye,
  Clank o'er our fields his hateful chain ?
And toss his fettered arms on high,
  And groan for Freedom's gift, in vain ?

Oh, say, shall Prussia's banner be
  A refuge for the stricken slave ?   50
And shall the Russian serf go free
  By Baikal's lake and Neva's wave ?
And shall the wintry-bosomed Dane
  Relax the iron hand of pride,

And bid his bondmen cast the chain
From fettered soul and limb aside ?

Shall every flap of England's flag
Proclaim that all around are free,
From farthest Ind to each blue crag
That beetles o'er the Western Sea ?   60
And shall we scoff at Europe's kings,
When Freedom's fire is dim with us,
And round our country's altar clings
The damning shade of Slavery's curse ?

Go, let us ask of Constantine
To loose his grasp on Poland's throat;
And beg the lord of Mahmoud's line
To spare the struggling Suliote;
Will not the scorching answer come
From turbaned Turk, and scornful Russ:
'Go, loose your fettered slaves at home,   71
Then turn and ask the like of us ! '

Just God ! and shall we calmly rest,
The Christian's scorn,the heathen's mirth,
Content to live the lingering jest
And by-word of a mocking Earth ?
Shall our own glorious land retain
That curse which Europe scorns to bear ?
Shall our own brethren drag the chain
Which not even Russia's menials wear ?

Up, then, in Freedom's manly part,   81
From graybeard eld to fiery youth,
And on the nation's naked heart
Scatter the living coals of Truth !
Up ! while ye slumber, deeper yet
The shadow of our fame is growing !
Up ! while ye pause, our sun may set
In blood around our altars flowing !

Oh ! rouse ye, ere the storm comes forth,
The gathered wrath of God and man,   90
Like that which wasted Egypt's earth,
When hail and fire above it ran.
Hear ye no warnings in the air ?
Feel ye no earthquake underneath ?
Up, up ! why will ye slumber where
The sleeper only wakes in death ?

Rise now for Freedom ! not in strife
Like that your sterner fathers saw,
The awful waste of human life,
The glory and the guilt of war: 100
But break the chain, the yoke remove,
And smite to earth Oppression's rod,

With those mild arms of Truth and Love,
Made mighty through the living God !

Down let the shrine of Moloch sink,
And leave no traces where it stood;
Nor longer let its idol drink
His daily cup of human blood;
But rear another altar there,
To Truth and Love and Mercy given,   110
And Freedom's gift, and Freedom's prayer,
Shall call an answer down from Heaven !
1834.   1834.

THE FAREWELL [1]

OF A VIRGINIA SLAVE MOTHER TO HER
DAUGHTERS SOLD INTO SOUTHERN
BONDAGE

Gone, gone, — sold and gone,
To the rice-swamp dank and lone.
Where the slave-whip ceaseless swings,
Where the noisome insect stings,
Where the fever demon strews
Poison with the falling dews,
Where the sickly sunbeams glare
Through the hot and misty air;
Gone, gone, — sold and gone,
To the rice-swamp dank and lone,   10
From Virginia's hills and waters;
Woe is me, my stolen daughters !

Gone, gone, — sold and gone,
To the rice-swamp dank and lone.
There no mother's eye is near them,
There no mother's ear can hear them;
Never, when the torturing lash
Seams their back with many a gash,
Shall a mother's kindness bless them,
Or a mother's arms caress them.   20
Gone, gone, — sold and gone,
To the rice-swamp dank and lone,
From Virginia's hills and waters;
Woe is me, my stolen daughters !

Gone, gone, — sold and gone,
To the rice-swamp dank and lone.
Oh, when weary, sad, and slow,
From the fields at night they go,
Faint with toil, and racked with pain,
To their cheerless homes again,   30
There no brother's voice shall greet them,

[1] Of all Whittier's anti-slavery poems this approaches
nearest to the half-romantic style of Longfellow's
' Poems on Slavery.'

There no father's welcome meet them.
  Gone, gone, — sold and gone,
  To the rice-swamp dank and lone,
  From Virginia's hills and waters;
  Woe is me, my stolen daughters!

  Gone, gone, — sold and gone,
  To the rice-swamp dank and lone.
From the tree whose shadow lay
On their childhood's place of play;   40
From the cool spring where they drank;
Rock, and hill, and rivulet bank;
From the solemn house of prayer,
And the holy counsels there;
  Gone, gone, — sold and gone,
  To the rice-swamp dank and lone,
  From Virginia's hills and waters;
  Woe is me, my stolen daughters!

  Gone, gone, — sold and gone,
  To the rice-swamp dank and lone;   50
Toiling through the weary day,
And at night the spoiler's prey.
Oh, that they had earlier died,
Sleeping calmly, side by side,
Where the tyrant's power is o'er,
And the fetter galls no more!
  Gone, gone, — sold and gone,
  To the rice-swamp dank and lone,
  From Virginia's hills and waters;
  Woe is me, my stolen daughters!   60

  Gone, gone, — sold and gone,
  To the rice-swamp dank and lone.
By the holy love He beareth;
By the bruisèd reed He spareth;
Oh, may He, to whom alone
All their cruel wrongs are known,
Still their hope and refuge prove,
With a more than mother's love.
  Gone, gone, — sold and gone,
  To the rice-swamp dank and lone,   70
  From Virginia's hills and waters;
  Woe is me, my stolen daughters!
                                      1838.

THE MERRIMAC

STREAM of my fathers! sweetly still
The sunset rays thy valley fill;
Poured slantwise down the long defile,
Wave, wood, and spire beneath them smile.
I see the winding Powow fold
The green hill in its belt of gold,
And following down its wavy line,

Its sparkling waters blend with thine.
There's not a tree upon thy side,
Nor rock, which thy returning tide   10
As yet hath left abrupt and stark
Above thy evening water-mark;
No calm cove with its rocky hem,
No isle whose emerald swells begem
Thy broad, smooth current; not a sail
Bowed to the freshening ocean gale;
No small boat with its busy oars,
Nor gray wall sloping to thy shores;
Nor farm-house with its maple shade,
Or rigid poplar colonnade,   20
But lies distinct and full in sight,
Beneath this gush of sunset light.
Centuries ago, that harbor-bar,
Stretching its length of foam afar,
And Salisbury's beach of shining sand,
And yonder island's wave-smoothed strand,
Saw the adventurer's tiny sail
Flit, stooping from the eastern gale;
And o'er these woods and waters broke
The cheer from Britain's hearts of oak,   30
As brightly on the voyager's eye
Weary of forest, sea, and sky,
Breaking the dull continuous wood,
The Merrimac rolled down his flood;
Mingling that clear pellucid brook,
Which channels vast Agioochook
When spring-time's sun and shower unlock
The frozen fountains of the rock,
And more abundant waters given
From that pure lake, 'The Smile of
     Heaven,' [1]   40
Tributes from vale and mountain-side, —
With ocean's dark, eternal tide!

On yonder rocky cape, which braves
The stormy challenge of the waves,
Midst tangled vine and dwarfish wood,
The hardy Anglo-Saxon stood, [2]
Planting upon the topmost crag
The staff of England's battle-flag;
And, while from out its heavy fold
Saint George's crimson cross unrolled,   50
Midst roll of drum and trumpet blare,
And weapons brandishing in air,
He gave to that lone promontory [3]

[1] Winnipesaukee. The Indian name was thought to
mean 'The Smile of the Great Spirit.' See 'The Lakeside' and 'Summer by the Lakeside.'
[2] The celebrated Captain Smith, after resigning the
government of the Colony in Virginia, in his capacity
of 'Admiral of New England,' made a careful survey
of the coast from Penobscot to Cape Cod, in the summer of 1614. (WHITTIER.)
[3] Captain Smith gave to the promontory now called

The sweetest name in all his story;
Of her, the flower of Islam's daughters,
Whose harems look on Stamboul's wa-
          ters, —
Who, when the chance of war had bound
The Moslem chain his limbs around,
Wreathed o'er with silk that iron chain,
Soothed with her smiles his hours of pain,
And fondly to her youthful slave   60
A dearer gift than freedom gave.

But look ! the yellow light no more
Streams down on wave and verdant shore;
And clearly on the calm air swells
The twilight voice of distant bells.
From Ocean's bosom, white and thin,
The mists come slowly rolling in;
Hills, woods, the river's rocky rim,
Amidst the sea-like vapor swim,   70
While yonder lonely coast-light, set
Within its wave-washed minaret,
Half quenched, a beamless star and pale,
Shines dimly through its cloudy veil !

Home of my fathers ! — I have stood
Where Hudson rolled his lordly flood:
Seen sunrise rest and sunset fade
Along his frowning Palisade;
Looked down the Appalachian peak
On Juniata's silver streak;   80
Have seen along his valley gleam
The Mohawk's softly winding stream;
The level light of sunset shine
Through broad Potomac's hem of pine;
And autumn's rainbow-tinted banner
Hang lightly o'er the Susquehanna;
Yet wheresoe'er his step might be,
Thy wandering child looked back to thee !
Heard in his dreams thy river's sound
Of murmuring on its pebbly bound,   90
The unforgotten swell and roar
Of waves on thy familiar shore;
And saw, amidst the curtained gloom
And quiet of his lonely room,
Thy sunset scenes before him pass;
As, in Agrippa's magic glass,
The loved and lost arose to view,
Remembered groves in greenness grew,
Bathed still in childhood's morning dew,
Along whose bowers of beauty swept   100
Whatever Memory's mourners wept,

Cape Ann, the name of Tragabizanda, in memory of
his young and beautiful mistress of that name, who,
while he was a captive at Constantinople, like Desde-
mona, 'loved him for the dangers he had passed.'
(WHITTIER.)

Sweet faces, which the charnel kept,
Young, gentle eyes, which long had slept;
And while the gazer leaned to trace,
More near, some dear familiar face,
He wept to find the vision flown, —
A phantom and a dream alone !

                                      1841.

MEMORIES [1]

A BEAUTIFUL and happy girl, [2]
    With step as light as summer air,
Eyes glad with smiles, and brow of pearl,
Shadowed by many a careless curl
    Of unconfined and flowing hair ;
A seeming child in everything,
    Save thoughtful brow and ripening
        charms,
As Nature wears the smile of Spring
    When sinking into Summer's arms.

A mind rejoicing in the light   10
    Which melted through its graceful
        bower,
Leaf after leaf, dew-moist and bright,
And stainless in its holy white,
    Unfolding like a morning flower:
A heart, which, like a fine-toned lute,
    With every breath of feeling woke,
And, even when the tongue was mute,
    From eye and lip in music spoke.

How thrills once more the lengthening
        chain
    Of memory, at the thought of thee ! 20
Old hopes which long in dust have lain,
Old dreams, come thronging back again,
    And boyhood lives again in me;
I feel its glow upon my cheek,

[1] It was not without thought and deliberation, that
in 1888 he directed this poem to be placed at the head
of his Poems Subjective and Reminiscent. He had never
before publicly acknowledged how much of his heart
was wrapped up in this delightful play of poetic fancy.
The poem was written in 1841, and although the romance it embalms lies far back of this date, possibly
there is a heart still beating which fully understands
its meaning. The biographer can do no more than
make this suggestion, which has the sanction of the
poet's explicit word. To a friend who told him that
Memories was her favorite poem, he said, 'I love it
too; but I hardly knew whether to publish it, it was
so personal and near my heart.' (Pickard's Life of
Whittier, vol. i, p. 276.)
    See also Pickard's Whittier-Land, pp. 66-67, and the
poem ' My Playmate.'
[2] Whittier was especially fond of these two opening
stanzas. He had already used the lines to describe an
ideal character in ' Moll Pitcher,' published in 1832, but
not now included in his collected works.

Its fulness of the heart is mine,
As when I leaned to hear thee speak,
Or raised my doubtful eye to thine.

I hear again thy low replies,
I feel thy arm within my own,
And timidly again uprise   30
The fringèd lids of hazel eyes,
With soft brown tresses overblown.
Ah! memories of sweet summer eves,
Of moonlit wave and willowy way,
Of stars and flowers, and dewy leaves,
And smiles and tones more dear than
they!

Ere this, thy quiet eye hath smiled
My picture of thy youth to see,
When, half a woman, half a child,
Thy very artlessness beguiled,   40
And folly's self seemed wise in thee;
I too can smile, when o'er that hour
The lights of memory backward stream,
Yet feel the while that manhood's power
Is vainer than my boyhood's dream.

Years have passed on, and left their trace,
Of graver care and deeper thought;
And unto me the calm, cold face
Of manhood, and to thee the grace
Of woman's pensive beauty brought.   50
More wide, perchance, for blame than
praise,
The school-boy's humble name has flown;
Thine, in the green and quiet ways
Of unobtrusive goodness known.

And wider yet in thought and deed
Diverge our pathways, one in youth;
Thine the Genevan's sternest creed,
While answers to my spirit's need
The Derby dalesman's simple truth.
For thee, the priestly rite and prayer,   60
And holy day, and solemn psalm;
For me, the silent reverence where
My brethren gather, slow and calm.

Yet hath thy spirit left on me
An impress Time has worn not out,
And something of myself in thee,
A shadow from the past, I see,
Lingering, even yet, thy way about;
Not wholly can the heart unlearn
That lesson of its better hours,   70
Not yet has Time's dull footstep worn
To common dust that path of flowers.

Thus, while at times before our eyes
The shadows melt, and fall apart,
And, smiling through them, round us lies
The warm light of our morning skies, —
The Indian Summer of the heart!
In secret sympathies of mind,
In founts of feeling which retain
Their pure, fresh flow, we yet may find   80
Our early dreams not wholly vain!
1841.   1843.

HAMPTON BEACH

THE sunlight glitters keen and bright,
Where, miles away,
Lies stretching to my dazzled sight
A luminous belt, a misty light,
Beyond the dark pine bluffs and wastes of
sandy gray.

The tremulous shadow of the Sea!
Against its ground
Of silvery light, rock, hill, and tree,
Still as a picture, clear and free,
With varying outline mark the coast for
miles around.   10

On — on — we tread with loose-flung rein
Our seaward way,
Through dark-green fields and blossom-
ing grain,
Where the wild brier-rose skirts the lane,
And bends above our heads the flowering
locust spray.

Ha! like a kind hand on my brow
Comes this fresh breeze,
Cooling its dull and feverish glow,
While through my being seems to flow
The breath of a new life, the healing of the
seas!   20

Now rest we, where this grassy mound
His feet hath set
In the great waters, which have bound
His granite ankles greenly round
With long and tangled moss, and weeds
with cool spray wet.

Good-by to Pain and Care! I take
Mine ease to-day:
Here where these sunny waters break,
And ripples this keen breeze, I shake
All burdens from the heart, all weary
thoughts away.   30

I draw a freer breath, I seem
    Like all I see —
Waves in the sun, the white-winged gleam
Of sea-birds in the slanting beam,
And far-off sails which flit before the
    southwind free.

So when Time's veil shall fall asunder,
    The soul may know
No fearful change, nor sudden wonder,
Nor sink the weight of mystery under,
But with the upward rise, and with the
    vastness grow.   40

And all we shrink from now may seem
    No new revealing;
Familiar as our childhood's stream,
Or pleasant memory of a dream
The loved and cherished Past upon the new
    life stealing.

Serene and mild the untried light
    May have its dawning;
And, as in summer's northern night
The evening and the dawn unite,
The sunset hues of Time blend with the
    soul's new morning.   50

I sit alone; in foam and spray
    Wave after wave
Breaks on the rocks which, stern and gray,
Shoulder the broken tide away,
Or murmurs hoarse and strong through
    mossy cleft and cave.

What heed I of the dusty land
    And noisy town?
I see the mighty deep expand
From its white line of glimmering sand
To where the blue of heaven on bluer
    waves shuts down!   60

In listless quietude of mind,
    I yield to all
The change of cloud and wave and wind;
And passive on the flood reclined,
I wander with the waves, and with them
    rise and fall.

But look, thou dreamer! wave and shore
    In shadow lie;
The night-wind warns me back once more
To where, my native hill-tops o'er,
Bends like an arch of fire the glowing sun-
    set sky.   70

So then, beach, bluff, and wave, farewell!
    I bear with me
No token stone nor glittering shell,
But long and oft shall Memory tell
Of this brief thoughtful hour of musing by
    the Sea.

                                1843.

CASSANDRA SOUTHWICK[1]

To the God of all sure mercies let my bless-
    ing rise to-day,
From the scoffer and the cruel He hath
    plucked the spoil away;
Yea, He who cooled the furnace around the
    faithful three,
And tamed the Chaldean lions, hath set
    his handmaid free!

Last night I saw the sunset melt through
    my prison bars,
Last night across my damp earth-floor fell
    the pale gleam of stars;
In the coldness and the darkness all through
    the long night-time,
My grated casement whitened with au-
    tumn's early rime.

Alone, in that dark sorrow, hour after hour
    crept by;
Star after star looked palely in and sank
    adown the sky;   10
No sound amid night's stillness, save that
    which seemed to be
The dull and heavy beating of the pulses
    of the sea;

All night I sat unsleeping, for I knew that
    on the morrow
The ruler and the cruel priest would mock
    me in my sorrow,
Dragged to their place of market, and bar-
    gained for and sold,
Like a lamb before the shambles, like a
    heifer from the fold!

[1] In 1658 two young persons, son and daughter of
Lawrence Southwick of Salem, who had himself been
imprisoned and deprived of nearly all his property for
having entertained Quakers at his house, were fined
for non-attendance at church. They being unable to pay
the fine, the General Court issued an order empowering
'The Treasurer of the County to sell the said persons
to any of the English nation of *Virginia* or *Barbadoes*,
to answer said fines.' An attempt was made to carry
this order into execution, but no shipmaster was found
willing to convey them to the West Indies. (WHITTIER.)

Oh, the weakness of the flesh was there, —
    the shrinking and the shame;
And the low voice of the Tempter like
    whispers to me came:
'Why sit'st thou thus forlornly,' the
    wicked murmur said,
Damp walls thy bower of beauty, cold
    earth thy maiden bed ?   20

'Where be the smiling faces, and voices
    soft and sweet,
Seen in thy father's dwelling, heard in the
    pleasant street ?
Where be the youths whose glances, the
    summer Sabbath through,
Turned tenderly and timidly unto thy
    father's pew ?

'Why sit'st thou here, Cassandra ? — Be-
    think thee with what mirth
The happy schoolmates gather around the
    warm, bright hearth;
How the crimson shadows tremble on fore-
    heads white and fair,
On eyes of merry girlhood, half hid in
    golden hair.

'Not for thee the hearth-fire brightens,
    not for thee kind words are spoken,
Not for thee the nuts of Wenham woods
    by laughing boys are broken;   30
No first-fruits of the orchard within thy
    lap are laid,
For thee no flowers of autumn the youth-
    ful hunters braid.

'O weak, deluded maiden ! — by crazy
    fancies led,
With wild and raving railers an evil path
    to tread;
To leave a wholesome worship, and teach-
    ing pure and sound,
And mate with maniac women, loose-
    haired and sackcloth bound, —

'Mad scoffers of the priesthood, who mock
    at things divine,
Who rail against the pulpit, and holy bread
    and wine;
Sore from their cart-tail scourgings, and
    from the pillory lame,
Rejoicing in their wretchedness, and glory-
    ing in their shame.   40

'And what a fate awaits thee ! — a sadly
    toiling slave,

Dragging the slowly lengthening chain of
    bondage to the grave !
Think of thy woman's nature, subdued in
    hopeless thrall,
The easy prey of any, the scoff and scorn
    of all !'

Oh, ever as the Tempter spoke, and feeble
    Nature's fears
Wrung drop by drop the scalding flow of
    unavailing tears,
I wrestled down the evil thoughts, and
    strove in silent prayer,
To feel, O Helper of the weak ! that Thou
    indeed wert there !

I thought of Paul and Silas, within Phi-
    lippi's cell,
And how from Peter's sleeping limbs the
    prison shackles fell,   50
Till I seemed to hear the trailing of an
    angel's robe of white,
And to feel a blessed presence invisible to
    sight.

Bless the Lord for all his mercies ! — for
    the peace and love I felt,
Like dew of Hermon's holy hill, upon my
    spirit melt ;
When 'Get behind me, Satan !' was the
    language of my heart,
And I felt the Evil Tempter with all his
    doubts depart.

Slow broke the gray cold morning; again
    the sunshine fell,
Flecked with the shade of bar and grate
    within my lonely cell;
The hoar-frost melted on the wall, and up-
    ward from the street
Came careless laugh and idle word, and
    tread of passing feet.   60

At length the heavy bolts fell back, my
    door was open cast,
And slowly at the sheriff's side, up the
    long street I passed;
I heard the murmur round me, and felt,
    but dared not see,
How, from every door and window, the
    people gazed on me.

And doubt and fear fell on me, shame
    burned upon my cheek,
Swam earth and sky around me, my trem-
    bling limbs grew weak:

'O Lord! support thy handmaid; and from
  her soul cast out
The fear of man, which brings a snare, the
  weakness and the doubt.'

Then the dreary shadows scattered, like a
  cloud in morning's breeze,
And a low deep voice within me seemed
  whispering words like these: 70
'Though thy earth be as the iron, and thy
  heaven a brazen wall,
Trust still his loving-kindness whose power
  is over all.'

We paused at length, where at my feet the
  sunlit waters broke
On glaring reach of shining beach, and
  shingly wall of rock;
The merchant-ships lay idly there, in hard
  clear lines on high,
Tracing with rope and slender spar their
  network on the sky.

And there were ancient citizens, cloak-
  wrapped and grave and cold,
And grim and stout sea-captains with faces
  bronzed and old,
And on his horse, with Rawson, his cruel
  clerk at hand,
Sat dark and haughty Endicott, the ruler
  of the land. 80

And poisoning with his evil words the
  ruler's ready ear,
The priest leaned o'er his saddle, with laugh
  and scoff and jeer;
It stirred my soul, and from my lips the
  seal of silence broke,
As if through woman's weakness a warning
  spirit spoke.

I cried, 'The Lord rebuke thee, thou smiter
  of the meek,
Thou robber of the righteous, thou trampler
  of the weak!
Go light the dark, cold hearth-stones,—
  go turn the prison lock
Of the poor hearts thou hast hunted, thou
  wolf amid the flock!'

Dark lowered the brows of Endicott, and
  with a deeper red
O'er Rawson's wine-empurpled cheek the
  flush of anger spread; 90

'Good people,' quoth the white-lipped priest,
  'heed not her words so wild,
Her Master speaks within her,—the Devil
  owns his child!'

But gray heads shook, and young brows
  knit, the while the sheriff read
That law the wicked rulers against the poor
  have made,
Who to their house of Rimmon and idol
  priesthood bring
No bended knee of worship, nor gainful
  offering.

Then to the stout sea-captains the sheriff,
  turning, said,—
'Which of ye, worthy seamen, will take this
  Quaker maid?
In the Isle of fair Barbadoes, or on Vir-
  ginia's shore,
You may hold her at a higher price than
  Indian girl or Moor.' 100

Grim and silent stood the captains; and when
  again he cried,
'Speak out, my worthy seamen!'— no
  voice, no sign replied;
But I felt a hard hand press my own, and
  kind words met my ear,—
'God bless thee, and preserve thee, my
  gentle girl and dear!'

A weight seemed lifted from my heart, a
  pitying friend was nigh,—
I felt it in his hard, rough hand, and saw it
  in his eye;
And when again the sheriff spoke, that
  voice, so kind to me,
Growled back its stormy answer like the
  roaring of the sea,—

'Pile my ship with bars of silver, pack with
  coins of Spanish gold,
From keel-piece up to deck-plank, the room-
  age of her hold, 110
By the living God who made me!— I
  would sooner in your bay
Sink ship and crew and cargo, than bear
  this child away!'

'Well answered, worthy captain, shame on
  their cruel laws!'
Ran through the crowd in murmurs loud
  the people's just applause.

'Like the herdsmen of Tekoa, in Israel of
  old,
Shall we see the poor and righteous again
  for silver sold ?'

I looked on haughty Endicott; with weapon
  half-way drawn,
Swept round the throng his lion glare of
  bitter hate and scorn;
Fiercely he drew his bridle-rein, and turned
  in silence back,
And sneering priest and baffled clerk rode
  murmuring in his track.   120

Hard after them the sheriff looked, in bitterness of soul;
Thrice smote his staff upon the ground, and
  crushed his parchment roll.
'Good friends,' he said, ' since both have
  fled, the ruler and the priest,
Judge ye, if from their further work I be
  not well released.'

Loud was the cheer which, full and clear,
  swept round the silent bay,
As, with kind words and kinder looks, he
  bade me go my way;
For He who turns the courses of the streamlet of the glen,
And the river of great waters, had turned
  the hearts of men.

Oh, at that hour the very earth seemed
  changed beneath my eye,
A holier wonder round me rose the blue
  walls of the sky,   130
A lovelier light on rock and hill and stream
  and woodland lay,
And softer lapsed on sunnier sands the waters of the bay.

Thanksgiving to the Lord of life ! to Him
  all praises be,
Who from the hands of evil men hath set
  his handmaid free;
All praise to Him before whose power the
  mighty are afraid,
Who takes the crafty in the snare which
  for the poor is laid !

Sing, O my soul, rejoicingly, on evening's
  twilight calm
Uplift the loud thanksgiving, pour forth
  the grateful psalm;

Let all dear hearts with me rejoice, as did
  the saints of old,
When of the Lord's good angel the rescued
  Peter told.   140

And weep and howl, ye evil priests and
  mighty men of wrong,
The Lord shall smite the proud, and lay
  His hand upon the strong.
Woe to the wicked rulers in his avenging
  hour !
Woe to the wolves who seek the flocks to
  raven and devour !

But let the humble ones arise, the poor in
  heart be glad,
And let the mourning ones again with robes
  of praise be clad.
For He who cooled the furnace, and
  smoothed the stormy wave,
And tamed the Chaldean lions, is mighty
  still to save !
                              1843.

MASSACHUSETTS TO VIRGINIA[1]

THE blast from Freedom's Northern hills,
  upon its Southern way,
Bears greeting to Virginia from Massachusetts Bay:
No word of haughty challenging, nor battle
  bugle's peal,
Nor steady tread of marching files, nor
  clang of horsemen's steel,

No trains of deep-mouthed cannon along
  our highways go;
Around our silent arsenals untrodden lies
  the snow;

[1] Written on reading an account of the proceedings
of the citizens of Norfolk, Va., in reference to George
Latimer, the alleged fugitive slave, who was seized in
Boston without warrant at the request of James B.
Grey, of Norfolk, claiming to be his master. The case
caused great excitement North and South, and led to
the presentation of a petition to Congress, signed by
more than fifty thousand citizens of Massachusetts,
calling for such laws and proposed amendments to the
Constitution as should relieve the Commonwealth from
all further participation in the crime of oppression.
George Latimer himself was finally given free papers
for the sum of four hundred dollars. (WHITTIER.)
    When the excitement was at its height, conventions
were held simultaneously in every county in Massachusetts, and this poem was read at the Essex County convention. The most intense enthusiasm was aroused by
those stanzas in which all the counties of the State
speak successively, each in its own character.

And to the land-breeze of our ports, upon
    their errands far,
A thousand sails of commerce swell, but
    none are spread for war.

We hear thy threats, Virginia! thy stormy
    words and high
Swell harshly on the Southern winds which
    melt along our sky;   10
Yet not one brown, hard hand foregoes its
    honest labor here,
No hewer of our mountain oaks suspends
    his axe in fear.

Wild are the waves which lash the reefs
    along St. George's bank;
Cold on the shores of Labrador the fog lies
    white and dank;
Through storm, and wave, and blinding
    mist, stout are the hearts which
    man
The fishing-smacks of Marblehead, the sea-
    boats of Cape Ann.

The cold north light and wintry sun glare
    on their icy forms,
Bent grimly o'er their straining lines or
    wrestling with the storms;
Free as the winds they drive before, rough
    as the waves they roam,
They laugh to scorn the slaver's threat
    against their rocky home.   20

What means the Old Dominion? Hath
    she forgot the day
When o'er her conquered valleys swept the
    Briton's steel array?
How, side by side with sons of hers, the
    Massachusetts men
Encountered Tarleton's charge of fire, and
    stout Cornwallis, then?

Forgets she how the Bay State, in answer
    to the call
Of her old House of Burgesses, spoke out
    from Faneuil Hall?
When, echoing back her Henry's cry, came
    pulsing on each breath
Of Northern winds the thrilling sounds of
    'Liberty or Death!'

What asks the Old Dominion? If now
    her sons have proved
False to their fathers' memory, false to the
    faith they loved;   30

If she can scoff at Freedom, and its great
    charter spurn,
Must we of Massachusetts from truth and
    duty turn?

We hunt your bondmen, flying from Sla-
    very's hateful hell;
Our voices, at your bidding, take up the
    bloodhound's yell;
We gather, at your summons, above our
    fathers' graves,
From Freedom's holy altar-horns to tear
    your wretched slaves!

Thank God! not yet so vilely can Massa-
    chusetts bow;
The spirit of her early time is with her even
    now;
Dream not because her Pilgrim blood moves
    slow and calm and cool,
She thus can stoop her chainless neck, a sis-
    ter's slave and tool!   40

All that a sister State should do, all that a
    free State may,
Heart, hand, and purse we proffer, as in our
    early day;
But that one dark loathsome burden ye
    must stagger with alone,
And reap the bitter harvest which ye your-
    selves have sown!

Hold, while ye may, your struggling slaves,
    and burden God's free air
With woman's shriek beneath the lash, and
    manhood's wild despair;
Cling closer to the 'cleaving curse' that
    writes upon your plains
The blasting of Almighty wrath against a
    land of chains.

Still shame your gallant ancestry, the cava-
    liers of old,
By watching round the shambles where hu-
    man flesh is sold;   50
Gloat o'er the new-born child, and count
    his market value, when
The maddened mother's cry of woe shall
    pierce the slaver's den!

Lower than plummet soundeth, sink the
    Virginia name;
Plant, if ye will, your fathers' graves with
    rankest weeds of shame;

Be, if ye will, the scandal of God's fair universe;
We wash our hands forever of your sin and shame and curse.

A voice from lips whereon the coal from Freedom's shrine hath been,
Thrilled, as but yesterday, the hearts of Berkshire's mountain men:
The echoes of that solemn voice are sadly lingering still
In all our sunny valleys, on every wind-swept hill.   60

And when the prowling man-thief came hunting for his prey
Beneath the very shadow of Bunker's shaft of gray,
How, through the free lips of the son, the father's warning spoke;
How, from its bonds of trade and sect, the Pilgrim city broke !

A hundred thousand right arms were lifted up on high,
A hundred thousand voices sent back their loud reply;
Through the thronged towns of Essex the startling summons rang,
And up from bench and loom and wheel her young mechanics sprang !

The voice of free, broad Middlesex, of thousands as of one,
The shaft of Bunker calling to that of Lexington;   70
From Norfolk's ancient villages, from Plymouth's rocky bound
To where Nantucket feels the arms of ocean close her round;

From rich and rural Worcester, where through the calm repose
Of cultured vales and fringing woods the gentle Nashua flows,
To where Wachuset's wintry blasts the mountain larches stir,
Swelled up to Heaven the thrilling cry of 'God save Latimer !'

And sandy Barnstable rose up, wet with the salt sea spray;
And Bristol sent her answering shout down Narragansett Bay !

Along the broad Connecticut old Hampden felt the thrill,
And the cheer of Hampshire's woodmen swept down from Holyoke Hill.   80

The voice of Massachusetts ! Of her free sons and daughters,
Deep calling unto deep aloud, the sound of many waters !
Against the burden of that voice what tyrant power shall stand ?
No fetters in the Bay State ! No slave upon her land !

Look to it well, Virginians ! In calmness we have borne,
In answer to our faith and trust, your insult and your scorn;
You 've spurned our kindest counsels; you 've hunted for our lives;
And shaken round our hearths and homes your manacles and gyves !

We wage no war, we lift no arm, we fling no torch within
The fire-damps of the quaking mine beneath your soil of sin;   90
We leave ye with your bondmen, to wrestle, while ye can,
With the strong upward tendencies and godlike soul of man !

But for us and for our children, the vow which we have given
For freedom and humanity is registered in heaven;
No slave-hunt in our borders, — no pirate on our strand !
No fetters in the Bay State, — no slave upon our land !
December, 1842.   *January, 1843.*

THE CHRISTIAN SLAVE [1]

A CHRISTIAN ! going, gone !
Who bids for God's own image ? for his grace,
Which that poor victim of the market-place
Hath in her suffering won ?

[1] In a publication of L. F. Tasistro, *Random Shots and Southern Breezes*, is a description of a slave auction at New Orleans, at which the auctioneer recommended the woman on the stand as 'A GOOD CHRISTIAN !' It was not uncommon to see advertisements of slaves for sale, in which they were described as pious or as members of the church. In one advertisement a slave was noted as 'a Baptist preacher.' (WHITTIER.)

My God ! can such things be ?
Hast Thou not said that whatsoe'er is done
Unto thy weakest and thy humblest one
    Is even done to Thee ?

In that sad victim, then,
Child of thy pitying love, I see Thee
    stand;   10
Once more the jest-word of a mocking.
    band,
    Bound, sold, and scourged again !

A Christian up for sale !
Wet with her blood your whips, o'ertask
    her frame,
Make her life loathsome with your wrong
    and shame,
    Her patience shall not fail !

A heathen hand might deal
Back on your heads the gathered wrong of
    years
But her low, broken prayer and nightly
    tears
    Ye neither heed nor feel.   20

Con well thy lesson o'er,
Thou prudent teacher, tell the toiling slave
No dangerous tale of Him who came to
    save
    The outcast and the poor.

But wisely shut the ray
Of God's free Gospel from her simple
    heart,
And to her darkened mind alone impart
    One stern command, Obey !

So shalt thou deftly raise
The market price of human flesh;[1] and
    while   30
On thee, their pampered guest, the planters
    smile,
    Thy church shall praise.

Grave, reverend men shall tell
From Northern pulpits how thy work was
    blest,

While in that vile South Sodom first and
    best,
    Thy poor disciples sell.

Oh, shame ! the Moslem thrall,
Who, with his master, to the Prophet
    kneels,
While turning to the sacred Kebla feels
    His fetters break and fall.   40

Cheers for the turbaned Bey
Of robber-peopled Tunis ! he hath torn
The dark slave-dungeons open, and hath
    borne
    Their inmates into day:

But our poor slave in vain
Turns to the Christian shrine his aching
    eyes;
Its rites will only swell his market price,
    And rivet on his chain.

God of all right ! how long
Shall priestly robbers at thine altar
    stand,   50
Lifting in prayer to Thee the bloody hand
    And haughty brow of wrong ?

Oh, from the fields of cane,
From the low rice-swamp, from the trader's
    cell;
From the black slave-ship's foul and loath-
    some hell,
    And coffle's weary chain;

Hoarse, horrible, and strong,
Rises to Heaven that agonizing cry,
Filling the arches of the hollow sky,
    How long, O God, how long ?   60
1843.   1842.

THE SHOEMAKERS [1]

Ho ! workers of the old time styled
    The Gentle Craft of Leather !

---

[1] There was at the time when this poem was written an Association in Liberty County, Georgia, for the religious instruction of negroes. One of their annual reports contains an address by the Rev. Josiah Spry Law, in which the following passage occurs : 'There is a growing interest in this community in the religious instruction of negroes. There is a conviction that religious instruction promotes the quiet and order of the people, and the pecuniary interest of the owners.' (WHITTIER.)

[1] In his *Songs of Labor*, though Whittier wrote with most sympathy of the two trades at which he had himself worked, shoemaking (cf. Carpenter's *Whittier*, pp. 39–41) and farming (see 'The Huskers,' p. 278), there are lines in others of the *Songs* which cannot be spared from any selection of his poetry. Such are these from 'The Lumbermen : ' —

> Keep who will the city's alleys,
>   Take the smooth-shorn plain ;
> Give to us the cedarn valleys,
>   Rocks and hills of Maine !

Young brothers of the ancient guild,
　Stand forth once more together !
Call out again your long array,
　In the olden merry manner !
Once more, on gay St. Crispin's day,
　Fling out your blazoned banner !

Rap, rap ! upon the well-worn stone
　How falls the polished hammer !　　10
Rap, rap ! the measured sound has grown
　A quick and merry clamor.
Now shape the sole ! now deftly curl
　The glossy vamp around it,
And bless the while the bright-eyed girl
　Whose gentle fingers bound it !

For you, along the Spanish main
　A hundred keels are ploughing ,
For you, the Indian on the plain
　His lasso-coil is throwing ;　　20
For you, deep glens with hemlock dark
　The woodman's fire is lighting ;
For you, upon the oak's gray bark,
　The woodman's axe is smiting.

For you, from Carolina's pine
　The rosin-gum is stealing ;
For you, the dark-eyed Florentine
　Her silken skein is reeling ;
For you, the dizzy goatherd roams
　His rugged Alpine ledges ;　　30
For you, round all her shepherd homes,
　Bloom England's thorny hedges.

The foremost still, by day or night,
　On moated mound or heather,
Where'er the need of trampled right
　Brought toiling men together ;
Where the free burghers from the wall
　Defied the mail-clad master,
Than yours, at Freedom's trumpet-call,
　No craftsmen rallied faster.　　40

Let foplings sneer, let fools deride,
　Ye heed no idle scorner ;
Free hands and hearts are still your pride,

　　In our North-land, wild and woody,
　　　Let us still have part :
　　Rugged nurse and mother sturdy,
　　　Hold us to thy heart !
　r the beginning of ' The Drovers : ' —

　　Through heat and cold, and shower and sun,
　　　Still onward cheerly driving !
　　There 's life alone in duty done,
　　　And rest alone in striving.

　See also the beautiful ' Dedication ' of the *Songs of Labor*, p. 282.

　　And duty done your honor.
Ye dare to trust, for honest fame,
　The jury Time empanels,
And leave to truth each noble name
　Which glorifies your annals.

Thy songs, Hans Sachs, are living yet,
　In strong and hearty German;　　50
And Bloomfield's lay, and Gifford's wit,
　And patriot fame of Sherman;
Still from his book, a mystic seer,
　The soul of Behmen teaches,
And England's priestcraft shakes to hear
　Of Fox's leathern breeches.

The foot is yours ; where'er it falls,
　It treads your well-wrought leather,
On earthern floor, in marble halls
　On carpet, or on heather.　　60
Still there the sweetest charm is found
　Of matron grace or vestal's,
As Hebe's foot bore nectar round
　Among the old celestials !

Rap, rap ! — your stout and bluff bro-
　　gan,
　With footsteps slow and weary,
May wander where the sky's blue span
　Shuts down upon the prairie.
On Beauty's foot your slippers glance,
　By Saratoga's fountains,　　70
Or twinkle down the summer dance
　Beneath the Crystal Mountains !

The red brick to the mason's hand,
　The brown earth to the tiller's,
The shoe in yours shall wealth com-
　　mand,
　Like fairy Cinderella's !
As they who shunned the household
　　maid
　Beheld the crown upon her,
So all shall see your toil repaid
　With hearth and home and honor.　　80

Then let the toast be freely quaffed,
　In water cool and brimming, —
' All honor to the good old Craft,
　Its merry men and women !'
Call out again your long array,
　In the old time's pleasant manner:
Once more, on gay St. Crispin's day,
　Fling out his blazoned banner !

　　　　　　　　　　　　　　1845.

THE PINE TREE [1]

LIFT again the stately emblem on the Bay
    State's rusted shield,
Give to Northern winds the Pine-Tree on
    our banner's tattered field.
Sons of men who sat in council with their
    Bibles round the board,
Answering England's royal missive with a
    firm, 'Thus saith the Lord!'
Rise again for home and freedom! set the
    battle in array!
What the fathers did of old time we their
    sons must do to-day.

Tell us not of banks and tariffs, cease your
    paltry pedler cries;
Shall the good State sink her honor that
    your gambling stocks may rise?
Would ye barter man for cotton? That
    your gains may sum up higher,
Must we kiss the feet of Moloch, pass our
    children through the fire?
Is the dollar only real? God and truth and
    right a dream?
Weighed against your lying ledgers must
    our manhood kick the beam?

O my God! for that free spirit, which of
    old in Boston town
Smote the Province House with terror,
    struck the crest of Andros down!
For another strong-voiced Adams in the
    city's streets to cry,
'Up for God and Massachusetts! Set your
    feet on Mammon's lie!
Perish banks and perish traffic, spin your
    cotton's latest pound,
But in Heaven's name keep your honor, keep
    the heart o' the Bay State sound!'

Where's the man for Massachusetts?
    Where's the voice to speak her free?
Where's the hand to light up bonfires from
    her mountains to the sea?

Beats her Pilgrim pulse no longer? Sits
    she dumb in her despair?
Has she none to break the silence? Has
    she none to do and dare?
O my God! for one right worthy to lift up
    her rusted shield,
And to plant again the Pine-Tree in her
    banner's tattered field!

1846.   1846.

FORGIVENESS

MY heart was heavy, for its trust had been
Abused, its kindness answered with foul
    wrong;
So, turning gloomily from my fellow-men,
One summer Sabbath day I strolled among
The green mounds of the village burial-
    place;
Where, pondering how all human love and
    hate
Find one sad level; and how, soon or late,
Wronged and wrongdoer, each with meek-
    ened face,
And cold hands folded over a still heart,
Pass the green threshold of our common
    grave,
Whither all footsteps tend, whence none
    depart,
Awed for myself, and pitying my race,
Our common sorrow, like a mighty wave,
Swept all my pride away, and trembling I
    forgave!

1846?   (1849.)

BARCLAY OF URY [2]

UP the streets of Aberdeen,
By the kirk and college green,
    Rode the Laird of Ury;

[1] Written on hearing that the Anti-Slavery Resolves of Stephen C. Phillips had been rejected by the Whig Convention in Faneuil Hall, in 1846. (WHITTIER.) Whittier sent the poem to Sumner in a letter in which he said : 'I have just read the proceedings of your Whig convention, and the lines enclosed are a feeble expression of my feelings. I look upon the rejection of Stephen C. Phillips's resolutions as an evidence that the end and aim of the managers of the convention was to go just far enough to scare the party and no farther. All thanks for the free voices of thyself, Phillips, Allen, and Adams. Notwithstanding the result you have not spoken in vain.' (Quoted in Pickard's *Life*, vol. i, p. 316.)

[2] Among the earliest converts to the doctrines of Friends in Scotland was Barclay of Ury, an old and distinguished soldier, who had fought under Gustavus Adolphus, in Germany. As a Quaker, he became the object of persecution and abuse at the hands of the magistrates and the populace. None bore the indignities of the mob with greater patience and nobleness of soul than this once proud gentleman and soldier. One of his friends, on an occasion of uncommon rudeness, lamented that he should be treated so harshly in his old age who had been so honored before. 'I find more satisfaction,' said Barclay, 'as well as honor, in being thus insulted for my religious principles, than when, a few years ago, it was usual for the magistrates, as I passed the city of Aberdeen, to meet me on the road and conduct me to public entertainment in their hall, and then escort me out again, to gain my favor.' (WHITTIER.)

Close behind him, close beside,
Foul of mouth and evil-eyed,
  Pressed the mob in fury.

Flouted him the drunken churl,
Jeered at him the serving-girl,
  Prompt to please her master;
And the begging carlin, late   10
Fed and clothed at Ury's gate,
  Cursed him as he passed her.

Yet, with calm and stately mien,
Up the streets of Aberdeen
  Came he slowly riding;
And, to all he saw and heard,
Answering not with bitter word,
  Turning not for chiding.

Came a troop with broadswords swinging,
Bits and bridles sharply ringing,   20
  Loose and free and froward;
Quoth the foremost, 'Ride him down!
Push him! prick him! through the town
  Drive the Quaker coward!'

But from out the thickening crowd
Cried a sudden voice and loud:
  'Barclay! Ho! a Barclay!'
And the old man at his side
Saw a comrade, battle tried,
  Scarred and sunburned darkly,   30

Who with ready weapon bare,
Fronting to the troopers there,
  Cried aloud: 'God save us,
Call ye coward him who stood
Ankle deep in Lützen's blood,
  With the brave Gustavus?'

'Nay, I do not need thy sword,
Comrade mine,' said Ury's lord
  'Put it up, I pray thee:
Passive to his holy will,   40
Trust I in my Master still,
  Even though He slay me.

'Pledges of thy love and faith,
Proved on many a field of death,
  Not by me are needed.'
Marvelled much that henchman bold,
That his laird, so stout of old,
  Now so meekly pleaded.

'Woe's the day!' he sadly said,
With a slowly shaking head,   50

And a look of pity;
'Ury's honest lord reviled,
Mock of knave and sport of child,
  In his own good city!

'Speak the word, and, master mine,
As we charged on Tilly's line,[1]
  And his Walloon lancers,
Smiting through their midst we'll teach
Civil look and decent speech
  To these boyish prancers!'   60

'Marvel not, mine ancient friend,
Like beginning, like the end,'
  Quoth the Laird of Ury;
'Is the sinful servant more
Than his gracious Lord who bore
  Bonds and stripes in Jewry?

'Give me joy that in his name
I can bear, with patient frame,
  All these vain ones offer;
While for them He suffereth long,   70
Shall I answer wrong with wrong,
  Scoffing with the scoffer?

'Happier I, with loss of all,
Hunted, outlawed, held in thrall,
  With few friends to greet me,
Than when reeve and squire were seen,
Riding out from Aberdeen,
  With bared heads to meet me.

'When each goodwife, o'er and o'er,
Blessed me as I passed her door;   80
  And the snooded daughter,
Through her casement glancing down,
Smiled on him who bore renown
  From red fields of slaughter.

'Hard to feel the stranger's scoff,
Hard the old friend's falling off,
  Hard to learn forgiving;
But the Lord his own rewards,
And his love with theirs accords,
  Warm and fresh and living.   90

'Through this dark and stormy night
Faith beholds a feeble light
  Up the blackness streaking;

[1] The barbarities of Count De Tilly after the siege of Magdeburg made such an impression upon our forefathers that the phrase 'like old Tilly' is still heard sometimes in New England of any piece of special ferocity. (WHITTIER.)

Knowing God's own time is best,
In a patient hope I rest
    For the full day-breaking!'

So the Laird of Ury said,
Turning slow his horse's head
    Towards the Tolbooth prison,
Where, through iron gates, he heard   100
Poor disciples of the Word
    Preach of Christ arisen!

Not in vain, Confessor old,
Unto us the tale is told
    Of thy day of trial;
Every age on him who strays
From its broad and beaten ways
    Pours its seven-fold vial.

Happy he whose inward ear
Angel comfortings can hear,   110
    O'er the rabble's laughter;
And while Hatred's fagots burn,
Glimpses through the smoke discern
    Of the good hereafter.

Knowing this, that never yet
Share of Truth was vainly set
    In the world's wide fallow;
After hands shall sow the seed,
After hands from hill and mead
    Reap the harvests yellow.   120

Thus, with somewhat of the Seer,
Must the moral pioneer
    From the Future borrow;
Clothe the waste with dreams of grain,
And, on midnight's sky of rain,
    Paint the golden morrow!

              1847.

THE ANGELS OF BUENA VISTA [1]

SPEAK and tell us, our Ximena, looking
    northward far away,
O'er the camp of the invaders, o'er the
    Mexican array,

[1] A letter-writer from Mexico during the Mexican War, when detailing some of the incidents at the terrible fight of Buena Vista, mentioned that Mexican women were seen hovering near the field of death, for the purpose of giving aid and succor to the wounded. One poor woman was found surrounded by the maimed and suffering of both armies, ministering to the wants of Americans as well as Mexicans with impartial tenderness. (WHITTIER.)

Who is losing? who is winning? are they
    far or come they near?
Look abroad, and tell us, sister, whither
    rolls the storm we hear.

'Down the hills of Angostura still the storm
    of battle rolls;
Blood is flowing, men are dying; God have
    mercy on their souls!'
Who is losing? who is winning?   'Over
    hill and over plain,
I see but smoke of cannon clouding through
    the mountain rain.'

Holy Mother! keep our brothers!   Look,
    Ximena, look once more.
'Still I see the fearful whirlwind rolling
    darkly as before,   10
Bearing on, in strange confusion, friend and
    foeman, foot and horse,
Like some wild and troubled torrent sweep-
    ing down its mountain course.'

Look forth once more, Ximena! 'Ah! the
    smoke has rolled away;
And I see the Northern rifles gleaming
    down the ranks of gray.
Hark! that sudden blast of bugles! there
    the troop of Minon wheels;
There the Northern horses thunder, with
    the cannon at their heels.

'Jesu, pity! how it thickens! now retreat
    and now advance!
Right against the blazing cannon shivers
    Puebla's charging lance!
Down they go, the brave young riders;
    horse and foot together fall;
Like a ploughshare in the fallow, through
    them ploughs the Northern ball.'   20

Nearer came the storm and nearer, rolling
    fast and frightful on!
Speak, Ximena, speak and tell us, who has
    lost, and who has won?
'Alas! alas! I know not; friend and foe
    together fall,
O'er the dying rush the living: pray, my
    sisters, for them all!

'Lo! the wind the smoke is lifting.
    Blessed Mother, save my brain!
I can see the wounded crawling slowly out
    from heaps of slain.

Now they stagger, blind and bleeding; now
    they fall, and strive to rise;
Hasten, sisters, haste and save them, lest
    they die before our eyes !

'O my heart's love ! O my dear one ! lay
    thy poor head on my knee;
Dost thou know the lips that kiss thee ?
    Canst thou hear me ? canst thou
    see ?   30
O my husband, brave and gentle ! O my
    Bernal, look once more
On the blessed cross before thee ! Mercy !
    mercy ! all is o'er ! '

Dry thy tears, my poor Ximena; lay thy
    dear one down to rest;
Let his hands be meekly folded, lay the
    cross upon his breast;
Let his dirge be sung hereafter, and his
    funeral masses said;
To-day, thou poor bereaved one, the living
    ask thy aid.

Close beside her, faintly moaning, fair and
    young, a soldier lay,
Torn with shot and pierced with lances,
    bleeding slow his life away;
But, as tenderly before him the lorn Ximena
    knelt,
She saw the Northern eagle shining on his
    pistol-belt.   40

With a stifled cry of horror straight she
    turned away her head;
With a sad and bitter feeling looked she
    back upon her dead;
But she heard the youth's low moaning, and
    his struggling breath of pain,
And she raised the cooling water to his
    parching lips again.

Whispered low the dying soldier, pressed
    her hand and faintly smiled;
Was that pitying face his mother's ? did
    she watch beside her child ?
All his stranger words with meaning her
    woman's heart supplied;
With her kiss upon his forehead, 'Mother!'
    murmured he, and died !

'A bitter curse upon them, poor boy, who
    led thee forth,
From some gentle, sad-eyed mother, weep-
    ing, lonely, in the North !'   50

Spake the mournful Mexic woman, as she
    laid him with her dead,
And turned to soothe the living, and bind
    the wounds which bled.

Look forth once more, Ximena ! 'Like a
    cloud before the wind
Rolls the battle down the mountains,
    leaving blood and death be-
    hind;
Ah ! they plead in vain for mercy; in the
    dust the wounded strive;
Hide your faces, holy angels ! O thou
    Christ of God, forgive ! '

Sink, O Night, among thy mountains ! let
    the cool, gray shadows fall;
Dying brothers, fighting demons, drop thy
    curtain over all !
Through the thickening winter twilight,
    wide apart the battle rolled,
In the sheath the sabre rested, and the can-
    non's lips grew cold.   60

But the noble Mexic women still their holy
    task pursued,
Through that long, dark night of sor-
    row, worn and faint and lacking
    food.
Over weak and suffering brothers, with a
    tender care they hung,
And the dying foeman blessed them in a
    strange and Northern tongue.

Not wholly lost, O Father ! is this evil
    world of ours;
Upward, through its blood and ashes, spring
    afresh the Eden flowers;
From its smoking hell of battle, Love and
    Pity send their prayer,
And still thy white-winged angels hover
    dimly in our air !
            1847

THE HUSKERS

IT was late in mild October, and the long
    autumnal rain
Had left the summer harvest-fields all
    green with grass again ;
The first sharp frosts had fallen, leaving all
    the woodlands gay
With the hues of summer's rainbow, or the
    meadow-flowers of May.

Through a thin, dry mist, that morning, the
   sun rose broad and red,
At first a rayless disk of fire, he brightened
   as he sped ;
Yet even his noontide glory fell chastened
   and subdued,
On the cornfields and the orchards and
   softly pictured wood.

And all that quiet afternoon, slow sloping
   to the night,
He wove with golden shuttle the haze with
   yellow light ;   10
Slanting through the painted beeches, he
   glorified the hill ;
And, beneath it, pond and meadow lay
   brighter, greener still.

And shouting boys in woodland haunts
   caught glimpses of that sky,
Flecked by the many-tinted leaves, and
   laughed, they knew not why ;
And school-girls, gay with aster-flowers,
   beside the meadow brooks,
Mingled the glow of autumn with the sunshine of sweet looks.

From spire and barn looked westerly the
   patient weathercocks ;
But even the birches on the hill stood motionless as rocks.
No sound was in the woodlands, save the
   squirrel's dropping shell,
And the yellow leaves among the boughs,
   low rustling as they fell.   20

The summer grains were harvested ; the
   stubble-fields lay dry,
Where June winds rolled, in light and
   shade, the pale green waves of
   rye ;
But still, on gentle hill-slopes, in valleys
   fringed with wood,
Ungathered, bleaching in the sun, the heavy
   corn crop stood.

Bent low, by autumn's wind and rain,
   through husks that, dry and sere,
Unfolded from their ripened charge, shone
   out the yellow ear ;
Beneath, the turnip lay concealed, in many
   a verdant fold,
And glistened in the slanting light the
   pumpkin's sphere of gold.

There wrought the busy harvesters ; and
   many a creaking wain
Bore slowly to the long barn-floor its load
   of husk and grain ;   30
Till broad and red, as when he rose, the
   sun sank down, at last,
And like a merry guest's farewell, the day
   in brightness passed.

And lo ! as through the western pines, on
   meadow, stream, and pond,
Flamed the red radiance of a sky, set all
   afire beyond,
Slowly o'er the eastern sea-bluffs a milder
   glory shone,
And the sunset and the moonrise were
   mingled into one !

As thus into the quiet night the twilight
   lapsed away,
And deeper in the brightening moon the
   tranquil shadows lay;
From many a brown old farm-house, and
   hamlet without name,
Their milking and their home-tasks done,
   the merry huskers came.   40

Swung o'er the heaped-up harvest, from
   pitchforks in the mow,
Shone dimly down the lanterns on the
   pleasant scene below;
The growing pile of husks behind, the
   golden ears before,
And laughing eyes and busy hands
   and brown cheeks glimmering
   o'er.

Half hidden, in a quiet nook, serene of look
   and heart,
Talking their old times over, the old men
   sat apart ;
While up and down the unhusked pile, or
   nestling in its shade,
At hide-and-seek, with laugh and shout,
   the happy children played.

Urged by the good host's daughter, a
   maiden young and fair,
Lifting to light her sweet blue eyes and
   pride of soft brown hair,   50
The master of the village school, sleek of
   hair and smooth of tongue,
To the quaint tune of some old psalm, a
   husking-ballad sung.

THE CORN SONG

Heap high the farmer's wintry hoard !
  Heap high the golden corn !
No richer gift has Autumn poured
  From out her lavish horn !

Let other lands, exulting, glean
  The apple from the pine,
The orange from its glossy green,
  The cluster from the vine ;   60

We better love the hardy gift
  Our rugged vales bestow,
To cheer us when the storm shall drift
  Our harvest-fields with snow.

Through vales of grass and meads of flowers
  Our ploughs their furrows made,
While on the hills the sun and showers
  Of changeful April played.

We dropped the seed o'er hill and plain
  Beneath the sun of May,   70
And frightened from our sprouting grain
  The robber crows away.

All through the long, bright days of June
  Its leaves grew green and fair,
And waved in hot midsummer's noon
  Its soft and yellow hair.

And now, with autumn's moonlit eves,
  Its harvest-time has come,
We pluck away the frosted leaves,
  And bear the treasure home.   80

There, when the snows about us drift,
  And winter winds are cold,
Fair hands the broken grain shall sift,
  And knead its meal of gold.

Let vapid idlers loll in silk
  Around their costly board;
Give us the bowl of samp and milk,
  By homespun beauty poured !

Where'er the wide old kitchen hearth
  Sends up its smoky curls,   90
Who will not thank the kindly earth,
  And bless our farmer girls !

Then shame on all the proud and vain,
  Whose folly laughs to scorn
The blessing of our hardy grain,
  Our wealth of golden corn !

Let earth withhold her goodly root,
  Let mildew blight the rye,
Give to the worm the orchard's fruit,
  The wheat-field to the fly :   100

But let the good old crop adorn
  The hills our fathers trod ;
Still let us, for his golden corn,
  Send up our thanks to God !

                  1847.

PROEM [1]

I love the old melodious lays
Which softly melt the ages through,
  The songs of Spenser's golden days,
  Arcadian Sidney's silvery phrase,
Sprinkling our noon of time with freshest
    morning dew.

Yet, vainly in my quiet hours
To breathe their marvellous notes I try;
  I feel them, as the leaves and flowers
  In silence feel the dewy showers,
And drink with glad, still lips the blessing
    of the sky.   10

The rigor of a frozen clime,
The harshness of an untaught ear,
  The jarring words of one whose rhyme
  Beat often Labor's hurried time,
Or Duty's rugged march through storm
    and strife, are here.

Of mystic beauty, dreamy grace,
No rounded art the lack supplies;
  Unskilled the subtle lines to trace,
  Or softer shades of Nature's face,
I view her common forms with unanointed
    eyes.   20

Nor mine the seer-like power to show
The secrets of the heart and mind;
  To drop the plummet-line below
  Our common world of joy and woe,
A more intense despair or brighter hope to
    find.

Yet here at least an earnest sense
Of human right and weal is shown;

[1] The first important collected edition of Whittier's poems was a large and beautiful volume published in 1848 (dated 1849). This 'Proem' was written to introduce it.

A hate of tyranny intense,
And hearty in its vehemence,
As if my brother's pain and sorrow were
   my own.   30

O Freedom ! if to me belong
Nor mighty Milton's gift divine,
   Nor Marvell's wit and graceful song,
   Still with a love as deep and strong
As theirs, I lay, like them, my best gifts on
   thy shrine !
1847.   *1848.*

THE LAKESIDE

THE shadows round the inland sea
   Are deepening into night;
Slow up the slopes of Ossipee
   They chase the lessening light.
Tired of the long day's blinding heat,
   I rest my languid eye,
Lake of the Hills ! where, cool and sweet,
   Thy sunset waters lie ! [1]

Along the sky, in wavy lines,
   O'er isle and reach and bay,   10
Green-belted with eternal pines,
   The mountains stretch away.
Below, the maple masses sleep
   Where shore with water blends,
While midway on the tranquil deep
   The evening light descends.

So seemed it when yon hill's red crown,[2]
   Of old, the Indian trod,
And, through the sunset air, looked down
   Upon the Smile of God.[3]   20
To him of light and shade the laws
   No forest skeptic taught;

[1] The 'Lake of the Hills' is Lake Winnipesaukee. One of Whittier's favorite resorts was West Ossipee, at the foot of the Ossipee Mountains, just northeast of the lake. See Pickard's *Whittier-Land*, pp. 109–115; his *Life of Whittier*, vol. ii, p. 669; and Whittier's 'Among the Hills' and 'Summer by the Lakeside.'

[2] Mt. Chocorua, north of West Ossipee, the most picturesque, though by no means the highest, of the mountains of New England. Its cone is formed of a peculiar reddish stone known as 'Chocorua granite.' For the legend of the Indian chief from whom it was named, see Thomas Starr King's *The White Hills*, or Sweetser's *White Mountains*, p. 341. See also Whittier's 'How They Climbed Chocorua' in *Whittier-Land*, pp. 111–114. One of Longfellow's early poems, 'Jeckoyva,' had the Indian chief Chocorua for its hero.

[3] The name Winnipesaukee is popularly thought to mean 'The Smile of the Great Spirit.' Students of the Indian languages, however, agree that its real meaning is 'Beautiful Water in a High Place.'

Their living and eternal Cause
   His truer instinct sought.

He saw these mountains in the light
   Which now across them shines ;
This lake, in summer sunset bright,
   Walled round with sombering pines.
God near him seemed; from earth and skies
   His loving voice he heard,   30
As, face to face, in Paradise,
   Man stood before the Lord.

Thanks, O our Father ! that, like him,
   Thy tender love I see,
In radiant hill and woodland dim,
   And tinted sunset sea.
For not in mockery dost Thou fill
   Our earth with light and grace;
Thou hid'st no dark and cruel will
   Behind Thy smiling face !   40
                        1849.

OUR STATE [1]

THE South-land boasts its teeming cane,
The prairied West its heavy grain,
And sunset's radiant gates unfold
On rising marts and sands of gold !

Rough, bleak, and hard, our little State
Is scant of soil, of limits strait;
Her yellow sands are sands alone,
Her only mines are ice and stone !

From Autumn frost to April rain,
Too long her winter woods complain;
From budding flower to falling leaf,
Her summer time is all too brief.

Yet, on her rocks, and on her sands,
And wintry hills, the school-house stands,
And what her rugged soil denies,
The harvest of the mind supplies.

The riches of the Commonwealth
Are free, strong minds, and hearts of health;
And more to her than gold or grain,
The cunning hand and cultured brain.

For well she keeps her ancient stock,
The stubborn strength of Pilgrim Rock;
And still maintains, with milder laws,
And clearer light, the Good Old Cause !

[1] Originally called 'Dedication of a School-house.'

Nor heeds the skeptic's puny hands,
While near her school the church-spire
    stands;
Nor fears the blinded bigot's rule,
While near her church-spire stands the
    school.

                                    1849.

ICHABOD [1]

So fallen! so lost! the light withdrawn
    Which once he wore!
The glory from his gray hairs gone
    Forevermore!

Revile him not, the Tempter hath
    A snare for all;

[1] This poem was the outcome of the surprise and grief and forecast of evil consequences which I felt on reading the Seventh of March speech of Daniel Webster in support of the 'Compromise,' and the Fugitive Slave Law. No partisan or personal enmity dictated it. On the contrary my admiration of the splendid personality and intellectual power of the great senator was never stronger than when I laid down his speech, and, in one of the saddest moments of my life, penned my protest. . . .

But death softens all resentments, and the consciousness of a common inheritance of frailty and weakness modifies the severity of judgment. Years after, in 'The Lost Occasion,' I gave utterance to an almost universal regret that the great statesman did not live to see the flag which he loved trampled under the feet of Slavery, and, in view of this desecration, make his last days glorious in defence of 'Liberty and Union, one and inseparable.' (WHITTIER.)

'Ichabod' and 'The Lost Occasion' (p. 348) should necessarily be read together. The best possible comment on the two poems, from the point of view of to-day, is that of Professor Carpenter: 'Those whom Whittier knew best in later life relate that he came eventually to feel that Webster was perhaps right and he wrong; that compromise meant weary years of waiting, but that the further and consistent pursuit of such a policy might have successfully avoided the evils of war and of reconstruction. However that may be, the verses [of 'Ichabod'] are, in their awful scorn, the most powerful that he ever wrote. Right or wrong, he spoke for a great part of the North and West, nay, for the world. For the poem, in much the same fashion as Browning's 'Lost Leader,' is becoming disassociated with any special name, and may thus remain a most remarkable expression — the most terrible in our literature — of the aversion which any mass of people may feel, especially in a democracy, for the once-worshipped leader whose acts and words, in matters of the greatest public weal, seem to retrograde.' (Carpenter's *Whittier*, pp. 221-222.)

Compare Emerson's 'Webster,' p. 61, and the note on it; and Holmes's 'The Statesman's Secret,' and 'The Birthday of Daniel Webster.' See also Pickard's *Life of Whittier*, vol. i, pp. 327-328.

For the meaning of the title, see 1 Samuel iv, 19-22: 'And she named the child Ichabod, saying, The glory is departed from Israel.' It may have been suggested by an anonymous article of Lowell's on Daniel Webster, in the *Anti-Slavery Standard* (June, 1846), in which he says: 'Shall not the Recording Angel write *Ichabod* after the name of this man in the great book of Doom?' (Scudder's *Life of Lowell*, vol. i, p. 201.)

And pitying tears, not scorn and wrath,
    Befit his fall!

Oh, dumb be passion's stormy rage,
    When he who might   10
Have lighted up and led his age,
    Falls back in night.

Scorn! would the angels laugh, to mark
    A bright soul driven,
Fiend-goaded, down the endless dark,
    From hope and heaven!

Let not the land once proud of him
    Insult him now,
Nor brand with deeper shame his dim,
    Dishonored brow.   20

But let its humbled sons, instead,
    From sea to lake,
A long lament, as for the dead,
    In sadness make.

Of all we loved and honored, naught
    Save power remains;
A fallen angel's pride of thought,
    Still strong in chains.

All else is gone; from those great eyes
    The soul has fled: 30
When faith is lost, when honor dies,
    The man is dead!

Then pay the reverence of old days
    To his dead fame;
Walk backward, with averted gaze,
    And hide the shame!
1850.   1850.

SONGS OF LABOR, DEDICATION

I WOULD the gift I offer here
    Might graces from thy favor take,
And, seen through Friendship's atmo-
        sphere,
On softened lines and coloring, wear
The unaccustomed light of beauty, for thy
        sake.

Few leaves of Fancy's spring remain:
    But what I have I give to thee,
The o'er-sunned bloom of summer's plain,
And paler flowers, the latter rain
Calls from the westering slope of life's
        autumnal lea.   10

Above the fallen groves of green,
   Where youth's enchanted forest stood
Dry root and mossèd trunk between,
   A sober after-growth is seen,
As springs the pine where falls the gay-
     leafed maple wood !

Yet birds will sing, and breezes play
   Their leaf-harps in the sombre tree;
And through the bleak and wintry
     day
It keeps its steady green alway, —
So, even my after-thoughts may have a
     charm for thee.   20

Art's perfect forms no moral need,
   And beauty is its own excuse; [1]
But for the dull and flowerless weed
   Some healing virtue still must plead,
And the rough ore must find its honors in
     its use.

So haply these, my simple lays
   Of homely toil, may serve to show
The orchard bloom and tasselled maize
   That skirt and gladden duty's ways,
The unsung beauty hid life's common
     things below.   30

Haply from them the toiler, bent
   Above his forge or plough, may gain
A manlier spirit of content,
   And feel that life is wisest spent
Where the strong working hand makes
     strong the working brain.

The doom which to the guilty pair
   Without the walls of Eden came,
Transforming sinless ease to care
   And rugged toil, no more shall bear
The burden of old crime, or mark of pri-
     mal shame.   40

A blessing now, a curse no more ;
   Since He, whose name we breathe with
     awe,
The coarse mechanic vesture wore,
   A poor man toiling with the poor,
In labor, as in prayer, fulfilling the same
     law.
                      1850.

[1] For the idea of this line, I am indebted to Emerson, in his inimitable sonnet to the Rhodora, —

   If eyes were made for seeing,
 Then Beauty is its own excuse for being.
                     (WHITTIER.)

WORDSWORTH

WRITTEN ON A BLANK LEAF OF HIS MEMOIRS

DEAR friends, who read the world aright,
   And in its common forms discern
A beauty and a harmony
   The many never learn !

Kindred in soul of him who found
   In simple flower and leaf and stone
The impulse of the sweetest lays
   Our Saxon tongue has known, —

Accept this record of a life
   As sweet and pure, as calm and good,
As a long day of blandest June
   In green field and in wood.

How welcome to our ears, long pained
   By strife of sect and party noise,
The brook-like murmur of his song
   Of nature's simple joys !

The violet by its mossy stone,
   The primrose by the river's brim,
And chance-sown daffodil, have found
   Immortal life through him.

The sunrise on his breezy lake,
   The rosy tints his sunset brought,
World-seen, are gladdening all the vales
   And mountain-peaks of thought.

Art builds on sand; the works of pride
   And human passion change and fall;
But that which shares the life of God
   With Him surviveth all.
                    1851

BENEDICITE

GOD's love and peace be with thee, where
Soe'er this soft autumnal air
Lifts the dark tresses of thy hair !

Whether through city casements comes
Its kiss to thee, in crowded rooms,
Or, out among the woodland blooms,

It freshens o'er thy thoughtful face,
Imparting, in its glad embrace,
Beauty to beauty, grace to grace !

Fair Nature's book together read,   10
The old wood-paths that knew our tread,
The maple shadows overhead, —

The hills we climbed, the river seen
By gleams along its deep ravine, —
All keep thy memory fresh and green.

Where'er I look, where'er I stray,
Thy thought goes with me on my way,
And hence the prayer I breathe to-day;

O'er lapse of time and change of scene,
The weary waste which lies between   20
Thyself and me, my heart I lean.

Thou lack'st not Friendship's spell-word, nor
The half-unconscious power to draw
All hearts to thine by Love's sweet law.

With these good gifts of God is cast
Thy lot, and many a charm thou hast
To hold the blessed angels fast.

If, then, a fervent wish for thee
The gracious heavens will heed from me,
What should, dear heart, its burden be ? 30

The sighing of a shaken reed, —
What can I more than meekly plead
The greatness of our common need ?

God's love, — unchanging, pure, and true, —
The Paraclete white-shining through
His peace, — the fall of Hermon's dew !

With such a prayer, on this sweet day,
As thou mayst hear and I may say,
I greet thee dearest, far away !

                                  1851.

APRIL

The spring comes slowly up this way. — *Christabel.*

'T is the noon of the spring-time, yet never
     a bird
In the wind-shaken elm or the maple is
     heard;
For green meadow-grasses wide levels of
     snow,
And blowing of drifts where the crocus
     should blow;
Where wind-flower and violet, amber and
     white,

On south-sloping brooksides should smile
     in the light,
O'er the cold winter-beds of their late-
     waking roots
The frosty flake eddies, the ice-crystal
     shoots;
And, longing for light, under wind-driven
     heaps,
Round the boles of the pine-wood the
     ground-laurel creeps,   10
Unkissed of the sunshine, unbaptized of
     showers,
With buds scarcely swelled, which should
     burst into flowers !
We wait for thy coming, sweet wind of the
     south !
For the touch of thy light wings, the kiss
     of thy mouth;
For the yearly evangel thou bearest from
     God,
Resurrection and life to the graves of the
     sod !
Up our long river-valley, for days, have not
     ceased
The wail and the shriek of the bitter north-
     east,
Raw and chill, as if winnowed through ices
     and snow,
All the way from the land of the wild Es-
     quimau,   20
Until all our dreams of the land of the
     blest,
Like that red hunter's, turn to the sunny
     southwest.
O soul of the spring-time, its light and its
     breath,
Bring warmth to this coldness, bring life
     to this death;
Renew the great miracle; let us behold
The stone from the mouth of the sepulchre
     rolled,
And Nature, like Lazarus, rise, as of old !
Let our faith, which in darkness and cold-
     ness has lain,
Revive with the warmth and the brightness
     again,
And in blooming of flower and budding of
     tree   30
The symbols and types of our destiny
     see;
The life of the spring-time, the life of the
     whole,
And, as sun to the sleeping earth, love to
     the soul !
                                  1852.

ASTRÆA

Jove means to settle
Astræa in her seat again,
And let down from his golden chain
An age of better metal.
BEN JONSON, 1615.

O POET rare and old !
    Thy words are prophecies;
Forward the age of gold,
    The new Saturnian lies.

The universal prayer
    And hope are not in vain;
Rise, brothers ! and prepare
    The way for Saturn's reign.

Perish shall all which takes
    From labor's board and can;
Perish shall all which makes
    A spaniel of the man !

Free from its bonds the mind,
    The body from the rod;
Broken all chains that bind
    The image of our God.

Just men no longer pine
    Behind their prison-bars;
Through the rent dungeon shine
    The free sun and the stars.

Earth own, at last, untrod
    By sect, or caste, or clan,
The fatherhood of God,
    The brotherhood of man !

Fraud fail, craft perish, forth
    The money-changers driven,
And God's will done on earth,
    As now in heaven !
                            1852.

FIRST-DAY THOUGHTS

IN calm and cool and silence, once again
I find my old accustomed place among
    My brethren, where, perchance, no hu-
        man tongue
    Shall utter words ; where never hymn is
        sung,
    Nor deep-toned organ blown, nor censer
        swung,
Nor dim light falling through the pictured
        pane !

There, syllabled by silence, let me hear
The still small voice which reached the
        prophet's ear;
Read in my heart a still diviner law
Than Israel's leader on his tables saw !
There let me strive with each besetting
        sin,
    Recall my wandering fancies, and re-
        strain
    The sore disquiet of a restless brain;
And, as the path of duty is made plain,
May grace be given that I may walk
        therein,
    Not like the hireling, for his selfish
        gain,
With backward glances and reluctant tread,
Making a merit of his coward dread,
    But, cheerful, in the light around me
        thrown,
    Walking as one to pleasant service led;
Doing God's will as if it were my own,
Yet trusting not in mine, but in his strength
        alone !
                            1852.

THE POOR VOTER ON ELECTION DAY

THE proudest now is but my peer,
    The highest not more high ;
To-day, of all the weary year,
    A king of men am I.
To-day alike are great and small,
    The nameless and the known;
My palace is the people's hall,
    The ballot-box my throne !

Who serves to-day upon the list
    Beside the served shall stand;   10
Alike the brown and wrinkled fist,
    The gloved and dainty hand !
The rich is level with the poor,
    The weak is strong to-day;
And sleekest broadcloth counts no more
    Than homespun frock of gray.

To-day let pomp and vain pretence
    My stubborn right abide;
I set a plain man's common sense
    Against the pedant's pride.   20
To-day shall simple manhood try
    The strength of gold and land ;
The wide world has not wealth to buy
    The power in my right hand !

While there's a grief to seek redress,
  Or balance to adjust,
Where weighs our living manhood less
  Than Mammon's vilest dust, —
While there's a right to need my vote,
  A wrong to sweep away,   30
Up! clouted knee and ragged coat!
  A man's a man to-day!

                                    1852.

SUMMER BY THE LAKESIDE [1]

LAKE WINNIPESAUKEE

I. NOON

WHITE clouds, whose shadows haunt the
    deep,
Light mists, whose soft embraces keep
The sunshine on the hills asleep!

O isles of calm! O dark, still wood!
And stiller skies that overbrood
Your rest with deeper quietude!

O shapes and hues, dim beckoning, through
Yon mountain gaps, my longing view
Beyond the purple and the blue,

To stiller sea and greener land,   10
And softer lights and airs more bland,
And skies, — the hollow of God's hand!

Transfused through you, O mountain
    friends!
With mine your solemn spirit blends,
And life no more hath separate ends.

I read each misty mountain sign,
I know the voice of wave and pine,
And I am yours, and ye are mine.

Life's burdens fall, its discords cease,
I lapse into the glad release   20
Of Nature's own exceeding peace.

O welcome calm of heart and mind!
As falls yon fir-tree's loosened rind
To leave a tenderer growth behind,

So fall the weary years away;
A child again, my head I lay
Upon the lap of this sweet day.

[1] See the note on 'The Lakeside,' p. 281.

This western wind hath Lethean powers,
Yon noonday cloud nepenthe showers,
The lake is white with lotus-flowers!   30

Even Duty's voice is faint and low,
And slumberous Conscience, waking slow,
Forgets her blotted scroll to show.

The Shadow which pursues us all,
Whose ever-nearing steps appall,
Whose voice we hear behind us call, —

That Shadow blends with mountain gray,
It speaks but what the light waves say, —
Death walks apart from Fear to-day!

Rocked on her breast, these pines and I   40
Alike on Nature's love rely;
And equal seems to live or die.

Assured that He whose presence fills
With light the spaces of these hills
No evil to His creatures wills,

The simple faith remains, that He
Will do, whatever that may be,
The best alike for man and tree,

What mosses over one shall grow,
What light and life the other know,   50
Unanxious, leaving Him to show.

II. EVENING

Yon mountain's side is black with night,
  While, broad-orbed, o'er its gleaming
    crown
The moon, slow-rounding into sight,
  On the hushed inland sea looks down.

How start to light the clustering isles,[1]
  Each silver - hemmed! How sharply
    show
The shadows of their rocky piles,
  And tree-tops in the wave below!

How far and strange the mountains seem,   60
  Dim - looming through the pale, still
    light!
The vague, vast grouping of a dream,
  They stretch into the solemn night.

Beneath, lake, wood, and peopled vale,
  Hushed by that presence grand and grave,

[1] There are some three hundred islands in Lake Winnipesaukee.

Are silent, save the cricket's wail,
  And low response of leaf and wave.

Fair scenes ! whereto the Day and Night
  Make rival love, I leave ye soon,
What time before the eastern light   70
  The pale ghost of the setting moon

Shall hide behind yon rocky spines,   /
  And the young archer, Morn, shall
      break
His arrows on the mountain pines,
  And, golden-sandalled, walk the lake !

Farewell ! around this smiling bay
  Gay-hearted Health, and Life in bloom,
With lighter steps than mine, may stray
  In radiant summers yet to come.

But none shall more regretful leave   80
  These waters and these hills than I:
Or, distant, fonder dream how eve
  Or dawn is painting wave and sky;

How rising moons shine sad and mild
  On wooded isle and silvering bay;
Or setting suns beyond the piled
  And purple mountains lead the day;

Nor laughing girl, or bearding boy,
  Nor full-pulsed manhood, lingering
     here,
Shall add, to life's abounding joy,   90
  The charmed repose to suffering dear.

Still waits kind Nature to impart
  Her choicest gifts to such as gain
An entrance to her loving heart
  Through the sharp discipline of pain.

Forever from the Hand that takes
  One blessing from us others fall;
And, soon or late, our Father makes
  His perfect recompense to all !

Oh, watched by Silence and the Night,   100
  And folded in the strong embrace
Of the great mountains, with the light
  Of the sweet heavens upon thy face,

Lake of the Northland ! keep thy dower
  Of beauty still, and while above
Thy solemn mountains speak of power,
  Be thou the mirror of God's love.
                     1853.

BURNS [1]

ON RECEIVING A SPRIG OF HEATHER IN BLOSSOM

No more these simple flowers belong
  To Scottish maid and lover;
Sown in the common soil of song,
  They bloom the wide world over.

In smiles and tears, in sun and showers,
  The minstrel and the heather,
The deathless singer and the flowers
  He sang of live together.

Wild heather-bells and Robert Burns !
  The moorland flower and peasant !   10
How, at their mention, memory turns
  Her pages old and pleasant !

The gray sky wears again its gold
  And purple of adorning,
And manhood's noonday shadows hold
  The dews of boyhood's morning.

The dews that washed the dust and soil
  From off the wings of pleasure,
The sky, that flecked the ground of toil
  With golden threads of leisure.   20

I call to mind the summer day,
  The early harvest mowing,
The sky with sun and clouds at play,
  And flowers with breezes blowing.

[1] When I was fourteen years old my first school-master, Joshua Coffin, the able, eccentric historian of Newbury, brought with him to our house a volume of Burns's poems, from which he read, greatly to my delight. I begged him to leave the book with me, and set myself at once to the task of mastering the glossary of the Scottish dialect at its close. This was about the first poetry I had ever read (with the exception of that of the Bible, of which I had been a close student), and it had a lasting influence upon me. I began to make rhymes myself, and to imagine stories and adventures. (WHITTIER, in his *Autobiographical Letter ;* Carpenter's *Whittier,* pp. 298–299.)

One day we had a call from a 'pawky auld carle' of a wandering Scotchman. To him I owe my first introduction to the songs of Burns. After eating his bread and cheese and drinking his mug of cider he gave us 'Bonny Doon,' 'Highland Mary' and 'Auld Lang Syne.' He had a rich, full voice, and entered heartily into the spirit of his lyrics. I have since listened to the same melodies from the lips of Dempster, than whom the Scottish bard has had no sweeter or truer interpreter ; but the skilful performance of the artist lacked the novel charm of the gaberlunzie's singing in the old farmhouse kitchen. (WHITTIER, 'Yankee Gypsies,' in his *Prose Works,* vol. i, pp. 336–337 ; also quoted in Carpenter's *Whittier,* p. 30.)

I hear the blackbird in the corn,
The locust in the haying;
And, like the fabled hunter's horn,
Old tunes my heart is playing.

How oft that day, with fond delay,
I sought the maple's shadow, 30
And sang with Burns the hours away,
Forgetful of the meadow !

Bees hummed, birds twittered, overhead
I heard the squirrels leaping,
The good dog listened while I read,
And wagged his tail in keeping.

I watched him while in sportive mood
I read 'The Twa Dogs'' story,
And half believed he understood
The poet's allegory. 40

Sweet day, sweet songs ! The golden hours
Grew brighter for that singing,
From brook and bird and meadow flowers
A dearer welcome bringing.

New light on home-seen Nature beamed,
New glory over Woman;
And daily life and duty seemed
No longer poor and common.

I woke to find the simple truth
Of fact and feeling better 50
Than all the dreams that held my youth
A still repining debtor:

That Nature gives her handmaid, Art,
The themes of sweet discoursing;
The tender idyls of the heart
In every tongue rehearsing.

Why dream of lands of gold and pearl,
Of loving knight and lady,
When farmer boy and barefoot girl
Were wandering there already ? 60

I saw through all familiar things
The romance underlying;
The joys and griefs that plume the wings
Of Fancy skyward flying.

I saw the same blithe day return,
The same sweet fall of even,
That rose on wooded Craigie-burn,
And sank on crystal Devon.

I matched with Scotland's heathery hills
The sweetbrier and the clover; 70
With Ayr and Doon, my native rills,
Their wood hymns chanting over.

O'er rank and pomp, as he had seen,
I saw the Man uprising;
No longer common or unclean,
The child of God's baptizing !

With clearer eyes I saw the worth
Of life among the lowly;
The Bible at his Cotter's hearth
Had made my own more holy. 80

And if at times an evil strain,
To lawless love appealing,
Broke in upon the sweet refrain
Of pure and healthful feeling,

It died upon the eye and ear,
No inward answer gaining;
No heart had I to see or hear
The discord and the staining.

Let those who never erred forget
His worth, in vain bewailings; 90
Sweet Soul of Song ! I own my debt
Uncancelled by his failings !

Lament who will the ribald line
Which tells his lapse from duty,
How kissed the maddening lips of wine
Or wanton ones of beauty;

But think, while falls that shade between
The erring one and Heaven,
That he who loved like Magdalen,
Like her may be forgiven. 100

Not his the song whose thunderous chime
Eternal echoes render;
The mournful Tuscan's haunted rhyme,
And Milton's starry splendor !

But who his human heart has laid
To Nature's bosom nearer ?
Who sweetened toil like him, or paid
To love a tribute dearer?

Through all his tuneful art, how strong
The human feeling gushes ! 110
The very moonlight of his song
Is warm with smiles and blushes !

And on a ground of sombre fir,
And azure-studded juniper,
The silver birch its buds of purple shows,
And scarlet berries tell where bloomed the
    sweet wild-rose !

III

With mingled sound of horns and bells,
    A far-heard clang, the wild geese fly,
Storm-sent, from Arctic moors and fells,
    Like a great arrow through the sky, 20
Two dusky lines converged in one,
Chasing the southward-flying sun;
While the brave snow-bird and the hardy
    jay
Call to them from the pines, as if to bid
    them stay.

IV

I passed this way a year ago:
    The wind blew south; the noon of day
Was warm as June's; and save that snow
    Flecked the low mountains far away,
And that the vernal-seeming breeze
Mocked faded grass and leafless trees, 30
I might have dreamed of summer as I lay,
Watching the fallen leaves with the soft
    wind at play.

V

Since then, the winter blasts have piled
    The white pagodas of the snow
On these rough slopes, and, strong and
    wild,
    Yon river, in its overflow
Of spring-time rain and sun, set free,
Crashed with its ices to the sea;
And over these gray fields, then green and
    gold,
The summer corn has waved, the thunder's
    organ rolled.   40

VI

Rich gift of God ! A year of time !
    What pomp of rise and shut of day,
What hues wherewith our Northern
    clime
    Makes autumn's dropping woodlands
    gay,
What airs outblown from ferny dells,
And clover-bloom and sweetbrier smells,
What songs of brooks and birds, what
    fruits and flowers,
Green woods and moonlit snows, have in
    its round been ours !

VII [1]

I know not how, in other lands,
    The changing seasons come and go; 50
What splendors fall on Syrian sands,
    What purple lights on Alpine snow !
Nor how the pomp of sunrise waits
On Venice at her watery gates;
A dream alone to me is Arno's vale,
And the Alhambra's halls are but a travel-
    ler's tale.

VIII

Yet, on life's current, he who drifts
    Is one with him who rows or sails;
And he who wanders widest lifts
    No more of beauty's jealous veils   60
Than he who from his doorway sees
The miracle of flowers and trees,
Feels the warm Orient in the noonday air,
And from cloud minarets hears the sunset
    call to prayer !

IX

The eye may well be glad that looks
    Where Pharpar's fountains rise and fall;
But he who sees his native brooks
    Laugh in the sun, has seen them all.
The marble palaces of Ind
Rise round him in the snow and wind; 70
From his lone sweetbrier Persian Hafiz
    smiles,
And Rome's cathedral awe is in his wood-
    land aisles.

X

And thus it is my fancy blends
    The near at hand and far and rare;

[1] With this and the following stanzas, compare Emerson's ' Written in Naples,' and the note on it ; Lowell's
' An Invitation ; ' Holmes's ' After a Lecture on Wordsworth ; ' and Whittier's ' To —— ':

> No sweeter bowers the bee delayed,
> In wild Hymettus' scented shade,
> Than those you dwell among ;
> Snow-flowered azaleas, intertwined
> With roses, over banks inclined
> With trembling harebells hung !
>
> A charmed life unknown to death,
> Immortal freshness Nature hath ;
> Her fabled fount and glen
> Are now and here : Dodona's shrine
> Still murmurs in the wind-swept pine,—
> All is that e'er hath been.
>
> The Beauty which old Greece or Rome
> Sung, painted, wrought, lies close at home ;
> We need but eye and ear
> In all our daily walks to trace
> The outlines of incarnate grace,
> The hymns of gods to hear !

See also Whittier's Introduction to the *Poems of
J. G. C. Brainard*, quoted in Carpenter's *Whittier*, pp.
86–87 ; and further, in Whittier's own poems, ' Our
River,' and the Prelude to ' Among the Hills.'

And while the same horizon bends
   Above the silver-sprinkled hair
Which flashed the light of morning skies
On childhood's wonder-lifted eyes,
Within its round of sea and sky and field,
Earth wheels with all her zones, the Kosmos
   stands revealed.   80

XI

And thus the sick man on his bed,
   The toiler to his task-work bound,
Behold their prison-walls outspread,
   Their clipped horizon widen round !
While freedom-giving fancy waits,
Like Peter's angel at the gates,
The power is theirs to baffle care and pain,
To bring the lost world back, and make it
   theirs again !

XII

What lack of goodly company,
   When masters of the ancient lyre   90
Obey my call, and trace for me
   Their words of mingled tears and fire !
I talk with Bacon, grave and wise,
I read the world with Pascal's eyes;
And priest and sage, with solemn brows
   austere,
And poets, garland-bound, the Lords of
   Thought, draw near.

XIII

Methinks, O friend, I hear thee say,
   ' In vain the human heart we mock;
Bring living guests who love the day,
   Not ghosts who fly at crow of cock !   100
The herbs we share with flesh and blood
Are better than ambrosial food
With laurelled shades.' I grant it, nothing
   loath,
But doubly blest is he who can partake of
   both.

XIV [1]

He who might Plato's banquet grace,
   Have I not seen before me sit,
And watched his puritanic face,
   With more than Eastern wisdom lit ?
Shrewd mystic ! who, upon the back
Of his Poor Richard's Almanac   110
Writing the Sufi's song, the Gentoo's
   dream,
Links Manu's age of thought to Fulton's
   age of steam !

[1] Stanzas xiv–xvi, Emerson, Bayard Taylor, Sumner.

XV

Here too, of answering love secure,
   Have I not welcomed to my hearth
The gentle pilgrim troubadour,
   Whose songs have girdled half the
   earth;
Whose pages, like the magic mat
Whereon the Eastern lover sat,
Have borne me over Rhine-land's purple
   vines,
And Nubia's tawny sands, and Phrygia's
   mountain pines !   120

XVI

And he, who to the lettered wealth
   Of ages adds the lore unpriced,
The wisdom and the moral health,
   The ethics of the school of Christ;
The statesman to his holy trust,
As the Athenian archon, just,
Struck down, exiled like him for truth
   alone,
Has he not graced my home with beauty all
   his own ?

XVII

What greetings smile, what farewells
   wave,
   What loved ones enter and depart !   130
The good, the beautiful, the brave,
   The Heaven-lent treasures of the
   heart !
How conscious seems the frozen sod
And beechen slope whereon they trod !
The oak-leaves rustle, and the dry grass
   bends
Beneath the shadowy feet of lost or absent
   friends.

XVIII

Then ask not why to these bleak hills
   I cling, as clings the tufted moss,
To bear the winter's lingering chills,   139
   The mocking spring's perpetual loss.
I dream of lands where summer smiles,
And soft winds blow from spicy isles,
But scarce would Ceylon's breath of flow-
   ers be sweet,
Could I not feel thy soil, New England, at
   my feet !

XIX

At times I long for gentler skies,
   And bathe in dreams of softer air,
But homesick tears would fill the eyes

That saw the Cross without the Bear.
The pine must whisper to the palm,
The north-wind break the tropic
  calm;   150
And with the dreamy languor of the
  Line,
The North's keen virtue blend, and strength
  to beauty join.

XX

Better to stem with heart and hand
  The roaring tide of life, than lie,
Unmindful, on its flowery strand,
  Of God's occasions drifting by !
Better with naked nerve to bear
  The needles of this goading air,
Than, in the lap of sensual ease, forego
The godlike power to do, the godlike aim
  to know.   160

XXI

Home of my heart ! to me more fair
  Than gay Versailles or Windsor's halls,
The painted, shingly town-house where
  The freeman's vote for Freedom falls !
The simple roof where prayer is made,
Than Gothic groin and colonnade;
The living temple of the heart of man,
Than Rome's sky-mocking vault, or many-
  spired Milan !

XXII

More dear thy equal village schools,
  Where rich and poor the Bible
    read,   170
Than classic halls where Priestcraft rules,
  And Learning wears the chains of
    Creed;
Thy glad Thanksgiving, gathering in
The scattered sheaves of home and kin,
Than the mad license ushering Lenten
  pains,
Or holidays of slaves who laugh and dance
  in chains.

XXIII

And sweet homes nestle in these dales,
  And perch along these wooded swells;
And, blest beyond Arcadian vales,
  They hear the sound of Sabbath bells !
Here dwells no perfect man sublime,   181
  Nor woman winged before her time,
But with the faults and follies of the race,
Old home-bred virtues hold their not un-
  honored place.

XXIV

Here manhood struggles for the sake
  Of mother, sister, daughter, wife,
The graces and the loves which make
  The music of the march of life;
And woman, in her daily round
  Of duty, walks on holy ground.   190
No unpaid menial tills the soil, nor here
Is the bad lesson learned at human rights
  to sneer.

XXV

Then let the icy north-wind blow
  The trumpets of the coming storm,
To arrowy sleet and blinding snow
  Yon slanting lines of rain transform.
Young hearts shall hail the drifted cold,
  As gayly as I did of old;
And I, who watch them through the frosty
  pane,
Unenvious, live in them my boyhood o'er
  again.   200

XXVI

And I will trust that He who heeds
  The life that hides in mead and wold,
Who hangs yon alder's crimson beads,
  And stains these mosses green and
    gold,
Will still, as He hath done, incline
  His gracious care to me and mine;
Grant what we ask aright, from wrong de-
  bar,
And, as the earth grows dark, make brighter
  every star !

XXVII

I have not seen, I may not see,
  My hopes for man take form in fact,
But God will give the victory   211
  In due time; in that faith I act.
And he who sees the future sure,
  The baffling present may endure,
And bless, meanwhile, the unseen Hand
  that leads
The heart's desires beyond the halting step
  of deeds.

XXVIII

And thou, my song, I send thee forth,
  Where harsher songs of mine have
    flown;
Go, find a place at home and hearth
  Where'er thy singer's name is
    known;   220

Revive for him the kindly thought
Of friends; and they who love him not,
Touched by some strain of thine, perchance
    may take
The hand he proffers all, and thank him for
    thy sake.

1856.   1857.

SKIPPER IRESON'S RIDE [1]

OF all the rides since the birth of time,
Told in story or sung in rhyme, —
On Apuleius's Golden Ass,
Or one-eyed Calender's horse of brass,
Witch astride of a human back,
Islam's prophet on Al-Borák, —
The strangest ride that ever was sped
Was Ireson's, out from Marblehead !
  Old Floyd Ireson, for his hard heart,
  Tarred and feathered and carried in a
    cart   10
    By the women of Marblehead !

Body of turkey, head of owl,
Wings a-droop like a rained-on fowl,
Feathered and ruffled in every part,
Skipper Ireson stood in the cart.
Scores of women, old and young,
Strong of muscle, and glib of tongue,
Pushed and pulled up the rocky lane,
Shouting and singing the shrill refrain:
  ' Here 's Flud Oirson, fur his horrd
    horrt,   20
  Torr'd an' futherr'd an' corr'd in a corrt
    By the women o' Morble'ead ! '

[1] The story of Skipper Ireson was told to Whittier by
a schoolmate from Marblehead, when he was a student
in Haverhill Academy (see Pickard's *Life*, vol. ii, p.
409, and the poem ' A Sea Dream '), and he began to
write the ballad at that time, in 1828. It was finished,
and published in the second number of the *Atlantic
Monthly*, in 1857. Lowell, then editor of the *Atlantic*,
suggested the use of dialect in the refrain (see Scudder's *Life of Lowell*, vol. i, pp. 417–418, and Lowell's
Letters, the letter to Whittier of Nov. 4, 1857).

Mr. Samuel Roads, Jr., in his *History of Marblehead*,
published in 1879, tried to show that Captain Ireson
was not responsible for the abandonment of the disabled ship. Whittier characteristically wrote to Mr.
Roads : —

' . . . I have now no doubt that thy version of Skipper Ireson's ride is the correct one. My verse was
founded solely on a fragment of rhyme which I heard
from one of my early schoolmates, a native of Marblehead. I supposed the story to which it referred dated
back at least a century. I knew nothing of the partici-
pators, and the narrative of the ballad was pure fancy.
I am glad for the sake of truth and justice that the
real facts are given in thy book. I certainly would not
knowingly do injustice to any one, dead or living.

' I am very truly thy friend, JOHN G. WHITTIER.'

Wrinkled scolds with hands on hips,
Girls in bloom of cheek and lips,
Wild-eyed, free-limbed, such as chase
Bacchus round some antique vase,
Brief of skirt, with ankles bare,
Loose of kerchief and loose of hair,
With conch-shells blowing and fish-horns'
    twang,
Over and over the Mænads sang: 30
  ' Here 's Flud Oirson, fur his horrd
    horrt,
  Torr'd an' futherr'd an' corr'd in a corrt
    By the women o' Morble'ead ! '

Small pity for him ! — He sailed away
From a leaking ship in Chaleur Bay, —
Sailed away from a sinking wreck,
With his own town's-people on her deck !
' Lay by ! lay by ! ' they called to him.
Back he answered, ' Sink or swim !
Brag of your catch of fish again ! '   40
And off he sailed through the fog and
    rain !
  Old Floyd Ireson, for his hard heart,
  Tarred and feathered and carried in a
    cart
    By the women of Marblehead !

Fathoms deep in dark Chaleur
That wreck shall lie forevermore.
Mother and sister, wife and maid,
Looked from the rocks of Marblehead
Over the moaning and rainy sea, —
Looked for the coming that might not
    be !   50
What did the winds and the sea-birds
    say
Of the cruel captain who sailed away ? —
  Old Floyd Ireson, for his hard heart,
  Tarred and feathered and carried in a
    cart
    By the women of Marblehead !

Through the street, on either side,
Up flew windows, doors swung wide;
Sharp-tongued spinsters, old wives gray,
Treble lent the fish-horn's bray.
Sea-worn grandsires, cripple-bound,   60
Hulks of old sailors run aground,
Shook head, and fist, and hat, and cane,
And cracked with curses the hoarse re-
    frain :
  ' Here 's Flud Oirson, fur his horrd horrt,
  Torr'd an' futherr'd an' corr'd in a corrt
    By the women o' Morble'ead ! '

Sweetly along the Salem road
Bloom of orchard and lilac showed.
Little the wicked skipper knew
Of the fields so green and the sky so blue.
Riding there in his sorry trim, 71
Like an Indian idol glum and grim,
Scarcely he seemed the sound to hear
Of voices shouting, far and near :
   'Here 's Flud Oirson, fur his horrd horrt,
   Torr'd an' futherr'd an' corr'd in a corrt
     By the women o' Morble'ead ! '

'Hear me, neighbors ! ' at last he cried, —
'What to me is this noisy ride ?
What is the shame that clothes the skin 80
To the nameless horror that lives within ?
Waking or sleeping, I see a wreck,
And hear a cry from a reeling deck !
Hate me and curse me, — I only dread
The hand of God and the face of the dead ! '
   Said old Floyd Ireson, for his hard heart,
   Tarred and feathered and carried in a cart
     By the women of Marblehead !

Then the wife of the skipper lost at sea
Said, 'God has touched him ! why should we ! ' 90
Said an old wife mourning her only son,
'Cut the rogue's tether and let him run ! '
So with soft relentings and rude excuse,
Half scorn, half pity, they cut him loose,
And gave him a cloak to hide him in,
And left him alone with his shame and sin.
   Poor Floyd Ireson, for his hard heart,
   Tarred and feathered and carried in a cart
     By the women of Marblehead !
1828, 1857. 1857.

THE GARRISON OF CAPE ANN

FROM the hills of home forth looking, far
   beneath the tent-like span
Of the sky, I see the white gleam of the
   headland of Cape Ann.
Well I know its coves and beaches to the
   ebb-tide glimmering down,
And the white-walled hamlet children of
   its ancient fishing-town.

Long has passed the summer morning, and
   its memory waxes old,
When along yon breezy headlands with a
   pleasant friend I strolled.

Ah ! the autumn sun is shining, and the
   ocean wind blows cool,
And the golden-rod and aster bloom around
   thy grave, Rantoul !

With the memory of that morning by the
   summer sea I blend
A wild and wondrous story, by the younger
   Mather penned, 10
In that quaint *Magnalia Christi*, with all
   strange and marvellous things,
Heaped up huge and undigested, like the
   chaos Ovid sings.

Dear to me these far, faint glimpses of the
   dual life of old,
Inward, grand with awe and reverence;
   outward, mean and coarse and cold;
Gleams of mystic beauty playing over dull
   and vulgar clay,
Golden-threaded fancies weaving in a web
   of hodden gray.

The great eventful Present hides the Past;
   but through the din
Of its loud life hints and echoes from the
   life behind steal in;
And the lore of home and fireside, and the
   legendary rhyme,
Make the task of duty lighter which the
   true man owes his time. 20

So, with something of the feeling which the
   Covenanter knew,
When with pious chisel wandering Scot-
   land's moorland graveyards through,
From the graves of old traditions I part
   the blackberry-vines,
Wipe the moss from off the headstones,
   and retouch the faded lines.

Where the sea-waves back and forward,
   hoarse with rolling pebbles, ran,
The garrison-house stood watching on the
   gray rocks of Cape Ann;
On its windy site uplifting gabled roof and
   palisade,
And rough walls of unhewn timber with
   the moonlight overlaid.

On his slow round walked the sentry, south
   and eastward looking forth
O'er a rude and broken coast-line, white
   with breakers stretching north, — 30

Wood and rock and gleaming sand-drift,
    jagged capes, with bush and tree,
Leaning inland from the smiting of the
    wild and gusty sea.

Before the deep-mouthed chimney, dimly
    lit by dying brands,
Twenty soldiers sat and waited, with their
    muskets in their hands;
On the rough-hewn oaken table the venison
    haunch was shared,
And the pewter tankard circled slowly
    round from beard to beard.

Long they sat and talked together, —
    talked of wizards Satan-sold;
Of all ghostly sights and noises, — signs
    and wonders manifold;
Of the spectre-ship of Salem, with the dead
    men in her shrouds,
Sailing sheer above the water, in the loom
    of morning clouds;   40

Of the marvellous valley hidden in the
    depths of Gloucester woods,
Full of plants that love the summer, —
    blooms of warmer latitudes;
Where the Arctic birch is braided by the
    tropic's flowery vines,
And the white magnolia-blossoms star the
    twilight of the pines !

But their voices sank yet lower, sank to
    husky tones of fear,
As they spake of present tokens of the
    powers of evil near; —
Of a spectral host, defying stroke of steel
    and aim of gun;
Never yet was ball to slay them in the
    mould of mortals run !

Thrice, with plumes and flowing scalp-locks,
    from the midnight wood they
    came, —
Thrice around the block-house marching,
    met, unharmed, its volleyed flame; 50
Then, with mocking laugh and gesture,
    sunk in earth or lost in air,
All the ghostly wonder vanished, and the
    moonlit sands lay bare.

Midnight came; from out the forest moved
    a dusky mass that soon
Grew to warriors, plumed and painted,
    grimly marching in the moon.

'Ghosts or witches,' said the captain, 'thus
    I foil the Evil One !'
And he rammed a silver button, from his
    doublet, down his gun.

Once again the spectral horror moved the
    guarded wall about;
Once again the levelled muskets through
    the palisades flashed out,
With that deadly aim the squirrel on his
    tree-top might not shun,
Nor the beach-bird seaward flying with his
    slant wing to the sun.   60

Like the idle rain of summer sped the harm-
    less shower of lead.
With a laugh of fierce derision, once again
    the phantoms fled;
Once again, without a shadow on the sands
    the moonlight lay,
And the white smoke curling through it
    drifted slowly down the bay !

'God preserve us !' said the captain ; 'never
    mortal foes were there;
They have vanished with their leader,
    Prince and Power of the air !
Lay aside your useless weapons; skill and
    prowess naught avail;
They who do the Devil's service wear their
    master's coat of mail !'

So the night grew near to cock-crow, when
    again a warning call
Roused the score of weary soldiers watch-
    ing round the dusky hall: 70
And they looked to flint and priming,
    and they longed for break of
    day;
But the captain closed his Bible: 'Let us
    cease from man, and pray !'

To the men who went before us, all the
    unseen powers seemed near,
And their steadfast strength of courage
    struck its roots in holy fear.
Every hand forsook the musket, every head
    was bowed and bare,
Every stout knee pressed the flag-stones,
    as the captain led in prayer.

Ceased thereat the mystic marching of the
    spectres round the wall,
But a sound abhorred, unearthly, smote the
    ears and hearts of all, —

Howls of rage and shrieks of anguish!
   Never after mortal man
Saw the ghostly leaguers marching round
   the block-house of Cape Ann.   80

So to us who walk in summer through the
   cool and sea-blown town,
From the childhood of its people comes the
   solemn legend down.
Not in vain the ancient fiction, in whose
   moral lives the youth
And the fitness and the freshness of an
   undecaying truth.

Soon or late to all our dwellings come the
   spectres of the mind,
Doubts and fears and dread forebodings,
   in the darkness undefined;
Round us throng the grim projections of
   the heart and of the brain,
And our pride of strength is weakness, and
   the cunning hand is vain.

In the dark we cry like children; and no
   answer from on high
Breaks the crystal spheres of silence, and
   no white wings downward fly;   90
But the heavenly help we pray for comes
   to faith, and not to sight,
And our prayers themselves drive backward
   all the spirits of the night!

                 1857.

THE PIPES AT LUCKNOW[1]

PIPES of the misty moorlands,
   Voice of the glens and hills;
The droning of the torrents,
   The treble of the rills!
Not the braes of bloom and heather,
   Nor the mountains dark with rain,
Nor maiden bower, nor border tower,
   Have heard your sweetest strain!

Dear to the Lowland reaper,
   And plaided mountaineer, —   10
To the cottage and the castle
   The Scottish pipes are dear; —
Sweet sounds the ancient pibroch
   O'er mountain, loch, and glade;
But the sweetest of all music
   The pipes at Lucknow played.

[1] An incident of the Siege of Lucknow, during the
mutiny of the native troops in India, 1857. See Tennyson's superb ballad, 'The Relief of Lucknow.'

Day by day the Indian tiger
   Louder yelled, and nearer crept;
Round and round the jungle-serpent
   Near and nearer circles swept.   20
'Pray for rescue, wives and mothers, —
   Pray to-day!' the soldier said;
'To-morrow, death's between us
   And the wrong and shame we dread.'

Oh, they listened, looked, and waited,
   Till their hope became despair;
And the sobs of low bewailing
   Filled the pauses of their prayer.
Then up spake a Scottish maiden,
   With her ear unto the ground: 30
'Dinna ye hear it? — dinna ye hear it?
   The pipes o' Havelock sound!'

Hushed the wounded man his groaning:
   Hushed the wife her little ones;
Alone they heard the drum-roll
   And the roar of Sepoy guns.
But to sounds of home and childhood
   The Highland ear was true; —
As her mother's cradle-crooning
   The mountain pipes she knew.   40

Like the march of soundless music
   Through the vision of the seer,
More of feeling than of hearing,
   Of the heart than of the ear,
She knew the droning pibroch,
   She knew the Campbell's call:
'Hark! hear ye no MacGregor's,
   The grandest o' them all!'

Oh, they listened, dumb and breath-
     less,
   And they caught the sound at last;   50
Faint and far beyond the Goomtee
   Rose and fell the piper's blast!
Then a burst of wild thanksgiving
   Mingled woman's voice and man's;
'God be praised! — the march of Have-
     lock!
   The piping of the clans!'

Louder, nearer, fierce as vengeance,
   Sharp and shrill as swords at strife,
Came the wild MacGregor's clan-call,
   Stinging all the air to life.   60
But when the far-off dust-cloud
   To plaided legions grew,
Full tenderly and blithesomely
   The pipes of rescue blew!

Round the silver domes of Lucknow,
  Moslem mosque and Pagan shrine,
Breathed the air to Britons dearest,
  The air of Auld Lang Syne. [1]
O'er the cruel roll of war-drums
  Rose that sweet and homelike strain;
And the tartan clove the turban,   71
  As the Goomtee cleaves the plain.

Dear to the corn-land reaper
  And plaided mountaineer, —
To the cottage and the castle
  The piper's song is dear.
Sweet sounds the Gaelic pibroch
  O'er mountain, glen, and glade;
But the sweetest of all music   80
  The Pipes at Lucknow played !

1857–1858.   1858.

TELLING THE BEES [2]

HERE is the place; right over the hill
  Runs the path I took;
You can see the gap in the old wall still,
  And the stepping-stones in the shallow
    brook.

There is the house, with the gate red-
    barred,
  And the poplars tall;

[1] It is in strict accordance with the facts of the rescue. In the distance the beleaguered garrison heard the stern and vengeful slogan of the MacGregors, but when the troops of Havelock came in view of the English flag still floating from the Residency, the pipers struck up the immortal air of Burns, 'Should Auld Acquaintance be Forgot.' (WHITTIER, in a letter to Lowell, April 10, 1858.)

[2] A remarkable custom, brought from the Old Country, formerly prevailed in the rural districts of New England. On the death of a member of the family, the bees were at once informed of the event, and their hives dressed in mourning. This ceremonial was supposed to be necessary to prevent the swarms from leaving their hives and seeking a new home. (WHITTIER.)
  The place Whittier had in mind in writing 'Telling the Bees' was his birthplace. There were bee-hives on the garden terrace near the well-sweep, occupied perhaps by the descendants of Thomas Whittier's bees. The approach to the house from over the northern shoulder of Job's Hill by a path that was in constant use in his boyhood and is still in existence, is accurately described in the poem. The 'gap in the old wall' is still to be seen, and 'the stepping-stones in the shallow brook' are still in use. His sister's garden was down by the brook-side in front of the house, and her daffodils are perpetuated and may now be found in their season each year in that place. The red-barred gate, the poplars, the cattle yard with 'the white horns tossing above the wall,' these were all part of Whittier's boy life on the old farm. (Pickard's *Life of Whittier*, vol. ii, pp. 414–415.)
  See also Pickard's *Whittier-Land*, pp. 17–18.

And the barn's brown length, and the cattle-
    yard,
  And the white horns tossing above the
    wall.

There are the beehives ranged in the sun;
  And down by the brink   10
Of the brook are her poor flowers, weed-
    o'errun,
  Pansy and daffodil, rose and pink.

A year has gone, as the tortoise goes,
  Heavy and slow;
And the same rose blows, and the same sun
    glows,
  And the same brook sings of a year ago.

There 's the same sweet clover-smell in the
    breeze;
  And the June sun warm
Tangles his wings of fire in the trees,
  Setting, as then, over Fernside farm.   20

I mind me how with a lover's care
  From my Sunday coat
I brushed off the burrs, and smoothed my
    hair,
  And cooled at the brookside my brow
    and throat.

Since we parted, a month had passed, —
  To love, a year;
Down through the beeches I looked at
    last
  On the little red gate and the well-sweep
    near.

I can see it all now, — the slantwise rain
  Of light through the leaves,   30
The sundown's blaze on her window-pane,
  The bloom of her roses under the eaves.

Just the same as a month before, —
  The house and the trees,
The barn's brown gable, the vine by the
    door, —
  Nothing changed but the hives of bees.

Before them, under the garden wall,
  Forward and back,
Went drearily singing the chore-girl small,
  Draping each hive with a shred of black.

Trembling, I listened: the summer sun   41
  Had the chill of snow;

For I knew she was telling the bees of one
    Gone on the journey we all must go !

Then I said to myself, ' My Mary weeps
    For the dead to-day;
Haply her blind old grandsire sleeps
    The fret and the pain of his age away.'

But her dog whined low; on the doorway
    sill,
    With his cane to his chin,   50
The old man sat; and the chore-girl still
    Sung to the bees stealing out and in.

And the song she was singing ever since
    In my ear sounds on: —
' Stay at home, pretty bees, fly not hence !
    Mistress Mary is dead and gone ! '

                              1858.

THE CABLE HYMN

O LONELY bay of Trinity,
    O dreary shores, give ear !
Lean down unto the white-lipped sea
    The voice of God to hear !

From world to world his couriers fly,
    Thought-winged and shod with fire;
The angel of his stormy sky
    Rides down the sunken wire.

What saith the herald of the Lord ?
    ' The world's long strife is done;   10
Close wedded by that mystic cord,
    Its continents are one.

' And one in heart, as one in blood,
    Shall all her peoples be;
The hands of human brotherhood
    Are clasped beneath the sea.

' Through Orient seas, o'er Afric's plain
    And Asian mountains borne,
The vigor of the Northern brain
    Shall nerve the world outworn.   20

' From clime to clime, from shore to shore,
    Shall thrill the magic thread;
The new Prometheus steals once more
    The fire that wakes the dead.'

Throb on, strong pulse of thunder! beat
    From answering beach to beach;

Fuse nations in thy kindly heat,
    And melt the chains of each !

Wild terror of the sky above,
    Glide tamed and dumb below !   30
Bear gently, Ocean's carrier-dove,
    Thy errands to and fro.

Weave on, swift shuttle of the Lord,
    Beneath the deep so far,
The bridal robe of earth's accord,
    The funeral shroud of war !

For lo ! the fall of Ocean's wall
    Space mocked and time outrun;
And round the world the thought of all
    Is as the thought of one !   40

The poles unite, the zones agree,
    The tongues of striving cease;
As on the Sea of Galilee
    The Christ is whispering, Peace !
1858.   1858.

MY PSALM

I MOURN no more my vanished years:
    Beneath a tender rain,
An April rain of smiles and tears,
    My heart is young again.

The west-winds blow, and, singing low,
    I hear the glad streams run;
The windows of my soul I throw
    Wide open to the sun.

No longer forward nor behind
    I look in hope or fear;   10
But, grateful, take the good I find,
    The best of now and here.

I plough no more a desert land,
    To harvest weed and tare;
The manna dropping from God's hand
    Rebukes my painful care.

I break my pilgrim staff, I lay
    Aside the toiling oar;
The angel sought so far away
    I welcome at my door.   20

The airs of spring may never play
    Among the ripening corn,
Nor freshness of the flowers of May
    Blow through the autumn morn;

Yet shall the blue-eyed gentian look
    Through fringèd lids to heaven,
And the pale aster in the brook
    Shall see its image given; —

The woods shall wear their robes of praise,
    The south-wind softly sigh,   30
And sweet, calm days in golden haze
    Melt down the amber sky.

Not less shall manly deed and word
    Rebuke an age of wrong;
The graven flowers that wreathe the sword
    Make not the blade less strong.

But smiting hands shall learn to heal, —
    To build as to destroy;
Nor less my heart for others feel
    That I the more enjoy.   40

All as God wills, who wisely heeds
    To give or to withhold,
And knoweth more of all my needs
    Than all my prayers have told !

Enough that blessings undeserved
    Have marked my erring track;
That whereso'er my feet have swerved,
    His chastening turned me back;

That more and more a Providence
    Of love is understood,   50
Making the springs of time and sense
    Sweet with eternal good; —

That death seems but a covered way
    Which opens into light,
Wherein no blinded child can stray
    Beyond the Father's sight;

That care and trial seem at last,
    Through Memory's sunset air,
Like mountain-ranges overpast,
    In purple distance fair;   60

That all the jarring notes of life
    Seem blending in a psalm,
And all the angles of its strife
    Slow rounding into calm.

And so the shadows fall apart,
    And so the west-winds play;
And all the windows of my heart
    I open to the day.

                         1859.

BROWN OF OSSAWATOMIE

John Brown of Ossawatomie spake on his
    dying day:
'I will not have to shrive my soul a priest
    in Slavery's pay.
But let some poor slave-mother whom I
    have striven to free,
With her children, from the gallows-stair
    put up a prayer for me !'

John Brown of Ossawatomie, they led him
    out to die;
And lo ! a poor slave-mother with her little
    child pressed nigh.
Then the bold, blue eye grew tender, and
    the old harsh face grew mild,
As he stooped between the jeering ranks
    and kissed the negro's child !

The shadows of his stormy life that moment
    fell apart;
And they who blamed the bloody hand for-
    gave the loving heart.
That kiss from all its guilty means re-
    deemed the good intent,
And round the grisly fighter's hair the mar-
    tyr's aureole bent !

Perish with him the folly that seeks through
    evil good !
Long live the generous purpose unstained
    with human blood !
Not the raid of midnight terror, but the
    thought which underlies;
Not the borderer's pride of daring, but the
    Christian's sacrifice.

Nevermore may yon Blue Ridges the North-
    ern rifle hear,
Nor see the light of blazing homes flash on
    the negro's spear.
But let the free-winged angel Truth their
    guarded passes scale,
To teach that right is more than might, and
    justice more than mail !

So vainly shall Virginia set her battle in
    array;
In vain her trampling squadrons knead the
    winter snow with clay.
She may strike the pouncing eagle, but she
    dares not harm the dove;
And every gate she bars to Hate shall open
    wide to Love !   1859.

MY PLAYMATE [1]

THE pines were dark on Ramoth hill,
　　Their song was soft and low;
The blossoms in the sweet May wind
　　Were falling like the snow.

The blossoms drifted at our feet,
　　The orchard birds sang clear;
The sweetest and the saddest day
　　It seemed of all the year.

For, more to me than birds or flowers,
　　My playmate left her home, 　　　10
And took with her the laughing spring,
　　The music and the bloom.

She kissed the lips of kith and kin,
　　She laid her hand in mine:
What more could ask the bashful boy
　　Who fed her father's kine ?

She left us in the bloom of May:
　　The constant years told o'er
Their seasons with as sweet May morns,
　　But she came back no more. 　　　20

I walk, with noiseless feet, the round
　　Of uneventful years;
Still o'er and o'er I sow the spring
　　And reap the autumn ears.

She lives where all the golden year
　　Her summer roses blow;
The dusky children of the sun
　　Before her come and go.

There haply with her jewelled hands
　　She smooths her silken gown, — 　　30
No more the homespun lap wherein
　　I shook the walnuts down.

The wild grapes wait us by the brook,
　　The brown nuts on the hill,
And still the May-day flowers make sweet
　　The woods of Follymill.

The lilies blossom in the pond,
　　The bird builds in the tree,
The dark pines sing on Ramoth hill
　　The slow song of the sea. 　　　40

I wonder if she thinks of them,
　　And how the old time seems, —
If ever the pines of Ramoth wood
　　Are sounding in her dreams.

I see her face, I hear her voice;
　　Does she remember mine ?
And what to her is now the boy
　　Who fed her father's kine ?

What cares she that the orioles build
　　For other eyes than ours, — 　　50
That other hands with nuts are filled,
　　And other laps with flowers ?

O playmate in the golden time !
　　Our mossy seat is green,
Its fringing violets blossom yet,
　　The old trees o'er it lean.

The winds so sweet with birch and fern
　　A sweeter memory blow;
And there in spring the veeries sing
　　The song of long ago. 　　　60

And still the pines of Ramoth wood
　　Are moaning like the sea, —
The moaning of the sea of change
　　Between myself and thee !

1859–1860. 　　　　　　　　　　1860.

TO WILLIAM H. SEWARD [2]

STATESMAN, I thank thee ! and, if yet dissent
Mingles, reluctant, with my large content,
I cannot censure what was nobly meant.
But, while constrained to hold even Union less
Than Liberty and Truth and Righteousness,
I thank thee in the sweet and holy name
Of peace, for wise calm words that put to shame
Passion and party. Courage may be shown
Not in defiance of the wrong alone;
He may be bravest who, unweaponed, bears

---

[1] Compare the poem ' Memories,' and see Pickard's *Life of Whittier*, vol. i, p. 276, vol. ii, pp. 426–428, and *Whittier-Land*, pp. 66–67.

　Tennyson said of this poem and of Whittier, ' It is a perfect poem ; in some of his descriptions of scenery and wild-flowers, he would rank with Wordsworth.'

[2] On the 12th of January, 1861, Mr. Seward delivered in the Senate chamber a speech on ' The State of the Union,' in which he urged the paramount duty of preserving the Union, and went as far as it was possible to go, without surrender of principles, in concessions to the Southern party. (WHITTIER.)

The olive branch, and, strong in justice,
        spares
The rash wrong-doer, giving widest scope
To Christian charity and generous hope.
If, without damage to the sacred cause
Of Freedom and the safeguard of its laws —
If, without yielding that for which alone
We prize the Union, thou canst save it now
From a baptism of blood, upon thy brow
A wreath whose flowers no earthly soil
        have known,
Woven of the beatitudes, shall rest,
And the peacemaker be forever blest !
1861.   1861.

OUR RIVER

FOR A SUMMER FESTIVAL AT 'THE
    LAURELS' ON THE MERRIMAC

ONCE more on yonder laurelled height
    The summer flowers have budded;
Once more with summer's golden light
    The vales of home are flooded;
And once more, by the grace of Him
    Of every good the Giver,
We sing upon its wooded rim
    The praises of our river:

Its pines above, its waves below,
    The west-wind down it blowing,   10
As fair as when the young Brissot
    Beheld it seaward flowing, —
And bore its memory o'er the deep,
    To soothe the martyr's sadness,
And fresco, in his troubled sleep,
    His prison-walls with gladness.

We know the world is rich with streams
    Renowned in song and story,
Whose music murmurs through our dreams
    Of human love and glory: 20
We know that Arno's banks are fair,
    And Rhine has castled shadows,
And, poet-tuned, the Doon and Ayr
    Go singing down their meadows.

But while, unpictured and unsung
    By painter or by poet,
Our river waits the tuneful tongue
    And cunning hand to show it, —
We only know the fond skies lean
    Above it, warm with blessing,   30
And the sweet soul of our Undine
    Awakes to our caressing.

No fickle sun-god holds the flocks
    That graze its shores in keeping;
No icy kiss of Dian mocks
    The youth beside it sleeping :
Our Christian river loveth most
    The beautiful and human;
The heathen streams of Naiads boast,
    But ours of man and woman.   40

The miner in his cabin hears
    The ripple we are hearing;
It whispers soft to homesick ears
    Around the settler's clearing:
In Sacramento's vales of corn,
    Or Santee's bloom of cotton,
Our river by its valley-born
    Was never yet forgotten.

The drum rolls loud, the bugle fills
    The summer air with clangor;   50
The war-storm shakes the solid hills
    Beneath its tread of anger;
Young eyes that last year smiled in ours
    Now point the rifle's barrel,
And hands then stained with fruit and
        flowers
    Bear redder stains of quarrel.

But blue skies smile, and flowers bloom
        on,
    And rivers still keep flowing,
The dear God still his rain and sun
    On good and ill bestowing.   60
His pine-trees whisper, 'Trust and wait !'
    His flowers are prophesying
That all we dread of change or fate
    His love is underlying.

And thou, O Mountain-born ! — no more
    We ask the wise Allotter
Than for the firmness of thy shore,
    The calmness of thy water,
The cheerful lights that overlay
    Thy rugged slopes with beauty,   70
To match our spirits to our day
    And make a joy of duty.
1861.   1861.

AMY WENTWORTH

HER fingers shame the ivory keys
    They dance so light along;
The bloom upon her parted lips
    Is sweeter than the song.

O perfumed suitor, spare thy smiles !
  Her thoughts are not of thee;
She better loves the salted wind,
  The voices of the sea.

Her heart is like an outbound ship
  That at its anchor swings;   10
The murmur of the stranded shell
  Is in the song she sings.

She sings, and, smiling, hears her praise,
  But dreams the while of one
Who watches from his sea-blown deck
  The icebergs in the sun.

She questions all the winds that blow,
  And every fog-wreath dim,
And bids the sea-birds flying north
  Bear messages to him.   20

She speeds them with the thanks of
      men
  He perilled life to save,
And grateful prayers like holy oil
  To smooth for him the wave.

Brown Viking of the fishing-smack
  Fair toast of all the town ! —
The skipper's jerkin ill beseems
  The lady's silken gown !

But ne'er shall Amy Wentworth wear
  For him the blush of shame   30
Who dares to set his manly gifts
  Against her ancient name.

The stream is brightest at its spring,
  And blood is not like wine;
Nor honored less than he who heirs
  Is he who founds a line.

Full lightly shall the prize be won,
  If love be Fortune's spur;
And never maiden stoops to him
  Who lifts himself to her.   40

Her home is brave in Jaffrey Street,
  With stately stairways worn
By feet of old Colonial knights
  And ladies gentle-born.

Still green about its ample porch
  The English ivy twines,
Trained back to show in English oak
  The herald's carven signs.

And on her, from the wainscot old,
  Ancestral faces frown, —   50
And this has worn the soldier's sword,
  And that the judge's gown.

But, strong of will and proud as they,
  She walks the gallery floor
As if she trod her sailor's deck
  By stormy Labrador !

The sweetbrier blooms on Kittery-side,
  And green are Elliot's bowers;
Her garden is the pebbled beach,
  The mosses are her flowers.   60

She looks across the harbor-bar
  To see the white gulls fly;
His greeting from the Northern sea
  Is in their clanging cry.

She hums a song, and dreams that he,
  As in its romance old,
Shall homeward ride with silken sails
  And masts of beaten gold !

Oh, rank is good, and gold is fair,
  And high and low mate ill;   70
But love has never known a law
  Beyond its own sweet will !

                                          1862.

THE WAITING

I WAIT and watch: before my eyes
  Methinks the night grows thin and gray;
I wait and watch the eastern skies
To see the golden spears uprise
  Beneath the oriflamme of day !

Like one whose limbs are bound in
      trance
  I hear the day-sounds swell and grow,
And see across the twilight glance,
Troop after troop, in swift advance,
  The shining ones with plumes of snow ! 10

I know the errand of their feet,
  I know what mighty work is theirs;
I can but lift up hands unmeet
The threshing-floors of God to beat,
  And speed them with unworthy prayers

I will not dream in vain despair
  The steps of progress wait for me:

The puny leverage of a hair
The planet's impulse well may spare,
  A drop of dew the tided sea.   20

The loss, if loss there be, is mine,
  And yet not mine if understood;
For one shall grasp and one resign,
One drink life's rue, and one its wine,
  And God shall make the balance good.

Oh power to do ! Oh baffled will !
  Oh prayer and action ! ye are one.
Who may not strive, may yet fulfil
The harder task of standing still,   29
  And good but wished with God is done !
                                    1862.[1]

THE WATCHERS

BESIDE a stricken field I stood ;
On the torn turf, on grass and wood,
Hung heavily the dew of blood.

Still in their fresh mounds lay the slain,
But all the air was quick with pain
And gusty sighs and tearful rain.

Two angels, each with drooping head
And folded wings and noiseless tread,
Watched by that valley of the dead.

The one, with forehead saintly bland   10
And lips of blessing, not command,
Leaned, weeping, on her olive wand.

The other's brows were scarred and knit,
His restless eyes were watch-fires lit,
His hands for battle-gauntlets fit.

'How long !' — I knew the voice of
                                    Peace, —
'Is there no respite ? no release ?
When shall the hopeless quarrel cease ?

'O Lord, how long ! One human soul
Is more than any parchment scroll,   20
Or any flag thy winds unroll.

'What price was Ellsworth's, young and
                                    brave ?
How weigh the gift that Lyon gave,
Or count the cost of Winthrop's grave ?

[1] The physical limitations which made it impossible
for Whittier to take an active part in public affairs
were especially hard for him to bear during these
years. Compare Milton's Sonnet ' On his Blindness.'

'O brother ! if thine eye can see,
Tell how and when the end shall be,
What hope remains for thee and me.'

Then Freedom sternly said : 'I shun
No strife nor pang beneath the sun,
When human rights are staked and won.   30

'I knelt with Ziska's hunted flock,
I watched in Toussaint's cell of rock,
I walked with Sidney to the block.

'The moor of Marston felt my tread,
Through Jersey snows the march I led,
My voice Magenta's charges sped.

'But now, through weary day and night,
I watch a vague and aimless fight
For leave to strike one blow aright.

'On either side my foe they own :   40
One guards through love his ghastly throne,
And one through fear to reverence grown.

'Why wait we longer, mocked, betrayed,
By open foes, or those afraid
To speed thy coming through my aid ?

'Why watch to see who win or fall ?
I shake the dust against them all,
I leave them to their senseless brawl.'

'Nay,' Peace implored: 'yet longer wait;
The doom is near, the stake is great: 50
God knoweth if it be too late.

'Still wait and watch; the way prepare
Where I with folded wings of prayer
May follow, weaponless and bare.'

'Too late !' the stern, sad voice replied,
'Too late !' its mournful echo sighed.
In low lament the answer died.

A rustling as of wings in flight,
An upward gleam of lessening white,
So passed the vision, sound and sight.   60

But round me, like a silver bell
Rung down the listening sky to tell
Of holy help, a sweet voice fell.

'Still hope and trust,' it sang; 'the rod
Must fall, the wine-press must be trod,
But all is possible with God !'   1862.

ANDREW RYKMAN'S PRAYER[1]

ANDREW RYKMAN 's dead and gone;
  You can see his leaning slate
In the graveyard, and thereon
  Read his name and date.

' *Trust is truer than our fears,*'
  Runs the legend through the moss,
' *Gain is not in added years,*
  Nor in death is loss.'

Still the feet that thither trod,
  All the friendly eyes are dim;   10
Only Nature, now, and God
  Have a care for him.

There the dews of quiet fall,
  Singing birds and soft winds stray:
Shall the tender Heart of all
  Be less kind than they ?

What he was and what he is
  They who ask may haply find,
If they read this prayer of his
  Which he left behind.   20

———

Pardon, Lord, the lips that dare
Shape in words a mortal's prayer !
Prayer, that, when my day is done,
And I see its setting sun,
Shorn and beamless, cold and dim,
Sink beneath the horizon's rim, —
When this ball of rock and clay
Crumbles from my feet away,
And the solid shores of sense
Melt into the vague immense,   30
Father ! I may come to Thee
Even with the beggar's plea,
As the poorest of thy poor,
With my needs, and nothing more.

Not as one who seeks his home
With a step assured I come;
Still behind the tread I hear
Of my life-companion, Fear;
Still a shadow deep and vast
From my westering feet is cast,   40

[1] In June, 1862, Whittier wrote to Fields, then editor of the *Atlantic :* ' I have by me a poem upon which I have bestowed much thought, and which I think is in some respects the best thing I have ever written. I will bring it or send it soon.' This poem was ' Andrew Rykman's Prayer.'

Wavering, doubtful, undefined,
Never shapen nor outlined:
From myself the fear has grown,
And the shadow is my own.
Yet, O Lord, through all a sense
Of thy tender providence
Stays my failing heart on Thee,
And confirms the feeble knee;
And, at times, my worn feet press
Spaces of cool quietness,   50
Lilied whiteness shone upon
Not by light of moon or sun.
Hours there be of inmost calm,
Broken but by grateful psalm,
When I love Thee more than fear Thee,
And thy blessed Christ seems near me,
With forgiving look, as when
He beheld the Magdalen.
Well I know that all things move
To the spheral rhythm of love, —   60
That to Thee, O Lord of all !
Nothing can of chance befall:
Child and seraph, mote and star,
Well Thou knowest what we are !
Through thy vast creative plan
Looking, from the worm to man,
There is pity in thine eyes,
But no hatred nor surprise.
Not in blind caprice of will,
Not in cunning sleight of skill,   70
Not for show of power, was wrought
Nature's marvel in thy thought.
Never careless hand and vain
Smites these chords of joy and pain;
No immortal selfishness
Plays the game of curse and bless:
Heaven and earth are witnesses
That thy glory goodness is.
Not for sport of mind and force
Hast Thou made thy universe,   80
But as atmosphere and zone
Of thy loving heart alone.
Man, who walketh in a show,
Sees before him, to and fro,
Shadow and illusion go;
All things flow and fluctuate,
Now contract and now dilate.
In the welter of this sea,
Nothing stable is but Thee;
In this whirl of swooning trance,   90
Thou alone art permanence;
All without Thee only seems,
All beside is choice of dreams.
Never yet in darkest mood
Doubted I that Thou wast good,

Nor mistook my will for fate,
Pain of sin for heavenly hate, —
Never dreamed the gates of pearl
Rise from out the burning marl,
Or that good can only live   100
Of the bad conservative,
And through counterpoise of hell
Heaven alone be possible.

For myself alone I doubt;
All is well, I know, without;
I alone the beauty mar,
I alone the music jar.
Yet, with hands by evil stained,
And an ear by discord pained,
I am groping for the keys   110
Of the heavenly harmonies;
Still within my heart I bear
Love for all things good and fair.
Hands of want or souls in pain
Have not sought my door in vain;
I have kept my fealty good
To the human brotherhood;
Scarcely have I asked in prayer
That which others might not share.
I, who hear with secret shame   120
Praise that paineth more than blame,
Rich alone in favors lent,
Virtuous by accident,
Doubtful where I fain would rest,
Frailest where I seem the best,
Only strong for lack of test, —
What am I, that I should press
Special pleas of selfishness,
Coolly mounting into heaven
On my neighbor unforgiven?   130
Ne'er to me, howe'er disguised,
Comes a saint unrecognized;
Never fails my heart to greet
Noble deed with warmer beat;
Halt and maimed, I own not less
All the grace of holiness;
Nor, through shame or self-distrust,
Less I love the pure and just.
Lord, forgive these words of mine:
What have I that is not Thine?   140
Whatsoe'er I fain would boast
Needs thy pitying pardon most.
Thou, O Elder Brother! who
In thy flesh our trial knew,
Thou, who hast been touched by these
Our most sad infirmities,
Thou alone the gulf canst span
In the dual heart of man,
And between the soul and sense

Reconcile all difference,   150
Change the dream of me and mine
For the truth of Thee and thine,
And, through chaos, doubt, and strife,
Interfuse thy calm of life.
Haply, thus by Thee renewed,
In thy borrowed goodness good,
Some sweet morning yet in God's
Dim, æonian periods,
Joyful I shall wake to see
Those I love who rest in Thee   160
And to them in Thee allied,
Shall my soul be satisfied.

Scarcely Hope hath shaped for me
What the future life may be.
Other lips may well be bold;
Like the publican of old,
I can only urge the plea,
'Lord, be merciful to me!'
Nothing of desert I claim,
Unto me belongeth shame.   170
Not for me the crowns of gold,
Palms, and harpings manifold;
Not for erring eye and feet
Jasper wall and golden street.
What Thou wilt, O Father, give!
All is gain that I receive.
If my voice I may not raise
In the elders' song of praise,
If I may not, sin-defiled,
Claim my birthright as a child,   180
Suffer it that I to Thee
As an hired servant be;
Let the lowliest task be mine,
Grateful, so the work be thine;
Let me find the humblest place
In the shadow of thy grace:
Blest to me were any spot
Where temptation whispers not.
If there be some weaker one,
Give me strength to help him on;   190
If a blinder soul there be,
Let me guide him nearer Thee.
Make my mortal dreams come true
With the work I fain would do;
Clothe with life the weak intent,
Let me be the thing I meant;
Let me find in thy employ
Peace that dearer is than joy;
Out of self to love be led
And to heaven acclimated,   200
Until all things sweet and good
Seem my natural habitude.

So we read the prayer of him
  Who, with John of Labadie,
Trod, of old, the oozy rim
  Of the Zuyder Zee.

Thus did Andrew Rykman pray.
  Are we wiser, better grown,
That we may not, in our day,
  Make his prayer our own ?   210
1862.   1863.

BARBARA FRIETCHIE[1]

UP from the meadows rich with corn,
Clear in the cool September morn,

The clustered spires of Frederick stand
Green-walled by the hills of Maryland.

Round about them orchards sweep,
Apple and peach tree fruited deep,

Fair as the garden of the Lord
To the eyes of the famished rebel horde,

On that pleasant morn of the early fall
When Lee marched over the mountain-
    wall;   10

Over the mountains winding down,
Horse and foot, into Frederick town.

Forty flags with their silver stars,
Forty flags with their crimson bars,

Flapped in the morning wind: the sun
Of noon looked down, and saw not one.

Up rose old Barbara Frietchie then,
Bowed with her fourscore years and ten;

Bravest of all in Frederick town,
She took up the flag the men hauled down; 20

In her attic window the staff she set,
To show that one heart was loyal yet.

Up the street came the rebel tread,
Stonewall Jackson riding ahead.

Under his slouched hat left and right
He glanced; the old flag met his sight.

[1] On the authenticity of the story see Pickard's *Life of Whittier*, vol. ii, pp. 454-459.

'Halt !' — the dust-brown ranks stood
    fast.
'Fire !' — out blazed the rifle-blast.

It shivered the window, pane and sash;
It rent the banner with seam and gash. 30

Quick, as it fell, from the broken staff
Dame Barbara snatched the silken scarf.

She leaned far out on the window-sill,
And shook it forth with a royal will.

'Shoot, if you must, this old gray head,
But spare your country's flag,' she
    said.

A shade of sadness, a blush of shame,
Over the face of the leader came;

The nobler nature within him stirred
To life at that woman's deed and
    word;   40

'Who touches a hair of yon gray head
Dies like a dog ! March on !' he said.

All day long through Frederick street
Sounded the tread of marching feet:

All day long that free flag tost
Over the heads of the rebel host.

Ever its torn folds rose and fell
On the loyal winds that loved it well;

And through the hill-gaps sunset light
Shone over it with a warm good-night. 50

Barbara Frietchie's work is o'er,
And the Rebel rides on his raids no
    more.

Honor to her ! and let a tear
Fall, for her sake, on Stonewall's bier.

Over Barbara Frietchie's grave,
Flag of Freedom and Union, wave !

Peace and order and beauty draw
Round thy symbol of light and law;

And ever the stars above look down
On thy stars below in Frederick town ! 60
1863.   1863.

THE WRECK OF RIVERMOUTH [1]

RIVERMOUTH Rocks are fair to see,
  By dawn or sunset shone across,
When the ebb of the sea has left them
    free
  To dry their fringes of gold-green moss:
For there the river comes winding down,
From salt sea-meadows and uplands brown,
And waves on the outer rocks afoam
Shout to its waters, ' Welcome home ! '

And fair are the sunny isles in view
  East of the grisly Head of the Boar,   10
And Agamenticus lifts its blue
  Disk of a cloud the woodlands o'er;
And southerly, when the tide is down,
'Twixt white sea-waves and sand-hills
    brown,
The beach-birds dance and the gray gulls
    wheel
Over a floor of burnished steel.

Once, in the old Colonial days,
  Two hundred years ago and more,
A boat sailed down through the winding
    ways
  Of Hampton River to that low shore,   20
Full of a goodly company
Sailing out on the summer sea,
Veering to catch the land-breeze light,
With the Boar to left and the Rocks to
    right.

In Hampton meadows, where mowers laid
  Their scythes to the swaths of salted
    grass,
' Ah, well-a-day ! our hay must be made ! '
  A young man sighed, who saw them pass.
Loud laughed his fellows to see him stand
Whetting his scythe with a listless hand,   30
Hearing a voice in a far-off song,
Watching a white hand beckoning long.

[1] The Goody Cole who figures in this poem and ' The Changeling ' was Eunice Cole, who for a quarter of a century or more was feared, persecuted, and hated as the witch of Hampton. She lived alone in a hovel a little distant from the spot where the Hampton Academy now stands, and there she died, unattended. When her death was discovered, she was hastily covered up in the earth near by, and a stake driven through her body, to exorcise the evil spirit. Rev. Stephen Bachiler or Batchelder was one of the ablest of the early New England preachers. His marriage late in life to a woman regarded by his church as disreputable induced him to return to England, where he enjoyed the esteem and favor of Oliver Cromwell during the Protectorate. (WHITTIER.)
See also Pickard's *Whittier-Land*, pp. 88-89.

' Fie on the witch ! ' cried a merry girl,
  As they rounded the point where Goody
    Cole
Sat by her door with her wheel atwirl,
  A bent and blear-eyed poor old soul.
' Oho ! ' she muttered, ' ye 're brave to-
    day !
But I hear the little waves laugh and say,
" The broth will be cold that waits at
    home;
For it 's one to go, but another to come ! " '

' She 's cursed,' said the skipper ; ' speak
    her fair: 41
I 'm scary always to see her shake
Her wicked head, with its wild gray hair,
  And nose like a hawk, and eyes like a
    snake.'
But merrily still, with laugh and shout,
From Hampton River the boat sailed out,
Till the huts and the flakes on Star seemed
    nigh,
And they lost the scent of the pines of Rye.

They dropped their lines in the lazy tide,
  Drawing up haddock and mottled cod; 50
They saw not the Shadow that walked be-
    side,
  They heard not the feet with silence shod.
But thicker and thicker a hot mist grew,
Shot by the lightnings through and through;
And muffled growls, like the growl of a
    beast,
Ran along the sky from west to east.

Then the skipper looked from the darken-
    ing sea
  Up to the dimmed and wading sun;
But he spake like a brave man cheerily,
  ' Yet there is time for our homeward
    run.'   60
Veering and tacking, they backward wore;
And just as a breath from the woods ashore
Blew out to whisper of danger past,
The wrath of the storm came down at last !

The skipper hauled at the heavy sail:
  ' God be our help ! ' he only cried,
As the roaring gale, like the stroke of a
    flail,
  Smote the boat on its starboard side.
The Shoalsmen looked, but saw alone
Dark films of rain-cloud slantwise blown, 70
Wild rocks lit up by the lightning's glare,
The strife and torment of sea and air.

Goody Cole looked out from her door:
  The Isles of Shoals were drowned and
    gone,
Scarcely she saw the Head of the Boar
  Toss the foam from tusks of stone.
She clasped her hands with a grip of pain,
The tear on her cheek was not of rain:
'They are lost,' she muttered, 'boat and
  crew!
Lord, forgive me! my words were true!' 80

Suddenly seaward swept the squall;
  The low sun smote through cloudy rack;
The Shoals stood clear in the light, and all
  The trend of the coast lay hard and black.
But far and wide as eye could reach,
No life was seen upon wave or beach;
The boat that went out at morning never
Sailed back again into Hampton River.

O mower, lean on thy bended snath,
  Look from the meadows green and low: 90
The wind of the sea is a waft of death,
  The waves are singing a song of woe!
By silent river, by moaning sea,
Long and vain shall thy watching be:
Never again shall the sweet voice call,
Never the white hand rise and fall!

O Rivermouth Rocks, how sad a sight
  Ye saw in the light of breaking day!
Dead faces looking up cold and white
  From sand and seaweed where they lay.
The mad old witch-wife wailed and wept, 101
And cursed the tide as it backward crept:
'Crawl back, crawl back, blue water-snake!
Leave your dead for the hearts that break!'

Solemn it was in that old day
  In Hampton town and its log-built church,
Where side by side the coffins lay
  And the mourners stood in aisle and
    porch.
In the singing-seats young eyes were dim,
The voices faltered that raised the hymn, 110
And Father Dalton, grave and stern,
Sobbed through his prayer and wept in turn.

But his ancient colleague did not pray;
  Under the weight of his fourscore years
He stood apart with the iron-gray
  Of his strong brows knitted to hide his
    tears;
And a fair-faced woman of doubtful fame,
Linking her own with his honored name,

Subtle as sin, at his side withstood
The felt reproach of her neighborhood. 120

Apart with them, like them forbid,
  Old Goody Cole looked drearily round,
As, two by two, with their faces hid,
  The mourners walked to the burying-
    ground.
She let the staff from her clasped hands
    fall:
'Lord, forgive us! we're sinners all!'
And the voice of the old man answered
    her:
'Amen!' said Father Bachiler.

So, as I sat upon Appledore
  In the calm of a closing summer day, 130
And the broken lines of Hampton shore
  In purple mist of cloudland lay,
The Rivermouth Rocks their story told;
And waves aglow with sunset gold,
Rising and breaking in steady chime,
Beat the rhythm and kept the time.

And the sunset paled, and warmed once
    more
  With a softer, tenderer after-glow;
In the east was moon-rise, with boats off-
    shore
  And sails in the distance drifting slow. 140
The beacon glimmered from Portsmouth
    bar,
The White Isle kindled its great red star;
And life and death in my old-time lay
Mingled in peace like the night and day!
                                    1864.

THE VANISHERS [1]

SWEETEST of all childlike dreams
  In the simple Indian lore
Still to me the legend seems
  Of the shapes who flit before.

Flitting, passing, seen and gone,
  Never reached nor found at rest,
Baffling search, but beckoning on
  To the Sunset of the Blest.

[1] Whittier wrote to Fields, September 27, 1864: 'I take the liberty of inclosing a little poem of mine which has beguiled some weary hours. I hope thee will like it. How strange it seems not to read it to my sister! If thee have read Schoolcraft thee will remember what he says of the Puck-wud-jinnies, or "Little Vanishers." The legend is very beautiful, and I hope I have done it justice in some sort.'

From the clefts of mountain rocks,
  Through the dark of lowland firs,   10
Flash the eyes and flow the locks
  Of the mystic Vanishers !

And the fisher in his skiff,
  And the hunter on the moss,
Hear their call from cape and cliff,
  See their hands the birch-leaves toss.

Wistful, longing, through the green
  Twilight of the clustered pines,
In their faces rarely seen
  Beauty more than mortal shines.   20

Fringed with gold their mantles flow
  On the slopes of westering knolls;
In the wind they whisper low
  Of the Sunset Land of Souls.

Doubt who may, O friend of mine !
  Thou and I have seen them too;
On before with beck and sign
  Still they glide, and we pursue.

More than clouds of purple trail
  In the gold of setting day;   30
More than gleams of wing or sail
  Beckon from the sea-mist gray.

Glimpses of immortal youth,
  Gleams and glories seen and flown,
Far-heard voices sweet with truth,
  Airs from viewless Eden blown;

Beauty that eludes our grasp,
  Sweetness that transcends our taste,
Loving hands we may not clasp,
  Shining feet that mock our haste;   40

Gentle eyes we closed below,
  Tender voices heard once more,
Smile and call us, as they go
  On and onward, still before.

Guided thus, O friend of mine !
  Let us walk our little way,
Knowing by each beckoning sign
  That we are not quite astray.

Chase we still, with baffled feet,
  Smiling eye and waving hand,   50
Sought and seeker soon shall meet,
  Lost and found, in Sunset Land !
1864.   1864.

BRYANT ON HIS BIRTHDAY [1]

WE praise not now the poet's art,
  The rounded beauty of his song;
Who weighs him from his life apart
  Must do his nobler nature wrong.

Not for the eye, familiar grown
  With charms to common sight denied, —
The marvellous gift he shares alone
  With him who walked on Rydal-side;

Not for rapt hymn nor woodland lay,
  Too grave for smiles, too sweet for tears;
We speak his praise who wears to-day
  The glory of his seventy years.

When Peace brings Freedom in her train,
  Let happy lips his songs rehearse;
His life is now his noblest strain,
  His manhood better than his verse !

Thank God ! his hand on Nature's keys
  Its cunning keeps at life's full span;
But, dimmed and dwarfed, in times like
    these,
  The poet seems beside the man !

So be it ! let the garlands die,
  The singer's wreath, the painter's meed,
Let our names perish, if thereby
  Our country may be saved and freed !
1864.   1865.

LAUS DEO ! [2]

  IT is done !
  Clang of bell and roar of gun
Send the tidings up and down.
  How the belfries rock and reel !
  How the great guns, peal on peal,
Fling the joy from town to town !

[1] Written for the celebration of Bryant's seventieth birthday at the Century Club in New York.

[2] On hearing the bells ring on the passage of the constitutional amendment abolishing slavery. The resolution was adopted by Congress, January 31, 1865. The ratification by the requisite number of States was announced December 18, 1865. (WHITTIER.)

The suggestion came to the poet as he sat in the Friends' Meeting-house in Amesbury, where he was present at the regular Fifth-day meeting. All sat in silence, but on his return to his home, he recited a portion of the poem, not yet committed to paper, to his housemates in the garden room. 'It wrote itself, or rather sang itself, while the bells rang,' he wrote to Lucy Larcom. (*Cambridge Edition* of Whittier.) See also Pickard's *Life of Whittier*, vol. ii, pp. 488–489.

Ring, O bells!
Every stroke exulting tells
Of the burial hour of crime.
    Loud and long, that all may hear,   10
    Ring for every listening ear
Of Eternity and Time!

    Let us kneel:
God's own voice is in that peal,
And this spot is holy ground.
    Lord, forgive us! What are we,
    That our eyes this glory see,
That our ears have heard the sound!

    For the Lord
On the whirlwind is abroad;   20
In the earthquake He has spoken;
    He has smitten with his thunder
    The iron walls asunder,
And the gates of brass are broken!

    Loud and long
Lift the old exulting song;
Sing with Miriam by the sea,
    He has cast the mighty down;
    Horse and rider sink and drown;
'He hath triumphed gloriously!'   30

    Did we dare,
In our agony of prayer,
Ask for more than He has done?
    When was ever his right hand
    Over any time or land
Stretched as now beneath the sun?

    How they pale,
Ancient myth and song and tale,
In this wonder of our days,
    When the cruel rod of war   40
    Blossoms white with righteous law,
And the wrath of man is praise!

    Blotted out!
All within and all about
Shall a fresher life begin;
    Freer breathe the universe
    As it rolls its heavy curse
On the dead and buried sin!

    It is done!
In the circuit of the sun   50
Shall the sound thereof go forth.
    It shall bid the sad rejoice,
    It shall give the dumb a voice,
It shall belt with joy the earth!

    Ring and swing,
    Bells of joy! On morning's wing
Send the song of praise abroad!
    With a sound of broken chains
    Tell the nations that He reigns,
Who alone is Lord and God!   60

1865.   1865.

HYMN

FOR THE CELEBRATION OF EMANCIPA-
TION AT NEWBURYPORT

Not unto us who did but seek
The word that burned within to speak,
Not unto us this day belong
The triumph and exultant song.

Upon us fell in early youth
The burden of unwelcome truth,
And left us, weak and frail and few,
The censor's painful work to do.

Thenceforth our life a fight became,
The air we breathed was hot with blame; 10
For not with gauged and softened tone
We made the bondman's cause our own.

We bore, as Freedom's hope forlorn,
The private hate, the public scorn;
Yet held through all the paths we trod
Our faith in man and trust in God.

We prayed and hoped; but still, with awe,
The coming of the sword we saw;
We heard the nearing steps of doom,
We saw the shade of things to come.   20

In grief which they alone can feel
Who from a mother's wrong appeal,
With blended lines of fear and hope
We cast our country's horoscope.

For still within her house of life
We marked the lurid sign of strife,
And, poisoning and imbittering all,
We saw the star of Wormwood fall.

Deep as our love for her became
Our hate of all that wrought her shame, 30
And if, thereby, with tongue and pen
We erred, — we were but mortal men.

We hoped for peace; our eyes survey
The blood-red dawn of Freedom's day·

We prayed for love to loose the chain;
'T is shorn by battle's axe in twain !

Nor skill nor strength nor zeal of ours
Has mined and heaved the hostile towers;
Not by our hands is turned the key
That sets the sighing captives free.   40

A redder sea than Egypt's wave
Is piled and parted for the slave;
A darker cloud moves on in light;
A fiercer fire is guide by night !

The praise, O Lord ! is thine alone,
In thy own way thy work is done !
Our poor gifts at thy feet we cast,
To whom be glory, first and last !
1865.   1865.

THE ETERNAL GOODNESS

O FRIENDS ! with whom my feet have trod
    The quiet aisles of prayer,
Glad witness to your zeal for God
    And love of man I bear.

I trace your lines of argument;
    Your logic linked and strong
I weigh as one who dreads dissent,
    And fears a doubt as wrong.

But still my human hands are weak
    To hold your iron creeds: 10
Against the words ye bid me speak
    My heart within me pleads.

Who fathoms the Eternal Thought ?
    Who talks of scheme and plan ?
The Lord is God ! He needeth not
    The poor device of man.

I walk with bare, hushed feet the ground
    Ye tread with boldness shod;
I dare not fix with mete and bound
    The love and power of God.   20

Ye praise his justice; even such
    His pitying love I deem:
Ye seek a king; I fain would touch
    The robe that hath no seam.

Ye see the curse which overbroods
    A world of pain and loss;
I hear our Lord's beatitudes
    And prayer upon the cross.

More than your schoolmen teach, with-
        in
    Myself, alas ! I know: 30
Too dark ye cannot paint the sin,
    Too small the merit show.

I bow my forehead to the dust,
    I veil mine eyes for shame,
And urge, in trembling self-distrust,
    A prayer without a claim.

I see the wrong that round me lies,
    I feel the guilt within;
I hear, with groan and travail-cries,
    The world confess its sin.   40

Yet, in the maddening maze of things,
    And tossed by storm and flood,
To one fixed trust my spirit clings;
    I know that God is good !

Not mine to look where cherubim
    And seraphs may not see,
But nothing can be good in Him
    Which evil is in me.

The wrong that pains my soul below
    I dare not throne above,   50
I know not of his hate, — I know
    His goodness and his love.

I dimly guess from blessings known
    Of greater out of sight,
And, with the chastened Psalmist, own
    His judgments too are right.

I long for household voices gone,
    For vanished smiles I long,
But God hath led my dear ones on,
    And He can do no wrong.   60

I know not what the future hath
    Of marvel or surprise,
Assured alone that life and death
    His mercy underlies.

And if my heart and flesh are weak
    To bear an untried pain,
The bruisèd reed He will not break,
    But strengthen and sustain.

No offering of my own I have,
    Nor works my faith to prove;   70
I can but give the gifts He gave,
    And plead his love for love.

And so beside the Silent Sea
  I wait the muffled oar;
No harm from Him can come to me
  On ocean or on shore.

I know not where his islands lift
  Their fronded palms in air;
I only know I cannot drift
  Beyond his love and care.   80

O brothers ! if my faith is vain,
  If hopes like these betray,
Pray for me that my feet may gain
  The sure and safer way.

And Thou, O Lord ! by whom are seen
  Thy creatures as they be,
Forgive me if too close I lean
  My human heart on Thee !

                                      1865 ?

SNOW–BOUND [1]

A WINTER IDYL

TO THE MEMORY OF THE HOUSEHOLD IT DESCRIBES

THIS POEM IS DEDICATED BY THE AUTHOR

As the Spirits of Darkness be stronger in the dark, so Good Spirits, which be Angels of Light, are augmented not only by the Divine light of the Sun, but also by our common VVood Fire: and as the Celestial Fire drives away dark spirits, so also this our Fire of VVood doth the same. — COR. AGRIPPA, *Occult Philosophy*, Book I. ch. v.

Announced by all the trumpets of the sky,
Arrives the snow, and, driving o'er the fields,
Seems nowhere to alight : the whited air
Hides hills and woods, the river and the heaven,
And veils the farm-house at the garden's end.
The sled and traveller stopped, the courier's feet
Delayed, all friends shut out, the housemates sit
Around the radiant fireplace, enclosed
In a tumultuous privacy of storm.
            EMERSON. *The Snow Storm.*

THE sun that brief December day
Rose cheerless over hills of gray,
And, darkly circled, gave at noon
A sadder light than waning moon.

[1] The inmates of the family at the Whittier homestead who are referred to in the poem were my father, mother, my brother and two sisters, and my uncle and aunt, both unmarried. In addition, there was the district school-master, who boarded with us. The 'not unfeared, half-welcome guest' was Harriet Livermore, daughter of Judge Livermore, of New Hampshire, a young woman of fine natural ability, enthusiastic, eccentric, with slight control over her violent temper, which sometimes made her religious profession doubtful. She was equally ready to exhort in school-house prayer-meetings and dance in a Washington ball-room, while her father was a member of Congress. She early embraced the doctrine of the Second Advent, and felt it her duty to proclaim the Lord's speedy coming. With this message she crossed the Atlantic and spent the greater part of a long life in travelling over Europe and Asia. She lived some time with Lady Hester Stanhope, a woman as fantastic and mentally strained as herself, on the slope of Mt. Lebanon, but finally quarrelled with her in regard to two white horses with red marks on their backs which suggested the idea of saddles, on which her titled hostess expected to ride into

Slow tracing down the thickening sky
Its mute and ominous prophecy,
A portent seeming less than threat,
It sank from sight before it set.

Jerusalem with the Lord. A friend of mine found her, when quite an old woman, wandering in Syria with a tribe of Arabs, who with the Oriental notion that madness is inspiration, accepted her as their prophetess and leader. At the time referred to in ' Snow-Bound ' she was boarding at the Rocks Village, about two miles from us.

In my boyhood, in our lonely farm-house, we had scanty sources of information; few books and only a small weekly newspaper. Our only annual was the Almanac. Under such circumstances story-telling was a necessary resource in the long winter evenings. My father when a young man had traversed the wilderness to Canada, and could tell us of his adventures with Indians and wild beasts, and of his sojourn in the French villages. My uncle was ready with his record of hunting and fishing and, it must be confessed, with stories, which he at least half believed, of witchcraft and apparitions. My mother, who was born in the Indian-haunted region of Somersworth, New Hampshire, between Dover and Portsmouth, told us of the inroads of the savages, and the narrow escape of her ancestors. She described strange people who lived on the Piscataqua and Cocheco, among whom was Bantam the sorcerer. I have in my possession the wizard's ' conjuring book,' which he solemnly opened when consulted. It is a copy of Cornelius Agrippa's *Magic*, printed in 1651, dedicated to Dr. Robert Child, who, like Michael Scott, had learned

                the art of glammorie
          In Padua beyond the sea,

and who is famous in the annals of Massachusetts, where he was at one time a resident, as the first man who dared petition the General Court for liberty of conscience. The full title of the book is *Three Books of Occult Philosophy, by Henry Cornelius Agrippa, Knight, Doctor of both Laws, Counsellor to Cæsar's Sacred Majesty and Judge of Prerogative Court.* (WHITTIER.)

See also Pickard's *Life of Whittier*, vol. i, pp. 27–36, and vol. ii, pp. 494–500; and *Whittier-Land*, pp. 12, 24, 39, 74.

A chill no coat, however stout,
Of homespun stuff could quite shut out, 10
A hard, dull bitterness of cold,
That checked, mid-vein, the circling race
Of life-blood in the sharpened face,
The coming of the snow-storm told.
The wind blew east; we heard the roar
Of Ocean on his wintry shore,
And felt the strong pulse throbbing there
Beat with low rhythm our inland air.

Meanwhile we did our nightly chores, —
Brought in the wood from out of doors, 20
Littered the stalls, and from the mows
Raked down the herd's-grass for the cows:
Heard the horse whinnying for his corn;
And, sharply clashing horn on horn,
Impatient down the stanchion rows
The cattle shake their walnut bows;
While, peering from his early perch
Upon the scaffold's pole of birch,
The cock his crested helmet bent
And down his querulous challenge sent. 30

Unwarmed by any sunset light
The gray day darkened into night,
A night made hoary with the swarm
And whirl-dance of the blinding storm,
As zigzag, wavering to and fro,
Crossed and recrossed the wingèd snow:
And ere the early bedtime came
The white drift piled the window-frame,
And through the glass the clothes-line posts
Looked in like tall and sheeted ghosts. 40

So all night long the storm roared on:
The morning broke without a sun;
In tiny spherule traced with lines
Of Nature's geometric signs,
In starry flake, and pellicle,
All day the hoary meteor fell;
And, when the second morning shone,
We looked upon a world unknown,
On nothing we could call our own.
Around the glistening wonder bent 50
The blue walls of the firmament,
No cloud above, no earth below, —
A universe of sky and snow !
The old familiar sights of ours
Took marvellous shapes; strange domes and towers
Rose up where sty or corn-crib stood,
Or garden-wall, or belt of wood;
A smooth white mound the brush - pile showed,

A fenceless drift what once was road;
The bridle-post an old man sat 60
With loose-flung coat and high cocked hat,
The well-curb had a Chinese roof;
And even the long sweep, high aloof,
In its slant splendor, seemed to tell
Of Pisa's leaning miracle.

A prompt, decisive man, no breath
Our father wasted: ' Boys, a path !'
Well pleased (for when did farmer boy
Count such a summons less than joy ?)
Our buskins on our feet we drew; 70
With mittened hands, and caps drawn low,
To guard our necks and ears from snow,
We cut the solid whiteness through.
And, where the drift was deepest, made
A tunnel walled and overlaid
With dazzling crystal: we had read
Of rare Aladdin's wondrous cave,
And to our own his name we gave,
With many a wish the luck were ours
To test his lamp's supernal powers. 80
We reached the barn with merry din,
And roused the prisoned brutes within.
The old horse thrust his long head out,
And grave with wonder gazed about;
The cock his lusty greeting said,
And forth his speckled harem led;
The oxen lashed their tails, and hooked,
And mild reproach of hunger looked;
The hornèd patriarch of the sheep,
Like Egypt's Amun roused from sleep, 90
Shook his sage head with gesture mute,
And emphasized with stamp of foot.

All day the gusty north-wind bore
The loosening drift its breath before;
Low circling round its southern zone,
The sun through dazzling snow-mist shone.
No church-bell lent its Christian tone
To the savage air, no social smoke
Curled over woods of snow-hung oak.
A solitude made more intense 100
By dreary-voicèd elements,
The shrieking of the mindless wind,
The moaning tree-boughs swaying blind,
And on the glass the unmeaning beat
Of ghostly finger-tips of sleet.
Beyond the circle of our hearth
No welcome sound of toil or mirth
Unbound the spell, and testified
Of human life and thought outside.
We minded that the sharpest ear 110
The buried brooklet could not hear,

The music of whose liquid lip
Had been to us companionship,
And, in our lonely life, had grown
To have an almost human tone.

As night drew on, and, from the crest
Of wooded knolls that ridged the west,
The sun, a snow-blown traveller, sank
From sight beneath the smothering bank,
We piled, with care, our nightly stack   120
Of wood against the chimney-back, —
The oaken log, green, huge, and thick,
And on its top the stout back-stick;
The knotty forestick laid apart,
And filled between with curious art
The ragged brush; then, hovering near,
We watched the first red blaze appear,
Heard the sharp crackle, caught the gleam
On whitewashed wall and sagging beam,
Until the old, rude-furnished room   130
Burst, flower-like, into rosy bloom;
While radiant with a mimic flame
Outside the sparkling drift became,
And through the bare-boughed lilac-tree
Our own warm hearth seemed blazing free.
The crane and pendent trammels showed,
The Turks' heads on the andirons glowed;
While childish fancy, prompt to tell
The meaning of the miracle,
Whispered the old rhyme: ' *Under the tree,*
When fire outdoors burns merrily,   141
There the witches are making tea.'

The moon above the eastern wood
Shone at its full; the hill-range stood
Transfigured in the silver flood,
Its blown snows flashing cold and keen,
Dead white, save where some sharp ravine
Took shadow, or the sombre green
Of hemlocks turned to pitchy black
Against the whiteness at their back.   150
For such a world and such a night
Most fitting that unwarming light,
Which only seemed where'er it fell
To make the coldness visible.

Shut in from all the world without,
We sat the clean-winged hearth about,
Content to let the north-wind roar
In baffled rage at pane and door,
While the red logs before us beat
The frost-line back with tropic heat;   160
And ever, when a louder blast
Shook beam and rafter as it passed,
The merrier up its roaring draught

The great throat of the chimney laughed;
The house-dog on his paws outspread
Laid to the fire his drowsy head,
The cat's dark silhouette on the wall
A couchant tiger's seemed to fall;
And, for the winter fireside meet,
Between the andirons' straddling feet,   170
The mug of cider simmered slow,
The apples sputtered in a row,
And, close at hand, the basket stood
With nuts from brown October's wood.

What matter how the night behaved ?
What matter how the north-wind raved ?
Blow high, blow low, not all its snow
Could quench our hearth-fire's ruddy glow.
O Time and Change ! — with hair as gray
As was my sire's that winter day,   180
How strange it seems, with so much gone
Of life and love, to still live on !
Ah, brother ! only I and thou [1]
Are left of all that circle now, —
The dear home faces whereupon
That fitful firelight paled and shone.
Henceforward, listen as we will,
The voices of that hearth are still;
Look where we may, the wide earth o'er
Those lighted faces smile no more.   190
We tread the paths their feet have worn,
  We sit beneath their orchard trees,
  We hear, like them, the hum of bees
And rustle of the bladed corn;
We turn the pages that they read,
  Their written words we linger o'er,
But in the sun they cast no shade,
No voice is heard, no sign is made,
  No step is on the conscious floor !
Yet Love will dream, and Faith will trust   200
(Since He who knows our need is just)
That somehow, somewhere, meet we must.
Alas for him who never sees
The stars shine through his cypress-trees !
Who, hopeless, lays his dead away,
Nor looks to see the breaking day
Across the mournful marbles play !
Who hath not learned, in hours of faith,
  The truth to flesh and sense unknown,
That Life is ever lord of Death,   210
  And Love can never lose its own !

We sped the time with stories old,
Wrought puzzles out, and riddles told,

[1] Whittier's only brother, Matthew, was born in 1812
and died in 1883. See Pickard's *Life of Whittier*, vol. i.
pp. 31-32.

Or stammered from our school-book lore
' The Chief of Gambia's golden shore.' [1]
How often since, when all the land
Was clay in Slavery's shaping hand,
As if a far-blown trumpet stirred
The languorous sin-sick air, I heard:
' *Does not the voice of reason cry,*   220
   Claim the first right which Nature gave,
From the red scourge of bondage fly,
   Nor deign to live a burdened slave!'

Our father rode again his ride
On Memphremagog's wooded side;
Sat down again to moose and samp
In trapper's hut and Indian camp;
Lived o'er the old idyllic ease
Beneath St. François' hemlock-trees;
Again for him the moonlight shone   230
On Norman cap and bodiced zone;
Again he heard the violin play
Which led the village dance away.
And mingled in its merry whirl
The grandam and the laughing girl.
Or, nearer home, our steps he led
Where Salisbury's level marshes spread
   Mile-wide as flies the laden bee;
Where merry mowers, hale and strong,
Swept, scythe on scythe, their swaths
         along   240
   The low green prairies of the sea.
We shared the fishing off Boar's Head,
   And round the rocky Isles of Shoals
The hake-broil on the drift-wood coals;
The chowder on the sand-beach made,
Dipped by the hungry, steaming hot
With spoons of clam-shell from the pot.
We heard the tales of witchcraft old,
And dream and sign and marvel told
To sleepy listeners as they lay   250
Stretched idly on the salted hay,
Adrift along the winding shores,
When favoring breezes deigned to blow
The square sail of the gundelow
And idle lay the useless oars.

Our mother, while she turned her wheel
Or run the new-knit stocking-heel,
Told how the Indian hordes came down
At midnight on Cocheco town,
And how her own great-uncle bore   260
His cruel scalp-mark to fourscore.

[1] ' The African Chief' was the title of a poem by Mrs. Sarah Wentworth Morton, wife of the Hon. Perez Morton, a former attorney-general of Massachusetts. Mrs. Morton's *nom de plume* was *Philenia*. The school-book in which ' The African Chief' was printed was Caleb Bingham's *The American Preceptor*. (WHITTIER.)

Recalling, in her fitting phrase,
   So rich and picturesque and free
   (The common unrhymed poetry
Of simple life and country ways),
The story of her early days, —
She made us welcome to her home;
Old hearths grew wide to give us room;
We stole with her a frightened look
At the gray wizard's conjuring-book,   270
The fame whereof went far and wide
Through all the simple country-side;
We heard the hawks at twilight play,
The boat-horn on Piscataqua,
The loon's weird laughter far away;
We fished her little trout-brook, knew
What flowers in wood and meadow grew,
What sunny hillsides autumn-brown
She climbed to shake the ripe nuts down,
Saw where in sheltered cove and bay   280
The ducks' black squadron anchored lay,
And heard the wild-geese calling loud
Beneath the gray November cloud.

Then, haply, with a look more grave,
And soberer tone, some tale she gave
From painful Sewel's ancient tome, [2]
Beloved in every Quaker home,
Of faith fire-winged by martyrdom,
Or Chalkley's Journal, old and quaint,[3] —
Gentlest of skippers, rare sea-saint! —   290
Who, when the dreary calms prevailed,
And water-butt and bread-cask failed,

[2] ' Painful Sewel's ancient tome' . . . is the *History of the Christian People called Quakers*, by William Sewel, a Dutchman . . . He died about 1725. . . . It was originally written in Low Dutch, and translated into English by Sewel himself. . . . It is devoted mostly to the persecutions of the Friends in Great Britain and in America. (Pickard's *Life of Whittier*.)

[3] Chalkley's own narrative of this incident, as given in his *Journal*, is as follows : ' To stop their murmuring, I told them they should not need to cast lots, which was usual in such cases, which of us should die first, for I would freely offer up my life to do them good. One said, " God bless you ! I will not eat any of you." Another said, " He would die before he would eat any of me," and so said several. I can truly say, on that occasion, at that time, my life was not dear to me, and that I was serious and ingenuous in my proposition : and as I was leaning over the side of the vessel, thoughtfully considering my proposal to the company, and looking in my mind to Him that made me, a very large dolphin came up towards the top or surface of the water, and looked me in the face ; and I called the people to put a hook into the sea, and take him, for here is one come to redeem me (I said to them). And they put a hook into the sea, and the fish readily took it and they caught him. He was longer than myself. I think he was about six feet long, and the largest that ever I saw. This plainly showed us that we ought not to distrust the providence of the Almighty. The people were quieted by this act of Providence, and murmured no more. We caught enough to eat plentifully of, till we got into the capes of Delaware.' (WHITTIER.)

And cruel, hungry eyes pursued
His portly presence mad for food,
With dark hints muttered under breath
Of casting lots for life or death,
Offered, if Heaven withheld supplies,
To be himself the sacrifice.
Then, suddenly, as if to save
The good man from his living grave,   300
A ripple on the water grew,
A school of porpoise flashed in view.
'Take, eat,' he said, 'and be content;
These fishes in my stead are sent
By Him who gave the tangled ram
To spare the child of Abraham.'

Our uncle, innocent of books,
Was rich in lore of fields and brooks,[1]
The ancient teachers never dumb
Of Nature's unhoused lyceum.   310
In moons and tides and weather wise,
He read the clouds as prophecies,
And foul or fair could well divine,
By many an occult hint and sign,
Holding the cunning-warded keys
To all the woodcraft mysteries;
Himself to Nature's heart so near
That all her voices in his ear
Of beast or bird had meanings clear,
Like Apollonius of old,   320
Who knew the tales the sparrows told,
Or Hermes, who interpreted
What the sage cranes of Nilus said;
A simple, guileless, childlike man,
Content to live where life began;
Strong only on his native grounds,
The little world of sights and sounds
Whose girdle was the parish bounds,
Whereof his fondly partial pride
The common features magnified,   330
As Surrey hills to mountains grew
In White of Selborne's loving view, —
He told how teal and loon he shot,
And how the eagle's eggs he got,
The feats on pond and river done,
The prodigies of rod and gun;
Till, warming with the tales he told,
Forgotten was the outside cold,
The bitter wind unheeded blew,
From ripening corn the pigeons flew,   340
The partridge drummed i' the wood, the mink
Went fishing down the river-brink;

[1] Compare Emerson's 'Wood-Notes.' On Whittier's uncle, see Pickard's *Life of Whittier*, vol. i, pp. 32–33, and Whittier's *Prose Works*, vol. i, pp. 323–325, 'The Fish I did n't Catch.'

In fields with bean or clover gay,
The woodchuck, like a hermit gray,
  Peered from the doorway of his cell;
The muskrat plied the mason's trade,
And tier by tier his mud-walls laid;
And from the shagbark overhead
  The grizzled squirrel dropped his shell.

Next, the dear aunt, whose smile of cheer   350
And voice in dreams I see and hear —
The sweetest woman ever Fate
Perverse denied a household mate,
Who, lonely, homeless, not the less
Found peace in love's unselfishness,
And welcome whereso'er she went,
A calm and gracious element,
Whose presence seemed the sweet income
And womanly atmosphere of home —
Called up her girlhood memories,   360
The huskings and the apple-bees,
The sleigh-rides and the summer sails,
Weaving through all the poor details
And homespun warp of circumstance
A golden woof-thread of romance.
For well she kept her genial mood
And simple faith of maidenhood;
Before her still a cloud-land lay,
The mirage loomed across her way;
The morning dew, that dries so soon   370
With others, glistened at her noon;
Through years of toil and soil and care,
From glossy tress to thin gray hair,
All unprofaned she held apart
The virgin fancies of the heart.
Be shame to him of woman born
Who hath for such but thought of scorn.

There, too, our elder sister [2] plied
Her evening task the stand beside;
A full, rich nature, free to trust,   380
Truthful and almost sternly just,
Impulsive, earnest, prompt to act,
And make her generous thought a fact,
Keeping with many a light disguise
The secret of self-sacrifice.
O heart sore-tried ! thou hast the best,
That Heaven itself could give thee, — rest,
Rest from all bitter thoughts and things !
  How many a poor one's blessing went
  With thee beneath the low green tent   390
Whose curtain never outward swings !

[2] Mary Whittier. 1806–1860. Pickard's *Life*, i, 29.

As one who held herself a part [1]
Of all she saw, and let her heart
 Against the household bosom lean,
Upon the motley-braided mat
Our youngest and our dearest sat,
Lifting her large, sweet, asking eyes,
 Now bathed in the unfading green
And holy peace of Paradise.
Oh, looking from some heavenly hill,   400
 Or from the shade of saintly palms,
 Or silver reach of river calms,
Do those large eyes behold me still?
With me one little year ago: —
The chill weight of the winter snow
 For months upon her grave has lain;
And now, when summer south-winds blow
 And brier and harebell bloom again,
I tread the pleasant paths we trod,
I see the violet-sprinkled sod   410
Whereon she leaned, too frail and weak
The hillside flowers she loved to seek,
Yet following me where'er I went
With dark eyes full of love's content.
The birds are glad; the brier-rose fills
The air with sweetness; all the hills
Stretch green to June's unclouded sky;
But still I wait with ear and eye
For something gone which should be nigh,
A loss in all familiar things,   420
In flower that blooms, and bird that sings.
And yet, dear heart ! remembering thee,
 Am I not richer than of old?
Safe in thy immortality,
  What change can reach the wealth I
   hold?
 What chance can mar the pearl and gold
Thy love hath left in trust with me?
And while in life's late afternoon,
 Where cool and long the shadows grow,
I walk to meet the night that soon   430
 Shall shape and shadow overflow,
I cannot feel that thou art far,
Since near at need the angels are;
And when the sunset gates unbar,
 Shall I not see thee waiting stand,
And, white against the evening star,
 The welcome of thy beckoning hand?

Brisk wielder of the birch and rule,
The master of the district school

[1] On Whittier's sister Elizabeth, his household companion and his closest friend until her death, in 1864,
see Pickard's *Life*, vol. i, pp. 29-31 ; *Whittier-Land*,
p. 74 ; Whittier's poems ' To My Sister,' and ' The Last
Eve of Summer ;' and her own poems, in the Riverside
and Cambridge Editions of Whittier's *Works*.

Held at the fire his favored place,   440
Its warm glow lit a laughing face
Fresh-hued and fair, where scarce appeared
The uncertain prophecy of beard.
He teased the mitten-blinded cat,
Played cross-pins on my uncle's hat,
Sang songs, and told us what befalls
In classic Dartmouth's college halls.
Born the wild Northern hills among,
From whence his yeoman father wrung
By patient toil subsistence scant,   450
Not competence and yet not want,
He early gained the power to pay
His cheerful, self-reliant way;
Could doff at ease his scholar's gown
To peddle wares from town to town;
Or through the long vacation's reach
In lonely lowland districts teach,
Where all the droll experience found
At stranger hearths in boarding round,
The moonlit skater's keen delight,   460
The sleigh-drive through the frosty night,
The rustic-party, with its rough
Accompaniment of blind-man's-buff,
And whirling-plate, and forfeits paid,
His winter task a pastime made.
Happy the snow-locked homes wherein
He tuned his merry violin,
Or played the athlete in the barn,
Or held the good dame's winding-yarn,
Or mirth-provoking versions told   470
Of classic legends rare and old,
Wherein the scenes of Greece and Rome
Had all the commonplace of home,
And little seemed at best the odds
'Twixt Yankee pedlers and old gods;
Where Pindus-born Arachthus took
The guise of any grist-mill brook,
And dread Olympus at his will
Became a huckleberry hill.

A careless boy that night he seemed;   480
 But at his desk he had the look
And air of one who wisely schemed,
  And hostage from the future took
  In trainèd thought and lore of book.
Large-brained, clear-eyed, of such as he
Shall Freedom's young apostles be,
Who, following in War's bloody trail,
Shall every lingering wrong assail;
All chains from limb and spirit strike,
Uplift the black and white alike;   490
Scatter before their swift advance
The darkness and the ignorance,
The pride, the lust, the squalid sloth,

Which nurtured Treason's monstrous
    growth,
Made murder pastime, and the hell
Of prison-torture possible;
The cruel lie of caste refute,
Old forms remould, and substitute
For Slavery's lash the freeman's will,
For blind routine, wise-handed skill;   500
A school-house plant on every hill,
Stretching in radiate nerve-lines thence
The quick wires of intelligence;
Till North and South together brought
Shall own the same electric thought,
In peace a common flag salute,
And, side by side in labor's free
And unresentful rivalry,
Harvest the fields wherein they fought.

Another guest that winter night [1]   510
Flashed back from lustrous eyes the light.
Unmarked by time, and yet not young,
The honeyed music of her tongue
And words of meekness scarcely told
A nature passionate and bold,
Strong, self-concentred, spurning guide,
Its milder features dwarfed beside
Her unbent will's majestic pride.
She sat among us, at the best,
A not unfeared, half-welcome guest,   520
Rebuking with her cultured phrase
Our homeliness of words and ways.
A certain pard-like, treacherous grace
Swayed the lithe limbs and dropped the
    lash,
Lent the white teeth their dazzling flash;
And under low brows, black with night,
Rayed out at times a dangerous light;
The sharp heat-lightnings of her face
Presaging ill to him whom Fate
Condemned to share her love or hate.   530
A woman tropical, intense
In thought and act, in soul and sense,
She blended in a like degree
The vixen and the devotee,
Revealing with each freak or feint
    The temper of Petruchio's Kate,
The raptures of Siena's saint.
Her tapering hand and rounded wrist
Had facile power to form a fist;

The warm, dark languish of her eyes   540
Was never safe from wrath's surprise.
Brows saintly calm and lips devout
Knew every change of scowl and pout;
And the sweet voice had notes more high
And shrill for social battle-cry.

Since then what old cathedral town
Has missed her pilgrim staff and gown,
What convent-gate has held its lock
Against the challenge of her knock!
Through Smyrna's plague-hushed thorough-
    fares,   550
Up sea-set Malta's rocky stairs,
Gray olive slopes of hills that hem
    Thy tombs and shrines, Jerusalem,
Or startling on her desert throne
The crazy Queen of Lebanon [2]
With claims fantastic as her own,
Her tireless feet have held their way;
And still, unrestful, bowed, and gray,
She watches under Eastern skies,
    With hope each day renewed and fresh,
    The Lord's quick coming in the flesh,   561
Whereof she dreams and prophesies!

Where'er her troubled path may be,
    The Lord's sweet pity with her go!
The outward wayward life we see,
    The hidden springs we may not know.
Nor is it given us to discern
    What threads the fatal sisters spun,
    Through what ancestral years has run
The sorrow with the woman born,   570
What forged her cruel chain of moods,
What set her feet in solitudes,
    And held the love within her mute,
What mingled madness in the blood,
    A life-long discord and annoy,
    Water of tears with oil of joy,
And hid within the folded bud
    Perversities of flower and fruit.
It is not ours to separate
    The tangled skein of will and fate,   580
To show what metes and bounds should
    stand
Upon the soul's debatable land,
And between choice and Providence
Divide the circle of events;
But He who knows our frame is just,
Merciful and compassionate,
And full of sweet assurances

---

[1] See Whittier's introductory note to 'Snow-Bound.'
He wrote to Fields in sending him the poem : 'The portrait of that strange pilgrim, Harriet Livermore. . .
who used to visit us, is as near the life as I can give
it.' An amusing anecdote of how Miss Livermore
found and read this characterization of herself is told
in Pickard's *Whittier-Land*, p. 39.

[2] An interesting account of Lady Hester Stanhope
may be found in Kinglake's *Eothen*, chap. viii.
(WHITTIER.)

And hope for all the language is,
That He remembereth we are dust!

At last the great logs, crumbling low,   590
Sent out a dull and duller glow,
The bull's-eye watch that hung in view,
Ticking its weary circuit through,
Pointed with mutely warning sign
Its black hand to the hour of nine.
That sign the pleasant circle broke:
My uncle ceased his pipe to smoke,
Knocked from its bowl the refuse gray,
And laid it tenderly away;
Then roused himself to safely cover   600
The dull red brands with ashes over.
And while, with care, our mother laid
The work aside, her steps she stayed
One moment, seeking to express
Her grateful sense of happiness
For food and shelter, warmth and health,
And love's contentment more than wealth,
With simple wishes (not the weak,
Vain prayers which no fulfilment seek,
But such as warm the generous heart,   610
O'er-prompt to do with Heaven its part)
That none might lack, that bitter night,
For bread and clothing, warmth and light.

Within our beds awhile we heard
The wind that round the gables roared,
With now and then a ruder shock,
Which made our very bedsteads rock.
We heard the loosened clapboards tost,
The board-nails snapping in the frost;
And on us, through the unplastered wall,
Felt the light sifted snow-flakes fall.   621
But sleep stole on, as sleep will do
When hearts are light and life is new;
Faint and more faint the murmurs grew,
Till in the summer-land of dreams
They softened to the sound of streams,
Low stir of leaves, and dip of oars,
And lapsing waves on quiet shores.

Next morn we wakened with the shout
Of merry voices high and clear;   630
And saw the teamsters drawing near
To break the drifted highways out.
Down the long hillside treading slow
We saw the half-buried oxen go,
Shaking the snow from heads uptost,
Their straining nostrils white with frost.
Before our door the straggling train
Drew up, an added team to gain.
The elders threshed their hands a-cold,

Passed, with the cider-mug, their jokes
From lip to lip; the younger folks   641
Down the loose snow-banks, wrestling,
        rolled,
Then toiled again the cavalcade
O'er windy hill, through clogged ravine,
And woodland paths that wound between
Low drooping pine-boughs winter-weighed.
From every barn a team afoot,
At every house a new recruit,
Where, drawn by Nature's subtlest law,
Haply the watchful young men saw   650
Sweet doorway pictures of the curls
And curious eyes of merry girls,
Lifting their hands in mock defence
Against the snow-ball's compliments,
And reading in each missive tost
The charm with Eden never lost.

We heard once more the sleigh-bells' sound;
And, following where the teamsters led,
The wise old Doctor went his round,
Just pausing at our door to say,   660
In the brief autocratic way
Of one who, prompt at Duty's call,
Was free to urge her claim on all,
That some poor neighbor sick abed
At night our mother's aid would need.
For, one in generous thought and deed,
What mattered in the sufferer's sight
The Quaker matron's inward light,
The Doctor's mail of Calvin's creed?
All hearts confess the saints elect   670
Who, twain in faith, in love agree,
And melt not in an acid sect
The Christian pearl of charity!

So days went on: a week had passed
Since the great world was heard from last.
The Almanac we studied o'er,
Read and reread our little store
Of books and pamphlets, scarce a score;
One harmless novel, mostly hid
From younger eyes, a book forbid,   680
And poetry (or good or bad,
A single book was all we had),
Where Ellwood's meek, drab-skirted Muse,
A stranger to the heathen Nine,
Sang, with a somewhat nasal whine,
The wars of David and the Jews.[1]

---

[1] Thomas Ellwood, one of the Society of Friends, a
contemporary and friend of Milton, and the suggester
of *Paradise Regained*, wrote an epic poem in five
books, called *Davideis*, the life of King David of Israel. He wrote the book, we are told, for his own diver-
sion, so it was not necessary that others should be

At last the floundering carrier bore
The village paper to our door.
Lo ! broadening outward as we read,
To warmer zones the horizon spread;   690
In panoramic length unrolled
We saw the marvels that it told.
Before us passed the painted Creeks,
    And daft McGregor on his raids
    In Costa Rica's everglades.
And up Taygetos winding slow
Rode Ypsilanti's Mainote Greeks,
A Turk's head at each saddle-bow !
Welcome to us its week-old news,
Its corner for the rustic Muse,   700
    Its monthly gauge of snow and rain,
Its record, mingling in a breath
The wedding bell and dirge of death:
Jest, anecdote, and love-lorn tale,
The latest culprit sent to jail;
Its hue and cry of stolen and lost,
Its vendue sales and goods at cost,
    And traffic calling loud for gain.
We felt the stir of hall and street,
The pulse of life that round us beat;   710
The chill embargo of the snow
Was melted in the genial glow;
Wide swung again our ice-locked door,
And all the world was ours once more !

Clasp, Angel of the backward look
    And folded wings of ashen gray
    And voice of echoes far away,
The brazen covers of thy book;
The weird palimpsest old and vast,
Wherein thou hid'st the spectral past;   720
Where, closely mingling, pale and glow
The characters of joy and woe;
The monographs of outlived years,
Or smile-illumed or dim with tears,
Green hills of life that slope to death,
And haunts of home, whose vistaed trees
Shade off to mournful cypresses
    With the white amaranths underneath.
Even while I look, I can but heed
    The restless sands' incessant fall,   730
Importunate hours that hours succeed,
Each clamorous with its own sharp need,
    And duty keeping pace with all.
Shut down and clasp the heavy lids;
I hear again the voice that bids
The dreamer leave his dream midway
For larger hopes and graver fears;
Life greatens in these later years,
The century's aloe flowers to-day !

Yet, haply, in some lull of life,   740
Some Truce of God which breaks its
        strife,
The worldling's eyes shall gather dew,
    Dreaming in throngful city ways
Of winter joys his boyhood knew;
And dear and early friends — the few
Who yet remain — shall pause to view
    These Flemish pictures of old days;
Sit with me by the homestead hearth,
And stretch the hands of memory forth 749
    To warm them at the wood-fire's blaze !
And thanks untraced to lips unknown
Shall greet me like the odors blown
From unseen meadows newly mown,
Or lilies floating in some pond,
Wood - fringed, the wayside gaze be-
        yond;
The traveller owns the grateful sense
Of sweetness near, he knows not whence,
And, pausing, takes with forehead bare
The benediction of the air.
1865.   1866.

ABRAHAM DAVENPORT [1]

In the old days (a custom laid aside
With breeches and cocked hats) the people
    sent

diverted by it. Ellwood's autobiography, a quaint and
delightful book, may be found in Howells's series of
Choice Autobiographies. (*Riverside Literature Series.*)
[1] The famous Dark Day of New England, May 19,
1780, was a physical puzzle for many years to our ancestors, but its occurrence brought something more than
philosophical speculation into the minds of those who
passed through it. The incident of Colonel Abraham
Davenport's sturdy protest is a matter of history.
(Whittier.)

Their wisest men to make the public laws.
And so, from a brown homestead, where
        the Sound
Drinks the small tribute of the Mianas,
Waved over by the woods of Rippowams,
And hallowed by pure lives and tranquil
        deaths,
Stamford sent up to the councils of the
        State
Wisdom and grace in Abraham Davenport.

'T was on a May-day of the far old year
Seventeen hundred eighty, that there fell 11

Over the bloom and sweet life of the
    Spring,
Over the fresh earth and the heaven of
    noon,
A horror of great darkness, like the night
In day of which the Norland sagas tell, —
The Twilight of the Gods. The low-hung
    sky
Was black with ominous clouds, save where
    its rim
Was fringed with a dull glow, like that
    which climbs
The crater's sides from the red hell below.
Birds ceased to sing, and all the barn-yard
    fowls   20
Roosted; the cattle at the pasture bars
Lowed, and looked homeward ; bats on
    leathern wings
Flitted abroad; the sounds of labor died;
Men prayed, and women wept; all ears grew
    sharp
To hear the doom-blast of the trumpet
    shatter
The black sky, that the dreadful face of
    Christ
Might look from the rent clouds, not as He
    looked
A loving guest at Bethany, but stern
As Justice and inexorable Law.

Meanwhile in the old State House, dim
    as ghosts,   30
Sat the lawgivers of Connecticut,
Trembling beneath their legislative robes.
' It is the Lord's Great Day ! Let us ad-
    journ,'
Some said; and then, as if with one accord,
All eyes were turned to Abraham Daven-
    port.
He rose, slow cleaving with his steady voice
The intolerable hush. ' This well may be
The Day of Judgment which the world
    awaits;
But be it so or not, I only know
My present duty, and my Lord's command
To occupy till He come. So at the post 41
Where He hath set me in his providence,
I choose, for one, to meet Him face to
    face, —
No faithless servant frightened from my
    task,
But ready when the Lord of the harvest
    calls;
And therefore, with all reverence, I would
    say,

Let God do his work, we will see to
    ours.
Bring in the candles.' And they brought
    them in.

Then by the flaring lights the Speaker
    read,
Albeit with husky voice and shaking hands,
An act to amend an act to regulate   51
The shad and alewive fisheries. Where-
    upon
Wisely and well spake Abraham Daven-
    port,
Straight to the question, with no figures of
    speech
Save the ten Arab signs, yet not without
The shrewd dry humor natural to the man:
His awe-struck colleagues listening all the
    while,
Between the pauses of his argument,
To hear the thunder of the wrath of God
Break from the hollow trumpet of the
    cloud.   60

And there he stands in memory to this
    day,
Erect, self-poised, a rugged face, half seen
Against the background of unnatural dark,
A witness to the ages as they pass,
That simple duty hath no place for fear.
                     1866.

THE DEAD SHIP OF HARPS-WELL

WHAT flecks the outer gray beyond
    The sundown's golden trail ?
The white flash of a sea-bird's wing,
    Or gleam of slanting sail ?
Let young eyes watch from Neck and Point,
    And sea-worn elders pray, —
The ghost of what was once a ship
    Is sailing up the bay !

From gray sea-fog, from icy drift,
    From peril and from pain,   10
The home-bound fisher greets thy lights,
    O hundred-harbored Maine !
But many a keel shall seaward turn,
    And many a sail outstand,
When, tall and white, the Dead Ship looms
    Against the dusk of land.

She rounds the headland's bristling pines;
    She threads the isle-set bay;

No spur of breeze can speed her on
  Nor ebb of tide delay.   20
Old men still walk the Isle of Orr
  Who tell her date and name,
Old shipwrights sit in Freeport yards
  Who hewed her oaken frame.

What weary doom of baffled quest,
  Thou sad sea-ghost, is thine ?
What makes thee in the haunts of home
  A wonder and a sign ?
No foot is on thy silent deck,
  Upon thy helm no hand;   30
No ripple hath the soundless wind
  That smites thee from the land !

For never comes the ship to port,
  Howe'er the breeze may be;
Just when she nears the waiting shore
  She drifts again to sea.
No tack of sail, nor turn of helm,
  Nor sheer of veering side,
Stern-fore she drives to sea and night,
  Against the wind and tide.   40

In vain o'er Harpswell Neck the star
  Of evening guides her in;
In vain for her the lamps are lit
  Within thy tower, Seguin !
In vain the harbor-boat shall hail,
  In vain the pilot call;
No hand shall reef his spectral sail,
  Or let her anchor fall.

Shake, brown old wives, with dreary joy,
  Your gray-head hints of ill;   50
And, over sick-beds whispering low,
  Your prophecies fulfil.
Some home amid yon birchen trees
  Shall drape its door with woe;
And slowly where the Dead Ship sails,
  The burial boat shall row !

From Wolf Neck and from Flying Point,
  From island and from main,
From sheltered cove and tided creek,
  Shall glide the funeral train.   60
The dead-boat with the bearers four,
  The mourners at her stern, —
And one shall go the silent way
  Who shall no more return !

And men shall sigh, and women weep,
  Whose dear ones pale and pine,
And sadly over sunset seas

Await the ghostly sign.
They·know not that its sails are filled
  By pity's tender breath,   70
Nor see the Angel at the helm
  Who steers the Ship of Death !

                         1866.

OUR MASTER [1]

IMMORTAL Love, forever full,
  Forever flowing free,
Forever shared, forever whole,
  A never-ebbing sea !

Our outward lips confess the name
  All other names above;
Love only knoweth whence it came
  And comprehendeth love.

Blow, winds of God, awake and blow
  The mists of earth away !   10
Shine out, O Light Divine, and show
  How wide and far we stray !

Hush every lip, close every book,
  The strife of tongues forbear;
Why forward reach, or backward look,
  For love that clasps like air ?

We may not climb the heavenly steeps
  To bring the Lord Christ down:
In vain we search the lowest deeps,
  For Him no depths can drown.   20

Nor holy bread, nor blood of grape,
  The lineaments restore
Of Him we know in outward shape
  And in the flesh no more.

He cometh not a king to reign;
  The world's long hope is dim;
The weary centuries watch in vain
  The clouds of heaven for Him.

Death comes, life goes; the asking eye
  And ear are answerless;   30
The grave is dumb, the hollow sky
  Is sad with silentness.

The letter fails, and systems fall,
  And every symbol wanes;

[1] Five of the best-known hymns by Whittier are
taken from this poem, beginning with the first, seventh,
sixteenth, twenty-fourth, and thirty-fifth stanzas.

The Spirit over-brooding all
  Eternal Love remains.

And not for signs in heaven above
  Or earth below they look,
Who know with John his smile of love,
  With Peter his rebuke.   40

In joy of inward peace, or sense
  Of sorrow over sin,
He is his own best evidence,
  His witness is within.

No fable old, nor mythic lore,
  Nor dream of bards and seers,
No dead fact stranded on the shore
  Of the oblivious years; —

But warm, sweet, tender, even yet
  A present help is He;   50
And faith has still its Olivet,
  And love its Galilee.

The healing of his seamless dress
  Is by our beds of pain;
We touch Him in life's throng and press,
  And we are whole again.

Through Him the first fond prayers are said
  Our lips of childhood frame,
The last low whispers of our dead
  Are burdened with his name.   60

Our Lord and Master of us all !
  Whate'er our name or sign,
We own thy sway, we hear thy call,
  We test our lives by thine.

Thou judgest us; thy purity
  Doth all our lusts condemn;
The love that draws us nearer Thee
  Is hot with wrath to them.

Our thoughts lie open to thy sight,
  And, naked to thy glance,   70
Our secret sins are in the light
  Of thy pure countenance.

Thy healing pains, a keen distress
  Thy tender light shines in;
Thy sweetness is the bitterness,
  Thy grace the pang of sin.

Yet, weak and blinded though we be,
  Thou dost our service own;

We bring our varying gifts to Thee,
  And Thou rejectest none.   80

To Thee our full humanity,
  Its joys and pains, belong;
The wrong of man to man on Thee
  Inflicts a deeper wrong.

Who hates, hates Thee, who loves becomes
  Therein to Thee allied;
All sweet accords of hearts and homes
  In Thee are multiplied.

Deep strike thy roots, O heavenly Vine,
  Within our earthly sod,   90
Most human and yet most divine,
  The flower of man and God !

O Love ! O Life !   Our faith and sight
  Thy presence maketh one,
As through transfigured clouds of white
  We trace the noon-day sun.

So, to our mortal eyes subdued,
  Flesh-veiled, but not concealed,
We know in Thee the fatherhood
  And heart of God revealed.   100

We faintly hear, we dimly see,
  In differing phrase we pray;
But, dim or clear, we own in Thee
  The Light, the Truth, the Way !

The homage that we render Thee
  Is still our Father's own;
No jealous claim or rivalry
  Divides the Cross and Throne.

To do thy will is more than praise,
  As words are less than deeds,   110
And simple trust can find thy ways
  We miss with chart of creeds.

No pride of self thy service hath,
  No place for me and mine;
Our human strength is weakness, death
  Our life, apart from thine.

Apart from Thee all gain is loss,
  All labor vainly done;
The solemn shadow of thy Cross
  Is better than the sun.   120

Alone, O Love ineffable !
  Thy saving name is given;

To turn aside from Thee is hell,
  To walk with Thee is heaven!

How vain, secure in all Thou art,
  Our noisy championship!
The sighing of the contrite heart
  Is more than flattering lip.

Not thine the bigot's partial plea,
  Nor thine the zealot's ban;   130
Thou well canst spare a love of Thee
  Which ends in hate of man.

Our Friend, our Brother, and our Lord,
  What may thy service be? —
Nor name, nor form, nor ritual word,
  But simply following Thee.

We bring no ghastly holocaust,
  We pile no graven stone;
He serves Thee best who loveth most
  His brothers and thy own.   140

Thy litanies, sweet offices
  Of love and gratitude;
Thy sacramental liturgies
  The joy of doing good.

In vain shall waves of incense drift
  The vaulted nave around,
In vain the minster turret lift
  Its brazen weights of sound.

The heart must ring thy Christmas bells,
  Thy inward altars raise;   150
Its faith and hope thy canticles,
  And its obedience praise!

                          1866?

THE WORSHIP OF NATURE

The harp at Nature's advent strung
  Has never ceased to play;
The song the stars of morning sung
  Has never died away.

And prayer is made, and praise is given,
  By all things near and far;
The ocean looketh up to heaven,
  And mirrors every star.

Its waves are kneeling on the strand,
  As kneels the human knee,   10
Their white locks bowing to the sand,
  The priesthood of the sea!

They pour their glittering treasures forth,
  Their gifts of pearl they bring,
And all the listening hills of earth
  Take up the song they sing.

The green earth sends her incense up
  From many a mountain shrine;
From folded leaf and dewy cup
  She pours her sacred wine.   20

The mists above the morning rills
  Rise white as wings of prayer;
The altar-curtains of the hills
  Are sunset's purple air.

The winds with hymns of praise are loud,
  Or low with sobs of pain, —
The thunder-organ of the cloud,
  The dropping tears of rain.

With drooping head and branches crossed
  The twilight forest grieves,   30
Or speaks with tongues of Pentecost
  From all its sunlit leaves.

The blue sky is the temple's arch,
  Its transept earth and air,
The music of its starry march
  The chorus of a prayer.

So Nature keeps the reverent frame
  With which her years began,
And all her signs and voices shame
  The prayerless heart of man.   40
                          1867.

THE MEETING

The elder folks shook hands at last,
Down seat by seat the signal passed.
To simple ways like ours unused,
Half solemnized and half amused,
With long-drawn breath and shrug, my
          guest
His sense of glad relief expressed.
Outside, the hills lay warm in sun;
The cattle in the meadow-run
Stood half-leg deep; a single bird
The green repose above us stirred.   10
'What part or lot have you,' he said,
'In these dull rites of drowsy-head?
Is silence worship? Seek it where
It soothes with dreams the summer air,
Not in this close and rude-benched hall,

But where soft lights and shadows fall,
And all the slow, sleep-walking hours
Glide soundless over grass and flowers !
From time and place and form apart,
Its holy ground the human heart,   20
Nor ritual-bound nor templeward
Walks the free spirit of the Lord !
Our common Master did not pen
His followers up from other men;
His service liberty indeed,
He built no church, He framed no creed;
But while the saintly Pharisee
Made broader his phylactery,
As from the synagogue was seen
The dusty-sandalled Nazarene   30
Through ripening cornfields lead the way
Upon the awful Sabbath day,
His sermons were the healthful talk
That shorter made the mountain-walk,
His wayside texts were flowers and birds,
Where mingled with his gracious words
The rustle of the tamarisk-tree
And ripple-wash of Galilee.'

' Thy words are well, O friend,' I said;
' Unmeasured and unlimited,   40
With noiseless slide of stone to stone,
The mystic Church of God has grown.
Invisible and silent stands
The temple never made with hands,
Unheard the voices still and small
Of its unseen confessional.
He needs no special place of prayer
Whose hearing ear is everywhere;
He brings not back the childish days
That ringed the earth with stones of praise,
Roofed Karnak's hall of gods, and laid   51
The plinths of Philæ's colonnade.
Still less He owns the selfish good
And sickly growth of solitude, —
The worthless grace that, out of sight,
Flowers in the desert anchorite,
Dissevered from the suffering whole,
Love hath no power to save a soul.
Not out of Self, the origin
And native air and soil of sin,   60
The living waters spring and flow,
The trees with leaves of healing grow.

' Dream not, O friend, because I seek
This quiet shelter twice a week,
I better deem its pine-laid floor
Than breezy hill or sea-sung shore;
But nature is not solitude:
She crowds us with her thronging wood;

Her many hands reach out to us,
Her many tongues are garrulous;   70
Perpetual riddles of surprise
She offers to our ears and eyes;
She will not leave our senses still,
But drags them captive at her will:
And, making earth too great for heaven,
She hides the Giver in the given.

' And so I find it well to come
For deeper rest to this still room,
For here the habit of the soul
Feels less the outer world's control;   80
The strength of mutual purpose pleads
More earnestly our common needs;
And from the silence multiplied
By these still forms on either side,
The world that time and sense have known
Falls off and leaves us God alone.

' Yet rarely through the charmed repose
Unmixed the stream of motive flows,
A flavor of its many springs,
The tints of earth and sky it brings;   90
In the still waters needs must be
Some shade of human sympathy;
And here, in its accustomed place,
I look on memory's dearest face;
The blind by-sitter guesseth not
What shadow haunts that vacant spot;
No eyes save mine alone can see
The love wherewith it welcomes me !
And still, with those alone my kin,
In doubt and weakness, want and sin,   100
I bow my head, my heart I bare,
As when that face was living there,
And strive (too oft, alas ! in vain)
The peace of simple trust to gain,
Fold fancy's restless wings, and lay
The idols of my heart away.

' Welcome the silence all unbroken,
Nor less the words of fitness spoken, —
Such golden words as hers for whom
Our autumn flowers have just made
          room;   110
Whose hopeful utterance through and
          through
The freshness of the morning blew;
Who loved not less the earth that light
Fell on it from the heavens in sight,
But saw in all fair forms more fair
The Eternal beauty mirrored there.
Whose eighty years but added grace
And saintlier meaning to her face, —

The look of one who bore away
Glad tidings from the hills of day,　120
While all our hearts went forth to meet
The coming of her beautiful feet !
Or haply hers, whose pilgrim tread
Is in the paths where Jesus led;
Who dreams her childhood's sabbath dream
By Jordan's willow-shaded stream,
And, of the hymns of hope and faith,
Sung by the monks of Nazareth,
Hears pious echoes, in the call
To prayer, from Moslem minarets fall,　130
Repeating where his works were wrought
The lesson that her Master taught,
Of whom an elder Sibyl gave,
The prophecies of Cumæ's cave !

' I ask no organ's soulless breath
To drone the themes of life and death,
No altar candle-lit by day,
No ornate wordsman's rhetoric-play,
No cool philosophy to teach
Its bland audacities of speech　140
To double-tasked idolaters
Themselves their gods and worshippers,
No pulpit hammered by the fist
Of loud-asserting dogmatist,
Who borrows for the Hand of love
The smoking thunderbolts of Jove.
I know how well the fathers taught,
What work the later schoolmen wrought;
I reverence old-time faith and men,
But God is near us now as then;　150
His force of love is still unspent,
His hate of sin as imminent;
And still the measure of our needs
Outgrows the cramping bounds of creeds;
The manna gathered yesterday
Already savors of decay;
Doubts to the world's child-heart unknown
Question us now from star and stone;
Too little or too much we know,
And sight is swift and faith is slow;　160
The power is lost to self-deceive
With shallow forms of make-believe.
We walk at high noon, and the bells
Call to a thousand oracles,
But the sound deafens, and the light
Is stronger than our dazzled sight;
The letters of the sacred Book
Glimmer and swim beneath our look;
Still struggles in the Age's breast
With deepening agony of quest　170
The old entreaty : " Art thou He,
Or look we for the Christ to be ? "

' God should be most where man is least:
So, where is neither church nor priest,
And never rag of form or creed
To clothe the nakedness of need, —
Where farmer-folk in silence meet, —
I turn my bell-unsummoned feet;
I lay the critic's glass aside,
I tread upon my lettered pride,　180
And, lowest-seated, testify
To the oneness of humanity;
Confess the universal want,
And share whatever Heaven may grant.
He findeth not who seeks his own,
The soul is lost that 's saved alone.
Not on one favored forehead fell
Of old the fire-tongued miracle,
But flamed o'er all the thronging host
The baptism of the Holy Ghost;　190
Heart answers heart: in one desire
The blending lines of prayer aspire;
" Where, in my name, meet two or three,"
Our Lord hath said, " I there will be ! "

' So sometimes comes to soul and sense
The feeling which is evidence
That very near about us lies
The realm of spiritual mysteries.
The sphere of the supernal powers
Impinges on this world of ours.　200
The low and dark horizon lifts,
To light the scenic terror shifts;
The breath of a diviner air
Blows down the answer of a prayer:
That all our sorrow, pain, and doubt
A great compassion clasps about,
And law and goodness, love and force,
Are wedded fast beyond divorce.
Then duty leaves to love its task,
The beggar Self forgets to ask;　210
With smile of trust and folded hands,
The passive soul in waiting stands
To feel, as flowers the sun and dew,
The One true Life its own renew.

' So to the calmly gathered thought
The innermost of truth is taught,
The mystery dimly understood,
That love of God is love of good,
And, chiefly, its divinest trace
In Him of Nazareth's holy face;　220
That to be saved is only this, —
Salvation from our selfishness,
From more than elemental fire,
The soul's unsanctified desire,
From sin itself, and not the pain

That warns us of its chafing chain;
That worship's deeper meaning lies
In mercy, and not sacrifice,
Not proud humilities of sense
And posturing of penitence,   230
But love's unforced obedience;
That Book and Church and Day are given
For man, not God, — for earth, not
    heaven, —
The blessed means to holiest ends,
Not masters, but benignant friends;
That the dear Christ dwells not afar,
The king of some remoter star,
Listening, at times, with flattered ear
To homage wrung from selfish fear,
But here, amidst the poor and blind,   240
The bound and suffering of our kind,
In works we do, in prayers we pray,
Life of our life, He lives to-day.'

                                        1868.

AMONG THE HILLS [1]

PRELUDE

ALONG the roadside, like the flowers of
    gold
That tawny Incas for their gardens wrought,
Heavy with sunshine droops the golden-rod,
And the red pennons of the cardinal-flowers
Hang motionless upon their upright staves.
The sky is hot and hazy, and the wind,
Wing-weary with its long flight from the
    south,
Unfelt; yet, closely scanned, yon maple
    leaf
With faintest motion, as one stirs in dreams,
Confesses it. The locust by the wall   10
Stabs the noon-silence with his sharp alarm.
A single hay-cart down the dusty road
Creaks slowly, with its driver fast asleep
On the load's top. Against the neighbor-
    ing hill,
Huddled along the stone wall's shady side,
The sheep show white, as if a snowdrift
    still

[1] The lady of the poem 'Among the Hills' was purely imaginary. I was charmed with the scenery in Tam-worth and West Ossipee, and tried to call attention to it in a story. . . . With the long range of the Sandwich Mountains and Chocorua on one hand, and the rugged masses of Ossipee on the other, it is really one of the most picturesque situations in the State. (WHITTIER, in a letter of May 11, 1881, quoted in Pickard's *Life*, vol. ii, p. 669. See also pp. 536-538.) The poem was at first called 'A Summer Idyl,' and planned as a com-panion piece to the 'Snow-Bound, a Winter Idyl.'

Defied the dog-star. Through the open
    door
A drowsy smell of flowers — gray helio-
    trope,
And white sweet clover, and shy mignon-
    ette —
Comes faintly in, and silent chorus lends 20
To the pervading symphony of peace.

No time is this for hands long over-worn
To task their strength: and (unto Him be
    praise
Who giveth quietness!) the stress and
    strain
Of years that did the work of centuries
Have ceased, and we can draw our breath
    once more
Freely and full. So, as yon harvesters
Make glad their nooning underneath the
    elms
With tale and riddle and old snatch of song,
I lay aside grave themes, and idly turn   30
The leaves of memory's sketch-book, dream-
    ing o'er
Old summer pictures of the quiet hills,
And human life, as quiet, at their feet.

And yet not idly all. A farmer's son,
Proud of field-lore and harvest craft, and
    feeling
All their fine possibilities, how rich
And restful even poverty and toil
Become when beauty, harmony, and love
Sit at their humble hearth as angels sat
At evening in the patriarch's tent, when
    man   40
Makes labor noble, and his farmer's frock
The symbol of a Christian chivalry
Tender and just and generous to her
Who clothes with grace all duty; still, I
    know
Too well the picture has another side, —
How wearily the grind of toil goes on
Where love is wanting, how the eye and
    ear
And heart are starved amidst the plenitude
Of nature, and how hard and colorless
Is life without an atmosphere. I look   50
Across the lapse of half a century,
And call to mind old homesteads, where no
    flower
Told that the spring had come, but evil
    weeds,
Nightshade and rough-leaved burdock in
    the place

Of the sweet doorway greeting of the rose
And honeysuckle, where the house walls
    seemed
Blistering in sun, without a tree or vine
To cast the tremulous shadow of its leaves
Across the curtainless windows, from whose
    panes
Fluttered the signal rags of shiftlessness. 60
Within, the cluttered kitchen floor, un-
    washed
(Broom-clean I think they called it) ; the
    best room
Stifling with cellar-damp, shut from the air
In hot midsummer, bookless, pictureless
Save the inevitable sampler hung
Over the fireplace, or a mourning piece,
A green-haired woman, peony-cheeked, be-
    neath
Impossible willows; the wide-throated
    hearth
Bristling with faded pine-boughs half con-
    cealing
The piled-up rubbish at the chimney's
    back;   70
And, in sad keeping with all things about
    them,
Shrill, querulous women, sour and sullen
    men,
Untidy, loveless, old before their time,
With scarce a human interest save their
    own
Monotonous round of small economies,
Or the poor scandal of the neighborhood;
Blind to the beauty everywhere revealed,
Treading the May-flowers with regardless
    feet;
For them the song-sparrow and the bobolink
Sang not, nor winds made music in the
    leaves;   80
For them in vain October's holocaust
Burned, gold and crimson, over all the hills,
The sacramental mystery of the woods.
Church-goers, fearful of the unseen Powers,
But grumbling over pulpit-tax and pew-
    rent,
Saving, as shrewd economists, their souls
And winter pork with the least possible
    outlay
Of salt and sanctity; in daily life
Showing as little actual comprehension
Of Christian charity and love and duty 90
As if the Sermon on the Mount had been
Outdated like a last year's almanac:
Rich in broad woodlands and in half-tilled
    fields,

And yet so pinched and bare and comfort-
    less,
The veriest straggler limping on his rounds,
The sun and air his sole inheritance,
Laughed at a poverty that paid its taxes,
And hugged his rags in self-complacency !

Not such should be the homesteads of a land
Where whoso wisely wills and acts may
    dwell   100
As king and lawgiver, in broad-acred state,
With beauty, art, taste, culture, books, to
    make
His hour of leisure richer than a life
Of fourscore to the barons of old time.
Our yeoman should be equal to his home
Set in the fair, green valleys, purple walled,
A man to match his mountains, not to creep
Dwarfed and abased below them. I would
    fain
In this light way (of which I needs must
    own
With the knife-grinder of whom Canning
    sings,   110
' Story, God bless you ! I have none to tell
    you ! ')
Invite the eye to see and heart to feel
The beauty and the joy within their reach, —
Home, and home loves, and the beatitudes
Of nature free to all. Haply in years
That wait to take the places of our own,
Heard where some breezy balcony looks
    down
On happy homes, or where the lake in the
    moon
Sleeps dreaming of the mountains, fair as
    Ruth,
In the old Hebrew pastoral, at the feet 120
Of Boaz, even this simple lay of mine
May seem the burden of a prophecy,
Finding its late fulfilment in a change
Slow as the oak's growth, lifting manhood up
Through broader culture, finer manners,
    love,
And reverence, to the level of the hills.

O Golden Age whose light is of the dawn,
And not of sunset, forward, not behind,
Flood the new heavens and earth, and with
    thee bring
All the old virtues, whatsoever things 130
Are pure and honest and of good repute,
But add thereto whatever bard has sung
Or seer has told of when in trance and dream
They saw the Happy Isles of prophecy !

Let Justice hold her scale, and Truth divide
Between the right and wrong; but give the
          heart
The freedom of its fair inheritance;
Let the poor prisoner, cramped and starved
          so long,
At Nature's table feast his ear and eye
With joy and wonder; let all harmonies 140
Of sound, form, color, motion, wait upon
The princely guest, whether in soft attire
Of leisure clad, or the coarse frock of toil,
And, lending life to the dead form of faith,
Give human nature reverence for the sake
Of One who bore it, making it divine
With the ineffable tenderness of God;
Let common need, the brotherhood of
          prayer,
The heirship of an unknown destiny,   149
The unsolved mystery round about us, make
A man more precious than the gold of Ophir.
Sacred, inviolate, unto whom all things
Should minister, as outward types and signs
Of the eternal beauty which fulfils
The one great purpose of creation, Love,
The sole necessity of Earth and Heaven!

For weeks the clouds had raked the hills
    And vexed the vales with raining,
And all the woods were sad with mist,
    And all the brooks complaining.   160

At last, a sudden night-storm tore
    The mountain veils asunder,
And swept the valleys clean before
    The besom of the thunder.

Through Sandwich notch the west-wind
          sang
    Good morrow to the cotter;
And once again Chocorua's horn
    Of shadow pierced the water.

Above his broad lake, Ossipee,
    Once more the sunshine wearing,   170
Stooped, tracing on that silver shield
    His grim armorial bearing.

Clear drawn against the hard blue sky,
    The peaks had winter's keenness;
And, close on autumn's frost, the vales
    Had more than June's fresh greenness.

Again the sodden forest floors
    With golden lights were checkered,

Once more rejoicing leaves in wind
    And sunshine danced and flickered.   180

It was as if the summer's late
    Atoning for its sadness
Had borrowed every season's charm
    To end its days in gladness.

I call to mind those banded vales
    Of shadow and of shining,
Through which, my hostess at my side,
    I drove in day's declining.

We held our sidelong way above
    The river's whitening shallows,   190
By homesteads old, with wide-flung barns
    Swept through and through by swallows;

By maple orchards, belts of pine
    And larches climbing darkly
The mountain slopes, and, over all,
    The great peaks rising starkly.

You should have seen that long hill-range
    With gaps of brightness riven, —
How through each pass and hollow streamed
    The purpling lights of heaven, —   200

Rivers of gold-mist flowing down
    From far celestial fountains, —
The great sun flaming through the rifts
    Beyond the wall of mountains!

We paused at last where home-bound cows
    Brought down the pasture's treasure,
And in the barn the rhythmic flails
    Beat out a harvest measure.

We heard the night-hawk's sullen plunge,
    The crow his tree-mates calling: 210
The shadows lengthening down the slopes
    About our feet were falling.

And through them smote the level sun
    In broken lines of splendor,
Touched the gray rocks and made the green
    Of the shorn grass more tender.

The maples bending o'er the gate,
    Their arch of leaves just tinted
With yellow warmth, the golden glow
    Of coming autumn hinted.   220

Keen white between the farm-house showed,
    And smiled on porch and trellis

The fair democracy of flowers
  That equals cot and palace.

And weaving garlands for her dog,
  'Twixt chidings and caresses,
A human flower of childhood shook
  The sunshine from her tresses.

On either hand we saw the signs
  Of fancy and of shrewdness,   230
Where taste had wound its arms of vines
  Round thrift's uncomely rudeness.

The sun-brown farmer in his frock
  Shook hands, and called to Mary:
Bare-armed, as Juno might, she came,
  White-aproned from her dairy.

Her air, her smile, her motions, told
  Of womanly completeness;
A music as of household songs
  Was in her voice of sweetness.   240

Not fair alone in curve and line,
  But something more and better,
The secret charm eluding art,
  Its spirit, not its letter; —

An inborn grace that nothing lacked
  Of culture or appliance, —
The warmth of genial courtesy,
  The calm of self-reliance.

Before her queenly womanhood
  How dared our hostess utter   250
The paltry errand of her need
  To buy her fresh-churned butter ?

She led the way with housewife pride,
  Her goodly store disclosing,
Full tenderly the golden balls
  With practised hands disposing.

Then, while along the western hills
  We watched the changeful glory
Of sunset, on our homeward way,
  I heard her simple story.   260

The early crickets sang; the stream
  Plashed through my friend's narration:
Her rustic patois of the hills
  Lost in my free translation.

'More wise,' she said, 'than those who swarm
  Our hills in middle summer,

She came, when June's first roses blow,
  To greet the early comer.

'From school and ball and rout she came,
  The city's fair, pale daughter,   270
To drink the wine of mountain air
  Beside the Bearcamp Water.

'Her step grew firmer on the hills
  That watch our homesteads over;
On cheek and lip, from summer fields,
  She caught the bloom of clover.

'For health comes sparkling in the streams
  From cool Chocorua stealing:
There 's iron in our northern winds;
  Our pines are trees of healing.   280

'She sat beneath the broad-armed elms
  That skirt the mowing meadow,
And watched the gentle west-wind weave
  The grass with shine and shadow.

'Beside her, from the summer heat
  To share her grateful screening,
With forehead bared, the farmer stood,
  Upon his pitchfork leaning.

'Framed in its damp, dark locks, his face
  Had nothing mean or common, —   290
Strong, manly, true, the tenderness
  And pride beloved of woman.

'She looked up, glowing with the health
  The country air had brought her,
And, laughing, said: " You lack a wife,
  Your mother lacks a daughter.

' " To mend your frock and bake your bread
  You do not need a lady:
Be sure among these brown old homes
  Is some one waiting ready, —   300

' " Some fair, sweet girl with skilful hand
  And cheerful heart for treasure,
Who never played with ivory keys,
  Or danced the polka's measure."

'He bent his black brows to a frown,
  He set his white teeth tightly.
" 'T is well," he said, " for one like you
  To choose for me so lightly.

' " You think because my life is rude
  I take no note of sweetness: 310

I tell you love has naught to do
  With meetness or unmeetness.

' " Itself its best excuse, it asks
  No leave of pride or fashion
When silken zone or homespun frock
  It stirs with throbs of passion.

' " You think me deaf and blind: you bring
  Your winning graces hither
As free as if from cradle-time
  We two had played together.   320

' " You tempt me with your laughing eyes,
  Your cheek of sundown's blushes,
A motion as of waving grain,
  A music as of thrushes.

' " The plaything of your summer sport,
  The spells you weave around me
You cannot at your will undo,
  Nor leave me as you found me.

' " You go as lightly as you came,
  Your life is well without me;   330
What care you that these hills will close
  Like prison-walls about me ?

' " No mood is mine to seek a wife,
  Or daughter for my mother:
Who loves you loses in that love
  All power to love another !

' " I dare your pity or your scorn,
  With pride your own exceeding;
I fling my heart into your lap
  Without a word of pleading."   340

' She looked up in his face of pain
  So archly, yet so tender:
" And if I lend you mine," she said,
  " Will you forgive the lender ?

' " Nor frock nor tan can hide the man;
  And see you not, my farmer,
How weak and fond a woman waits
  Behind the silken armor ?

' " I love you: on that love alone,
  And not my worth, presuming,   350
Will you not trust for summer fruit
  The tree in May-day blooming ? "

' Alone the hangbird overhead,
  His hair-swung cradle straining,

Looked down to see love's miracle, —
  The giving that is gaining.

' And so the farmer found a wife,
  His mother found a daughter:
There looks no happier home than hers
  On pleasant Bearcamp Water.   360

' Flowers spring to blossom where she walks
  The careful ways of duty;
Our hard, stiff lines of life with her
  Are flowing curves of beauty.

' Our homes are cheerier for her sake,
  Our door-yards brighter blooming,
And all about the social air
  Is sweeter for her coming.

' Unspoken homilies of peace
  Her daily life is preaching;   370
The still refreshment of the dew
  Is her unconscious teaching.

' And never tenderer hand than hers
  Unknits the brow of ailing;
Her garments to the sick man's ear
  Have music in their trailing.

' And when, in pleasant harvest moons,
  The youthful huskers gather,
Or sleigh-drives on the mountain ways
  Defy the winter weather, —   380

' In sugar-camps, when south and warm
  The winds of March are blowing,
And sweetly from its thawing veins
  The maple's blood is flowing, —

' In summer, where some lilied pond
  Its virgin zone is baring,
Or where the ruddy autumn fire
  Lights up the apple-paring, —

' The coarseness of a ruder time
  Her finer mirth displaces,   390
A subtler sense of pleasure fills
  Each rustic sport she graces.

' Her presence lends its warmth and health
  To all who come before it.
If woman lost us Eden, such
  As she alone restore it.

' For larger life and wiser aims
  The farmer is her debtor;

Who holds to his another's heart
   Must needs be worse or better.   400

' Through her his civic service shows
   A purer-toned ambition;
No double consciousness divides
   The man and politician.

' In party's doubtful ways he trusts
   Her instincts to determine;
At the loud polls, the thought of her
   Recalls Christ's Mountain Sermon.

' He owns her logic of the heart,
   And wisdom of unreason,   410
Supplying, while he doubts and weighs,
   The needed word in season.

' He sees with pride her richer thought,
   Her fancy's freer ranges;
And love thus deepened to respect
   Is proof against all changes.

' And if she walks at ease in ways
   His feet are slow to travel,
And if she reads with cultured eyes
   What his may scarce unravel,   420

' Still clearer, for her keener sight
   Of beauty and of wonder,
He learns the meaning of the hills
   He dwelt from childhood under.

' And higher, warmed with summer lights,
   Or winter-crowned and hoary,
The ridged horizon lifts for him
   Its inner veils of glory.

' He has his own free, bookless lore,
   The lessons nature taught him,   430
The wisdom which the woods and hills
   And toiling men have brought him:

' The steady force of will whereby
   Her flexile grace seems sweeter;
The sturdy counterpoise which makes
   Her woman's life completer;

' A latent fire of soul which lacks
   No breath of love to fan it;
And wit, that, like his native brooks,
   Plays over solid granite.   440

' How dwarfed against his manliness
   She sees the poor pretension,

The wants, the aims, the follies, born
   Of fashion and convention !

' How life behind its accidents
   Stands strong and self-sustaining,
The human fact transcending all
   The losing and the gaining.

' And so in grateful interchange
   Of teacher and of hearer,   450
Their lives their true distinctness keep
   While daily drawing nearer.

' And if the husband or the wife
   In home's strong light discovers
Such slight defaults as failed to meet
   The blinded eyes of lovers,

' Why need we care to ask ? — who dreams
   Without their thorns of roses,
Or wonders that the truest steel
   The readiest spark discloses ?   460

' For still in mutual sufferance lies
   The secret of true living;
Love scarce is love that never knows
   The sweetness of forgiving.

' We send the Squire to General Court,
   He takes his young wife thither;
No prouder man election day
   Rides through the sweet June weather.

' He sees with eyes of manly trust
   All hearts to her inclining;   470
Not less for him his household light
   That others share its shining.'

Thus, while my hostess spake, there grew
   Before me, warmer tinted
And outlined with a tenderer grace,
   The picture that she hinted.

The sunset smouldered as we drove
   Beneath the deep hill-shadows.
Below us wreaths of white fog walked
   Like ghosts the haunted meadows.   480

Sounding the summer night, the stars
   Dropped down their golden plummets;
The pale arc of the Northern lights
   Rose o'er the mountain summits,

Until, at last, beneath its bridge,
   We heard the Bearcamp flowing,

And saw across the mapled lawn
  The welcome home-lights glowing.

And, musing on the tale I heard,
  'T were well, thought I, if often   490
To rugged farm-life came the gift
  To harmonize and soften;

If more and more we found the troth
  Of fact and fancy plighted,
And culture's charm and labor's strength
  In rural homes united, —

The simple life, the homely hearth,
  With beauty's sphere surrounding,
And blessing toil where toil abounds
  With graces more abounding.   500
1867–1868.   1868.

MARGUERITE [1]

THE robins sang in the orchard, the buds
    into blossoms grew;
Little of human sorrow the buds and the
    robins knew !

Sick, in an alien household, the poor French
    neutral lay;
Into her lonesome garret fell the light of
    the April day,

Through the dusty window, curtained by
    the spider's warp and woof,
On the loose-laid floor of hemlock, on oaken
    ribs of roof,

The bedquilt's faded patchwork, the tea-
    cups on the stand,
The wheel with flaxen tangle, as it dropped
    from her sick hand !

What to her was the song of the robin, or
    warm morning light,
As she lay in the trance of the dying, heed-
    less of sound or sight ?   10

[1] See the note on Longfellow's ' Evangeline,' p. 121.
Whittier wrote to Mrs. Fields in November, 1870 : ' You
know that a thousand of the Acadians were distributed
among the towns of Massachusetts, where they were
mostly treated as paupers.' In the letter already
quoted in the note on Evangeline, he says : ' The children were bound out to the families in the localities in
which they resided; and I wrote a poem upon finding, in
the records of Haverhill, the indenture that bound an
Acadian girl as a servant in one of the families of that
neighborhood. Gathering the story of her death, I wrote
" Marguerite." '

Done was the work of her hands, she had
    eaten her bitter bread;
The world of the alien people lay behind
    her dim and dead.

But her soul went back to its child-time;
    she saw the sun o'erflow
With gold the Basin of Minas, and set over
    Gaspereau;

The low, bare flats at ebb-tide, the rush of
    the sea at flood,
Through inlet and creek and river, from
    dike to upland wood;

The gulls in the red of morning, the fish-
    hawk's rise and fall,
The drift of the fog in moonshine, over the
    dark coast-wall.

She saw the face of her mother, she heard
    the song she sang;
And far off, faintly, slowly, the bell for
    vespers rang !   20

By her bed the hard-faced mistress sat,
    smoothing the wrinkled sheet,
Peering into the face, so helpless, and feel-
    ing the ice-cold feet.

With a vague remorse atoning for her greed
    and long abuse,
By care no longer heeded and pity too late
    for use.

Up the stairs of the garret softly the son of
    the mistress stepped,
Leaned over the head-board, covering his
    face with his hands, and wept.

Outspake the mother, who watched him
    sharply, with brow a-frown:
' What ! love you the Papist, the beggar,
    the charge of the town ? '

' Be she Papist or beggar who lies here, I
    know and God knows
I love her, and fain would go with her
    wherever she goes !   30

' O mother ! that sweet face came pleading,
    for love so athirst.
You saw but the town-charge; I knew her
    God's angel at first.'

shaking her gray head, the mistress hushed
    down a bitter cry;
And awed by the silence and shadow of
    death drawing nigh, -

She murmured a psalm of the Bible; but
    closer the young girl pressed,
With the last of her life in her fingers, the
    cross to her breast.

My son, come away,' cried the mother,
    her voice cruel grown.
She is joined to her idols, like Ephraim;
    let her alone !'

But he knelt with his hand on her forehead,
    his lips to her ear,
And he called back the soul that was pass-
    ing: 'Marguerite, do you hear ?' 40

She paused on the threshold of heaven;
    love, pity, surprise,
Wistful, tender, lit up for an instant the
    cloud of her eyes.

With his heart on his lips he kissed her,
    but never her cheek grew red,
And the words the living long for he spake
    in the ear of the dead.

And the robins sang in the orchard, where
    buds to blossoms grew;
Of the folded hands and the still face never
    the robins knew !
869.   1871.

IN SCHOOL–DAYS [1]

STILL sits the school-house by the road,
    A ragged beggar sleeping;
Around it still the sumachs grow,
    And blackberry-vines are creeping.

Within, the master's desk is seen,
    Deep scarred by raps official;
The warping floor, the battered seats,
    The jack-knife's carved initial;

The charcoal frescoes on its wall;
    Its door's worn sill, betraying 10

[1] See Pickard's *Whittier-Land*, pp. 32, 33. For Long-
fellow's comment on the poem, see Samuel Longfellow's
Life of H. W. Longfellow, vol. iii, p. 287; and for
Holmes's, Pickard's *Life of Whittier*, vol. ii, pp. 641, 642.
'You have written,' said Holmes to Whittier, 'the most
beautiful school-boy poem in the English language.'

The feet that, creeping slow to school,
    Went storming out to playing !

Long years ago a winter sun
    Shone over it at setting;
Lit up its western window-panes,
    And low eaves' icy fretting.

It touched the tangled golden curls,
    And brown eyes full of grieving,
Of one who still her steps delayed
    When all the school were leaving. 20

For near her stood the little boy
    Her childish favor singled:
His cap pulled low upon a face
    Where pride and shame were mingled.

Pushing with restless feet the snow
    To right and left, he lingered; —
As restlessly her tiny hands
    The blue-checked apron fingered.

He saw her lift her eyes; he felt
    The soft hand's light caressing, 30
And heard the tremble of her voice,
    As if a fault confessing.

'I 'm sorry that I spelt the word:
    I hate to go above you,
Because,' — the brown eyes lower fell, —
    'Because, you see, I love you !'

Still memory to a gray-haired man
    That sweet child-face is showing.
Dear girl ! the grasses on her grave
    Have forty years been growing ! 40

He lives to learn, in life's hard school,
    How few who pass above him
Lament their triumph and his loss,
    Like her, — because they love him.
1869.   1870.

MY TRIUMPH

THE autumn-time has come;
On woods that dream of bloom,
And over purpling vines
The low sun fainter shines.

The aster-flower is failing,
The hazel's gold is paling;
Yet overhead more near
The eternal stars appear !

And present gratitude
Insures the future's good,   10
And for the things I see,
I trust the things to be;

That in the paths untrod,
And the long days of God,
My feet shall still be led,
My heart be comforted.

O living friends who love me!
O dear ones gone above me!
Careless of other fame,
I leave to you my name.   20

Hide it from idle praises,
Save it from evil phrases:
Why, when dear lips that spake it
Are dumb, should strangers wake
    it?

Let the thick curtain fall;
I better know than all
How little I have gained,
How vast the unattained.

Not by the page word-painted
Let life be banned or sainted: 30
Deeper than written scroll
The colors of the soul.

Sweeter than any sung
My songs that found no tongue;
Nobler than any fact
My wish that failed of act.

Others shall sing the song,
Others shall right the wrong, —
Finish what I begin,
And all I fail of win.   40

What matter, I or they?
Mine or another's day,
So the right word be said
And life the sweeter made?

Hail to the coming singers!
Hail to the brave light-bringers!
Forward I reach and share
All that they sing and dare.

The airs of heaven blow o'er me;
A glory shines before me   50
Of what mankind shall be, —
Pure, generous, brave, and free.

A dream of man and woman
Diviner but still human,
Solving the riddle old,
Shaping the Age of Gold!

The love of God and neighbor;
An equal-handed labor;
The richer life, where beauty
Walks hand in hand with duty.

Ring, bells in unreared steeples,
The joy of unborn peoples!
Sound, trumpets far off blown,
Your triumph is my own!

Parcel and part of all,
I keep the festival,
Fore-reach the good to be,
And share the victory.

I feel the earth move sunward,
I join the great march onward,
And take, by faith, while living,
My freehold of thanksgiving.

1870

MY BIRTHDAY

BENEATH the moonlight and the snow
    Lies dead my latest year;
The winter winds are wailing low
    Its dirges in my ear.

I grieve not with the moaning wind
    As if a loss befell;
Before me, even as behind,
    God is, and all is well!

His light shines on me from above,
    His low voice speaks within, —
The patience of immortal love
    Outwearying mortal sin.

Not mindless of the growing years
    Of care and loss and pain,
My eyes are wet with thankful tears
    For blessings which remain.

If dim the gold of life has grown,
    I will not count it dross,
Nor turn from treasures still my own
    To sigh for lack and loss.

The years no charm from Nature take;
    As sweet her voices call,

As beautiful her mornings break,
  As fair her evenings fall.

Love watches o'er my quiet ways,
  Kind voices speak my name,
And lips that find it hard to praise
  Are slow, at least, to blame.

How softly ebb the tides of will !
  How fields, once lost or won,   30
Now lie behind me green and still
  Beneath a level sun !

How hushed the hiss of party hate,
  The clamor of the throng !
How old, harsh voices of debate
  Flow into rhythmic song !

Methinks the spirit's temper grows
  Too soft in this still air;
Somewhat the restful heart foregoes
  Of needed watch and prayer.   40

The bark by tempest vainly tossed
  May founder in the calm,
And he who braved the polar frost
  Faint by the isles of balm.

Better than self-indulgent years
  The outflung heart of youth,
Than pleasant songs in idle ears
  The tumult of the truth.

Rest for the weary hands is good,
  And love for hearts that pine,   50
But let the manly habitude
  Of upright souls be mine.

Let winds that blow from heaven refresh,
  Dear Lord, the languid air;
And let the weakness of the flesh
  Thy strength of spirit share.

And, if the eye must fail of light,
  The ear forget to hear,
Make clearer still the spirit's sight,
  More fine the inward ear !   60

Be near me in mine hours of need
  To soothe, or cheer, or warn,
And down these slopes of sunset lead
  As up the hills of morn !

                1871.

THE SISTERS

Annie and Rhoda, sisters twain,
Woke in the night to the sound of rain,

The rush of wind, the ramp and roar
Of great waves climbing a rocky shore.

Annie rose up in her bed-gown white,
And looked out into the storm and night.

' Hush, and hearken !' she cried in fear,
' Hearest thou nothing, sister dear ? '

' I hear the sea, and the plash of rain,
And roar of the northeast hurricane.   10

' Get thee back to the bed so warm,
No good comes of watching a storm.

' What is it to thee, I fain would know,
That waves are roaring and wild winds blow ?

' No lover of thine 's afloat to miss
The harbor-lights on a night like this.'

' But I heard a voice cry out my name,
Up from the sea on the wind it came !

' Twice and thrice have I heard it call,
And the voice is the voice of Estwick Hall ! '   20

On her pillow the sister tossed her head.
' Hall of the Heron is safe,' she said.

' In the tautest schooner that ever swam
He rides at anchor in Annisquam.

' And, if in peril from swamping sea
Or lee shore rocks, would he call on thee ? '

But the girl heard only the wind and tide,
And wringing her small white hands she cried:

' O sister Rhoda, there 's something wrong;
I hear it again, so loud and long.   30

' " Annie ! Annie ! " I hear it call,
And the voice is the voice of Estwick Hall ! '

Up sprang the elder, with eyes aflame,
' Thou liest ! He never would call thy name !

' If he did, I would pray the wind and sea
To keep him forever from thee and me ! '

Then out of the sea blew a dreadful blast;
Like the cry of a dying man it passed.

The young girl hushed on her lips a groan,
But through her tears a strange light
    shone, —   40

The solemn joy of her heart's release
To own and cherish its love in peace.

' Dearest ! ' she whispered, under breath,
' Life was a lie, but true is death.

' The love I hid from myself away
Shall crown me now in the light of day.

' My ears shall never to wooer list,
Never by lover my lips be kissed.

' Sacred to thee am I henceforth,
Thou in heaven and I on earth ! '   50

She came and stood by her sister's bed:
' Hall of the Heron is dead ! ' she said.

' The wind and the waves their work have
    done,
We shall see him no more beneath the sun.

' Little will reck that heart of thine;
It loved him not with a love like mine.

' I, for his sake, were he but here,
Could hem and 'broider thy bridal gear,

' Though hands should tremble and eyes
    be wet,
And stitch for stitch in my heart be set. 60

' But now my soul with his soul I wed;
Thine the living, and mine the dead ! '
                    1871.

THE THREE BELLS

BENEATH the low-hung night cloud
    That raked her splintering mast
The good ship settled slowly,
    The cruel leak gained fast.

Over the awful ocean
    Her signal guns pealed out.

Dear God ! was that thy answer
    From the horror round about ?

A voice came down the wild wind,
    ' Ho ! ship ahoy ! ' its cry: 10
' Our stout Three Bells of Glasgow
    Shall lay till daylight by ! '

Hour after hour crept slowly,
    Yet on the heaving swells
Tossed up and down the ship-lights,
    The lights of the Three Bells !

And ship to ship made signals,
    Man answered back to man,
While oft, to cheer and hearten,
    The Three Bells nearer ran;   20

And the captain from her taffrail
    Sent down his hopeful cry:
' Take heart ! Hold on ! ' he shouted !
    ' The Three Bells shall lay by ! '

All night across the waters
    The tossing lights shone clear;
All night from reeling taffrail
    The Three Bells sent her cheer.

And when the dreary watches
    Of storm and darkness passed,   30
Just as the wreck lurched under,
    All souls were saved at last.

Sail on, Three Bells, forever,
    In grateful memory sail !
Ring on, Three Bells of rescue,
    Above the wave and gale !

Type of the Love eternal,
    Repeat the Master's cry,
As tossing through our darkness
    The lights of God draw nigh !   40
                    1872.

CONDUCTOR BRADLEY[1]

CONDUCTOR BRADLEY (always may his
    name
Be said with reverence !), as the swift doom
    came,
Smitten to death, a crushed and mangled
    frame,

[1] A railway conductor who lost his life in an accident
on a Connecticut railway, May 9, 1873. (WHITTIER.)

Sank, with the brake he grasped just where
    he stood
To do the utmost that a brave man could,
And die, if needful, as a true man should.

Men stooped above him; women dropped
    their tears
On that poor wreck beyond all hopes or
    fears,
Lost in the strength and glory of his years.

What heard they? Lo! the ghastly lips
    of pain,   10
Dead to all thought save duty's, moved
    again:
' Put out the signals for the other train ! '

No nobler utterance since the world be-
    gan
From lips of saint or martyr ever ran,
Electric, through the sympathies of man.

Ah me ! how poor and noteless seem to
    this
The sick-bed dramas of self-conscious-
    ness,
Our sensual fears of pain and hopes of
    bliss !

Oh, grand, supreme endeavor ! Not in
    vain
That last brave act of failing tongue and
    brain!   20
Freighted with life the downward rushing
    train,

Following the wrecked one, as wave follows
    wave,
Obeyed the warning which the dead lips
    gave.
Others he saved, himself he could not
    save.

Nay, the lost life *was* saved. He is not
    dead
Who in his record still the earth shall
    tread
With God's clear aureole shining round
    his head.

We bow as in the dust, with all our pride
Of virtue dwarfed the noble deed beside.
God give us grace to live as Bradley
    died !   30
1873.   1873.

A MYSTERY [1]

THE river hemmed with leaning trees
    Wound through its meadows green;
A low, blue line of mountains showed
    The open pines between.

One sharp, tall peak above them all
    Clear into sunlight sprang:
I saw the river of my dreams,
    The mountains that I sang !

No clew of memory led me on,
    But well the ways I knew;   10
A feeling of familiar things
    With every footstep grew.

Not otherwise above its crag
    Could lean the blasted pine;
Not otherwise the maple hold
    Aloft its red ensign.

So up the long and shorn foot-hills
    The mountain road should creep;
So, green and low, the meadow fold
    Its red-haired kine asleep.   20

The river wound as it should wind;
    Their place the mountains took;
The white torn fringes of their clouds
    Wore no unwonted look.

Yet ne'er before that river's rim
    Was pressed by feet of mine,
Never before mine eyes had crossed
    That broken mountain line.

A presence, strange at once and known,
    Walked with me as my guide;   30
The skirts of some forgotten life
    Trailed noiseless at my side.

Was it a dim-remembered dream ?
    Or glimpse through æons old ?
The secret which the mountains kept
    The river never told.

But from the vision ere it passed
    A tender hope I drew,
And, pleasant as a dawn of spring,
    The thought within me grew,   40

That love would temper every change,
    And soften all surprise,

[1] Compare Lowell's ' In the Twilight.'

And, misty with the dreams of earth,
  The hills of Heaven arise.
                                    1873.

THE PRAYER OF AGASSIZ [1]

On the isle of Penikese,
Ringed about by sapphire seas,
Fanned by breezes salt and cool,
Stood the Master with his school.
Over sails that not in vain
Wooed the west-wind's steady strain,
Line of coast that low and far
Stretched its undulating bar,
Wings aslant across the rim
Of the waves they stooped to skim,   10
Rock and isle and glistening bay,
Fell the beautiful white day.

Said the Master to the youth:
'We have come in search of truth,
Trying with uncertain key
Door by door of mystery;
We are reaching, through his laws,
To the garment-hem of Cause,
Him, the endless, unbegun,
The Unnamable, the One   20
Light of all our light the Source,
Life of life, and Force of force.

As with fingers of the blind,
We are groping here to find
What the hieroglyphics mean
Of the Unseen in the seen,
What the Thought which underlies
Nature's masking and disguise,
What it is that hides beneath
Blight and bloom and birth and death.   30
By past efforts unavailing,
Doubt and error, loss and failing,
Of our weakness made aware,

[1] The island of Penikese in Buzzard's Bay was given by
Mr. John Anderson to Agassiz for the uses of a summer
school of natural history. A large barn was cleared
and improvised as a lecture-room. Here, on the first
morning of the school, all the company was gathered.
'Agassiz had arranged no programme of exercises,'
says Mrs. Agassiz, in *Louis Agassiz; his Life and Correspondence*, 'trusting to the interest of the occasion
to suggest what might best be said or done. But, as he
looked upon his pupils gathered there to study nature
with him, by an impulse as natural as it was unpremeditated, he called upon them to join in silently asking God's blessing on their work together. The pause
was broken by the first words of an address no less
fervent than its unspoken prelude.' This was in the
summer of 1873, and Agassiz died the December following. (Whittier.)

On the threshold of our task
Let us light and guidance ask,
Let us pause in silent prayer!'

Then the Master in his place
Bowed his head a little space,
And the leaves by soft airs stirred,
Lapse of wave and cry of bird,   40
Left the solemn hush unbroken
Of that wordless prayer unspoken,
While its wish, on earth unsaid,
Rose to heaven interpreted.
As, in life's best hours, we hear
By the spirit's finer ear
His low voice within us, thus
The All-Father heareth us;
And his holy ear we pain
With our noisy words and vain.   50
Not for Him our violence
Storming at the gates of sense,
His the primal language, his
The eternal silences!

Even the careless heart was moved,
And the doubting gave assent,
With a gesture reverent,
To the Master well-beloved.
As thin mists are glorified
By the light they cannot hide,   60
All who gazed upon him saw,
Through its veil of tender awe,
How his face was still uplit
By the old sweet look of it,
Hopeful, trustful, full of cheer,
And the love that casts out fear.
Who the secret may declare
Of that brief, unuttered prayer?
Did the shade before him come
Of th' inevitable doom,   70
Of the end of earth so near,
And Eternity's new year?

In the lap of sheltering seas
Rests the isle of Penikese;
But the lord of the domain
Comes not to his own again:
Where the eyes that follow fail,
On a vaster sea his sail
Drifts beyond our beck and hail.
Other lips within its bound   80
Shall the laws of life expound;
Other eyes from rock and shell
Read the world's old riddles well:
But when breezes light and bland
Blow from Summer's blossomed land,

When the air is glad with wings,
And the blithe song-sparrow sings,
Many an eye with his still face
Shall the living ones displace,
Many an ear the word shall seek   90
He alone could fitly speak.
And one name forevermore
Shall be uttered o'er and o'er
By the waves that kiss the shore,
By the curlew's whistle sent
Down the cool, sea-scented air;
In all voices known to her,
Nature owns her worshipper,
Half in triumph, half lament.
Thither Love shall tearful turn,   100
Friendship pause uncovered there,
And the wisest reverence learn
From the Master's silent prayer.

1874.   1874.

A SEA DREAM [1]

WE saw the slow tides go and come,
  The curving surf-lines lightly drawn,
The gray rocks touched with tender
    bloom
  Beneath the fresh-blown rose of dawn.

We saw in richer sunsets lost
  The sombre pomp of showery noons;
And signalled spectral sails that crossed
  The weird, low light of rising moons.

On stormy eves from cliff and head
  We saw the white spray tossed and
    spurned;   10
While over all, in gold and red,
  Its face of fire the lighthouse turned.

The rail-car brought its daily crowds,
  Half curious, half indifferent,
Like passing sails or floating clouds,
  We saw them as they came and went.

But, one calm morning, as we lay
  And watched the mirage-lifted wall
Of coast, across the dreamy bay,
  And heard afar the curlew call,   20

And nearer voices, wild or tame,
  Of airy flock and childish throng,
Up from the water's edge there came
  Faint snatches of familiar song.

[1] See Pickard's *Whittier-Land*, pp. 67-72.

Careless we heard the singer's choice
  Of old and common airs; at last
The tender pathos of his voice
  In one low chanson held us fast.

A song that mingled joy and pain,
  And memories old and sadly sweet;   30
While, timing to its minor strain,
  The waves in lapsing cadence beat.

The waves are glad in breeze and sun;
  The rocks are fringed with foam;
I walk once more a haunted shore,
  A stranger, yet at home,
  A land of dreams I roam.

Is this the wind, the soft sea-wind
  That stirred thy locks of brown?
Are these the rocks whose mosses knew
  The trail of thy light gown,   41
  Where boy and girl sat down?

I see the gray fort's broken wall, [2]
  The boats that rock below;
And, out at sea, the passing sails
  We saw so long ago
  Rose-red in morning's glow.

The freshness of the early time
  On every breeze is blown;
As glad the sea, as blue the sky, —   50
  The change is ours alone;
  The saddest is my own.

A stranger now, a world-worn man,
  Is he who bears my name;
But thou, methinks, whose mortal life
  Immortal youth became,
  Art evermore the same.

Thou art not here, thou art not there,
  Thy place I cannot see;
I only know that where thou art   60
  The blessed angels be,
  And heaven is glad for thee.

Forgive me if the evil years
  Have left on me their sign;
Wash out, O soul so beautiful,
  The many stains of mine
  In tears of love divine!

[2] The place that was in the mind of the poet when he wrote this stanza was on the rocks at Marblehead, where he had spent an early morning more than forty years before. (*Cambridge Edition* of Whittier's Poems.)

I could not look on thee and live,
　If thou wert by my side;
The vision of a shining one,   70
　The white and heavenly bride,
　Is well to me denied.

But turn to me thy dear girl-face
　Without the angel's crown,
The wedded roses of thy lips,
　Thy loose hair rippling down
　In waves of golden brown.

Look forth once more through space and
　time,
　And let thy sweet shade fall
In tenderest grace of soul and form   80
　On memory's frescoed wall,
　A shadow, and yet all !

Draw near, more near, forever dear !
　Where'er I rest or roam,
Or in the city's crowded streets,
　Or by the blown sea foam,
　The thought of thee is home !

At breakfast hour the singer read
　The city news, with comment wise,
Like one who felt the pulse of trade   90
　Beneath his finger fall and rise.

His look, his air, his curt speech, told
　The man of action, not of books,
To whom the corners made in gold
　And stocks were more than seaside
　　nooks.

Of life beneath the life confessed
　His song had hinted unawares;
Of flowers in traffic's ledgers pressed,
　Of human hearts in bulls and bears.

But eyes in vain were turned to watch   100
　That face so hard and shrewd and strong;
And ears in vain grew sharp to catch
　The meaning of that morning song.

In vain some sweet-voiced querist sought
　To sound him, leaving as she came;
Her baited album only caught
　A common, unromantic name.

No word betrayed the mystery fine,
　That trembled on the singer's tongue;

He came and went, and left no sign   110
　Behind him save the song he sung.
　　　　　　　　　　　　　1874.

SUNSET ON THE BEARCAMP

A GOLD fringe on the purpling hem
　Of hills the river runs,
As down its long, green valley falls
　The last of summer's suns.
Along its tawny gravel-bed
　Broad-flowing, swift, and still,
As if its meadow levels felt
　The hurry of the hill,
Noiseless between its banks of green
　From curve to curve it slips;   10
The drowsy maple-shadows rest
　Like fingers on its lips.

A waif from Carroll's wildest hills,
　Unstoried and unknown;
The ursine legend of its name
　Prowls on its banks alone.
Yet flowers as fair its slopes adorn
　As ever Yarrow knew,
Or, under rainy Irish skies,
　By Spenser's Mulla grew;   20
And through the gaps of leaning trees
　Its mountain cradle shows:
The gold against the amethyst,
　The green against the rose.

Touched by a light that hath no name,
　A glory never sung,
Aloft on sky and mountain wall
　Are God's great pictures hung.
How changed the summits vast and old !
　No longer granite-browed,   30
They melt in rosy mist; the rock
　Is softer than the cloud;
The valley holds its breath; no leaf
　Of all its elms is twirled:
The silence of eternity
　Seems falling on the world.

The pause before the breaking seals
　Of mystery is this;
Yon miracle-play of night and day
　Makes dumb its witnesses.   40
What unseen altar crowns the hills
　That reach up stair on stair ?
What eyes look through, what white wings
　fan
　These purple veils of air ?

What Presence from the heavenly heights
  To those of earth stoops down ?
Not vainly Hellas dreamed of gods
  On Ida's snowy crown !

Slow fades the vision of the sky,
  The golden water pales,   50
And over all the valley-land
  A gray-winged vapor sails.
I go the common way of all;
  The sunset fires will burn,
The flowers will blow, the river flow,
  When I no more return.
No whisper from the mountain pine
  Nor lapsing stream shall tell
The stranger, treading where I tread,
  Of him who loved them well.   60

But beauty seen is never lost,
  God's colors all are fast;
The glory of this sunset heaven
  Into my soul has passed,
A sense of gladness unconfined
  To mortal date or clime;
As the soul liveth, it shall live
  Beyond the years of time.
Beside the mystic asphodels
  Shall bloom the home-born flowers,   70
And new horizons flush and glow
  With sunset hues of ours.

Farewell ! these smiling hills must wear
  Too soon their wintry frown,
And snow-cold winds from off them
      shake
  The maple's red leaves down.
But I shall see a summer sun
  Still setting broad and low;
The mountain slopes shall blush and bloom,
  The golden water flow.   80
A lover's claim is mine on all
  I see to have and hold, —
The rose-light of perpetual hills,
  And sunsets never cold !
1875.   1876.

LEXINGTON

1775

No Berserk thirst of blood had they,
  No battle-joy was theirs, who set
    Against the alien bayonet
  Their homespun breasts in that old day.

Their feet had trodden peaceful ways;
  They loved not strife, they dreaded
      pain;
  They saw not, what to us is plain,
That God would make man's wrath his
      praise.

No seers were they, but simple men;
  Its vast results the future hid: 10
  The meaning of the work they did
Was strange and dark and doubtful then.

Swift as their summons came they left
  The plough mid-furrow standing still,
  The half - ground corn grist in the
      mill,
The spade in earth, the axe in cleft.

They went where duty seemed to call,
  They scarcely asked the reason why;
  They only knew they could but die,
And death was not the worst of all !   20

Of man for man the sacrifice,
  All that was theirs to give, they gave.
  The flowers that blossomed from their
      grave
Have sown themselves beneath all skies.

Their death-shot shook the feudal tower,
  And shattered slavery's chain as well;
  On the sky's dome, as on a bell,
Its echo struck the world's great hour.

That fateful echo is not dumb:
  The nations listening to its sound   30
  Wait, from a century's vantage-ground,
The holier triumphs yet to come, —

The bridal time of Law and Love,
  The gladness of the world's release,
  When, war-sick, at the feet of Peace
The hawk shall nestle with the dove ! —

The golden age of brotherhood
  Unknown to other rivalries
  Than of the mild humanities,
And gracious interchange of good,   40

When closer strand shall lean to strand,
  Till meet, beneath saluting flags,
  The eagle of our mountain-crags,
The lion of our Motherland !
1875.   1875.

CENTENNIAL HYMN [1]

I

Our fathers' God! from out whose hand
The centuries fall like grains of sand,
We meet to-day, united, free,
And loyal to our land and Thee,
To thank Thee for the era done,
And trust Thee for the opening one.

II

Here, where of old, by thy design,
The fathers spake that word of thine
Whose echo is the glad refrain
Of rended bolt and falling chain,   10
To grace our festal time, from all
The zones of earth our guests we call.

III

Be with us while the New World greets
The Old World thronging all its streets,
Unveiling all the triumphs won
By art or toil beneath the sun;
And unto common good ordain
This rivalship of hand and brain.

IV

Thou, who hast here in concord furled
The war flags of a gathered world,   20
Beneath our Western skies fulfil
The Orient's mission of good-will,
And, freighted with love's Golden Fleece,
Send back its Argonauts of peace.

V

For art and labor met in truce,
For beauty made the bride of use,
We thank Thee; but, withal, we crave
The austere virtues strong to save,
The honor proof to place or gold,
The manhood never bought nor sold!   30

VI

Oh make Thou us, through centuries
    long,
In peace secure, in justice strong;
Around our gift of freedom draw
The safeguards of thy righteous law:
And, cast in some diviner mould,
Let the new cycle shame the old!
1876.   1876.

[1] Written for the opening of the International Exhibition, Philadelphia, May 10, 1876. The music for the hymn was written by John K. Paine, and may be found in *The Atlantic Monthly* for June, 1876.

(WHITTIER.)

THE PROBLEM

I

Not without envy Wealth at times must
    look
On their brown strength who wield the
    reaping-hook
    And scythe, or at the forge-fire shape
        the plough
Or the steel harness of the steeds of steam;
    All who, by skill and patience, anyhow
Make service noble, and the earth redeem
From savageness. By kingly accolade
Than theirs was never worthier knighthood
    made.
Well for them, if, while demagogues their
    vain
And evil counsels proffer, they maintain 10
    Their honest manhood unseduced, and
        wage
No war with Labor's right to Labor's gain
Of sweet home-comfort, rest of hand and
    brain,
    And softer pillow for the head of Age.

II

And well for Gain if it ungrudging yields
    Labor its just demand; and well for
        Ease
    If in the uses of its own, it sees
No wrong to him who tills its pleasant
    fields
    And spreads the table of its luxuries.
The interests of the rich man and the poor
Are one and same, inseparable evermore; 21
And, when scant wage or labor fail to give
Food, shelter, raiment, wherewithal to live,
Need has its rights, necessity its claim.
Yea, even self-wrought misery and shame
Test well the charity suffering long and
    kind.
The home-pressed question of the age can
    find
No answer in the catch-words of the blind
Leaders of blind. Solution there is none
Save in the Golden Rule of Christ alone. 30
1876?   (1878.)

RESPONSE [2]

Beside that milestone where the level sun,
Nigh unto setting, sheds his last, low rays

[2] Written in response to the many tokens of esteem which Whittier received on his seventieth birthday.

On word and work irrevocably done,
Life's blending threads of good and ill out-
    spun,
I hear, O friends ! your words of cheer and
    praise,
Half doubtful if myself or otherwise.
Like him who, in the old Arabian joke,
A beggar slept and crownèd Caliph woke.
Thanks not the less. With not unglad sur-
    prise
I see my life-work through your partial
    eyes;
Assured, in giving to my home-taught
    songs
A higher value than of right belongs,
You do but read between the written
    lines
The finer grace of unfulfilled designs.
1877.   1877.

AT EVENTIDE

POOR and inadequate the shadow-play
    Of gain and loss, of waking and of
        dream,
    Against life's solemn background needs
        must seem
At this late hour. Yet, not unthankfully,
I call to mind the fountains by the way,
The breath of flowers, the bird-song on the
    spray,
Dear friends, sweet human loves, the joy
    of giving
And of receiving, the great boon of liv-
    ing
    In grand historic years when Liberty
Had need of word and work, quick sympa-
    thies
For all who fail and suffer, song's relief,
Nature's uncloying loveliness; and chief,
    The kind restraining hand of Provi-
        dence,
    The inward witness, the assuring sense
Of an Eternal Good which overlies
The sorrow of the world, Love which out-
    lives
All sin and wrong, Compassion which for-
    gives
To the uttermost, and Justice whose clear
    eyes
Through lapse and failure look to the in-
    tent,
And judge our frailty by the life we meant.
                                    1878.

THE TRAILING ARBUTUS

I WANDERED lonely where the pine-trees
    made
Against the bitter East their barricade,
    And, guided by its sweet
Perfume, I found, within a narrow dell,
The trailing spring flower tinted like a
    shell
    Amid dry leaves and mosses at my feet.

From under dead boughs, for whose loss
    the pines
Moaned ceaseless overhead, the blossoming
    vines
    Lifted their glad surprise,
While yet the bluebird smoothed in leafless
    trees
His feathers ruffled by the chill sea-breeze,
    And snow-drifts lingered under April
        skies.

As, pausing, o'er the lonely flower I bent,
I thought of lives thus lowly, clogged and
    pent,
    Which yet find room,
Through care and cumber, coldness and
    decay,
To lend a sweetness to the ungenial day,
    And make the sad earth happier for their
        bloom.
                                    1879 ?

OUR AUTOCRAT [1]

HIS laurels fresh from song and lay,
    Romance, art, science, rich in all,
And young of heart, how dare we say
    We keep his seventieth festival ?

No sense is here of loss or lack;
    Before his sweetness and his light
The dial holds its shadow back,
    The charmèd hours delay their flight.

His still the keen analysis
    Of men and moods, electric wit,   10
Free play of mirth, and tenderness
    To heal the slightest wound from it.

And his the pathos touching all
    Life's sins and sorrows and regrets,

[1] Read at the breakfast given in honor of Holmes's
seventieth birthday.

Its hopes and fears, its final call
   And rest beneath the violets.

His sparkling surface scarce betrays
   The thoughtful tide beneath it rolled,
The wisdom of the latter days,
   And tender memories of the old.   20

What shapes and fancies, grave or gay,
   Before us at his bidding come !
The Treadmill tramp, the One-Horse
     Shay,
   The dumb despair of Elsie's doom !

The tale of Avis and the Maid,
   The plea for lips that cannot speak,
The holy kiss that Iris laid
   On Little Boston's pallid cheek!

Long may he live to sing for us
   His sweetest songs at evening time,   30
And, like his Chambered Nautilus,
   To holier heights of beauty climb !

Though now unnumbered guests surround
   The table that he rules at will,
Its Autocrat, however crowned,
   Is but our friend and comrade still.

The world may keep his honored name,
   The wealth of all his varied powers;
A stronger claim has love than fame,
   And he himself is only ours !   40
1879.   1879.

GARRISON [1]

THE storm and peril overpast,
   The hounding hatred shamed and still,
Go, soul of freedom ! take at last
   The place which thou alone canst fill.

Confirm the lesson taught of old —
   Life saved for self is lost, while they
Who lose it in his service hold
   The lease of God's eternal day.

Not for thyself, but for the slave
   Thy words of thunder shook the world; 10

[1] My poetical service in the cause of freedom is almost synchronous with his life of devotion to the same cause. (WHITTIER.)
   See Pickard's *Life of Whittier*, vol. ii, p. 668 ; and the article on Garrison in Whittier's *Prose Works*, vol. iii, pp. 189–192.

No selfish griefs or hatred gave
   The strength wherewith thy bolts were
     hurled.

From lips that Sinai's trumpet blew
   We heard a tender under song;
Thy very wrath from pity grew,
   From love of man thy hate of wrong.

Now past and present are as one;
   The life below is life above;
Thy mortal years have but begun
   Thy immortality of love.   20

With somewhat of thy lofty faith
   We lay the outworn garment by,
Give death but what belongs to death,
   And life the life that cannot die !

Not for a soul like thine the calm
   Of selfish ease and joys of sense;
But duty, more than crown or palm,
   Its own exceeding recompense.

Go up and on ! thy day well done,
   Its morning promise well fulfilled,   30
Arise to triumphs yet unwon,
   To holier tasks that God has willed.

Go, leave behind thee all that mars
   The work below of man for man;
With the white legions of the stars
   Do service such as angels can.

Wherever wrong shall right deny
   Or suffering spirits urge their plea,
Be thine a voice to smite the lie,
   A hand to set the captive free !   40
1879.   1879.

THE LOST OCCASION [2]

SOME die too late and some too soon,
At early morning, heat of noon,
Or the chill evening twilight. Thou,
Whom the rich heavens did so endow
With eyes of power and Jove's own brow,
With all the massive strength that fills
Thy home-horizon's granite hills,
With rarest gifts of heart and head
From manliest stock inherited,
New England's stateliest type of man,   10
In port and speech Olympian;

[2] See the note on ' Ichabod,' p. 282.

Whom no one met, at first, but took
A second awed and wondering look
(As turned, perchance, the eyes of Greece
On Phidias' unveiled masterpiece);
Whose words in simplest homespun clad,
The Saxon strength of Cædmon's had,
With power reserved at need to reach
The Roman forum's loftiest speech,
Sweet with persuasion, eloquent   20
In passion, cool in argument,
Or, ponderous, falling on thy foes
As fell the Norse god's hammer blows,
Crushing as if with Talus' flail
Through Error's logic-woven mail,
And failing only when they tried
The adamant of the righteous side, —
Thou, foiled in aim and hope, bereaved
Of old friends, by the new deceived,
Too soon for us, too soon for thee,   30
Beside thy lonely Northern sea,
Where long and low the marsh-lands spread,
Laid wearily down thy august head.

Thou shouldst have lived to feel below
Thy feet Disunion's fierce upthrow;
The late-sprung mine that underlaid
Thy sad concessions vainly made.
Thou shouldst have seen from Sumter's wall
The star-flag of the Union fall,
And armed rebellion pressing on   40
The broken lines of Washington !
No stronger voice than thine had then
Called out the utmost might of men,
To make the Union's charter free
And strengthen law by liberty.
How had that stern arbitrament
To thy gray age youth's vigor lent,
Shaming ambition's paltry prize
Before thy disillusioned eyes;
Breaking the spell about thee wound   50
Like the green withes that Samson bound;
Redeeming in one effort grand,
Thyself and thy imperilled land !
Ah, cruel fate, that closed to thee,
O sleeper by the Northern sea,
The gates of opportunity !
God fills the gaps of human need,
Each crisis brings its word and deed.
Wise men and strong we did not lack;
But still, with memory turning back,   60
In the dark hours we thought of thee,
And thy lone grave beside the sea.
Above that grave the east winds blow,
And from the marsh-lands drifting slow
The sea-fog comes, with evermore

The wave-wash of a lonely shore,
And sea-bird's melancholy cry,
As Nature fain would typify
The sadness of a closing scene,
The loss of that which should have been.   70
But, where thy native mountains bare
Their foreheads to diviner air,
Fit emblem of enduring fame,
One lofty summit keeps thy name.
For thee the cosmic forces did
The rearing of that pyramid,
The prescient ages shaping with
Fire, flood, and frost thy monolith.
Sunrise and sunset lay thereon
With hands of light their benison,   80
The stars of midnight pause to set
Their jewels in its coronet.
And evermore that mountain mass
Seems climbing from the shadowy pass [1]
To light, as if to manifest
Thy nobler self, thy life at best !

                                        1880.

STORM ON LAKE ASQUAM

A CLOUD, like that the old-time Hebrew saw
    On Carmel prophesying rain, began
    To lift itself o'er wooded Cardigan,
Growing and blackening. Suddenly, a flaw

Of chill wind menaced; then a strong blast
        beat
    Down the long valley's murmuring pines,
        and woke
    The noon-dream of the sleeping lake, and
        broke
Its smooth steel mirror at the mountains'
        feet.

Thunderous and vast, a fire-veined darkness
        swept
    Over the rough pine-bearded Asquam
        range;
    A wraith of tempest, wonderful and
        strange,
From peak to peak the cloudy giant stepped.

One moment, as if challenging the storm,
    Chocorua's tall, defiant sentinel
    Looked from his watch-tower; then the
        shadow fell,
And the wild rain-drift blotted out his form.

[1] Mt. Webster stands next the White Mountain Notch,
at the southern end of the Presidential Range.

And over all the still unhidden sun,
  Weaving its light through slant-blown
    veils of rain,
  Smiled on the trouble, as hope smiles on
    pain;
And, when the tumult and the strife were
    done,

With one foot on the lake, and one on
    land,
  Framing within his crescent's tinted
    streak
  A far-off picture of the Melvin peak,
Spent broken clouds the rainbow's angel
    spanned.
                                    1882.

THE POET AND THE CHILDREN

LONGFELLOW

With a glory of winter sunshine
  Over his locks of gray,
In the old historic mansion
  He sat on his last birthday;

With his books and his pleasant pic-
    tures,
  And his household and his kin,
While a sound as of myriads singing
  From far and near stole in.

It came from his own fair city,
  From the prairie's boundless plain,   10
From the Golden Gate of sunset,
  And the cedarn woods of Maine.

And his heart grew warm within him,
  And his moistening eyes grew dim,
For he knew that his country's children
  Were singing the songs of him:

The lays of his life's glad morning,
  The psalms of his evening time,
Whose echoes shall float forever
  On the winds of every clime.   20

All their beautiful consolations,
  Sent forth like birds of cheer,
Came flocking back to his windows,
  And sang in the Poet's ear.

Grateful, but solemn and tender,
  The music rose and fell

With a joy akin to sadness
  And a greeting like farewell.

With a sense of awe he listened
  To the voices sweet and young;   30
The last of earth and the first of heaven
  Seemed in the songs they sung.

And waiting a little longer
  For the wonderful change to come,
He heard the Summoning Angel,
  Who calls God's children home!

And to him in a holier welcome
  Was the mystical meaning given
Of the words of the blessed Master:
  'Of such is the kingdom of heaven!'   40
                                    1882.

AN AUTOGRAPH

I write my name as one,
  On sands by waves o'errun
Or winter's frosted pane,
  Traces a record vain.

Oblivion's blankness claims
  Wiser and better names,
And well my own may pass
  As from the strand or glass.

Wash on, O waves of time!
  Melt, noons, the frosty rime!
Welcome the shadow vast,
  The silence that shall last!

When I and all who know
  And love me vanish so,
What harm to them or me
  Will the lost memory be?

If any words of mine,
  Through right of life divine,
Remain, what matters it
  Whose hand the message writ?   20

Why should the 'crowner's quest'
  Sit on my worst or best?
Why should the showman claim
  The poor ghost of my name?

Yet, as when dies a sound
  Its spectre lingers round,
Haply my spent life will
  Leave some faint echo still.

A whisper giving breath
Of praise or blame to death, 30
Soothing or saddening such
As loved the living much.

Therefore with yearnings vain
And fond I still would fain
A kindly judgment seek,
A tender thought bespeak.

And, while my words are read,
Let this at least be said:
'Whate'er his life's defeatures,
He loved his fellow-creatures. 40

'If, of the Law's stone table,
To hold he scarce was able
The first great precept fast,
He kept for man the last.

'Through mortal lapse and dulness
What lacks the Eternal Fulness,
If still our weakness can
Love Him in loving man?

'Age brought him no despairing
Of the world's future faring; 50
In human nature still
He found more good than ill.

'To all who dumbly suffered,
His tongue and pen he offered;
His life was not his own,
Nor lived for self alone.

'Hater of din and riot
He lived in days unquiet;
And, lover of all beauty,
Trod the hard ways of duty. 60

'He meant no wrong to any
He sought the good of many,
Yet knew both sin and folly, —
May God forgive him wholly!'
1882?

UNITY[1]

FORGIVE, O Lord, our severing ways,
The separate altars that we raise,
The varying tongues that speak thy praise!

Suffice it now. In time to be
Shall one great temple rise to Thee,
Thy church our broad humanity.

White flowers of love its walls shall
climb,
Sweet bells of peace shall ring its chime,
Its days shall all be holy time.

The hymn, long sought, shall then be
heard,
The music of the world's accord,
Confessing Christ, the inward word!

That song shall swell from shore to shore,
One faith, one love, one hope restore
The seamless garb that Jesus wore!
1883.

SWEET FERN

THE subtle power in perfume found
Nor priest nor sibyl vainly learned;
On Grecian shrine or Aztec mound
No censer idly burned.

That power the old-time worships knew,
The Corybantes' frenzied dance,
The Pythian priestess swooning through
The wonderland of trance.

And Nature holds, in wood and field,
Her thousand sunlit censers still; 10
To spells of flower and shrub we yield
Against or with our will.

I climbed a hill path strange and new
With slow feet, pausing at each turn;
A sudden waft of west wind blew
The breath of the sweet fern.

That fragrance from my vision swept
The alien landscape; in its stead,
Up fairer hills of youth I stepped,
As light of heart as tread. 20

I saw my boyhood's lakelet shine
Once more through rifts of woodland
shade;
I knew my river's winding line
By morning mist betrayed.

---

[1] This poem was written by Mr. Whittier while he was a guest at the Asquam House. A fair was being held in aid of the little Episcopal church at Holderness, and people at the hotel were asked to contribute. These lines were Whittier's contribution, and the ladies in charge of the fair received ten dollars for them. They were written in an album now in the possession of a niece of Whittier's Philadelphia friend, Joseph Liddon Pennock. (PICKARD.)

With me June's freshness, lapsing brook,
  Murmurs of leaf and bee, the call
Of birds, and one in voice and look
  In keeping with them all.

A fern beside the way we went
  She plucked, and, smiling, held it up, 30
While from her hand the wild, sweet
      scent
  I drank as from a cup.

O potent witchery of smell !
  The dust-dry leaves to life return,
And she who plucked them owns the
      spell
  And lifts her ghostly fern.

Or sense or spirit ?   Who shall say
  What touch the chord of memory thrills ?
It passed, and left the August day
  Ablaze on lonely hills.
                                    40
                                  1884.

SAMUEL J. TILDEN

GREYSTONE, AUGUST 4, 1886

ONCE more, O all-adjusting Death !
  The nation's Pantheon opens wide;
Once more a common sorrow saith
  A strong, wise man has died.

Faults doubtless had he. Had we not
  Our own, to question and asperse
The worth we doubted or forgot
  Until beside his hearse ?

Ambitious, cautious, yet the man
  To strike down fraud with resolute
      hand;
A patriot, if a partisan,
  He loved his native land.

So let the mourning bells be rung,
  The banner droop its folds half way,
And while the public pen and tongue
  Their fitting tribute pay,

Shall we not vow above his bier
  To set our feet on party lies,
And wound no more a living ear
  With words that Death denies ?
1886.   1886.

THE BARTHOLDI STATUE

1886

THE land, that, from the rule of kings,
  In freeing us, itself made free,
Our Old World Sister, to us brings
  Her sculptured Dream of Liberty:

Unlike the shapes on Egypt's sands
  Uplifted by the toil-worn slave,
On Freedom's soil with freemen's hands
  We rear the symbol free hands gave.

O France, the beautiful ! to thee
  Once more a debt of love we owe:
In peace beneath thy Colors Three,
  We hail a later Rochambeau !

Rise, stately Symbol ! holding forth
  Thy light and hope to all who sit
In chains and darkness ! Belt the earth
  With watch-fires from thy torch uplit !

Reveal the primal mandate still
  Which Chaos heard and ceased to be,
Trace on mid-air th' Eternal Will
  In signs of fire: ' Let man be free ! '

Shine far, shine free, a guiding light
  To Reason's ways and Virtue's aim,
A lightning-flash the wretch to smite
  Who shields his license with thy name !
1886.   1887.

TO E. C. S.[1]

POET and friend of poets, if thy glass
Detects no flower in winter's tuft of
      grass,
Let this slight token of the debt I owe
  Outlive for thee December's frozen
      day,
And, like the arbutus budding under
      snow,
  Take bloom and fragrance from some
      morn of May
When he who gives it shall have gone the
      way
Where faith shall see and reverent trust
  shall know.
                                  1890.

[1] The dedication of Whittier's last volume, *At Sundown*, to Edmund Clarence Stedman.

THE LAST EVE OF SUMMER

SUMMER'S last sun nigh unto setting shines
    Through yon columnar pines,
And on the deepening shadows of the
    lawn
    Its golden lines are drawn.

Dreaming of long gone summer days like
    this,
    Feeling the wind's soft kiss,
Grateful and glad that failing ear and
    sight
    Have still their old delight,

I sit alone, and watch the warm, sweet
    day
    Lapse tenderly away;   10
And, wistful, with a feeling of forecast,
    I ask, ' Is this the last ?

' Will nevermore for me the seasons run
    Their round, and will the sun
Of ardent summers yet to come forget
    For me to rise and set ? '

Thou shouldst be here, or I should be with
    thee
    Wherever thou mayst be,
Lips mute, hands clasped, in silences of
    speech
    Each answering unto each.   20

For this still hour, this sense of mystery
    far
    Beyond the evening star,
No words outworn suffice on lip or scroll:
    The soul would fain with soul

Wait, while these few swift-passing days
    fulfil
    The wise-disposing Will,
And, in the evening as at morning, trust
    The All-Merciful and Just.

The solemn joy that soul-communion feels
    Immortal life reveals;   30
And human love, its prophecy and sign,
    Interprets love divine.

Come then, in thought, if that alone may be,
    O friend ! and bring with thee
Thy calm assurance of transcendent Spheres
    And the Eternal Years !
1890.   1890.

JAMES RUSSELL LOWELL

FROM purest wells of English undefiled
None deeper drank than he, the New
    World's child,
Who in the language of their farm-fields
    spoke
The wit and wisdom of New England folk,
Shaming a monstrous wrong. The world-
    wide laugh
Provoked thereby might well have shaken
    half
The walls of Slavery down, ere yet the ball
And mine of battle overthrew them all.
1891.   1891.

TO OLIVER WENDELL HOLMES

8TH MO. 29TH, 1892

AMONG the thousands who with hail and
    cheer
    Will welcome thy new year,
How few of all have passed, as thou and I,
    So many milestones by !

We have grown old together ; we have
    seen,
    Our youth and age between,
Two generations leave us, and to-day
    We with the third hold way,

Loving and loved. If thought must back-
    ward run
    To those who, one by one,   10
In the great silence and the dark beyond
    Vanished with farewells fond,

Unseen, not lost ; our grateful memories
    still
    Their vacant places fill,
And with the full-voiced greeting of new
    friends
    A tenderer whisper blends.

Linked close in a pathetic brotherhood
    Of mingled ill and good,
Of joy and grief, of grandeur and of shame,
    For pity more than blame,—   20

The gift is thine the weary world to make
    More cheerful for thy sake,
Soothing the ears its Miserere pains,
    With the old Hellenic strains,

Lighting the sullen face of discontent
　　With smiles for blessing sent.
Enough of selfish wailing has been had,
　　Thank God ! for notes more glad.

Life is indeed no holiday; therein
　　Are want, and woe, and sin,　　　30
Death and its nameless fears, and over all
　　Our pitying tears must fall.

Sorrow is real; but the counterfeit
　　Which folly brings to it,
We need thy wit and wisdom to resist,
　　O rarest Optimist !

Thy hand, old friend ! the service of our
　　days,
　　In differing moods and ways
May prove to those who follow in our train
　　Not valueless nor vain.　　　40

Far off, and faint as echoes of a dream,
　　The songs of boyhood seem,
Yet on our autumn boughs, unflown with
　　spring,
　　The evening thrushes sing.

The hour draws near, howe'er delayed and
　　late,
　　When at the Eternal Gate
We leave the words and works we call our
　　own,
　　And lift void hands alone

For love to fill. Our nakedness of
　　soul
　　Brings to that Gate no toll;　　　50
Giftless we come to Him, who all things
　　gives,
　　And live because He lives.

1892.　　　　　　　　　　　　　　　　1892.

OLIVER WENDELL HOLMES

OLD IRONSIDES [1]

AY, tear her tattered ensign down !
  Long has it waved on high,
And many an eye has danced to see
  That banner in the sky;
Beneath it rung the battle shout,
  And burst the cannon's roar; —
The meteor of the ocean air
  Shall sweep the clouds no more.

Her deck, once red with heroes' blood,
  Where knelt the vanquished foe,
When winds were hurrying o'er the flood,
  And waves were white below,
No more shall feel the victor's tread,
  Or know the conquered knee; —
The harpies of the shore shall pluck
  The eagle of the sea !

Oh, better that her shattered hulk
  Should sink beneath the wave;

Her thunders shook the mighty deep,
  And there should be her grave;
Nail to the mast her holy flag,
  Set every threadbare sail,
And give her to the god of storms,
  The lightning and the gale !

1830.   1830.

THE BALLAD OF THE OYSTER-MAN [2]

IT was a tall young oysterman lived by the
  river-side,
His shop was just upon the bank, his boat
  was on the tide;
The daughter of a fisherman, that was so
  straight and slim,
Lived over on the other bank, right opposite to him.

It was the pensive oysterman that saw a
  lovely maid,
Upon a moonlight evening, a-sitting in the
  shade;
He saw her wave her handkerchief, as much
  as if to say,
' I 'm wide awake, young oysterman, and all
  the folks away.'

Then up arose the oysterman, and to himself said he,
' I guess I 'll leave the skiff at home, for
  fear that folks should see;
I read it in the story-book, that, for to kiss
  his dear,
Leander swam the Hellespont, — and I will
  swim this here.'

[1] One genuine lyric outburst, however, done in this year of the law, almost made him in a way actually famous. The frigate Constitution, historic indeed, but old and unseaworthy, then lying in the navy yard at Charlestown, was condemned by the Navy Department to be destroyed. Holmes read this in a newspaper paragraph, and it stirred him. On a scrap of paper, with a lead pencil, he rapidly shaped the impetuous stanzas of ' Old Ironsides,' and sent them to the *Daily Advertiser*, of Boston. Fast and far they travelled through the newspaper press of the country ; they were even printed in hand-bills and circulated about the streets of Washington. An occurrence, which otherwise would probably have passed unnoticed, now stirred a national indignation. The astonished Secretary made haste to retrace a step which he had taken quite innocently in the way of business. The Constitution's tattered ensign was *not* torn down. The ringing, spirited verses gave the gallant ship a reprieve, which satisfied sentimentality, and a large part of the people of the United States had heard of O. W. Holmes, law student at Cambridge, who had only come of age a month ago. (Morse's *Life of Holmes*, vol. i, pp. 79, 80.)

This is probably the only case in which a government policy was changed by the verses of a college student.

The frigate Constitution was launched in 1797, first served in the war against the pirates in the Mediterranean, and made a brilliant record in the war of 1812. In 1834 she was almost entirely rebuilt, and continued in commission until 1881. From that time she was kept at the navy yard at Portsmouth, N. H., until in 1897 she was taken to the Charlestown Navy Yard for the celebration of the centenary of her launching.

[2] Except for the ballad of ' Old Ironsides,' the ' Metrical Essay on Poetry ' written for the Phi Beta Kappa meeting in 1836, and a few other occasional poems, Holmes wrote little but humorous verse from 1830 to 1848 ; most of this he excluded from the later editions of his work. ' The Ballad of the Oysterman,' and ' The Spectre Pig,' are the best of his parodies on the pseudo-ballads so popular at that time.

And he has leaped into the waves, and
    crossed the shining stream,
And he has clambered up the bank, all in
    the moonlight gleam;
Oh there were kisses sweet as dew, and
    words as soft as rain, —
But they have heard her father's step, and
    in he leaps again !

Out spoke the ancient fisherman, — 'Oh,
    what was that, my daughter ? '
' 'T was nothing but a pebble, sir, I threw
    into the water.'
' And what is that, pray tell me, love, that
    paddles off so fast ? '
' It 's nothing but a porpoise, sir, that 's been
    a-swimming past.'

Out spoke the ancient fisherman, — ' Now
    bring me my harpoon !
I 'll get into my fishing-boat, and fix the
    fellow soon.'
Down fell that pretty innocent, as falls a
    snow-white lamb,
Her hair drooped round her pallid cheeks,
    like seaweed on a clam.

Alas for those two loving ones ! she waked
    not from her swound,
And he was taken with the cramp, and in
    the waves was drowned;
But Fate has metamorphosed them, in pity
    of their woe,
And now they keep an oyster-shop for mer-
    maids down below.

                    1830 ?

THE HEIGHT OF THE RIDICU-
LOUS

I WROTE some lines once on a time
    In wondrous merry mood,
And thought, as usual, men would say
    They were exceeding good.

They were so queer, so very queer,
    I laughed as I would die;
Albeit, in the general way,
    A sober man am I.

I called my servant, and he came;
    How kind it was of him   10
To mind a slender man like me,
    He of the mighty limb !

' These to the printer,' I exclaimed,
    And, in my humorous way,
I added (as a trifling jest),
    ' There 'll be the devil to pay.'

He took the paper, and I watched,
    And saw him peep within;
At the first line he read, his face
    Was all upon the grin.   20

He read the next; the grin grew broad,
    And shot from ear to ear;
He read the third; a chuckling noise
    I now began to hear.

The fourth; he broke into a roar;
    The fifth; his waistband split;
The sixth; he burst five buttons off,
    And tumbled in a fit.

Ten days and nights, with sleepless eye,
    I watched that wretched man,   30
And since, I never dare to write
    As funny as I can.

                    1830.

TO AN INSECT

I LOVE to hear thine earnest voice,
    Wherever thou art hid,
Thou testy little dogmatist,
    Thou pretty Katydid !
Thou mindest me of gentlefolks, —
    Old gentlefolks are they, —
Thou say'st an undisputed thing
    In such a solemn way.

Thou art a female, Katydid !
    I know it by the trill   10
That quivers through thy piercing notes,
    So petulant and shrill;
I think there is a knot of you
    Beneath the hollow tree, —
A knot of spinster Katydids, —
    Do Katydids drink tea ?

Oh, tell me where did Katy live,
    And what did Katy do ?
And was she very fair and young,
    And yet so wicked, too ?   20
Did Katy love a naughty man,
    Or kiss more cheeks than one ?

I warrant Katy did no more
    Than many a Kate has done.

Dear me! I 'll tell you all about
    My fuss with little Jane,
And Ann, with whom I used to walk
    So often down the lane,
And all that tore their locks of black,
    Or wet their eyes of blue, —   30
Pray tell me, sweetest Katydid,
    What did poor Katy do?

Ah no! the living oak shall crash,
    That stood for ages still,
The rock shall rend its mossy base
    And thunder down the hill,
Before the little Katydid
    Shall add one word, to tell
The mystic story of the maid
    Whose name she knows so well.   40

Peace to the ever-murmuring race!
    And when the latest one
Shall fold in death her feeble wings
    Beneath the autumn sun,
Then shall she raise her fainting voice,
    And lift her drooping lid,
And then the child of future years
    Shall hear what Katy did.

                                   1831.

L'INCONNUE

Is thy name Mary, maiden fair?
    Such should, methinks, its music be;
The sweetest name that mortals bear
    Were best befitting thee;
And she to whom it once was given,
Was half of earth and half of heaven.

I hear thy voice, I see thy smile,
    I look upon thy folded hair;
Ah! while we dream not they beguile,
    Our hearts are in the snare;
And she who chains a wild bird's wing
Must start not if her captive sing.

So, lady, take the leaf that falls,
    To all but thee unseen, unknown:
When evening shades thy silent walls,
    Then read it all alone;
In stillness read, in darkness seal,
Forget, despise, but not reveal!

                                   1831.

MY AUNT

My aunt! my dear unmarried aunt!
    Long years have o'er her flown;
Yet still she strains the aching clasp
    That binds her virgin zone;
I know it hurts her, — though she looks
    As cheerful as she can;
Her waist is ampler than her life,
    For life is but a span.

My aunt! my poor deluded aunt!
    Her hair is almost gray;   10
Why will she train that winter curl
    In such a spring-like way?
How can she lay her glasses down,
    And say she reads as well,
When through a double convex lens
    She just makes out to spell?

Her father — grandpapa! forgive
    This erring lip its smiles —
Vowed she should make the finest girl
    Within a hundred miles;   2
He sent her to a stylish school;
    'T was in her thirteenth June;
And with her, as the rules required,
    'Two towels and a spoon.'

They braced my aunt against a board,
    To make her straight and tall;
They laced her up, they starved her down,
    To make her light and small;
They pinched her feet, they singed her hair,
    They screwed it up with pins; —   30
Oh, never mortal suffered more
    In penance for her sins.

So, when my precious aunt was done,
    My grandsire brought her back
(By daylight, lest some rabid youth
    Might follow on the track);
'Ah!' said my grandsire, as he shook
    Some powder in his pan,
'What could this lovely creature do
    Against a desperate man!'   40

Alas! nor chariot, nor barouche,
    Nor bandit cavalcade,
Tore from the trembling father's arms
    His all-accomplished maid.
For her how happy had it been!
    And Heaven had spared to me
To see one sad, ungathered rose
    On my ancestral tree.

                                   1831.

THE LAST LEAF[1]

I SAW him once before,
As he passed by the door,
    And again
The pavement stones resound,
As he totters o'er the ground
    With his cane.

They say that in his prime,
Ere the pruning-knife of Time
    Cut him down,
Not a better man was found   10
By the Crier on his round
    Through the town.

But now he walks the streets,
And he looks at all he meets
    Sad and wan,

[1] The poem was suggested by the sight of a figure well known to Bostonians [in 1831 or 1832], that of Major Thomas Melville, 'the last of the cocked hats,' as he was sometimes called. The Major had been a personable young man, very evidently, and retained evidence of it in

        The monumental pomp of age —

which had something imposing and something odd about it for youthful eyes like mine. He was often pointed at as one of the 'Indians' of the famous 'Boston Tea-Party' of 1774. His aspect among the crowds of a later generation reminded me of a withered leaf which had held to its stem through the storms of autumn and winter, and finds itself still clinging to its bough while the new growths of spring are bursting their buds and spreading their foliage all around it. I make this explanation for the benefit of those who have been puzzled by the lines,

        The last leaf upon the tree
          In the spring.

The way in which it came to be written in a somewhat singular measure was this. I had become a little known as a versifier, and I thought that one or two other young writers were following my efforts with imitations, not meant as parodies and hardly to be considered improvements on their models. I determined to write in a measure which would at once betray any copyist. So far as it was suggested by any previous poem, the echo must have come from Campbell's 'Battle of the Baltic,' with its short terminal lines, such as the last of these two,

        By thy wild and stormy steep,
          Elsinore.

But I do not remember any poem in the same measure, except such as have been written since its publication. (HOLMES.)

Holmes wrote to his publishers in 1894: 'I have lasted long enough to serve as an illustration of my own poem. . . . It was with a smile on my lips that I wrote it; I cannot read it without a sigh of tender remembrance. I hope it will not sadden my older readers, while it may amuse some of the younger ones to whom its experiences are as yet only floating fancies.'

Lincoln called the poem 'inexpressibly touching,' and knew it by heart. Holmes possessed a copy of it written out by Edgar Allan Poe. Whittier (Prose Works, vol. iii, p. 381) called it a 'unique compound of humor and pathos.'

And he shakes his feeble head,
That it seems as if he said,
    They are gone.'

The mossy marbles rest
On the lips that he has prest   20
    In their bloom,
And the names he loved to hear
Have been carved for many a year
    On the tomb.

My grandmamma has said —
Poor old lady, she is dead
    Long ago —
That he had a Roman nose,
And his cheek was like a rose
    In the snow;   30

But now his nose is thin,
And it rests upon his chin
    Like a staff,
And a crook is in his back,
And a melancholy crack
    In his laugh.

I know it is a sin
For me to sit and grin
    At him here;
But the old three-cornered hat,   40
And the breeches, and all that,
    Are so queer !

And if I should live to be
The last leaf upon the tree
    In the spring,
Let them smile, as I do now,
At the old forsaken bough
    Where I cling.

1831 or 1832.   1833.[2]

LA GRISETTE

AH, Clemence ! when I saw thee last
    Trip down the Rue de Seine,
And turning, when thy form had past,
    I said, 'We meet again,' —
I dreamed not in that idle glance
    Thy latest image came,

[2] Just when it was written I cannot exactly say, nor in what paper or periodical it was first published. It must have been written before April, 1833; probably in 1831 or 1832. It was republished in the first edition of my poems in 1836. (HOLMES.) It was in fact published in *The Harbinger*, Boston, 1833.

And only left to memory's trance
　　A shadow and a name.

The few strange words my lips had taught
　　Thy timid voice to speak,   10
Their gentler signs, which often brought
　　Fresh roses to thy cheek,
The trailing of thy long loose hair
　　Bent o'er my couch of pain,
All, all returned, more sweet, more fair;
　　Oh, had we met again !

I walked where saint and virgin keep
　　The vigil lights of Heaven,
I knew that thou hadst woes to weep,
　　And sins to be forgiven;   20
I watched where Genevieve was laid,
　　I knelt by Mary's shrine,
Beside me low, soft voices prayed;
　　Alas ! but where was thine ?

And when the morning sun was bright,
　　When wind and wave were calm,
And flamed, in thousand-tinted light,
　　The rose of Notre Dame,
I wandered through the haunts of men,
　　From Boulevard to Quai,   30
Till, frowning o'er Saint Etienne,
　　The Pantheon's shadow lay.

In vain, in vain; we meet no more,
　　Nor dream what fates befall;
And long upon the stranger's shore
　　My voice on thee may call,
When years have clothed the line in
　　moss
　　That tells thy name and days,
And withered, on thy simple cross,
　　The wreaths of Père-la-Chaise !   40
                                          1836.

OUR YANKEE GIRLS

Let greener lands and bluer skies,
　　If such the wide earth shows,
With fairer cheeks and brighter eyes,
　　Match us the star and rose;
The winds that lift the Georgian's veil,
　　Or wave Circassia's curls,
Waft to their shores the sultan's sail, — .
　　Who buys our Yankee girls ?

The gay grisette, whose fingers touch
　　Love's thousand chords so well;   10

The dark Italian, loving much,
　　But more than *one* can tell;
And England's fair-haired, blue-eyed dame,
　　Who binds her brow with pearls; —
Ye who have seen them, can they shame
　　Our own sweet Yankee girls ?

And what if court or castle vaunt
　　Its children loftier born ?
Who heeds the silken tassel's flaunt
　　Beside the golden corn ?   20
They ask not for the dainty toil
　　Of ribboned knights and earls,
The daughters of the virgin soil,
　　Our freeborn Yankee girls !

By every hill whose stately pines
　　Wave their dark arms above
The home where some fair being shines,
　　To warm the wilds with love,
From barest rock to bleakest shore
　　Where farthest sail unfurls,   20
That stars and stripes are streaming o'er, —
　　God bless our Yankee girls !
                                          1836.

ON LENDING A PUNCH-BOWL [1]

This ancient silver bowl of mine, it tells of
　　good old times,
Of joyous days and jolly nights, and merry
　　Christmas chimes;
They were a free and jovial race, but
　　honest, brave, and true,
Who dipped their ladle in the punch when
　　this old bowl was new.

A Spanish galleon brought the bar, — so
　　runs the ancient tale;
'T was hammered by an Antwerp smith,
　　whose arm was like a flail;
And now and then between the strokes, for
　　fear his strength should fail,
He wiped his brow and quaffed a cup of
　　good old Flemish ale.

'T was purchased by an English squire to
　　please his loving dame,

[1] This 'punch-bowl' was, according to old family
tradition, a *caudle-cup*. It is a massive piece of silver,
its cherubs and other ornaments of coarse repoussé
work, and has two handles like a loving-cup, by which
it was held, or passed from guest to guest. (Holmes.)

Who saw the cherubs, and conceived a
    longing for the same;   10
And oft as on the ancient stock another
    twig was found,
'T was filled with caudle spiced and hot,
    and handed smoking round.

But, changing hands, it reached at length a
    Puritan divine,
Who used to follow Timothy, and take a
    little wine,
But hated punch and prelacy; and so it
    was, perhaps,
He went to Leyden, where he found con-
    venticles and schnapps.

And then, of course, you know what 's
    next: it left the Dutchman's shore
With those that in the Mayflower came, —
    a hundred souls and more, —
Along with all the furniture, to fill their
    new abodes, —
To judge by what is still on hand, at least
    a hundred loads.   20

'T was on a dreary winter's eve, the night
    was closing dim,
When brave Miles Standish took the bowl,
    and filled it to the brim ;
The little Captain stood and stirred the
    posset with his sword,
And all his sturdy men-at-arms were
    ranged about the board.

He poured the fiery Hollands in, — the
    man that never feared, —
He took a long and solemn draught, and
    wiped his yellow beard;
And one by one the musketeers — the men
    that fought and prayed —
All drank as 't were their mother's milk,
    and not a man afraid.

That night, affrighted from his nest, the
    screaming eagle flew,
He heard the Pequot's ringing whoop, the
    soldier's wild halloo;   30
And there the sachem learned the rule he
    taught to kith and kin:
'Run from the white man when you find
    he smells of Holland's gin !'

A hundred years, and fifty more, had
    spread their leaves and snows,

A thousand rubs had flattened down each
    little cherub's nose,
When once again the bowl was filled, but
    not in mirth or joy, —
'T was mingled by a mother's hand to
    cheer her parting boy.

Drink, John, she said, 't will do you good,
    — poor child, you 'll never bear
This working in the dismal trench, out in
    the midnight air;
And if — God bless me ! — you were hurt,
    't would keep away the chill.
So John did drink, — and well he wrought
    that night at Bunker's Hill !   40

I tell you, there was generous warmth in
    good old English cheer;
I tell you, 't was a pleasant thought to
    bring its symbol here.
'T is but the fool that loves excess; hast
    thou a drunken soul ?
Thy bane is in thy shallow skull, not in my
    silver bowl !

I love the memory of the past, — its
    pressed yet fragrant flowers, —
The moss that clothes its broken walls, the
    ivy on its towers;
Nay, this poor bauble it bequeathed, —
    my eyes grow moist and dim,
To think of all the vanished joys that
    danced around its brim.

Then fill a fair and honest cup, and bear it
    straight to me;
The goblet hallows all it holds, whate'er
    the liquid be;   50
And may the cherubs on its face protect
    me from the sin
That dooms one to those dreadful words,
    — 'My dear, where have you
    been ?'

           (1848.)

THE STETHOSCOPE SONG

A PROFESSIONAL BALLAD

THERE was a young man in Boston town,
    He bought him a stethoscope nice and
    new,
All mounted and finished and polished
    down,
    With an ivory cap and a stopper too.

It happened a spider within did crawl,
   And spun him a web of ample size,
Wherein there chanced one day to fall
   A couple of very imprudent flies.

The first was a bottle-fly, big and blue,
   The second was smaller, and thin and
      long;   10
So there was a concert between the two,
   Like an octave flute and a tavern gong.

Now being from Paris but recently,
   This fine young man would show his
      skill;
And so they gave him, his hand to try,
   A hospital patient extremely ill.

Some said that his *liver* was short of *bile*,
   And some that his *heart* was over size,
While some kept arguing, all the while,
   He was crammed with *tubercles* up to his
      eyes.   20

This fine young man then up stepped he,
   And all the doctors made a pause;
Said he, The man must die, you see,
   By the fifty-seventh of Louis's laws.

But since the case is a desperate one,
   To explore his chest it may be well;
For if he should die and it were not done,
   You know the *autopsy* would not tell.

Then out his stethoscope he took,
   And on it placed his curious ear;   30
Mon Dieu! said he, with a knowing look,
   Why, here is a sound that's mighty
      queer!

The *bourdonnement* is very clear, —
   Amphoric buzzing, as I'm alive!
Five doctors took their turn to hear;
   Amphoric buzzing, said all the five.

There's *empyema* beyond a doubt;
   We'll plunge a *trocar* in his side.
The diagnosis was made out, —
   They tapped the patient; so he died.   40

Now such as hate new-fashioned toys
   Began to look extremely glum;
They said that *rattles* were made for
      boys,
And vowed that his *buzzing* was all a
      hum.

There was an old lady had long been sick,
   And what was the matter none did
      know:
Her pulse was slow, though her tongue was
      quick;
   To her this knowing youth must go.

So there the nice old lady sat,
   With phials and boxes all in a row;   50
She asked the young doctor what he was
      at,
   To thump her and tumble her ruffles
      so.

Now, when the stethoscope came out,
   The flies began to buzz and whiz:
Oh, ho! the matter is clear, no doubt;
   An *aneurism* there plainly is.

The *bruit de râpe* and the *bruit de scie*
   And the *bruit de diable* are all combined;
How happy Bouillaud would be,
   If he a case like this could find!   60

Now, when the neighboring doctors found
   A case so rare had been descried,
They every day her ribs did pound
   In squads of twenty; so she died.

Then six young damsels, slight and frail,
   Received this kind young doctor's cares;
They all were getting slim and pale,
   And short of breath on mounting stairs.

They all made rhymes with 'sighs' and
      'skies,'
   And loathed their puddings and buttered
      rolls,   70
And dieted, much to their friends' surprise,
   On pickles and pencils and chalk and
      coals.

So fast their little hearts did bound,
   The frightened insects buzzed the more;
So over all their chests he found
   The *râle sifflant* and the *râle sonore*.

He shook his head. There's grave dis-
      ease, —
   I greatly fear you all must die;
A slight *post-mortem*, if you please,
   Surviving friends would gratify.   80

The six young damsels wept aloud,
   Which so prevailed on six young men

That each his honest love avowed,
  Whereat they all got well again.

This poor young man was all aghast;
  The price of stethoscopes came down;
And so he was reduced at last
  To practise in a country town.

The doctors being very sore,
  A stethoscope they did devise   90
That had a rammer to clear the bore,
  With a knob at the end to kill the flies.

Now use your ears, all you that can,
  But don't forget to mind your eyes,
Or you may be cheated, like this young
    man,
  By a couple of silly, abnormal flies.

                                    (1848.)

THE STATESMAN'S SECRET [1]

  WHO of all statesmen is his country's
      pride,
Her councils' prompter and her leaders'
    guide ?
He speaks; the nation holds its breath to
    hear;
He nods, and shakes the sunset hemisphere.
Born where the primal fount of Nature
    springs
By the rude cradles of her throneless
    kings,
In his proud eye her royal signet flames,
By his own lips her Monarch she pro-
    claims.
  Why name his countless triumphs, whom
      to meet
Is to be famous, envied in defeat ?   10
The keen debaters, trained to brawls and
    strife,
Who fire one shot, and finish with the
    knife,
Tried him but once, and, cowering in their
    shame,
Ground their hacked blades to strike at
    meaner game.
The lordly chief, his party's central stay,
Whose lightest word a hundred votes obey,
Found a new listener seated at his side,
Looked in his eye, and felt himself defied,

  [1] Originally called 'The Disappointed Statesman.'
See the notes on Emerson's 'Webster,' p. 61, and Whittier's 'Ichabod,' p. 282.

Flung his rash gauntlet on the startled
    floor,
Met the all-conquering, fought, — and
    ruled no more.   20
  See where he moves, what eager crowds
      attend !
What shouts of thronging multitudes as-
    cend !
If this is life, — to mark with every hour
The purple deepening in his robes of
    power,
To see the painted fruits of honor fall
Thick at his feet, and choose among them
    all,
To hear the sounds that shape his spread-
    ing name
Peal through the myriad organ-stops of
    fame,
Stamp the lone isle that spots the seaman's
    chart,
And crown the pillared glory of the mart, 30
To count as peers the few supremely
    wise
Who mark their planet in the angels'
    eyes, —
If this is life —
                    What savage man is he
Who strides alone beside the sounding
    sea?
Alone he wanders by the murmuring shore,
His thoughts as restless as the waves that
    roar;
Looks on the sullen sky as stormy-browed
As on the waves yon tempest-brooding
    cloud,
Heaves from his aching breast a wailing
    sigh,
Sad as the gust that sweeps the clouded
    sky.   40
Ask him his griefs; what midnight demons
    plough
The lines of torture on his lofty brow;
Unlock those marble lips, and bid them
    speak
The mystery freezing in his bloodless
    cheek.
  His secret ? Hid beneath a flimsy word;
One foolish whisper that ambition heard;
And thus it spake: 'Behold yon gilded
    chair,
The world's one vacant throne, — thy place
    is there !'
  Ah, fatal dream ! What warning spec-
    tres meet
In ghastly circle round its shadowy seat ! 50

Yet still the Tempter murmurs in his
 ear
The maddening taunt he cannot choose but
 hear:
'Meanest of slaves, by gods and men ac-
 curst,
He who is second when he might be first !
Climb with bold front the ladder's topmost
 round,
Or chain thy creeping footsteps to the
 ground ! '
 Illustrious Dupe ! Have those majestic
  eyes
Lost their proud fire for such a vulgar
 prize?
Art thou the last of all mankind to know
That party-fights are won by aiming low?
Thou, stamped by Nature with her royal
 sign,   61
That party-hirelings hate a look like thine?
Shake from thy sense the wild delusive
 dream !
Without the purple, art thou not su-
 preme ?
And soothed by love unbought, thy heart
 shall own
A nation's homage nobler than its throne !
1850 ?   (1861.)

AFTER A LECTURE ON WORDS-
WORTH [1]

Come, spread your wings, as I spread mine,
 And leave the crowded hall
For where the eyes of twilight shine
 O'er evening's western wall.

These are the pleasant Berkshire hills,
 Each with its leafy crown;
Hark ! from their sides a thousand rills
 Come singing sweetly down.

A thousand rills; they leap and shine,
 Strained through the shadowy nooks, 10
Till, clasped in many a gathering twine,
 They swell a hundred brooks.

A hundred brooks, and still they run
 With ripple, shade, and gleam,

[1] This and the following poem were read by Holmes
as postludes to lectures given by him at the Lowell
Institute in Boston, in 1853, on English Poetry of the
Nineteenth Century. Two years later Lowell lectured
at the same Institute on English Poetry from its Origins
to Wordsworth.

Till, clustering all their braids in one,
 They flow a single stream.

A bracelet spun from mountain mist,
 A silvery sash unwound,
With ox-bow curve and sinuous twist
 It writhes to reach the Sound. 20

This is my bark, — a pygmy's ship;
 Beneath a child it rolls;
Fear not, — one body makes it dip,
 But not a thousand souls.

Float we the grassy banks between;
 Without an oar we glide;
The meadows, drest in living green,
 Unroll on either side.

Come, take the book we love so well,
 And let us read and dream 30
We see whate'er its pages tell,
 And sail an English stream.

Up to the clouds the lark has sprung,
 Still trilling as he flies;
The linnet sings as there he sung;
 The unseen cuckoo cries,

And daisies strew the banks along,
 And yellow kingcups shine,
With cowslips, and a primrose throng,
 And humble celandine. 40

Ah foolish dream ! when Nature nursed
 Her daughter in the West,
The fount was drained that opened first;
 She bared her other breast.

On the young planet's orient shore
 Her morning hand she tried;
Then turned the broad medallion o'er
 And stamped the sunset side.

Take what she gives, her pine's tall stem,
 Her elm with hanging spray; 50
She wears her mountain diadem
 Still in her own proud way.

Look on the forests' ancient kings,
 The hemlock's towering pride:
Yon trunk had thrice a hundred rings,
 And fell before it died.

Nor think that Nature saves her bloom
 And slights our grassy plain;

For us she wears her court costume, —
  Look on its broidered train;   60

The lily with the sprinkled dots,
  Brands of the noontide beam;
The cardinal, and the blood-red spots,
  Its double in the stream,

As if some wounded eagle's breast,
  Slow throbbing o'er the plain,
Had left its airy path impressed
  In drops of scarlet rain.

And hark ! and hark ! the woodland rings;
  There thrilled the thrush's soul;   70
And look ! that flash of flamy wings, —
  The fire-plumed oriole !

Above, the hen-hawk swims and swoops,
  Flung from the bright, blue sky;
Below, the robin hops, and whoops
  His piercing Indian cry.

Beauty runs virgin in the woods
  Robed in her rustic green,
And oft a longing thought intrudes,
  As if we might have seen   80

Her every finger's every joint
  Ringed with some golden line,
Poet whom Nature did anoint !
  Had our wild home been thine.

Yet think not so; Old England's blood
  Runs warm in English veins;
But wafted o'er the icy flood
  Its better life remains:

Our children know each wildwood smell,
  The bayberry and the fern,   90
The man who does not know them well
  Is all too old to learn.

Be patient ! On the breathing page
  Still pants our hurried past;
Pilgrim and soldier, saint and sage, —
  The poet comes the last !

Though still the lark-voiced matins ring
  The world has known so long;
The wood-thrush of the West shall sing
  Earth's last sweet even-song !   100
1853.   (1861.)

AFTER A LECTURE ON SHELLEY

One broad, white sail in Spezzia's treacher-
    ous bay;
  On comes the blast; too daring bark, be-
    ware !
The cloud has clasped her; lo ! it melts
    away;
  The wide, waste waters, but no sail
    there.

Morning: a woman looking on the sea;
  Midnight: with lamps the long veranda
    burns;
Come, wandering sail, they watch, they
    burn for thee !
  Suns come and go, alas! no bark returns.

And feet are thronging on the pebbly
    sands,
  And torches flaring in the weedy caves, 10
Where'er the waters lay with icy hands
  The shapes uplifted from their coral
    graves.

Vainly they seek; the idle quest is o'er;
  The coarse, dark women, with their hang-
    ing locks,
And lean, wild children gather from the
    shore
To the black hovels bedded in the rocks.

But Love still prayed, with agonizing wail,
  ' One, one last look, ye heaving waters,
    yield ! '
Till Ocean, clashing in his jointed mail,
  Raised the pale burden on his level
    shield.   20

Slow from the shore the sullen waves re-
    tire;
  His form a nobler element shall claim;
Nature baptized him in ethereal fire,
  And Death shall crown him with a wreath
    of flame.

Fade, mortal semblance, never to return;
  Swift is the change within thy crimson
    shroud;
Seal the white ashes in the peaceful urn;
  All else has risen in yon silvery cloud.

Sleep where thy gentle Adonais lies,
  Whose open page lay on thy dying
    heart,   30

Both in the smile of those blue-vaulted skies,
Earth's fairest dome of all divinest art.

Breathe for his wandering soul one passing
sigh,
O happier Christian, while thine eye
grows dim, —
In all the mansions of the house on high,
Say not that Mercy has not one for him !
1853. (1861.)

THE HUDSON [1]

AFTER A LECTURE AT ALBANY

'T WAS a vision of childhood that came
with its dawn,
Ere the curtain that covered life's day-star
was drawn;
The nurse told the tale when the shadows
grew long,
And the mother's soft lullaby breathed it in
song.

'There flows a fair stream by the hills of
the West,' —
She sang to her boy as he lay on her breast;
'Along its smooth margin thy fathers
have played;
Beside its deep waters their ashes are laid.'

I wandered afar from the land of my birth,
I saw the old rivers, renowned upon earth,
But fancy still painted that wide-flowing
stream
With the many-hued pencil of infancy's
dream.

I saw the green banks of the castle-crowned
Rhine,
Where the grapes drink the moonlight and
change it to wine;

[1] See the notes on Whittier's ' The Last Walk in Autumn,' p. 292, and on Emerson's ' Written in Naples,'
p. 60, and compare a recent sonnet on the Hudson by
Mr. George S. Hellman : —

Where in its old historic splendor stands
The home of England's far-famed Parliament,
And waters of the Thames in calm content
At England's fame flow slowly o'er their sands ;
And where the Rhine past vine-entwined lands
Courses in castled beauty, there I went ;
And far to Southern rivers, flower-besprent ;
And to the icy streams of Northern strands.
Then mine own native shores I trod once more,
And, gazing on thy waters' majesty,
The memory, O Hudson, came to me
Of one who went to seek the wide world o'er
For Love, but found it not.   Then home turned he
And saw his mother waiting at the door.

I stood by the Avon, whose waves as they
glide
Still whisper his glory who sleeps at their
side.

But my heart would still yearn for the
sound of the waves
That sing as they flow by my forefathers'
graves;
If manhood yet honors my cheek with a tear,
I care not who sees it, — nor blush for it
here !

Farewell to the deep-bosomed stream of
the West !
I fling this loose blossom to float on its
breast;
Nor let the dear love of its children grow
cold,
Till the channel is dry where its waters
have rolled !
1854. (1861.)

TO AN ENGLISH FRIEND

THE seed that wasteful autumn cast
To waver on its stormy blast,
Long o'er the wintry desert tost,
Its living germ has never lost.
Dropped by the weary tempest's wing,
It feels the kindling ray of spring,
And, starting from its dream of death,
Pours on the air its perfumed breath.

So, parted by the rolling flood,
The love that springs from common blood
Needs but a single sunlit hour
Of mingling smiles to bud and flower;
Unharmed its slumbering life has flown,
From shore to shore, from zone to zone,
Where summer's falling roses stain
The tepid waves of Pontchartrain,
Or where the lichen creeps below
Katahdin's wreaths of whirling snow.

Though fiery sun and stiffening cold
May change the fair ancestral mould,
No winter chills, no summer drains
The life-blood drawn from English veins,
Still bearing wheresoe'er it flows
The love that with its fountain rose,
Unchanged by space, unwronged by time,
From age to age, from clime to clime !
(1861.)

THE OLD MAN DREAMS [1]

OH for one hour of youthful joy !
　　Give back my twentieth spring !
I 'd rather laugh, a bright-haired boy,
　　Than reign, a gray-beard king.

Off with the spoils of wrinkled age !
　　Away with Learning's crown !
Tear out life's Wisdom-written page,
　　And dash its trophies down !

One moment let my life-blood stream
　　From boyhood's fount of flame !　　10
Give me one giddy, reeling dream
　　Of life all love and fame !

My listening angel heard the prayer,
　　And, calmly smiling, said,
' If I but touch thy silvered hair
　　Thy hasty wish hath sped.

' But is there nothing in thy track
　　To bid thee fondly stay,
While the swift seasons hurry back
　　To find the wished-for day ? '　　20

' Ah, truest soul of womankind !
　　Without thee what were life ?
One bliss I cannot leave behind:
　　I 'll take — my — precious — wife ! '

The angel took a sapphire pen
　　And wrote in rainbow dew,
The man would be a boy again,
　　And be a husband too !

' And is there nothing yet unsaid,
　　Before the change appears ?　　30
Remember, all their gifts have fled
　　With those dissolving years.'

' Why, yes;' for memory would recall
　　My fond paternal joys;
' I could not bear to leave them all —
　　I 'll take — my — girl — and — boys.'

The smiling angel dropped his pen, —
　　' Why, this will never do;
The man would be a boy again,
　　And be a father too ! '　　40

[1] Written for a reunion of Holmes's college class.
See the note on ' The Boys,' p. 374.

And so I laughed, — my laughter woke
　　The household with its noise, —
And wrote my dream, when morning broke,
　　To please the gray-haired boys.
1854.　　　　　　　　　　　　(1861.)

BIRTHDAY OF DANIEL WEB-
STER

JANUARY 18, 1856

WHEN life hath run its largest round
　　Of toil and triumph, joy and woe,
How brief a storied page is found
　　To compass all its outward show !

The world-tried sailor tires and droops;
　　His flag is rent, his keel forgot;
His farthest voyages seem but loops
　　That float from life's entangled knot.

But when within the narrow space
　　Some larger soul hath lived and
　　　　wrought,　　10
Whose sight was open to embrace
　　The boundless realms of deed and
　　　　thought, —

When, stricken by the freezing blast,
　　A nation's living pillars fall,
How rich the storied page, how vast,
　　A word, a whisper, can recall !

No medal lifts its fretted face,
　　Nor speaking marble cheats your eye,
Yet, while these pictured lines I trace,
　　A living image passes by:　　20

A roof beneath the mountain pines;
　　The cloisters of a hill-girt plain;
The front of life's embattled lines;
　　A mound beside the heaving main.

These are the scenes: a boy appears;
　　Set life's round dial in the sun,
Count the swift arc of seventy years,
　　His frame is dust; his task is done.

Yet pause upon the noontide hour,
　　Ere the declining sun has laid　　30
His bleaching rays on manhood's power,
　　And look upon the mighty shade.

No gloom that stately shape can hide,
　　No change uncrown its brow; behold !

Dark, calm, large-fronted, lightning-eyed,
  Earth has no double from its mould !

Ere from the fields by valor won
  The battle-smoke had rolled away,
And bared the blood-red setting sun,
  His eyes were opened on the day.   40

His land was but a shelving strip
  Black with the strife that made it free;
He lived to see its banners dip
  Their fringes in the Western sea.

The boundless prairies learned his name,
  His words the mountain echoes knew.
The Northern breezes swept his fame
  From icy lake to warm bayou.

In toil he lived; in peace he died;
  When life's full cycle was complete   50
Put off his robes of power and pride,
  And laid them at his Master's feet.

His rest is by the storm-swept waves
  Whom life's wild tempests roughly tried,
Whose heart was like the streaming caves
  Of ocean, throbbing at his side.

Death's cold white hand is like the snow
  Laid softly on the furrowed hill,
It hides the broken seams below,
  And leaves the summit brighter still.   60

In vain the envious tongue upbraids;
  His name a nation's heart shall keep
Till morning's latest sunlight fades
  On the blue tablet of the deep !

1855–56.   (1861.)

FOR THE MEETING OF THE BURNS CLUB

1856

THE mountains glitter in the snow
  A thousand leagues asunder;
Yet here, amid the banquet's glow,
  I hear their voice of thunder;
Each giant's ice-bound goblet clinks;
  A flowing stream is summoned;
Wachusett to Ben Nevis drinks;
  Monadnock to Ben Lomond !

Though years have clipped the eagle's
    plume

That crowned the chieftain's bonnet,   10
The sun still sees the heather bloom,
  The silver mists lie on it;
With tartan kilt and philibeg,
  What stride was ever bolder
Than his who showed the naked leg
  Beneath the plaided shoulder ?

The echoes sleep on Cheviot's hills,
  That heard the bugles blowing
When down their sides the crimson rills
  With mingled blood were flowing;   20
The hunts where gallant hearts were
    game,
  The slashing on the border,
The raid that swooped with sword and
    flame,
  Give place to ' law and order.'

Not while the rocking steeples reel
  With midnight tocsins ringing,
Not while the crashing war-notes peal,
  God sets his poets singing;
The bird is silent in the night,
  Or shrieks a cry of warning   30
While fluttering round the beacon-light, —
  But hear him greet the morning !

The lark of Scotia's morning sky !
  Whose voice may sing his praises ?
With Heaven's own sunlight in his eye,
  He walked among the daisies,
Till through the cloud of fortune's wrong
  He soared to fields of glory;
But left his land her sweetest song
  And earth her saddest story.   40

'T is not the forts the builder piles
  That chain the earth together;
The wedded crowns, the sister isles,
  Would laugh at such a tether;
The kindling thought, the throbbing words,
  That set the pulses beating,
Are stronger than the myriad swords
  Of mighty armies meeting.

Thus while within the banquet glows,
  Without, the wild winds whistle,   50
We drink a triple health, — the Rose,
  The Shamrock, and the Thistle !
Their blended hues shall never fade
  Till War has hushed his cannon, —
Close-twined as ocean-currents braid
  The Thames, the Clyde, the Shannon !

1856.   (1861.)

LATTER–DAY WARNINGS[1]

WHEN legislators keep the law,
  When banks dispense with bolts and locks,
When berries — whortle, rasp, and straw —
  Grow bigger *downwards* through the
    box, —

When he that selleth house or land
  Shows leak in roof or flaw in right,
When haberdashers choose the stand
  Whose window hath the broadest light, —

When preachers tell us all they think,
  And party leaders all they mean, —   10
When what we pay for, that we drink,
  From real grape and coffee-bean, —

When lawyers take what they would give,
  And doctors give what they would take,—
When city fathers eat to live,
  Save when they fast for conscience'
    sake, —

When one that hath a horse on sale
  Shall bring his merit to the proof,
Without a lie for every nail
  That holds the iron on the hoof, —   20

When in the usual place for rips
  Our gloves are stitched with special care,
And guarded well the whalebone tips
  Where first umbrellas need repair, —

When Cuba's weeds have quite forgot
  The power of suction to resist,
And claret-bottles harbor not
  Such dimples as would hold your fist, —

When publishers no longer steal,
  And pay for what they stole before, — 30
When the first locomotive's wheel
  Rolls through the Hoosac Tunnel's
    bore; —

Till then let Cumming blaze away,
  And Miller's saints blow up the globe;
But when you see that blessed day,
  Then order your ascension robe !
                                    1857.

[1] I should have felt more nervous about the late comet, if I had thought the world was ripe. But it is very green yet, if I am not mistaken ; and besides, there is a great deal of coal to use up, which I cannot bring myself to think was made for nothing. . . . (HOLMES, introducing the poem, in the *Autocrat of the Breakfast Table*.)
This and the six following poems first appeared in the *Autocrat* papers, in the *Atlantic Monthly*.

THE CHAMBERED NAUTILUS[2]

THIS is the ship of pearl, which, poets feign,
  Sails the unshadowed main, —
  The venturous bark that flings
On the sweet summer wind its purpled
    wings
In gulfs enchanted, where the Siren sings,
  And coral reefs lie bare,
Where the cold sea-maids rise to sun their
    streaming hair.

Its webs of living gauze no more unfurl;
  Wrecked is the ship of pearl !
  And every chambered cell,   10
Where its dim dreaming life was wont to
    dwell,
As the frail tenant shaped his growing
    shell,
  Before thee lies revealed, —
Its irised ceiling rent, its sunless crypt un-
    sealed !

Year after year beheld the silent toil
  That spread his lustrous coil;
  Still, as the spiral grew,
He left the past year's dwelling for the
    new,
Stole with soft step its shining archway
    through,
  Built up its idle door,   20
Stretched in his last-found home, and knew
    the old no more.

Thanks for the heavenly message brought
    by thee,
  Child of the wandering sea,
  Cast from her lap, forlorn !
From thy dead lips a clearer note is born
Than ever Triton blew from wreathèd horn !
  While on mine ear it rings,
Through the deep caves of thought I hear
    a voice that sings: —

Build thee more stately mansions, O my
    soul,
  As the swift seasons roll !   30
  Leave thy low-vaulted past !
Let each new temple, nobler than the last,

[2] Suggested by looking at a section of one of those chambered shells to which is given the name of Pearly Nautilus. . . . If you will look into Roget's *Bridgewater Treatise* you will find a figure of one of these shells and a section of it. The last will show you the series of enlarging compartments successively dwelt in by the animal that inhabits the shell, which is built in a widening spiral. (HOLMES, in the *Autocrat*.)

Shut thee from heaven with a dome more
        vast,
    Till thou at length art free,
Leaving thine outgrown shell by life's un-
        resting sea !

                                        1858.

THE LIVING TEMPLE [1]

Not in the world of light alone,
Where God has built his blazing throne,
Nor yet alone in earth below,
With belted seas that come and go,
And endless isles of sunlit green,
Is all thy Maker's glory seen:
Look in upon thy wondrous frame, —
Eternal wisdom still the same !

The smooth, soft air with pulse-like waves
Flows murmuring through its hidden
        caves,   10
Whose streams of brightening purple rush,
Fired with a new and livelier blush,
While all their burden of decay
The ebbing current steals away,
And red with Nature's flame they start
From the warm fountains of the heart.

No rest that throbbing slave may ask,
Forever quivering o'er his task,
While far and wide a crimson jet
Leaps forth to fill the woven net   20
Which in unnumbered crossing tides
The flood of burning life divides,
Then, kindling each decaying part,
Creeps back to find the throbbing heart.

But warmed with that unchanging flame
Behold the outward moving frame,
Its living marbles jointed strong
With glistening band and silvery thong,
And linked to reason's guiding reins
By myriad rings in trembling chains,   30
Each graven with the threaded zone
Which claims it as the master's own.

See how yon beam of seeming white
Is braided out of seven-hued light,

[1] Having read our company so much of the Professor's talk about age and other subjects connected
with physical life, I took the next Sunday morning to
repeat to them the following poem of his, which I have
had by me for some time. He calls it — I suppose for
his professional friends — 'The Anatomist's Hymn,'
but I shall name it 'The Living Temple.' (HOLMES, introducing the poem, in the *Autocrat*.)

Yet in those lucid globes no ray
By any chance shall break astray.
Hark how the rolling surge of sound,
Arches and spirals circling round,
Wakes the hushed spirit through thine
        ear
With music it is heaven to hear.   40

Then mark the cloven sphere that holds
All thought in its mysterious folds;
That feels sensation's faintest thrill,
And flashes forth the sovereign will;
Think on the stormy world that dwells
Locked in its dim and clustering cells !
The lightning gleams of power it sheds
Along its hollow glassy threads !

O Father ! grant thy love divine
To make these mystic temples thine !   50
When wasting age and wearying strife
Have sapped the leaning walls of life,
When darkness gathers over all,
And the last tottering pillars fall,
Take the poor dust thy mercy warms,
And mould it into heavenly forms !

                                        1858.

THE DEACON'S MASTERPIECE

OR, THE WONDERFUL 'ONE-HOSS SHAY'

A LOGICAL STORY

Have you heard of the wonderful one-hoss
        shay,
That was built in such a logical way
It ran a hundred years to a day,
And then, of a sudden, it — ah, but stay,
I 'll tell you what happened without delay,
Scaring the parson into fits,
Frightening people out of their wits, —
Have you ever heard of that, I say ?

Seventeen hundred and fifty-five.
Georgius Secundus was then alive, —   10
Snuffy old drone from the German hive.
That was the year when Lisbon-town
Saw the earth open and gulp her down,
And Braddock's army was done so brown,
Left without a scalp to its crown.
It was on the terrible Earthquake-day
That the Deacon finished the one-hoss shay.

Now in building of chaises, I tell you what,
There is always *somewhere* a weakest spot, —

In hub, tire, felloe, in spring or thill,   20
In panel, or crossbar, or floor, or sill,
In screw, bolt, thoroughbrace, — lurking
    still,
Find it somewhere you must and will, —
Above or below, or within or without, —
And that's the reason, beyond a doubt,
That a chaise *breaks down*, but does n't *wear
    out.*

But the Deacon swore (as deacons do,
With an 'I dew vum,' or an 'I tell *yeou* ')
He would build one shay to beat the taown
'N' the keounty 'n' all the kentry raoun'; 30
It should be so built that it *could* n' break
    daown:
'Fur,' said the Deacon, ''t's mighty plain
Thut the weakes' place mus' stan' the
    strain;
'N' the way t' fix it, uz I maintain,
       Is only jest
T' make that place uz strong uz the rest.'

So the Deacon inquired of the village
    folk
Where he could find the strongest oak,
That could n't be split nor bent nor broke, —
That was for spokes and floor and sills;   40
He sent for lancewood to make the thills;
The crossbars were ash, from the straight-
    est trees,
The panels of white-wood, that cuts like
    cheese,
But lasts like iron for things like these;
The hubs of logs from the 'Settler's el-
    lum,' —
Last of its timber, — they could n't sell 'em,
Never an axe had seen their chips,
And the wedges flew from between their
    lips,
Their blunt ends frizzled like celery-tips;
Step and prop-iron, bolt and screw,   50
Spring, tire, axle, and linchpin too,
Steel of the finest, bright and blue;
Thoroughbrace bison-skin, thick and wide;
Boot, top, dasher, from tough old hide
Found in the pit when the tanner died.
That was the way he 'put her through.'
'There!' said the Deacon, 'naow she 'll
    dew!'

Do! I tell you, I rather guess
She was a wonder, and nothing less!
Colts grew horses, beards turned gray,   60
Deacon and deaconess dropped away,

Children and grandchildren — where were
    they?
But there stood the stout old one-hoss shay
As fresh as on Lisbon-earthquake-day!

EIGHTEEN HUNDRED; — it came and found
The Deacon's masterpiece strong and
    sound.
Eighteen hundred increased by ten; —
'Hahnsum kerridge' they called it then.
Eighteen hundred and twenty came; —
Running as usual; much the same.   70
Thirty and forty at last arrive,
And then come fifty, and FIFTY-FIVE.

Little of all we value here
Wakes on the morn of its hundredth year
Without both feeling and looking queer.
In fact, there's nothing that keeps its youth,
So far as I know, but a tree and truth.
(This is a moral that runs at large;
Take it. — You're welcome. — No extra
    charge.)

FIRST OF NOVEMBER, — the earthquake-
    day, —   80
There are traces of age in the one-hoss
    shay,
A general flavor of mild decay,
But nothing local, as one may say.
There could n't be, — for the Deacon's art
Had made it so like in every part
That there was n't a chance for one to
    start.
For the wheels were just as strong as the
    thills,
And the floor was just as strong as the
    sills,
And the panels just as strong as the floor,
And the whipple-tree neither less nor more,
And the back crossbar as strong as the
    fore,   91
And spring and axle and hub *encore.*
And yet, *as a whole*, it is past a doubt
In another hour it will be *worn out!*

First of November, 'Fifty-five!
This morning the parson takes a drive.
Now, small boys, get out of the way!
Here comes the wonderful one-hoss shay,
Drawn by a rat-tailed, ewe-necked bay.
'Huddup!' said the parson. — Off went
    they.   100
The parson was working his Sunday's
    text, —

Had got to *fifthly*, and stopped perplexed
At what the — Moses — was coming next.
All at once the horse stood still,
Close by the meet'n'-house on the hill.
First a shiver, and then a thrill,
Then something decidedly like a spill, —
And the parson was sitting upon a rock,
At half past nine by the meet'n'-house
    clock, —
Just the hour of the Earthquake shock ! 110
What do you think the parson found,
When he got up and stared around ?
The poor old chaise in a heap or mound,
As if it had been to the mill and ground !
You see, of course, if you 're not a dunce,
How it went to pieces all at once, —
All at once, and nothing first, —
Just as bubbles do when they burst.

End of the wonderful one-hoss shay
Logic is logic. That 's all I say.   120
                        1858.

CONTENTMENT

'Man wants but little here below.'

LITTLE I ask; my wants are few;
    I only wish a hut of stone
(A *very plain* brown stone will do)
    That I may call my own; —
And close at hand is such a one,
In yonder street that fronts the sun.

Plain food is quite enough for me;
    Three courses are as good as ten; —
If Nature can subsist on three,
    Thank Heaven for three. Amen !   10
I always thought cold victual nice; —
My *choice* would be vanilla-ice.

I care not much for gold or land; —
    Give me a mortgage here and there, —
Some good bank-stock, some note of hand,
    Or trifling railroad share, —
I only ask that Fortune send
A *little* more than I shall spend.

Honors are silly toys, I know,
    And titles are but empty names;   20
I would, *perhaps*, be Plenipo, —
    But only near St. James;
I 'm very sure I should not care
To fill our Gubernator's chair.

Jewels are baubles; 't is a sin
    To care for such unfruitful things; —

One good-sized diamond in a pin, —
    Some, *not so large*, in rings, —
A ruby, and a pearl, or so,
Will do for me; — I laugh at show.   30

My dame should dress in cheap attire
    (Good, heavy silks are never dear); —
I own perhaps I *might* desire
    Some shawls of true Cashmere, —
Some marrowy crapes of China silk,
Like wrinkled skins on scalded milk.

I would not have the horse I drive
    So fast that folks must stop and stare;
An easy gait — two forty-five —
    Suits me; I do not care; —   40
Perhaps, for just a *single spurt*,
Some seconds less would do no hurt.

Of pictures, I should like to own
    Titians and Raphaels three or four, —
I love so much their style and tone,
    One Turner, and no more
(A landscape, — foreground golden dirt, —
The sunshine painted with a squirt).

Of books but few, — some fifty score
    For daily use, and bound for wear;   50
The rest upon an upper floor; —
    Some *little* luxury *there*
Of red morocco's gilded gleam
And vellum rich as country cream.

Busts, cameos, gems, — such things as
    these,
    Which others often show for pride,
I value for their power to please,
    And selfish churls deride; —
One Stradivarius, I confess,
Two Meerschaums, I would fain possess. 60

Wealth's wasteful tricks I will not learn,
    Nor ape the glittering upstart fool: —
Shall not carved tables serve my turn,
    But *all* must be of buhl ?
Give grasping pomp its double share, —
I ask but *one* recumbent chair.

Thus humble let me live and die,
    Nor long for Midas' golden touch;
If Heaven more generous gifts deny,
    I shall not miss them *much*, —   70
Too grateful for the blessing lent
Of simple tastes and mind content !

                        1858.

PARSON TURELL'S LEGACY

OR, THE PRESIDENT'S OLD ARM-CHAIR

A MATHEMATICAL STORY

FACTS respecting an old arm-chair,
At Cambridge. Is kept in the College
    there.
Seems but little the worse for wear.
That 's remarkable when I say
It was old in President Holyoke's day.
(One of his boys, perhaps you know,
Died, *at one hundred*, years ago.)
He took lodgings for rain or shine
Under green bed-clothes in '69.

Know old Cambridge? Hope you do. — 10
Born there? Don't say so ! I was, too.
(Born in a house with a gambrel-roof, —
Standing still, if you must have proof. —
'Gambrel ? — Gambrel ? ' — Let me beg
You 'll look at a horse's hinder leg, —
First great angle above the hoof, —
That 's the gambrel : hence gambrel-
    roof.)
Nicest place that ever was seen, —
Colleges red and Common green,
Sidewalks brownish with trees between. 20
Sweetest spot beneath the skies
When the canker-worms don't rise, —
When the dust, that sometimes flies
Into your mouth and ears and eyes,
In a quiet slumber lies,
Not in the shape of unbaked pies
Such as barefoot children prize.

A kind of harbor it seems to be,
Facing the flow of a boundless sea.
Rows of gray old Tutors stand   30
Ranged like rocks above the sand;
Rolling beneath them, soft and green,
Breaks the tide of bright sixteen, —
One wave, two waves, three waves, four, —
Sliding up the sparkling floor:
Then it ebbs to flow no more,
Wandering off from shore to shore
With its freight of golden ore !
Pleasant place for boys to play; —
Better keep your girls away;   40
Hearts get rolled as pebbles do
Which countless fingering waves pursue,
And every classic beach is strown
With heart-shaped pebbles of blood-red
    stone.

But this is neither here nor there;
I 'm talking about an old arm-chair.
You 've heard, no doubt, of PARSON TU-
    RELL ?
Over at Medford he used to dwell;
Married one of the Mathers' folk;
Got with his wife a chair of oak, —   50
Funny old chair with seat like wedge,
Sharp behind and broad front edge, —
One of the oddest of human things,
Turned all over with knobs and rings, —
But heavy, and wide, and deep, and
    grand, —
Fit for the worthies of the land, —
Chief Justice Sewall a cause to try in,
Or Cotton Mather to sit — and lie —
    in.
Parson Turell bequeathed the same
To a certain student, — SMITH by name;   60
These were the terms, as we are told:
' Saide Smith saide Chaire to have and
    holde;
When he doth graduate, then to passe
To yᵉ oldest Youth in yᵉ Senior Classe.
On payment of ' — (naming a certain
    sum) —
' By him to whom yᵉ Chaire shall come;
He to yᵉ oldest Senior next,
And soe forever ' (thus runs the text), —
' But one Crown lesse than he gave to
    claime,
That being his Debte for use of same.'   70

Smith transferred it to one of the BROWNS,
And took his money, — five silver crowns.
Brown delivered it up to MOORE,
Who paid, it is plain, not five, but four.
Moore made over the chair to LEE,
Who gave him crowns of silver three.
Lee conveyed it unto DREW,
And now the payment, of course, was two.
Drew gave up the chair to DUNN, —
All he got, as you see, was one.   80
Dunn released the chair to HALL,
And got by the bargain no crown at all.

And now it passed to a second BROWN,
Who took it and likewise *claimed a crown.*
When *Brown* conveyed it unto WARE,
Having had one crown, to make it fair,
He paid him two crowns to take the chair;
And *Ware*, being honest (as all Wares be),
He paid one POTTER, who took it, three.
Four got ROBINSON; five got DIX;   90
JOHNSON *primus* demanded six;

And so the sum kept gathering still
Till after the battle of Bunker's Hill.

When paper money became so cheap,
Folks would n't count it, but said 'a heap,'
A certain RICHARDS, — the books de-
    clare
(A. M. in '90 ?   I 've looked with care
Through the Triennial, — *name not there*),—
This person, Richards, was offered then
Eightscore pounds, but would have ten;   100
Nine, I think, was the sum he took, —
Not quite certain, — but see the book.
By and by the wars were still,
But nothing had altered the Parson's will.
The old arm-chair was solid yet,
But saddled with such a monstrous debt !
Things grew quite too bad to bear,
Paying such sums to get rid of the chair !
But dead men's fingers hold awful tight,
And there was the will in black and white,
Plain enough for a child to spell.   111
What should be done no man could tell,
For the chair was a kind of nightmare
    curse,
And every season but made it worse.

As a last resort, to clear the doubt,
They got old GOVERNOR HANCOCK out.
The Governor came with his Lighthorse
    Troop
And his mounted truckmen, all cock-a-
    hoop;
Halberds glittered and colors flew,
French horns whinnied and trumpets blew,
The yellow fifes whistled between their
    teeth,   121
And the bumble-bee bass-drums boomed
    beneath;
So he rode with all his band,
Till the President met him, cap in hand.
The Governor 'hefted' the crowns, and
    said, —
' A will is a will, and the Parson 's dead.'
The Governor hefted the crowns.   Said
    he, —
' There is your p'int.   And here 's my fee.
These are the terms you must fulfil, —
On such conditions I BREAK THE WILL ! '   130
The Governor mentioned what these should
    be.
(Just wait a minute and then you 'll see.)
The President prayed.   Then all was still,
And the Governor rose and BROKE THE
    WILL !

' About those conditions ? '   Well, now you
    go
And do as I tell you, and then you 'll know.
Once a year, on Commencement day,
If you 'll only take the pains to stay,
You 'll see the President in the CHAIR,
Likewise the Governor sitting there.   140
The President rises; both old and young
May hear his speech in a foreign tongue,
The meaning whereof, as lawyers swear,
Is this: Can I keep this old arm-chair ?
And then his Excellency bows,
As much as to say that he allows.
The Vice-Gub. next is called by name;
He bows like t' other, which means the
    same.
And all the officers round 'em bow,
As much as to say that *they* allow.   150
And a lot of parchments about the chair
Are handed to witnesses then and there,
And then the lawyers hold it clear
That the chair is safe for another year.

God bless you, Gentlemen !   Learn to give
Money to colleges while you live.
Don't be silly and think you 'll try
To bother the colleges, when you die,
With codicil this, and codicil that,
That Knowledge may starve while Law
    grows fat;   160
For there never was pitcher that would n't
    spill,
And there 's always a flaw in a donkey's
    will !

1858.

THE VOICELESS

WE count the broken lyres that rest
    Where the sweet wailing singers slum-
        ber,
But o'er their silent sister's breast
    The wild-flowers who will stoop to num-
        ber ?
A few can touch the magic string,
    And noisy Fame is proud to win them: —
Alas for those that never sing,
    But die with all their music in them !

Nay, grieve not for the dead alone
    Whose song has told their hearts' sad
        story, —
Weep for the voiceless, who have known
    The cross without the crown of glory !

Not where Leucadian breezes sweep
  O'er Sappho's memory-haunted billow,
But where the glistening night-dews weep
  On nameless sorrow's churchyard pillow.

O hearts that break and give no sign
  Save whitening lip and fading tresses,
Till Death pours out his longed-for wine
  Slow-dropped from Misery's crushing
    presses, —
If singing breath or echoing chord
  To every hidden pang were given,
What endless melodies were poured,
  As sad as earth, as sweet as heaven !

                    1858.

FOR THE BURNS CENTENNIAL
CELEBRATION

JANUARY 25, 1859

His birthday. — Nay, we need not speak
  The name each heart is beating, —
Each glistening eye and flushing cheek
  In light and flame repeating !

We come in one tumultuous tide, —
  One surge of wild emotion, —
As crowding through the Frith of Clyde
  Rolls in the Western Ocean;

As when yon cloudless, quartered moon
  Hangs o'er each storied river,   10
The swelling breasts of Ayr and Doon
  With sea-green wavelets quiver.

The century shrivels like a scroll, —
  The past becomes the present, —
And face to face, and soul to soul,
  We greet the monarch-peasant.

While Shenstone strained in feeble flights
  With Corydon and Phillis, —
While Wolfe was climbing Abraham's
    heights
  To snatch the Bourbon lilies, —   20

Who heard the wailing infant's cry,
  The babe beneath the sheeling,
Whose song to-night in every sky
  Will shake earth's starry ceiling, —

Whose passion-breathing voice ascends
  And floats like incense o'er us,
Whose ringing lay of friendship blends
  With labor's anvil chorus ?

We love him, not for sweetest song,
  Though never tone so tender;   30
We love him, even in his wrong, —
  His wasteful self-surrender.

We praise him, not for gifts divine, —
  His Muse was born of woman, —
His manhood breathes in every line, —
  Was ever heart more human ?

We love him, praise him, just for this:
  In every form and feature,
Through wealth and want, through woe
    and bliss,
  He saw his fellow-creature !   40

No soul could sink beneath his love, —
  Not even angel blasted;
No mortal power could soar above
  The pride that all outlasted !

Ay ! Heaven had set one living man
  Beyond the pedant's tether, —
His virtues, frailties, He may scan,
  Who weighs them all together !

I fling my pebble on the cairn
  Of him, though dead, undying;   50
Sweet Nature's nursling, bonniest bairn
  Beneath her daisies lying.

The waning suns, the wasting globe,
  Shall spare the minstrel's story, —
The centuries weave his purple robe,
  The mountain-mist of glory !
1859.   (1861.)

THE BOYS [1]

Has there any old fellow got mixed with
    the boys ?
If there has, take him out, without making
    a noise.

----

[1] For nearly forty years, from 1851 to 1889, Holmes
never failed to bring a poem to the annual reunion of
his college class. These poems, merely 'occasional,'
and local as they were in origin, form a section in his
collected works which is perhaps the most important,
and, except for his best humorous narratives and his
two finest lyrics, the most likely to survive; for, with
all Holmes's characteristic wit and humor, they celebrate feelings that are broadly and typically American
— class loyalty and college loyalty, and growing out of
these, the loyalty of man's enduring friendship, and
loyalty to country.

The 'famous class of '29' counted among its members
a chief-justice of Massachusetts, George T. Bigelow
(the 'Judge' of this poem) ; a justice of the United

Hang the Almanac's cheat and the Catalogue's spite !
Old Time is a liar ! We 're twenty to-night !

We 're twenty ! We 're twenty ! Who says we are more ?
He 's tipsy, — young jackanapes ! — show him the door !
'Gray temples at twenty ?' — Yes ! *white* if we please;
Where the snow-flakes fall thickest there 's nothing can freeze !

Was it snowing I spoke of ? Excuse the mistake !
Look close, — you will see not a sign of a flake !   10
We want some new garlands for those we have shed, —
And these are white roses in place of the red.

We 've a trick, we young fellows, you may have been told,
Of talking (in public) as if we were old: —
That boy we call 'Doctor,' and this we call 'Judge;'
It 's a neat little fiction, — of course it 's all fudge.

That fellow 's the 'Speaker,' [1] — the one on the right;
'Mr. Mayor,' [2] my young one, how are you to-night ?
That 's our 'Member of Congress,' [3] we say when we chaff;
There 's the 'Reverend' What 's his name ? — don't make me laugh.   20

That boy with the grave mathematical look
Made believe he had written a wonderful book,
And the ROYAL SOCIETY thought it was *true !*
So they chose him right in; a good joke it was, too !

States Supreme Court, B. R. Curtis (the 'boy with the three-decker brain'); the great preacher, James Freeman Clarke ; Professor Benjamin Peirce ('that boy with the grave mathematical look'); and the author of 'America,' S. F. Smith. For a full list of members of the class, see the Cambridge Edition of Holmes's *Poetical Works*, p. 340.
[1] Hon. Francis B. Crowninshield, Speaker of the Massachusetts House of Representatives.
[2] G. W. Richardson, of Worcester, Massachusetts.
[3] Hon. George L. Davis.

There 's a boy, we pretend, with a three-decker brain,
That could harness a team with a logical chain;
When he spoke for our manhood in syllabled fire,
We called him 'The Justice,' but now he 's 'The Squire.'

And there 's a nice youngster of excellent pith, —
Fate tried to conceal him by naming him Smith;   30
But he shouted a song for the brave and the free, —
Just read on his medal, 'My country,' 'of thee !'

You hear that boy laughing ? — You think he 's all fun;
But the angels laugh, too, at the good he has done;
The children laugh loud as they troop to his call,
And the poor man that knows him laughs loudest of all !

Yes, we 're boys, — always playing with tongue or with pen, —
And I sometimes have asked, — Shall we ever be men ?
Shall we always be youthful, and laughing, and gay,
Till the last dear companion drops smiling away ?   40

Then here 's to our boyhood, its gold and its gray !
The stars of its winter, the dews of its May !
And when we have done with our life-lasting toys,
Dear Father, take care of thy children, THE BOYS !

1859.   1859.

AT A MEETING OF FRIENDS

AUGUST 29, 1859 [4]

I REMEMBER — why, yes ! God bless me ! and was it so long ago ?
I fear I 'm growing forgetful, as old folks do, you know;

[4] Holmes's fiftieth birthday.

It must have been in 'forty — I would say
  'thirty-nine —
We talked this matter over, I and a friend
  of mine.

He said, 'Well now, old fellow, I'm
  thinking that you and I,
If we act like other people, shall be older
  by and by;
What though the bright blue ocean is
  smooth as a pond can be,
There is always a line of breakers to fringe
  the broadest sea.

'We're taking it mighty easy, but that is
  nothing strange,
For up to the age of thirty we spend our
  years like change;   10
But creeping up towards the forties, as fast
  as the old years fill,
And Time steps in for payment, we seem to
  change a bill.'

'I know it,' I said, 'old fellow; you speak
  the solemn truth;
A man can't live to a hundred and likewise
  keep his youth;
But what if the ten years coming shall
  silver-streak my hair,
You know I shall then be forty; of course
  I shall not care.

'At forty a man grows heavy and tired of
  fun and noise;
Leaves dress to the five-and-twenties and
  love to the silly boys;
No foppish tricks at forty, no pinching of
  waists and toes,
But high-low shoes and flannels and good
  thick worsted hose.'   20

But one fine August morning I found myself awake:
My birthday: — By Jove, I'm forty! Yes,
  forty and no mistake!
Why, this is the very milestone, I think I
  used to hold,
That when a fellow had come to, a fellow
  would then be old!

But that is the young folks' nonsense;
  they're full of their foolish stuff;
A man's in his prime at forty, — I see that
  plain enough;

At *fifty* a man *is* wrinkled, and *may be* bald
  or gray ;
I call men old at fifty, in spite of all they
  say.

At last comes another August with mist
  and rain and shine;
Its mornings are slowly counted and creep
  to twenty-nine,   30
And when on the western summits the fading light appears,
It touches with rosy fingers the last of my
  fifty years.

There have been both men and women
  whose hearts were firm and bold,
But there never was one of fifty that loved
  to say 'I'm old;'
So any elderly person that strives to shirk
  his years,
Make him stand up at a table and try him
  by his peers.

Now here I stand at fifty, my jury gathered
  round;
Sprinkled with dust of silver, but not yet
  silver-crowned,
Ready to meet your verdict, waiting to hear
  it told;
Guilty of fifty summers; speak! Is the
  verdict *old?*   40

No! say that his hearing fails him; say
  that his sight grows dim;
Say that he's getting wrinkled and weak in
  back and limb,
Losing his wits and temper, but pleading,
  to make amends,
The youth of his fifty summers he finds in
  his twenty friends.

1859.   (1877.)

THE TWO STREAMS [1]

BEHOLD the rocky wall
That down its sloping sides
Pours the swift rain-drops, blending, as
  they fall,
In rushing river-tides!

Yon stream, whose sources run
Turned by a pebble's edge,

[1] This and the three following poems are from the
Professor at the Breakfast Table. 'The Boys' also is
included in that volume.

Is Athabasca, rolling toward the sun
  Through the cleft mountain-ledge.

The slender rill had strayed,
  But for the slanting stone,
To evening's ocean, with the tangled braid
  Of foam-flecked Oregon.

· So from the heights of Will
  Life's parting stream descends,
And, as a moment turns its slender rill,
  Each widening torrent bends, —

From the same cradle's side,
  From the same mother's knee, —
One to long darkness and the frozen tide,
  One to the Peaceful Sea !

                                  1859.

UNDER THE VIOLETS

HER hands are cold; her face is white;
  No more her pulses come and go;
Her eyes are shut to life and light; —
  Fold the white vesture, snow on snow,
  And lay her where the violets blow.

But not beneath a graven stone,
  To plead for tears with alien eyes;
A slender cross of wood alone
  Shall say, that here a maiden lies
  In peace beneath the peaceful skies.   10

And gray old trees of hugest limb
  Shall wheel their circling shadows round
To make the scorching sunlight dim
  That drinks the greenness from the
      ground,
  And drop their dead leaves on her mound.

When o'er their boughs the squirrels run,
  And through their leaves the robins call,
And, ripening in the autumn sun,
  The acorns and the chestnuts fall,
  Doubt not that she will heed them all.   20

For her the morning choir shall sing
  Its matins from the branches high,
And every minstrel-voice of Spring,
  That trills beneath the April sky,
  Shall greet her with its earliest cry.

When, turning round their dial-track,
  Eastward the lengthening shadows pass,
Her little mourners, clad in black,

The crickets, sliding through the grass,
  Shall pipe for her an evening mass.   30

At last the rootlets of the trees
  Shall find the prison where she lies,
And bear the buried dust they seize
  In leaves and blossoms to the skies.
  So may the soul that warmed it rise !

If any, born of kindlier blood,
  Should ask, What maiden lies below ?
Say only this: A tender bud,
  That tried to blossom in the snow,
  Lies withered where the violets blow.   40

                                  1859.

HYMN OF TRUST

O LOVE Divine, that stooped to share
  Our sharpest pang, our bitterest tear,
On Thee we cast each earth-born care,
  We smile at pain while Thou art near !

Though long the weary way we tread,
  And sorrow crown each lingering year,
No path we shun, no darkness dread,
  Our hearts still whispering, Thou art
      near !

When drooping pleasure turns to grief,
  And trembling faith is changed to fear,
The murmuring wind, the quivering leaf,
  Shall softly tell us, Thou art near !

On Thee we fling our burdening woe,
  O Love Divine, forever dear,
Content to suffer while we know,
  Living and dying, Thou art near !

                                  1859.

A SUN-DAY HYMN

LORD of all being ! throned afar,
  Thy glory flames from sun and star;
Centre and soul of every sphere,
  Yet to each loving heart how near !

Sun of our life, thy quickening ray
  Sheds on our path the glow of day;
Star of our hope, thy softened light
  Cheers the long watches of the night.

Our midnight is thy smile withdrawn;
  Our noontide is thy gracious dawn;

Our rainbow arch thy mercy's sign;
All, save the clouds of sin, are thine !

Lord of all life, below, above,
Whose light is truth, whose warmth is
    love,
Before thy ever-blazing throne
We ask no lustre of our own.

Grant us thy truth to make us free,
And kindling hearts that burn for thee,
Till all thy living altars claim
One holy light, one heavenly flame !
                              1859.

PROLOGUE TO 'SONGS IN MANY KEYS'

THE piping of our slender, peaceful reeds
Whispers uncared for while the trumpets
    bray;
Song is thin air; our hearts' exulting play
Beats time but to the tread of marching
    deeds,
Following the mighty van that Freedom
    leads,
Her glorious standard flaming to the day !
The crimsoned pavement where a hero
    bleeds
Breathes nobler lessons than the poet's lay.
Strong arms, broad breasts, brave hearts,
    are better worth
Than strains that sing the ravished echoes
    dumb.
Hark ! 't is the loud reverberating drum
Rolls o'er the prairied West, the rock-bound
    North:
The myriad-handed Future stretches forth
Its shadowy palms. Behold, we come, —
    we come !

Turn o'er these idle leaves. Such toys as
    these
Were not unsought for, as, in languid
    dreams,
We lay beside our lotus-feeding streams,
And nursed our fancies in forgetful ease.
It matters little if they pall or please,
Dropping untimely, while the sudden
    gleams
Glare from the mustering clouds whose
    blackness seems
Too swollen to hold its lightning from the
    trees.

Yet, in some lull of passion, when at last
These calm revolving moons that come and
    go —
Turning our months to years, they creep so
    slow —
Have brought us rest, the not unwelcome
    past
May flutter to thee through these leaflets,
    cast
On the wild winds that all around us blow.
1861.   1861.

BROTHER JONATHAN'S LAMENT FOR SISTER CAROLINE

MARCH 25, 1861

SHE has gone, — she has left us in passion
    and pride, —
Our stormy-browed sister, so long at our
    side !
She has torn her own star from our firma-
    ment's glow,
And turned on her brother the face of a foe !

Oh, Caroline, Caroline, child of the sun,
We can never forget that our hearts have
    been one, —
Our foreheads both sprinkled in Liberty's
    name,
From the fountain of blood with the finger
    of flame !

You were always too ready to fire at a
    touch;
But we said, 'She is hasty, — she does not
    mean much.'   10
We have scowled, when you uttered some
    turbulent threat;
But Friendship still whispered, 'Forgive
    and forget !'

Has our love all died out ? Have its altars
    grown cold ?
Has the curse come at last which the fathers
    foretold ?
Then Nature must teach us the strength of
    the chain
That her petulant children would sever in
    vain.

They may fight till the buzzards are gorged
    with their spoil,
Till the harvest grows black as it rots in
    the soil,

Till the wolves and the catamounts troop
    from their caves,
And the shark tracks the pirate, the lord of
    the waves: 20

In vain is the strife ! When its fury is past,
Their fortunes must flow in one channel at
    last,
As the torrents that rush from the moun-
    tains of snow
Roll mingled in peace through the valleys
    below.

Our Union is river, lake, ocean, and sky:
Man breaks not the medal, when God cuts
    the die !
Though darkened with sulphur, though
    cloven with steel,
The blue arch will brighten, the waters will
    heal !

Oh, Caroline, Caroline, child of the sun,
There are battles with Fate that can never
    be won !   30
The star-flowering banner must never be
    furled,
For its blossoms of light are the hope of
    the world !

Go, then, our rash sister ! afar and aloof,
Run wild in the sunshine away from our
    roof;
But when your heart aches and your feet
    have grown sore,
Remember the pathway that leads to our
    door !
March, 1861.   May, 1861.

PARTING HYMN

' DUNDEE '

FATHER of Mercies, Heavenly Friend,
    We seek thy gracious throne;
To Thee our faltering prayers ascend,
    Our fainting hearts are known!

From blasts that chill, from suns that
    smite,
    From every plague that harms;
In camp and march, in siege and fight,
    Protect our men-at-arms !

Though from our darkened lives they take
    What makes our life most dear,

We yield them for their country's sake
    With no relenting tear.

Our blood their flowing veins will shed,
    Their wounds our breasts will share;
Oh, save us from the woes we dread,
    Or grant us strength to bear !

Let each unhallowed cause that brings
    The stern destroyer cease,
Thy flaming angel fold his wings,
    And seraphs whisper Peace !

Thine are the sceptre and the sword,
    Stretch forth thy mighty hand, —
Reign Thou our kingless nation's Lord,
    Rule Thou our throneless land !
1861.   August, 1861.

UNION AND LIBERTY

FLAG of the heroes who left us their glory,
    Borne through their battle-fields' thun-
        der and flame,
Blazoned in song and illumined in story,
    Wave o'er us all who inherit their
        fame!
        Up with our banner bright,
        Sprinkled with starry light,
    Spread its fair emblems from mountain
        to shore,
        While through the sounding sky
        Loud rings the Nation's cry, —
    UNION AND LIBERTY ! ONE EVER-
    MORE !   10

Light of our firmament, guide of our Na-
    tion,
    Pride of her children, and honored
        afar,
Let the wide beams of thy full constella-
    tion
    Scatter each cloud that would darken a
        star !
        Up with our banner bright, etc.

Empire unsceptred ! what foe shall assail
    thee,
Bearing the standard of Liberty's van ?
Think not the God of thy fathers shall fail
    thee,
    Striving with men for the birthright of
        man !
        Up with our banner bright, etc.   20

Yet if, by madness and treachery blighted,
  Dawns the dark hour when the sword
      thou must draw,
Then with the arms of thy millions united,
  Smite the bold traitors to Freedom and
      Law !
    Up with our banner bright, etc.

Lord of the Universe ! shield us and guide
      us,
  Trusting Thee always, through shadow
      and sun !
Thou hast united us, who shall divide us ?
  Keep us, oh keep us the MANY IN ONE !
    Up with our banner bright,   30
    Sprinkled with starry light,
  Spread its fair emblems from mountain
      to shore,
    While through the sounding sky
    Loud rings the Nation's cry, —
  UNION AND LIBERTY ! ONE EVER-
      MORE !

1861.   December, 1861.

J. D. R.[1]

1862

THE friends that are, and friends that were,
  What shallow waves divide !
I miss the form for many a year
  Still seated at my side.

I miss him, yet I feel him still
  Amidst our faithful band,
As if not death itself could chill
  The warmth of friendship's hand.

His story other lips may tell, —
  For me the veil is drawn;
I only know he loved me well,
  He loved me — and is gone !
1862.   1862.

TO MY READERS [2]

NAY, blame me not; I might have spared
  Your patience many a trivial verse,
Yet these my earlier welcome shared,
  So, let the better shield the worse.

  [1] James D. Russell, a classmate of Holmes.
  [2] Written as a prologue to the collected edition of
Holmes's poems published in 1862.

And some might say, ' Those ruder songs
  Had freshness which the new have lost;
To spring the opening leaf belongs,
  The chestnut-burs await the frost.'

When those I wrote, my locks were brown,
  When these I write — ah, well-a-day ! 10
The autumn thistle's silvery down
  Is not the purple bloom of May !

Go, little book, whose pages hold
  Those garnered years in loving trust;
How long before your blue and gold
  Shall fade and whiten in the dust ?

O sexton of the alcoved tomb,
  Where souls in leathern cerements lie,
Tell me each living poet's doom !
  How long before his book shall die ? 20

It matters little, soon or late,
  A day, a month, a year, an age, —
I read oblivion in its date,
  And Finis on its title-page.

Before we sighed, our griefs were told;
  Before we smiled, our joys were sung;
And all our passions shaped of old
  In accents lost to mortal tongue.

In vain a fresher mould we seek, —
  Can all the varied phrases tell   30
That Babel's wandering children speak
  How thrushes sing or lilacs smell ?

Caged in the poet's lonely heart,
  Love wastes unheard its tenderest tone;
The soul that sings must dwell apart,
  Its inward melodies unknown.

Deal gently with us, ye who read !
  Our largest hope is unfulfilled, —
The promise still outruns the deed, —
  The tower, but not the spire, we build. 40

Our whitest pearl we never find;
  Our ripest fruit we never reach;
The flowering moments of the mind
  Drop half their petals in our speech.

These are my blossoms; if they wear
  One streak of morn or evening's glow,
Accept them; but to me more fair
  The buds of song that never blow.
1862.   1862.

VOYAGE OF THE GOOD SHIP UNION [1]

1862

'T IS   midnight : through   my   troubled
  dream
 Loud wails the tempest's cry;
Before the gale, with tattered sail,
 A ship goes plunging by.
What name ? Where bound ? — The rocks
  around
 Repeat the loud halloo.
— The good ship Union, Southward bound:
 God help her and her crew !

And is the old flag flying still
 That o'er your fathers flew,   10
With bands of white and rosy light,
 And field of starry blue ?
— Ay ! look aloft ! its folds full oft
 Have braved the roaring blast,
And still shall fly when from the sky
 This black typhoon has past !

Speak, pilot of the storm-tost bark !
 May I thy peril share ?
— O landsman, there are fearful seas
 The brave alone may dare ! 20
— Nay, ruler of the rebel deep,
 What matters wind or wave ?
The rocks that wreck your reeling deck
 Will leave me naught to save !

O landsman, art thou false or true ?
 What sign hast thou to show ?
— The crimson stains from loyal veins
 That hold my heart-blood's flow !
— Enough ! what more shall honor claim ?
 I know the sacred sign;   30
Above thy head our flag shall spread,
 Our ocean path be thine !

The bark sails on; the Pilgrim's Cape
 Lies low along her lee,
Whose headland crooks its anchor-flukes
 To lock the shore and sea.
No treason here ! it cost too dear
 To win this barren realm !
And true and free the hands must be
 That hold the whaler's helm ! 40

Still on ! Manhattan's narrowing bay
 No rebel cruiser scars;

[1] Written for a reunion of the class of '29.

Her waters feel no pirate's keel
 That flaunts the fallen stars !
— But watch the light on yonder height, —
 Ay, pilot, have a care !
Some lingering cloud in mist may shroud
 The capes of Delaware !

Say, pilot, what this fort may be,
 Whose sentinels look down 50
From moated walls that show the sea
 Their deep embrasures' frown ?
The Rebel host claims all the coast,
 But these are friends, we know,
Whose footprints spoil the ' sacred soil,'
 And this is ? — Fort Monroe !

The breakers roar, — how bears the shore ?
 — The traitorous wreckers' hands
Have quenched the blaze that poured its
  rays
 Along the Hatteras sands. 60
— Ha ! say not so ! I see its glow !
 Again the shoals display
The beacon light that shines by night,
 The Union Stars by day !

The good ship flies to milder skies,
 The wave more gently flows,
The softening breeze wafts o'er the seas
 The breath of Beaufort's rose.
What fold is this the sweet winds kiss,
 Fair-striped and many-starred, 70
Whose shadow palls these orphaned walls,
 The twins of Beauregard ?

What ! heard you not Port Royal's doom ?
 How the black war-ships came
And turned the Beaufort roses' bloom
 To redder wreaths of flame ?
How from Rebellion's broken reed
 We saw his emblem fall,
As soon his cursed poison-weed
 Shall drop from Sumter's wall ? 80

On ! on ! Pulaski's iron hail
 Falls harmless on Tybee !
The good ship feels the freshening gales,
 She strikes the open sea;
She rounds the point, she threads the keys
 That guard the Land of Flowers,
And rides at last where firm and fast
 Her own Gibraltar towers !

The good ship Union's voyage is o'er,
 At anchor safe she swings, 90

And loud and clear with cheer on cheer
Her joyous welcome rings:
Hurrah ! Hurrah ! it shakes the wave,
It thunders on the shore, —
One flag, one land, one heart, one hand,
One Nation, evermore !

1862.   March, 1862.

BRYANT'S SEVENTIETH BIRTH-DAY

NOVEMBER 3, 1864

O EVEN-HANDED Nature ! we confess
This life that men so honor, love, and bless
Has filled thine olden measure. Not the less

We count the precious seasons that remain;
Strike not the level of the golden grain,
But heap it high with years, that earth may gain

What heaven can lose, — for heaven is rich in song:
Do not all poets, dying, still prolong
Their broken chants amid the seraph throng,

Where, blind no more, Ionia's bard is seen,   10
And England's heavenly minstrel sits between
The Mantuan and the wan-cheeked Florentine ?

This was the first sweet singer in the cage
Of our close-woven life.   A new-born age
Claims in his vesper song its heritage:

Spare us, oh spare us long our heart's desire !
Moloch, who calls our children through the fire,
Leaves us the gentle master of the lyre.

We count not on the dial of the sun
The hours, the minutes, that his sands have run;   20
Rather, as on those flowers that one by one

From earliest dawn their ordered bloom display
Till evening's planet with her guiding ray
Leads in the blind old mother of the day,

We reckon by his songs, each song a flower,
The long, long daylight, numbering hour by hour,
Each breathing sweetness like a bridal bower.

His morning glory shall we e'er forget ?
His noontide's full-blown lily coronet ?
His evening primrose has not opened yet;   30

Nay, even if creeping Time should hide the skies
In midnight from his century-laden eyes,
Darkened like his who sang of Paradise,

Would not some hidden song-bud open bright
As the resplendent cactus of the night
That floods the gloom with fragrance and with light ?

How can we praise the verse whose music flows
With solemn cadence and majestic close,
Pure as the dew that filters through the rose ?

How shall we thank him that in evil days   40
He faltered never, — nor for blame, nor praise,
Nor hire, nor party, shamed his earlier lays ?

But as his boyhood was of manliest hue,
So to his youth his manly years were true,
All dyed in royal purple through and through !

He for whose touch the lyre of Heaven is strung
Needs not the flattering toil of mortal tongue:
Let not the singer grieve to die unsung !

Marbles forget their message to mankind:
In his own verse the poet still we find,   50
In his own page his memory lives enshrined,

As in their amber sweets the smothered bees, —
As the fair cedar, fallen before the breeze,
Lies self-embalmed amidst the mouldering trees.

Poets, like youngest children, never grow
Out of their mother's fondness. Nature so
Holds their soft hands, and will not let
    them go,

Till at the last they track with even feet
Her rhythmic footsteps, and their pulses
    beat
Twinned with her pulses, and their lips re-
    peat   60

The secrets she has told them, as their
    own:
Thus is the inmost soul of Nature known,
And the rapt minstrel shares her awful
    throne !

O lover of her mountains and her woods,
Her bridal chamber's leafy solitudes,
Where Love himself with tremulous step
    intrudes,

Her snows fall harmless on thy sacred
    fire:
Far be the day that claims thy sounding
    lyre
To join the music of the angel choir !

Yet, since life's amplest measure must be
    filled,   70
Since throbbing hearts must be forever
    stilled,
And all must fade that evening sunsets gild,

Grant, Father, ere he close the mortal eyes
That see a Nation's reeking sacrifice,
Its smoke may vanish from these blackened
    skies !

Then, when his summons comes, since come
    it must,
And, looking heavenward with unfaltering
    trust,
He wraps his drapery round him for the
    dust,

His last fond glance will show him o'er his
    head
The Northern fires beyond the zenith
    spread   80
In lambent glory, blue and white and
    red, —

The Southern cross without its bleeding
    load.

The milky way of peace all freshly strowed,
And every white-throned star fixed in its
    lost abode !

1864.   1864.

MY ANNUAL[1]

1866

How long will this harp which you once
    loved to hear
Cheat your lips of a smile or your eyes of
    a tear ?
How long stir the echoes it wakened of old,
While its strings were unbroken, untar-
    nished its gold ?

Dear friends of my boyhood, my words do
    you wrong;
The heart, the heart only, shall throb in
    my song;
It reads the kind answer that looks from
    your eyes, —
' We will bid our old harper play on till
    he dies.'

Though Youth, the fair angel that looked
    o'er the strings,
Has lost the bright glory that gleamed on
    his wings,   10
Though the freshness of morning has
    passed from its tone,
It is still the old harp that was always
    your own.

I claim not its music, — each note it affords
I strike from your heart-strings, that lend
    me its chords;
I know you will listen and love to the last,
For it trembles and thrills with the voice
    of your past.

Ah, brothers ! dear brothers ! the harp
    that I hold
No craftsman could string and no artisan
    mould;
He shaped it, He strung it, who fashioned
    the lyres
That ring with the hymns of the seraphim
    choirs.   20

Not mine are the visions of beauty it brings,
Not mine the faint fragrance around it that
    clings;

[1] For a reunion of the class of '29.

Those shapes are the phantoms of years
    that are fled,
Those sweets breathe from roses your sum-
    mers have shed.

Each hour of the past lends its tribute to
    this,
Till it blooms like a bower in the Garden
    of Bliss;
The thorn and the thistle may grow as they
    will,
Where Friendship unfolds there is Paradise
    still.

The bird wanders careless while summer
    is green,
The leaf-hidden cradle that rocked him un-
    seen;   30
When Autumn's rude fingers the woods
    have undressed,
The boughs may look bare, but they show
    him his nest.

Too precious these moments! the lustre
    they fling
Is the light of our year, is the gem of its
    ring,
So brimming with sunshine, we almost for-
    get
The rays it has lost, and its border of jet.

While round us the many-hued halo is shed,
How dear are the living, how near are the
    dead!
One circle, scarce broken, these waiting be-
    low,
Those walking the shores where the aspho-
    dels blow!   40

Not life shall enlarge it nor death shall
    divide, —
No brother new-born finds his place at my
    side;
No titles shall freeze us, no grandeurs in-
    fest,
His Honor, His Worship, are boys like the
    rest.

Some won the world's homage, their names
    we hold dear, —
But Friendship, not Fame, is the counter-
    sign here;
Make room by the conqueror crowned in
    the strife
For the comrade that limps from the battle
    of life!

What tongue talks of battle? Too long we
    have heard
In sorrow, in anguish, that terrible word;
It reddened the sunshine, it crimsoned the
    wave,   51
It sprinkled our doors with the blood of
    our brave.

Peace, Peace comes at last, with her garland
    of white;
Peace broods in all hearts as we gather to-
    night;
The blazon of Union spreads full in the sun;
We echo its words, — We are one! We
    are one!

1866.   1866.

ALL HERE [1]

IT is not what we say or sing,
    That keeps our charm so long unbroken,
Though every lightest leaf we bring
    May touch the heart as friendship's token;
Not what we sing or what we say
    Can make us dearer to each other;
We love the singer and his lay,
    But love as well the silent brother.

Yet bring whate'er your garden grows,
    Thrice welcome to our smiles and
        praises;   10
Thanks for the myrtle and the rose,
    Thanks for the marigolds and daisies;
One flower ere long we all shall claim,
    Alas! unloved of Amaryllis —
Nature's last blossom — need I name
    The wreath of threescore's silver lilies?

How many, brothers, meet to-night
    Around our boyhood's covered embers?
Go read the treasured names aright
    The old triennial list remembers;   20
Though twenty wear the starry sign
    That tells a life has broke its tether,
The fifty-eight of 'twenty-nine —
    God bless THE BOYS! — are all together!

These come with joyous look and word,
    With friendly grasp and cheerful greet-
        ing, —
Those smile unseen, and move unheard,
    The angel guests of every meeting;
They cast no shadow in the flame
    That flushes from the gilded lustre,   30

[1] For the class reunion, 1867.

But count us — we are still the same;
  One earthly band, one heavenly clus-
    ter!

Love dies not when he bows his head
  To pass beyond the narrow portals, —
The light these glowing moments shed
  Wakes from their sleep our lost immor-
    tals;
They come as in their joyous prime,
  Before their morning days were num-
    bered, —
Death stays the envious hand of Time, —
  The eyes have not grown dim that slum-
    bered!   40

The paths that loving souls have trod
  Arch o'er the dust where worldlings
    grovel
High as the zenith o'er the sod, —
  The cross above the sexton's shovel!
We rise beyond the realms of day;
  They seem to stoop from spheres of
    glory
With us one happy hour to stray,
  While youth comes back in song and
    story.

Ah! ours is friendship true as steel
  That war has tried in edge and temper;
It writes upon its sacred seal   51
  The priest's *ubique* — *omnes* — *semper!*
It lends the sky a fairer sun
  That cheers our lives with rays as steady
As if our footsteps had begun
  To print the golden streets already!

The tangling years have clinched its knot
  Too fast for mortal strength to sunder;
The lightning bolts of noon are shot;
  No fear of evening's idle thunder!   60
Too late! too late! — no graceless hand
  Shall stretch its cords in vain endeavor
To rive the close encircling band
  That made and keeps us one forever!

So when upon the fated scroll
  The falling stars have all descended,
And, blotted from the breathing roll,
  Our little page of life is ended,
We ask but one memorial line
  Traced on thy tablet, Gracious Mother:
'My children. Boys of '29.   71
  In pace. How they loved each other!'

1867.   1867.

BILL AND JOE[1]

COME, dear old comrade, you and I
Will steal an hour from days gone by,
The shining days when life was new,
And all was bright with morning dew,
The lusty days of long ago,
When you were Bill and I was Joe.

Your name may flaunt a titled trail
Proud as a cockerel's rainbow tail,
And mine as brief appendix wear
As Tam O'Shanter's luckless mare;   10
To-day, old friend, remember still
That I am Joe and you are Bill.

You 've won the great world's envied prize,
And grand you look in people's eyes,
With H O N. and L L. D.
In big brave letters, fair to see, —
Your fist, old fellow! off they go! —
How are you, Bill? How are you, Joe?

You 've worn the judge's ermined robe;
You 've taught your name to half the globe;
You 've sung mankind a deathless strain; 21
You 've made the dead past live again:
The world may call you what it will,
But you and I are Joe and Bill.

The chaffing young folks stare and say
'See those old buffers, bent and gray, —
They talk like fellows in their teens!
Mad, poor old boys! That 's what it
  means,' —
And shake their heads; they little know
The throbbing hearts of Bill and Joe! — 30

How Bill forgets his hour of pride,
While Joe sits smiling at his side;
How Joe, in spite of time's disguise,
Finds the old schoolmate in his eyes, —
Those calm, stern eyes that melt and fill
As Joe looks fondly up at Bill.

Ah, pensive scholar, what is fame?
A fitful tongue of leaping flame;
A giddy whirlwind's fickle gust,
That lifts a pinch of mortal dust;   40
A few swift years, and who can show
Which dust was Bill and which was Joe?

The weary idol takes his stand,
Holds out his bruised and aching hand,

[1] For the class reunion, 1868.

While gaping thousands come and go, —
How vain it seems, this empty show !
Till all at once his pulses thrill; —
'T is poor old Joe's 'God bless you, Bill ! '

And shall we breathe in happier spheres
The names that pleased our mortal ears; 50
In some sweet lull of harp and song
For earth-born spirits none too long,
Just whispering of the world below
Where this was Bill and that was Joe ?

No matter; while our home is here
No sounding name is half so dear;
When fades at length our lingering day,
Who cares what pompous tombstones say ?
Read on the hearts that love us still,
Hic jacet Joe.   *Hic jacet* Bill.   60
1868.   1868.

NEARING THE SNOW-LINE

SLOW toiling upward from the misty vale,
I leave the bright enamelled zones below;
No more for me their beauteous bloom shall
    glow,
Their lingering sweetness load the morning
    gale;
Few are the slender flowerets, scentless, pale,
That on their ice-clad stems all trembling
    blow
Along the margin of unmelting snow;
Yet with unsaddened voice thy verge I hail,
White realm of peace above the flowering
    line;
Welcome thy frozen domes, thy rocky
    spires !
O'er thee undimmed the moon-girt planets
    shine,
On thy majestic altars fade the fires
That filled the air with smoke of vain de-
    sires,
And all the unclouded blue of heaven is
    thine !
1870.   1870.

DOROTHY Q [1]

A FAMILY PORTRAIT

GRANDMOTHER'S mother: her age, I guess,
Thirteen summers, or something less;

[1] I cannot tell the story of Dorothy Q. more simply
in prose than I have told it in verse, but I can add
something to it.

Girlish bust, but womanly air;
Smooth, square forehead with uprolled
    hair;
Lips that lover has never kissed;
Taper fingers and slender wrist;
Hanging sleeves of stiff brocade;
So they painted the little maid.

On her hand a parrot green
Sits unmoving and broods serene.   10
Hold up the canvas full in view, —
Look ! there 's a rent the light shines
    through,
Dark with a century's fringe of dust, —
That was a Red-Coat's rapier-thrust !
Such is the tale the lady old,
Dorothy's daughter's daughter, told.

Who the painter was none may tell, —
One whose best was not over well;
Hard and dry, it must be confessed,
Flat as a rose that has long been pressed; 20
Yet in her cheek the hues are bright,
Dainty colors of red and white,
And in her slender shape are seen
Hint and promise of stately mien.

Look not on her with eyes of scorn, —
Dorothy Q. was a lady born !
Ay ! since the galloping Normans came,
England's annals have known her name;
And still to the three-hilled rebel town
Dear is that ancient name's renown,   30
For many a civic wreath they won,
The youthful sire and the gray-haired son.

O Damsel Dorothy ! Dorothy Q. !
Strange is the gift that I owe to you ;
Such a gift as never a king
Save to daughter or son might bring, —
All my tenure of heart and hand,
All my title to house and land;
Mother and sister and child and wife
And joy and sorrow and death and life ! 40

Dorothy was the daughter of Judge Edmund Quincy,
and the niece of Josiah Quincy, junior, the young
patriot and orator who died just before the American
Revolution, of which he was one of the most eloquent
and effective promoters. The son of the latter, Josiah
Quincy, the first mayor of Boston bearing that name,
lived to a great age, one of the most useful and honored
citizens of his time.

The canvas of the painting was so much decayed that
it had to be replaced by a new one, in doing which the
rapier thrust was of course filled up.   (HOLMES.)

See Morse's *Life of Holmes*, vol. i, pp. 17 and 231-
232.

For a reproduction of the portrait, see *Scribner's
Magazine*, May, 1879.

What if a hundred years ago
Those close-shut lips had answered No,
When forth the tremulous question came
That cost the maiden her Norman name,
And under the folds that look so still
The bodice swelled with the bosom's thrill ?
Should I be I, or would it be
One tenth another, to nine tenths me ?

Soft is the breath of a maiden's YES:
Not the light gossamer stirs with less;   50
But never a cable that holds so fast
Through all the battles of wave and blast,
And never an echo of speech or song
That lives in the babbling air so long !
There were tones in the voice that whis-
        pered then
You may hear to-day in a hundred men.

O lady and lover, how faint and far
Your images hover, — and here we are,
Solid and stirring in flesh and bone, —
Edward's and Dorothy's — all their own, —
A goodly record for Time to show   61
Of a syllable spoken so long ago ! —
Shall I bless you, Dorothy, or forgive
For the tender whisper that bade me live ?

It shall be a blessing, my little maid !
I will heal the stab of the Red-Coat's blade,
And freshen the gold of the tarnished
        frame,
And gild with a rhyme your household
        name;
So you shall smile on us brave and bright
As first you greeted the morning's light,   70
And live untroubled by woes and fears
Through a second youth of a hundred
        years.

                              1871.

EPILOGUE TO THE BREAK-FAST-TABLE SERIES

AUTOCRAT — PROFESSOR — POET

AT A BOOKSTORE

Anno Domini 1972

A CRAZY bookcase, placed before
A low-price dealer's open door;
Therein arrayed in broken rows
A ragged crew of rhyme and prose,
The homeless vagrants, waifs, and strays
Whose low estate this line betrays

(Set forth the lesser birds to lime)
YOUR CHOICE AMONG THESE BOOKS
        1 DIME !

Ho ! dealer; for its motto's sake
This scarecrow from the shelf I take;   10
Three starving volumes bound in one,
Its covers warping in the sun.
Methinks it hath a musty smell,
I like its flavor none too well,
But Yorick's brain was far from dull,
Though Hamlet pah ! 'd, and dropped his
        skull.

Why, here comes rain ! The sky grows
        dark, —
Was that the roll of thunder ? Hark !
The shop affords a safe retreat,
A chair extends its welcome seat,   20
The tradesman has a civil look
(I 've paid, impromptu, for my book),
The clouds portend a sudden shower, —
I 'll read my purchase for an hour.

.   .   .   .

What have I rescued from the shelf ?
A Boswell, writing out himself !
For though he changes dress and name,
The man beneath is still the same,
Laughing or sad, by fits and starts,
One actor in a dozen parts,   30
And whatsoe'er the mask may be,
The voice assures us, *This is he.*

I say not this to cry him down;
I find my Shakespeare in his clown,
His rogues the selfsame parent own;
Nay ! Satan talks in Milton's tone !
Where'er the ocean inlet strays,
The salt sea wave its source betrays;
Where'er the queen of summer blows,
She tells the zephyr, ' I 'm the rose ! '   40

And his is not the playwright's page;
His table does not ape the stage;
What matter if the figures seen
Are only shadows on a screen,
He finds in them his lurking thought,
And on their lips the words he sought,
Like one who sits before the keys
And plays a tune himself to please.

And was he noted in his day ?
Read, flattered, honored ? Who shall say ?
Poor wreck of time the wave has cast   51
To find a peaceful shore at last,

Once glorying in thy gilded name
And freighted deep with hopes of fame,
Thy leaf is moistened with a tear,
The first for many a long, long year !

For be it more or less of art
That veils the lowliest human heart
Where passion throbs, where friendship
		glows,
Where pity's tender tribute flows,		60
Where love has lit its fragrant fire,
And sorrow quenched its vain desire,
For me the altar is divine,
Its flame, its ashes, — all are mine !

And thou, my brother, as I look
And see thee pictured in thy book,
Thy years on every page confessed
In shadows lengthening from the west,
Thy glance that wanders, as it sought
Some freshly opening flower of thought, 70
Thy hopeful nature, light and free,
I start to find myself in thee !

.   .   .   .

Come, vagrant, outcast, wretch forlorn
In leather jerkin stained and torn,
Whose talk has filled my idle hour
And made me half forget the shower,
I 'll do at least as much for you,
Your coat I 'll patch, your gilt renew,
Read you —perhaps — some other time.
Not bad, my bargain ! Price one dime ! 80
1872.					1872.

PROGRAMME [1]

OCTOBER 7, 1874

READER — gentle — if so be
Such still live, and live for me,
Will it please you to be told
What my tenscore pages hold ?

Here are verses that in spite
Of myself I needs must write,
Like the wine that oozes first
When the unsqueezed grapes have burst.

Here are angry lines, ' too hard ! '
Says the soldier, battle-scarred.		10

[1] Written to introduce the *Songs of Many Seasons*,
which contained a large number of Holmes's ' occasional' poems.

Could I smile his scars away
I would blot the bitter lay,

Written with a knitted brow,
Read with placid wonder now.
Throbbed such passion in my heart ?
Did his wounds once really smart ?

Here are varied strains that sing
All the changes life can bring,
Songs when joyous friends have met,
Songs the mourner's tears have wet.	20

See the banquet's dead bouquet,
Fair and fragrant in its day;
Do they read the selfsame lines, —
He that fasts and he that dines ?

Year by year, like milestones placed,
Mark the record Friendship traced.
Prisoned in the walls of time
Life has notched itself in rhyme:

As its seasons slid along,
Every year a notch of song,		30
From the June of long ago,
When the rose was full in blow,

Till the scarlet sage has come
And the cold chrysanthemum.
Read, but not to praise or blame;
Are not all our hearts the same ?

For the rest, they take their chance, —
Some may pay a passing glance,
Others, — well, they served a turn, —
Wherefore written, would you learn ? 40

Not for glory, not for pelf,
Not, be sure, to please myself,
Not for any meaner ends, —
Always ' by request of friends.'

Here 's the cousin of a king, —
Would I do the civil thing ?
Here 's the first-born of a queen:
Here 's a slant-eyed Mandarin.

Would I polish off Japan ?
Would I greet this famous man,		50
Prince or Prelate, Sheik or Shah ? —
Figaro çi and Figaro là !

Would I just this once comply ? —
So they teased and teased till I

(Be the truth at once confessed)
Wavered — yielded — did my best.

Turn my pages, — never mind
If you like not all you find;
Think not all the grains are gold
Sacramento's sand-banks hold.   60

Every kernel has its shell,
Every chime its harshest bell,
Every face its weariest look,
Every shelf its emptiest book,

Every field its leanest sheaf,
Every book its dullest leaf,
Every leaf its weakest line, —
Shall it not be so with mine ?

Best for worst shall make amends,
Find us, keep us, leave us friends   70
Till, perchance, we meet again.
Benedicite. — Amen !

1874.   *1874.*

GRANDMOTHER'S STORY OF BUNKER-HILL BATTLE[1]

AS SHE SAW IT FROM THE BELFRY

'T IS like stirring living embers when, at
    eighty, one remembers
All the achings and the quakings of ' the
    times that tried men's souls;'[2]

[1] The story of Bunker Hill battle is told as literally in accordance with the best authorities as it would have been if it had been written in prose instead of in verse. I have often been asked what steeple it was from which the little group I speak of looked upon the conflict. To this I answer that I am not prepared to speak authoritatively, but that the reader may take his choice among all the steeples standing at that time in the northern part of the city. Christ Church in Salem Street is the one I always think of, but I do not insist upon its claim. As to the personages who made up the small company that followed the old corporal, it would be hard to identify them, but by ascertaining where the portrait by Copley is now to be found, some light may be thrown on their personality.
Daniel Malcolm's gravestone, splintered by British bullets, may be seen in the Copp's Hill burial-ground. (HOLMES.)
This poem was first published in 1875, in connection with the centenary of the battle of Bunker Hill. The belfry could hardly have been that of Christ Church, since tradition says that General Gage was stationed there watching the battle, and we may make it to be what was known as the New Brick Church, built in 1721, on Hanover, corner of Richmond Street, Boston, rebuilt of stone in 1845, and pulled down at the widening of Hanover Street in 1871. There are many narratives of the battle of Bunker Hill. Frothingham's *History of the Siege of Boston* is one of the most com-

When I talk of *Whig* and *Tory*, when I tell
    the *Rebel* story,
To you the words are ashes, but to me
    they 're burning coals.

I had heard the muskets' rattle of the
    April running battle;
Lord Percy's hunted soldiers, I can see
    their red coats still;
But a deadly chill comes o'er me, as the
    day looms up before me,
When a thousand men lay bleeding on the
    slopes of Bunker's Hill.

'T was a peaceful summer's morning, when
    the first thing gave us warning
Was the booming of the cannon from the
    river and the shore: 10
' Child,' says grandma, ' what 's the matter,
    what is all this noise and clatter ?
Have those scalping Indian devils come to
    murder us once more ? '

Poor old soul ! my sides were shaking in
    the midst of all my quaking,
To hear her talk of Indians when the guns
    began to roar:
She had seen the burning village, and the
    slaughter and the pillage,
When the Mohawks killed her father with
    their bullets through his door.

Then I said, ' Now, dear old granny, don't
    you fret and worry any,
For I 'll soon come back and tell you
    whether this is work or play;
There can't be mischief in it, so I won't
    be gone a minute ' —
For a minute then I started. I was gone
    the livelong day.   20

No time for bodice-lacing or for looking-
    glass grimacing;

prehensive accounts, and has furnished material for many popular narratives. (*Riverside Literature Series.*)
[2] In December, 1776, Thomas Paine, whose *Common Sense* had so remarkable a popularity as the first homely expression of public opinion on Independence, began issuing a series of tracts called *The Crisis*, eighteen numbers of which appeared. The familiar words quoted by the grandmother must often have been heard and used by her. They begin the first number of *The Crisis:* ' These are the times that try men's souls: the summer soldier and the sunshine patriot will, in this crisis, shrink from the service of his country; but he that stands it NOW deserves the love and thanks of man and woman.' (*Riverside Literature Series.*)

Down my hair went as I hurried, tumbling
    half-way to my heels;
God forbid your ever knowing, when
    there's blood around her flowing,
How the lonely, helpless daughter of a
    quiet household feels !

In the street I heard a thumping; and I
    knew it was the stumping
Of the Corporal, our old neighbor, on that
    wooden leg he wore,
With a knot of women round him, — it was
    lucky I had found him,
So I followed with the others, and the Cor-
    poral marched before.

They were making for the steeple, — the
    old soldier and his people;
The pigeons circled round us as we climbed
    the creaking stair.   30
Just across the narrow river — oh, so close
    it made me shiver ! —
Stood a fortress on the hill-top that but
    yesterday was bare.

Not slow our eyes to find it; well we knew
    who stood behind it,
Though the earthwork hid them from us,
    and the stubborn walls were dumb:
Here were sister, wife, and mother, looking
    wild upon each other,
And their lips were white with terror as
    they said, THE HOUR HAS COME !

The morning slowly wasted, not a morsel
    had we tasted,
And our heads were almost splitting with
    the cannon's deafening thrill,
When a figure tall and stately round the
    rampart strode sedately;
It was PRESCOTT, one since told me; he
    commanded on the hill.   40

Every woman's heart grew bigger when we
    saw his manly figure,
With the banian buckled round it, standing
    up so straight and tall;
Like a gentleman of leisure who is strolling
    out for pleasure,
Through the storm of shells and cannon-
    shot he walked around the wall.

At eleven the streets were swarming, for
    the redcoats' ranks were forming;

At noon in marching order they were mov-
    ing to the piers;
How the bayonets gleamed and glistened,
    as we looked far down, and listened
To the trampling and the drum-beat of the
    belted grenadiers !

At length the men have started, with a
    cheer (it seemed faint-hearted),
In their scarlet regimentals, with their
    knapsacks on their backs,   50
And the reddening, rippling water, as after
    a sea-fight's slaughter,
Round the barges gliding onward blushed
    like blood along their tracks.

So they crossed to the other border, and
    again they formed in order;
And the boats came back for soldiers,
    came for soldiers, soldiers still:
The time seemed everlasting to us women
    faint and fasting, —
At last they're moving, marching, marching
    proudly up the hill.

We can see the bright steel glancing all
    along the lines advancing, —
Now the front rank fires a volley, — they
    have thrown away their shot;
For behind their earthwork lying, all the
    balls above them flying,
Our people need not hurry; so they wait
    and answer not.   60

Then the Corporal, our old cripple (he would
    swear sometimes and tipple) —
He had heard the bullets whistle (in the
    old French war) before —
Calls out in words of jeering, just as if they
    all were hearing, —
And his wooden leg thumps fiercely on the
    dusty belfry floor: —

· Oh ! fire away, ye villains, and earn King
    George's shillin's,
But ye'll waste a ton of powder afore a
    'rebel' falls;
You may bang the dirt and welcome,
    they're as safe as Dan'l Malcolm,
Ten foot beneath the gravestone that
    you've splintered with your balls !'[1]

---

[1] The following epitaph is still to be read on a tall
gravestone, standing as yet undisturbed among the
transplanted monuments of the dead in Copp's Hill
Burial Ground, one of the three city [Boston] ceme-

In the hush of expectation, in the awe and
   trepidation
Of the dread approaching moment, we are
   well-nigh breathless all;   70
Though the rotten bars are failing on the
   rickety belfry railing,
We are crowding up against them like the
   waves against a wall.

Just a glimpse (the air is clearer), they are
   nearer, — nearer, — nearer,
When a flash — a curling smoke-wreath —
   then a crash — the steeple shakes —
The deadly truce is ended; the tempest's
   shroud is rended;
Like a morning mist it gathered, like a
   thundercloud it breaks !

Oh the sight our eyes discover as the blue-
   black smoke blows over !
The red-coats stretched in windrows as a
   mower rakes his hay;
Here a scarlet heap is lying, there a headlong crowd is flying
Like a billow that has broken and is shivered into spray.   80

Then we cried, 'The troops are routed !
   they are beat — it can't be doubted !
God be thanked, the fight is over !' — Ah !
   the grim old soldier's smile !
'Tell us, tell us why you look so ?' (we
   could hardly speak, we shook so), —
'Are they beaten ? *Are* they beaten?
   ARE they beaten?' — 'Wait a
   while.'

Oh the trembling and the terror ! for too
   soon we saw our error:
They are baffled, not defeated; we have
   driven them back in vain;
And the columns that were scattered, round
   the colors that were tattered,
Toward the sullen, silent fortress turn their
   belted breasts again.

teries which have been desecrated and ruined within
my own remembrance : —

     Here lies buried in a
     Stone Grave 10 feet deep
        Capt. DANIEL MALCOLM Mercht
     Who departed this Life
      October 23, 1769,
      Aged 44 years,
     A true son of Liberty,
    A Friend to the Publick,
    An Enemy to oppression,
    And one of the foremost
       In opposing the Revenue Acts
    On America.
                      (HOLMES.)

All at once, as we are gazing, lo the roofs
   of Charlestown blazing !
They have fired the harmless village; in an
   hour it will be down !   90
The Lord in heaven confound them, rain
   his fire and brimstone round them, —
The robbing, murdering red-coats, that
   would burn a peaceful town !

They are marching, stern and solemn; we
   can see each massive column
As they near the naked earth-mound with
   the slanting walls so steep.
Have our soldiers got faint-hearted, and in
   noiseless haste departed ?
Are they panic-struck and helpless ? Are
   they palsied or asleep ?

Now ! the walls they 're almost under !
   scarce a rod the foes asunder !
Not a firelock flashed against them ! up
   the earthwork they will swarm !
But the words have scarce been spoken,
   when the ominous calm is broken,
And a bellowing crash has emptied all the
   vengeance of the storm !   100

So again, with murderous slaughter, pelted
   backwards to the water,
Fly Pigot's running heroes and the frightened braves of Howe;
And we shout, 'At last they 're done for,
   it 's their barges they have run for:
They are beaten, beaten, beaten; and the
   battle 's over now !'

And we looked, poor timid creatures, on
   the rough old soldier's features,
Our lips afraid to question, but he knew
   what we would ask:
'Not sure,' he said; 'keep quiet, — once
   more, I guess, they 'll try it —
Here 's damnation to the cut-throats !' —
   then he handed me his flask,

Saying, 'Gal, you 're looking shaky; have
   a drop of old Jamaiky;
I 'm afeard there 'll be more trouble afore
   the job is done;'   110
So I took one scorching swallow; dreadful
   faint I felt and hollow,
Standing there from early morning when
   the firing was begun.

All through those hours of trial I had
   watched a calm clock dial,

As the hands kept creeping, creeping, —
  they were creeping round to four,
When the old man said, 'They're forming
  with their bagonets fixed for storming:
It's the death-grip that's a-coming, — they
  will try the works once more.'

With brazen trumpets blaring, the flames
  behind them glaring,
The deadly wall before them, in close array
  they come;
Still onward, upward toiling, like a dragon's
  fold uncoiling, —
Like the rattlesnake's shrill warning the
  reverberating drum !   120

Over heaps all torn and gory — shall I tell
  the fearful story,
How they surged above the breastwork, as
  a sea breaks over a deck;
How, driven, yet scarce defeated, our worn-
  out men retreated,
With their powder-horns all emptied, like
  the swimmers from a wreck ?

It has all been told and painted; as for me,
  they say I fainted,
And the wooden-legged old Corporal
  stumped with me down the stair:
When I woke from dreams affrighted the
  evening lamps were lighted, —
On the floor a youth was lying; his bleeding breast was bare.

And I heard through all the flurry, 'Send
  for WARREN ! hurry ! hurry !
Tell him here's a soldier bleeding, and he'll
  come and dress his wound !'   130
Ah, we knew not till the morrow told its
  tale of death and sorrow,
How the starlight found him stiffened on
  the dark and bloody ground.

Who the youth was, what his name was,
  where the place from which he came
  was,
Who had brought him from the battle, and
  had left him at our door,
He could not speak to tell us; but 't was
  one of our brave fellows,
As the homespun plainly showed us which
  the dying soldier wore.

For they all thought he was dying, as they
  gathered round him crying, —

And they said, 'Oh, how they'll miss him!
  and, 'What *will* his mother do ?'
Then, his eyelids just unclosing like a child's
  that has been dozing,
He faintly murmured, 'Mother!' — and
  — I saw his eyes were blue.   140

'Why, grandma, how you're winking!' Ah,
  my child, it sets me thinking
Of a story not like this one. Well, he somehow lived along;
So we came to know each other, and I
  nursed him like a — mother,
Till at last he stood before me, tall, and
  rosy-cheeked, and strong.

And we sometimes walked together in the
  pleasant summer weather, —
'Please to tell us what his name was?'
  Just your own, my little dear, —
There's his picture Copley painted: we be-
  came so well acquainted,
That — in short, that's why I'm grandma,
  and you children all are here !
                              1875.

HOW THE OLD HORSE WON THE BET

DEDICATED BY A CONTRIBUTOR TO THE
COLLEGIAN, 1830, TO THE EDITORS OF
THE HARVARD ADVOCATE, 1876 [1]

'T WAS on the famous trotting-ground,
The betting men were gathered round
From far and near; the 'cracks' were there
Whose deeds the sporting prints declare:
The swift g. m., Old Hiram's nag,
The fleet s. h., Dan Pfeiffer's brag,
With these a third — and who is he
That stands beside his fast b. g. ?
Budd Doble, whose catarrhal name
So fills the nasal trump of fame.   10
There too stood many a noted steed
Of Messenger and Morgan breed;
Green horses also, not a few;
Unknown as yet what they could do;
And all the hacks that know so well
The scourgings of the Sunday swell.

Blue are the skies of opening day;
The bordering turf is green with May;

[1] The poem was read at a dinner of the editors of the
Harvard Advocate, a literary magazine published by
undergraduates.

The sunshine's golden gleam is thrown
On sorrel, chestnut, bay, and roan;   20
The horses paw and prance and neigh,
Fillies and colts like kittens play,
And dance and toss their rippled manes
Shining and soft as silken skeins;
Wagons and gigs are ranged about,
And fashion flaunts her gay turn-out;
Here   stands — each   youthful   Jehu's
      dream —
The jointed tandem, ticklish team !
And there in ampler breadth expand
The splendors of the four-in-hand;   30
On faultless ties and glossy tiles
The lovely bonnets beam their smiles;
(The style 's the man, so books avow;
The style 's the woman, anyhow);
From flounces frothed with creamy lace
Peeps out the pug-dog's smutty face,
Or spaniel rolls his liquid eye,
Or stares the wiry pet of Skye, —
O woman, in your hours of ease
So shy with us, so free with these !   40

'Come on !   I 'll bet you two to one
I 'll   make   him   do   it !'   'Will   you ?
      Done !'

What was it who was bound to do?
I did not hear and can't tell you, —
Pray listen till my story 's through.
Scarce noticed, back behind the rest,
By cart and wagon rudely prest,
The parson's lean and bony bay
Stood harnessed in his one-horse shay —
Lent to his sexton for the day   50
(A funeral — so the sexton said;
His mother's uncle's wife was dead).

Like Lazarus bid to Dives' feast,
So looked the poor forlorn old beast;
His coat was rough, his tail was bare,
The gray was sprinkled in his hair;
Sportsmen and jockeys knew him not,
And yet they say he once could trot
Among the fleetest of the town,
Till something cracked and broke him
      down, —   60
The steed's, the statesman's, common
      lot !
'And are we then so soon forgot ?
Ah me !   I doubt if one of you
Has ever heard the name 'Old Blue,'
Whose fame through all this region rung
In those old days when I was young !

'Bring forth the horse !'   Alas ! he showed
Not like the one Mazeppa rode;
Scant-maned,   sharp-backed,   and   shaky-
      kneed,
The wreck of what was once a steed,   70
Lips thin, eyes hollow, stiff in joints;
Yet not without his knowing points.
The sexton laughing in his sleeve,
As if 't were all a make-believe,
Led forth the horse, and as he laughed
Unhitched the breeching from a shaft,
Unclasped the rusty belt beneath,
Drew forth the snaffle from his teeth,
Slipped off his head-stall, set him free
From strap and rein, — a sight to see !   80

So worn, so lean in every limb,
It can't be they are saddling him !
It is !   his back the pig-skin strides
And flaps his lank, rheumatic sides;
With look of mingled scorn and mirth
They buckle round the saddle-girth;
With horsy wink and saucy toss
A youngster throws his leg across,
And so, his rider on his back,
They lead him, limping, to the track,   90
Far up behind the starting-point,
To limber out each stiffened joint.

As through the jeering crowd he past,
One pitying look Old Hiram cast;
'Go it, ye cripple, while ye can !'
Cried out unsentimental Dan;
'A Fast-Day dinner for the crows !'
Budd Doble's scoffing shout arose.

Slowly, as when the walking-beam
First feels the gathering head of steam,   100
With   warning   cough   and   threatening
      wheeze
The stiff old charger crooks his knees;
At first with cautious step sedate,
As if he dragged a coach of state;
He 's not a colt; he knows full well
That time is weight and sure to tell;
No horse so sturdy but he fears
The handicap of twenty years.

As through the throng on either hand
The old horse nears the judges' stand,   110
Beneath his jockey's feather-weight
He warms a little to his gait,
And now and then a step is tried
That hints of something like a stride.

'Go!'—Through his ear the summons stung
As if a battle-trump had rung;
The slumbering instincts long unstirred
Start at the old familiar word;
It thrills like flame through every limb, —
What mean his twenty years to him?   120
The savage blow his rider dealt
Fell on his hollow flanks unfelt;
The spur that pricked his staring hide
Unheeded tore his bleeding side;
Alike to him are spur and rein, —
He steps a five-year-old again!

Before the quarter pole was past,
Old Hiram said, 'He's going fast.'
Long ere the quarter was a half,
The chuckling crowd had ceased to laugh;
Tighter his frightened jockey clung   131
As in a mighty stride he swung,
The gravel flying in his track,
His neck stretched out, his ears laid back,
His tail extended all the while
Behind him like a rat-tail file!
Off went a shoe, — away it spun,
Shot like a bullet from a gun;
The quaking jockey shapes a prayer
From scraps of oaths he used to swear;   140
He drops his whip, he drops his rein,
He clutches fiercely for a mane;
He'll lose his hold — he sways and reels —
He'll slide beneath those trampling heels!
The knees of many a horseman quake,
The flowers on many a bonnet shake,
And shouts arise from left and right,
'Stick on! Stick on!' 'Hould tight!
    Hould tight!'
'Cling round his neck and don't let go —
That pace can't hold — there! steady!
    whoa!'   150
But like the sable steed that bore
The spectral lover of Lenore,
His nostrils snorting foam and fire,
No stretch his bony limbs can tire;
And now the stand he rushes by,
And 'Stop him! — stop him!' is the cry.
Stand back! he's only just begun —
He's having out three heats in one!

'Don't rush in front! he'll smash your
    brains;
But follow up and grab the reins!'   160
Old Hiram spoke. Dan Pfeiffer heard,
And sprang impatient at the word;
Budd Doble started on his bay,
Old Hiram followed on his gray,

And off they spring, and round they go,
The fast ones doing 'all they know.'
Look! twice they follow at his heels,
As round the circling course he wheels,
And whirls with him that clinging boy
Like Hector round the walls of Troy,   170
Still on, and on, the third time round!
They're tailing off! they're losing ground!
Budd Doble's nag begins to fail!
Dan Pfeiffer's sorrel whisks his tail!
And see! in spite of whip and shout,
Old Hiram's mare is giving out!
Now for the finish! at the turn,
The old horse — all the rest astern —
Comes swinging in, with easy trot;
By Jove! he's distanced all the lot!   180

That trot no mortal could explain;
Some said, 'Old Dutchman come again!'
Some took his time, — at least they tried,
But what it was could none decide;
One said he could n't understand
What happened to his second hand;
One said 2.10; that could n't be —
More like two twenty-two or three;
Old Hiram settled it at last;
'The time was two — too dee-vel-ish fast!'

The parson's horse had won the bet;   191
It cost him something of a sweat;
Back in the one-horse shay he went;
The parson wondered what it meant,
And murmured, with a mild surprise
And pleasant twinkle of the eyes,
'That funeral must have been a trick,
Or corpses drive at double-quick;
I should n't wonder, I declare,
If brother — Jehu — made the prayer!'   200

And this is all I have to say
About that tough old trotting bay,
Huddup! Huddup! G'lang! Good day!

Moral for which this tale is told:
A horse can trot, for all he's old.

                                    1876.

FOR WHITTIER'S SEVENTIETH BIRTHDAY

DECEMBER 17, 1877

I BELIEVE that the copies of verses I've
    spun,
Like Scheherezade's tales, are a thousand
    and one;

You remember the story, — those mornings
    in bed, —
'T was the turn of a copper, — a tale or a
    head.

A doom like Scheherezade's falls upon me
In a mandate as stern as the Sultan's
    decree:
I 'm a florist in verse, and what *would* peo-
    ple say
If I came to a banquet without my bou-
    quet ?

It is trying, no doubt, when the company
    knows
Just the look and the smell of each lily and
    rose,   10
The green of each leaf in the sprigs that I
    bring,
And the shape of the bunch and the knot
    of the string.

Yes, — 'the style is the man,' and the nib
    of one's pen
Makes the same mark at twenty, and three-
    score and ten;
It is so in all matters, if truth may be told;
Let one look at the cast, he can tell you
    the mould.

How we all know each other ! no use in
    disguise;
Through the holes in the mask comes the
    flash of the eyes;
We can tell by his — somewhat — each one
    of our tribe,
As we know the old hat which we cannot
    describe.   20

Though in Hebrew, in Sanscrit, in Choctaw
    you write,
Sweet singer who gave us the 'Voices of
    Night,'
Though in buskin or slipper your song may
    be shod,
Or the velvety verse that Evangeline trod,

We shall say, ' You can't cheat us, — we
    know it is you,'
There is one voice like that, but there can-
    not be two,
Maëstro, whose chant like the dulcimer
    rings:
And the woods will be hushed while the
    nightingale sings.

And he, so serene, so majestic, so true,
Whose temple hypæthral the planets shine
    through,   30
Let us catch but five words from that mys-
    tical pen,
We should know our one sage from all
    children of men.

And he whose bright image no distance can
    dim,
Through a hundred disguises we can't mis-
    take him,
Whose play is all earnest, whose wit is the
    edge
(With a beetle behind) of a sham-splitting
    wedge.

Do you know whom we send you, Hidalgos
    of Spain?
Do you know your old friends when you
    see them again ?
Hosea was Sancho ! you Dons of Madrid,
But Sancho that wielded the lance of the
    Cid !   40

And the wood-thrush of Essex, — you know
    whom I mean,
Whose song echoes round us while he sits
    unseen,
Whose heart-throbs of verse through our
    memories thrill
Like a breath from the wood, like a breeze
    from the hill,

So fervid, so simple, so loving, so pure,
We hear but one strain and our verdict is
    sure, —
Thee cannot elude us, — no further we
    search, —
'T is Holy George Herbert cut loose from
    his church !

We think it the voice of a seraph that
    sings, —
Alas ! we remember that angels have
    wings, —   50
What story is this of the day of his
    birth ?
Let him live to a hundred ! we want him
    on earth !

One life has been paid him (in gold) by
    the sun;
One account has been squared and another
    begun;

But he never will die if he lingers below
Till we 've paid him in love half the bal-
    ance we owe !

1877.   1877.

VERITAS [1]

TRUTH: So the frontlet's older legend ran,
On the brief record's opening page dis-
    played;
Not yet those clear-eyed scholars were
    afraid
Lest the fair fruit that wrought the woe of
    man
By far Euphrates — where our sire began
His search for truth, and, seeking, was
    betrayed —
Might work new treason in their forest
    shade,
Doubling the curse that brought life's
    shortened span.

Nurse of the future, daughter of the past,
That stern phylactery best becomes thee
    now :
Lift to the morning star thy marble
    brow !
Cast thy brave truth on every warring
    blast !
Stretch thy white hand to that forbidden
    bough,
And let thine earliest symbol be thy last !
1878.   1878.

THE SILENT MELODY

'BRING me my broken harp,' he said;
  'We both are wrecks, — but as ye
will, —
Though all its ringing tones have fled,
  Their echoes linger round it still;
It had some golden strings, I know,
But that was long — how long ! — ago.

[1] The original motto on the seal of Harvard College,
adopted in 1643. In a letter enclosing this sonnet and
another entitled 'Christo et Ecclesiae,' to be read at a
meeting of the New York Harvard Club, Holmes says :
'At the first meeting of the Governors of the College
under the Charter of 1642, held in the year 1643, it was
"ordered that there shall be a College seale in forme
following," namely, a shield with three open books
bearing the word *Veritas*. This motto was soon ex-
changed for *In Christi gloriam;* and this again shortly
superseded by the one so long used, *Christo et Ecclesiae.*'

Holmes's sonnet was meant as a plea that the older
and broader motto, *Veritas*, be restored. (See Morse's
Life of Holmes, vol. i, pp. 236-240. This has now been
done, but without displacing the other motto, *Christo
et Ecclesiae.*

'I cannot see its tarnished gold,
  I cannot hear its vanished tone,
Scarce can my trembling fingers hold
  The pillared frame so long their own; 10
We both are wrecks, — awhile ago
It had some silver strings, I know,

'But on them Time too long has played
  The solemn strain that knows no change,
And where of old my fingers strayed
  The chords they find are new and
    strange, —
Yes ! iron strings, — I know, — I know, —
We both are wrecks of long ago.

'We both are wrecks, — a shattered
    pair, —
  Strange to ourselves in time's dis-
    guise . . . 20
What say ye to the lovesick air
  That brought the tears from Marian's
    eyes ?
Ay ! trust me, — under breasts of snow
Hearts could be melted long ago !

'Or will ye hear the storm-song's crash
  That from his dreams the soldier woke,
And bade him face the lightning flash
  When battle's cloud in thunder
    broke ? . . .
Wrecks, — nought but wrecks ! — the time
    was when
We two were worth a thousand men !' 30

And so the broken harp they bring
  With pitying smiles that none could
    blame;
Alas ! there 's not a single string
  Of all that filled the tarnished frame !
But see ! like children overjoyed,
His fingers rambling through the void !

'I clasp thee ! Ay . . . mine ancient
    lyre . . .
  Nay, guide my wandering fingers. . . .
    There !
They love to dally with the wire
  As Isaac played with Esau's hair. . . . 40
Hush ! ye shall hear the famous tune
That Marian called the Breath of June !'

And so they softly gather round:
  Rapt in his tuneful trance he seems:
His fingers move: but not a sound !
  A silence like the song of dreams. . . .

'There! ye have heard the air,' he cries,
'That brought the tears from Marian's
  eyes!'

Ah, smile not at his fond conceit,
  Nor deem his fancy wrought in vain; 50
To him the unreal sounds are sweet, —
  No discord mars the silent strain
Scored on life's latest, starlit page —
The voiceless melody of age.

Sweet are the lips of all that sing,
  When Nature's music breathes unsought,
But never yet could voice or string
  So truly shape our tenderest thought
As when by life's decaying fire
Our fingers sweep the stringless lyre! 60

                                   1878.

THE IRON GATE [1]

WHERE is this patriarch you are kindly
    greeting?
  Not unfamiliar to my ear his name,
Nor yet unknown to many a joyous meet-
    ing
  In days long vanished, — is he still the
    same,

Or changed by years, forgotten and for-
    getting,
  Dull-eared, dim-sighted, slow of speech
    and thought,
Still o'er the sad, degenerate present fret-
    ting,
  Where all goes wrong, and nothing as it
    ought?

Old age, the graybeard! Well, indeed, I
    know him, —
  Shrunk, tottering, bent, of aches and ills
    the prey; 10
In sermon, story, fable, picture, poem,
  Oft have I met him from my earliest
    day:

In my old Æsop, toiling with his bundle, —
  His load of sticks, — politely asking
    Death,
Who comes when called for, — would he
    lug or trundle
  His fagot for him? — he was scant of
    breath.

Read by Holmes at the celebration of his seventieth
birthday.

And sad 'Ecclesiastes, or the Preacher,' —
  Has he not stamped the image on my
    soul,
In that last chapter, where the worn-out
    Teacher
  Sighs o'er the loosened cord, the broken
    bowl? 20

Yes, long, indeed, I've known him at a dis-
    tance,
  And now my lifted door-latch shows him
    here;
I take his shrivelled hand without resist-
    ance,
  And find him smiling as his step draws
    near.

What though of gilded baubles he bereaves
    us,
  Dear to the heart of youth, to manhood's
    prime;
Think of the calm he brings, the wealth he
    leaves us,
  The hoarded spoils, the legacies of time!

Altars once flaming, still with incense fra-
    grant,
  Passion's uneasy nurslings rocked asleep,
Hope's anchor faster, wild desire less va-
    grant, 31
  Life's flow less noisy, but the stream
    how deep!

Still as the silver cord gets worn and
    slender,
  Its lightened task-work tugs with lessen-
    ing strain,
Hands get more helpful, voices, grown more
    tender,
  Soothe with their softened tones the
    slumberous brain.

Youth longs and manhood strives, but age
    remembers,
  Sits by the raked-up ashes of the past,
Spreads its thin hands above the whitening
    embers
  That warm its creeping life-blood till
    the last. 40

Dear to its heart is every loving token
  That comes unbidden ere its pulse grows
    cold,
Ere the last lingering ties of life are broken.
  Its labors ended and its story told.

Ah, while around us rosy youth rejoices,
  For us the sorrow-laden breezes sigh,
And through the chorus of its jocund
    voices
  Throbs the sharp note of misery's hope-
    less cry.

As on the gauzy wings of fancy flying
  From some far orb I track our watery
    sphere,   50
Home of the struggling, suffering, doubt-
    ing, dying,
  The silvered globule seems a glistening
    tear.

But Nature lends her mirror of illusion
  To win from saddening scenes our age-
    dimmed eyes,
And misty day-dreams blend in sweet con-
    fusion
  The wintry landscape and the summer
    skies.

So when the iron portal shuts behind us,
  And life forgets us in its noise and
    whirl,
Visions that shunned the glaring noonday
    find us,
  And glimmering starlight shows the
    gates of pearl.   60

I come not here your morning hour to sad-
    den,
  A limping pilgrim, leaning on his staff, —
I, who have never deemed it sin to glad-
    den
  This vale of sorrows with a wholesome
    laugh.

If word of mine another's gloom has
    brightened,
  Through my dumb lips the heaven-sent
    message came;
If hand of mine another's task has light-
    ened,
  It felt the guidance that it dares not
    claim.

But, O my gentle sisters, O my brothers,
  These thick-sown snow-flakes hint of
    toil's release;   70
These feebler pulses bid me leave to oth-
    ers
  The tasks once welcome; evening asks
    for peace.

Time claims his tribute; silence now is
    golden;
  Let me not vex the too long suffering
    lyre;
Though to your love untiring still beholden,
  The curfew tells me —cover up the fire.

And now with grateful smile and accents
    cheerful,
  And warmer heart than look or word
    can tell,
In simplest phrase —these traitorous eyes
    are tearful —
  Thanks, Brothers, Sisters, — Children,
    — and farewell!   80
1879.   1879.

THE SHADOWS[1]

' How many have gone ? ' was the question
    of old
  Ere Time our bright ring of its jewels
    bereft;
Alas ! for too often the death-bell has tolled,
  And the question we ask is, ' How many
    are left ? '

Bright sparkled the wine; there were *fifty*
    that quaffed;
  For a decade had slipped and had taken
    but three.
How they frolicked and sung, how they
    shouted and laughed,
  Like a school full of boys from their
    benches set free !

There were speeches and toasts, there were
    stories and rhymes,
  The hall shook its sides with their mer-
    riment's noise;   10
As they talked and lived over the college
    day times, —
  No wonder they kept their old nam
    ' The Boys' !

The seasons moved on in their rhyt
    flow
  With mornings like maidens that
    or smiled,
With the bud and the leaf and t
    and the snow,
  And the year-books of Time i
    coves were piled.

[1] For the class reunion, 1880.

There were *forty* that gathered where fifty
    had met;
  Some locks had got silvered, some lives
    had grown sere,
But the laugh of the laughers was lusty as
    yet,
  And the song of the singers rose ringing
    and clear.   20

Still flitted the years; there were *thirty* that
    came;
  'The Boys' they were still, and they an-
    swered their call;
There were foreheads of care, but the smiles
    were the same,
  And the chorus rang loud through the
    garlanded hall.

The hour-hand moved on, and they gath-
    ered again;
  There were *twenty* that joined in the
    hymn that was sung;
But ah! for our song-bird we listened in
    vain, —
  The crystalline tones like a seraph's that
    rung!

How narrow the circle that holds us to-
    night!
  How many the loved ones that greet us
    no more,   30
As we meet like the stragglers that come
    from the fight,
  Like the mariners flung from a wreck
    on the shore!

We look through the twilight for those we
    have lost;
  The stream rolls between us, and yet
    they seem near;
Already outnumbered by those who have
    crossed,
  Our band is transplanted, its home is not
    here!

They smile on us still — is it only a
    dream? —
  While fondly or proudly their names we
    recall;
They beckon — they come — they are cross-
    ing the stream —
  Lo! the Shadows! the Shadows! room
    — room for them all!   40

1880.   1880.

AT THE SATURDAY CLUB [1]

THIS is our place of meeting; opposite
That towered and pillared building: look
    at it;
King's Chapel in the Second George's day,
Rebellion stole its regal name away, —
Stone Chapel sounded better; but at last
The poisoned name of our provincial past
Had lost its ancient venom; then once more
Stone Chapel was King's Chapel as before.
(So let rechristened North Street, when it
    can,
Bring back the days of Marlborough and
    Queen Anne!)   10

[1] About the time when these papers [*The Autocrat*] were published, the Saturday Club was founded, or, rather, found itself in existence, without any organization, almost without parentage. It was natural enough that such men as Emerson, Longfellow, Agassiz, Peirce, with Hawthorne, Motley, Sumner, when within reach, and others who would be good company for them, should meet and dine together once in a while, as they did, in point of fact, every month, and as some who are still living, with other and newer members, still meet and dine. If some of them had not admired each other they would have been exceptions in the world of letters and science. [Holmes here alludes to the fact that the profane sometimes called this club 'The Mutual Admiration Society.' It is related that when a book by one of its members was reviewed by another member in the 'North American Review,' some outsider wrote below the heading of the article, 'Insured in the Mutual.'] The club deserves being remembered for having no constitution or by-laws, for making no speeches, reading no papers, observing no ceremonies, coming and going at will without remark, and acting out, though it did not proclaim the motto, 'Shall I not take mine ease in mine inn?' (HOLMES.)

Outside the sacred *penetralia* which were shut within his own front door, nothing else in Dr. Holmes's life gave him so much pleasure as did this Club. He loved it; he hugged the thought of it. When he was writing to Lowell and Motley in Europe, he seemed to think that merely to name '*The Club*' was enough to give a genial flavor to his page. He would tell who were present at the latest meeting, and where they sat. He would recur to those who used to come, and mention their habitual seats, — matters which his correspondents already knew perfectly well. But the names were sweet things in his mouth; and, in fact, he was doing one of the deepest acts of intimacy in thus touching the chord of the dearest reminiscence which their memories held in common. By this he seemed sure that he would make his letter welcome, however little else of news or interest it might convey. In the later days there came to be something pathetic about his attachment to that which still had existence and yet for him was almost all a memory. In 1883 he wrote to Lowell: 'I go to the Saturday Club quite regularly, but the company is more of ghosts than of flesh and blood for me. I carry a stranger there now and then, introduce him to the members who happen to be there, and then say: There at that end used to sit Agassiz; here at this end Longfellow; Emerson used to be there, and Lowell often next him; on such an occasion Hawthorne was with us, at another time Motley and Sumner, and smaller constellations, — nebulæ if you will, but luminous more or less in the provincial firmament.' (Morse's *Life of Holmes*, vol. i, pp. 243, 244.)

Cf. Lowell's 'Agassiz,' and Holmes's *Life of Emerson*.

Next the old church your wandering eye
    will meet —
A granite pile that stares upon the street —
Our civic temple; slanderous tongues have
    said
Its shape was modelled from St. Botolph's
    head,
Lofty, but narrow; jealous passers-by
Say Boston always held her head too high.
    Turn half-way round, and let your look
    survey
The white façade that gleams across the
    way, —
The many-windowed building, tall and
    wide,
The palace-inn that shows its northern
    side   20
In grateful shadow when the sunbeams
    beat
The granite wall in summer's scorching
    heat.
This is the place; whether its name you
    spell
Tavern, or caravansera, or hotel.
Would I could steal its echoes ! you should
    find
Such store of vanished pleasures brought
    to mind:
Such feasts ! the laughs of many a jocund
    hour
That shook the mortar from King George's
    tower;
Such guests ! What famous names its re-
    cord boasts,
Whose owners wander in the mob of
    ghosts !   30
Such stories ! Every beam and plank is
    filled
With juicy wit the joyous talkers spilled,
Ready to ooze, as once the mountain pine
The floors are laid with oozed its turpen-
    tine !

    A month had flitted since The Club had
    met;
The day came round; I found the table set,
The waiters lounging round the marble
    stairs,
Empty as yet the double row of chairs.
I was a full half hour before the rest,
Alone, the banquet-chamber's single guest.
So from the table's side a chair I took, 41
And having neither company nor book
To keep me waking, by degrees there crept
A torpor over me, — in short, I slept.

Loosed from its chain, along the wreck-
    strown track
Of the dead years my soul goes travelling
    back;
My ghosts take on their robes of flesh; it
    seems
Dreaming is life; nay, life less life than
    dreams,
So real are the shapes that meet my eyes.
They bring no sense of wonder, no sur-
    prise,   50
No hint of other than an earth-born source;
All seems plain daylight, everything of
    course.
    How dim the colors are, how poor and
    faint
This palette of weak words with which I
    paint !
Here sit my friends; if I could fix them so
As to my eyes they seem, my page would
    glow
Like a queen's missal, warm as if the
    brush
Of Titian or Velasquez brought the flush
Of life into their features. *Ay de mi!*
If syllables were pigments, you should
    see   60
Such breathing portraitures as never man
Found in the Pitti or the Vatican.

    Here sits our POET, Laureate, if you will.
Long has he worn the wreath, and wears it
    still.
Dead ? Nay, not so; and yet they say his
    bust
Looks down on marbles covering royal dust,
Kings by the Grace of God, or Nature's
    grace;
Dead ! No ! Alive ! I see him in his place,
Full-featured, with the bloom that heaven
    denies
Her children, pinched by cold New England
    skies,   70
Too often, while the nursery's happier few
Win from a summer cloud its roseate hue.
Kind, soft-voiced, gentle, in his eye there
    shines
The ray serene that filled Evangeline's.
    Modest he seems, not shy; content to
    wait
Amid the noisy clamor of debate
The looked-for moment when a peaceful
    word
Smooths the rough ripples louder tongues
    have stirred.

In every tone I mark his tender grace
And all his poems hinted in his face;   80
What tranquil joy his friendly presence
        gives !
How could I think him dead ? He lives !
        He lives !

There, at the table's further end I see
In his old place our Poet's *vis-à-vis*,
The great PROFESSOR, strong, broad-shoul-
        dered, square,
In life's rich noontide, joyous, debonair.
His social hour no leaden care alloys,
His laugh rings loud and mirthful as a
        boy's, —
That lusty laugh the Puritan forgot, —
What ear has heard it and remembers
        not ?   90
How often, halting at some wide crevasse
Amid the windings of his Alpine pass,
High up the cliffs, the climbing moun-
        taineer,
Listening the far-off avalanche to hear,
Silent, and leaning on his steel-shod staff,
Has heard that cheery voice, that ringing
        laugh,
From the rude cabin whose nomadic walls
Creep with the moving glacier as it crawls !
    How does vast Nature lead her living
        train
In ordered sequence through that spacious
        brain,   100
As in the primal hour when Adam named
The new-born tribes that young creation
        claimed ! —
How will her realm be darkened, losing
        thee,
Her darling, whom we call *our* AGASSIZ !

But who is he whose massive frame belies
The maiden shyness of his downcast eyes ?
Who broods in silence till, by questions
        pressed,
Some answer struggles from his laboring
        breast ?
An artist Nature meant to dwell apart,   109
Locked in his studio with a human heart,
Tracking its caverned passions to their lair,
And all its throbbing mysteries laying bare.
    Count it no marvel that he broods alone
Over the heart he studies, — 't is his own;
So in his page, whatever shape it wear,
The Essex wizard's shadowed self is there,—
The great ROMANCER, hid beneath his veil
Like the stern preacher of his sombre tale;

Virile in strength, yet bashful as a girl,
Prouder than Hester, sensitive as Pearl. 12

    From his mild throng of worshippers
        released,
Our Concord Delphi sends its chosen priest,
Prophet or poet, mystic, sage, or seer,
By every title always welcome here.
Why that ethereal spirit's frame describe ?
You know the race-marks of the Brahmin
        tribe, —
The spare, slight form, the sloping shoul-
        der's droop,
The calm, scholastic mien, the clerkly
        stoop,
The lines of thought the sharpened features
        wear,
Carved by the edge of keen New England
        air.   130
    List ! for he speaks ! As when a king
        would choose
The jewels for his bride, he might refuse
This diamond for its flaw, — find that less
        bright
Than those, its fellows, and a pearl less
        white
Than fits her snowy neck, and yet at last,
The fairest gems are chosen, and made fast
In golden fetters; so, with light delays
He seeks the fittest word to fill his phrase;
Nor vain nor idle his fastidious quest,
His chosen word is sure to prove the best.
    Where in the realm of thought, whose
        air is song,   141
Does he, the Buddha of the West, belong ?
He seems a wingèd Franklin, sweetly wise,
Born to unlock the secrets of the skies;
And which the nobler calling, — if 't is fair
Terrestrial with celestial to compare, —
To guide the storm-cloud's elemental flame,
Or walk the chambers whence the light-
        ning came,
Amidst the sources of its subtile fire,
And steal their effluence for his lips and
        lyre ?   150
    If lost at times in vague aerial flights,
None treads with firmer footstep when he
        lights;
A soaring nature, ballasted with sense,
Wisdom without her wrinkles or pretence,
In every Bible he has faith to read,
And every altar helps to shape his creed.
Ask you what name this prisoned spirit bears
While with ourselves this fleeting breath it
        shares ?   158

Till angels greet him with a sweeter one
In heaven, on earth we call him EMERSON.

I start; I wake; the vision is withdrawn;
Its figures fading like the stars at dawn;
Crossed from the roll of life their cher-
    ished names,
And memory's pictures fading in their
    frames;
Yet life is lovelier for these transient
    gleams
Of buried friendships; blest is he who
    dreams!
                                    1884.

THE GIRDLE OF FRIENDSHIP [1]

SHE gathered at her slender waist
    The beauteous robe she wore;
Its folds a golden belt embraced,
    One rose-hued gem it bore.

The girdle shrank; its lessening round
    Still kept the shining gem,
But now her flowing locks it bound,
    A lustrous diadem.

And narrower still the circlet grew;
    Behold! a glittering band,
Its roseate diamond set anew,
    Her neck's white column spanned.

Suns rise and set; the straining clasp
    The shortened links resist,
Yet flashes in a bracelet's grasp
    The diamond, on her wrist.

At length, the round of changes past
    The thieving years could bring,
The jewel, glittering to the last,
    Still sparkles in a ring.

So, link by link, our friendships part,
    So loosen, break, and fall,
A narrowing zone; the loving heart
    Lives changeless through them all.
1884.   1884.

TO JAMES RUSSELL LOWELL [2]

THIS is your month, the month of 'perfect
    days,'
Birds in full song and blossoms all ablaze.

[1] For the class reunion, 1884.
[2] On his return from England.

Nature herself your earliest welcome
    breathes,
Spreads every leaflet, every bower in-
    wreathes;
Carpets her paths for your returning feet,
Puts forth her best your coming steps to
    greet;
And Heaven must surely find the earth in
    tune
When Home, sweet Home, exhales the
    breath of June.

These blessed days are waning all too fast,
And June's bright visions mingling with
    the past;   10
Lilacs have bloomed and faded, and the rose
Has dropped its petals, but the clover blows,
And fills its slender tubes with honeyed
    sweets;
The fields are pearled with milk-white
    margarites;
The dandelion, which you sang of old,
Has lost its pride of place, its crown of gold,
But still displays its feathery-mantled
    globe,
Which children's breath or wandering
    winds unrobe.
These were your humble friends; your
    opened eyes
Nature had trained her common gifts to
    prize;   20
Not Cam nor Isis taught you to despise
Charles, with his muddy margin and the
    harsh,
Plebeian grasses of the reeking marsh.
New England's home-bred scholar, well
    you knew
Her soil, her speech, her people, through
    and through,
And loved them ever with the love that
    holds
All sweet, fond memories in its fragrant
    folds.
Though far and wide your wingèd words
    have flown,
Your daily presence kept you all our own,
Till, with a sorrowing sigh, a thrill of
    pride,   30
We heard your summons, and you left our
    side
For larger duties and for tasks untried.

How pleased the Spaniards for a while to
    claim
This frank Hidalgo with the liquid name,

Who stored their classics on his crowded
    shelves
And loved their Calderon as they did
    themselves !
Before his eyes what changing pageants
    pass !
The bridal feast how near the funeral
    mass !
The death-stroke falls, — the Misereres
    wail;
The joy - bells ring, — the tear - stained
    cheeks unveil,   40
While, as the playwright shifts his pictured
    scene,
The royal mourner crowns his second
    queen.

From Spain to Britain is a goodly stride, —
Madrid and London long-stretched leagues
    divide.
What if I send him, 'Uncle S., says he,'
To my good cousin whom he calls ' J. B.'?
A nation's servants go where they are
    sent, —
He heard his Uncle's orders, and he went.
  By what enchantments, what alluring
    arts,
Our truthful James led captive British
    hearts, —   50
Whether his shrewdness made their states-
    men halt,
Or if his learning found their Dons at fault,
Or if his virtue was a strange surprise,
Or if his wit flung star-dust in their eyes, —
Like honest Yankees we can simply guess;
But that he did it all must needs confess.
England herself without a blush may
    claim
Her only conqueror since the Norman
    came.
  Eight years an exile ! What a weary
    while
Since first our herald sought the mother
    isle !   60
His snow-white flag no churlish wrong has
    soiled, —
He left unchallenged, he returns unspoiled.

Here let us keep him, here he saw the
    light, —
His genius, wisdom, wit, are ours by right;
And if we lose him our lament will be
We have ' five hundred ' — *not* ' as good
    as he.'

1885.   (1888.)

THE LYRE OF ANACREON [1]

THE minstrel of the classic lay
  Of love and wine who sings
Still found the fingers run astray
  That touched the rebel strings.

Of Cadmus he would fain have sung,
  Of Atreus and his line;
But all the jocund echoes rung
  With songs of love and wine.

Ah, brothers ! I would fain have caught
  Some fresher fancy's gleam;   10
My truant accents find, unsought,
  The old familiar theme.

Love, Love ! but not the sportive child
  With shaft and twanging bow,
Whose random arrows drove us wild
  Some threescore years ago;

Not Eros, with his joyous laugh,
  The urchin blind and bare,
But Love, with spectacles and staff,
  And scanty, silvered hair.   20

Our heads with frosted locks are white,
  Our roofs are thatched with snow,
But red, in chilling winter's spite,
  Our hearts and hearthstones glow.

Our old acquaintance, Time, drops in,
  And while the running sands
Their golden thread unheeded spin,
  He warms his frozen hands.

Stay, wingèd hours, too swift, too sweet,
  And waft this message o'er   30
To all we miss, from all we meet
  On life's fast-crumbling shore:

Say that, to old affection true,
  We hug the narrowing chain
That binds our hearts, — alas, how few
  The links that yet remain !

The fatal touch awaits them all
  That turns the rocks to dust;
From year to year they break and fall, —
  They break, but never rust.   40

Say if one note of happier strain
  This worn-out harp afford, —

    [1] For the class reunion, 1885.

One throb that trembles, not in vain, —
  Their memory lent its chord.

Say that when Fancy closed her wings
  And Passion quenched his fire,
Love, Love, still echoed from the strings
  As from Anacreon's lyre !
1885.   (1888.)

AFTER THE CURFEW [1]

THE Play is over.   While the light
  Yet lingers in the darkening hall,
I come to say a last Good-night
  Before the final *Exeunt all.*

We gathered once, a joyous throng:
  The jovial toasts went gayly round;
With jest, and laugh, and shout, and song,
  We made the floors and walls resound.

We come with feeble steps and slow,
  A little band of four or five,   10
Left from the wrecks of long ago,
  Still pleased to find ourselves alive.

Alive !   How living, too, are they
  Whose memories it is ours to share !
Spread the long table's full array, —
  There sits a ghost in every chair !

One breathing form no more, alas !
  Amid our slender group we see; [2]
With him we still remained ' The Class,' —
  Without his presence what are we ?   20

The hand we ever loved to clasp, —
  That tireless hand which knew no rest, —
Loosed from affection's clinging grasp,
  Lies nerveless on the peaceful breast.

[1] The last of the poems written for the class of '29.
See the letter from Samuel May to F. J. Garrison,
quoted in Morse's *Life of Holmes*, vol. i, p. 78 : ' " After
the Curfew " was positively *the last*.   " Farewell ! I let
the curtain fall."   The curtain never rose again for
" '29."   We met once more — a year later — at Parker's.
But three were present, Smith, Holmes, and myself.
No poem — very quiet — something very like tears.
The following meetings — all at Dr. H.'s house — were
quiet, social, *talking* meetings — the Doctor of course
doing the *live* talking. . . . At one of these meetings
four were present, all the survivors but one ; and there
was more *general* talk.   But never another *Class
Poem.*'
  This poem, and the three following, appeared in *Over
the Teacups.*
[2] The personal reference is to our greatly beloved
and honored classmate, James Freeman Clarke.
(HOLMES.)

The beaming eye, the cheering voice,
  That lent to life a generous glow,
Whose every meaning said ' Rejoice,'
  We see, we hear, no more below.

The air seems darkened by his loss,
  Earth's shadowed features look less fair,
And heavier weighs the daily cross   31
  His willing shoulders helped us bear.

Why mourn that we, the favored few
  Whom grasping Time so long has spared
Life's sweet illusions to pursue,
  The common lot of age have shared ?

In every pulse of Friendship's heart
  There breeds unfelt a throb of pain, —
One hour must rend its links apart,
  Though years on years have forged the
    chain.   40

So ends ' The Boys,' — a lifelong play.
  We too must hear the Prompter's call
To fairer scenes and brighter day :
  Farewell !   I let the curtain fall.
1889.   1890.

LA MAISON D'OR

(BAR HARBOR)

FROM this fair home behold on either side
  The restful mountains or the restless sea:
So the warm sheltering walls of life divide
  Time and its tides from still eternity.

Look on the waves: their stormy voices
    teach
  That not on earth may toil and struggle
    cease.
Look on the mountains: better far than
    speech
  Their silent promise of eternal peace.
1890.   1890.

TOO YOUNG FOR LOVE

    Too young for love ?
    Ah, say not so !
Tell reddening rosebuds not to blow !
Wait not for spring to pass away, —
Love's summer months begin with May !

Too young for love ?
Ah, say not so !
Too young ? Too young ?
Ah, no ! no ! no !

Too young for love ?
Ah, say not so,
While daisies bloom and tulips glow !
June soon will come with lengthened day
To practise all love learned in May.
    Too young for love ?
    Ah, say not so !
    Too young ? Too young ?
    Ah, no ! no ! no !

1890.   1890.

THE BROOMSTICK TRAIN; OR, THE RETURN OF THE WITCHES [1]

LOOK out ! Look out, boys ! Clear the track !
The witches are here ! They 've all come back !
They hanged them high, — No use ! No use !
What cares a witch for a hangman's noose ?
They buried them deep, but they would n't lie still,
For cats and witches are hard to kill ;
They swore they should n't and would n't die, —
Books said they did, but they lie ! they lie !

A couple of hundred years, or so,
They had knocked about in the world below,   10
When an Essex Deacon dropped in to call,
And a homesick feeling seized them all ;

For he came from a place they knew full well,
And many a tale he had to tell.
They longed to visit the haunts of men,
To see the old dwellings they knew again,
And ride on their broomsticks all around
Their wide domain of unhallowed ground.

In Essex county there 's many a roof
Well known to him of the cloven hoof ; 20
The small square windows are full in view
Which the midnight hags went sailing through,
On their well-trained broomsticks mounted high,
Seen like shadows against the sky ;
Crossing the track of owls and bats,
Hugging before them their coal-black cats.

Well did they know, those gray old wives,
The sights we see in our daily drives :
Shimmer of lake and shine of sea,
Browne's bare hill with its lonely tree, 30
(It was n't then as we see it now,
With one scant scalp-lock to shade its brow ;)
Dusky nooks in the Essex woods,
Dark, dim, Dante-like solitudes,
Where the tree-toad watches the sinuous snake
Glide through his forests of fern and brake ;
Ipswich River ; its old stone bridge ;
Far off Andover's Indian Ridge,
And many a scene where history tells
Some shadow of bygone terror dwells, — 40
Of 'Norman's Woe' with its tale of dread,
Of the Screeching Woman of Marblehead,
(The fearful story that turns men pale :
Don't bid me tell it, — my speech would fail.)

Who would not, will not, if he can,
Bathe in the breezes of fair Cape Ann, —
Rest in the bowers her bays enfold,
Loved by the sachems and squaws of old ?
Home where the white magnolias bloom,
Sweet with the bayberry's chaste perfume,
Hugged by the woods and kissed by the sea ! 51
Where is the Eden like to thee ?
For that 'couple of hundred years, or so,'
There had been no peace in the world below ;
The witches still grumbling, 'It is n't fair ;
Come, give us a taste of the upper air !

[1] Look here ! There are crowds of people whirled through our streets on these new-fashioned cars, with their witch-broomsticks overhead, — if they don't come from Salem, they ought to, — and not more than one in a dozen of these fish-eyed bipeds thinks or cares a nickel's worth about the miracle which is wrought for their convenience. They know that without hands or feet, without horses, without steam, so far as they can see, they are transported from place to place, and that there is nothing to account for it except the witch-broomstick and the iron or copper cobweb which they see stretched above them. What do they know or care about this last revelation of the omnipresent spirit of the material universe ? We ought to go down on our knees when one of these mighty caravans, car after car, spins by us, under the mystic impulse which seems to know not whether its train is loaded or empty. (HOLMES, in *Over the Teacups.*) The first electric trolley-cars had just been introduced when this poem was written, in 1890.

We 've had enough of your sulphur springs,
And the evil odor that round them clings;
We long for a drink that is cool and
   nice, —
Great buckets of water with Wenham ice;
We 've served you well up-stairs, you
   know;   61
You 're a good old — fellow — come, let us
   go !'

I don't feel sure of his being good,
But he happened to be in a pleasant
   mood, —
As fiends with their skins full sometimes
   are
(He 'd been drinking with 'roughs' at a
   Boston bar).
So what does he do but up and shout
To a graybeard turnkey, 'Let 'em out !'

To mind his orders was all he knew;
The gates swung open, and out they flew. 70
'Where are our broomsticks ?' the beldams
   cried.
'Here are your broomsticks,' an imp re-
   plied.
'They 've been in — the place you know —
   so long
They smell of brimstone uncommon strong;
But they 've gained by being left alone, —
Just look, and you 'll see how tall they 've
   grown.'
'And where is my cat ?' a vixen squalled.
'Yes, where are our cats ?' the witches
   bawled,
And began to call them all by name:
As fast as they called the cats, they came:
There was bob-tailed Tommy and long-
   tailed Tim,   81
And wall-eyed Jacky and green-eyed Jim,
And splay-foot Benny and slim-legged
   Beau,
And Skinny and Squally, and Jerry and
   Joe,
And many another that came at call, —
It would take too long to count them all.
All black, — one could hardly tell which
   was which,
But every cat knew his own old witch;
And she knew hers as hers knew her, —
Ah, did n't they curl their tails and purr ! 90

No sooner the withered hags were free
Than out they swarmed for a midnight
   spree;

I could n't tell all they did in rhymes,
But the Essex people had dreadful times.
The Swampscott fishermen still relate
How a strange sea-monster stole their bait;
How their nets were tangled in loops and
   knots,
And they found dead crabs in their lobster-
   pots.
Poor Danvers grieved for her blasted crops,
And Wilmington mourned over mildewed
   hops.   100
A blight played havoc with Beverly
   beans, —
It was all the work of those hateful queans !
A dreadful panic began at 'Pride's,'
Where the witches stopped in their mid-
   night rides,
And there rose strange rumors and vague
   alarms
'Mid the peaceful dwellers at Beverly
   Farms.

Now when the Boss of the Beldams found
That without his leave they were ramping
   round,
He called, — they could hear him twenty
   miles,   109
From Chelsea beach to the Misery Isles;
The deafest old granny knew his tone
Without the trick of the telephone.
'Come here, you witches ! Come here !'
   says he, —
'At your games of old, without asking me !
I 'll give you a little job to do
That will keep you stirring, you godless
   crew !'

They came, of course, at their master's call,
The witches, the broomsticks, the cats, and
   all;
He led the hags to a railway train
The horses were trying to drag in vain. 120
'Now, then,' says he, 'you 've had your
   fun,
And here are the cars you 've got to run.
The driver may just unhitch his team,
We don't want horses, we don't want
   steam;
You may keep your old black cats to hug,
But the loaded train you 've got to lug.'

Since then on many a car you 'll see
A broomstick plain as plain can be;
On every stick there 's a witch astride, —
The string you see to her leg is tied. 130

She will do a mischief if she can,
But the string is held by a careful man,
And whenever the evil-minded witch
Would cut some caper, he gives a twitch.
As for the hag, you can't see her,
But hark ! you can hear her black cat's
    purr,
And now and then, as a car goes by,
You may catch a gleam from her wicked
    eye.
Often you 've looked on a rushing train,
But just what moved it was not so plain.
It could n't be those wires above,   141
For they could neither pull nor shove;
Where was the motor that made it go
You could n't guess, *but now you know.*

Remember my rhymes when you ride again
On the rattling rail by the broomstick
    train !
1890.   1890.

INVITA MINERVA [1]

VEX not the Muse with idle prayers, —
    She will not hear thy call;
She steals upon thee unawares,
    Or seeks thee not at all.

Soft as the moonbeams when they sought
    Endymion's fragrant bower,
She parts the whispering leaves of thought
    To show her full-blown flower.

For thee her wooing hour has passed,
    The singing birds have flown,
And winter comes with icy blast
    To chill thy buds unblown.

Yet, though the woods no longer thrill
    As once their arches rung,

[1] I find the burden and restrictions of rhyme more
and more troublesome as I grow older. There are
times when it seems natural enough to employ that
form of expression, but it is only occasionally ; and the
use of it as a vehicle of the commonplace is so prevalent that one is not much tempted to select it as the
medium for his thoughts and emotions. The art of
rhyming has almost become a part of a high-school
education, and its practice is far from being an evidence of intellectual distinction. Mediocrity is as
much forbidden to the poet in our days as it was in
those of Horace, and the immense majority of the
verses written are stamped with hopeless mediocrity.
    When one of the ancient poets found he was trying
to grind out verses which came unwillingly, he said he
was writing *Invita Minerva.* (HOLMES, in *Over the
Tea-Cups,* introducing the poem.)

Sweet echoes hover round thee still
    Of songs thy summer sung.

Live in thy past; await no more
    The rush of heaven-sent wings;
Earth still has music left in store
    While Memory sighs and sings.
1890.   1890.

JAMES RUSSELL LOWELL

1819–1891

THOU shouldst have sung the swan-song
        for the choir
    That filled our groves with music till the
        day
Lit the last hilltop with its reddening fire,
    And evening listened for thy lingering
        lay.

But thou hast found thy voice in realms
        afar
    Where strains celestial blend their notes
        with thine;
Some cloudless sphere beneath a happier
        star
    Welcomes the bright-winged spirit we
        resign.

How Nature mourns thee in the still re-
        treat
    Where passed in peace thy love-enchanted
        hours !   10
Where shall she find an eye like thine to
        greet
    Spring's earliest footprints on her open-
        ing flowers ?

Have the pale wayside weeds no fond re-
        gret
    For him who read the secrets they en-
        fold ?
Shall the proud spangles of the field forget
    The verse that lent new glory to their
        gold ?

And ye whose carols wooed his infant
        ear,
    Whose chants with answering woodnotes
        he repaid,
Have ye no song his spirit still may hear
    From Elmwood's vaults of overarching
        shade ?   20

Friends of his studious hours, who thronged
　　to teach
　　The deep-read scholar all your varied
　　　lore,
Shall he no longer seek your shelves to
　　reach
　　The treasure missing from his world-
　　　wide store ?

This singer whom we long have held so dear
　　Was Nature's darling, shapely, strong,
　　　and fair;
Of keenest wit, of judgment crystal-clear,
　　Easy of converse, courteous, debonair,

Fit for the loftiest or the lowliest lot,
　　Self-poised, imperial, yet of simplest
　　　ways;　　　　　　　　　　　　　30
At home alike in castle or in cot,
　　True to his aim, let others blame or
　　　praise.

Freedom he found an heirloom from his
　　sires;
　　Song, letters, statecraft, shared his years
　　　in turn;
All went to feed the nation's altar-fires
　　Whose mourning children wreathe his
　　　funeral urn.

He loved New England, — people, lan-
　　guage, soil,
　　Unweaned by exile from her arid breast.
Farewell awhile, white-handed son of toil,
　　Go with her brown-armed laborers to thy
　　　rest.　　　　　　　　　　　　　40

Peace to thy slumber in the forest shade !
　　Poet and patriot, every gift was thine;
Thy name shall live while summers bloom
　　and fade,
　　And grateful Memory guard thy leafy
　　　shrine !

1891.　　　　　　　　　　　　　　1891.

IN MEMORY OF JOHN GREEN-
LEAF WHITTIER

DECEMBER 17, 1807–SEPTEMBER 7, 1892

THOU, too, hast left us.　While with heads
　　bowed low,
　　And sorrowing hearts, we mourned our
　　summer's dead,

The flying season bent its Parthian bow,
　　And yet again our mingling tears were
　　shed.

Was Heaven impatient that it could not
　　wait
　　The blasts of winter for earth's fruits to
　　fall ?
Were angels crowding round the open gate
　　To greet the spirits coming at their call ?

Nay, let not fancies, born of old be-
　　liefs,
　　Play with the heart-beats that are throb-
　　bing still,　　　　　　　　　　　　10
And waste their outworn phrases on the
　　griefs,
　　The silent griefs that words can only
　　chill.

For thee, dear friend, there needs no high-
　　·　wrought lay,
　　To shed its aureole round thy cherished
　　name, —
Thou whose plain, home-born speech of
　　Yea and Nay
　　Thy truthful nature ever best became.

Death reaches not a spirit such as thine, —
　　It can but steal the robe that hid thy
　　wings;
Though thy warm breathing presence we
　　resign,
　　Still in our hearts its loving semblance
　　clings.　　　　　　　　　　　　　20

Peaceful thy message, yet for struggling
　　right, —
　　When Slavery's gauntlet in our face was
　　flung, —
While timid weaklings watched the dubi-
　　ous fight
　　No herald's challenge more defiant rung.

Yet was thy spirit tuned to gentle themes
　　Sought in the haunts thy humble youth
　　had known.
Our stern New England's hills and vales
　　and streams, —
　　Thy tuneful idyls made them all their own.

The wild flowers springing from thy native
　　sod
　　Lent all their charms thy new-world
　　song to fill, —　　　　　　　　　　30

Gave thee the mayflower and the golden-
rod
To match the daisy and the daffodil.

In the brave records of our earlier time
A hero's deed thy generous soul inspired,
And many a legend, told in ringing rhyme,
The youthful soul with high resolve has
fired.

Not thine to lean on priesthood's broken
reed;
No barriers caged thee in a bigot's fold;
Did zealots ask to syllable thy creed,
Thou saidst 'Our Father,' and thy creed
was told.   40

Best loved and saintliest of our singing
train,
Earth's noblest tributes to thy name belong.
A lifelong record closed without a stain,
A blameless memory shrined in deathless
song.

Lift from its quarried ledge a flawless
stone;
Smooth the green turf and bid the tablet
rise,
And on its snow-white surface carve alone
These words, — he needs no more, —
HERE WHITTIER LIES.

1892.   1892.

JAMES RUSSELL LOWELL

'FOR THIS TRUE NOBLENESS I SEEK IN VAIN'

'FOR this true nobleness I seek in vain,
In woman and in man I find it not;
I almost weary of my earthly lot,
My life-springs are dried up with burning
    pain.'
Thou find'st it not ? I pray thee look
    again,
Look *inward* through the depths of thine
    own soul.
How is it with thee ?   Art thou sound and
    whole ?
Doth narrow search show thee no earthly
    stain ?
BE NOBLE ! and the nobleness that lies
In other men, sleeping, but never dead,
Will rise in majesty to meet thine own;
Then wilt thou see it gleam in many
    eyes,
Then will pure light around thy path be
    shed,
And thou wilt nevermore be sad and lone.
1840.   1840.

MY LOVE[1]

NOT as all other women are
Is she that to my soul is dear;
Her glorious fancies come from far,
Beneath the silver evening-star,
And yet her heart is ever near.

Great feelings hath she of her own,
Which lesser souls may never know;
God giveth them to her alone,
And sweet they are as any tone
Wherewith the wind may choose to blow. 10

Yet in herself she dwelleth not,
Although no home were half so fair;
No simplest duty is forgot,

[1] On the poems of 1840 and 1841, see Scudder's *Life of Lowell*, vol. i, pp. 76–97.

Life hath no dim and lowly spot
That doth not in her sunshine share.

She doeth little kindnesses,
Which most leave undone, or despise:
For naught that sets one heart at ease,
And giveth happiness or peace,
Is low-esteemèd in her eyes.   20

She hath no scorn of common things,
And, though she seem of other birth,
Round us her heart intwines and clings,
And patiently she folds her wings
To tread the humble paths of earth.

Blessing she is: God made her so,
And deeds of week-day holiness
Fall from her noiseless as the snow,
Nor hath she ever chanced to know
That aught were easier than to bless. 30

She is most fair, and thereunto
Her life doth rightly harmonize;
Feeling or thought that was not true
Ne'er made less beautiful the blue
Unclouded heaven of her eyes.

She is a woman: one in whom
The spring-time of her childish years
Hath never lost its fresh perfume,
Though knowing well that life hath room
For many blights and many tears.   40

I love her with a love as still
As a broad river's peaceful might,
Which, by high tower and lowly mill,
Seems following its own wayward will,
And yet doth ever flow aright.

And, on its full, deep breast serene,
Like quiet isles my duties lie;
It flows around them and between,
And makes them fresh and fair and
    green,
Sweet homes wherein to live and die.   50
1840.   1840.

'MY LOVE, I HAVE NO FEAR THAT THOU SHOULDST DIE'

MY Love, I have no fear that thou shouldst
die;
Albeit I ask no fairer life than this,
Whose numbering-clock is still thy gentle
kiss,
While Time and Peace with hands en-
lockèd fly;
Yet care I not where in Eternity
We live and love, well knowing that there is
No backward step for those who feel the
bliss
Of Faith as their most lofty yearnings
high:
Love hath so purified my being's core,
Meseems I scarcely should be startled, even,
To find, some morn, that thou hadst gone
before;
Since, with thy love, this knowledge too
was given,
Which each calm day doth strengthen
more and more,
That they who love are but one step from
Heaven.

1841. (1843.)

'I ASK NOT FOR THOSE THOUGHTS, THAT SUDDEN LEAP'

I ASK not for those thoughts, that sudden
leap
From being's sea, like the isle-seeming
Kraken,
With whose great rise the ocean all is
shaken
And a heart-tremble quivers through the
deep;
Give me that growth which some perchance
deem sleep,
Wherewith the steadfast coral-stems uprise,
Which, by the toil of gathering energies,
Their upward way into clear sunshine keep,
Until, by Heaven's sweetest influences,
Slowly and slowly spreads a speck of green
Into a pleasant island in the seas,
Where, 'mid tall palms, the cane-roofed
home is seen,
And wearied men shall sit at sunset's hour,
Hearing the leaves and loving God's dear
power.

1841. (1843.)

'GREAT TRUTHS ARE PORTIONS OF THE SOUL OF MAN'

GREAT Truths are portions of the soul of
man;
Great souls are portions of Eternity;
Each drop of blood that e'er through true
heart ran
With lofty message, ran for thee and
me;
For God's law, since the starry song
began,
Hath been, and still forevermore must
be,
That every deed which shall outlast Time's
span
Must spur the soul to be erect and free;
Slave is no word of deathless lineage
sprung;
Too many noble souls have thought and
died,
Too many mighty poets lived and sung,
And our good Saxon, from lips purified
With martyr-fire, throughout the world
hath rung
Too long to have God's holy cause denied.

1841. 1842.

. TO THE SPIRIT OF KEATS

GREAT soul, thou sittest with me in my
room,
Uplifting me with thy vast, quiet eyes,
On whose full orbs, with kindly lustre,
lies
The twilight warmth of ruddy ember-
gloom:
Thy clear, strong tones will oft bring sud-
den bloom
Of hope secure, to him who lonely cries,
Wrestling with the young poet's agonies,
Neglect and scorn, which seem a certain
doom:
Yes! the few words which, like great
thunder-drops,
Thy large heart down to earth shook doubt-
fully,
Thrilled by the inward lightning of its
might,
Serene and pure, like gushing joy of light,
Shall track the eternal chords of Des-
tiny,
After the moon-led pulse of ocean stops.

1841. 1842.

'OUR LOVE IS NOT A FADING EARTHLY FLOWER'

OUR love is not a fading earthly flower:
Its wingèd seed dropped down from Para-
     dise,
And, nursed by day and night, by sun and
     shower,
Doth momently to fresher beauty rise:
To us the leafless autumn is not bare,
Nor winter's rattling boughs lack lusty
     green.
Our summer hearts make summer's ful-
     ness, where
No leaf, or bud, or blossom may be seen:
For nature's life in love's deep life doth lie,
Love, — whose forgetfulness is beauty's
     death,
Whose mystic key these cells of Thou and I
Into the infinite freedom openeth,
And makes the body's dark and narrow
     grate
The wide-flung leaves of Heaven's own
     palace-gate.

1842.   1843.

'BELOVED, IN THE NOISY CITY HERE'

BELOVED, in the noisy city here,
The thought of thee can make all turmoil
     cease;
Around my spirit, folds thy spirit clear
Its still, soft arms, and circles it with peace;
There is no room for any doubt or fear
In souls so overfilled with love's increase,
There is no memory of the bygone year
But growth in heart's and spirit's perfect
     ease:
How hath our love, half nebulous at first,
Rounded itself into a full-orbed sun !
How have our lives and wills (as haply erst
They were, ere this forgetfulness begun)
Through all their earthly distances out-
     burst,
And melted, like two rays of light in one !

1842.   (1843.)

SONG

O MOONLIGHT deep and tender,
     A year and more agone,
Your mist of golden splendor
     Round my betrothal shone !

O elm-leaves dark and dewy,
     The very same ye seem,
The low wind trembles through ye,
     Ye murmur in my dream !

O river, dim with distance,
     Flow thus forever by,
A part of my existence
     Within your heart doth lie !

O stars, ye saw our meeting,
     Two beings and one soul,
Two hearts so madly beating
     To mingle and be whole !

O happy night, deliver
     Her kisses back to me,
Or keep them all, and give her
     A blissful dream of me !

1842.   (1843.)

THE SHEPHERD OF KING AD-
METUS

THERE came a youth upon the earth,
     Some thousand years ago,
Whose slender hands were nothing worth,
Whether to plough, or reap, or sow.

Upon an empty tortoise-shell
     He stretched some chords, and drew
Music that made men's bosoms swell
Fearless, or brimmed their eyes with dew.

Then King Admetus, one who had
     Pure taste by right divine,   10
Decreed his singing not too bad
To hear between the cups of wine:

And so, well pleased with being soothed
     Into a sweet half-sleep,
Three times his kingly beard he smoothed,
And made him viceroy o'er his sheep.

His words were simple words enough,
     And yet he used them so,
That what in other mouths was rough
In his seemed musical and low.   20

Men called him but a shiftless youth,
     In whom no good they saw;
And yet, unwittingly, in truth,
They made his careless words their law.

They knew not how he learned at all,
  For idly, hour by hour,
He sat and watched the dead leaves fall,
Or mused upon a common flower.

It seemed the loveliness of things
  Did teach him all their use,   30
For, in mere weeds, and stones, and springs,
He found a healing power profuse.

Men granted that his speech was wise,
  But, when a glance they caught
Of his slim grace and woman's eyes,
They laughed, and called him good-for-
    naught.

Yet after he was dead and gone,
  And e'en his memory dim,
Earth seemed more sweet to live upon,
More full of love, because of him.   40

And day by day more holy grew
  Each spot where he had trod,
Till after-poets only knew
Their first-born brother as a god.

                1842.

AN INCIDENT IN A RAILROAD CAR

HE spoke of Burns: men rude and rough
Pressed round to hear the praise of one
Whose heart was made of manly, simple
    stuff,
  As homespun as their own.

And, when he read, they forward leaned,
  Drinking, with thirsty hearts and ears,
His brook-like songs whom glory never
    weaned
  From humble smiles and tears.

Slowly there grew a tender awe,
  Sun-like, o'er faces brown and hard,   10
As if in him who read they felt and saw
  Some presence of the bard.

It was a sight for sin and wrong
  And slavish tyranny to see,
A sight to make our faith more pure and
    strong
  In high humanity.

I thought, these men will carry hence
Promptings their former life above,

And something of a finer reverence
  For beauty, truth, and love.   20

God scatters love on every side
  Freely among his children all,
And always hearts are lying open wide,
  Wherein some grains may fall.

There is no wind but soweth seeds
  Of a more true and open life,
Which burst, unlooked for, into high-souled
    deeds,
  With wayside beauty rife.

We find within these souls of ours
  Some wild germs of a higher birth,   30
Which in the poet's tropic heart bear flowers
  Whose fragrance fills the earth.

Within the hearts of all men lie
  These promises of wider bliss,
Which blossom into hopes that cannot die,
  In sunny hours like this.

All that hath been majestical
  In life or death, since time began,
Is native in the simple heart of all,
  The angel heart of man.   40

And thus, among the untaught poor,
  Great deeds and feelings find a home,
That cast in shadow all the golden lore
  Of classic Greece and Rome.

O mighty brother-soul of man,
  Where'er thou art, in low or high,
Thy skyey arches with exulting span
  O'er-roof infinity !

All thoughts that mould the age begin
  Deep down within the primitive soul,   50
And from the many slowly upward win
  To one who grasps the whole:

In his wide brain the feeling deep
  That struggled on the many's tongue
Swells to a tide of thought, whose surges
    leap
  O'er the weak thrones of wrong.

All thought begins in feeling, — wide
  In the great mass its base is hid,
And, narrowing up to thought, stands
    glorified,
  A moveless pyramid.   60

Nor is he far astray, who deems
That every hope, which rises and grows
      broad
In the world's heart, by ordered impulse
      streams
      From the great heart of God.

God wills, man hopes: in common souls
Hope is but vague and undefined,
Till from the poet's tongue the message
      rolls
      A blessing to his kind.

Never did Poesy appear
So full of heaven to me, as when   70
I saw how it would pierce through pride
      and fear
      To the lives of coarsest men.

It may be glorious to write .
Thoughts that shall glad the two or
      three
High souls, like those far stars that come
      in sight
      Once in a century; —

But better far it is to speak
One simple word, which now and then
Shall waken their free nature in the weak
      And friendless sons of men;   80

To write some earnest verse or line,
Which, seeking not the praise of art,
Shall make a clearer faith and manhood
      shine
      In the untutored heart.

He who doth this, in verse or prose,
May be forgotten in his day,
But surely shall be crowned at last with
      those
      Who live and speak for aye.
1842.   1842.

STANZAS ON FREEDOM [1]

MEN! whose boast it is that ye
Come of fathers brave and free,

[1] It is to be remembered that in publicly espousing
the cause of abolition so early as 1843 Lowell made personal and social sacrifices even greater than Whittier's.
See his passage on Whittier, and that on himself, in the
'Fable for Critics;' and Scudder's *Life of Lowell,*
vol. i, pp. 105, 168–175, 211 and following, and especially
183, 184, where Lowell speaks in particular of these
'Stanzas on Freedom,' which were written for an anti-

If there breathe on earth a slave,
Are ye truly free and brave?
If ye do not feel the chain,
When it works a brother's pain,
Are ye not base slaves indeed,
Slaves unworthy to be freed?

Women! who shall one day bear
Sons to breathe New England air,   10
If ye hear, without a blush,
Deeds to make the roused blood rush
Like red lava through your veins,
For your sisters now in chains, —
Answer! are ye fit to be
Mothers of the brave and free?

Is true Freedom but to break
Fetters for our own dear sake,
And, with leathern hearts, forget
That we owe mankind a debt?   20
No! true freedom is to share
All the chains our brothers wear,
And, with heart and hand, to be
Earnest to make others free!

They are slaves who fear to speak
For the fallen and the weak;
They are slaves who will not choose
Hatred, scoffing, and abuse,
Rather than in silence shrink
From the truth they needs must think;
They are slaves who dare not be   3'
In the right with two or three.
1843.   1843.

WENDELL PHILLIPS

HE stood upon the world's broad thresh-
      old; wide
The din of battle and of slaughter rose;

slavery reunion held on the anniversary of West Indian
Emancipation, and were first printed under the title
given in this letter: 'This puts me in mind of Longfellow's suppression of his anti-slavery pieces. [These
had been omitted in one edition of Longfellow's poems,
published at Philadelphia.] Sydney Gay wishes to
know whether I think he spoke too harshly of the affair. I think he *did* . . . and this not because I agree
with what he tells me is your notion of the matter . . .
— .for I do not think that an author has a right to
suppress anything that *God* has given him — but because I believe that Longfellow esteemed them of inferior quality to his other poems. For myself, when I
was printing my second volume of poems, Owen wished
to suppress a certain "Song sung at an Anti-Slavery
Picnic." I never saw him, but he urged me with I
know not what worldly arguments. My only answer
was: "Let all the others be suppressed if you will —
that I will never suppress."'

He saw God stand upon the weaker side,
That sank in seeming loss before its foes:
Many there were who made great haste
    and sold
Unto the cunning enemy their swords,
He scorned their gifts of fame, and power,
    and gold,
And, underneath their soft and flowery
    words,
Heard the cold serpent hiss; therefore he
    went
And humbly joined him to the weaker
    part,
Fanatic named, and fool, yet well content
So he could be the nearer to God's heart,
And feel its solemn pulses sending blood
Through all the widespread veins of end-
    less good.

                                    (1843.)

RHŒCUS [1]

GOD sends his teachers unto every age,
To every clime, and every race of men,
With revelations fitted to their growth
And shape of mind, nor gives the realm of
    Truth
Into the selfish rule of one sole race:
Therefore each form of worship that hath
    swayed
The life of man, and given it to grasp
The master-key of knowledge, reverence,
Infolds some germs of goodness and of
    right;
Else never had the eager soul, which
    loathes   10
The slothful down of pampered ignorance,
Found in it even a moment's fitful rest.

    There is an instinct in the human heart
Which makes that all the fables it hath
    coined,
To justify the reign of its belief
And strengthen it by beauty's right divine,
Veil in their inner cells a mystic gift,
Which, like the hazel twig, in faithful
    hands,
Points surely to the hidden springs of truth.
For, as in nature naught is made in vain, 20
But all things have within their hull of
    use
A wisdom and a meaning which may speak
Of spiritual secrets to the ear
Of spirit; so, in whatso'er the heart

[1] Compare Landor's 'The Hamadryad.'

Hath fashioned for a solace to itself,
To make its inspirations suit its creed,
And from the niggard hands of falsehood
    wring
Its needful food of truth, there ever is
A sympathy with Nature, which reveals,
Not less than her own works, pure gleams
    of light   30
And earnest parables of inward lore.
Hear now this fairy legend of old Greece,
As full of gracious youth, and beauty still
As the immortal freshness of that grace
Carved for all ages on some Attic frieze.

    A youth named Rhœcus, wandering in
    the wood,
Saw an old oak just trembling to its fall,
And, feeling pity of so fair a tree,
He propped its gray trunk with admiring
    care,
And with a thoughtless footstep loitered
    on.   40
But, as he turned, he heard a voice behind
That murmured 'Rhœcus!' 'T was as if
    the leaves,
Stirred by a passing breath, had murmured
    it,
And, while he paused bewildered, yet again
It murmured 'Rhœcus!' softer than a
    breeze.
He started and beheld with dizzy eyes
What seemed the substance of a happy
    dream
Stand there before him, spreading a warm
    glow
Within the green glooms of the shadowy
    oak.
It seemed a woman's shape, yet far too
    fair   50
To be a woman, and with eyes too meek
For any that were wont to mate with gods.
All naked like a goddess stood she there,
And like a goddess all too beautiful
To feel the guilt-born earthliness of shame.
'Rhœcus, I am the Dryad of this tree,'
Thus she began, dropping her low-toned
    words
Serene, and full, and clear, as drops of
    dew,
'And with it I am doomed to live and die;
The rain and sunshine are my caterers, 60
Nor have I other bliss than simple life;
Now ask me what thou wilt, that I can
    give,
And with a thankful joy it shall be thine.'

Then Rhœcus, with a flutter at the heart,
Yet by the prompting of such beauty bold,
Answered: ' What is there that can satisfy
The endless craving of the soul but love ?
Give me thy love, or but the hope of that
Which must be evermore my nature's goal.'
After a little pause she said again,   70
But with a glimpse of sadness in her tone,
' I give it, Rhœcus, though a perilous gift;
An hour before the sunset meet me here.'
And straightway there was nothing he
          could see
But the green glooms beneath the shadowy
          oak,
And not a sound came to his straining ears
But the low trickling rustle of the leaves,
And far away upon an emerald slope
The falter of an idle shepherd's pipe.

Now, in those days of simpleness and
          faith,   80
Men did not think that happy things were
          dreams
Because they overstepped the narrow bourn
Of likelihood, but reverently deemed
Nothing too wondrous or too beautiful
To be the guerdon of a daring heart.
So Rhœcus made no doubt that he was blest,
And all along unto the city's gate
Earth seemed to spring beneath him as he
          walked,
The clear, broad sky looked bluer than its
          wont,
And he could scarce believe he had not
          wings,   90
Such sunshine seemed to glitter through
          his veins
Instead of blood, so light he felt and
          strange.

Young Rhœcus had a faithful heart
          enough,
But one that in the present dwelt too
          much,
And, taking with blithe welcome whatso-
          e'er
Chance gave of joy, was wholly bound in
          that,
Like the contented peasant of a vale,
Deemed it the world, and never looked
          beyond.
So, haply meeting in the afternoon
Some comrades who were playing at the
          dice,   100
He joined them, and forgot all else beside.

The dice were rattling at the merriest,
And Rhœcus, who had met but sorry luck,
Just laughed in triumph at a happy throw,
When through the room there hummed a
          yellow bee
That buzzed about his ear with down-
          dropped legs
As if to light. And Rhœcus laughed and
          said,
Feeling how red and flushed he was with
          loss,
' By Venus ! does he take me for a rose ? '
And brushed him off with rough, impatient
          hand.   110
But still the bee came back, and thrice
          again
Rhœcus did beat him off with growing
          wrath.
Then through the window flew the wounded
          bee,
And Rhœcus, tracking him with angry
          eyes,
Saw a sharp mountain-peak of Thessaly
Against the red disk of the setting sun, —
And instantly the blood sank from his
          heart,
As if its very walls had caved away.
Without a word he turned, and, rushing
          forth,
Ran madly through the city and the gate,
And o'er the plain, which now the wood's
          long shade,   121
By the low sun thrown forward broad and
          dim,
Darkened wellnigh unto the city's wall.

Quite spent and out of breath he reached
          the tree,
And, listening fearfully, he heard once
          more
The low voice murmur ' Rhœcus ! ' close at
          hand:
Whereat he looked around him, but could
          see
Naught but the deepening glooms beneath
          the oak.
Then sighed the voice, ' O Rhœcus ! never-
          more
Shalt thou behold me or by day or night,
Me, who would fain have blessed thee with
          a love   131
More ripe and bounteous than ever yet
Filled up with nectar any mortal heart:
But thou didst scorn my humble mes-
          senger,

And sent'st him back to me with bruisèd
    wings.
We spirits only show to gentle eyes,
We ever ask an undivided love,
And he who scorns the least of Nature's
    works
Is thenceforth exiled and shut out from all.
Farewell! for thou canst never see me
    more.'   140

Then Rhœcus beat his breast, and
    groaned aloud,
And cried, ' Be pitiful ! forgive me yet
This once, and I shall never need it more ! '
' Alas ! ' the voice returned, ' 't is thou art
    blind,
Not I unmerciful; I can forgive,
But have no skill to heal thy spirit's eyes;
Only the soul hath power o'er itself.'
With that again there murmured ' Never-
    more ! '
And Rhœcus after heard no other sound,
Except the rattling of the oak's crisp
    leaves,   150
Like the long surf upon a distant shore,
Raking the sea-worn pebbles up and down.
The night had gathered round him: o'er
    the plain
The city sparkled with its thousand lights,
And sounds of revel fell upon his ear
Harshly and like a curse; above, the sky,
With all its bright sublimity of stars,
Deepened, and on his forehead smote the
    breeze:
Beauty was all around him and delight,
But from that eve he was alone on earth. 160
           (1843.)

TO THE DANDELION

DEAR common flower, that grow'st be-
    side the way,
Fringing the dusty road with harmless
    gold,
    First pledge of blithesome May,
Which children pluck, and full of pride
    uphold,
    High-hearted buccaneers, o'erjoyed that
      they
An Eldorado in the grass have found,
    Which not the rich earth's ample round
    May match in wealth, thou art more dear
      to me
    Than all the prouder summer-blooms
      may be.

Gold such as thine ne'er drew the Span-
    ish prow   10
Through the primeval hush of Indian seas,
    Nor wrinkled the lean brow
Of age, to rob the lover's heart of ease;
    'T is the Spring's largess, which she scat-
    ters now
To rich and poor alike, with lavish hand,
    Though most hearts never understand
    To take it at God's value, but pass by
    The offered wealth with unrewarded eye.

Thou art my tropics and mine Italy;
To look at thee unlocks a warmer clime; 20
    The eyes thou givest me
Are in the heart, and heed not space or
    time:
Not in mid June the golden-cuirassed bee
Feels a more summer-like warm ravish-
    ment
    In the white lily's breezy tent,
    His fragrant Sybaris, than I, when first
    From the dark green thy yellow circles
    burst.

Then think I of deep shadows on the
    grass,
Of meadows where in sun the cattle graze,
    Where, as the breezes pass,   30
The gleaming rushes lean a thousand ways,
    Of leaves that slumber in a cloudy mass,
Or whiten in the wind, of waters blue
    That from the distance sparkle through
    Some woodland gap, and of a sky above,
    Where one white cloud like a stray lamb
    doth move.

My childhood's earliest thoughts are
    linked with thee;
The sight of thee calls back the robin's
    song,
    Who, from the dark old tree
Beside the door, sang clearly all day long, 40
    And I, secure in childish piety,
Listened as if I heard an angel sing
    With news from heaven, which he
    could bring
    Fresh every day to my untainted ears
    When birds and flowers and I were
    happy peers.

How like a prodigal doth nature seem,
When thou, for all thy gold, so common
    art !
    Thou teachest me to deem

More sacredly of every human heart,
　　Since each reflects in joy its scanty
　　　gleam   50
Of heaven, and could some wondrous secret
　　show,
　　Did we but pay the love we owe,
　　And with a child's undoubting wisdom
　　look
　　On all these living pages of God's book.
1844 ?   1845.

COLUMBUS

THE cordage creaks and rattles in the
　　wind,
With whims of sudden hush; the reeling
　　sea
Now thumps like solid rock beneath the
　　stern,
Now leaps with clumsy wrath, strikes
　　short, and falling,
Crumbled to whispery foam, slips rustling
　　down
The broad backs of the waves, which jostle
　　and crowd
To fling themselves upon that unknown
　　shore,
Their used familiar since the dawn of
　　time,
Whither this foredoomed life is guided on
To sway on triumph's hushed, aspiring
　　poise   10
One glittering moment, then to break ful-
　　filled.

How lonely is the sea's perpetual swing,
The melancholy wash of endless waves,
The sigh of some grim monster undescried,
Fear-painted on the canvas of the dark,
Shifting on his uneasy pillow of brine !
Yet night brings more companions than the
　　day
To this drear waste; new constellations
　　burn,
And fairer stars, with whose calm height
　　my soul
Finds nearer sympathy than with my herd 20
Of earthen souls, whose vision's scanty ring
Makes me its prisoner to beat my wings
Against the cold bars of their unbelief,
Knowing in vain my own free heaven be-
　　yond.
O God ! this world, so crammed with eager
　　life,

That comes and goes and wanders back to
　　silence
Like the idle wind, which yet man's shap-
　　ing mind
Can make his drudge to swell the longing
　　sails
Of highest endeavor, — this mad, unthrift
　　world,
Which, every hour, throws life enough
　　away   30
To make her deserts kind and hospitable,
Lets her great destinies be waved aside
By smooth, lip-reverent, formal infidels,
Who weigh the God they not believe with
　　gold,
And find no spot in Judas, save that he,
Driving a duller bargain than he ought,
Saddled his guild with too cheap precedent.
O Faith ! if thou art strong, thine opposite
Is mighty also, and the dull fool's sneer
Hath ofttimes shot chill palsy through the
　　arm   40
Just lifted to achieve its crowning deed,
And made the firm-based heart, that would
　　have quailed
The rack or fagot, shudder like a leaf
Wrinkled with frost, and loose upon its
　　stem.
The wicked and the weak, by some dark
　　law,
Have a strange power to shut and rivet
　　down
Their own horizon round us, to unwing
Our heaven-aspiring visions, and to blur
With surly clouds the Future's gleaming
　　peaks,
Far seen across the brine of thankless
　　years.   50
If the chosen soul could never be alone
In deep mid-silence, open-doored to God,
No greatness ever had been dreamed or
　　done;
Among dull hearts a prophet never grew;
The nurse of full-grown souls is solitude.

The old world is effete; there man with
　　man
Jostles, and, in the brawl for means to live,
Life is trod underfoot, — Life, the one
　　block
Of marble that 's vouchsafed wherefrom to
　　carve
Our great thoughts, white and godlike, to
　　shine down   60
The future, Life, the irredeemable block,

Which one o'er-hasty chisel-dint oft mars,
Scanting our room to cut the features out
Of our full hope, so forcing us to crown
With a mean head the perfect limbs, or
        leave
The god's face glowing o'er a satyr's trunk,
Failure's brief epitaph.

                    Yes, Europe's world
Reels on to judgment; there the common
        need,
Losing God's sacred use, to be a bond
'Twixt Me and Thee, sets each one scowl-
        ingly   70
O'er his own selfish hoard at bay; no state,
Knit strongly with eternal fibres up
Of all men's separate and united weals,
Self-poised and sole as stars, yet one as
        light,
Holds up a shape of large Humanity
To which by natural instinct every man
Pays loyalty exulting, by which all
Mould their own lives, and feel their pulses
        filled
With the red, fiery blood of the general
        life,
Making them mighty in peace, as now in
        war   80
They are, even in the flush of victory,
        weak,
Conquering that manhood which should
        them subdue.
And what gift bring I to this untried
        world?
Shall the same tragedy be played anew,
And the same lurid curtain drop at last
On one dread desolation, one fierce crash
Of that recoil which on its makers God
Lets Ignorance and Sin and Hunger make,
Early or late? Or shall that common-
        wealth
Whose potent unity and concentric force
Can draw these scattered joints and parts
        of men   91
Into a whole ideal man once more,
Which sucks not from its limbs the life
        away,
But sends it flood-tide and creates itself
Over again in every citizen,
Be there built up? For me, I have no
        choice;
I might turn back to other destinies,
For one sincere key opes all Fortune's doors;
But whoso answers not God's earliest call
Forfeits or dulls that faculty supreme   100

Of lying open to his genius
Which makes the wise heart certain of its
        ends.

Here am I; for what end God knows, not I;
Westward still points the inexorable soul:
Here am I, with no friend but the sad sea,
The beating heart of this great enterprise,
Which, without me, would stiffen in swift
        death;
This have I mused on, since mine eye could
        first   108
Among the stars distinguish and with joy
Rest on that God-fed Pharos of the north,
On some blue promontory of heaven lighted
That juts far out into the upper sea;
To this one hope my heart hath clung for
        years,
As would a foundling to the talisman
Hung round his neck by hands he knew
        not whose;
A poor, vile thing and dross to all beside,
Yet he therein can feel a virtue left
By the sad pressure of a mother's hand,
And unto him it still is tremulous   119
With palpitating haste and wet with tears,
The key to him of hope and humanness,
The coarse shell of life's pearl, Expectancy
This hope hath been to me for love and
        fame,
Hath made me wholly lonely on the earth,
Building me up as in a thick-ribbed tower,
Wherewith enwalled my watching spirit
        burned,
Conquering its little island from the Dark,
Sole as a scholar's lamp, and heard men's
        steps,
In the far hurry of the outward world,
Pass dimly forth and back, sounds heard in
        dream.   130
As Ganymede by the eagle was snatched
        up
From the gross sod to be Jove's cup-bearer,
So was I lifted by my great design:
And who hath trod Olympus, from his eye
Fades not that broader outlook of the gods;
His life's low valleys overbrow earth's
        clouds,
And that Olympian spectre of the past
Looms towering up in sovereign memory,
Beckoning his soul from meaner heights of
        doom.
Had but the shadow of the Thunderer's
        bird,   140
Flashing athwart my spirit, made of me

A swift-betraying vision's Ganymede,
Yet to have greatly dreamed precludes low
        ends;
Great days have ever such a morning-red,
On such a base great futures are built up,
And aspiration, though not put in act,
Comes back to ask its plighted troth again,
Still watches round its grave the unlaid
        ghost
Of a dead virtue, and makes other hopes,
Save that implacable one, seem thin and
        bleak   150
As shadows of bare trees upon the snow,
Bound freezing there by the unpitying
        moon.

While other youths perplexed their mando-
        lins,
Praying that Thetis would her fingers twine
In the loose glories of her lover's hair,
And wile another kiss to keep back day,
I, stretched beneath the many-centuried
        shade
Of some writhed oak, the wood's Laocoön,
Did of my hope a dryad mistress make,
Whom I would woo to meet me privily, 160
Or underneath the stars, or when the moon
Flecked all the forest floor with scattered
        pearls.
O days whose memory tames to fawning
        down
The surly fell of Ocean's bristled neck !

I know not when this hope enthralled me
        first,
But from my boyhood up I loved to hear
The tall pine-forests of the Apennine
Murmur their hoary legends of the sea,
Which hearing, I in vision clear beheld
The sudden dark of tropic night shut
        down   170
O'er the huge whisper of great watery
        wastes,
The while a pair of herons trailingly
Flapped inland, where some league-wide
        river hurled
The yellow spoil of unconjectured realms
Far through a gulf's green silence, never
        scarred
By any but the North-wind's hurrying
        keels.
And not the pines alone ; all sights and
        sounds
To my world-seeking heart paid fealty,
And catered for it as the Cretan bees

Brought honey to the baby Jupiter,   180
Who in his soft hand crushed a violet,
Godlike foremusing the rough thunder's
        gripe;
Then did I entertain the poet's song,
My great Idea's guest, and, passing o'er
That iron bridge the Tuscan built to hell,
I heard Ulysses tell of mountain-chains
Whose adamantine links, his manacles,
The western main shook growling, and still
        gnawed.
I brooded on the wise Athenian's tale
Of happy Atlantis, and heard Björne's
        keel   190
Crunch the gray pebbles of the Vinland
        shore:
I listened, musing, to the prophecy
Of Nero's tutor-victim; lo, the birds
Sing darkling, conscious of the climbing
        dawn.
And I believed the poets; it is they
Who utter wisdom from the central deep,
And, listening to the inner flow of things,
Speak to the age out of eternity.

Ah me ! old hermits sought for solitude
In caves and desert places of the earth, 200
Where their own heart-beat was the only
        stir
Of living thing that comforted the year;
But the bald pillar-top of Simeon,
In midnight's blankest waste, were popu-
        lous,
Matched with the isolation drear and deep
Of him who pines among the swarm of
        men,
At once a new thought's king and pris-
        oner,
Feeling the truer life within his life,
The fountain of his spirit's prophecy,
Sinking away and wasting, drop by drop, 210
In the ungrateful sands of sceptic ears.
He in the palace-aisles of untrod woods
Doth walk a king ; for him the pent-up
        cell
Widens beyond the circles of the stars,
And all the sceptred spirits of the past
Come thronging in to greet him as their
        peer;
But in the market-place's glare and throng
He sits apart, an exile, and his brow
Aches with the mocking memory of its
        crown.
Yet to the spirit select there is no choice;
He cannot say, This will I do, or that, 221

For the cheap means putting Heaven's ends
in pawn,
And bartering his bleak rocks, the freehold
stern
Of destiny's first-born, for smoother fields
That yield no crop of self-denying will;
A hand is stretched to him from out the
dark,
Which grasping without question, he is led
Where there is work that he must do for
God.
The trial still is the strength's complement,
And the uncertain, dizzy path that scales 230
The sheer heights of supremest purposes
Is steeper to the angel than the child.
Chances have laws as fixed as planets have,
And disappointment's dry and bitter root,
Envy's harsh berries, and the choking pool
Of the world's scorn, are the right mother-
milk
To the tough hearts that pioneer their kind,
And break a pathway to those unknown
realms
That in the earth's broad shadow lie en-
thralled;
Endurance is the crowning quality,   240
And patience all the passion of great hearts;
These are their stay, and when the leaden
world
Sets its hard face against their fateful
thought,
And brute strength, like the Gaulish con-
queror,
Clangs his huge glaive down in the other
scale,
The inspired soul but flings his patience in,
And slowly that outweighs the ponderous
globe, —
One faith against a whole earth's unbelief,
One soul against the flesh of all mankind.

Thus ever seems it when my soul can hear
The voice that errs not; then my triumph
gleams,   251
O'er the blank ocean beckoning, and all
night
My heart flies on before me as I sail;
Far on I see my lifelong enterprise,
That rose like Ganges 'mid the freezing
snows
Of a world's solitude, sweep broadening
down,
And, gathering to itself a thousand streams,
Grow sacred ere it mingle with the sea;
I see the ungated wall of chaos old,

With blocks Cyclopean hewn of solid night,
Fade like a wreath of unreturning mist 261
Before the irreversible feet of light; —
And lo, with what clear omen in the east
On day's gray threshold stands the eager
dawn,
Like young Leander rosy from the sea
Glowing at Hero's lattice !

                              One day more
These muttering shoalbrains leave the
helm to me:
God, let me not in their dull ooze be
stranded;
Let not this one frail bark, to hollow
which
I have dug out the pith and sinewy heart
Of my aspiring life's fair trunk, be so   271
Cast up to warp and blacken in the sun,
Just as the opposing wind 'gins whistle off
His cheek-swollen pack, and from the lean-
ing mast
Fortune's full sail strains forward !

                             One poor day ! —
Remember whose and not how short it is !
It is God's day, it is Columbus's.
A lavish day ! One day, with life and
heart,   278
Is more than time enough to find a world.
1844.   (1847.) [1]

THE PRESENT CRISIS [2]

WHEN a deed is done for Freedom, through
the broad earth's aching breast
Runs a thrill of joy prophetic, trembling
on from east to west,

[1] Lowell's *Poems, Second Series*, dated 1848, was
really published in 1847.
[2] Written when the annexation of Texas was being
discussed, but universal in its application.
For twenty years the solemn monitory music of this
poem never ceased to reëcho in public halls. In the
Lowell Memorial Address which George William Curtis
delivered before the Brooklyn Institute, February 22,
1892, he said in his heightened way of some passages
of 'The Present Crisis :' 'Wendell Phillips winged
with their music and tipped with their flame the dart
of his fervid appeal and manly scorn. As he quoted
them with suppressed emotion in his low, melodious,
penetrating voice, the white plume of the resistless
Navarre of eloquence gained a loftier grace, that relentless sword of invective a more flashing edge.' And
the stanza of ' The Present Crisis' beginning ' For humanity sweeps onward ' was made by Sumner the text
and motif of that famous ' Crime against Speech ' oration that provoked the assault of Preston Brooks
(Greenslet's *Lowell*, pp. 79, 80.)

And the slave, where'er he cowers, feels
        the soul within him climb
To the awful verge of manhood, as the
        energy sublime
Of a century bursts full-blossomed on the
        thorny stem of Time.

Through the walls of hut and palace shoots
        the instantaneous throe,
When the travail of the Ages wrings
        earth's systems to and fro;
At the birth of each new Era, with a recog-
        nizing start,
Nation wildly looks at nation, standing
        with mute lips apart,
And glad Truth's yet mightier man-child
        leaps beneath the Future's heart. 10

So the Evil's triumph sendeth, with a ter-
        ror and a chill,
Under continent to continent, the sense of
        coming ill,
And the slave, where'er he cowers, feels
        his sympathies with God
In hot tear-drops ebbing earthward, to be
        drunk up by the sod,
Till a corpse crawls round unburied, delv-
        ing in the nobler clod.

For mankind are one in spirit, and an in-
        stinct bears along,
Round the earth's electric circle, the swift
        flash of right or wrong;
Whether conscious or unconscious, yet Hu-
        manity's vast frame
Through its ocean-sundered fibres feels the
        gush of joy or shame; —
In the gain or loss of one race all the rest
        have equal claim.   20

Once to every man and nation comes the
        moment to decide,
In the strife of Truth with Falsehood, for
        the good or evil side;
Some great cause, God's new Messiah,
        offering each the bloom or blight,
Parts the goats upon the left hand, and the
        sheep upon the right,
And the choice goes by forever 'twixt that
        darkness and that light.

Hast thou chosen, O my people, on whose
        party thou shalt stand,
Ere the Doom from its worn sandals shakes
        the dust against our land ?

Though the cause of Evil prosper, yet 't is
        Truth alone is strong,
And, albeit she wander outcast now, I see
        around her throng
Troops of beautiful, tall angels, to enshield
        her from all wrong.   30

Backward look across the ages and the
        beacon-moments see,
That, like peaks of some sunk continent,
        jut through Oblivion's sea;
Not an ear in court or market for the low
        foreboding cry
Of those Crises, God's stern winnowers,
        from whose feet earth's chaff must
        fly;
Never shows the choice momentous till the
        judgment hath passed by.

Careless seems the great Avenger; history's
        pages but record
One death-grapple in the darkness 'twixt
        old systems and the Word;
Truth forever on the scaffold, Wrong for-
        ever on the throne, —
Yet that scaffold sways the future, and, be-
        hind the dim unknown,
Standeth God within the shadow, keeping
        watch above his own.   40

We see dimly in the Present what is small
        and what is great,
Slow of faith how weak an arm may turn
        the iron helm of fate,
But the soul is still oracular; amid the
        market's din,
List the ominous stern whisper from the
        Delphic cave within, —
' They enslave their children's children who
        make compromise with sin.'

Slavery, the earth-born Cyclops, fellest of
        the giant brood,
Sons of brutish Force and Darkness, who
        have drenched the earth with blood,
Famished in his self-made desert, blinded
        by our purer day,
Gropes in yet unblasted regions for his
        miserable prey; —
Shall we guide his gory fingers where our
        helpless children play ?   50

Then to side with Truth is noble when we
        share her wretched crust,

Ere her cause bring fame and profit, and
   't is prosperous to be just;
Then it is the brave man chooses, while the
   coward stands aside,
Doubting in his abject spirit, till his Lord
   is crucified,
And the multitude make virtue of the faith
   they had denied.

Count me o'er earth's chosen heroes, —
   they were souls that stood alone,
While the men they agonized for hurled
   the contumelious stone,
Stood serene, and down the future saw the
   golden beam incline
To the side of perfect justice, mastered by
   their faith divine,
By one man's plain truth to manhood and
   to God's supreme design.   60

By the light of burning heretics Christ's
   bleeding feet I track,
Toiling up new Calvaries ever with the
   cross that turns not back,
And these mounts of anguish number how
   each generation learned
One new word of that grand *Credo* which
   in prophet-hearts hath burned
Since the first man stood God-conquered
   with his face to heaven upturned.

For Humanity sweeps onward: where to-
   day the martyr stands,
On the morrow crouches Judas with the
   silver in his hands;
Far in front the cross stands ready and the
   crackling fagots burn,
While the hooting mob of yesterday in
   silent awe return
To glean up the scattered ashes into History's golden urn.   70

'T is as easy to be heroes as to sit the idle
   slaves
Of a legendary virtue carved upon our
   father's graves,
Worshippers of light ancestral make the
   present light a crime; —
Was the Mayflower launched by cowards,
   steered by men behind their time ?
Turn those tracks toward Past or Future,
   that make Plymouth Rock sublime?

They were men of present valor, stalwart
   old iconoclasts,

Unconvinced by axe or gibbet that all virtue was the Past's;
But we make their truth our falsehood,
   thinking that hath made us free,
Hoarding it in mouldy parchments, while
   our tender spirits flee
The rude grasp of that great Impulse which
   drove them across the sea.   80

They have rights who dare maintain them;
   we are traitors to our sires,
Smothering in their holy ashes Freedom's
   new-lit altar-fires;
Shall we make their creed our jailer ?
   Shall we, in our haste to slay,
From the tombs of the old prophets steal
   the funeral lamps away
To light up the martyr-fagots round the
   prophets of to-day ?

New occasions teach new duties; Time
   makes ancient good uncouth;
They must upward still, and onward, who
   would keep abreast of Truth;
Lo, before us gleam her camp-fires ! we
   ourselves must Pilgrims be,
Launch our Mayflower, and steer boldly
   through the desperate winter sea,
Nor attempt the Future's portal with the
   Past's blood-rusted key.   90

December, 1844.   1845.

A CONTRAST

THY love thou sentest oft to me,
   And still as oft I thrust it back;
Thy messengers I could not see
   In those who everything did lack,
   The poor, the outcast and the black.

Pride held his hand before mine eyes,
   The world with flattery stuffed mine
    ears;
I looked to see a monarch's guise,
   Nor dreamed thy love would knock for
    years,
   Poor, naked, fettered, full of tears.

Yet, when I sent my love to thee,
   Thou with a smile didst take it in,
And entertain'dst it royally,
   Though grimed with earth, with hunger
    thin,
   And leprous with the taint of sin.

Now every day thy love I meet,
  As o'er the earth it wanders wide,
With weary step and bleeding feet,
  Still knocking at the heart of pride
  And offering grace, though still denied.
                1845.

AN INDIAN-SUMMER REVERIE [1]

WHAT visionary tints the year puts on,
When falling leaves falter through mo-
    tionless air
  Or humbly cling and shiver to be gone !
How shimmer the low flats and pastures
    bare,
  As with her nectar Hebe Autumn fills
  The bowl between me and those distant
    hills,
And smiles and shakes abroad her misty,
    tremulous hair !

No more the landscape holds its wealth
    apart,
Making me poorer in my poverty,
  But mingles with my senses and my
    heart;   10
My own projected spirit seems to me
  In her own reverie the world to steep;
  'T is she that waves to sympathetic sleep,
Moving, as she is moved, each field and hill
    and tree.

How fuse and mix, with what unfelt
    degrees,
Clasped by the faint horizon's languid arms,
  Each into each, the hazy distances !
The softened season all the landscape
    charms;
  Those hills, my native village that embay,
  In waves of dreamier purple roll away, 20
And floating in mirage seem all the glim-
    mering farms.

Far distant sounds the hidden chickadee
Close at my side; far distant sound the
    leaves;

The fields seem fields of dream, where
    Memory
Wanders like gleaning Ruth; and as the
    sheaves
  Of wheat and barley wavered in the eye
  Of Boaz as the maiden's glow went by,
So tremble and seem remote all things the
    sense receives.

The cock's shrill trump that tells of
    scattered corn,
Passed breezily on by all his flapping
    mates,   30
  Faint and more faint, from barn to barn
    is borne,
Southward, perhaps to far Magellan's
    Straits;
  Dimly I catch the throb of distant flails;
  Silently overhead the hen-hawk sails,
With watchful, measuring eye, and for his
    quarry waits.

The sobered robin, hunger-silent now,
Seeks cedar-berries blue, his autumn cheer;
  The chipmunk, on the shingly shagbark's
    bough
Now saws, now lists with downward eye
    and ear,
  Then drops his nut, and, cheeping, with
    a bound   40
  Whisks to his winding fastness under-
    ground;
The clouds like swans drift down the
    streaming atmosphere.

O'er yon bare knoll the pointed cedar
    shadows
Drowse on the crisp, gray moss; the
    ploughman's call
  Creeps faint as smoke from black, fresh-
    furrowed meadows;
The single crow a single caw lets fall;
  And all around me every bush and tree
  Says Autumn 's here, and Winter soon
    will be,
Who snows his soft, white sleep and silence
    over all.

The birch, most shy and ladylike of
    trees,   50
Her poverty, as best she may, retrieves,
  And hints at her foregone gentilities
With some saved relics of her wealth of
    leaves;
  The swamp-oak, with his royal purple on,

Glares red as blood across the sinking
    sun,
As one who proudlier to a falling fortune
    cleaves.

He looks a sachem, in red blanket wrapt,
Who, 'mid some council of the sad-garbed
    whites,
    Erect and stern, in his own memories
      lapt,
With distant eye broods over other
    sights,   60
    Sees the hushed wood the city's flare re-
      place,
    The wounded turf heal o'er the railway's
      trace,
And roams the savage Past of his un-
    dwindled rights.

The red-oak, softer-grained, yields all for
    lost,
And, with his crumpled foliage stiff and
    dry,
After the first betrayal of the frost,
Rebuffs the kiss of the relenting sky;
    The chestnuts, lavish of their long-hid
      gold,
    To the faint Summer, beggared now and
      old,
Pour back the sunshine hoarded 'neath her
    favoring eye.   70

The ash her purple drops forgivingly
And sadly, breaking not the general hush;
    The maple-swamps glow like a sunset
      sea,
Each leaf a ripple with its separate flush;
    All round the wood's edge creeps the
      skirting blaze
Of bushes low, as when, on cloudy days,
Ere the rain fall, the cautious farmer burns
    his brush.

O'er yon low wall, which guards one un-
    kempt zone,
Where vines and weeds and scrub-oaks
    intertwine
    Safe from the plough, whose rough, dis-
      cordant stone   80
Is massed to one soft gray by lichens fine,
    The tangled blackberry, crossed and re-
      crossed, weaves
    A prickly network of ensanguined leaves;
Hard by, with coral beads, the prim black-
    alders shine.

Pillaring with flame this crumbling bound-
    ary,
Whose loose blocks topple 'neath the plough-
    boy's foot,
    Who, with each sense shut fast except
      the eye,
Creeps close and scares the jay he hoped to
    shoot,
    The woodbine up the elm's straight stem
      aspires,
    Coiling it, harmless, with autumnal
      fires;   90
In the ivy's paler blaze the martyr oak
    stands mute.

Below, the Charles, a stripe of nether
    sky,
Now hid by rounded apple-trees between,
    Whose gaps the misplaced sail sweeps
      bellying by,
Now flickering golden through a woodland
    screen,
    Then spreading out, at his next turn be-
      yond,
    A silver circle like an inland pond —
Slips seaward silently through marshes
    purple and green.

Dear marshes! vain to him the gift of
    sight
Who cannot in their various incomes
    share,   100
    From every season drawn, of shade and
      light,
Who sees in them but levels brown and
    bare;
    Each change of storm or sunshine scatters
      free
    On them its largess of variety,
For Nature with cheap means still works
    her wonders rare.

In Spring they lie one broad expanse of
    green,
O'er which the light winds run with glim-
    mering feet:
    Here, yellower stripes track out the creek
      unseen,
There, darker growths o'er hidden ditches
    meet;
    And purpler stains show where the blos-
      soms crowd,   110
    As if the silent shadow of a cloud
Hung there becalmed, with the next breath
    to fleet.

All round, upon the river's slippery edge,
Witching to deeper calm the drowsy tide,
    Whispers and leans the breeze-entangling
        sedge;
Through emerald glooms the lingering
        waters slide,
    Or, sometimes wavering, throw back the
        sun,
And the stiff banks in eddies melt and run
Of dimpling light, and with the current
        seem to glide.

    In Summer 't is a blithesome sight to
        see,   120
As, step by step, with measured swing, they
        pass,
    The wide-ranked mowers wading to the
        knee,
Their sharp scythes panting through the
        wiry grass;
    Then, stretched beneath a rick's shade in
        a ring,
    Their nooning take, while one begins to
        sing
A stave that droops and dies 'neath the
        close sky of brass.

    Meanwhile that devil-may-care, the bobo-
        link,
Remembering duty, in mid-quaver stops
    Just ere he sweeps o'er rapture's tremu-
        lous brink,
And 'twixt the winrows most demurely
        drops,   130
    A decorous bird of business, who provides
    For his brown mate and fledglings six
        besides,
And looks from right to left, a farmer 'mid
        his crops.

    Another change subdues them in the Fall,
But saddens not; they still show merrier
        tints,
    Though sober russet seems to cover all;
When the first sunshine through their dew-
        drops glints,
    Look how the yellow clearness, streamed
        across,
    Redeems with rarer hues the season's
        loss,
As Dawn's feet there had touched and left
        their rosy prints.   140

    Or come when sunset gives its freshened
        zest,

Lean o'er the bridge and let the ruddy
        thrill,
    While the shorn sun swells down the hazy
        west,
Glow opposite; — the marshes drink their
        fill
    And swoon with purple veins, then slowly
        fade
    Through pink to brown, as eastward
        moves the shade,
Lengthening with stealthy creep, of Si-
        mond's darkening hill.

    Later, and yet ere Winter wholly shuts,
Ere through the first dry snow the runner
        grates,
    And the loath cart-wheel screams in
        slippery ruts,   150
While firmer ice the eager boy awaits,
    Trying each buckle and strap beside the
        fire,
    And until bedtime plays with his desire,
Twenty times putting on and off his new-
        bought skates; —

    Then, every morn, the river's banks shine
        bright
With smooth plate-armor, treacherous and
        frail,
    By the frost's clinking hammers forged
        at night,
'Gainst which the lances of the sun prevail,
    Giving a pretty emblem of the day
    When guiltier arms in light shall melt
        away,   160
And states shall move free-limbed, loosed
        from war's cramping mail.

    And now those waterfalls the ebbing
        river
Twice every day creates on either side
    Tinkle, as through their fresh-sparred
        grots they shiver
In grass-arched channels to the sun denied;
    High flaps in sparkling blue the far-
        heard crow,
    The silvered flats gleam frostily below,
Suddenly drops the gull and breaks the
        glassy tide.

    But crowned in turn by vying seasons
        three,
Their winter halo hath a fuller ring;   170
    This glory seems to rest immovably, —

The others were too fleet and vanishing;
  When the hid tide is at its highest flow,
  O'er marsh and stream one breathless
    trance of snow
With brooding fulness awes and hushes
  everything.

The sunshine seems blown off by the bleak
    wind,
As pale as formal candles lit by day;
  Gropes to the sea the river dumb and
    blind;
The brown ricks, snow-thatched by the
    storm in play,
  Show pearly breakers combing o'er their
    lee,   180
  White crests as of some just enchanted
    sea,
Checked in their maddest leap and hanging
  poised midway.

But when the eastern blow, with rain
    aslant,
From mid-sea's prairies green and rolling
    plains
  Drives in his wallowing herds of billows
    gaunt,
And the roused Charles remembers in his
    veins
  Old Ocean's blood and snaps his gyves of
    frost,
  That tyrannous silence on the shores is
    tost
In dreary wreck, and crumbling desolation
  reigns.

Edgewise or flat, in Druid-like device, 190
With leaden pools between or gullies
    bare,
  The blocks lie strewn, a bleak Stonehenge
    of ice;
No life, no sound, to break the grim de-
    spair,
  Save sullen plunge, as through the sedges
    stiff
  Down crackles riverward some thaw-
    sapped cliff,
Or when the close-wedged fields of ice
  crunch here and there.

But let me turn from fancy - pictured
    scenes
To that whose pastoral calm before me lies:
  Here nothing harsh or rugged inter-
    venes;

The early evening with her misty dyes 200
  Smooths off the ravelled edges of the
    nigh,
  Relieves the distant with her cooler sky,
And tones the landscape down, and soothes
  the wearied eyes.

There gleams my native village, dear to
    me,
Though higher change's waves each day
    are seen,
  Whelming fields famed in boyhood's his-
    tory,
Sanding with houses the diminished
    green;
  There, in red brick, which softening time
    defies,
  Stand square and stiff the Muses' fac-
    tories; —
How with my life knit up is every well-
  known scene !   210

Flow on, dear river ! not alone you flow
To outward sight, and through your marshes
    wind;
  Fed from the mystic springs of long-
    ago, •
Your twin flows silent through my world
    of mind: [1]
  Grow dim, dear marshes, in the evening's
    gray !
  Before my inner sight ye stretch away,
And will forever, though these fleshly eyes
  grow blind.

Beyond the hillock's house-bespotted
    swell,
Where Gothic chapels house the horse and
    chaise,
  Where quiet cits in Grecian temples
    dwell,   220
Where Coptic tombs resound with prayer
    and praise,
  Where dust and mud the equal year di-
    vide,
  There gentle Allston lived, and wrought,
    and died,
Transfiguring street and shop with his illu-
  mined gaze.

Virgilium vidi tantum, — I have seen
But as a boy, who looks alike on all,
  That misty hair, that fine Undine-like
    mien,

[1] Compare Emerson's ' Two Rivers,' p. 87.

Tremulous as down to feeling's faintest
        call; —
    Ah, dear old homestead ! count it to thy
        fame
That thither many times the Painter
        came; —   230
One elm yet bears his name, a feathery tree
        and tall.

    Swiftly the present fades in memory's
        glow, —
Our only sure possession is the past; —
    The village blacksmith died a month ago,
And dim to me the forge's roaring blast;
    Soon fire-new mediævals we shall see
    Oust the black smithy from its chestnut-
        tree,
And that hewn down, perhaps, the beehive
        green and vast. [1]

    How many times, prouder than king on
        throne,
Loosed from the village school-dame's A's
        and B's,   240
    Panting have I the creaky bellows blown,
And watched the pent volcano's red in-
        crease,
    Then paused to see the ponderous sledge,
        brought down
    By that hard arm voluminous and brown,
From the white iron swarm its golden van-
        ishing bees.

    Dear native town ! whose choking elms
        each year
With eddying dust before their time turn
        gray,
    Pining for rain, — to me thy dust is dear;
It glorifies the eve of summer day,
    And when the westering sun half sunken
        burns,   250
    The mote-thick air to deepest orange
        turns,
The westward horseman rides through
        clouds of gold away,

    So palpable, I 've seen those unshorn few,
The six old willows at the causey's end
    (Such trees Paul Potter never dreamed
        nor drew),
Through this dry mist their checkering
        shadows send,

[1] The tree was cut down by the city authorities in
1876. See the note on Longfellow's 'Village Blacksmith,' p. 108.

Striped, here and there, with many a
        long-drawn thread,
Where streamed through leafy chinks the
        trembling red,
Past which, in one bright trail, the hang-
        bird's flashes blend.

    Yes, dearer far thy dust than all that
        e'er,   260
Beneath the awarded crown of victory,
    Gilded the blown Olympic charioteer;
Though lightly prized the ribboned parch-
        ments three,
    Yet *collegisse juvat*, I am glad
    That here what colleging was mine I
        had, —
It linked another tie, dear native town, with
        thee !

    Nearer art thou than simply native earth,
My dust with thine concedes a deeper tie,
    A closer claim thy soil may well put
        forth,
Something of kindred more than sympa-
        thy;   270
    For in thy bounds I reverently laid away
    That blinding anguish of forsaken clay,
That title I seemed to have in earth and
        sea and sky,

    That portion of my life more choice to
        me
(Though brief, yet in itself so round and
        whole)
    Than all the imperfect residue can be; —
The Artist saw his statue of the soul
    Was perfect; so, with one regretful
        stroke,
    The earthen model into fragments broke,
And without her the impoverished seasons
        roll.   280

1847.   1847.

HEBE

    I saw the twinkle of white feet,
    I saw the flash of robes descending;
    Before her ran an influence fleet,
    That bowed my heart like barley bending

    As, in bare fields, the searching bees
    Pilot to blooms beyond our finding,
    It led me on, by sweet degrees
    Joy's simple honey-cells unbinding.

Those Graces were that seemed grim
    Fates;
With nearer love the sky leaned o'er me;
    The long-sought Secret's golden gates
On musical hinges swung before me.

I saw the brimmed bowl in her grasp
Thrilling with godhood; like a lover
    I sprang the proffered life to clasp; —
The beaker fell; the luck was over.

The Earth has drunk the vintage up;
What boots it patch the goblet's splinters ?
    Can Summer fill the icy cup,
Whose treacherous crystal is but Winter's ?

O spendthrift haste ! await the Gods;
The nectar crowns the lips of Patience;
    Haste scatters on unthankful sods
The immortal gift in vain libations.

Coy Hebe flies from those that woo,
And shuns the hands would seize upon
    her;
    Follow thy life, and she will sue
To pour for thee the cup of honor.

                                    1847.

THE CHANGELING [1]

I HAD a little daughter,
    And she was given to me
To lead me gently backward
    To the Heavenly Father's knee,
That I, by the force of nature,
    Might in some dim wise divine
The depth of his infinite patience
    To this wayward soul of mine.

I know not how others saw her,
    But to me she was wholly fair,   10
And the light of the heaven she came
    from
    Still lingered and gleamed in her hair;
For it was as wavy and golden,
    And as many changes took,
As the shadows of sun-gilt ripples
    On the yellow bed of a brook.

To what can I liken her smiling
    Upon me, her kneeling lover,

[1] Lowell's first child, Blanche, was born December
31, 1845, and died March 19, 1847. The sorrow of her
loss was softened by the birth of a second daughter in
the autumn of 1847. See ' The First Snow-Fall.'

How it leaped from her lips to her eye-
    lids,
    And dimpled her wholly over,   20
Till her outstretched hands smiled also,
    And I almost seemed to see
The very heart of her mother
    Sending sun through her veins to me !

She had been with us scarce a twelve-
    month,
    And it hardly seemed a day,
When a troop of wandering angels
    Stole my little daughter away;
Or perhaps those heavenly Zingari
    But loosed the hampering strings,   30
And when they had opened her cage-
    door,
    My little bird used her wings.

But they left in her stead a changeling,
    A little angel child,
That seems like her bud in full blossom,
    And smiles as she never smiled:
When I wake in the morning, I see it
    Where she always used to lie,
And I feel as weak as a violet
    Alone 'neath the awful sky.   40

As weak, yet as trustful also;
    For the whole year long I see
All the wonders of faithful Nature
    Still worked for the love of me;
Winds wander, and dews drip earth-
    ward,
    Rain falls, suns rise and set,
Earth whirls, and all but to prosper
    A poor little violet.

This child is not mine as the first was,
    I cannot sing it to rest,   50
I cannot lift it up fatherly
    And bliss it upon my breast:
Yet it lies in my little one's cradle
    And sits in my little one's chair,
And the light of the heaven she 's gone to
    Transfigures its golden hair.
1847.   1847.

SHE CAME AND WENT

As a twig trembles, which a bird
    Lights on to sing, then leaves unbent,
So is my memory thrilled and stirred; —
    I only know she came and went.

As clasps some lake, by gusts unriven,
  The blue dome's measureless content,
So my soul held that moment's heaven; —
  I only know she came and went.

As, at one bound, our swift spring heaps
  The orchards full of bloom and scent,
So clove her May my wintry sleeps; —
  I only know she came and went.

An angel stood and met my gaze,
  Through the low doorway of my tent;
The tent is struck, the vision stays; —
  I only know she came and went.

Oh, when the room grows slowly dim,
  And life's last oil is nearly spent,
One gush of light these eyes will brim,
  Only to think she came and went.

1847 ?   (1849.)

'I THOUGHT OUR LOVE AT FULL, BUT I DID ERR'

I THOUGHT our love at full, but I did err;
Joy's wreath drooped o'er mine eyes; I
    could not see
That sorrow in our happy world must be
Love's deepest spokesman and interpreter:
But, as a mother feels her child first stir
Under her heart, so felt I instantly
Deep in my soul another bond to thee
Thrill with that life we saw depart from her;
O mother of our angel child ! twice dear !
Death knits as well as parts, and still, I wis,
Her tender radiance shall infold us here,
Even as the light, borne up by inward bliss,
Threads the void glooms of space without
    a fear,
To print on farthest stars her pitying kiss.

                                    (1849.)

THE BIGLOW PAPERS [1]

FIRST SERIES

No. I

A LETTER [2]

FROM MR. EZEKIEL BIGLOW OF JAALAM TO THE HON. JOSEPH T. BUCKINGHAM, EDITOR OF THE BOSTON COURIER, INCLOSING A POEM OF HIS SON, MR. HOSEA BIGLOW

JAYLEM, june 1846.

MISTER EDDYTER, — Our Hosea wuz down to Boston last week, and he see a cruetin Sarjunt a struttin round as popler as a hen with 1 chicking, with 2 fellers a

[1] Cumberland in his Memoirs tells us that when, in the midst of Admiral Rodney's great sea-fight, Sir Charles Douglas said to him, 'Behold, Sir George, the Greeks and Trojans contending for the body of Patroclus!' the Admiral answered, peevishly, 'Damn the Greeks and damn the Trojans! I have other things to think of.' After the battle was won, Rodney thus to Sir Charles, 'Now, my dear friend, I am at the service of your Greeks and Trojans, and the whole of Homer's Iliad, or as much of it as you please!' I had some such feeling of the impertinence of our pseudo-classicality when I chose our homely dialect to work in. Should we be nothing, because somebody had contrived to be something (and that perhaps in a provincial dialect) ages ago? and be nothing by our very attempt to be that something, which they had already been, and which therefore nobody could be again without being a bore? Is there no way left, then, I thought, of being natural, of being *naïf*, which means nothing more than native, of belonging to the age and country in which you are born? The Yankee, at least, is a new phenomenon; let us try to be *that*. . . . To me the dialect was native, was spoken all about me when a boy, at a time when an Irish day-laborer was as rare as an Ameri-

can one now. Since then I have made a study of it so far as opportunity allowed. But when I write in it, it is as in a mother tongue, and I am carried back far beyond any studies of it to long-ago noonings in my father's hay-fields, and to the talk of Sam and Job over their jug of *blackstrap* under the shadow of the ash-tree which still dapples the grass whence they have been gone so long. (LOWELL, in the 'Introduction' to the *Biglow Papers*, 1866.)

I only know that I believed our war with Mexico (though we had as just ground for it as a strong nation ever has against a weak one) to be essentially a war of false pretences, and that it would result in widening the boundaries and so prolonging the life of slavery. . . . Against these and many other things I thought all honest men should protest. I was born and bred in the country, and the dialect was homely to me. I tried my first *Biglow Paper* in a newspaper, and found that it had a great run. So I wrote the others from time to time during the year which followed, always very rapidly, and sometimes (as with 'What Mr. Robinson thinks') at one sitting.

When I came to collect them and publish them in a volume, I conceived my parson-editor with his pedantry and verbosity, his amiable vanity and superiority to the verses he was editing, as a fitting artistic background and soil. It gave me the chance, too, of glancing obliquely at many things which were beyond the horizon of my other characters. (LOWELL, in a letter on the first series of the *Biglow Papers*, September 13, 1859, to Thomas Hughes, who was planning an English reprint of them. *Lowell's Letters*, vol. i, pp. 296, 297. Quoted by the kind permission of Messrs. Harper & Bros.) On the political effect of the *Biglow Papers*, see Greenslet's *Lowell*, pp. 84–86.

[2] The act of May 13, 1846, authorized President Polk to employ the militia, and call out 50,000 volunteers, if

drummin and fifin arter him like all nater.
the sarjunt he thout Hosea hed n't gut his
i teeth cut cos he looked a kindo 's though
he 'd jest com down, so he cal'lated to hook
him in, but Hosy wood n't take none o' his
sarse for all he hed much as 20 Rooster's
tales stuck onto his hat and eenamost enuf
brass a bobbin up and down on his shoulders and figureed onto his coat and trousis,
let alone wut nater hed sot in his featers,
to make a 6 pounder out on.

   wal, Hosea he com home considerabal
riled, and arter I 'd gone to bed I heern
Him a thrashin round like a short-tailed
Bull in fli-time. The old Woman ses she
to me ses she, Zekle, ses she, our Hosee 's
gut the chollery or suthin anuther ses she,
don't you Bee skeered, ses I, he 's oney
amakin pottery [1] ses i, he 's ollers on hand
at that ere busynes like Da & martin, and
shure enuf, cum mornin, Hosy he cum down
stares full chizzle, hare on eend and cote
tales flyin, and sot rite of to go reed his
varses to Parson Wilbur bein he haint aney
grate shows o' book larnin himself, bimeby
he cum back and sed the parson wuz dreffle
tickled with 'em as i hoop you will Be, and
said they wuz True grit.

   Hosea ses taint hardly fair to call 'em
hisn now, cos the parson kind o' slicked off
sum o' the last varses, but he told Hosee
he did n't want to put his ore in to tetch to
the Rest on 'em, bein they wuz verry well
As thay wuz, and then Hosy ses he sed
suthin a nuther about Simplex Mundishes
or sum sech feller, but I guess Hosea kind
o' did n't hear him, for I never hearn o'
nobody o' that name in this villadge, and
I 've lived here man and boy 76 year cum
next tater diggin, and thair aint no wheres
a kitting spryer 'n I be.

necessary. He immediately called for the full number
of volunteers, asking Massachusetts for 777 men. On
May 26 Governor Briggs issued a proclamation for the
enrolment of the regiment. As the President's call was
merely a request and not an order, many Whigs and
the Abolitionists were for refusing it. *The Liberator*
for June 5 severely censured the governor for comply-
ing, and accused him of not carrying out the resolutions of the last Whig Convention, which had pledged
the party ' to present as firm a front of opposition to
the institution as was consistent with their allegiance
to the Constitution.' (Note by Mr. Frank Beverly Williams, in the *Riverside* and *Cambridge Editions* of
Lowell's *Poetical Works*.)
   [1] *Aut insanit, aut versos facit.* — H. W. (The com-
ments signed H. W. are made by the Rev. Homer Wilbur, A. M., pastor of the First Church in Jaalam,
who edits the poems of his young parishioner Hosea
Biglow.)

   If you print 'em I wish you 'd jest let
folks know who hosy's father is, cos my ant
Keziah used to say it 's nater to be curus
ses she, she aint livin though and he 's
a likely kind o' lad.
            EZEKIEL BIGLOW.

———

THRASH away, you 'll *hev* to rattle
   On them kittle-drums o' yourn, —
'T aint a knowin' kind o' cattle
   Thet is ketched with mouldy corn;
Put in stiff, you fifer feller,
   Let folks see how spry you be, —
Guess you 'll toot till you are yeller
   'Fore you git ahold o' me !

Thet air flag 's a leetle rotten,
   Hope it aint your Sunday's best; —   10
Fact ! it takes a sight o' cotton
   To stuff out a soger's chest:
Sence we farmers hev to pay fer 't,
   Ef you must wear humps like these,
S'posin' you should try salt hay fer 't,
   It would du ez slick ez grease.

'T would n't suit them Southun fellers,
   They 're a dreffle graspin' set,
We must ollers blow the bellers
   Wen they want their irons het;   20
May be it 's all right ez preachin',
   But *my* narves it kind o' grates,
Wen I see the overreachin'
   O' them nigger-drivin' States.

Them thet rule us, them slave-traders,
   Haint they cut a thunderin' swarth
(Helped by Yankee renegaders),
   Thru the vartu o' the North !
We begin to think it 's nater
   To take sarse an' not be riled; —   30
Who 'd expect to see a tater
   All on eend at bein' biled ?

Ez fer war, I call it murder, —
   There you hev it plain an' flat;
I don't want to go no furder
   Than my Testyment fer that;
God hez sed so plump an' fairly,
   It 's ez long ez it is broad,
An' you 've gut to git up airly
   Ef you want to take in God.   40

'T aint your eppyletts an' feathers
   Make the thing a grain more right;

'T aint afollerin' your bell-wethers
  Will excuse ye in His sight;
Ef you take a sword an' dror it,
  An' go stick a feller thru,
Guv'ment aint to answer for it,
  God 'll send the bill to you.

Wut 's the use o' meetin'-goin'
  Every Sabbath, wet or dry,   50
Ef it 's right to go amowin'
  Feller-men like oats an' rye?
I dunno but wut it 's pooty
  Trainin' round in bobtail coats, —
But it 's curus Christian dooty
  This 'ere cuttin' folks's throats.

They may talk o' Freedom's airy
  Tell they 're pupple in the face, —
It 's a grand gret cemetary
  Fer the barthrights of our race;   60
They jest want this Californy
  So 's to lug new slave-States in
To abuse ye, an' to scorn ye,
  An' to plunder ye like sin.

Aint it cute to see a Yankee
  Take sech everlastin' pains,
All to get the Devil's thankee
  Helpin' on 'em weld their chains?
Wy, it 's jest ez clear ez figgers,
  Clear ez one an' one make two,   70
Chaps thet make black slaves o' niggers
  Want to make wite slaves o' you.

Tell ye jest the eend I 've come to
  Arter cipherin' plaguy smart,
An' it makes a handy sum, tu,
  Any gump could larn by heart;
Laborin' man an' laborin' woman
  Hev 'one glory an' one shame.
Ev'y thin' thet 's done inhuman
  Injers all on 'em the same.   80

'T aint by turnin' out to hack folks
  You 're agoin' to git your right,
Nor by lookin' down on black folks
  Coz you 're put upon by wite;
Slavery aint o' nary color,
  'T aint the hide thet makes it wus,
All it keers fer in a feller
  'S jest to make him fill its pus.

Want to tackle *me* in, du ye?
  I expect you 'll hev to wait;   90

Wen cold lead puts daylight thru ye
  You 'll begin to kal'late;
S'pose the crows wun't fall to pickin'
  All the carkiss from your bones,
Coz you helped to give a lickin'
  To them poor half-Spanish drones?

Jest go home an' ask our Nancy
  Wether I 'd be sech a goose
Ez to jine ye, — guess you 'd fancy
  The etarnal bung wuz loose!   100
She wants me fer home consumption,
  Let alone the hay 's to mow, —
Ef you 're arter folks o' gumption,
  You 've a darned long row to hoe.

Take them editors thet 's crowin'
  Like a cockerel three months old, —
Don't ketch any on 'em goin',
  Though they *be* so blasted bold;
Aint they a prime lot o' fellers?
  'Fore they think on 't guess they 'll sprout   110
(Like a peach thet 's got the yellers),
  With the meanness bustin' out.

Wal, go 'long to help 'em stealin'
  Bigger pens to cram with slaves,
Help the men thet 's ollers dealin'
  Insults on your fathers' graves;
Help the strong to grind the feeble,
  Help the many agin the few,
Help the men thet call your people
  Witewashed slaves an' peddlin' crew!   120

Massachusetts, God forgive her,
  She 's akneelin' with the rest,[1]
She, thet ough' to ha' clung ferever
  In her grand old eagle-nest;
She thet ough' to stand so fearless
  W'ile the wracks are round her hurled,
Holdin' up a beacon peerless
  To the oppressed of all the world!

[1] An allusion to the governor's call for troops as well as to the vote on the War Bill. On May 11, 1846, the President sent to the House of Representatives his well-known message declaring the existence of war brought on 'by the act of Mexico,' and asking for a supply of $10,000,000. Of the seven members from Massachusetts, all Whigs, two, Robert C. Winthrop, of Boston, and Amos Abbott, of Andover, voted for the bill. The Whigs throughout the country, remembering the fate of the party which had opposed the last war with England, sanctioned the measure as necessary for the preservation of the army, then in peril by the unauthorized acts of the President. (F. B. Williams, in *Riverside* and *Cambridge Editions*.)

Ha'n't they sold your colored seamen ?
  Ha'n't they made your env'ys w'iz ? [1]
Wut 'll make ye act like freemen ?   131
  Wut 'll git your dander riz ?
Come, I 'll tell ye wut I 'm thinkin'
  Is our dooty in this fix,
They 'd ha' done 't ez quick ez winkin'
  In the days o' seventy-six.

Clang the bells in every steeple,
  Call all true men to disown
The tradoocers of our people,
  The enslavers o' their own;   140
Let our dear old Bay State proudly
  Put the trumpet to her mouth,
Let her ring this messidge loudly
  In the ears of all the South : —

' I 'll return ye good fer evil
  Much ez we frail mortils can,
But I wun't go help the Devil
  Makin' man the cus o' man;
Call me coward, call me traiter,
  Jest ez suits your mean idees, —   150
Here I stand a tyrant-hater,
  An' the friend o' God an' Peace ! '

Ef I 'd *my* way I hed ruther
  We should go to work an' part, [2]
They take one way, we take t' other,
  Guess it would n't break my heart;

[1] South Carolina, Louisiana, and several other Southern States at an early date passed acts to prevent free persons of color from entering their jurisdictions. These acts bore with particular severity upon colored seamen, who were imprisoned, fined, or whipped, and often sold into slavery. On the petition of the Massachusetts Legislature, Governor Briggs, in 1844, appointed Mr. Samuel Hoar agent to Charleston, and Mr. George Hubbard to New Orleans, to act on behalf of oppressed colored citizens of the Bay State. Mr. Hoar was expelled from South Carolina by order of the Legislature of that State, and Mr. Hubbard was forced by threats of violence to leave Louisiana. The obnoxious acts remained in force until after the Civil War. F. B. Williams, in *Riverside* and *Cambridge Editions*.)

[2] Propositions to secede were not uncommon in New England at this time. The rights of the States had been strongly asserted on the acquisition of Louisiana in 1803, and on the admission of the State of that name in 1812. Among the resolutions of the Massachusetts Legislature adopted in 1845, relative to the proposed annexation of Texas, was one declaring that ' such an act of admission would have no binding force whatever on the people of Massachusetts.'
John Quincy Adams, in a discourse before the New York Historical Society in 1839, claimed a right for the States ' to part in friendship with each other . . . when the fraternal spirit shall give way,' etc. The Garrisonian wing of the Abolitionists notoriously advocated secession. There were several other instances of an expression of this sentiment, but for the most part they were not evoked by opposition to slavery. (F. B. Williams in *Riverside* and *Cambridge Editions*.)

Man hed ough' to put asunder
  Them thet God has noways jined;
An' I should n't gretly wonder
  Ef there 's thousands o' my mind.
               June 17, 1846.

[The first recruiting sergeant on record I conceive to have been that individual who is mentioned in the Book of Job as *going to and fro in the earth, and walking up and down in it.* Bishop Latimer will have him to have been a bishop, but to me that other calling would appear more congenial. The sect of Cainites is not yet extinct, who esteemed the first-born of Adam to be the most worthy, not only because of that privilege of primogeniture, but inasmuch as he was able to overcome and slay his younger brother. That was a wise saying of the famous Marquis Pescara to the Papal Legate, that *it was impossible for men to serve Mars and Christ at the same time.* Yet in time past the profession of arms was judged to be κατ' ἐξοχήν that of a gentleman, nor does this opinion want for strenuous upholders even in our day. Must we suppose, then, that the profession of Christianity was only intended for losels, or, at best, to afford an opening for plebeian ambition ? Or shall we hold with that nicely metaphysical Pomeranian, Captain Vratz, who was Count Königsmark's chief instrument in the murder of Mr. Thynne, that the Scheme of Salvation has been arranged with an especial eye to the necessities of the upper classes, and that ' God would consider *a gentleman* and deal with him suitably to the condition and profession he had placed him in' ? It may be said of us all, *Exemplo plus quam ratione vivimus.* — H. W.]

No. III

WHAT MR. ROBINSON THINKS

GUVENER B. is a sensible man; [3]
  He stays to his home an' looks arter his
    folks;

[3] George Nixon Briggs was the Whig governor of Massachusetts from 1844 to 1851. The campaign referred to here is that of 1847. Governor Briggs was renominated by acclamation and supported by his party with great enthusiasm. His opponent was Caleb Cushing, then in Mexico, and raised by President Polk to the rank of Brigadier-General. Cushing was defeated by a majority of 14,060. (F. B. Williams.)

He draws his furrer ez straight ez he can,
    An' into nobody's tater-patch pokes;
            But John P. [1]
            Robinson he
    Sez he wunt vote fer Guvener B.

My! aint it terrible? Wut shall we du?
    We can't never choose him o' course, —
        thet 's flat;
Guess we shall hev to come round (don't
        you?)   10
    An' go in fer thunder an' guns, an' all
        that;
            Fer John P.
            Robinson he
    Sez he wunt vote fer Guvener B.

Gineral C. is a dreffle smart man: [2]
    He 's ben on all sides thet give places or
        pelf;
But consistency still wuz a part of his
        plan, —
    He 's ben true to *one* party, — an' thet is
        himself; —
            So John P.
            Robinson he   20
    Sez he shall vote fer Gineral C.

Gineral C. he goes in fer the war;
    He don't vally princerple more 'n an old
        cud;
Wut did God make us raytional creeturs fer,
    But glory an' gunpowder, plunder an'
        blood?
            So John P.
            Robinson he
    Sez he shall vote fer Gineral C.

We were gittin' on nicely up here to our
        village,
    With good old idees o' wut 's right an'
        wut aint,   30
We kind o' thought Christ went agin war
        an' pillage,

[1] John Paul Robinson (1799–1864) was a resident of Lowell, a lawyer of considerable ability, and a thorough classical scholar. He represented Lowell in the State Legislature in 1829, 1830, 1831, 1833, and 1842, and was Senator from Middlesex in 1836. Late in the gubernatorial contest of 1847 it was rumored that Robinson, heretofore a zealous Whig, and a delegate to the recent Springfield Convention, had gone over to the Democratic or, as it was then styled, the 'Loco' camp. The editor of the *Boston Palladium* wrote to him to learn the truth, and Robinson replied in an open letter avowing his intention to vote for Cushing. (F. B. Williams.)
[2] General Caleb Cushing.

An' thet eppyletts worn't the best mark
        of a saint;
            But John P.
            Robinson he
    Sez this kind o' thing 's an exploded
        idee.

The side of our country must ollers be took,
    An' President Polk, you know, *he* is our
        country.
An' the angel thet writes all our sins in a
        book
    Puts the *debit* to him, an' to us the *per*
        contry;
            An' John P.   40
            Robinson he
    Sez this is his view o' the thing to a T.

Parson Wilbur he calls all these argimunts
        lies;
    Sez they 're nothin' on airth but jest
        fee, faw, fum;
An' thet all this big talk of our destinies
    Is half on it ign'ance, an' t' other half
        rum;
            But John P.
            Robinson he
    Sez it aint no sech thing; an', of course,
        so must we.

Parson Wilbur sez *he* never heerd in his
        life   50
    Thet th' Apostles rigged out in their
        swaller-tail coats,
An' marched round in front of a drum an'
        a fife,
    To git some on 'em office, an' some on
        'em votes;
            But John P.
            Robinson he
    Sez they did n't know everythin' down
        in Judee.

Wal, it 's a marcy we 've gut folks to tell us
    The rights an' the wrongs o' these mat-
        ters, I vow, —
God sends country lawyers, an' other wise
        fellers,
    To start the world's team wen it gits in
        a slough;   60
            Fer John P.
            Robinson he
    Sez the world 'll go right, ef he hollers
        out Gee!

                            November 2, 1847

[The attentive reader will doubtless have perceived in the foregoing poem an allusion to that pernicious sentiment, 'Our country, right or wrong.' It is an abuse of language to call a certain portion of land, much more, certain personages, elevated for the time being to high station, our country. I would not sever nor loosen a single one of those ties by which we are united to the spot of our birth, nor minish by a tittle the respect due to the Magistrate. I love our own Bay State too well to do the one, and as for the other, I have myself for nigh forty years exercised, however unworthily, the function of Justice of the Peace, having been called thereto by the unsolicited kindness of that most excellent man and upright patriot, Caleb Strong. *Patriae fumus igne alieno luculentior* is best qualified with this, — *Ubi libertas, ibi patria.* We are inhabitants of two worlds, and owe a double, not a divided, allegiance. In virtue of our clay, this little ball of earth exacts a certain loyalty of us, while, in our capacity as spirits, we are admitted citizens of an invisible and holier fatherland. There is a patriotism of the soul whose claim absolves us from our other and terrene fealty. Our true country is that ideal realm which we represent to ourselves under the names of religion, duty, and the like. Our terrestrial organizations are but far-off approaches to so fair a model, and all they are verily traitors who resist not any attempt to divert them from this their original intendment. When, therefore, one would have us to fling up our caps and shout with the multitude, 'Our country, *however bounded* !' [1] he demands of us that we sacrifice the larger to the less, the higher to the lower, and that we yield to the imaginary claims of a few acres of soil our duty and privilege as liegemen of Truth. Our true country is bounded on the north and the south, on the east and the west, by Justice, and when she oversteps that invisible boundary-line by so much as a hair's-breadth, she ceases to be our mother,

and chooses rather to be looked upon *quasi noverca.* That is a hard choice when our earthly love of country calls upon us to tread one path and our duty points us to another. We must make as noble and becoming an election as did Penelope between Icarius and Ulysses. Veiling our faces, we must take silently the hand of Duty to follow her. . . . H. W.]

No. VI

THE PIOUS EDITOR'S CREED

I DU believe in Freedom's cause,
   Ez fur away ez Payris is; [2]
I love to see her stick her claws
   In them infarnal Phayrisees;
It 's wal enough agin a king
   To dror resolves an' triggers, —
But libbaty 's a kind o' thing
   Thet don't agree with niggers.

I du believe the people want
   A tax on teas an' coffees,
Thet nothin' aint extravygunt, —   10
   Purvidin' I 'm in office;
Fer I hev loved my country sence
   My eye-teeth filled their sockets,
An' Uncle Sam I reverence,
   Partic'larly his pockets.

I du believe in *any* plan
   O' levyin' the texes,
Ez long ez, like a lumberman,
   I git jest wut I axes;   20
I go free-trade thru thick an' thin,
   Because it kind o' rouses
The folks to vote, — an' keeps us in
   Our quiet custom-houses.

I du believe it 's wise an' good
   To sen' out furrin missions,
Thet is, on sartin understood
   An' orthydox conditions; —
I mean nine thousan' dolls. per ann.,
   Nine thousan' more fer outfit,   30
An' me to recommend a man
   The place 'ould jest about fit.

I du believe in special ways
   O' prayin' an' convartin';
The bread comes back in many days,

[1] Mr. R. C. Winthrop, M. C., in a speech at Faneuil Hall, July 4, 1845, said in deprecation of secession : 'Our country — bounded by the St. John's and the Sabine, or however otherwise bounded or described, and be the measurements more or less — still our country — to be cherished in all our hearts, to be defended by all our hands.' The sentiment was at once taken up and used effectively by the 'Cotton' Whigs, those who inclined to favor the Mexican War. (F. B. Williams.)

[2] This was written just after the Revolution of 1848 in France, when the monarchy of Louis Philippe was overthrown.

An' buttered, tu, fer sartin;
I mean in preyin' till one busts
On wut the party chooses,
An' in convartin' public trusts
    To very privit uses.   40

I du believe hard coin the stuff
    Fer 'lectioneers to spout on;
The people 's ollers soft enough
    To make hard money out on;
Dear Uncle Sam pervides fer his,
    An' gives a good-sized junk to all, —
I don't care *how* hard money is,
    Ez long ez mine 's paid punctooal.

I du believe with all my soul
    In the gret Press's freedom,   50
To pint the people to the goal
    An' in the traces lead 'em;
Palsied the arm thet forges yokes
    At my fat contracts squintin',
An' withered be the nose thet pokes
    Inter the gov'ment printin' !

I du believe thet I should give
    Wut 's his'n unto Cæsar,
Fer it 's by him I move an' live,
    Frum him my bread an' cheese air;   60
I du believe thet all o' me
    Doth bear his superscription, —
Will, conscience, honor, honesty,
    An' things o' thet description.

I du believe in prayer an' praise
    To him thet hez the grantin'
O' jobs, — in every thin' thet pays,
    But most of all in Cantin' ;
This doth my cup with marcies fill,
    This lays all thought o' sin to rest, 70
I *don't* believe in princerple,
    But oh, I *du* in interest.

I du believe in bein' this
    Or thet, ez it may happen
One way or 't other hendiest is
    To ketch the people nappin' ;
It aint by princerples nor men
    My preudunt course is steadied, —
I scent wich pays the best, an' then
    Go into it baldheaded.   80

I du believe thet holdin' slaves
    Comes nat'ral to a Presidunt,
Let 'lone the rowdedow it saves
    To hev a wal-broke precedunt;

Fer any office, small or gret,
    I could n't ax with no face,
'uthout I 'd ben, thru dry an' wet,
    Th' unrizzest kind o' doughface.

I du believe wutever trash
    'll keep the people in blindness,   90
Thet we the Mexicuns can thrash
    Right inter brotherly kindness,
Thet bombshells, grape, an' powder 'n' ball
    Air good-will's strongest magnets,
Thet peace, to make it stick at all,
    Must be druv in with bagnets.

In short, I firmly du believe
    In Humbug generally,
Fer it 's a thing thet I perceive
    To hev a solid vally;   100
This heth my faithful shepherd ben,
    In pasturs sweet heth led me,
An' this 'll keep the people green
    To feed ez they hev fed me.

                                May 4, 1848.

No. VIII

A SECOND LETTER FROM B. SAWIN, ESQ. [1]

I spose you wonder ware I be; I can't tell,
        fer the soul o' me,
Exacly ware I be myself, — meanin' by
        thet the holl o' me.
Wen I left hum, I hed two legs, an' they
        worn't bad ones neither
(The scaliest trick they ever played wuz
        bringin' on me hither),
Now one on 'em 's I dunno ware; — they
        thought I wuz adyin',
An' sawed it off because they said 't wuz
        kin' o' mortifyin';
I 'm willin' to believe it wuz, an' yit I don't
        see, nuther,
Wy one shoud take to feelin' cheap a min-
        nit sooner 'n t' other.
Sence both wuz equilly to blame; but
        things is ez they be:
It took on so they took it off, an' thet 's
        enough fer me: 10
There 's one good thing, though, to be said
        about my wooden new one, —

[1] ' Birdofredum Sawin ' is a fellow-townsman of Hosea
Biglow, who ' wuz cussed fool enuff to goe atrottin inter
Miss Chiff arter a Drum and fife,' beguiled by the
' cruetin sarjunt' of Biglow Paper No. I. His first letter
is given in No. II.

The liquor can't git into it ez 't used to in
    the true one;
So it saves drink; an' then, besides, a feller
    could n't beg
A gretter blessin' then to hev one ollers
    sober peg;
It 's true a chap 's in want o' two fer follerin'
    a drum,
But all the march I 'm up to now is jest to
    Kingdom Come.

I 've lost one eye, but thet 's a loss it 's easy
    to supply
Out o' the glory thet I 've gut, fer thet is all
    my eye;
An' one is big enough, I guess, by dili-
    gently usin' it,
To see all I shall ever git by way o' pay fer
    losin' it;   20
Off'cers I notice, who git paid fer all our
    thumps an' kickins,
Du wal by keepin' single eyes arter the fat-
    test pickins;
So, ez the eye 's put fairly out, I 'll larn to
    go without it,
An' not allow *myself* to be no gret put out
    about it.
Now, le' me see, thet is n't all; I used, 'fore
    leavin' Jaalam,
To count things on my finger-eends, but
    sutthin' seems to ail 'em:
Ware 's my left hand? Oh, darn it, yes, I
    recollect wut 's come on 't;
I haint no left arm but my right, an' thet 's
    gut jest a thumb on 't;
It aint so hendy ez it wuz to cal'late a sum
    on 't.
I 've hed some ribs broke, — six (I b'lieve),
    —I haint kep' no account on 'em; 30
Wen pensions git to be the talk, I 'll settle
    the amount on 'em.
An' now I 'm speakin' about ribs, it kin' o'
    brings to mind
One thet I could n't never break, — the one
    I lef' behind;
Ef you should see her, jest clear out the
    spout o' your invention
An' pour the longest sweetnin' in about an
    annooal pension,
An' kin' o' hint (in case, you know, the
    critter should refuse to be
Consoled) I aint so 'xpensive now to keep
    ez wut I used to be;
There 's one arm less, ditto one eye, an'
    then the leg thet 's wooden

Can be took off an' sot away wenever ther 's
    a puddin'.

I spose you think I 'm comin' back ez op-
    perlunt ez thunder,   40
With shiploads o' gold images an' varus
    sorts o' plunder;
Wal, 'fore I vullinteered, I thought this
    country wuz a sort o'
Canaan, a reg'lar Promised Land flowin'
    with rum an' water,
Ware propaty growed up like time, without
    no cultivation,
An' gold wuz dug ez taters be among our
    Yankee nation,
Ware nateral advantages were pufficly
    amazin',
Ware every rock there wuz about with pre-
    cious stuns wuz blazin',
Ware mill-sites filled the country up ez
    thick ez you could cram 'em,
An' desput rivers run about a beggin' folks
    to dam 'em;
Then there were meetinhouses, tu, chockful
    o' gold an' silver   50
Thet you could take, an' no one could n't
    hand ye in no bill fer; —
Thet 's wut I thought afore I went, thet 's
    wut them fellers told us
Thet stayed to hum an' speechified an' to
    the buzzards sold us;
I thought thet gold-mines could be gut
    cheaper than Chiny asters,
An' see myself acomin' back like sixty Ja-
    cob Astors;
But sech idees soon melted down an' did n't
    leave a grease-spot;
I vow my holl sheer o' the spiles would n't
    come nigh a V spot;
Although, most anywares we 've ben, you
    need n't break no locks,
Nor run no kin' o' risks, to fill your pocket
    full o' rocks.
I 'xpect I mentioned in my last some o' the
    nateral feeturs   60
O' this all-fiered buggy hole in th' way o'
    awfle creeturs,
But I fergut to name (new things to speak
    on so abounded)
How one day you 'll most die o' thust, an'
    'fore the next git drownded.
The clymit seems to me jest like a teapot
    made o' pewter
Our Preudence hed, thet would n't pour
    (all she could du) to suit her;

Fust place the leaves 'ould choke the
  spout, so 's not a drop 'ould dreen
  out,
Then Prude 'ould tip an' tip an' tip, till the
  holl kit bust clean out,
The kiver-hinge-pin bein' lost, tea-leaves
  an' tea an' kiver
'ould all come down *kerswosh* ! ez though
  the dam bust in a river.
Jest so 't is here; holl months there aint a
  day o' rainy weather,   70
An' jest ez th' officers 'ould be a layin'
  heads together
Ez t' how they 'd mix their drink at sech a
  milingtary deepot, —
'T would pour ez though the lid wuz off the
  everlastin' teapot.

The cons'quence is, thet I shall take, wen
  I 'm allowed to leave here,
One piece o' propaty along, an' thet 's the
  shakin' fever;
It 's reggilar employment, though, an' thet
  aint thought to harm one,
Nor 't aint so tiresome ez it wuz with
  t' other leg an' arm on;
An' it 's a consolation, tu, although it doos
  n't pay,
To hev it said you 're some gret shakes in
  any kin' o' way.
'T worn't very long, I tell ye wut, I thought
  o' fortin-makin', —   80
One day a reg'lar shiver-de-freeze, an' next
  ez good ez bakin', —
One day abrilin' in the sand, then smoth'rin'
  in the mashes, —
Git up all sound, be put to bed a mess o'
  hacks an' smashes.
But then, thinks I, at any rate there 's glory
  to be hed, —
Thet 's an investment, arter all, thet may n't
  turn out so bad;
But somehow, wen we 'd fit an' licked, I
  ollers found the thanks
Gut kin' o' lodged afore they come ez low
  down ez the ranks;
The Gin'rals gut the biggest sheer, the
  Cunnles next, an' so on, —
We never gut a blasted mite o' glory ez I
  know on;
An' spose we hed, I wonder how you 're
  goin' to contrive its   90
Division so 's to give a piece to twenty
  thousand privits;
Ef you should multiply by ten the portion
  o' the brav'st one,

You would n't git more 'n half enough to
  speak of on a grave-stun;
We git the licks, — we 're jest the grist
  thet 's put into War's hoppers;
Leftenants is the lowest grade thet helps
  pick up the coppers.
It may suit folks thet go agin a body with
  a soul in't,
An' aint contented with a hide without a
  bagnet hole in't;
But glory is a kin' o' thing *I* sha'n't pursue
  no furder,
Coz thet 's the off'cers' parquisite, — yourn 's
  on'y jest the murder.

Wal, arter I gin glory up, thinks I at least
  there 's one   100
Thing in the bills we aint hed yit, an' thet 's
  the GLORIOUS FUN:
Ef once we git to Mexico, we fairly may
  persume we
All day an' night shall revel in the halls o'
  Montezumy.
I 'll tell ye wut *my* revels wuz, an' see how
  you would like 'em;
We never gut inside the hall: the nighest
  ever *I* come
Wuz stan'in' sentry in the sun (an', fact, it
  seemed a cent'ry)
A ketchin' smells o' biled an' roast thet
  come out thru the entry,
An' hearin' ez I sweltered thru my passes
  an' repasses,
A rat-tat-too o' knives an' forks, a clinkty-
  clink o' glasses:
I can't tell off the bill o' fare the Gin'rals
  hed inside;   110
All I know is, thet out o' doors a pair o'
  soles wuz fried,
An' not a hunderd miles away frum ware
  this child wuz posted,
A Massachusetts citizen wuz baked an'
  biled an' roasted;
The on'y thing like revellin' thet ever come
  to me
Wuz bein' routed out o' sleep by thet darned
  revelee.

They say the quarrel 's settled now; fer my
  part I 've some doubt on 't,
't 'll take more fish-skin than folks
  think to take the rile clean out
  on 't;
At any rate I 'm so used up I can't do no
  more fightin',

The on'y chance thet's left to me is politics
or writin';
Now, ez the people's gut to hev a miling-
tary man, 120
An' I aint nothin' else jest now, I 've hit
upon a plan;
The can'idatin' line, you know, 'ould suit
me to a T,
An' ef I lose, 't wunt hurt my ears to lodge
another flea;
So I 'll set up ez can'idate fer any kin' o' office
(I mean fer any thet includes good easy-
cheers an' soffies;
Fer ez tu runnin' fer a place ware work 's
the time o' day,
You know thet's wut I never did, — ex-
cept the other way);
Ef it 's the Presidential cheer fer wich I 'd
better run,
Wut two legs anywares about could keep
up with my one ?
There aint no kin' o' quality in can'idates,
it 's said, 130
So useful ez a wooden leg, — except a
wooden head;
There 's nothin' aint so poppylar (wy, it 's
a parfect sin
To think wut Mexico hez paid fer Santy
Anny's pin);
Then I haint gut no princerples, an', sence
I wuz knee-high,
I never *did* hev any gret, ez you can testify;
I 'm a decided peace-man, tu, an' go agin
the war, —
Fer now the holl on 't 's gone an' past, wut
is there to go *for*?
Ef, wile you 're 'lectioneerin' round, some
curus chaps should beg
To know my views o' state affairs, jest
answer WOODEN LEG !
Ef they aint settisfied with thet, an' kin' o'
pry an' doubt 140
An' ax fer sutthin' deffynit, jest say ONE
EYE PUT OUT !
Thet kin' o' talk I guess you 'll find 'll
answer to a charm,
An' wen you 're druv tu nigh the wall, hol'
up my missin' arm;
Ef they should nose round fer a pledge, put
on a vartoous look
An' tell 'em thet 's percisely wut I never
gin nor — took !

Then you can call me 'Timbertoes,' —
thet 's wut the people likes;

Sutthin' combinin' morril truth with phrases
sech ez strikes;
Some say the people 's fond o' this, or thet,
or wut you please, —
I tell ye wut the people want is jest correct
idees;
'Old Timbertoes,' you see, 's a creed it 's
safe to be quite bold on, 150
There 's nothin' in 't the other side can any
ways git hold on;
It 's a good tangible idee, a sutthin' to embody
Thet valooable class o' men who look thru
brandy-toddy;
It gives a Party . Platform, tu, jest level
with the mind
Of all right-thinkin', honest folks thet
mean to go it blind;
Then there air other good hooraws to dror
on ez you need 'em,
Sech ez the ONE-EYED SLARTERER, the
BLOODY BIRDOFREDUM:
Them 's wut takes hold o' folks thet think,
ez well ez o' the masses,
An' makes you sartin o' the aid o' good
men of all classes.

There 's one thing I 'm in doubt about; in
order to be Presidunt, 160
It 's absolutely ne'ssary to be a Southern
residunt;
The Constitution settles thet, an' also thet
a feller
Must own a nigger o' some sort, jet black,
or brown, or yeller.
Now I haint no objections agin particklar
climes,
Nor agin ownin' anythin' (except the truth
sometimes),
But, ez I haint no capital, up there among
ye, maybe,
You might raise funds enough fer me to
buy a low-priced baby,
An' then to suit the No'thern folks, who
feel obleeged to say
They hate an' cus the very thing they vote
fer every day,
Say you 're assured I go full but fer Lib-
baty's diffusion 170
An' made the purchis on'y jest to spite the
Institootion; —
But, golly ! there 's the currier's hoss upon
the pavement pawin' !
I 'll be more 'xplicit in my next.
 Yourn, BIRDOFREDUM SAWIN.
 July 6, 1848.

A FABLE FOR CRITICS [1]

Reader! walk up at once (it will soon be too late),
and buy at a perfectly ruinous rate

A FABLE FOR CRITICS:

OR, BETTER,

(I LIKE, AS A THING THAT THE READER'S FIRST
FANCY MAY STRIKE, AN OLD-FASHIONED TITLE-
PAGE, SUCH AS PRESENTS A TABULAR VIEW OF
THE VOLUME'S CONTENTS),

A GLANCE AT A FEW OF OUR LIT-
ERARY PROGENIES

(MRS. MALAPROP'S WORD)

FROM THE TUB OF DIOGENES;

A VOCAL AND MUSICAL MEDLEY,

THAT IS,

A SERIES OF JOKES

𝔅𝔶 𝔄 𝔚𝔬𝔫𝔡𝔢𝔯𝔣𝔲𝔩 𝔔𝔲𝔦𝔷,

WHO ACCOMPANIES HIMSELF WITH A RUB-A-
DUB-DUB, FULL OF SPIRIT AND GRACE, ON THE
TOP OF THE TUB.

Set forth in October, the 31st day,
In the year '48, G. P. Putnam, Broadway.

---

[1] This *jeu d'esprit* was extemporized, I may fairly say, so rapidly was it written, purely for my own amusement and with no thought of publication. I sent daily instalments of it to a friend in New York, the late Charles F. Briggs. He urged me to let it be printed, and I at last consented to its anonymous publication. The secret was kept till after several persons had laid claim to its authorship. (LOWELL.)

On the writing of the 'Fable,' its progress from week to week, and Lowell's presentation of the copyright to his friend Briggs, see Scudder's *Life of Lowell*, vol. i, pp. 238-255.

Holmes said of it: 'It is capital — crammed full and rammed down hard — powder (lots of it) — shot slugs — bullets — very little wadding, and that is gun-cotton — all crowded into a rusty looking sort of a blunder-buss barrel as it were — capped with a percussion pre-face — and cocked with a title-page as apropos as a wink to a joke.' (Morse's *Life of Holmes*, vol. ii, p. 107.)

The original title-page is given above.

It being the commonest mode of proce-dure, I premise a few candid remarks

TO THE READER: —

This trifle, begun to please only myself and my own private fancy, was laid on the shelf. But some friends, who had seen it, induced me, by dint of saying they liked it, to put it in print. That is, having come to that very conclusion, I asked their advice when 't would make no confusion. For though (in the gentlest of ways) they had hinted it was scarce worth the while, I should doubtless have printed it.

I began it, intending a Fable, a frail, slender thing, rhyme-ywinged, with a sting in its tail. But, by addings and alterings not previously planned, digressions chance-hatched, like birds' eggs in the sand, and dawdlings to suit every whimsey's demand (always freeing the bird which I held in my hand, for the two perched, perhaps out of reach, in the tree), — it grew by degrees to the size which you see. I was like the old woman that carried the calf, and my neighbors, like hers, no doubt, wonder and laugh; and when, my strained arms with their grown burthen full, I call it my Fable, they call it a bull.

Having scrawled at full gallop (as far as that goes) in a style that is neither good verse nor bad prose, and being a person whom nobody knows, some people will say I am rather more free with my readers than it is becoming to be, that I seem to expect them to wait on my leisure in fol-lowing wherever I wander at pleasure, that, in short, I take more than a young author's lawful ease, and laugh in a queer way so like Mephistopheles, that the Pub-lic will doubt, as they grope through my rhythm, if in truth I am making fun *of* them or *with* them.

So the excellent Public is hereby assured that the sale of my book is already secured. For there is not a poet throughout the whole land but will purchase a copy or two out of hand, in the fond expectation of being amused in it, by seeing his betters cut up and abused in it. Now, I find, by a pretty exact calculation, there are something like ten thousand bards in the nation, of that special variety whom the Review and Magazine critics call *lofty* and *true*, and about thirty thousand (*this* tribe is increasing) of the kinds who are termed *full of promise* and *pleasing*. The Public will see by a glance at this schedule, that they cannot expect me to be over-sedulous about courting *them*, since it seems I have got enough fuel made sure of for boiling my pot.

As for such of our poets as find not their names mentioned once in my pages, with praises or blames, let them SEND IN THEIR CARDS, without further DELAY, to my friend G. P. PUTNAM, Esquire, in Broadway, where a LIST will be kept with the strictest regard to the day and the hour of receiving the card. Then, taking them up as I chance to have time (that is, if their names can be twisted in rhyme), I will honestly give each his PROPER POSITION, at the rate of ONE AUTHOR to each NEW EDITION. Thus a PREMIUM is offered sufficiently HIGH (as the magazines say when they tell their best lie) to induce bards to CLUB their resources and buy the balance of every edition, until they have all of them fairly been run through the mill.

One word to such readers (judicious and wise) as read books with something behind the mere eyes, of whom in the country, perhaps, there are two, including myself, gentle reader, and you. All the characters sketched in this slight *jeu d' esprit*, though, it may be, they seem, here and there, rather free, and drawn from a somewhat too cynical standpoint, are *meant* to be faithful, for that is the grand point, and none but an owl would feel sore at a rub from a jester who tells you, without any subterfuge, that he sits in Diogenes' tub.

PHŒBUS, sitting one day in a laurel-tree's shade,
Was reminded of Daphne, of whom it was made,
For the god being one day too warm in his wooing,
She took to the tree to escape his pursuing;
Be the cause what it might, from his offers she shrunk,
And, Ginevra-like, shut herself up in a trunk;
And, though 't was a step into which he had driven her,

He somehow or other had never forgiven her;
Her memory he nursed as a kind of a tonic,
Something bitter to chew when he 'd play the Byronic,   10
And I can't count the obstinate nymphs that he brought over
By a strange kind of smile he put on when he thought of her.
' My case is like Dido's,' he sometimes remarked;
' When I last saw my love, she was fairly embarked
In a laurel, as *she* thought — but (ah, how Fate mocks !)
She has found it by this time a very bad box;
Let hunters from me take this saw when they need it, —
You 're not always sure of your game when you 've treed it.
Just conceive such a change taking place in one's mistress !
What romance would be left ? — who can flatter or kiss trees ?   20
And, for mercy's sake, how could one keep up a dialogue
With a dull wooden thing that will live and will die a log, —
Not to say that the thought would forever intrude
That you 've less chance to win her the more she is wood ?
Ah ! it went to my heart, and the memory still grieves,
To see those loved graces all taking their leaves;
Those charms beyond speech, so enchanting but now,
As they left me forever, each making its bough !
If her tongue *had* a tang sometimes more than was right,
Her new bark is worse than ten times her old bite.'   30

. . . .

Apollo looked up, hearing footsteps approaching,
And slipped out of sight the new rhymes he was broaching, —
' Good day, Mr. D——,[1] I 'm happy to meet

---

[1] Duyckinck. Evert A. Duyckinck, with his brother George L. Duyckinck, published a ' Cyclopædia of American Literature, embracing personal and critical notices of authors, and selections from their writings.'

With a scholar so ripe, and a critic so neat,
Who through Grub Street the soul of a
    gentleman carries;
What news from that suburb of London
    and Paris
Which latterly makes such shrill claims to
    monopolize
The credit of being the New World's me-
    tropolis ? '

    ' Why, nothing of consequence, save this
        attack
On my friend there, behind, by some pitiful
    hack,   40
Who thinks every national author a poor
    one,
That is n't a copy of something that 's for-
    eign,
And assaults the American Dick— '
            ' Nay, 't is clear
That your Damon there 's fond of a flea in
    his ear,
And, if no one else furnished them gratis,
    on tick
He would buy some himself, just to hear
    the old click;
Why, I honestly think, if some fool in
    Japan
Should turn up his nose at the " Poems on
    Man "
(Which contain many verses as fine, by the
    bye,
As any that lately came under my eye),   50
Your friend there by some inward instinct
    would know it,
Would get it translated, reprinted, and show
    it;
As a man might take off a high stock to
    exhibit
The autograph round his own neck of the
    gibbet;
Nor would let it rest so, but fire column
    after column,
Signed Cato, or Brutus, or something as
    solemn,
By way of displaying his critical crosses,
And tweaking that poor transatlantic pro-
    boscis,
His broadsides resulting (this last there 's
    no doubt of)
In successively sinking the craft they 're
    fired out of.   60
Now nobody knows when an author is
    hit,
If he have not a public hysterical fit;

Let him only keep close in his snug garret's
    dim ether,
And nobody 'd think of his foes — or of
    him either;
If an author have any least fibre of worth
    in him,
Abuse would but tickle the organ of mirth
    in him;
All the critics on earth cannot crush with
    their ban
One word that 's in tune with the nature of
    man.'

.   .   .   .

    ' But stay, here comes Tityrus Griswold,[1]
        and leads on
The flocks whom he first plucks alive, and
    then feeds on, —   70
A loud-cackling swarm, in whose feathers
    warm drest,
He goes for as perfect a — swan as the
    rest.

    'There comes Emerson first, whose rich
        words, every one,
Are like gold nails in temples to hang tro-
    phies on,
Whose prose is grand verse, while his
    verse, the Lord knows,
Is some of it pr— No, 't is not even
    prose;
I 'm speaking of metres; some poems have
    welled
From those rare depths of soul that have
    ne'er been excelled;
They 're not epics, but that does n't matter
    a pin,
In creating, the only hard thing 's to begin;
A grass-blade 's no easier to make than an
    oak;   81
If you 've once found the way, you 've
    achieved the grand stroke;
In the worst of his poems are mines of rich
    matter,
But thrown in a heap with a crash and a
    clatter,
Now it is not one thing nor another alone
Makes a poem, but rather the general
    tone,
The something pervading, uniting the
    whole,
The before unconceived, unconceivable soul,

[1] Rev. R. W. Griswold published in 1842 *The Poets and Poetry of America*, in 1846 *The Prose Writers of America*, and in 1848 *The Female Poets of America*.

So that just in removing this trifle or that, you
Take away, as it were, a chief limb of the statue; 90
Roots, wood, bark, and leaves singly perfect may be,
But, clapt hodge-podge together, they don't make a tree.

'But, to come back to Emerson (whom, by the way,
I believe we left waiting), — his is, we may say,
A Greek head on right Yankee shoulders, whose range
Has Olympus for one pole, for t' other the Exchange;
He seems, to my thinking (although I'm afraid
The comparison must, long ere this, have been made),
A Plotinus-Montaigne, where the Egyptian's gold mist
And the Gascon's shrewd wit cheek-by-jowl coexist; 100
All admire, and yet scarcely six converts he's got
To I don't (nor they either) exactly know what;
For though he builds glorious temples, 't is odd
He leaves never a doorway to get in a god.
'T is refreshing to old-fashioned people like me
To meet such a primitive Pagan as he,
In whose mind all creation is duly respected
As parts of himself — just a little projected;
And who's willing to worship the stars and the sun,
A convert to — nothing but Emerson. 110
So perfect a balance there is in his head,
That he talks of things sometimes as if they were dead;
Life, nature, love, God, and affairs of that sort,
He looks at as merely ideas; in short,
As if they were fossils stuck round in a cabinet,
Of such vast extent that our earth's a mere dab in it;
Composed just as he is inclined to conjecture her,
Namely, one part pure earth, ninety-nine parts pure lecturer;

You are filled with delight at his clear demonstration,
Each figure, word, gesture, just fits the occasion, 120
With the quiet precision of science he'll sort 'em,
But you can't help suspecting the whole a post mortem.

'There are persons, mole-blind to the soul's make and style,
Who insist on a likeness 'twixt him and Carlyle;
To compare him with Plato would be vastly fairer,
Carlyle's the more burly, but E. is the rarer;
He sees fewer objects, but clearlier, truelier,
If C.'s as original, E.'s more peculiar;
That he's more of a man you might say of the one,
Of the other he's more of an Emerson; 130
C.'s the Titan, as shaggy of mind as of limb, —
E. the clear-eyed Olympian, rapid and slim;
The one's two thirds Norseman, the other half Greek,
Where the one's most abounding, the other's to seek;
C.'s generals require to be seen in the mass, —
E.'s specialties gain if enlarged by the glass;
C. gives nature and God his own fits of the blues,
And rims common-sense things with mystical hues, —
E. sits in a mystery calm and intense,
And looks coolly around him with sharp common-sense; 140
C. shows you how every-day matters unite
With the dim transdiurnal recesses of night, —
While E., in a plain, preternatural way,
Makes mysteries matters of mere every day;
C. draws all his characters quite à la Fuseli, —
Not sketching their bundles of muscles and thews illy,
He paints with a brush so untamed and profuse
They seem nothing but bundles of muscles and thews;

E. is rather like Flaxman, lines strait and
    severe,
And a colorless outline, but full, round, and
    clear; —   150
To the men he thinks worthy he frankly
    accords
The design of a white marble statue in
    words.
C. labors to get at the centre, and then
Take a reckoning from there of his actions
    and men;
E. calmly assumes the said centre as
    granted,
And, given himself, has whatever is wanted.

   'He has imitators in scores, who omit
No part of the man but his wisdom and
    wit, —
Who go carefully o'er the sky-blue of his
    brain,
And when he has skimmed it once, skim it
    again;   160
If at all they resemble him, you may be sure
    it is
Because their shoals mirror his mists and
    obscurities,
As a mud-puddle seems deep as heaven for
    a minute,
While a cloud that floats o'er is reflected
    within it.

   'There comes ——, for instance; to see
    him's rare sport,
Tread in Emerson's tracks with legs pain-
    fully short;
How he jumps, how he strains, and gets red
    in the face,
To keep step with the mystagogue's natural
    pace !
He follows as close as a stick to a rocket,
His fingers exploring the prophet's each
    pocket.   170
Fie, for shame, brother bard; with good fruit
    of your own,
Can't you let Neighbor Emerson's orchards
    alone ?
Besides, 't is no use, you 'll not find e'en a
    core, —
—— has picked up all the windfalls before.
They might strip every tree, and E. never
    would catch 'em,
His Hesperides have no rude dragon to
    watch 'em;
When they send him a dishful, and ask him
    to try 'em,

He never suspects how the sly rogues came
    by 'em;
He wonders why 't is there are none such
    his trees on,
And thinks 'em the best he has tasted this
    season.   180

  .   .   .   .

   'There is Bryant,[1] as quiet, as cool, and
    as dignified,
As a smooth, silent iceberg, that never is
    ignified,
Save when by reflection 't is kindled o'
    nights
With a semblance of flame by the chill
    Northern Lights.
He may rank (Griswold says so) first bard
    of your nation
(There 's no doubt that he stands in su-
    preme iceolation),
Your topmost Parnassus he may set his
    heel on,
But no warm applauses come, peal follow-
    ing peal on, —
He's too smooth and too polished to hang
    any zeal on:
Unqualified merits, I 'll grant, if you
    choose, he has 'em,   190
But he lacks the one merit of kindling
    enthusiasm;
If he stir you at all, it is just, on my soul,
Like being stirred up with the very North
    Pole.

   'He is very nice reading in summer,
    but *inter*
Nos, we don't want *extra* freezing in winter;
Take him up in the depth of July, my ad-
    vice is,

---

[1] Compare three passages in *Lowell's Letters* (quoted
by permission of Messrs. Harper and Brothers) : —
  'The Bryant is funny, and as fair as I could make it,
immitigably just. Indeed I have endeavored to be so
in all. . . . The only verses I shall add regarding him
are some complimentary ones which I left for a happier
mood after I had written the comic part.' . . . *May
12, 1848.* See the whole passage, *Lowell's Letters*, vol.
i, p. 131.
  'I am quite sensible that I did not do Mr. Bryant
justice in the "Fable." But there was no personal feeling in what I said — though I have regretted what I
did say because it might seem personal. I am now
asked to write a review of his poems for the *North
American*. If I do, I shall try to do him justice.' *January 11, 1855;* vol. i, p. 221.
  'I am all the gladder I wrote my poem for Bryant's
birthday [" On Board the Seventy-Six,"] — a kind of
palinode to what I said of him in the "Fable for Critics," which has something of youth's infallibility in it,
or at any rate of youth's irresponsibility.' *February 9,
1887.* See the whole letter (to Mr. Richard Watson
Gilder), *Lowell's Letters*, vol. ii, p. 334.

When you feel an Egyptian devotion to
    ices.
But, deduct all you can, there's enough
    that's right good in him,
He has a true soul for field, river, and
    wood in him;
And his heart, in the midst of brick walls,
    or where'er it is,   200
Glows, softens, and thrills with the tender-
    est charities —
To you mortals that delve in this trade-
    ridden planet ?
No, to old Berkshire's hills, with their
    limestone and granite.
If you're one who *in loco* (add *foco* here)
    desipis,
You will get of his outermost heart (as I
    guess) a piece;
But you'd get deeper down if you came as
    a precipice,
And would break the last seal of its in-
    wardest fountain,
If you only could palm yourself off for a
    mountain.
Mr. Quivis, or somebody quite as discerning,
Some scholar who's hourly expecting his
    learning,   210
Calls B. the American Wordsworth; but
    Wordsworth
May be rated at more than your whole
    tuneful herd's worth.
No, don't be absurd, he's an excellent
    Bryant;
But, my friends, you'll endanger the life
    of your client,
By attempting to stretch him up into a
    giant:
If you choose to compare him, I think
    there are two per-
-sons fit for a parallel — Thomson and
    Cowper; [1]
I don't mean exactly, — there's something
    of each,
There's T.'s love of nature, C.'s penchant
    to preach;
Just mix up their minds so that C.'s spice
    of craziness   220
Shall balance and neutralize T.'s turn for
    laziness,
And it gives you a brain cool, quite fric-
    tionless, quiet,

[1] To demonstrate quickly and easily how per-
-versely absurd 't is to sound this name *Cowper*,
As people in general call him named *super*,
I remark that he rhymes it himself with horse-
trooper

Whose internal police nips the buds of all
    riot, —
A brain like a permanent strait-jacket put
    on
The heart that strives vainly to burst off a
    button, —
A brain which, without being slow or me-
    chanic,
Does more than a larger less drilled, more
    volcanic;
He's a Cowper condensed, with no crazi-
    ness bitten,
And the advantage that Wordsworth be-
    fore him had written.

'But, my dear little bardlings, don't
    prick up your ears   230
Nor suppose I would rank you and Bryant
    as peers;
If I call him an iceberg, I don't mean to say
There is nothing in that which is grand in
    its way;
He is almost the one of your poets that
    knows
How much grace, strength, and dignity lie
    in Repose;
If he sometimes fall short, he is too wise
    to mar
His thought's modest fulness by going too
    far;
'T would be well if your authors should all
    make a trial
Of what virtue there is in severe self-
    denial,
And measure their writings by Hesiod's
    staff,   240
Which teaches that all has less value than
    half.

'There is Whittier, whose swelling and
    vehement heart
Strains the strait-breasted drab of the
    Quaker apart,
And reveals the live Man, still supreme
    and erect,
Underneath the bemummying wrappers of
    sect;
There was ne'er a man born who had more
    of the swing
Of the true lyric bard and all that kind of
    thing;
And his failures arise (though he seem not
    to know it)
From the very same cause that has made
    him a poet, —

A fervor of mind which knows no separa-
tion   250
'Twixt simple excitement and pure inspira-
tion,
As my Pythoness erst sometimes erred
· from not knowing
If 't were I or mere wind through her tripod
was blowing;
Let his mind once get head in its favorite
direction
And the torrent of verse bursts the dams
of reflection,
While, borne with the rush of the metre
along,
The poet may chance to go right or go
wrong,
Content with the whirl and delirium of
song;
Then his grammar's not always correct,
nor his rhymes,
And he 's prone to repeat his own lyrics
sometimes,   260
Not his best, though, for those are struck
off at white-heats
When the heart in his breast like a trip-
hammer beats,
And can ne'er be repeated again any more
Than they could have been carefully plot-
ted before:
Like old what 's-his-name there at the bat-
tle of Hastings
(Who, however, gave more than mere
rhythmical bastings),
Our Quaker leads off metaphorical fights
For reform and whatever they call human
rights,
Both singing and striking in front of the war,
And hitting his foes with the mallet of
Thor;   270
Anne haec, one exclaims, on beholding his
knocks,
Vestis filii tui, O leather-clad Fox ?
Can that be thy son, in the battle's mid din,
Preaching brotherly love and then driving
it in
To the brain of the tough old Goliath of sin,
With the smoothest of pebbles from Cas-
taly's spring
Impressed on his hard moral sense with a
sling ?

  ' All honor and praise to the right-hearted
bard
Who was true to The Voice when such service was hard,

Who himself was so free he dared sing for
the slave   280
When to look but a protest in silence was
brave;
All honor and praise to the women and men
Who spoke out for the dumb and the
down-trodden then !
It needs not to name them, already for
each
I see History preparing the statue and
niche;
They were harsh, but shall *you* be so shocked
at hard words
Who have beaten your pruning-hooks up
into swords,
Whose rewards and hurrahs men are surer
to gain
By the reaping of men and of women than
grain ?
Why should *you* stand aghast at their fierce
wordy war, if   290
You scalp one another for Bank or for
Tariff ?
Your calling them cut-throats and knaves
all day long
Does n't prove that the use of hard lan-
guage is wrong;
While the World's heart beats quicker to
think of such men
As signed Tyranny's doom with a bloody
steel-pen,
While on Fourth-of-Julys beardless orators
fright one
With hints at Harmodius and Aristogeiton,
You need not look shy at your sisters and
brothers
Who stab with sharp words for the free-
dom of others; —
No, a wreath, twine a wreath for the loyal
and true   300
Who, for sake of the many, dared stand
with the few,
Not of blood-spattered laurel for enemies
braved,
But of broad, peaceful oak-leaves for citizens saved !

  .   .   .   .

  'There is Hawthorne, with genius so
shrinking and rare
That you hardly at first see the strength
that is there;
A frame so robust, with a nature so sweet,
So earnest, so graceful, so lithe and so fleet,
Is worth a descent from Olympus to meet;

'T is as if a rough oak that for ages had
stood,
With his gnarled bony branches like ribs of
the wood, 310
Should bloom, after cycles of struggle and
scathe,
With a single anemone trembly and rathe;
His strength is so tender, his wildness so
meek,
That a suitable parallel sets one to seek, —
He 's a John Bunyan Fouqué, a Puritan
Tieck;
When Nature was shaping him, clay was
not granted
For making so full-sized a man as she
wanted,
So, to fill out her model, a little she spared
From some finer-grained stuff for a woman
prepared,
And she could not have hit a more excellent
plan 320
For making him fully and perfectly man.

. . . .

'Here 's Cooper, who 's written six vol-
umes to show
He 's as good as a lord: well, let 's grant
that he 's so;
If a person prefer that description of praise,
Why, a coronet 's certainly cheaper than
bays;
But he need take no pains to convince us
he 's not
(As his enemies say) the American Scott.
Choose any twelve men, and let C. read
aloud
That one of his novels of which he 's most
proud,
And I 'd lay any bet that, without ever
quitting 330
Their box, they 'd be all, to a man, for ac-
quitting.
He has drawn you one character, though,
that is new,
One wildflower he 's plucked that is wet
with the dew
Of this fresh Western world, and, the thing
not to mince,
He has done naught but copy it ill ever
since;
His Indians, with proper respect be it said,
Are just Natty Bumppo, daubed over with
red,
And his very Long Toms are the same
useful Nat,

Rigged up in duck pants and a sou'wester
hat
(Though once in a Coffin, a good chance
was found 340
To have slipped the old fellow away under-
ground).
All his other men-figures are clothes upon
sticks,
The *dernière chemise* of a man in a fix
(As a captain besieged, when his garrison 's
small,
Sets up caps upon poles to be seen o'er the
wall);
And the women he draws from one model
don't vary,
All sappy as maples and flat as a prairie.
When a character 's wanted, he goes to the
task
As a cooper would do in composing a
cask;
He picks out the staves, of their qualities
heedful, 350
Just hoops them together as tight as is
needful,
And, if the best fortune should crown the
attempt, he
Has made at the most something wooden
and empty.

'Don't suppose I would underrate Coop-
er's abilities;
If I thought you 'd do that, I should feel
very ill at ease;
The men who have given to *one* character life
And objective existence are not very rife;
You may number them all, both prose-
writers and singers,
Without overrunning the bounds of your
fingers,
And Natty won't go to oblivion quicker 360
Than Adams the Parson or Primrose the
vicar.

'There is one thing in Cooper I like,
too, and that is
That on manners he lectures his country-
men gratis;
Not precisely so either, because, for a
rarity,
He is paid for his tickets in unpopularity.
Now he may overcharge his American pic-
tures,
But you 'll grant there 's a good deal of
truth in his strictures;
And I honor the man who is willing to sink

Half his present repute for the freedom to
    think,
And, when he has thought, be his cause
    strong or weak,   370
Will risk t' other half for the freedom to
    speak,
Caring naught for what vengeance the mob
    has in store,
Let that mob be the upper ten thousand or
    lower.

   'There are truths you Americans need to
    be told,
And it never 'll refute them to swagger and
    scold;
John Bull, looking o'er the Atlantic, in
    choler
At your aptness for trade, says you worship
    the dollar;
But to scorn such eye-dollar-try 's what
    very few do,
And John goes to that church as often as
    you do.
No matter what John says, don't try to
    outcrow him,   380
'T is enough to go quietly on and outgrow
    him;
Like most fathers, Bull hates to see Num-
    ber One
Displacing himself in the mind of his son,
And detests the same faults in himself
    he 'd neglected
When he sees them again in his child's
    glass reflected;
To love one another you 're too like by half;
If he is a bull, you 're a pretty stout calf,
And tear your own pasture for naught but
    to show
What a nice pair of horns you 're begin-
    ning to grow.

   'There are one or two things I should
    just like to hint,   390
For you don't often get the truth told you
    in print;
The most of you (this is what strikes all
    beholders)
Have a mental and physical stoop in the
    shoulders;
Though you ought to be free as the winds
    and the waves,
You 've the gait and the manners of run-
    away slaves;
Though you brag of your New World, you
    don't half believe in it;

And as much of the Old as is possible
    weave in it;
Your goddess of freedom, a tight, buxom
    girl,
With lips like a cherry and teeth like a
    pearl,
With eyes bold as Herë's, and hair floating
    free,   400
And full of the sun as the spray of the sea,
Who can sing at a husking or romp at a
    shearing,
Who can trip through the forests alone
    without fearing,
Who can drive home the cows with a song
    through the grass,
Keeps glancing aside into Europe's cracked
    glass,
Hides her red hands in gloves, pinches up
    her lithe waist,
And makes herself wretched with transma-
    rine taste;
She loses her fresh country charm when
    she takes
Any mirror except her own rivers and
    lakes.

   'You steal Englishmen's books and think
    Englishmen's thought,   410
With their salt on her tail your wild eagle
    is caught;
Your literature suits its each whisper and
    motion
To what will be thought of it over the
    ocean;
The cast clothes of Europe your statesman-
    ship tries
And mumbles again the old blarneys and
    lies; —
Forget Europe wholly, your veins throb
    with blood,
To which the dull current in hers is but
    mud:
Let her sneer, let her say your experiment
    fails,
In her voice there 's a tremble e'en now
    while she rails,
And your shore will soon be in the nature
    of things   420
Covered thick with gilt drift-wood of cast-
    away kings,
Where alone, as it were in a Longfellow's
    Waif,
Her fugitive pieces will find themselves safe.
O my friends, thank your god, if you have
    one, that he

'Twixt the Old World and you set the gulf
  of a sea;
Be strong-backed, brown-handed, upright
  as your pines,
By the scale of a hemisphere shape your
  designs,
Be true to yourselves and this new nine-
  teenth age,
As a statue by Powers, or a picture by Page,
Plough, sail, forge, build, carve, paint,
  make all over new,   430
To your own New-World instincts contrive
  to be true,
Keep your ears open wide to the Future's
  first call,
Be whatever you will, but yourselves first
  of all,
Stand fronting the dawn on Toil's heaven-
  scaling peaks,
And become my new race of more practical
  Greeks.'

.   .   .   .

Here Miranda[1] came up, and said, 'Phœ-
  bus! you know
That the Infinite Soul has its infinite woe,
As I ought to know, having lived cheek by
  jowl,
Since the day I was born, with the Infinite
  Soul;
I myself introduced, I myself, I alone,   440
To my Land's better life authors solely my
  own,
Who the sad heart of earth on their shoul-
  ders have taken,
Whose works sound a depth by Life's
  quiet unshaken,
Such as Shakespeare, for instance, the
  Bible, and Bacon,
Not to mention my own works; Time's
  nadir is fleet,
And, as for myself, I 'm quite out of con-
  ceit ' —

[1] Margaret Fuller. Lowell wrote to Briggs, March
26, 1848: 'I think I shall say nothing about Margaret
Fuller (though she offer so fair a target), because she
has done me an ill-natured turn. I shall revenge myself
amply upon her by writing better. She is a very foolish, conceited woman, who has got together a great deal
of information, but not enough *knowledge* to save her
from being ill-tempered. However, the temptation may
be too strong for me. It certainly would have been if
she had never said anything about me. Even Maria
thinks I ought to give her a line or two.' (*Lowell's
Letters*, vol. i, p. 128. Quoted by permission of Messrs.
Harper and Brothers.) See Margaret Fuller's *Papers
on Literature and Art*, or Greenslet's *Lowell*, p. 63;
and Poe's review of the *Fable for Critics*, in his *Works*,
vol. xiii, pp. 165-175.

' Quite out of conceit! I 'm enchanted to
  hear it,'
Cried Apollo aside. 'Who 'd have thought
  she was near it?
To be sure, one is apt to exhaust those
  commodities
One uses too fast, yet in this case as odd
  it is   450
As if Neptune should say to his turbots
  and whitings,
" I 'm as much out of salt as Miranda's own
  writings "
(Which, as she in her own happy manner
  has said,
Sound a depth, for 't is one of the functions
  of lead).
She often has asked me if I could not find
A place somewhere near me that suited her
  mind;
I know but a single one vacant, which she,
With her rare talent that way, would fit to
  a T.
And it would not imply any pause or cessa-
  tion
In the work she esteems her peculiar voca-
  tion, —   460
She may enter on duty to-day, if she chooses,
And remain Tiring-woman for life to the
  Muses.'

.   .   .   .

' There comes Poe, with his raven, like
  Barnaby Rudge,
Three fifths of him genius and two fifths
  sheer fudge,
Who talks like a book of iambs and pen-
  tameters,
In a way to make people of common sense
  damn metres,
Who has written some things quite the
  best of their kind,
But the heart somehow seems all squeezed
  out by the mind,
Who—   But hey-day!   What 's this?
  Messieurs Mathews and Poe,
You must n't fling mud-balls at Longfellow
  so,   470
Does it make a man worse that his charac-
  ter 's such
As to make his friends love him (as you
  think) too much?
Why, there is not a bard at this moment
  alive
More willing than he that his fellows
  should thrive;

While you are abusing him thus, even now
He would help either one of you out of a
   slough;
You may say that he 's smooth and all that
   till you 're hoarse,
But remember that elegance also is force;
After polishing granite as much as you
   will,
The heart keeps its tough old persistency
   still;   480
Deduct all you can, *that* still keeps you at
   bay;
Why, he 'll live till men weary of Collins
   and Gray.
I 'm not over-fond of Greek metres in Eng-
   lish,
To me rhyme 's a gain, so it be not too jin-
   glish,
And your modern hexameter verses are no
   more
Like Greek ones than sleek Mr. Pope is
   like Homer;
As the roar of the sea to the coo of a pigeon
   is,
So, compared to your moderns, sounds old
   Melesigenes;
I may be too partial, the reason, perhaps,
   o 't is
That I 've heard the old blind man recite
   his own rhapsodies,   490
And my ear with that music impregnate
   may be,
Like the poor exiled shell with the soul of
   the sea,
Or as one can't bear Strauss when his na-
   ture is cloven
To its deeps within deeps by the stroke of
   Beethoven;
But, set that aside, and 't is truth that I
   speak,
Had Theocritus written in English, not
   Greek,
I believe that his exquisite sense would
   scarce change a line
In that rare, tender, virgin-like pastoral
   Evangeline.
That 's not ancient nor modern, its place is
   apart
Where time has no sway, in the realm of
   pure Art,   500
'T is a shrine of retreat from Earth's hub-
   bub and strife
As quiet and chaste as the author's own
   life.

.   ,   ,   ,   .   .   .

'What! Irving? thrice welcome, warm
   heart and fine brain,
You bring back the happiest spirit from
   Spain,
And the gravest sweet humor, that ever
   were there
Since Cervantes met death in his gentle
   despair;
Nay, don't be embarrassed, nor look so be-
   seeching,
I sha'n't run directly against my own
   preaching,
And, having just laughed at their Raphaels
   and Dantes,
Go to setting you up beside matchless Cer-
   vantes;   510
But allow me to speak what I honestly
   feel, —
To a true poet-heart add the fun of Dick
   Steele,
Throw in all of Addison, *minus* the chill,
With the whole of that partnership's stock
   and good-will,
Mix well, and while stirring, hum o'er, as
   a spell,
The fine *old* English Gentleman, simmer it
   well,
Sweeten just to your own private liking,
   then strain,
That only the finest and clearest re-
   main,
Let it stand out of doors till a soul it re-
   ceives
From the warm lazy sun loitering down
   through green leaves,   520
And you 'll find a choice nature, not wholly
   deserving
A name either English or Yankee, — just
   Irving.'

.   .   .   .

Here, 'Forgive me, Apollo,' I cried,
   'while I pour
My heart out to my birthplace:[1] O loved
   more and more
Dear Baystate, from whose rocky bosom
   thy sons
Should suck milk, strong-will-giving, brave,
   such as runs

[1] 'The only passage in "A Fable for Critics" which he [later] dwelt upon with genuine delight was his apostrophe to Massachusetts, and that is almost out of key with the rest of the poem.' (Scudder's *Life of Lowell*, vol. i, p. 266.) The passage should now be read as an apostrophe to America rather than to Massachusetts. It is far more true of the West than of New England, and of America as a whole than of any section.

In the veins of old Graylock — who is it
that dares
Call thee pedler, a soul wrapped in bank-
books and shares ?
It is false ! She 's a Poet ! I see, as I
write,
Along the far railroad the steam - snake
glide white, 530
The cataract-throb of her mill-hearts I
hear,
The swift strokes of trip-hammers weary
my ear,
Sledges ring upon anvils, through logs the
saw screams,
Blocks swing to their place, beetles drive
home the beams: —
It is songs such as these that she croons to
the din
Of her fast-flying shuttles, year out and
year in,
While from earth's farthest corner there
comes not a breeze
But wafts her the buzz of her gold-glean-
ing bees:
What though those horn hands have as yet
found small time
For painting and sculpture and music and
rhyme ? 540
These will come in due order; the need
that pressed sorest
Was to vanquish the seasons, the ocean, the
forest,
To bridle and harness the rivers, the
steam,
Making those whirl her mill-wheels, this
tug in her team,
To vassalize old tyrant Winter, and
make
Him delve surlily for her on river and
lake; —
When this New World was parted, she
strove not to shirk
Her lot in the heirdom, the tough, silent
Work,
The hero-share ever from Herakles down
To Odin, the Earth's iron sceptre and
crown: 550
Yes, thou dear, noble Mother ! if ever
men's praise
Could be claimed for creating heroical
lays,
Thou hast won it; if ever the laurel
divine
Crowned the Maker and Builder, that glory
is thine !

Thy songs are right epic, they tell how this
rude
Rock-rib of our earth here was tamed and
subdued;
Thou hast written them plain on the face
of the planet
In brave, deathless letters of iron and
granite;
Thou hast printed them deep for all time;
they are set
From the same runic type-fount and alpha-
bet 560
With thy stout Berkshire hills and the
arms of thy Bay, —
They are staves from the burly old May-
flower lay.
If the drones of the Old World, in queru-
lous ease,
Ask thy Art and thy Letters, point proudly
to these,
Or, if they deny these are Letters and
Art,
Toil on with the same old invincible
heart;
Thou art rearing the pedestal broad-based
and grand
Whereon the fair shapes of the Artist shall
stand,
And creating, through labors undaunted
and long,
The theme for all Sculpture and Painting
and Song ! 570

' But my good mother Baystate wants no
praise of mine,
She learned from *her* mother a precept divine
About something that butters no parsnips,
her *forte*
In another direction lies, work is her
sport
(Though she 'll curtsey and set her cap
straight, that she will,
If you talk about Plymouth and red Bunker's hill).
Dear, notable goodwife ! by this time of
night,
Her hearth is swept neatly, her fire burning
bright,
And she sits in a chair (of home plan and
make) rocking,
Musing much, all the while, as she darns on
a stocking, 580
Whether turkeys will come pretty high
next Thanksgiving,

Whether flour 'll be so dear, for, as sure
    as she 's living,
She will use rye-and-injun then, whether
    the pig
By this time ain't got pretty tolerable
    big,
And whether to sell it outright will be
    best,
Or to smoke hams and shoulders and salt
    down the rest, —
At this minute, she 'd swop all my verses,
    ah, cruel !
For the last patent stove that is saving of
    fuel;
So I 'll just let Apollo go on, for his
    phiz
Shows I 've kept him awaiting too long as
    it is.'   590

' If our friend, there, who seems a re-
    porter, is done
With his burst of emotion, why, *I* will go
    on,'
Said Apollo; some smiled, and, indeed, I
    must own
There was something sarcastic, perhaps, in
    his tone: —

' There 's Holmes, who is matchless
    among you for wit;
A Leyden-jar always full-charged, from
    which flit
The electrical tingles of hit after hit;
In long poems 't is painful sometimes, and
    invites
A thought of the way the new Telegraph
    writes,
Which pricks down its little sharp sentences
    spitefully   600
As if you got more than you 'd title to
    rightfully,
And you find yourself hoping its wild father
    Lightning
Would flame in for a second and give you a
    fright'ning.
He has perfect sway of what I call a sham
    metre,
But many admire it, the English pentame-
    ter,
And Campbell, I think, wrote most com-
    monly worse,
With less nerve, swing, and fire in the same
    kind of verse,

Nor e'er achieved aught in 't so worthy of
    praise
As the tribute of Holmes to the grand
    Marseillaise.
You went crazy last year over Bulwer's
    New Timon; —   610
Why, if B., to the day of his dying, should
    rhyme on,
Heaping verses on verses and tomes upon
    tomes,
He could ne'er reach the best point and
    vigor of Holmes.
His are just the fine hands, too, to weave
    you a lyric
Full of fancy, fun, feeling, or spiced with
    satiric
In a measure so kindly you doubt if the
    toes
That are trodden upon are your own or
    your foes'.

' There is Lowell, who 's striving Par-
    nassus to climb
With a whole bale of *isms* tied together
    with rhyme,
He might get on alone, spite of brambles
    and boulders,   620
But he can't with that bundle he has on his
    shoulders,
The top of the hill he will ne'er come nigh
    reaching
Till he learns the distinction 'twixt singing
    and preaching;
His lyre has some chords that would ring
    pretty well,
But he 'd rather by half make a drum of
    the shell,
And rattle away till he 's old as Methusa-
    lem,
At the head of a march to the last new
    Jerusalem.'

.   .   .   .

Here Miranda came up and began, ' As
    to that — '
Apollo at once seized his gloves, cane, and
    hat,
And, seeing the place getting rapidly
    cleared,   630
I too snatched my notes and forthwith
    disappeared.
1847-48.   1848.

THE VISION OF SIR LAUNFAL [1]

PRELUDE TO PART FIRST [2]

OVER his keys the musing organist,
  Beginning doubtfully and far away,
First lets his fingers wander as they list,
  And builds a bridge from Dreamland for
    his lay:
Then, as the touch of his loved instrument
  Gives hope and fervor, nearer draws his
    theme,
First guessed by faint auroral flushes sent
  Along the wavering vista of his dream.
Not only around our infancy
Doth heaven with all its splendors lie; [3] 10
Daily, with souls that cringe and plot,
We Sinais climb and know it not. [4]

Over our manhood bend the skies;
  Against our fallen and traitor lives
The great winds utter prophecies;
  With our faint hearts the mountain
    strives;
Its arms outstretched, the druid wood
  Waits with its benedicite;

And to our age's drowsy blood
  Still shouts the inspiring sea. 20

Earth gets its price for what Earth gives
    us;
  The beggar is taxed for a corner to die
    in,
The priest hath his fee who comes and
    shrives us,
  We bargain for the graves we lie in;
At the devil's booth are all things sold,
Each ounce of dross costs its ounce of
    gold;
For a cap and bells our lives we pay,
Bubbles we buy with a whole soul's task-
    ing:
'T is heaven alone that is given away,
'T is only God may be had for the ask-
    ing; 30
No price is set on the lavish summer;
June may be had by the poorest comer.

And what is so rare as a day in June?
  Then, if ever, come perfect days;
Then Heaven tries earth if it be in tune,
  And over it softly her warm ear lays;
Whether we look, or whether we listen,
We hear life murmur, or see it glisten;
Every clod feels a stir of might,
  An instinct within it that reaches and
    towers, 40
And, groping blindly above it for light,
  Climbs to a soul in grass and flowers;
The flush of life may well be seen
  Thrilling back over hills and valleys;
The cowslip startles in meadows green,
  The buttercup catches the sun in its
    chalice,
And there 's never a leaf nor a blade too
    mean
  To be some happy creature's palace;
The little bird sits at his door in the sun,
  Atilt like a blossom among the leaves, 50
And lets his illumined being o'errun
  With the deluge of summer it receives;
His mate feels the eggs beneath her wings,
And the heart in her dumb breast flutters
    and sings;
He sings to the wide world, and she to her
    nest, —
In the nice ear of Nature which song is the
    best?

[1] According to the mythology of the Romancers, the San Greal, or Holy Grail, was the cup out of which Jesus partook of the Last Supper with his disciples. It was brought into England by Joseph of Arimathea, and remained there, an object of pilgrimage and adoration, for many years in the keeping of his lineal descendants. It was incumbent upon those who had charge of it to be chaste in thought, word, and deed; but one of the keepers having broken this condition, the Holy Grail disappeared. From that time it was a favorite enterprise of the knights of Arthur's court to go in search of it. Sir Galahad was at last successful in finding it, as may be read in the seventeenth book of the Romance of King Arthur. Tennyson has made Sir Galahad the subject of one of the most exquisite of his poems.

The plot (if I may give that name to anything so slight) of the following poem is my own, and, to serve its purposes, I have enlarged the circle of competition in search of the miraculous cup in such a manner as to include, not only other persons than the heroes of the Round Table, but also a period of time subsequent to the supposed date of King Arthur's reign. (LOWELL.)

[2] Holmes begins a poem of welcome to Lowell on his return from England: —

This is your month, the month of 'perfect days.'

June was indeed Lowell's month. Not only in the famous passage of this 'Prelude,' but in 'Under the Willows' (originally called 'A June Idyl'), 'Al Fresco' (originally 'A Day in June'), 'Sunthin' in the Pastoral Line' of the *Biglow Papers*, and 'The Nightingale in the Study,' he has made it peculiarly his own.

[3] Heaven lies about us in our Infancy! (WORDSWORTH, in the fifth stanza of the 'Ode: Intimations of Immortality.')

[4] See Lowell's letter, of Sunday, September 3, 1848, to his friend C. F. Briggs.

Now is the high-tide of the year,
  And whatever of life hath ebbed away
Comes flooding back with a ripply cheer,
  Into every bare inlet and creek and
    bay; 60
Now the heart is so full that a drop over-
    fills it,
We are happy now because God wills it;
No matter how barren the past may have
    been,
'T is enough for us now that the leaves are
    green;
We sit in the warm shade and feel right
    well
How the sap creeps up and the blossoms
    swell;
We may shut our eyes, but we cannot help
    knowing
That skies are clear and grass is grow-
    ing;
The breeze comes whispering in our ear,
That dandelions are blossoming near, 70
  That maize has sprouted, that streams
    are flowing,
That the river is bluer than the sky,
That the robin is plastering his house hard
    by;
And if the breeze kept the good news
    back,
For other couriers we should not lack;
  We could guess it all by yon heifer's
    lowing, —
And hark ! how clear bold chanticleer,
Warmed with the new wine of the year,
  Tells all in his lusty crowing !

Joy comes, grief goes, we know not how; 80
Everything is happy now,
  Everything is upward striving;
'T is as easy now for the heart to be
    true
As for grass to be green or skies to be
    blue, —
  'T is the natural way of living:
Who knows whither the clouds have fled ?
  In the unscarred heaven they leave no
    wake;
And the eyes forget the tears they have
    shed,
  The heart forgets its sorrow and ache;
The soul partakes the season's youth, 90
  And the sulphurous rifts of passion and
    woe
Lie deep 'neath a silence pure and smooth,
  Like burnt-out craters healed with snow.

What wonder if Sir Launfal now
Remembered the keeping of his vow ?

PART FIRST

I

' MY golden spurs now bring to me,
  And bring to me my richest mail,
For to-morrow I go over land and sea
  In search of the Holy Grail;
Shall never a bed for me be spread, 100
Nor shall a pillow be under my head,
Till I begin my vow to keep;
Here on the rushes will I sleep,
And perchance there may come a vision
    true
Ere day create the world anew.'
  Slowly Sir Launfal's eyes grew dim,
  Slumber fell like a cloud on him,
And into his soul the vision flew.

II

The crows flapped over by twos and threes,
In the pool drowsed the cattle up to their
    knees, 110
  The little birds sang as if it were
  The one day of summer in all the year,
And the very leaves seemed to sing on the
    trees:
The castle alone in the landscape lay
Like an outpost of winter, dull and gray:
'T was the proudest hall in the North
    Countree,
And never its gates might opened be,
Save to lord or lady of high degree;
Summer besieged it on every side,
But the churlish stone her assaults defied;
She could not scale the chilly wall, 121
Though around it for leagues her pavilions
    tall
Stretched left and right,
Over the hills and out of sight;
  Green and broad was every tent,
  And out of each a murmur went
Till the breeze fell off at night.

III

The drawbridge dropped with a surly clang,
And through the dark arch a charger sprang,
Bearing Sir Launfal, the maiden knight, 130
In his gilded mail, that flamed so bright
It seemed the dark castle had gathered all
Those shafts the fierce sun had shot over
    its wall

In his siege of three hundred summers
    long,
And, binding them all in one blazing sheaf,
    Had cast them forth: so, young and
        strong,
And lightsome as a locust-leaf,
Sir Launfal flashed forth in his maiden
    mail,
To seek in all climes for the Holy Grail.

IV

It was morning on hill and stream and
    tree,   140
    And morning in the young knight's heart;
Only the castle moodily
Rebuffed the gifts of the sunshine free,
    And gloomed by itself apart;
The season brimmed all other things up
Full as the rain fills the pitcher-plant's cup.

V

As Sir Launfal made morn through the
    darksome gate,
    He was 'ware of a leper, crouched by the
        same,
Who begged with his hand and moaned as
    he sate;
And a loathing over Sir Launfal came;
The sunshine went out of his soul with a
    thrill,   151
    The flesh 'neath his armor 'gan shrink
        and crawl,
And midway its leap his heart stood still
    Like a frozen waterfall;
For this man, so foul and bent of stature,
Rasped harshly against his dainty nature,
And seemed the one blot on the summer
    morn, —
So he tossed him a piece of gold in scorn.

VI

The leper raised not the gold from the
    dust:
' Better to me the poor man's crust,   160
Better the blessing of the poor,
Though I turn me empty from his door;
That is no true alms which the hand can
    hold;
He gives only the worthless gold
    Who gives from a sense of duty;
But he who gives but a slender mite,
And gives to that which is out of sight,
    That thread of the all-sustaining Beauty
Which runs through all and doth all
    unite, —

The hand cannot clasp the whole of his
    alms,   170
The heart outstretches its eager palms,
For a god goes with it and makes it store
To the soul that was starving in darkness
    before.'

PRELUDE TO PART SECOND [1]

DOWN swept the chill wind from the moun-
    tain peak,
    From the snow five thousand summers
        old;
On open wold and hilltop bleak
    It had gathered all the cold,
And whirled it like sleet on the wanderer's
    cheek;
It carried a shiver everywhere
From the unleafed boughs and pastures
    bare;   180
The little brook heard it and built a roof
'Neath which he could house him, winter-
    proof;
All night by the white stars' frosty gleams
He groined his arches and matched his
    beams;
Slender and clear were his crystal spars
As the lashes of light that trim the stars:
He sculptured every summer delight
In his halls and chambers out of sight;
Sometimes his tinkling waters slipt
Down through a frost-leaved forest-crypt,
Long, sparkling aisles of steel-stemmed
    trees   191
Bending to counterfeit a breeze;
Sometimes the roof no fretwork knew
But silvery mosses that downward grew;
Sometimes it was carved in sharp relief
With quaint arabesques of ice-fern leaf;
Sometimes it was simply smooth and clear
For the gladness of heaven to shine
    through, and here

---

[1] Last night . . . I walked to Watertown over the
snow with the new moon before me and a sky exactly
like that in Page's evening landscape. Orion was rising
behind me, and, as I stood on the hill just before you
enter the village, the stillness of the fields around me
was delicious, broken only by the tinkle of a little brook
which runs too swiftly for Frost to catch it. My picture of the brook in *Sir Launfal* was drawn from it.
But why do I send you this description — like the bones
of a chicken I had picked? Simply because I was so
happy as I stood there, and felt so sure of doing something that would justify my friends. (LOWELL, to
Briggs, in a letter of December, 1848, just after the
publication of *Sir Launfal*. Quoted by permission of
Messrs. Harper and Brothers.)

He had caught the nodding bulrush-tops
And hung them thickly with diamond
    drops,   200
That crystalled the beams of moon and
    sun,
And made a star of every one:
No mortal builder's most rare device
Could match this winter-palace of ice;
'T was as if every image that mirrored
    lay
In his depths serene through the summer
    day,
Each fleeting shadow of earth and sky,
    Lest the happy model should be lost,
Had been mimicked in fairy masonry
    By the elfin builders of the frost.   210

Within the hall are song and laughter,
    The cheeks of Christmas glow red and
        jolly,
And sprouting is every corbel and rafter
    With lightsome green of ivy and holly;
Through the deep gulf of the chimney
    wide
Wallows the Yule-log's roaring tide;
The broad flame-pennons droop and flap
    And belly and tug as a flag in the wind;
Like a locust shrills the imprisoned sap,
    Hunted to death in its galleries blind;   220
And swift little troops of silent sparks,
    Now pausing, now scattering away as in
        fear,
Go threading the soot-forest's tangled darks
Like herds of startled deer.

But the wind without was eager and sharp,
Of Sir Launfal's gray hair it makes a harp,
    And rattles and wrings
        The icy strings,
Singing, in dreary monotone,
    A Christmas carol of its own,   230
Whose burden still, as he might guess,
    Was 'Shelterless, shelterless, shelter-
        less!'
The voice of the seneschal flared like a
    torch
As he shouted the wanderer away from the
    porch,
And he sat in the gateway and saw all
    night
    The great hall-fire, so cheery and bold,
    Through the window-slits of the castle
        old,
Build out its piers of ruddy light
Against the drift of the cold.

PART SECOND

I

THERE was never a leaf on bush or tree,
The bare boughs rattled shudderingly;   241
The river was dumb and could not speak,
    For the weaver Winter its shroud had
        spun;
A single crow on the tree-top bleak
    From his shining feathers shed off the
        cold sun;
Again it was morning, but shrunk and cold,
As if her veins were sapless and old,
And she rose up decrepitly
For a last dim look at earth and sea.

II

Sir Launfal turned from his own hard
    gate,   250
For another heir in his earldom sate;
An old, bent man, worn out and frail,
He came back from seeking the Holy Grail;
Little he recked of his earldom's loss,
No more on his surcoat was blazoned the
    cross,
But deep in his soul the sign he wore,
The badge of the suffering and the poor.

III

Sir Launfal's raiment thin and spare
Was idle mail 'gainst the barbèd air,
For it was just at the Christmas time;   260
So he mused, as he sat, of a sunnier clime,
And sought for a shelter from cold and
    snow
In the light and warmth of long-ago;
He sees the snake-like caravan crawl
O'er the edge of the desert, black and
    small,
Then nearer and nearer, till, one by one,
He can count the camels in the sun,
As over the red-hot sands they pass
To where, in its slender necklace of grass,
The little spring laughed and leapt in the
    shade,   270
And with its own self like an infant played,
And waved its signal of palms.

IV

'For Christ's sweet sake, I beg an alms;'
The happy camels may reach the spring,
But Sir Launfal sees only the grewsome
    thing,
The leper, lank as the rain-blanched bone,
That cowers beside him, a thing as lone

And white as the ice-isles of Northern
    seas
In the desolate horror of his disease.

V

And Sir Launfal said, 'I behold in thee 280
An image of Him who died on the tree;
Thou also hast had thy crown of thorns,
Thou also hast had the world's buffets and
    scorns,
And to thy life were not denied
The wounds in the hands and feet and side:
Mild Mary's Son, acknowledge me;
Behold, through him, I give to thee!'

VI

Then the soul of the leper stood up in his
    eyes
    And looked at Sir Launfal, and straight-
    way he
Remembered in what a haughtier guise 290
    He had flung an alms to leprosie,
When he girt his young life up in gilded
    mail
And set forth in search of the Holy Grail.
The heart within him was ashes and dust;
He parted in twain his single crust,
He broke the ice on the streamlet's brink,
And gave the leper to eat and drink,
'Twas a mouldy crust of coarse brown
    bread,
'Twas water out of a wooden bowl, —
Yet with fine wheaten bread was the leper
    fed, 300
    And 't was red wine he drank with his
    thirsty soul.

VII

As Sir Launfal mused with a downcast
    face,
A light shone round about the place;
The leper no longer crouched at his side,
But stood before him glorified,
Shining and tall and fair and straight
As the pillar that stood by the Beautiful
    Gate, —
Himself the Gate whereby men can
Enter the temple of God in Man.

VIII

His words were shed softer than leaves
    from the pine, 310
And they fell on Sir Launfal as snows on
    the brine,

That mingle their softness and quiet in
    one
With the shaggy unrest they float down
    upon;
And the voice that was softer than silence
    said,
'Lo, it is I, be not afraid!
In many climes, without avail,
Thou hast spent thy life for the Holy
    Grail;
Behold, it is here, — this cup which thou
Didst fill at the streamlet for me but
    now;
This crust is my body broken for thee, 320
This water his blood that died on the
    tree;
The Holy Supper is kept, indeed,
In whatso we share with another's need;
Not what we give, but what we share,
For the gift without the giver is bare;
Who gives himself with his alms feeds
    three,
Himself, his hungering neighbor, and me.'

IX

Sir Launfal awoke as from a swound:
'The Grail in my castle here is found!
Hang my idle armor up on the wall, 330
Let it be the spider's banquet-hall;
He must be fenced with stronger mail
Who would seek and find the Holy Grail.'

X

The castle gate stands open now,
    And the wanderer is welcome to the
    hall
As the hangbird is to the elm-tree bough;
    No longer scowl the turrets tall,
The Summer's long siege at last is o'er;
When the first poor outcast went in at the
    door,
She entered with him in disguise, 340
And mastered the fortress by surprise;
There is no spot she loves so well on
    ground,
She lingers and smiles there the whole year
    round;
The meanest serf on Sir Launfal's land
Has hall and bower at his command;
And there's no poor man in the North
    Countree
But is lord of the earldom as much as
    he.

1848.   **1848.**

BEAVER BROOK [1]

HUSHED with broad sunlight lies the hill,
  And, minuting the long day's loss,
The cedar's shadow, slow and still,
  Creeps o'er its dial of gray moss.

Warm noon brims full the valley's cup,
  The aspen's leaves are scarce astir;
Only the little mill sends up
  Its busy, never-ceasing burr.

Climbing the loose-piled wall that hems
  The road along the mill-pond's brink, 10
From 'neath the arching barberry-stems,
  My footstep scares the shy chewink.

Beneath a bony buttonwood
  The mill's red door lets forth the din;
The whitened miller, dust-imbued,
  Flits past the square of dark within.

No mountain torrent's strength is here;
  Sweet Beaver, child of forest still,
Heaps its small pitcher to the ear,
  And gently waits the miller's will. 20

Swift slips Undine along the race
  Unheard, and then, with flashing bound,
Floods the dull wheel with light and grace,
  And, laughing, hunts the loath drudge
    round.

The miller dreams not at what cost
  The quivering millstones hum and whirl,
Nor how for every turn are tost
  Armfuls of diamond and of pearl.

But Summer cleared my happier eyes
  With drops of some celestial juice, 30
To see how Beauty underlies
  Forevermore each form of use.

And more; methought I saw that flood,
  Which now so dull and darkling steals,
Thick, here and there, with human blood,
  To turn the world's laborious wheels.

No more than doth the miller there,
  Shut in our several cells, do we
Know with what waste of beauty rare
  Moves every day's machinery. 40

Surely the wiser time shall come
  When this fine overplus of might,
No longer sullen, slow, and dumb,
  Shall leap to music and to light.

In that new childhood of the Earth
  Life of itself shall dance and play,
Fresh blood in Time's shrunk veins make
    mirth,
  And labor meet delight half-way.
1848.   1849.

BIBLIOLATRES

BOWING thyself in dust before a Book,
And thinking the great God is thine alone,
O rash iconoclast, thou wilt not brook
What gods the heathen carves in wood and
    stone,
As if the Shepherd who from the outer
    cold
Leads all his shivering lambs to one sure
    fold
Were careful for the fashion of his crook.

There is no broken reed so poor and base,
No rush, the bending tilt of swamp-fly
    blue,
But He therewith the ravening wolf can
    chase,   10
And guide his flock to springs and pastures
    new;
Through ways unlooked for, and through
    many lands,
Far from the rich folds built with human
    hands,
The gracious footprints of his love I trace.

And what art thou, own brother of the clod,
That from his hand the crook wouldst
    snatch away
And shake instead thy dry and sapless rod,
To scare the sheep out of the wholesome
    day?
Yea, what art thou, blind, unconverted
    Jew,
That with thy idol-volume's covers two 20
Wouldst make a jail to coop the living
    God?

---

[1] The little mill stands in a valley between one of the spurs of Wellington Hill and the main summit, just on the edge of Waltham. It is surely one of the loveliest spots in the world. It is one of my lions, and if you will make me a visit this spring I will take you up to hear it roar, and I will show you 'the oaks' — the largest, I fancy, left in the country. (LOWELL, in a letter of January 5, 1849. Quoted by permission of Messrs. Harper and Brothers.)

The poem was originally called 'The Mill.'

Thou hear'st not well the mountain organ-
tones
By prophet ears from Hor and Sinai caught,
Thinking the cisterns of those Hebrew
brains
Drew dry the springs of the All-knower's
thought,
Nor shall thy lips be touched with living
fire,
Who blow'st old altar-coals with sole de-
sire
To weld anew the spirit's broken châins.

God is not dumb, that He should speak no
more;
If thou hast wanderings in the wilder-
ness   30
And find'st not Sinai, 't is thy soul is poor;
There towers the Mountain of the Voice no
less,
Which whoso seeks shall find, but he who
bends,
Intent on manna still and mortal ends,
Sees it not, neither hears its thundered
lore.

Slowly the Bible of the race is writ,
And not on paper leaves nor leaves of
stone;
Each age, each kindred, adds a verse to
it,
Texts of despair or hope, of joy or moan.
While swings the sea, while mists the
mountains shroud,   40
While thunder's surges burst on cliffs of
cloud,
Still at the prophets' feet the nations sit.
                                        1849.

THE FIRST SNOW-FALL [1]

THE snow had begun in the gloaming,
  And busily all the night
Had been heaping field and highway
  With a silence deep and white.

Every pine and fir and hemlock
  Wore ermine too dear for an earl,

[1] See 'The Changeling' and 'She came and went.'
In sending this poem to the *Standard* Lowell wrote:
'Print *that* as if you loved it. Let not a comma be
blundered. Especially I fear they will put *gloaming*
for *gloaming* in the first line unless you look to it. May
you never have the key which shall unlock the whole
meaning of the poem to you!' (*Lowell's Letters*, Harper
and Brothers, letter of December 22, 1849.)

And the poorest twig on the elm-tree
  Was ridged inch deep with pearl.

From sheds new-roofed with Carrara
  Came Chanticleer's muffled crow,   10
The stiff rails softened to swan's-down,
  And still fluttered down the snow.

I stood and watched by the window
  The noiseless work of the sky,
And the sudden flurries of snow-birds,
  Like brown leaves whirling by.

I thought of a mound in sweet Auburn
  Where a little headstone stood;
How the flakes were folding it gently,
  As did robins the babes in the wood.   20

Up spoke our own little Mabel,
  Saying, ' Father, who makes it snow ? '
And I told of the good All-father
  Who cares for us here below.

Again I looked at the snow-fall,
  And thought of the leaden sky
That arched o'er our first great sorrow,
  When that mound was heaped so high.

I remembered the gradual patience
  That fell from that cloud like snow,   30
Flake by flake, healing and hiding
  The scar that renewed our woe.

And again to the child I whispered,
  ' The snow that husheth all,
Darling, the merciful Father
  Alone can make it fall ! '

Then, with eyes that saw not, I kissed
    her;
  And she, kissing back, could not know
That *my* kiss was given to her sister,
  Folded close under deepening snow.   40
1849.   1849.

THE SINGING LEAVES

A BALLAD

I

' WHAT fairings will ye that I bring ? '
  Said the King to his daughters three;
' For I to Vanity Fair am boun,
  Now say what shall they be ? '

Then up and spake the eldest daughter,
  That lady tall and grand:
' Oh, bring me pearls and diamonds great,
  And gold rings for my hand.'

Thereafter spake the second daughter,
  That was both white and red: 10
' For me bring silks that will stand alone,
  And a gold comb for my head.'

Then came the turn of the least daughter,
  That was whiter than thistle-down,
And among the gold of her blithesome hair
  Dim shone the golden crown.

' There came a bird this morning,
  And sang 'neath my bower eaves,
Till I dreamed, as his music made me,
  " Ask thou for the Singing Leaves." '   20

Then the brow of the King swelled crimson
  With a flush of angry scorn:
' Well have ye spoken, my two eldest,
  And chosen as ye were born;

' But she, like a thing of peasant race,
  That is happy binding the sheaves; '
Then he saw her dead mother in her face,
  And said, ' Thou shalt have thy leaves.'

II

He mounted and rode three days and nights
  Till he came to Vanity Fair,   30
And 't was easy to buy the gems and the silk,
  But no Singing Leaves were there.

Then deep in the greenwood rode he,
  And asked of every tree,
' Oh, if you have ever a Singing Leaf,
  I pray you give it me ! '

But the trees all kept their counsel,
  And never a word said they,
Only there sighed from the pine-tops
  A music of seas far away.   40

Only the pattering aspen
  Made a sound of growing rain,
That fell ever faster and faster,
  Then faltered to silence again.

' Oh, where shall I find a little foot-page
  That would win both hose and shoon,

And will bring to me the Singing Leaves
  If they grow under the moon ? '

Then lightly turned him Walter the page,
  By the stirrup as he ran: 50
' Now pledge you me the truesome word
  Of a king and gentleman,

' That you will give me the first, first thing
  You meet at your castle-gate,
And the Princess shall get the Singing Leaves,
  Or mine be a traitor's fate.'

The King's head dropt upon his breast
  A moment, as it might be;
'T will be my dog, he thought, and said,
  ' My faith I plight to thee.'   60

Then Walter took from next his heart
  A packet small and thin,
' Now give you this to the Princess Anne,
  The Singing Leaves are therein.'

III

As the King rode in at his castle-gate,
  A maiden to meet him ran,
And ' Welcome, father ! ' she laughed and cried
  Together, the Princess Anne.

' Lo, here the Singing Leaves,' quoth he,
  ' And woe, but they cost me dear ! '   70
She took the packet, and the smile
  Deepened down beneath the tear.

It deepened down till it reached her heart,
  And then gushed up again,
And lighted her tears as the sudden sun
  Transfigures the summer rain.

And the first Leaf, when it was opened,
  Sang: ' I am Walter the page,
And the songs I sing 'neath thy window
  Are my only heritage.'   80

And the second Leaf sang: ' But in the land
  That is neither on earth nor sea,
My lute and I are lords of more
  Than thrice this kingdom's fee.'

And the third Leaf sang, ' Be mine ! Be mine ! '
  And ever it sang, ' Be mine ! '

Then sweeter it sang and ever sweeter,
  And said, 'I am thine, thine, thine !'

At the first Leaf she grew pale enough,
  At the second she turned aside,   90
At the third, 't was as if a lily flushed
  With a rose's red heart's tide.

'Good counsel gave the bird,' said she,
  'I have my hope thrice o'er,
For they sing to my very heart,' she said,
  'And it sings to them evermore.'

She brought to him her beauty and truth,
  But and broad earldoms three,
And he made her queen of the broader lands
  He held of his lute in fee.   100
                                    1854.

WITHOUT AND WITHIN

My coachman, in the moonlight there,
  Looks through the side-light of the door;
I hear him with his brethren swear,
  As I could do, — but only more.

Flattening his nose against the pane,
  He envies me my brilliant lot,
Breathes on his aching fists in vain,
  And dooms me to a place more hot.

He sees me in to supper go,
  A silken wonder by my side,   10
Bare arms, bare shoulders, and a row
  Of flounces, for the door too wide.

He thinks how happy is my arm
  'Neath its white-gloved and jewelled
    load;
And wishes me some dreadful harm,
  Hearing the merry corks explode.

Meanwhile I inly curse the bore
  Of hunting still the same old coon,
And envy him, outside the door,
  In golden quiets of the moon.   20

The winter wind is not so cold
  As the bright smile he sees me win,
Nor the host's oldest wine so old
  As our poor gabble sour and thin.

I envy him the ungyved prance
  With which his freezing feet he warms,

And drag my lady's-chains and dance
  The galley-slave of dreary forms.

Oh, could he have my share of din,
  And I his quiet ! — past a doubt   30
'T would still be one man bored within,
  And just another bored without.

Nay, when, once paid my mortal fee,
  Some idler on my headstone grim
Traces the moss-blurred name, will he
  Think me the happier, or I him ?
                                    1854.

AUF WIEDERSEHEN [1]

SUMMER

The little gate was reached at last,
  Half hid in lilacs down the lane;
She pushed it wide, and, as she past,
A wistful look she backward cast,
  And said, — 'Auf wiedersehen !'

With hand on latch, a vision white
  Lingered reluctant, and again
Half doubting if she did aright,
Soft as the dews that fell that night,
  She said, — 'Auf wiedersehen !'

The lamp's clear gleam flits up the
    stair;
  I linger in delicious pain;
Ah, in that chamber, whose rich air
To breathe in thought I scarcely dare,
  Thinks she, — 'Auf wiedersehen ?' . . .

'T is thirteen years; once more I press
  The turf that silences the lane;
I hear the rustle of her dress,
I smell the lilacs, and — ah, yes,
  I hear 'Auf wiedersehen !'

Sweet piece of bashful maiden art !
  The English words had seemed too
    fain,
But these — they drew us heart to heart,
Yet held us tenderly apart;
  She said, 'Auf wiedersehen !'
                                    1854.

[1] Mrs. Lowell died October 27, 1853. See Longfellow's ' The Two Angels,' Scudder's *Life of Lowell*, vol. i, pp. 356-362, and *The Poems of Maria White Lowell*.

PALINODE

AUTUMN

STILL thirteen years: 't is autumn now
  On field and hill, in heart and brain;
The naked trees at evening sough;
The leaf to the forsaken bough
  Sighs not, — ' Auf wiedersehen !'

Two watched yon oriole's pendent dome,
  That now is void, and dank with rain,
And one, — oh, hope more frail than foam !
The bird to his deserted home
  Sings not, — ' Auf wiedersehen !'

The loath gate swings with rusty creak;
  Once, parting there, we played at pain;
There came a parting, when the weak
And fading lips essayed to speak
  Vainly, — ' Auf wiedersehen !'

Somewhere is comfort, somewhere faith,
  Though thou in outer dark remain;
One sweet sad voice ennobles death,
And still, for eighteen centuries saith
  Softly, — ' Auf wiedersehen !'

If earth another grave must bear,
  Yet heaven hath won a sweeter strain,
And something whispers my despair,
That, from an orient chamber there,
  Floats down, ' Auf wiedersehen !'

                                      1854.

THE WIND-HARP [1]

I TREASURE in secret some long, fine hair
  Of tenderest brown, but so inwardly
    golden
I half used to fancy the sunshine there,
So shy, so shifting, so waywardly rare,
  Was only caught for the moment and
    holden

---

[1] It is dreary enough sometimes, for a mountain-peak on whose snow your foot makes the first mortal print is not so lonely as a room full of happy faces from which *one* is missing forever. This was originally the fifth stanza of ' The Windharp: ' —

O tress ! that so oft in my heart hast lain,
  Rocked to rest within rest by its thankful beating,
Say, which is harder — to bear the pain
Of laughter and light, or to wait in vain
  'Neath the unleaved tree the impossible meeting ?
If Death's lips be icy, Life gives, iwis,
Some kisses more clay-cold and darkening than his !

(LOWELL, in a letter of December 7, 1854.)

While I could say *Dearest!* and kiss it,
    and then
In pity let go to the summer again.

I twisted this magic in gossamer strings
  Over a wind-harp's Delphian hollow;
Then called to the idle breeze that swings
All day in the pine-tops, and clings, and
    sings
  'Mid the musical leaves, and said, ' Oh,
    follow
The will of those tears that deepen my
    words,
And fly to my window to waken these
    chords.'

So they trembled to life, and, doubtfully
  Feeling their way to my sense, sang,
    ' Say whether
They sit all day by the greenwood tree,
The lover and loved, as it wont to be,
  When we — ' But grief conquered, and
    all together
They swelled such weird murmur as haunts
    a shore
Of some planet dispeopled, — ' Never-
    more !'

Then from deep in the past, as seemed to
    me,
  The strings gathered sorrow and sang
    forsaken,
' One lover still waits 'neath the green-
    wood tree,
But 't is dark,' and they shuddered, ' where
    lieth she
  Dark and cold ! Forever must one be
    taken ?'
But I groaned, ' O harp of all ruth bereft,
This Scripture is sadder, — " the other
    left " !'

There murmured, as if one strove to speak,
  And tears came instead; then the sad
    tones wandered
And faltered among the uncertain chords
In a troubled doubt between sorrow and
    words;
  At last with themselves they questioned
    and pondered,
' Hereafter ? — who knoweth ?' and so they
    sighed
Down the long steps that lead to silence
    and died.

1854.   1854.

AFTER THE BURIAL [1]

YES, faith is a goodly anchor;
   When skies are sweet as a psalm,
At the bows it lolls so stalwart,
   In its bluff, broad-shouldered calm.

And when over breakers to leeward
   The tattered surges are hurled,
It may keep our head to the tempest,
   With its grip on the base of the world.

But, after the shipwreck, tell me
   What help in its iron thews,   10
Still true to the broken hawser,
   Deep down among sea-weed and ooze ?

In the breaking gulfs of sorrow,
   When the helpless feet stretch out
And find in the deeps of darkness
   No footing so solid as doubt,

Then better one spar of Memory,
   One broken plank of the Past,

[1] A threefold sorrow has here found for itself a single expression. Part of the poem was written in 1850, after the death of Lowell's third daughter, Rose, only six months and a half old. 'I shall never forget,' he said at this time, 'the feeling I had when little Blanche's coffin was brought into the house. It was refreshed again lately. But for Rose I would have no funeral. .·. She was a lovely child — we think the loveliest of our three. She was more like Blanche than Mabel. . . . Her illness lasted a week, but I never had any hope, so that she died to me the first day the doctor came. She was very beautiful — fair, with large dark-gray eyes and fine features. . . . Dear little child! she had never spoken, only smiled.' There follow, in Lowell's letter, six stanzas of this poem, in an earlier form. Into it is interwoven the memory of his oldest child, Blanche, especially perhaps in the last stanza. 'After Blanche was buried' says Scudder in his *Life of Lowell*, 'her father took her tiny shoes, the only ones she had ever worn, and hung them in his chamber. There they stayed till his own death.' But it was the death of Lowell's wife that gave to the poem its real intensity. The second to fourth stanzas, and the seventh to twelfth, were written in a mood which made Lowell say later: 'Something broke my life in two, and I cannot piece it together again. . . . I hope you may never have reason to like "After the Burial" better than you do.'

The same interweaving is found in 'Under the Willows,' of which Lowell says: 'Something more than half of it was written more than twenty years ago, on the death of our eldest daughter; but when I came to complete it, that other death, which broke my life in two, *would* come in against my will.'

Lowell said of this poem later, 'A living verse can only be made of a living experience — and that our own. One of my most personal poems, "After the Burial," has roused strange echoes in men who assured me they were generally insensible to poetry. After all, the only stuff a solitary man has to spin is himself.' (The extracts from *Lowell's Letters* are quoted by permission of Messrs. Harper and Brothers.)

That our human heart may cling to,
   Though hopeless of shore at last!   20

To the spirit its splendid conjectures,
   To the flesh its sweet despair,
Its tears o'er the thin-worn locket
   With its anguish of deathless hair !

Immortal ? I feel it and know it,
   Who doubts it of such as she ?
But that is the pang's very secret, —
   Immortal away from me.

There's a narrow ridge in the graveyard
   Would scarce stay a child in his race,   30
But to me and my thought it is wider
   Than the star-sown vague of Space.

Your logic, my friend, is perfect,
   Your moral most drearily true;
But, since the earth clashed on *her* coffin,
   I keep hearing that, and not you.

Console if you will, I can bear it;
   'T is a well-meant alms of breath;
But not all the preaching since Adam
   Has made Death other than Death.   40

It is pagan ; but wait till you feel it, —
   That jar of our earth, that dull shock
When the ploughshare of deeper passion
   Tears down to our primitive rock.

Communion in spirit ! Forgive me,
   But I, who am earthly and weak,
Would give all my incomes from dreamland
   For a touch of her hand on my cheek.

That little shoe in the corner,
   So worn and wrinkled and brown,   50
With its emptiness confutes you,
   And argues your wisdom down.

1850, 1854, 1868.   **1868.**

L'ENVOI

TO THE MUSE [1]

WHITHER ?   Albeit I follow fast,
   In all life's circuit I but find,

[1] Passed an hour with Lowell this morning. He read me a poem, 'The Muse,' — very beautiful. It reminded me of Emerson's 'Forerunners.' (Longfellow's *Journal*, May 3. 1855.)

Not where thou art, but where thou wast,
  Sweet beckoner, more fleet than wind !
I haunt the pine-dark solitudes,
  With soft brown silence carpeted,
And plot to snare thee in the woods:
  Peace I o'ertake, but thou art fled !
I find the rock where thou didst rest,
The moss thy skimming foot hath prest; 10
  All Nature with thy parting thrills,
Like branches after birds new-flown;
Thy passage hill and hollow fills
With hints of virtue not their own;
In dimples still the water slips
Where thou has dipt thy finger-tips;
  Just, just beyond, forever burn
  Gleams of a grace without return;
Upon thy shade I plant my foot,
And through my frame strange raptures
      shoot;   20
All of thee but thyself I grasp;
  I seem to fold thy luring shape,
And vague air to my bosom clasp,
  Thou lithe, perpetual Escape !

One mask and then another drops,
And thou art secret as before:
  Sometimes with flooded ear I list,
  And hear thee, wondrous organist,
From mighty continental stops
A thunder of new music pour;   30
Through pipes of earth and air and stone
Thy inspiration deep is blown;
Through mountains, forests, open downs,
Lakes, railroads, prairies, states, and towns,
Thy gathering fugue goes rolling on
From Maine to utmost Oregon;
The factory-wheels in cadence hum,
From brawling parties concords come;
All this I hear, or seem to hear,
But when, enchanted, I draw near   40
To mate with words the various theme,
Life seems a whiff of kitchen steam,
History an organ-grinder's thrum,
  For thou hast slipt from it and me
And all thine organ-pipes left dumb,
  Most mutable Perversity !

Not weary yet, I still must seek,
And hope for luck next day, next week;
I go to see the great man ride,
Shiplike, the swelling human tide   50
That floods to bear him into port,
Trophied from Senate-hall and Court;
Thy magnetism, I feel it there,
Thy rhythmic presence fleet and rare,

Making the Mob a moment fine
With glimpses of their own Divine,
As in their demigod they see
  Their cramped ideal soaring free;
'T was thou didst bear the fire about,
  That, like the springing of a mine, 60
Sent up to heaven the street-long shout;
Full well I know that thou wast here,
It was thy breath that brushed my ear;
But vainly in the stress and whirl
I dive for thee, the moment's pearl.

Through every shape thou well canst run,
Proteus, 'twixt rise and set of sun,
Well pleased with logger-camps in Maine
  As where Milan's pale Duomo lies
A stranded glacier on the plain,   70
  Its peaks and pinnacles of ice
  Melted in many a quaint device,
And sees, above the city's din,
Afar its silent Alpine kin:
I track thee over carpets deep
To wealth's and beauty's inmost keep;
Across the sand of bar-room floors
'Mid the stale reek of boosing boors;
Where browse the hay-field's fragrant
      heats,
Or the flail-heart of Autumn beats;   80
I dog thee through the market's throngs
To where the sea with myriad tongues
Laps the green edges of the pier,
And the tall ships that eastward steer,
Curtsy their farewells to the town,
O'er the curved distance lessening down;
I follow allwhere for thy sake,
Touch thy robe's hem, but ne'er o'ertake,
Find where, scarce yet unmoving, lies,
Warm from thy limbs, thy last disguise; 90
But thou another shape hast donned,
And lurest still just, just beyond !

But here a voice, I know not whence,
Thrills clearly through my inward sense,
Saying: 'See where she sits at home
While thou in search of her dost roam !
All summer long her ancient wheel
  Whirls humming by the open door,
Or, when the hickory's social zeal
  Sets the wide chimney in a roar,   100
Close-nestled by the tinkling hearth,
It modulates the household mirth
With that sweet serious undertone
Of duty, music all her own;
Still as of old she sits and spins
Our hopes, our sorrows, and our sins;

With equal care she twines the fates
Of cottages and mighty states;
She spins the earth, the air, the sea,
The maiden's unschooled fancy free,   110
The boy's first love, the man's first grief,
The budding and the fall o' the leaf;
The piping west-wind's snowy care
For her their cloudy fleeces spare,
Or from the thorns of evil times
She can glean wool to twist her rhymes;
Morning and noon and eve supply
To her their fairest tints for dye,
But ever through her twirling thread
There spires one line of warmest red,   120
Tinged from the homestead's genial heart,
The stamp and warrant of her art;
With this Time's sickle she outwears,
And blunts the Sisters' baffled shears.

'Harass her not: thy heat and stir
But greater coyness breed in her;
Yet thou mayst find, ere Age's frost,
Thy long apprenticeship not lost,
Learning at last that Stygian Fate
Unbends to him that knows to wait.   130
The Muse is womanish, nor deigns
Her love to him that pules and plains;
With proud, averted face she stands
To him that wooes with empty hands.
Make thyself free of Manhood's guild;
Pull down thy barns and greater build;
The wood, the mountain, and the plain
Wave breast-deep with the poet's grain;
Pluck thou the sunset's fruit of gold,
Glean from the heavens and ocean old;   140
From fireside lone and trampling street
Let thy life garner daily wheat;
The epic of a man rehearse,
Be something better than thy verse;
Make thyself rich, and then the Muse
Shall court thy precious interviews,
Shall take thy head upon her knee,
And such enchantment lilt to thee,
That thou shalt hear the life-blood flow
From farthest stars to grass-blades low,   150
And find the Listener's science still
Transcends the Singer's deepest skill!'
1855?   1860.

MASACCIO

IN THE BRANCACCI CHAPEL

HE came to Florence long ago,
And painted here these walls, that shone

For Raphael and for Angelo,
With secrets deeper than his own,
Then shrank into the dark again,
And died, we know not how or when.

The shadows deepened, and I turned
Half sadly from the fresco grand;
'And is this,' mused I, 'all ye earned,
High-vaulted brain and cunning hand,   10
That ye to greater men could teach
The skill yourselves could never reach?'

'And who were they,' I mused, 'that
            wrought
Through pathless wilds, with labor long,
The highways of our daily thought?
Who reared those towers of earliest song
That lift us from the crowd to peace
Remote in sunny silences?'

Out clanged the Ave Mary bells,
And to my heart this message came: 20
Each clamorous throat among them tells
What strong-souled martyrs died in flame
To make it possible that thou
Shouldst here with brother sinners bow.

Thoughts that great hearts once broke for,
            we
Breathe cheaply in the common air;
The dust we trample heedlessly
Throbbed once in saints and heroes rare,
Who perished, opening for their race
New pathways to the commonplace.   30

Henceforth, when rings the health to those
Who live in story and in song,
O nameless dead, that now repose
Safe in Oblivion's chambers strong,
One cup of recognition true
Shall silently be drained to you!
1856?   (1868.)

THE ORIGIN OF DIDACTIC
POETRY

WHEN wise Minerva still was young
      And just the least romantic,
Soon after from Jove's head she flung
      That preternatural antic,
'T is said, to keep from idleness
      Or flirting, those twin curses,
She spent her leisure, more or less,
      In writing po——, no, verses.

How nice they were ! to rhyme with *far*
  A kind *star* did not tarry;   10
The metre, too, was regular
  As schoolboy's dot and carry;
And full they were of pious plums,
  So extra-super-moral, —
For sucking Virtue's tender gums
  Most tooth-enticing coral.

A clean, fair copy she prepares,
  Makes sure of moods and tenses,
With her own hand, — for prudence spares
  A man-(or woman-)-uensis;   20
Complete, and tied with ribbons proud,
  She hinted soon how cosy a
Treat it would be to read them loud
  After next day's Ambrosia.

The Gods thought not it would amuse
  So much as Homer's Odyssees,
But could not very well refuse
  The properest of Goddesses;
So all sat round in attitudes
  Of various dejection,   30
As with a *hem !* the queen of prudes
  Began her grave prelection.

At the first pause Zeus said, 'Well sung ! —
  I mean — ask Phœbus, — *he* knows.'
Says Phœbus, 'Zounds ! a wolf 's among
  Admetus's merinos !
Fine ! very fine ! but I must go;
  They stand in need of me there;
Excuse me ! ' snatched his stick, and so
  Plunged down the gladdened ether.   40

With the next gap, Mars said, 'For me
  Don't wait, — naught could be finer,
But I 'm engaged at half past three, —
  A fight in Asia Minor ! '
Then Venus lisped, 'I 'm sorely tried,
  These duty-calls are vip'rous;
But I *must* go; I have a bride
  To see about in Cyprus.'

Then Bacchus, — 'I must say good-by,
  Although my peace it jeopards;   50
I meet a man at four, to try
  A well-broke pair of leopards.'
His words woke Hermes. 'Ah ! ' he said,
  'I *so* love moral theses ! '
Then winked at Hebe, who turned red,
  And smoothed her apron's creases.

Just then Zeus snored, — the Eagle drew
  His head the wing from under;

Zeus snored, — o'er startled Greece there
    flew
  The many-volumed thunder.   60
Some augurs counted nine, some, ten;
  Some said 't was war, some, famine,
And all, that other-minded men
  Would get a precious ——.

Proud Pallas sighed, 'It will not do;
  Against the Muse I 've sinned, oh ! '
And her torn rhymes sent flying through
  Olympus's back window.
Then, packing up a peplus clean,
  She took the shortest path thence,   70
And opened, with a mind serene,
  A Sunday-school in Athens.

The verses ? Some in ocean swilled,
  Killed every fish that bit to 'em;
Some Galen caught, and, when distilled,
  Found morphine the residuum;
But some that rotted on the earth
  Sprang up again in copies,
And gave two strong narcotics birth,
  Didactic verse and poppies.   80

Years after, when a poet asked
  The Goddess's opinion,
As one whose soul its wings had tasked
  In Art's clear-aired dominion,
'Discriminate,' she said, 'betimes;
  The Muse is unforgiving;
Put all your beauty in your rhymes,
  Your morals in your living.'

                         1857. [1]

THE DEAD HOUSE [2]

HERE once my step was quickened,
  Here beckoned the opening door,
And welcome thrilled from the threshold
  To the foot it had known before.

[1] In the first number of the *Atlantic Monthly*, of which Lowell was editor.

[2] I have a notion that the inmates of a house should never be changed. When the first occupants go out it should be burned, and a stone set up with ' *Sacred to the memory of a HOME* ' on it. Suppose the body were eternal, and that when one spirit went out another took the lease. How frightful the strange expression of the eyes would be ! I fancy sometimes that the look in the eyes of a familiar house changes when aliens have come into it. For certainly a dwelling adapts itself to its occupants. The front door of a hospitable man opens easily and looks broad, and you can read Welcome ! on every step that leads to it. (*Lowell's Letters*, vol. i, pp. 283, 284. Quoted by permission of Messrs. Harper and Brothers.)

For the first form of the poem, see Scudder's *Life of Lowell*, vol. i, pp. 435-437.

A glow came forth to meet me
  From the flame that laughed in the grate,
And shadows adance on the ceiling,
  Danced blither with mine for a mate.

'I claim you, old friend,' yawned the arm-
    chair,
  'This corner, you know, is your seat;' 10
'Rest your slippers on me,' beamed the
    fender,
  'I brighten at touch of your feet.'

'We know the practised finger,'
  Said the books, 'that seems like brain;'
And the shy page rustled the secret
  It had kept till I came again.

Sang the pillow, 'My down once quivered
  On nightingales' throats that flew
Through moonlit gardens of Hafiz
  To gather quaint dreams for you.'   20

Ah me, where the Past sowed heart's-ease,
  The Present plucks rue for us men !
I come back: that scar unhealing
  Was not in the churchyard then.

But, I think, the house is unaltered,
  I will go and beg to look
At the rooms that were once familiar
  To my life as its bed to a brook.

Unaltered ! Alas for the sameness
  That makes the change but more !   30
'T is a dead man I see in the mirrors,
  'T is his tread that chills the floor !

To learn such a simple lesson,
  Need I go to Paris and Rome,
That the many make the household,
  But only one the home ?

'T was just a womanly presence,
  An influence unexprest,
But a rose she had worn, on my grave-sod
  Were more than long life with the rest !

'T was a smile, 't was a garment's rustle, 41
  'T was nothing that I can phrase,
But the whole dumb dwelling grew con-
    scious,
  And put on her looks and ways.

Were it mine I would close the shutters,
  Like lids when the life is fled,

And the funeral fire should wind it,
  This corpse of a home that is dead.

For it died that autumn morning
  When she, its soul, was borne   50
To lie all dark on the hillside
  That looks over woodland and corn.
1858.   1858.

AT THE BURNS CENTENNIAL

JANUARY, 1859

I

A HUNDRED years ! they 're quickly fled,
  With all their joy and sorrow;
Their dead leaves shed upon the dead,
  Their fresh ones sprung by morrow !
And still the patient seasons bring
  Their change of sun and shadow;
New birds still sing with every spring,
  New violets spot the meadow.

II

A hundred years ! and Nature's powers
  No greater grown nor lessened !   10
They saw no flowers more sweet than
    ours,
  No fairer new moon's crescent.
Would she but treat us poets so,
  So from our winter free us,
And set our slow old sap aflow
  To sprout in fresh ideas !

III

Alas, think I, what worth or parts
  Have brought me here competing,
To speak what starts in myriad hearts
  With Burns's memory beating !   20
Himself had loved a theme like this;
  Must I be its entomber ?
No pen save his but 's sure to miss
  Its pathos or its humor.

IV

As I sat musing what to say,
  And how my verse to number,
Some elf in play passed by that way,
  And sank my lids in slumber;
And on my sleep a vision stole,
  Which I will put in metre,   30
Of Burns's soul at the wicket-hole
  Where sits the good Saint Peter.

V

The saint, methought, had left his post
  That day to Holy Willie,
Who swore, 'Each ghost that comes shall
    toast
  In brunstane, will he, nill he;
There's nane need hope with phrases
    fine
  Their score to wipe a sin frae;
I 'll chalk a sign, to save their tryin', —
  A hand (☞) and " *Vide infra!* " '   40

VI

Alas! no soil 's too cold or dry
  For spiritual small potatoes,
Scrimped natures, spry the trade to ply
  Of *diaboli advocatus;*
Who lay bent pins in the penance-stool
  Where Mercy plumps a cushion,
Who 've just one rule for knave and fool,
  It saves so much confusion!

VII

So when Burns knocked, Will knit his
    brows,
  His window gap made scanter,   50
And said, 'Go rouse the other house;
  We lodge no Tam O'Shanter!'
'*We* lodge!' laughed Burns. 'Now well
    I see
  Death cannot kill old nature;
No human flea but thinks that he
  May speak for his Creator!'

VIII

'But, Willie, friend, don't turn me forth,
  Auld Clootie needs no gauger;
And if on earth I had small worth,
  You 've let in worse, I 'se wager!'   60
'Na, nane has knockit at the yett
  But found me hard as whunstane;
There 's chances yet your bread to get
  Wi Auld Nick, gaugin' brunstane.'

IX

Meanwhile, the Unco' Guid had ta'en
  Their place to watch the process,
Flattening in vain on many a pane
  Their disembodied noses.
Remember, please, 't is all a dream;
  One can't control the fancies   70
Through sleep that stream with wayward
    gleam,
  Like midnight's boreal dances.

X

Old Willie's tone grew sharp 's a knife:
  '*In primis,* I indite ye,
For makin' strife wi' the water o' life,
  And preferrin' *aqua vitæ!*'
Then roared a voice with lusty din,
  Like a skipper's when 't is blowy,
'If *that* 's a sin, *I* 'd ne'er got in,
  As sure as my name 's Noah!'   80

XI

Baulked, Willie turned another leaf, —
  'There 's many here have heard ye,
To the pain and grief o' true belief,
  Say hard things o' the clergy!'
Then rang a clear tone over all, —
  'One plea for him allow me:
I once heard call from o'er me, " Saul,
  Why persecutest thou me? " '

XII

To the next charge vexed Willie turned,
  And, sighing, wiped his glasses: 90
'I 'm much concerned to find ye yearned
  O'er-warmly tow'rd the lasses!'
Here David sighed; poor Willie's face
  Lost all its self-possession:
'I leave this case to God's own grace;
  It baffles *my* discretion!'

XIII

Then sudden glory round me broke,
  And low melodious surges
Of wings whose stroke to splendor woke
  Creation's farthest verges;   100
A cross stretched, ladder-like, secure
  From earth to heaven's own portal,
Whereby God's poor, with footing sure,
  Climbed up to peace immortal.

XIV

I heard a voice serene and low
  (With my heart I seemed to hear it)
Fall soft and slow as snow on snow,
  Like grace of the heavenly spirit;
As sweet as over new-born son
  The croon of new-made mother,   110
The voice begun, 'Sore tempted one!'
  Then, pausing, sighed, 'Our brother!

XV

'If not a sparrow fall, unless
  The Father sees and knows it,
Think! recks He less his form express,
  The soul his own deposit?

If only dear to Him the strong,
  That never trip nor wander,
Where were the throng whose morning
    song
  Thrills his blue arches yonder ?   120

XVI

' Do souls alone clear-eyed, strong-kneed,
  To Him true service render,
And they who need his hand to lead,
  Find they his heart untender ?
Through all your various ranks and fates
  He opens doors to duty,
And he that waits there at your gates
  Was servant of his Beauty.

XVII

' The Earth must richer sap secrete
  (Could ye in time but know it !),   130
Must juice concrete with fiercer heat,
  Ere she can make her poet;
Long generations go and come,
  At last she bears a singer,
For ages dumb of senses numb
  The compensation-bringer !

XVIII

' Her cheaper broods in palaces
  She raises under glasses,
But souls like these, heav'n's hostages,
  Spring shelterless as grasses: 140
They share Earth's blessing and her bane,
  The common sun and shower;
What makes your pain to them is gain,
  Your weakness is their power.

XIX

' These larger hearts must feel the rolls
  Of stormier-waved temptation;
These star-wide souls between their poles
  Bear zones of tropic passion.
He loved much ! — that is gospel good,
  Howe'er the text you handle;   150
From common wood the cross was hewed,
  By love turned priceless sandal.

XX

' If scant his service at the kirk,
  He *paters* heard and *aves*
From choirs that lurk in hedge and birk,
  From blackbird and from mavis;
The cowering mouse, poor unroofed thing,
  In him found Mercy's angel;
The daisy's ring brought every spring
  To him Love's fresh evangel !   160

XXI

' Not he the threatening texts who deals
  Is highest 'mong the preachers,
But he who feels the woes and weals
  Of all God's wandering creatures.
He doth good work whose heart can find
  The spirit 'neath the letter;
Who makes his kind of happier mind,
  Leaves wiser men and better.

XXII

' They make Religion be abhorred
  Who round with darkness gulf her,   170
And think no word can please the Lord
  Unless it smell of sulphur.
Dear Poet-heart, that childlike guessed
  The Father's loving kindness,
Come now to rest ! Thou didst his hest,
  If haply 't was in blindness !'

XXIII

Then leapt heaven's portals wide apart,
  And at their golden thunder
With sudden start I woke, my heart
  Still throbbing-full of wonder.   180
' Father,' I said, ' 't is known to Thee
  How Thou thy Saints preparest;
But this I see, — Saint Charity
  Is still the first and fairest !'

XXIV

Dear Bard and Brother ! let who **may**
  Against thy faults be railing
(Though far, I pray, from us be they
  That never had a failing !),
One toast I 'll give, and that not long,
  Which thou wouldst pledge if present, —
To him whose song, in nature strong,   191
  Makes man of prince and peasant !

                    1859 ?

THE WASHERS OF THE SHROUD [1]

OCTOBER, 1861

ALONG a river-side, I know not where,
I walked one night in mystery of dream;

[1] Lowell wrote to Professor Charles Eliot Norton, October 12, 1861 : ' I had just two days allowed me by Fields for the November *Atlantic*, and I got it done. It had been in my head some time, and when you see it you will remember my having spoken to you about it. Indeed, I owe it to you, for the hint came from one of those books of Souvestre's you lent me — the Breton legends. The writing took hold of me enough to leave

A chill creeps curdling yet beneath my hair,
To think what chanced me by the pallid gleam
Of a moon-wraith that waned through haunted air.

Pale fireflies pulsed within the meadow-mist
Their halos, wavering thistle downs of light;
The loon, that seemed to mock some goblin tryst,
Laughed; and the echoes, huddling in affright,
Like Odin's hounds, fled baying down the night.　10

Then all was silent, till there smote my ear
A movement in the stream that checked my breath:
Was it the slow plash of a wading deer?
But something said, ' This water is of Death!
The Sisters wash a shroud, — ill thing to hear!'

I, looking then, beheld the ancient Three
Known to the Greek's and to the Northman's creed,
That sit in shadow of the mystic Tree,
Still crooning, as they weave their endless brede,
One song: ' Time was, Time is, and Time shall be.'　20

No wrinkled crones were they, as I had deemed,
But fair as yesterday, to-day, to-morrow,
To mourner, lover, poet, ever seemed;
Something too high for joy, too deep for sorrow,
Thrilled in their tones, and from their faces gleamed.

me tired out and to satisfy me entirely as to what was
the original of my head and back pains. But whether
it is good or not, I am not yet far enough off to say.
But *do* like it, if you can. Fields says it is "splendid,"
with tears in his eyes — but then I read it to him, which
is half the battle. I began it as a lyric, but it *would*
be too aphoristic for that, and finally flatly refused to
sing at any price. So I submitted, took to pentameters,
and only hope the thoughts are good enough to be preserved in the ice of the colder and almost glacier-slow
measure. I think I have done well — in some stanzas
at least — and not wasted words. It is about present
matters.' (*Lowell's Letters*, vol. i, p. 318. Quoted by
permission of Messrs. Harper and Brothers.)

' Still men and nations reap as they have strawn,'
So sang they, working at their task the while;
' The fatal raiment must be cleansed ere dawn:
For Austria? Italy? the Sea - Queen's isle?
O'er what quenched grandeur must our shroud be drawn?　30

' Or is it for a younger, fairer corse,
That gathered States like children round his knees,
That tamed the wave to be his posting horse,
Feller of forests, linker of the seas,
Bridge-builder, hammerer, youngest son of Thor's?

' What make we, murmur'st thou? and what are we?
When empires must be wound, we bring the shroud,
The time-old web of the implacable Three:
Is it too coarse for him, the young and proud?
Earth's mightiest deigned to wear it, — why not he?'　40

' Is there no hope?' I moaned, ' so strong, so fair!
Our Fowler whose proud bird would brook erewhile
No rival's swoop in all our western air!
Gather the ravens, then, in funeral file
For him, life's morn yet golden in his hair?

' Leave me not hopeless, ye unpitying dames!
I see, half seeing. Tell me, ye who scanned
The stars, Earth's elders, still must noblest aims
Be traced upon oblivious ocean-sands?
Must Hesper join the wailing ghosts of names?'　50

' When grass-blades stiffen with red battle-dew,
Ye deem we choose the victor and the slain:
Say, choose we them that shall be leal and true
To the heart's longing, the high faith of brain?
Yet there the victory lies, if ye but knew.

'Three roots bear up Dominion: Know-
        ledge, Will, —
These twain are strong, but stronger yet
        the third, —
Obedience, — 't is the great tap-root that
        still,
Knit round the rock of Duty, is not stirred,
Though Heaven-loosed tempests spend their
        utmost skill.   60

' Is the doom sealed for Hesper? 'T is not
        we
Denounce it, but the Law before all time:
The brave makes danger opportunity;
The waverer, paltering with the chance sub-
        lime,
Dwarfs it to peril: which shall Hesper be?

' Hath he let vultures climb his eagle's
        seat
To make Jove's bolts purveyors of their
        maw?
Hath he the Many's plaudits found more
        sweet
Than Wisdom? held Opinion's wind for
        Law?
Then let him hearken for the doomster's
        feet !   70

' Rough are the steps, slow-hewn in flintiest
        rock,
States climb to power by ; slippery those
        with gold
Down which they stumble to eternal mock:
No chafferer's hand shall long the sceptre
        hold,
Who, given a Fate to shape, would sell the
        block.

' We sing old Sagas, songs of weal and
        . woe,
Mystic because too cheaply understood;
Dark sayings are not ours; men hear and
        know,
See Evil weak, see strength alone in Good,
Yet hope to stem God's fire with walls of
        tow.   80

' Time Was unlocks the riddle of Time
        Is,
That offers choice of glory or of gloom;
The solver makes Time Shall Be surely
        his.

But hasten, Sisters ! for even now the tomb
Grates its slow hinge and calls from the
        abyss.'

' But not for him,' I cried, ' not yet for
        him,
Whose large horizon, westering, star by
        star
Wins from the void to where on Ocean's
        rim
The sunset shuts the world with golden
        bar,
Not yet his thews shall fail, his eye grow
        dim!   90

' His shall be larger manhood, saved for
        those
That walk unblenching through the trial-
        fires;
Not suffering, but faint heart, is worst of
        woes,
And he no base-born son of craven sires,
Whose eye need blench confronted with his
        foes.

' Tears may be ours, but proud, for those
        who win
Death's royal purple in the foeman's lines;
Peace, too, brings tears; and 'mid the battle-
        din,
The wiser ear some text of God divines,
For the sheathed blade may rust with
        darker sin.   100

' God, give us peace ! not such as lulls to
        sleep,
But sword on thigh, and brow with purpose
        knit !
And let our Ship of State to harbor sweep,
Her ports all up, her battle-lanterns lit,
And her leashed thunders gathering for
        their leap !'

So cried I with clenched hands and passion-
        ate pain,
Thinking of dear ones by Potomac's side;
Again the loon laughed mocking, and
        again
The echoes bayed far down the night and
        died,
While waking I recalled my wandering
        brain.   110

1861.   1861.

THE BIGLOW PAPERS

SECOND SERIES

THE COURTIN' [1]

GOD makes sech nights, all white an' still
  Fur 'z you can look or listen,
Moonshine an' snow on field an' hill,
  All silence an' all glisten.

Zekle crep' up quite unbeknown
  An' peeked in thru' the winder,
An' there sot Huldy all alone,
  'ith no one nigh to hender.

A fireplace filled the room's one side
  With half a cord o' wood in —   10
There war n't no stoves (tell comfort died)
  To bake ye to a puddin'.

The wa'nut logs shot sparkles out
  Towards the pootiest, bless her,
An' leetle flames danced all about
  The chiny on the dresser.

Agin the chimbley crook-necks hung,
  An' in amongst 'em rusted
The ole queen's-arm thet gran'ther Young
  Fetched back f'om Concord busted.   20

The very room, coz she was in,
  Seemed warm f'om floor to ceilin',
An' she looked full ez rosy agin
  Ez the apples she was peelin'.

[1] The only attempt I had ever made at anything like a pastoral (if that may be called an attempt which was the result almost of pure accident) was in 'The Courtin'.' While the Introduction to the First Series was going through the press, I received word from the printer that there was a blank page left which must be filled. I sat down at once and improvised another fictitious 'notice of the press,' in which, because verse would fill up space more cheaply than prose, I inserted an extract from a supposed ballad of Mr. Biglow. I kept no copy of it, and the printer, as directed, cut it off when the gap was filled. Presently I began to receive letters asking for the rest of it, sometimes for the *balance* of it. I had none,' but to answer such demands, I patched a conclusion upon it in a later edition. Those who had only the first continued to importune me. Afterward, being asked to write it out as an autograph for the Baltimore Sanitary Commission Fair, I added other verses, into some of which I infused a little more sentiment in a homely way, and after a fashion completed it by sketching in the characters and making a connected story. Most likely I have spoiled it, but I shall put it at the end of this Introduction, to answer once for all those kindly importunings. (LOWELL, in the 'Introduction' to the *Biglow Papers*, 1866.)

'T was kin' o' kingdom-come to look
  On sech a blessed cretur,
A dogrose blushin' to a brook
  Ain't modester nor sweeter.

He was six foot o' man, A 1,
  Clear grit an' human natur',   30
None could n't quicker pitch a ton
  Nor dror a furrer straighter.

He 'd sparked it with full twenty gals,
  Hed squired 'em, danced 'em, druv 'em,
Fust this one, an' then thet, by spells —
  All is, he could n't love 'em.

But long o' her his veins 'ould run
  All crinkly like curled maple,
The side she breshed felt full o' sun
  Ez a south slope in Ap'il.   40

She thought no v'ice hed sech a swing
  Ez hisn in the choir;
My! when he made Ole Hunderd ring,
  She *knowed* the Lord was nigher.

An' she 'd blush scarlit, right in prayer,
  When her new meetin'-bunnet
Felt somehow thru' its crown a pair
  O' blue eyes sot upun it.

Thet night, I tell ye, she looked *some!*
  She seemed to 've gut a new soul,   50
For she felt sartin-sure he 'd come,
  Down to her very shoe-sole.

She heered a foot, an' knowed it tu,
  A-raspin' on the scraper, —
All ways to once her feelins flew
  Like sparks in burnt-up paper.

He kin' o' l'itered on the mat,
  Some doubtfle o' the sekle,
His heart kep' goin' pity-pat,
  But hern went pity Zekle.   60

An' yit she gin her cheer a jerk
  Ez though she wished him furder,
An' on her apples kep' to work,
  Parin' away like murder.

'You want to see my Pa, I s'pose?'
    'Wal . . . no . . . I come dasignin''—
'To see my Ma? She's sprinklin' clo'es
    Agin to-morrer's i'nin'.'

To say why gals acts so or so,
    Or don't, 'ould be persumin';   70
Mebby to mean *yes* an' say *no*
    Comes nateral to women.

He stood a spell on one foot fust,
    Then stood a spell on t' other,
An' on which one he felt the wust
    He could n't ha' told ye nuther.

Says he, 'I'd better call agin;'
    Says she, 'Think likely, Mister:'
Thet last word pricked him like a pin,
    An' . . . Wal, he up an' kist her.   80

When Ma bimeby upon 'em slips,
    Huldy sot pale ez ashes,
All kin' o' smily roun' the lips
    An' teary roun' the lashes.

For she was jes' the quiet kind
    Whose naturs never vary,
Like streams that keep a summer mind
    Snowhid in Jenooary.

The blood clost roun' her heart felt glued
    Too tight for all expressin',   90
Tell mother see how metters stood,
    An' gin 'em both her blessin'.

Then her red come back like the tide
    Down to the Bay o' Fundy,
An' all I know is they was cried
    In meetin' come nex' Sunday.
1848, ?, 1866.   1848, 1866.

No. II

MASON AND SLIDELL: A YAN-
KEE IDYLL[1]

I love to start out arter night's begun,
An' all the chores about the farm are done,
The critters milked an' foddered, gates
    shet fast,
Tools cleaned aginst to-morrer, supper
    past,
An' Nancy darnin' by her ker'sene lamp,—
I love, I say, to start upon a tramp,
To shake the kinkles out o' back an' legs,
An' kind o' rack my life off from the dregs
Thet's apt to settle in the buttery-hutch
Of folks thet foller in one rut too much: 10
Hard work is good an' wholesome, past all
    doubt;
But 't ain't so, ef the mind gits tuckered
    out.
Now, bein' born in Middlesex, you know,
There's certin spots where I like best to
    go:
The Concord road, for instance (I, for one,
Most gin'lly ollers call it *John Bull's Run*),
The field o' Lexin'ton where England tried
The fastest colours thet she ever dyed,
An' Concord Bridge, thet Davis, when he
    came,
Found was the bee-line track to heaven an'
    fame,   20
Ez all roads be by natur', ef your soul
Don't sneak thru shun-pikes so 's to save
    the toll.

They 're 'most too fur away, take too much
    time
To visit of'en, ef it ain't in rhyme;
But the' 's a walk thet 's hendier, a sight,
An' suits me fust-rate of a winter's night,—

[1] In the latter part of 1861 President Davis undertook to send agents or commissioners to England and France to represent the Southern cause. The men chosen were James M. Mason, of Virginia, and John Slidell, of Louisiana. On the 12th of October they left Charleston, eluded the blockading squadron, and landed at Havana. Thence they embarked for St. Thomas on the British mail-steamer Trent. On the way the Trent was stopped by Captain Wilkes, of the American man-of-war San Jacinto, and the Confederate agents were transferred as prisoners to the latter vessel. The British Government at once proclaimed the act 'a great outrage,' and sent a peremptory demand for the release of the prisoners and reparation. At the same time, without waiting for any explanation, it made extensive preparations for hostilities. It seemed and undoubtedly was expedient for the United States to receive Lord Russell's demand as an admission that impressment of British seamen found on board neutral vessels was unwarrantable. Acting on the demand as an admission of the principle so long contended for by the United States, Mr. Seward disavowed the act of Wilkes and released the commissioners. But it was held then and has since been stoutly maintained by many jurists that the true principles of international law will not justify a neutral vessel in transporting the agents of a belligerent on a hostile mission. On the analogy of despatches they should be contraband. The difficulty of amicable settlement at that time, however, lay not so much in the point of law as in the intensity of popular feeling on both sides of the Atlantic. (F. B. Williams, in the *Riverside* and *Cambridge Editions* of Lowell's *Poetical Works*.) See also the long introductory letter of the Rev. Homer Wilbur, in the *Cambridge Edition*, pp. 228–233, and the *Riverside Edition*, vol. ii, pp 240–253.

I mean the round whale's-back o' Prospect Hill.
I love to l'iter there while night grows still,
An' in the twinklin' villages about,
Fust here, then there, the well-saved lights goes out, 30
An' nary sound but watch-dogs' false alarms,
Or muffled cock-crows from the drowsy farms,
Where some wise rooster (men act jest thet way)
Stands to 't thet moon-rise is the break o' day
(So Mister Seward sticks a three-months' pin
Where the war 'd oughto eend, then tries agin;
My gran'ther's rule was safer 'n 't is to crow:
Don't never prophesy — onless ye know).
I love to muse there till it kind o' seems
Ez ef the world went eddyin' off in dreams; 40
The northwest wind thet twitches at my baird
Blows out o' sturdier days not easy scared,
An' the same moon thet this December shines
Starts out the tents an' booths o' Putnam's lines;
The rail-fence posts, acrost the hill thet runs,
Turn ghosts o' sogers should'rin' ghosts o' guns;
Ez wheels the sentry, glints a flash o' light,
Along the firelock won at Concord Fight,
An', 'twixt the silences, now fur, now nigh,
Rings the sharp chellenge, hums the low reply. 50

Ez I was settin' so, it warn't long sence,
Mixin' the puffict with the present tense,
I heerd two voices som'ers in the air,
Though, ef I was to die, I can't tell where:
Voices I call 'em: 't was a kind o' sough
Like pine-trees thet the wind's ageth'rin' through;
An', fact, I thought it *was* the wind a spell,
Then some misdoubted, could n't fairly tell,
Fust sure, then not, jest as you hold an eel,
I knowed, an' did n't, — fin'lly seemed to feel 60
'T was Concord Bridge a talkin' off to kill

With the Stone Spike thet 's druv thru Bunker's Hill;
Whether 't was so, or ef I on'y dreamed,
I could n't say; I tell it ez it seemed.

THE BRIDGE

Wal, neighbor, tell us wut 's turned up thet 's new ?
You 're younger 'n I be, — nigher Boston, tu:
An' down to Boston, ef you take their showin',
Wut they don't know ain't hardly wuth the knowin'.
There 's *sunthin'* goin' on, I know: las' night
The British sogers killed in our gret fight 70
(Nigh fifty year they hed n't stirred nor spoke)
Made sech a coil you 'd thought a dam hed broke:
Why, one he up an' beat a revellee
With his own crossbones on a holler tree,
Till all the graveyards swarmed out like a hive
With faces I hain't seen sence Seventy-five.
Wut *is* the news ? 'T ain't good, or they 'd be cheerin'.
Speak slow an' clear, for I 'm some hard o' hearin'.

THE MONIMENT

I don't know hardly ef it 's good or bad, —

THE BRIDGE

At wust, it can't be wus than wut we 've had. 80

THE MONIMENT

You know them envys thet the Rebbles sent,
An' Cap'n Wilkes he borried o' the Trent ?

THE BRIDGE

Wut ! they ha'n't hanged 'em ? Then their wits is gone !
Thet 's the sure way to make a goose a swan !

THE MONIMENT

No: England she *would* hev 'em, *Fee, Faw, Fum !*
(Ez though she hed n't fools enough to home),
So they 've returned 'em —

THE BRIDGE

   Hev they ? Wal, by heaven,
Thet 's the wust news I 've heerd sence
  Seventy-seven !
By George, I meant to say, though I declare
It 's 'most enough to make a deacon swear.

THE MONIMENT

Now don't go off half-cock: folks never
  gains   91
By usin' pepper-sarse instid o' brains.
Come, neighbor, you don't understan' —

THE BRIDGE

     How ? Hey ?
Not understan' ? Why, wut 's to hender,
  pray ?
Must I go huntin' round to find a chap
To tell me when my face hez hed a slap ?

THE MONIMENT

See here: the British they found out a flaw
In Cap'n Wilkes's readin' o' the law
(They *make* all laws, you know, an' so, o'
  course,
It 's nateral they should understan' their
  force):   100
He 'd oughto ha' took the vessel into port,
An' hed her sot on by a reg'lar court;
She was a mail-ship, an' a steamer, tu,
An' thet, they say, hez changed the pint o'
  view,
Coz the old practice, bein' meant for sails,
Ef tried upon a steamer, kind o' fails;
You *may* take out despatches, but you
  mus' n't
Take nary man —

THE BRIDGE

   You mean to say, you dus' n't !
Changed pint o' view ! No, no, — it 's
  overboard
With law an' gospel, when their ox is
  gored !   110
I tell ye, England's law, on sea an' land,
Hez ollers ben, ' *I 've gut the heaviest hand.*'
Take nary man ? Fine preachin' from *her*
  lips !
Why, she hez taken hunderds from our
  ships,
An' would agin, an' swear she had a right to,
Ef we warn't strong enough to be perlite to.
Of all the sarse thet I can call to mind,
England *doos* make the most onpleasant
  kind:

It 's you 're the sinner ollers, she 's the
  saint;
Wut 's good 's all English, all thet is n't
  ain't;   120
Wut profits her is ollers right an' just,
An' ef you don't read Scriptur so, you
  must;
She 's praised herself ontil she fairly thinks
There ain't no light in Natur when she
  winks;
Hain't she the Ten Comman'ments in her
  pus ?
Could the world stir 'thout she went, tu,
  ez nus ?
She ain't like other mortals, thet 's a fact:
She never stopped the habus-corpus act,
Nor specie payments, nor she never yet
Cut down the int'rest on her public debt; 130
She don't put down rebellions, lets 'em
  breed,
An' 's ollers willin' Ireland should secede;
She 's all thet 's honest, honnable, an' fair,
An' when the vartoos died they made her
  heir.

THE MONIMENT

Wal, wal, two wrongs don't never make a
  right;
Ef we 're mistaken, own up, an' don't
  fight:
For gracious' sake, ha'n't we enough to du
'thout gettin' up a fight with England, tu ?
She thinks we 're rabble-rid —

THE BRIDGE

     An' so we can't
Distinguish 'twixt *You oughtn' t* an' *You
  sha'n' t !*   140
She jedges by herself; she 's no idear
How 't stiddies folks to give 'em their fair
  sheer:
The odds 'twixt her an' us is plain 's a
  steeple, —
Her People 's turned to Mob, our Mob 's
  turned People.

THE MONIMENT

She 's riled jes' now —

THE BRIDGE

  Plain proof her cause ain't strong, —
The one thet fust gits mad 's 'most ollers
  wrong.
Why, sence she helped in lickin' Nap the
  Fust
An' pricked a bubble jest agoin' to bust,

With Rooshy, Prooshy, Austry, all assistin',
Th' ain't nut a face but wut she 's shook
    her fist in,   150
Ez though she done it all, an' ten times
    more,
An' nothin' never hed gut done afore,
Nor never could agin, 'thout she wuz spliced
On to one eend an' gin th' old airth a hoist.
She *is* some punkins, thet I wun't deny
(For ain't she some related to you 'n' I ?),
But there 's a few small intrists here be-
    low
Outside the counter o' John Bull an' Co,
An' though they can't conceit how 't
    should be so,
I guess the Lord druv down Creation's
    spiles   160
'thout no *gret* helpin' from the British Isles,
An' could contrive to keep things pooty
    stiff
Ef they withdrawed from business in a
    miff;
I ha'n't no patience with sech swellin' fel-
    lers ez
Think God can't forge 'thout them to blow
    the bellerses.

THE MONIMENT

You 're ollers quick to set your back aridge,
Though 't suits a tom-cat more 'n a sober
    bridge:
Don't you git het: they thought the thing
    was planned;
They 'll cool off when they come to under-
    stand.

THE BRIDGE

Ef *thet* 's wut you expect, you 'll *hev* to
    wait;   170
Folks never understand the folks they hate:
She 'll fin' some other grievance jest ez
    good,
'fore the month 's out, to git misunderstood.
England cool off !   She 'll do it, ef she sees
She 's run her head into a swarm o' bees.
I ain't so prejudiced ez wut you spose:
I hev thought England was the best thet
    goes;
Remember (no, you can't), when *I* was
    reared,
God save the King was all the tune you
    heerd:
But it 's enough to turn Wachuset roun' 180
This stumpin' fellers when you think
    they 're down.

THE MONIMENT

But, neighbor, ef they prove their claim at
    law,
The best way is to settle, an' not jaw.
An' don't le' 's mutter 'bout the awfle bricks
We 'll give 'em, ef we ketch 'em in a
    fix:
That 'ere 's most frequently the kin' o' talk
Of critters can't be kicked to toe the chalk;
Your ' You 'll see *nex*' time !' an' 'Look
    out bumby !'
'Most ollers ends in eatin' umble-pie.
'T wun't pay to scringe to England : will
    it pay   190
To fear thet meaner bully, old 'They 'll
    say ' ?
Suppose they *du* say: words are dreffle
    bores,
But they ain't quite so bad ez seventy-fours.
Wut England wants is jest a wedge to fit
Where it 'll help to widen out our split:
She 's found her wedge, an' 't ain't for us
    to come
An' lend the beetle thet 's to drive it home.
For growed-up folks like us 't would be a
    scandle,
When we git sarsed, to fly right off the
    handle.
England ain't *all* bad, coz she thinks us
    blind: 200
Ef she can't change her skin, she can her
    mind;
An' we shall see her change it double-quick,
Soon ez we 've proved thet we 're a-goin'
    to lick.
She an' Columby 's gut to be fas' friends:
For the world prospers by their privit
    ends:
'T would put the clock back all o' fifty
    years
Ef they should fall together by the ears.

THE BRIDGE

I 'gree to thet; she 's nigh us to wut France
    is;
But then she 'll hev to make the fust ad-
    vances;
We 've gut pride, tu, an' gut it by good
    rights,   210
An' ketch *me* stoopin' to pick up the mites
O' condescension she 'll be lettin' fall
When she finds out we ain't dead arter all !
I tell ye wut, it takes more 'n one good
    week
Afore *my* nose forgits it 's hed a tweak.

THE MONIMENT

She'll come out right bumby, thet I'll
    engage,
Soon ez she gits to seein' we're of age;
This talkin' down o' hers ain't wuth a fuss;
It's nat'ral ez nut likin' 't is to us;   219
Ef we're agoin' to prove we *be* growed-up,
'T wun't be by barkin' like a tarrier pup,
But turnin' to an' makin' things ez good
Ez wut we're ollers braggin' that we could;
We're boun' to be good friends, an' so
    we'd oughto,
In spite of all the fools both sides the water.

THE BRIDGE

I b'lieve thet's so; but harken in your
    ear, —
I'm older'n you, — Peace wun't keep house
    with Fear:
Ef you want peace, the thing you've gut tu
    du
Is jes' to show you're up to fightin', tu.
I recollect how sailors' rights was won, 230
Yard locked in yard, hot gun-lip kissin'
    gun:
Why, afore thet, John Bull sot up thet he
Hed gut a kind o' mortgage on the sea;
You'd thought he held by Gran'ther
    Adam's will,
An' ef you knuckle down, *he*'ll think so
    still.
Better thet all our ships an' all their crews
Should sink to rot in ocean's dreamless
    ooze,
Each torn flag wavin' chellenge ez it went,
An' each dumb gun a brave man's moni-
    ment,
Than seek sech peace ez only cowards
    crave: 240
Give *me* the peace of dead men or of brave!

THE MONIMENT

I say, ole boy, it ain't the Glorious Fourth:
You'd oughto larned 'fore this wut talk
    wuz worth.
It ain't *our* nose thet gits put out o' jint;
It's England thet gives up her dearest pint.
We've gut, I tell ye now, enough to du
In our own fem'ly fight, afore we're thru.
I hoped, las' spring, jest arter Sumter's
    shame,
When every flag-staff flapped its tethered
    flame,
An' all the people, startled from their
    doubt,   250

Come must'rin' to the flag with sech a
    shout, —
I hoped to see things settled 'fore this fall,
The Rebbles licked, Jeff Davis hanged, an'
    all;
Then come Bull Run, an' *sence* then I've
    ben waitin'
Like boys in Jennooary thaw for skatin',
Nothin' to du but watch my shadder's trace
Swing, like a ship at anchor, roun' my base,
With daylight's flood an' ebb: it's gittin'
    slow,
An' I'most think we'd better let 'em go.
I tell ye wut, this war's a-goin' to cost —

THE BRIDGE

An' I tell *you* it wun't be money lost; 261
Taxes milks dry, but, neighbor, you'll allow
Thet havin' things onsettled kills the cow:
We've gut to fix this thing for good an' all;
It's no use buildin' wut's a-goin' to fall.
I'm older'n you, an' I've seen things an'
    men,
An' *my* experunce, — tell ye wut it's ben:
Folks thet worked thorough was the ones
    thet thriv,
But bad work follers ye ez long's ye live;
You can't git red on 't; jest ez sure ez sin,
It's ollers askin' to be done agin: 271
Ef we should part, it would n't be a week
'Fore your soft-soddered peace would spring
    aleak.
We've turned our cuffs up, but, to put her
    thru,
We must git mad an' off with jackets, tu;
'T wun't du to think thet killin' ain't per-
    lite, —
You've gut to be in airnest, ef you fight;
Why, two thirds o' the Rebbles 'ould cut
    dirt,
Ef they once thought thet Guv'ment meant
    to hurt;
An' I *du* wish our Gin'rals hed in mind 280
The folks in front more than the folks be-
    hind;
You wun't do much ontil you think it's God,
An' not constitoounts, thet holds the rod;
We want some more o' Gideon's sword, I
    jedge,
For proclamations ha'n't no gret of edge;
There's nothin' for a cancer but the knife,
Onless you set by 't more than by your life.
I've seen hard times; I see a war begun
Thet folks thet love their bellies never'd
    won;

Pharo's lean kine hung on for seven long
    year;   290
But when 't was done, we did n't count it
    dear;
Why, law an' order, honor, civil right,
Ef they *ain't* wuth it, wut *is* wuth a fight ?
I 'm older 'n you: the plough, the axe, the
    mill,
All kin's o' labor an' all kin's o' skill,
Would be a rabbit in a wile-cat's claw,
Ef 't warn't for thet slow critter, 'stablished
    law;
Onsettle *thet*, an' all the world goes whiz,
A screw 's gut loose in everythin' there is:
Good buttresses once settled, don't you fret
An' stir 'em; take a bridge's word for thet!
Young folks are smart, but all ain't good
    thet 's new;   302
I guess the gran'thers they knowed sunthin',
    tu.

THE MONIMENT

Amen to thet ! build sure in the beginnin':
An' then don't never tech the underpinnin':
Th' older a guv'ment is, the better 't suits;
New ones hunt folks's corns out like new
    boots:
Change jes' for change, is like them big
    hotels
Where they shift plates, an' let ye live on
    smells.

THE BRIDGE

Wal, don't give up afore the ship goes
    down: 310
It 's a stiff gale, but Providence wun't
    drown;
An' God wun't leave us yit to sink or swim,
Ef we don't fail to du wut 's right by Him.
This land o' ourn, I tell ye, 's gut to be
A better country than man ever see.
I feel my sperit swellin' with a cry
Thet seems to say, 'Break forth an' pro-
    phesy !'
O strange New World, thet yit wast never
    young,
Whose youth from thee by gripin' need
    was wrung,
Brown foundlin' o' the woods, whose baby-
    bed   320
Was prowled roun' by the Injun's cracklin'
    tread,
An' who grew'st strong thru shifts an' wants
    an' pains,
Nussed by stern men with empires in their
    brains,

Who saw in vision their young Ishmel
    strain
With each hard hand a vassal ocean's mane,
Thou, skilled by Freedom an' by gret events
To pitch new States ez Old-World men
    pitch tents,
Thou, taught by Fate to know Jehovah's
    plan
Thet man's devices can't unmake a man,
An' whose free latch-string never was
    drawed in   330
Against the poorest child of Adam's kin, —
The grave 's not dug where traitor hands
    shall lay
In fearful haste thy murdered corse away !
I see —

Jest here some dogs begun to bark,
So thet I lost old Concord's last remark:
I listened long, but all I seemed to hear
Was dead leaves gossipin' on some birch-
    trees near;
But ez they hed n't no gret things to say,
An' sed 'em often, I come right away,
An', walkin' home'ards, jest to pass the
    time,   340
I put some thoughts thet bothered me in
    rhyme;
I hain't hed time to fairly try 'em on,
But here they be — it 's

JONATHAN TO JOHN

It don't seem hardly right, John,
    When both my hands was full,
To stump me to a fight, John, —
    Your cousin, tu, John Bull !
        Ole Uncle S. sez he, 'I guess
        We know it now,' sez he,
'The lion's paw is all the law,   350
    Accordin' to J. B.,
    Thet 's fit for you an' me !'

You wonder why we 're hot, John ?
    Your mark wuz on the guns,
The neutral guns, thet shot, John,
    Our brothers an' our sons:
        Ole Uncle S. sez he, 'I guess
        There 's human blood,' sez he,
'By fits an' starts, in Yankee hearts,
    Though 't may surprise J. B.   360
    More 'n it would you an' me.'

Ef *I* turned mad dogs loose, John,
    On *your* front-parlor stairs,

Would it jest meet your views, John,
　To wait an' sue their heirs?
　　Ole Uncle S. sez he, 'I guess,
　　　I on'y guess,' sez he,
'Thet ef Vattel on *his* toes fell,
　　'T would kind o' rile J. B.,
　　Ez wal ez you an' me!'　　　370

Who made the law thet hurts, John,
　Heads I win, — *ditto tails?*
'*J. B.*' was on his shirts, John,
　Onless my memory fails.
　　Ole Uncle S. sez he, 'I guess
　　　(I'm good at thet),' sez he,
'Thet sauce for goose ain't *jest* the juice
　For ganders with J. B.,
　　No more 'n with you or me!'

When your rights was our wrongs, John,
　You did n't stop for fuss, —　　　381
Britanny's trident prongs, John,
　Was good 'nough law for us.
　　Ole Uncle S. sez he, 'I guess,
　　　Though physic's good,' sez he,
'It does n't foller thet he can swaller
　Prescriptions signed "J. B.,"
　　Put up by you an' me!'

We own the ocean, tu, John:
　You mus' n' take it hard,　　　390
Ef we can't think with you, John,
　It's jest your own back-yard.
　　Ole Uncle S. sez he, 'I guess,
　　　Ef *thet*'s his claim,' sez he,
'The fencin'-stuff 'll cost enough
　To bust up friend J. B.,
　　Ez wal ez you an' me!'

Why talk so dreffle big, John,
　Of honor when it meant
You did n't care a fig, John,　　　400
　But jest for *ten per cent?*
　　Ole Uncle S. sez he, 'I guess
　　　He's like the rest,' sez he:
'When all is done, it's number one
　Thet's nearest to J. B.,
　　Ez wal ez t' you an' me!'

We give the critters back, John,
　Cos Abram thought 't was right;
It warn't your bullyin' clack, John,
　Provokin' us to fight.　　　410
　　Ole Uncle S. sez he, 'I guess
　　　We 've a hard row,' sez he,
'To hoe jest now; but thet, somehow,

May happen to J. B.,
　Ez wal ez you an' me!'

We ain't so weak an' poor, John,
　With twenty million people,
An' close to every door, John,
　A school-house an' a steeple.
　　Ole Uncle S. sez he, 'I guess,　　　420
　　　It is a fact,' sez he,
'The surest plan to make a Man
　Is, think him so, J. B.,
　　Ez much ez you or me!'

Our folks believe in Law, John;
　An' it's for her sake, now,
They 've left the axe an' saw, John,
　The anvil an' the plough.
　　Ole Uncle S. sez he, 'I guess,
　　　Ef 't warn't for law,' sez he,　　　430
'There 'd be one shindy from here to Indy;
　An' thet don't suit J. B.
　　(When 't ain't 'twixt you an' me!)'

We know we 've got a cause, John,
　Thet's honest, just, an' true;
We thought 't would win applause, John,
　Ef nowheres else, from you.
　　Ole Uncle S. sez he, 'I guess
　　　His love of right,' sez he,
'Hangs by a rotten fibre o' cotton:　　　440
　There 's natur' in J. B.,
　　Ez wal 'z in you an' me!'

The South says, '*Poor folks down!*' John,
　An' '*All men up!*' say we, —
White, yaller, black, an' brown, John:
　Now which is your idee?
　　Ole Uncle S. sez he, 'I guess,
　　　John preaches wal,' sez he;
'But, sermon thru, an' come to *du,*
　Why, there 's the old J. B.　　　450
　　A-crowdin' you an' me!'

Shall it be love, or hate, John?
　It 's you thet's to decide;
Ain't *your* bonds held by Fate, John
　Like all the world's beside?
　　Ole Uncle S. sez he, 'I guess
　　　Wise men forgive,' sez he,
'But not forgit; an' some time yit
　Thet truth may strike J. B.,
　　Ez wal ez you an' me!'　　　460

God means to make this land, John,
　Clear thru, from sea to sea,

Believe an' understand, John,
The *wuth* o' bein' free.
    Ole Uncle S. sez he, ' I guess,
    God's price is high,' sez he;
' But nothin' else than wut He sells
    Wears long, an' thet J. B.
    May larn, like you an' me ! '

December, 1861.   February, 1862.

No. VI

SUNTHIN' IN THE PASTORAL LINE [1]

ONCE git a smell o' musk into a draw,
An' it clings hold like precerdents in law:
Your gra'ma'am put it there, — when, good-
        ness knows, —
To jes' this-worldify her Sunday-clo'es ;
But the old chist wun't sarve her gran'son's
        wife
(For, 'thout new funnitoor, wut good in
        life?),
An' so ole clawfoot, from the precinks
        dread
O' the spare chamber, slinks into the shed,
Where, dim with dust, it fust or last sub-
        sides
To holdin' seeds an' fifty things besides; 10
But better days stick fast in heart an' husk,
An' all you keep in 't gits a scent o' musk.

Jes' so with poets: wut they 've airly read
Gits kind o' worked into their heart an'
        head,
So 's 't they can't seem to write but jest on
        sheers
With furrin countries or played-out ideers,
Nor hev a feelin', ef it doos n't smack
O' wut some critter chose to feel 'way
        back:
This makes 'em talk o' daisies, larks, an'
        things,
Ez though we 'd nothin' here that blows an'
        sings   20

[1] He [Arthur Hugh Clough] often suggested that I
should try my hand at some Yankee Pastorals, which
would admit of more sentiment and a higher tone without foregoing the advantage offered by the dialect. I
have never completed anything of the kind, but, in this
Second Series, both my remembrance of his counsel
and the deeper feeling called up by the great interests
at stake, led me to venture some passages nearer to
what is called poetical than could have been admitted
without incongruity into the former series. (LOWELL, in
the ' Introduction' to the *Biglow Papers*, 1866.)

(Why, I 'd give more for one live bobolink
Than a square mile o' larks in printer's
        ink), —
This makes 'em think our fust o' May is
        May,
Which 't ain't, for all the almanicks can
        say.

O little city-gals, don't never go it
Blind on the word o' noospaper or poet !
They 're apt to puff, an' May-day seldom
        looks
Up in the country ez 't doos in books;
They 're no more like than hornets'-nests
        an' hives,
Or printed sarmons be to holy lives.   30
I, with my trouses perched on cowhide
        boots,
Tuggin' my foundered feet out by the roots,
Hev seen ye come to fling on April's hearse
Your muslin nosegays from the milliner's,
Puzzlin' to find dry ground your queen to
        choose,
An' dance your throats sore in morocker
        shoes:
I 've seen ye an' felt proud, thet, come wut
        would,
Our Pilgrim stock wuz pethed with hardi-
        hood.
Pleasure doos make us Yankees kind o'
        winch,
Ez though 't wuz sunthin' paid for by the
        inch;   40
But yit we du contrive to worry thru,
Ef Dooty tells us thet the thing 's to du,
An' kerry a hollerday, ef we set out,
Ez stiddily ez though 't wuz a redoubt.

I, country-born an' bred, know where to find
Some blooms thet make the season suit the
        mind,
An' seem to metch the doubtin' bluebird's
        notes, —
Half-vent'rin' liverworts in furry coats,
Bloodroots, whose rolled-up leaves ef you
        oncurl,
Each on 'em 's cradle to a baby-pearl, — 50
But these are jes' Spring's pickets; sure ez
        sin,
The rebble frosts 'll try to drive 'em in;
For half our May 's so awfully like May n't,
't would rile a Shaker or an evrige saint;
Though I own up I like our back'ard springs
Thet kind o' haggle with their greens an'
        things,

An' when you 'most give up, 'uthout more
    words
Toss the fields full o' blossoms, leaves, an'
    birds;
Thet 's Northun natur', slow an' apt to
    doubt,
But when it *doos* git stirred, ther' 's no gin-
    out !   60

Fust come the blackbirds clatt'rin' in tall
    trees,
An' settlin' things in windy Congresses, —
Queer politicians, though, for I 'll be
    skinned
Ef all on 'em don't head aginst the wind.
'fore long the trees begin to show belief, —
The maple crimsons to a coral-reef,
Then saffern swarms swing off from all the
    willers
So plump they look like yaller caterpillars,
Then gray hossches'nuts leetle hands un-
    fold
Softer 'n a baby's be at three days old: 70
Thet 's robin - redbreast's almanick; he
    knows
Thet arter this ther' 's only blossom-snows;
So, choosin' out a handy crotch an' spouse,
He goes to plast'rin' his adobë house.

Then seems to come a hitch, — things lag
    behind,
Till some fine mornin' Spring makes up her
    mind,
An' ez, when snow-swelled rivers cresh
    their dams
Heaped-up with ice thet dovetails in an'
    jams,
A leak comes spirtin' thru some pin-hole
    cleft,
Grows stronger, fercer, tears out right an'
    left,   80
Then all the waters bow themselves an'
    come,
Suddin, in one gret slope o' shedderin' foam,
Jes' so our Spring gits everythin' in tune
An' gives one leap from Aperl into June:
Then all comes crowdin' in; afore you
    think,
Young oak-leaves mist the side-hill woods
    with pink;
The catbird in the laylock-bush is loud;
The orchards turn to heaps o' rosy cloud;
Red-cedars blossom tu, though few folks
    know it,
An' look all dipt in sunshine like a poet; 90

The lime-trees pile their solid stacks o'
    shade
An' drows'ly simmer with the bees' sweet
    trade;
In ellum-shrouds the flashin' hangbird
    clings
An' for the summer vy'ge his hammock
    slings;
All down the loose-walled lanes in archin'
    bowers
The barb'ry droops its strings o' golden
    flowers,
Whose shrinkin' hearts the school-gals love
    to try
With pins, — they 'll worry yourn so, boys,
    bimeby !
But I don't love your cat'logue style, — do
    you ? —
Ez ef to sell off Natur' by vendoo; 100
One word with blood in 't 's twice ez good
    ez two:
'nuff sed, June's bridesman, poet o' the year,
Gladness on wings, the bobolink, is here;
Half-hid in tip-top apple-blooms he swings,
Or climbs aginst the breeze with quiverin'
    wings,
Or, givin' way to 't in a mock despair,
Runs down, a brook o' laughter, thru the
    air.

I ollus feel the sap start in my veins
In Spring, with curus heats an' prickly
    pains,
Thet drive me, when I git a chance, to
    walk   110
Off by myself to hev a privit talk
With a queer critter thet can't seem to
    'gree
Along o' me like most folks, — Mister Me.
Ther' 's times when I 'm unsoshle ez a stone,
An' sort o' suffercate to be alone, —
I 'm crowded jes' to think thet folks are
    nigh,
An' can't bear nothin' closer than the sky;
Now the wind 's full ez shifty in the mind
Ez wut it is ou'-doors, ef I ain't blind,
An' sometimes, in the fairest sou'west
    weather,   120
My innard vane pints east for weeks to-
    gether,
My natur' gits all goose-flesh, an' my sins
Come drizzlin' on my conscience sharp ez
    pins:
Wal, et sech times I jes' slip out o' sight
An' take it out in a fair stan'-up fight

With the one cuss I can't lay on the shelf,
The crook'dest stick in all the heap, — Myself.

'T wuz so las' Sabbath arter meetin'-time:
Findin' my feelin's would n't noways rhyme
With nobody's, but off the hendle flew   130
An' took things from an east-wind pint o'
view,
I started off to lose me in the hills
Where the pines be, up back o' 'Siah's
Mills:
Pines, ef you 're blue, are the best friends
I know,
They mope an' sigh an' sheer your feelin's
so, —
They hesh the ground beneath so, tu, I
swan,
You half-forgit you 've gut a body on.
Ther' 's a small school'us' there where four
roads meet,
The door-steps hollered out by little feet,
An' side-posts carved with names whose
owners grew   140
To gret men, some on 'em, an' deacons, tu;
't ain't used no longer, coz the town hez gut
A high-school, where they teach the Lord
knows wut:
Three-story larnin' 's pop'lar now; I guess
We thriv' ez wal on jes' two stories less,
For it strikes me ther' 's sech a thing ez
sinnin'
By overloadin' children's underpinnin':
Wal, here it wuz I larned my A B C,
An' it 's a kind o' favorite spot with me.

We 're curus critters: Now ain't jes' the
minute   150
Thet ever fits us easy while we 're in it;
Long ez 't wuz futur', 't would be perfect
bliss, —
Soon ez it 's past, *thet* time 's wuth ten o'
this;
An' yit there ain't a man thet need be told
Thet Now 's the only bird lays eggs o' gold.
A knee-high lad, I used to plot an' plan
An' think 't wuz life's cap-sheaf to be a
man;
Now, gittin' gray, there 's nothin' I enjoy
Like dreamin' back along into a boy:
So the ole school'us' is a place I choose   160
Afore all others, ef I want to muse;
I set down where I used to set, an' git
My boyhood back, an' better things with
it, —

Faith, Hope, an' sunthin', ef it is n't Cher-
rity,
It 's want o' guile, an' thet 's ez gret a rer-
rity, —
While Fancy's cushin', free to Prince and
Clown,
Makes the hard bench ez soft ez milk-
weed-down.

Now, 'fore I knowed, thet Sabbath arter-
noon
When I sot out to tramp myself in tune,
I found me in the school'us' on my seat,   170
Drummin' the march to No-wheres with
my feet.
Thinkin' o' nothin', I 've heerd ole folks
say
Is a hard kind o' dooty in its way:
It 's thinkin' everythin' you ever knew,
Or ever hearn, to make your feelin's blue.
I sot there tryin' thet on for a spell:
I thought o' the Rebellion, then o' Hell,
Which some folks tell ye now is jest a met-
terfor
(A the'ry, p'raps, it wun't *feel* none the bet-
ter for);
I thought o' Reconstruction, wut we 'd
win   180
Patchin' our patent self-blow-up agin:
I thought ef this 'ere milkin' o' the wits,
So much a month, warn't givin' Natur'
fits, —
Ef folks warn't druv, findin' their own milk
fail,
To work the cow thet hez an iron tail,
An' ef idees 'thout ripenin' in the pan
Would send up cream to humor ary man:
From this to thet I let my worryin' creep,
Till finally I must ha' fell asleep.

Our lives in sleep are some like streams
thet glide   190
'twixt flesh an' sperrit boundin' on each
side, —
Where both shores' shadders kind o' mix
an' mingle
In sunthin' thet ain't jes' like either single;
An' when you cast off moorin's from To-
day,
An' down towards To-morrer drift away,
The imiges thet tengle on the stream
Make a new upside-down'ard world o'
dream:
Sometimes they seem like sunrise-streaks
an' warnin's

O' wut 'll be in Heaven on Sabbath-morn-
 in's,
An', mixed right in ez ef jest out o'
 spite,   200
Sunthin' thet says your supper ain't gone
 right.
I 'm gret on dreams, an' often when I wake,
I 've lived so much it makes my mem'ry
 ache,
An' can't skurce take a cat-nap in my
 cheer
'thout hevin' 'em, some good, some bad, all
 queer.

Now I wuz settin' where I 'd ben, it
 seemed,
An' ain't sure yit whether I r'ally dreamed,
Nor, ef I did, how long I might ha' slep',
When I hearn some un stompin' up the
 step,
An' lookin' round, ef two an' two make
 four,   210
I see a Pilgrim Father in the door.
He wore a steeple-hat, tall boots, an' spurs
With rowels to 'em big ez ches'nut-burrs,
An' his gret sword behind him sloped away
Long 'z a man's speech thet dunno wut to
 say. —
'Ef your name 's Biglow, an' your given-
 name
Hosee,' sez he, 'it 's arter you I came;
I 'm your gret-gran'ther multiplied by
 three.' —
'My wut?' sez I. — 'Your gret-gret-gret,'
 sez he:
'You would n't ha' never ben here but for
 me.   220
Two hundred an' three year ago this May
The ship I come in sailed up Boston Bay;
I 'd been a cunnle in our Civil War, —
But wut on airth hev you gut up one for?
Coz we du things in England, 't ain't for
 you
To git a notion you can du 'em tu:
I 'm told you write in public prints: ef
 true,
It 's nateral you should know a thing or
 two.' —
'Thet air 's an argymunt I can't en-
 dorse, —
't would prove, coz you wear spurs, you kep'
 a horse;   230
For brains,' sez I, 'wutever you may think,
Ain't boun' to cash the drafs o' pen-an'-
 ink, —

Though mos' folks write ez ef they hoped
 jes' quickenin'
The churn would argoo skim-milk into
 thickenin';
But skim-milk ain't a thing to change its
 view
O' wut it 's meant for more 'n a smoky
 flue.
But du pray tell me, 'fore we furder go,
How in all Natur' did you come to know
'bout our affairs,' sez I, 'in Kingdom-
 Come?' —
'Wal, I worked round at sperrit-rappin'
 some,   240
An' danced the tables till their legs wuz
 gone,
In hopes o' larnin' wut wuz goin' on,'
Sez he, 'but mejums lie so like all-split
Thet I concluded it wuz best to quit.
But, come now, ef you wun't confess to
 knowin',
You 've some conjectures how the thing 's
 a-goin'.' —
'Gran'ther,' sez I, 'a vane warn't never
 known
Nor asked to hev a jedgment of its own;
An' yit, ef 't ain't gut rusty in the jints,
It 's safe to trust its say on certin pints: 250
It knows the wind's opinions to a T,
An' the wind settles wut the weather 'll be.'
'I never thought a scion of our stock
Could grow the wood to make a weather-
 cock;
When I wuz younger 'n you, skurce more 'n
 a shaver,
No airthly wind,' sez he, 'could make me
 waver!'
(Ez he said this, he clinched his jaw an'
 forehead,
Hitchin' his belt to bring his sword-hilt
 forrard.) —
'Jes so it wuz with me,' sez I, 'I swow,
When I wuz younger 'n wut you see me
 now,   260
Nothin' from Adam's fall to Huldy's bon-
 net,
Thet I warn't full-cocked with my jedg-
 ment on it;
But now I 'm gittin' on in life, I find
It 's a sight harder to make up my mind, —
Nor I don't often try tu, when events
Will du it for me free of all expense.
The moral question 's ollus plain enough, —
It 's jes' the human-natur' side thet 's
 tough;

Wut 's best to think may n't puzzle me nor
you, —
The pinch comes in decidin' wut to *du;* 270
Ef you *read* History, all runs smooth ez
grease,
Coz there the men ain't nothin' more 'n
idees, —
But come to *make* it, ez we must to-day,
Th' idees hev arms an' legs an' stop the way:
It 's easy fixin' things in facts an' figgers, —
They can't resist, nor warn't brought up
with niggers;
But come to try your the'ry on, — why, then
Your facts an' figgers change to ign'ant
men
Actin' ez ugly — ' — ' Smite 'em hip an'
thigh ! '
Sez gran'ther, 'and let every man-child
die ! 280
Oh for three weeks o' Cromwle an' the
Lord !
Up, Isr'el, to your tents an' grind the
sword ! ' —
' Thet kind o' thing worked wal in ole
Judee,
But you forgit how long it 's ben A. D. ;
You think thet 's ellerkence, — I call it
shoddy,
A thing,' sez I, ' wun't cover soul nor body;
I like the plain all-wool o' common-sense,
Thet warms ye now, an' will a twelve-
month hence.
You took to follerin' where the Prophets
beckoned,
An', fust you knowed on, back come Charles
the Second; 290
Now wut I want 's to hev all *we* gain stick,
An' not to start Millennium too quick;
We hain't to punish only, but to keep,
An' the cure 's gut to go a cent'ry deep.'
' Wall, milk-an'-water ain't the best o' glue,'
Sez he, ' an' so you 'll find afore you 're
thru;
Ef reshness venters sunthin', shilly-shally
Loses ez often wut 's ten times the vally.
Thet exe of ourn, when Charles's neck gut
split,
Opened a gap thet ain't bridged over yit: 300
Slav'ry 's your Charles, the Lord hez gin
the exe ' —
' Our Charles,' sez I, ' hez gut eight mil-
lion necks.
The hardest question ain't the black man's
right,
The trouble is to 'mancipate the white;

One 's chained in body an' can be sot free,
But t' other 's chained in soul to an idee:
It 's a long job, but we shall worry thru it;
Ef bagnets fail, the spellin'-book must du
it.'
' Hosee,' sez he, ' I think you 're goin to fail:
The rettlesnake ain't dangerous in the
tail; 310
This 'ere rebellion 's nothing but the ret-
tle, —
You 'll stomp on thet an' think you 've won
the bettle;
It 's Slavery thet 's the fangs an' thinkin'
head,
An' ef you want selvation, cresh it dead, —
An' cresh it suddin, or you 'll larn by
waitin'
Thet Chance wun't stop to listen to de-
batin' ! ' —
' God's truth ! ' sez I, — ' an' ef *I* held the
club,
An' knowed jes' where to strike, — but
there 's the rub ! ' —
' Strike soon,' sez he, ' or you 'll be deadly
ailin', —
Folks thet 's afeared to fail are sure o'
failin'; 320
God hates your sneakin' creturs thet believe
He 'll settle things they run away an'
leave ! '
He brought his foot down fercely, ez he
spoke,
An' give me sech a startle thet I woke.
1862. June, 1862.

No. VII

LATEST VIEWS OF MR. BIGLOW

Ef I a song or two could make
  Like rockets druv by their own burnin',
All leap an' light, to leave a wake
  Men's hearts an' faces skyward turn-
    in' ! —
But, it strikes me, 't ain't jest the time
  Fer stringin' words with settisfaction:
Wut 's wanted now 's the silent rhyme
  'Twixt upright Will an' downright Ac-
    tion.

Words, ef you keep 'em, pay their keep,
  But gabble 's the short cut to ruin; 10
It 's gratis (gals half-price), but cheap
  At no rate, ef it henders doin';

Ther' 's nothin' wuss, 'less 't is to set
  A martyr-prem'um upon jawrin':
Teapots git dangerous, ef you shet
  Their lids down on 'em with Fort War-
    ren.

'Bout long enough it 's ben discussed
  Who sot the magazine afire,
An' whether, ef Bob Wickliffe bust,
  'T would scare us more or blow us
    higher.   20
D' ye s'pose the Gret Foreseer's plan
  Wuz settled fer him in town-meetin' ?
Or thet ther' 'd ben no Fall o' Man,
  Ef Adam 'd on'y bit a sweetin' ?

Oh, Jon'than, ef you want to be
  A rugged chap agin an' hearty,
Go fer wutever 'll hurt Jeff D.,
  Nut wut 'll boost up ary party.
Here 's hell broke loose, an' we lay flat
  With half the univarse a-singein',   30
Till Sen'tor This an' Gov'nor Thet
  Stop squabblin' fer the garding-ingin.

It 's war we 're in, not politics;
  It 's systems wrastlin' now, not parties;
An' victory in the eend 'll fix
  Where longest will an' truest heart is.
An' wut 's the Guv'ment folks about ?
  Tryin' to hope ther' 's nothin' doin',
An' look ez though they did n't doubt
  Sunthin' pertickler wuz a-brewin'.   40

Ther' 's critters yit thet talk an' act
  Fer wut they call Conciliation;
They 'd hand a buff'lo-drove a tract
  When they wuz madder than all Ba-
    shan.
Conciliate ? it jest means *be kicked*,
  No metter how they phrase an' tone it;
It means thet we 're to set down licked,
  Thet we 're poor shotes an' glad to own
    it !

A war on tick 's ez dear 'z the deuce,
  But it wun't leave no lastin' traces,   50
Ez 't would to make a sneakin' truce
  Without no moral specie-basis:
Ef greenbacks ain't nut jest the cheese,
  I guess ther' 's evils thet 's extremer, —
Fer instance, — shinplaster idees
  Like them put out by Gov'nor Seymour.[1]

[1] Horatio Seymour (1810–1886), of Utica, New York,
was one of the most prominent and respected men in

Last year, the Nation, at a word,
  When tremblin' Freedom cried to shield
    her,
Flamed weldin' into one keen sword
  Waitin' an' longin' fer a wielder: 60
A splendid flash ! — but how 'd the grasp
  With sech a chance ez thet wuz tally ?
Ther' warn't no meanin' in our clasp, —
  Half this, half thet, all shilly-shally.

More men ? More Man ! It 's there we fail;
  Weak plans grow weaker yit by length-
    enin':
Wut use in addin' to the tail,
  When it 's the head 's in need o' strength-
    enin' ?
We wanted one thet felt all Chief
  From roots o' hair to sole o' stockin',   70
Square-sot with thousan'-ton belief
  In him an' us, ef earth went rockin' !

Ole Hick'ry would n't ha' stood see-saw
  'Bout doin' things till they wuz done
    with, —
He 'd smashed the tables o' the Law
  In time o' need to load his gun with;
He could n't see but jest one side, —
  Ef his, 't wuz God's, an' thet wuz plenty;
An' so his ' *Forrards !* ' multiplied
  An army's fightin' weight by twenty.   80

But this 'ere histin', creak, creak, creak,
  Your cappen's heart up with a derrick,
This tryin' to coax a lightnin'-streak
  Out of a half-discouraged hay-rick,
This hangin' on mont' arter mont'
  Fer one sharp purpose 'mongst the
    twitter, —
I tell ye, it doos kind o' stunt
  The peth and sperit of a critter.

In six months where 'll the People be,
  Ef leaders look on revolution   90
Ez though it wuz a cup o' tea, —
  Jest social el'ments in solution ?
This weighin' things doos wal enough
  When war cools down, an' comes to
    writin';

the Democratic party, and a bitter opponent of Lincoln.
He had at this time been recently elected governor of
New York on a platform that denounced almost every
measure the government had found it necessary to
adopt for the suppression of the Rebellion. His influence contributed not a little to the encouragement of
that spirit which inspired the Draft Riot in the city of
New York in July, 1863. (F. B. Williams, in *Riverside*
and *Cambridge Editions*.)

But while it 's makin', the true stuff
  Is pison-mad, pig-headed fightin'.

Democ'acy gives every man
  The right to be his own oppressor ;
But a loose Gov'ment ain't the plan,
  Helpless ez spilled beans on a dresser: 100
I tell ye one thing we might larn
  From them smart critters, the Seced-
    ers, —
Ef bein' right 's the fust consarn,
  The 'fore-the-fust 's cast-iron leaders.

But 'pears to me I see some signs
  Thet we 're a-goin' to use our senses:
Jeff druv us into these hard lines,
  An' ough' to bear his half th' expenses;
Slavery 's Secession's heart an' will,
  South, North, East, West, where'er you
    find it, 110
An' ef it drors into War's mill,
  D' ye say them thunder-stones sha'n't
    grind it ?

D' ye s'pose, ef Jeff giv *him* a lick,
  Ole Hick'ry 'd tried his head to sof'n
So 's 't would n't hurt thet ebony stick
  Thet 's made our side see stars so
    of'n ?
' No ! ' he 'd ha' thundered, ' on your knees,
  An' own one flag, one road to glory !
Soft-heartedness, in times like these,
  Shows sof'ness in the upper story ! ' 120

An' why should we kick up a muss
  About the Pres'dunt's proclamation ? [1]
It ain't a-goin' to lib'rate us,
  Ef we don't like emancipation:
The right to be a cussed fool
  Is safe from all devices human,
It 's common (ez a gin'l rule)
  To every critter born o' woman.

So *we* 're all right, an' I, fer one,
  Don't think our cause 'll lose in vally 130
By rammin' Scriptur in our gun,
  An' gittin' Natur' fer an ally:
Thank God, say I, fer even a plan
  To lift one human bein's level,
Give one more chance to make a man,
  Or, anyhow, to spile a devil !

Not thet I 'm one thet much expec'
  Millennium by express to-morrer;

[1] The Emancipation Proclamation.

They *will* miscarry, — I rec'lec'
  Tu many on 'em, to my sorrer: 140
Men ain't made angels in a day,
  No matter how you mould an' labor
    'em,
Nor 'riginal ones, I guess, don't stay
  With Abe so of'n ez with Abraham.

The'ry thinks Fact a pooty thing,
  An' wants the banns read right ensuin';
But fact wun't noways wear the ring,
  'Thout years o' settin' up an' wooin':
Though, arter all, Time's dial-plate
  Marks cent'ries with the minute-finger,
An' Good can't never come tu late, 151
  Though it doos seem to try an' linger.

An' come wut will, I think it 's grand
  Abe 's gut his will et last bloom-fur-
    naced
In trial-flames till it 'll stand
  The strain o' bein' in deadly earnest:
Thet 's wut we want, — we want to know
  The folks on our side hez the bravery
To b'lieve ez hard, come weal, come woe,
  In Freedom ez Jeff doos in Slavery. 160

Set the two forces foot to foot,
  An' every man knows who 'll be winner,
Whose faith in God hez ary root
  Thet goes down deeper than his dinner:
Then 't will be felt from pole to pole,
  Without no need o' proclamation,
Earth's biggest Country 's gut her soul
  An' risen up Earth's Greatest Nation!
                              February, 1863.

No. X

MR. HOSEA BIGLOW TO THE EDITOR OF THE ATLANTIC MONTHLY

DEAR SIR, — Your letter come to han'
  Requestin' me to please be funny;
But I ain't made upon a plan
  Thet knows wut 's comin', gall or honey:
Ther' 's times the world doos look so queer
  Odd fancies come afore I call 'em;
An' then agin, for half a year,
  No preacher 'thout a call 's more solemn

You 're 'n want o' sunthin' light an' cute,
  Rattlin' an' shrewd an' kin' o' jingle-
    ish, 10

An' wish, pervidin' it 'ould suit,
  I 'd take an' citify my English.
I *ken* write long-tailed, ef I please, —
  But when I 'm jokin', no, I thankee;
Then, 'fore I know it, my idees
  Run helter-skelter into Yankee.

Sence I begun to scribble rhyme,
  I tell ye wut, I hain't ben foolin';
The parson's books, life, death, an' time
  Hev took some trouble with my school-
    in';   20
Nor th' airth don't git put out with me,
  Thet love her 'z though she wuz a
    woman;
Why, th' ain't a bird upon the tree
  But half forgives my bein' human.

An' yit I love th' unhighschooled way
  Ol' farmers hed when I wuz younger;
Their talk wuz meatier, an' 'ould stay,
  While book-froth seems to whet your
    hunger;
For puttin' in a downright lick
  'twixt Humbug's eyes, ther' 's few can
    metch it,   30
An' then it helves my thoughts ez slick
  Ez stret-grained hickory doos a hetchet.

But when I can't, I can't, thet 's all,
  For Natur' won't put up with gullin';
Idees you hev to shove an' haul
  Like a druv pig ain't wuth a mullein:
Live thoughts ain't sent for; thru all
    rifts
  O' sense they pour an' resh ye onwards,
Like rivers when south-lyin' drifts
  Feel thet th' old airth 's a-wheelin' sun-
    wards.   40

Time wuz, the rhymes come crowdin' thick
  Ez office-seekers arter 'lection,
An' into ary place 'ould stick
  Without no bother nor objection;
But sence the war my thoughts hang
    back
  Ez though I wanted to enlist 'em,
An' subs'tutes, — *they* don't never lack,
  But then they 'll slope afore you 've
    mist 'em.

Nothin' don't seem like wut it wuz;
  I can't see wut there is to hender,   50
An' yit my brains jes' go buzz, buzz,
  Like bumblebees agin a winder;

'fore these times come, in all airth's row,
  Ther' wuz one quiet place, my head in,
Where I could hide an' think, — but now
  It 's all one teeter, hopin', dreadin'.

Where 's Peace ? I start, some clear-blown
    night,
  When gaunt stone walls grow numb an'
    number,
An', creakin' 'cross the snow-crus' white,
  Walk the col' starlight into summer; 60
Up grows the moon, an' swell by swell
  Thru the pale pasturs silvers dimmer
Than the last smile thet strives to tell
  O' love gone heavenward in its shim-
    mer.

I hev been gladder o' sech things
  Than cocks o' spring or bees o' clover,
They filled my heart with livin' springs,
  But now they seem to freeze 'em over;
Sights innercent ez babes on knee,
  Peaceful ez eyes o' pastur'd cattle, 70
Jes' coz they be so, seem to me
  To rile me more with thoughts o' battle.

Indoors an' out by spells I try;
  Ma'am Natur' keeps her spin-wheel
    goin',
But leaves my natur' stiff and dry
  Ez fiel's o' clover arter mowin';
An' her jes' keepin' on the same,
  Calmer 'n a clock, an' never carin',
An' findin' nary thing to blame,
  Is wus than ef she took to swearin'. 80

Snow-flakes come whisperin' on the pane
  The charm makes blazin' logs so plea-
    sant,
But I can't hark to wut they 're say'n',
  With Grant or Sherman ollers present;
The chimbleys shudder in the gale,
  Thet lulls, then suddin takes to flappin'
Like a shot hawk, but all 's ez stale
  To me ez so much sperit-rappin'.

Under the yaller-pines I house,
  When sunshine makes 'em all sweet-
    scented,   90
An' hear among their furry boughs
  The baskin' west-wind purr contented,
While 'way o'erhead, ez sweet an' low
  Ez distant bells thet ring for meetin',
The wedged wil' geese their bugles blow,
  Further an' further South retreatin'.

Or up the slippery knob I strain
　An' see a hundred hills like islan's
Lift their blue woods in broken chain
　Out o' the sea o' snowy silence;　　　100
The farm-smokes, sweetes' sight on airth,
　Slow thru the winter air a-shrinkin'
Seem kin' o' sad, an' roun' the hearth
　Of empty places set me thinkin'.

Beaver roars hoarse with meltin' snows,
　An' rattles di'mon's from his granite;
Time wuz, he snatched away my prose,
　An' into psalms or satires ran it;
But he, nor all the rest thet once
　Started my blood to country-dances,　110
Can't set me goin' more 'n a dunce
　Thet hain't no use for dreams an' fan-
　　cies.

Rat-tat-tat-tattle thru the street
　I hear the drummers makin' riot,
An' I set thinkin' o' the feet
　Thet follered once an' now are quiet, —
White feet ez snowdrops innercent,
　Thet never knowed the paths o' Satan,
Whose comin' step ther' 's ears thet won't,
　No, not lifelong, leave off awaitin'.　120

Why, hain't I held 'em on my knee ?[1]
　Did n't I love to see 'em growin',
Three likely lads ez wal could be,
　Hahnsome an' brave an' not tu knowin' ?
I set an' look into the blaze
　Whose natur', jes' like theirn, keeps
　　climbin',
Ez long 'z it lives, in shinin' ways,
　An' half despise myself for rhymin'.

---

[1] Of Lowell's three nephews one, William Lowell
Putnam, was killed, and another, James Jackson
Lowell, seriously wounded, at the battle of Ball's Bluff,
the same battle in which Holmes's son was wounded
(see ' My Hunt After the Captain '); the third, Charles
Russell Lowell, died October 20, 1864, of wounds received the previous day at the battle of Cedar Creek.
James Jackson Lowell recovered from the wounds
received at Ball's Bluff, but was killed in the battle
of Seven Pines. See Lowell's Letters, vol. i, pp. 162–
166 ; and Scudder's Life of Lowell, vol. ii, pp. 29–31.
　See also the note on Emerson's ' Sacrifice,' p. 95, note
1 ; and Colonel Henry Lee Higginson's Four Addresses,
there referred to. Emerson wrote to Carlyle, October
15, 1870 : ' The Lowell race, again, in our War yielded
three or four martyrs so able and tender and true, that
James Russell Lowell cannot allude to them in verse or
prose but the public is melted anew.' (Carlyle-Emerson
Correspondence, vol. ii, p. 374.) See also Lowell's
' Commemoration Ode,' p. 490, and ' Under the Old
Elm,' p. 512, with the passages from his letters there
quoted.

Wut 's words to them whose faith an'
　　truth
　On War's red techstone rang true metal,
Who ventered life an' love an' youth　　131
　For the gret prize o' death in battle ?
To him who, deadly hurt, agen
　Flashed on afore the charge's thunder,[2]
Tippin' with fire the bolt of men
　Thet rived the Rebel line asunder ?

'T ain't right to hev the young go fust,
　All throbbin' full o' gifts an' graces,
Leavin' life's paupers dry ez dust
　To try an' make b'lieve fill their places:
Nothin' but tells us wut we miss,　　141
　Ther' 's gaps our lives can't never fay
　　in,
An' thet world seems so fur from this
　Lef' for us loafers to grow gray in !

My eyes cloud up for rain; my mouth
　Will take to twitchin' roun' the cor-
　　ners;
I pity mothers, tu, down South,
　For all they sot among the scorners:
I 'd sooner take my chance to stan'
　At Jedgment where your meanest slave
　　is,　　　　　　　　　　　　150
Than at God's bar hol' up a han'
　Ez drippin' red ez yourn, Jeff Davis !

Come, Peace ! not like a mourner bowed
　For honor lost an' dear ones wasted,
But proud, to meet a people proud,
　With eyes thet tell o' triumph tasted !
Come, with han' grippin' on the hilt,
　An' step thet proves ye Victory's daugh-
　　ter !
Longin' for you, our sperits wilt
　Like shipwrecked men's on raf's for
　　water.　　　　　　　　　　160

Come, while our country feels the lift
　Of a gret instinct shoutin' ' Forwards !'
An' knows thet freedom ain't a gift
　Thet tarries long in han's o' cowards !
Come, sech ez mothers prayed for, when
　They kissed their cross with lips thet
　　quivered,
An' bring fair wages for brave men,
　A nation saved, a race delivered !

　　　　　　　　　　　　April, 1865.

[2] General Charles Russell Lowell, at the battle of
Cedar Creek.

ON BOARD THE '76 [1]

WRITTEN FOR MR. BRYANT'S SEVEN-
TIETH BIRTHDAY

NOVEMBER 3, 1864

OUR ship lay tumbling in an angry sea,
 Her rudder gone, her mainmast o'er the
  side;
Her scuppers, from the waves' clutch stag-
  gering free,
 Trailed threads · of priceless crimson
  through the tide;
Sails, shrouds, and spars with pirate cannon
  torn,
  We lay, awaiting morn.

Awaiting morn, such morn as mocks de-
  spair;
 And she that bare the promise of the
  world
Within her sides, now hopeless, helmless,
  bare,
 At random o'er the wildering waters
  hurled;   10
The reek of battle drifting slow alee
  Not sullener than we.

Morn came at last to peer into our woe,
 When lo, a sail ! Now surely help was
  nigh;
The red cross flames aloft, Christ's pledge;
  but no,
 Her black guns grinning hate, she rushes
  by
And hails us: — 'Gains the leak ! Ay, so
  we thought !
  Sink, then, with curses fraught !'

I leaned against my gun still angry-hot,
 And my lids tingled with the tears held
  back: 20
This scorn methought was crueller than
  shot:
 The manly death-grip in the battle-wrack,
Yard-arm to yard-arm, were more friendly
  far
  Than such fear-smothered war.

There our foe wallowed, like a wounded
  brute
 The fiercer for his hurt. What now
  were best ?

[1] See the third quotation from *Lowell's Letters*, in
note on p. 444.

Once more tug bravely at the peril's root,
 Though death came with it ?   Or evade
  the test
If right or wrong in this God's world of ours
 Be leagued with mightier powers ?   30

Some, faintly loyal, felt their pulses lag
 With the slow beat that doubts and
  then despairs;
Some, caitiff, would have struck the starry
  flag
 That knits us with our past, and makes
  us heirs
Of deeds high-hearted as were ever done
  'Neath the all-seeing sun.

But there was one, the Singer of our crew,
 Upon whose head Age waved his peace-
  ful sign,
But whose red heart's-blood no surrender
  knew;
 And couchant under brows of massive
  line,   40
The eyes, like guns beneath a parapet,
  Watched, charged with lightnings yet.

The voices of the hills did his obey;
 The torrents flashed and tumbled in his
  song;
He brought our native fields from far
  away,
Or set us 'mid the innumerable throng
Of dateless woods, or where we heard the
  calm
  Old homestead's evening psalm.

But now he sang of faith to things unseen,
 Of freedom's birthright given to us in
  trust;   50
And words of doughty cheer he spoke be-
  tween,
 That made all earthly fortune seem as
  dust,
Matched with that duty, old as Time and
  new,
  Of being brave and true.

We, listening, learned what makes the
  might of words, —
 Manhood to back them, constant as a
  star;
His voice rammed home our cannon, edged
  our swords,
 And sent our boarders shouting; shroud
  and spar

Heard him and stiffened; the sails heard,
  and wooed
  The winds with loftier mood. 60

In our dark hours he manned our guns
  again;
  Remanned ourselves from his own man-
   hood's stores;
Pride, honor, country, throbbed through
  all his strain;
  And shall we praise? God's praise was
   his before;
And on our futile laurels he looks down,
  Himself our bravest crown.

1864.   1865.

ODE RECITED AT THE HARVARD COMMEMORATION [1]

JULY 21, 1865

I

WEAK-WINGED is song,
Nor aims at that clear-ethered height
Whither the brave deed climbs for light:
 We seem to do them wrong,

Bringing our robin's-leaf to deck their
  hearse
Who in warm life-blood wrote their nobler
  verse,
Our trivial song to honor those who
  come
With ears attuned to strenuous trump and
  drum,
And shaped in squadron-strophes their de-
  sire,
Live battle-odes whose lines were steel and
  fire: 10
  Yet sometimes feathered words are
   strong,
A gracious memory to buoy up and save
From Lethe's dreamless ooze, the common
  grave
  Of the unventurous throng.

[1] The Commemoration services (July 21, 1865) took place in the open air, in the presence of a great assembly. Prominent among the speakers were Major-General Meade, the hero of Gettysburg, and Major-General Devens. The wounds of the war were still fresh and bleeding, and the interest of the occasion was deep and thrilling. The summer afternoon was drawing to its close when the poet began the recital of the ode. No living audience could for the first time follow with intelligent appreciation the delivery of such a poem. To be sure, it had its obvious strong points and its sonorous charms; but, like all the later poems of the author, it is full of condensed thought and requires study. The reader to-day finds many passages whose force and beauty escaped him during the recital, yet the effect of the poem at the time was overpowering. The face of the poet, always singularly expressive, was on this occasion almost transfigured, — glowing, as if with an inward light. It was impossible to look away from it. Our age has furnished many great historic scenes, but this Commemoration combined the elements of grandeur and pathos, and produced an impression as lasting as life. (Underwood's *James Russell Lowell,* quoted in the *Riverside Literature Series.*)

The passage about Lincoln was not in the Ode as originally recited, but added immediately after. More than eighteen months before, however, I had written about Lincoln in the *North American Review,* — an article which pleased him. I *did* divine him earlier than most men of the Brahmin caste. The Ode itself was an improvisation. Two days before the Commemoration I had told my friend Child that it was impossible, — that I was dull as a door-mat. But the next day something gave me a jog and the whole thing came out of me with a rush. I sat up all night writing it out clear, and took it on the morning of the day to Child. 'I have something, but don't yet know what it is, or whether it will do. Look at it and tell

me.' He went a little way apart with it under an elm-tree in the college yard. He read a passage here and there, brought it back to me, and said, 'Do? I should think so! Don't you be scared.' And I was n't, but virtue enough had gone out of me to make me weak for a fortnight after. (LOWELL, in a letter to Richard Watson Gilder, January 16, 1886. *Letters,* Harper and Brothers, vol. ii, pp. 305–306.)

I don't know how to answer your queries about my 'Ode.' I *guess* I am right, for it was a matter of pure instinct — except the strophe you quote, which I added for balance both of measure and thought. I am not sure if I understand what you say about the tenth strophe. You will observe that it leads naturally to the eleventh, and that I there justify a certain narrowness in it as an expression of the popular feeling as well as my own. I confess I have never got over the feeling of wrath with which (just after the death of my nephew Willie) I read in an English paper that nothing was to be hoped of an army officered by tailors' apprentices and butcher-boys. The poem was written with a vehement speed, which I thought I had lost in the skirts of my professor's gown. Till within two days of the celebration I was hopelessly dumb, and then it all came with a rush, literally making me lean (*mi fece magro*) and so nervous that I was weeks in getting over it. I was longer in getting the new (eleventh) strophe to my mind than in writing the rest of the poem. In *that* I hardly changed a word, and it was so undeliberate that I did not find out till after it was printed that some of the verses lacked corresponding rhymes. All the 'War Poems' were improvisations as it were. My blood was up, and you would hardly believe me if I were to tell how few hours intervened between conception and completion, even in so long a one as 'Mason and Slidell.' So I have a kind of faith that the 'Ode' is right because it was *there,* I hardly knew how. I doubt you are right in wishing it more historical. But then I could not have written it. I had put the ethical and political view so often in prose that I was weary of it. The motives of the war? I had impatiently argued them again and again — but for an ode they must be in the blood and not the memory. (LOWELL, in a letter of December 8, 1868. *Letters,* Harper and Brothers, vol. ii, pp. 9–10.) See also Lowell's letter to Miss Norton, July 25, 1865; and Scudder's *Life of Lowell,* vol. ii, pp. 1–73, especially 63–73.

For a noble description of the Commemoration procession and the exercises, see W. G. Brown's *The Foe of Compromise and other Essays,* pp. 197–199; quoted in Greenslet's *Lowell,* pp. 161–163.

II

To-day our Reverend Mother welcomes back
  Her wisest Scholars, those who under-
    stood
The deeper teaching of her mystic tome,
  And offered their fresh lives to make it
    good:
      No lore of Greece or Rome.
No science peddling with the names of
  things,   20
Or reading stars to find inglorious fates,
    Can lift our life with wings
Far from Death's idle gulf that for the
  many waits,
    And lengthen out our dates
With that clear fame whose memory sings
In manly hearts to come, and nerves them
  and dilates:
Nor such thy teaching, Mother of us all!
    Not such the trumpet-call
    Of thy diviner mood,
    That could thy sons entice   30
From happy homes and toils, the fruitful
  nest
Of those half-virtues which the world calls
  best,
    Into War's tumult rude;
    But rather far that stern device
The sponsors chose that round thy cradle
  stood
    In the dim, unventured wood,
    The VERITAS that lurks beneath [1]
    The letter's unprolific sheath,
Life of whate'er makes life worth living,
Seed-grain of high emprise, immortal food,
One heavenly thing whereof earth hath
  the giving.   41

III

Many loved Truth, and lavished life's best
  oil
  Amid the dust of books to find her,
Content at last, for guerdon of their toil,
  With the cast mantle she hath left be-
    hind her.
    Many in sad faith sought for her,
    Many with crossed hands sighed for
    her;
    But these, our brothers, fought for her,
    At life's dear peril wrought for her,
    So loved her that they died for her, 50

[1] VERITAS, the motto on the seal of Harvard University, inscribed upon three open books. See Holmes's poem ' Veritas,' p. 396.

    Tasting the raptured fleetness
    Of her divine completeness:
    Their higher instinct knew
Those love her best who to themselves are
  true,
And what they dare to dream of, dare to
  do;
    They followed her and found her
    Where all may hope to find,
Not in the ashes of the burnt-out mind,
But beautiful, with danger's sweetness
  round her.
    Where faith made whole with deed 60
    Breathes its awakening breath
    Into the lifeless creed,
    They saw her plumed and mailed,
    With sweet, stern face unveiled,
And all-repaying eyes, look proud on them
  in death.

IV

Our slender life runs rippling by, and
  glides
  Into the silent hollow of the past;
    What is there that abides
  To make the next age better for the
    last?
    Is earth too poor to give us   70
  Something to live for here that shall out-
    live us?
    Some more substantial boon
Than such as flows and ebbs with Fortune's
  fickle moon?
    The little that we see
    From doubt is never free;
    The little that we do
    Is but half-nobly true;
    With our laborious hiving
What men call treasure, and the gods call
  dross,
  Life seems a jest of Fate's contriving, 80
  Only secure in every one's conniving,
A long account of nothings paid with loss,
Where we poor puppets, jerked by unseen
  wires,
  After our little hour of strut and rave,
With all our pasteboard passions and de-
  sires,
Loves, hates, ambitions, and immortal fires,
  Are tossed pell-mell together in the
  grave.
  But stay! no age was e'er degenerate,
  Unless men held it at too cheap a rate,
  For in our likeness still we shape our
    fate.   90

Ah, there is something here
Unfathomed by the cynic's sneer,
Something that gives our feeble light
A high immunity from Night,
Something that leaps life's narrow bars
To claim its birthright with the hosts of
    heaven;
A seed of sunshine that can leaven
Our earthly dullness with the beams of
    stars,
    And glorify our clay
With light from fountains elder than the
    Day;   100
    A conscience more divine than we,
    A gladness fed with secret tears,
    A vexing, forward-reaching sense
    Of some more noble permanence;
    A light across the sea,
Which haunts the soul and will not let it
    be,
Still beaconing from the heights of unde-
    generate years.

V

    Whither leads the path
    To ampler fates that leads?
    Not down through flowery meads,
    To reap an aftermath   111
    Of youth's vainglorious weeds,
But up the steep, amid the wrath
And shock of deadly-hostile creeds,
Where the world's best hope and stay
By battle's flashes gropes a desperate
    way,
And every turf the fierce foot clings to
    bleeds.
Peace hath her not ignoble wreath,
Ere yet the sharp, decisive word
Light the black lips of cannon, and the
    sword   120
    Dreams in its easeful sheath;
But some day the live coal behind the
    thought,
    Whether from Baäl's stone obscene,
    Or from the shrine serene
    Of God's pure altar brought,
Bursts up in flame; the war of tongue and
    pen
Learns with what deadly purpose it was
    fraught,
And, helpless in the fiery passion caught,
Shakes all the pillared state with shock of
    men:
Some day the soft Ideal that we wooed   130
Confronts us fiercely, foe-beset, pursued,

And cries reproachful: 'Was it, then, my
    praise,
And not myself was loved? Prove now
    thy truth;
I claim of thee the promise of thy youth;
Give me thy life, or cower in empty phrase,
The victim of thy genius, not its mate!'
    Life may be given in many ways,
    And loyalty to Truth be sealed
As bravely in the closet as the field,
    So bountiful is Fate;   140
    But then to stand beside her,
    When craven churls deride her,
To front a lie in arms and not to yield,
    This shows, methinks, God's plan
    And measure of a stalwart man,
    Limbed like the old heroic breeds,
    Who stands self-poised on manhood's
        solid earth,
    Not forced to frame excuses for his birth,
Fed from within with all the strength he
    needs.

VI

Such was he, our Martyr-Chief,   150
    Whom late the Nation he had led,
    With ashes on her head,
Wept with the passion of an angry grief:
Forgive me, if from present things I
    turn
To speak what in my heart will beat and
    burn,
And hang my wreath on his world-honored
    urn.
    Nature, they say, doth dote,
    And cannot make a man
    Save on some worn-out plan,
    Repeating us by rote: 160
For him her Old-World moulds aside she
    threw,
    And choosing sweet clay from the
        breast
    Of the unexhausted West,
With stuff untainted shaped a hero new,
Wise, steadfast in the strength of God, and
    true.
    How beautiful to see
Once more a shepherd of mankind indeed,
Who loved his charge, but never loved to
    lead;
One whose meek flock the people joyed to
    be,
    Not lured by any cheat of birth,   170
    But by his clear-grained human worth,
And brave old wisdom of sincerity!

They knew that outward grace is dust;
They could not choose but trust
In that sure-footed mind's unfaltering skill,
And supple-tempered will
That bent like perfect steel to spring again
    and thrust.
  His was no lonely mountain-peak of
    mind,
  Thrusting to thin air o'er our cloudy
    bars,
A sea-mark now, now lost in vapors
    blind;   180
Broad prairie rather, genial, level-
    lined,
Fruitful and friendly for all human
    kind,
Yet also nigh to heaven and loved of lofti-
    est stars.
        Nothing of Europe here,
Or, then, of Europe fronting mornward still,
  Ere any names of Serf and Peer
  Could Nature's equal scheme deface
  And thwart her genial will;
  Here was a type of the true elder race,
And one of Plutarch's men talked with us
    face to face.   190
I praise him not; it were too late;
And some innative weakness there must be
In him who condescends to victory
Such as the Present gives, and cannot wait,
  Safe in himself as in a fate.
    So always firmly he:
    He knew to bide his time,
    And can his fame abide,
Still patient in his simple faith sublime,
    Till the wise years decide.   200
  Great captains, with their guns and
    drums,
  Disturb our judgment for the hour,
    But at last silence comes;
These all are gone, and, standing like a
    tower,
Our children shall behold his fame.
  The kindly-earnest, brave, foreseeing
    man,
Sagacious, patient, dreading praise, not
    blame,
New birth of our new soil, the first Amer-
    ican.

VII

Long as man's hope insatiate can discern
  Or only guess some more inspiring
    goal   210
  Outside of Self, enduring as the pole,

Along whose course the flying axles burn
Of spirits bravely-pitched, earth's man-
    lier brood;
  Long as below we cannot find
The meed that stills the inexorable mind;
So long this faith to some ideal Good,
Under whatever mortal names it masks,
Freedom, Law, Country, this ethereal
    mood
That thanks the Fates for their severer
    tasks,
  Feeling its challenged pulses leap,   220
  While others skulk in subterfuges cheap,
And, set in Danger's van, has all the boon
    it asks,
Shall win man's praise and woman's love,
Shall be a wisdom that we set above
All other skills and gifts to culture dear,
  A virtue round whose forehead we in-
    wreathe
Laurels that with a living passion breathe
When other crowns grow, while we twine
    them, sear.
  What brings us thronging these high rites
    to pay,
And seal these hours the noblest of our year,
  Save that our brothers found this better
    way ?   231

VIII

We sit here in the Promised Land
  That flows with Freedom's honey and
    milk;
  But 't was they won it, sword in hand,
Making the nettle danger soft for us as silk.
  We welcome back our bravest and our
    best; —
  Ah me ! not all! some come not with the
    rest,
Who went forth brave and bright as any
    here !
I strive to mix some gladness with my strain,
    But the sad strings complain,   240
    And will not please the ear:
I sweep them for a pæan, but they wane
    Again and yet again
Into a dirge, and die away, in pain.
In these brave ranks I only see the gaps,
Thinking of dear ones whom the dumb
    turf wraps,
Dark to the triumph which they died to gain:
  Fitlier may others greet the living,
  For me the past is unforgiving;
    I with uncovered head   250
    Salute the sacred dead,

Who went, and who return not. — Say not
so!
'T is not the grapes of Canaan that repay,
But the high faith that failed not by the
way;
Virtue treads paths that end not in the
grave;
No ban of endless night exiles the brave;
 And to the saner mind
We rather seem the dead that stayed be-
hind.

Blow, trumpets, all your exultations blow!
For never shall their aureoled presence lack:
I see them muster in a gleaming row, 261
With ever-youthful brows that nobler show;
We find in our dull road their shining
track;
 In every nobler mood
We feel the orient of their spirit glow,
Part of our life 's unalterable good,
Of all our saintlier aspiration;
 They come transfigured back,
Secure from change in their high-hearted
ways,
Beautiful evermore, and with the rays 270
Of morn on their white Shields of Expecta-
tion !

IX

But is there hope to save
Even this ethereal essence from the
grave ?
What ever 'scaped Oblivion's subtle
wrong
Save a few clarion names, or golden threads
of song ?
 Before my musing eye
The mighty ones of old sweep by,
Disvoicèd now and insubstantial things,
As noisy once as we; poor ghosts of kings,
Shadows of empire wholly gone to dust,
And many races, nameless long ago, 281
To darkness driven by that imperious
gust
Of ever-rushing Time that here doth
blow:
O visionary world, condition strange,
Where naught abiding is but only Change,
Where the deep-bolted stars themselves
still shift and range!
Shall we to more continuance make pre-
tence ?
Renown builds tombs; a life-estate is Wit;
 And, bit by bit,
The cunning years steal all from us but woe;

Leaves are we, whose decays no harvest
sow. 291
 But, when we vanish hence,
Shall they lie forceless in the dark be-
low,
Save to make green their little length
of sods,
Or deepen pansies for a year or two,
Who now to us are shining-sweet as
gods ?
Was dying all they had the skill to do ?
That were not fruitless: but the Soul
resents
Such short-lived service, as if blind
events
Ruled without her, or earth could so
endure; 300
She claims a more divine investiture
Of longer tenure than Fame's airy rents;
Whate'er she touches doth her nature
share;
Her inspiration haunts the ennobled air,
 Gives eyes to mountains blind,
Ears to the deaf earth, voices to the
wind,
And her clear trump sings succor every-
where
By lonely bivouacs to the wakeful mind;
For soul inherits all that soul could dare:
 Yea, Manhood hath a wider span
And larger privilege of life than man. 311
The single deed, the private sacrifice,
So radiant now through proudly-hidden
tears,
Is covered up erelong from mortal eyes
With thoughtless drift of the deciduous
years;
But that high privilege that makes all
men peers,
That leap of heart whereby a people rise
 Up to a noble anger's height,
And, flamed on by the Fates, not shrink,
but grow more bright,
 That swift validity in noble veins, 320
 Of choosing danger and disdaining
shame,
  Of being set on flame
 By the pure fire that flies all contact
base
But wraps its chosen with angelic might,
 These are imperishable gains,
 Sure as the sun, medicinal as light,
 These hold great futures in their lusty
reins
And certify to earth a new imperial race.

X

Who now shall sneer ?
Who dare again to say we trace   330
Our lines to a plebeian race ?
Roundhead and Cavalier !
Dumb are those names erewhile in battle
    loud;
Dream-footed as the shadow of a cloud,
    They flit across the ear:
That is best blood that hath most iron
    in 't,
To edge resolve with, pouring without stint
    For what makes manhood dear.
    Tell us not of Plantagenets,
Hapsburgs, and Guelfs, whose thin bloods
    crawl   340
Down from some victor in a border-brawl !
    How poor their outworn coronets,
Matched with one leaf of that plain civic
    wreath
Our brave for honor's blazon shall be-
    queath,
    Through whose desert a rescued Nation
        sets
Her heel on treason, and the trumpet hears
Shout victory, tingling Europe's sullen ears
    With vain resentments and more vain
        regrets !

XI

Not in anger, not in pride,
Pure from passion's mixture rude   350
Ever to base earth allied,
But with far-heard gratitude,
Still with heart and voice renewed,
To heroes living and dear martyrs dead,
The strain should close that consecrates
    our brave.
Lift the heart and lift the head !
    Lofty be its mood and grave,
    Not without a martial ring,
    Not without a prouder tread
And a peal of exultation: 360
Little right has he to sing
Through whose heart in such an hour
Beats no march of conscious power,
Sweeps no tumult of elation !
'T is no Man we celebrate,
By his country's victories great,
A hero half, and half the whim of Fate,
But the pith and marrow of a Nation
Drawing force from all her men,
Highest, humblest, weakest, all,   370
For her time of need, and then
Pulsing it again through them,

Till the basest can no longer cower,
Feeling his soul spring up divinely tall,
Touched but in passing by her mantle-
    hem.
Come back, then, noble pride, for 't is
    her dower !
    How could poet ever tower,
    If his passions, hopes, and fears,
    If his triumphs and his tears,
    Kept not measure with his people ? 380
Boom, cannon, boom to all the winds and
    waves !
Clash out, glad bells, from every rocking
    steeple !
Banners, adance with triumph, bend your
    staves !
    And from every mountain-peak
    Let beacon-fire to answering beacon
        speak,
    Katahdin tell Monadnock, Whiteface
        he,
And so leap on in light from sea to sea,
        Till the glad news be sent
        Across a kindling continent,
Making earth feel more firm and air breathe
    braver: 390
' Be proud ! for she is saved, and all have
    helped to save her !
    She that lifts up the manhood of the
        poor,
    She of the open soul and open door,
    With room about her hearth for all
        mankind !
    The fire is dreadful in her eyes no
        more;
    From her bold front the helm she doth
        unbind,
    Sends all her handmaid armies back to
        spin,
    And bids her navies, that so lately
        hurled
    Their crashing battle, hold their thun-
        ders in,
    Swimming like birds of calm along the
        unharmful shore.   400
    No challenge sends she to the elder
        world,
    That looked askance and hated; a light
        scorn
    Plays o'er her mouth, as round her
        mighty knees
    She calls her children back, and waits
        the morn
Of nobler day, enthroned between her sub-
    ject seas.'

XII

Bow down, dear Land, for thou hast found
    release !
    Thy God, in these distempered days,
    Hath taught thee the sure wisdom of
      His ways,
And through thine enemies hath wrought
    thy peace !
    Bow down in prayer and praise !   410
No poorest in thy borders but may now
Lift to the juster skies a man's enfran-
    chised brow.
O Beautiful ! my country ! ours once
    more !
Smoothing thy gold of war-dishevelled hair
O'er such sweet brows as never other wore,
    And letting thy set lips,
    Freed from wrath's pale eclipse,
The rosy edges of their smile lay bare,
What words divine of lover or of poet
Could tell our love and make thee know it,
Among the Nations bright beyond com-
    pare ?   421
    What were our lives without thee ?
    What all our lives to save thee ?
    We reck not what we gave thee;
    We will not dare to doubt thee,
But ask whatever else, and we will dare !
1865.   1865.

THE MINER

Down 'mid the tangled roots of things
    That coil about the central fire,
I seek for that which giveth wings
    To stoop, not soar, to my desire.

Sometimes I hear, as 't were a sigh,
    The sea's deep yearning far above,
' Thou hast the secret not,' I cry,
    ' In deeper deeps is hid my Love.'

They think I burrow from the sun,
    In darkness, all alone, and weak;   10
Such loss were gain if He were won,
    For 't is the sun's own Sun I seek.

' The earth,' they murmur, ' is the tomb
    That vainly sought his life to prison;
Why grovel longer in the gloom ?
    He is not here; he hath arisen.'

More life for me where he hath lain
    Hidden while ye believed him dead,

Than in cathedrals cold and vain,
    Built on loose sands of *It is said*.   20

My search is for the living gold;
    Him I desire who dwells recluse,
And not his image worn and old,
    Day-servant of our sordid use.

If him I find not, yet I find
    The ancient joy of cell and church,
The glimpse, the surety undefined,
    The unquenched ardor of the search.

Happier to chase a flying goal
    Than to sit counting laurelled gains,
To guess the Soul within the soul   31
    Than to be lord of what remains.

Hide still, best Good, in subtile wise,
    Beyond my nature's utmost scope;
Be ever absent from mine eyes
    To be twice present in my hope !
                       1866.

TO H. W. L.[1]

ON HIS BIRTHDAY, 27TH FEBRUARY, 1867

I NEED not praise the sweetness of his song,
    Where limpid verse to limpid verse suc-
      ceeds
Smooth as our Charles, when, fearing lest
    he wrong
The new moon's mirrored skiff, he slides
    along,
    Full without noise, and whispers in his
      reeds.

With loving breath of all the winds his
    name
    Is blown about the world, but to his
      friends
A sweeter secret hides behind his fame,
And Love steals shyly through the loud
    acclaim
    To murmur a *God bless you !* and there
      ends.   10

[1] See Lowell's letter sent with these verses, February 27, 1867, in the *Letters*, vol. i, pp. 378, 379. In this
letter a stanza was added to the poem : —

    A gift of symbol-flowers I meant to bring,
    White for thy candor, for thy kindness red ;
    But Nature here denies them to the Spring,
    And in forced blooms an odorous warmth will cling
    Not artless : take this bunch of verse instead.

           (*Life of Longfellow*, vol. iii, p. 84.)

As I muse backward up the checkered years
　　Wherein so much was given, so much was
　　　　lost,
Blessings in both kinds, such as cheapen
　　　　tears, —
But hush! this is not for profaner ears;
　　Let them drink molten pearls nor dream
　　　　the cost.

Some suck up poison from a sorrow's core,
　　As naught but nightshade grew upon
　　　　earth's ground;
Love turned all his to heart's-ease, and the
　　more
Fate tried his bastions, she but forced a door
　　Leading to sweeter manhood and more
　　　　sound.   20

Even as a wind-waved fountain's swaying
　　shade
　　Seems of mixed race, a gray wraith shot
　　　　with sun,
So through his trial faith translucent rayed
Till darkness, half disnatured so, betrayed
　　A heart of sunshine that would fain o'er-
　　　　run.

Surely if skill in song the shears may stay
　　And of its purpose cheat the charmed
　　　　abyss,
If our poor life be lengthened by a lay,
He shall not go, although his presence may,
　　And the next age in praise shall double
　　　　this.   30

Long days be his, and each as lusty-sweet
　　As gracious natures find his song to be;
May Age steal on with softly-cadenced feet
Falling in music, as for him were meet
　　Whose choicest verse is harsher-toned
　　　　than he!

　　　　　　　　　　　　　　　　　　1867.

THE NIGHTINGALE IN THE STUDY[1]

'Come forth!' my catbird calls to me,
　　'And hear me sing a cavatina

---

[1] I have not felt in the mood to do much during my imprisonment. One little poem I have written, 'The Nightingale in the Study.' . . . 'T is a dialogue between my catbird and me — he calling me out of doors, I giving my better reasons for staying within. Of course my nightingale is Calderon. (LOWELL, in a letter to Professor C. E. Norton, July 8, 1867. *Lowell's Letters*, Harper and Brothers, vol. i, p. 390.)

That, in this old familiar tree,
　　Shall hang a garden of Alcina.

'These buttercups shall brim with wine
　　Beyond all Lesbian juice or Massic;
May not New England be divine?
　　My ode to ripening summer classic?

'Or, if to me you will not hark,
　　By Beaver Brook a thrush is ringing   10
Till all the alder-coverts dark
　　Seem sunshine-dappled with his singing.

'Come out beneath the unmastered sky,
　　With its emancipating spaces,
And learn to sing as well as I,
　　Without premeditated graces.

'What boot your many-volumed gains,
　　Those withered leaves forever turning,
To win, at best, for all your pains,
　　A nature mummy-wrapt in learning?   20

'The leaves wherein true wisdom lies
　　On living trees the sun are drinking;
Those white clouds, drowsing through the
　　　　skies,
　　Grew not so beautiful by thinking.

'"Come out!" with me the oriole cries,
　　Escape the demon that pursues you!
And, hark, the cuckoo weatherwise,
　　Still hiding farther onward, wooes you.'

'Alas, dear friend, that, all my days,
　　Hast poured from that syringa thicket 30
The quaintly discontinuous lays
　　To which I hold a season-ticket,

'A season-ticket cheaply bought
　　With a dessert of pilfered berries,
And who so oft my soul hast caught
　　With morn and evening voluntaries,

'Deem me not faithless, if all day
　　Among my dusty books I linger,
No pipe, like thee, for June to play
　　With fancy-led, half-conscious finger. 40

'A bird is singing in my brain
　　And bubbling o'er with mingled fancies,
Gay, tragic, rapt, right heart of Spain
　　Fed with the sap of old romances.

'I ask no ampler skies than those
　　His magic music rears above me,

No falser friends, no truer foes, —
   And does not Doña Clara love me ?

‘Cloaked shapes, a twanging of guitars,
   A rush of feet, and rapiers clashing,   50
Then silence deep with breathless stars,
   And overhead a white hand flashing.

‘O music of all moods and climes,
   Vengeful, forgiving, sensuous, saintly,
Where still, between the Christian chimes,
   The Moorish cymbal tinkles faintly !

‘O life borne lightly in the hand,
   For friend or foe with grace Castilian !
O valley safe in Fancy’s land,
   Not tramped to mud yet by the million !

‘Bird of to-day, thy songs are stale   61
   To his, my singer of all weathers,
My Calderon, my nightingale,
   My Arab soul in Spanish feathers.

‘Ah, friend, these singers dead so long,
   And still, God knows, in purgatory,
Give its best sweetness to all song,
   To Nature’s self her better glory.’
1867.   1867.

AN EMBER PICTURE

How strange are the freaks of memory !
   The lessons of life we forget,
While a trifle, a trick of color,
   In the wonderful web is set, —

Set by some mordant of fancy,
   And, spite of the wear and tear
Of time or distance or trouble,
   Insists on its right to be there.

A chance had brought us together;
   Our talk was of matters-of-course;   10
We were nothing, one to the other,
   But a short half-hour’s resource.

We spoke of French acting and actors,
   And their easy, natural way:
Of the weather, for it was raining
   As we drove home from the play.

We debated the social nothings
   We bore ourselves so to discuss;
The thunderous rumors of battle
   Were silent the while for us.   20

Arrived at her door, we left her
   With a drippingly hurried adieu,
And our wheels went crunching the gravel
   Of the oak-darkened avenue.

As we drove away through the shadow,
   The candle she held in the door
From rain-varnished tree-trunk to tree-trunk
   Flashed fainter, and flashed no more; —

Flashed fainter, then wholly faded
   Before we had passed the wood;   30
But the light of the face behind it
   Went with me and stayed for good.

The vision of scarce a moment,
   And hardly marked at the time,
It comes unbidden to haunt me,
   Like a scrap of ballad-rhyme.

Had she beauty ? Well, not what they call
   so;
   You may find a thousand as fair;
And yet there ’s her face in my memory
   With no special claim to be there.   40

As I sit sometimes in the twilight,
   And call back to life in the coals
Old faces and hopes and fancies
   Long buried (good rest to their souls !),

Her face shines out in the embers;
   I see her holding the light,
And hear the crunch of the gravel
   And the sweep of the rain that night.

’T is a face that can never grow older,
   That never can part with its gleam,   50
’T is a gracious possession forever,
   For is it not all a dream ?
                         1867.

IN THE TWILIGHT

MEN say the sullen instrument,
   That, from the Master’s bow,
   With pangs of joy or woe,
Feels music’s soul through every fibre sent
   Whispers the ravished strings
More than he knew or meant;
   Old summers in its memory glow;
   The secrets of the wind it sings;
   It hears the April-loosened springs;

And mixes with its mood   10
All it dreamed when it stood
In the murmurous pine-wood
    Long ago !

The magical moonlight then
  Steeped every bough and cone;
The roar of the brook in the glen
Came dim from the distance blown;
The wind through its glooms sang low,
  And it swayed to and fro
    With delight as it stood,   20
    In the wonderful wood,
      Long ago !

O my life, have we not had seasons
  That only said, Live and rejoice ?
That asked not for causes and reasons,
  But made us all feeling and voice ?
When we went with the winds in their
    blowing,
  When Nature and we were peers,
And we seemed to share in the flowing
  Of the inexhaustible years ?   30
  Have we not from the earth drawn juices
Too fine for earth's sordid uses ?
    Have I heard, have I seen
      All I feel, all I know ?
    Doth my heart overween ?
    Or could it have been
      Long ago ?

Sometimes a breath floats by me,
  An odor from Dreamland sent,
That makes the ghost seem nigh me   40
  Of a splendor that came and went,
Of a life lived somewhere, I know not
  In what diviner sphere,
Of memories that stay not and go not,
  Like music heard once by an ear
    That cannot forget or reclaim it,
A something so shy, it would shame it
    To make it a show,
A something too vague, could I name it,
  For others to know,   50
As if I had lived it or dreamed it,
As if I had acted or schemed it,
    Long ago !

And yet, could I live it over,
  This life that stirs in my brain,
Could I be both maiden and lover,
Moon and tide, bee and clover,
  As I seem to have been, once again,
Could I but speak it and show it,

This pleasure more sharp than pain,   60
  That baffles and lures me so,
The world should once more have a poet,
    Such as it had
    In the ages glad,
      Long ago !

                1868.

FOR AN AUTOGRAPH

THOUGH old the thought and oft exprest,
'T is his at last who says it best, —
I 'll try my fortune with the rest.

Life is a leaf of paper white
Whereon each one of us may write
His word or two, and then comes night.

'Lo, time and space enough,' we cry,
'To write an epic !' so we try
Our nibs upon the edge, and die.

Muse not which way the pen to hold,
Luck hates the slow and loves the bold,
Soon come the darkness and the cold.

Greatly begin ! though thou have time
But for a line, be that sublime, —
Not failure, but low aim, is crime.

Ah, with what lofty hope we came !
But we forget it, dream of fame,
And scrawl, as I do here, a name.

              (1868.)

THE FOOT-PATH

IT mounts athwart the windy hill
  Through sallow slopes of upland bare,
And Fancy climbs with foot-fall still
  Its narrowing curves that end in air.

By day, a warmer-hearted blue
  Stoops softly to that topmost swell;
Its thread-like windings seem a clue
  To gracious climes where all is well.

By night, far yonder, I surmise
  An ampler world than clips my ken,   10
Where the great stars of happier skies
  Commingle nobler fates of men.

I look and long, then haste me home,
  Still master of my secret rare;

Once tried, the path would end in Rome,
 But now it leads me everywhere.

Forever to the new it guides,
 From former good, old overmuch;
What Nature for her poets hides,
 'T is wiser to divine than clutch. 20

The bird I list hath never come
 Within the scope of mortal ear;
My prying step would make him dumb,
 And the fair tree, his shelter, sear.

Behind the hill, behind the sky,
 Behind my inmost thought, he sings;
No feet avail; to hear it nigh,
 The song itself must lend the wings.

Sing on, sweet bird close hid, and raise
 Those angel stairways in my brain, 30
That climb from these low-vaulted days
 To spacious sunshines far from pain.

Sing when thou wilt, enchantment fleet,
 I leave thy covert haunt untrod,
And envy Science not her feat
 To make a twice-told tale of God.

They said the fairies tript no more,
 And long ago that Pan was dead;
'T was but that fools preferred to bore
 Earth's rind inch-deep for truth instead.

Pan leaps and pipes all summer long, 41
 The fairies dance each full-mooned night,
Would we but doff our lenses strong,
 And trust our wiser eyes' delight.

City of Elf-land, just without
 Our seeing, marvel ever new,
Glimpsed in fair weather, a sweet doubt
 Sketched-in, mirage-like, on the blue,

I build thee in yon sunset cloud,
 Whose edge allures to climb the height;
I hear thy drowned bells, inly-loud, 51
 From still pools dusk with dreams of
  night.

Thy gates are shut to hardiest will,
 Thy countersign of long-lost speech, —
Those fountained courts, those chambers
  still,
 Fronting Time's far East, who shall
  reach ?

I know not, and will never pry,
 But trust our human heart for all;
Wonders that from the seeker fly
 Into an open sense may fall. 60

Hide in thine own soul, and surprise
 The password of the unwary elves;
Seek it, thou canst not bribe their spies;
 Unsought, they whisper it themselves.
        1868.

ALADDIN

When I was a beggarly boy,
 And lived in a cellar damp,
I had not a friend nor a toy,
 But I had Aladdin's lamp;
When I could not sleep for the cold,
 I had fire enough in my brain,
And builded, with roofs of gold,
 My beautiful castles in Spain !

Since then I have toiled day and night,
 I have money and power good store,
But I 'd give all my lamps of silver bright
 For the one that is mine no more;
Take, Fortune, whatever you choose,
 You gave, and may snatch again;
I have nothing 't would pain me to lose,
 For I own no more castles in Spain !
       1853, 1868.

TO CHARLES ELIOT NORTON[1]

AGRO DOLCE

The wind is roistering out of doors,
My windows shake and my chimney roars;
My Elmwood chimneys seem crooning to
 me,
As of old, in their moody, minor key,
And out of the past the hoarse wind blows,
As I sit in my arm-chair, and toast my toes.

'Ho! ho! nine-and-forty,' they seem to
 sing,
'We saw you a little toddling thing.
We knew you child and youth and man,
A wonderful fellow to dream and plan, 10
With a great thing always to come, — who
 knows ?
Well, well! 't is some comfort to toast
 one's toes.

[1] Written as dedication of the volume *Under the Willows and other Poems*.

'How many times have you sat at gaze
Till the mouldering fire forgot to blaze,
Shaping among the whimsical coals
Fancies and figures and shining goals !
What matters the ashes that cover those ?
While hickory lasts you can toast your toes.

' O dream-ship-builder ! where are they all,
Your grand three-deckers, deep-chested
          and tall,   20
That should crush the waves under canvas
          piles,
And anchor at last by the Fortunate Isles ?
There 's gray in your beard, the years turn
          foes,
While you muse in your arm-chair, and
          toast your toes.'

I sit and dream that I hear, as of yore,
My Elmwood chimneys' deep-throated
          roar;
If much be gone, there is much remains;
By the embers of loss I count my gains,
You and yours with the best, till the old
          hope glows
In the fanciful flame, as I toast my toes. 30

Instead of a fleet of broad-browed ships,
To send a child's armada of chips !
Instead of the great guns, tier on tier,
A freight of pebbles and grass-blades
          sere !
' Well, maybe more love with the less gift
          goes,'
I growl, as, half moody, I toast my toes.
1868.   1868.

AGASSIZ [1]

                              Come
Dicesti *egli ebbe ?* non viv' egli ancora ?
Non fiere gli occhi suoi lo dolce lome ?

I

1

THE electric nerve, whose instantaneous
          thrill
Makes next-door gossips of the antipodes,

[1] See Lowell's letters to Professor Charles Eliot
Norton, February 2, and February 26, 1874, especially
the second letter. Lowell was in Florence when Agassiz
died. 'His death,' he says, ' came home to me in a
singular way, growing into my consciousness from day
to day as if it were a graft new-set, that by degrees became part of my own wood and drew a greater share of
my sap than belonged to it, as grafts sometimes will.'
(*Lowell's Letters*, Harper and Brothers, vol. ii, pp. 115–
116.) See also the references in note on p. 211.

Confutes poor Hope's last fallacy of ease, —
The distance that divided her from ill:
Earth sentient seems again as when of old
          The horny foot of Pan
Stamped, and the conscious horror ran
Beneath men's feet through all her fibres
          cold:
Space's blue walls are mined; we feel the
          throe
From underground of our night-mantled
          foe :   10
          The flame-winged feet
Of Trade's new Mercury, that dry-shod run
Through briny abysses dreamless of the
          sun,
          Are mercilessly fleet,
          And at a bound annihilate
Ocean's prerogative of short reprieve;
          Surely ill news might wait,
And man be patient of delay to grieve:
          Letters have sympathies
          And tell-tale faces that reveal,   20
          To senses finer than the eyes,
Their errand's purport ere we break the
          seal;
They wind a sorrow round with circum-
          stance
To stay its feet, nor all unwarned displace
The veil that darkened from our sidelong
          glance
          The inexorable face:
          But now Fate stuns as with a mace;
The savage of the skies, that men have
          caught
          And some scant use of language
          taught,
          Tells only what he must, —   30
The steel-cold fact in one laconic thrust.

2

So thought I, as, with vague, mechanic eyes,
I scanned the festering news we half de-
          spise
          Yet scramble for no less,
And read of public scandal, private fraud,
Crime flaunting scot-free while the mob
          applaud,
Office made vile to bribe unworthiness,
          And all the unwholesome mess
The Land of Honest Abraham serves of
          late
          To teach the Old World how to wait,
          When suddenly,   41
As happens if the brain, from overweight
          Of blood, infect the eye,

Three tiny words grew lurid as I read,
And reeled commingling: *Agassiz is dead*.
As when, beneath the street's familiar jar,
An earthquake's alien omen rumbles far,
Men listen and forebode, I hung my head,
    And strove the present to recall,
As if the blow that stunned were yet to
    fall.   50

3

    Uprooted is our mountain oak,
That promised long security of shade
And brooding-place for many a wingèd
    thought;
    Not by Time's softly-cadenced stroke
With pauses of relenting pity stayed,
But ere a root seemed sapt, a bough de-
    cayed,
From sudden ambush by the whirlwind
    caught
And in his broad maturity betrayed !

4

Well might I, as of old, appeal to you,
    O mountains, woods, and streams,   60
To help us mourn him, for ye loved him
    too;
    But simpler moods befit our modern
    themes,
And no less perfect birth of nature can,
Though they yearn tow'rd him, sympathize
    with man,
Save as dumb fellow-prisoners through a
    wall;
    Answer ye rather to my call,
Strong poets of a more unconscious day,
When Nature spake nor sought nice rea-
    sons why,
Too much for softer arts forgotten since
That teach our forthright tongue to lisp
    and mince,   70
And drown in music the heart's bitter cry !
Lead me some steps in your directer way,
Teach me those words that strike a solid
    root
    Within the ears of men;
Ye chiefly, virile both to think and feel,
Deep-chested Chapman and firm-footed
    Ben,
For he was masculine from head to heel.
Nay, let himself stand undiminished by
With those clear parts of him that will not
    die.
Himself from out the recent dark I claim
To hear, and, if I flatter him, to blame;   81

To show himself, as still I seem to see,
A mortal, built upon the antique plan,
Brimful of lusty blood as ever ran,
And taking life as simply as a tree !
To claim my foiled good-by let him ap-
    pear,
Large-limbed and human as I saw him
    near,
Loosed from the stiffening uniform of
    fame:
And let me treat him largely: I should fear
(If with too prying lens I chanced to err,
Mistaking catalogue for character),   91
His wise forefinger raised in smiling blame.
Nor would I scant him with judicial
    breath
And turn mere critic in an epitaph;
I choose the wheat, incurious of the chaff
That swells fame living, chokes it after
    death,
And would but memorize the shining half
Of his large nature that was turned to me:
Fain had I joined with those that honored
    him
With eyes that darkened because his were
    dim,   100
And now been silent: but it might not be.

II

I

In some the genius is a thing apart,
    A pillared hermit of the brain,
Hoarding with incommunicable art
        Its intellectual gain;
    Man's web of circumstance and fate
    They from their perch of self observe,
Indifferent as the figures on a slate
        Are to the planet's sun-swung curve
    Whose bright returns they calculate;
    Their nice adjustment, part to part,
Were shaken from its serviceable mood 112
By unpremeditated stirs of heart
        Or jar of human neighborhood:
Some find their natural selves, and only
    then,
In furloughs of divine escape from men,
And when, by that brief ecstasy left bare,
        Driven by some instinct of desire,
They wander worldward, 't is to blink and
    stare,
Like wild things of the wood about a fire,
Dazed by the social glow they cannot
    share;   121

His nature brooked no lonely lair,
But basked and bourgeoned in copartnery,
Companionship, and open-windowed glee:
    He knew, for he had tried,
Those speculative heights that lure
The unpractised foot, impatient of a guide,
Tow'rd ether too attenuately pure
For sweet unconscious breath, though dear
    to pride,
But better loved the foothold sure 130
Of paths that wind by old abodes of men
Who hope at last the churchyard's peace
    secure,
And follow time-worn rules, that them
    suffice,
Learned from their sires, traditionally wise,
Careful of honest custom's how and when;
His mind, too brave to look on Truth
    askance,
No more those habitudes of faith could
    share,
But, tinged with sweetness of the old Swiss
    manse,
Lingered around them still and fain would
    spare.
Patient to spy a sullen egg for weeks, 140
The enigma of creation to surprise,
His truer instinct sought the life that
    speaks
Without a mystery from kindly eyes;
In no self-spun cocoon of prudence wound,
He by the touch of men was best inspired,
And caught his native greatness at rebound
From generosities itself had fired;
Then how the heat through every fibre ran,
Felt in the gathering presence of the man,
While the apt word and gesture came un-
    bid! 150
Virtues and faults it to one metal wrought,
    Fined all his blood to thought,
And ran the molten man in all he said or
    did.
All Tully's rules and all Quintilian's too
He by the light of listening faces knew,
And his rapt audience all unconscious lent
Their own roused force to make him elo-
    quent;
Persuasion fondled in his look and tone;
Our speech (with strangers prudish) he
    could bring
To find new charm in accents not her own;
Her coy constraints and icy hindrances 161
Melted upon his lips to natural ease,
As a brook's fetters swell the dance of
    spring.

Nor yet all sweetness: not in vain he wore,
Nor in the sheath of ceremony, controlled
By velvet courtesy or caution cold,
That sword of honest anger prized of old,
    But, with two-handed wrath,
If baseness or pretension crossed his path,
    Struck once nor needed to strike more.

2

His magic was not far to seek, — 171
He was so human! Whether strong or
    weak,
Far from his kind he neither sank nor
    soared,
But sate an equal guest at every board:
No beggar ever felt him condescend,
No prince presume; for still himself he bare
At manhood's simple level, and where'er
He met a stranger, there he left a friend.
How large an aspect! nobly unsevere,
With freshness round him of Olympian
    cheer, 180
Like visits of those earthly gods he came;
His look, wherever its good-fortune fell,
Doubled the feast without a miracle,
And on the hearthstone danced a happier
    flame;
Philemon's crabbed vintage grew benign;
Amphitryon's gold-juice humanized to wine.

III

1

The garrulous memories
Gather again from all their far-flown
    nooks,
Singly at first, and then by twos and threes,
Then in a throng innumerable, as the rooks
    Thicken their twilight files 191
Tow'rd Tintern's gray repose of roofless
    aisles:
Once more I see him at the table's head
When Saturday her monthly banquet
    spread
    To scholars, poets, wits,
All choice, some famous, loving things, not
    names,
And so without a twinge at others' fames;
Such company as wisest moods befits,
Yet with no pedant blindness to the worth
    Of undeliberate mirth, 200
Natures benignly mixed of air and earth,
Now with the stars and now with equal zest
Tracing the eccentric orbit of a jest.

2

I see in vision the warm-lighted hall,
The living and the dead I see again,
And but my chair is empty; 'mid them all
'T is I that seem the dead: they all remain
Immortal, changeless creatures of the brain:
Wellnigh I doubt which world is real
    most,
Of sense or spirit, to the truly sane;   210
In this abstraction it were light to deem
Myself the figment of some stronger
    dream;
They are the real things, and I the ghost
That glide unhindered through the solid
    door,
Vainly for recognition seek from chair to
    chair,
And strive to speak and am but futile air,
As truly most of us are little more.

3

Him most I see whom we most dearly miss,
    The latest parted thence,
His features poised in genial armistice   220
And armed neutrality of self-defence
Beneath the forehead's walled preëminence,
While Tyro, plucking facts with careless
    reach,
Settles off-hand our human how and
    whence;
The long-trained veteran scarcely wincing
    hears
The infallible strategy of volunteers
Making through Nature's walls its easy
    breach,
And seems to learn where he alone could
    teach.
Ample and ruddy, the board's end he fills
As he our fireside were, our light and
    heat,   230
Centre where minds diverse and various
    skills
Find their warm nook and stretch unham-
    pered feet;
I see the firm benignity of face,
Wide-smiling champaign, without tameness
    sweet,
The mass Teutonic toned to Gallic grace,
The eyes whose sunshine runs before the
    lips
While Holmes's rockets curve their long
    ellipse,
    And burst in seeds of fire that burst
        again
        To drop in scintillating rain.

4

There too the face half-rustic, half-divine,
Self-poised, sagacious, freaked with hu-
    mor fine,   241
Of him who taught us not to mow and
    mope
About our fancied selves, but seek our
    scope
In Nature's world and Man's, nor fade to
    hollow trope,
Content with our New World and timely
    bold
To challenge the o'ermastery of the Old;
Listening with eyes averse I see him sit
Pricked with the cider of the Judge's wit
(Ripe-hearted homebrew, fresh and fresh
    again),
While the wise nose's firm-built aquiline
    Curves sharper to restrain   251
The merriment whose most unruly moods
Pass not the dumb laugh learned in lis-
    tening woods
    Of silence-shedding pine:
Hard by is he whose art's consoling spell
Hath given both worlds a whiff of aspho-
    del,
His look still vernal 'mid the wintry ring
Of petals that remember, not foretell,
The paler primrose of a second spring.

5

And more there are: but other forms
    arise   260
And seen as clear, albeit with dimmer
    eyes:
First he from sympathy still held apart
By shrinking over-eagerness of heart,
Cloud charged with searching fire, whose
    shadow's sweep
Heightened mean things with sense of
    brooding ill,
And steeped in doom familiar field and
    hill, —
New England's poet, soul reserved and
    deep,
November nature with a name of May,
Whom high o'er Concord plains we laid
    to sleep,
While the orchards mocked us in their
    white array   270
And building robins wondered at our
    tears,
Snatched in his prime, the shape august
That should have stood unbent 'neath
    fourscore years,

The noble head, the eyes of furtive trust,
   All gone to speechless dust.
   And he our passing guest,[1]
Shy nature, too, and stung with life's
   unrest,
Whom we too briefly had but could not
   hold,
Who brought ripe Oxford's culture to
   our board,
   The Past's incalculable hoard, 280
Mellowed by scutcheoned panes in clois-
   ters old,
Seclusions, ivy-hushed, and pavements
   sweet
With immemorial lisp of musing feet;
Young head time-tonsured smoother than
   a friar's,
Boy face, but grave with answerless de-
   sires,
Poet in all that poets have of best,
But foiled with riddles dark and cloudy
   aims,
   Who now hath found sure rest,
Not by still Isis or historic Thames,
Nor by the Charles he tried to love with
   me, 290
But, not misplaced, by Arno's hallowed
   brim,
Nor scorned by Santa Croce's neighbor-
   ing fames,
   Haply not mindless, wheresoe'er he
   be,
Of violets that to-day I scattered over
   him.[2]
   He, too, is there,[3]
After the good centurion fitly named,
Whom learning dulled not, nor conven-
   tion tamed,
Shaking with burly mirth his hyacinthine
   hair,
Our hearty Grecian of Homeric ways,
Still found the surer friend where least he
   hoped the praise. 300

[1] Arthur Hugh Clough, who lived in Cambridge from 1852 to 1853. Lowell speaks of him in the 'Introduction' to the *Biglow Papers*, 1866, as among those whose opinion and encouragement he most valued : ' With a feeling too tender and grateful to be mixed with any vanity, I mention as one of these the late A. H. Clough, who more than any one of those I have known (no longer living), except Hawthorne, impressed me with the constant presence of that indefinable thing we call genius.'

[2] Clough's grave is in the little Protestant Cemetery at Florence, near that of Elizabeth Barrett Browning, and not far from Walter Savage Landor's.

[3] Cornelius C. Felton. See Longfellow's ' Three Friends of Mine.'

6

   Yea truly, as the sallowing years
Fall from us faster, like frost-loosened
   leaves
Pushed by the misty touch of shortening
   days,
   And that unwakened winter nears,
'T is the void chair our surest guest re-
   ceives,
'T is lips long cold that give the warm-
   est kiss,
'T is the lost voice comes oftenest to our
   ears;
We count our rosary by the beads we
   miss:
   To me, at least, it seemeth so,
An exile in the land once found divine, 310
   While my starved fire burns low,
And homeless winds at the loose case-
   ment whine
Shrill ditties of the snow-roofed Apen-
   nine.

IV

1

Now forth into the darkness all are gone,
But memory, still unsated, follows on,
Retracing step by step our homeward walk,
With many a laugh among our serious
   talk,
Across the bridge where, on the dimpling
   tide,
The long red streamers from the windows
   glide,
   Or the dim western moon 320
Rocks her skiff's image on the broad lagoon,
And Boston shows a soft Venetian side
In that Arcadian light when roof and tree,
Hard prose by daylight, dream in Italy;
Or haply in the sky's cold chambers wide
Shivered the winter stars, while all below,
As if an end were come of human ill,
The world was wrapt in innocence of snow
And the cast-iron bay was blind and still;
These were our poetry; in him perhaps 330
Science had barred the gate that lets in
   dream,
And he would rather count the perch and
   bream
Than with the current's idle fancy lapse;
And yet he had the poet's open eye
That takes a frank delight in all it sees,
Nor was earth voiceless, nor the mystic
   sky,

To him the life-long friend of fields and
trees:
Then came the prose of the suburban street,
Its silence deepened by our echoing feet,
And converse such as rambling hazard
finds; 340
Then he who many cities knew and many
minds,
And men once world-noised, now mere
Ossian forms
Of misty memory, bade them live anew
As when they shared earth's manifold de-
light,
In shape, in gait, in voice, in gesture true,
And, with an accent heightening as he
warms,
Would stop forgetful of the shortening
night,
Drop my confining arm, and pour profuse
Much worldly wisdom kept for others'
use,
Not for his own, for he was rash and free, 350
His purse or knowledge all men's, like the
sea.
Still can I hear his voice's shrilling might
(With pauses broken, while the fitful spark
He blew more hotly rounded on the dark
To hint his features with a Rembrandt
light)
Call Oken back, or Humboldt, or Lamarck,
Or Cuvier's taller shade, and many more
Whom he had seen, or knew from others'
sight,
And make them men to me as ne'er be-
fore:
Not seldom, as the undeadened fibre stirred
Of noble friendships knit beyond the sea, 361
German or French thrust by the lagging
word,
For a good leash of mother-tongues had
he.
At last, arrived at where our paths divide,
'Good night!' and, ere the distance grew
too wide,
'Good night!' again; and now with cheated
ear
I half hear his who mine shall never hear.

2

Sometimes it seemed as if New England
air
For his large lungs too parsimonious
were,
As if those empty rooms of dogma
drear 370

Where the ghost shivers of a faith austere
Counting the horns o'er of the Beast,
Still scaring those whose faith in it is
least,
As if those snaps o' th' moral atmosphere
That sharpen all the needles of the East,
Had been to him like death,
Accustomed to draw Europe's freer
breath
 In a more stable element;
Nay, even our landscape, half the year
morose,
Our practical horizon grimly pent, 380
Our air, sincere of ceremonious haze,
Forcing hard outlines mercilessly close,
Our social monotone of level days,
 Might make our best seem banishment;
 But it was nothing so;
 Haply his instinct might divine,
Beneath our drift of puritanic snow,
 The marvel sensitive and fine
Of sanguinaria over-rash to blow
And trust its shyness to an air malign; 390
Well might he prize truth's warranty and
pledge
In the grim outcrop of our granite edge,
Or Hebrew fervor flashing forth at need
In the gaunt sons of Calvin's iron breed,
As prompt to give as skilled to win and
keep;
But, though such intuitions might not
cheer,
Yet life was good to him, and, there or
here,
With that sufficing joy, the day was never
cheap;
Thereto his mind was its own ample
sphere,
And, like those buildings great that
through the year 400
Carry one temperature, his nature large
Made its own climate, nor could any
marge
Traced by convention stay him from his
bent:
He had a habitude of mountain air;
He brought wide outlook where he went,
And could on sunny uplands dwell
Of prospect sweeter than the pastures
fair
 High-hung of viny Neufchâtel;
 Nor, surely, did he miss
 Some pale, imaginary bliss 410
Of earlier sights whose inner landscape still
 was Swiss.

V

1

I cannot think he wished so soon to die
With all his senses full of eager heat,
And rosy years that stood expectant by
To buckle the winged sandals on their
    feet,
He that was friends with Earth, and
    all her sweet
Took with both hands unsparingly:
Truly this life is precious to the root,
And good the feel of grass beneath the
    foot;
To lie in buttercups and clover-bloom, 420
    Tenants in common with the bees,
And watch the white clouds drift through
    gulfs of trees,
Is better than long waiting in the tomb;
Only once more to feel the coming spring
As the birds feel it, when it bids them
    sing,
    Only once more to see the moon
Through leaf-fringed abbey-arches of the
    elms
    Curve her mild sickle in the West
Sweet with the breath of hay-cocks, were
    a boon
Worth any promise of soothsayer
    realms   430
Or casual hope of being elsewhere blest;
    To take December by the beard
And crush the creaking snow with springy
    foot,
While overhead the North's dumb stream-
    ers shoot,
Till Winter fawn upon the cheek en-
    deared,
    Then the long evening-ends
    Lingered by cosy chimney-nooks,
With high companionship of books
    Or slippered talk of friends
    And sweet habitual looks,   440
Is better than to stop the ears with dust:
Too soon the spectre comes to say, 'Thou
    must!'

2

When toil-crooked hands are crost upon
    the breast,
    They comfort us with sense of rest;
They must be glad to lie forever still;
    Their work is ended with their day;
Another fills their room; 't is the World's
    ancient way,

Whether for good or ill;
But the deft spinners of the brain,
Who love each added day and find it
    gain,   450
    Them overtakes the doom
To snap the half-grown flower upon the
    loom
(Trophy that was to be of life-long pain),
The thread no other skill can ever knit
    again.
'T was so with him, for he was glad to
    live,
'T was doubly so, for he left work begun;
Could not this eagerness of Fate forgive
    Till all the allotted flax were spun?
It matters not; for, go at night or noon,
A friend, whene'er he dies, has died too
    soon,   460
And, once we hear the hopeless *He is
    dead*,
So far as flesh hath knowledge, all is
    said.

VI

1

I seem to see the black procession go:
That crawling prose of death too well I
    know,
The vulgar paraphrase of glorious woe;
I see it wind through that unsightly
    grove,
    Once beautiful, but long defaced
With granite permanence of cockney
    taste
And all those grim disfigurements we
    love:
There, then, we leave him: Him? such
    costly waste   470
Nature rebels at: and it is not true
Of those most precious parts of him we
    knew:
Could we be conscious but as dreamers be,
'T were sweet to leave this shifting life
    of tents
Sunk in the changeless calm of Deity;
Nay, to be mingled with the elements,
The fellow-servant of creative powers,
Partaker in the solemn year's events,
To share the work of busy-fingered
    hours,
To be night's silent almoner of dew, 480
To rise again in plants and breathe and
    grow,

To stream as tides the ocean caverns
    through,
Or with the rapture of great winds to
    blow
About earth's shaken coignes, were not a
    fate
    To leave us all-disconsolate;
Even endless slumber in the sweetening
    sod
    Of charitable earth
That takes out all our mortal stains,
And makes us cleanlier neighbors of the
    clod,
    Methinks were better worth   490
Than the poor fruit of most men's wake-
    ful pains,
    The heart's insatiable ache:
    But such was not his faith,
Nor mine: it may be he had trod
Outside the plain old path of *God thus
    spake,*
    But God to him was very God,
    And not a visionary wraith
Skulking in murky corners of the mind,
    And he was sure to be   499
Somehow, somewhere, imperishable as He,
Not with His essence mystically combined,
As some high spirits long, but whole and
    free,
A perfected and conscious Agassiz.
And such I figure him: the wise of old
Welcome and own him of their peaceful
    fold,
    Not truly with the guild enrolled
    Of him who seeking inward guessed
    Diviner riddles than the rest,
    And groping in the darks of thought
Touched the Great Hand and knew it
    not;   510
    Rather he shares the daily light,
    From reason's charier fountains won,
Of his great chief, the slow-paced Stagy-
    rite,
And Cuvier clasps once more his long-lost
    son.

2

The shape erect is prone: forever stilled
The winning tongue; the forehead's high-
    piled heap,
A cairn which every science helped to
    build,
Unvalued will its golden secrets keep:
He knows at last if Life or Death be
    best:

Wherever he be flown, whatever vest   520
The being hath put on which lately here
So many-friended was, so full of cheer
To make men feel the Seeker's noble zest,
We have not lost him all; he is not gone
To the dumb herd of them that wholly
    die;
The beauty of his better self lives on
In minds he touched with fire, in many an
    eye
He trained to Truth's exact severity;
He was a Teacher: why be grieved for
    him
Whose living word still stimulates the   529
    air?
In endless file shall loving scholars come
The glow of his transmitted touch to share,
And trace his features with an eye less
    dim
Than ours whose sense familiar wont
    makes numb.

1874.   1874.

SONNET [1]

SCOTTISH BORDER

As sinks the sun behind yon alien hills
Whose heather-purpled slopes, in glory
    rolled,
Flush all my thought with momentary
    gold,
What pang of vague regret my fancy
    thrills?
Here 't is enchanted ground the peasant
    tills,
Where the shy ballad dared its blooms un-
    fold,
And memory's glamour makes new sights
    seem old,
As when our life some vanished dream
    fulfils.
Yet not to thee belong these painless tears,
Land loved ere seen: before my darkened
    eyes,
From far beyond the waters and the years,
Horizons mute that wait their poet rise;
The stream before me fades and disap-
    pears,
And in the Charles the western splendor
    dies.

    1875.

[1] See Lowell's letter to Howells, March 21, 1875.
Letters, vol. ii, p. 137.

THREE MEMORIAL POEMS

'Coscienza fusca
O della propria o dell' altrui vergogna
Pur sentirà la tua parola brusca.'

If I let fall a word of bitter mirth [1]
When public shames more shameful pardon won,
Some have misjudged me, and my service done,
If small, yet faithful, deemed of little worth:
Through veins that drew their life from Western earth
Two hundred years and more my blood hath run
In no polluted course from sire to son;
And thus was I predestined ere my birth
To love the soil wherewith my fibres own
Instinctive sympathies; yet love it so
As honor would, nor lightly to dethrone
Judgment, the stamp of manhood, nor forego
The son's right to a mother dearer grown
With growing knowledge and more chaste than snow.

ODE [2]

READ AT THE ONE HUNDREDTH ANNI-
VERSARY OF THE FIGHT AT CONCORD
BRIDGE

19TH APRIL, 1875

I

WHO cometh over the hills,
Her garments with morning sweet,
The dance of a thousand rills
Making music before her feet?
Her presence freshens the air;
Sunshine steals light from her face;
The leaden footstep of Care
Leaps to the tune of her pace,
Fairness of all that is fair,
Grace at the heart of all grace,   10
Sweetener of hut and of hall,
Bringer of life out of naught,
Freedom, oh, fairest of all
The daughters of Time and Thought!

II

She cometh, cometh to-day:
Hark! hear ye not her tread,
Sending a thrill through your clay,
Under the sod there, ye dead,
Her nurslings and champions?
Do ye not hear, as she comes,   20
The bay of the deep-mouthed guns,
The gathering rote of the drums?

[1] Alluding to the lines in the second stanza of Lowell's 'Agassiz,' which were written in 1874, when the
political corruption of that time was being revealed and
in many cases condoned,— lines which were at the
time severely criticised as 'unpatriotic.'
[2] See Lowell's letter to James B. Thayer, January
4, 1877. *Letters*, vol. ii, pp. 188–191.

The bells that called ye to prayer,
How wildly they clamor on her,
Crying, 'She cometh! prepare
Her to praise and her to honor,
That a hundred years ago
Scattered here in blood and tears
Potent seeds wherefrom should grow
Gladness for a hundred years!'   30

III

Tell me, young men, have ye seen
Creature of diviner mien
For true hearts to long and cry for,
Manly hearts to live and die for?
What hath she that others want?
Brows that all endearments haunt,
Eyes that make it sweet to dare,
Smiles that cheer untimely death,
Looks that fortify despair,
Tones more brave than trumpet's breath;
Tell me, maidens, have ye known   41
Household charm more sweetly rare,
Grace of woman ampler blown,
Modesty more debonair,
Younger heart with wit full grown?
Oh for an hour of my prime,
The pulse of my hotter years,
That I might praise her in rhyme
Would tingle your eyelids to tears,
Our sweetness, our strength, and our star,
Our hope, our joy, and our trust,   51
Who lifted us out of the dust,
And made us whatever we are!

IV

Whiter than moonshine upon snow
Her raiment is, but round the hem

Crimson stained; and, as to and fro
Her sandals flash, we see on them,
And on her instep veined with blue,
Flecks of crimson, on those fair feet,
High-arched, Diana-like, and fleet,   60
Fit for no grosser stain than dew:
Oh, call them rather chrisms than stains,
Sacred and from heroic veins !
For, in the glory-guarded pass,
Her haughty and far-shining head
She bowed to shrive Leonidas
With his imperishable dead;
Her, too, Morgarten saw,
Where the Swiss lion fleshed his icy paw;
She followed Cromwell's quenchless star
Where the grim Puritan tread   71
Shook Marston, Naseby, and Dunbar:
Yea, on her feet are dearer dyes
Yet fresh, not looked on with untearful
          eyes.

V

Our fathers found her in the woods
Where Nature meditates and broods,
The seeds of unexampled things
Which Time to consummation brings
Through life and death and man's unstable
          moods;
They met her here, not recognized,   80
A sylvan huntress clothed in furs,
To whose chaste wants her bow sufficed,
Nor dreamed what destinies were hers:
She taught them bee-like to create
Their simpler forms of Church and State;
She taught them to endue
The past with other functions than it knew,
And turn in channels strange the uncertain
          stream of Fate;
Better than all, she fenced them in their
          need
With iron-handed Duty's sternest creed, 90
'Gainst Self's lean wolf that ravens word
          and deed.

VI

Why cometh she hither to-day
To this low village of the plain
Far from the Present's loud highway,
From Trade's cool heart and seething
          brain ?
Why cometh she ? She was not far away.
Since the soul touched it, not in vain,
With pathos of immortal gain,
'T is here her fondest memories stay.
She loves yon pine-bemurmured ridge   100

Where now our broad-browed poet sleeps
Dear to both Englands; near him he
Who wore the ring of Canace;
But most her heart to rapture leaps
Where stood that era-parting bridge,
O'er which, with footfall still as dew,
The Old Time passed into the New;
Where, as your stealthy river creeps,
He whispers to his listening weeds
Tales of sublimest homespun deeds.   110
Here English law and English thought
'Gainst the self-will of England fought;
And here were men (coequal with their
          fate),
Who did great things, unconscious they
          were great.
They dreamed not what a die was cast
With that first answering shot; what then
There was their duty; they were men
Schooled the soul's inward gospel to obey,
Though leading to the lion's den.
They felt the habit-hallowed world give
          way   120
Beneath their lives, and on went they,
Unhappy who was last.
When Buttrick gave the word,
That awful idol of the unchallenged Past,
Strong in their love, and in their lineage
          strong,
Fell crashing: if they heard it not,
Yet the earth heard,
Nor ever hath forgot,
As on from startled throne to throne,
Where Superstition sate or conscious
          Wrong,   130
A shudder ran of some dread birth un-
          known.
Thrice venerable spot !
River more fateful than the Rubicon !
O'er those red planks, to snatch her diadem
Man's Hope, star - girdled, sprang with
          them,
And over ways untried the feet of Doom
          strode on.

VII

Think you these felt no charms
In their gray homesteads and embowered
          farms ?
In household faces waiting at the door
Their evening step should lighten up no
          more ?   140
In fields their boyish feet had known ?
In trees their fathers' hands had set,
And which with them had grown,

Widening each year their leafy coronet ?
Felt they no pang of passionate regret
For those unsolid goods that seem so much
    our own ?
These things are dear to every man that
    lives,
And life prized more for what it lends than
    gives.
Yea, many a tie, through iteration sweet,
Strove to detain their fatal feet;   150
And yet the enduring half they chose,
Whose choice decides a man life's slave or
    king,
The invisible things of God before the seen
    and known:
Therefore their memory inspiration blows
With echoes gathering on from zone to
    zone;
For manhood is the one immortal thing
Beneath Time's changeful sky,
And, where it lightened once, from age to
    age,
Men come to learn, in grateful pilgrimage,
That length of days is knowing when to
    die.   160

VIII

What marvellous change of things and
    men !
She, a world-wandering orphan then,
So mighty now ! Those are her streams
That whirl the myriad, myriad wheels
Of all that does, and all that dreams,
Of all that thinks, and all that feels,
Through spaces stretched from sea to sea;
By idle tongues and busy brains,
By who doth right, and who refrains,
Hers are our losses and our gains;   170
Our maker and our victim she.

IX

Maiden half mortal, half divine,
We triumphed in thy coming; to the brinks
Our hearts were filled with pride's tumul-
    tuous wine;
Better to-day who rather feels than thinks.
Yet will some graver thoughts intrude,
And cares of sterner mood;
They won thee: who shall keep thee ? From
    the deeps
Where discrowned empires o'er their ruins
    brood,
And many a thwarted hope wrings its weak
    hands and weeps,   180
I hear the voice as of a mighty wind

From all heaven's caverns rushing uncon-
    fined,
' I, Freedom, dwell with Knowledge: I
    abide
With men whom dust of faction cannot
    blind
To the slow tracings of the Eternal Mind;
With men by culture trained and fortified,
Who bitter duty to sweet lusts prefer,
Fearless to counsel and obey.
Conscience my sceptre is, and law my
    sword,
Not to be drawn in passion or in play,   190
But terrible to punish and deter;
Implacable as God's word,
Like it, a shepherd's crook to them that
    blindly err.
Your firm-pulsed sires, my martyrs and my
    saints,
Offshoots of that one stock whose patient
    sense
Hath known to mingle flux with perma-
    nence,
Rated my chaste denials and restraints
Above the moment's dear-paid paradise:
Beware lest, shifting with Time's gradual
    creep,
The light that guided shine into your
    eyes.   200
The envious Powers of ill nor wink nor
    sleep:
Be therefore timely wise,
Nor laugh when this one steals, and that
    one lies,
As if your luck could cheat those sleepless
    spies,
Till the deaf Fury comes your house to
    sweep ! '
I hear the voice, and unaffrighted bow;
Ye shall not be prophetic now,
Heralds of ill, that darkening fly
Between my vision and the rainbowed sky,
Or on the left your hoarse forebodings
    croak   210
From many a blasted bough
On Yggdrasil's storm-sinewed oak,
That once was green, Hope of the West, as
    thou:
Yet pardon if I tremble while I boast;
For I have loved as those who pardon most.

X

Away, ungrateful doubt, away !
At least she is our own to-day.
Break into rapture, my song,

Verses, leap forth in the sun,
Bearing the joyance along   220
Like a train of fire as ye run!
Pause not for choosing of words,
Let them but blossom and sing
Blithe as the orchards and birds
With the new coming of spring!
Dance in your jollity, bells;
Shout, cannon; cease not, ye drums;
Answer, ye hillside and dells;
Bow, all ye people!   She comes,
Radiant, calm-fronted, as when   230
She hallowed that April day.
Stay with us! Yes, thou shalt stay,
Softener and strengthener of men,
Freedom, not won by the vain,
Not to be courted in play,
Not to be kept without pain.
Stay with us! Yes, thou wilt stay,
Handmaid and mistress of all,
Kindler of deed and of thought,
Thou that to hut and to hall   240
Equal deliverance brought!
Souls of her martyrs, draw near,
Touch our dull lips with your fire,
That we may praise without fear
Her our delight, our desire,
Our faith's inextinguishable star,
Our hope, our remembrance, our trust,
Our present, our past, our to be,
Who will mingle her life with our dust
And makes us deserve to be free!   250

1875.   1875.

UNDER THE OLD ELM [1]

POEM READ AT CAMBRIDGE ON THE
HUNDREDTH ANNIVERSARY OF WASH-
INGTON'S TAKING COMMAND OF THE
AMERICAN ARMY, 3D JULY, 1775

I

1

WORDS pass as wind, but where great
     deeds were done
A power abides transfused from sire to
     son:

[1] I think the 'Old Elm' the best of the three
[memorial poems], mainly because it was composed
after my college duties were over, though even in that
I was distracted by the intervention of the Commencement dinner. (LOWELL, letter of January 14, 1877.)
  We, too, here in my birthplace, having found out

The boy feels deeper meanings thrill his
     ear,
That tingling through his pulse life-long
     shall run,
With sure impulsion to keep honor clear,
When, pointing down, his father whispers,
     'Here,
Here, where we stand, stood he, the purely
     great,
Whose soul no siren passion could un-
     sphere,
Then nameless, now a power and mixed
     with fate.'
Historic town, thou holdest sacred dust, 10
Once known to men as pious, learnèd,
     just,
And one memorial pile that dares to
     last;
But Memory greets with reverential kiss
No spot in all thy circuit sweet as this,
Touched by that modest glory as it past,
O'er which yon elm hath piously displayed
These hundred years its monumental shade.

2

Of our swift passage through this scenery
Of life and death, more durable than we,
What landmark so congenial as a tree   20
Repeating its green legend every spring,
And, with a yearly ring,
Recording the fair seasons as they flee,
Type of our brief but still-renewed mortal-
     ity?
We fall as leaves: the immortal trunk re-
     mains,
Builded with costly juice of hearts and
     brains
Gone to the mould now, whither all that
     be
Vanish returnless, yet are procreant still
In human lives to come of good or ill,
And feed unseen the roots of Destiny.   30

that something happened here a hundred years ago,
must have our centennial; and, since my friend and
townsman Dr. Holmes could n't be had, I felt bound
to do the poetry for the day. We have still standing
the elm under which Washington took command of the
American (till then *provincial*) army, and under which
also Whitefield had preached some thirty years before.
I took advantage of the occasion to hold out a hand of
kindly reconciliation to Virginia. I could do it with the
profounder feeling, that no family lost more than mine
by the Civil War. Three nephews (the hope of our race)
were killed in one or other of the Virginia battles,
and three cousins on other of those bloody fields.
(LOWELL, letter of July 6, 1875. Quoted by permission
of Messrs. Harper & Brothers.)
  See also the letters of October 16, 1875, and February
22, 1877.

II

1

Men's monuments, grown old, forget their
        names
They should eternize, but the place
Where shining souls have passed imbibes a
        grace
Beyond mere earth; some sweetness of
        their fames
Leaves in the soil its unextinguished trace,
Pungent, pathetic, sad with nobler aims,
That penetrates our lives and heightens
        them or shames.
This insubstantial world and fleet
Seems solid for a moment when we stand
On dust ennobled by heroic feet   40
Once mighty to sustain a tottering land,
And mighty still such burthen to upbear,
Nor doomed to tread the path of things
        that merely were:
Our sense, refined with virtue of the spot,
Across the mists of Lethe's sleepy stream
Recalls him, the sole chief without a blot,
No more a pallid image and a dream,
But as he dwelt with men decorously su-
        preme.

2

Our grosser minds need this terrestrial
        hint
To raise long-buried days from tombs of
        print: 50
'Here stood he,' softly we repeat,
And lo, the statue shrined and still
In that gray minster-front we call the Past,
Feels in its frozen veins our pulses thrill,
Breathes living air and mocks at Death's
        deceit.
It warms, it stirs, comes down to us at last,
Its features human with familiar light,
A man, beyond the historian's art to kill,
Or sculptor's to efface with patient chisel-
        blight.

3

Sure the dumb earth hath memory, nor for
        naught   60
Was Fancy given, on whose enchanted loom
Present and Past commingle, fruit and
        bloom
Of one fair bough, inseparably wrought
Into the seamless tapestry of thought.
So charmed, with undeluded eye we see
In history's fragmentary tale

Bright clues of continuity,
Learn that high natures over Time prevail,
And feel ourselves a link in that entail
That binds all ages past with all that are
        to be.   70

III

1

Beneath our consecrated elm
A century ago he stood,
Famed vaguely for that old fight in the
        wood
Whose red surge sought, but could not
        overwhelm
The life foredoomed to wield our rough-
        hewn helm: [1] —
From colleges, where now the gown
To arms had yielded,[2] from the town,
Our rude self-summoned levies flocked to
        see
The new-come chiefs and wonder which
        was he.
No need to question long; close-lipped and
        tall,   80
Long trained in murder-brooding forests
        lone
To bridle others' clamors and his own,
Firmly erect, he towered above them all,
The incarnate discipline that was to free
With iron curb that armed democracy.

2

A motley rout was that which came to
        stare,
In raiment tanned by years of sun and
        storm,
Of every shape that was not uniform,
Dotted with regimentals here and there;
An army all of captains, used to pray   90
And stiff in fight, but serious drill's despair,
Skilled to debate their orders, not obey;
Deacons were there, selectmen, men of note
In half-tamed hamlets ambushed round
        with woods,
Ready to settle Freewill by a vote,

[1] After the defeat of Braddock, Washington wrote to
his brother: 'By the all-powerful dispensations of Providence I have been protected beyond all human probability or expectation; for I had four bullets through
my coat, and two horses shot under me, yet I escaped
unhurt, although death was levelling my companions
on every side of me.' (Quoted in the *Riverside Literature Series*.)
[2] Harvard, Hollis, and Massachusetts Halls were used
as barracks, and the President's house was for a time
Washington's headquarters.

But largely liberal to its private moods;
Prompt to assert by manners, voice, or pen,
Or ruder arms, their rights as Englishmen,
Nor much fastidious as to how and when:
Yet seasoned stuff and fittest to create   100
A thought-staid army or a lasting state:
Haughty they said he was, at first; severe;
But owned, as all men own, the steady hand
Upon the bridle, patient to command,
Prized, as all prize, the justice pure from
    fear,
And learned to honor first, then love him,
    then revere.
Such power there is in clear-eyed self-
    restraint
And purpose clean as light from every
    selfish taint.

3

Musing beneath the legendary tree,
The years between furl off: I seem to see   110
The sun-flecks, shaken the stirred foliage
    through,
Dapple with gold his sober buff and blue
And weave prophetic aureoles round the
    head
That shines our beacon now nor darkens
    with the dead.
O man of silent mood,
A stranger among strangers then,
How art thou since renowned the Great,
    the Good,
Familiar as the day in all the homes of men !
The wingèd years, that winnow praise to
    blame,
Blow many names out: they but fan and
    flame   120
The self-renewing splendors of thy fame.

IV

1

How many subtlest influences unite,
With spiritual touch of joy or pain,
Invisible as air and soft as light,
To body forth that image of the brain
We call our Country, visionary shape,
Loved more than woman, fuller of fire than
    wine,
Whose charm can none define,
Nor any, though he flee it, can escape !   129
All party-colored threads the weaver Time
Sets in his web, now trivial, now sublime,
All memories, all forebodings, hopes and
    fears,

Mountain and river, forest, prairie, sea,
A hill, a rock, a homestead, field, or tree,
The casual gleanings of unreckoned years,
Take goddess-shape at last and there is She,
Old at our birth, new as the springing
    hours,
Shrine of our weakness, fortress of our
    powers,
Consoler, kindler, peerless 'mid her peers,
A force that 'neath our conscious being
    stirs,   140
A life to give ours permanence, when we
Are borne to mingle our poor earth with
    hers,
And all this glowing world goes with us on
    our biers.

2

Nations are long results, by ruder ways
Gathering the might that warrants length
    of days;
They may be pieced of half-reluctant
    shares
Welded by hammer-strokes of broad-
    brained kings,
Or from a doughty people grow, the heirs
Of wise traditions widening cautious rings;
At best they are computable things,   150
A strength behind us making us feel bold
In right, or, as may chance, in wrong;
Whose force by figures may be summed
    and told,
So many soldiers, ships, and dollars strong,
And we but drops that bear compulsory
    part
In the dumb throb of a mechanic heart;
But Country is a shape of each man's
    mind
Sacred from definition, unconfined
By the cramped walls where daily drudger-
    ies grind;
An inward vision, yet an outward birth   160
Of sweet familiar heaven and earth;
A brooding Presence that stirs motions
    blind
Of wings within our embryo being's shell
That wait but her completer spell
To make us eagle-natured, fit to dare
Life's nobler spaces and untarnished air.

3

You, who hold dear this self-conceived
    ideal,
Whose faith and works alone can make it
    real,

Bring all your fairest gifts to deck her
    shrine
Who lifts our lives away from Thine and
    Mine   170
And feeds the lamp of manhood more di-
    vine
With fragrant oils of quenchless constancy.
When all have done their utmost, surely he
Hath given the best who gives a character
Erect and constant, which nor any shock
Of loosened elements, nor the forceful sea
Of flowing or of ebbing fates, can stir
From its deep bases in the living rock
Of ancient manhood's sweet security:
And this he gave, serenely far from pride
As baseness, boon with prosperous stars
    allied,   181
Part of what nobler seed shall in our loins
    abide.

4

No bond of men as common pride so
    strong,
In names time-filtered for the lips of song,
Still operant, with the primal Forces bound
Whose currents, on their spiritual round,
Transfuse our mortal will nor are gainsaid:
These are their arsenals, these the exhaust-
    less mines
That give a constant heart in great de-
    signs;
These are the stuff whereof such dreams
    are made   190
As make heroic men: thus surely he
Still holds in place the massy blocks he
    laid
'Neath our new frame, enforcing soberly
The self-control that makes and keeps a
    people free.

V

1

Oh, for a drop of that Cornelian ink
Which gave Agricola dateless length of
    days,
To celebrate him fitly, neither swerve
To phrase unkempt, nor pass discretion's
    brink,
With him so statue-like in sad reserve,
So diffident to claim, so forward to de-
    serve !   200
Nor need I shun due influence of his fame
Who, mortal among mortals, seemed as
    now

The equestrian shape with unimpassioned
    brow,
That paces silent on through vistas of ac-
    claim.

2

What figure more immovably august
Than that grave strength so patient and so
    pure,
Calm in good fortune, when it wavered,
    sure,
That mind serene, impenetrably just,
Modelled on classic lines so simple they
    endure ?
That soul so softly radiant and so white 210
The track it left seems less of fire than
    light,
Cold but to such as love distemperature ?
And if pure light, as some deem, be the
    force
That drives rejoicing planets on their
    course,
Why for his power benign seek an impurer
    source ?
His was the true enthusiasm that burns
    long,
Domestically bright,
Fed from itself and shy of human sight,
The hidden force that makes a lifetime
    strong,
And not the short-lived fuel of a song. 220
Passionless, say you ? What is passion for
But to sublime our natures and control
To front heroic toils with late return,
Or none, or such as shames the conqueror ?
That fire was fed with substance of the
    soul
And not with holiday stubble, that could
    burn,
Unpraised of men who after bonfires run,
Through seven slow years of unadvancing
    war,
Equal when fields were lost or fields were
    won,
With breath of popular applause or blame,
Nor fanned nor damped, unquenchably the
    same,   231
Too inward to be reached by flaws of idle
    fame.

3

Soldier and statesman, rarest unison;
High-poised example of great duties done
Simply as breathing, a world's honors worn
As life's indifferent gifts to all men born,

Dumb for himself, unless it were to God,
But for his barefoot soldiers eloquent,
Tramping the snow to coral where they
    trod,
Held by his awe in hollow-eyed content; 240
Modest, yet firm as Nature's self; un-
    blamed
Save by the men his nobler temper
    shamed;
Never seduced through show of present
    good
By other than unsetting lights to steer
New-trimmed in Heaven, nor than his
    steadfast mood
More steadfast, far from rashness as from
    fear;
Rigid, but with himself first, grasping
    still
In swerveless poise the wave-beat helm of
    will;
Not honored then or now because he
    wooed
The popular voice, but that he still with-
    stood;   250
Broad-minded, higher-souled, there is but
    one,
Who was all this and ours, and all men's,
    — WASHINGTON.

4

Minds strong by fits, irregularly great,
That flash and darken like revolving lights,
Catch more the vulgar eye unschooled to
    wait
On the long curve of patient days and
    nights
Rounding a whole life to the circle fair
Of orbed fulfilment; and this balanced
    soul,
So simple in its grandeur, coldly bare
Of draperies theatric, standing there   260
In perfect symmetry of self-control,
Seems not so great at first, but greater
    grows
Still as we look, and by experience learn
How grand this quiet is, how nobly stern
The discipline that wrought through life-
    long throes
That energetic passion of repose.

5

A nature too decorous and severe,
Too self-respectful in its griefs and joys,
For ardent girls and boys
Who find no genius in a mind so clear   270

That its grave depths seem obvious and
    near,
Nor a soul great that made so little noise.
They feel no force in that calm-cadenced
    phrase,
The habitual full-dress of his well-bred
    mind,
That seems to pace the minuet's courtly
    maze
And tell of ampler leisures, roomier length
    of days.
His firm-based brain, to self so little kind
That no tumultuary blood could blind,
Formed to control men, not amaze,
Looms not like those that borrow height of
    haze: 280
It was a world of statelier movement then
Than this we fret in, he a denizen
Of that ideal Rome that made a man for
    men.

VI

1

The longer on this earth we live
And weigh the various qualities of men,
Seeing how most are fugitive,
Or fitful gifts, at best, of now and then,
Wind-wavered corpse-lights, daughters of
    the fen,
The more we feel the high stern-featured
    beauty
Of plain devotedness to duty,   290
Steadfast and still, nor paid with mortal
    praise,
But finding amplest recompense
For life's ungarlanded expense
In work done squarely and unwasted days.
For this we honor him, that he could
    know
How sweet the service and how free
Of her, God's eldest daughter here below,
And choose in meanest raiment which was
    she.

2

Placid completeness, life without a fall
From faith or highest aims, truth's breach-
    less wall,   300
Surely if any fame can bear the touch,
His will say 'Here!' at the last trumpet's
    call,
The unexpressive man whose life expressed
    so much.

VII

1

Never to see a nation born
Hath been given to mortal man,
Unless to those who, on that summer morn,
Gazed silent when the great Virginian
Unsheathed the sword whose fatal flash
Shot union through the incoherent clash
Of our loose atoms, crystallizing them ₃₁₀
Around a single will's unpliant stem,
And making purpose of emotion rash.
Out of that scabbard sprang, as from its womb,
Nebulous at first but hardening to a star,
Through mutual share of sunburst and of gloom,
The common faith that made us what we are.

2

That lifted blade transformed our jangling clans,
Till then provincial, to Americans,
And made a unity of wildering plans;
Here was the doom fixed: here is marked the date ₃₂₀
When this New World awoke to man's estate,
Burnt its last ship and ceased to look behind:
Nor thoughtless was the choice; no love or hate
Could from its poise move that deliberate mind,
Weighing between too early and too late
Those pitfalls of the man refused by Fate:
His was the impartial vision of the great
Who see not as they wish, but as they find.
He saw the dangers of defeat, nor less
The incomputable perils of success; ₃₃₀
The sacred past thrown by, an empty rind;
The future, cloud-land, snare of prophets blind;
The waste of war, the ignominy of peace;
On either hand a sullen rear of woes,
Whose garnered lightnings none could guess,
Piling its thunder-heads and muttering 'Cease!'
Yet drew not back his hand, but gravely chose
The seeming-desperate task whence our new nation rose.

3

A noble choice and of immortal seed !
Nor deem that acts heroic wait on chance
Or easy were as in a boy's romance;   ₃₄₁
The man's whole life preludes the single deed
That shall decide if his inheritance
Be with the sifted few of matchless breed,
Our race's sap and sustenance,
Or with the unmotived herd that only sleep and feed.
Choice seems a thing indifferent; thus or so,
What matters it ? The Fates with mocking face
Look on inexorable, nor seem to know
Where the lot lurks that gives life's foremost place.   ₃₅₀
Yet Duty's leaden casket holds it still,
And but two ways are offered to our will,
Toil with rare triumph, ease with safe disgrace,
The problem still for us and all of human race.
He chose, as men choose, where most danger showed,
Nor ever faltered 'neath the load
Of petty cares, that gall great hearts the most,
But kept right on the strenuous up-hill road,
Strong to the end, above complaint or boast:
The popular tempest on his rock-mailed coast   ₃₆₀
Wasted its wind-borne spray,
The noisy marvel of a day;
His soul sate still in its unstormed abode.

VIII

Virginia gave us this imperial man
Cast in the massive mould
Of those high-statured ages old
Which into grander forms our mortal metal ran;
She gave us this unblemished gentleman:
What shall we give her back but love and praise
As in the dear old unestrangèd days   ₃₇₀
Before the inevitable wrong began ?
Mother of States and undiminished men,
Thou gavest us a country, giving him,
And we owe alway what we owed thee then:
The boon thou wouldst have snatched from us agen
Shines as before with no abatement dim,

A great man's memory is the only thing
With influence to outlast the present whim
And bind us as when here he knit our
    golden ring.   379
All of him that was subject to the hours
Lies in thy soil and makes it part of ours:
Across more recent graves,
Where unresentful Nature waves
Her pennons o'er the shot-ploughed sod,
Proclaiming the sweet Truce of God,
We from this consecrated plain stretch out
Our hands as free from afterthought or
    doubt
As here the united North
Poured her embrownèd manhood forth
In welcome of our savior and thy son.   390
Through battle we have better learned thy
    worth,
The long-breathed valor and undaunted
    will,
Which, like his own, the day's disaster
    done,
Could, safe in manhood, suffer and be still.
Both thine and ours the victory hardly
    won;
If ever with distempered voice or pen
We have misdeemed thee, here we take it
    back,
And for the dead of both don common
    black.
Be to us evermore as thou wast then,
As we forget thou hast not always been,
Mother of States and unpolluted men,   401
Virginia, fitly named from England's manly
    queen !
1875.   *1875.*

AN ODE

FOR THE FOURTH OF JULY, 1876

I

1

ENTRANCED I saw a vision in the cloud
That loitered dreaming in yon sunset sky,
Full of fair shapes, half creatures of the
    eye,
Half chance-evoked by the wind's fantasy
In golden mist, an ever-shifting crowd:
There, 'mid unreal forms that came and
    went
In air-spun robes, of evanescent dye,
A woman's semblance shone preëminent;
Not armed like Pallas, not like Hera proud,

But as on household diligence intent,   10
Beside her visionary wheel she bent
Like Aretë or Bertha, nor than they
Less queenly in her port: about her knee
Glad children clustered confident in play:
Placid her pose, the calm of energy;
And over her broad brow in many a round
(That loosened would have gilt her gar-
    ment's hem),
Succinct, as toil prescribes, the hair was
    wound
In lustrous coils, a natural diadem.
The cloud changed shape, obsequious to the
    whim   20
Of some transmuting influence felt in me,
And, looking now, a wolf I seemed to see
Limned in that vapor, gaunt and hunger-
    bold,
Threatening her charge: resolve in every
    limb,
Erect she flamed in mail of sun-wove gold,
Penthesilea's self for battle dight;
One arm uplifted braced a flickering spear,
And one her adamantine shield made light;
Her face, helm-shadowed, grew a thing to
    fear,
And her fierce eyes, by danger challenged,
    took   30
Her trident - sceptred mother's dauntless
    look.
'I know thee now, O goddess-born !' I
    cried,
And turned with loftier brow and firmer
    stride;
For in that spectral cloud-work I had seen
Her image, bodied forth by love and pride,
The fearless, the benign, the mother-eyed,
The fairer world's toil-consecrated queen.

2

What shape by exile dreamed elates the
    mind
Like hers whose hand, a fortress of the
    poor,
No blood in vengeance spilt, though lawful,
    stains ?   40
Who never turned a suppliant from her
    door ?
Whose conquests are the gains of all man-
    kind ?
To-day her thanks shall fly on every wind,
Unstinted, unrebuked, from shore to shore,
One love, one hope, and not a doubt be-
    hind !
Cannon to cannon shall repeat her praise

Banner to banner flap it forth in flame;
Her children shall rise up to bless her
    name,
And wish her harmless length of days,
The mighty mother of a mighty brood,   50
Blessed in all tongues and dear to every
    blood,
The beautiful, the strong, and, best of all,
    the good.

3

Seven years long was the bow
Of battle bent, and the heightening
Storm-heaps convulsed with the throe
Of their uncontainable lightning;
Seven years long heard the sea
Crash of navies and wave-borne thunder;
Then drifted the cloud-rack a-lee,
And new stars were seen, a world's won-
    der;   60
Each by her sisters made bright,
All binding all to their stations,
Cluster of manifold light
Startling the old constellations:
Men looked up and grew pale:
Was it a comet or star,
Omen of blessing or bale,
Hung o'er the ocean afar ?

4

Stormy the day of her birth:
Was she not born of the strong,   70
She, the last ripeness of earth,
Beautiful, prophesied long ?
Stormy the days of her prime:
Hers are the pulses that beat
Higher for perils sublime,
Making them fawn at her feet.
Was she not born of the strong ?
Was she not born of the wise ?
Daring and counsel belong
Of right to her confident eyes: 80
Human and motherly they,
Careless of station or race:
Hearken ! her children to-day
Shout for the joy of her face.

II

1

No praises of the past are hers,
No fanes by hallowing time caressed,
No broken arch that ministers
To Time's sad instinct in the breast:

She has not gathered from the years
Grandeur of tragedies and tears,   90
Nor from long leisure the unrest
That finds repose in forms of classic grace:
These may delight the coming race
Who haply shall not count it to our crime
That we who fain would sing are here
    before our time.
She also hath her monuments;
Not such as stand decrepitly resigned
To ruin-mark the path of dead events
That left no seed of better days behind,
The tourist's pensioners that show their
    scars   100
And maunder of forgotten wars;
She builds not on the ground, but in the
    mind,
Her open-hearted palaces
For larger-thoughted men with heaven and
    earth at ease:
Her march the plump mow marks, the
    sleepless wheel,
The golden sheaf, the self-swayed com-
    monweal;
The happy homesteads hid in orchard trees
Whose sacrificial smokes through peaceful
    air
Rise lost in heaven, the household's silent
    prayer;
What architect hath bettered these ?   110
With softened eye the westward traveller
    sees
A thousand miles of neighbors side by side,
Holding by toil-won titles fresh from God
The lands no serf or seigneur ever trod,
With manhood latent in the very sod,
Where the long billow of the wheatfield's
    tide
Flows to the sky across the prairie wide,
A sweeter vision than the castled Rhine,
Kindly with thoughts of Ruth and Bible-
    days benign.

2

O ancient commonwealths, that we revere
Haply because we could not know you
    near,   121
Your deeds like statues down the aisles of
    Time
Shine peerless in memorial calm sublime,
And Athens is a trumpet still, and Rome;
Yet which of your achievements is not foam
Weighed with this one of hers (below you
    far
In fame, and born beneath a milder star),

That to Earth's orphans, far as curves the
    dome
Of death-deaf sky, the bounteous West
    means home,
With dear precedency of natural ties   130
That stretch from roof to roof and make
    men gently wise ?
And if the nobler passions wane,
Distorted to base use, if the near goal
Of insubstantial gain
Tempt from the proper race-course of the
    soul
That crowns their patient breath
Whose feet, song-sandalled, are too fleet
    for Death,
Yet may she claim one privilege urbane
And haply first upon the civic roll,
That none can breathe her air nor grow
    humane.   140

3

Oh, better far the briefest hour
Of Athens self-consumed, whose plastic
    power
Hid Beauty safe from Death in words or
    stone;
Of Rome, fair quarry where those eagles
    crowd
Whose fulgurous vans about the world had
    blown
Triumphant storm and seeds of polity;
Of Venice, fading o'er her shipless sea,
Last iridescence of a sunset cloud;
Than this inert prosperity,
This bovine comfort in the sense alone ! 150
Yet art came slowly even to such as those,
Whom no past genius cheated of their
    own
With prudence of o'ermastering precedent;
Petal by petal spreads the perfect rose,
Secure of the divine event;
And only children rend the bud half-blown
To forestall Nature in her calm intent:
Time hath a quiver full of purposes
Which miss not of their aim, to us un-
    known,
And brings about the impossible with ease:
Haply for us the ideal dawn shall break 161
From where in legend-tinted line
The peaks of Hellas drink the morning's
    wine,
To tremble on our lids with mystic sign
Till the drowsed ichor in our veins awake
And set our pulse in tune with moods
    divine:

Long the day lingered in its sea-fringed
    nest,
Then touched the Tuscan hills with golden
    lance
And paused; then on to Spain and France
The splendor flew, and Albion's misty
    crest: 170
Shall Ocean bar him from his destined
    West ?
Or are we, then, arrived too late,
Doomed with the rest to grope disconsolate,
Foreclosed of Beauty by our modern date ?

III

1

Poets, as their heads grow gray,
Look from too far behind the eyes,
Too long-experienced to be wise
In guileless youth's diviner way;
Life sings not now, but prophesies;
Time's shadows they no more behold,   180
But, under them, the riddle old
That mocks, bewilders, and defies:
In childhood's face the seed of shame,
In the green tree an ambushed flame,
In Phosphor a vaunt-guard of Night,
They, though against their will, divine,
And dread the care-dispelling wine
Stored from the Muse's vintage bright,
By age imbued with second-sight.
From Faith's own eyelids there peeps out,
Even as they look, the leer of doubt;   191
The festal wreath their fancy loads
With care that whispers and forebodes:
Nor this our triumph-day can blunt Me-
    gæra's goads.

2

Murmur of many voices in the air
Denounces us degenerate,
Unfaithful guardians of a noble fate,
And prompts indifference or despair:
Is this the country that we dreamed in
    youth,
Where wisdom and not numbers should
    have weight,   200
Seed-field of simpler manners, braver
    truth,
Where shams should cease to dominate
In household, church, and state ?
Is this Atlantis ? This the unpoisoned soil,
Sea-whelmed for ages and recovered late,
Where parasitic greed no more should coil

Round Freedom's stem to bend awry and
   blight
What grew so fair, sole plant of love and
   light ?
Who sit where once in crowned seclusion
   sate
The long-proved athletes of debate   210
Trained from their youth, as none thinks
   needful now ?
Is this debating club where boys dispute,
And wrangle o'er their stolen fruit,
The Senate, erewhile cloister of the few,
Where Clay once flashed and Webster's
   cloudy brow
Brooded those bolts of thought that all the
   horizon knew ?

3

Oh, as this pensive moonlight blurs my
   pines,
Here while I sit and meditate these lines,
To gray-green dreams of what they are by
   day,
So would some light, not reason's sharp-
   edged ray,   220
Trance me in moonshine as before the
   flight
Of years had won me this unwelcome right
To see things as they are, or shall be
   soon,
In the frank prose of undissembling noon !

4

Back to my breast, ungrateful sigh !
Whoever fails, whoever errs,
The penalty be ours, not hers!
The present still seems vulgar, seen too
   nigh;
The golden age is still the age that 's past:
I ask no drowsy opiate   230
To dull my vision of that only state
Founded on faith in man, and therefore
   sure to last.
For, O my country, touched by thee,
The gray hairs gather back their gold;
Thy thought sets all my pulses free;
The heart refuses to be old;
The love is all that I can see.
Not to thy natal-day belong
Time's prudent doubt or age's wrong,
But gifts of gratitude and song: 240
Unsummoned crowd the thankful words,
As sap in spring-time floods the tree,
Foreboding the return of birds,
For all that thou hast been to me !

IV

1

Flawless his heart and tempered to the
   core
Who, beckoned by the forward-leaning
   wave,
First left behind him the firm-footed shore,
And, urged by every nerve of sail and
   oar,
Steered for the Unknown which gods to
   mortals gave,   249
Of thought and action the mysterious door,
Bugbear of fools, a summons to the brave:
Strength found he in the unsympathizing
   sun,
And strange stars from beneath the horizon
   won,
And the dumb ocean pitilessly grave:
High-hearted surely he;
But bolder they who first off-cast
Their moorings from the habitable Past
And ventured chartless on the sea
Of storm-engendering Liberty:
For all earth's width of waters is a span, 260
And their convulsed existence mere re-
   pose,
Matched with the unstable heart of man,
Shoreless in wants, mist-girt in all it
   knows,
Open to every wind of sect or clan,
And sudden-passionate in ebbs and flows.

2

They steered by stars the elder shipmen
   knew,
And laid their courses where the currents
   draw
Of ancient wisdom channelled deep in law,
The undaunted few
Who changed the Old World for the
   New,   270
And more devoutly prized
Than all perfection theorized
The more imperfect that had roots and
   grew.
They founded deep and well,
Those danger-chosen chiefs of men
Who still believed in Heaven and Hell,
Nor hoped to find a spell,
In some fine flourish of a pen,
To make a better man
Than long-considering Nature will or can,
Secure against his own mistakes,   281
Content with what life gives or takes,

And acting still on some fore-ordered plan,
A cog of iron in an iron wheel,
Too nicely poised to think or feel,
Dumb motor in a clock-like common-
　　weal.
They wasted not their brain in schemes
Of what man might be in some bubble-
　　sphere,
As if he must be other than he seems
Because he was not what he should be
　　here,   290
Postponing Time's slow proof to petulant
　　dreams:
Yet herein they were great
Beyond the incredulous lawgivers of yore,
And wiser than the wisdom of the shelf,
That they conceived a deeper-rooted state,
Of hardier growth, alive from rind to
　　core,
By making man sole sponsor of himself.

3
God of our fathers, Thou who wast,
Art, and shalt be when those eye-wise who
　　flout
Thy secret presence shall be lost   300
In the great light that dazzles them to
　　doubt,
We, sprung from loins of stalwart men
Whose strength was in their trust
That Thou wouldst make thy dwelling in
　　their dust
And walk with those a fellow-citizen
Who build a city of the just,
We, who believe Life's bases rest
Beyond the probe of chemic test,
Still, like our fathers, feel Thee near,
Sure that, while lasts the immutable decree,
The land to Human Nature dear   311
Shall not be unbeloved of Thee.
1876.   `   1876.

DEATH OF QUEEN MERCEDES [1]

HERS all that Earth could promise or be-
　　stow, —
Youth, Beauty, Love, a crown, the beckon-
　　ing years,
Lids never wet, unless with joyous tears,
A life remote from every sordid woe,
And by a nation's swelled to lordlier flow.
What lurking-place, thought we, for doubts
　　or fears,
When, the day's swan, she swam along the
　　cheers
Of the Alcalá, five happy months ago ?
The guns were shouting Io Hymen then
That, on her birthday, now denounce her
　　doom;
The same white steeds that tossed their
　　scorn of men
To-day as proudly drag her to the tomb.
Grim jest of fate ! Yet who dare call it
　　blind,
Knowing what life is, what our human-kind?
1878.   (1888.)

[1] Anything more tragic than the circumstances of
her death it would be hard to imagine. She was actually receiving extreme unction while the guns were
firing in honor of her eighteenth birthday, and four
days later we saw her dragged to her dreary tomb at
the Escorial, followed by the coach and its eight white
horses in which she had driven in triumph from the
church to the palace on the day of her wedding. The
poor brutes tossed their snowy plumes as haughtily
now as then. (LOWELL, in a letter to his daughter,
Mabel Lowell Burnett, July 26, 1878. Quoted by permission of Messrs. Harper and Brothers.)

PHŒBE [2]

ERE pales in Heaven the morning star
　　A bird, the loneliest of its kind,
Hears Dawn's faint footfall from afar
　　While all its mates are dumb and blind.

It is a wee sad-colored thing,
　　As shy and secret as a maid,
That, ere in choir the robins sing,
　　Pipes its own name like one afraid.

It seems pain-prompted to repeat
　　The story of some ancient ill,   10
But *Phœbe! Phœbe!* sadly sweet
　　Is all it says, and then is still.

It calls and listens. Earth and sky,
　　Hushed by the pathos of its fate,
Listen: no whisper of reply
　　Comes from its doom-dissevered mate.

Phœbe! it calls and calls again,
　　And Ovid, could he but have heard,
Had hung a legendary pain
　　About the memory of the bird;   20

A pain articulate so long,
　　In penance of some mouldered crime

[2] For Lowell's careful revision of this poem, see his
letters to Mr. Richard Watson Gilder, September 4, 5,
6, 8, and 12, and October 24, 1881; quoted in the *Cambridge Edition* of Lowell, pp. 480-481.

Whose ghost still flies the Furies' thong
  Down the waste solitudes of time.

Waif of the young World's wonder-hour,
  When gods found mortal maidens fair,
And will malign was joined with power
  Love's kindly laws to overbear,

Like Progne, did it feel the stress
  And coil of the prevailing words   30
Close round its being, and compress
  Man's ampler nature to a bird's ?

One only memory left of all
  The motley crowd of vanished scenes,
Hers, and vain impulse to recall
  By repetition what it means.

Phœbe ! is all it has to say
  In plaintive cadence o'er and o'er,
Like children that have lost their way,
  And know their names, but nothing more.

Is it a type, since Nature's Lyre   41
  Vibrates to every note in man,
Of that insatiable desire,
  Meant to be so since life began ?

I, in strange lands at gray of dawn,
  Wakeful, have heard that fruitless plaint
Through Memory's chambers deep withdrawn
  Renew its iterations faint.

So nigh ! yet from remotest years
  It summons back its magic, rife   50
With longings unappeased, and tears
  Drawn from the very source of life.
1881.   1881.

TO WHITTIER

ON HIS SEVENTY-FIFTH BIRTHDAY

NEW ENGLAND's poet, rich in love as years,
  Her hills and valleys praise thee, her swift
      brooks
Dance in thy verse; to her grave sylvan
      nooks
Thy steps allure us, which the wood-thrush
      hears
As maids their lovers', and no treason fears;
Through thee her Merrimacs and Agiochooks

And many a name uncouth win gracious
      looks,
Sweetly familiar to both Englands' ears:

Peaceful by birthright as a virgin lake,
The lily's anchorage, which no eyes behold
Save those of stars, yet for thy brother's
      sake
That lay in bonds, thou blewst a blast as
      bold
As that wherewith the heart of Roland
      brake,
Far heard across the New World and the
      Old.
1882.   1882.

TO HOLMES

ON HIS SEVENTY-FIFTH BIRTHDAY

DEAR Wendell, why need count the years
  Since first your genius made me thrill,
If what moved then to smiles or tears,
  Or both contending, move me still ?

What has the Calendar to do
  With poets ? What Time's fruitless tooth
With gay immortals such as you
  Whose years but emphasize your youth ?

One air gave both their lease of breath;
  The same paths lured our boyish feet;   10
One earth will hold us safe in death
  With dust of saints and scholars sweet.

Our legends from one source were drawn,
  I scarce distinguish yours from mine,
And *don't* we make the Gentiles yawn
  With ' You remembers ? ' o'er our wine !

If I, with too senescent air,
  Invade your elder memory's pale,
You snub me with a pitying ' Where
  Were you in the September Gale ? '   20

Both stared entranced at Lafayette,
  Saw Jackson dubbed with LL. D.
What Cambridge saw not strikes us yet
  As scarcely worth one's while to see.

Ten years my senior, when my name
  In Harvard's entrance-book was writ,
Her halls still echoed with the fame
  Of you, her poet and her wit.

'T is fifty years from then to now:
But your Last Leaf renews its green,   30
Though, for the laurels on your brow
(So thick they crowd), 't is hardly seen.

The oriole's fledglings fifty times
Have flown from our familiar elms;
As many poets with their rhymes
Oblivion's darkling dust o'erwhelms.

The birds are hushed, the poets gone
Where no harsh critic's lash can reach,
And still your wingèd brood sing on
To all who love our English speech.   40

Nay, let the foolish records be
That make believe you 're seventy-five:
You 're the old Wendell still to me, —
And that 's the youngest man alive.

The gray-blue eyes, I see them still,
The gallant front with brown o'erhung,
The shape alert, the wit at will,
The phrase that stuck, but never stung.

You keep your youth as yon Scotch firs,
Whose gaunt line my horizon hems,   50
Though twilight all the lowland blurs,
Hold sunset in their ruddy stems.

You with the elders? Yes, 't is true,
But in no sadly literal sense,
With elders and coevals too,
Whose verb admits no preterite tense.

Master alike in speech and song
Of fame's great antiseptic — Style,
You with the classic few belong
Who tempered wisdom with a smile.   60

Outlive us all! Who else like you
Could sift the seedcorn from our chaff,
And make us with the pen we knew
Deathless at least in epitaph?
1884.   1884.

INTERNATIONAL COPYRIGHT

IN vain we call old notions fudge,
And bend our conscience to our deal-
ing;
The Ten Commandments will not budge,
And stealing will continue stealing.
1885.   1886.

SIXTY-EIGHTH BIRTHDAY

As life runs on, the road grows strange
With faces new, and near the end
The milestones into headstones change,
'Neath every one a friend.
1887.

INSCRIPTION

PROPOSED FOR A SOLDIERS' AND SAILORS' MONUMENT IN BOSTON

To those who died for her on land and
sea,
That she might have a country great and
free,
Boston builds this: build ye her monument
In lives like theirs, at duty's summons
spent.
                              1887.

ENDYMION [1]

A MYSTICAL COMMENT ON TITIAN'S 'SACRED AND PROFANE LOVE'

I

MY day began not till the twilight fell,
And, lo, in ether from heaven's sweetest
well,
The New Moon swam divinely isolate
In maiden silence, she that makes my fate
Haply not knowing it, or only so
As I the secrets of my sheep may know;
Nor ask I more, entirely blest if she,
In letting me adore, ennoble me
To height of what the Gods meant making
man,
As only she and her best beauty can.   10
Mine be the love that in itself can find
Seed of white thoughts, the lilies of the
mind,
Seed of that glad surrender of the will
That finds in service self's true purpose
still;
Love that in outward fairness sees the tent
Pitched for an inmate far more excellent;
Love with a light irradiate to the core,
Lit at her lamp, but fed from inborn store;

[1] See Scudder's *Life of Lowell*, vol. ii, pp. 371, 372, and also two letters from Lowell to Mr. Garrison, on ' Endymion,' quoted in Greenslet's *Lowell*, pp. 217, 218.

Love thrice-requited with the single joy 19
Of an immaculate vision naught could cloy,
Dearer because, so high beyond my scope,
My life grew rich with her, unbribed by
   hope
Of other guerdon save to think she knew
One grateful votary paid her all her due;
Happy if she, high-radiant there, resigned
To his sure trust her image in his mind.
O fairer even than Peace is when she
   comes
Hushing War's tumult, and retreating
   drums
Fade to a murmur like the sough of bees
Hidden among the noon-stilled linden-trees,
Bringer of quiet, thou that canst allay   31
The dust and din and travail of the day,
Strewer of Silence, Giver of the dew
That doth our pastures and our souls re-
   new,
Still dwell remote, still on thy shoreless sea
Float unattained in silent empery,
Still light my thoughts, nor listen to a
   prayer
Would make thee less imperishably fair !

II

Can, then, my twofold nature find content
In vain conceits of airy blandishment ?   40
Ask I no more ? Since yesterday I task
My storm-strewn thoughts to tell me what
   I ask:
Faint premonitions of mutation strange
Steal o'er my perfect orb, and, with the
   change,
Myself am changed; the shadow of my
   earth
Darkens the disk of that celestial worth
Which only yesterday could still suffice
Upwards to waft my thoughts in sacrifice;
My heightened fancy with its touches
   warm
Moulds to a woman's that ideal form;   50
Nor yet a woman's wholly, but divine
With awe her purer essence bred in mine.
Was it long brooding on their own surmise,
Which, of the eyes engendered, fools the
   eyes,
Or have I seen through that translucent air
A Presence shaped in its seclusions bare,
My Goddess looking on me from above
As look our russet maidens when they love,
But high-uplifted o'er our human heat
And passion-paths too rough for her pearl
   feet ?   60

Slowly the Shape took outline as I gazed
At her full-orbed or crescent, till, bedazed
With wonder-working light that subtly
   wrought
My brain to its own substance, steeping
   thought
In trances such as poppies give, I saw
Things shut from vision by sight's sober
   law,
Amorphous, changeful, but defined at last
Into the peerless Shape mine eyes hold fast.
This, too, at first I worshipt: soon, like
   wine,
Her eyes, in mine poured, frenzy-philtred
   mine;   70
Passion put Worship's priestly raiment on
And to the woman knelt, the Goddess gone.
Was I, then, more than mortal made ? or
   she
Less than divine that she might mate with
   me ?
If mortal merely, could my nature cope
With such o'ermastery of maddening hope ?
If Goddess, could she feel the blissful woe
That women in their self-surrender know ?

III

Long she abode aloof there in her heaven,
Far as the grape-bunch of the Pleiad seven
Beyond my madness' utmost leap ; but
   here   81
Mine eyes have feigned of late her rapture
   near,
Moulded of mind-mist that broad day dis-
   pels,
Here in these shadowy woods and brook-
   lulled dells.

Have no heaven-habitants e'er felt a void
In hearts sublimed with ichor unalloyed ?
E'er longed to mingle with a mortal fate
Intense with pathos of its briefer date ?
Could she partake, and live, our human
   stains ?
Even with the thought there tingles through
   my veins   90
Sense of unwarned renewal; I, the dead,
Receive and house again the ardor fled,
As once Alcestis; to the ruddy brim
Feel masculine virtue flooding every limb,
And life, like Spring returning, brings the
   key
That sets my senses from their winter free,
Dancing like naked fauns too glad for
   shame.

Her passion, purified to palest flame,
Can it thus kindle ? Is her purpose this ?
I will not argue, lest I lose a bliss   100
That makes me dream Tithonus' fortune
  mine
(Or what of it was palpably divine
Ere came the fruitlessly immortal gift);
I cannot curb my hope's imperious drift
That wings with fire my dull mortality;
Though fancy-forged, 't is all I feel or see.

IV

My Goddess sinks; round Latmos' darken-
  ing brow
Trembles the parting of her presence now,
Faint as the perfume left upon the grass
By her limbs' pressure or her feet that
  pass   110
By me conjectured, but conjectured so
As things I touch far fainter substance
  show.
Was it mine eyes' imposture I have seen
Flit with the moonbeams on from shade to
  sheen
Through the wood-openings ? Nay, I see
  her now
Out of her heaven new-lighted, from her
  brow
The hair breeze-scattered, like loose mists
  that blow
Across her crescent, goldening as they go
High-kirtled for the chase, and what was
  shown,
Of maiden rondure, like the rose half-
  blown.   120
If dream, turn real ! If a vision, stay !
Take mortal shape, my philtre's spell obey !
If hags compel thee from thy secret sky
With gruesome incantations, why not I,
Whose only magic is that I distil
A potion, blent of passion, thought, and
  will,
Deeper in reach, in force of fate more
  rich,
Than e'er was juice wrung by Thessalian
  witch
From moon-enchanted herbs, — a potion
  brewed
Of my best life in each diviner mood ?   130
Myself the elixir am, myself the bowl
Seething and mantling with my soul of soul.
Taste and be humanized: what though the
  cup,
With thy lips frenzied, shatter ? Drink it
  up !

If but these arms may clasp, o'erquited so,
My world, thy heaven, all life means I
  shall know.

V

Sure she hath heard my prayer and granted
  half,
As Gods do who at mortal madness laugh.
Yet if life's solid things illusion seem,
Why may not substance wear the mask of
  dream ?   140
In sleep she comes; she visits me in
  dreams,
And, as her image in a thousand streams,
So in my veins, that her obey, she sees,
Floating and flaming there, her images
Bear to my little world's remotest zone
Glad messages of her, and her alone.
With silence-sandalled Sleep she comes to
  me
(But softer-footed, sweeter-browed, than
  she),
In motion gracious as a seagull's wing,
And all her bright limbs, moving, seem to
  sing.   150
Let me believe so, then, if so I may
With the night's bounty feed my beggared
  day.
In dreams I see her lay the goddess down
With bow and quiver, and her crescent-
  crown
Flicker and fade away to dull eclipse
As down to mine she deigns her longed-for
  lips;
And as her neck my happy arms enfold,
Flooded and lustred with her loosened gold,
She whispers words each sweeter than a
  kiss:
Then, wakened with the shock of sudden
  bliss,   160
My arms are empty, my awakener fled,
And, silent in the silent sky o'erhead,
But coldly as on ice-plated snow, she
  gleams,
Herself the mother and the child of dreams.

VI

Gone is the time when phantasms could
  appease
My quest phantasmal and bring cheated
  ease;
When, if she glorified my dreams, I felt
Through all my limbs a change immortal
  melt
At touch of hers illuminate with soul.

Not long could I be stilled with Fancy's
    dole; 170
Too soon the mortal mixture in me caught
Red fire from her celestial flame, and
    fought
For tyrannous control in all my veins:
My fool's prayer was accepted; what re-
    mains ?
Or was it some eidolon merely, sent
By her who rules the shades in banishment,
To mock me with her semblance ? Were
    it thus,
How 'scape I shame, whose will was trai-
    torous ?
What shall compensate an ideal dimmed ?
How blanch again my statue virgin-limbed,
Soiled with the incense-smoke her chosen
    priest 181
Poured more profusely as within decreased
The fire unearthly, fed with coals from far
Within the soul's shrine ? Could my fallen
    star
Be set in heaven again by prayers and tears
And quenchless sacrifice of all my years,
How would the victim to the flamen leap,
And life for life's redemption paid hold
    cheap !

But what resource when she herself de-
    scends
From her blue throne, and o'er her vassal
    bends 190
That shape thrice-deified by love, those eyes
Wherein the Lethe of all others lies ?
When my white queen of heaven's remote-
    ness tires,
Herself against her other self conspires,
Takes woman's nature, walks in mortal
    ways,
And finds in my remorse her beauty's
    praise ?
Yet all would I renounce to dream again
The dream in dreams fulfilled that made
    my pain,
My noble pain that heightened all my years
With crowns to win and prowess-breeding
    tears; 200
Nay, would that dream renounce once more
    to see
Her from her sky there looking down at me !

VII

Goddess, reclimb thy heaven, and be once
    more
An inaccessible splendor to adore,

A faith, a hope of such transcendent worth
As bred ennobling discontent with earth;
Give back the longing, back the elated
    mood
That, fed with thee, spurned every meaner
    good;
Give even the spur of impotent despair
That, without hope, still bade aspire and
    dare; 210
Give back the need to worship, that still
    pours
Down to the soul the virtue it adores !

Nay, brightest and most beautiful, deem
    naught
These frantic words, the reckless wind of
    thought:
Still stoop, still grant, — I live but in thy
    will;
Be what thou wilt, but be a woman still !
Vainly I cried, nor could myself believe
That what I prayed for I would fain re-
    ceive.
My moon is set; my vision set with her;
No more can worship vain my pulses stir.
Goddess Triform, I own thy triple spell, 221
My heaven's queen, — queen, too, of my
    earth and hell !

1887. [1]   1888.

AUSPEX

My heart, I cannot still it,
Nest that had song-birds in it;
And when the last shall go,
The dreary days, to fill it,
Instead of lark or linnet,
Shall whirl dead leaves and snow.

Had they been swallows only,
Without the passion stronger
That skyward longs and sings, —
Woe 's me, I shall be lonely
When I can feel no longer
The impatience of their wings !

A moment, sweet delusion,
Like birds the brown leaves hover;
But it will not be long
Before the wild confusion
Fall wavering down to cover
The poet and his song.

                               (1888.)

[1] Parts of the poem were written much earlier.

THE PREGNANT COMMENT

OPENING one day a book of mine,
I absent, Hester found a line
Praised with a pencil-mark, and this
She left transfigured with a kiss.

When next upon the page I chance,
Like Poussin's nymphs my pulses dance,
And whirl my fancy where it sees
Pan piping 'neath Arcadian trees,
Whose leaves no winter-scenes rehearse,
Still young and glad as Homer's verse.
'What mean,' I ask, 'these sudden joys?
This feeling fresher than a boy's?
What makes this line, familiar long,
New as the first bird's April song?
I could, with sense illumined thus,
Clear doubtful texts in Æschylus!'

Laughing, one day she gave the key,
My riddle's open-sesame;
Then added, with a smile demure,
Whose downcast lids veiled triumph sure,
'If what I left there give you pain,
You — you — can take it off again;
'T was for *my* poet, not for him,
Your Doctor Donne there!'

                           Earth grew dim
And wavered in a golden mist,
As rose, not paper, leaves I kissed.
Donne, you forgive? I let you keep
Her precious comment, poet deep.

                              (1888.)

TELEPATHY

'AND how could you dream of meeting?'
  Nay, how can you ask me, sweet?
All day my pulse had been beating
  The tune of your coming feet.

And as nearer and ever nearer
  I felt the throb of your tread,
To be in the world grew dearer,
  And my blood ran rosier red.

Love called, and I could not linger,
  But sought the forbidden tryst,
As music follows the finger
  Of the dreaming lutanist.

And though you had said it and said it,
  'We must not be happy to-day,'

Was I not wiser to credit
  The fire in my feet than your Nay?

                              (1888.)

THE SECRET

I HAVE a fancy: how shall I bring it
Home to all mortals wherever they be?
Say it or sing it? Shoe it or wing it,
So it may outrun or outfly ME,
Merest cocoon-web whence it broke free?

Only one secret can save from disaster,
Only one magic is that of the Master:
Set it to music; give it a tune, —
Tune the brook sings you, tune the breeze
      brings you,
Tune the wild columbines nod to in June!

This is the secret: so simple, you see!
Easy as loving, easy as kissing,
Easy as — well, let me ponder — as miss-
      ing,
Known, since the world was, by scarce two
      or three.

                                   1888.

MONNA LISA

SHE gave me all that woman can,
Nor her soul's nunnery forego,
A confidence that man to man
Without remorse can never show.

Rare art, that can the sense refine
Till not a pulse rebellious stirs,
And, since she never can be mine,
Makes it seem sweeter to be hers!

                              (1888.)

THE NOBLER LOVER

IF he be a nobler lover, take him!
  You in you I seek, and not myself;
Love with men 's what women choose to
      make him,
  Seraph strong to soar, or fawn-eyed elf:
All I am or can, your beauty gave it,
  Lifting me a moment nigh to you,
And my bit of heaven, I fain would save
      it —
  Mine I thought it was, I never knew.

What you take of me is yours to serve
    you,
  All I give, you gave to me before;
Let him win you! If I but deserve you,
  I keep all you grant to him and more:
You shall make me dare what others dare
    not,
  You shall keep my nature pure as snow,
And a light from you that others share
    not
  Shall transfigure me where'er I go.

Let me be your thrall! However lowly
  Be the bondsman's service I can do,
Loyalty shall make it high and holy;
  Naught can be unworthy, done for you.
Men shall say, 'A lover of this fashion
  Such an icy mistress well beseems.'
Women say, 'Could we deserve such pas-
    sion,
  We might be the marvel that he dreams.'
                                (1895.)

'FRANCISCUS DE VERULAMIO SIC COGITAVIT'

THAT'S a rather bold speech, my Lord
    Bacon,
  For, indeed, is 't so easy to know
Just how much we from others have
    taken,
  And how much our own natural flow?

Since your mind bubbled up at its foun-
    tain,
  How many streams made it elate,
While it calmed to the plain from the
    mountain,
  As every mind must that grows great?

While you thought 't was You thinking as
    newly
  As Adam still wet with God's dew,   10
You forgot in your self-pride that truly
  The whole Past was thinking through
    you.

Greece, Rome, nay, your namesake, old
    Roger,
  With Truth's nameless delvers who
    wrought
In the dark mines of Truth, helped to prod
    your
  Fine brain with the goad of their thought.

As mummy was prized for a rich hue
  The painter no elsewhere could find,
So 't was buried men's thinking with which
    you
  Gave the ripe mellow tone to your
    mind.   20

I heard the proud strawberry saying,
  'Only look what a ruby I 've made!'
It forgot how the bees in their maying
  Had brought it the stuff for its trade.

And yet there 's the half of a truth in it,
  And my Lord might his copyright sue;
For a thought 's his who kindles new youth
    in it,
  Or so puts it as makes it more true.

The birds but repeat without ending
  The same old traditional notes,   30
Which some, by more happily blending,
  Seem to make over new in their throats;

And we men through our old bit of song
    run,
  Until one just improves on the rest,
And we call a thing his, in the long run,
  Who utters it clearest and best.
                                1888.

IN A COPY OF OMAR KHAYYÁM

THESE pearls of thought in Persian gulfs
    were bred,
  Each softly lucent as a rounded moon;
The diver Omar plucked them from their
    bed,
  Fitzgerald strung them on an English
    thread.

Fit rosary for a queen, in shape and hue,
  When Contemplation tells her pensive
    beads
Of mortal thoughts, forever old and new.
  Fit for a queen? Why, surely then for
    you!

The moral? Where Doubt's eddies toss
    and twirl
  Faith's slender shallop till her footing reel,
Plunge: if you find not peace beneath the
    whirl,
  Groping, you may like Omar grasp a pearl.
                                1888.

TURNER'S OLD TÉMÉRAIRE

UNDER A FIGURE SYMBOLIZING THE CHURCH

THOU wast the fairest of all man-made
  things;
The breath of heaven bore up thy cloudy
  wings,
And, patient in their triple rank,
The thunders crouched about thy flank,
Their black lips silent with the doom of
  kings.

The storm-wind loved to rock him in thy
  pines,
And swell thy vans with breath of great
  designs;
Long-wildered pilgrims of the main
By thee relaid their course again,
Whose prow was guided by celestial signs.

How didst thou trample on tumultuous
  seas,   11
Or, like some basking sea-beast stretched
  at ease,
Let the bull-fronted surges glide
Caressingly along thy side,
Like glad hounds leaping by the hunts-
  man's knees !

Heroic feet, with fire of genius shod,
In battle's ecstasy thy deck have trod,
While from their touch a fulgor ran
Through plank and spar, from man to man,
Welding thee to a thunderbolt of God.   20

Now a black demon, belching fire and
  steam,
Drags thee away, a pale, dismantled
  dream,
And all thy desecrated hulk
Must landlocked lie, a helpless bulk,
To gather weeds in the regardless stream.

Woe 's me, from Ocean's sky-horizoned air
To this ! Better, the flame-cross still aflare,
Shot-shattered to have met thy doom
Where thy last lightnings cheered the
  gloom,
Than here be safe in dangerless despair. 30

Thy drooping symbol to the flagstaff
  clings,
Thy rudder soothes the tide to lazy rings,

Thy thunders now but birthdays greet,
Thy planks forget the martyrs' feet,
Thy masts what challenges the sea-wind
  brings.

Thou a mere hospital, where human
  wrecks,
Like winter-flies, crawl those renownèd
  decks,
Ne'er trodden save by captive foes,
And wonted sternly to impose
God's will and thine on bowed imperial
  necks !   40

Shall nevermore, engendered of thy fame,
A new sea-eagle heir thy conqueror name,
And with commissioned talons wrench
From thy supplanter's grimy clench
His sheath of steel, his wings of smoke
  and flame ?

This shall the pleased eyes of our children
  see;
For this the stars of God long even as
  we;
Earth listens for his wings; the Fates
Expectant lean; Faith cross-propt waits,
And the tired waves of Thought's insur-
  gent sea.   50
                                        1888.

ON A BUST OF GENERAL GRANT [1]

STRONG, simple, silent are the [steadfast]
  laws
That sway this universe, of none withstood,
Unconscious of man's outcries or applause,
Or what man deems his evil or his good;

[1] This poem is the last, so far as is known, written by
Mr. Lowell. He laid it aside for revision, leaving two
of the verses incomplete. In a pencilled fragment of
the poem the first verse appears as follows : —

Strong, simple, silent, such are Nature's Laws.

In the final copy, from which the poem is now printed,
the verse originally stood : —

Strong, steadfast, silent are the   laws.

but 'steadfast' is crossed out, and 'simple' written
above.
  A similar change is made in the ninth verse of the
stanza, where 'simpleness' is substituted for 'stead-
fastness.' The change from 'steadfast' to 'simple'
was not made, probably through oversight, in the first
verse of the second stanza. There is nothing to indicate what epithet Mr. Lowell would have chosen to
complete the first verse of the third stanza. (Note by
Professor C. E. Norton, in Last Poems of James Russell Lowell.)

And when the Fates ally them with a cause
That wallows in the sea-trough and seems
    lost,
Drifting in danger of the reefs and sands
Of shallow counsels, this way, that way,
    tost,
Strength, silence, simpleness, of these three
    strands
They twist the cable shall the world hold
    fast   10
To where its anchors clutch the bed-rock
    of the Past.

Strong, simple, silent, therefore such was
    he
Who helped us in our need; the eternal law
That who can saddle Opportunity
Is God's elect, though many a mortal flaw
May minish him in eyes that closely see,
Was verified in him: what need we say
Of one who made success where others
    failed,
Who, with no light save that of common
    day,
Struck hard, and still struck on till For-
    tune quailed,   20
But that (so sift the Norns) a desperate
    van
Ne'er fell at last to one who was not wholly
    man.

A face all prose where Time's [benignant]
    haze
Softens no raw edge yet, nor makes all fair
With the beguiling light of vanished days;
This is relentless granite, bleak and bare,
Roughhewn, and scornful of æsthetic
    phrase;
Nothing is here for fancy, nought for
    dreams,
The Present's hard uncompromising light
Accents all vulgar outlines, flaws, and
    seams,   30
Yet vindicates some pristine natural right
O'ertopping that hereditary grace
Which marks the gain or loss of some time-
    fondled race.

So Marius looked, methinks, and Crom-
    well so,
Not in the purple born, to those they led
Nearer for that and costlier to the foe,
New moulders of old forms, by nature
    bred

The exhaustless life of manhood's seeds to
    show,
Let but the ploughshare of portentous
    times
Strike deep enough to reach them where
    they lie: 40
Despair and danger are their fostering
    climes,
And their best sun bursts from a stormy
    sky:
He was our man of men, nor would abate
The utmost due manhood could claim of
    fate.

Nothing ideal, a plain-people's man
At the first glance, a more deliberate
    ken
Finds type primeval, theirs in whose veins
    ran
Such blood as quelled the dragon in his
    den,
Made harmless fields, and better worlds
    began:
He came grim-silent, saw and did the
    deed   50
That was to do; in his master-grip
Our sword flashed joy; no skill of words
    could breed
Such sure conviction as that close-clamped
    lip;
He slew our dragon, nor, so seemed it,
    knew
He had done more than any simplest man
    might do.

Yet did this man, war-tempered, stern as
    steel
Where steel opposed, prove soft in civil
    sway;
The hand hilt-hardened had lost tact to
    feel
The world's base coin, and glozing knaves
    made prey
Of him and of the entrusted Common-
    weal;   60
So Truth insists and will not be denied.
We turn our eyes away, and so will
    Fame,
As if in his last battle he had died
Victor for us and spotless of all blame,
Doer of hopeless tasks which praters shirk
One of those still plain men that do the
    world's rough work.

1891.   1892.

WALT WHITMAN

[The selections from Whitman are printed by the kind permission of Messrs. Small, Maynard & Co., the authorized publishers of his works; and of Messrs. Horace L. Traubel and Thomas B. Harned, his literary executors.]

THERE WAS A CHILD WENT FORTH [1]

THERE was a child went forth every day,
And the first object he look'd upon, that object he became,
And that object became part of him for the day or a certain part of the day,
Or for many years or stretching cycles of years.

The early lilacs became part of this child,
And grass and white and red morning-glories, and white and red clover, and the song of the phœbe-bird,
And the Third-month lambs and the sow's pink-faint litter, and the mare's foal and the cow's calf,
And the noisy brood of the barnyard or by the mire of the pond-side,
And the fish suspending themselves so curiously below there, and the beautiful curious liquid,
And the water-plants with their graceful flat heads, all became part of him. 10

The field-sprouts of Fourth-month and Fifth-month became part of him,
Winter-grain sprouts and those of the light-yellow corn, and the esculent roots of the garden,
And the apple-trees cover'd with blossoms and the fruit afterward, and wood-berries, and the commonest weeds by the road,
And the old drunkard staggering home from the outhouse of the tavern whence he had lately risen,
And the schoolmistress that pass'd on her way to the school,

And the friendly boys that pass'd, and the quarrelsome boys,
And the tidy and fresh-cheek'd girls, and the barefoot negro boy and girl,
And all the changes of city and country wherever he went.
His own parents, he that had father'd him and she that had conceiv'd him in her womb and birth'd him,
They gave this child more of themselves than that, 20
They gave him afterward every day, they became part of him.

The mother at home quietly placing the dishes on the supper-table,
The mother with mild words, clean her cap and gown, a wholesome odor falling off her person and clothes as she walks by,
The father, strong, self-sufficient, manly, mean, anger'd, unjust,
The blow, the quick loud word, the tight bargain, the crafty lure,
The family usages, the language, the company, the furniture, the yearning and swelling heart,
Affection that will not be gainsay'd, the sense of what is real, the thought if after all it should prove unreal,
The doubts of day-time and the doubts of night-time, the curious whether and how,
Whether that which appears so is so, or is it all flashes and specks?
Men and women crowding fast in the streets, if they are not flashes and specks what are they? 30
The streets themselves and the façades of houses, and goods in the windows,
Vehicles, teams, the heavy-plank'd wharves, the huge crossing at the ferries,
The village on the highland seen from afar at sunset, the river between,
Shadows, aureola and mist, the light falling on roofs and gables of white or brown two miles off,

[1] In the first edition, 1855, without title. In the second edition, 1856, called 'Poem of The Child That Went Forth and Always Goes Forth Forever and Forever.'

The schooner near by sleepily dropping
down the tide, the little boat slack-tow'd
astern,
The hurrying tumbling waves, quick-broken
crests, slapping,
The strata of color'd clouds, the long bar of
maroon-tint away solitary by itself, the
spread of purity it lies motionless in,
The horizon's edge, the flying sea-crow, the
fragrance of salt marsh and shore mud,
These became part of that child who went
forth- every day, and who now goes, and
will always go forth every day.[1]

1855.

SONG OF MYSELF [2]

1

I CELEBRATE myself, and sing myself,
And what I assume you shall assume,
For every atom belonging to me as good
belongs to you.

[1] In the early editions, the following line was added
at the end of the poem: —

And these become part of him or her that peruses them now.

[2] In 1855, without title. In 1856, as the 'Poem of
Walt Whitman, an American.' In the third edition, 1860,
with the title, ' Walt Whitman,' and so in the following
editions until 1881, when the present title was first
used.

The sections were first numbered in 1867.

It must be noted from the beginning that Whitman
celebrates himself not as an isolated individual, but
as the type of all individual selves, claiming for them
all absolute equality. Compare the poem beginning: —

One's-self I sing, a simple separate person,
Yet utter the word Democratic, the word En-Masse.

One of Whitman's early fragments (Notes and Fragments, p. 36, no. 112) reads : —

I celebrate myself to celebrate you ;
I say the same word for every man and woman living.

Compare also Whitman's Preface to the 1876 edition
of Leaves of Grass : ' Then I meant " Leaves of Grass,"
as published, to be the Poem of average Identity (of
yours, whoever you are, now reading these lines). . . .
All serves, helps — but in the centre of all, absorbing
all, giving, for your purpose, the only meaning and vitality to all, master or mistress of all, under the law,
stands Yourself. To sing the Song of that law of average Identity, and of Yourself, consistently with the
divine law of the universal, is a main intention of these
" Leaves." '

In his ' myself ' he means to picture the typical democratic self. It was both by temperament, and also with
a definite purpose in view, that he chose to speak in
the first person. One of his early fragmentary notes
reads : ' Ego-style. First-person-style. Style of composition an animated ego-style — " I do not think " " I
perceive " — or something involving self-esteem, decision, authority — as opposed to the current third person style, essayism, didactic, removed from animation,
stating general truths in a didactic, well-smoothed . . .'
(Notes and Fragments, p. 179.)

I loafe and invite my soul,
I lean and loafe at my ease observing a
spear of summer grass.

My tongue, every atom of my blood, form'd
from this soil, this air,
Born here of parents born here from parents the same, and their parents the same,
I, now thirty-seven years old in perfect
health begin,
Hoping to cease not till death.

Creeds and schools in abeyance,   10
Retiring back a while sufficed at what they
are, but never forgotten,
I harbor for good or bad, I permit to speak
at every hazard,
Nature without check with original energy. [3]

. . . .

6

A child said What is the grass ? fetching it
to me with full hands;
How could I answer the child ? I do not
know what it is any more than he.

I guess it must be the flag of my disposition,
out of hopeful green stuff woven.

Or I guess it is the handkerchief of the
Lord,
A scented gift and remembrancer design-
edly dropt,
Bearing the owner's name someway in the
corners, that we may see and remark, and
say Whose ?

Or I guess the grass is itself a child, the
produced babe of the vegetation.

Or I guess it is a uniform hieroglyphic,
And it means, Sprouting alike in broad
zones and narrow zones,
Growing among black folks as among white,
Kanuck, Tuckahoe, Congressman, Cuff, I
give them the same, I receive them the
same.   11

And now it seems to me the beautiful uncut
hair of graves.

Tenderly will I use you curling grass,
It may be you transpire from the breasts of
young men,

[3] The last eight lines of section 1 are not found in
the earlier editions, and were not added until 1881.

It may be if I had known them I would
have loved them,
It may be you are from old people, or from
offspring taken soon out of their mothers'
laps,
And here you are the mothers' laps.

This grass is very dark to be from the
white heads of old mothers,
Darker than the colorless beards of old men,
Dark to come from under the faint red
roofs of mouths.   20

O I perceive after all so many uttering
tongues,
And I perceive they do not come from the
roofs of mouths for nothing.

I wish I could translate the hints about the
dead young men and women,
And the hints about old men and mothers,
and the offspring taken soon out of their
laps.

What do you think has become of the young
and old men?
And what do you think has become of the
women and children?

They are alive and well somewhere,
The smallest sprout shows there is really
no death,
And if ever there was it led forward life,
and does not wait at the end to arrest it,
And ceas'd the moment life appear'd.   30

All goes onward and outward, nothing col-
lapses,
And to die is different from what any one
supposed, and luckier.

7

Has any one supposed it lucky to be born?
I hasten to inform him or her it is just as
lucky to die, and I know it.

I pass death with the dying and birth with
the new-wash'd babe, and am not contain'd between my hat and boots,
And peruse manifold objects, no two alike
and every one good,
The earth good and the stars good, and their
adjuncts all good.

I am not an earth nor an adjunct of an
earth,

I am the mate and companion of people, all
just as immortal and fathomless as myself,
(They do not know how immortal, but I
know.)

Every kind for itself and its own, for me
mine male and female,
For me those that have been boys and that
love women,   10
For me the man that is proud and feels how
it stings to be slighted,
For me the sweet-heart and the old maid,
for me mothers and the mothers of
mothers,
For me lips that have smiled, eyes that have
shed tears,
For me children and the begetters of children.

Undrape! you are not guilty to me, nor
stale nor discarded,
I see through the broadcloth and gingham
whether or no,
And am around, tenacious, acquisitive, tireless, and cannot be shaken away.

8

The little one sleeps in its cradle,
I lift the gauze and look a long time, and
silently brush away flies with my hand.

The youngster and the red-faced girl turn
aside up the bushy hill,
I peeringly view them from the top.

The suicide sprawls on the bloody floor of
the bedroom,
I witness the corpse with its dabbled hair,
I note where the pistol has fallen.

.   .   .   .

9

The big doors of the country barn stand
open and ready,
The dried grass of the harvest-time loads
the slow-drawn wagon,
The clear light plays on the brown gray
and green intertinged,
The armfuls are pack'd to the sagging
mow.

I am there, I help, I came stretch'd atop
of the load,
I felt its soft jolts, one leg reclined on the
other,

I jump from the cross-beams and seize the clover and timothy,
And roll head over heels and tangle my hair full of wisps.

10.

Alone far in the wilds and mountains I hunt,
Wandering amazed at my own lightness and glee,
In the late afternoon choosing a safe spot to pass the night,
Kindling a fire and broiling the fresh-kill'd game,
Falling asleep on the gather'd leaves with my dog and gun by my side.

The Yankee clipper is under her sky-sails, she cuts the sparkle and scud,
My eyes settle the land, I bend at her prow or shout joyously from the deck.

The boatmen and clam-diggers arose early and stopt for me,
I tuck'd my trowser-ends in my boots and went and had a good time;
You should have been with us that day round the chowder-kettle. 10

I saw the marriage of the trapper in the open air in the far west, the bride was a red girl,
Her father and her friends sat near cross-legged and dumbly smoking, they had moccasins to their feet and large thick blankets hanging from their shoulders,
On a bank lounged the trapper, he was drest mostly in skins, his luxuriant beard and curls protected his neck, he held his bride by the hand,
She had long eyelashes, her head was bare, her coarse straight locks descended upon her voluptuous limbs and reach'd to her feet.

The runaway slave came to my house and stopt outside,
I heard his motions crackling the twigs of the woodpile,
Through the swung half-door of the kitchen I saw him limpsy and weak,
And went where he sat on a log and led him in and assured him,
And brought water and fill'd a tub for his sweated body and bruis'd feet,

And gave him a room that enter'd from my own, and gave him some coarse clean clothes, 20
And remember perfectly well his revolving eyes and his awkwardness,
And remember putting plasters on the galls of his neck and ankles;
He staid with me a week before he was recuperated and pass'd north,
I had him sit next me at table, my fire-lock lean'd in the corner.

. . . .

14

The wild gander leads his flock through the cool night,
Ya-honk he says, and sounds it down to me like an invitation,
The pert may suppose it meaningless, but I, listening close,
Find its purpose and place up there toward the wintry sky.
The sharp-hoof'd moose of the north, the cat on the house-sill, the chickadee, the prairie-dog,
The litter of the grunting sow as they tug at her teats,
The brood of the turkey-hen and she with her half-spread wings,
I see in them and myself the same old law.

The press of my foot to the earth springs a hundred affections,
They scorn the best I can do to relate them.

I am enamour'd of growing out-doors, 11
Of men that live among cattle or taste of the ocean or woods,
Of the builders and steerers of ships and the wielders of axes and mauls, and the drivers of horses,
I can eat and sleep with them week in and week out.

What is commonest, cheapest, nearest, easiest, is Me,
Me going in for my chances, spending for vast returns,
Adorning myself to bestow myself on the first that will take me,
Not asking the sky to come down to my good will,
Scattering it freely forever.

. . . .

16

I am of old and young, of the foolish as
much as the wise,
Regardless of others, ever regardful of
others,
Maternal as well as paternal, a child as well
as a man,
Stuff'd with the stuff that is coarse and
stuff'd with the stuff that is fine,
One of the Nation of many nations, the
smallest the same and the largest the
same,
A Southerner soon as a Northerner, a
planter nonchalant and hospitable down
by the Oconee I live,
A Yankee bound my own way ready for
trade, my joints the limberest joints on
earth and the sternest joints on earth,
A Kentuckian walking the vale of the Elk-
horn in my deer-skin leggings, a Louisi-
anian or Georgian,
A boatman over lakes or bays or along
coasts, a Hoosier, Badger, Buckeye;
At home on Kanadian snow-shoes or up in
the bush, or with fishermen off Newfoundland,   10
At home in the fleet of ice-boats, sailing
with the rest and tacking,
At home on the hills of Vermont or in the
woods of Maine, or the Texan ranch,
Comrade of Californians, comrade of free
North-Westerners (loving their big proportions),
Comrade of raftsmen and coalmen, comrade of all who shake hands and welcome
to drink and meat,
A learner with the simplest, a teacher of
the thoughtfullest,
A novice beginning yet experient of myriads
of seasons,
Of every hue and caste am I, of every rank
and religion,
A farmer, mechanic, artist, gentleman,
sailor, quaker,
Prisoner, fancy-man, rowdy, lawyer, physician, priest.

I resist any thing better than my own
diversity,   20
Breathe the air but leave plenty after me,
And am not stuck up, and am in my
place.

(The moth and the fish-eggs are in their
place,
The bright suns I see and the dark suns I
cannot see are in their place,
The palpable is in its place and the impalpable is in its place.)

17

These are really the thoughts of all men in
all ages and lands, they are not original
with me,
If they are not yours as much as mine they
are nothing, or next to nothing,
If they are not the riddle and the untying
of the riddle they are nothing,
If they are not just as close as they are
distant they are nothing.

This is the grass that grows wherever the
land is and the water is,
This the common air that bathes the
globe.

18

With music strong I come, with my cornets
and my drums,
I play not marches for accepted victors
only, I play marches for conquer'd and
slain persons.[1]

Have you heard that it was good to gain
the day?
I also say it is good to fall, battles are lost
in the same spirit in which they are
won.

I beat and pound for the dead,
I blow through my embouchures my loudest and gayest for them.[2]

Vivas to those who have fail'd!
And to those whose war-vessels sank in the
sea!
And to those themselves who sank in the
sea!

---

[1] Instead of these two lines, the original edition has:

This is the breath of laws and songs and behaviour,
This is the tasteless water of souls . . . this is the true sustenance,
It is for the illiterate . . . it is for the judges of the supreme
court . . . it is for the federal capitol and the state capitols,
It is for the admirable communes of literary men and com-
posers and singers and lecturers and engineers and savans,
It is for the endless races of working people and farmers and
seamen.
This is the trill of a thousand clear cornets and scream of the
octave flute and strike of triangles.
I play not a march for victors only . . . I play great marches
for conquered and slain persons.

[2] I sound triumphal drums for the dead.
I fling through my embouchures the loudest and gayest
music to them. (1855.)

And to all generals that lost engagements,
and all overcome heroes !
And the numberless unknown heroes equal
to the greatest heroes known !

20

. . . .

In all people I see myself, none more and
not one a barley-corn less,
And the good or bad I say of myself I say
of them.

I know I am solid and sound,
To me the converging objects of the universe perpetually flow,
All are written to me, and I must get what
the writing means.

I know I am deathless,
I know this orbit of mine cannot be swept
by a carpenter's compass,
I know I shall not pass like a child's carla-
cue cut with a burnt stick at night.

I know I am august,
I do not trouble my spirit to vindicate itself
or be understood,   10
I see that the elementary laws never apolo-
gize,
(I reckon I behave no prouder than the
level I plant my house by, after all.)

I exist as I am, that is enough,
If no other in the world be aware I sit
content,
And if each and all be aware I sit content.

One world is aware and by far the largest
to me, and that is myself,
And whether I come to my own to-day or
in ten thousand or ten million years,
I can cheerfully take it now, or with equal
cheerfulness I can wait.

My foothold is tenon'd and mortis'd in
granite,
I laugh at what you call dissolution,   20
And I know the amplitude of time.

21

I am the poet of the Body and I am the
poet of the Soul,
The pleasures of heaven are with me and
the pains of hell are with me,

The first I graft and increase upon myself,
the latter I translate into a new tongue.

I am the poet of the woman the same as
the man,
And I say it is as great to be a woman as
to be a man,
And I say there is nothing greater than the
mother of men.

I chant the chant of dilation or pride,[1]
We have had ducking and deprecating
about enough,
I show that size is only development.

Have you outstript the rest ? are you the
President ?   10
It is a trifle, they will more than arrive
there every one, and still pass on.

I am he that walks with the tender and
growing night,[2]
I call to the earth and sea half-held by the
night.
Press close bare-bosom'd night — press
close magnetic nourishing night !
Night of south winds — night of the large
few stars !
Still nodding night — mad naked summer
night.

Smile O voluptuous cool-breath'd earth !
Earth of the slumbering and liquid trees !
Earth of departed sunset — earth of the
mountains misty-topt !

[1] Among Whitman's early memoranda of the essential things not to be omitted from *Leaves of Grass* we
find : ' Boldness — *Nonchalant ease* and indifference.
To encourage me or any one else continually to strike
out alone.' (*Notes and Fragments*, p. 57.)
[2] The original form of this beautiful apostrophe to
Night is to be found in *Notes and Fragments*, p. 17 : —

Night of south winds — night of the large few stars !
Still slumberous night — mad, naked summer night !

Smile, O voluptuous, procreant earth !
Earth of the nodding and liquid trees !
Earth of the mountains, misty-top't
Earth of departed sunset — Earth of shine and dark, mottling
the tide of the river !
Earth of the vitreous fall of the full moon just tinged with
blue !
Earth of the limpid gray of clouds purer and clearer for my
sake !
Earth of far arms — rich, apple-blossomed earth !
Smile, for your lover comes !

Spread round me earth ! Spread with your curtained hours;
Take me as many a time you 've taken ;
Till springing up in . . .

Prodigal, you have given me love ;
Sustenance, happiness, health have given ;
Therefore I to you give love ;
O unspeakable, passionate love !

Earth of the vitreous pour of the full moon
    just tinged with blue !   20
Earth of shine and dark mottling the tide
    of the river !
Earth of the limpid gray of clouds brighter
    and clearer for my sake !
Far-swooping elbow'd earth — rich apple-
    blossom'd earth !
Smile, for your lover comes.

Prodigal, you have given me love — there-
    fore I to you give love !
O unspeakable passionate love !

22

You sea ! I resign myself to you also — I
    guess what you mean,
I behold from the beach your crooked in-
    viting fingers,
I believe you refuse to go back without
    feeling of me,
We must have a turn together, I undress,
    hurry me out of sight of the land,
Cushion me soft, rock me in billowy
    drowse,
Dash me with amorous wet, I can repay
    you.

Sea of stretch'd ground-swells,
Sea breathing broad and convulsive breaths,
Sea of the brine of life and of unshovell'd
    yet always-ready graves,
Howler and scooper of storms, capricious
    and dainty sea,
I am integral with you, I too am of one
    phase and of all phases.

. . . .

30

All truths wait in all things,
They neither hasten their own delivery nor
    resist it,
They do not need the obstetric forceps of
    the surgeon,
The insignificant is as big to me as any,
(What is less or more than a touch ?)

Logic and sermons never convince,
The damp of the night drives deeper into
    my soul.

(Only what proves itself to every man and
    woman is so,
Only what nobody denies is so.)

A minute and a drop of me settle my
    brain,
I believe the soggy clods shall become
    lovers and lamps,
And a compend of compends is the meat of
    a man or woman,
And a summit and flower there is the feel-
    ing they have for each other,
And they are to branch boundlessly out of
    that lesson until it becomes omnific,
And until one and all shall delight us, and
    we them.

31

I believe a leaf of grass is no less than the
    journey-work of the stars,
And the pismire is equally perfect, and a
    grain of sand, and the egg of the wren,
And the tree-toad is a chef-d'œuvre for the
    highest,
And the running blackberry would adorn
    the parlors of heaven,
And the narrowest hinge in my hand puts
    to scorn all machinery,
And the cow crunching with depress'd head
    surpasses any statue,
And a mouse is miracle enough to stagger
    sextillions of infidels.

. . . .

33

Space and Time ! now I see it is true, what
    I guess'd at,
What I guess'd when I loaf'd on the grass,
What I guess'd while I lay alone in my bed,
And again as I walk'd the beach under the
    paling stars of the morning.

My ties and ballasts leave me, my elbows
    rest in sea-gaps,
I skirt sierras, my palms cover continents,
I am afoot with my vision.

By the city's quadrangular houses — in log
    huts, camping with lumbermen,
Along the ruts of the turnpike, along the dry
    gulch and rivulet bed,
Weeding my onion-patch or hoeing rows of
    carrots and parsnips, crossing savannas,
    trailing in forests,   10
Prospecting, gold-digging, girdling the trees
    of a new purchase,
Scorch'd ankle-deep by the hot sand, haul-
    ing my boat down the shallow river,

Where the panther walks to and fro on a limb overhead, where the buck turns furiously at the hunter,

Where the rattlesnake suns his flabby length on a rock, where the otter is feeding on fish,

Where the alligator in his tough pimples sleeps by the bayou,

Where the black bear is searching for roots or honey, where the beaver pats the mud with his paddle-shaped tail;

Over the growing sugar, over the yellow-flower'd cotton plant, over the rice in its low moist field,

Over the sharp-peak'd farm house, with its scallop'd scum and slender shoots from the gutters,

Over the western persimmon, over the long-leav'd corn, over the delicate blue-flower flax,

Over the white and brown buckwheat, a hummer and buzzer there with the rest,

Over the dusky green of the rye as it ripples and shades in the breeze;   21

Scaling mountains, pulling myself cautiously up, holding on by low scragged limbs,

Walking the path worn in the grass and beat through the leaves of the brush,

Where the quail is whistling betwixt the woods and the wheat-lot,

Where the bat flies in the Seventh-month eve, where the great gold-bug drops through the dark,

Where the brook puts out of the roots of the old tree and flows to the meadow,

Where cattle stand and shake away flies with the tremulous shuddering of their hides,

Where the cheese-cloth hangs in the kitchen, where andirons straddle the hearth-slab, where cobwebs fall in festoons from the rafters;

Where trip-hammers crash, where the press is whirling its cylinders,

Wherever the human heart beats with terrible throes under its ribs,   30

Where the pear-shaped balloon is floating aloft (floating in it myself and looking composedly down),

Where the life-car is drawn on the slip-noose, where the heat hatches pale-green eggs in the dented sand,

Where the she-whale swims with her calf and never forsakes it,

Where the steam-ship trails hind-ways its long pennant of smoke,

Where the fin of the shark cuts like a black chip out of the water,

Where the half-burn'd brig is riding on unknown currents,

Where shells grow to her slimy deck, where the dead are corrupting below;

Where the dense-starr'd flag is borne at the head of the regiments,

Approaching Manhattan up by the long-stretching island,

Under Niagara, the cataract falling like a veil over my countenance,   40

Upon a door-step, upon the horse-block of hard wood outside,

Upon the race-course, or enjoying picnics or jigs or a good game of base-ball,

At he-festivals, with blackguard gibes, ironical license, bull-dances, drinking, laughter,

At the cider-mill tasting the sweets of the brown mash, sucking the juice through a straw,

At apple-peelings wanting kisses for all the red fruit I find,

At musters, beach-parties, friendly bees, huskings, house-raisings;

Where the mocking-bird sounds his delicious gurgles, cackles, screams, weeps,

Where the hay-rick stands in the barn-yard, where the dry-stalks are scatter'd, where the brood-cow waits in the hovel,

Where the bull advances to do his masculine work, where the stud to the mare, where the cock is treading the hen,

Where the heifers browse, where geese nip their food with short jerks,   50

Where sun-down shadows lengthen over the limitless and lonesome prairie,

Where herds of buffalo make a crawling spread of the square miles far and near,

Where the humming-bird shimmers, where the neck of the long-lived swan is curving and winding,

Where the laughing-gull scoots by the shore, where she laughs her near-human laugh,

Where bee-hives range on a gray bench in the garden half hid by the high weeds,

Where band-neck'd partridges roost in a ring on the ground with their heads out,

Where burial coaches enter the arch'd gates of a cemetery,

Where winter wolves bark amid wastes of
snow and icicled trees,
Where the yellow-crown'd heron comes to
the edge of the marsh at night and feeds
upon small crabs,
Where the splash of swimmers and divers
cools the warm noon,   60
Where the katy-did works her chromatic
reed on the walnut-tree over the well,
Through patches of citrons and cucumbers
with silver-wired leaves,
Through the salt-lick or orange glade, or
under conical firs,
Through the gymnasium, through the curtain'd saloon, through the office or public
hall;
Pleas'd with the native and pleas'd with the
foreign, pleas'd with the new and old,
Pleas'd with the homely woman as well as
the handsome,
Pleas'd with the quakeress as she puts off
her bonnet and talks melodiously,
Pleas'd with the tune of the choir of the
whitewash'd church,
Pleas'd with the earnest words of the sweat-
ing Methodist preacher, impress'd seriously at the camp-meeting;
Looking in at the shop-windows of Broadway the whole forenoon, flatting the flesh
of my nose on the thick plate glass,   70
Wandering the same afternoon with my
face turn'd up to the clouds, or down a
lane or along the beach,
My right and left arms round the sides of
two friends, and I in the middle;
Coming home with the silent and dark-
cheek'd bush-boy, (behind me he rides at
the drape of the day,)
Far from the settlements studying the
print of animals' feet, or the moccasin
print,
By the cot in the hospital reaching lemon-
ade to a feverish patient,
Nigh the coffin'd corpse when all is still,
examining with a candle;
Voyaging to every port to dicker and adventure,
Hurrying with the modern crowd as eager
and fickle as any,
Hot toward one I hate, ready in my madness to knife him,
Solitary at midnight in my back yard, my
thoughts gone from me a long while,   80
Walking the old hills of Judæa with the
beautiful gentle God by my side,

Speeding through space, speeding through
heaven and the stars,
Speeding amid the seven satellites and the
broad ring, and the diameter of eighty
thousand miles,
Speeding with tail'd meteors, throwing fire-
balls like the rest,
Carrying the crescent child that carries its
own full mother in its belly, [1]
Storming, enjoying, planning, loving, cau-
tioning,
Backing and filling, appearing and disappearing,
I tread day and night such roads.

I visit the orchards of spheres and look at
the product, [2]
And look at quintillions ripen'd and look at
quintillions green.   90

I fly those flights of a fluid and swallowing
soul,
My course runs below the soundings of
plummets.

I help myself to material and immate-
rial,
No guard can shut me off, no law prevent
me.

I anchor my ship for a little while only,
My messengers continually cruise away or
bring their returns to me.

I go hunting polar furs and the seal, leaping
chasms with a pike pointed staff, clinging
to topples of brittle and blue.

I ascend to the foretruck,
I take my place late at night in the crow's-
nest,
We sail the arctic sea, it is plenty light
enough,   100
Through the clear atmosphere I stretch
around on the wonderful beauty,
The enormous masses of ice pass me and
I pass them, the scenery is plain in all
directions,
The white-topt mountains show in the dis-
tance, I fling out my fancies toward them,

[1] Compare the old ballad: —

> I saw the new moon late yestreen
> With the old moon in her arms.

[2] I visit the orchards of God and look at the spheric product. (1855.)

We are approaching some great battle-
field in which we are soon to be engaged,
We pass the colossal outposts of the encampment, we pass with still feet and
caution, .
Or we are entering by the suburbs some vast
and ruin'd city,
The blocks and fallen architecture more
than all the living cities of the globe.

. . . .

I understand the large hearts of heroes,
The courage of present times and all times,
How the skipper saw the crowded and rud-
derless wreck of the steam-ship, and
Death chasing it up and down the storm,
How he knuckled tight and gave not back
an inch, and was faithful of days and
faithful of nights,　　　　　III
And chalk'd in large letters on a board, *Be
of good cheer, we will not desert you ;*
How he follow'd with them and tack'd with
them three days and would not give it
up,
How he saved the drifting company at
last,
How the lank loose-gown'd women look'd
when boated from the side of their prepared graves,
How the silent old-faced infants and the
lifted sick, and the sharp-lipp'd unshaved
men;
All this I swallow, it tastes good, I like it
well, it becomes mine,
I am the man, I suffer'd, I was there.

The disdain and calmness of martyrs,
The mother of old, condemn'd for a witch,
burnt with dry wood, her children gazing
on,　　　　　120
The hounded slave that flags in the race,
leans by the fence, blowing, cover'd with
sweat,
The twinges that sting like needles his legs
and neck, the murderous buckshot and
the bullets,
All these I feel or am.

I am the hounded slave, I wince at the bite
of the dogs,
Hell and despair are upon me, crack and
again crack the marksmen,
I clutch the rails of the fence, my gore
dribs, thinn'd with the ooze of my skin,
I fall on the weeds and stones,

The riders spur their unwilling horses, haul
close,
Taunt my dizzy ears and beat me violently
over the head with whip-stocks.

Agonies are one of my changes of garments,　　　　　130
I do not ask the wounded person how he
feels, I myself become the wounded person,
My hurts turn livid upon me as I lean on a
cane and observe.

I am the mash'd fireman with breast-bone
broken,
Tumbling walls buried me in their débris,
Heat and smoke I inspired, I heard the yell-
ing shouts of my comrades,
I heard the distant click of their picks and
shovels,
They have clear'd the beams away, they
tenderly lift me forth.

I lie in the night air in my red shirt, the
pervading hush is for my sake,
Painless after all I lie exhausted but not so
unhappy,
White and beautiful are the faces around
me, the heads are bared of their fire-caps,
The kneeling crowd fades with the light of
the torches.　　　　　141

Distant and dead resuscitate,
They show as the dial or move as the hands
of me, I am the clock myself.

I am an old artillerist, I tell of my fort's
bombardment,
I am there again.

Again the long roll of the drummers,
Again the attacking cannon, mortars,
Again to my listening ears the cannon re-
sponsive.

I take part, I see and hear the whole,
The cries, curses, roar, the plaudits for well-
aim'd shots,　　　　　150
The ambulanza slowly passing trailing its
red drip,
Workmen searching after damages, making
indispensable repairs,
The fall of grenades through the rent roof,
the fan-shaped explosion,
The whizz of limbs, heads, stone, wood, iron,
high in the air.

Again gurgles the mouth of my dying
general, he furiously waves with his
hand,
He gasps through the clot *Mind not me —
mind — the entrenchments.*

34

Now I tell what I knew in Texas in my
early youth,[1]
(I tell not the fall of Alamo,
Not one escaped to tell the fall of Alamo,
The hundred and fifty are dumb yet at
Alamo,)
'T is the tale of the murder in cold blood of
four hundred and twelve young men.

Retreating they had form'd in a hollow
square with their baggage for breast-
works,
Nine hundred lives out of the surrounding
enemies, nine times their number, was
the price they took in advance,
Their colonel was wounded and their am-
munition gone,
They treated for an honorable capitulation,
receiv'd writing and seal, gave up their
arms and march'd back prisoners of war.

They were the glory of the race of ran-
gers,   10
Matchless with horse, rifle, song, supper,
courtship,
Large, turbulent, generous, handsome,
proud, and affectionate,
Bearded, sunburnt, drest in the free costume of hunters,
Not a single one over thirty years of age.

The second First-day morning they were
brought out in squads and massacred, it
was beautiful early summer,
The work commenced about five o'clock and
was over by eight.

None obey'd the command to kneel,
Some made a mad and helpless rush, some
stood stark and straight,
A few fell at once, shot in the temple or
heart, the living and dead lay together,

The maim'd and mangled dug in the dirt,
the new-comers saw them there,   20
Some half-kill'd attempted to crawl away,
These were despatch'd with bayonets or
batter'd with the blunts of muskets,
A youth not seventeen years old seiz'd his
assassin till two more came to release
him,
The three were all torn and cover'd with
the boy's blood.

At eleven o'clock began the burning of the
bodies;
That is the tale of the murder of the four
hundred and twelve young men.[2]

35

Would you hear of an old-time sea-
fight?[3]
Would you learn who won by the light of
the moon and stars?
List to the yarn, as my grandmother's
father the sailor told it to me.

Our foe was no skulk in his ship I tell you
(said he),
His was the surly English pluck, and there
is no tougher or truer, and never was,
and never will be;
Along the lower'd eve he came horribly
raking us.

We closed with him, the yards entangled,
the cannon touch'd,
My captain lash'd fast with his own hands.

We had receiv'd some eighteen pound shots
under the water,
On our lower-gun-deck two large pieces
had burst at the first fire, killing all
around and blowing up overhead.   10

Fighting at sun-down, fighting at dark,
Ten o'clock at night, the full moon well up,
our leaks on the gain, and five feet of
water reported,
The master-at-arms loosing the prisoners
confined in the after-hold to give them a
chance for themselves.

---

[1] Instead of the first five lines of this section, the
original edition has: —

I tell not the fall of Alamo . . . not one escaped to tell the
fall of Alamo,
The hundred and fifty are dumb yet at Alamo.

Hear now the tale of a jet-black sunrise,
Hear of the murder in cold-blood of four hundred and twelve
young men.

[2] In the original edition there was added the line: —

And that was a jet-black sunrise.

[3] Did you read in the sea-books of the old-fashioned **frigate**
fight? (1855.)

The transit to and from the magazine is
now stopt by the sentinels,
They see so many strange faces they do
not know whom to trust.

Our frigate takes fire,
The other asks if we demand quarter ?
If our colors are struck and the fighting
done ?

Now I laugh content, for I hear the voice
of my little captain,
We have not struck, he composedly cries,
*we have just begun our part of the fight-
ing.*

Only three guns are in use,   21
One is directed by the captain himself
against the enemy's mainmast,
Two well serv'd with grape and canister
silence his musketry and clear his decks.

The tops alone second the fire of this little
battery, especially the main-top,
They hold out bravely during the whole of
the action.

Not a moment's cease,
The leaks gain fast on the pumps, the fire
eats toward the powder-magazine.

One of the pumps has been shot away, it is
generally thought we are sinking.

Serene stands the little captain,
He is not hurried, his voice is neither high
nor low,   30
His eyes give more light to us than our
battle-lanterns.

Toward twelve there in the beams of the
moon they surrender to us.

36

Stretch'd and still lies the midnight,
Two great hulls motionless on the breast of
the darkness,
Our vessel riddled and slowly sinking,
preparations to pass to the one we have
conquer'd,
The captain on the quarter-deck coldly
giving his orders through a countenance
white as a sheet,
Near by the corpse of the child that serv'd
in the cabin,

The dead face of an old salt with long white
hair and carefully curl'd whiskers,
The flames spite of all that can be done
flickering aloft and below,
The husky voices of the two or three officers yet fit for duty,
Formless stacks of bodies and bodies by
themselves, dabs of flesh upon the masts
and spars,
Cut of cordage, dangle of rigging, slight
shock of the soothe of waves,
Black and impassive guns, litter of pow-
der-parcels, strong scent,
A few large stars overhead, silent and
mournful shining,
Delicate sniffs of sea-breeze, smells of sedgy
grass and fields by the shore, death-mes-
sages given in charge to survivors,
The hiss of the surgeon's knife, the gnawing teeth of his saw,
Wheeze, cluck, swash of falling blood, short
wild scream, and long, dull, tapering
groan,
These so, these irretrievable.

. . . .

44

It is time to explain myself — let us stand
up.

What is known I strip away,
I launch all men and women forward with
me into the Unknown.

The clock indicates the moment — but what
does eternity indicate ? [1]

We have thus far exhausted trillions of
winters and summers,
There are trillions ahead, and trillions
ahead of them.

Births have brought us richness and variety,
And other births will bring us richness and
variety.

I do not call one greater and one smaller,
That which fills its period and place is equal
to any.   10

[1] After this line there followed, in the original edition, another paragraph of two lines : —

Eternity lies in bottomless reservoirs . . . its buckets are
rising forever and ever,
They pour and they pour and they exhale away.

Were mankind murderous or jealous upon
 you, my brother, my sister?
I am sorry for you, they are not murderous or jealous upon me,
All has been gentle with me, I keep no account with lamentation,
(What have I to do with lamentation?)

I am an acme of things accomplish'd, and
 I an encloser of things to be.

My feet strike an apex of the apices of the
 stairs,
On every step bunches of ages, and larger
 bunches between the steps,
All below duly travel'd, and still I mount
 and mount.

Rise after rise bow the phantoms behind
 me,
Afar down I see the huge first Nothing, I
 know I was even there,   20
I waited unseen and always, and slept
 through the lethargic mist,[1]
And took my time, and took no hurt from
 the fetid carbon.

Long I was hugg'd close — long and long.

Immense have been the preparations for
 me,
Faithful and friendly the arms that have
 help'd me.

Cycles ferried my cradle, rowing and rowing like cheerful boatmen,
For room to me stars kept aside in their
 own rings,
They sent influences to look after what was
 to hold me.

Before I was born out of my mother generations guided me,
My embryo has never been torpid, nothing
 could overlay it.   30

For it the nebula cohered to an orb,
The long slow strata piled to rest it on,
Vast vegetables gave it sustenance,
Monstrous sauroids transported it in their
 mouths and deposited it with care.

[1] I waited unseen and always, and slept while God carried me through the lethargic mist. (1855.)

All forces have been steadily employ'd to
 complete and delight me,
Now on this spot I stand with my robust
 soul.

.   .   .   .

46

I know I have the best of time and space,
 and was never measured and never will
 be measured.

I tramp a perpetual journey, (come listen
 all!)
My signs are a rain-proof coat, good shoes,
 and a staff cut from the woods,
No friend of mine takes his ease in my
 chair,
I have no chair, no church, no philosophy,
I lead no man to a dinner-table, library,
 exchange,
But each man and each woman of you I
 lead upon a knoll,
My left hand hooking you round the waist,
My right hand pointing to landscapes of
 continents and the public road.

Not I, not any one else can travel that road
 for you,   10
You must travel it for yourself.

It is not far, it is within reach,
Perhaps you have been on it since you were
 born and did not know,
Perhaps it is everywhere on water and on
 land.

Shoulder your duds, dear son, and I will
 mine, and let us hasten forth,
Wonderful cities and free nations we shall
 fetch as we go.

If you tire, give me both burdens, and rest
 the chuff of your hand on my hip,
And in due time you shall repay the same
 service to me,
For after we start we never lie by again.

This day before dawn I ascended a hill and
 look'd at the crowded heaven,   20
And I said to my spirit *When we become
 the enfolders of those orbs, and the pleasure and knowledge of every thing in them,
 shall we be fill'd and satisfied then?*
And my spirit said *No, we but level that lift
 to pass and continue beyond.*

You are also asking me questions and I hear
you,
I answer that I cannot answer, you must
find out for yourself.

Sit a while dear son,
Here are biscuits to eat and here is milk
to drink,
But as soon as you sleep and renew yourself in sweet clothes, I kiss you with a
good-by kiss and open the gate for your
egress hence.

Long enough have you dream'd contempt-
ible dreams,
Now I wash the gum from your eyes,
You must habit yourself to the dazzle of
the light and of every moment of your
life.   30

Long have you timidly waded holding a
plank by the shore,
Now I will you to be a bold swimmer,
To jump off in the midst of the sea, rise
again, nod to me, shout, and laughingly
dash with your hair.

47

I am the teacher of athletes,
He that by me spreads a wider breast
than my own proves the width of my
own,
He most honors my style who learns under
it to destroy the teacher.

The boy I love, the same becomes a man
not through derived power, but in his
own right,
Wicked rather than virtuous out of conformity or fear,
Fond of his sweetheart, relishing well his
steak,
Unrequited love or a slight cutting him
worse than sharp steel cuts,
First-rate to ride, to fight, to hit the bull's
eye, to sail a skiff, to sing a song or play
on the banjo,
Preferring scars and the beard and faces
pitted with small-pox over all lather-
ers,
And those well-tann'd to those that keep
out of the sun.   10

I teach straying from me, yet who can
stray from me ?

I follow you whoever you are from the
present hour,
My words itch at your ears till you understand them.

I do not say these things for a dollar or to
fill up the time while I wait for a boat,
(It is you talking just as much as myself,
I act as the tongue of you,
Tied in your mouth, in mine it begins to be
loosen'd.)

I swear I will never again mention love or
death inside a house,
And I swear I will never translate myself
at all, only to him or her who privately
stays with me in the open air.

If you would understand me go to the
heights or water-shore,
The nearest gnat is an explanation, and a
drop or motion of waves a key,   20
The maul, the oar, the hand-saw, second
my words.

No shutter'd room or school can commune
with me,
But roughs and little children better than
they.

The young mechanic is closest to me, he
knows me well,
The woodman that takes his axe and jug
with him shall take me with him all day,
The farm-boy ploughing in the field feels
good at the sound of my voice,
In vessels that sail my words sail, I go with
fishermen and seamen and love them.

The soldier camp'd or upon the march is
mine,
On the night ere the pending battle many
seek me, and I do not fail them,
On that solemn night (it may be their last)
those that know me seek me.[1]   30

My face rubs to the hunter's face when he
lies down alone in his blanket,
The driver thinking of me does not mind
the jolt of his wagon,
The young mother and old mother comprehend me,
The girl and the wife rest the needle a
moment and forget where they are,
They and all would resume what I have
told them.

[1] These three lines appeared first in the edition of 1867.

48

I have said that the soul is not more than
the body,[1]
And I have said that the body is not more
than the soul,
And nothing, not God, is greater to one than
óne's self is,
And whoever walks a furlong without sympathy walks to his own funeral drest in
his shroud,
And I or you pocketless of a dime may
purchase the pick of the earth,
And to glance with an eye or show a bean
in its pod confounds the learning of all
times,
And there is no trade or employment but
the young man following it may become
a hero,
And there is no object so soft but it makes
a hub for the wheel'd universe,
And I say to any man or woman, Let your
soul stand cool and composed before a
million universes.

[1] Compare, in *Notes and Fragments*, p. 36, No. 112 of
the 'First Drafts and Rejected Lines' for *Leaves of
Grass*. Compare also, as the best possible commentary
on this section, two passages of Whitman's prose, the
first a note written probably between 1850 and 1855, the
second from the Preface to the 1876 edition of *Leaves of
Grass* : —

All through writings preserve the equilibrium of the
truth that the material world, and all its laws, are as
grand and superb as the spiritual world and all its laws.
Most writers have disclaimed the physical world, and
they have not over-estimated the other, or soul, but
have under-estimated the corporeal. How shall my eye
separate the beauty of the blossoming buckwheat field
from the stalks and heads of tangible matter ? How
shall I know what the life is except as I see it in the
flesh ? I will not praise one without the other or more
than the other.

Do not argue at all or compose proofs to demonstrate
things. State nothing which it will not do to state as
apparent to all eyes. (*Notes and Fragments*, p. 56.)

. . . .

It was originally my intention, after chanting in
'Leaves of Grass' the songs of the body and existence, to then compose a further, equally needed volume, based on those convictions of perpetuity and con-
servation which, enveloping all precedents, make the
unseen soul govern absolutely at last. I meant, while
in a sort continuing the theme of my first chants, to
shift the slides, and exhibit the problem and paradox of
the same ardent and fully appointed personality entering the sphere of the resistless gravitation of spiritual
law, and with cheerful face estimating death, not at all
as the cessation, but as somehow what I feel it must
be, the entrance upon by far the greatest part of existence, and something that life is at least as much for, as
it is for itself. But the full construction of such a
work is beyond my powers, and must remain for some
bard in the future. The physical and the sensuous, in
themselves or in their immediate continuations, retain
holds upon me which I think are never entirely re-
leas'd ; and those holds I have not only not denied, but
hardly wish'd to weaken. (*Complete Prose Works*, pp.
273, 274.)

And I say to mankind, Be not curious about
God,[2]
For I who am curious about each am not
curious about God,
(No array of terms can say how much I am
at peace about God and about death.)

I hear and behold God in every object, yet
understand God not in the least,
Nor do I understand who there can be
more wonderful than myself.

Why should I wish to see God better than
this day ?
I see something of God each hour of the
twenty-four, and each moment then,
In the faces of men and women I see God,
and in my own face in the glass,
I find letters from God dropt in the street,
and every one is sign'd by God's name,
And I leave them where they are, for I
know that wheresoe'er I go,
Others will punctually come for ever and
ever.

. . . . . .

51 •

The past and present wilt — I have fill'd
them, emptied them,
And proceed to fill my next fold of the
future.

Listener up there ! what have you to con-
fide to me ?
Look in my face while I snuff the sidle of
evening.
(Talk honestly, no one else hears you, and
I stay only a minute longer.)

[2] Compare the original sketch for these lines in
Notes and Fragments, p. 24 : —

There is no word in any tongue,
No array, no form of symbol,
To tell his infatuation
Who would define the scope and purpose of God.

Mostly this we have of God ; we have man.
Lo, the Sun ;
Its glory floods the moon
Which of a night shines in some turbid pool,
Shaken by soughing winds :
And there are sparkles mad and tossed and broken
And their archetype is the sun.

Of God I know not ;
But this I know :
I can comprehend no being more wonderful than man;
Man, before the rage of whose passions the storms of Heaven
are but a breath :
Before whose caprices the lightning is slow and less fatal ;
Man, microcosm of all Creation's wildness, terror, beauty and
power,
And whose folly and wickedness are in nothing else ex-
istent.

Do I contradict myself?
Very well then I contradict myself,
(I am large, I contain multitudes.)

I concentrate toward them that are nigh, I
wait on the door-slab.

Who has done his day's work? who will
soonest be through with his supper?
Who wishes to walk with me?

Will you speak before I am gone? will
you prove already too late?

52

The spotted hawk swoops by and accuses
me, he complains of my gab and my
loitering.

I too am not a bit tamed, I too am untrans-
latable,
I sound my barbaric yawp over the roofs
of the world.[1]

The last scud of day holds back for me,
It flings my likeness after the rest and true
as any on the shadow'd wilds,
It coaxes me to the vapor and the dusk.

I depart as air, I shake my white locks at
the runaway sun,
I effuse my flesh in eddies, and drift it in
lacy jags.

I bequeath myself to the dirt to grow from
the grass I love,
If you want me again look for me under
your boot-soles.

You will hardly know who I am or what I
mean,
But I shall be good health to you neverthe-
less,
And filter and fibre your blood.

Failing to fetch me at first keep encour-
aged,
Missing me one place search another,
I stop somewhere waiting for you.
                                        1855.

[1] Compare the original sketch for these lines, in
Notes and Fragments, p. 36 : —
The spotted hawk salutes the approaching night ;
He sweeps by me and rebukes me hoarsely with his invita-
tion ;
He complains with sarcastic voice of my lagging.

I feel apt to clip it and go ;
I am not half tamed yet.

SONG OF THE OPEN ROAD [2]

I

AFOOT and light-hearted I take to the open
road,
Healthy, free, the world before me,
The long brown path before me leading
wherever I choose.

Henceforth I ask not good-fortune, I myself am good-fortune,
Henceforth I whimper no more, postpone
no more, need nothing,
Done with indoor complaints, libraries,
querulous criticisms, [3]
Strong and content I travel the open road.

The earth, that is sufficient,
I do not want the constellations any nearer,
I know they are very well where they are,
I know they suffice for those who belong to
them.   11

(Still here I carry my old delicious burdens,
I carry them, men and women, I carry
them with me wherever I go,
I swear it is impossible for me to get rid of
them,
I am fill'd with them, and I will fill them
in return.)

2

You road I enter upon and look around, I
believe you are not all that is here,
I believe that much unseen is also here.[4]

Here the profound lesson of reception, nor
preference nor denial,
The black with his woolly head, the felon,
the diseas'd, the illiterate person, are not
denied ;
The birth, the hasting after the physician,
the beggar's tramp, the drunkard's stagger, the laughing party of mechanics, 20

[2] A great recreation, the past three years, has been
in taking long walks out from Washington, five, seven,
perhaps ten miles and back ; generally with my friend
Peter Doyle, who is as fond of it as I am. Fine moonlight nights, over the perfect military roads, hard and
smooth — or Sundays — we had these delightful walks,
never to be forgotten. (WHITMAN, *Specimen Days*,
December 10th, 1865. Complete Prose Works, p. 70.)
This poem first appeared in 1856, with the title ' Poem
of the Road.'
[3] This line was added in the edition of 1881.
[4] In the first form of the poem, 1856, this line read ·
I believe that something unseen is also here.

The escaped youth, the rich person's carriage, the fop, the eloping couple,
The early market-man, the hearse, the moving of furniture into the town, the return back from the town,
They pass, I also pass, any thing passes, none can be interdicted,
None but are accepted, none but shall be dear to me.

3

You air that serves me with breath to speak !
You objects that call from diffusion my meanings and give them shape !
You light that wraps me and all things in delicate equable showers ! [1]
You paths worn in the irregular hollows by the roadsides !
I believe you are latent with unseen existences, you are so dear to me.

You flagg'd walks of the cities ! you strong curbs at the edges !   30
You ferries ! you planks and posts of wharves ! you timber-lined sides ! you distant ships !
You rows of houses ! you window-pierc'd façades ! you roofs !
You porches and entrances! you copings and iron guards !
You windows whose transparent shells might expose so much !
You doors and ascending steps ! you arches !
You gray stones of interminable pavements ! you trodden crossings !
From all that has touch'd you I believe you have imparted to yourselves, and now would impart the same secretly to me,
From the living and the dead you have peopled your impassive surfaces, and the spirits thereof would be evident and amicable with me.

4

The earth expanding right hand and left hand,
The picture alive, every part in its best light,   40

The music falling in where it is wanted, and stopping where it is not wanted,
The cheerful voice of the public road, the gay fresh sentiment of the road.

O highway I travel, do you say to me *Do not leave me ?*
Do you say *Venture not — if you leave me you are lost ?*
Do you say *I am already prepared, I am well-beaten and undenied, adhere to me ?*

O public road, I say back I am not afraid to leave you, yet I love you,
You express me better than I can express myself,
You shall be more to me than my poem.

I think heroic deeds were all conceiv'd in the open air, and all free poems also,
I think I could stop here myself and do miracles,   50
I think whatever I shall meet on the road I shall like, and whoever beholds me shall like me,
I think whoever I see must be happy.

5

From this hour I ordain myself loos'd of limits and imaginary lines,[2]
Going where I list, my own master total and absolute,
Listening to others, considering well what they say,
Pausing, searching, receiving, contemplating,
Gently, but with undeniable will, divesting myself of the holds that would hold me.

I inhale great draughts of space,
The east and the west are mine, and the north and the south are mine.

I am larger, better than I thought,   60
I did not know I held so much goodness.

All seems beautiful to me,
I can repeat over to men and women You have done such good to me I would do the same to you,
I will recruit for myself and you as I go,

---

[1] In the first form of the poem there followed here three lines which were omitted in 1871 and in the following editions : —

You animals moving serenely over the earth !
You birds that wing yourselves through the air ! you insects !
You sprouting growths from the farmers' fields ! you stalks and weeds by the fences !

[2] In the edition of 1856 this section began : —

From this hour, freedom !
From this hour I ordain myself loos'd of limits, etc.

I will scatter myself among men and women as I go,
I will toss a new gladness and roughness
among them,
Whoever denies me it shall not trouble me,
Whoever accepts me he or she shall be
blessed and shall bless me.

6

Now if a thousand perfect men were to appear it would not amaze me,
Now if a thousand beautiful forms of women appear'd it would not astonish me. 70

Now I see the secret of the making of the
best persons,
It is to grow in the open air and to eat and
sleep with the earth.

Here a great personal deed has room, [1]
(Such a deed seizes upon the hearts of the
whole race of men,
Its effusion of strength and will overwhelms
law and mocks all authority and all
argument against it.)

Here is the test of wisdom,
Wisdom is not finally tested in schools,
Wisdom cannot be pass'd from one having
it to another not having it,
Wisdom is of the soul, is not susceptible of
proof, is its own proof,
Applies to all stages and objects and quali-
ties and is content,   80
Is the certainty of the reality and immortal-
ity of things, and the excellence of things;
Something there is in the float of the sight
of things that provokes it out of the soul.

Now I re-examine philosophies and religions,
They may prove well in lecture-rooms, yet
not prove at all under the spacious clouds
and along the landscape and flowing currents.

Here is realization,
Here is a man tallied — he realizes here
what he has in him,
The past, the future, majesty, love — if
they are vacant of you, you are vacant of
them. [2]

Only the kernel of every object nourishes;
Where is he who tears off the husks for
you and me ?
Where is he that undoes stratagems and
envelopes for you and me ?   90

Here is adhesiveness, it is not previously
fashion'd, it is apropos;
Do you know what it is as you pass to be
loved by strangers ?
Do you know the talk of those turning eye-
balls ?

7

Here is the efflux of the soul,
The efflux of the soul comes from within
through embower'd gates, ever provok-
ing questions,
These yearnings why are they ? these
thoughts in the darkness why are they ?
Why are there men and women that while
they are nigh me the sunlight expands
my blood ?
Why when they leave me do my pennants
of joy sink flat and lank ?
Why are there trees I never walk under
but large and melodious thoughts descend
upon me ?
(I think they hang there winter and summer on those trees and always drop fruit
as I pass ;)   100
What is it I interchange so suddenly with
strangers ?
What with some driver as I ride on the
seat by his side ?
What with some fisherman drawing his
seine by the shore as I walk by and pause ?
What gives me to be free to a woman's and
man's good-will ? what gives them to be
free to mine ?

8

The efflux of the soul is happiness, here is
happiness,
I think it pervades the open air, waiting at
all times,
Now it flows unto us, we are rightly
charged.

Here rises the fluid and attaching character,
The fluid and attaching character is the
freshness and sweetness of man and woman,

---

[1] Here is space — here a great personal deed has
room. (1856.)
[2] The animals, the past, the future, light, space,
majesty, love. if they are vacant of you, you are
vacant of them. (1856.)

(The herbs of the morning sprout no fresher and sweeter every day out of the roots of themselves, than it sprouts fresh and sweet continually out of itself.)   110

Toward the fluid and attaching character exudes the sweat of the love of young and old,
From it falls distill'd the charm that mocks beauty and attainments,
Toward it heaves the shuddering longing ache of contact.

9

Allons ! whoever you are come travel with me !
Traveling with me you find what never tires.

The earth never tires,
The earth is rude, silent, incomprehensible at first, Nature is rude and incomprehensible at first,
Be not discouraged, keep on, there are divine things well envelop'd,
I swear to you there are divine things more beautiful than words can tell.

Allons ! we must not stop here,   120
However sweet these laid-up stores, however convenient this dwelling we cannot remain here,
However shelter'd this port and however calm these waters we must not anchor here,
However welcome the hospitality that surrounds us we are permitted to receive it but a little while.

10

Allons ! the inducements shall be greater,
We will sail pathless and wild seas,
We will go where winds blow, waves dash, and the Yankee clipper speeds by under full sail.

Allons ! with power, liberty, the earth, the elements,
Health, defiance, gayety, self-esteem, curiosity;
Allons ! from all formules !
From your formules, O bat-eyed and materialistic priests. [1]   130

[1] The 1856 edition has ' formulas ' in both these lines.

The stale cadaver blocks up the passage — the burial waits no longer.

Allons ! yet take warning !
He traveling with me needs the best blood, thews, endurance,
None may come to the trial till he or she bring courage and health,
Come not here if you have already spent the best of yourself,
Only those may come who come in sweet and determin'd bodies,
No diseas'd person, no rum-drinker or venereal taint is permitted here.

(I and mine do not convince by arguments, similes, rhymes,
We convince by our presence.)

11

Listen ! I will be honest with you,   140
I do not offer the old smooth prizes, but offer rough new prizes,
These are the days that must happen to you:
You shall not heap up what is call'd riches,
You shall scatter with lavish hand all that you earn or achieve,
You but arrive at the city to which you were destin'd, you hardly settle yourself to satisfaction before you are call'd by an irresistible call to depart,
You shall be treated to the ironical smiles and mockings of those who remain behind you,
What beckonings of love you receive you shall only answer with passionate kisses of parting,
You shall not allow the hold of those who spread their reach'd hands toward you.

12

Allons ! after the great Companions, and to belong to them !
They too are on the road — they are the swift and majestic men — they are the greatest women, [2]   150
Enjoyers of calms of seas and storms of seas,
Sailors of many a ship, walkers of many a mile of land,

[2] Here began in the 1856 edition a new paragraph :

Over that which hindered them, over that which retarded,
  passing impediments large or small,
Committers of crimes, committers of many beautiful virtues,
Enjoyers of calms of seas and storms of seas, . . .

The first two lines were omitted from 1881 on.

Habitués of many distant countries, habitues of far-distant dwellings,

Trusters of men and women, observers of cities, solitary toilers,

Pausers and contemplators of tufts, blossoms, shells of the shore,

Dancers at wedding-dances, kissers of brides, tender helpers of children, bearers of children,

Soldiers of revolts, standers by gaping graves, lowerers-down of coffins,

Journeyers over consecutive seasons, over the years, the curious years each emerging from that which preceded it,

Journeyers as with companions, namely their own diverse phases,

Forth-steppers from the latent unrealized baby-days, 160

Journeyers gayly with their own youth, journeyers with their bearded and well-grain'd manhood,

Journeyers with their womanhood, ample, unsurpass'd, content,

Journeyers with their own sublime old age of manhood or womanhood,

Old age, calm, expanded, broad with the haughty breadth of the universe,

Old age, flowing free with the delicious near-by freedom of death.

13

Allons! to that which is endless as it was beginningless,

To undergo much, tramps of days, rests of nights,

To merge all in the travel they tend to, and the days and nights they tend to,

Again to merge them in the start of superior journeys,

To see nothing anywhere but what you may reach it and pass it, 170

To conceive no time, however distant, but what you may reach it and pass it,

To look up or down no road but it stretches and waits for you, however long but it stretches and waits for you,

To see no being, not God's or any, but you also go thither,

To see no possession but you may possess it, enjoying all without labor or purchase, abstracting the feast yet not abstracting one particle of it,

To take the best of the farmer's farm and the rich man's elegant villa, and the chaste blessings of the well-married

couple, and the fruits of orchards and flowers of gardens,

To take to your use out of the compact cities as you pass through,

To carry buildings and streets with you afterward wherever you go,

To gather the minds of men out of their brains as you encounter them, to gather the love out of their hearts,

To take your lovers on the road with you, for all that you leave them behind you,

To know the universe itself as a road, as many roads, as roads for traveling souls. [1]

All parts away for the progress of souls, 181

All religion, all solid things, arts, governments — all that was or is apparent upon this globe, or any globe falls into niches and corners before the procession of souls along the grand roads of the universe.

Of the progress of the souls of men and women along the grand roads of the universe, all other progress is the needed emblem and sustenance.

Forever alive, forever forward,

Stately, solemn, sad, withdrawn, baffled, mad, turbulent, feeble, dissatisfied,

Desperate, proud, fond, sick, accepted by men, rejected by men,

They go! they go! I know that they go, but I know not where they go,

But I know that they go toward the best — toward something great.

Whoever you are, come forth! or man or woman come forth!

You must not stay sleeping and dallying there in the house, though you built it, or though it has been built for you. 190

Out of the dark confinement! out from behind the screen!

It is useless to protest, I know all and expose it.

Behold through you as bad as the rest,

Through the laughter, dancing, dining, supping, of people,

[1] In the early editions, down to 1881, there follows here another brief paragraph : —

The soul travels,
The body does not travel as much as the soul,
The body has just as great a work as the soul, and parts away at last for the journeys of the soul.

Inside of dresses and ornaments, inside of those wash'd and trimm'd faces,
Behold a secret silent loathing and despair.

No husband, no wife, no friend, trusted to hear the confession,
Another self, a duplicate of every one, skulking and hiding it goes,
Formless and wordless through the streets of the cities, polite and bland in the parlors,
In the cars of railroads, in steamboats, in the public assembly,   200
Home to the houses of men and women, at the table, in the bedroom, everywhere,
Smartly attired, countenance smiling, form upright, death under the breast-bones, hell under the skull-bones,
Under the broadcloth and gloves, under the ribbons and artificial flowers,
Keeping fair with the customs, speaking not a syllable of itself,
Speaking of any thing else but never of itself.

14

Allons! through struggles and wars!
The goal that was named cannot be countermanded.

Have the past struggles succeeded?
What has succeeded? yourself? your nation? Nature?
Now understand me well — it is provided in the essence of things that from any fruition of success, no matter what, shall come forth something to make a greater struggle necessary.   210

My call is the call of battle, I nourish active rebellion,
He going with me must go well arm'd,
He going with me goes often with spare diet, poverty, angry enemies, desertions.

15

Allons! the road is before us!
It is safe — I have tried it — my own feet have tried it well — be not detain'd!

Let the paper remain on the desk unwritten, and the book on the shelf unopen'd!
Let the tools remain in the workshop! let the money remain unearn'd!
Let the school stand! mind not the cry of the teacher!

Let the preacher preach in his pulpit! let the lawyer plead in the court, and the judge expound the law.

Camerado, I give you my hand!   220
I give you my love more precious than money,
I give you myself before preaching or law;
Will you give me yourself? will you come travel with me?
Shall we stick by each other as long as we live?

                                        1856.

MIRACLES [1]

WHY, who makes much of a miracle?
As to me I know of nothing else but miracles,
Whether I walk the streets of Manhattan,
Or dart my sight over the roofs of houses toward the sky,
Or wade with naked feet along the beach just in the edge of the water,
Or stand under trees in the woods,
Or talk by day with any one I love, or sleep in the bed at night with any one I love,
Or sit at table at dinner with the rest,
Or look at strangers opposite me riding in the car,
Or watch honey-bees busy around the hive of a summer forenoon,
Or animals feeding in the fields,
Or birds, or the wonderfulness of insects in the air,
Or the wonderfulness of the sundown, or of stars shining so quiet and bright,
Or the exquisite delicate thin curve of the new moon in spring;
These with the rest, one and all, are to me miracles,
The whole referring, yet each distinct and in its place. [2]

[1] In the 1856 edition, with the title 'Poem of Perfect Miracles.' In its first form the poem began with a paragraph since omitted : —

Realism is mine, my miracles,
Take all of the rest — take freely — I keep but my own — I give only of them,
I offer them without end — I offer them to you wherever your feet can carry you, or your eyes reach.

[2] Compare the original Preface to *Leaves of Grass*, the first edition, 1855 : '. . . every motion and every spear of grass, and the frames and spirits of men and women and all that concerns them, are unspeakably perfect miracles, all referring to all, and each distinct and in its place.'
See also the longer passage at the end of the fifth paragraph of this Preface, on the miracle of eyesight.

To me every hour of the light and dark is
a miracle,
Every cubic inch of space is a miracle,
Every square yard of the surface of the
earth is spread with the same,
Every foot of the interior swarms with the
same.

To me the sea is a continual miracle,
The fishes that swim — the rocks — the
motion of the waves — the ships with
men in them,
What stranger miracles are there ?

1856.

ASSURANCES [1]

I NEED no assurances, I am a man who is
pre-occupied of his own soul; [2]
I do not doubt that from under the feet and
beside the hands and face I am cognizant of, are now looking faces I am not
cognizant of, calm and actual faces,
I do not doubt but the majesty and beauty
of the world are latent in any iota of the
world, [3]
I do not doubt I am limitless, and that the
universes are limitless, in vain I try to
think how limitless,
I do not doubt that the orbs and the systems of orbs play their swift sports
through the air on purpose, and that I
shall one day be eligible to do as much
as they, and more than they, [4]
I do not doubt that temporary affairs keep
on and on millions of years,
I do not doubt interiors have their interiors,
and exteriors have their exteriors, and
that the eyesight has another eyesight,

[1] In the 1856 edition, with the title ' Faith Poem ; ' in
1860 as No. vii, *Leaves of Grass*.
[2] In the 1856 edition there followed the line (omitted
in 1867) : —

I do not doubt that whatever I know at a given time, there
waits for me more which I do not know.

[3] In the 1856 edition there followed the line (omitted
in 1867) : —

I do not doubt there are realizations I have no idea of, waiting for me through time and through the universes — also
upon this earth.

[4] Here followed, in the 1856 edition, the lines (omitted
in 1867) : —

I do not doubt there is far more in trivialities, insects, vulgar
persons, slaves, dwarfs, weeds, rejected refuse, than I have
supposed ;
I do not doubt there is more in myself than I have supposed
— and more in all men and women — and more in my poems
than I have supposed.

and the hearing another hearing, and the
voice another voice,
I do not doubt that the passionately-wept
deaths of young men are provided for,
and that the deaths of young women and
the deaths of little children are provided
for,
(Did you think Life was so well provided
for, and Death, the purport of all Life, is
not well provided for ?)
I do not doubt that wrecks at sea, no
matter what the horrors of them, no
matter whose wife, child, husband, father,
lover, has gone down, are provided for,
to the minutest points, [5]
I do not doubt that whatever can possibly
happen anywhere at any time, is provided for in the inherences of things,
I do not think Life provides for all and for
Time and Space, but I believe Heavenly
Death provides for all.[6]

1856.

CROSSING BROOKLYN FERRY [7]

I

FLOOD-TIDE below me ! I see you face to
face !
Clouds of the west — sun there half an
hour high — I see you also face to face.

[5] Here followed, in 1856, the lines (omitted in 1871) :

I do not doubt that shallowness, meanness, malignance, are
provided for;
I do not doubt that cities, you, America, the remainder of the
earth, politics, freedom, degradations, are carefully provided for.

[6] The last line of the poem, and the fourth line from
the end; in parenthesis, appeared first in the edition of
1871, where the poem was included among the *Whispers
of Heavenly Death*.
[7] Living in Brooklyn or New York city from this
time forward, my life, then, and still more the following years, was curiously identified with Fulton ferry,
already becoming the greatest of its sort in the world
for general importance, volume, variety, rapidity, and
picturesqueness. Almost daily, later ('50 to '60), I
cross'd on the boats, often up in the pilot-houses where
I could get a full sweep, absorbing shows, accompani-
ments, surroundings. What oceanic currents, eddies,
underneath — the great tides of humanity also, with
ever-shifting movements ! Indeed, I have always had a
passion for ferries; to me they afford inimitable, streaming, never-failing, living poems. The river and bay
scenery, all about New York island, any time of a fine
day — the hurrying, splashing sea-tides — the changing
panorama of steamers, all sizes, often a string of big
ones outward bound to distant ports — the myriads of
white sail'd schooners, sloops, skiffs, and the marvel-
lously beautiful yachts — the majestic Sound boats as
they rounded the Battery and came along towards 5,
afternoon, eastward bound — the prospect off towards
Staten Island, or down the Narrows, or the other way
up the Hudson — what refreshment of spirit such sights

Crowds of men and women attired in the usual costumes, how curious you are to me !

On the ferry-boats the hundreds and hundreds that cross, returning home, are more curious to me than you suppose,

And you that shall cross from shore to shore years hence are more to me, and more in my meditations, than you might suppose.

2

The impalpable sustenance of me from all things at all hours of the day,

The simple, compact, well-join'd scheme, myself disintegrated, every one disintegrated yet part of the scheme,

The similitudes of the past and those of the future,

The glories strung like beads on my smallest sights and hearings, on the walk in the street and the passage over the river,

The current rushing so swiftly and swimming with me far away,   10

The others that are to follow me, the ties between me and them,

The certainty of others, the life, love, sight, hearing of others.

Others will enter the gates of the ferry and cross from shore to shore,

Others will watch the run of the flood-tide,

Others will see the shipping of Manhattan north and west, and the heights of Brooklyn to the south and east,

Others will see the islands large and small;

Fifty years hence, others will see them as they cross, the sun half an hour high,

A hundred years hence, or ever so many hundred years hence, others will see them,

Will enjoy the sunset, the pouring-in of the flood-tide, the falling-back to the sea of the ebb-tide.

3

It avails not, time nor place — distance avails not,   20

and experiences gave me years ago (and many a time since)! My old pilot friends, the Balsirs, Johnny Cole, Ira Smith, William White, and my young ferry friend, Tom Gere — how well I remember them all ! (WHITMAN, Specimen Days. Complete Prose Works, Small, Maynard & Co., p. 11.)

In 1856 the poem was entitled ' Sun-down Poem,' and the first line read: —

Flood-tide of the river, flow on! I watch you, face to face!

I am with you, you men and women of a generation, or ever so many generations hence,

Just as you feel when you look on the river and sky, so I felt,

Just as any of you is one of a living crowd, I was one of a crowd,

Just as you are refresh'd by the gladness of the river and the bright flow, I was refresh'd,

Just as you stand and lean on the rail, yet hurry with the swift current, I stood yet was hurried,

Just as you look on the numberless masts of ships and the thick-stemm'd pipes of steamboats, I look'd.

I too many and many a time cross'd the river of old,

Watched the Twelfth-month sea-gulls, saw them high in the air floating with motionless wings, oscillating their bodies,

Saw how the glistening yellow lit up parts of their bodies and left the rest in strong shadow,

Saw the slow-wheeling circles and the gradual edging toward the south,   30

Saw the reflection of the summer sky in the water,

Had my eyes dazzled by the shimmering track of beams,

Look'd at the fine centrifugal spokes of light round the shape of my head in the sunlit water,

Look'd on the haze on the hills southward and south-westward,

Look'd on the vapor as it flew in fleeces tinged with violet,

Look'd toward the lower bay to notice the vessels arriving,

Saw their approach, saw aboard those that were near me,

Saw the white sails of schooners and sloops, saw the ships at anchor,

The sailors at work in the rigging or out astride the spars,

The round masts, the swinging motion of the hulls, the slender serpentine pennants,   40

The large and small steamers in motion, the pilots in their pilot-houses,

The white wake left by the passage, the quick tremulous whirl of the wheels,

The flags of all nations, the falling of them at sunset,

The scallop-edged waves in the twilight, the ladled cups, the frolicsome crests and glistening,
The stretch afar growing dimmer and dimmer, the gray walls of the granite storehouses by the docks,
On the river the shadowy group, the big steam-tug closely flank'd on each side by the barges, the hay-boat, the belated lighter,
On the neighboring shore the fires from the foundry chimneys burning high and glaringly into the night,
Casting their flicker of black contrasted with wild red and yellow light over the tops of houses, and down into the clefts of streets.

4

These and all else were to me the same as they are to you,
I loved well those cities, loved well the stately and rapid river, 50
The men and women I saw were all near to me,
Others the same — others who look back on me because I look'd forward to them
(The time will come, though I stop here today and to-night).

5

What is it then between us ?
What is the count of the scores or hundreds of years between us ?

Whatever it is, it avails not — distance avails not, and place avails not,
I too lived, Brooklyn of ample hills was mine,
I too walk'd the streets of Manhattan island, and bathed in the waters around it,
I too felt the curious abrupt questionings stir within me,
In the day among crowds of people sometimes they came upon me, 60
In my walks home late at night or as I lay in my bed they came upon me,
I too had been struck from the float forever held in solution,
I too had receiv'd identity by my body,
That I was I knew was of my body, and what I should be I knew I should be of my body.

6

It is not upon you alone the dark patches fall,

The dark threw its patches down upon me also,
The best I had done seem'd to me blank and suspicious,
My great thoughts as I supposed them, were they not in reality meagre ?
Nor is it you alone who know what it is to be evil,
I am he who knew what it was to be evil, 70
I too knitted the old knot of contrariety,
Blabb'd, blush'd, resented, lied, stole, grudg'd,
Had guile, anger, lust, hot wishes I dared not speak,
Was wayward, vain, greedy, shallow, sly, cowardly, malignant,
The wolf, the snake, the hog, not wanting in me,
The cheating look, the frivolous word, the adulterous wish, not wanting,
Refusals, hates, postponements, meanness, laziness, none of these wanting,
Was one with the rest, the days and haps of the rest,[1]
Was call'd by my nighest name by clear loud voices of young men as they saw me approaching or passing,
Felt their arms on my neck as I stood, or the negligent leaning of their flesh against me as I sat, 80
Saw many I loved in the street or ferry-boat or public assembly, yet never told them a word,
Lived the same life with the rest, the same old laughing, gnawing, sleeping,
Play'd the part that still looks back on the actor or actress,
The same old rôle, the rôle that is what we make it, as great as we like,
Or as small as we like, or both great and small.

7

Closer yet I approach you,
What thought you have of me now, I had as much of you — I laid in my stores in advance,
I consider'd long and seriously of you before you were born.

Who was to know what should come home to me ?
Who knows but I am enjoying this ? 90

[1] Instead of this line the 1856 edition has : —
But I was a Manhattanese, free, friendly, and proud !
and this line begins a new paragraph.

Who knows, for all the distance, but I am as good as looking at you now, for all you cannot see me ?[1]

8

Ah, what can ever be more stately and admirable to me than mast-hemm'd Manhattan ?
River and sunset and scallop-edg'd waves of flood-tide ?
The sea-gulls oscillating their bodies, the hay-boat in the twilight, and the belated lighter ?

What gods can exceed these that clasp me by the hand, and with voices I love call me promptly and loudly by my nighest name as I approach ?
What is more subtle than this which ties me to the woman or man that looks in my face ?
Which fuses me into you now, and pours my meaning into you ?[2]

We understand, then, do we not ?
What I promis'd without mentioning it, have you not accepted ?
What the study could not teach — what the preaching could not accomplish is accomplish'd, is it not ?[3]   100

9

Flow on, river ! flow with the flood-tide, and ebb with the ebb-tide !
Frolic on, crested and scallop-edg'd waves !
Gorgeous clouds of the sunset ! drench with your splendor me, or the men and women generations after me !
Cross from shore to shore, countless crowds of passengers !

Stand up, tall masts of Mannahatta ! stand up, beautiful hills of Brooklyn !
Throb, baffled and curious brain ! throw out questions and answers !
Suspend here and everywhere, eternal float of solution !
Gaze, loving and thirsting eyes, in the house or street or public assembly !
Sound out, voices of young men ! loudly and musically call me by my nighest name !
Live, old life ! play the part that looks back on the actor or actress !   110
Play the old rôle, the rôle that is great or small according as one makes it !
Consider, you who peruse me, whether I may not in unknown ways be looking upon you;
Be firm, rail over the river, to support those who lean idly, yet haste with the hasting current;
Fly on, sea-birds ! fly sideways, or wheel in large circles high in the air;
Receive the summer sky, you water, and faithfully hold it till all downcast eyes have time to take it from you !
Diverge, fine spokes of light, from the shape of my head, or any one's head, in the sunlit water !
Come on, ships from the lower bay ! pass up or down, white-sail'd schooners, sloops, lighters !
Flaunt away, flags of all nations ! be duly lower'd at sunset !
Burn high your fires, foundry chimneys ! cast black shadows at nightfall ! cast red and yellow light over the tops of the houses !
Appearances, now or henceforth, indicate what you are,   120
You necessary film, continue to envelop the soul,
About my body for me, and your body for you, be hung our divinest aromas,
Thrive, cities — bring your freight, bring your shows, ample and sufficient rivers,
Expand, being than which none else is perhaps more spiritual,
Keep your places, objects than which none else is more lasting.[4]

---

[1] There follow at this point in the 1856 edition two other brief paragraphs : —

It is not you alone, nor I alone,
Not a few races, not a few generations, not a few centuries,
It is that each came, or comes, or shall come, from its due emission, either now, or then, or henceforth.

Everything indicates — the smallest does, and the largest does,
A necessary film envelops all, and envelops the soul for a proper time.

These lines seem necessary to the understanding of line 121, which has been retained in all editions.

[2] Remember, the book arose out of my life in Brooklyn and New York from 1838 to 1855, absorbing a million people with an intimacy, an eagerness, an abandon, probably never equalled. (WHITMAN, Bucke's *Life*, p. 67.)

[3] In the 1856 edition this paragraph ends with a line unhappily omitted from the latest editions : —

What the push of reading could not start is started by me personally, is it not ?

[4] At this point a paragraph has been omitted from the 1881 and later editions : —

We descend upon you and all things, we arrest you all,
We realize the soul only by you, you faithful solids and fluids,
Through you color, form, location, sublimity, ideality,
Through you every proof, comparison, and all the suggestions and determinations of ourselves.

You have waited, you always wait, you
 dumb, beautiful ministers,
We receive you with free sense at last, and
 are insatiate henceforward,
Not you any more shall be able to foil us,
 or withhold yourselves from us,
We use you, and do not cast you aside — we
 plant you permanently within us,
We fathom you not — we love you — there
 is perfection in you also,   130
You furnish your parts toward eternity,
Great or small, you furnish your parts toward the soul.

                                      1856.

OUT OF THE CRADLE END-
LESSLY ROCKING [1]

OUT of the cradle endlessly rocking,
Out of the mocking-bird's throat, the musi-
 cal shuttle,
Out of the Ninth-month midnight,
Over the sterile sands and the fields be-
 yond, where the child leaving his bed
 wander'd alone, bareheaded, barefoot,
Down from the shower'd halo,
Up from the mystic play of shadows twin-
 ing and twisting as if they were alive,
Out from the patches of briers and black-
 berries,
From the memories of the bird that chanted
 to me,
From your memories sad brother, from the
 fitful risings and fallings I heard,
From under that yellow half-moon late-
 risen and swollen as if with tears,   10
From those beginning notes of yearning
 and love there in the mist,
From the thousand responses of my heart
 never to cease,
From the myriad thence-arous'd words,
From the word stronger and more delicious
 than any,
From such as now they start the scene re-
 visiting,
As a flock, twittering, rising, or overhead
 passing,

[1] First published in the New York *Saturday Press*,
December 24, 1859, with the title 'A Child's Reminiscence.' In 1860 it appears with the new title, 'A Word
Out of the Sea,' for the whole poem, and with the sub-
title, 'Reminiscences,' for the part beginning with the
second paragraph.
   In the earlier versions, up to 1871, the first line
read : —

           Out of the rocked cradle.

Borne hither, ere all eludes me, hurriedly,
A man, yet by these tears a little boy
 again,
Throwing myself on the sand, confronting
 the waves,
I, chanter of pains and joys, uniter of here
 and hereafter,   20
Taking all hints to use them, but swiftly
 leaping beyond them,
A reminiscence sing.

Once Paumanok,
When the lilac-scent was in the air [2] and
 Fifth-month grass was growing,
Up this seashore in some briers,
Two feather'd guests from Alabama, two
 together,
And their nest, and four light-green eggs
 spotted with brown,
And every day the he-bird to and fro near
 at hand,
And every day the she-bird crouch'd on her
 nest, silent, with bright eyes,
And every day I, a curious boy, never too
 close, never disturbing them,   30
Cautiously peering, absorbing, translating.

Shine ! shine ! shine !
Pour down your warmth, great sun !
While we bask, we two together.

Two together !
Winds blow south, or winds blow north,
Day come white, or night come black,
Home, or rivers and mountains from home,
Singing all time, minding no time,
While we two keep together.   40

Till of a sudden,
May-be kill'd, unknown to her mate,
One forenoon the she-bird crouch'd not on
 the nest,
Nor return'd that afternoon, nor the next,
Nor ever appear'd again.

And thenceforward all summer in the
 sound of the sea,
And at night under the full of the moon
 in calmer weather,
Over the hoarse surging of the sea,
Or flitting from brier to brier by day,
I saw, I heard at intervals the remaining
 one, the he-bird,   50
The solitary guest from Alabama.

[2] When the snows had melted. (1859-60.)

Blow! blow! blow!
Blow up sea-winds along Paumanok's shore;
I wait and I wait till you blow my mate to
    me.

Yes, when the stars glisten'd,
All night long on the prong of a moss-scal-
    lop'd stake,
Down almost amid the slapping waves,
Sat the lone singer wonderful causing tears.

He call'd on his mate,
He pour'd forth the meanings which I of
    all men know.   60

Yes my brother I know,
The rest might not, but I have treasur'd
    every note,
For more than once dimly down to the
    beach gliding,
Silent, avoiding the moonbeams, blending
    myself with the shadows,
Recalling now the obscure shapes, the
    echoes, the sounds and sights after their
    sorts,
The white arms out in the breakers tire-
    lessly tossing,
I, with bare feet, a child, the wind wafting
    my hair,
Listen'd long and long.

Listen'd to keep, to sing, now translating
    the notes,
Following you my brother.   70

Soothe! soothe! soothe!
Close on its wave soothes the wave behind,
And again another behind embracing and lap-
    ping, every one close,
But my love soothes not me, not me.

Low hangs the moon, it rose late,
It is lagging — O I think it is heavy with love,
    with love.

O madly the sea pushes upon the land,
With love, with love.

O night! do I not see my love fluttering out
    among the breakers?
What is that little black thing I see there in
    the white?   80

Loud! loud! loud!
Loud I call to you, my love!

High and clear I shoot my voice over the
    waves,
Surely you must know who is here, is here,
You must know who I am, my love.

Low-hanging moon!
What is that dusky spot in your brown yellow?
O it is the shape, the shape of my mate!
O moon do not keep her from me any longer.

Land! land! O land!   90
Whichever way I turn, O I think you could
    give me my mate back again if you only
    would,
For I am almost sure I see her dimly which-
    ever way I look.

O rising stars!
Perhaps the one I want so much will rise, will
    rise with some of you.

O throat! O trembling throat!
Sound clearer through the atmosphere!
Pierce the woods, the earth,
Somewhere listening to catch you must be the
    one I want.

Shake out carols!
Solitary here, the night's carols!   100
Carols of lonesome love! death's carols!
Carols under that lagging, yellow, waning
    moon!
O under that moon where she droops almost
    down into the sea!
O reckless despairing carols.

But soft! sink low!
Soft! let me just murmur,
And do you wait a moment you husky-nois'd
    sea,
For somewhere I believe I heard my mate re-
    sponding to me,
So faint, I must be still, be still to listen,
But not altogether still, for then she might not
    come immediately to me.   110

Hither my love!
Here I am! here!
With this just-sustain'd note I announce my-
    self to you,
This gentle call is for you my love, for you.

Do not be decoy'd elsewhere,
That is the whistle of the wind, it is not my
    voice,

*That is the fluttering, the fluttering of the
    spray,*
Those are the shadows of leaves.

O darkness! O in vain!
O I am very sick and sorrowfuu.   120

*O brown halo in the sky near the moon,
    drooping upon the sea!*
O troubled reflection in the sea!
O throat! O throbbiny heart!
*And I singing uselessly, uselessly all the
    night.*

O past! O happy life! O songs of joy!
In the air, in the woods, over fields,
Loved! loved! loved! loved! loved!
But my mate no more, no more with me!
We two together no more.

The aria sinking,   130
All else continuing, the stars shining,
The winds blowing, the notes of the bird
    continuous echoing,
With angry moans the fierce old mother in-
    cessantly moaning,
On the sands of Paumanok's shore gray
    and rustling,
The yellow half-moon enlarged, sagging
    down, drooping, the face of the sea al-
    most touching,
The boy ecstatic, with his bare feet the
    waves, with his hair the atmosphere dal-
    lying,
The love in the heart long pent, now loose,
    now at last tumultuously bursting,
The aria's meaning, the ears, the soul,
    swiftly depositing,
The strange tears down the cheeks
    coursing,
The colloquy there, the trio, each uttering,
The undertone, the savage old mother in-
    cessantly crying,   141
To the boy's soul's questions sullenly
    timing, some drown'd secret hissing,
To the outsetting bard.

Demon or bird (said the boy's soul)!
Is it indeed toward your mate you sing?
    or is it really to me?
For I, that was a child, my tongue's use
    sleeping, now I have heard you,
Now in a moment I know what I am for, I
    awake,
And already a thousand singers, a thousand

songs, clearer, louder and more sorrowful
    than yours,
A thousand warbling echoes have started
    to life within me, never to die.

O you singer solitary, singing by yourself,
    projecting me,   150
O solitary me listening, never more shall I
    cease perpetuating you,
Never more shall I escape, never more the
    reverberations,
Never more the cries of unsatisfied love be
    absent from me,
Never again leave me to be the peaceful
    child I was before what there in the night,
By the sea under the yellow and sagging
    moon,
The messenger there arous'd, the fire, the
    sweet hell within,
The unknown want, the destiny of me.

O give me the clew (it lurks in the night
    here somewhere)!
O if I am to have so much, let me have more!

A word then (for I will conquer it),   160
The word final, superior to all,
Subtle, sent up — what is it? — I listen;
Are you whispering it, and have been all
    the time, you sea-waves?
Is that it from your liquid rims and wet
    sands?

Whereto answering, the sea,
Delaying not, hurrying not,
Whisper'd me through the night, and very
    plainly before daybreak,
Lisp'd to me the low and delicious word
    death,
And again death, death, death, death,
Hissing melodious, neither like the bird nor
    like my arous'd child's heart,   170
But edging near as privately for me rus-
    tling at my feet,
Creeping thence steadily up to my ears and
    laving me softly all over,
Death, death, death, death, death.

Which I do not forget,
But fuse the song of my dusky demon and
    brother,
That he sang to me in the moonlight on
    Paumanok's gray beach,
With the thousand responsive songs at ran-
    dom,

My own songs awaked from that hour,
And with them the key, the word up from
the waves,
The word of the sweetest song and all
songs,   180
That strong and delicious word which,
creeping to my feet,
(Or like some old crone rocking the cradle,
swathed in sweet garments, bending
aside,)
The sea whisper'd me.

                              1859. (1860.) [1]

FACING WEST FROM CALIFOR-NIA'S SHORES [2]

FACING west from California's shores,
Inquiring, tireless, seeking what is yet unfound,
I, a child, very old, over waves, towards
the house of maternity, the land of mi-
grations, look afar,
Look off the shores of my Western sea, the
circle almost circled;
For starting westward from Hindustan,
from the vales of Kashmere,
From Asia, from the north, from the God,
the sage, and the hero,
From the south, from the flowery peninsulas and the spice islands,
Long having wander'd since, round the
earth having wander'd,
Now I face home again, very pleas'd and
joyous.
(But where is what I started for so long
ago?
And why is it yet unfound?)

                                           1860.

I HEAR AMERICA SINGING

I HEAR America singing, the varied carols
I hear,
Those of mechanics, each one singing his as
it should be blithe and strong,
The carpenter singing his as he measures his
plank or beam,

The mason singing his as he makes ready
for work, or leaves off work,
The boatman singing what belongs to him
in his boat, the deckhand singing on the
steamboat deck,
The shoemaker singing as he sits on his
bench, the hatter singing as he stands,
The wood-cutter's song, the ploughboy's on
his way in the morning, or at noon inter-
mission or at sundown,
The delicious singing of the mother, or of
the young wife at work, or of the girl
sewing or washing,
Each singing what belongs to him or her
and to none else,
The day what belongs to the day — at
night the party of young fellows, robust,
friendly,
Singing with open mouths their strong melodious songs.

                                           1860.

POETS TO COME

POETS to come! orators, singers, musicians
to come!
Not to-day is to justify me and answer what
I am for,
But you, a new brood, native, athletic, con-
tinental, greater than before known,
Arouse! for you must justify me.

I myself but write one or two indicative
words for the future,
I but advance a moment only to wheel and
hurry back in the darkness.

I am a man who, sauntering along without
fully stopping, turns a casual look upon
you and then averts his face,
Leaving it to you to prove and define it,
Expecting the main things from you.

                                           1860.

ME IMPERTURBE

ME imperturbe, standing at ease in Nature,
Master of all or mistress of all, aplomb in
the midst of irrational things,
Imbued as they, passive, receptive, silent
as they,
Finding my occupation, poverty, notoriety,
foibles, crimes, less important than I
thought,

---

[1] For Whitman the date of publication in book form
is the most important. This has therefore been added,
in parentheses, when the poem was published earlier
in a periodical.

[2] In the 1860 edition, without separate sub-title, as
No. 10 of the section entitled *Enfans d'Adam*. In
this edition the poem began with what is now the second line. The first line was added in 1867.

Me toward the Mexican sea, or in the Mannahatta or the Tennessee, or far north or
inland,
A river man, or a man of the woods or of
any farm-life of these States or of the
coast, or the lakes of Kanada,
Me wherever my life is lived, O to be self-
balanced for contingencies,
To confront night, storms, hunger, ridicule,
accidents, rebuffs, as the trees and animals do.

1860.

FOR YOU O DEMOCRACY[1]

COME, I will make the continent indissoluble,
I will make the most splendid race the sun
ever shone upon,

[1] This and the eight following poems belong to the
section of Whitman's work devoted to the celebration
of 'the dear love of comrades,' and entitled 'Calamus.'
'The Sweet Flag or Calamus,' says W. S. Kennedy, in
explaining Whitman's use of this title, 'belongs among
the grasses, and like them suggests equality and brotherhood. It is found in vast masses in marshy ground,
growing in fascicles of three, four, or five blades,
which cling together for support, shoulder to shoulder
and back to back, the delicate "pink-tinged" roots
exhaling a faint fragrance, not only when freshly
gathered, but after having been kept many years.'
With these poems should be read the volume entitled
*Calamus, a Series of Letters written during the Years
1868–1880 by Walt Whitman to a Young Friend.*
'For you O Democracy' is a revised and improved
version of the last lines of a much longer poem with the
title 'States,' in the 1860 edition, the whole of which is
worth preserving : —

STATES !
Were you looking to be held together by the lawyers ?
By an agreement on a paper ? Or by arms ?

Away !
I arrive, bringing these, beyond all the forces of courts and
arms,
These ! to hold you together as firmly as the earth itself is
held together.

The old breath of life, ever new,
Here ! I pass it by contact to you, America.

O mother ! have you done much for me ?
Behold, there shall from me be much done for you.

There shall from me be a new friendship — It shall be called
after my name,
It shall circulate through The States, indifferent of place,
It shall twist and intertwist them through and around each
other — Compact shall they be, showing new signs,
Affection shall solve every one of the problems of freedom,
Those who love each other shall be invincible,
They shall finally make America completely victorious, in
my name.

One from Massachusetts shall be comrade to a Missourian,
One from Maine or Vermont, and a Carolinian and an Ore-
gonese, shall be friends triune, more precious to each other
than all the riches of the earth.
To Michigan shall be wafted perfume from Florida,
To the Mannahatta from Cuba or Mexico,
Not the perfume of flowers, but sweeter, and wafted beyond
death.

No danger shall balk Columbia's lovers,
If need be, a thousand shall sternly immolate themselves
for one,

I will make divine magnetic lands,
With the love of comrades,
With the life-long love of comrades.

I will plant companionship thick as trees
along all the rivers of America, and
along the shores of the great lakes, and
all over the prairies,
I will make inseparable cities with their
arms about each other's necks,
By the love of comrades,
By the manly love of comrades.

For you these from me, O Democracy, to
serve you ma femme !
For you, for you I am trilling these songs.

1860.

RECORDERS AGES HENCE

RECORDERS ages hence,[2]
Come, I will take you down underneath
this impassive exterior, I will tell you
what to say of me,
Publish my name and hang up my picture
as that of the tenderest lover,
The friend the lover's portrait, of whom
his friend his lover was fondest,
The Kanuck shall be willing to lay down his life for the
Kansian, and the Kansian for the Kanuck, on due need.

It shall be customary in all directions, in the houses and
streets, to see manly affection,
The departing brother or friend shall salute the remaining
brother or friend with a kiss.

There shall be innovations,
There shall be countless linked hands — namely, the North-
easterner's, and the Northwesterner's, and the South-
westerner's, and those of the interior, and all their brood,
These shall be masters of the world under a new power,
They shall laugh to scorn the attacks of all the remainder of
the world.

The most dauntless and rude shall touch face to face lightly,
The dependence of Liberty shall be lovers,
The continuance of Equality shall be comrades.

These shall tie and band stronger than hoops of iron,
I, ecstatic, O partners ! O lands ! henceforth with the love of
lovers tie you.

I will make the continent indissoluble,
I will make the most splendid race the sun ever yet shone
upon,
I will make divine magnetic lands

I will plant companionship thick as trees along all the rivers
of America, and along the shores of the great lakes, and all
over the prairies,
I will make inseparable cities, with their arms about each
other's necks.

For you these, from me, O Democracy, to serve you ma
femme !
For you ! for you, I am trilling these songs.

[2] Instead of this line, the edition of 1860 reads : —

You bards of ages hence ! when you refer to me, mind not so
much my poems,
Nor speak of me that I prophesied of The States, and led
them the way of their glories.

Who was not proud of his songs, but of the
measureless ocean of love within him,
and freely pour'd it forth,
Who often walk'd lonesome walks thinking
of his dear friends, his lovers,
Who pensive away from one he lov'd often
lay sleepless and dissatisfied at night,
Who knew too well the sick, sick dread lest
the one he lov'd might secretly be indifferent to him,
Whose happiest days were far away through
fields, in woods, on hills, he and another
wandering hand in hand, they twain apart
from other men,
Who oft as he saunter'd the streets curv'd
with his arm the shoulder of his friend,
while the arm of his friend rested upon
him also.

1860.

WHEN I HEARD AT THE CLOSE
OF THE DAY

WHEN I heard at the close of the day how
my name had been receiv'd with plaudits
in the capitol, still it was not a happy
night for me that follow'd,
And else when I carous'd, or when my
plans were accomplish'd, still I was not
happy,
But the day when I rose at dawn from the
bed of perfect health, refresh'd, singing,
inhaling the ripe breath of autumn,
When I saw the full moon in the west
grow pale and disappear in the morning
light,
When I wander'd alone over the beach,
and undressing bathed, laughing with the
cool waters, and saw the sun rise,
And when I thought how my dear friend
my lover was on his way coming, O then
I was happy,
O then each breath tasted sweeter, and all
that day my food nourish'd me more, and
the beautiful day pass'd well,
And the next came with equal joy, and with
the next at evening came my friend,
And that night while all was still I heard
the waters roll slowly continually up the
shores,
I heard the hissing rustle of the liquid and
sands as directed to me whispering to
congratulate me,
For the one I love most lay sleeping by me
under the same cover in the cool night,

In the stillness in the autumn moonbeams
his face was inclined toward me,
And his arm lay lightly around my breast
— and that night I was happy.

1860.

I SAW IN LOUISIANA A LIVE-
OAK GROWING

I SAW in Louisiana a live-oak growing,
All alone stood it and the moss hung down
from the branches,
Without any companion it grew there uttering joyous leaves of dark green,
And its look, rude, unbending, lusty, made
me think of myself,
But I wonder'd how it could utter joyous
leaves standing alone there without its
friend near, for I knew I could not,
And I broke off a twig with a certain number of leaves upon it, and twined around
it a little moss,
And brought it away, and I have placed
it in sight in my room,
It is not needed to remind me as of my
own dear friends,
(For I believe lately I think of little else
than of them,)
Yet it remains to me a curious token, it
makes me think of manly love;
For all that, and though the live-oak glis-
tens there in Louisiana solitary in a wide
flat space,
Uttering joyous leaves all its life without a
friend a lover near,
I know very well I could not.

1860.

I HEAR IT WAS CHARGED
AGAINST ME

I HEAR it was charged against me that I
sought to destroy institutions,
But really I am neither for nor against institutions,
(What indeed have I in common with them?
or what with the destruction of them?)
Only I will establish in the Mannahatta
and in every city of these States inland
and seaboard,
And in the fields and woods, and above
every keel little or large that dents the
water,

Without edifices or rules or trustees or any
argument,
The institution of the dear love of comrades.

1860.

THE PRAIRIE-GRASS DIVIDING

THE prairie-grass dividing, its special odor
breathing,
I demand of it the spiritual corresponding,
Demand the most copious and close com-
panionship of men,
Demand the blades to rise of words, acts,
beings,
Those of the open atmosphere, coarse, sun-
lit, fresh, nutritious,
Those that go their own gait, erect, step-
ping with freedom and command, leading
not following,
Those with a never-quell'd audacity, those
with sweet and lusty flesh clear of taint,
Those that look carelessly in the faces of
Presidents and governors, as to say *Who
are you?*
Those of earth-born passion, simple, never
constrain'd, never obedient,
Those of inland America.[1]

1860.

[1] If you care to have a word from me, I should speak
it about these very prairies; they impress me most, of
all the objective shows I have seen on this, my first
real visit to the West. . . . As I have . . . launch'd
my view across broad expanses of living green, in every
direction — I have again been most impress'd, I say,
and shall remain for the rest of my life most impress'd,
with . . . that vast Something, stretching out on its
own unbounded scale, unconfined, which there is in
these prairies, combining the real and the ideal, and
beautiful as dreams.
I wonder indeed if the people of this continental inland West know how much of first-class *art* they have
in these prairies — how original and all your own —
how much of the influences of a character for your future humanity, broad, patriotic, heroic, and new? how
entirely they tally on land the grandeur and superb
monotony of the skies of heaven, and the ocean with
its waters? how freeing, soothing, nourishing they are
to the soul?
Then is it not subtly they who have given us our leading modern Americans, Lincoln and Grant? — vast-
spread, average men — their foregrounds of character
altogether practical and real, yet (to those who have
eyes to see) with finest backgrounds of the ideal, towering high as any. And do we not see, in them, fore-
shadowings of the future races that shall fill these
prairies?
Not but what the Yankee and Atlantic States, and
every other part — Texas, and the States flanking the
south-east and the Gulf of Mexico — the Pacific shore
empire — the Territories and Lakes, and the Canada
line (the day is not yet, but it will come, including
Canada entire) — are equally and integrally and indis-

WHEN I PERUSE THE CON-QUER'D FAME

WHEN I peruse the conquer'd fame of heroes and the victories of mighty generals,
I do not envy the generals,
Nor the President in his Presidency, nor
the rich in his great house,
But when I hear of the brotherhood of lovers, how it was with them,
How together through life, through dangers, odium, unchanging, long and long,
Through youth and through middle and old
age, how unfaltering, how affectionate
and faithful they were,
Then I am pensive — I hastily walk away
fill'd with the bitterest envy.

1860.

I DREAM'D IN A DREAM[2]

I DREAM'D in a dream I saw a city invincible to the attacks of the whole of the
rest of the earth,
I dream'd that was the new city of Friends,

solubly this Nation, the *sine qua non* of the human, political and commercial New World. But this favor'd
central area of (in round numbers) two thousand miles
square seems fated to be the home both of what I would
call America's distinctive ideas and distinctive realities.
(WHITMAN, *Specimen Days*, 'The Prairies.' Complete
Prose Works, Small, Maynard & Co., pp. 134, 135.)
[2] Intense and loving comradeship, the personal and
passionate attachment of man to man — which, hard to
define, underlies the lessons and ideals of the profound
saviours of every land and age, and which seems to
promise, when thoroughly develop'd, cultivated and
recognized in manners and literature, the most substantial hope and safety of the future of these States,
will then [when the true poet comes] be fully express'd.
A strong fibred joyousness and faith, and the sense
of health *al fresco*, may well enter into the preparation
of future noble American authorship. . . .
It is to the development, identification, and general
prevalence of that fervid comradeship (the adhesive
love, at least rivaling the amative love hitherto possess-
ing imaginative literature, if not going beyond it), that
I look for the counterbalance and offset of our materialistic and vulgar American democracy, and for the
spiritualization thereof. Many will say it is a dream,
and will not follow my inferences : but I confidently
expect a time when there will be seen, running like a
half-hid warp through all the myriad audible and visible worldly interests of America, threads of manly
friendship, fond and loving, pure and sweet, strong and
life-long, carried to degrees hitherto unknown — not
only giving tone to individual character, and making
it unprecedently emotional, muscular, heroic, and refined, but having the deepest relations to general politics. I say democracy infers such loving comradeship,
as its most inevitable twin or counterpart, without
which it will be incomplete, in vain, and incapable of
perpetuating itself. . . . .
In my opinion, it is by a fervent, accepted develop-

Nothing was greater there than the quality
of robust love, it led the rest,
It was seen every hour in the actions of the
men of that city,
And in all their looks and words.

1860.

FULL OF LIFE NOW

FULL of life now, compact, visible,
I, forty years old the eighty-third year of
the States,
To one a century hence or any number of
centuries hence,
To you yet unborn these, seeking you.

When you read these I that was visible am
become invisible,
Now it is you, compact, visible, realizing
my poems, seeking me,
Fancying how happy you were if I could be
with you and become your comrade;
Be it as if I were with you. (Be not too
certain but I am now with you.)

1860.

TO ONE SHORTLY TO DIE

FROM all the rest I single out you, having
a message for you,
You are to die — let others tell you what
they please, I cannot prevaricate,
I am exact and merciless, but I love you —
there is no escape for you.

Softly I lay my right hand upon you, you
just feel it,
I do not argue, I bend my head close and
half envelop it,
I sit quietly by, I remain faithful,
I am more than nurse, more than parent or
neighbor,
I absolve you from all except yourself
spiritual bodily, that is eternal, you yourself will surely escape,
The corpse you will leave will be but
excrementitious.

ment of comradeship, the beautiful and sane affection of
man for man, latent in all the young fellows, north and
south, east and west — it is by this, I say, and by what
goes directly and indirectly along with it, that the
United States of the future (I cannot too often repeat),
are to be most effectually welded together, intercalated,
anneal'd into a living union. (WHITMAN, in his Preface
to the 1876 edition of *Leaves of Grass.* Complete
Prose Works, Small, Maynard & Co., pp. 239, 240, and
277, 278.)

The sun bursts through in unlooked-for
directions,
Strong thoughts fill you and confidence,
you smile,
You forget you are sick, as I forget you
are sick,
You do not see the medicines, you do not
mind the weeping friends, I am with
you,
I exclude others from you, there is nothing
to be commiserated,
I do not commiserate, I congratulate you.

1860.

NIGHT ON THE PRAIRIES [1]

NIGHT on the prairies,
The supper is over, the fire on the ground
burns low,
The wearied emigrants sleep, wrapt in their
blankets;
I walk by myself — I stand and look at the
stars, which I think now I never realized
before.

Now I absorb immortality and peace,
I admire death and test propositions.

How plenteous! how spiritual! how re-
sumé!
The same old man and soul — the same old
aspirations, and the same content.

I was thinking the day most splendid till I
saw what the not-day exhibited,
I was thinking this globe enough till there
sprang out so noiseless around me myriads of other globes.

Now while the great thoughts of space and
eternity fill me I will measure myself by
them,

[1] The germ of this poem is found in a loose note of
Whitman's: 'Idea of poem. Day and night. Namely,
celebrate the beauty of Day, with all its splendor, the
sun — life — action — Love — strength. The Night with
its beauty. . .'
Compare also the passages from Whitman's Prose
Works quoted or referred to in the note on 'When I
heard the learn'd astronomer;' especially the passage
in *Specimen Days* under date of July 22, 1878. Complete Prose Works, pp. 111, 112.
Whitman was acquainted with Blanco White's famous sonnet on this same idea. Among his clippings
he preserved a copy of it, on the margin of which he
had written: 'What life hides too!' (*Notes and Fragments,* p. 104.)

And now touch'd with the lives of other
globes arrived as far along as those of
the earth,
Or waiting to arrive, or pass'd on farther
than those of the earth,
I henceforth no more ignore them than I
ignore my own life,
Or the lives of the earth arrived as far as
mine, or waiting to arrive.

O I see now that life cannot exhibit all to
me, as the day cannot,
I see that I am to wait for what will be
exhibited by death.

1860.

O MAGNET-SOUTH [1]

O MAGNET-SOUTH ! O glistening perfumed
South ! my South !
O quick mettle, rich blood, impulse and
love ! good and evil ! O all dear to
me !
O dear to me my birth-things — all moving
things and the trees where I was born
— the grains, plants, rivers,
Dear to me my own slow sluggish rivers
where they flow, distant, over flats of
silvery sands or through swamps,
Dear to me the Roanoke, the Savannah, the
Altamahaw, the Pedee, the Tombigbee,
the Santee, the Coosa and the Sabine,
O pensive, far away wandering, I return with
my soul to haunt their banks again,
Again in Florida I float on transparent
lakes, I float on the Okeechobee, I cross
the hummock-land or through pleasant
openings or dense forests,
I see the parrots in the woods, I see the
papaw-tree and the blossoming titi;
Again, sailing in my coaster on deck, I
coast off Georgia, I coast up the Caro-
linas,
I see where the live-oak is growing, I see
where the yellow-pine, the scented bay-
tree, the lemon and orange, the cypress,
the graceful palmetto,
I pass rude sea-headlands and enter Pam-
lico sound through an inlet, and dart my
vision inland;
O the cotton plant ! the growing fields of
rice, sugar, hemp !

[1] In the 1860 edition, with the title 'Longings for
Home.'

The cactus guarded with thorns, the laurel-
tree with large white flowers,
The range afar, the richness and barrenness,
the old woods charged with mistletoe and
trailing moss,
The piney odor and the gloom, the awful
natural stillness, (here in these dense
swamps the freebooter carries his gun,
and the fugitive has his conceal'd hut;)
O the strange fascination of these half-
known half-impassable swamps, infested
by reptiles, resounding with the bellow of
the alligator, the sad noises of the night-
owl and the wild-cat, and the whirr of
the rattlesnake,
The mocking-bird, the American mimi,
singing all the forenoon, singing through
the moon-lit night,
The humming-bird, the wild turkey, the
raccoon, the opossum;
A Kentucky corn-field, the tall, graceful,
long-leav'd corn, slender, flapping, bright
green, with tassels, with beautiful ears
each well-sheath'd in its husk;
O my heart ! O tender and fierce pangs, I
can stand them not, I will depart;
O to be a Virginian where I grew up ! O to
be a Carolinian !
O longings irrepressible ! O I will go back
to old Tennessee and never wander more.

1860.

MANNAHATTA [2]

I WAS asking for something specific and
perfect for my city,
Whereupon lo ! upsprang the aboriginal
name.

[2] Compare ' Crossing Brooklyn Ferry,' ' A Broadway
Pageant,' ' Give me the Splendid Silent Sun,' and the
following passages from Whitman's *Specimen Days :* —
June 25. — Returned to New York last night. Out to-
day on the waters for a sail in the wide bay, southeast
of Staten island, — a rough, tossing ride, and a free
sight — the long stretch of Sandy Hook, the highlands
of Navesink, and the many vessels outward and inward
bound. We came up through the midst of all, in the full
sun. I especially enjoy'd the last hour or two. A moderate sea-breeze had set in; yet over the city, and the
waters adjacent, was a thin haze, concealing nothing
only adding to the beauty. From my point of view, as
I write amid the soft breeze, with a sea-temperature,
surely nothing on earth of its kind can go beyond this
show. To the left the North river with its far vista —
nearer, three or four war-ships, anchor'd peacefully —
the Jersey side, the banks of Weehawken, the Palisades,
and the gradually receding blue, lost in the distance —
to the right the East river — the mast-hemm'd shores

Now I see what there is in a name, a word,
    liquid, sane, unruly, musical, self-suffi-
    cient,
I see that the word of my city is that word
    from of old,

—the grand obelisk-like towers of the bridge, one on either side, in haze, yet plainly defin'd, giant brothers twain, throwing free graceful interlinking loops high across the tumbled tumultuous current below (the tide is just changing to its ebb)—the broad water-spread everywhere crowded—no, not crowded, but thick as stars in the sky—with all sorts and sizes of sail and steam vessels, plying ferry-boats, arriving and departing coasters, great ocean Dons, iron-black, modern, magnificent in size and power, fill'd with their incalculable value of human life and precious merchandise—with here and there, above all, those daring, careening things of grace and wonder, those white and shaded swift-darting fish-birds (I wonder if shore or sea elsewhere can outvie them), ever with their slanting spars, and fierce, pure, hawk-like beauty and motion—first-class New York sloop or schooner yachts, sailing, this fine day, the free sea in a good wind. And rising out of the midst, tall-topt, ship-hemm'd, modern, American, yet strangely oriental, V-shaped Manhattan, with its compact mass, its spires, its cloud-touching edifices group'd at the centre—the green of the trees, and all the white, brown and gray of the architecture well blended, as I see it, under a miracle of limpid sky, delicious light of heaven above, and June haze on the surface below.

HUMAN AND HEROIC NEW YORK.—The general subjective view of New York and Brooklyn (will not the time hasten when the two shall be municipally united in one, and named Manhattan?)—what I may call the human interior and exterior of these great seething oceanic populations, as I get it in this visit, is to me best of all. After an absence of many years (I went away at the outbreak of the secession war, and have never been back to stay since), again I resume with curiosity the crowds, the streets, I knew so well, Broadway, the ferries, the west side of the city, democratic Bowery—human appearances and manners as seen in all these, and along the wharves, and in the perpetual travel of the horse-cars, or the crowded excursion steamers, or in Wall and Nassau streets by day—in the places of amusement at night—bubbling and whirling and moving like its own environment of waters—endless humanity in all phases—Brooklyn also—taken in for the last three weeks. No need to specify minutely—enough to say that (making all allowances for the shadows and side-streaks of a million-headed-city) the brief total of the impressions, the human qualities, of these vast cities, is to me comforting, even heroic, beyond statement. Alertness, generally fine physique, clear eyes that look straight at you, a singular combination of reticence and self-possession, with good nature and friendliness—a prevailing range of according manners, taste and intellect, surely beyond any elsewhere upon earth—and a palpable out-cropping of that personal comradeship I look forward to as the subtlest, strongest future hold of this many-item'd Union—are not only constantly visible here in these mighty channels of men, but they form the rule and average. To-day, I should say—defiant of cynics and pessimists, and with a full knowledge of all their exceptions—an appreciative and perceptive study of the current humanity of New York gives the directest proof yet of successful Democracy, and of the solution of that paradox, the eligibility of the free and fully developed individual with the paramount aggregate. In old age, lame and sick, pondering for years on many a doubt and danger for this republic of ours—fully aware of all that can be said on the other side—I find in this

Because I see that word nested in nests of
    water-bays, superb,
Rich, hemm'd thick all around with sailships
    and steamships, an island sixteen miles
    long, solid-founded,
Numberless crowded streets, high growths
    of iron, slender, strong, light, splendidly
    uprising toward clear skies,
Tides swift and ample, well-loved by me,
    toward sundown,
The flowing sea-currents, the little islands,
    larger adjoining islands, the heights, the
    villas,
The countless masts, the white shore-steam-
    ers, the lighters, the ferry-boats, the black
    sea-steamers well-model'd,
The down-town streets, the jobbers' houses
    of business, the houses of business of the
    ship-merchants and money-brokers, the
    river-streets,
Immigrants arriving, fifteen or twenty thou-
    sand in a week,
The carts hauling goods, the manly race
    of drivers of horses, the brown-faced
    sailors,
The summer air, the bright sun shining, and
    the sailing clouds aloft,
The winter snows, the sleigh-bells, the
    broken ice in the river, passing along up
    or down with the flood-tide or ebb-tide,
The mechanics of the city, the masters,
    well-form'd, beautiful-faced, looking you
    straight in the eyes,
Trottoirs throng'd, vehicles, Broadway, the
    women, the shops and shows,
A million people—manners free and superb
    —open voices—hospitality—the most
    courageous and friendly young men,
City of hurried and sparkling waters! city
    of spires and masts!
City nested in bays! my city!

                         1860.

visit to New York, and the daily contact and rapport with its myriad people, on the scale of the oceans and tides, the best, most effective medicine my soul has yet partaken—the grandest physical habitat and surroundings of land and water the globe affords—namely, Manhattan island and Brooklyn, which the future shall join in one city—city of superb democracy, amid superb surroundings. (Complete Prose Works, Small, Maynard & Co., pp. 109-111.)

See also *Specimen Days*, May 24, 1879, 'Two City Areas, Certain Hours,' Prose Works, pp. 126, 127 ; May 16 to 22, 'Central Park Walks and Talks,' Prose Works, pp. 128, 129 ; July 29, 1881, 'My Passion for Ferries,' 'Broadway Sights,' 'Omnibus Jaunts,' Prose Works, pp. 11-13 ; and also the *Collect*, Prose Works, pp. 205, 206, quoted in part in the note on 'Give me the splendid silent sun,' p. 578.

MYSELF AND MINE

MYSELF and mine gymnastic ever,
To stand the cold or heat, to take good aim
  with a gun, to sail a boat, to manage
  horses, to beget superb children,
To speak readily and clearly, to feel at
  home among common people,
And to hold our own in terrible positions
  on land and sea.

Not for an embroiderer,
(There will always be plenty of embroider-
  ers, I welcome them also,)
But for the fibre of things and for inherent
  men and women.

Not to chisel ornaments,
But to chisel with free stroke the heads
  and limbs of plenteous supreme Gods,
  that the States may realize them walking
  and talking.

Let me have my own way,   10
Let others promulge the laws, I will make
  no account of the laws,
Let others praise eminent men and hold up
  peace, I hold up agitation and conflict,
I praise no eminent man, I rebukĕ to his
  face the one that was thought most worthy.

(Who are you ? and what are you secretly
  guilty of all your life ?
Will you turn aside all your life ? will you
  grub and chatter all your life ?
And who are you, blabbing by rote, years,
  pages, languages, reminiscences,
Unwitting to-day that you do not know
  how to speak properly a single word ?)

Let others finish specimens, I never finish
  specimens,
I start them by exhaustless laws as Nature
  does, fresh and modern continually.

I give nothing as duties,   20
What others give as duties I give as living
  impulses,
(Shall I give the heart's action as a duty ?)

Let others dispose of questions, I dispose of
  nothing, I arouse unanswerable questions,
Who are they I see and touch, and what
  about them ?

What about these likes of myself that draw
  me so close by tender directions and in-
  directions ?

I call to the world to distrust the accounts
  of my friends, but listen to my enemies,
  as I myself do,
I charge you forever reject those who would
  expound me, for I cannot expound myself,
I charge that there be no theory or school
  founded out of me,
I charge you to leave all free, as I have left
  all free.

After me, vista !   30
O I see life is not short, but immeasurably
  long,
I henceforth tread the world chaste, tem-
  perate, an early riser, a steady grower,
Every hour the semen of centuries, and
  still of centuries.

I must follow up these continual lessons of
  the air, water, earth,
I perceive I have no time to lose.

                                   1860.

A BROADWAY PAGEANT

I

OVER the Western sea hither from Niphon [1]
  come,
Courteous, the swart-cheek'd two-sworded
  envoys,
Leaning back in their open barouches, bare-
  headed, impassive,
Ride to-day through Manhattan.[2]

Libertad ! I do not know whether others be-
  hold what I behold,
In the procession along with the nobles of
  Niphon, the errand-bearers,
Bringing up the rear, hovering above,
  around, or in the ranks marching,
But I will sing you a song of what I behold
  Libertad.

[1] Nippon, the native name of Japan.
[2] In the edition of 1865 the poem begins : —

        A BROADWAY PAGEANT
   (Reception Japanese Embassy, June 16, 1860.)

Over sea, hither from Niphon,
Courteous, the Princes of Asia, swart-cheek'd princes,
First-comers, guests, two-sworded princes,
Lesson-giving princes, leaning back in their open barouches,
  bare-headed, impassive,
This day they ride through Manhattan

When million-footed Manhattan unpent
descends to her pavements,
When the thunder-cracking guns arouse me
with the proud roar I love,   10
When the round-mouth'd guns out of the
smoke and smell I love spit their salutes,
When the fire-flashing guns have fully
alerted me, and heaven-clouds canopy my
city with a delicate thin haze,
When gorgeous the countless straight stems,
the forests at the wharves, thicken with
colors,
When every ship richly drest carries her
flag at the peak,
When pennants trail and street-festoons
hang from the windows,
When Broadway is entirely given up to
foot-passengers and foot-standers, when
the mass is densest,
When the façades of the houses are alive
with people, when eyes gaze riveted tens
of thousands at a time,
When the guests from the islands advance,
when the pageant moves forward visible,
When the summons is made, when the answer that waited thousands of years answers,
I too arising, answering, descend to the
pavements, merge with the crowd, and
gaze with them.   20

2

Superb-faced Manhattan !
Comrade Americanos ! to us, then at last
the Orient comes.

To us, my city,
Where our tall-topt marble and iron beauties range on opposite sides, to walk in
the space between,
To-day our Antipodes comes.

The Originatress comes, [1]
The nest of languages, the bequeather of
poems, the race of eld,
Florid with blood, pensive, rapt with mus-
ings, hot with passion,
Sultry with perfume, with ample and flow-
ing garments,
With sunburnt visage, with intense soul and
glittering eyes,   30
The race of Brahma comes.

[1] Here follows, in the original edition : —
The land of Paradise — land of the Caucasus — the nest of
birth, . . .

See my cantabile ! these and more are flashing to us from the procession,
As it moves changing, a kaleidoscope divine
it moves changing before us.

For not the envoys nor the tann'd Japanee
from his island only,[2]
Lithe and silent the Hindoo appears, the
Asiatic continent itself appears, the past,
the dead,
The murky night-morning of wonder and
fable inscrutable,
The envelop'd mysteries, the old and unknown hive-bees,
The north, the sweltering south, eastern
Assyria, the Hebrews, the ancient of
ancients,
Vast desolated cities, the gliding present,
all of these and more are in the pageant-
procession.

Geography, the world, is in it,   40
The Great Sea, the brood of islands, Poly-
nesia, the coast beyond,
The coast you henceforth are facing —
you Libertad ! from your Western golden
shores,
The countries there with their populations, the millions en-masse are curiously
here,
The swarming market-places, the temples
with idols ranged along the sides or at
the end, bonze, brahmin, and llama,
Mandarin, farmer, merchant, mechanic, and
fisherman,
The singing-girl and the dancing-girl, the
ecstatic persons, the secluded emperors,
Confucius himself, the great poets and
heroes, the warriors, the castes, all,[3]
Trooping up, crowding from all directions,
from the Altay mountains,
From Thibet, from the four winding and
far-flowing rivers of China,
From the southern peninsulas and the demi-
continental islands, from Malaysia,   50
These and whatever belongs to them palpable show forth to me, and are seiz'd
by me,

[2] In the original edition this line reads : —

Not the errand-bearing princes only, nor the tann'd Japanee
only.

[3] In the original edition these two lines read: —

The singing-girl and the dancing-girl — the ecstatic person
— the divine Buddha;
The secluded Emperors — Confucius himself — the great
poets and heroes — the warriors, the castes, all.

And I am seiz'd by them, and friendlily
held by them,
Till as here them all I chant, Libertad!
for themselves and for you.

For I too raising my voice join the ranks
of this pageant,
I am the chanter, I chant aloud over the
pageant,
I chant the world on my Western sea,
I chant copious the islands beyond, thick
as stars in the sky,
I chant the new empire grander than any
before, as in a vision it comes to me,
I chant America the mistress, I chant a
greater supremacy,
I chant projected a thousand blooming
cities yet in time on those groups of sea-
islands,   60
My sail-ships and steam-ships threading
the archipelagoes,
My stars and stripes fluttering in the wind,
Commerce opening, the sleep of ages having done its work, races reborn, refresh'd,
Lives, works resumed — the object I know
not — but the old, the Asiatic renew'd as
it must be,
Commencing from this day surrounded by
the world.

3

And you Libertad of the world!
You shall sit in the middle well-pois'd
thousands and thousands of years,
As to-day from one side the nobles of Asia
come to you,
As to-morrow from the other side the
queen of England sends her eldest son
to you,
The sign is reversing, the orb is enclosed, 70
The ring is circled, the journey is done,
The box-lid is but perceptibly open'd, never-
theless the perfume pours copiously out
of the whole box.

Young Libertad! with the venerable Asia,
the all-mother,
Be considerate with her now and ever hot
Libertad, for you are all,
Bend your proud neck to the long-off
mother now sending messages over the
archipelagoes to you,
Bend your proud neck low for once, young
Libertad.

Were the children straying westward so
long? so wide the tramping?
Were the precedent dim ages debouching
westward from Paradise so long?
Were the centuries steadily footing it that
way, all the while unknown, for you, for
reasons?

They are justified, they are accomplish'd,
they shall now be turn'd the other way
also, to travel toward you thence,   80
They shall now also march obediently eastward for your sake Libertad.[1]
1860.   *1865.*

PIONEERS! O PIONEERS!

COME my tan-faced children,
Follow well in order, get your weapons
ready,
Have you your pistols? have you your
sharp-edged axes?
Pioneers! O pioneers!

For we cannot tarry here,
We must march my darlings, we must bear
the brunt of danger,
We the youthful sinewy races, all the rest
on us depend,
Pioneers! O pioneers!

O you youths, Western youths,
So impatient, full of action, full of manly
pride and friendship,   10
Plain I see you Western youths, see you
tramping with the foremost,
Pioneers! O pioneers!

Have the elder races halted?
Do they droop and end their lesson, wearied
over there beyond the seas?

---

[1] THE EAST. — What a subject for a poem! Indeed,
where else a more pregnant, more splendid one?
Where one more idealistic-real, more subtle, more sen-
suous-delicate? The East, answering all lands, all
ages, peoples; touching all senses, here, immediate,
now — and yet so indescribably far off — such retrospect! The East — long-stretching — so losing itself —
the orient, the gardens of Asia, the womb of history
and song — forth-issuing all those strange, dim caval-
cades —
Florid with blood, pensive, rapt with musings, hot with
passion,
Sultry with perfume, with ample and flowing garments,
With sunburnt visage, intense soul and glittering eyes.
Always the East — old, how incalculably old! And
yet here the same — ours yet, fresh as a rose, to every
morning, every life, to-day — and always will be.
(WHITMAN, *Specimen Days.* Complete Prose Works,
pp. 112, 113.)

We take up the task eternal, and the burden and the lesson,
  Pioneers! O pioneers!

All the past we leave behind,
We debouch upon a newer mightier world, varied world,
Fresh and strong the world we seize, world of labor and the march,
  Pioneers! O pioneers!   20

We detachments steady throwing,
Down the edges, through the passes, up the mountains steep,
Conquering, holding, daring, venturing as we go the unknown ways,
  Pioneers! O pioneers!

We primeval forests felling,
We the rivers stemming, vexing we and piercing deep the mines within,
We the surface broad surveying, we the virgin soil upheaving,
  Pioneers! O pioneers!

Colorado men are we,
From the peaks gigantic, from the great sierras and the high plateaus,   30
From the mine and from the gully, from the hunting trail we come,
  Pioneers! O pioneers!

From Nebraska, from Arkansas,
Central inland race are we, from Missouri, with the continental blood intervein'd,
All the hands of comrades clasping, all the Southern, all the Northern,
  Pioneers! O pioneers!.

O resistless restless race!
O beloved race in all! O my breast aches with tender love for all!
O I mourn and yet exult, I am rapt with love for all,
  Pioneers! O pioneers!   40

Raise the mighty mother mistress,
Waving high the delicate mistress, over all the starry mistress (bend your heads all),
Raise the fang'd and warlike mistress, stern, impassive, weapon'd mistress,
  Pioneers! O pioneers!

See my children, resolute children,
By those swarms upon our rear we must never yield or falter,

Ages back in ghostly millions frowning there behind us urging,
  Pioneers! O pioneers!

On and on the compact ranks,
With accessions ever waiting, with the places of the dead quickly fill'd,   50
Through the battle, through defeat, moving yet and never stopping,
  Pioneers! O pioneers!

O to die advancing on!
Are there some of us to droop and die? has the hour come?
Then upon the march we fittest die, soon and sure the gap is fill'd,
  Pioneers! O pioneers!

All the pulses of the world,
Falling in they beat for us, with the Western movement beat,
Holding single or together, steady moving to the front, all for us,
  Pioneers! O pioneers!   60

Life's involv'd and varied pageants,
All the forms and shows, all the workmen at their work,
All the seamen and the landsmen, all the masters with their slaves,
  Pioneers! O pioneers!

All the hapless silent lovers,
All the prisoners in the prisons, all the righteous and the wicked,
All the joyous, all the sorrowing, all the living, all the dying,
  Pioneers! O pioneers!

I too with my soul and body,
We, a curious trio, picking, wandering on our way,   70
Through these shores amid the shadows, with the apparitions pressing,
  Pioneers! O pioneers!

Lo, the darting bowling orb!
Lo, the brother orbs around, all the clustering suns and planets,
All the dazzling days, all the mystic nights with dreams,
  Pioneers! O pioneers!

These are of us, they are with us,
All for primal needed work, while the followers there in embryo wait behind,

We to-day's procession heading, we the
.   route for travel clearing,
      Pioneers ! O pioneers !   80

O you daughters of the West !
O you young and elder daughters ! O you
  mothers and you wives !
Never must you be divided, in our ranks
  you move united,
      Pioneers ! O pioneers !

Minstrels latent on the prairies !
(Shrouded bards of other lands, you may
  rest, you have done your work,)
Soon I hear you coming warbling, soon you
  rise and tramp amid us,
      Pioneers ! O pioneers !

Not for delectations sweet,
Not the cushion and the slipper, not the
  peaceful and the studious,   90
Not the riches safe and palling, not for us
  the tame enjoyment,
      Pioneers ! O pioneers !

Do the feasters gluttonous feast ?
Do the corpulent sleepers sleep ? have they
  lock'd and bolted doors ?
Still be ours the diet hard, and the blanket
  on the ground,
      Pioneers ! O pioneers !

Has the night descended ?
Was the road of late so toilsome ? did we
  stop discouraged nodding on our way ?
Yet a passing hour I yield you in your
  tracks to pause oblivious,
      Pioneers ! O pioneers !   100

Till with sound of trumpet,
Far, far off the daybreak call — hark !
  how loud and clear I hear it wind,
Swift ! to the head of the army ! — swift !
  spring to your places,
      Pioneers ! O pioneers !

                   1865.

FROM PAUMANOK STARTING I FLY LIKE A BIRD

FROM Paumanok starting I fly like a
  bird,
Around and around to soar to sing the idea
  of all,

To the north betaking myself to sing there
  arctic songs,
To Kanada till I absorb Kanada in myself,
  to Michigan then,
To Wisconsin, Iowa, Minnesota, to sing
  their songs (they are inimitable);
Then to Ohio and Indiana to sing theirs, to
  Missouri and Kansas and Arkansas to
  sing theirs,
To Tennessee and Kentucky, to the Caro-
  linas and Georgia to sing theirs,
To Texas and so along up toward California,
  to roam accepted everywhere;
To sing first (to the tap of the war-drum
  if need be),
The idea of all, of the Western world one
  and inseparable,
And then the song of each member of these
  States.

                   1865.

EIGHTEEN SIXTY-ONE

ARM'D year — year of the struggle,
No dainty rhymes or sentimental love
  verses for you terrible year,
Not you as some pale poetling seated at a
  desk lisping cadenzas piano,
But as a strong man erect, clothed in blue
  clothes, advancing, carrying a rifle on
  your shoulder,
With well-gristled body and sunburnt face
  and hands, with a knife in the belt at
  your side,
As I heard you shouting loud, your sonorous voice ringing across the continent,
Your masculine voice O year, as rising
  amid the great cities,
Amid the men of Manhattan I saw you as
  one of the workmen, the dwellers in
  Manhattan,
Or with large steps crossing the prairies
  out of Illinois and Indiana,
Rapidly crossing the West with springy
  gait and descending the Alleghanies,
Or down from the great lakes or in Pennsylvania, or on deck along the Ohio river,
Or southward along the Tennessee or Cumberland rivers, or at Chattanooga on the
  mountain top,
Saw I your gait and saw I your sinewy
  limbs clothed in blue, bearing weapons,
  robust year,
Heard your determin'd voice launch'd forth
  again and again,

Year that suddenly sang by the mouths of the round-lipp'd cannon,
I repeat you, hurrying, crashing, sad, distracted year.

1865.

BEAT! BEAT! DRUMS!

BEAT! beat! drums! — blow! bugles! blow!
Through the windows — through doors — burst like a ruthless force,
Into the solemn church, and scatter the congregation,
Into the school where the scholar is studying;
Leave not the bridegroom quiet — no happiness must he have now with his bride,
Nor the peaceful farmer any peace, ploughing his field or gathering his grain,
So fierce you whirr and pound you drums — so shrill you bugles blow.

Beat! beat! drums! — blow! bugles! blow!
Over the traffic of cities — over the rumble of wheels in the streets;
Are beds prepared for sleepers at night in the houses? no sleepers must sleep in those beds,
No bargainers' bargains by day — no brokers or speculators — would they continue?
Would the talkers be talking? would the singer attempt to sing?
Would the lawyer rise in the court to state his case before the judge?
Then rattle quicker, heavier drums — you bugles wilder blow.

Beat! beat! drums! — blow! bugles! blow!
Make no parley — stop for no expostulation,
Mind not the timid — mind not the weeper or prayer,
Mind not the old man beseeching the young man,
Let not the child's voice be heard, nor the mother's entreaties,
Make even the trestles to shake the dead where they lie awaiting the hearses,
So strong you thump O terrible drums — so loud you bugles blow.

1865.

CAVALRY CROSSING A FORD

A LINE in long array where they wind betwixt green islands,
They take a serpentine course, their arms flash in the sun — hark to the musical clank,
Behold the silvery river, in it the splashing horses loitering stop to drink,
Behold the brown-faced men, each group, each person a picture, the negligent rest on the saddles,
Some emerge on the opposite bank, others are just entering the ford — while,
Scarlet and blue and snowy white,
The guidon flags flutter gayly in the wind.

1865.

BIVOUAC ON A MOUNTAIN SIDE [1]

I SEE before me now a traveling army halting,
Below a fertile valley spread, with barns and the orchards of summer,
Behind, the terraced sides of a mountain, abrupt, in places rising high,
Broken, with rocks, with clinging cedars, with tall shapes dingily seen,
The numerous camp-fires scatter'd near and far, some away up on the mountain,
The shadowy forms of men and horses, looming, large-sized, flickering,
And over all the sky — the sky! far, far out of reach, studded, breaking out, the eternal stars.

1865.

BY THE BIVOUAC'S FITFUL FLAME

By the bivouac's fitful flame,
A procession winding around me, solemn and sweet and slow — but first I note,
The tents of the sleeping army, the fields' and woods' dim outline,
The darkness lit by spots of kindled fire, the silence,
Like a phantom far or near an occasional figure moving,
The shrubs and trees (as I lift my eyes they seem to be stealthily watching me),

[1] Compare *Specimen Days*, July 4, 6, 10, 1863. Complete Prose Works, p. 11.

While wind in procession thoughts, O tender and wondrous thoughts,
Of life and death, of home and the past
and loved, and of those that are far
away;
A solemn and slow procession there as I sit
on the ground,
By the bivouac's fitful flame.

1865.

I SAW OLD GENERAL AT BAY

I SAW old General at bay,
(Old as he was, his gray eyes yet shone out
in battle like stars,)
His small force was now completely hemm'd
in, in his works,
He call'd for volunteers to run the enemy's
lines, a desperate emergency,
I saw a hundred and more step forth from
the ranks, but two or three were selected,
I saw them receive their orders aside, they
listen'd with care, the adjutant was very
grave,
I saw them depart with cheerfulness, freely
risking their lives.

1865.

VIGIL STRANGE I KEPT ON THE
FIELD ONE NIGHT

VIGIL strange I kept on the field one night;
When you my son and my comrade dropt at
my side that day,
One look I but gave which your dear eyes
return'd with a look I shall never forget,
One touch of your hand to mine O boy,
reach'd up as you lay on the ground,
Then onward I sped in the battle, the even-
contested battle,
Till late in the night reliev'd to the place at
last again I made my way,
Found you in death so cold dear comrade,
found your body son of responding kisses
(never again on earth responding),
Bared your face in the starlight, curious the
scene, cool blew the moderate night-wind,
Long there and then in vigil I stood, dimly
around me the battle-field spreading,
Vigil wondrous and vigil sweet there in the
fragrant silent night,
But not a tear fell, not even a long-drawn
sigh, long, long I gazed,

Then on the earth partially reclining sat by
your side leaning my chin in my hands,
Passing sweet hours, immortal and mystic
hours with you dearest comrade — not a
tear, not a word,
Vigil of silence, love and death, vigil for you
my son and my soldier,
As onward silently stars aloft, eastward new
ones upward stole,
Vigil final for you brave boy, (I could not
save you, swift was your death,
I faithfully loved you and cared for you
living, I think we shall surely meet
again,)
Till at latest lingering of the night, indeed
just as the dawn appear'd,
My comrade I wrapt in his blanket, envelop'd well his form,
Folded the blanket well, tucking it carefully over head and carefully under
feet,
And there and then and bathed by the rising
sun, my son in his grave, in his rude-dug
grave I deposited,
Ending my vigil strange with that, vigil of
night and battle-field dim,
Vigil for boy of responding kisses (never
again on earth responding),
Vigil for comrade swiftly slain, vigil I never
forget, how as day brighten'd,
I rose from the chill ground and folded my
soldier well in his blanket,
And buried him where he fell.

1865.

COME UP FROM THE FIELDS
FATHER

COME up from the fields father, here's a
letter from our Pete,
And come to the front door mother, here's
a letter from thy dear son.

Lo, 't is autumn,
Lo, where the trees, deeper green, yellower
and redder,
Cool and sweeten Ohio's villages with
leaves fluttering in the moderate wind,
Where apples ripe in the orchards hang
and grapes on the trellis'd vines,
(Smell you the smell of the grapes on the
vines?
Smell you the buckwheat where the bees
were lately buzzing?)

Above all, lo, the sky so calm, so transparent after the rain, and with wondrous
clouds,   .
Below too, all calm, all vital and beautiful,
and the farm prospers well.   10

Down in the fields all prospers well,
But now from the fields come father, come
at the daughter's call,
And come to the entry mother, to the front
door come right away.

Fast as she can she hurries, something
ominous, her steps trembling,
She does not tarry to smooth her hair nor
adjust her cap.

Open the envelope quickly,
O this is not our son's writing, yet his
name is sign'd,
O a strange hand writes for our dear son,
O stricken mother's soul !
All swims before her eyes, flashes with
black, she catches the main words only,
Sentences broken, *gunshot wound in the
breast, cavalry skirmish, taken to hospital,*
At present low, but will soon be better.   21

Ah now the single figure to me,
Amid all teeming and wealthy Ohio with
all its cities and farms,
Sickly white in the face and dull in the
head, very faint,
By the jamb of a door leans.

Grieve not so, dear mother (the just-grown
daughter speaks through her sobs,
The little sisters huddle around speechless
and dismay'd),
*See, dearest mother, the letter says Pete will
soon be better.*

Alas poor boy, he will never be better
(nor may-be needs to be better, that
brave and simple soul),
While they stand at home at the door he is
dead already,   30
The only son is dead.

But the mother needs to be better,
She with thin form presently drest in black,
By day her meals untouch'd, then at night
fitfully sleeping, often waking,
In the midnight waking, weeping, longing
with one deep longing,

O that she might withdraw unnoticed, silent
from life escape and withdraw,
To follow, to seek, to be with her dear
dead son.

                              1865.

A SIGHT IN CAMP IN THE DAY-
BREAK GRAY AND DIM

A SIGHT in camp in the daybreak gray and
dim,
As from my tent I emerge so early sleepless,
As slow I walk in the cool fresh air the
path near by the hospital tent,
Three forms I see on stretchers lying,
brought out there untended lying,
Over each the blanket spread, ample
brownish woolen blanket,
Gray and heavy blanket, folding, covering
all.

Curious I halt and silent stand,
Then with light fingers I from the face of
the nearest the first just lift the blanket;
Who are you elderly man so gaunt and
grim, with well-gray'd hair and flesh all
sunken about the eyes ?
Who are you my dear comrade ?

Then to the second I step — and who are
you my child and darling ?
Who are you sweet boy with cheeks yet
blooming ?

Then to the third — a face nor child nor
old, very calm, as of beautiful yellow-
white ivory;
Young man I think I know you — I think
this face is the face of the Christ himself,
Dead and divine and brother of all, and
here again he lies.

                              1865.

AS TOILSOME I WANDER'D VIR-
GINIA'S WOODS

As toilsome I wander'd Virginia's woods,
To the music of rustling leaves kick'd by
my feet (for 't was autumn),
I mark'd at the foot of a tree the grave of
a soldier;
Mortally wounded he and buried on the retreat (easily all could I understand),

The halt of a mid-day hour, when up ! no
time to lose — yet this sign left,
On a tablet scrawl'd and nail'd on the tree
by the grave,
Bold, cautious, true, and my loving comrade.

Long, long I muse, then on my way go
wandering,
Many a changeful season to follow, and
many a scene of life,
Yet at times through changeful season and
scene, abrupt, alone, or in the crowded
street,
Comes before me the unknown soldier's
grave, comes the inscription rude in Virginia's woods,
Bold, cautious, true, and my loving comrade.
1865.

THE WOUND-DRESSER [1]

I

An old man bending I come among new
faces,
Years looking backward resuming in
answer to children,

[1] See the letter in Bucke's *Whitman*, pp. 38–40.
With this, and all the poems relating to the Civil
War, should be read the book entitled *The Wound-
Dresser,* a collection of letters written from the field
and from the hospitals in Washington ; and the parts of
Specimen Days picturing Whitman's experiences in the
war and in the hospitals, in his Complete Prose Works,
pp. 15–75. A few passages may be quoted: —
' The men, whatever their condition, lie there, and
patiently wait till their turn comes to be taken up.
Near by, the ambulances are now arriving in clusters,
and one after another is call'd to back up and take its
load. Extreme cases are sent off on stretchers. The
men generally make little or no ado, whatever their
sufferings. A few groans that cannot be suppress'd,
and occasionally a scream of pain as they lift a man
into the ambulance. To-day, as I write, hundreds more
are expected, and to-morrow and the next day more,
and so on for many days. Quite often they arrive at
the rate of 1000 a day. . . .
' It is Sunday afternoon, middle of summer, hot and
oppressive, and very silent through the ward. I am
taking care of a critical case, now lying in a half
lethargy. Near where I sit is a suffering rebel, from the
8th Louisiana; his name is Irving. He has been here a
long time, badly wounded, and lately had his leg amputated; it is not doing very well. Right opposite me
is a sick soldier-boy, laid down with his clothes on,
sleeping, looking much wasted, his pallid face on his
arm. I see by the yellow trimming on his jacket that
he is a cavalry boy. I step softly over and find by his
card that he is named William Cone, of the 1st Maine
cavalry, and his folks live in Skowhegan.
' One hot day toward the middle of June, I gave the
inmates of Carver hospital a general ice cream treat,
purchasing a large quantity, and, under convoy of the
doctor or head nurse, going around personally through
the wards to see to its distribution.
' . . . I do not see that I do much good to these

Come tell us old man, as from young men
and maidens that love me,
(Arous'd and angry, I'd thought to beat the
alarum, and urge relentless war,

wounded and dying; but I cannot leave them. Once in
a while some youngster holds on to me convulsively,
and I do what I can for him; at any rate, stop with him
and sit near him for hours, if he wishes it. . . .
' . . . I soon get acquainted anywhere in camp,
with officers or men, and am always well used. Sometimes I go down on picket with the regiments I know
best. . . .
' . . . In these wards, or on the field, as I thus continue to go round, I have come to adapt myself to each
emergency, after its kind or call, however trivial, however solemn, every one justified and made real under
its circumstances — not only visits and cheering talk
and little gifts — not only washing and dressing
wounds (I have some cases where the patient is unwilling any one should do this but me) — but passages
from the Bible, expounding them, prayer at the bedside, explanations of doctrine, &c. (I think I see my
friends smiling at this confession, but I was never
more in earnest in my life.) In camp and everywhere, I was in the habit of reading or giving recitations to the men. . . .
' . . . I went through the rooms, downstairs and up,
Some of the men were dying. I had nothing to give
at that visit, but wrote a few letters to folks home,
mothers, &c. Also talk'd to three or four, who seem'd
most susceptible to it, and needing it. . . .
' In one bed a young man, Marcus Small, company K,
7th Maine — sick with dysentery and typhoid fever —
pretty critical case — I talk with him often — he thinks
he will die — looks like it indeed. I write a letter for
him home to East Livermore, Maine — I let him talk to
me a little, but not much, advise him to keep very
quiet — do most of the talking myself —stay quite a
while with him, as he holds on to my hand — talk to
him in a cheering, but slow, low, and measured manner — talk about his furlough, and going home as soon
as he is able to travel.'
[From a letter to a dead soldier's mother] ; . . .
I will write you a few lines — as a casual friend that
sat by his death-bed. Your son, Corporal Frank H. Ir-
win, was wounded near Fort Fisher, Virginia, March
25th, 1865 — the wound was in the left knee, pretty
bad . . . I visited and sat by him frequently, as he
was fond of having me. The last ten or twelve days of
April I saw that his case was critical. He previously
had some fever, with cold spells. The last week in
April he was much of the time flighty — but always
mild and gentle. He died first of May. The actual
cause of death was pyæmia (the absorption of the matter in the system instead of its discharge). Frank, as
far as I saw, had everything requisite in surgical treatment, nursing, &c. He had watches much of the time.
He was so good and well-behaved and affectionate, I
myself liked him very much. I was in the habit of
coming in afternoons and sitting by him, and soothing
him, and he liked to have me — liked to put his arm
out and lay his hand on my knee — would keep it so a
long while. Toward the last he was more restless and
flighty at night. . . . All the time he was out of his
head not one single bad word or idea escaped him. It
was remark'd that many a man's conversation in his
senses was not half as good as Frank's delirium. He
seem'd quite willing to die — he had become very weak
and had suffer'd a good deal, and was perfectly resign'd,
poor boy. I do not know his past life, but I feel as if it
must have been good. At any rate what I saw of him
here, under the most trying circumstances, with a
painful wound, and among strangers, I can say that he
behaved so brave, so composed, and so sweet and af-

But soon my fingers fail'd me, my face
    droop'd and I resign'd myself,
To sit by the wounded and soothe them, or
    silently watch the dead;)
Years hence of these scenes, of these fu-
    rious passions, these chances,
Of unsurpass'd heroes (was one side so
    brave? the other was equally brave;) [1]
Now be witness again, paint the mightiest
    armies of earth,
Of those armies so rapid so wondrous what
    saw you to tell us?   10
What stays with you latest and deepest?
    of curious panics,
Of hard-fought engagements or sieges tre-
    mendous what deepest remains?

2

O maidens and young men I love and that
    love me,
What you ask of my days those the
    strangest and sudden your talking recalls,
Soldier alert I arrive after a long march
    cover'd with sweat and dust,
In the nick of time I come, plunge in the
    fight, loudly shout in the rush of success-
    ful charge,
Enter the captur'd works — yet lo, like a
    swift-running river they fade,
Pass and are gone they fade — I dwell not
    on soldiers' perils or soldiers' joys
(Both I remember well — many the hard-
    ships, few the joys, yet I was content).

But in silence, in dreams' projections,   20
While the world of gain and appearance
    and mirth goes on,

fectionate, it could not be surpass'd. And now like
many other noble and good men, after serving his
country as a soldier, he has yielded up his young life
at the very outset in her service. Such things are
gloomy — yet here is a text, ' God doeth all things
well ' — the meaning of which, after due time, appears to the soul.
    I thought perhaps a few words, though from a
stranger, about your son, from one who was with him
at the last, might be worth while — for I loved the
young man, though I but saw him immediately to lose
him. . . .   W. W.
    [1] The grand soldiers are not comprised in those of one
side, any more than the other. Here is a sample of an
unknown Southerner, a lad of seventeen. At the War
Department, a few days ago, I witness'd a presentation
of captured flags to the Secretary. Among others a
soldier named Gant, of the 104th Ohio Volunteers, presented a rebel battle-flag, which one of the officers
stated to me was borne to the mouth of our cannon
and planted there by a boy but seventeen years of age,
who actually endeavor'd to stop the muzzle of the gun
with fence-rails. He was kill'd in the effort, and the
flag-staff was sever'd by a shot from one of our men.
(Specimen Days, p. 27.)

So soon what is over forgotten, and waves
    wash the imprints off the sand,
With hinged knees returning I enter the
    doors (while for you up there,
Whoever you are, follow without noise and
    be of strong heart).

Bearing the bandages, water and sponge,
Straight and swift to my wounded I go,
Where they lie on the ground after the
    battle brought in,
Where their priceless blood reddens the
    grass the ground,
Or to the rows of the hospital tent, or
    under the roof'd hospital,
To the long rows of cots up and down each
    side I return,   30
To each and all one after another I draw
    near, not one do I miss,
An attendant follows holding a tray, he
    carries a refuse pail,
Soon to be fill'd with clotted rags and blood,
    emptied, and fill'd again.

I onward go, I stop,
With hinged knees and steady hand to
    dress wounds,
I am firm with each, the pangs are sharp
    yet unavoidable,
One turns to me his appealing eyes — poor
    boy! I never knew you,
Yet I think I could not refuse this moment
    to die for you, if that would save you.

3

On, on I go, (open doors of time! open
    hospital doors!)
The crush'd head I dress (poor crazed hand
    tear not the bandage away),   40
The neck of the cavalry-man with the bul-
    let through and through I examine,
Hard the breathing rattles, quite glazed
    already the eye, yet life struggles hard
(Come sweet death! be persuaded O
    beautiful death!
In mercy come quickly).

From the stump of the arm, the amputated
    hand,
I undo the clotted lint, remove the slough,
    wash off the matter and blood,
Back on his pillow the soldier bends with
    curv'd neck and side-falling head,
His eyes are closed, his face is pale, he
    dares not look on the bloody stump,
And has not yet look'd on it.

I dress a wound in the side, deep, deep, 50
But a day or two more, for see the frame
all wasted and sinking,
And the yellow-blue countenance see.

I dress the perforated shoulder, the foot
with the bullet-wound,
Cleanse the one with a gnawing and putrid
gangrene, so sickening, so offensive,
While the attendant stands behind aside
me holding the tray and pail.

I am faithful, I do not give out,
The fractur'd thigh, the knee, the wound
in the abdomen,
These and more I dress with impassive
hand (yet deep in my breast a fire, a
burning flame).

4

Thus in silence in dreams' projections,
Returning, resuming, I thread my way
through the hospitals, 60
The hurt and wounded I pacify with soothing hand,
I sit by the restless all the dark night,
some are so young,
Some suffer so much, I recall the experience sweet and sad,
(Many a soldier's loving arms about this
neck have cross'd and rested,
Many a soldier's kiss dwells on these
bearded lips).

1865.

GIVE ME THE SPLENDID SILENT SUN

1

GIVE me the splendid silent sun with all his
beams full-dazzling,
Give me juicy autumnal fruit ripe and red
from the orchard,
Give me a field where the unmow'd grass
grows,
Give me an arbor, give me the trellis'd
grape,
Give me fresh corn and wheat, give me se-
rene-moving animals teaching content,
Give me nights perfectly quiet as on high
plateaus west of the Mississippi, and I
looking up at the stars,
Give me odorous at sunrise a garden of
beautiful flowers where I can walk un-
disturb'd,

Give me for marriage a sweet-breath'd
woman of whom I should never tire,
Give me a perfect child, give me away aside
from the noise of the world a rural domestic life,
Give me to warble spontaneous songs recluse
by myself, for my own ears only, 10
Give me solitude, give me Nature, give me
again O Nature your primal sanities !

These demanding to have them (tired with
ceaseless excitement, and rack'd by the
war-strife),
These to procure incessantly asking, rising
in cries from my heart,
While yet incessantly asking still I adhere
to my city,
Day upon day and year upon year O city,
walking your streets,
Where you hold me enchain'd a certain
time refusing to give me up,
Yet giving to make me glutted, enrich'd of
soul, you give me forever faces;
(Oh I see what I sought to escape, confronting, reversing my cries,
I see my own soul trampling down what it
ask'd for.)

2

Keep your splendid silent sun, 20
Keep your woods O Nature, and the quiet
places by the woods,
Keep your fields of clover and timothy, and
your corn-fields and orchards,
Keep the blossoming buckwheat fields
where the Ninth-month bees hum;
Give me faces and streets — give me these
phantoms incessant and endless along the
trottoirs !
Give me interminable eyes — give me
women — give me comrades and lovers
by the thousand !
Let me see new ones every day — let me
hold new ones by the hand every day !
Give me such shows — give me the streets
of Manhattan !
Give me Broadway, with the soldiers marching — give me the sound of the trumpets
and drums !
(The soldiers in companies or regiments —
some starting away, flush'd and reckless,
Some, their time up, returning with thinn'd
ranks, young, yet very old, worn, marching, noticing nothing;) 30

Give me the shores and wharves heavy-fringed with black ships !
O such for me ! O an intense life, full to repletion and varied !
The life of the theatre, bar-room, huge hotel, for me !
The saloon of the steamer ! the crowded excursion for me ! the torchlight procession !
The dense brigade bound for the war, with high piled military wagons following;
People, endless, streaming, with strong voices, passions, pageants,
Manhattan streets with their powerful throbs, with beating drums as now,
The endless and noisy chorus, the rustle and clank of muskets (even the sight of the wounded),
Manhattan crowds, with their turbulent musical chorus !
Manhattan faces and eyes forever for me.[1] 39
1865.

LONG, TOO LONG AMERICA [2]

LONG, too long America,
Traveling roads all even and peaceful you learn'd from joys and prosperity only,
But now, ah now, to learn from crises of anguish, advancing, grappling with direst fate and recoiling not,
And now to conceive and show to the world what your children en-masse really are,
(For who except myself has yet conceiv'd what your children en-masse really are ?)
1865.

OVER THE CARNAGE ROSE PROPHETIC A VOICE

OVER the carnage rose prophetic a voice,
Be not dishearten'd, affection shall solve the problems of freedom yet,

[1] Compare Whitman's *Collect* (Complete Prose Works, Small, Maynard & Co., p. 205) : —
' Always and more and more, as I cross the East and North rivers, the ferries, or with the pilots in their pilot-houses, or pass an hour in Wall Street, or the gold exchange, I realize (if we must admit such partialisms), that not Nature alone is great in her fields of freedom and the open air, in her storms, the shows of night and day, the mountains, forests, seas — but in the artificial, the work of man too is equally great — in this profusion of teeming humanity — in these ingenuities, streets, goods, houses, ships — these hurrying, feverish, electric crowds of men, their complicated business genius, (not least among the geniuses), and all this mighty, many-threaded wealth and industry concentrated here.'
[2] In the original edition the title and first line read:
Long, too long, O land.

Those who love each other shall become invincible,
They shall yet make Columbia victorious.

Sons of the Mother of All, you shall yet be victorious,
You shall yet laugh to scorn the attacks of all the remainder of the earth.

No danger shall balk Columbia's lovers,
If need be a thousand shall sternly immolate themselves for one.

One from Massachusetts shall be a Missourian's comrade,
From Maine and from hot Carolina, and another an Oregonese, shall be friends triune,
More precious to each other than all the riches of the earth.

To Michigan, Florida perfumes shall tenderly come,
Not the perfumes of flowers, but sweeter, and wafted beyond death.

It shall be customary in the houses and streets to see manly affection,
The most dauntless and rude shall touch face to face lightly,
The dependence of Liberty shall be lovers,
The continuance of Equality shall be comrades.[3]

These shall tie you and band you stronger than hoops of iron,
I, ecstatic, O partners ! O lands ! with the love of lovers tie you.

(Were you looking to be held together by lawyers ?
Or by an agreement on a paper ? or by arms ?
Nay, nor the world, nor any living thing, will so cohere.)
1865.

OUT OF THE ROLLING OCEAN THE CROWD [4]

OUT of the rolling ocean the crowd came a drop gently to me,
Whispering *I love you, before long I die*,

[3] Taken in part from the poem ' States,' of the 1860 edition, quoted in the note on p. 561.
[4] Originally in *Drum-Taps*, but now included in the ' Children of Adam ' section of *Leaves of Grass*.

*I have travel'd a long way merely to look on
 you to touch you,
For I could not die till I once look'd on you,
For I fear'd I might afterward lose you.*

Now we have met, we have look'd, we are
 safe,
Return in peace to the ocean my love,
I too am part of that ocean my love, we are
 not so much separated,
Behold the great rondure, the cohesion of
 all, how perfect!
But as for me, for you, the irresistible sea
 is to separate us,
As for an hour carrying us diverse, yet cannot carry us diverse forever;
Be not impatient — a little space — know
 you I salute the air, the ocean and the
 land,
Every day at sundown for your dear sake
 my love.

                                      1865.

WHEN I HEARD THE LEARN'D ASTRONOMER [1]

WHEN I heard the learn'd astronomer,
When the proofs, the figures, were ranged
 in columns before me,

[1] To-night, after leaving the hospital at 10 o'clock (I had been on self-imposed duty some five hours, pretty closely confined), I wander'd a long time around Washington. The night was sweet, very clear, sufficiently cool, a voluptuous half-moon, slightly golden, the space near it of a transparent blue-gray tinge. I walk'd up Pennsylvania avenue, and then to Seventh street, and a long while around the Patent-office. Somehow it look'd rebukefully strong, majestic, there in the delicate moonlight. The sky, the planets, the constellations all so bright, so calm, so expressively silent, so soothing, after those hospital scenes. I wander'd to and fro till the moist moon set, long after midnight. (*Specimen Days,* October 20, 1863. Complete Prose Works, p. 41.)

See also *Specimen Days,* July 22, 1878, Prose Works, pp. 111, 112; April 5, 1879, Prose Works, pp. 118–121; February 10, 1881, Prose Works, pp. 162, 163.

Compare one of Whitman's 'Notes on the Meaning and Intention of *Leaves of Grass,*' in *Notes and Fragments,* p. 58: —

Book learning is good, let none dispense with it, but a man may [be] of great excellence and effect with very little of it. Washington had but little. Andrew Jackson also. Fulton also. Frequently it stands in the way of real manliness and power. Powerful persons and the first inventors and poets of the earth never come from the depths of the schools — never. There is a man who is no chemist, nor linguist, nor antiquary, nor mathematician — yet he takes very easily the perfection of these sciences, or of the belles lettres, and eats of the fruit of all. Erudition is low among the glories of humanity. I think if those who best embody it were collected together this day in the public assembly it would be grand. But powerful unlearned persons are also grand.

When I was shown the charts and diagrams,
 to add, divide, and measure them,
When I sitting heard the astronomer where
 he lectured with much applause in the
 lecture-room,
How soon unaccountable I became tired and
 sick,
Till rising and gliding out I wander'd off
 by myself,
In the mystical moist night-air, and from
 time to time,
Look'd up in perfect silence at the stars.

                                      1865.

SHUT NOT YOUR DOORS

SHUT not your doors to me proud libraries,
For that which was lacking on all your well-
 fill'd shelves, yet needed most, I bring,
Forth from the war emerging, a book I have
 made,
The words of my book nothing, the drift of
 it every thing,
A book separate, not link'd with the rest
 nor felt by the intellect,
But you ye untold latencies will thrill to
 every page. [2]

                                      1865.

TO A CERTAIN CIVILIAN [3]

DID you ask dulcet rhymes from me?
Did you seek the civilian's peaceful and
 languishing rhymes?

But all book knowledge is important as helping one's personal qualities, and the use and power of a man. Let a man learn to run, leap, swim, wrestle, fight, to take good aim, to manage horses, to speak readily and clearly and without mannerism, to feel at home among common people and able to hold his own in terrible positions. With these . . .

Behind — Eluding — Mocking all the text-books and professor's expositions and proofs and diagrams and practical show, stand or lie millions of all the most beautiful and common facts. We are so proud of our learning! As if it were anything to analyze fluids and call certain parts oxygen or hydrogen, or to map out stars and call . . .

[2] In the original version this poem reads: —

Shut not your doors to me, proud libraries,
For that which was lacking among you all, yet needed most,
 I bring;
A book I have made for your dear sake, O soldiers,
And for you, O soul of man, and you, love of comrades;
The words of my book nothing, the life of it everything;
A book separate, not link'd with the rest, nor felt by the
 intellect;
But you will feel every word, O Libertad! arm'd Libertad!
It shall pass by the intellect to swim the sea, the air,
With joy with you, O soul of man.

[3] Compare the opening stanzas of Emerson's 'Merlin.'

Did you find what I sang erewhile so hard
  to follow ?
Why I was not singing erewhile for you to
  follow, to understand — nor am I now
(I have been born of the same as the war
  was born,
The drum-corps' rattle is ever to me sweet
  music, I love well the martial dirge,
With slow wail and convulsive throb lead-
  ing the officer's funeral);
What to such as you anyhow such a poet as
  I ? therefore leave my works,
And go lull yourself with what you can
  understand, and with piano-tunes,
For I lull nobody, and you will never un-
  derstand me. [1]

                                        1865.

[1] This is a poem which some of Whitman's admirers
are fond of quoting to those who fail to appreciate him.
It is hardly fair to him, however, to take it apart
from his own more modest expression of the same ideas,
in ' A Backward Glance o'er Travel'd Roads : — '
  ' And whether my friends claim it for me or not, I
know well enough, too, that in respect to pictorial
talent, dramatic situations, and especially in verbal
melody and all the conventional technique of poetry, not
only the divine works that to-day stand ahead in the
world's reading, but dozens more, transcend (some of
them immeasurably transcend) all I have done, or
could do. . . .
  ' Plenty of songs had been sung — beautiful, matchless songs — adjusted to other lands than these — another spirit and stage of evolution ; but I would sing,
and leave out or put in, quite solely with reference to
America and to-day. Modern science and democracy
seem'd to be throwing out their challenge to poetry to
put them in its statements in contradistinction to the
songs and myths of the past. As I see it now (perhaps
too late), I have unwittingly taken up that challenge
and made an attempt at such statements — which I
certainly would not assume to do now, knowing more
clearly what it means. . . .
  ' Behind all else that can be said, I consider "Leaves
of Grass " and its theory experimental — as, in the
deepest sense, I consider our American republic itself
to be, with its theory. (I think I have at least enough
philosophy not to be too absolutely certain of any thing,
or any results.) . . .
  ' I have allow'd the stress of my poems from beginning
to end to bear upon American individuality. . . . Defiant of ostensible literary and other conventions, I
avowedly chant " the great pride of man in himself,"
and permit it to be more or less a *motif* of nearly all
my verse. I think this pride indispensable to an American. I think it not inconsistent with obedience, humil-
ity, deference, and self-questioning. . . .
  ' Let me not dare, here or anywhere, for my own purposes, or any purposes, to attempt the definition of
Poetry, nor answer the question what it is. Like Religion, Love, Nature, while those terms are indispensable,
and we all give a sufficiently accurate meaning to them,
in my opinion no definition that has ever been made
sufficiently encloses the name Poetry ; nor can any
rule or convention ever so absolutely obtain but some
great exception may arise and disregard and overturn it.
  ' But it is not on "Leaves of Grass " distinctively as
literature, or a specimen thereof, that I feel to dwell,
or advance claims. No one will get at my verses who
insists upon viewing them as a literary performance,

QUICKSAND YEARS

QUICKSAND years that whirl me I know
  not whither,
Your schemes, politics, fail, lines give way,
  substances mock and elude me,
Only the theme I sing, the great and
  strong-possess'd soul, eludes not,
One's-self must never give way — that is
  the final substance — that out of all is
  sure,
Out of politics, triumphs, battles, life, what
  at last finally remains ?
When shows break up what but One's-Self
  is sure ?

                                        1865.

HERS   MAY   PRAISE   WHAT
          THEY LIKE

OTHERS may praise what they like;
But I, from the banks of the running Missouri, praise nothing in art or aught
  else,
Till it has well inhaled the atmosphere
  of this river, also the western prairie-
  scent,
And exudes it all again.

                                        1865.

THICK-SPRINKLED BUNTING [2]

THICK-SPRINKLED bunting ! flag of stars !
Long yet your road, fateful flag — long yet
  your road, and lined with bloody death,
For the prize I see at issue at last is the
  world,
All its ships and shores I see interwoven
  with your threads greedy banner;
Dream'd again the flags of kings, highest
  borne, to flaunt unrival'd ?
O hasten flag of man — O with sure and
  steady step, passing highest flags of
  kings,
Walk supreme to the heavens mighty
  symbol — run up above them all,
Flag of stars ! thick-sprinkled bunting !

                                        1865.

or attempt at such performance, or as aiming mainly
toward art or æstheticism.'
  [2] In the original edition both the title and the first
line read : —

        Flag of stars, thick-sprinkled bunting

BATHED IN WAR'S PERFUME [1]

BATHED in war's perfume — delicate flag !
O to hear you call the sailors and the soldiers ! flag like a beautiful woman !
O to hear the tramp, tramp, of a million
answering men ! O the ships they arm
with joy !
O to see you leap and beckon from the tall
masts of ships !
O to see you peering down on the sailors
on the decks !
Flag like the eyes of women.

                                        1865.

O CAPTAIN ! MY CAPTAIN !

O CAPTAIN ! my Captain ! our fearful trip
is done,
The ship has weather'd every rack, the
prize we sought is won,
The port is near, the bells I hear, the people all exulting,
While follow eyes the steady keel, the vessel grim and daring;
      But O heart ! heart ! heart !
            O the bleeding drops of red,[2]
            Where on the deck my Captain
                  lies,
            Fallen cold and dead.

O Captain ! my Captain ! rise up and hear
the bells;
Rise up — for you the flag is flung — for
you the bugle trills,
For you bouquets and ribbon'd wreaths —
for you the shores a-crowding,
For you they call, the swaying mass, their
eager faces turning;
      Here Captain ! dear father ![3]
            This arm beneath your head ![3]
            It is some dream that on the
                  deck,
            You 've fallen cold and dead.

My Captain does not answer, his lips are
pale and still,
My father does not feel my arm, he has no
pulse nor will,
The ship is anchor'd safe and sound,[4] its
voyage closed and done,

1 Omitted from the 1871 and later editions.
2 Leave you not the little spot. (1865.)
3 O Captain ! dear father
   This arm I push beneath you. (1865.)
4 But the ship, the ship is anchored safe. (1865.)

From fearful trip the victor ship comes in
with object won;
      Exult O shores, and ring O bells !
      But I with mournful tread,
            Walk the deck my Captain lies,[5]
            Fallen cold and dead.

                                        1865.

WHEN LILACS LAST IN THE DOORYARD BLOOM'D [6]

1

WHEN lilacs last in the dooryard bloom'd,
And the great star early droop'd in the
western sky in the night,
I mourn'd, and yet shall mourn with ever-
returning spring.

5 But I with silent tread
   Walk the spot my Captain lies. (1865.)
6 The most sonorous anthem ever chanted in the
church of the world. (SWINBURNE.) See Swinburne's
comparison of this poem with Lowell's 'Commemoration Ode,' in *Under the Microscope.*
   — I see the President almost every day, as I happen
to live where he passes to or from his lodgings out of
town. . . . I see very plainly ABRAHAM LINCOLN's dark
brown face, with the deep-cut lines, the eyes, always to
me with a deep latent sadness in the expression. We
have got so that we exchange bows, and very cordial
ones. . . . None of the artists or pictures has caught
the deep, though subtle and indirect expression of this
man's face. There is something else there. One of the
great portrait painters of two or three centuries ago
is needed. (WHITMAN, *Specimen Days,* August 12, 1863.
Complete *Prose Works,* p. 37.)
   I saw him on his return, at three o'clock, after the
performance was over. He was in his plain two-horse
barouche, and look'd very much worn and tired; the
lines, indeed, of vast responsibilities, intricate questions, and demands of life and death, cut deeper than
ever upon his dark brown face ; yet all the old goodness, tenderness, sadness, and canny shrewdness, underneath the furrows. (I never see that man without
feeling that he is one to become personally attach'd to,
for his combination of purest, heartiest tenderness, and
native western form of manliness.) By his side sat his
little boy, of ten years. There were no soldiers. (*Specimen Days,* March 4, 1865. *Prose Works,* p. 57.)
   He leaves for America's history and biography, so
far, not only its most dramatic reminiscence — he
leaves, in my opinion, the greatest, best, most characteristic, artistic, moral personality. Not but that he
had faults, and show'd them in the Presidency ; but
honesty, goodness, shrewdness, conscience, and (a new
virtue, unknown to other lands, and hardly yet really
known here, but the foundation and tie of all, as the
future will grandly develop), UNIONISM, in its truest
and amplest sense, form'd the hard-pan of his character. These he seal'd with his life. (*Specimen Days,*
April 16, 1865. *Prose Works,* pp. 61, 62.)
   See also in Whitman's *Collect* ' The Death of Abraham
Lincoln.' Complete *Prose Works,* pp. 308, 309; and ' A
Lincoln Reminiscence,' p. 331 ; also, in *November
Boughs,* ' Abraham Lincoln,' *Prose Works,* pp. 436–438.
   It is not out of place to add here Lincoln's comment
on Whitman. Seeing him walk by the White House,
' Mr. Lincoln ' (says a witness of the scene, whose let-
ter is quoted in Bucke's *Life of Whitman,* p. 42) ' asked

Ever-returning spring, trinity sure to me
  you bring,
Lilac blooming perennial and drooping star
  in the west,
And thought of him I love.

2

O powerful western fallen star !
O shades of night — O moody, tearful
  night !
O great star disappear'd — O the black
  murk that hides the star !
O cruel hands that hold me powerless — O
  helpless soul of me !   10
O harsh surrounding cloud that will not
  free my soul.

3

In the dooryard fronting an old farm-house
  near the white-wash'd palings,
Stands the lilac-bush tall-growing with
  heart-shaped leaves of rich green,
With many a pointed blossom rising delicate, with the perfume strong I love,
With every leaf a miracle — and from this
  bush in the dooryard,
With delicate-color'd blossoms and heart-
  shaped leaves of rich green,
A sprig with its flower I break.

4

In the swamp in secluded recesses,
A shy and hidden bird is warbling a song.

Solitary the thrush,   20
The hermit withdrawn to himself, avoiding
  the settlements,
Sings by himself a song.

Song of the bleeding throat,
Death's outlet song of life (for well dear
  brother I know,
If thou wast not granted to sing thou
  would'st surely die.)

5

Over the breast of the spring, the land,
  amid cities,

who that was, or something of the kind. I spoke up,
mentioning the name Walt Whitman, and said he was
the author of *Leaves of Grass*. Mr. Lincoln did not
say anything, but took a good look, till Whitman was
quite gone by. Then he said (I cannot give you his
way of saying it, but it was quite emphatic and odd),
" Well, *he* looks like a MAN." He said it pretty loud,
but in a sort of absent way, and with the emphasis on
the words I have underscored.' This was probably in
the winter of 1864–1865.

Amid lanes and through old woods, where
  lately the violets peep'd from the ground,
  spotting the gray debris,
Amid the grass in the fields each side of the
  lanes, passing the endless grass,
Passing the yellow-spear'd wheat, every
  grain from its shroud in the dark-brown
  fields uprisen,
Passing the apple-tree blows of white and
  pink in the orchards,   30
Carrying a corpse to where it shall rest in
  the grave,
Night and day journeys a coffin.

6

Coffin that passes through lanes and streets,
Through day and night with the great cloud
  darkening the land,
With the pomp of the inloop'd flags with
  the cities draped in black,
With the show of the States themselves as
  of crape-veil'd women standing,
With processions long and winding and the
  flambeaus of the night,
With the countless torches lit, with the si-
  lent sea of faces and the unbared heads,
With the waiting depot, the arriving coffin,
  and the sombre faces,
With dirges through the night, with the
  thousand voices rising strong and solemn,   40
With all the mournful voices of the dirges
  pour'd around the coffin,
The dim-lit churches and the shuddering
  organs — where amid these you journey,
With the tolling tolling bells' perpetual
  clang,
Here, coffin that slowly passes,
I give you my sprig of lilac.

7

(Nor for you, for one alone,
Blossoms and branches green to coffins all
  I bring,
For fresh as the morning, thus would I
  chant a song for you O sane and sacred
  death.

All over bouquets of roses,
O death, I cover you over with roses and
  early lilies,   50
But mostly and now the lilac that blooms
  the first,
Copious I break, I break the sprigs from
  the bushes,

With loaded arms I come, pouring for
you,
For you and the coffins all of you O
death.)

8

O western orb sailing the heaven,
Now I know what you must have meant as
a month since I walk'd,
As I walk'd in silence the transparent
shadowy night,
As I saw you had something to tell as you
bent to me night after night,
As you droop'd from the sky low down as
if to my side (while the other stars all
look'd on),
As we wander'd together the solemn night
(for something I know not what kept me
from sleep),   60
As the night advanced, and I saw on the
rim of the west how full you were of
woe,
As I stood on the rising ground in the
breeze in the cool transparent night,
As I watch'd where you pass'd and was lost
in the netherward black of the night,
As my soul in its trouble dissatisfied sank,
as where you sad orb,
Concluded, dropt in the night, and was gone.

9

Sing on there in the swamp,
O singer bashful and tender, I hear your
notes, I hear your call,
I hear, I come presently, I understand you,
But a moment I linger, for the lustrous star
has detain'd me,
The star my departing comrade holds and
detains me.   70

10

O how shall I warble myself for the dead
one there I loved?
And how shall I deck my song for the large
sweet soul that has gone?
And what shall my perfume be for the grave
of him I love?

Sea-winds blown from east and west,
Blown from the Eastern sea and blown from
the Western sea, till there on the prairies
meeting,
These and with these and the breath of my
chant,
I 'll perfume the grave of him I love.

11

O what shall I hang on the chamber walls?
And what shall the pictures be that I hang
on the walls,
To adorn the burial-house of him I love? 80

Pictures of growing spring and farms and
homes,
With the Fourth-month eve at sundown,
and the gray smoke lucid and bright,
With floods of the yellow gold of the gorgeous, indolent, sinking sun, burning, expanding the air,
With the fresh sweet herbage under foot,
and the pale green leaves of the trees
prolific,
In the distance the flowing glaze, the breast
of the river, with a wind-dapple here and
there,
With ranging hills on the banks, with many
a line against the sky, and shadows,
And the city at hand with dwellings so
dense, and stacks of chimneys,
And all the scenes of life and the workshops,
and the workmen homeward returning.

12

Lo, body and soul — this land,
My own Manhattan with spires, and the
sparkling and hurrying tides, and the
ships,   90
The varied and ample land, the South and
the North in the light, Ohio's shores and
flashing Missouri,
And ever the far-spreading prairies cover'd
with grass and corn.

Lo, the most excellent sun so calm and
haughty,
The violet and purple morn with just-felt
breezes,
The gentle soft-born measureless light,
The miracle spreading bathing all, the ful-
fill'd noon,
The coming eve delicious, the welcome
night and the stars,
Over my cities shining all, enveloping man
and land.

13

Sing on, sing on you gray-brown bird,
Sing from the swamps, the recesses, pour
your chant from the bushes,   100
Limitless out of the dusk, out of the cedars
and pines.

Sing on dearest brother, warble your reedy
   song,
Loud human song, with voice of uttermost
   woe.

O liquid and free and tender !
O wild and loose to my soul — O wondrous
   singer !
You only I hear — yet the star holds me
   (but will soon depart),
Yet the lilac with mastering odor holds me.

14

Now while I sat in the day and look'd
   forth,
In the close of the day with its light and
   the fields of spring, and the farmers preparing their crops,
In the large unconscious scenery of my land
   with its lakes and forests,   110
In the heavenly aerial beauty (after the
   perturb'd winds and the storms),
Under the arching heavens of the afternoon
   swift passing, and the voices of children
   and women,
The many-moving sea-tides, and I saw the
   ships how they sail'd,
And the summer approaching with richness,
   and the fields all busy with labor,
And the infinite separate houses, how they
   all went on, each with its meals and
   minutia of daily usages,
And the streets how their throbbings
   throbb'd, and the cities pent — lo, then
   and there,
Falling upon them all and among them all,
   enveloping me with the rest,
Appear'd the cloud, appear'd the long
   black trail,
And I knew death, its thought, and the
   sacred knowledge of death.

Then with the knowledge of death as walking one side of me,   120
And the thought of death close-walking
   the other side of me,
And I in the middle as with companions,
   and as holding the hands of companions,
I fled forth to the hiding receiving night
   that talks not,
Down to the shores of the water, the path
   by the swamp in the dimness,
To the solemn shadowy cedars and ghostly
   pines so still.

And the singer so shy to the rest receiv'd
   me,
The gray-brown bird I know receiv'd us
   comrades three,
And he sang the carol of death, and a verse
   for him I love.

From deep secluded recesses,
From the fragrant cedars and the ghostly
   pines so still,   130
Came the carol of the bird.

And the charm of the carol rapt me,
As I held as if by their hands my comrades
   in the night,
And the voice of my spirit tallied the song
   of the bird.

Come lovely and soothing death,
Undulate round the world, serenely arriving,
   arriving,
In the day, in the night, to all, to each,
Sooner or later delicate death.

Prais'd be the fathomless universe,
For life and joy, and for objects and know-
   ledge curious,   140
And for love, sweet love — but praise ! praise !
   praise !
For the sure-enwinding arms of cool-enfold-
   ing death.

Dark mother always gliding near with soft
   feet,
Have none chanted for thee a chant of fullest
   welcome ?
Then I chant it for thee, I glorify thee above
   all,
I bring thee a song that when thou must in-
   deed come, come unfalteringly.

Approach strong deliveress,
When it is so, when thou hast taken them I
   joyously sing the dead,
Lost in the loving floating ocean of thee,
Laved in the flood of thy bliss O death.   150

From me to thee glad serenades,
Dances for thee I propose saluting thee, adorn-
   ments and feastings for thee,
And the sights of the open landscape and the
   high-spread sky are fitting,
And life and the fields, and the huge and
   thoughtful night.

The night in silence under many a star,
The ocean shore and the husky whispering
wave whose voice I know,
And the soul turning to thee O vast and well-
veil'd death,
And the body gratefully nestling close to thee.

Over the tree-tops I float thee a song,
Over the rising and sinking waves, over the
myriad fields and the prairies wide,   160
Over the dense-pack'd cities all and the teem-
ing wharves and ways,
I float this carol with joy, with joy to thee O
death.

15

To the tally of my soul,
Loud and strong kept up the gray-brown
bird,
With pure deliberate notes spreading filling
the night.

Loud in the pines and cedars dim,
Clear in the freshness moist and the swamp-
perfume,
And I with my comrades there in the night.

While my sight that was bound in my eyes
unclosed,
As to long panoramas of visions.   170

And I saw askant the armies,
I saw as in noiseless dreams hundreds of
battle-flags,
Borne through the smoke of the battles
and pierc'd with missiles I saw them,
And carried hither and yon through the
smoke, and torn and bloody,
And at last but a few shreds left on the
staffs (and all in silence),
And the staffs all splinter'd and broken.

I saw battle-corpses, myriads of them,
And the white skeletons of young men, I
saw them,
I saw the débris and débris of all the slain
soldiers of the war,
But I saw they were not as was thought, 180
They themselves were fully at rest, they
suffer'd not,
The living remain'd and suffer'd, the mother
suffer'd,
And the wife and the child and the musing
comrade suffer'd,
And the armies that remain'd suffer'd.

16

Passing the visions, passing the night,
Passing, unloosing the hold of my comrades' hands,
Passing the song of the hermit bird and the
tallying song of my soul,
Victorious song, death's outlet song, yet
varying ever-altering song,
As low and wailing, yet clear the notes,
rising and falling, flooding the night,
Sadly sinking and fainting, as warning and
warning, and yet again bursting with
joy,   190
Covering the earth and filling the spread of
the heaven,
As that powerful psalm in the night I heard
from recesses,
Passing, I leave thee lilac with heart-
shaped leaves,
I leave thee there in the door-yard, blooming, returning with spring.

I cease from my song for thee,
From my gaze on thee in the west, fronting
the west, communing with thee,
O comrade lustrous with silver face in the
night.

Yet each to keep and all, retrievements out
of the night,
The song, the wondrous chant of the gray-
brown bird,
And the tallying chant, the echo arous'd
in my soul,   200
With the lustrous and drooping star with
the countenance full of woe,
With the holders holding my hand nearing
the call of the bird,
Comrades mine and I in the midst, and
their memory ever to keep, for the dead
I loved so well,
For the sweetest, wisest soul of all my days
and lands — and this for his dear sake,
Lilac and star and bird twined with the
chant of my soul,
There in the fragrant pines and the cedars
dusk and dim.

1865.

HUSH'D BE THE CAMPS TO-DAY

MAY 4, 1865

Hush'd be the camps to-day,
And soldiers let us drape our war-worn
weapons,

And each with musing soul retire to celebrate,
Our dear commander's death.

No more for him life's stormy conflicts,
Nor victory, nor defeat — no more time's
dark events,
Charging like ceaseless clouds across the
sky.

But sing poet in our name,
Sing of the love we bore him — because
you, dweller in camps, know it truly.

As they invault the coffin there,
Sing — as they close the doors of earth
upon him — one verse,[1]
For the heavy hearts of soldiers.

1865.

OLD WAR-DREAMS [2]

IN midnight sleep of many a face of anguish,
Of the look at first of the mortally wounded
(of that indescribable look),
Of the dead on their backs with arms extended wide,
    I dream, I dream, I dream.

Of scenes of Nature, fields and mountains,
Of skies so beauteous after a storm, and at
night the moon so unearthly bright,
Shining sweetly, shining down, where we
dig the trenches and gather the heaps,
    I dream, I dream, I dream.

Long have they pass'd, faces and trenches
and fields,
Where through the carnage I moved with
a callous composure, or away from the
fallen,
Onward I sped at the time — but new of
their forms at night,
    I dream, I dream, I dream.

1865.

---

[1] In the original version, 1865, these two lines read : —

Sing, to the lower'd coffin there;
Sing, with the shovel'd clods that fill the grave — a verse, . . .

The change was made in the edition of 1881.

[2] In the original version, 1865, the first line of the
poem read : —

In clouds descending, in midnight sleep, of many a face of
anguish,

and the first half of this line was used as title for the
poem.

RECONCILIATION

WORD over all, beautiful as the sky,
Beautiful that war and all its deeds of car-
nage must in time be utterly lost,
That the hands of the sisters Death and
Night incessantly softly wash again, and
ever again, this soil'd world;
For my enemy is dead, a man divine as my-
self is dead,
I look where he lies white-faced and still in
the coffin — I draw near,
Bend down and touch lightly with my lips
the white face in the coffin.

1865.

AS I LAY WITH MY HEAD IN YOUR LAP CAMERADO

As I lay with my head in your lap camerado,
The confession I made I resume, what I
said to you and the open air I resume,
I know I am restless and make others so,
I know my words are weapons full of danger, full of death,[3]
For I confront peace, security, and all the
settled laws, to unsettle them,
I am more resolute because all have denied
me than I could ever have been had all
accepted me,
I heed not and have never heeded either
experience, cautions, majorities, nor ridicule,
And the threat of what is call'd hell is little
or nothing to me,
And the lure of what is call'd heaven is
little or nothing to me;
Dear camerado! I confess I have urged
you onward with me, and still urge you,
without the least idea what is our desti-
nation,
Or whether we shall be victorious, or utterly quell'd and defeated.

1865.

ABOARD AT A SHIP'S HELM

ABOARD at a ship's helm,
A young steersman steering with care.

---

[3] In the original edition there followed here two
lines since omitted : —

(Indeed I am myself the real soldier;
It is not he, there, with his bayonet, and not the red-striped
artilleryman);

Through fog on a sea-coast dolefully ringing,
An ocean-bell — O a warning bell, rock'd
by the waves.

O you give good notice indeed, you bell by
the sea-reefs ringing,
Ringing, ringing, to warn the ship from its
wreck-place.

For as on the alert O steersman, you mind
the loud admonition,
The bows turn, the freighted ship tacking
speeds away under her gray sails,
The beautiful and noble ship with all her
precious wealth speeds away gayly and
safe.

But O the ship, the immortal ship! O ship
aboard the ship!
Ship of the body, ship of the soul, voyaging,
voyaging, voyaging.

1867.

NOT THE PILOT [1]

NOT the pilot has charged himself to bring
his ship into port, though beaten back
and many times baffled;
Not the pathfinder penetrating inland weary
and long,
By deserts parch'd, snows chill'd, rivers
wet, perseveres till he reaches his desti-
nation,
More than I have charged myself, heeded
or unheeded, to compose a march for
these States,
For a battle-call, rousing to arms if need
be, years, centuries hence.

1867.

[1] Compare Whitman's *Democratic Vistas*, in the
Complete Prose Works, pp. 197-250; especially pp. 199,
200, 202, 203 : —
Our fundamental want to-day in the United States,
with closest, amplest reference to present conditions,
and to the future, is of a class, and the clear idea of a
class, of native authors, . . . fit to cope with our occasions, lands, permeating the whole mass of American
mentality, taste, belief, breathing into it a new breath
of life, giving it decision. . . . For, I say, the true nationality of the States, the genuine union, when we
come to a moral crisis, is, and is to be, after all, neither
the written law nor, (as is generally supposed), either
self-interest, or common pecuniary or material objects
— but the fervid and tremendous Idea, melting everything else with resistless heat, and solving all lesser
and definite distinctions in vast, indefinite, spiritual,
emotional power.

ONE'S-SELF I SING [2]

ONE'S-SELF I sing, a simple separate per-
son,
Yet utter the word Democratic, the word
En-Masse.

Of physiology from top to toe I sing,
Not physiognomy alone nor brain alone is
worthy for the Muse — I say the Form
complete is worthier far,
The Female equally with the Male I sing.

Of Life immense in passion, pulse, and
power,
Cheerful, for freest action form'd under
the laws divine,
The Modern Man I sing.

1867, 1871.

TEARS

TEARS! tears! tears!
In the night, in solitude, tears,
On the white shore dripping, dripping,
suck'd in by the sand,
Tears, not a star shining, all dark and
desolate,
Moist tears from the eyes of a muffled
head;
O who is that ghost? that form in the
dark, with tears?
What shapeless lump is that, bent, crouch'd
there on the sand?
Streaming tears, sobbing tears, throes,
choked with wild cries;
O storm, embodied, rising, careering with
swift steps along the beach!

[2] This poem is now placed first in the standard editions of Whitman's Poems. In its original form, as the
Inscription of the 1867 edition, it read : —
SMALL is the theme of the following Chant, yet the greatest
— namely, ONE'S-SELF — that wondrous thing, a simple,
separate person. That, for the use of the New World, I
sing.
Man's physiology complete, from top to toe, I sing. Not
physiognomy alone, nor brain alone, is worthy for the
muse; — I say the Form complete is worthier far. The
female equally with the male, I sing.
Nor cease at the theme of One's-Self. I speak the word of the
modern, the word EN-MASSE.
My Days I sing, and the Lands — with interstice I knew of
hapless War.
O friend, whoe'er you are, at last arriving hither to commence, I feel through every leaf the pressure of your hand,
which I return. And thus upon our journey link'd together let us go.

This version, in a slightly revised form, beginning
'Small the theme of my chant,' is now printed as a
separate poem in the final edition of *Leaves of Grass*,
p. 397.

O wild and dismal night storm, with wind
— O belching and desperate !
O shade so sedate and decorous by day, with
calm countenance and regulated pace,
But away at night as you fly, none looking
— O then the unloosen'd ocean,
Of tears ! tears ! tears !

                                    1867.

WHISPERS OF HEAVENLY DEATH

WHISPERS of heavenly death murmur'd I
hear,
Labial gossip of night, sibilant chorals,
Footsteps gently ascending, mystical
breezes' wafted soft and low,
Ripples of unseen rivers, tides of a current
flowing, forever flowing,
(Or is it the plashing of tears ? the mea-
sureless waters of human tears ?)
I see, just see skyward, great cloud-masses,
Mournfully slowly they roll, silently swell-
ing and mixing,
With at times a half-dimm'd sadden'd far-
off star,
Appearing and disappearing.

(Some parturition rather, some solemn im-
mortal birth;
On the frontiers to eyes impenetrable,
Some soul is passing over.)

                          1868. (1871.)

THE SINGER IN THE PRISON

I

O sight of pity, shame and dole ! [1]
O fearful thought — a convict soul.

RANG the refrain along the hall, the prison,
Rose to the roof, the vaults of heaven above,
Pouring in floods of melody in tones so pensive sweet and strong the like whereof was
never heard,
Reaching the far-off sentry and the armed
guards, who ceas'd their pacing,
Making the hearer's pulses stop for ecstasy
and awe.

2 [2]

The sun was low in the west one winter day,
When down a narrow aisle amid the thieves
and outlaws of the land,

[1] *O sight of shame, and pain, and dole !* (1869, 1871.)
[2] In the early editions this section begins : —

   O sight of pity, gloom, and dole !
   O pardon me, a hapless Soul !

(There by the hundreds seated, sear-faced
murderers, wily counterfeiters,   10
Gather'd to Sunday church in prison walls,
the keepers round,
Plenteous, well-armed, watching with vigi-
lant eyes,)
Calmly a lady walk'd holding a little innocent child by either hand,
Whom seating on their stools beside her on
the platform,
She, first preluding with the instrument a
low and musical prelude,
In voice surpassing all, sang forth a quaint
old hymn.

A soul confined by bars and bands, [3]
Cries, help ! O help ! and wrings her hands,
Blinded her eyes, bleeding her breast,
Nor pardon finds, nor balm of rest.   20

Ceaseless she paces to and fro,
O heart-sick days ! O nights of woe !
Nor hand of friend, nor loving face,
Nor favor comes, nor word of grace.

It was not I that sinn'd the sin,
The ruthless body dragg'd me in;
Though long I strove courageously,
The body was too much for me.

Dear prison'd soul bear up a space,
For soon or late the certain grace;   30
To set thee free and bear thee home,
The heavenly pardoner death shall come.

   Convict no more, nor shame, nor dole !
   Depart — a God-enfranchis'd soul !

3

The singer ceas'd,
One glance swept from her clear calm eyes
o'er all those upturn'd faces,
Strange sea of prison faces, a thousand varied, crafty, brutal, seam'd and beauteous
faces,
Then rising, passing back along the narrow
aisle between them,
While her gown touch'd them rustling in
the silence,
She vanish'd with her children in the dusk.

[3] In the early editions these stanzas have a sub-title
' The Hymn,' and each stanza is followed by a refrain,
in italics : after the first stanza, the same as at the beginning of Section 1 ; after the second stanza, the same
as at the beginning of Section 2 ; after the third stanza:

       O life ! no life, but bitter dole !
       O burning, beaten, baffled Soul !

While upon all, convicts and armed keepers
  ere they stirr'd   41
(Convict forgetting prison, keeper his
  loaded pistol),
A hush and pause fell down a wondrous
  minute,
With deep half-stifled sobs and sound of
  bad men bow'd and moved to weeping,
And youth's convulsive breathings, memories of home,
The mother's voice in lullaby, the sister's
  care, the happy childhood,
The long-pent spirit rous'd to reminiscence;
A wondrous minute then — but after in the
  solitary night, to many, many there,
Years after, even in the hour of death, the
  sad refrain, the tune, the voice, the words,
Resumed, the large calm lady walks the
  narrow aisle,   50
The wailing melody again, the singer in the
  prison sings,

    O sight of pity, shame and dole ! [1]
    O fearful thought — a convict soul.
                 1869. (1871.)

ETHIOPIA SALUTING THE COLORS

WHO are you dusky woman, so ancient
  hardly human,
With your woolly-white and turban'd head,
  and bare bony feet ?
Why rising by the roadside here, do you
  the colors greet ?

('T is while our army lines Carolina's sands
  and pines,
Forth from thy hovel door thou Ethiopia
  com'st to me,
As under doughty Sherman I march toward the sea.)

Me master years a hundred since from my
  parents sunder'd,
A little child, they caught me as the savage
  beast is caught,
Then hither me across the sea the cruel slaver
  brought.

No further does she say, but lingering all
  the day,

[1] The early editions have the same variant reading
here as in the first line.

Her high-borne turban'd head she wags,
  and rolls her darkling eye,
And courtesies to the regiments, the guid-
  ons moving by.

What is it fateful woman, so blear, hardly
  human ?
Why wag your head with turban bound,
  yellow, red and green ?
Are the things so strange and marvelous
  you see or have seen ?
                 1871.

DELICATE CLUSTER

DELICATE cluster ! flag of teeming life !
Covering all my lands — all my seashores
  lining !
Flag of death ! (how I watch'd you through
  the smoke of battle pressing !
How I heard you flap and rustle, cloth
  defiant !)
Flag cerulean — sunny flag, with the orbs
  of night dappled !
Ah my silvery beauty — ah my woolly
  white and crimson !
Ah to sing the song of you, my matron
  mighty !
My sacred one, my mother.
                 1871.

THE BASE OF ALL META-PHYSICS

AND now gentlemen,
A word I give to remain in your memories
  and minds,
As base and finale too for all metaphysics.

(So to the students the old professor,
At the close of his crowded course.)

Having studied the new and antique, the
  Greek and Germanic systems,
Kant having studied and stated, Fichte and
  Schelling and Hegel,
Stated the lore of Plato, and Socrates
  greater than Plato,
And greater than Socrates sought and
  stated, Christ divine having studied long,
I see reminiscent to-day those Greek and
  Germanic systems,
See the philosophies all, Christian churches
  and tenets see,

Yet underneath Socrates clearly see, and
  underneath Christ the divine I see,
The dear love of man for his comrade, the
  attraction of friend to friend,
Of the well-married husband and wife, of
  children and parents,
Of city for city and land for land.
                          1871.

ON THE BEACH AT NIGHT

ON the beach at night,
Stands a child with her father,
Watching the east, the autumn sky.

Up through the darkness,
While ravening clouds, the burial clouds, in
  black masses spreading,
Lower sullen and fast athwart and down
  the sky,
Amid a transparent clear belt of ether yet
  left in the east,
Ascends large and calm the lord-star Jupi-
  ter,
And nigh at hand, only a very little above,
Swim the delicate sisters the Pleiades.   10

From the beach the child holding the hand
  of her father,
Those burial-clouds that lower victorious
  soon to devour all,
Watching, silently weeps.

Weep not, child,
Weep not, my darling,
With these kisses let me remove your tears,
The ravening clouds shall not long be vic-
  torious,
They shall not long possess the sky, they
  devour the stars only in apparition,
Jupiter shall emerge, be patient, watch
  again another night, the Pleiades shall
  emerge,
They are immortal, all those stars both
  silvery and golden shall shine out again,
The great stars and the little ones shall
  shine out again, they endure,   21
The vast immortal suns and the long-
  enduring pensive moons shall again shine.

Then dearest child mournest thou only for
  Jupiter?
Considerest thou alone the burial of the
  stars?

Something there is,
(With my lips soothing thee, adding I
  whisper,
I give thee the first suggestion, the prob-
  lem and indirection,)
Something there is more immortal even
  than the stars,
(Many the burials, many the days and
  nights, passing away,)
Something that shall endure longer even
  than lustrous Jupiter,   30
Longer than sun or any revolving satellite,
Or the radiant sisters the Pleiades.
                          1871.

A NOISELESS PATIENT SPIDER

A NOISELESS patient spider,
I mark'd where on a little promontory it
  stood isolated,
Mark'd how to explore the vacant vast surrounding,
It launch'd forth filament, filament, filament, out of itself,
Ever unreeling them, ever tirelessly speeding them.

And you O my soul where you stand,
Surrounded, detached, in measureless oceans
  of space,
Ceaselessly musing, venturing, throwing,
  seeking the spheres to connect them,
Till the bridge you will need be form'd, till
  the ductile anchor hold,
Till the gossamer thread you fling catch
  somewhere, O my soul.
                          1871.

'PASSAGE TO INDIA [1]

1

SINGING my days,
Singing the great achievements of the present,

[1] Compare the passage from Whitman's Prose Work
quoted in a note at the end of 'A Broadway Pageant,'
and also, especially (among many other passages), *Specimen Days*, July 22 and 23, 1878, Complete Prose Works,
pp. 111, 112; and the following paragraphs from the
note on 'Passage to India' in the Preface of the 1876
edition (Complete Prose Works, pp. 272-274): —
  I am not sure but the last inclosing sublimation of
race or poem is, what it thinks of death. After the rest
has been comprehended and said, even the grandest —
after those contributions to mightiest nationality, or to

Singing the strong light works of engineers,
Our modern wonders (the antique ponderous Seven outvied),
In the Old World the east the Suez canal,
The New by its mighty railroad spann'd,
The seas inlaid with eloquent gentle wires;
Yet first to sound, and ever sound, the cry
with thee O soul,
The Past! the Past! the Past!

The Past—the dark unfathom'd retrospect!
The teeming gulf—the sleepers and the
shadows!   11
The past—the infinite greatness of the
past!
For what is the present after all but a
growth out of the past?
(As a projectile form'd, impell'd, passing a
certain line, still keeps on,
So the present, utterly form'd, impell'd by
the past.)

2

Passage O soul to India!
Eclaircise the myths Asiatic, the primitive
fables.

sweetest song, or to the best personalism, male or female,
have been glean'd from the rich and varied themes of
tangible life, and have been fully accepted and sung,
and the pervading fact of visible existence, with the
duty it devolves, is rounded and apparently completed,
it still remains to be really completed by suffusing
through the whole and several, that other pervading
invisible fact, so large a part (is it not the largest
part?) of life here, combining the rest, and furnishing,
for person or State, the only permanent and unitary
meaning to all, even the meanest life, consistently with
the dignity of the universe, in Time. As from the eligibility to this thought, and the cheerful conquest of this
fact, flash forth the first distinctive proofs of the soul,
so to me (extending it only a little further), the ultimate Democratic purports, the ethereal and spiritual
ones, are to concentrate here, and as fixed stars, radiate
hence. For, in my opinion, it is no less than this idea
of immortality, above all other ideas, that is to enter
into, and vivify, and give crowning religious stamp, to
democracy in the New World.
    [Here follows the paragraph already quoted at the
end of note 1 on p. 546; then, after speaking of his
own paralysis and his mother's death, Whitman con-
cludes:—]
    Under these influences, therefore, I still feel to keep
·Passage to India' for last words. . . . Not as, in antiquity, at highest festival of Egypt, the noisome skeleton
of death was sent on exhibition to the revelers, for zest
and shadow to the occasion's joy and light—but as the
marble statue of the normal Greeks at Elis, suggesting
death in the form of a beautiful and perfect young
man, with closed eyes, leaning on an inverted torch—
emblem of rest and aspiration after action—of crown
and point which all lives and poems should steadily
have reference to, namely, the justified and noble ter-
mination of our identity, this grade of it, and outlet-
preparation to another grade.

Not you alone proud truths of the world,
Not you alone ye facts of modern science,
But myths and fables of eld, Asia's, Africa's
fables,   20
The far-darting beams of the spirit, the
unloos'd dreams,
The deep diving bibles and legends,
The daring plots of the poets, the elder
religions,
O you temples fairer than lilies pour'd over
by the rising sun!
O you fables spurning the known, eluding
the hold of the known, mounting to
heaven!
You lofty and dazzling towers, pinnacled,
red as roses, burnish'd with gold!
Towers of fables immortal fashion'd from
mortal dreams!
You too I welcome and fully the same as
the rest!
You too with joy I sing.

Passage to India!   30
Lo, soul, seest thou not God's purpose from
the first?
The earth to be spann'd, connected by net-
work,[2]
The races, neighbors, to marry and be given
in marriage,
The oceans to be cross'd, the distant brought
near,
The lands to be welded together.

A worship new I sing,
You captains, voyagers, explorers, yours,
You engineers, you architects, machinists,
yours,
You, not for trade or transportation only,
But in God's name, and for thy sake O soul.

3

Passage to India!   41
Lo soul for thee of tableaus twain,
I see in one the Suez canal initiated, open'd,
I see the procession of steamships, the Em-
press Eugenie's leading the van,
I mark from on deck the strange landscape,
the pure sky, the level sand in the dis-
tance,
I pass swiftly the picturesque groups, the
workmen gather'd,
The gigantic dredging machines.

[1] Here follows, in the original edition, the line:—
        The people to become brothers and sisters.

In one again, different (yet thine, all thine,
   O soul, the same),
I see over my own continent the Pacific
   railroad surmounting every barrier,
I see continual trains of cars winding along
   the Platte carrying freight and pas-
   sengers,   50
I hear the locomotives rushing and roaring,
   and the shrill steam-whistle,
I hear the echoes reverberate through the
   grandest scenery in the world,
I cross the Laramie plains, I note the rocks
   in grotesque shapes, the buttes,
I see the plentiful larkspur and wild onions,
   the barren, colorless, sage-deserts,
I see in glimpses afar or towering immediately above me the great mountains,
I see the Wind river and the Wahsatch
   mountains,
I see the Monument mountain and the
   Eagle's Nest, I pass the Promontory, I
   ascend the Nevadas,
I scan the noble Elk mountain and wind
   around its base,
I see the Humboldt range, I thread the
   valley and cross the river,
I see the clear waters of lake Tahoe, I see
   forests of majestic pines,
Or crossing the great desert, the alkaline
   plains, I behold enchanting mirages of
   waters and meadows,   60
Marking through these and after all, in
   duplicate slender lines,
Bridging the three or four thousand miles
   of land travel,
Tying the Eastern to the Western sea,
The road between Europe and Asia.

(Ah Genoese thy dream! thy dream!
Centuries after thou art laid in thy grave,
The shore thou foundest verifies thy
   dream.)

4

Passage to India!
Struggles of many a captain, tales of many
   a sailor dead,
Over my mood stealing and spreading they
   come,   70
Like clouds and cloudlets in the unreach'd
   sky.

Along all history, down the slopes,
As a rivulet running, sinking now, and now
   again to the surface rising,

A ceaseless thought, a varied train — lo,
   soul, to thee, thy sight, they rise,
The plans, the voyages again, the expedi-
   tions;
Again Vasco de Gama sails forth,
Again the knowledge gain'd, the mariner's
   compass,
Lands found and nations born, thou born
   America,
For purpose vast, man's long probation
   fill'd,
Thou rondure of the world at last accom-
   plish'd.   80

5

O vast Rondure, swimming in space,
Cover'd all over with visible power and
   beauty,
Alternate light and day and the teeming
   spiritual darkness,
Unspeakable high processions of sun and
   moon and countless stars above,
Below, the manifold grass and waters, animals, mountains, trees,
With inscrutable purpose, some hidden
   prophetic intention,
Now first it seems my thought begins to
   span thee.

Down from the gardens of Asia descending
   radiating,
Adam and Eve appear, then their myriad
   progeny after them,
Wandering, yearning, curious, with restless
   explorations,   90
With questionings, baffled, formless, feverish, with never-happy hearts,
With that sad incessant refrain, *Wherefore
   unsatisfied soul?* and *Whither O mocking
   life?*

Ah who shall soothe these feverish chil-
   dren?
Who justify these restless explorations?
Who speak the secret of impassive earth?
Who bind it to us? what is this separate
   Nature so unnatural?
What is this earth to our affections? (un-
   loving earth, without a throb to answer
   ours,
Cold earth, the place of graves.)

Yet soul be sure the first intent remains,
   and shall be carried out,
Perhaps even now the time has arrived. 100

After the seas are all cross'd (as they seem
  already cross'd),
After the great captains and engineers
  have accomplish'd their work,
After the noble inventors, after the scientists, the chemist, the geologist, ethnolo-
  gist,
Finally shall come the poet worthy that
  name,
The true son of God shall come singing his
  songs.

Then not your deeds only O voyagers, O
  scientists and inventors, shall be justified,
All these hearts as of fretted children shall
  be sooth'd,
All affection shall be fully responded to,
  the secret shall be told,
All these separations and gaps shall be taken
  up and hook'd and link'd together,
The whole earth, this cold, impassive, voiceless earth, shall be completely justified,   110
Trinitas divine shall be gloriously accomplish'd and compacted by the true son of
  God, the poet,
(He shall indeed pass the straits and conquer the mountains,
He shall double the cape of Good Hope to
  some purpose,)
Nature and Man shall be disjoin'd and diffused no more,
The true son of God shall absolutely fuse
  them.

6

Year at whose wide-flung door I sing!
Year of the purpose accomplish'd!
Year of the marriage of continents, climates
  and oceans!
(No mere doge of Venice now wedding the
  Adriatic,)
I see O year in you the vast terraqueous
  globe given and giving all,   120
Europe to Asia, Africa join'd, and they to
  the New World,
The lands, geographies, dancing before you,
  holding a festival garland,
As brides and bridegrooms hand in hand.

Passage to India!
Cooling airs from Caucasus far, soothing
  cradle of man,
The river Euphrates flowing, the past lit up
  again.

Lo soul, the retrospect brought forward,
The old, most populous, wealthiest of
  earth's lands,
The streams of the Indus and the Ganges
  and their many affluents,
(I my shores of America walking to-day
  behold, resuming all,)   130
The tale of Alexander on his warlike
  marches suddenly dying,
On one side China and on the other side
  Persia and Arabia,
To the south the great seas and the bay of
  Bengal,
The flowing literatures, tremendous epics,
  religions, castes,
Old occult Brahma interminably far back,
  the tender and junior Buddha,
Central and southern empires and all their
  belongings, possessors,
The wars of Tamerlane, the reign of Au-
  rungzebe,
The traders, rulers, explorers, Moslems,
  Venetians, Byzantium, the Arabs, Portu-
  guese,
The first travelers famous yet, Marco Polo,
  Batouta the Moor,
Doubts to be solv'd, the map incognita,
  blanks to be fill'd,   140
The foot of man unstay'd, the hands never
  at rest,
Thyself O soul that will not brook a chal-
  lenge.

The mediæval navigators rise before me,
The world of 1492, with its awaken'd enterprise,
Something swelling in humanity now like
  the sap of the earth in spring,
The sunset splendor of chivalry declining.

And who art thou sad shade?
Gigantic, visionary, thyself a visionary,
With majestic limbs and pious beaming
  eyes,
Spreading around with every look of thine
  a golden world,   150
Enhuing it with gorgeous hues.

As the chief histrion
Down to the footlights walks in some great
  scena,
Dominating the rest I see the Admiral him-
  self,
(History's type of courage, action, faith,)

Behold him sail from Palos leading his
little fleet,
His voyage behold, his return, his great
fame,
His misfortunes, calumniators, behold him
a prisoner, chain'd,
Behold his dejection, poverty, death.

(Curious in time I stand, noting the efforts
of heroes,   160
Is the deferment long? bitter the slander,
poverty, death?
Lies the seed unreck'd for centuries in the
ground? lo, to God's due occasion,
Uprising in the night, it sprouts, blooms,
And fills the earth with use and beauty.)

7

Passage indeed O soul to primal thought,
Not lands and seas alone, thy own clear
freshness,
The young maturity of brood and bloom,
To realms of budding bibles.

O soul, repressless, I with thee and thou
with me,
Thy circumnavigation of the world begin, 170
Of man, the voyage of his mind's return,
To reason's early paradise,
Back, back to wisdom's birth, to innocent
intuitions,
Again with fair creation.

8

O we can wait no longer,
We too take ship O soul,
Joyous we too launch out on trackless
seas,
Fearless for unknown shores on waves of
ecstasy to sail,
Amid the wafting winds (thou pressing me
to thee, I thee to me, O soul),
Caroling free, singing our song of God, 180
Chanting our chant of pleasant explora-
tion.

With laugh and many a kiss
(Let others deprecate, let others weep for
sin, remorse, humiliation),
O soul thou pleasest me, I thee.

Ah more than any priest O soul we too
believe in God,
But with the mystery of God we dare not
dally.

O soul thou pleasest me, I thee,
Sailing these seas or on the hills, or waking
in the night,
Thoughts, silent thoughts, of Time and
Space and Death, like waters flowing,
Bear me indeed as through the regions in-
finite,   190
Whose air I breathe, whose ripples hear,
lave me all over,
Bathe me O God in thee, mounting to thee,
I and my soul to range in range of thee.

O Thou transcendent,
Nameless, the fibre and the breath,
Light of the light, shedding forth universes,
thou centre of them,
Thou mightier centre of the true, the good,
the loving,
Thou moral, spiritual fountain — affection's
source — thou reservoir,
(O pensive soul of me — O thirst unsatis-
fied — waitest not there?
Waitest not haply for us somewhere there
the Comrade perfect?)   200
Thou pulse — thou motive of the stars,
suns, systems,
That, circling, move in order, safe, harmo-
nious,
Athwart the shapeless vastnesses of space,
How should I think, how breathe a single
breath, how speak, if, out of myself,
I could not launch, to those, superior universes?

Swiftly I shrivel at the thought of God,
At Nature and its wonders, Time and
Space and Death,
But that I, turning, call to thee O soul,
thou actual Me,
And lo, thou gently masterest the orbs,
Thou matest Time, smilest content at Death,
And fillest, swellest full the vastnesses of
Space.   211

Greater than stars or suns,
Bounding O soul thou journeyest forth;
What love than thine and ours could wider
amplify?
What aspirations, wishes, outvie thine and
ours O soul?
What dreams of the ideal? what plans of
purity, perfection, strength?
What cheerful willingness for others' sake
to give up all?
For others' sake to suffer all?

Reckoning ahead O soul, when thou, the
time achiev'd,
The seas all cross'd, weather'd the capes,
the voyage done,   220
Surrounded, copest, frontest God, yieldest,
the aim attain'd,
As fill'd with friendship, love complete, the
· Elder Brother found,
The Younger melts in fondness in his
arms.

9

Passage to more than India !
Are thy wings plumed indeed for such far
flights ?
O soul, voyagest thou indeed on voyages
like those ?
Disportest thou on waters such as those ?
Soundest below the Sanscrit and the Vedas ?
Then have thy bent unleash'd.

Passage to you, your shores, ye aged fierce
enigmas !   230
Passage to you, to mastership of you, ye
strangling problems !
You, strew'd with the wrecks of skeletons,
that, living, never reach'd you.

Passage to more than India !
O secret of the earth and sky !
Of you O waters of the sea ! O winding
creeks and rivers !
Of you O woods and fields ! of you strong
mountains of my land !
Of you O prairies ! of you gray rocks !
O morning red ! O clouds ! O rain and
snows !
O day and night, passage to you !

O sun and moon and all you stars ! Sirius
and Jupiter !   240
Passage to you !

Passage, immediate passage ! the blood
burns in my veins !
Away O soul ! hoist instantly the anchor !
Cut the hawsers — haul out — shake out
every sail !
Have we not stood here like trees in the
ground long enough ?
Have we not grovel'd here long enough,
eating and drinking like mere brutes ?
Have we not darken'd and dazed ourselves
with books long enough ?

Sail forth — steer for the deep waters only,
Reckless O soul, exploring, I with thee,
and thou with me,
For we are bound where mariner has not
yet dared to go,   250
And we will risk the ship, ourselves and all.

O my brave soul !
O farther farther sail !
O daring joy, but safe ! are they not all the
seas of God ?
O farther, farther, farther sail !

                                     1871.

DAREST THOU NOW O SOUL

DAREST thou now O soul,
Walk out with me toward the unknown
region,
Where neither ground is for the feet nor
any path to follow ?

No map there, nor guide,
Nor voice sounding, nor touch of human
hand,
Nor face with blooming flesh, nor lips, nor
eyes, are in that land.

I know it not O soul,
Nor dost thou, all is a blank before us,
All waits undream'd of in that region, that
inaccessible land.

Till when the ties loosen,
All but the ties eternal, Time and Space,
Nor darkness, gravitation, sense, nor any
bounds bounding us.

Then we burst forth, we float,
In Time and Space O soul, prepared for
them,
Equal, equipt at last (O joy ! O fruit of
all !) them to fulfil O soul.

                                     1871.

THE LAST INVOCATION

AT the last, tenderly,
From the walls of the powerful fortress'd
house,
From the clasp of the knitted locks, from
the keep of the well-closed doors,
Let me be wafted.

Let me glide noiselessly forth;
With the key of softness unlock the locks
  — with a whisper,
Set ope the doors O soul.

Tenderly — be not impatient,
(Strong is your hold O mortal flesh,
Strong is your hold O love.)

1871.

JOY, SHIPMATE, JOY!

Joy, shipmate, joy!
(Pleas'd to my soul at death I cry,)
Our life is closed, our life begins,
The long, long anchorage we leave,
The ship is clear at last, she leaps!
She swiftly courses from the shore,
Joy, shipmate, joy.

1871.

O STAR OF FRANCE[1]

1870-71

O star of France,
The brightness of thy hope and strength
  and fame,
Like some proud ship that led the fleet so
  long,
Beseems to-day a wreck driven by the
  gale, a mastless hulk,
And 'mid its teeming madden'd half-
  drown'd crowds,
Nor helm nor helmsman.

Dim smitten star,
Orb not of France alone, pale symbol of my
  soul, its dearest hopes,
The struggle and the daring, rage divine
  for liberty,
Of aspirations toward the far ideal, enthu-
  siast's dreams of brotherhood,   10
Of terror to the tyrant and the priest.

Star crucified — by traitors sold,
Star panting o'er a land of death, heroic
  land,
Strange, passionate, mocking, frivolous land.

Miserable! yet for thy errors, vanities,
  sins, I will not now rebuke thee,

[1] Compare Whitman's *Specimen Days*, April 18, 1881.
Complete Prose Works, p. 174.

Thy unexampled woes and pangs have
  quell'd them all,
And left thee sacred.

In that amid thy many faults thou ever
  aimedst highly,
In that thou wouldst not really sell thyself
  however great the price,
In that thou surely wakedst weeping
  from thy drugg'd sleep,   20
In that alone among thy sisters thou,
  giantess, didst rend the ones that shamed
  thee,
In that thou couldst not, wouldst not, wear
  the usual chains,
This cross, thy livid face, thy pierced hands
  and feet,
The spear thrust in thy side.

O star! O ship of France, beat back and
  baffled long!
Bear up O smitten orb! O ship continue
  on!

Sure as the ship of all, the Earth itself,
Product of deathly fire and turbulent
  chaos,
Forth from its spasms of fury and its
  poisons,
Issuing at last in perfect power and beauty,
Onward beneath the sun following its
  course,   31
So thee O ship of France!

Finish'd the days, the clouds dispel'd,
The travail o'er, the long-sought extrica-
  tion,
When lo! reborn, high o'er the European
  world,
(In gladness answering thence, as face afar
  to face, reflecting ours Columbia,)
Again thy star O France, fair lustrous star,
In heavenly peace, clearer, more bright
  than ever,
Shall beam immortal.

1871. (1872.)

THE MYSTIC TRUMPETER

1

Hark, some wild trumpeter, some strange
  musician,
Hovering unseen in air, vibrates capricious
  tunes to-night.

I hear thee trumpeter, listening alert I
    catch thy notes,
Now pouring, whirling like a tempest round
    me,
Now low, subdued, now in the distance lost.

2

Come nearer bodiless one, haply in thee
    resounds
Some dead composer, haply thy pensive life
Was fill'd with aspirations high, unform'd
    ideals,
Waves, oceans musical, chaotically surging,
That now ecstatic ghost, close to me bend-
    ing, thy cornet echoing, pealing,   10
Gives out to no one's ears but mine, but
    freely gives to mine,
That I may thee translate.

3

Blow trumpeter free and clear, I follow
    thee,
While at thy liquid prelude, glad, serene,
The fretting world, the streets, the noisy
    hours of day withdraw,
A holy calm descends like dew upon me,
I walk in cool refreshing night the walks of
    Paradise,
I scent the grass, the moist air and the roses;
Thy song expands my numb'd imbonded
    spirit, thou freest, launchest me,
Floating and basking upon heaven's lake. 20

4

Blow again trumpeter! and for my sensu-
    ous eyes,
Bring the old pageants, show the feudal
    world.

What charm thy music works! thou makest
    pass before me,
Ladies and cavaliers long dead, barons are
    in their castle halls, the troubadours are
    singing,
Arm'd knights go forth to redress wrongs,
    some in quest of the holy Graal;
I see the tournament, I see the contestants
    incased in heavy armor seated on stately
    champing horses,
I hear the shouts, the sounds of blows and
    smiting steel;
I see the Crusaders' tumultuous armies —
    hark, how the cymbals clang,
Lo, where the monks walk in advance,
    bearing the cross on high.

5

Blow again trumpeter! and for thy theme,
Take now the enclosing theme of all, the
    solvent and the setting,   31
Love, that is pulse of all, the sustenance
    and the pang,
The heart of man and woman all for love,
No other theme but love — knitting, enclos-
    ing, all-diffusing love.

O how the immortal phantoms crowd
    around me!
I see the vast alembic ever working, I
    see and know the flames that heat the
    world,
The glow, the blush, the beating hearts of
    lovers,
So blissful happy some, and some so silent,
    dark, and nigh to death;
Love, that is all the earth to lovers — love,
    that mocks time and space,
Love, that is day and night — love, that is
    sun and moon and stars,   40
Love, that is crimson, sumptuous, sick with
    perfume,
No other words but words of love, no other
    thought but love.

6

Blow again trumpeter — conjure war's
    alarums.

Swift to thy spell a shuddering hum like
    distant thunder rolls,
Lo, where the arm'd men hasten — lo, 'mid
    the clouds of dust the glint of bayonets,
I see the grime-faced cannoneers, I mark the
    rosy flash amid the smoke, I hear the
    cracking of the guns;
Nor war alone — thy fearful music-song,
    wild player, brings every sight of fear,
The deeds of ruthless brigands, rapine,
    murder — I hear the cries for help!
I see ships foundering at sea, I behold on
    deck and below deck the terrible tableaus.

7

O trumpeter, methinks I am myself the
    instrument thou playest,   50
Thou melt'st my heart, my brain — thou
    movest, drawest, changest them at will;
And now thy sullen notes send darkness
    through me,
Thou takest away all cheering light, all
    hope,

I see the enslaved, the overthrown, the hurt,
the opprest of the whole earth,
I feel the measureless shame and humiliation of my race, it becomes all mine,
Mine too the revenges of humanity, the
wrongs of ages, baffled feuds and hatreds,
Utter defeat upon me weighs — all lost —
the foe victorious,
(Yet 'mid the ruins Pride colossal stands
unshaken to the last,
Endurance, resolution to the last.)

8

Now trumpeter for thy close,   60
Vouchsafe a higher strain than any yet,
Sing to my soul, renew its languishing faith
and hope,
Rouse up my slow belief, give me some
vision of the future,
Give me for once its prophecy and joy.

O glad, exulting, culminating song !
A vigor more than earth's is in thy notes,
Marches of victory — man disenthral'd —
the conqueror at last,
Hymns to the universal God from universal
man — all joy !
A reborn race appears — a perfect world,
all joy !
Women and men in wisdom innocence and
health — all joy !   70
Riotous laughing bacchanals fill'd with joy !
War, sorrow, suffering gone — the rank
earth purged — nothing but joy left !
The ocean fill'd with joy — the atmosphere
all joy !
Joy ! joy ! in freedom, worship, love ! joy
in the ecstasy of life !
Enough to merely be ! enough to breathe !
Joy ! joy ! all over joy !

1872.

VIRGINIA — THE WEST

THE noble sire fallen on evil days,
I saw with hand uplifted, menacing, bran-
dishing
(Memories of old in abeyance, love and
faith in abeyance),
The insane knife toward the Mother of All.

The noble son on sinewy feet advancing,
I saw, out of the land of prairies, land of
Ohio's waters and of Indiana,

To the rescue the stalwart giant hurry his
plenteous offspring,
Drest in blue, bearing their trusty rifles on
their shoulders.

Then the Mother of All with calm voice
speaking,
As to you Rebellious (I seemed to hear her
say), why strive against me, and why seek
my life ?
When you yourself forever provide to defend me ?
For you provided me Washington — and
now these also.

1872.

THOU MOTHER WITH THY
EQUAL BROOD [1]

I

THOU Mother with thy equal brood,
Thou varied chain of different States, yet
one identity only,

[1] Read by Whitman at the Commencement of Dartmouth College, in 1872.
The poem originally began with what is now Section
2, and the title as well as the first line was 'As a strong
bird on pinions free.' What is now Section 1 was added
in the 1881 edition.
See the original Preface of this poem, in the Complete Prose Works, pp. 268–272. One of its chief ideas
is condensed in two paragraphs near the end : —
'The Four Years' War is over — and in the peaceful,
strong, exciting, fresh occasions of to-day, and of the
future, that strange, sad war is hurrying even now to
be forgotten. The camp, the drill, the lines of sentries,
the prisons, the hospitals — (ah ! the hospitals !) — all
have passed away — all seem now like a dream. A new
race, a young and lusty generation, already sweeps in
with oceanic currents, obliterating the war, and all its
scars, its mounded graves, and all its reminiscences of
hatred, conflict, death. So let it be obliterated. I say
the life of the present and the future makes undeniable
demands upon us each and all, south, north, east, west.
To help put the United States (even if only in imagination) hand in hand, in one unbroken circle in a chant
— to rouse them to the unprecedented grandeur of the
part they are to play, and are even now playing — to
the thought of their great future, and the attitude conform'd to it — especially their great esthetic, moral,
scientific future (of which their vulgar material and
political present is but as the preparatory tuning of instruments by an orchestra), these, as hitherto, are still,
for me, among my hopes, ambitions.
' "Leaves of Grass," already publish'd, is, in its intentions, the song of a great composite *democratic individual*, male or female. And following on and ampli-
fying the same purpose, I suppose I have in my mind
to run through the chants of this volume (if ever completed), the thread-voice, more or less audible, of an
aggregated, inseparable, unprecedented, vast, composite, electric *democratic nationality*.'
Compare also Whitman's *Democratic Vistas*, Complete Prose Works, pp. 197–250 ; "A Backward Glance

A special song before I go I 'd sing o'er all
   the rest,
For thee, the future.

I 'd sow a seed for thee of endless Nationality,
I 'd fashion thy ensemble including body
   and soul,
I 'd show away ahead thy real Union, and
   how it may be accomplish'd.

The paths to the house I seek to make,
But leave to those to come the house itself.

Belief I sing, and preparation;   10
As Life and Nature are not great with ref-
   erence to the present only,
But greater still from what is yet to
   come,
Out of that formula for thee I sing.

2

As a strong bird on pinions free,
Joyous, the amplest spaces heavenward
   cleaving,
Such be the thought I 'd think of thee
   America,
Such be the recitative I 'd bring for thee.

The conceits of the poets of other lands I 'd
   bring thee not,
Nor the compliments that have served their
   turn so long,
Nor rhyme, nor the classics, nor perfume
   of foreign court or indoor library;   20
But an odor I 'd bring as from forests of
   pine in Maine, or breath of an Illinois
   prairie,
With open airs of Virginia or Georgia or
   Tennessee, or from Texas uplands, or
   Florida's glades,
Or the Saguenay's black stream, or the
   wide blue spread of Huron,
With presentment of Yellowstone's scenes,
   or Yosemite,
And murmuring under, pervading all, I 'd
   bring the rustling sea-sound,
That endlessly sounds from the two Great
   Seas of the world.

o'er Travel'd Roads;" and, especially, one of Whitman's
early notes, in *Notes and Fragments*, p. 59: —
   ' In Poems — bring in the idea of Mother — the idea
of the mother with numerous children — all, great and
small, old and young, equal in her eyes — as the identity of America.'

And for thy subtler sense subtler refrains
   dread Mother,
Preludes of intellect tallying these and
   thee, mind-formulas fitted for thee, real
   and sane and large as these and thee,
Thou ! mounting higher, diving deeper than
   we knew, thou transcendental Union !
By thee fact to be justified, blended with
   thought,   30
Thought of man justified, blended with
   God,
Through thy idea, lo, the immortal reality !
Through thy reality, lo, the immortal idea !

3

Brain of the New World, what a task is
   thine,
To formulate the Modern — out of the peerless grandeur of the modern,
Out of thyself, comprising science, to recast
   poems, churches, art,
(Recast, may-be discard them, end them —
   may-be their work is done, who knows ?)
By vision, hand, conception, on the background of the mighty past, the dead,
To limn with absolute faith the mighty living present.

And yet thou living present brain, heir of
   the dead, the Old World brain,   40
Thou that lay folded like an unborn babe
   within its folds so long,
Thou carefully prepared by it so long —
   haply thou but unfoldest it, only maturest
   it,
It to eventuate in thee — the essence of the
   by-gone time contain'd in thee,
Its poems, churches, arts, unwitting to
   themselves, destined with reference to
   thee;
Thou but the apples, long, long, long a-grow-
   ing,
The fruit of all the Old ripening to-day in
   thee.

4

Sail, sail thy best, ship of Democracy,
Of value is thy freight, 't is not the Present
   only,
The Past is also stored in thee,
Thou holdest not the venture of thyself
   alone, not of the Western continent
   alone,   50
Earth's *résumé* entire floats on thy keel O
   ship, is steadied by thy spars,

With thee Time voyages in trust, the
antecedent nations sink or swim with
thee,
With all their ancient struggles, martyrs,
heroes, epics, wars, thou bear'st the other
continents,
Theirs, theirs as much as thine, the desti-
nation-port triumphant;
Steer then with good strong hand and wary
eye O helmsman, thou carriest great
companions,
Venerable priestly Asia sails this day with
thee,
And royal feudal Europe sails with thee.

5

Beautiful world of new superber birth that
rises to my eyes,
Like a limitless golden cloud filling the
western sky,
Emblem of general maternity lifted above
all,   60
Sacred shape of the bearer of daughters
and sons,
Out of thy teeming womb thy giant babes
in ceaseless procession issuing,
Acceding from such gestation, taking and
giving continual strength and life,
World of the real — world of the twain in
one,
World of the soul, born by the world of the
real alone, led to identity, body, by it
alone,
Yet in beginning only, incalculable masses
of composite precious materials,
By history's cycles forwarded, by every
nation, language, hither sent,
Ready, collected here, a freer, vast, electric world, to be constructed here
(The true New World, the world of orbic
science, morals, literatures to come),
Thou wonder world yet undefined, un-
form'd, neither do I define thee,   70
How can I pierce the impenetrable blank
of the future ?
I feel thy ominous greatness evil as well as
good,
I watch thee advancing, absorbing the
present, transcending the past,
I see thy light lighting, and thy shadow
shadowing, as if the entire globe,
But I do not undertake to define thee,
hardly to comprehend thee,
I but thee name, thee prophesy, as now,
I merely thee ejaculate !

Thee in thy future,
Thee in thy only permanent life, career, thy
own unloosen'd mind, thy soaring spirit,
Thee as another equally needed sun, radiant, ablaze, swift-moving, fructifying all,
Thee risen in potent cheerfulness and joy,
in endless great hilarity,   81
Scattering for good the cloud that hung so
long, that weigh'd so long upon the mind
of man,
The doubt, suspicion, dread, of gradual,
certain decadence of man;
Thee in thy larger, saner brood of female,
male — thee in thy athletes, moral,
spiritual, South, North, West, East,
(To thy immortal breasts, Mother of All,
thy every daughter, son, endear'd alike,
forever equal,)
Thee in thy own musicians, singers, artists,
unborn yet, but certain,
Thee in thy moral wealth and civilization,
(until which thy proudest material civilization must remain in vain,)
Thee in thy all-supplying, all-enclosing
worship — thee in no single bible, saviour,
merely,
Thy saviours countless, latent within thyself, thy bibles incessant within thyself,
equal to any, divine as any.
(Thy soaring course thee formulating, not
in thy two great wars, nor in thy century's visible growth,   90
But far more in these leaves and chants,
thy chants, great Mother !) [1]
Thee in an education grown of thee, in
teachers, studies, students, born of thee,
Thee in thy democratic fêtes en-masse, thy
high original festivals, operas, lecturers,
preachers,
Thee in thy ultimata (the preparations
only now completed, the edifice on sure
foundations tied),
Thee in thy pinnacles, intellect, thought,
thy topmost rational joys, thy love and
godlike aspiration,
In thy resplendent coming literati, thy full-
lung'd orators, thy sacerdotal bards, kos-
mic savans,
These ! these in thee (certain to come), to-
day I prophesy.

6

Land tolerating all, accepting all, not for
the good alone, all good for thee,

[1] The two lines in parenthesis were added in 1881.

Land in the realms of God to be a realm
  unto thyself,
Under the rule of God to be a rule unto
  thyself.   100

(Lo, where arise three peerless stars,
To be thy natal stars my country, Ensem-
  ble, Evolution, Freedom,
Set in the sky of Law.)

Land of unprecedented faith, God's faith,
Thy soil, thy very subsoil, all upheav'd,
The general inner earth so long so sedu-
  lously draped over, now hence for what
  it is boldly laid bare,
Open'd by thee to heaven's light for benefit
  or bale.

Not for success alone,
Not to fair-sail unintermitted always,
The storm shall dash thy face, the murk of
  war and worse than war shall cover thee
  all over,   110
(Wert capable of war, its tug and trials?
  be capable of peace, its trials,
For the tug and mortal strain of nations
  come at last in prosperous peace, not war ;)
In many a smiling mask death shall approach beguiling thee, thou in disease
  shalt swelter,
The livid cancer spread its hideous claws,
  clinging upon thy breasts, seeking to
  strike thee deep within,
Consumption of the worst, moral consumption, shall rouge thy face with hectic,[1]
But thou shalt face thy fortunes, thy diseases, and surmount them all,
Whatever they are to-day and whatever
  through time they may be,
They each and all shall lift and pass away
  and cease from thee,
While thou, Time's spirals rounding, out
  of thyself, thyself still extricating, fusing,
Equable, natural, mystical Union thou
  (the mortal with immortal blent),   120
Shalt soar toward the fulfilment of the future, the spirit of the body and the mind,
The soul, its destinies.

The soul, its destinies, the real real,
(Purport of all these apparitions of the
  real ;)
In thee America, the soul, its destinies,

[1] Compare *Democratic Vistas*, pp. 203-208 ; and *Two
Rivulets*, 1876, the prose section.

Thou globe of globes ! thou wonder nebulous !
By many a throe of heat and cold convuls'd
  (by these thyself solidifying),
Thou mental, moral orb — thou New, indeed new, Spiritual World !
The Present holds thee not — for such
  vast growth as thine,
For such unparallel'd flight as thine, such
  brood as thine,   130
The FUTURE only holds thee and can hold
  thee.
                                        1872.

PRAYER OF COLUMBUS [2]

A BATTER'D, wreck'd old man,
Thrown on this savage shore, far, far from
  home,
Pent by the sea and dark rebellious brows,
  twelve dreary months,
Sore, stiff with many toils, sicken'd and nigh
  to death,
I take my way along the island's edge,
Venting a heavy heart.

I am too full of woe !
Haply I may not live another day ;
I cannot rest O God, I cannot eat or drink
  or sleep,
Till I put forth myself, my prayer, once
  more to Thee,   10
Breathe, bathe myself once more in Thee,
  commune with Thee,
Report myself once more to Thee.

Thou knowest my years entire, my life,
My long and crowded life of active work,
  not adoration merely ;

[2] It was near the close of his indomitable and pious
life — on his last voyage when nearly 70 years of age —
that Columbus, to save his two remaining ships from
foundering in the Caribbean Sea in a terrible storm,
had to run them ashore on the Island of Jamaica —
where, laid up for a long and miserable year — 1503 —
he was taken very sick, had several relapses, his men
revolted, and death seem'd daily imminent ; though he
was eventually rescued, and sent home to Spain to die,
unrecognized, neglected and in want. . . . It is only
ask'd, as preparation and atmosphere for the following
lines, that the bare authentic facts be recall'd and realized, and nothing contributed by the fancy. See, the
Antillean Island, with its florid skies and rich foliage
and scenery, the waves beating the solitary sands, and
the hulls of the ships in the distance. See, the figure
of the great Admiral, walking the beach, as a stage, in
this sublimest tragedy — for what tragedy, what poem,
so piteous and majestic as the real scene ? — and hear
him uttering — as his mystical and religious soul surely
utter'd, the ideas following — perhaps, in their equiv-
alents, the very words. (WHITMAN.)

Thou knowest the prayers and vigils of my
youth,
Thou knowest my manhood's solemn and
visionary meditations,
Thou knowest how before I commenced I
devoted all to come to Thee,
Thou knowest I have in age ratified all
those vows and strictly kept them,
Thou knowest I have not once lost nor faith
nor ecstasy in Thee,
In shackles, prison'd, in disgrace, repining
not,   20
Accepting all from Thee, as duly come
from Thee.

All my emprises have been fill'd with Thee,
My speculations, plans, begun and carried
on in thoughts of Thee,
Sailing the deep or journeying the land for
Thee;
Intentions, purports, aspirations mine, leav-
ing results to Thee.

O I am sure they really came from Thee,
The urge, the ardor, the unconquerable
will,
The potent, felt, interior command, stronger
than words,
A message from the Heavens whispering
to me even in sleep,
These sped me on.   30

By me and these the work so far accomplish'd,
By me earth's elder cloy'd and stifled lands
uncloy'd, unloos'd,
By me the hemispheres rounded and tied,
the unknown to the known.

The end I know not, it is all in Thee,
Or small or great I know not — haply
what broad fields, what lands,
Haply the brutish measureless human un-
dergrowth I know,
Transplanted there may rise to stature,
knowledge worthy Thee,
Haply the swords I know may there indeed
be turn'd to reaping-tools,
Haply the lifeless cross I know, Europe's
dead cross, may bud and blossom there.

One effort more, my altar this bleak sand;
That Thou O God my life hast lighted,   41
With ray of light, steady, ineffable, vouch-
safed of Thee,

Light rare untellable, lighting the very
light,
Beyond all signs, descriptions, languages;
For that O God, be it my latest word, here
on my knees,
Old, poor, and paralyzed, I thank Thee.

My terminus near,
The clouds already closing in upon me,
The voyage balk'd, the course disputed,
lost,
I yield my ships to Thee.   50

My hands, my limbs grow nerveless,
My brain feels rack'd, bewilder'd,
Let the old timbers part, I will not part,
I will cling fast to Thee, O God, though
the waves buffet me,
Thee, Thee at least I know.

Is it the prophet's thought I speak, or am I
raving?
What do I know of life? what of myself?
I know not even my own work past or pre-
sent,
Dim ever-shifting guesses of it spread be-
fore me,
Of newer better worlds, their mighty
parturition,   60
Mocking, perplexing me.

And these things I see suddenly, what
mean they?
As if some miracle, some hand divine un-
seal'd my eyes,
Shadowy vast shapes smile through the air
and sky,
And on the distant waves sail countless
ships,
And anthems in new tongues I hear saluting me.

            1874. (1876.)

COME, SAID MY SOUL [1]

COME, SAID MY SOUL,
SUCH VERSES FOR MY BODY LET US
WRITE, (FOR WE ARE ONE),
THAT SHOULD I AFTER DEATH INVISIBLY
RETURN,
OR, LONG, LONG HENCE, IN OTHER SPHERES,

[1] The Inscription, signed with Whitman's autograph,
to the 1876 edition of *Leaves of Grass*, and to all the
following editions authorized by him.

THERE TO SOME GROUP OF MATES THE
CHANTS RESUMING,
(TALLYING EARTH'S SOIL, TREES, WINDS,
TUMULTUOUS WAVES,)
EVER WITH PLEAS'D SMILE I MAY KEEP
ON,
EVER AND EVER YET THE VERSES OWN-
ING — AS, FIRST, I HERE AND NOW,
SIGNING FOR SOUL AND BODY, SET TO
THEM MY NAME,
                    WALT WHITMAN.
                              1876.

WHEN THE FULL-GROWN POET CAME

WHEN the full-grown poet came,
Out spake pleased Nature (the round impassive globe, with all its shows of day
and night), saying, *He is mine;*
But out spake too the Soul of man, proud,
jealous and unreconciled, *Nay, he is mine
alone*;
— Then the full-grown poet stood between
the two, and took each by the hand;
And to-day and ever so stands, as blender,
uniter, tightly holding hands,
Which he will never release until he re-
conciles the two,
And wholly and joyously blends them.
                              1876.

TO THE MAN-OF-WAR-BIRD

THOU who hast slept all night upon the
storm,
Waking renew'd on thy prodigious pinions
(Burst the wild storm? above it thou ascended'st,
And rested on the sky, thy slave that
cradled thee),
Now a blue point, far, far in heaven floating,
As to the light emerging here on deck I
watch thee
(Myself a speck, a point on the world's
floating vast).

Far, far at sea,
After the night's fierce drifts have strewn
the shore with wrecks,
With reappearing day as now so happy
and serene,

The rosy and elastic dawn, the flashing sun,
The limpid spread of air cerulean,
Thou also reappearest.

Thou born to match the gale (thou art all
wings),
To cope with heaven and earth and sea and
hurricane,
Thou ship of air that never furl'st thy
sails,
Days, even weeks untired and onward,
through spaces, realms gyrating,
At dusk that look'st on Senegal, at morn
America,
That sport'st amid the lightning-flash and
thunder-cloud,
In them, in thy experiences, had'st thou
my soul,
What joys! what joys were thine!
                              1876.

THE OX-TAMER

IN a far-away northern county in the placid
pastoral region,
Lives my farmer friend, the theme of my
recitative, a famous tamer of oxen,
There they bring him the three-year-olds
and the four-year-olds to break them,
He will take the wildest steer in the world
and break him and tame him,
He will go fearless without any whip where
the young bullock chafes up and down
the yard,
The bullock's head tosses restless high in
the air with raging eyes,
Yet see you! how soon his rage subsides —
how soon this tamer tames him;
See you! on the farms hereabout a hundred oxen young and old, and he is the
man who has tamed them,
They all know him, all are affectionate to
him;
See you! some are such beautiful animals,
so lofty looking;
Some are buff-color'd, some mottled, one
has a white line running along his back,
some are brindled,
Some have wide flaring horns (a good sign)
— see you! the bright hides,
See, the two with stars on their foreheads
— see, the round bodies and broad
backs,
How straight and square they stand on
their legs — what fine sagacious eyes!

How they watch their tamer — they wish
him near them — how they turn to look
after him!
What yearning expression! how uneasy they
are when he moves away from them;
Now I marvel what it can be he appears to
them (books, politics, poems, depart —
all else departs),
I confess I envy only his fascination — my
silent, illiterate friend,
Whom a hundred oxen love there in his life
on farms,
In the northern county far, in the placid
pastoral region.

1876.

TO A LOCOMOTIVE IN WINTER [1]

THEE for my recitative,
Thee in the driving storm even as now, the
snow, the winter-day declining,
Thee in thy panoply, thy measur'd dual
throbbing and thy beat convulsive,
Thy black cylindric body, golden brass and
silvery steel,
Thy ponderous side-bars, parallel and connecting rods, gyrating, shuttling at thy
sides,
Thy metrical, now swelling pant and roar,
now tapering in the distance,
Thy great protruding head-light fix'd in
front,
Thy long, pale, floating vapor-pennants,
tinged with delicate purple,
The dense and murky clouds out-belching
from thy smoke-stack,
Thy knitted frame, thy springs and valves,
the tremulous twinkle of thy wheels,
Thy train of cars behind, obedient, merrily
following,
Through gale or calm, now swift, now
slack, yet steadily careering;
Type of the modern — emblem of motion
and power — pulse of the continent,

[1] Contrast Wordsworth's attitude toward the railroad and its invasion of natural scenes! And compare
Whitman's *Specimen Days*, April 29, 1879: —
'It was a happy thought to build the Hudson River
railroad right along the shore. . . . I see, hear, the
locomotives and cars, rumbling, roaring, flaming, smoking, constantly, away off there, night and day — less
than a mile distant, and in full view by day. I like
both sight and sound. Express trains thunder and
lighten along; of freight trains, most of them very
long, there cannot be less than a hundred a day. At
night far down you see the headlight approaching,
coming steadily on like a meteor. The river at night
has its special character-beauties.' 1876, vol. i, p. 369.

For once come serve the Muse and merge
in verse, even as here I see thee,
With storm and buffeting gusts of wind
and falling snow,
By day thy warning ringing bell to sound
its notes,
By night thy silent signal lamps to swing.

Fierce-throated beauty!
Roll through my chant with all thy lawless music, thy swinging lamps at night,
Thy madly-whistled laughter, echoing,
rumbling like an earthquake, rousing all,
Law of thyself complete, thine own track
firmly holding,
(No sweetness debonair of tearful harp or
glib piano thine,)
Thy trills of shrieks by rocks and hills
return'd,
Launch'd o'er the prairies wide, across the
lakes,
To the free skies unpent and glad and
strong.

1876.

AFTER AN INTERVAL

(NOVEMBER 22, 1875, MIDNIGHT — SATURN
AND MARS IN CONJUNCTION)

AFTER an interval, reading, here in the
midnight,
With the great stars looking on — all the
stars of Orion looking,
And the silent Pleiades — and the duo
looking of Saturn and ruddy Mars;
Pondering, reading my own songs, after a
long interval (sorrow and death familiar
now),
Ere closing the book, what pride! what
joy! to find them,
Standing so well the test of death and
night!
And the duo of Saturn and Mars!

1876.[1]

TO FOREIGN LANDS

I HEARD that you ask'd for something to
prove this puzzle the New World,
And to define America, her athletic Democracy,
Therefore I send you my poems that you
behold in them what you wanted.

1881.

[1] 1876 only. Omitted from later edition

WHAT BEST I SEE IN THEE [1]

TO U. S. G. RETURN'D FROM HIS WORLD'S TOUR

WHAT best I see in thee,
Is not that where thou mov'st down history's
great highways,
Ever undimm'd by time shoots warlike
victory's dazzle,
Or that thou sat'st where Washington sat,
ruling the land in peace,
Or thou the man whom feudal Europe fêted,
venerable Asia swarm'd upon,
Who walk'd with kings with even pace the
round world's promenade;
But that in foreign lands, in all thy walks
with kings,
Those prairie sovereigns of the West, Kan-
sas, Missouri, Illinois,
Ohio's, Indiana's millions, comrades, farm-
ers, soldiers, all to the front,
Invisibly with thee walking with kings with
even pace the round world's promenade,
Were all so justified.

1881.

[1] So General Grant, after circumambiating the world,
has arrived home again, landed in San Francisco yesterday, from the ship City of Tokio from Japan. What a
man he is! what a history! what an illustration — his
life — of the capacities of that American individuality
common to us all. Cynical critics are wondering 'what
the people can see in Grant' to make such a hubbub
about. They aver (and it is no doubt true) that he has
hardly the average of our day's literary and scholastic
culture, and absolutely no pronounc'd genius or conventional eminence of any sort. Correct : but he proves how
an average western farmer, mechanic, boatman, carried
by tides of circumstances, perhaps caprices, into a position of incredible military or civic responsibilities (history has presented none more trying, no born monarch's,
no mark more shining for attack or envy), may steer his
way fitly and steadily through them all, carrying the
country and himself with credit year after year — command over a million armed men — fight more than fifty
pitch'd battles — rule for eight years a land larger than
all the kingdoms of Europe combined — and then, retiring, quietly (with a cigar in his mouth), make the promenade of the whole world, through its courts and cote-
ries, and kings and czars and mikados, and splendidest
glitters and etiquettes, as phlegmatically as he ever
walk'd the portico of a Missouri hotel after dinner. I
say all this is what people like — and I am sure I like it.
Seems to me it transcends Plutarch. How those old
Greeks, indeed, would have seized on him ! A mere
plain man — no art, no poetry — only practical sense,
ability to do, or try his best to do, what devolv'd upon
him. A common trader, money-maker, tanner, farmer
of Illinois — general for the republic, in its terrific
struggle with itself, in the war of attempted secession —
President following (a task of peace, more difficult than
the war itself) — nothing heroic, as the authorities put
it — and yet the greatest hero. The gods, the destinies,
seem to have concentrated upon him. (*Specimen Days*,
September 27, 1879. Complete Prose Works, pp. 146,
147.) See also Whitman's poem: ' On the Death of
General Grant.'

SPIRIT THAT FORM'D THIS SCENE [2]

WRITTEN IN PLATTE CAÑON, COLORADO

SPIRIT that form'd this scene,
These tumbled rock-piles grim and red,
These reckless heaven-ambitious peaks,
These gorges, turbulent-clear streams, this
naked freshness,
These formless wild arrays, for reasons of
their own,
I know thee, savage spirit — we have com-
muned together,
Mine too such wild arrays, for reasons of
their own,
Was't charged against my chants they had
forgotten art ?
To fuse within themselves its rules precise
and delicatesse ?
The lyrist's measur'd beat, the wrought-out
temple's grace — column and polish'd
arch forgot ?
But thou that revelest here — spirit that
form'd this scene,
They have remember'd thee.   1881.

[2] Compare Whitman's entry in his journal during
his trip through Colorado : —
' I have found the law of my own poems,' was the
unspoken but more-and-more decided feeling that came
to me as I pass'd, hour after hour, amid all this grim
yet joyous elemental abandon — this plenitude of material, entire absence of art, untrammel'd play of primitive Nature — the chasm, the gorge, the crystal mountain stream, repeated scores, hundreds of miles — the
broad handling and absolute uncrampedness — the fantastic forms, bathed in transparent browns, faint reds
and grays, towering sometimes a thousand, sometimes
two or three thousand feet high — at their tops now
and then huge masses pois'd, and mixing with the
clouds, with only their outlines, hazed in misty lilac,
visible. (' In Nature's grandest shows,' says an old
Dutch writer, an ecclesiastic, ' amid the ocean's depth,
if so might be, or countless worlds rolling above at night,
a man thinks of them, weighs all, not for themselves or
the abstract, but with reference to his own personality,
and how they may affect him or color his destinies.')
We follow the stream of amber and bronze brawling
along its bed, with its frequent cascades and snow-white
foam. Through the cañon we fly — mountains not only
each side, but seemingly, till we get near, right in front
of us — every rood a new view flashing and each flash
defying description — on the almost perpendicular sides,
clinging pines, cedars, spruces, crimson sumach bushes,
spots of wild grass — but dominating all, those towering rocks, rocks, rocks, bathed in delicate vari-colors,
with the clear sky of autumn overhead. New senses,
new joys, seem develop'd. Talk as you like, a typical
Rocky Mountain cañon, or a limitless sea-like stretch
of the great Kansas or Colorado plains, under favoring
circumstances, tallies, perhaps expresses, certainly
awakes, those grandest and subtlest element-emotions
in the human soul, that all the marble temples and
sculptures from Phidias to Thorwaldsen — all paintings,
poems, reminiscences, or even music, probably never
can. (*Specimen Days*. Complete Prose Works, Small,
Maynard & Co., p. 136.)

YOUTH, DAY, OLD AGE AND NIGHT

YOUTH, large, lusty, loving — youth full of
grace, force, fascination,
Do you know that Old Age may come after
you with equal grace, force, fascination?

Day full-blown and splendid — day of the
immense sun, action, ambition, laughter,
The Night follows close with millions of
suns, and sleep and restoring darkness.[1]

1881.

A CLEAR MIDNIGHT

THIS is thy hour O Soul, thy free flight
into the wordless,
Away from books, away from art, the day
erased, the lesson done,
Thee fully forth emerging, silent, gazing,
pondering the themes thou lovest best,
Night, sleep, death and the stars.

1881.

WITH HUSKY-HAUGHTY LIPS, O SEA![2]

WITH husky-haughty lips, O sea!
Where day and night I wend thy surf-beat
shore,
Imaging to my sense thy varied strange
suggestions
(I see and plainly list thy talk and confer-
ence here),
Thy troops of white-maned racers racing to
the goal,
Thy ample, smiling face, dash'd with the
sparkling dimples of the sun,
Thy brooding scowl and murk — thy unloos'd hurricanes,

---

[1] Compare the passages in Whitman's Prose Works
referred to in the notes on pp. 564 and 579.
[2] *July 25, '81. Far Rockaway, L. I.* — A good day
here, on a jaunt, amid the sand and salt, a steady
breeze setting in from the sea, the sun shining, the
sedge-odor, the noise of the surf, a mixture of hissing
and booming, the milk-white crests curling over. I
had a leisurely bath and naked ramble as of old, on the
warm-gray shore-sands, my companions off in a boat in
deeper water — (I shouting to them Jupiter's menaces
against the gods, from Pope's Homer.) (*Specimen Days.*
Complete Prose Works, Small, Maynard & Co., pp. 176,
177.)

Thy unsubduedness, caprices, wilfulness;
Great as thou art above the rest, thy many
tears — a lack from all eternity in thy
content,
(Naught but the greatest struggles, wrongs,
defeats, could make thee greatest — no
less could make thee,)
Thy lonely state — something thou ever
seek'st and seek'st, yet never gain'st,
Surely some right withheld — some voice,
in huge monotonous rage, of freedom-
lover pent,
Some vast heart, like a planet's, chain'd and
chafing in those breakers,
By lengthen'd swell, and spasm, and pant-
ing breath,
And rhythmic rasping of thy sands and
waves,
And serpent hiss, and savage peals of
laughter,
And undertones of distant lion roar,
(Sounding, appealing to the sky's deaf ear
— but now, rapport for once,
A phantom in the night thy confidant for
once,)
The first and last confession of the globe,
Outsurging, muttering from thy soul's
abysms,
The tale of cosmic elemental passion,
Thou tellest to a kindred soul.

1884. (1888.)

OF THAT BLITHE THROAT OF THINE

[More than eighty-three degrees north — about a
good day's steaming distance to the Pole by one of our
fast oceaners in clear water — Greely the explorer heard
the song of a single snow-bird merrily sounding over
the desolation.]

OF that blithe throat of thine from arctic
bleak and blank,
I'll mind the lesson, solitary bird — let me
too welcome chilling drifts,
E'en the profoundest chill, as now — a
torpid pulse, a brain unnerv'd,
Old age land-lock'd within its winter bay
(cold, cold, O cold!) —
These snowy hairs, my feeble arm, my
frozen feet,
For them thy faith, thy rule I take, and
grave it to the last;
Not summer's zones alone — not chants of
youth, or south's warm tides alone,

But held by sluggish floes, pack'd in the northern ice, the cumulus of years,
These with gay heart I also sing.

1885. (1888.)

AS THE GREEK'S SIGNAL FLAME

[FOR WHITTIER'S EIGHTIETH BIRTHDAY, DECEMBER 17, 1887.]

As the Greek's signal flame, by antique records told,
Rose from the hill-top, like applause and glory,
Welcoming in fame some special veteran, hero,
With rosy tinge reddening the land he 'd served,
So I aloft from Mannahatta's ship-fringed shore,
Lift high a kindled brand for thee, Old Poet.

1887. (1888.)

TO THOSE WHO 'VE FAIL'D

To those who've fail'd, in aspiration vast,
To unnam'd soldiers fallen in front on the lead,
To calm, devoted engineers — to over-ardent travelers — to pilots on their ships,
To many a lofty song and picture without recognition — I 'd rear a laurel-cover'd monument,
High, high above the rest — To all cut off before their time,
Possess'd by some strange spirit of fire,
Quench'd by an early death.

1888.

A CAROL CLOSING SIXTY-NINE

A CAROL closing sixty-nine — a *résumé* — a repetition,
My lines in joy and hope continuing on the same,
Of ye, O God, Life, Nature, Freedom, Poetry;
Of you, my Land — your rivers, prairies, States — you, mottled Flag I love,

Your aggregate retain'd entire — O north, south, east and west, your items all;
Of me myself — the jocund heart yet beating in my breast,
The body wreck'd, old, poor and paralyzed — the strange inertia falling pall-like round me,
The burning fires down in my sluggish blood not yet extinct,
The undiminish'd faith — the groups of loving friends.[1]

1888.

THE FIRST DANDELION

SIMPLE and fresh and fair from winter's close emerging,
As if no artifice of fashion, business, politics, had ever been,
Forth from its sunny nook of shelter'd grass — innocent, golden, calm as the dawn,
The spring's first dandelion shows its trustful face.

1888.

THE VOICE OF THE RAIN

AND who art thou ? said I to the soft-falling shower,
Which, strange to tell, gave me an answer, as here translated:
I am the Poem of Earth, said the voice of the rain,
Eternal I rise impalpable out of the land and the bottomless sea,
Upward to heaven, whence, vaguely form'd, altogether changed, and yet the same,

[1] Compare, in Complete Prose Works, p. 190, the letter of May 31, 1882: 'From to-day I enter upon my 64th year. The paralysis that first affected me nearl' ten years ago, has since remain'd, with varying courf — seems to have settled quietly down, and will pr(bably continue. I easily tire, am very clumsy, canno walk far; but my spirits are first-rate. I go around in public almost every day — now and then take long trips, by railroad or boat, hundreds of miles — live largely in the open air — am sunburnt and stout (weigh 190), — keep up my activity and interest in life, people, progress, and the questions of the day. About two thirds of the time I am quite comfortable. What mentality I ever had remains entirely unaffected; though physically I am a half-paralytic, and likely to be so, long as I live. But the principal object of my life seems to have been accomplish'd — I have the most devoted and ardent of friends, and affectionate relatives — and of enemies I really make no account.'

I descend to lave the drouths, atomies, dust-
layers of the globe,
And all that in them without me were seeds
only, latent, unborn;
And forever, by day and night, I give back
life to my own origin, and make pure and
beautify it;
(For song, issuing from its birthplace, after
fulfilment, wandering,
Reck'd or unreck'd, duly with love returns.)

1888.

A PRAIRIE SUNSET

SHOT gold, maroon and violet, dazzling
silver, emerald, fawn,
The earth's whole amplitude and Nature's
multiform power consign'd for once to
colors;
The light, the general air possess'd by
them — colors till now unknown,
No limit, confine — not the Western sky
alone — the high meridian — North,
South, all,
Pure luminous color fighting the silent
shadows to the last.

1888.

THANKS IN OLD AGE

THANKS in old age — thanks ere I go,
For health, the midday sun, the impalpable
air — for life, mere life,
For precious ever-lingering memories, (of
you my mother dear — you, father —
you, brothers, sisters, friends,)
For all my days — not those of peace alone
— the days of war the same,
For gentle words, caresses, gifts from foreign lands,
For shelter, wine and meat — for sweet appreciation,
(You distant, dim unknown — or young or
old — countless, unspecified, readers be-
lov'd,
We never met, and ne'er shall meet — and
yet our souls embrace, long, close and
long;)
For beings, groups, love, deeds, words,
books — for colors, forms,
For all the brave strong men — devoted,
hardy men — who 've forward sprung in
freedom's help, all years, all lands,

For braver, stronger, more devoted men —
(a special laurel ere I go, to life's war's
chosen ones,
The cannoneers of song and thought — the
great artillerists — the foremost leaders,
captains of the soul:)
As soldier from an ended war return'd —
As traveler out of myriads, to the long
procession retrospective,
Thanks — joyful thanks! — a soldier's,
traveler's thanks.

1888.

MY 71ST YEAR

AFTER surmounting three-score and ten,
With all their chances, changes, losses, sorrows,
My parents' deaths, the vagaries of my
life, the many tearing passions of me,
the war of '63 and '4,
As some old broken soldier, after a long,
hot, wearying march, or haply after
battle,
To-day at twilight, hobbling, answering
company roll-call, *Here*, with vital voice,
Reporting yet, saluting yet the Officer over
all.

1891.

OLD AGE'S SHIP & CRAFTY DEATH'S

FROM east and west across the horizon's
edge,
Two mighty masterful vessels sailers steal
upon us:
But we 'll make race a-time upon the seas
— a battle-contest yet! bear lively
there!
(Our joys of strife and derring-do to the
last!)
Put on the old ship all her power to-day!
Crowd top-sail, top-gallant and royal stud-
ding-sails,
Out challenge and defiance — flags and
flaunting pennants added,
As we take to the open — take to the deepest, freest waters.

1891.

THE COMMONPLACE

THE commonplace I sing;
How cheap is health! how cheap nobility!

Abstinence, no falsehood, no gluttony, lust;
The open air I sing, freedom, toleration
(Take here the mainest lesson — less from
   books — less from the schools,)
The common day and night — the common
   earth and waters,
Your farm — your work, trade, occupation,
The democratic wisdom underneath, like
   solid ground for all.

1891.

L. OF G.'S PURPORT

Not to exclude or demarcate, or pick out
   evils from their formidable masses (even
   to expose them),
But add, fuse, complete, extend — and
   celebrate the immortal and the good.

Haughty this song, its words and scope,
To span vast realms of space and time,
Evolution — the cumulative — growths and
   generations.

Begun in ripen'd youth and steadily pursued,
Wandering, peering, dallying with all —
   war, peace, day and night absorbing,
Never even for one brief hour abandoning
   my task,
I end it here in sickness, poverty, and old
   age.

I sing of life, yet mind me well of death:
To-day shadowy Death dogs my steps, my
   seated shape, and has for years —
Draws sometimes close to me, as face to
   face.

1891.

THE UNEXPRESS'D

How dare one say it ?
After the cycles, poems, singers, plays,
Vaunted Ionia's, India's — Homer, Shakspere — the long, long times' thick dotted
   roads, areas,
The shining clusters and the Milky Ways
   of stars — Nature's pulses reap'd,
All retrospective passions, heroes, war,
   love, adoration,
All ages' plummets dropt to their utmost
   depths,
All human lives, throats, wishes, brains —
   all experiences' utterance;

After the countless songs, or long or short,
   all tongues, all lands,
Still something not yet told in poesy's voice
   or print — something lacking,
(Who knows ? the best yet unexpress'd and
   lacking.)

1891.

GOOD–BYE MY FANCY!

Good-bye my Fancy !
Farewell dear mate, dear love !
I 'm going away, I know not where,
Or to what fortune, or whether I may ever
   see you again,
So Good-bye my Fancy.

Now for my last — let me look back a
   moment;
The slower fainter ticking of the clock is
   in me,
Exit, nightfall, and soon the heart-thud
   stopping.

Long have we lived, joy'd, caress'd together;
Delightful ! — now separation — Good-bye
   my Fancy.

Yet let me not be too hasty,
Long indeed have we lived, slept, filter'd,
   become really blended into one;
Then if we die we die together (yes, we 'll
   remain one),
If we go anywhere we 'll go together to
   meet what happens,
May-be we 'll be better off and blither, and
   learn something,
May-be it is yourself now really ushering
   me to the true songs, (who knows ?)
May-be it is you the mortal knob really
   undoing, turning — so now finally,
Good-bye — and hail ! my Fancy.

1891.

DEATH'S VALLEY

To accompany a picture; by request. ' The Valley of
the Shadow of Death,' from the painting by George
Inness.

Nay, do not dream, designer dark,
Thou hast portray'd or hit thy theme entire;

I, hoverer of late by this dark valley, by
its confines, having glimpses of it,
Here enter lists with thee, claiming my
right to make a symbol too.
For I have seen many wounded soldiers
die,
After dread suffering — have seen their
lives pass off with smiles;
And I have watch'd the death-hours of the
old; and seen the infant die;
The rich, with all his nurses and his doctors;
And then the poor, in meagreness and
poverty;
And I myself for long, O Death, have
breath'd my every breath
Amid the nearness and the silent thought
of thee.

And out of these and thee,
I make a scene, a song (not fear of thee,
Nor gloom's ravines, nor bleak, nor dark
— for I do not fear thee,
Nor celebrate the struggle, or contortion,
or hard-tied knot),
Of the broad blessed light and perfect air,
with meadows, rippling tides, and trees
and flowers and grass,
And the low hum of living breeze — and
in the midst God's beautiful eternal right
hand,
Thee, holiest minister of Heaven — thee,
envoy, usherer, guide at last of all,
Rich, florid, loosener of the stricture-knot
call'd life,
Sweet, peaceful, welcome Death.

1896. (1897.)

SIDNEY LANIER

[The poems from Lanier are printed by the kind permission of Mrs. Sidney Lanier, and of Messrs. Charles Scribner's Sons, the authorized publishers of Lanier's Works.]

THE DYING WORDS OF STONE-WALL JACKSON

'Order A. P. Hill to prepare for battle.'
'Tell Major Hawks to advance the Commissary train.'
'Let us cross the river and rest in the shade.'

THE stars of Night contain the glittering
            Day
And rain his glory down with sweeter grace
Upon the dark World's grand, enchanted
            face —
        All loth to turn away.

And so the Day, about to yield his breath,
Utters the stars unto the listening Night,
To stand for burning fare-thee-wells of
            light
        Said on the verge of death.

O hero-life that lit us like the sun !
O hero-words that glittered like the stars
And stood and shone above the gloomy
            wars
        When the hero-life was done !

The phantoms of a battle came to dwell
I' the fitful vision of his dying eyes —
Yet even in battle-dreams, he sends sup-
            plies
        To those he loved so well.

His army stands in battle-line arrayed:
His couriers fly: all 's done: now God de-
            cide !
— And not till then saw he the Other Side
        Or would accept the shade.

Thou Land whose sun is gone, thy stars
            remain !
Still shine the words that miniature his
            deeds.
O thrice-beloved, where'er thy great heart
            bleeds,
        Solace hast thou for pain !

1865.   1884.

NIGHT AND DAY

THE innocent, sweet Day is dead.
Dark Night hath slain her in her bed.
O, Moors are as fierce to kill as to wed !
    — Put out the light, said he.

A sweeter light than ever rayed
From star of heaven or eye of maid
Has vanished in the unknown Shade.
    — She 's dead, she 's dead, said he.

Now, in a wild, sad after-mood
The tawny Night sits still to brood
Upon the dawn-time when he wooed.
    — I would she lived, said he.

Star-memories of happier times,
Of loving deeds and lovers' rhymes,
Throng forth in silvery pantomimes.
    — Come back, O Day ! said he.

1866.   1884.

SONG FOR 'THE JACQUERIE'[1]

THE hound was cuffed, the hound was
            kicked,
O' the ears was cropped, o' the tail was
            nicked,
(*All.*)   Oo-hoo-o, howled the hound.
The hound into his kennel crept;
He rarely wept, he never slept.

[1] One of Lanier's early plans was for a long poem in heroic couplets, with lyric interludes, on the insurrection of the French peasantry in the fourteenth century. 'Although,' says Mrs. Lanier, ' "The Jacquerie" remained a fragment for thirteen years, Mr. Lanier's interest in the subject never abated. Far on in this interval he is found planning for leisure to work out in romance the story of that savage insurrection of the French peasantry, which the Chronicles of Froissart had impressed upon his boyish imagination.' 'It was the first time,' says Lanier himself, in a letter of November 15, 1874, 'that the big hungers of *the People* appear in our modern civilization ; and it is full of significance.' Five chapters of the story, and three lyrics, were completed. See the *Poems*, pp. 191-214.

His mouth he always open kept
  Licking his bitter wound,
    The hound,
(*All.*)   U-lu-lo, *howled the hound.*

A star upon his kennel shone
That showed the hound a meat-bare bone.
(*All.*)   O hungry was the hound !
The hound had but a churlish wit.
He seized the bone, he crunched, he bit.
' An thou wert Master, I had slit
  Thy throat with a huge wound,'
    Quo' hound.
(*All.*)   O, angry was the hound.

The star in castle-window shone,
The Master lay abed, alone.
(*All.*)   Oh ho, why not ? quo' hound.
He leapt, he seized the throat, he tore
The Master, head from neck, to floor,
And rolled the head i' the kennel door,
  And fled and salved his wound,
    Good hound !
(*All.*)   U-lu-lo, *howled the hound.*
1868.   1884.

MY SPRINGS

IN the heart of the Hills of Life, I know
Two springs that with unbroken flow
Forever pour their lucent streams
Into my soul's far Lake of Dreams.

Not larger than two eyes, they lie
Beneath the many-changing sky
And mirror all of life and time,
— Serene and dainty pantomime.

Shot through with lights of stars and dawns,
And shadowed sweet by ferns and fawns,   10
— Thus heaven and earth together vie
Their shining depths to sanctify.

Always when the large Form of Love
Is hid by storms that rage above,
I gaze in my two springs and see
Love in his very verity.

Always when Faith with stifling stress
Of grief hath died in bitterness,
I gaze in my two springs and see
A Faith that smiles immortally.   20

Always when Charity and Hope,
In darkness bounden, feebly grope,

I gaze in my two springs and see
A Light that sets my captives free.

Always, when Art on perverse wing
Flies where I cannot hear him sing,
I gaze in my two springs and see
A charm that brings him back to me.

When Labor faints, and Glory fails.
And coy Reward in sighs exhales,   30
I gaze in my two springs and see
Attainment full and heavenly.

O Love, O Wife, thine eyes are they,
— My springs from out whose shining gray
Issue the sweet celestial streams
That feed my life's bright Lake of Dreams.

Oval and large and passion-pure
And gray and wise and honor-sure;
Soft as a dying violet-breath
Yet calmly unafraid of death;   40

Thronged, like two dove-cotes of gray
      doves,
With wife's and mother's and poor-folk's
      loves,
And home-loves and high glory-loves
And science-loves and story-loves,

And loves for all that God and man
In art and nature make or plan,
And lady-loves for spidery lace
And broideries and supple grace

And diamonds and the whole sweet round
Of littles that large life compound,   50
And loves for God and God's bare truth,
And loves for Magdalen and Ruth,

Dear eyes, dear eyes and rare complete —
Being heavenly-sweet and earthly-sweet,
— I marvel that God made you mine,
For when He frowns, 't is then ye shine !
1874.   1882.

THE SYMPHONY [1]

'O TRADE ! O Trade ! would thou wert
      dead !
The Time needs heart — 't is tired of
      head:

---

[1] I have so many fair dreams and hopes about music
in these days. It is a gospel whereof the people are in
great need. As Christ gathered up the ten command-

We 're all for love,' the violins said.[1]
' Of what avail the rigorous tale
Of bill for coin and box for bale ?
Grant thee, O Trade ! thine uttermost hope:
Level red gold with blue sky-slope,
And base it deep as devils grope:
When all 's done, what hast thou won
Of the only sweet that 's under the sun ? 10
Ay, canst thou buy a single sigh
Of true love's least, least ecstasy ? '
Then, with a bridegroom's heart-beats
 trembling,
All the mightier strings assembling
Ranged them on the violins' side
As when the bridegroom leads the bride,
And, heart in voice, together cried:
' Yea, what avail the endless tale
Of gain by cunning and plus by sale ?
Look up the land, look down the land, 20
The poor, the poor, the poor, they stand
Wedged by the pressing of Trade's hand
Against an inward-opening door
That pressure tightens evermore:
They sigh a monstrous foul-air sigh
For the outside leagues of liberty,
Where Art, sweet lark, translates the sky
Into a heavenly melody.
" Each day, all day " (these poor folks say),
" In the same old year-long, drear-long
 way, 30
We weave in the mills and heave in the
 kilns,
We sieve mine-meshes under the hills,
And thieve much gold from the Devil's
 bank tills,
To relieve, O God, what manner of ills ? —
The beasts, they hunger, and eat, and die;
And so do we, and the world 's a sty;
Hush, fellow-swine: why nuzzle and cry ?
Swinehood hath no remedy
Say many men, and hasten by,
Clamping the nose and blinking the eye. 40
But who said once, in the lordly tone,
Man shall not live by bread alone
But all that cometh from the Throne ?
Hath God said so ?
But Trade saith *No :*

ments and re-distilled them into the clear liquid of that
wondrous eleventh — Love God utterly, and thy neighbor as thyself — so I think the time will come when
music, rightly developed to its now-little-foreseen grandeur, will be found to be a later revelation of all gospels
in one. (LANIER, in a letter of March 12, 1875. *The
Letters of Sidney Lanier,* p. 113.)

[1] Music . . . is utterly unconscious of aught but
Love. (LANIER, in a letter of October, 1866. *The Letters
of Sidney Lanier,* p. 66.)

And the kilns and the curt-tongued mills
 say *Go !*
There 's plenty that can, if you can't: we
 know.
Move out, if you think you 're underpaid.
The poor are prolific ; we 're not afraid ;
Trade is trade." ' 50
Thereat this passionate protesting
Meekly changed, and softened till
It sank to sad requesting
And suggesting sadder still:
' And oh, if men might sometime see
How piteous-false the poor decree
That trade no more than trade must be !
Does business mean, *Die, you — live, I ?*
Then " Trade is trade " but sings a lie:
'T is only war grown miserly. 60
If business is battle, name it so:
War-crimes less will shame it so,
And widows less will blame it so.
Alas, for the poor to have some part
In yon sweet living lands of Art,
Makes problem not for head, but heart.
Vainly might Plato's brain revolve it:
Plainly the heart of a child could solve it.'

And then, as when from words that seem
 but rude
We pass to silent pain that sits abroad 70
Back in our heart's great dark and solitude,
So sank the strings to gentle throbbing
Of long chords change-marked with sob-
 bing —
Motherly sobbing, not distinctlier heard
Than half wing-openings of the sleeping
 bird,
Some dream of danger to her young hath
 stirred.
Then stirring and demurring ceased, and lo !
Every least ripple of the strings' song-flow
Died to a level with each level bow
And made a great chord tranquil-surfaced
 so, 80
As a brook beneath his curving bank doth
 go
To linger in the sacred dark and green
Where many boughs the still pool overlean
And many leaves make shadow with their
 sheen.
 But presently
A velvet flute-note fell down pleasantly
Upon the bosom of that harmony,
And sailed and sailed incessantly,
As if a petal from a wild-rose blown
Had fluttered down upon that pool of tone

And boatwise dropped o' the convex side 91
And floated down the glassy tide
And clarified and glorified
The solemn spaces where the shadows bide.
From the warm concave of that fluted
note
Somewhat, half song, half odor, forth did
float,
As if a rose might somehow be a throat:
' When Nature from her far-off glen
Flutes her soft messages to men,
 The flute can say them o'er again; 100
 Yea, Nature, singing sweet and lone,
Breathes through life's strident polyphone
The flute-voice in the world of tone.
 Sweet friends,
 Man's love ascends
To finer and diviner ends
Than man's mere thought e'er compre-
hends
For I, e'en I,
As here I lie,
A petal on a harmony, 110
Demand of Science whence and why
Man's tender pain, man's inward cry,
When he doth gaze on earth and sky ?
I am not overbold:
 I hold
Full powers from Nature manifold.
I speak for each no-tonguèd tree
That, spring by spring, doth nobler be,
And dumbly and most wistfully
His mighty prayerful arms outspreads 120
Above men's oft-unheeding heads,
And his big blessing downward sheds.
I speak for all-shaped blooms and leaves,
Lichens on stones and moss on eaves,
Grasses and grains in ranks and sheaves ;
Broad-fronded ferns and keen-leaved canes,
And briery mazes bounding lanes,
And marsh-plants, thirsty-cupped for rains,
And milky stems and sugary veins;
For every long-armed woman-vine 130
That round a piteous tree doth twine;
For passionate odors, and divine
Pistils, and petals crystalline;
All purities of shady springs,
All shynesses of film-winged things
That fly from tree-trunks and bark-rings;
All modesties of mountain-fawns
That leap to covert from wild lawns,
And tremble if the day but dawns;
All sparklings of small beady eyes 140
Of birds, and sidelong glances wise
Wherewith the jay hints tragedies;

All piquancies of prickly burs,
And smoothnesses of downs and furs,
Of eiders and of minevers;
All limpid honeys that do lie
At stamen-bases, nor deny
The humming-birds' fine roguery,
Bee-thighs, nor any butterfly;
All gracious curves of slender wings, 150
Bark-mottlings, fibre-spiralings,
Fern-wavings and leaf-flickerings;
Each dial-marked leaf and flower-bell
Wherewith in every lonesome dell
Time to himself his hours doth tell;
All tree-sounds, rustlings of pine-cones,
Wind-sighings, doves' melodious moans,
And night's unearthly under-tones;
All placid lakes and waveless deeps,
All cool reposing mountain-steeps, 160
Vale-calms and tranquil lotos-sleeps; —
Yea, all fair forms, and sounds, and lights,
And warmths, and mysteries, and mights,
Of Nature's utmost depths and heights,
— These doth my timid tongue present,
Their mouthpiece and leal instrument
And servant, all love-eloquent.
I heard, when "All for love" the violins
cried:
So, Nature calls through all her system
wide,
Give me thy love, O man, so long denied. 170
Much time is run, and man hath changed
his ways,
Since Nature, in the antique fable-days,
Was hid from man's true love by proxy
fays,
False fauns and rascal gods that stole her
praise.
The nymphs, cold creatures of man's colder
brain;
Chilled Nature's streams till man's warm
heart was fain
Never to lave its love in them again.
Later, a sweet Voice Love thy neighbor said,
Then first the bounds of neighborhood out-
spread
Beyond all confines of old ethnic dread. 180
Vainly the Jew might wag his covenant
head:
"All men are neighbors," so the sweet Voice
said.
So, when man's arms had circled all man's
race,
The liberal compass of his warm embrace
Stretched bigger yet in the dark bounds of
space;

With hands a-grope he felt smooth Nature's
    grace,
Drew her to breast and kissed her sweet-
    heart face:
Yea, man found neighbors in great hills and
    trees
And streams and clouds and suns and birds
    and bees,
And throbbed with neighbor-loves in loving
    these.   190
But oh, the poor ! the poor ! the poor !
That stand by the inward-opening door
Trade's hand doth tighten ever more,
And sigh their monstrous foul-air sigh
For the outside hills of liberty,
Where Nature spreads her wild blue sky
For Art to make into melody !
Thou Trade ! thou king of the modern days !
    Change thy ways,
    Change thy ways;   200
Let the sweaty laborers file
    A little while,
    A little while,
Where Art and Nature sing and smile.
Trade ! is thy heart all dead, all dead ?
And hast thou nothing but a head ?
I 'm all for heart,' the flute-voice said,
And into sudden silence fled,
Like as a blush that while 't is red
Dies to a still, still white instead.   210

    Thereto a thrilling calm succeeds,
Till presently the silence breeds
A little breeze among the reeds
That seems to blow by sea-marsh weeds:
Then from the gentle stir and fret
Sings out the melting clarionet,
Like as a lady sings while yet
Her eyes with salty tears are wet.
'O Trade ! O Trade !' the Lady said,
'I too will wish thee utterly dead   220
If all thy heart is in thy head.
For O my God ! and O my God !
What shameful ways have women trod
At beckoning of Trade's golden rod !
Alas when sighs are traders' lies,
And heart's-ease eyes and violet eyes
    Are merchandise !
O purchased lips that kiss with pain !
O cheeks coin-spotted with smirch and stain!
O trafficked hearts that break in twain! 230
— And yet what wonder at my sisters'
    crime ?
So hath Trade withered up Love's sinewy
    prime,

Men love not women as in olden time.
Ah, not in these cold merchantable days
Deem men their life an opal gray, where
    plays
The one red Sweet of gracious ladies'-praise.
Now, comes a suitor with sharp prying
    eye —
Says, *Here, you Lady, if you 'll sell, I 'll buy:*
Come, heart for heart — a trade ? What !
    weeping ? why ?
Shame on such wooers' dapper mercery !
I would my lover kneeling at my feet 241
In humble manliness should cry, *O sweet!*
I know not if thy heart my heart will greet:
I ask not if thy love my love can meet:
Whate'er thy worshipful soft tongue shall say,
I 'll kiss thine answer, be it yea or nay :
I do but know I love thee, and I pray
To be thy knight until my dying day.
Woe him that cunning trades in hearts con-
    trives !
Base love good women to base loving
    drives.   250
If men loved larger, larger were our lives;
And wooed they nobler, won they nobler
    wives.'

There thrust the bold straightforward horn
To battle for that lady lorn,
With heartsome voice of mellow scorn,
Like any knight in knighthood's morn.
'Now comfort thee,' said he,
    ' Fair Lady.
For God shall right thy grievous wrong,
And man shall sing thee a true-love song,
Voiced in act his whole life long,   261
    Yea, all thy sweet life long,
    Fair Lady.
Where 's he that craftily hath said,
The day of chivalry is dead ?
I 'll prove that lie upon his head,
    Or I will die instead,
    Fair Lady.
Is Honor gone into his grave ?
Hath Faith become a caitiff knave,   270
And Selfhood turned into a slave
    To work in Mammon's cave,
    Fair Lady ?
Will Truth's long blade ne'er gleam again ?
Hath Giant Trade in dungeons slain
All great contempts of mean-got gain
    And hates of inward stain,
    Fair Lady ?
For aye shall name and fame be sold,
And place be hugged for the sake of gold,

And smirch-robed Justice feebly scold   281
   At Crime all money-bold,
      Fair Lady?
Shall self-wrapt husbands aye forget
Kiss-pardons for the daily fret
Wherewith sweet wifely eyes are wet —
   Blind to lips kiss-wise set —
      Fair Lady?
Shall lovers higgle, heart for heart,
Till wooing grows a trading mart   290
Where much for little, and all for part,
   Make love a cheapening art,
      Fair Lady?
Shall woman scorch for a single sin
That her betrayer may revel in,
And she be burnt, and he but grin
   When that the flames begin,
      Fair Lady?
Shall ne'er prevail the woman's plea,
We maids would far, far whiter be   300
If that our eyes might sometimes see
   Men maids in purity,
      Fair Lady?
Shall Trade aye salve his conscience-aches
With jibes at Chivalry's old mistakes —
The wars that o'erhot knighthood makes
   For Christ's and ladies' sakes,
      Fair Lady?
Now by each knight that e'er hath prayed
To fight like a man and love like a maid, 310
Since Pembroke's life, as Pembroke's blade,
   I' the scabbard, death, was laid,
      Fair Lady,
I dare avouch my faith is bright
That God doth right and God hath might.
Nor mine hath changed His hair to white,
   Nor His dear love to spite,
      Fair Lady.
I doubt no doubts: I strive, and shrive my
   clay,
And fight my fight in the patient modern
   way   320
For true love and for thee — ah me! and
   pray
   To be thy knight until my dying day,
      Fair Lady.'
Made end that knightly horn, and spurred
   away
Into the thick of the melodious fray.

And then the hautboy played and smiled,
And sang like any large-eyed child,
Cool-hearted and all undefiled.
   'Huge Trade!' he said,
 'Would thou wouldst lift me on thy head

And run where'er my finger led!   33[...]
Once said a Man — and wise was He —
Never shalt thou the heavens see,
Save as a little child thou be.'
Then o'er sea-lashings of commingling
   tunes
The ancient wise bassoons,
   Like weird
   Gray-beard
Old harpers sitting on the high sea-dunes,
   Chanted runes: 340
'Bright-waved gain, gray-waved loss,
The sea of all doth lash and toss,
One wave forward and one across:
But now 't was trough, now 't is crest,
And worst doth foam and flash to best,
   And curst to blest.

'Life! Life! thou sea-fugue, writ from
   east to west,
   Love, Love alone can pore
   On thy dissolving score
   Of harsh half-phrasings,   350
      Blotted ere writ,
   And double erasings
      Of chords most fit.
Yea, Love, sole music-master blest,
May read thy weltering palimpsest.
To follow Time's dying melodies through,
And never to lose the old in the new,
And ever to solve the discords true —
   Love alone can do.
And ever Love hears the poor-folks' cry-
   ing,   360
And ever Love hears the women's sighing,
And ever sweet knighthood's death-defy-
   ing,
And ever wise childhood's deep implying,
But never a trader's glozing and lying.

'And yet shall Love himself be heard,
Though long deferred, though long de[...]
   ferred:
O'er the modern waste a dove hath whirred:
Music is Love in search of a word.'
1875.   1875.

EVENING SONG

Look off, dear Love, across the sallow
   sands,
   And mark yon meeting of the sun and
      sea,
How long they kiss in sight of all the lands.
   Ah! longer, longer, we.

Now in the sea's red vintage melts the
    sun,
  As Egypt's pearl dissolved in rosy wine,
And Cleopatra night drinks all. 'T is done,
  Love, lay thine hand in mine.

Come forth, sweet stars, and comfort
    heaven's heart;
  Glimmer, ye waves, round else unlighted
    sands.
O night ! divorce our sun and sky apart
  Never our lips, our hands.
1876.   1877.

THE WAVING OF THE CORN [1]

PLOUGHMAN, whose gnarly hand yet
    kindly wheeled
Thy plough to ring this solitary tree
 · With clover, whose round plat, reserved
    a-field,
In cool green radius twice my length may
    be —
  Scanting the corn thy furrows else might
    yield,
To pleasure August, bees, fair thoughts,
    and me,
    That here come oft together — daily I,
    Stretched prone in summer's mortal
      ecstasy,
Do stir with thanks to thee, as stirs this
    morn
    With waving of the corn.   10

Unseen, the farmer's boy from round the
    hill
Whistles a snatch that seeks his soul un-
    sought,
  And fills some time with tune, howbeit
    shrill;
The cricket tells straight on his simple
    thought —
  Nay, 't is the cricket's way of being still;
The peddler bee drones in, and gossips
    naught;
    Far down the wood, a one-desiring
    dove
    Times me the beating of the heart of
      love:
And these be all the sounds that mix, each
    morn,
    With waving of the corn.   20

[1] Compare the *Letters of Sidney Lanier*, p. 172, letter
from Bayard Taylor.

From here to where the louder passions
    dwell,
Green leagues of hilly separation roll:
  Trade ends where yon far clover ridges
    swell.
Ye terrible Towns, ne'er claim the trem-
    bling soul
  That, craftless all to buy or hoard or sell,
From out your deadly complex quarrel
    stole
    To company with large amiable trees,
    Suck honey summer with unjealous
      bees,
And take Time's strokes as softly as this
    morn
    Takes waving of the corn.   30
1876.   1877.

SONNETS ON COLUMBUS

FROM THE PSALM OF THE WEST

. . . .

COLUMBUS stands in the night alone, and,
    passing grave,
  Yearns o'er the sea as tones o'er under-
    silence yearn.
Heartens his heart as friend befriends his
    friend less brave,
  Makes burn the faiths that cool, and
    cools the doubts that burn: —

I

' 'Twixt this and dawn, three hours my
    soul will smite
With prickly seconds, or less tolerably
With dull-blade minutes flatwise slapping
    me.
Wait, Heart ! Time moves. — Thou lithe
    young Western Night,
Just-crownèd king, slow riding to thy right,
Would God that I might straddle mu-
    tiny   10
Calm as thou sitt'st yon never-managed
    sea,
Balk'st with his balking, fliest with his
    flight,
Giv'st supple to his rearings and his falls,
Nor dropp'st one coronal star about thy
    brow
    Whilst ever dayward thou art steadfast
    drawn !
Yea, would I rode these mad contentious
    brawls

No damage taking from their If and How,
Nor no result save galloping to my Dawn !

II

'My Dawn ? my Dawn ? How if it never
    break ?
How if this West by other Wests is
    pieced,   20
And these by vacant Wests on Wests in-
    creased —
One Pain of Space, with hollow ache on
    ache
Throbbing and ceasing not for Christ's own
    sake ? —
Big perilous theorem, hard for king and
    priest:
    Pursue the West but long enough, 't is
       East !
Oh, if this watery world no turning take !
Oh, if for all my logic, all my dreams,
Provings of that which is by that which
    seems,
Fears, hopes, chills, heats, hastes, patiences,
    droughts, tears,
Wife-grievings, slights on love, embezzled
    years,   30
Hates, treaties, scorns, upliftings, loss and
    gain, —
This earth, no sphere, be all one sickening
    plane !

III

' Or, haply, how if this contrarious West,
That me by turns hath starved, by turns
    hath fed,
Embraced, disgraced, beat back, solicited,
Have no fixed heart of Law within his
    breast,
Or with some different rhythm doth e'er
    contest
Nature in the East ? Why, 't is but three
    weeks fled
I saw my Judas needle shake his head
And flout the Pole that, east, he Lord con-
    fessed !   40
God ! if this West should own some other
    Pole,
And with his tangled way perplex my
    soul
Until the maze grow mortal, and I die
Where distraught Nature clean hath gone
    astray,
On earth some other wit than Time's at
    play,
Some other God than mine above the sky !

IV

' Now speaks mine other heart with cheer-
    ier seeming :
Ho, Admiral ! o'er-defalking to thy crew
Against thyself, thyself far overfew
To front yon multitudes of rebel scheming ? 50
Come, ye wild twenty years of heavenly
    dreaming !
Come, ye wild weeks since first this canvas
    drew
Out of vexed Palos ere the dawn was
    blue,
O'er milky waves about the bows full-
    creaming !
Come set me round with many faithful
    spears
Of confident remembrance — how I crushed
Cat-lived rebellions, pitfalled treasons,
    hushed
Scared husbands' heart-break cries on dis-
    tant wives,
Made cowards blush at whining for their
    lives,
Watered my parching souls, and dried their
    tears.   60

V

' Ere we Gomera cleared, a coward cried,
Turn, turn : here be three caravels ahead,
From Portugal, to take us : we are dead !
Hold Westward, pilot, calmly I replied.
So when the last land down the horizon
    died,
Go back, go back ! they prayed : our hearts
    are lead. —
Friends, we are bound into the West, I
    said.
Then passed the wreck of a mast upon our
    side.
See (so they wept) *God's Warning ! Admi-*
    ral, turn ! —
Steersman, I said, *hold straight into the*
    West.   70
Then down the night we saw the meteor
    burn.
So do the very heavens in fire protest :
Good Admiral, put about ! O Spain, dear
    Spain ! —
Hold straight into the West, I said again.

VI

' Next drive we o'er the slimy-weeded
    sea.
Lo ! herebeneath (another coward cries)
The cursèd land of sunk Atlantis lies:

*This slime will suck us down — turn while
 thou 'rt free ! —*
But no ! I said, Freedom bears West for me !
Yet when the long-time stagnant winds
 arise,   80
And day by day the keel to westward flies,
My Good my people's Ill doth come to
 be:
Ever the winds into the West do blow ;
*Never a ship, once turned, might homeward
 go ;*
Meanwhile we speed into the lonesome main.
*For Christ's sake, parley, Admiral ! Turn,
 before*
*We sail outside all bounds of help from
 pain ! —*
Our help is in the West, I said once more.

VII

'So when there came a mighty cry of
 Land !
And we clomb up and saw, and shouted
 strong   90
Salve Regina ! all the ropes along,
But knew at morn how that a counterfeit
 band
Of level clouds had aped a silver strand;
So when we heard the orchard-bird's small
 song,
And all the people cried, *A hellish throng
To tempt us onward by the Devil planned,
Yea, all from hell — keen heron, fresh green
 weeds,
Pelican, tunny-fish, fair tapering reeds,
Lie-telling lands that ever shine and die
In clouds of nothing round the empty sky.* 100
*Tired Admiral, get thee from this hell, and
 rest ! —*
Steersman, I said, *hold straight into the West.*

VIII

'I marvel how mine eye, ranging the Night,
From its big circling ever absently
Returns, thou large low Star, to fix on
 thee.
Maria ! Star ? No star: a Light, a Light !
Would'st leap ashore, Heart ? Yonder burns
 — a Light.
Pedro Gutierrez, wake ! come up to me.
I prithee stand and gaze about the sea:
What seest ? *Admiral, like as Land — a
 Light !*   110
Well ! Sanchez of Segovia, come and try :
What seest ? *Admiral, naught but sea and
 sky !*

Well ! But *I* saw It. Wait ! the Pinta's
 gun !
Why, look, 't is dawn, the land is clear :
 't is done !
Two dawns do break at once from Time's
 full hand —
God's, East — mine, West : good friends,
 behold my Land ! '
1876.   1876.

TO BEETHOVEN

IN o'er-strict calyx lingering,
 Lay music's bud too long unblown,
Till thou, Beethoven, breathed the spring :
 Then bloomed the perfect rose of tone.

O Psalmist of the weak, the strong,
 O Troubadour of love and strife,
Co-Litanist of right and wrong,
 Sole Hymner of the whole of life,

I know not how, I care not why, —
 Thy music sets my world at ease,   10
And melts my passion's mortal cry
 In satisfying symphonies.

It soothes my accusations sour
 'Gainst thoughts that fray the restless
  soul:
The stain of death; the pain of power;
 The lack of love 'twixt part and whole;

The yea-nay of Freewill and Fate,
 Whereof both cannot be, yet are;
The praise a poet wins too late
 Who starves from earth into a star; 20

The lies that serve great parties well,
 While truths but give their Christ a
  cross;
The loves that send warm souls to hell,
 While cold-blood neuters take no loss;

Th' indifferent smile that nature's grace
 On Jesus, Judas, pours alike;
Th' indifferent frown on nature's face
 When luminous lightnings strangely
  strike

The sailor praying on his knees   29
 And spare his mate that 's cursing God;
How babes and widows starve and freeze,
 Yet Nature will not stir a clod;

Why Nature blinds us in each act
  Yet makes no law in mercy bend,
No pitfall from our feet retract,
  No storm cry out, *Take shelter, friend;*

Why snakes that crawl the earth should ply
  Rattles, that whoso hears may shun,
While serpent lightnings in the sky,
  But rattle when the deed is done;   40

How truth can e'er be good for them
  That have not eyes to bear its strength,
And yet how stern our lights condemn
  Delays that lend the darkness length;

To know all things, save knowingness;
  To grasp, yet loosen, feeling's rein;
To waste no manhood on success;
  To look with pleasure upon pain;

Though teased by small mixt social claims,
  To lose no large simplicity, ·   50
And midst of clear-seen crimes and shames
  To move with manly purity;

To hold, with keen, yet loving eyes,
  Art's realm from Cleverness apart,
To know the Clever good and wise,
  Yet haunt the lonesome heights of Art;

O Psalmist of the weak, the strong,
  O Troubadour of love and strife,
Co-Litanist of right and wrong,
  Sole Hymner of the whole of life,   60

I know not how, I care not why,
  Thy music brings this broil at ease,
And melts my passion's mortal cry
  In satisfying symphonies.

Yea, it forgives me all my sins,
  Fits life to love like rhyme to rhyme,
And tunes the task each day begins
  By the last trumpet-note of Time.
1876-77.   *1877.*

THE MOCKING BIRD

SUPERB and sole, upon a plumèd spray
That o'er the general leafage boldly grew,
He summ'd the woods in song; or typic drew
The watch of hungry hawks, the lone dismay
Of languid doves when long their lovers stray,

And all birds' passion-plays that sprinkle dew
At morn in brake or bosky avenue.
Whate'er birds did or dreamed, this bird could say.
Then down he shot, bouncèd airily along
The sward, twitched in a grasshopper, made song
Midflight, perched, prinked, and to his art again.
Sweet Science, this large riddle read me plain:
How may the death of that dull insect be
The life of yon trim Shakspere on the tree?[1]

                            1877.

TAMPA ROBINS

THE robin laughed in the orange-tree:
'Ho, windy North, a fig for thee:
While breasts are red and wings are bold
And green trees wave us globes of gold,
  Time's scythe shall reap but bliss for me
  — Sunlight, song, and the orange-tree.

'Burn, golden globes in leafy sky,
My orange-planets: crimson I
Will shine and shoot among the spheres
(Blithe meteor that no mortal fears)
  And thrid the heavenly orange-tree
  With orbits bright of minstrelsy.

'If that I hate wild winter's spite —
The gibbet trees, the world in white,
The sky but gray wind over a grave —
Why should I ache, the season's slave?
  I'll sing from the top of the orange-tree
  Gramercy, winter's tyranny.

'I'll south with the sun, and keep my clime;
My wing is king of the summer-time;
My breast to the sun his torch shall hold;
And I'll call down through the green and gold
  Time, take thy scythe, reap bliss for me,
  Bestir thee under the orange-tree.'
1877.   *1877.*

      1 ... Yon trim Shakspere on the tree

leads back, almost twenty years from its writing, to
the poet's college note-book, where we find the boy reflecting: 'A poet is the mocking-bird of the spiritual
universe. In him are collected all the individual songs
of all individual natures.' (Mrs. LANIER, note, in the
Poems, 1884.)

FROM THE FLATS

WHAT heartache — ne'er a hill!
Inexorable, vapid, vague and chill
The drear sand-levels drain my spirit low.
With one poor word they tell me all they
      know;
Whereat their stupid tongues, to tease my
      pain,
Do drawl it o'er again and o'er again.
They hurt my heart with griefs I cannot
      name :
      Always the same, the same.

Nature hath no surprise,
No ambuscade of beauty 'gainst mine eyes
From brake or lurking dell or deep defile;
No humors, frolic forms — this mile, that
      mile;
No rich reserves or happy-valley hopes
Beyond the bend of roads, the distant slopes.
Her fancy fails, her wild is all run tame:
      Ever the same, the same.

Oh, might I through these tears
But glimpse some hill my Georgia high
      uprears,
Where white the quartz and pink the pebble
      shine,
The hickory heavenward strives, the mus-
      cadine
Swings o'er the slope, the oak's far-falling
      shade
Darkens the dogwood in the bottom glade,
And down the hollow from a ferny nook
Lull sings a little brook !

1877.   1877.

THE STIRRUP-CUP

DEATH, thou 'rt a cordial old and rare:
Look how compounded, with what care !
Time got his wrinkles reaping thee
Sweet herbs from all antiquity.

David to thy distillage went,
Keats, and Gotama excellent,
Omar Khayyám, and Chaucer bright,
And Shakspere for a king-delight.

Then, Time, let not a drop be spilt:
Hand me the cup whene'er thou wilt;
'T is thy rich stirrup-cup to me;
I 'll drink it down right smilingly.

1877.   1877.

SONG OF THE CHATTAHOO-CHEE

OUT of the hills of Habersham,
      Down the valleys of Hall,
I hurry amain to reach the plain,
Run the rapid and leap the fall,
Split at the rock and together again,
Accept my bed, or narrow or wide,
And flee from folly on every side
With a lover's pain to attain the plain
      Far from the hills of Habersham,
      Far from the valleys of Hall.   10

All down the hills of Habersham,
      All through the valleys of Hall,
The rushes cried *Abide, abide,*
The willful waterweeds held me thrall,
The laving laurel turned my tide,
The ferns and the fondling grass said *Stay,*
The dewberry dipped for to work delay,
And the little reeds sighed *Abide, abide,*
      Here in the hills of Habersham,
      Here in the valleys of Hall.   20

High o'er the hills of Habersham,
      Veiling the valleys of Hall,
The hickory told me manifold
Fair tales of shade, the poplar tall
Wrought me her shadowy self to hold,
The chestnut, the oak, the walnut, the
      pine,
Overleaning, with flickering meaning and
      sign,
Said, *Pass not, so cold, these manifold*
      Deep shades of the hills of Habersham,
      These glades in the valleys of Hall.   30

And oft in the hills of Habersham,
      And oft in the valleys of Hall,
The white quartz shone, and the smooth
      brook-stone
Did bar me of passage with friendly brawl,
And many a luminous jewel lone
— Crystals clear or a-cloud with mist,
Ruby, garnet and amethyst —
Made lures with the lights of streaming
      stone
      In the clefts of the hills of Habersham,
      In the beds of the valleys of Hall.   40

But oh, not the hills of Habersham,
      And oh, not the valleys of Hall
Avail: I am fain for to water the plain.
Downward the voices of Duty call —

Downward, to toil and be mixed with the
    main,
The dry fields burn, and the mills are to
    turn,
And a myriad flowers mortally yearn,
And the lordly main from beyond the plain
        Calls o'er the hills of Habersham,
        Calls through the valleys of Hall.   50
1877.   1877.

THE MARSHES OF GLYNN [1]

GLOOMS of the live-oaks, beautiful-braided
    and woven
With intricate shades of the vines that my-
    riad-cloven
    Clamber the forks of the multiform
        boughs, —
            Emerald twilights, —
            Virginal shy lights,
Wrought of the leaves to allure to the
    whisper of vows,
When lovers pace timidly down through
    the green colonnades
Of the dim sweet woods, of the dear dark
    woods,
Of the heavenly woods and glades,
That run to the radiant marginal sand-beach
    within   10
    The wide sea-marshes of Glynn; —

Beautiful glooms, soft dusks in the noon-
    day fire, —
Wildwood privacies, closets of lone desire,
Chamber from chamber parted with waver-
    ing arras of leaves, —
Cells for the passionate pleasure of prayer
    to the soul that grieves,
Pure with a sense of the passing of saints
    through the wood,
Cool for the dutiful weighing of ill with
    good; —

O braided dusks of the oak and woven
    shades of the vine,
While the riotous noon-day sun of the June-
    day long did shine
Ye held me fast in your heart and I held
    you fast in mine;   20

But now when the noon is no more, and
    riot is rest,
And the sun is a-wait at the ponderous gate
    of the West,
And the slant yellow beam down the wood-
    aisle doth seem
Like a lane into heaven that leads from a
    dream, —
Ay, now, when my soul all day hath drunken
    the soul of the oak,
And my heart is at ease from men, and the
    wearisome sound of the stroke
    Of the scythe of time and the trowel of
        trade is low,
    And belief overmasters doubt, and I know
        that I know,
    And my spirit is grown to a lordly great
        compass within,
That the length and the breadth and the
    sweep of the Marshes of Glynn   30
Will work me no fear like the fear they
    have wrought me of yore
When length was fatigue, and when breadth
    was but bitterness sore,
And when terror and shrinking and dreary
    unnamable pain
Drew over me out of the merciless miles of
    the plain, —

Oh, now, unafraid, I am fain to face
The vast sweet visage of space.
To the edge of the wood I am drawn, I am
    drawn,
Where the gray beach glimmering runs,
    as a belt of the dawn,
    For a mete and a mark
        To the forest-dark: —   4
            So:
Affable live-oak, leaning low, —
Thus — with your favor — soft, with a rev
    erent hand
(Not lightly touching your person, Lord of
    the land !),
Bending your beauty aside, with a step I
    stand
On the firm-packed sand,
        Free
By a world of marsh that borders a world
    of sea.
    Sinuous southward and sinuous northward
        the shimmering band
    Of the sand-beach fastens the fringe of
        the marsh to the folds of the land. 50
Inward and outward to northward and south-
    ward the beach-lines linger and curl

As a silver-wrought garment that clings to
    and follows the firm sweet limbs of
    a girl.
Vanishing, swerving, evermore curving
    again into sight,
Softly the sand-beach wavers away to a dim
    gray looping of light.
And what if behind me to westward the
    wall of the woods stands high ?
The world lies east: how ample, the marsh
    and the sea and the sky !
A league and a league of marsh-grass, waist-
    high, broad in the blade,
Green, and all of a height, and unflecked
    with a light or a shade,
Stretch leisurely off, in a pleasant plain,
To the terminal blue of the main.   60

Oh, what is abroad in the marsh and the
    terminal sea ?
    Somehow my soul seems suddenly free
From the weighing of fate and the sad
    discussion of sin,
By the length and the breadth and the
    sweep of the marshes of Glynn.

Ye marshes, how candid and simple and no-
    thing-withholding and free
Ye publish yourselves to the sky and offer
    yourselves to the sea !
Tolerant plains, that suffer the sea and the
    rains and the sun,
Ye spread and span like the catholic man
    who hath mightily won
God out of knowledge and good out of
    infinite pain
And sight out of blindness and purity out
    of a stain.   70

As the marsh-hen secretly builds on the
    watery sod,
Behold I will build me a nest on the great-
    ness of God:
I will fly in the greatness of God as the
    marsh-hen flies
In the freedom that fills all the space
    'twixt the marsh and the skies:
By so many roots as the marsh-grass sends
    in the sod
I will heartily lay me a-hold on the great-
    ness of God:
Oh, like to the greatness of God is the
    greatness within
The range of the marshes, the liberal
    marshes of Glynn.

And the sea lends large, as the marsh: lo,
    out of his plenty the sea
Pours fast: full soon the time of the flood-
    tide must be: 80
Look how the grace of the sea doth go
About and about through the intricate
    channels that flow
        Here and there,
            Everywhere,
Till his waters have flooded the uttermost
    creeks and the low-lying lanes,
And the marsh is meshed with a million
    veins,
That like as with rosy and silvery essences
    flow
    In the rose-and-silver evening glow.
        Farewell, my lord Sun !
The creeks overflow: a thousand rivulets
    run   90
'Twixt the roots of the sod; the blades of
    the marsh-grass stir;
Passeth a hurrying sound of wings that
    westward whirr;
Passeth, and all is still; and the currents
    cease to run;
And the sea and the marsh are one.

How still the plains of the waters be !
The tide is in his ecstasy.
The tide is at his highest height:
        And it is night.

And now from the Vast of the Lord will
    the waters of sleep
Roll in on the souls of men,   100
But who will reveal to our waking ken
The forms that swim and the shapes that
    creep
        Under the waters of sleep ?
And I would I could know what swimmeth
    below when the tide comes in
On the length and the breadth of the mar-
    vellous marshes of Glynn.
1878.   1878.

THE REVENGE OF HAMISH

It was three slim does and a ten-tined buck
    in the bracken lay;
    And all of a sudden the sinister smell of
    a man,
Awaft on a wind-shift, wavered and ran
Down the hillside and sifted along through
    the bracken and passed that way.

Then Nan got a-tremble at nostril; she was
   the daintiest doe;
  In the print of her velvet flank on the
    velvet fern
  She reared, and rounded her ears in turn.
Then the buck leapt up, and his head as a
   king's to a crown did go

Full high in the breeze, and he stood as if
   Death had the form of a deer;
  And the two slim does long lazily stretch-
    ing arose,   10
  For their day-dream slowlier came to a
    close,
Till they woke and were still, breath-bound
   with waiting and wonder and fear.

Then Alan the huntsman sprang over the
   hillock, the hounds shot by,
  The does and the ten-tined buck made a
    marvellous bound,
  The hounds swept after with never a
    sound,
But Alan loud winded his horn in sign that
   the quarry was nigh.

For at dawn of that day proud Maclean of
   Lochbuy to the hunt had waxed
   wild,
  And he cursed at old Alan till Alan fared
    off with the hounds
  For to drive him the deer to the lower
    glen-grounds:
'I will kill a red deer,' quoth Maclean,
   'in the sight of the wife and the
   child.'   20

So gayly he paced with the wife and the
   child to his chosen stand;
  But he hurried tall Hamish the hench-
    man ahead: 'Go turn,' —
  Cried Maclean, — 'if the deer seek to
    cross to the burn,
Do thou turn them to me: nor fail, lest thy
   back be red as thy hand.'

Now hard-fortuned Hamish, half blown of
   his breath with the height of the
   hill,
  Was white in the face when the ten-tined
    buck and the does
  Drew leaping to burn-ward; huskily rose
His shouts, and his nether lip twitched, and
   his legs were o'er-weak for his
   will.

So the deer darted lightly by Hamish and
   bounded away to the burn.
  But Maclean never bating his watch tar-
    ried waiting below;   30
  Still Hamish hung heavy with fear for
    to go
All the space of an hour; then he went, and
   his face was greenish and stern,

And his eye sat back in the socket, and
   shrunken the eye-balls shone,
  As withdrawn from a vision of deeds it
    were shame to see.
'Now, now, grim henchman, what is 't
   with thee?'
Brake Maclean, and his wrath rose red as
   a beacon the wind hath upblown.

'Three does and a ten-tined buck made
   out,' spoke Hamish, full mild,
'And I ran for to turn, but my breath it
   was blown, and they passed;
  I was weak, for ye called ere I broke me
    my fast.'
Cried Maclean: 'Now a ten-tined buck in
   the sight of the wife and the child 40

I had killed if the gluttonous kern had not
   wrought me a snail's own wrong!'
  Then he sounded, and down came kins-
    men and clansmen all:
'Ten blows, for ten tine, on his back let
   fall,
And reckon no stroke if the blood follow
   not at the bite of thong!'

So Hamish made bare, and took him his
   strokes; at the last he smiled.
'Now I'll to the burn,' quoth Maclean,
   'for it still may be,
  If a slimmer-paunched henchman will
    hurry with me,
I shall kill me the ten-tined buck for a gift
   to the wife and the child!'

Then the clansmen departed, by this path
   and that; and over the hill
  Sped Maclean with an outward wrath for
    an inward shame;   50
  And that place of the lashing full quiet
    became;
And the wife and the child stood sad; and
   bloody-backed Hamish sat still.

But look! red Hamish has risen; quick
   about and about turns he.

'There is none betwixt me and the crag-
  top !' he screams under breath.
Then, livid as Lazarus lately from death,
He snatches the child from the mother, and
  clambers the crag toward the sea.

Now the mother drops breath; she is dumb,
  and her heart goes dead for a space,
Till the motherhood, mistress of death,
  shrieks, shrieks through the glen,
And that place of the lashing is live with
  men,
And Maclean, and the gillie that told him,
  dash up in a desperate race.   60

Not a breath's time for asking; an eye-
  glance reveals all the tale untold.
They follow mad Hamish afar up the
  crag toward the sea,
  And the lady cries: 'Clansmen, run for
    a fee !
Yon castle and lands to the two first hands
  that shall hook him and hold

'Fast Hamish back from the brink !' — and
  ever she flies up the steep,
  And the clansmen pant, and they sweat,
    and they jostle and strain.
But, mother, 't is vain; but, father, 't is
  vain;
Stern Hamish stands bold on the brink, and
  dangles the child o'er the deep.

Now a faintness falls on the men that run,
  and they all stand still.
  And the wife prays Hamish as if he were
    God, on her knees,   70
    Crying: 'Hamish ! O Hamish ! but please,
      but please
For to spare him !' and Hamish still dangles
  the child, with a wavering will.

On a sudden he turns; with a sea-hawk
  scream, and a gibe, and a song,
  Cries: 'So; I will spare ye the child if, in
    sight of ye all,
  Ten blows on Maclean's bare back shall
    fall,
And ye reckon no stroke if the blood follow
  not at the bite of the thong !'

Then Maclean he set hardly his tooth to his
  lip that his tooth was red,
  Breathed short for a space, said: 'Nay,
    but it never shall be !

Let me hurl off the damnable hound in
  the sea !'
But the wife: 'Can Hamish go fish us the
  child from the sea, if dead ?   80

'Say yea ! — Let them lash me, Hamish ?'
  — 'Nay !' — 'Husband, the lashing
    will heal;
  But, oh, who will heal me the bonny
    sweet bairn in his grave ?
  Could ye cure me his heart with the
    death of a knave ?
Quick ! Love ! I will bare thee — so —
  kneel !' Then Maclean 'gan slowly
    to kneel

With never a word, till presently down-
  ward he jerked to the earth.
  Then the henchman — he that smote
    Hamish — would tremble and lag;
  'Strike, hard !' quoth Hamish, full stern,
    from the crag;
Then he struck him, and 'One !' sang
  Hamish, and danced with the child
    in his mirth.

And no man spake beside Hamish; he
  counted each stroke with a song.
  When the last stroke fell, then he moved
    him a pace down the height,   90
  And he held forth the child in the heart-
    aching sight
Of the mother, and looked all pitiful grave,
  as repenting a wrong.

And there as the motherly arms stretched
  out with the thanksgiving prayer —
  And there as the mother crept up with a
    fearful swift pace,
  Till her finger nigh felt of the bairn'e's
    face —
In a flash fierce Hamish turned round and
  lifted the child in the air,

And sprang with the child in his arms from
  the horrible height in the sea,
  Shrill screeching, 'Revenge !' in the
    wind-rush; and pallid Maclean,
  Age-feeble with anger and impotent pain,
Crawled up on the crag, and lay flat, and
  locked hold of dead roots of a tree,

And gazed hungrily o'er, and the blood
  from his back drip-dripped in the
    brine,   101

And a sea-hawk flung down a skeleton
  fish as he flew,
And the mother stared white on the
  waste of blue,
And the wind drove a cloud to seaward,
  and the sun began to shine.
1878.   1878.

HOW LOVE LOOKED FOR HELL [1]

To heal his heart of long-time pain
One day Prince Love for to travel was
  fain
    With Ministers Mind and Sense.
' Now what to thee most strange may be ? '
Quoth Mind and Sense. ' All things above,
One curious thing I first would see —
    Hell,' quoth Love.

Then Mind rode in and Sense rode out:
They searched the ways of man about.
    First frightfully groaneth Sense.   10
' 'T is here, 't is here,' and spurreth in fear
To the top of the hill that hangeth above
And plucketh the Prince : ' Come, come,
  't is here — '
    ' Where ? ' quoth Love —

' Not far, not far,' said shivering Sense
As they rode on. ' A short way hence,
    — But seventy paces hence:
Look, King, dost see where suddenly
This road doth dip from the height above ?
Cold blew a mouldy wind by me '   20
    (' Cold ? ' quoth Love)

' As I rode down, and the River was black,
And yon-side, lo ! an endless wrack
    And rabble of souls,' sighed Sense,
' Their eyes upturned and begged and
  burned
In brimstone lakes, and a Hand above
Beat back the hands that upward
  yearned — '
    ' Nay ! ' quoth Love —

' Yea, yea, sweet Prince ; thyself shalt see,
Wilt thou but down this slope with me;   30
    'T is palpable,' whispered Sense.
At the foot of the hill a living rill
Shone, and the lilies shone white above;

' But now 't was black, 't was a river, this
  rill,'
    (' Black ? ' quoth Love)

' Ay, black, but lo ! the lilies grow,
And yon-side where was woe, was woe, —
    Where the rabble of souls,' cried
  Sense,
' Did shrivel and turn and beg and burn,
Thrust back in the brimstone from above —
Is banked of violet, rose, and fern: '   41
    ' How ? ' quoth Love:

' For lakes of pain, yon pleasant plain
Of woods and grass and yellow grain
    Doth ravish the soul and sense:
And never a sigh beneath the sky,
And folk that smile and gaze above ' —
' But saw'st thou here, with thine own
  eye,
    Hell ? ' quoth Love.

' I saw true hell with mine own eye,   50
True hell, or light hath told a lie,
    True, verily,' quoth stout Sense.
Then Love rode round and searched the
  ground,
The caves below, the hills above;
' But I cannot find where thou hast found
    Hell,' quoth Love.

There, while they stood in a green wood
And marvelled still on Ill and Good,
    Came suddenly Minister Mind.
' In the heart of sin doth hell begin: 6
'T is not below, 't is not above,
It lieth within, it lieth within: '
    (' Where ? ' quoth Love)

' I saw a man sit by a corse;
Hell 's in the murderer's breast : remorse !
    Thus clamored his mind to his mind:
Not fleshly dole is the sinner's goal,
Hell 's not below, nor yet above,
'T is fixed in the ever-damnèd soul ' —
    ' Fixed ? ' quoth Love —   70

' Fixed: follow me, would'st thou but see:
He weepeth under yon willow tree,
    Fast chained to his corse,' quoth
  Mind.
Full soon they passed, for they rode fast,
Where the piteous willow bent above.
' Now shall I see at last, at last,
    Hell,' quoth Love.

[1] This poem is quoted, with interesting comment, in
Professor Josiah Royce's *Spirit of Modern Philosophy.*
In Lanier's *Poems* this is No. iii of ' Street-Cries.'

There when they came Mind suffered
    shame:
'These be the same and not the same,'
A-wondering whispered Mind.   80
Lo, face by face two spirits pace
Where the blissful willow waves above:
One saith: 'Do me a friendly grace' —
    ('Grace!' quoth Love)

'Read me two Dreams that linger long,
Dim as returns of old-time song
    That flicker about the mind.
I dreamed (how deep in mortal sleep!)
I struck thee dead, then stood above,
With tears that none but dreamers weep;'
    'Dreams,' quoth Love;   91

In dreams, again, I plucked a flower
That clung with pain and stung with
    power,
    Yea, nettled me, body and mind.'
''T was the nettle of sin, 't was medicine;
No need nor seed of it here Above;
In dreams of hate true loves begin.'
    'True,' quoth Love.

'Now strange,' quoth Sense, and 'Strange,'
    quoth Mind,
'We saw it, and yet 't is hard to find,   100
    — But we saw it,' quoth Sense and
    Mind.
Stretched   on   the   ground,   beautiful-
    crowned
Of the piteous willow that wreathed above,
'But I cannot find where ye have found
    Hell,' quoth Love.
1878-79.   1884.

TO BAYARD TAYLOR[1]

To range, deep-wrapt, along a heavenly
    height,
    O'erseeing all that man but under-
    sees;
To loiter down lone alleys of delight,
    And hear the beating of the hearts of
    trees,

[1] On Lanier's friendship with Bayard Taylor, see
Professor Mims's *Lanier* and the *Letters of Sidney
Lanier,* pp. 117-215.
    Lanier's beautiful picture of the Elysium of the
Poets should be compared with Richard Hovey's, in
'Seaward: a Threnody on the Death of Thomas William
Parsons.'

And think the thoughts that lilies speak in
    white
    By greenwood pools and pleasant pas-
    sages;

With healthy dreams a-dream in flesh and
    soul,
    To pace, in mighty meditations drawn,
From out the forest to the open knoll
    Where much thyme is, whence blissful
    leagues of lawn   10
Betwixt the fringing woods to southward
    roll
    By tender inclinations; mad with dawn,

Ablaze with fires that flame in silver dew
    When each small globe doth glass the
    morning-star,
Long ere the sun, sweet-smitten through
    and through
    With dappled revelations read afar,
Suffused with saintly ecstasies of blue
    As all the holy eastern heavens are, —

To fare thus fervid to what daily toil
    Employs thy spirit in that larger Land   20
Where thou art gone; to strive, but not to
    moil
    In nothings that do mar the artist's hand,
Not drudge unriched, as grain rots back to
    soil, —
    No profit out of death, — going, yet still
    at stand, —

Giving what life is here in hand to-day
    For that that 's in to-morrow's bush, per-
    chance, —
Of this year's harvest none in the barn to lay,
    All sowed for next year's crop, — a dull
    advance
In curves that come but by another way
    Back to the start, — a thriftless thrift of
    ants   30

Whose winter wastes their summer; O my
    Friend,
    Freely to range, to muse, to toil, is thine:
Thine, now, to watch with Homer sails that
    bend
    Unstained by Helen's beauty o'er the
    brine
Tow'rds some clean Troy no Hector need
    defend
    Nor flame devour; or, in some mild
    moon's shine,

Where amiabler winds the whistle heed,
  To sail with Shelley o'er a bluer sea,
And mark Prometheus, from his fetters
    freed,
  Pass with Deucalion over Italy,   40
While bursts the flame from out his eager
    reed
  Wild-stretching towards the West of
    destiny;

Or, prone with Plato, Shakspere, and a
    throng
  Of bards beneath some plane-tree's cool
    eclipse
To gaze on glowing meads where, lingering
    long,
  Psyche's large Butterfly her honey sips;
Or, mingling free in choirs of German
    song,
  To learn of Goethe's life from Goethe's
    lips;

These, these are thine, and we, who still are
    dead,
  Do yearn — nay, not to kill thee back
    again   50
Into this charnel life, this lowlihead,
  Not to the dark of sense, the blinking
    brain,
The hugged delusion drear, the hunger fed
  On husks of guess, the monarchy of pain,

The cross of love, the wrench of faith, the
    shame
  Of science that cannot prove proof is, the
    twist
Of blame for praise and bitter praise for
    blame,
  The silly stake and tether round the
    wrist
By fashion fixed, the virtue that doth claim
  The gains of vice, the lofty mark that 's
    missed   60

By all the mortal space 'twixt heaven and
    hell,
  The soul's sad growth o'er stationary
    friends
Who hear us from our height not well, not
    well,
  The slant of accident, the sudden bends
Of purpose tempered strong, the gambler's
    spell,
  The son's disgrace, the plan that e'er
    depends

On others' plots, the tricks that passion
    plays
  (I loving you, you him, he none at all),
The artist's pain — to walk his blood-stained
  · ways,
  A special soul, yet judged as general —
The endless grief of art, the sneer that
    slays,   71
  The war, the wound, the groan, the fu-
    neral pall —

Not into these, bright spirit, do we yearn
  To bring thee back, but oh, to be, to be
Unbound of all these gyves, to stretch, to
    spurn
  The dark from off our dolorous lids, to
    see
Our spark, Conjecture, blaze and sunwise
    burn,
  And suddenly to stand again by thee !

Ah, not for us, not yet, by thee to stand:
  For us, the fret, the dark, the thorn, the
    chill;   80
For us, to call across unto thy Land,
  'Friend, get thee to the minstrels' holy
    hill,
And kiss those brethren for us, mouth and
    hand,
  And make our duty to our master Will.'
1879.   1879.

MARSH SONG — AT SUNSET

OVER the monstrous shambling sea,
  Over the Caliban sea,
Bright Ariel-cloud, thou lingerest:
Oh wait, oh wait, in the warm red West, —
  Thy Prospero I 'll be.

Over the humped and fishy sea,
  Over the Caliban sea
O cloud in the West, like a thought in the
    heart
Of pardon, loose thy wing, and start,
  And do a grace for me.

Over the huge and huddling sea,
  Over the Caliban sea,
Bring hither my brother Antonio, — Man, —
My injurer: night breaks the ban:
  Brother, I pardon thee.
1879-80.   1882.

SUNRISE [1]

In my sleep I was fain of their fellowship,
        fain
    Of the live-oak, the marsh, and the
        main.
The little green leaves would not let me
    alone in my sleep;
Up-breathed from the marshes, a message
    of range and of sweep,
Interwoven with waftures of wild sea-
    liberties, drifting,
    Came through the lapped leaves sifting,
        sifting,
    Came to the gates of sleep.
Then my thoughts, in the dark of the
    dungeon-keep
Of the Castle of Captives hid in the City
    of Sleep,
Upstarted, by twos and by threes assem-
    bling: 10
    The gates of sleep fell a-trembling
Like as the lips of a lady that forth falter
    yes,
        Shaken with happiness:
    The gates of sleep stood wide.

I have waked, I have come, my beloved!
    I might not abide:
I have come ere the dawn, O beloved, my
    live-oaks, to hide
    In your gospelling glooms, — to be
As a lover in heaven, the marsh my marsh
    and the sea my sea.

Tell me, sweet burly-bark'd, man-bodied
    Tree
That mine arms in the dark are embracing,
    dost know   20
From what fount are these tears at thy feet
    which flow?
They rise not from reason, but deeper in-
    consequent deeps.
        Reason's not one that weeps.
    What logic of greeting lies

Betwixt dear over-beautiful trees and the
    rain of the eyes?

O cunning green leaves, little masters! like
    as ye gloss
All the dull-tissued dark with your lumi
    nous darks that emboss
The vague blackness of night into pattern
    and plan,
        So
(But would I could know, but would I
    could know),   30
With your question embroid'ring the dark
    of the question of man, —
So, with your silences purfling this silence
    of man
While his cry to the dead for some know-
    ledge is under the ban,
            Under the ban, —
        So, ye have wrought me
Designs on the night of our knowledge, —
    yea, ye have taught me,
        So,
    That haply we know somewhat more
        than we know.

    Ye lispers, whisperers, singers in storms,
    Ye consciences murmuring faiths un-
        der forms,   40
    Ye ministers meet for each passion
        that grieves,
    Friendly, sisterly, sweetheart leaves,
Oh, rain me down from your darks that
    contain me
Wisdoms ye winnow from winds that pain
    me, —
Sift down tremors of sweet-within-sweet
That advise me of more than they bring, —
    repeat
Me the woods-smell that swiftly but now
    brought breath
From the heaven-side bank of the river o'
    death, —
    Teach me the terms of silence, — preach
        me
    The passion of patience, — sift me, — im-
        peach me, —   50
            And there, oh there
As ye hang with your myriad palms up-
    turned in the air,
        Pray me a myriad prayer.

    My gossip, the owl, — is it thou
That out of the leaves of the low-hanging
    bough,

<hr/>

[1] 'Sunrise,' Mr. Lanier's latest completed poem, was
written while his sun of life seemed fairly at the setting, and the hand which first pencilled its lines had
not strength to carry nourishment to the lips. . . .
    'Sunrise,' the culminating poem, the highest vision
of Sidney Lanier, was dedicated through his latest request to that friend who indeed came into his life only
near its close, yet was at first meeting recognized by
the poet as 'the father of his spirit,' George Westfeldt.
When words were very few and the poem was unread,
even by any friend, the earnest bidding came: 'Send
him my "Sunrise," that he may know how entirely we
are one in thought.' (*Poems*, 1884.)

As I pass to the beach, art stirred?
Dumb woods, have ye uttered a bird?

. . . .

Reverend Marsh, low-couched along the sea,
Old chemist, rapt in alchemy,
   Distilling silence, — lo,   60
That which our father-age had died to
   know —
The menstruum that dissolves all matter
   — thou
Hast found it: for this silence, filling now
The globèd clarity of receiving space,
This solves us all: man, matter, doubt, dis-
   grace,
Death, love, sin, sanity,
Must in yon silence' clear solution lie.
Too clear! That crystal nothing who'll
   peruse?
The blackest night could bring us brighter
   news.
Yet precious qualities of silence haunt   70
Round these vast margins, ministrant.
Oh, if thy soul's at latter gasp for space,
With trying to breathe no bigger than thy
   race
Just to be fellow'd, when that thou hast
   found
No man with room, or grace enough of
   bound
To entertain that New thou tell'st, thou
   art, —
'T is here, 't is here thou canst unhand thy
   heart
And breathe it free, and breathe it free,
By rangy marsh, in lone sea-liberty.

The tide's at full: the marsh with flooded
   streams   80
Glimmers, a limpid labyrinth of dreams.
Each winding creek in grave entrancement
   lies
A rhapsody of morning-stars. The skies
Shine scant with one forked galaxy, —
The marsh brags ten: looped on his breast
   they lie.

Oh, what if a sound should be made!
Oh, what if a bound should be laid
To this bow-and-string tension of beauty
   and silence a-spring, —
To the bend of beauty the bow, or the hold
   of silence the string!
I fear me, I fear me yon dome of diapha-
   nous gleam   90

Will break as a bubble o'er-blown in a
   dream, —
Yon dome of too-tenuous tissues of space
   and of night,
Over-weighted with stars, over-freighted
   with light,
Over-sated with beauty and silence, will
   seem
But a bubble that broke in a dream,
If a bound of degree to this grace be
   laid,
Or a sound or a motion made.

But no: it is made: list! somewhere, —
   mystery, where?
            In the leaves? in the air?
In my heart? is a motion made: 100
'T is a motion of dawn, like a flicker of
   shade on shade.
In the leaves 't is palpable: low multitu-
   dinous stirring
Upwinds through the woods; the little ones,
   softly conferring,
Have settled my lord's to be looked for;
   so; they are still;
But the air and my heart and the earth are
   a-thrill, —
And look where the wild duck sails round
   the bend of the river, —
   And look where a passionate shiver
Expectant is bending the blades
Of the marsh-grass in serial shimmers and
   shades, —
And invisible wings, fast fleeting, fast
   fleeting,   110
            Are beating
The dark overhead as my heart beats, —
   and steady and free
Is the ebb-tide flowing from marsh to sea
   (Run home, little streams,
   With your lapfulls of stars and dreams),
And a sailor unseen is hoisting a-peak,
For list, down the inshore curve of the creek
   How merrily flutters the sail, —
And lo, in the East! Will the East unveil?
The East is unveiled, the East hath con-
   fessed   120
A flush: 't is dead; 't is alive: 't is dead, ere
   the West
Was aware of it: nay, 't is abiding, 't is un-
   withdrawn:
   Have a care, sweet Heaven! 'T is Dawn.

Now a dream of a flame through that dream
   of a flush is uprolled:

To the zenith ascending, a dome of un-
dazzling gold
Is builded, in shape as a bee-hive, from out
of the sea:
The hive is of gold undazzling, but oh, the
Bee,
The star-fed Bee, the build-fire Bee,
Of dazzling gold is the great Sun-
Bee
That shall flash from the hive-hole over the
sea. 130

Yet now the dew-drop, now the morning
gray,
Shall live their little lucid sober day ,
Ere with the sun their souls exhale
away.
Now in each pettiest personal sphere of
dew
The summ'd morn shines complete as in
the blue
Big dew-drop of all heaven: with these lit
shrines
O'er-silvered to the farthest sea-confines,
The sacramental marsh one pious plain
Of worship lies. Peace to the ante-reign
Of Mary Morning, blissful mother mild, 140
Minded of nought but peace, and of a
child.

Not slower than Majesty moves, for a mean
and a measure
Of motion, — not faster than dateless Olym-
pian leisure
Might pace with unblown ample garments
from pleasure to pleasure, —
The wave-serrate sea-rim sinks unjarring,
unreeling,
Forever revealing, revealing, reveal-
ing,
Edgewise, bladewise, halfwise, wholewise,
— 't is done !
Good-morrow, lord Sun !
With several voice, with ascription one,
The woods and the marsh and the sea and
my soul 150
Unto thee, whence the glittering stream of
all morrows doth roll,
Cry good and past-good and most heavenly
morrow, lord Sun.

O Artisan born in the purple, — Workman
Heat, —
Parter of passionate atoms that travail to
meet

And be mixed in the death-cold oneness, —
innermost Guest
At the marriage of elements, —fellow of
publicans, — blest
King in the blouse of flame, that loiterest
o'er
The idle skies yet laborest fast ever-
more, —
Thou, in the fine forge-thunder, thou, in the
beat
Of the heart of a man, thou Motive, —
Laborer Heat: 160
Yea, Artist, thou, of whose art yon sea 's all
news,
With his inshore greens and manifold mid-
sea blues,
Pearl-glint, shell-tint, ancientest perfectest
hues
Ever shaming the maidens, — lily and rose
Confess thee, and each mild flame that
glows
In the clarified virginal bosoms of stones
that shine,
It is thine, it is thine:

Thou chemist of storms, whether driving
the winds a-swirl
Or a-flicker the subtiler essences polar that
whirl
In the magnet earth, — yea, thou with a
storm for a heart, 170
Rent with debate, many-spotted with question, part
From part oft sundered, yet ever a globèd
light,
Yet ever the artist, ever more large and
bright
Than the eye of a man may avail of: —
manifold One,
I must pass from thy face, I must pass
from the face of the Sun:
Old Want is awake and agog, every wrinkle
a-frown;
The worker must pass to his work in the
terrible town:
But I fear not, nay, and I fear not the thing
to be done;
I am strong with the strength of my lord
the Sun:
How dark, how dark soever the race that
must needs be run, 180
I am lit with the Sun.

Oh, never the mast-high run of the seas
Of traffic shall hide thee,

Never the hell-colored smoke of the fac-
. tories
              Hide thee,
Never the reek of the time's fen-politics
              Hide thee,
And ever my heart through the night shall
    with knowledge abide thee,

And ever by day shall my spirit, as one
    that hath tried thee,
  Labor, at leisure, in art, — till yonder
      beside thee   190
  My soul shall float, friend Sun,
    The day being done.

December, 1880.   1882.

LIST OF REFERENCES

LIST OF REFERENCES [1]

BRYANT

EDITIONS

*THE LIFE AND WORKS OF WILLIAM CULLEN BRYANT, 6 volumes: vols. i and ii, Biography; vols. iii and iv, The Poetical Works; vols. v and vi, Prose Writings: D. Appleton & Co., 1883–84. (The standard edition, edited by Parke Godwin.) — *THE POETICAL WORKS, Roslyn Edition: D. Appleton & Co., 1903. (An excellent edition, complete — except the translations from Homer — in one volume; with chronologies, bibliography, etc.) — THE ILIAD OF HOMER, translated into English Blank Verse; THE ODYSSEY OF HOMER, translated into English Blank Verse: Roslyn Edition, 4 volumes; Students' Edition, 2 volumes: Houghton, Mifflin & Co.

BIOGRAPHY AND REMINISCENCES

*GODWIN (Parke), Biography of William Cullen Bryant, with extracts from his private correspondence, 1883. (The standard biography.) — *BIGELOW (John), William Cullen Bryant (American Men of Letters Series), 1890. — *BRADLEY (W. A.), Bryant (English Men of Letters Series), 1905.
BARTLETT (D. W.), Modern Agitators, or Pen Portraits of Living American Reformers, 1855. — BROWN (E. R.), The Life and Poems of John Howard Bryant, 1899. (Containing in the biographical sketch many allusions to William Cullen Bryant also.) — BUNGAY (George W.), Off-Hand Takings; or Crayon Sketches of the Noticeable Men of our Age: Biography of Bryant, 1854. — *CENTURY ASSOCIATION (N. Y.), The Bryant Festival at 'The Century,' Nov. 5, 1864. (An account of the celebration of Bryant's seventieth birthday, containing Lowell's poem On Board the Seventy-Six, poems by Holmes, Whittier, Bayard Taylor, George H. Boker, Thomas Buchanan Read, Julia Ward Howe, R. H. Stoddard, H. T. Tuckerman, etc., and addresses by Emerson, Bancroft, Samuel Osgood, etc.), 1865. — CENTURY ASSOCIATION (N. Y.), Bryant Memorial Meeting of the Century, Nov. 12, 1878. (Containing Stedman's The Death of Bryant, Bayard Taylor's Epicedium, R. H. Stoddard's The Dead Master, and an oration by John Bigelow.) — CUMMINGTON, Mass., Bryant Centennial Celebration. (Containing addresses by Parke Godwin, E. R. Brown, John Bigelow, Charles Dudley Warner, John White Chadwick, Charles Eliot Norton, G. Stanley Hall, etc., and poems by Julia Ward Howe and John H. Bryant), 1894. — *CURTIS (G. W.), Orations and Addresses, vol. iii: William Cullen Bryant: His Life, Character, and Writings. A Commemorative Address, Dec. 30, 1878. — DERBY (J. C.), Fifty Years among Authors, 1884. — FINLEY (John H.) and CALKINS (E. E.), The Bryant Centennial; a Book about a Day, Galesburg, 1894. — GODWIN (Parke), Commemorative Addresses. — GREER (F. H.), William Cullen Bryant, in Universal Biography of Men of Mark of the Nineteenth Century. — HAWTHORNE, Passages from French and Italian Note-Books: May 22, 1858. — HILL (D. J.), William Cullen Bryant (American Authors), 1879. — KIRKLAND (Mrs. C.), William Cullen Bryant: in Homes of American Authors, 1853; the same, in Little Journeys to the Homes of American Authors, 1896. — PALMER (Ray), Biography of Bryant, 1877. — POWERS (H. N.), William Cullen Bryant: in R. H. Stoddard's The Homes and Haunts of our Elder Poets. — SYMINGTON (A. J.), William Cullen Bryant, a biographical sketch, with selections, 1880. — TAYLOR (Mrs. Bayard), On Two Continents, 1905. — TUCKERMAN (H. T.), Thoughts on the Poets, 1846. — WALSH (William Shepard), Pen Pictures of Modern Authors, 1882. (Quotations from Hawthorne, John Bigelow, etc.) — WHITMAN, Specimen Days, June 13–14, 1878: Death of William Cullen Bryant. (Complete Prose Works, pp. 106–107.) — WILSON (J. G.), Bryant and his Friends: some reminiscences of the Knickerbocker writers, 1885. — *(The Diary of a Poet's Mother, a

---

[1] The more important books and essays are marked with an asterisk. For explanations regarding the arrangement of the Reference-Lists, see *Preface*.

daily record kept by Mrs. Bryant for fifty-three years, is announced for early publication; it is to be edited by Professor Richard Jones.)

CRITICISM

ALDEN (Joseph), Studies in Bryant, with an introduction by William Cullen Bryant. (An ele mentary school text, with questions on the poems.) — BURTON (R.), Literary Leaders. — CHENEY (J. V.), That Dome in Air. — *COLLINS (Churton), The Poetry and Poets of America. — HARTUNG (A. E. G.), Ueber Robert Burns poetische Episteln und über den nordamerikanischen Dichter William Cullen Bryant. — HOWE (M. A. DeW.), American Bookmen. — MATTHEWS (B.), Introduction to the Study of American Literature, chapter vi — MITCHELL (D. G.), American Lands and Letters. — NADAL (E. S.), Essays at Home and Elsewhere. — NEWCOMER (A. G.), American Literature. — NICHOL (John), American Literature, an Historical Sketch. — OSGOOD (Rev. Samuel), Bryant among his Countrymen: The Poet, the Patriot, the Man. — OTTO (W.), William Cullen Bryants poetische Werke und Uebersetzungen. — PALMER (G. H.), William Cullen Bryant : in Atlas Essays, New York, 1877. — PATTEE (Fred Lewis), History of American Literature. — POE (Edgar Allan), Works, Virginia Edition: vol. viii, pp. 1, 2, Poems, by William Cullen Bryant (January, 1835) ; vol. ix, pp. 268–305, Poems, by William Cullen Bryant, Fourth Edition (June, 1837) ; vol. x, pp. 85–96, A Notice of William Cullen Bryant (May, 1840) ; vol. xiii, pp. 125–141, William Cullen Bryant (April, 1846). — See also vol. xi, pp. 150, 194, 195, 223. — POET-LORE, How to Study Bryant's Thanatopsis, in Poet-Lore, vol. vi, pp. 520–526. — POWELL (Thomas), Living Authors of America, 1850. — RICHARDSON (C. F.), American Literature, vol. ii. — SAUNDERS (Frederic), Character Studies. — SHEPARD (W. S.), The Literary Life. — *STEDMAN (E. C.), Poets of America. — STEWART (George, Jr.), Evenings in the Library. — STODDARD (R. H.), Introduction to the 'Household' and 'Roslyn' editions. — TAYLOR (Bayard), Critical Essays and Literary Notes.— *THAYER (W. R.), Throne-makers and Portraits. — TRENT (W. P.), A History of American Literature. — VINCENT (L. H.), American Literary Masters, 1905. — WHIPPLE (E. P.), Literature and Life. — WHIPPLE (E. P.), Men of Mark.— *WHITMAN, Specimen Days, April 16, 1881 : My Tribute to Four Poets. (Complete Prose Works, pp. 173, 174.) — WILKINSON (W. C.), A Free Lance in the Field of Life and Letters : Mr. Bryant's Poetry. — WILSON (John), Essays, critical and imaginative : American Poetry, Bryant. (Originally in Blackwood's Magazine, 1832 ; vol. xxxi, pp. 646–664. A generous early appreciation of Bryant.) — WOODBERRY (G. E.), America in Literature, chapter ii.

TRIBUTES IN VERSE

BATES (Charlotte Fiske), Risk and Other Poems : The Poet's Birthplace ; The Poet's Death ; The Birthday after Death. — BOKER (G. H.), Bryant, Nov. 5, 1864.— *CHADWICK (J. W.), Later Poems, William Cullen Bryant : Read on the Hundredth Anniversary of his Birth. — HAYNE (Paul H.), Bryant Dead. — *HOLMES, Bryant's Seventieth Birthday. — HOWE (Julia Ward), A Leaf from the Bryant Chaplet. — *LOWELL, Fable for Critics. (Poetical Works, Cambridge Edition, pp. 131, 132.) — *LOWELL, On Board the Seventy-six. — READ (T. B.), To Bryant. — STEDMAN, The Death of Bryant. — *STODDARD (R. H.), Vates Patriae. — TAYLOR (Bayard), Epicedium, William Cullen Bryant.— TUCKERMAN (H. T.), To William Cullen Bryant on his Seventieth Birthday.— WHITTIER, To a Poetical Trio in the City of Gotham. (Satirical. Written in 1832. Poetical Works, Cambridge Edition, p. 510.) — *WHITTIER, Bryant on his Birthday, 1864.

POE

EDITIONS

*COMPLETE WORKS, Virginia Edition, 17 volumes (including Biography and Letters), edited by James A. Harrison : T. Y. Crowell & Co., 1902. (The standard edition, superseding all others, both by its completeness — especially in the section of criticism — and by its carefully edited text.) — WORKS, 4 volumes, edited, with a memoir, by R. W. Griswold, and with notices of Poe's life and genius by N. P. Willis and J. R. Lowell, New York, 1850–56, etc. (Badly arranged and unreliable. The Memoir in particular is not to be trusted.) — WORKS, 4 volumes, edited by John H. Ingram, Edinburgh, 1874–75, etc. (The best British edition.) — WORKS, 6 volumes, edited, with memoir, by R. H. Stoddard : New York, A. C. Armstrong & Son, 1884. (The memoir is unsatisfactory.) — *WORKS, 10 volumes, edited, with a memoir, critical introductions, and notes, by E. C. Stedman and G. E. Woodberry: Stone & Kimball, Chicago, 1894–95. — WORKS, 10 volumes, Knickerbocker Edition, with introduction by Charles F. Richardson: G. P. Putnam's Sons, New York, 1904.

THE RAVEN AND OTHER POEMS: Wiley & Putnam, New York, 1845. — POETICAL WORKS, with a notice of his life and genius, by James Hannay, London, 1852, etc. — POETICAL WORKS, with memoir by C. F. Briggs, London and New York, 1858, etc. — POEMS, with memoir by R. H. Stoddard, New York, 1872, etc. — POEMS, with an essay on his poetry by Andrew Lang, London, 1881, etc. — POEMS AND ESSAYS, edited, with memoir, by John H. Ingram, London, 1884. — POETICAL WORKS, Canterbury Poets' Edition, London, 1886. — THE RAVEN, THE FALL OF THE HOUSE OF USHER, AND OTHER POEMS AND TALES, edited by W. P. Trent, Riverside Literature Series, 1897. — THE BEST POEMS AND ESSAYS OF POE, edited, with a new biographical and critical study, by Sherwin Cody, 1903. — POEMS, edited by Charles W. Kent, Macmillan's Pocket Classics, 1904. — (There are many other one-volume editions of the poems, none of them to be fully trusted. Most of them follow the bad arrangement of the 1845 edition.)

BIOGRAPHY AND REMINISCENCES

See the Griswold, Hannay, Briggs, Ingram, Stoddard, Stedman-Woodberry, Lang, Richardson, Cody, and Kent editions mentioned above.

*HARRISON (J. A.), Life and Letters of Edgar Allan Poe, 2 volumes, 1903. (Also as vol. i and vol. xvii of the Virginia Edition of Poe's Works.) (The latest full biography. More than half of the Letters are here published for the first time.) — DIDIER (E. L.), The Life and Poems of Edgar Allan Poe, 1876. — INGRAM (John H.), Edgar Allan Poe, in Atlas Essays, no. 2, 1877. — GILL (W. F.), Life of Poe, London, 1878. — INGRAM (John H.), Edgar Allan Poe : His Life, Letters and Opinions. 2 volumes, London, 1880 ; second edition, 1 volume, 1886. (This biography is perhaps the fairest and best-balanced in its judgment of Poe, but is now somewhat out of date. In the second edition no account was taken of new facts brought out by Prof. Woodberry.) — *WOODBERRY (G. E.), Edgar Allan Poe (American Men of Letters Series), 1885. (The first life of Poe based on thorough investigation of the facts ; and still the best critically ; but unsympathetic.) — LAUVRIÈRE (E.), Edgar Poe, sa vie et son œuvre, 1904. (A thorough study ; emphasizing pathological considerations.) — *TRENT (W. P.), Edgar Allan Poe. (Soon to be published, in the English Men of Letters Series ; and likely to prove the best brief biography.)

BENTON (Joel), In the Poe Circle ; with some account of the Poe-Chivers controversy, and other Poe memorabilia, 1899. — DARGAN (Olive T.), Semiramis and Other Plays, 1904. (The third play, 'The Poet,' deals with Poe.) — GILDERSLEEVE (B. L.), Poe as a Lecturer : in Harrison's New Glimpses of Poe. — GRISWOLD (R. W.), Correspondence. — HARRISON (J. A.), New Glimpses of Poe, 1901. — KENT (Charles W.), The Unveiling of the Bust of Edgar Allan Poe in the Library of the University of Virginia, October 7, 1899 ; being an account of Poe's connection with the University of Virginia, etc. — MINOR (B. B.), The Southern Literary Messenger, 1834 to 1863, 1905. — MORAN (John J.), A Defense of Edgar Allan Poe, 1885. — RICE (Sara S.), Edgar Allan Poe : A Memorial Volume, 1877. — STODDARD (R. H.), Recollections, Personal and Literary, edited by Ripley Hitchcock, 1904. — WALSH (William Shepard), The Literary Life : Edgar Allan Poe. — WEISS (Susan A. T.), The Last Days of Edgar Allan Poe : in Scribner's, March, 1878. — WEISS (Susan A. T.), Reminiscences of Poe : in the Independent, May 5 and August 25, 1904 : vol. lvi, p. 1010 ; vol. lvii, p. 443. — *WHITMAN (Sarah Helen), Poe and his Critics, 1860 ; second edition, 1885. — WHITMAN (Walt), Specimen Days : Broadway Sights (Prose Works, p. 12.) — *WILLIS (N. P.), Hurrygraphs, 1851. (Also in Griswold's and other editions of Poe's Works.) — WILSON (J. G.), Bryant and his Friends. — WOODBERRY (G. E.), The Poe-Chivers Papers : in the Century, January and February, 1903 : vol. xliii, pp. 435–47, and 545–58. — NEWCOMER (A. G.), The Poe-Chivers Tradition reëxamined : in the Sewanee Review, January, 1904 : vol. xii, p. 20.

CRITICISM

BARBEY D'AUREVILLY (Jules), Littérature étrangère. — BARINE (Arvède) [Mme. Cécile Vincens], Névrosés : Hoffmann ; Quincey ; Edgar Poe ; Gérard de Nerval. — BARRETT (Elizabeth), in Horne's Letters of Elizabeth Barrett Browning, letter of May 12, 1845. — BAUDELAIRE (Charles), Edgar Poe, sa vie et ses œuvres : in his Histoires extraordinaires, translated from Poe. — BAUDELAIRE (Charles), Notes nouvelles : in his Nouvelles Histoires extraordinaires. —

BEERS (H. A.), Initial Studies in American Literature. — BENTON (Joel), Baudelaire and Poe : *in his* In the Poe Circle. — BETZ (L. P.), Poe in der französischen Litteratur. — BROWNING (E. B.), The Letters of Robert Browning and Elizabeth Barrett Browning : vol. i. p. 429. — BURTON (R.), Literary Leaders. — CHADWICK (J. W.), Poe : *in* Chambers's New Cyclopædia of English Literature, vol. iii. — COLLINS (Churton), The Poetry and Poets of America. — DESHLER (C. D.), Afternoons with Authors : Sonnets of Poe. — FRANCE (Anatole), La vie littéraire, vol. iv. — FRUIT (J. P.), The Mind and Art of Poe's Poetry. — FULLER-OSSOLI (Margaret), Life Without and Life Within. (A review of The Raven and other Poems, 1845.) — *GATES (L. E.), Studies and Appreciations. — *GOSSE (Edmund), Questions at Issue : Has America produced a poet ? — GRUENER (Gustav), Notes on the Influence of E. T. A. Hoffmann upon Edgar Allan Poe : *in the* Publications of the Modern Language Association, vol. xix, p. 1. — GRUENER (Gustav), Poe's Knowledge of German : *in* Modern Philology, vol. ii, p. 125. — HENNEQUIN (Émile), Écrivains francisés. — HOWE (M. A. DeW.), American Bookmen. — HUTTON (R. H.), Criticisms on Contemporary Thought and Thinkers. (Review of vol. i of Ingram's edition). — *KENT (C. W.), Poe the Poet. (Introduction to vol. vii of the Virginia Edition.) — LANG (A.), Letters to Dead Authors. — *LANG (A.), Preface to his edition of Poe's Poems, 1845. — LAWTON (W. C.), Introduction to the Study of American Literature. — LINTON (W. J.), Pot-pourri. (Parodies on Poe's poems, and — according to the author — definitive criticism on his work.) — LOWELL (J. R.), Edgar Allan Poe : *in* Graham's Magazine, February, 1845 ; reprinted in vol. iii of Griswold's edition of Poe's Works ; in vol. x of the Stedman-Woodberry Edition ; and in vol. i of the Virginia Edition. — *MABIE (H. W.), Poe's Place in American Literature. (Introduction to vol. ii of the Virginia Edition.) — MALLARMÉ (Stéphane), Divagations : Edgar Poe. — MATTHEWS (B.), Introduction to the Study of American Literature, chapter xii. — MATTHEWS (B.), Pen and Ink. (On the prose works.) — MAUCLAIR (Camille), L'art en silence : Edgar Poe idéologue. — MITCHELL (D. G.), American Lands and Letters, vol. ii. — MORE (P. E.), Shelburne Essays, First Series : The Origins of Hawthorne and Poe. — NENCIONI (E.), Letteratura inglese. (Review of Hennequin's essay.) — NICHOL (J.), American Literature, an historical study. — ONDERDONK (J. L.), History of American Verse. — *RICHARDSON (C. F.), American literature, vol. ii, chapter iv. — ROBERTSON (J. M.), New Essays towards a Critical Method : Poe. — SALT (H. S.), Literary Sketches. — *STEDMAN (E. C.), Poets of America. — *STEDMAN (E. C.), Introduction to vol. x of the Stedman-Woodberry edition of Poe's Works. — *SWINBURNE, Under the Microscope, pp. 54, 55. — TOLMAN (A. H.), The Views about Hamlet and other essays : Was Poe Accurate ? (Chiefly on ' The Gold Bug.') — TRENT (W. P.), A History of American Literature. — *TRENT (W. P.), Southern Writers : Introduction to the Selections from Poe. — VINCENT (L. H.), American Literary Masters. — WENDELL (B.), A Literary History of America. — WHITMAN, Specimen Days : Edgar Poe's Significance. (Complete Prose Works, p. 149.) — WOODBERRY (G. E.), America in Literature, chapter iv. — WYZEWA (T. de), Écrivains étrangers.

TRIBUTES IN VERSE

*BONER (John H.), Poe's Cottage at Fordham : *in the* Century, vol. xxxix, p. 85 ; *and in* Stedman's American Anthology, p. 487. — FAWCETT (Edgar), Edgar A. Poe : *in* Edgar Allan Poe, a Memorial Volume. — HAYNE (Paul H.), Poe : *in* Edgar Allan Poe, a Memorial Volume. — *LOWELL, A Fable for Critics. — MALLARMÉ (Stéphane), Vers et Prose : Le Tombeau d'Edgar Poe (Sonnet). — MALONE (Walter), Poems : Poe's Cottage at Fordham. — OSGOOD (Frances Sargent), Poems, 1850 : The Hand that Swept the Sounding Lyre. — *STOCKARD (A. J.), Fugitive Lines : Sonnets on Poe's Cottage. — *TABB (John B.), To Edgar Allan Poe : *in* The Unveiling of the Bust of Edgar Allan Poe. — TYRRELL (Henry), In the Ragged Mountains : *in* The Unveiling of the Bust of Edgar Allan Poe. — *WHITMAN (Sarah Helen), Poems, 1878, pp. 72–100, and 195–197. — WILSON (Robert Burns), Memorial Poem : *in* The Unveiling of the Bust of Edgar Allan Poe. — WINTER (William), At Poe's Grave : *in* Edgar Allan Poe, a Memorial Volume. — WINTER (William), The Wanderers : Poem read at the Dedication of the Actors' Monument to Poe.

EMERSON

EDITIONS

WORKS, Little Classic Edition, 12 volumes ; WORKS, Riverside Edition, 12 volumes ; *COMPLETE WORKS, Centenary Edition, 12 volumes : Houghton, Mifflin & Co. (In any of these editions the POEMS can be obtained separately in one volume. The *Centenary Edition has about fifty poems and fragments not contained in previous editions, and valuable notes by Dr. E. W. Emerson.) — POEMS, New Household Edition, 1 volume: Houghton, Mifflin & Co. — *CORRE-SPONDENCE OF CARLYLE AND EMERSON, 2 volumes. — CORRESPONDENCE OF JOHN STERLING AND EMERSON, 1 volume. — CORRESPONDENCE BETWEEN EMERSON AND HERMAN GRIMM, 1 volume. — *LETTERS FROM EMERSON TO A FRIEND, 1 volume. — SELECTED POEMS, edited by George H. Browne, Riverside Literature Series.

BIOGRAPHY AND REMINISCENCES

BOLTON (S. K.), Emerson (Chiswick Series).— *CABOT (J. E.), Memoir of Ralph Waldo Emerson, 2 volumes, 1887. (The authorized biography.) — CARY (E. L.), Ralph Waldo Emerson, Poet and Thinker, 1904. — *EMERSON (E. W.), Emerson in Concord: A Memoir. (Very important; a necessary supplement to Cabot's Memoir.)— GARNETT (Richard), Emerson (Great Writers Series).— HOLMES (O. W.), Ralph Waldo Emerson (American Men of Letters Series), 1885. — IRELAND (Alex.), Ralph Waldo Emerson: His Life, Genius, and Writings. Second Edition, augmented, 1882.— SANBORN (F. B.), Emerson (Beacon Biographies), 1901.

ALBEE (J.), Remembrances of Emerson, 1901. — ALCOTT (A. B.), Concord Days, 1872. — ALCOTT (A. B.), Emerson, 1865.— ALCOTT (A. B.), Ralph Waldo Emerson: An Estimate of his Character and Genius, in prose and verse, 1882. (Containing the preceding essay, and three poems.)— ALCOTT (A. B.), Ralph Waldo Emerson: Philosopher and Seer, 1888. (Identical with the preceding.)— ALCOTT (Louisa M.), Reminiscences of Ralph Waldo Emerson: in Parton's Some Noted Princes, Authors, and Statesmen, 1886. — BARTLETT (G. B.), Concord, Historic, Literary, and Picturesque.— *BREMER (Frederika), Homes of the New World; impressions of America. Translated by Mary Howitt, 1853.— BUNGAY (George W.), Off-Hand Takings, 1854. — CLARKE (Charles and Mary Cowden), Recollections of Writers: Emerson.— CLARKE (J. F.), Nineteenth Century Questions, 1897. — CONWAY (M. D.), Autobiography, Memories, and Experiences, 1904.— CONWAY (M. D.), Emerson at Home and Abroad.— COOKE (G. W.), Ralph Waldo Emerson: His Life, Writings, and Philosophy, 1881. — CURTIS (G. W.), Homes of American Authors, 1853; the same, in Little Journeys to the Homes of American Authors, 1896.— *CURTIS (G. W.), Literary and Social Essays.— CURTIS (G. W.), The Easy Chair: Emerson Lecturing.— FIELDS (Mrs. Annie), Authors and Friends, 1896. — FROTHINGHAM (O. B.), Memoir of William Henry Channing. — FROTHINGHAM (O. B.), Theodore Parker: A Biography, 1874. — GILMAN (Arthur), Poets' Homes. Pen and Pencil Sketches of American Poets and their Homes. Second Series, 1880. — GRISWOLD (H. T.), Home Life of Great Authors.— HALE (E. E.), Ralph Waldo Emerson; with two early essays of Emerson's, 1899.— HASKINS (D. G.), Ralph Waldo Emerson: His Maternal Ancestors; with Some Reminiscences of Emerson. — HAWTHORNE, Passages from the American Note-Books, 1868, vol. ii: Sept. 28, 1841; Aug. 5, 15, 22, Oct. 10, 1842; April 8, 11, 1843; May 14, 1850. — *HAWTHORNE, The Great Stone Face. — HAWTHORNE, Mosses from an Old Manse: The Old Manse. — HIGGINSON (T. W.), Contemporaries, 1899. — HOWE (Julia Ward), Reminiscences, 1819–1899, 1899.— IRELAND (Alex.), In Memoriam, Ralph Waldo Emerson.— LANDOR (W. S.), An Open Letter to Emerson: in Literary Anecdotes of the Nineteenth Century. — *LOWELL, Literary Essays: Emerson, the Lecturer. — MARTINEAU (Harriet), Autobiography, Period iv, Section iii. — ROBINSON (H. C.), Diary, vol. ii, chapter xxii. — SANBORN (F. B.), and HARRIS (W. T.), Life of A. Bronson Alcott, 1893. — SANBORN (F. B.), Emerson and his Friends in Concord, 1890.— SANBORN (F. B.), The Personality of Emerson, 1903.— SANBORN (F. B.), Ralph Waldo Emerson: in Stoddard's The Homes and Haunts of Our Elder Poets, 1881. — SCUDDER (H. E.), Men and Letters; Essays in Characterization and Criticism. Emerson's Self. — *STEARNS (F. P.), Sketches from Concord and Appledore: Emerson Himself. — THOREAU, Miscellanies. — TROWBRIDGE (J. T.), My Own Story, 1904. — WALSH (William Shepard), Pen Pictures of Modern Authors, 1882. (Quotations from N. P. Willis, Miss Bremer, and Hawthorne.)—WHIPPLE (E. P.), Recollections of Eminent Men.—*WHITMAN, Specimen Days: A Visit, at the Last, to Ralph Waldo Emerson; Boston Common — More of Emerson; By Emerson's Grave. (Complete Prose Works, pp. 181–184, 189–190.) — WILLIS (N. P.), Hurrygraphs, 1853.— WOLFE (T. F.), Literary Shrines; The Haunts of Some Famous American Authors, 1895.— *WOODBURY (C. J.), Talks with Ralph Waldo Emerson, 1890.

CRITICISM

AMES (Rev. C. G.), Memorial Address, April 30, 1882. — *ARNOLD, Discourses in America. — BARTOL (C. A.), Radical Problems: Transcendentalism. — BATES (Katharine Lee), American Literature. — *BEERS (H. A.), Points at Issue : Emerson's Transcendentalism. — BENTON (Joel), Emerson as a Poet.— BIJVANCK (W. G. C.), Poezie en leven in de 19de Eeuw : Emerson en Walt Whitman.— BIRRELL (Augustine), Obiter Dicta.— BURROUGHS (John), Birds and Poets, with Other Papers. — BURROUGHS (John), Emerson and the Superlative : in Essays from The Critic. — BURROUGHS (John), Indoor Studies : Matthew Arnold's View of Emerson. — BURTON (R.), Literary Leaders. — CHADWICK (J. W.), Emerson : in Chambers's New Cyclopædia of English Literature. — *CHAPMAN (John Jay), Emerson and Other Essays. — CHENEY (J. V.), That Dome in Air. — CONCORD, Mass., SOCIAL CIRCLE, The Centenary of the Birth of Ralph Waldo Emerson. — CROZIER (J. B.), The Religion of the Future.— DANA (W. F.), Optimism of Ralph Waldo Emerson. — DOWDEN (E.), Studies in Literature : The Transcendental Movement and Literature — EELLS (J.), Emerson. A Tribute, May 24, 1903.— ELIOT (C. W.), Emerson as Seer : in the Atlantic, June, 1903.— EVANS (E. P.), Beiträge zur amerikanischen Litteratur und Kulturgeschichte.— *EVERETT (C. C.), Essays Theological and Literary : The Poems of Emerson. — FEDERN (Karl), Essays zur amerikanischen Litteratur. — FORSTER (Joseph), Four Great Teachers.— FRANCKE (Kuno), Emerson and German Personality : in the International Quarterly, vol. viii, p. 93. — FRISWELL (J. H.), Modern Men of Letters Honestly Criticised. — FROTHING-HAM (O. B.), Transcendentalism in New England. — FROUDE (J. A.), Short Studies on Great Subjects, vol. iii : Representative Men. — FULLER-OSSOLI (Margaret), Life Without and Life Within : Emerson's Essays. — GARNETT (Richard), Essays of an ex-Librarian.— GIFFORD (Lord Adam), Lectures Delivered on Various Occasions.— GORDON (G. A.), Emerson as a Religious In-fluence : in the Atlantic, vol. xci, p. 577.— GRIERSON (Francis), The Celtic Temperament, and Other Essays. — *GRIMM (F. Hermann), Fünfzehn Essays, Erste Folge ; Ralph Waldo Emerson (Essay of 1861) ; same essay, in Neue Essays über Kunst und Litteratur.—GRIMM (F. Hermann), Fünfzehn Essays, Dritte Folge : Ralph Waldo Emerson. (Essay of 1882, on Emerson's Death.)— GRIMM (F. Hermann), Essays on Literature, translated by Sarah Adams. (Translations of both the preceding essays.) — GUERNSEY (A. H.), Ralph Waldo Emerson : Philosopher and Poet. — HAWTHORNE (J.), Confessions and Criticisms : Emerson as an American.— HIGGINSON (T. W.), and BOYNTON (H. W.), A Reader's History of American Literature. — HILL (A. S.), The Influ-ence of Emerson : in Studies and Notes in Philology and Literature, vol. v, Child Memorial Volume. — HUNT (T. W.), Studies in Literature and Style : Emerson's English Style. — *HUT-TON (R. H.), Criticisms on Contemporary Thought and Thinkers.— JAMES (Henry, Sr.), Literary Remains.— JAMES (Henry, Jr.), Partial Portraits : Cabot's Life of Emerson.— JOHNSON (C. F.), Three Americans and Three Englishmen. — KENNEDY (W. S.), Clews to Emerson's Mystic Verse : in the American Author, June, 1903. — KERNAHAN (C.), Wise Men and a Fool : A Poet who was not a Poet. — LÄLANA (P. F. K.), Emerson viewed with an Oriental Eye. — LANGHAM (J. J.), An Englishman's Appreciation of Emerson.— LAWTON (W. C.), Introduction to the Study of American Literature. — LAWTON (W. C.), The New England Poets. — LEE (G. S.), Emerson as a Poet : in the Critic, vol. xlii, p. 416 ; May, 1903. — LINDSAY (J.), Essays, Literary and Phi-losophical. — The LITERARY WORLD, Emerson Number, May 22, 1880. — LOCKWOOD (F. C.), Emerson as a Philosopher. A Thesis presented to the Northwestern University. — LOFORTE-RANDI (Andrea), Nelle letterature straniere. — MABIE (H. W.), Backgrounds of Literature. — *MAETERLINCK (Maurice), Le Trésor des Humbles : Emerson.— MANNING (J. M.), Half Truths and the Truth.— MASSACHUSETTS HISTORICAL SOCIETY, Tributes to Longfellow and Emerson.— MEAD (E. D.), The Influence of Emerson. — MITCHELL (D. G.), American Lands and Letters.— MONTÉGUT (Émile), Un penseur et poète américain : in the Revue des deux Mondes, Aug. 1, 1847, vol. xix, pp. 462–494. — MORE (P. E.), Shelburne Essays, First Series : The Influence of Emerson. — MORLEY (J.), Critical Miscellanies, vol. i. — NICHOL (J.), American Literature, an Historical Sketch. — ONDERDONK (J. L.), History of American Verse. — PATMORE (C.), Princi-ple in Art. — PATTEE (F. L.), History of American Literature. — POWELL (T.), The Living Authors of America, 1850.— RICHARDSON (C. F.), American Literature, vol. i, chapter ix (prose) ; vol. ii, chapter v (poetry). — ROZ (Firmin), L'idéalisme américain : in the Revue des deux Mondes, vol. lxix. — SANBORN (F. B.), The Genius and Character of Emerson. Lectures (by sev-eral authors) at the Concord School of Philosophy.— SANBORN (F. B.), Emerson and Contempo-raneous Poets : in the Critic, vol. xlii, p. 143 ; May, 1903. — *SCHMIDT (J.), Neue Essays : Ralph Waldo Emerson.—SANTAYANA (G.), Interpretations of Poetry and Religion.—SCHÖNBACH (A. E.), Ueber Lesen und Bildigung. — SEARLE (January) [George S. Phillips], Emerson, His Life and Writings.— SHARP (R. F.), Architects of English Literature. — * STEARNS (F. P.), The Real and Ideal in Literature : Emerson as a Poet.— STEARNS (F. P.), Cambridge Sketches : The Emer-son Centennial ; Emerson and the Greek Poets.—*STEDMAN (E. C.), Poets of America. — STE-PHEN (L.), Studies of a Biographer, vol. iv.— STEWART (George, Jr.), Evenings in the Library.— STEWART (George, Jr.), Essays from Reviews : Emerson the Thinker. — THAYER (W. R.), The

Influence of Emerson.— *Trent (W. P.), A History of American Literature. — Vincent (L. H.), American Literary Masters, 1905. — Whipple (E. P.), American Literature and Other Papers : Emerson as a Poet ; Emerson and Carlyle. — Whitman, Specimen Days, April 16, 1881 : My Tribute to Four Poets. (Complete Prose Works, p. 173.) — Whitman, Letters to William Sloane Kennedy : in Poet-Lore, February, 1895.

TRIBUTES IN VERSE

Alcott (A. B.), Ion ; A Monody : in his Ralph Waldo Emerson, etc., 1882 and 1888. — *Arnold (Matthew), Poetical Works : Sonnet, written in Emerson's Essays.— Chadwick (J. W.), Later Poems : Ralph Waldo Emerson, May 25, 1903. — Channing (Ellery), Poems : Ode, to Emerson. — Cone (Helen Gray), Oberon and Puck : Ralph Waldo Emerson.— Cranch (C. P.), Ariel and Caliban, with Other Poems : Ralph Waldo Emerson. — *Holmes, At the Saturday Club. — *Holmes, For Whittier's Seventieth Birthday. — *Hosmer (F. L.), Hymn for the Fiftieth Anniversary of Emerson's Divinity School Address. — Johnson (R. U.), The Winter Hour and Other Poems : To Ralph Waldo Emerson, September, 1881. — Johnson (R. U.), The Winter Hour : Written in Emerson's Poems. — Larcom (Lucy), Wild Roses of Cape Ann and Other Poems : R. W. E., May 25, 1880. — Lazarus (Emma), To R. W. E. : in Sanborn's The Genius and Character of Emerson. — *Lowell, A Fable for Critics. — Lowell, Agassiz, section iii, stanza iv. — Moulton (Louise Chandler), In the Garden of Dreams : Ralph Waldo Emerson. — Parsons (T. W.), Poems : Emerson.— Sanborn (F. B.), The Poet's Countersign. An Ode : in Alcott's Ralph Waldo Emerson, etc.— *Thomas (Edith), Emerson : in the Critic, May, 1903. — *Whittier, The Last Walk in Autumn, stanza xiv. — *Woodberry (G. E.), Poems, 1903 : Ode read at the Emerson Centenary.

LONGFELLOW

EDITIONS

*Complete Works, Riverside Edition, 11 volumes (vols. i–vi, Poetical Works ; vols. vii, viii, Prose Works ; vols. ix–xi, Translation of Dante) ; Craigie Edition, illustrated, 11 volumes ; Standard Library Edition, illustrated, 14 volumes (including the Life by Samuel Longfellow) : Houghton, Mifflin & Co. — Complete Poetical Works, *Riverside Edition, 6 volumes ; Handy-Volume Edition, 5 volumes ; *Cambridge Edition, 1 volume ; New Household Edition, 1 volume ; etc. : Houghton, Mifflin & Co.

BIOGRAPHY AND REMINISCENCES

*Longfellow (Samuel), Life of Henry Wadsworth Longfellow, with Extracts from his Journal and Correspondence, 3 volumes, 1891. (The standard biography, and in every way satisfactory. It combines and supersedes the Life, 2 volumes, 1886, and the Final Memorials, 1 volume, 1887.) — *Carpenter (G. R.), Henry Wadsworth Longfellow (Beacon Biographies), 1901. (The best brief biography.) — Robertson (Eric S.), Life of Longfellow (Great Writers Series), 1887. — Higginson (T. W.), Henry Wadsworth Longfellow (American Men of Letters Series), 1902.

Austin (G. L.), Henry Wadsworth Longfellow : His Life, his Works, his Friendships, 1883. — Conway (M. D.), Autobiography, Memories and Experiences, 1904. — Curtis (G. W.), Homes of American Authors, 1853 ; the same, in Little Journeys to the Homes of American Authors, 1896. — Davidson (Thomas), H. W. Longfellow, 1882 ; also in the Encyclopædia Britannica, 9th edition. — *Fields (Mrs. Annie), Authors and Friends : Longfellow, 1807–1882, 1896. — Greene (G. W.), Life of Nathaniel Greene (especially the *Dedication). — Hale (Rev. E. E.), Fireside Travels : Cambridge Thirty Years Ago. — Higginson (T. W.), Old Cambridge, 1899. — Holmes, in Tributes to Longfellow and Emerson, by the Massachusetts Historical Society. — *Howells (W. D.), My Literary Friends and Acquaintances. — Kennedy (W. S.), Henry Wadsworth Longfellow : Biography, Anecdote, Letters, Criticism, 1882. — Lanman (Chas.), Haphazard Personalities, 1886. — Macchetta (Blanche Roosevelt), The Home Life of Henry Wadsworth Longfellow : Reminiscences of many Visits at Cambridge and Nahant, during 1880, 1881 and 1882. — Maine Historical Society, Henry Wadsworth Longfellow, Seventy-fifth Birthday, 1882. — Massachusetts Historical Society, Tributes to Longfellow and

Emerson, 1882. — MITFORD (M. R.), Recollections of a Literary Life, 1851. — NORTON (C. E.), *in* Tributes to Longfellow and Emerson, by the Massachusetts Historical Society. — NORTON (C. E.), *in* Appleton's Cyclopedia of American Biography, vol. iv, 1888. — ROSSETTI (W. M.), Lives of Famous Poets, 1878. — SAUNDERS (Frederic), Character Studies, with some personal Recollections, 1894. — STEARNS (F. P.), Cambridge Sketches, 1905. — STODDARD (R. H.) Homes and Haunts of our Elder Poets, 1878. — TROWBRIDGE (J. T.), My Own Story, 1904. — UNDERWOOD (F. H.), Henry Wadsworth Longfellow, a Biographical Sketch, 1882.

CRITICISM

BADEAU (Adam), The Vagabond, 1859. — BANDOW (Karl), Die lyrischen und epischen Gedichte des Amerikaners Henry Wadsworth Longfellow, 1856. — BATES (K. L.), American Literature. — BAUMGARTNER (A.), Longfellow's Dichtungen : Ein literarisches Zeitbild aus dem Geistesleben Nordamerika's, 1887. — BECHGER (A.), Longfellow : Literarisch-biographische Studie, 1883. — BENT (S. A.), The Wayside Inn, its History and Literature, 1897. — BUNGAY (G. W.), Traits of Representative Men, 1882. — BURTON (R.), Literary Leaders, 1903. — CAMERINI (Eugenio), Nuovi profili letterari, 1875. — CHADWICK (J. W.), *in* Chambers's Cyclopædia of English Literature, vol. iii, 1904. — CHENEY (J. V.), That Dome in Air. — COLERIDGE (Sara), Memoir and Letters, vol. ii, chapter vi (on ' Evangeline ' and ' Hyperion '). — CURTIS (G. W.), Literary and Social Essays, 1894. — DÉPRET (Louis), La Poésie en Amérique, 1876. — DÉPRET (Louis), Chez les Anglais, 1879. — DESHLER (C. D.), Afternoons with Authors: The Sonnets of Longfellow, 1879. — DEVEY (J.), A Comparative Estimate of Modern English Poets, 1873. — FISKE (John), The Unseen World, and other Essays: Longfellow's Dante, 1902. — FRISWELL (J. H.), Modern Men of Letters Honestly Criticised, 1870. — GANNETT (W. C.), Studies in Longfellow (Riverside Literature Series). — GOSTWICK (Joseph), English Poets, 1875. — HATTON (Joseph), Old Lamps and New : Tennyson and Longfellow. — HAZELTINE (M. W.), Chats about Books, Poets and Novelists, 1883. — HENLEY (W. E.), Views and Reviews, 1890. — HUTTON (R. H.), Criticisms on Contemporary Thought and Thinkers. — JOHNSON (C. F.), Three Americans and Three Englishmen, 1886. — KNORTZ (Karl), Longfellow: Literar-historische Studie. — LANG (Andrew), Letters on Literature, 1889. — LAWTON (W. C.), Introduction to the Study of American Literature. — LAWTON (W. C.), The New England Poets. — MATTHEWS (B.), Introduction to the Study of American Literature. — NEWCOMER (A. G.), American Literature. — NICHOL (John), American Literature, an Historical Sketch, 1882. — PALMER (George Herbert), Henry Wadsworth Longfellow : *in* Atlas Essays, No. 2, 1877. — PÄTSCH (E.), Longfellow und seine Stellung in der nordamerikanischen Litteratur, 1883. — PATTEE (F. L.), A History of American Literature. — POE (Edgar Allan), Works, Virginia Edition: vol. x, pp. 39, 40, Hyperion (October, 1839) ; vol. x, pp. 71–80, Voices of the Night (February, 1840) ; vol. xi, pp. 64–85, Ballads and Other Poems (March, April, 1842) ; vol. xii, pp. 41–106, Imitation — Plagiarism — Mr. Poe's Reply to Outis' — The Longfellow War (March 8–April 5, 1845) ; vol. xiii, pp. 54–73, The Spanish Student (August, 1845). — PRINS (A. de), Études américaines, 1877. — *RICHARDSON (C. F.), American Literature, vol. ii, chapter iii. — SCHÖNBACH (A. E.), Gesammelte Aufsätze zur neueren Litteratur. — SHARP (R. F.), Architects of English Literature. — SPRENGER (R.), Zu Longfellow's poetischen Werken, 1903. — SIEMT (O.), Der Stabreim bei Longfellow, 1897. — *STEDMAN (E. C.), Poets of America. — STEWART (George, Jr.), Evenings in the Library, 1878. — STEWART (George, Jr.), Essays from Reviews, 1892. — TAYLOR (B.), Critical Essays and Literary Notes, 1880. — TRENT (W. P.), A History of American Literature. — VARNHAGEN (Hermann), Longfellow's Tales of A Wayside Inn und ihre Quellen, 1884. — VINCENT (L. H.), American Literary Masters, 1905. — WENDELL (B.), A Literary History of America. — WHIPPLE (E. P.), Essays and Reviews : Poets and Poetry of America. — WHITMAN, *in* Essays from the Critic : The Death of Longfellow. — *WHITMAN, Specimen Days : My Tribute to Four Poets ; The Death of Longfellow. (Complete Prose Works, pp. 173, 174 ; 186, 187.) — WHITTIER, Prose Works, vol. ii : Longfellow's Evangeline. — WILLIAMS (S. F.), Essays, Critical, Biographical, and Miscellaneous. — WINTER (William), English Rambles : In Memory of Longfellow. — WINTER (William), Old Shrines and Ivy. — WORDEN (J. Perry), Über Longfellow's Beziehungen zur deutschen Litteratur. — (For references, especially on ' Evangeline ' and ' Hiawatha,' see the notes at the beginning of those poems.)

TRIBUTES IN VERSE

BATES (Charlotte Fiske), Risk and Other Poems: The Craigie House; *the same, revised, in* Cambridge Sketches by Cambridge Authors. — *BATES (Katharine Lee), Longfellow: In Memoriam. — *BUNNER (H. C.), Airs from Arcady and Elsewhere: Longfellow. — CONE (Helen Gray), Oberon and Puck: Henry Wadsworth Longfellow. — *DOBSON (Austin), In Memoriam: *in the* London Athenæum, no. 2840, p. 411. — CRANCH (C. P.), Ariel and Caliban, with other Poems: Longfellow. — *FAWCETT (Edgar), Romance and Revery: Longfellow in Westminster Abbey. — FREELAND (H. W.), Elegy on the Death of Longfellow. — GILDER (R. W.), Lyrics: Longfellow's 'Book of Sonnets.' — *HAYNE (Paul H.), Complete Poems: Personal Sonnets, To Henry Wadsworth Longfellow; To Longfellow (On Hearing he was Ill); Longfellow Dead. — HOLMES, To Henry Wadsworth Longfellow, May 27, 1868. — *HOLMES, For Whittier's Seventieth Birthday. — *HOLMES, At the Saturday Club. — HOLMES, Our Dead Singer, H. W. L. — LOWELL, A Fable for Critics. — *LOWELL, To H. W. L. on his Birthday, 27th February, 1867. — LOWELL, Agassiz, section iii, stanza iv. — MIFFLIN (Lloyd), The Slopes of Helicon and Other Poems. — NICHOL (John), *in* Stedman's Victorian Anthology, p. 255. — RILEY (J. W.), Green Fields and Running Brooks: Longfellow. — SAVAGE (Minot J.), Poems: The People's Poet. — THOMAS (Edith M.), Vale et Salve: *in the* Critic, 1882. — WATSON (William), Wordsworth's Grave and Other Poems: On Longfellow's Death. — *WHITTIER, The Poet and the Children. — WHITTIER, On a Fly-Leaf of Longfellow's Poems. — WINTER (William), Wanderers: Longfellow. — (See also a large number of poems to Longfellow, pp. 307–339 of Kennedy's *Longfellow*, from The Literary World, The Critic, Baldwin's Monthly, etc., etc.)

WHITTIER

EDITIONS

*COMPLETE WORKS, Riverside Edition, 7 volumes (vols. i–iv, Poetical Works; vols. v–vii, Prose Works); Amesbury Edition, illustrated, 7 volumes; Standard Library Edition, illustrated, 9 volumes (including the *Life* by S. T. Pickard): Houghton, Mifflin & Co. — POETICAL WORKS, *Riverside Edition, 4 volumes; Handy-Volume Edition, 4 volumes; *Cambridge Edition, 1 volume; New Household Edition, 1 volume; etc.: Houghton, Mifflin & Co.

BIOGRAPHY AND REMINISCENCES

*PICKARD (Samuel T.), Life and Letters of John Greenleaf Whittier, 2 volumes, 1894. (The standard biography. Excellent.) — LINTON (W. J.), Life of John Greenleaf Whittier (Great Writers Series), 1893. (Of little value, except for its bibliography.) — BURTON (Richard), John Greenleaf Whittier (Beacon Biographies), 1901. — HIGGINSON (T. W.), John Greenleaf Whittier (English Men of Letters Series), 1902. — *CARPENTER (G. R.), John Greenleaf Whittier (American Men of Letters Series), 1903. (The best brief biography.)

BACON (E. M.), Literary Pilgrimages in New England: The Amesbury Home of Whittier; The Country of Whittier. — BREMER (Frederika), Homes of the New World, 1853. — BUNGAY (George W.), Off-Hand Takings, 1854. — BUTTERWORTH (H.), The Home of J. G. Whittier, *in* Parton's Some Noted Princes, Authors, and Statesmen. — *CLAFLIN (Mrs. M. B.), Personal Recollections of John Greenleaf Whittier, 1893. — DAVIS (Miss Rebecca T.), Gleanings from Merrimac Valley. — *FIELDS (Mrs. Annie), Whittier: Notes of his Life and of his Friendships, 1893: *the same, in* Authors and Friends, 1896. — GARRISON (Wm. Lloyd), John Greenleaf Whittier: An Address Delivered before the Brooklyn Institute of Arts and Sciences, December 17, 1892. — GARRISON (W. P. and F. J.), William Lloyd Garrison; the Story of his Life told by his Children, 1889. — GOSSE (Edmund), A Visit to Whittier: *in the* Bookman, 1899, vol. viii, p. 459. — GRIMKE (A. H.), William Lloyd Garrison, the Abolitionist, 1891. (Numerous allusions to Whittier.) — GRISWOLD (H. T.), Home Life of Great Authors. — HAVERHILL, Mass., A Memorial of John Greenleaf Whittier, 1893. — HIGGINSON (T. W.), Contemporaries. — HIGGINSON (T. W.), Cheerful Yesterdays, 1899. — KENNEDY (W. S.), John Greenleaf Whittier, the Poet of Freedom (American Reformers Series), 1892. — KENNEDY (W. S.), John Greenleaf Whittier, his Life, Genius, and Writings, 1882. — MAY (S. J.), Some Recollections of our Anti-slavery conflict, 1869. — MITFORD (M. R.), Recollections of a Literary Life, 1851. — *PICKARD (S. T.), Whittier-Land, 1904. — PICKARD (S. T.), Whittier as a Politician, Illustrated by his Letters to Prof. Elizur Wright,

1900. — PORTER (Maria S.), Recollections of L. M. Alcott, John Greenleaf Whittier, and Robert Browning, with Memorial Poems, 1893. — RANTOUL (R. S.), Some Personal Reminiscences of the Poet Whittier: *in the* Historical Collections of the Essex Institute, April, 1901. — SARGENT (Mrs. John T.), Sketches and Reminiscences of the Radical Club of Chestnut Street, 1880. — SPOFFORD (Harriet P.): *in* J. L. and J. B. Gilder's Authors at Home, 1888. — STEARNS (F. P.), Sketches from Concord and Appledore, 1895. — STODDARD (R. H.), Homes and Haunts of our Elder Poets, 1878. — TAYLOR (Mrs. Bayard) and SCUDDER (H. E.), Life and Letters of Bayard Taylor, 1884. (Numerous allusions to Whittier.) — TROWBRIDGE (J. T.), My Own Story, 1904. — *UNDERWOOD (F. H.), John Greenleaf Whittier, a Biography, 1883. — WARD (Elizabeth Stuart Phelps), Chapters from a Life. — WHITTIER (C. C.), Genealogy of the Whittier Family, 1622–1882, 1882. — WOLFE (T. F.), Literary Shrines: The Haunts of Some Famous American Authors.

CRITICISM

BATES (K. L.), American Literature. — BRACE (Donald G.), Whittier as an Anti-Slavery Poet: *in the* Columbia Monthly, April–May, 1904. — BURTON (R.), Literary Leaders, 1903. — COLLINS (Churton), The Poetry and Poets of America. — CHENEY (J. V.), That Dome in Air. — DALL (Mrs. Caroline Wells Healey), Barbara Frietchie, a Study, Boston, 1892. — FLOWER (B. O.), Whittier, Prophet, Seer and Man. — FRIENDS' SCHOOL, Providence, R. I., Proceedings at Presentation of Portrait of Whittier. — HAWKINS (C. J.), The Mind of Whittier, 1904. — HAZELTINE (M. W.), Chats about Books. — HOWE (M. A. DeW.), American Bookmen, 1898. — LAWTON (W. C.), The New England Poets. — LAWTON (W. C.), Introduction to the Study of American Literature. — MATTHEWS (B.), Introduction to the Study of American Literature. — MAULSBY (D. L.), Whittier's New Hampshire: *in the* New England Magazine, vol. xxii, p. 631, 1900. — MEAD (E. D.), The Eulogy: *in the* Haverhill Memorial of John Greenleaf Whittier. — MITCHELL (D. G.), American Lands and Letters, 1899. — NEWCOMER(A. G.), American Literature. — NICHOL (J.), American Literature. — ONDERDONK (J. L.), History of American Verse. — RICHARDSON (C. F.), American Literature, vol. ii, chapter vi. — STEDMAN (E. C.), Poets of America. — STEWART (George, Jr.), Evenings in the Library. — STEWART (George, Jr.), Essays from Reviews. — TAYLOR (B.), Critical Essays and Literary Notes, 1880. — TEINCET (Jean), Un poète américain: *in the* Revue britannique, 1899, vol. v, p. 5. — TRENT (W. P.), A History of American Literature. — VINCENT (L. H.), American Literary Masters, 1905. — WENDELL (B.), Stelligeri and Other Essays. — WHIPPLE (E. P.), American Literature and other Papers: American Literature. — WHIPPLE (E. P.), Essays and Reviews: Poets and Poetry of America. — WHITMAN (W.), Specimen Days, April 16, 1881. (Complete Prose Works, p. 173). — WOODBERRY (G. E.), Makers of Literature, 1900.

TRIBUTES IN VERSE

BATES (Charlotte Fiske), Risk and Other Poems: Oak Knoll, Danvers; On his Seventieth Birthday. — CARLETON (Will), Ode to Whittier: *in the* Haverhill Memorial of John Greenleaf Whittier. — CHADWICK (J. W.), Later Poems: John Greenleaf Whittier, Read before the Brooklyn Institute on the Anniversary of his Birthday, 1892. — CRANCH (C. P.), Ariel and Caliban, with Other Poems: To John Greenleaf Whittier, December 5, 1877. — GARRISON (Wm. L.), Verses Read at the Whittier Memorial Gathering, October 7, 1892: printed with his Address delivered before the Brooklyn Institute of Arts and Sciences, December 17, 1892. — HAYNE (Paul H.), Complete Poems: To the Poet Whittier on his Seventieth Birthday. — *HOLMES, For Whittier's Seventieth Birthday. — HOLMES, To John Greenleaf Whittier on his Eightieth Birthday. — *HOLMES, In Memory of John Greenleaf Whittier: December 17, 1807—September 7, 1892. — LARCOM (Lucy), Wild Roses of Cape Ann and Other Poems: John Greenleaf Whittier, December 17, 1877. — LONGFELLOW, The Three Silences of Molinos. — *LOWELL, A Fable for Critics. — *LOWELL, To Whittier on his Seventy-fifth Birthday. — PORTER (Maria S.), Recollections of L. M. Alcott, John Greenleaf Whittier, and Robert Browning: John Greenleaf Whittier. — SANGSTER (Margaret), Whittier: *in* Stedman's American Anthology. — SHURTLEFF (E. W.), Whittier, *in* Proceedings at the Presentation of Portrait of Whittier, Friends' School, Providence. — *STEDMAN, Poetical Works: Ad Vatem. — TAYLOR, Poetical Works: A Friend's Greeting, 1877. — *WHITMAN (W.), Leaves of Grass: As the Greek's Signal Flame (for Whittier's Eightieth Birthday).— WHITNEY (A. D. T.), White Memories: John Greenleaf Whittier. — (See also the ' Whittier Number' of the Literary World, December, 1877.)

HOLMES

EDITIONS

*COMPLETE WORKS, Riverside Edition, 14 volumes (vols. i–xi, Prose Works; vols. xii–xiv, Poems); Autocrat Edition, illustrated, 13 volumes (in this and the following edition the poems occupy only two volumes); Standard Library Edition, illustrated, 15 volumes (including the *Life* by John T. Morse, Jr.): Houghton, Mifflin & Co. — POETICAL WORKS, *Riverside Edition, 3 volumes; *Cambridge Edition, 1 volume; Household Edition, 1 volume; etc.: Houghton, Mifflin & Co.

BIOGRAPHY AND REMINISCENCES

*MORSE (John T., Jr.), Life and Letters of Oliver Wendell Holmes, 2 volumes, 1896. (The standard biography.) — CROTHERS (S. M.), Oliver Wendell Holmes. (To be published in 1906, in the American Men of Letters Series.)

BALL (James), Dr. Oliver Wendell Holmes and his Works; Being a brief Biographical and Critical Review, London, 1878. — FIELDS (Mrs. Annie), Authors and Friends, 1896. — GRISWOLD (H. T.), Home-Life of Great Authors. — HIGGINSON (T. W.), Old Cambridge. — *HOWELLS (W. D.), My Literary Friends and Acquaintances. — JERROLD (Walter), Oliver Wendell Holmes, London, 1893. (A compilation.) — KENNEDY (W. S.), Oliver Wendell Holmes, Poet, Littérateur, Scientist, 1883. — MITFORD (M. R.), Recollections of a Literary Life, 1851. — NOBLE (J. H.), Impressions and Memories: Oliver Wendell Holmes, 1895. — ROLLINS (A. W.), Oliver Wendell Holmes: *in* J. L. & J. B. Gilder's Authors at Home. — SMALLEY (G. W.), Studies of Men: Oliver Wendell Holmes, 1895. — SMITH (J. E. A.), The Poet among the Hills; Oliver Wendell Holmes in Berkshire, his Berkshire poems, etc., 1895. — TROWBRIDGE (J. T.), My Own Story, 1904.

CRITICISM

BURTON (R.), Literary Leaders, 1903. — *COLLINS (Churton), The Poetry and Poets of America. — The CRITIC, Holmes Number, August 30, 1884. — CURTIS (G. W.), Literary and Social Essays, 1895. — HAWEIS (H. R.), American Humorists. — HOWE (M. A. DeW.), American Bookmen. — LANG (A.), Adventures among Books: Oliver Wendell Holmes. — LAWTON (W. C.), Introduction to the Study of American Literature. — LAWTON (W. C.), The New England Poets. — LODGE (H. C.), Certain accepted Heroes, and Other Essays in Literature and Politics: Dr. Holmes, 1897. — MATTHEWS (Brander), Introduction to the Study of American Literature, chapter xiii. — MEYNELL (Alice), The Rhythm of Life and Other Essays: Dr. Oliver Wendell Holmes. — NEWCOMER (A. G.), American Literature. — ONDERDONK (J. L.), History of American Verse. — PAYNE (W. M.), Little Leaders, 1895. — RICHARDSON (C. F.), American Literature, vol. ii, chapter vi. — STEARNS (F. P.), Cambridge Sketches: Doctor Holmes. — *STEDMAN (E. C.), Poets of America. — *STEPHEN (L.), Studies of a Biographer, 1898. — STEWART (George, Jr.), Evenings in the Library. — STEWART (George, Jr.), Essays from Reviews. — TAYLOR (B.), Critical Essays and Literary Notes: Oliver Wendell Holmes, 1877. — TRENT (W. P.), A History of American Literature, 1903. — VINCENT (L. H.), American Literary Masters, 1905. — VOSSION (Louis), Un poète américain: Oliver Wendell Holmes, 1896. — WENDELL (B.), A Literary History of America, 1900. — WHIPPLE (E. P.), Essays and Reviews: Poets and Poetry of America, 1848. — WHITTIER, Prose Works, vol. iii: Mirth and Medicine. — WHITTIER, Prose Works, vol. ii: Oliver Wendell Holmes.

TRIBUTES IN VERSE

CRANCH (C. P.), Ariel and Caliban: To Oliver Wendell Holmes, æt. 70. — *GOSSE (Edmund), An Epistle to Dr. Oliver Wendell Holmes, on his Seventy-fifth Birthday, August 29, 1884. — LARCOM (Lucy), Wild Roses of Cape Ann: Oliver Wendell Holmes, August 29, 1879. — LATHROP (Geo. Parsons), Youth to the Poet (To Oliver Wendell Holmes): *in* Scribner's Monthly, vol. xix. — LOWELL, A Fable for Critics. — LOWELL, Agassiz, section iii, stanza iii. — *LOWELL, To Holmes on his Seventy-fifth Birthday. — *TROWBRIDGE (J. T.), Filling an Order. — *WHITTIER, Our Autocrat. — WHITTIER, Oliver Wendell Holmes on his Eightieth Birthday. — *WHITTIER, To Oliver Wendell Holmes. — *WINTER (William) Wanderers: Oliver Wendell Holmes, or the Chieftain. — (See also the CRITIC, Holmes Number, August 30, 1884, for Poems by Julia C. R. Dorr, R. W. Gilder, E. E. Hale, Bret Harte, Edith M. Thomas, etc.)

LOWELL

EDITIONS

*COMPLETE WORKS, Riverside Edition, 11 volumes; Standard Library Edition, illustrated, 11 volumes; Elmwood Edition, illustrated, 16 volumes (including the Letters of Lowell and the *Life* by H. E. Scudder) : Houghton, Mifflin & Co. — WORKS, Popular Edition, 6 volumes. Houghton, Mifflin & Co. — POETICAL WORKS, *Riverside Edition, 4 volumes ; *Cambridge Edition, 1 volume ; Household Edition, 1 volume : Houghton, Mifflin & Co. — *LETTERS, edited by Charles E. Norton, 2 volumes : Harper & Brothers ; *the same,* 3 volumes : Houghton, Mifflin & Co. (The three-volume edition of the Letters is sold only as a part of the Elmwood Edition of Lowell's Complete Works.) — IMPRESSIONS OF SPAIN, compiled by J. B. Gilder. (Official despatches, etc., during Lowell's ministry to Spain.)

BIOGRAPHY AND REMINISCENCES

*SCUDDER (H. E.), James Russell Lowell, a Biography, 1901. (The standard biography.) — *GREENSLET (F.), James Russell Lowell, his Life and Work, 1905. (The best brief biographical and critical study.) — HALE (E. E., Jr.), James Russell Lowell (Beacon Biographies), 1899. BREMER (Frederika), Homes of the New World, 1853. — BRIGGS (C. F.), James Russell Lowell : *in* Homes of American Authors, 1853 ; *the same, in* Little Journeys to the Homes of American Authors, 1896. — CONWAY (M. D.), Autobiography, Memories, and Experiences, 1904. — GRISWOLD (H. T.), Home Life of Great Authors. — HALE (Rev. E. E.), James Russell Lowell and his Friends. — HIGGINSON (T. W.), Book and Heart : Last Years in Cambridge. — HIGGINSON (T. W.), Old Cambridge. — HIGGINSON (T. W.), Cheerful Yesterdays. — HIGGINSON (T. W.), Contemporaries. — * HOWELLS (W. D.), Literary Friends and Acquaintances. — The LITERARY WORLD, Lowell Number, June 27, 1885. — LOWNDES (F. S. A.), Literary Associations of the American Embassy : *in the* Fortnightly Review, June, 1905. — POND (George E.), Lowell at Harvard : *in the* Liber Scriptorum of the New York Authors' Club. (Reminiscences of Lowell's class in Dante). — SANBORN (F. B.), James Russell Lowell : *in* Homes and Haunts of our Elder Poets, 1878. — SMALLEY (G. W.), London Letters and Some Others : Lowell in England, 1891. — STEAD (W. T.), Character Sketches, 1891. — STEARNS (F. P.), Cambridge Sketches, 1905. — TROWBRIDGE (J. T.), My Own Story, 1904. — UNDERWOOD (F. H.), James Russell Lowell, 1882. — UNDERWOOD (F. H.), The Poet and the Man, Recollections and Appreciations of James Russell Lowell, 1893. — WENDELL (B.), Stelligeri, and Other Essays Concerning America : Mr. Lowell as a Teacher.

CRITICISM

BEALS (S. B.), Outline Studies in James Russell Lowell, his Poetry and Prose. — BURTON (R.), Literary Leaders. — CHADWICK (J. W.), Lowell : *in* Chambers's New Cyclopædia of English Literature, vol. iii. — CHENEY (J. V.), That Dome in Air. — COLLINS (Churton), The Poetry and Poets of America. — CURTIS (G. W.), James Russell Lowell, an Address, 1892 ; *the same, in his* Orations and Addresses, vol. iii ; *also, in* Memorials of Two Friends, N. Y., 1902. — DESHLER (C. D.), Afternoons with the Poets : Sonnets of Lowell. — HAWEIS (H. R.), American Humorists. — HOWE (M. A. DeW.), American Bookmen. — *JAMES (Henry, Jr.), Essays in London and Elsewhere. — LAWTON (W. C.), The New England Poets. — LAWTON (W. C.), An Introduction to the Study of American Literature. — MABIE (H. W.), My Study Fire : the Letters of Lowell. — MACARTHUR (H.), Realism and Romance. — MATTHEWS (B.), Introduction to the Study of American Literature. — MEYNELL (A.), The Rhythm of Life and Other Essays. — NEWCOMER (A. G.), American Literature. — NICHOL (J.), American Literature. — POE, Complete Works, Virginia Edition, vol. xi : Poems by James Russell Lowell ; vol. xiii : The Fable for Critics. — RICHARDSON (C. F.), American Literature, vol. ii, chapter vii. — ROOSEVELT (Theodore), James Russell Lowell, *in the* Critic, vol. ix, p. 86. — STEDMAN (E. C.), Poets of America. — STEWART (George, Jr.), Essays from Reviews. — STEWART (George, Jr.), Evenings in the Library. — TAYLOR (B.), Critical Essays and Literary Notes. — *TRENT (W. P.), A History of American Literature. — VINCENT (L. H.), American Literary Masters, 1905. — WATSON (W.), Excursions in Criticism : Lowell as a Critic. — *WENDELL (B.), A Literary History of America. — WHIPPLE (E. P.), Essays and Reviews, 1861. — WHIPPLE (E. P.), Outlooks on Society, Literature and Politics: Lowell as a Prose Writer. — WHITMAN (W.), Letter to Sylvester Baxter, beginning, ' Camden, N. J., Aug. 13, '91. Let me send my little word too to James Russell Lowell's memory.' (Boston Public Library MS.) — WILKINSON (W. C.), A Free Lance in the Field of Life and Letters. — *WOODBERRY (G. E.), Makers of Literature.

TRIBUTES IN VERSE

ALDRICH (T. B.), Unguarded Gates and Other Poems: Elmwood. — BOLTON (Mrs. S. K.), The Inevitable and Other Poems: James Russell Lowell. — CONE (Helen Gray), The Ride to the Lady and Other Poems: The Gifts of the Oak. — CRANCH (C. P.), The Bird and the Bell, with Other Poems: J. R. L. on his Fiftieth Birthday. — CRANCH (C. P.), Ariel and Caliban, with Other Poems: J. R. L., on his Homeward Voyage. — EMERSON, in Greenslet's James Russell Lowell, p. 144. — FIELD (Eugene), James Russell Lowell. — GILDER (R. W.), Two Worlds and Other Poems: J. R. L., on his Birthday. — GILDER (R. W.), The Great Remembrance: Lowell. — HOLMES, Farewell to James Russell Lowell. — HOLMES, At a Birthday Festival: To James Russell Lowell. — HOLMES, To James Russell Lowell. — HOLMES, For Whittier's Seventieth Birthday. — HOLMES, To James Russell Lowell on his Seventieth Birthday. — *HOLMES, James Russell Lowell, 1819–1891. — *LONGFELLOW, The Herons of Elmwood. — PARSONS (T. W.), James Russell Lowell: in the Literary World, August 29, 1891. — SAVAGE (Rev. Minot J.), These Degenerate Days. — STORY (W. W.), To James Russell Lowell: in Blackwood's Magazine, October, 1891: also in the Critic, October 10, 1891. — *WHITTIER, A Welcome to Lowell. — *WHITTIER, James Russell Lowell. — (See also the Literary World, June 27, 1885, for poems by Wm. Everett, Rose Terry Cooke, Charlotte Fiske Bates, Will Carleton, Margaret J. Preston, Clinton Scollard, Oscar Fay Adams, etc.)

WHITMAN

EDITIONS

*LEAVES OF GRASS, including Sands at Seventy, Good-bye my Fancy, Old Age Echoes (Whitman's COMPLETE POETICAL WORKS), and A Backward Glance O'er Travel'd Roads, 1 volume; *COMPLETE PROSE WORKS, 1 volume; *CALAMUS, A Series of Letters Written during the Years 1868–1880, by Walt Whitman to a young friend (Peter Doyle), edited with an Introduction by R. M. Bucke; *THE WOUND DRESSER, A Series of Letters Written from the Hospitals in Washington during the War of the Rebellion, edited by R. M. Bucke: Small, Maynard & Co. — *NOTES AND FRAGMENTS: Left by Walt Whitman and now edited by Dr. R. M. Bucke: Privately Printed, 1899. (Also in the Camden Edition, below.) — IN RE WALT WHITMAN, edited by his Literary Executors: David McKay, 1893. (Contains nine articles by Whitman.) — *COMPLETE WORKS, Camden Edition, 10 volumes: G. P. Putnam's Sons. (Sold only by subscription.) — WALT WHITMAN'S DIARY IN CANADA, with Extracts from other of his Diaries and Literary Notebooks, edited by W. S. Kennedy, 1904: Small, Maynard & Co. — AN AMERICAN PRIMER, edited by Horace Traubel, 1904: Small, Maynard & Co. — (The above are the only authorized or in any way complete editions of Whitman's writings.) — LEAVES OF GRASS: T. Y. Crowell & Co. (A reprint of the 1860 edition.) — LEAVES OF GRASS: David McKay. (Containing only such poems as had appeared before 1872, with variorum readings — not always accurate — from earlier editions.) — *SELECTIONS FROM THE PROSE AND POETRY OF WALT WHITMAN, edited by O. L. Triggs. (The authorized volume of selections, and by far the best.) — *POEMS, selected and edited by W. M. Rossetti: London, 1868; new edition, 1886. — *LEAVES OF GRASS, Edition of 1860, a facsimile reproduction of Whitman's copy, with his notes for revision, is announced by Horace Traubel for publication by subscription.

BIOGRAPHY AND REMINISCENCES

*BUCKE (R. M.), Walt Whitman, 1883. (An authorized biography.) — *IN RE WALT WHITMAN, edited by his literary executors, 1893. (Designed to supplement and complete the authorized biography.) — *BUCKE (R. M.), HARNED (T. B.), and TRAUBEL (Horace), Life of Whitman: in vol. i of the Camden Edition of Whitman's Works. — *PLATT (I. H.), Walt Whitman (Beacon

Biographies), 1904. (The latest and best brief book on Whitman.) — *TRAUBEL (Horace), With Walt Whitman in Camden, 1905. (A diary record of Whitman's life and conversation during his last years.) — Volumes on Whitman are soon to be added to the American Men of Letters Series (by Bliss Perry), and to the English Men of Letters Series (by G. R. Carpenter).

ARNOLD (Edwin), Seas and Lands, 1891, pp. 78–84. — ASKHAM (Richard) [Henry Bryan BINNS], Life of Whitman, London, 1905. — BAZALGETTE (Léon), Walt Whitman, l'homme, l'œuvre, la prophétie, Paris, 1905 or 1906. — BUCKE (R. M.), The Man Walt Whitman : in In Re Walt Whitman. — *BURROUGHS (John), Notes on Walt Whitman as Poet and Person, 1867. — CAMDEN's Compliments to Walt Whitman, May 31, 1889, edited by Horace Traubel, 1889. (Containing Whitman's Autobiographic Note and Response; Poems by Rhys and Traubel; Addresses by R. W. Gilder, Julian Hawthorne, Hamlin Garland, etc.; and letters from Tennyson, Rossetti, Morris, Dowden, Stedman, Whittier, etc.) — CLARKE (Wm.), Walt Whitman, London, 1892. — The CONSERVATOR, many articles on Whitman. — DONALDSON (T. C.), Walt Whitman, the Man, 1896. — GILMAN (Arthur), Pen and Pencil Sketches of American Poets and their Homes, 1879. — GOULD (E. P.), Walt Whitman among the Soldiers : in Gems from Walt Whitman, 1889. — GOULD (E. P.), Anne Gilchrist and Walt Whitman, 1900. — HUBBARD (Elbert), Walt Whitman : in Little Journeys to the Homes of American Authors, 1896. — JOHNSTON (John), Diary Notes of a Visit to Walt Whitman and Some of His Friends, in 1890. Privately printed, 1890, published, 1898. — *KENNEDY (W. S.), Reminiscences of Walt Whitman, with Extracts from his Letters and Remarks on his Writings, 1896. — MORSE (Sidney H.), My Summer with Walt Whitman, 1887 : in In Re Walt Whitman. — O'CONNOR (W. D.), The Good Gray Poet, a Vindication, 1866. (Reprinted in Bucke's Walt Whitman.) — *O'CONNOR (W. D.), Three Tales. (*The Carpenter* represents Whitman.) — O'CONNOR (W. D.), The Good Gray Poet, Supplemental : in In Re Walt Whitman. — ROSSETTI (W. M.), Lives of Famous Poets, 1878. — SELWYN (George), Walt Whitman in Camden : in J. L. & J. B. Gilder's Authors at Home, 1888. — SKINNER (C. M.), Walt Whitman as an Editor : in the Atlantic, November, 1903, vol. xcii, p. 679. — STODDARD (R. H.), Homes and Haunts of our Elder Poets. — TRAUBEL (Horace), Walt Whitman at Date : in the New England Magazine, May, 1891, n. s. vol. iv, pp. 275–292 ; also in In Re Walt Whitman. — TRAUBEL (Horace), Walt Whitman : Poet and Philosopher and Man : in Lippincott's Magazine, vol. xlvii, p. 287, 1891 ; also in In Re Walt Whitman. — TRAUBEL (Horace), Lowell-Whitman, a Contrast : in Poet-Lore, January, 1892. — *TRAUBEL (Horace), Notes from Conversations with George W. Whitman, 1893 : in In Re Walt Whitman. — TRAUBEL (Horace), Conversations with Walt Whitman : in the Arena, January, 1896. — *TRAUBEL (Horace), editor, Walt Whitman Fellowship Papers. — TRAUBEL (Horace), editor, At the Grave-side of Walt Whitman. — *TROWBRIDGE (J. T.), Reminiscences of Walt Whitman : in the Atlantic, vol. lxxxix, p. 163, February, 1902. — *TROWBRIDGE (J. T.), My Own Story, 1904. — WOLFE (T. F.), Literary Shrines, the Homes of Some Famous American Authors : A Day with the Good Gray Poet, 1895.

CRITICISM

AUSTIN (A.), Poetry of the Period. — BIJVANCK (W. G. C.), Poezie en Leven in de 19de Eeuw : Emerson en Walt Whitman. — BORN (Helena), Whitman's Ideal Democracy and Other Writings, 1902. — BUCHANAN (R.), David Gray and Other Essays, 1868. — *BUCHANAN (R.), The Fleshly School of Poetry : note, on p. 96. — BUCHANAN (R.), A Look Round Literature : The American Socrates, 1886. — BUCKE (R. M.), Walt Whitman and the Cosmic Sense, in In Re Walt Whitman. — BUCKE (R. M.), Cosmic Consciousness, 1901. — BURKE (Charles Bell), The Open Road, or the Highway of the Spirit : An Inquiry into Whitman's Absolute Selfhood, a Thesis Presented to Cornell University. — BURROUGHS (John), Birds and Poets : The Flight of the Eagle, 1878. — BURROUGHS (John), Walt Whitman and his Recent Critics, in In Re Walt Whitman. — BURROUGHS (John), Art for Life's Sake, in the Dial, October, 1893. — *BURROUGHS (John), Whitman : A Study, 1896. — BURTON (R.), Literary Leaders, 1903. — CARPENTER (Edward), Angels' Wings : Wagner, Millet, and Whitman, 1898. — *CHAPMAN (J. J.), Emerson and Other Essays. — CHENEY (J. V.), That Dome in Air, 1895. — CHIMENTI (F.), Larghi Orizzonti : Walt Whitman e l'arte nuova. — CLIFFORD (W. K.), Lectures and Addresses : Cosmic Emotion. — The CONSERVATOR, many articles on Whitman. — CONWAY (M. D.), Walt Whitman, in the Fortnightly Review, October 15, 1865. (Quoted, in part, in Walsh's Pen Pictures of Modern Authors.) — *DOWDEN (Edward), Studies in Literature, 1789–1877 : The Poetry of Democracy, Walt Whitman. (From the Westminster Review, July, 1871). — *ELLIS (Havelock), The New Spirit, 1890. — *EMERSON, Letter to Whitman, quoted in Platt's Walt Whitman, pp. 27, 28. — *EMERSON, Letter to Carlyle, May 6, 1856 : The Correspondence of Carlyle and Emerson, vol. ii, p. 283. — EMERSON, *in* Woodbury's Talks with Ralph Waldo Emerson, pp. 62, 63. — FEDERN (Karl), Essays zur amerikanischen Litteratur, 1899. — FORMAN (H. B.), Our Living Poets : Introduction. — GAMBERALE (Luigi), Canti Scelti (Italian translation of selections from Leaves of Grass) : Introduction, 1887. — GAMBERALE (Luigi), La Vita e le Opere di Walt Whitman : *in the* Rivista d'Italia, vol. i, p. 181 ; translated in part in the Conservator, September, 1904. — GAY (William), Walt Whitman : His Relation to Science and Philosophy, Melbourne, 1895. — *GILCHRIST (Anne), An Englishwoman's Estimate of Walt Whitman ; from Late Letters to W. M. Rossetti : *in* H. H. Gilchrist's Anne Gilchrist, Her Life and Writings, 1887 ; *also in* In Re Walt Whitman. — *GILCHRIST (Anne), A Confession of Faith, *in* H. H. Gilchrist's Anne Gilchrist, Her Life and Writings, 1887 ; *also in* E. P. Gould's Anne Gilchrist and Walt Whitman. — *GOSSE (Edmund), Critical Kit-Kats, 1896. — GREG (Thomas T.), Walt Whitman : Man and Poet, 1888. — GUTHRIE (William Norman), Modern Poet-Prophets, Essays critical and interpretative : Walt Whitman the Camden Sage, 1897. — HARNED (T. B.), The Poet of Immortality : *in* In Re Walt Whitman. — HARNED (T. B.), Walt Whitman and Oratory ; Walt Whitman and Physique ; Walt Whitman and his Second Boston Publishers : *in* vol. viii of the Camden Edition. — HIGGINSON (T. W.), Contemporaries, 1899. — HOLMES (Edmond), Walt Whitman's Poetry, a Study and a Selection, 1902. — HOWE (M. A. DeW.), American Bookmen, 1898. — JAMES (H., Jr.), Walt Whitman's Letters to Peter Doyle : *in* Literature, April 16, 1898. — JAMES (H., Jr.), The War and Literature ; The Wound Dresser : *in* Literature, May 7, 1898. — JANNACONE (P.), La Poesia di Walt Whitman, e l'Evoluzione delle Forme Ritmiche, Turin, 1898. — KENNEDY (W. S.), The Poet as a Craftsman, 1886. — KNORTZ (Karl), Vorwort und Einleitung (introducing the German translation of selected poems, by Knortz and Rolleston), Zurich, 1889; *translated, in* In Re Walt Whitman. — KNORTZ (Karl), Walt Whitman ; Der Dichter der Demokratie, 1899. — LANIER (C. D.), Walt Whitman : *in the* Chautauquan, 1892, vol. xv, pp. 311-313. — *LANIER, Letters, 1866 to 1881 : To Bayard Taylor, February 3, 1878. — LANIER, The English Novel and its Development ; Lecture iii. — LE GALLIENNE (R.), Walt Whitman, an Address. — *MABIE (H. W.), Backgrounds of Literature : America in the Poems of Walt Whitman, 1903. — *MACPHAIL (Andrew), Essays in Puritanism, 1905. — MAYNARD (Mrs. M. T.), Walt Whitman, the Poet of the Wider Selfhood, 1903. — MAYNARD (Laurens), Walt Whitman's Comradeship : *in the* Whitman Fellowship Papers. — NENCIONI (E.), Letteratura inglese : Il Poeta della Guerra americana. — NEWCOMER (A. G.), American Literature. — NICHOL (John), American Literature, an Historical Sketch, 1882. — NOBLE (Charles), Studies in American Literature, 1898. — *NOEL (Roden), Essays on Poetry and Poets : A Study of Walt Whitman, 1886. — NOYES (Carleton E.), Whitman's Message to a Young Man : *in the* Conservator, January, 1905. — ONDERDONK (J. L.), History of American Verse, 1901. — RAYMOND (G. L.), Art in Theory : Whitman as a Romanticist. — RHYS (E.), Poems by Walt Whitman (The Canterbury Poets) : Introduction, 1886. — RICHARDSON (C. F.), American Literature. — ROBERTSON (J. M.), Walt Whitman, Poet and Democrat, Edinburgh, 1884. — ROLLESTON (T. W.), Ueber Wordsworth und Walt Whitman, Dresden, 1883; *translated, in* In Re Walt Whitman. — *ROSSETTI (W. M.), Poems of Whitman, Selected and Edited : Prefatory Notice, 1868. — ROSSETTI (W. M.), Ruskin, Rossetti, Pre-Raphaelitism. (Allusions to Whitman, pp. 134, 147, 159-160.) — SALTER (W. M.), Walt Whitman, Two Addresses : The Great Side of Walt Whitman ; The Questionable Side of Walt Whitman, 1899. — SANTAYANA (George), Walt Whitman, A Dialogue : *in the* Harvard Monthly, May, 1890. — *SANTAYANA (George), Interpretations of Poetry and Religion : The Poetry of Barbarism, 1900. — SANTAYANA (George), Introduction to the Selections from Walt Whitman : *in* G. R. Carpenter's American Prose. — SARRAZIN (Gabriel), La Renaissance de la poésie anglaise, 1798-1889 : Walter Whitman ; *the same*, translated by Harrison S. Morris : *in* In Re Walt Whitman. — SCHLAF (Johannes), Walt Whitman, Lyrik des chat noir, Paul Verlaine. — SCHMIDT (Rudolf), Buster og Masker ; Litteratur-Studier, Copenhagen, 1882 ; *translated, in* In Re Walt Whitman. — *STEDMAN (E. C.), Poets of America, 1885. — *STEVENSON (R. L.), Familiar Studies of Men and Books, 1882. — STEVENSON, Miscellanies, vol. ii. — SWINBURNE, William Blake, A Critical Essay, 1868. — *SWINBURNE, Under the Microscope, 1872. — *SWINBURNE, Studies in Prose and Poetry : Whitmania, 1894. (From the Fortnightly Review, August 1, 1887.) — *SYMONDS (J. A.), Essays, 1890, vol. ii : Democratic Art, with Special Reference to Walt Whitman ; *the same*, *in* Essays Speculative and Suggestive. — *SYMONDS (J. A.), Walt Whitman, a Study, 1893. — *THAYER (W. R.), Throne-Makers and Portraits. — *TRENT (W. P.), A History of American Literature. — TRIGGS (O. L.), Browning and Whitman, a Study in Democracy, 1893. — TRIGGS (O. L.), Selections from Whitman's Prose and Poetry : Introduction, 1898. — TRIMBLE (W. H.), Walt Whitman and Leaves of Grass : An Introduction, London, 1905. — VINCENT (L. H.), American Literary Masters, 1905. — VON ENDE (A.), Walt Whitman and Arno Holz : *in* Poet-

Lore, June, 1905. — WENDELL (B.), A Literary History of America, 1900. — *WHITMAN, Walt Whitman and his Poems; Leaves of Grass; An English and an American Poet: in In Re Walt Whitman. — Prefaces to Leaves of Grass: in Complete Prose Works. — A Backward Glance o'er Travel'd Roads: in Leaves of Grass, final edition. — WILKIE (James), The Democratic Movement in Literature, 1886. — WYZEWA (T. de), Écrivains étrangers, 1899.

TRIBUTES IN VERSE

*BARKER (Elsa), To Walt Whitman: in the Conservator, 1903. — BARLOW (George), From Dawn to Sunset: Walt Whitman. — BLOCK (L. J.), The New World and Other Verse: Walt Whitman. — *BUNNER (H. C.), Airs from Arcady and Elsewhere: Home, Sweet Home, with Variations: vi, Walt Whitman. (The best of all parodies on Whitman's style, and at the same time a genuine tribute to him.) — BROWN (J. H.), Poems Lyrical and Dramatic: To Walt Whitman. — D'ANNUNZIO (Gabriele), Poema Paradisiaco, p. 216. — GARLAND (Hamlin), Walt Whitman: in In Re Walt Whitman. — *GILDER (R. W.), A Wondrous Song: in the Conservator, June, 1905. — HORTON (George), in In Re Walt Whitman, p. 22. — LAW (James D.), Dreams o' Hame and Other Scotch Poems: A Few Words to Walt Whitman. — LLOYD (J. William), Wind-Harp Songs: Mount Walt Whitman. — MAYNARD (Laurens), For Whitman's Birthday, 1895: in the Conservator, June, 1895. — MORRIS (H. S.), Madonna and Other Poems: Walt Whitman; also in Stedman's American Anthology. — PIATT (J. J.), To Walt Whitman the Man: in the Cosmopolitan, November, 1892. — RHYS (Ernest), A London Rose and Other Poems: To Walt Whitman on his Seventieth Birthday: also in Camden's Compliments to Walt Whitman. — *STEDMAN (E. C.), Walt Whitman, March 30, 1892. — *SYMONDS (J. A.), Life and Death, a Symphony: in In Re Walt Whitman, pp. 1–12. — *SWINBURNE, Songs before Sunrise: To Walt Whitman in America, 1871. — WILLIAMS (F. H.), The Flute Player and Other Poems: Walt Whitman, May 31, 1886; Walt Whitman, March 26, 1892: the second is also in Stedman's American Anthology.

LANIER

EDITIONS

*POEMS, edited by his wife, with a memorial by William Hayes Ward, 1 volume: Charles Scribner's Sons. — *THE SCIENCE OF ENGLISH VERSE, 1 volume: Charles Scribner's Sons. — RETROSPECTS AND PROSPECTS, Descriptive and Historical Essays; MUSIC AND POETRY, a Volume of Essays; THE ENGLISH NOVEL, A Study in the Development of Personality: Charles Scribner's Sons. — SHAKSPERE AND HIS FORERUNNERS, Studies in Elizabethan Poetry and its Development from Early English, edited by H. W. Lanier, 2 volumes: Doubleday, Page & Co. — *LETTERS OF SIDNEY LANIER, Selections from his Correspondence 1866–1881, 1 volume: Charles Scribner's Sons. — SELECT POEMS, edited with an Introduction and Notes by Morgan Callaway, Jr.: Charles Scribner's Sons.

BIOGRAPHY AND REMINISCENCES

WARD (W. H.), Memorial: in Poems of Sidney Lanier, 1884. — *MIMS (Edwin), Sidney Lanier (American Men of Letters Series), 1905.
BASKERVILL (W. M.), Sidney Lanier: in Southern Writers, Biographical and Critical Studies, 1896–1897. — BOYKIN (Laurette), Home Life of Sidney Lanier, 1889. — BROWNE (William H.), Memorial Address before the Johns Hopkins University, October 22, 1881 (privately printed). — GILMAN (D. C.), editor, The Forty-sixth Birthday of Sidney Lanier, February 3, 1888. (Containing poems by John B. Tabb, Richard Burton, Edith Thomas, etc.; letters from Lowell, Stedman, Gilder, etc.; and a bibliography by Richard Burton.) — *GILMAN (D. C.), Sidney Lanier, Reminiscences and Letters: in the South Atlantic Quarterly, April, 1905. — HAYNE (Paul H.), A Poet's Letters to a Friend: in the Critic, vol. v, pp. 77, 78, 89, 90, February 13, 20, 1886: also in The Letters of Sidney Lanier. — NEWELL (A. C.), Lanier's Life at Oglethorpe College: in the Atlanta Constitution, February 27, 1894. — *NORTHRUP (M. H.), Sidney Lanier, Recollections and Letters, in Lippincott's Magazine, March, 1905. — TURNBULL (Mrs. Lawrence), The Catholic Man: A Study, 1890. (The character of Paul represents Sidney Lanier.) — WEST (C. N.), A Brief Sketch of the Life and Writings of Sidney Lanier, 1888. —

WILLS (George S.), Sidney Lanier: *in the* Publications of the Southern History Association, vol. iii, pp. 190–211, 1899. (With a complete bibliography of Lanier's writings.)

CRITICISM

*BENTZON (Th.) [Mme. Thérèse Blanc], Choses et gens d'Amérique: Un musicien poète Sidney Lanier, 1898: *translated*, *in* Littell's Living Age, May 14, 21, 1898. — GOSSE (Edmund) Questions at Issue, 1893. — HIGGINSON (T. W.), Women and Men: The Victory of the Weak, 1888. — *HIGGINSON (T. W.), Contemporaries, 1899. — HIGGINSON (T. W.), and BOYNTON (H. W.), A Reader's History of American Literature, 1903. — *KENT (Charles W.), A Study of Lanier's Poems: *in the* Publications of the Modern Language Association, vol. vii, pp. 33–63, 1892. — MORRIS (H. S.), The Poetry of Sidney Lanier: *in the* American, Philadelphia, February 18, 1888. — NEWCOMER (A. G.), American Literature. — STEDMAN (E. C.), Poets of America, 1885. — *THAYER (W. R.), Letters of Sidney Lanier to Mr. and Mrs. Peacock, Introduction: *in the* Atlantic, vol. 74, pp. 14–17, 1894; *also*, *in the* Letters of Sidney Lanier, pp. 3–9. — THAYER (W. R.), *in the* Independent, June 12, 1884, Sidney Lanier and his Poetry; December 18, 1884, Lanier's Poems. — THAYER (W. R.), Sidney Lanier's Poems: *in the* American, Philadelphia, December 20, 1884. — TOLMAN (A. H.), The Views about Hamlet and Other Essays: Lanier's Science of English Verse, 1904. — TRENT (W. P.), Southern Writers: Introduction to the Selections from Lanier, 1905. — WARD (W. H.), Sidney Lanier, Poet: *in the* Century, April, 1888. — WENDELL (B.), A Literary History of America. — WILKINSON (W. C.), *in the* Independent, September, 1886.

TRIBUTES IN VERSE

BARBE (W.), Ashes and Incense. — BURROUGHS (Ellen), *in the* Literary World, vol. xxi, p. 40, February 1, 1890. — BURTON (Richard), To Sidney Lanier: *in* The Forty-sixth Birthday of Sidney Lanier. — CUMMINGS (James), The Stranger's Invocation before the Bust of Lanier: *in* The Forty-sixth Birthday of Sidney Lanier. — FISKE (Isabella H.), Sidney Lanier: *in the* New York Times Saturday Review, September 2, 1905. — GARLAND (Hamlin), *in the* Southern Bivouac, vol. ii, p. 759, May, 1887. — HAYNE (Paul H.), Complete Poems: The Pole of Death, In Memory of Sidney Lanier. — HAYNE (William H.), Sylvan Lyrics and Other Verses: Sidney Lanier. — *HOVEY (Richard), The Laurel, an Ode: To Mary Day Lanier. — REESE (Lizette W.), *in the* Southern Bivouac, vol. ii, p. 488, January, 1887. — REESE (Lizette W.), With a Copy of Lanier's Poems: *in the* Independent, vol. 44, p. 322, March 3, 1892. — ROBERTS (Charles G. D.), In Divers Tones: To the Memory of Sidney Lanier; On Reading the Poems of Sidney Lanier. — ROBERTS (Charles G. D.), For a Bust of Lanier: *in the* Independent, vol. xlii, p. 625, April 30, 1891. — *TABB (J. B.), Poems: p. 116, To Sidney Lanier; p. 117, On the Forthcoming Volume of Sidney Lanier's Poems. — THOMAS (Edith M.), Sidney Lanier: *in* The Forty-sixth Birthday of Sidney Lanier. — TURNBULL (Mrs. Lawrence), In Memoriam, Sidney Lanier, died September 7, 1881: *in* The Forty-sixth Birthday of Sidney Lanier.

BIOGRAPHICAL SKETCHES

BIOGRAPHICAL SKETCHES

WILLIAM CULLEN BRYANT

WILLIAM CULLEN BRYANT was born at Cummington, Mass., November 3, 1794. Of what sturdy New England stock he came may be guessed from the entry in his mother's diary (which she kept for fifty-three years without missing a day), under that date: 'Stormy wind N E — churned — unwell, seven at Night a Son Born.' Two days later the entry reads : 'Clear Wind N W — Made Austin a coat. . . .' Bryant's mother, like Longfellow's, was a descendant of John and Priscilla Alden of the Plymouth Colony. His earliest American ancestor on his father's side is said, like so many others, to have come over in the Mayflower. It is at least certain that he was at Plymouth in 1632, and he was constable of the colony in 1663. Bryant's father, his grandfather, and his grandmother's father were all New England country doctors. His father was a genial and generous man, a lover of poetry, especially that of the school of Pope. He encouraged his boy to read Pope's Iliad, and to act the old story over again with wooden shields and swords and mock-heroic costume; and also encouraged him in his early writing and in his later devotion to poetry, though not always in sympathy with the style and manner of his work. In all these points he reminds us of Browning's father.

Bryant began to write verses when he was eight years old. He showed similar precocity in other ways. Though he was never a strong child, yet 'On my first birthday,' he says, 'there is a record that I could already go alone, and on the 28th of March, 1796, when but a few days more than sixteen months old, there is another record that I knew all the letters of the alphabet.' He was sent to school at three years old, and could read well at four. His early verses were mostly in heroic couplets, and include school poems and versions of a part of the Book of Job and the first book of the Æneid, etc. They are much like the verses written in colonial days by worthy Puritan divines. Like Elizabeth Barrett, he published his first volume at the age of thirteen. This was a satire on the political events of the time, and it actually had a second edition the following year — a thing which probably has happened to no other poet when so young.

Bryant was prepared for college, as was usual in those times, by studying in the families of country ministers. From one he learned Latin, from another Greek. It took him eight months to go through the Latin grammar, the New Testament in Latin, Virgil's Æneid, Eclogues, and Georgics, and a volume of Cicero's orations. After a summer's work on the farm he then attacked Greek, and 'at the end of two calendar months,' according to his own testimony, 'knew the Greek Testament from end to end almost as if it had been English.' This was when he was fourteen years old. The following year he mastered his mathematics, and entered the sophomore class of Williams College at the age of fifteen.

Before he had quite completed the year at Williams, he withdrew from college, intending to prepare himself for the junior class at Yale. But when the time came for entering there in the fall, it was found that the family means would not allow Bryant to finish a college course, and he accordingly turned to the study of the law as the quickest way to prepare himself for earning a living. He passed his preliminary bar examinations in 1814, was admitted as attorney in 1816, and practised for nine years.

In the meantime 'Thanatopsis' and the 'Inscription for the Entrance to a Wood,' at first called 'A Fragment,' had been published in the *North American Review* for September, 1817. The story of how 'Thanatopsis' had been written when Bryant was only sixteen or seventeen years old, and how his father, having received a letter asking for contributions to the *Review*, found these unfinished poems in a desk and submitted them to the editors, who were at first unable to believe that they had been written by so young a man as Bryant, or even by any one ' on this side of the Atlantic,' has often been told. (See the notes on ' Thanatopsis,' pp. 1, 2; Bigelow's *Bryant*, pp. 38–41; or Bradley's *Bryant*, pp. 27–33.) Bryant was asked to be a regular contributor to the *North American*, and his next important poem published there was the lines ' To a Waterfowl.' A collection of his *Poems* was published in September, 1821, containing eight pieces, five of which are included in the present volume. The slight success of this book, of which only 270 copies were sold in five years, showed that an audience for the best poetry had still to be created in America. Bryant's name was already known, however, as that of the most promising of the younger poets, and he had been invited to deliver the annual Phi Beta Kappa poem at Harvard in 1821. It was for this occasion that ' The Ages,' the longest poem in the volume of 1821, had been written.

Bryant wrote very little from the time when he was admitted to the bar, in 1816, until 1821, except the noble ' Hymn to Death,' which he took up and completed at the time when his father died, in March, 1820. Soon after this a new impulse came into his life, in his love for Miss Frances Fairchild, whom he married June 11, 1821. Of the many poems written for her at this time, Bryant preserved only one, ' O fairest of the rural maids.' Throughout his life he was very severe in his criticism of his own verses, and is said to have destroyed more than he printed.

Bryant was weary of the law (see the last stanza of ' Green River '), but the sale of his volume of *Poems* was not such as to give him hope of making a living by purely literary work. During the five years following its publication his total profit from the sale had been $14.92. In 1825, however, after two visits to New York, he found employment there as associate editor of the *New York Review and Athenæum Magazine*, just about to be established. The first number appeared in June, 1825, and Bryant moved to New York to take up the editorial work which was to keep him there for the rest of his life. New York was then a village of 150,000 inhabitants, with the northern city limits at what is now Canal Street. The part of New York still known as Greenwich Village, south of Washington Square, was then a summer resort.

Bryant's first magazine, like so many others at that time, was not successful, and lived for only a year. At the beginning of 1826 he again took up the practice of the law for a short time. Later in the year, however, he was asked to be assistant editor of the New York *Evening Post*, and three years later became editor-in-chief. His connection with the paper as editor and part owner lasted for fifty-two years.

Bryant was so engrossed with his editorial work (for many years he kept office hours from seven in the morning till four in the afternoon), and with the many demands of life in a growing metropolitan and cosmopolitan city, that he gave little time to poetry. In 1832 he visited the West (accidentally seeing Lincoln, who was leading a company of Illinois volunteers across the prairie to the Black Hawk war), and wrote his poem ' The Prairies; ' he wrote no other poem of importance for three years. A new collection of his poems had been published in 1831, both in America and in England (see the note on the ' Song of Marion's Men,' p. 17), which considerably increased his reputation. In 1834 to 1836 he took his first trip to Europe, visiting England, France, Italy, and Germany, where, at Heidelberg, he met Longfellow, then preparing himself for his professorship at Harvard.

Bryant was always fond of travelling, and visited Europe again in 1845, in 1849, in 1852–53, when he saw something of the Oriental countries also, in 1857, and again in 1858, when he met, at Rome and Florence, the Brownings, W. W. Story, Crawford, Page, Miss Hosmer (the sculptress), Frederika Bremer, Hawthorne, and Landor, whom he greatly admired; and still again in 1866. His impressions were recorded in letters to the *Evening Post*, some of which have been collected in his *Letters from a Traveller*, *Letters from the East*, and *Letters from Spain and other Countries*. He also travelled extensively in America at various times. His life, during all these years, was uneventful; the time which he could give to writing was almost wholly filled with editorial work, and he produced only a few poems from year to year. New editions of his poems were, however, published, always with some additions, in 1834, 1836, 1842, 1844, and a collection in two volumes in 1854.

Bryant was an active worker in the formation of the Republican party in 1855. In 1859 he presided at a lecture given by Lincoln. Lincoln said: 'It was worth the journey to the East to see such a man,' and Bryant was so impressed with Lincoln's personality that he threw the whole influence of the *Post* in favor of his nomination for the Presidency in the following year, and was himself presidential elector on the Republican ticket. The *Post* was always a distinct power in national life, and especially so during the Civil War. Bryant had never been an abolitionist, but he was one of the strongest supporters of the Union, and, once the war had begun, of the policy of emancipation. His criticism of the administration was sometimes severe, especially in the matter of its greenback policy, but he retained close relations with Lincoln and was one of his most valued advisers. The struggle of these years had but few echoes in his poetry, except in two poems of 1861, 'Our Country's Call' and 'Not Yet,' and in three later poems, 'My Autumn Walk,' 'The Death of Lincoln,' and the 'Death of Slavery.' He seems rather to have sought a refuge in poetry from the strain of his daily work and the anxiety of the time. It was in 1862–63 that he wrote 'Sella' and the 'Little People of the Snow,' which have more lightness and charm than anything else in his work, and made a translation of the Fifth Book of the Odyssey. A collection of his later work was published in 1863, with the title *Thirty Poems*.

Already Bryant had long been recognized as the chief of our elder poets, and was called the 'Father of American Song.' This position, and still more the service which he had done and was doing as a man and a citizen, almost to the exclusion of further poetical work, were practically recognized by a meeting at the Century Club in New York, of which Bryant was for many years President. To this meeting the American republic of letters sent its best representatives, men of a generation just younger than Bryant, yet whose literary reputation was already greater than his, to do him honor on his seventieth birthday. Whittier wrote, —

> Who weighs him from his life apart
> Must do his nobler nature wrong,

and

> His life is now his noblest strain,
> His manhood better than his verse.

Holmes sent the finest of his many poetical tributes to contemporaries, and Lowell wrote for this occasion 'On Board the '76 ;' but perhaps the greatest tribute was Emerson's address. This was the culminating point in Bryant's career. He spoke of himself as 'one who has carried a lantern in the night, and who perceives that its beams are no longer visible in the glory which the morning pours around him.' It is true that Bryant is inferior to his younger contemporaries in the scope, the abundance, and the beauty of his poetical work. But he remains the pioneer of American poetry, and neither in the high nobility of his writing, nor in his dignity and his faithful work as a man, has he been surpassed.

In 1866 Mrs. Bryant died. Bryant's feeling of his loss is expressed only in the one poem 'A Life-Time.' He gave himself up during the following years to his translation of Homer. The Iliad was completed and published in 1870, the Odyssey in 1872. During the last years of his life he wrote a few poems, characterized by the same high dignity of expression which marks all his best work, and showing no loss of power. 'The Flood of Years' comes as the conclusion of his work and as a fitting pendent to 'Thanatopsis' at its commencement. This and 'A Life-Time' were the last poems he wrote.

He continued his editorial work till the last year of his life, walking daily to his office and back, a distance of three miles. Many New Yorkers still remember his impressive personality, the large, high forehead, flowing white hair, deep-set clear-seeing eyes under shaggy brows, and erect carriage. During these last years he was more and more in request as a public speaker, and was often called 'the old man eloquent.' Though he was not an orator in the usual sense of the word, his addresses were always impressive, appropriate, and full of well-knit thought. The best have been preserved in his prose works, and deal with Fitz-Greene Halleck, Shakspere, Scott, Burns, Franklin, Goethe, etc. His earlier addresses, especially those on Irving (1860) and Cooper (1852), must not be forgotten. When he was in his eighty-fourth year he paid a noble tribute to Mazzini in an oration at the unveiling of the statue in Central Park. He was somewhat exhausted by the effort and by the heat of the day ; and on returning to the home of his friend, General Wilson, he fell at the doorstep, receiving injuries which resulted in his death, June 12, 1878.

Bryant's life extended from the administration of Washington to that of Hayes — from the first presidency until after the centennial of the country. For more than fifty years during the formative period of the nation, he was a strong though quiet influence in its development. It is therefore impossible, as it would be unjust, to 'judge him from his life apart.' A keen judge, and never too generous a critic — Edgar Allan Poe — wrote of him so early as 1846 : 'In character, no man stands more loftily than Bryant. . . . His soul is charity itself, in all respects generous and noble.' It was this generous and noble character that Bryant freely gave to his times. He entered into all the life of a great material city, the centre of the country, as editor, orator, and public man. His life was too full for him to devote much of it to poetry, the most lasting part of his life-work, and to take that permanently high rank among American poets which some think he might have attained. Yet it is doubtful whether, if he had given more time to poetry, his limitations rather than his power might not have become more evident. His was not a genius of overflowing richness, of passion, of imagination. His range is narrow. But within his range he is supreme. What he gives us is the expression of simple and noble thought on life, and still more on death; and our first, and still the greatest, expression of American Nature in poetry. Whether or not he is the 'American Wordsworth' (see Lowell's *Fable for Critics*), he is the first and greatest poet of Nature in America ; not of larks and nightingales and English primroses would he write, like most of the provincial poets who preceded him, but of the bobolink, and the veerie, and the fringed gentian ; not of the English ponds and hills, but of the American lakes and mountains. This was America's 'Declaration of Independence' in poetry. Then too, in the highest of poetic forms in English, he is perhaps the greatest master since Milton. The blank verse of even Wordsworth, Landor, or Browning has not the power or the convoluted richness of expression through long interwoven rhythmic periods that Bryant's has. In 'Thanatopsis,' the 'Inscription for the Entrance to a Wood,' 'A Winter Piece,' the 'Hymn to Death,' 'Monument Mountain' (the best of his poems on Indian subjects), 'A Forest Hymn,' 'The Prairies,' the 'Antiquity of Freedom,' and the 'Flood of Years,' this noble rhythmic form fitly expresses the high dignity of his thought, and these together fitly represent his character and his life.

EDGAR ALLAN POE

EDGAR ALLAN POE was born at Boston, January 19, 1809, in the same year as Holmes and Tennyson, Lincoln and Gladstone, Mendelssohn and Chopin, and Charles Darwin. On his father's side he came of a good Maryland family, going back to John Poe, who emigrated from the north of Ireland to Pennsylvania about the middle of the eighteenth century, and soon moved to Maryland. The poet's grandfather, General David Poe, was Assistant-Quartermaster-General in the Revolution, and a close friend of Lafayette's. His son, David Poe, Jr., studied law, but soon abandoned it for acting, and in 1805 married Elizabeth Arnold, who had been born and brought up to the stage. Her mother was an English actress, and she had been first married to C. D. Hopkins, a comedian, who died in 1805. It seems that David Poe proved to have little talent as an actor, and his wife, delicate, beautiful, strong-willed, and versatile, was the support of the family. They had three children, of whom Edgar was the second. The little troop wandered up and down from Maine to So. Carolina, but found their best patrons and friends in Richmond.

It was at Richmond that Poe's mother died, of consumption, in December, 1811. His father had probably died some months before.

Poe was adopted by Mr. John Allan, a Scotch tobacco merchant of Richmond, not at all a rich man as has so often been stated. It is of record that he made an assignment for the benefit of creditors in 1822. In 1825, however, just before Poe left home for the University of Virginia, Mr. Allan received an inheritance from his uncle, one of the rich men of the State, which made him well-to-do. In the meantime he had attempted to extend his business to London. The most important result of this was that he took Poe to England and placed him for five years in the Manor House School, Stoke-Newington. Poe's story 'William Wilson' is full of reminiscences from this period, and much of his work is colored by it. Probably on some vacation trip to Scotland with his adopted parents he saw that lake among the hills which is the subject of one of his earliest yet most characteristic poems — one of those which he says were written before he was twelve years old : —

THE LAKE

In youth's spring it was my lot
To haunt of the wide earth a spot
The which I could not love the less ;
So lovely was the loneliness
Of a wild lake, with black rock bound,
And the tall pines that tower'd around.
But when the night had thrown her pall
Upon that spot — as upon all,
And the wind would pass me by
In its stilly melody,
My infant spirit would awake
To the terror of the lone lake.
Yet that terror was not fright —
But a tremulous delight,
And a feeling undefined,
Springing from a darken'd mind.
Death was in the poison'd wave
And in its gulf a fitting grave
For him who thence could solace bring
To his dark imagining ;
Whose wildering thought could even make
An Eden of that dim lake.

The poem was published in this form in his first volume, when he was eighteen years old, and was retained in every subsequent edition of his poems, in the edition of 1831 being inserted as a part of 'Tamerlane.' In the successive editions he made less changes in this than in any other of his earliest poems. The memory of a mystic lake of poisoned waves 'with black rock bound' reappears often in others of his works, until it becomes the 'dim lake of Auber' in his greatest poem. The love of loneliness and of night, the tremulous delight in terror, the thought of a darkened mind that seeks for death and finds in it an Eden, all remain characteristic of his later writing.

In 1820 the Allans returned to Richmond, and until 1825 Poe was at school there; he distinguished himself in athletics (especially swimming), in declamation, and in French. It was natural enough that his first school-boy love should be for a woman older than himself, but perhaps hardly natural that this should be the mother of one of his school-mates, and certainly not so that a healthy boy should haunt her grave for months, as is recorded of Poe ; for she died in 1824, the first of his many Helens and Lenores. Just before going away to the University he had a somewhat more normal love affair with a girl nearly two years younger than he (he was sixteen himself), a Miss Royster. They became 'engaged,' at least according to the lady's later account. Poe wrote to her from the University, but the letters were intercepted by her father, and she was soon married to a Mr. Shelton. Perhaps in this simple story is to be found the whole basis of Poe's 'Tamerlane,' almost certainly written during the following year.

The University of Virginia had been opened under Jefferson's patronage in March, 1825. Poe registered as a student there on February 14, 1826, and remained for one year. During this time he obtained distinction in Latin, French, and Italian, and was fairly regular in his attendance, but sometimes (not habitually) drank, and gambled with passionate recklessness. His gambling debts at the end of the year are said to have been about $2000. Mr. Allan refused to pay these debts of honor, withdrew Poe from the University, and set him to work at a desk in his own counting-room.

Poe did not submit to this employment long, but ran away, somehow reached Boston, and soon published there (1827) his first volume: *Tamerlane and Other Poems, By a Bostonian*. (See note 1 on page 36, and note 2 on page 39.) By the time the book was published, Poe, perhaps unable to find any other means of subsistence, had already (May 26, 1827) enlisted in the United States army, under the name of Edgar A. Perry. He served for nearly two years. He seems to have served faithfully; on January 1, 1829, he was promoted for merit to be Sergeant-Major. Early in 1829 Mrs. Allan died. Poe had been recalled to Richmond to see her, but arrived too late. There was, however, a partial reconciliation with Mr. Allan, who obtained a substitute for him in the army, and after some effort secured his nomination to West Point.

While waiting for this appointment he had published at Richmond (1829) *Al Aaraaf, Tamerlane, and Minor Poems*. For this volume he re-wrote, condensed, and for the most part greatly improved the 'Tamerlane.' (See the notes on pages 37 and 38.) 'Al Aaraaf' is on the whole a less successful production than 'Tamerlane.' In 'Tamerlane' he had deplored the triumph of ambition over love, in 'Al Aaraaf' he seems to be celebrating the claims of beauty as superior to all others, even those of love. The poem, however, has not, as 'Tamerlane' has, any clear thread of narrative on which to string its ideas and pictures, and even these are entirely vague and almost meaningless. 'Al Aaraaf' seems to show the influence of Shelley, as 'Tamerlane' (in the first form of which there occurs, unquoted, 'A sound of revelry by night') shows that of Byron. 'Al Aaraaf' also suffers from the fact that Poe never took the time to re-write it as he did 'Tamerlane.' There is in it, however, one supremely beautiful 'Burst of Melody' (as Professor Trent has entitled it in his *Selections from Poe*), the song to Ligeia. There are also in the volume of 1829 two exquisite lyrics, both entitled 'To ——,' and an early form of the poem 'A Dream within a Dream.' When we remember that Poe was barely twenty when this volume was published, and that Keats was twenty-two when his first volume (not containing any of his greatest work except the 'Sonnet on Chapman's Homer') appeared, we feel that Lowell was almost justified in writing to Poe (May 8, 1843) : 'Your early poems display a maturity which astonished me, and I recollect no individual (and I believe I have read all the poetry that ever was written) whose early poems were anything like as good.'

Poe entered West Point July 1, 1830. His work there was at first fairly good. He ranked third in French and seventeenth in mathematics, in a class of eighty-seven. Late in this year Mr. Allan married again, and Poe seems to have felt that he had no more to expect from him in the way of support or inheritance. In January of 1831 he deliberately neglected all duties at the academy for two weeks, was court-marshalled, and dismissed.

'When in doubt, publish a volume of poems,' seems, says some one, to have been the rule of Poe's life. After his dismissal from West Point, he went to New York and brought out his third volume, entitled simply *Poems*. This volume contained (and Poe was still only twenty-two years old) what is, perhaps, his most beautiful lyric, the first 'To Helen,' and the poems 'Israfel,' 'The City in the Sea,' 'The Sleeper,' 'Lenore' in its earliest form, and 'The Valley of Unrest.' His fellow cadets at West Point, to whom he dedicated the volume, and through whose subscriptions he had been enabled to publish it, were naturally disappointed at receiving such poems as these, instead of the satirical verses on their professors which they had expected.

For the next two years practically nothing is known of Poe's life. We find him in Baltimore in 1833, living with his father's sister, Mrs. Clemm. He had written six *Tales of the Folio Club*, and one of these, 'The Manuscript found in a Bottle,' won him a prize of one hundred dollars and the friendship of John P. Kennedy. The second prize of fifty dollars, offered for the best poem submitted, would have been awarded to Poe's 'Coliseum,' except that the judges felt unwilling to give both prizes to one competitor. This success gave Poe a practical start in literature, or rather journalism, and Mr. Kennedy secured for him a position on *The Southern Literary Messenger*, published at Richmond.

Meanwhile there had come to Poe the one genuine, deep, and lasting love of his lifetime, that for his child-cousin, Virginia Clemm. A license for marriage was obtained on September 22, 1834, when Virginia was barely twelve years old. There seems to have been no marriage at this time. In any case, after Poe moved to Richmond a new license was obtained, in May, 1836, and the marriage took place, while Virginia was still only in her fourteenth year.

Poe showed great ability as an editor and journalistic writer. He made the magazine famous, and greatly increased its circulation. But he was irregular in his habits and not to be depended upon. He had not learned to master the tendency against which he later struggled — at least for many months and even years of his life — so successfully. 'No man is safe,' his employer wrote to him, 'that drinks before breakfast.' He lost his position in January, 1837, went to New York, where he published in 1838 the *Narrative of Arthur Gordon Pym*, and then to Philadelphia, where he lived for the next six years.

During these years he did a great amount of literary hack-work, and did it well, and also wrote some of his best stories and criticism. His *Tales of the Grotesque and Arabesque* were published, in two volumes, at the end of 1839 (dated 1840). He was editor for a while of the *Gentleman's Magazine* and later of *Graham's Magazine*, two of the most important periodicals of the time. It has repeatedly been assumed that he lost his positions on both these magazines through incapacity caused by drinking, but the weight of evidence seems to disprove this. Mrs. Clemm stated positively, speaking of the period from 1837 to 1841, that 'for years I know he did not taste even a glass of wine' (Harrison's *Life of Poe*, p. 161), and this testimony is so strongly confirmed by others who knew him well during this time, that we may perhaps accept fully his own statement of the matter as made in a letter of 1841 : 'At no period of my life was I ever what men call intemperate, — I never was in the *habit* of intoxication. . . . But, for a period, while I resided in Richmond and edited the *Messenger*, I certainly did give way, at long intervals, to the temptation held out on all sides by the spirit of Southern conviviality. My sensitive temperament could not stand an excitement which was an every-day matter to my companions, — in short it sometimes happened that I was completely intoxicated. For some days after each excess I was invariably confined to bed. But it is now quite four years since I have abandoned every kind of alcoholic drink — four years, with the exception of a single deviation. . . .'

A few facts seem now to be clearly established after the years of controversy over this disagreeable question. It is certain that Poe was not, as has so often been stated, an abandoned or habitual drunkard. It is also certain that the effect of even small quantities of alcohol was, in his case, especially severe ; that he was to some extent the victim of a hereditary tendency ('There is one thing,' his cousin William Poe wrote to him, 'I am anxious to caution you against, and which has been a great enemy to our family . . . a too free use of the bottle '); and that the surroundings of his early life and the habits of the University and of West Point in those times did much to strengthen this tendency. It is also certain, and this has not been sufficiently recognized, that for many years Poe struggled manfully against this tendency, and succeeded, in spite of occasional relapses, and in the midst of all kinds of difficulties, discouragements, anxiety, poverty, and physical weakness, in doing an amount of work, and of highly intellectual work, that would have been impossible for a man so weak as he has usually been represented.

Two strong motives governed his life, so far as it could be governed : his devotion to his beautiful child-wife and to her mother, whom he calls his 'more than mother' in the beautiful sonnet which is the simple expression of his genuine feeling for her ; and his passionate desire for literary fame, which, at its worst, showed itself in petty envy and carping criticism of his contemporaries, but which, at its best, became a noble devotion to the ideal of beauty.

Every point in Poe's life and character has been the subject of controversy and conflicting statements, except one, — the genuineness, simplicity, and, until his wife's death, constancy, of his devotion to the two women who made his home. 'I shall never forget,' wrote the owner of *Graham's Magazine*, within a year after Poe's death, when the attacks upon him were bitterest, 'how solicitous of their happiness he was. . . . His whole efforts seemed to be to procure the comfort and welfare of his home. Except for their happiness, and the natural ambition of having a magazine of his own, I never heard him deplore the want of wealth. . . . His love for his wife was a sort of rapturous worship of the spirit of beauty, which he felt was fading before his eyes. I have seen him hovering around her when she was ill, with all the fond fear and tender anxiety of a mother for her first-born, — her slightest cough causing in him a shudder, a breast chill, that was visible. I rode out one summer evening with them, and the remembrance of his watchful eyes, eagerly bent upon the slightest change of hue in that loved face, haunts me yet as the memory of a sad strain.'

Virginia is described as of wonderful delicate loveliness, like that of Ligeia. She was a beautiful singer. In 1842, while singing for her husband, she broke a blood vessel in her throat, and this resulted in serious hemorrhages, which afterward recurred often, and sometimes brought her almost to the point of death. It was to Poe as if she had died many times, — as often, even, as he has expressed in his poetry that one theme which he calls the highest of all, the death of a beautiful woman.

Early in 1844 the little family moved to New York, Poe still hoping to found there a magazine of his own. For some time he worked on the staff of the *Evening Mirror*, under N. P. Willis, whose description of his faithfulness, industry, and courtesy must not be overlooked by any one trying to estimate his character during these years. 1845 was the year that gave Poe his national reputation. 'The Raven' appeared in the *Evening Mirror* on January 29, and was immediately copied by newspapers throughout the country, just as the first of Lowell's *Biglow Papers* was to be, a little more than a year later. His *Tales* were published by Wiley and Putnam, and had considerable success. He became associate-editor of the *Broadway Journal*, in which he republished, in their final perfected form, many of his earlier poems. And finally, all the poems which he wished to preserve were collected and published, toward the end of the year, in a volume entitled *The Raven and Other Poems*.

Meantime, Poe was involved in many bitter controversies, through his severe criticism of his contemporaries. The *Broadway Journal*, of which he had finally obtained exclusive control in October, 1845, failed to prove a financial success, and involved him in considerable debt; its publication had to be discontinued at the end of the year. Early in 1846 Poe moved, with his family, to the cottage at Fordham, in what is now the Borough of the Bronx, New York City. Here the little family lived through a year of wretchedness. Poe's strength, both of body and of character, was seriously impaired. Virginia's illness became more and more serious, until she died on January 30, 1847. Poe was seriously ill for a long time, but gradually recovered. It was at the end of this 'most immemorial year' that he wrote his 'Ulalume.'

In the year and a half that followed, all Poe's weaknesses were accentuated, and a new weakness, which is comprehensible, but not pleasant to contemplate, was added, in his abject appeal for the sympathy and sometimes for the hand of one woman after another. Yet his intellect and genius shone out at intervals almost more brightly than before. During this time he wrote 'Eureka' and 'The Bells,' the strange and wonderful lyric 'For Annie,' and 'Annabel Lee' — the last certainly a reminiscence of his child-wife Virginia. He became engaged to Sarah Helen Whitman, a poetess of extreme romantic temperament, his first meeting with whom is described in the second 'To Helen;' but the engagement was broken through the efforts of her friends. Her loyal defence of Poe against his critics after his death is to be remembered. Poe was in Richmond in 1848, and again in 1849, hoping to get help there for the establishment of the new magazine which he was still planning; he found there the Mrs. Shelton who, as Miss Royster, had been his first love, and who was now a widow. He became engaged to her, his friends in Richmond raised a fund to help him start anew in life, and he left Richmond on September 30, to return to New York and settle up his affairs. It will never be known what happened on the following days, but he was found, October 3, in the back room of a saloon in Baltimore which was being used as a polling place. It has been suggested that he was drugged by an electioneering gang and made to serve as a repeater; and also that he had been drugged by robbers, for his money was gone. He was taken to a hospital, and died there, four days later, on Sunday, October 7, without having recovered consciousness. The attending physician testified that he was not under the influence of liquor, but this does not seem to be important, though it may refute the repeated statement that his death was caused by delirium tremens.

Poe's character has often been judged harshly, but the case is one rather for human pity than for harsh judgment. His life was a tragedy, and in part a tragedy of hereditary fate, against which his human will struggled as best it could. He should be judged with the same charity which his New England contemporaries showed in their many beautiful tributes to Burns, whose life and character have points of resemblance with Poe's, though Burns's poetry is so much more human and less strange.

In many ways Poe is unique among the chief American poets : in his life, for he is the only one who lived in extreme poverty and loneliness ; the only one of weak character and ill-repute ; the only one (except Lanier) who died young. He is unique in his hatred of commonplace and of convention, in his intense devotion to poetry, in his love of mere music in verse, in his power to express emotion and his inability to express character, in his comparative blindness to Nature (except that strange unreal region of Nature which he creates for himself ' out of place, out of time '), in his exaltation of love, in his strange visionary conceptions of death. He is the only American who has been *intensely a poet*, and the only American poet (as Hawthorne is our only prose writer) who can justly be said, in any strict and narrow use of the word, to have had genius.

RALPH WALDO EMERSON

THE story of Emerson's life, so far as its external events are related to his poetry, can be told briefly. He was the last of nine successive generations of ministers. Thomas Emerson emigrated from England to Ipswich, Mass., about 1635. At about the same time, Emerson's first American ancestor in another line, Peter Bulkeley (see the beginning of ' Hamatreya '), settled in Concord as the first minister of that parish. Emerson's grandfather, William Emerson, was minister in Concord at the beginning of the Revolution, and on April 19, 1775, urged the minute-men to stand their ground near his parsonage, the ' Old Manse.' In 1776 he left Concord to join the troops at Ticonderoga, but caught a fever on his way there, and died in the same year. Emerson's father was minister of the First Church, Boston, which had already become Unitarian.

Ralph Waldo Emerson was born in Boston, May 25, 1803. His father died when he was eight years old, and the family was left in comparative poverty. Yet his mother, with devoted help from her sons, succeeded in obtaining an education for all of them. His eldest brother, William, graduated at Harvard in 1818, and studied for two years in Germany. Ralph Waldo graduated at Harvard in 1821, and his younger brothers, Edward and Charles, in 1824 and 1828.

Ralph was prepared for Harvard at the Boston Latin School, where, in his eleventh year, he made a brief verse translation from Virgil's Eclogues, which has been preserved and published. He entered college in 1817, with the appointment of ' President's Freshman,' receiving free lodging for the work of carrying official messages ; and he saved three-fourths of the cost of his board by waiting at table in the college Commons, and in the last years of his course earned something by tutoring. He did not especially distinguish himself in his studies, being generally thought the least brilliant of the brothers, but he was well liked by both teachers and students, and was elected class poet at the end of his course, as Lowell was later. He was only eighteen when he graduated, but immediately began work as a school-teacher, and when his older brother, William, went to

Germany, took charge of his school for young ladies in Boston. He wrote long after : ' I was nineteen, had grown up without sisters, and, in my solitary and secluded way of living, had no acquaintance with girls. I still recall my terrors at entering the school.' It was on the occasion of his weekly escape from these ' terrors ' to his home in Roxbury, which was then the country (and not at his retirement to Concord, as has often been said), that he wrote the poem 'Good-bye, proud world.'

He soon entered the Divinity School at Harvard, where he studied under Dr. W. E. Channing and Professor Andrews Norton ; and was ' approbated to preach ' in October, 1826. He had no settled parish, and had not as yet much confidence in himself, his doctrines, or his power to speak. ' Whatever Heaven has given me or withheld,' he wrote at this time, ' my feelings, or the expression of them, is very cold, my understanding and my tongue slow and ineffective.' His feelings were soon to be roused and quickened, however, and his expression vivified. In December, 1827, he was preaching at Concord, N. H., and met there Miss Ellen Tucker, then sixteen years old, to whom he became engaged just a year later. Of the beautiful lyrics written for her, one, beginning ' And Ellen, when the graybeard years,' which was written in 1829, but remained unpublished for seventy-five years, deserves to stand beside anything even of Landor's for its simplicity and condensation, and for that peculiar feeling of the eternal which a brief and perfect poem can give.

In 1829 he was appointed assistant pastor of the Hanover Street Church, Boston (the church of the Mathers). In September he was married. His wife was already frail from consumption, and she died two years later. Emerson found even the liberal doctrines and simple forms of the Unitarian Church somewhat too strict for him, and felt himself compelled, in the following year, 1832, to give up his pastorate. He still preached occasionally for a few years, but for the rest of his life the public lecture platform was his chief pulpit ; for he never ceased to be, in a way, a preacher.

In December, 1832, Emerson sailed for Europe, going by the then unusual southern route, and visited first Sicily and Italy. The fragments ' Written in Naples,' and ' Written at Rome,' are significant of his mood and thoughts at this time. The first, with its remembrance of

> beauty in the fogs
> Of close low pinewoods in a river town,

foreshadows the idea which is primarily Emerson's, but for which Whittier found its most perfect expression in his

> He who wanders widest, lifts
> No more of Beauty's jealous veils
> Than he who from his doorway sees
> The miracle of flowers and trees,

and reminds us that Emerson was to be the poet of ' Woodnotes,' and, after Bryant, the chief poet of Nature in America, with its own peculiar and distinctive beauties. The second, ' Written at Rome,' with its

> And ever in the strife of your own thoughts
> Obey the nobler impulse ; that is Rome,

shows that Emerson was already on the track of his answer to the Sphinx's riddle.

He sought in Europe not things but men, not relics of the past but living thoughts. For him Florence seems to have meant Landor, in his villa at the foot of the Fiesolan hill. He passed through France uncomprehending, thinking it a land ' where poet never grew,' and went to visit the almost unknown Carlyle on his Scotch hillside, and Wordsworth by his English Lakes. His friendship for Carlyle lasted till the end of his life, and he did Carlyle great service in introducing his works to America, taking charge of all the material details of their publication here. He seems to have been much amused at first to see Wordsworth pause in his garden walks and stand apart to declaim his own sonnets, but on second thought recollected that that was what he had come for, and listened with reverence.

On his return, Emerson settled in Concord. He had been through his *Lehrjahre* and

Wanderjahre, had found his own place, intellectually and spiritually, in the universe, and had acquired confidence in his own thought and his right and power to deliver a message to the world. He now abandoned, as unimportant, the negative side of his earlier Unitarianism and of his revolt from the forms and formal beliefs even of Unitarianism itself; and insisted on what is the positive side of Unitarianism, and, more broadly, of idealistic philosophy, — the thought that every man (as well as the Christ, though not in the same degree) has in himself something of the divine, is himself a part of the ' World-Soul,' and therefore has within himself, and himself is, the measure of all things ; and so can meet fearlessly all the Sphinx-riddles of the universe. The other side of this conception is his thought that all Nature is but another manifestation, or another part of the same manifestation, of the ' World-Soul;' and that Nature is thus most closely related to the central reality in man. Hardly more than this need be said, I think, in elucidation of the so-called obscure and mystic poems of Emerson, and in elementary statement of his much-discussed 'transcendentalism.'

Strong in this belief in the intellectual independence of himself and of every individual man, Emerson prepared that famous address on ' The American Scholar,' which was given before the Phi Beta Kappa of Harvard University in 1837. That and his little book called *Nature*, published in the previous year, give us the two sides of his thought just stated. In the Phi Beta Kappa address, however, he stated this thought more especially as related to the intellectual attitude of America in 1837, and as a protest against its provincialism. ' Our day of dependence, our long apprenticeship to the learning of other lands, draws to a close . . . We will walk on our own feet ; we will work with our own hands; we will speak our own minds . . . a nation of men will for the first time exist, because each believes himself inspired by the Divine Will, which also inspires all men.' This address was America's Declaration of Independence in the intellectual life. His Divinity School address, in the following year, was a spiritual declaration of independence : ' Let me admonish you, first of all, to go alone; to refuse the good models, even those which are sacred in the imagination of men, and dare to love God without mediator or veil . . . Thank God for these good men, but say, "I am also a man." . . . Yourself a new-born bard of the Holy Ghost, cast behind you all conformity, and acquaint yourself at first hand with the Deity.' These two addresses aroused great opposition, but Emerson entirely disregarded it, and went quietly on his way. He seems to have regretted it only so far as he felt that opposition to him personally might injure the success in America of Carlyle's works, for which he stood sponsor.

In the years of this (as it then seemed) revolutionary thinking and speaking, Emerson was living a quiet, simple, practical life at Concord, taking his part in the affairs of the village, even accepting an election as hog-reeve of the township, delivering the Bi-Centennial Address in 1835, and writing the Hymn for the Completion of the Battle Monument in 1837. In 1834 his brother Edward died, and in 1836 his youngest brother, Charles. It was in 1838, ' at the mid-point of life's pathway,' as Dante expresses it in the first line of his *Divina Commedia*, that Emerson wrote the beautiful ' Dirge ' for them : —

> I reached the middle of the mount
> Up which the incarnate soul must climb,
> And paused for them, and looked around,
> With me who walked through space and time.
>
> Five rosy boys with morning light
> Had leaped from one fair mother's arms,
> Fronted the sun with hope as bright,
> And greeted God with childhood's psalms.
>
> . . . .
>
> The winding Concord gleamed below,
> Pouring as wide a flood
> As when my brothers, long ago,
> Came with me to the wood.
>
> But they are gone, — the holy ones
> Who trod with me this lovely vale;
> The strong, star-bright companions
> Are silent, low, and pale.

My good, my noble, in their prime,
  Who made this world the feast it was,
Who learned with me the lore of time,
  Who loved this dwelling-place !

They took this valley for their toy,
  They played with it in every mood ;
A cell for prayer, a hall for joy, —
  They treated Nature as they would.

They colored the horizon round ;
  Stars flamed and faded as they bade,
All echoes hearkened for their sound, —
  They made the woodlands glad or mad.

I touch this flower of silken leaf,
  Which once our childhood knew ;
Its soft leaves wound me with a grief
  Whose balsam never grew.

From this time on, Emerson's life was diversified only by home joys and sorrows. He married in 1835 Miss Lidian Jackson of Plymouth. In October, 1836, was born the beautiful boy who died in January, 1842, the ' wondrous child ' of his ' Threnody.' Some of his most important poems were published in the *Dial* in 1840 and 1841, and he was editor of that short-lived transcendentalist magazine from 1842 to 1844. The first series of his *Essays* was published in 1841, the second in 1844, the second edition of *Nature* in 1849, *Representative Men* in 1850, and *English Traits* in 1856. He had taken a second brief trip to Europe in 1847–48. The only important collections of his verse during his lifetime were the *Poems* of 1846 (dated 1847), *May Day and Other Pieces*, 1867, and a selection in the *Little Classics* edition, 1876, including a few poems not previously collected. The editions of the *Poems*, 1883, and 1904 (*Centenary Edition*), both contain very important additions. His lecture field was extended in 1843 to New York and Philadelphia, in 1847–48 to England and Scotland, in 1854 to the States of the new Northwest, Michigan and Wisconsin, in 1862 to Washington, where Lincoln attended his lecture on ' American Civilization.' From 1854 to 1868 he gave many lecture courses in the West, and in 1871 went as far as the Pacific coast, but the larger part of his lectures were still given in New England, especially at Boston and Concord. In 1870 he gave a regular course in the Graduate School of Harvard, then just established. During these years his life in Concord was enriched by the friendships with Thoreau, Alcott, and Ellery Channing, as well as by his acquaintance in Boston and Cambridge with Longfellow, Agassiz, Holmes, and Lowell ; he and Hawthorne were good neighbors, but never intimate friends. Concord became a shrine of pilgrimage, and many of the best and ablest minds of the time, as well as many unbalanced and vague idealists, made themselves, like Lowell, Emerson's faithful ' liegemen.'

Emerson always refused to be drawn into the anti-slavery contest as an active worker. He gives his reasons in full in the ' Ode to W. H. Channing.' He advocated the purchase of the slaves, for two billion dollars, — less than the war ultimately cost, in mere money expenditure, to the North alone. But though he did not identify himself with the abolitionists, he never hesitated on occasion to express his views clearly. His first speech on American Slavery was given at Concord in 1837, and his address on Emancipation in 1844; he voted with the Free-Soil party in 1850, joined in the mistaken opposition to Webster in 1851, denounced the Fugitive Slave Law and the assault on Charles Sumner, and took part in the memorial service for John Brown of Ossawatomie. In January, 1861, with Wendell Phillips, he was mobbed at the Tremont Temple in Boston. During the war he was a strong advocate of unconditional emancipation. But that he did wisely in keeping for the most part to ' his chosen work,' was proved by the outcome. His political idealism, his belief in man, which finds its perfect expression in the famous quatrain of ' Voluntaries,' became a pervading influence. To this influence, more than to anything else, said Lowell, ' the young martyrs of our Civil War owe the astounding strength of thoughtful heroism that is so touching in every record of their lives.' It was Emerson who was chosen to give the address at the Harvard Commemoration for which Lowell's great Ode was written.

The last ten years of Emerson's life were somewhat clouded by a gradual failure of his mental powers, especially of the memory, but he was always, as Whitman has described him in his reminiscences, beautiful in old age. Holmes tells us of the last time he saw Emerson, at Longfellow's funeral, in 1882. Twice he rose, and looked intently on the face of the dead poet, and the last time turned and said to a friend near him, ' That gentleman was a sweet, beautiful soul, but I have entirely forgotten his name.' Emerson died just a month after Longfellow, April 24, 1882.

' I am born a poet,' wrote Emerson in 1835 ; ' of a low class, without doubt, yet a poet. That is my nature and vocation. My singing, to be sure, is very husky, and is for the most part in prose. Still, I am a poet in the sense of a perceiver and true lover of the harmonies that are in the soul and in matter, and specially of the correspondences between these and those.' At other times, Emerson said of himself, ' I am *not* a great poet.' On the other hand, Mr. Stedman calls him ' our most typical and inspiring poet.' It has often been said that he could not write poetry at all, and as often replied that he could write nothing else. Of course the question is largely one of definitions. Emerson's own dictum, ' The great poets are judged by the frame of mind they induce,' which has often been quoted in settlement of the question, is too vague to be of any real help. It would apply equally well as a standard for the judgment of great prose writers, or great orators. Confusion arises on the one hand from identifying poetry with whatever is noble and imaginative in thought or feeling, and on the other hand, from narrowing it to the mere singing faculty. The lyric is only one of the many poetic forms ; and the lyric element in poetry is only one of its important elements. In the nineteenth century, to be sure, the lyric almost usurped to itself the whole domain and conception of poetry. But this error can be only a passing one. What lasts from century to century in poetry is even more often those words or phrases which condense thought or feeling or vision into simple and well-shaped rhythmic form, than the verse that merely appeals to the senses with easy-flowing or even haunting melody. We may even admit that Emerson was not a born singer, — many of the greatest poets have not been, in the narrow lyric sense of the word, — and still maintain, without falling into the opposite error of identifying poetry with that nobility of thought and originality of imagination which are merely possible material for poetry, that he was a born poet. For he proved himself a poet in the form as well as in the substance of his work. That he did not altogether lack the lyric note, the ' Earth Song ' in ' Hamatreya,' a few passages in ' Woodnotes ' and ' May Day,' and many stanzas of ' My Garden,' of ' Waldeinsamkeit,' and of the ' Concord Ode,' at once show. But, what is far more important, he has in a supreme degree the faculty of fitting thought to the *form* of verse rather than merely to its melody. Many a line, many a quatrain, many brief passages, and a few complete poems, stand, and are beginning more and more to stand out, in Emerson's work, like those lines of which Holmes said that a moment after they were written it seemed ' as if they had been carved on marble for a thousand years.'

HENRY WADSWORTH LONGFELLOW

HENRY WADSWORTH LONGFELLOW was born at Portland, Maine, February 27, 1807, the second of eight children. He came of an old New England family. His father and his great-grandfather were graduates of Harvard College. On his mother's side he was descended from John and Priscilla Alden of Plymouth, and his maternal grandfather, General Peleg Wadsworth, was a distinguished officer in the Revolution. He spent a happy boyhood in Portland, the memory of which returns often in his poems, especially in ' My Lost Youth.' The first book that he remembered with delight was Irving's *Sketch Book*, which he read in numbers when it appeared. His first published verses, the ' Battle of Lovell's Pond,' were printed in the *Portland Gazette* when he was thirteen years old.

It might have been expected that he would go to Harvard College, as his father had done. But his father was now a trustee of Bowdoin, the chief college of Maine, which had only recently been set apart from Massachusetts as a separate state. Longfellow entered the sophomore class at Bowdoin in 1822, and graduated in 1825, ranking second in his class. Hawthorne was in the same class; and Franklin Pierce, later President of the United States, and Hawthorne's close friend, was in the next preceding class.

In his last year at college, when the question of choosing a career in life became pressing, Longfellow wrote to his father (December 5, 1824) : ' I take this early opportunity to write to you, because I wish to know fully your inclination with regard to the profession I am to pursue when I leave college. For my part, I have already hinted to you what would best please me. I want to spend one year at Cambridge for the purpose of reading history, and of becoming familiar with the best authors in polite literature ; whilst at the same time I can be acquiring a knowledge of the Italian language, without an acquaintance with which I shall be shut out from one of the most beautiful departments of letters. The French I mean to understand pretty thoroughly before I leave college. After leaving Cambridge, I would attach myself to some literary periodical publication, by which I could maintain myself and still enjoy the advantages of reading. Now, I do not think that there is anything visionary or chimerical in my plan thus far. The fact is — and I will not disguise it in the least, for I think I ought not — the fact is, I most eagerly aspire after future eminence in literature ; my whole soul burns most ardently for it, and every earthly thought centres in it. There may be something visionary in *this*, but I flatter myself that I have prudence enough to keep my enthusiasm from defeating its object by too great haste. Surely, there never was a better opportunity offered for the exertion of literary talent in our own country than is now offered. To be sure, most of our literary men thus far have not been professedly so, until they have studied and entered the practice of Theology, Law, or Medicine. But this is evidently lost time. . . . Whether Nature has given me any capacity for knowledge or not, she has at any rate given me a very strong predilection for literary pursuits, and I am almost confident in believing, that, if I can ever rise in the world, it must be by the exercise of my talent in the wide field of literature. With such a belief, I must say that I am unwilling to engage in the study of the law.'

On the last day of the year he wrote again: ' I am very desirous to hear your opinion of my project of residing a year at Cambridge. Even if it should be found necessary for me to study a profession, I should think a twelve-months' residence at Harvard before commencing the study would be exceedingly useful. Of divinity, medicine, and law, I should choose the last. Whatever I do study ought to be engaged in with all my soul, — for I *will be eminent* in something. The question then is, whether I could engage in the law with all that eagerness which in these times is necessary to success. I fear that I could not. . . . Let me then reside one year at Cambridge; let me study belles-lettres; and after that time it will not require a spirit of prophecy to predict with some degree of certainty what kind of a figure I could make in the literary world.' His father answered: ' A literary life, to one who has the means of support, must be very pleasant. But there is not enough wealth in this country to afford encouragement and patronage to merely literary men. And as you have not had the fortune (I will not say whether good or ill) to be born rich, you must adopt a profession which will afford you subsistence as well as reputation. I am happy to observe that my ambition has never been to accumulate wealth for my children, but to cultivate their minds in the best possible manner, and to imbue them with correct moral, political, and religious principles, — believing that a person thus educated will with proper diligence be certain of attaining all the wealth which is necessary to happiness. With regard to your spending a year at Cambridge, I have always thought it might be beneficial; and if my health should not be impaired and my finances should allow, I should be very happy to gratify you.' The letter goes on with a kindly criticism of some verses by Longfellow which had just been published.

Longfellow regretfully accepted his father's decision, choosing, among the three possible professions, the law. ' I can be a lawyer,' he says. ' This will support my real existence, literature my *ideal* one.' Just at the right moment, however, there came an apparent solution of the difficulty in the shape of an offer from the trustees of Bowdoin to establish for Longfellow a professorship of modern languages, on condition that he should spend some time in Europe preparing for the position. His father provided the necessary money for foreign travel and study. The season of the year was not favorable for sailing, so it was not until the following May (1826), that he began the long voyage from New York to Havre. Meanwhile he spent some time in reading law in his father's office, and more in writing verses, some of which were printed in the *Atlantic Souvenir* of Philadelphia, and others in the *United States Literary Gazette* of Boston, to which he had already contributed during his last year in college. A few of these pieces were preserved in the section entitled ' Earlier Poems ' of Longfellow's first volume of original verse, published fourteen years later.

On arriving in Europe, in June, 1826, he went first to Paris, and spent about eight months there; then to Spain (where he met Washington Irving), for nearly a year; then to Italy for almost another year (1828); and to Germany for his last six months, returning home in August, 1829. He had acquired a good practical knowledge of French, Spanish, and Italian, but had found German more difficult, and made comparatively little progress in it.

Longfellow entered on his work as a teacher of modern languages and literatures in September, 1829. The idea that study of the modern languages could form any serious part of a college curriculum was at that time a new one. Only one important professorship in the subject existed. There were not even any elementary text-books for English speaking students, and Longfellow had to begin by making his own. He published a translation of L'Homond's French Grammar ; an elementary reading book in French, called *Manuel de Proverbes Dramatiques ;* and a similar book for Spanish; he wrote in French a syllabus of the elements of Italian grammar, and edited a collection of extracts from Italian writers, writing his preface in Italian. He attended carefully and thoroughly to his work, hearing recitations, composing and correcting exercises, etc., and found time to write, outside of his text-books, only a few articles for the *North American Review,* dealing in elementary fashion with the French, Italian, and Spanish languages and literatures. He found the profession which he had chosen no less exacting than the law would have been, and almost more so; since, by employing him on work closely similar in kind to that which he most desired to do, it left him little freshness of mind for original composition. His work was well and faithfully done, however; he had the respect and liking of his students; and in 1834 the most important position within the field of his chosen work was offered to him, the ' Smith Professorship of the French and Spanish Languages and Literatures and of Belles Lettres,' at Harvard, previously held, since its foundation in 1816, by Ticknor. With the offer came a suggestion from the President of the University: 'Should it be your wish, previously to entering upon the duties of the office, to reside in Europe, at your own expense, a year or eighteen months, for the purpose of a more perfect attainment of the German, Mr. Ticknor will retain his office till your return.'

Longfellow eagerly accepted this offer. He had been married in 1831 to Mary Potter of Portland, and they sailed for Europe in April, 1835. They went first to England, then to Holland, where Mrs. Longfellow fell ill, and died in November. Longfellow was more than most men one for whom it was ' not good that he should be alone.' The rest of his year in Europe was spent in the shadow of sorrow and loneliness. He studied faithfully, mastered the German language, and buried himself in the reading of the modern German romantic literature, the influence of which is so strong in his prose romance, *Hyperion.* This romance was in part inspired by Miss Frances Appleton, whom he met the following summer in Switzerland, and who appears in it as Mary Ashburton.

On his return to America in the autumn (1836), he entered on the duties of his professorship at Harvard. He had somewhat less of routine work to do than at Bowdoin, and more lecturing. He had one assistant for each of the foreign languages taught, but still retained personal oversight of the work of each student, and often was confined to his classroom work for three whole days in each week. He now formed broader and richer friendships than he had known before, particularly with Charles Sumner, then teaching in the Harvard Law School, with C. C. Felton, professor of Greek, and later President, with George S. Hillard, and others; and renewed his college friendship with Hawthorne. He had grown with the experiences of life, and now found the mechanical duties which filled so much of his time more irksome than before. 'Perhaps the worst thing in college life,' he wrote in his *Journal*, 'is this having your mind constantly a playmate for boys, constantly adapting itself to them, instead of stretching out and grappling with *men's* minds;' and again: 'Lecturing is all well enough, and in my history is an evident advance upon the past. But now one of my French teachers is gone, and this dragooning of schoolboys in lessons is like going backward.' On the whole, however, he believed in his work : 'Have I been wise to give up three whole days (in the week) to college classes ? I think I have; for thus I make my presence felt here, and have no idle time to mope and grieve;' and again: 'After all Cambridge delighteth my heart exceedingly. I have fallen upon books with a most voracious appetite; . . . no doubt, if I could bring myself to give up all my time to the college . . . I could get along very comfortably, but the idea of standing still or going backward is not to be entertained.' Constantly the memory of his early ambitions, and of how little he has done to achieve them, returns to him: 'I could live very happily here if I could chain myself down to college duties and be nothing but a professor. I should then have work enough, and recreation enough. But I am too restless for this. What should I be at fifty ? A fat mill-horse, grinding round with blinkers on. . . . This will not do. It is too much for one's daily bread when one can live on so little.'

These extracts are from his *Journal* of 1838–39 ; and it is in these same years that he is writing the few brief and simple poems that are the real beginning of his poetical work : the 'Psalm of Life,' the 'Light of Stars,' the 'Hymn to the Night,' 'Footsteps of Angels,' and the 'Beleaguered City.' These five poems and four others almost equally well known, with seven 'Earlier Poems,' were collected and published in a slender volume called *Voices of the Night*, in 1839. *Hyperion* was published in the same year. Two years later he published another small collection entitled *Ballads and Other Poems*, containing the 'Skeleton in Armor,' the 'Wreck of the Hesperus,' the 'Village Blacksmith,' 'Endymion,' the 'Rainy Day,' 'Maidenhood,' and 'Excelsior.' In 1842 the 'Spanish Student' appeared, as a serial, in *Graham's Magazine*.

Longfellow was now thirty-five years old. His health was somewhat impaired by his years of close work, and he found himself compelled to take a half-year's leave of absence, which he spent mostly at Marienberg, in Germany. Here began his lasting friendship with Freiligrath, who later translated 'Hiawatha.' On his way home he passed through England, met Landor and Dickens, read Dickens's *American Notes*, and was particularly impressed with 'the grand chapter on slavery,' as he calls it. During the return voyage, being confined to his cabin for about a fortnight, he wrote the seven brief *Poems on Slavery*. These, with one additional poem, were published in a little volume of thirty-one pages, in December, 1842, and were hailed with delight by the abolitionists, who felt that a very strong ally had joined their forces. Longfellow, however, declined to accept the congressional nomination which was offered him through Whittier by the Liberty party, or to take any further part in the anti-slavery contest. He even omitted the poems on slavery from the first collected edition of his poems, an act for which he has been severely blamed. Yet even Lowell, ardent abolitionist as he was at the time, and uncompromising as he was on the question of omitting any of his own anti-slavery poems, felt that Longfellow was justified in doing so, since he might well consider these poems to be the least valuable part of his work. It is probable, also, that the gentle Longfellow, who did not lack courage, but who did lack 'the fighting edge,' omitted the poems rather from a genuine desire to avoid wounding any of his readers than from mere policy. In any case, the poems are unimportant. 'I have attempted only to invest the subject with a poetic coloring,' wrote Longfellow to John Forster; and that is all he succeeded in doing; many will say, with a false poetic coloring. The *Poems on Slavery* have none of the deep conviction and intensity of Whittier's or Lowell's, and are more closely related to German literary romanticism than to American social conditions.

Longfellow had not even yet 'found himself,' and had barely begun, in a few ballads, his real poetical work. He had written in his *Journal* in 1840, speaking of a visit to Mr. Norton: 'There I beheld what perfect happiness may exist on this earth, and felt how I stood alone in life, cut off for a while from those dearest sympathies for which I long.' It was at Marienberg that he wrote the sonnet 'Mezzo Cammin,' oppressed with a feeling that, though he was the author of a few brief and popular poems, yet he had spent half of man's allotted years without having begun that 'tower of song with lofty parapet,' which it had been his ambition to build. He was almost entirely dependent upon home life and home affection; and when he at last found these, in his marriage with Miss Frances Appleton, in 1843, his maturity and the creative period of his life really began. He finished his work as a mere editor and compiler (except for the *Poems of Places*, much later) with the *Poets and Poetry of Europe*, in 1845. At the end of that year was published the *Belfry of Bruges and Other Poems*, dated 1846, which closes the first period of his work, and already shows a great advance in artistic quality over the crude moralizing and vaguely romantic commonplace of his earliest work. The first collected edition of his poems had been published in a sumptuous volume by Carey and Hart of Philadelphia, in 1845, and 'Evangeline' was just begun.

The characteristics of all Longfellow's work, which are especially marked in its first period, are not such as appeal either to the intellectual critic or to the lover of art for art's sake. A good deal of its romantic imagery strikes us now as false, and its simplicity as bathos. 'Excelsior' is a truly imaginative conception, but in expression it degenerates into 'A tear stood in his bright blue eye. But still he answered with a sigh,' etc. The expression is truly imaginative in that French passage from which he took the idea of the 'Old Clock on the Stairs,' yet Longfellow makes of it such lines as 'Some are married, some are dead,' which is almost as bad as the line that Tennyson declared to be typical Wordsworthian blank verse, 'A Mr. Wilkinson, a clergyman.' But it is the very triumph of these early poems that most of their lines seem more commonplace than they really are, because they have become, by their simplicity and genuineness, a part of the universal feeling of the race. Simple and genuine they are, except for the false romantic imagery already spoken of, such as is found in the 'Reaper and the Flowers.' Their appeal is universal; and to each individual it may at some time be new, as it was to all the young America of 1840. Even in our sophisticated times, it would be a pretty poor sort of youth who would not still be thrilled at his first reading of the 'Psalm of Life.' 'The Day is Done,' hackneyed as it is, is still full of simple and restful beauty.

On the last day of 1845, Longfellow wrote in his *Journal* : 'Peace to the embers of burnt-out things ; fears, anxieties, doubts, all gone ! I see them now as a thin blue smoke, hanging in the bright heaven of the past year, vanishing away into utter nothingness. Not many hopes deceived, not many illusions scattered, not many anticipations disappointed ; but love fulfilled, the heart comforted, the soul enriched with affection !' The first period of his life and writing was in fact finished, and his next fifteen years were to contain the largest and the most important part of his poetical work. In the earlier period he had been growing, experimenting, preluding ; in the third and last period, which was to follow 1861, he touched deeper notes sometimes, and attained to greater artistic beauty and condensation ; but he produced no such large body of lasting work as in the middle period.

This middle period, from the end of 1845 to the beginning of 1861, contains 'Evangeline' (1847) ; 'Hiawatha' (1855) ; the 'Courtship of Miles Standish' (1858); the 'Building of the Ship,' and other poems, especially of the home, in *The Seaside and the Fireside* (dated 1850, published 1849); the *Golden Legend* (1851); the 'Saga of King Olaf' and others of the best *Tales of a Wayside Inn*, not published until later ; 'My Lost Youth ;' the 'Fiftieth Birthday of Agassiz ;' and some of Longfellow's most beautiful poems of childhood, including 'Children,' and 'The Children's Hour.' Longfellow's own home was made complete in these years by the coming of his five children, three girls and two boys, and his outside life was broadened by his growing friendship with Agassiz, Lowell, and Mr. Charles Eliot Norton, and by his continued close relations with Sumner. The duties of his professorship, however, were becoming more and more irksome to him. 'What vexes me most,' he wrote in 1847, 'is being cribbed and shut up in college, not that I dislike work, but that I have other work to do than this;' and again later: 'I seem to be quite banished from all literary work save that of my professorship. . . . I am tired, not of work, but of the sameness of work . . . these hours in the lecture-room, like a schoolmaster ! It is pleasant enough when the mind gets engaged in it, — but " art is long and life is short. "' In 1853 he wrote nothing except the brief poem to Lowell, 'The Two Angels.' In 1854, realizing that his means were quite adequate for his support without a college salary, — they had been so since his second marriage, — he finally decided to resign his professorship and devote himself entirely to literature. The next few years were full of work. 'Hiawatha' was written immediately after his retirement from the professorship, the *Courtship of Miles Standish and other Poems* was published in 1858, and in the next three years were written many of his best shorter poems and some of the *Tales of a Wayside Inn*.

Longfellow had his greatest success as a narrative poet. For the average reader 'the tale's the thing,' and Longfellow possessed the surprisingly rare faculty of telling a simple story well. For him too the tale was the thing ; he realized by instinct the simple and essential first point that it must be constantly interesting, and he had the faculty of making it so. In local flavor and truth of detail his work is vastly inferior to Whittier's. Some score of years after he wrote the 'Wreck of the Hesperus,' he still vaguely wondered just where the Reef of Norman's Woe might be, though it was not fifteen miles from his own summer home. He knew the country of 'Hiawatha' only through books, and for 'Evangeline' he formed his ideas of the Mississippi from reading (perhaps mostly in Chateaubriand), and from a pictorial diorama which was exhibited at Boston while he was writing the poem, and which he enthusiastically welcomed as a great help. Yet his narrative, as such, is better even than Whittier's, whether in the ringing ballads of the Northland, from the 'Skeleton in Armor' to the 'Saga of King Olaf,' or in the gentler, easily flowing tales that are more characteristic of his own mood, from 'Evangeline' to 'King Robert of Sicily' or the 'Birds of Killingworth.' And in 'Hiawatha,' by some wondrous alchemy due to the true simplicity of his own mind, he did catch the true local color, even in detail as well as in mood, of a life that he had never seen. 'Hiawatha' has worn surprisingly well, and has stood the test of being judged even by the people whose life and legends it describes. It stands out, more and more, as Longfellow's most important work. This is anything but the fate predicted for it by those intellectual critics who (with the exception of Emerson) judged it so severely at its first appearance. In the 'Courtship of Miles Standish,' Longfellow was dealing with a life that he knew more intimately, by its partial survival and by its traditions living all about him, as well as from books; though he did not take the trouble to visit Plymouth until the poem had been completed. His treatment of this theme is entirely happy and true. The 'Golden Legend' is naturally much less so, though it is by far the best part of the ambitious trilogy which he planned, under the title of *Christus: a Mystery*. It has charm and the glamour of mediæval story, but Longfellow was manifestly unfitted for any real dramatic composition, or for the broad picturing of a great period like the Middle Ages.

In 1861 came the tragic break in Longfellow's life. It was in July. Mrs. Longfellow's light summer dress caught fire, and she was so severely burned that she died the next morning. Longfellow also was seriously burned in trying to smother the flames, and could not leave his room on the day of her funeral, — the anniversary of their wedding day.

The story of his next few years is completely told in the first of the 'Divina Commedia' sonnets. That of the later years is suggested in the 'Cross of Snow.' 'I have taken refuge in this translation of the Divina Commedia,' he wrote to his friend Freiligrath. For a while he wrote little else, except to complete and publish, at the end of 1863, the first part of *Tales of a Wayside Inn ;* the second and third parts were published in

1872 and 1873. The two *New England Tragedies*, the first of which had been written in 1856–57, were published in 1868, the *Divine Tragedy* was written and published in 1871, and the completed *Christus* in 1872. He wrote 'Morituri Salutamus,' for the fiftieth anniversary of his college class, and this was published in 1875, in the *Masque of Pandora and Other Poems*, together with the 'Hanging of the Crane,' which was written for Thomas Bailey Aldrich, and which holds a peculiar place in Longfellow's work, as summing up within itself so many of the different aspects of home life, of all of which he was the poet laureate.

During this last period of his life, he wrote often in a form which he had hardly more than once or twice tried before, except for translations, — the sonnet. In much of the work of this period, especially the sonnets, his feeling is deeper and stronger (it could not be truer), and his expression richer and more condensed, than before. Longfellow was always a true artist and careful of the form of his work, as few of our American poets, except Poe, have been. The little lyric 'Sea-Weed,' of an earlier period, shows how carefully and well he could fit the form of his idea to a somewhat intricate stanza. But his art was never rich or varied, and he lacked most of all that tenseness of expression which is the mark of any very strong artistic or imaginative feeling for language. In the sonnets, however, his feeling, now deepened and strengthened by the experiences of his constantly growing life, and by his communion with Dante, was confined within the narrow walls of a form that did not allow it to flow out thin over the marshes of the commonplace, as it had so often done before, and as it did still in the 'Hanging of the Crane.' There is much of this same strength and condensation in his noble 'Morituri Salutamus.'

Longfellow's last years were made happier by the devotion of his own children, and by the love of all children who knew him — and it would seem that few in America, or even in England or Germany, did not know him. The story of his gift from the Cambridge schoolchildren on his seventy-second birthday, and of their constant visits to his home, is too well known to be repeated. His seventy-fifth birthday was celebrated in the schools throughout the United States, and was made memorable also by Whittier's poem, 'The Poet and the Children.' He died not quite a month later, March 24, 1882.

Longfellow's life was that of a simple, faithful, true man and gentleman, kindly and home-loving. And that is what he has put into his verse. He has been well called 'the laureate of the common human heart.' He is first and most of all the poet of the home. There is not an aspect of home life that he has not touched and beautified. If much of his poetry is mere commonplace, it is always the making beautiful of the commonplace. Bryant's poetry often — as in the well-known lines from 'The Battle-Field,' — and Emerson's still oftener, are the making noble of the commonplace. Whittier's is the simple and true rendering of it. Whitman's is the apotheosis of it. Poe is the only one of our chief elder poets who is not commonplace, who detests and despises the commonplace.

Next, Longfellow is the only American who has successfully written poems of any considerable length. The long poem is different from the short poem, as the novel is from the short story, not only in quantity, but in kind. For those who can conceive only that kind or class of poetry which finds fit expression in the short poem, Poe's dictum that 'there is no such thing as a long poem' is true; for the poem which by its nature belongs to the short poem class, yet tries to extend itself to greater length, is, as Poe saw, inevitably a failure. The long poem is an entirely different literary class or genre. It is Longfellow's distinctive glory that he had the patience and the sustained artistic power to win success in this difficult form, — a kind of success which is almost the rarest in literature, and second only to success in the true dramatic presentation of character and life. Without comparing Longfellow's achievement in this field with that of greater foreign poets, we may say that it alone would give him an unanswerable claim to the largest space in any fully representative collection of our chief American poets.

JOHN GREENLEAF WHITTIER

WHITTIER is the poet of New England country life, almost as truly and fully as Burns is of the country life of Scotland. For this he was fitted by all the circumstances of his own life. He was born and bred a farmer's boy, on the same farm which his first American ancestor, Thomas Whittier, had taken up and cleared in 1647, and in the very house which this Thomas Whittier had built for himself in 1688. This sturdy pioneer came to New England in 1638, when he was eighteen years old, and so was nearly seventy when he built the house which was to be Whittier's birthplace. Of his ten children, five were boys, and each of the five boys, like his father, was over six feet tall, and strong correspondingly. The youngest son, Joseph, Whittier's great-grandfather, had nine children, of whom the youngest, Whittier's grandfather, married Sarah Greenleaf, and had eleven children, of whom the youngest but one was Whittier's father. There was naturally but little property to divide among so many children, and the older sons usually went out and made their own way in the world, while the farm was left to the youngest — in the last case, to the two youngest, Whittier's father and his uncle, Moses Whittier, who is one of the family group in 'Snow-Bound.'

John Greenleaf Whittier was born December 17. 1807. He lived and worked on the farm, but he lacked the sturdy strength of his ancestors, and the hard work of his early boyhood resulted in physical injury and weakness which lasted for the rest of his life. His education was that of a typical country boy in those days ; he attended the district school in the outskirts of the town where he lived, and later earned for himself two short terms at the neighboring academy. Only once in his boyhood did he go so far away from home as to visit Boston. Thus, in ancestry and training, Whittier differs from the other New England poets, who were all college bred, and spent their youth in a city or an academic town. One other important point is to be noted, — that Whittier's family were devout Quakers.

Books were naturally scarce in the household, except for the Bible and the lives of Quaker worthies. He read all the poetry he could get hold of, from the dry 'Davideis' spoken of in 'Snow-Bound' to something of Gray and Cowper. He wrote rhymes on his slate after the 'nightly chores' were done. But his real awakening to poetry came through Burns, as he has told us so vividly and beautifully in his tribute to the Scotch peasant-poet.

Whittier's first printed verses appeared when he was eighteen years old, in the local newspaper, edited by William Lloyd Garrison, then only twenty. Garrison at once sought out his new contributor, and urged the necessity of further education and cultivation of his talent. 'Sir,' replied Whittier's father, 'poetry will not give him bread.' Whittier, however, earned enough by shoemaking to support himself for one term at Haverhill Academy in 1827, and by school-teaching enough for another term in 1828. During these two years he wrote for the local papers, especially the *Haverhill Gazette*, something like a hundred poems.

A college education seemed out of the question, but Whittier obtained employment in the following winter as hack editor of a Boston trade journal, the *American Manufacturer*. The following summer his father fell seriously ill, and he had to return home and take charge of the farm. But here he found an opportunity for continuing his other work, in the editorship of the chief local paper, the *Haverhill Gazette*. His father died in June, 1830. In July he went to Hartford, Conn., to be editor of the *New England Review*, and continued to conduct it until the end of 1831, although he was compelled to spend a good deal of that year at home in Haverhill, and ultimately to give up his editorial position, on account of serious illness.

In these excursions into the outside world, at Boston, and particularly at Hartford, which was then somewhat of a literary centre, and where he held an important position, Whittier's outlook had of course been greatly broadened, and his literary ambition strengthened. His letters at the time show a strong desire and even hope of winning fame as a poet. His editorial work had also drawn him into politics, and when he returned to Haverhill, in spite of his ill health, he took an important practical part in the local contests. In September, 1832, he wrote : ' Even if my health was restored, I should not leave this place. I have too many friends around me, and my prospects are too good to be sacrificed for any uncertainty.' The prospect which he was unwilling to sacrifice was that of being elected to Congress in the following year. It appears that he could probably have been elected in 1832, but he was not yet of the required age.

Both his literary and political ambitions, however, seemed to be once for all sacrificed when, almost by a sort of religious conversion, he devoted himself to the abolition cause. The abolitionists were at that time a small and persecuted band, despised by all ' respectable ' people in church, state, or university, and generally looked on much as an avowed anarchist is now. They were, in fact, setting themselves in opposition to what was then the law of the land, and to what seemed, to Northerners as well as Southerners, part of the very basis of its social and economic system. Whittier had far more common sense and balance than most of the abolitionists in 1833. ' He counted the cost with Quaker coolness of judgment,' says Pickard, ' before taking a step that closed to him the gates of both political and literary preferment. He realized more fully than did most of the early abolitionists that the institution of slavery would not fall at the first blast of their horns. When he decided to enter upon this contest, he understood that his cherished ambitions must be laid aside, and that an entire change in his plans was involved. He took the step deliberately and after serious consideration.' What induced Whittier to take this step, even while realizing its cost so clearly, was an intense idealistic belief, a belief amounting almost to religious fervor, in the principle of universal liberty and equality. Late in life, giving counsel to a boy of fifteen, Whittier said, ' My lad, if thou wouldest win success, join thyself to some unpopular but noble cause.'

This is not the place to give any extended account of Whittier's work in the abolition movement. It has been treated with admirable completeness and fairness in Professor Carpenter's *Whittier*. Strange as this seems to us now, Whittier was, aside from his poetry, one of the most able workers in practical politics on the abolition side. He held together a small band of followers in his own congressional district, and kept the balance of power in such a way as often to force anti-slavery declarations from any candidate who wished to be elected. He had taken no part in founding the New England Anti-Slavery Society in 1832; but in 1833 he was a delegate from Massachusetts to the Convention at Philadelphia which founded the American Anti-Slavery Society. (See note on page 260.) He later became somewhat estranged from the purely idealistic faction of the abolitionists, led by Garrison, who refused to have anything to do with a government based, as it seemed to them, on false principles, or even to vote under it, and who advocated immediate dissolution of the Union in order to break away from the slave power. Whittier was elected as representative to the Massachusetts Legislature in 1835, and again in 1836, but could not serve his second term on account of ill health, and was unable, for the same reason, to take office himself at any subsequent time. He still continued to play an active part in politics, however, even to the end of his life. He is described in a letter quoted by Professor Carpenter, as ' one of the greatest workers, politically, even, in all our State. I sometimes wonder how so fine a mind can stoop to such drudgery. But Whittier has as much benevolence as he has ideality. He knows the drudgery must be done, and, since no one else does it, will do it himself. May Heaven bless him.' Whittier was largely instrumental in securing the nomination of Charles Sumner to the Senate, and in persuading him to accept the nomination. His correspondence with Sumner, from 1840 on, is very important for the history of that period. Toward the end of Sumner's life, when he had been censured by the Massachusetts Legislature for advocating the proposal that the names of battles fought against fellow-citizens should no longer be inscribed on regimental flags, it was Whittier who aroused public opinion to compel the repeal of this vote of censure. In 1834 Whittier was instrumental in bringing the English abolitionist, George Thompson, to New England, and this caused bitter personal opposition. He accompanied Thompson to New Hampshire, and at Concord they were stoned and shot at by a mob, and barely escaped. Whittier went to Philadelphia in 1838, to edit the *Pennsylvania Freeman;* Pennsylvania Hall, where he had his office, was burned by a mob without interference from the authorities. He took part, from 1835 to 1850, in the editing of several anti-slavery papers, and in many anti-slavery conventions.

During all this time, he was a great influence by his poetry also. The ringing lines of 'Expostulation,' and of 'Massachusetts to Virginia,' were declaimed again and again through the North and West. The anti-slavery movement rapidly grew, and won the allegiance of men like Dr. Channing in 1836, and Lowell in 1841. But it was still the unpopular cause, and abolitionists were mobbed in Massachusetts as late as 1861.

Whittier's anti-slavery poems form the larger part of his work for all this period. His earliest volumes were almost entirely made up of them, — the *Poems,* of 1837, the *Ballads, Anti-Slavery Poems, etc.,* of 1838, and the *Voices of Freedom,* of 1841. Of course little of this verse can survive, except for its historic interest. Sometimes, however, though local and temporary in its origin, it expresses something universal and eternal, as with the idea of freedom in 'Expostulation,' of truth and honor and the shame of their betrayal, in 'Ichabod,' of loathing at the triumph of wrong, in 'The Christian Slave' and 'The Rendition.' 'Massachusetts to Virginia' is one of the greatest of 'poems of places,' making the very rocks arise and speak. ·

In the meantime, Whittier was writing other poems, more enduring than the mass of his anti-slavery work. The *Lays of my Home* was published in 1843, the first collected edition of his *Poems* in 1849, *Songs of Labor* in 1850, the *Chapel of the Hermits and Other Poems* in 1853, the 'blue and gold' edition of his *Poetical Works* in 1857. Except for the publication of his works, there is little to note in his life-story. He had given up the farm, and moved to a little house in the near-by village of Amesbury, where he lived until 1876. His income was very small, until after the publication of 'Snow-Bound,' in 1866, for in the earlier years he could necessarily earn but little by his writings. 'For twenty years,' he said, 'I was shut out from the favor of booksellers and magazine editors; but I was enabled, by rigid economy, to live in spite of them, and to see the end of the institution that proscribed me.' 'Snow-Bound,' and all his later works, brought him large profits.

During the war Whittier wrote little. His feeling is expressed intensely in 'The Waiting' and 'The Watchers,' and he wrote the best ballad of the war in 'Barbara Frietchie.' He hailed the coming of emancipation in 'Laus Deo' and the 'Emancipation Hymn.' In 1866 came 'Snow-Bound,' in 1867 the 'Tent on the Beach,' in 1869 'Among the Hills,' in 1870 the *Ballads of New England.* These are his most important volumes, and mark his late maturity as a poet, which came only with his freedom from the partisan struggle that had filled the best years of his life.

> Hater of din and riot
> He lived in days unquiet ;
> And lover of all beauty,
> Trod the hard ways of duty,

he says truly of himself in 'An Autograph ;' while in his Prelude to the 'Tent on the Beach,' he expresses more fully this feeling of what his life had been : —

> And one there was, a dreamer born,
>   Who, with a mission to fulfil,
> Had left the Muses' haunts to turn
>   The crank of an opinion-mill,
> Making his rustic reed of song
> A weapon in the war with wrong,
> Yoking his fancy to the breaking-plough
> That beam-deep turned the soil for truth to spring and grow.
>
> Too quiet seemed the man to ride
>   The wingèd Hippogriff Reform ;
> Was his a voice from side to side
>   To pierce the tumult of the storm ?
> A silent, shy, peace-loving man,
> He seemed no fiery partisan

To hold his way against the public frown,
The ban of Church and State, the fierce mob's hounding down.

For while he wrought with strenuous will
　　The work his hands had found to do,
He heard the fitful music still
　　Of winds that out of dream-land blew.
The din about him could not drown
What the strange voices whispered down ;
Along his task-field weird processions swept,
The visionary pomp of stately phantoms stepped.

The common air was thick with dreams, —
　　He told them to the toiling crowd ;
Such music as the woods and streams
　　Sang in his ear he sang aloud ;
In still, shut bays, on windy capes,
　　He heard the call of beckoning shapes,
And, as the gray old shadows prompted him,
To homely moulds of rhyme he shaped their legends grim.

Whittier never married. 'Circumstances,' he wrote, — 'the care of an aged mother, and the duty owed to a sister in delicate health for many years, must be my excuse for living the lonely life which has called out thy pity. . . . I have learned to look into happiness through the eyes of others.' Still more cogent reasons for not marrying were his comparative poverty, his ill health, and especially the strong feeling of the Quakers that it was not permissible to marry out of their own sect. There are beautiful memories of his school-boy loves in poems like 'My Playmate,' 'Benedicite,' 'A Sea Dream,' 'Memories,' and 'In School-Days,' and these poems of dim and delicate reminiscence, untouched by the realities of life, sometimes seem more beautiful than any songs of living passion. His home, for many years, was made by his younger sister, Elizabeth, until her death, in 1864 ; then by his niece, Elizabeth Whittier, till her marriage, in 1876. After this he lived most of the time with three sisters, his cousins, at Oak Knoll, Danvers. His faculties remained unimpaired to the last, and he died at the age of eighty-four, September 7, 1892.

Whittier was primarily the poet of abolition ; but enough has already been said on that part of his work. Next, he was the poet of Nature in New England. His poems of the Merrimac Valley, of Lake Winnipesaukee and the mountains near it, of Hampton Beach and the Marblehead coast, are unsurpassed in simple truth and love. But most of all he is the poet of country life in New England. This means more than at first appears, for it was from these New England homes that the larger number and the more energetic of the young men, like the older brothers of Whittier's father and grandfather, went out to take and make the great Northwest and then the greater West ; moreover Whittier, in speaking for his own section, often expresses what the whole of America is and means as contrasted with the Old World, — in 'The Last Walk in Autumn,' for instance. There are two or three other points to be noted in summary. One is the simple beauty, truth, and modesty of Whittier's own nature, constantly and unconsciously showing itself in his many personal poems, and in his modest estimate of his own work, as in the 'Proem.' Another is that he ranks as our truest, though not our greatest, narrative poet. This has already been touched on in speaking of Longfellow ; as a writer of ballads, Whittier surpasses Longfellow in everything except that which is after all the first essential, but only one essential, — spirited movement. And finally, he is our chief religious poet.

OLIVER WENDELL HOLMES

HOLMES was a great believer in ancestry, and very proud of his own. Through his mother he was connected with the Phillipses, and was a cousin of Wendell Phillips ; with the Bradstreets, and was a direct descendant of Anne Bradstreet, the first American poetess ; with the Quincys, and was the great-grandson of 'Dorothy Q.;' with the Hancocks, one of whom had married the second Dorothy Quincy, niece of the first; and with the Wendells, one of the old Dutch families who came to America about 1646. He was named for his maternal grandfather, the Honorable Oliver Wendell. On the other side of the family his great-great-grandfather, John Holmes, of Puritan stock, settled in Woodstock, Conn., in 1686. His grandfather, David Holmes, the ' Deacon ' who built the ' One-Hoss Shay,' was a captain in the French and Indian wars, and surgeon in the Revolutionary army. His father, Rev. Abiel Holmes, graduated at Yale in 1782, preached in Georgia for six years, and then came to settle in Cambridge, Mass., where for forty years he was pastor of the First Church. He was also an author and lecturer, and wrote the *Annals of America*, the first important history after the Revolution. He lived in the ' house with the gambrel-roof,' which stood near the site of the present Harvard Gymnasium, and which is so often alluded to in Holmes's writings and so lovingly described in the *Poet at the Breakfast Table*. Here Holmes was born, almost under the shadow of the elms in the Harvard College yard, August 29, 1809. He went to school first in Cambridge, then at Phillips Academy, Andover. While at the Academy, he made a translation in heroic couplets of the first book of Virgil's Æneid. He entered Harvard with the ' famous class of '29 ' (see notes on ' The Boys,' pages 374, 375). Beside his own classmates who later became illustrious, he knew in college Charles Sumner, of the class of 1830, and Wendell Phillips and John Lothrop Motley, of 1831.

After graduation he spent a year in the Law School, and published during this year more than a score of poems, many of them in a college periodical, the *Collegian*. Most of these were humorous skits, but there ring out among them the thrilling lines of ' Old Ironsides.' Thus from the beginning, as throughout his life, love of fun and love of country were two chief elements in Holmes's poetry. At the end of the year he abandoned the law and took up the study of medicine. From 1833 to 1835 he spent a little more than two years in study abroad, mostly at Paris, and came back to take his degree at the Harvard Medical School in 1836. At the same Commencement he read his Phi Beta Kappa poem: ' Poetry; A Metrical Essay.' This was published later in the year, with other poems, among them the ' Last Leaf,' which had already appeared in a miscellaneous collection, the *Harbinger*, in 1833. We may say that he ' commenced ' doctor and poet at the same time; and his profession and his poetry were to be the two chief interests of his life, neither ever crowding out the other.

During the following years he published or edited a number of important medical books, was professor of anatomy at Dartmouth College for a short time, settled in Boston in 1840 to the practice of his profession, and was married in that year to Miss Amelia Lee Jackson. In 1846 he published his second volume of collected *Poems*, and in 1847 was appointed professor of anatomy and physiology at Harvard, a position which he held as an active teacher until 1882, and as professor emeritus until his death, in 1894, in all forty-seven years.

Like the other New England poets, Holmes came rather late to his maturity as a writer. It was not until he began the *Breakfast Table* series, on which, even more than on his verse, will depend his ultimate fame, that he began also to write his best poetry. ' The Chambered Nautilus,' the ' One-Hoss Shay,' ' Latter-Day Warnings,' ' Contentment,' ' Parson Turell's Legacy,' ' The Living Temple,' ' The Voiceless,' all appeared first with the *Autocrat* papers (1857–58). Among these are two of his best humorous narratives, and two of his best serious lyrics. In the *Professor at the Breakfast Table* (1859) appeared ' The Boys,' ' Under the Violets,' and Holmes's two best hymns. The Civil War period called out some of his strongest verse, notably ' Union and Liberty,' ' The Voyage of the Good Ship Union,' and the poem on Bryant's seventieth birthday. Meanwhile he had begun that series of poems for his class reunions, in which there is not a break for thirty-nine years, and which thus forms one of the largest and most characteristic sections of his work. Occasional poetry is usually doomed to sure and quick oblivion. Holmes had the rare faculty of giving it a touch of greater vitality, while at the same time fitting it closely to the occasion. Class loyalty, and college loyalty, and the lasting reality of men's friendships, are not merely local and occasional things. Holmes has expressed these in his class poems, and in others like ' At a Meeting of Friends,' and ' At the Saturday Club,' and in his tributes to his fellow poets. In these and others of his occasional poems (the 'Voyage of the Good Ship Union' is one of the class poems) he has expressed also the broader loyalty of patriotism, both local and national. And in his later class poems the charm of mellow, genial, and youthful old age has found unique expression.

There is little further to be said of the external facts of Holmes's life, or of his work. This is not the place to speak of his novels and other prose work, or of how he gave to the *Atlantic Monthly* its name and its character. Lowell was willing to accept the editorship only on condition that Holmes should be a constant contributor, and later he said: 'You see the Doctor is like a bright mountain stream that has been dammed up among the hills, and is waiting for an outlet into the Atlantic.' His later volumes of verse were published, *Songs in Many Keys* in 1861, *Humorous Poems* in 1865, *Songs of Many Seasons* in 1874, *Bunker Hill Battle, etc.* in 1875, *The Iron Gate, etc.* in 1880, *Before the Curfew* in 1888. He died October 7, 1894, the oldest, and the 'last survivor,' of our elder poets.

If Whittier is the poet of a single section, New England, Holmes is the poet of a single city, Boston. It is a pity that he, instead of Emerson, did not write the quatrain

> What care though rival cities soar
> Along the stormy coast,
> Penn's town, New York, and Baltimore,
> If Boston knew the most?

Holmes would have written it better, and with some peculiar quaint touch of his own humor. He makes one of his characters in the *Autocrat* say: 'Boston State House is the hub of the Solar System. You could n't pry that out of a Boston man if you had the tire of all creation straightened out for a crowbar.' He says it in satire, but he has a subtle feeling that it is true. On the whole his verse, however, is to a less degree merely local in flavor than his prose.

Holmes seldom strikes the deeper notes or touches on the higher themes of poetry, except that of patriotism. He is one of the chief poets of friendship and loyalty, as we have seen, but he expresses friendship rather in its social aspect, and chooses only to suggest its deeper feelings. So always, it is his own choice to touch but lightly on the surface of things. But if he is not among the great poets, he is among the rare. It is even one of the rarest things to make real poetry out of mere wit and humor, as he has so often done. In his humorous narratives, from the 'One-Hoss Shay' to the 'Broomstick Train,' and perhaps most of all in 'How the Old Horse won the Bet,' his verse sparkles and crackles in every line. And he has written two lyrics that are sure to live, the one serious, and the other so interwoven of fun and pathos that we shall never know whether it be serious or not: the 'Chambered Nautilus,' and the 'Last Leaf.'

JAMES RUSSELL LOWELL

JAMES RUSSELL LOWELL was born February 22, 1819, in Cambridge, at 'Elmwood,' the house which he occupied during so large a part of his life. The Lowells were an old New England family, going back, in Massachusetts Colony, to 1639. The poet's father, grandfather, and great-grandfather were graduates of Harvard College. It was John Lowell, his grandfather, who as a member of the Constitutional Convention of Massachusetts in 1780 introduced into the Bill of Rights of the State a clause abolishing slavery — 'a good sort of grandfather for the author of the *Biglow Papers*,' as Dr. Edward Everett Hale says. The great-grandfather was a clergyman, the grandfather a lawyer, and the father again a clergyman, pastor of the First Church in Boston. The family had always been distinguished for ability and public spirit. An uncle of the poet, Francis Cabot Lowell, was one of the first successful manufacturers of New England, and for him the city of Lowell was named. Another uncle, John Lowell, Jr., founded the Lowell Institute in Boston.

Lowell's mother was of Orkney descent. Both her father, Keith Spence, and her mother's father, Robert Traill, were New England merchants who had come from the

Orkney Islands. Her mother's mother, Mary Whipple, was, however, of New England ancestry. Mary Whipple's father, William Whipple, was one of the signers of the Declaration of Independence, and her mother belonged to another old New England family, the Cutts, going back to the first half of the seventeenth century in New England.

James Russell Lowell was the youngest of six brothers and sisters. His home training, as in the case of Holmes, was that of a scholarly minister's family, illuminated in his case by his mother's strong imaginative temperament and skill in music. As a child, he was read to sleep from Spenser's *Faerie Queene.* He was surrounded by books and by nature (Elmwood being then at a considerable distance from other houses, among the woods and meadows), and from the first he showed an almost passionate love of both.

After fitting for college in a Cambridge school, he entered Harvard in 1834, and had among his teachers there C. C. Felton, professor of Greek and later president of the college (celebrated by Longfellow in ' Three Friends of Mine '), Benjamin Peirce, the mathematician of Holmes's ' famous Class of '29,' George Ticknor, Longfellow's predecessor in the Smith professorship of Belles Lettres, and, in the last half of his course, Longfellow himself. Lowell read in college, he tells us, ' almost everything except the text-books prescribed by the faculty.' He had already devoured Scott's novels before entering college. Now he read Dante, Tasso, Montaigne, the old English dramatists, Butler, Cowper, Burns, Landor, Byron, Coleridge, Keats, Carlyle, and Milton, and, under the impulse of his study of Milton, something of the classics. As Dr. Hale tells us in his reminiscences, the college boys of those days were passionately devoted to literature, and Lowell's knowledge and ability made him a leader among them. He was an editor of *Harvardiana*, and was elected class poet. During his senior year he became so much more devoted to reading than to studying, and so regardless of prescribed exercises, including chapel, that he was suspended ' on account of continued neglect of his college duties,' as it was expressed in the vote of the faculty ; and was rusticated at Concord, where he lived and studied in the household of the Rev. Barzillai Frost. During this rustication he perhaps found models both for the Rev. Homer Wilbur and for Hosea Biglow.

In any case, he met Emerson, and walked and talked with him, but at first was influenced more toward opposition than toward discipleship. In his class poem, which he was not allowed to deliver, but which he printed for distribution among his classmates, he ridiculed the transcendentalists and the abolitionists, and, in a mild way, Emerson himself. He loyally sent a copy of the poem to Emerson, with a note excusing himself for these liberties, but stoutly maintaining his own opinions. Emerson's influence gradually ' struck in,' however, and Lowell became, though not a disciple, an ardent admirer. Late in life he signed himself Emerson's ' liegeman,' and said that he for one must ' Obey the voice at eve obeyed at prime.' We also find the anti-slavery feeling growing in him during this same year, and beginning to dominate his thought at least a year before he first met Miss Maria White, to whose influence it has usually been attributed. ' The abolitionists,' he wrote in November, 1838, ' are the only ones with whom I sympathize of the present extant parties.'

He had been allowed to return to Cambridge just in time to graduate with his class in 1838. Not knowing what else to do, he, like Holmes, began the study of the law, and graduated from the Law School in 1840. During these two years he continued his eager reading, and now paid much more attention to the classics than he had done in college when they were prescribed subjects. Ovid, Theocritus, and the Greek dramatists seem to have been his favorites. In August, 1840, he graduated from the Law School, and became engaged to Miss Maria White, whom he had met late in the previous year. He entered a law office in Boston, but spent most of his time in reading and in writing verse, and seems never to have had, on his own account, that ' First Client' whose imaginary existence offered the material of his later humorous sketch. Late in this year (1840) he published his first book of verse, *A Year's Life*, dated 1841 ; and in 1841–1842 he published many poems and essays in the magazines of the time. Among his poems of this period are the beautiful lyrics, 'My Love,' 'Irene,' and the song 'O Moonlight deep and tender;' and in many of the sonnets there is a personal sincerity and a fineness of poetic quality to be found in few other American sonnets. These poems express his feeling for Miss White, whose influence upon him was strong and always ideal. It was partly through her influence, and partly through his own natural development, that Lowell had now openly joined forces with the extreme abolitionists, at a time when abolition seemed mere quixotism, was despised by almost all conservative people, even in New England, and shut out its devotees from the social circles to which Lowell was born, and from many of the most important literary magazines and publishing houses.

At the end of 1842 Lowell entirely gave up the law, and with Robert Carter attempted to start a new magazine, *The Pioneer*. This was not a success financially, and left Lowell considerably in debt by its failure after the third number had been published. The list of contributors to the three numbers which did appear included most of the chief contemporary writers, — Hawthorne, Whittier, Poe, W. W. Story, Thomas William Parsons, and Lowell. Lowell was in New York during the winter of 1842–43, and made many acquaintances and friends among the men of letters there. He published a new volume of *Poems* in December, 1843 (dated 1844), which contained 'Rhœcus,' 'An Incident in a Railroad Car,' 'The Shepherd of King Admetus,' the 'Stanzas on Freedom,' etc. A year later, in December, 1844, he published *Conversations on Some of the Old Poets*. Both these volumes were republished in London, and they brought Lowell considerable reputation in England and in America.

Lowell was married to Miss White in December, 1844, and for some months after his marriage lived in Philadelphia, where he was employed as editorial writer on the *Pennsylvania Freeman* at the munificent salary of ten dollars a month. In May, 1845, he returned to Elmwood, where he lived until his first trip to Europe, in 1851. These were the busiest and poetically the most productive years of his life, and they were years full of both joy and sorrow in his home life, and of growing friendships with his chief contemporaries, most of them, like Holmes and Longfellow, his elders by ten years or more. His first child, Blanche, was born December 31, 1845, and died March 19, 1847. The second daughter, Mabel, was born September 9, 1847. Lowell is not so popular a poet of the home as Longfellow, but in 'The First Snowfall,' 'The Changeling,' 'She Came and Went,' 'I thought our love at full, but I did err,' and later, in 'After the Burial,' 'The Dead House,' 'The Wind-Harp,' and 'Auf Wiedersehen,' he has written poems of home joys and sorrows that have a deeper and more intimate appeal.

The year 1848 has been called by Lowell's latest biographer his 'annus mirabilis.' Just at the end of 1847 appeared his *Poems, Second Series* (dated 1848), containing the noble poem 'Columbus;' the characteristic 'Indian Summer Reverie;' 'The Present Crisis,' as strong and as universal in its truth as the very best of Whittier's work; 'To the Dandelion;' and other important short poems. In 1848 were published the *Biglow Papers, First Series*, the *Fable for Critics*, and the *Vision of Sir Launfal*, besides some forty articles and poems in various periodicals. From 1846 to 1850 Lowell was a regular contributor to the *National Anti-Slavery Standard*. In July, 1851, he sailed for Europe, spent nearly a year in Italy, and returned home through Switzerland, Germany, France, and England, having for companions on the return voyage Thackeray and Clough. The journey had been undertaken partly on account of Mrs. Lowell's health, but she continued to fail, and died October 21, 1853.

Holmes had given his lectures on the English Poets of the Nineteenth Century at the Lowell Institute in 1853. In the winter of 1854–55 Lowell gave there a general course on poetry, which marked the beginning of his mature criticism, and which seems to have impressed its hearers as the best lecture-course ever given at this famous Institute. Three weeks after the beginning of the course he was appointed to the Smith Professorship at Harvard (which Longfellow had just resigned), with a year's leave of absence for study and travel abroad. He held this professorship, except for an interval of two years, until his appointment as Minister to Spain in 1877. Since Lowell's resignation of it no appointment has been made, and it remains distinguished by the names of its three holders, Ticknor, Longfellow, Lowell.

During his year of preparation Lowell went to Paris (and to Chartres, where he received the impressions out of which grew his poem 'The Cathedral'); then to London, where he visited Thackeray and Leigh Hunt; then to Dresden for the winter, where he attended lectures at the University. There is something pathetic — or even tragic — in the idea of putting the poet to school again after he has reached middle age, to make of him a professor ! — even so distinguished a professor as Lowell was. In the spring he escaped for another visit to Italy, and returned to America in August.

He taught regularly from 1856 to 1872, giving courses on Dante, German Literature, Spanish Literature (especially Don Quixote), and later on old French; and public lectures on English Poetry and Belles Lettres. He was not so faithful a routine teacher as Longfellow, but many students have borne witness to the inspiration received from him. He was not of course a scholar in the narrow modern sense of the word, except to a certain extent in old French; but he was an omnivorous reader, and his general knowledge of literature was probably not surpassed in breadth or intimacy by that of any teacher in his time.

Lowell was the first editor-in-chief of the *Atlantic Monthly* from its foundation in 1857 until 1861. From 1864 to 1872 he was editor, with his close friend, Mr. Charles Eliot Norton, of the *North American Review*. Leaving out of account the second series of the *Biglow Papers*, all of which appeared in the *Atlantic Monthly* from 1862 to 1866, his contributions to both of these reviews were much more important in prose than in verse. During the first part of the period, his articles dealt particularly with public affairs, and were notable for his strong support of Lincoln. (See note on page 490.) In the later part of the period appeared some of Lowell's best literary essays, which were collected in *Among My Books* (1870), *My Study Windows* (1871), and *Among My Books, Second Series* (1876). In 1869 was published *Under the Willows and Other Poems*, and in 1870 *The Cathedral*.

In 1872, Lowell asked the Harvard authorities for leave of absence with half pay, which is now granted to most college professors every seventh year. After his sixteen years of continuous teaching, however, this was refused him, and he resigned his position. The years 1872–74 he spent in Europe, mostly at Paris, Rome, and Florence. While in England he received the degrees of D. C. L. from Oxford and LL. D. from Cambridge. On his return in 1874 he again took up his professorship.

Lowell's poems of the war period, even if we were to leave out of account the second series of the *Biglow Papers*, which stand by themselves and are incomparable, must still be considered more important than those of any other poet except Whitman. They include 'The Washers of the Shroud' (1861), the memorial poem to Robert Gould Shaw (1864), 'On Board the '76' (1865), and culminate in the 'Commemoration Ode,' which seems by almost universal consent to be ranked as the greatest single poem yet written in America. Lowell had the right to speak as he did in these poems and in the *Biglow Papers*. He had not, like Longfellow and Holmes, any son of his own to send to the war (though it is certain that if there had been a son in Lowell's family, he would have gone), but his nephews, 'the hope of our race,' as he calls them, whom he loved almost as if they were his own sons, — three as noble young men as fought on either side, — all won their death-wounds in battle. Lowell's 'Commemoration Ode,' the *Biglow Papers*, and the *Three Memorial Poems*, make him unquestionably our greatest poet of patriotism.

Yet, when he was aroused to bitter denunciation of the corruption in public life revealed under Grant's administration, and in his 'Agassiz' wrote a few stinging lines about the spectacle which 'The land of honest Abraham' (or, as he first wrote it, the 'land of broken promise') was then offering to the world, he naturally received a storm of abuse from the party press of the time. His sufficient answer was the three memorial poems of 1875 and 1876. In his Epistle to George William Curtis, written in 1874, but not published till 1888, he answered for himself more directly: —

> Was I too bitter ? Who his phrase can choose
> That sees the life-blood of his dearest ooze ?

> I loved my Country so as only they
> Who love a mother fit to die for may;
> I loved her old renown, her stainless fame, —
> What better proof than that I loathed her shame ?

Lowell was delegate to the Republican Convention, and presidential elector, in 1876. In 1877 he was appointed Minister to Spain, where he at once won the sympathies of the Spanish people. His coming was looked on as a revival of the days when Irving was minister. Among other honors, he received that of an election to the Spanish Academy. In January, 1880, he was transferred to London, the most important post in the American diplomatic service. Here he was equally successful in his larger field. He did more than any other minister has done to interpret to England the character and the strength of America, and to lay the foundations of that friendship, based on mutual respect, which has since been built up between the two chief branches of the English-speaking race. It has been said that he was the most popular man in England. Certainly no one was more in demand on every public occasion, especially where speech-making was in order. Lowell's speeches were clever, witty, always fitted to the occasion, and, wherever this was appropriate, were weighty and important ; and they were almost as numerous as the days of the year. In these speeches he was always, on occasion, strongly American and strongly democratic. There is no better exposition of the American idea than his address on ' Democracy ' at Manchester. And he conducted public affairs with absolute firmness, never yielding anything so far as America was in the right. ' With all his grace,' it has been well said, ' there was a plainness of purpose that could not be mistaken.' Yet during his mission, and after his return to America, he was again bitterly assailed by the partisan press, who blamed him for his very success and for the respect which he had won. Because he was a gentleman and a man of the world, and had conducted affairs with courtesy as well as firmness, he was accused of being un-American, and of toadying to the British nobility. Nothing could be more unjust or farther from the truth. It was precisely because he was always and strongly American that he won the respect of the English. In many other Americans of culture, as for instance Washington Irving and Mr. Charles Eliot Norton, they had thought they found simply Englishmen transferred to an unfortunate environment and making the best of it. Lowell compelled them to feel that he was always, as one of them has expressed it, 'a scrappy Yankee,' and a typical Yankee. It was Lowell's great service to prove that a thoroughly typical American could be also a thorough gentleman, a man of broad culture, and, in every best sense, a man of the world.

He returned to America in 1885. Shortly before his return the second Mrs. Lowell died. He had married, in September, 1857, the sister of a close friend of his first wife, who had been chosen by her to care for her only daughter. He came back to find many of his best friends gone, — among them Longfellow and Emerson, — but younger friends still remained to him, like George William Curtis, Mr. Norton, and Mr. Howells. He wrote in the ' Postscript ' (1887) of his ' Epistle to George William Curtis: ' —

> Home am I come : not, as I hoped might be,
> To the old haunts, too full of ghosts for me,
> But to the olden dreams that time endears,
> And the loved books that younger grow with years ;
> To country rambles, timing with my tread
> Some happier verse that carols in my head,
> Yet all with sense of something vainly missed,
> Of something lost, but when I never wist.
> How empty seems to me the populous street,
> One figure gone I daily loved to meet, —
> The clear, sweet singer with the crown of snow
> Not whiter than the thoughts that housed below !
> And, ah, what absence feel I at my side,
> Like Dante when he missed his laurelled guide,
> What sense of diminution in the air
> Once so inspiring, Emerson not there !
> But life is sweet, though all that makes it sweet
> Lessen like sound of friends' departing feet,
> And Death is beautiful as feet of friend

> Coming with welcome at our journey's end;
> For me Fate gave, whate'er she else denied,
> A nature sloping to the southern side;
> I thank her for it, though when clouds arise
> Such natures double-darken gloomy skies.
>
> . . . .
>
> Little I ask of Fate; will she refuse
> Some days of reconcilement with the Muse?
> I take my reed again and blow it free
> Of dusty silence, murmuring, 'Sing to me!'

These lines describe his last years. He returned to poetry; he completed his 'Endymion,' which has in it a quality rare in Lowell's work, the poetic suggestion of more than is expressed; and he wrote some exquisite lyrics, with a lightness of touch he had not possessed before, and some poems full of his best strength, like those on 'Turner's Old Téméraire' and on Grant. His last years gave us also important addresses like those on 'The Independent in Politics,' and 'Our Literature,' and charming essays like that on 'Izaak Walton.' He died at Elmwood, August 12, 1891.

Lowell is the largest and best rounded personality that our literature yet possesses. He has unquestionably written our best literary essays, and perhaps also our best political essays in literary form. In his poetry he has all but surpassed the other poets, each in his own field. He is as true a nature poet as Bryant; though he has nothing to compare with the higher ranges of Bryant's nature poetry, like the 'Forest Hymn,' yet his treatment of Nature in her gentler aspects can well meet the comparison. 'To a Dandelion,' for instance, may be set beside 'To the Fringed Gentian.' What is more important, he writes of Nature with a happy intimacy which Bryant never had, as in the 'Indian Summer Reverie' and 'Sunthin' in the Pastoral Line,' and in many of the essays, like 'My Garden Acquaintance' and 'A Good Word for Winter.' There is a personal genuineness in his early work, especially the sonnets, which we do not find elsewhere except in Longfellow or Whittier, and in them it hardly has Lowell's deeper poetic quality; while in his later work, there is a high dignity which we do not find elsewhere except in Bryant. He is a true poet of New England country life, once at least, in 'The Courtin',' surpassing Whittier in his own field. He has written poems of sincere thought, though without the condensation and the fitness of form of Emerson at his best, in 'Bibliolatres,' 'The Lesson,' 'Masaccio,' 'The Miner,' 'Turner's Old Téméraire,' etc.; and these poems are somewhat more human in quality than Emerson's. He is our greatest humorist; the Biglow Papers have far broader and more significant power than the best of Holmes's humor, and the 'Fable for Critics' is almost as sparkling as the best wit of Holmes. If he is not a greater poet of occasions than Holmes, he is certainly a poet of greater occasions, and adequate to them. He has a lightness of touch in familiar verse that no one of our greater poets had (though it is to be found in Thomas Bailey Aldrich and others), as in 'Hebe,' 'The Pregnant Comment,' 'An Ember Picture' and 'Telepathy.' Yet there is something lacking in most of his work, something of charm, especially of rhythmic charm, something of poetic suggestiveness, something which he seems always striving after (see 'L'Envoi to the Muse,' 'Auspex,' and 'The Secret'), and which now and then he does almost attain, as in 'In the Twilight.' He lacks, usually, just that last touch of genius, that 'St. Elmo's Fire' playing over all, which he so well describes in his own essay on Keats. His life and character possessed something of this charm which did not quite get expression in his verse. He had a genius for friendship; he was one of the best talkers, and by far the best letter-writer, we have had; and we feel that uncaptured charm hovering near some of his poems of personal moods, like 'My Study Fire,' 'To Charles Eliot Norton,' or the 'Envoi to the Muse' and the others just mentioned. In personality, he was the fine flower of American society. Noble and varied as his verse is, he lived out his own motto, —

> The Epic of a man rehearse,
> Be something better than thy verse.

He is our noblest patriot-poet, and our most complete and well-rounded man.

WALT WHITMAN

WHITMAN, like Holmes, was of combined Connecticut and Dutch ancestry. His immediate ancestors, like Whittier's, were farmers, but more prosperous, his father owning five hundred acres of good land on Long Island, which Whitman preferred to call by its Indian name of Paumanok. His mother's family were also prosperous farmers. On his father's side, the first American ancestor, Rev. Zachariah Whitman, came to this country in 1635 and settled at Milford, Conn. In the last part of the seventeenth century Long Island was settled, largely from Connecticut, and the son of Rev. Zachariah Whitman crossed the Sound with the others. At about the same time Whitman's ancestors on his mother's side, a family of Dutch origin, the Van Velsors, settled in Long Island a little further to the west, nearer New York. There was also Quaker blood in Whitman's veins, coming from his maternal grandmother.

Whitman's father, Walter Whitman, was a carpenter and builder as well as a farmer, and lived at Huntington, Long Island. There Walt Whitman was born, May 31, 1819, the second of nine children. He was christened Walter, but to distinguish him from his father was called Walt, and he kept this name throughout his life. When he was four years old the family moved to Brooklyn, and there Walt attended the public schools. He was still almost as much a country as a city boy, however. He tells of his expeditions with his comrades on the ice of the Long Island bays in the winter, and of his own walks on the bare shores of Coney Island in summer, which then, he says, 'I had all to myself.' These expeditions to deserted Coney Island lasted until he was more than thirty years old, and he tells how, in its solitudes, he 'loved after bathing to race up and down the hard sand, and declaim Homer and Shakspere to the surf and sea-gulls by the hour.' In 1833–34 he was in printing offices in Brooklyn, learning the trade, and until 1837 worked as compositor in Brooklyn and New York. For the following year or two he taught school in country towns on Long Island, and 'boarded round.' 'This,' he says, 'I consider one of my best experiences and deepest lessons in human nature behind the scenes and in the masses.' In the following year (1839–40), he started and published a weekly paper in his native town, probably doing both the writing and the typesetting himself. 'All these years,' he says, 'I was down Long Island more or less every summer, now east, now west, sometimes months at a stretch.' For the five years following 1840, all the time, and off and on for the next fifteen years, he lived winters in Brooklyn, working more or less as a compositor in New York city. He tells how his life was 'curiously identified with Fulton Ferry' (see the passage quoted in full in the note on 'Crossing Brooklyn Ferry'), how he crossed almost daily, often in the pilot-house, familiar with all the pilots, as he was in New York with all the omnibus drivers, with whom he spent many hours riding the length of Broadway. He passionately loved the great city and its sights and its people, and no one has given so vivid a picture of it either in verse or in prose. He had a passion for music also, spent night after night at the opera, and went much to the theatre. In 1848–49 he was editor of the *Brooklyn Eagle*. He had written more or less since 1839 for newspapers and magazines, among others the *Democratic Review*. A few specimens of this early writing, both in prose and verse, are preserved in his *Complete Prose Works* (pages 334–374). The 'Dough-Face Song' is good ordinary rhyme, and in both substance and form reminds us a little of the first series of the *Biglow Papers*, though it is dated earlier. His prose, so far as preserved, consists of story-sketches, which hold the reader's interest but are in no way remarkable. Among other things he wrote at this time a temperance tract, *Franklin Evans*.

In 1849 he broke away from all regular employment, and started off on a leisurely and apparently purposeless excursion, which was to be of great importance in forming the character of his later work. He calls it 'a leisurely journey and working expedition.' It must be described in his own words of brief summary. He went, he says, with his brother Jeff, 'through all the Middle States, and down the Ohio and Mississippi rivers. Lived awhile in New Orleans, and work'd there on the editorial staff of "daily Crescent" newspaper.   After a time plodded back northward, up the Mississippi, and around to and by way of the Great Lakes, Michigan, Huron, and Erie, to Niagara falls and lower Canada, finally returning through central New York and down the Hudson ; traveling altogether probably 8,000 miles this trip, to and fro.'   From what we know of his life in New York and Brooklyn, we can infer what this expedition was to him.   Speaking of the origin of *Leaves of Grass*, he once said, ' Remember, the book arose out of my life in Brooklyn and New York from 1838 to 1853, absorbing a million people, for fifteen years, with an intimacy, an eagerness, an abandon, probably never equalled.'   With the same passion he must have absorbed the sights and the life of the country he passed through — almost the whole of the United States at that time — on this 8,000 mile excursion, making his own way, working here and there at his trade, living the life of the people.   There are vivid reminiscences of the South constantly recurring in his later writing, as in the poem of the live-oak; and there is everywhere present the feeling of bigness, freedom, and heartiness, of the life of the West.

On his return, he took up for a little while his former occupations, editing and printing a daily and weekly paper, the *Freeman*, and engaging, with his father, as he had done before going away, in the business of building and selling houses in Brooklyn.   But he had now conceived the work which he was to do, to chant the songs of democracy as he understood it, to ' Compose a march for these States.'   According to his first biographer, Dr. Bucke, he experienced a sort of conversion, and, like other mystics, felt his life-work given him as a mission.   At any rate, he lost interest in other occupations, except so far as was necessary for simple self-support, gave up the successful house-building business, and devoted himself to the composition of his *Leaves of Grass*.   This was issued without any publisher, the typesetting and printing having been done partly by Whitman himself, in 1855.

Apparently the last specimen we possess of Whitman's earlier style is the poem 'Sailing the Mississippi at Midnight,' probably written in 1849, and given, as by a rather pleasant irony are all the specimens which we have of his regular verse, in the *Prose Works*.   I quote from what seems to be its original form, in the *Notes and Fragments:* —

> How solemn ! sweeping this dense black tide !
>   No friendly lights i' the heaven o'er us ;
> A murky darkness on either side,
>   And kindred darkness all before us !
>
> Now, drawn nearer the shelving rim,
>   Weird-like shadows suddenly rise ;
> Shapes of mist and phantoms dim
>   Baffle the gazer's straining eyes.
> . . . .
> Then, by the trick of our own swift motion,
>   Straight, tall giants, an army vast,
> Rank by rank, like the waves of ocean,
>   On the shore march stilly past.
>
> How solemn ! the river a trailing pall,
>   Which takes, but never again gives back ;
> And moonless and starless the heaven's arch'd wall,
>   Responding an equal black !
>
> O, tireless waters ! like Life's quick dream,
>   Onward and onward ever hurrying —
> Like death in this midnight hour you seem,
>   Life in your chill drops greedily burying !
> . . . .
> Unlike time you begin and end,
>   Unlike life you 've a pathway steady,
> Unlike earth's are your numberless graves
>   Ever undug, yet ever ready.

The change from this style to that of the first edition of *Leaves of Grass* is so great that it seems as though some connecting links must be found in his newspaper writing of the time.   Yet this is doubtful.   The first edition of *Leaves of Grass*, he says, was printed ' after many MS. doings and undoings,' and possibly all the transition stages were lost in this repeated revision. The section of 'First Drafts and Rejected Lines and Passages' given in the *Notes and Fragments* does not show this transition, but is entirely in the style of *Leaves of Grass* itself. All that we know of the development of Whitman's peculiar style is what he tells us in one brief sentence: 'I had great trouble in leaving out the stock "poetical" touches, but succeeded at last.'

The first edition of *Leaves of Grass* had practically no sale. Some copies were sent out for review, which received little attention, and some were given away. Only one copy, so far as we know, won a real response, and that was the one sent to Emerson. His letter to Whitman must be quoted in full : —

'I am not blind to the worth of the wonderful gift of " Leaves of Grass." I find it the most extraordinary piece of wit and wisdom that America has yet contributed. I am very happy in reading it, as great power makes us happy. It meets the demand I am always making of what seems the sterile and stingy Nature, as if too much handiwork or too much lymph in the temperament were making our western wits fat and mean. I give you joy of your free and brave thought. I have great joy in it. I find incomparable things said incomparably well, as they must be. I find the courage of treatment which so delights us, and which large perception only can inspire.

'I greet you at the beginning of a great career, which yet must have had a long foreground somewhere for such a start. I rubbed my eyes a little to see if this sunbeam were no illusion; but the solid sense of the book is a sober certainty. It has the best merits, namely of fortifying and encouraging.

'I did not know until I, last night, saw the book advertised in a newspaper, that I could trust the name as real and available for a post-office. I wish to see my benefactor, and have felt much like striking my tasks and visiting New York to pay you my respects.'

Whitman published this letter, together with his own long reply to it, in the second edition of *Leaves of Grass*, which appeared in 1856. On the back of this edition was printed, over Emerson's name, 'I greet you at the beginning of a great career.' All this was at least in somewhat doubtful taste, but Emerson was above resenting it or retracting anything he had said, though naturally in a private letter, acknowledging the gift of a book from its author, he perhaps expressed himself somewhat otherwise than he would have done in writing for public print. In 1856 he wrote to Carlyle, 'One book last summer came out in New York, a non-descript monster which yet had terrible eyes and buffalo strength, and was indisputably American.' (See the whole letter in the *Carlyle-Emerson Correspondence*, volume ii, page 283.) He visited Whitman in New York, as he had spoken of doing, and friendly relations were kept up between the two till the end of Emerson's life. In 1856 Thoreau also visited Whitman, and wrote of him soon after: 'That Walt Whitman . . . is the most interesting fact to me at present. I have just read his second edition (which he gave me), and it has done me more good than any reading for a long time. . . . There are two or three pieces in the book which are disagreeable, to say the least; simply sensual. . . . . On the whole it sounds to me very brave and American, after whatever deductions. I do not believe that all the sermons, so called, that have been preached in this land, put together, are equal to it for preaching. We ought to rejoice greatly in him. . . . Though rude and sometimes ineffectual, it is a great primitive poem, an alarum or trumpet-note ringing through the American camp. . . . Since I have seen him, I find that I am not disturbed by any brag or egotism in his book. He may turn out the least of a braggart of all, having a better right to be confident. He is a great fellow.'

The personal impression Whitman made upon all who ever saw him seems to have been such as to counteract any previous notions they may have had of his work as being either 'egotistic' or 'sensual.' Howells, not a judge prejudiced in his favor, met him in New York in 1860, and speaks of 'the spiritual purity which I felt in him, no less than the dignity.' Howells had previously conceived him as 'the apostle of the rough, the uncouth.' Now he found him to be 'the gentlest person; his barbaric yawp, translated into terms of social encounter, was an address of singular quiet, delivered in a voice of winning and endearing friendliness.'

There are in Whitman's work passages which, though Thoreau's word 'sensual' is by no means the right one to describe them, are anything but fit reading for young ladies' seminaries. Such passages he has in common with nearly all the greatest writers. But naturally at their first appearance they aroused bitter opposition to him, and from time to time this opposition took serious practical form. When the third edition of *Leaves of Grass* was being printed at Boston in 1860, Emerson tried to persuade Whitman to omit these parts of his work. Whitman owns that 'each point of Emerson's statement was unanswerable,' but his own 'unmistakable conviction' that he must leave his work complete, as he understood completeness, was unshaken.

The 1856 edition of *Leaves of Grass* contained more than twice as many poems as the edition of 1855. The edition of 1860 was still further augmented, especially by the important collection of poems on men's friendship entitled *Calamus*. Neither of these editions, however, had much sale, and the firm which published the Boston edition failed at the beginning of the war.

Whitman's younger brother, George, enlisted in the Union army, and served throughout the war, rising to the rank of Lieutenant-Colonel. He was in most of the important battles in Virginia. In 1862 he was wounded at the first battle of Fredericksburg. The wound was thought to be serious (though it did not prove so), and Whitman at an hour's notice started for the army. He spent a considerable part of that winter with the Army of the Potomac, and began the attendance on wounded soldiers which he did not give up until the last hospitals at Washington were closed.

These were the central years of Whitman's life. He gave them almost wholly to his work for the soldiers, living as simply and cheaply as he could, and working in the hospitals almost daily till the end of the war. He assisted constantly in dressing the soldiers' wounds, but he did far more by ministering to their wants in many other ways, and most of all by the health and strength and courage of his own personality. 'A surgeon who throughout the war had charge of one of the largest army hospitals in Washington,' says Dr. Bucke, in his *Life of Whitman*, 'has told the present writer that (without personal acquaintance or any other than professional interest), he watched for many months Walt Whitman's ministerings to the sick and wounded, and was satisfied that he saved many lives.' There are few records, even in those years, of such simple and unselfish devotion as can be found in Whitman's *Specimen Days*, and in his unpremeditated letters, which have now been collected under the title *The Wound-Dresser*. At least one passage must be quoted from an eye-witness, Mr. John Swinton, telling of his hospital visits : 'I first heard of him among the sufferers on the Peninsula after a battle there. Subsequently I saw him, time and again, in the Washington hospitals, or wending his way there with basket or haversack on his arm, and the strength of beneficence suffusing his face. His devotion surpassed the devotion of woman. It would take a volume to tell of his kindness, tenderness, and thoughtfulness.

'Never shall I forget one night when I accompanied him on his rounds through a hospital, filled with those wounded young Americans whose heroism he has sung in deathless numbers. There were three rows of cots, and each cot bore its man. When he appeared, in passing along, there was a smile of affection and welcome on every face, however wan, and his presence seemed to light up the place as it might be lit by the presence of the Son of Love. From cot to cot they called him, often in tremulous tones or in whispers ; they embraced him, they touched his hand, they gazed at him. To one he gave a few words of cheer, for another he wrote a letter home, to others he gave an orange, a few comfits, a cigar, a pipe and tobacco, a sheet of paper or a postage stamp, all of which and many other things were in his capacious haversack. From another he would receive a dying message for mother, wife, or sweetheart ; for another he would promise to go on an errand ; to another, some special friend, very low, he would give a manly farewell kiss. He did the things for them which no nurse or doctor could do, and he seemed to leave a benediction at every cot as he passed along. The lights had gleamed for hours in the hospital that night before he left it, and as he took his way towards the door, you could hear the voice of many a stricken hero calling, "Walt, Walt, Walt, come again ! come again !"'

Drum Taps, Whitman's poems of the war, was published in 1865, and the *Sequel to Drum Taps*, containing his memorial poems on Lincoln, and a few more war poems, later in the year. It is surprising that these attracted so little attention as they did. Yet we must remember that it has always taken at least a generation for the general public to accept any original form of rhythmic expression, especially a form so different from accepted standards, and apparently so uncouth, as Whitman's. Of the substance of the poems, their vividness and truth, it is unnecessary to speak here. But it may be noted in passing, that, while there is more of the war in his work than in that of any other poet, there is nowhere any touch of bitterness or even of hostility.

Toward the end of the war Whitman obtained a position as clerk in the Department of the Interior. Not long afterward the Secretary of the Interior, James Harlan, came across Whitman's copy of *Leaves of Grass* (the 1860 edition) which he was revising for republication, and at once discharged Whitman as 'the author of an indecent book.' Whitman soon obtained an equally good position in the office of the Attorney-General, but the incident called out a famous defence of Whitman and arraignment of Harlan, in W. D. O'Connor's pamphlet *The Good Gray Poet*. This defence and arraignment are so exaggerated in tone that they have probably done Whitman's reputation more harm than good, and have made people feel that anything written by a disciple of his must be taken with very large allowances. Yet the pamphlet is admirable at least for its intense loyalty, and for its title, which was a creation of genius. Whitman has been called ever since, and deservedly, 'The Good Gray Poet.'

The new and revised edition (the fourth) of *Leaves of Grass*, with *Drum Taps* added, was published in 1867. In 1871 was published the fifth edition, with 'Passage to India' and other important additions. In 1872 Whitman was asked to give the Commencement poem at Dartmouth College, and he delivered 'As a strong bird on pinions free' (now 'Thou mother with thy equal brood'). In 'Passage to India' and in the later poems that group themselves with it, we have Whitman's work under a somewhat new aspect. From the beginning he had said, 'I am the poet of the Body and I am the poet of the Soul,' and had insisted always on the unity of the two and on their equal claims. But both by temperament and by fixed intention he had expressed primarily the material side of things and of man (as he said, the side most neglected by other poets), glorying in the triumphs of modern industrialism and in the joys of physical health. Now (see the passages quoted in notes on pages 546 and 590, and the whole of his own note on 'Passage to India' in the *Complete Prose Works*, pages 272–274, as well as the poem itself and those that follow), he insists most on the other aspect of the dual unity, on the spirit, that 'laughs at what you call dissolution,' and knows it has the best of time and space. The changes which he made in the brief poem 'Assurances' (page 553) from one edition to another, until it found its final form as given in the 1871 edition with 'Passage to India,' are typical of this development.

Whitman was one of the healthiest of men. Those who have described his work in the hospitals say that health and strength seemed to radiate from his presence. All his life he had lived a great deal in the open air, and in the hospital years he depended on his long walks about Washington as his chief delight and relief. But by 1864 his health began to be broken down. He had the first illness of his life, called at first 'hospital malaria,' in the hot summer of that year. Dr. Platt, in his life of Whitman, says also that through a scratch in his hand he was infected with septic poisoning from a wound he was helping to dress. This seemed to have only a temporary effect, but he was never entirely well afterward. In January, 1873, he had a paralytic stroke, which for a while disabled his left side completely. After a time he recovered somewhat, but could never move freely. For the first two years he suffered severely, and he was an invalid for the nineteen years that followed. His work at Washington was of course ended, and he had no source of income but his books, which hardly brought him anything.

During these years he lived at Camden, N. J., the home of George Whitman. Almost in poverty, until 1881, when the sale of his works began to bring him a small income, — which enabled him to live with some slight degree of comfort in a home of his own, —

and in constant weakness and much of the time helplessness, he underwent a test such as few men have been subjected to, and one which was particularly severe for him, the lover of all physical joys and especially of free movement in the open air. He met this test with complete triumph. All who saw him at Camden — and his home became to some degree a goal of pilgrimage, especially in the last ten years of his life — bear witness to the sweetness and strength of the character that revealed itself in him.

The so-called 'Centennial Edition' of *Leaves of Grass* was issued in 1876, with a second volume, composed partly of prose and partly of verse. By 1879 Whitman had partially recovered from his paralysis, and was able to take a journey through the Western States in that year, and in the following year to Canada. In 1881 the seventh edition of *Leaves of Grass* was published by James R. Osgood & Co. of Boston, but six months after its publication, when some two thousand copies had been sold, the firm was threatened with prosecution by the Massachusetts District Attorney, and declined to continue the sale of the book. It was immediately after published at Philadelphia. In 1888 was added the collection called *November Boughs*, in 1891 were published *Good-bye My Fancy* and the tenth edition of *Leaves of Grass*, including these last two additions. Whitman's health had been steadily declining again since 1885; he suffered a second shock of paralysis in 1888, but lived on, still cheerful and mentally active, and happy in a few devoted friends, until 1892, when he died, March 26. The small collection, *Old Age Echoes*, was added to his *Leaves of Grass* in the 1897 edition, *Calamus* (letters to his friend Peter Doyle) was published in 1897, *The Wound Dresser* in 1898, *An American Primer* and the *Diary in Canada* in 1904.

The question whether Walt Whitman's work is properly to be called poetry at all or not still exists only in a few academic circles. It has always been largely a question of academic definitions. And while we must have some definiteness of conception, in order that our ideas may not become entirely vague and our words meaningless, it would be well in this case to imitate Whitman's own modesty when he says: 'Let me not dare, here or anywhere, for my own purposes, or any purposes, to attempt the definition of Poetry, nor answer the question what it is. Like Religion, Love, Nature, while those terms are indispensable, and we all give a sufficiently accurate meaning to them, in my opinion no definition that has ever been made sufficiently encloses the name Poetry.' It may be added that one of the chief functions of any strongly original poet — or thinker — is to compel us to enlarge our definitions.

But even without departing greatly from the traditional conceptions of poetry, and certainly without abandoning the idea that material for poetry, however noble or beautiful, does not truly become poetry until it has been put into rhythmic form, we are now beginning frankly to accept Whitman's work as poetry. We no longer need the excellent authority of John Addington Symonds, a critic competent above most others and especially devoted to beauty of form in verse, to tell us that Whitman's verse is wonderfully rhythmical, and that his rhythms are truly and often delicately fitted to what he has to express. It is only needful really to read Whitman, a thing which is often at first difficult to do and which people in general have not even yet learned to do — to read him in the mass — and above all to read him aloud, which is the final test of poetry — in order to feel the strength and fitness of his rhythms, and to realize that they are not the rhythms of prose, nor of that bastard form called poetic prose, but are distinctly metrical rhythms, that is, the rhythms of verse. For the most part, they hold among verse-rhythms somewhat the same place as the recitative and the chant (names which he often gives to his poems) hold in music. He has also, when he chooses, the lyric note. The distinction between his recitative and his lyric, when he uses them together, as in 'Out of the cradle endlessly rocking,' or 'When lilacs last in the dooryard bloom'd,' is just the same and just as clearly marked as that between regular lyrics and regular blank verse.

It has taken people so long, however, to settle for themselves, consciously or uncon-sciously, this preliminary question of whether Whitman's work was poetry at all or not, that they have only just begun to appreciate his power and to give him his true rank.

Professor Trent, in his recent *History of American Literature* (1903), calls him ' too large a man and poet for adequate comprehension at present.' Moreover, Americans have been somewhat alienated from Whitman by the attitude of the best foreign critics, who have found in him the one and only poet truly characteristic of America. Not really having taken the trouble to know Whitman, but having conceived of him and his work as something rough, rowdyish, uncultured and altogether materialistic and sensual, Americans were naturally offended that he, rather than men like Longfellow, Lowell, and Emerson, should be taken as typical of America. We felt that all the chief American poets (except Poe, the only one whose work could have been written elsewhere than in America) were typical; and that the breadth of culture in such men as Longfellow and Lowell made them only the more completely typical. We naturally sought in the typical American poet an expression of our whole life and character, including (as Whitman himself has said somewhere) our inheritance of all the best from past ages and foreign lands; while the foreign critic, as naturally, sought in him the expression of only that part of our life which is entirely new and strange — and if uncouth and rude, so much the better. We have now come to know Whitman more truly; to know that he was anything but the rowdy and materialist of our first conceptions; to know that while he did not lack culture in the narrower sense (having read and thoroughly digested Emerson, having understood Carlyle and in his own thought refuted and gone beyond him, having won some genuine knowledge of Fichte's thought and Hegel's, if not directly of Plato's, and having nourished himself on the few greatest writers, Shakspere, the Bible, and Homer — even though in translation, some genuine knowledge of which is better than our usual pretence at knowledge of the original) he also had that broader and better first-hand culture which comes from true human relations with many living men and women, forming out of them a character which stood some of the hardest tests of life. We have also become more ready to admit that those material aspects of our life which primarily, though by no means exclusively, he tried to express, are in their crudeness and power truly characteristic of America. And now, knowing him better, we see that he has expressed not only some material aspects, but also some essential ideals of America, as no other poet has: among them, our sense of freedom and independence (his work is the logical outcome of Emerson's address on 'The American Scholar'), our conception of real democratic equality, our intense individualism yet sense of union one with another in a great whole.

SIDNEY LANIER

SIDNEY LANIER was born at Macon, Ga., February 3, 1842. He came of a family of musicians, the earliest known ancestor having been attached to the court of Queen Elizabeth, and his son and grandson having been directors of music under Charles I and Charles II. The grandson was one of the incorporators and the first Marshal of the Society of Musicians under Charles II, and there were four others of the name of Lanier among the incorporators. Thomas Lanier came to America in 1716, and settled in Virginia. Lanier's father was a lawyer, living at Macon, Ga., and his mother was a Virginian of Scotch descent, of a family distinguished in politics and also skilled in music.

Sidney Lanier had from his childhood a strong ambition, and we may even say genius, for music. As a boy he seemed able to learn any instrument without instruction, and could play the flute, violin, organ, piano, and guitar before he could fairly read. His greatest passion was for the violin, but his father persuaded him to abandon it. His sensitive nature was hardly able to bear the exaltation produced in him by its notes. In deference to his father's wishes, he devoted himself chiefly to the flute.

When he was fourteen years old, he entered Oglethorpe College (or ' University,' as it called itself), in the sophomore class. After losing a year by outside work, he graduated at the age of eighteen, sharing the highest honors for scholarship with one of his classmates, and was immediately appointed tutor in the college. This was in 1860. In 1861 he gave up his position to volunteer as a private in the Confederate army. He was in the battles of

Seven Pines, Malvern Hill, and others. The following year his younger brother, Clifford, joined him, and both served as privates (though promotion was offered to each at different times, and to Sidney Lanier three times), in order not to be separated from each other. They were transferred to the Signal Service in 1862, and in 1863 their company was mounted and served in Virginia and North Carolina. Finally they were appointed signal officers on blockade-runners, and thus necessarily separated. Sidney Lanier was captured, with his vessel, and imprisoned for five months at Point Lookout. In February, 1865, he was released, and returned home to Georgia on foot, with his flute, from which he had never been separated. His strength was seriously impaired, and though he recovered from a dangerous illness of six weeks, the beginning of consumption, from which his mother had just died, was already upon him. The rest of his life was a struggle against the disease.

He was still only twenty-three years old, and had not found his vocation in life, though strong musical and literary ambitions were already awake in him. But he was led to think that music was not a serious career, not worth devoting his life to. While working as clerk in a hotel, he took up and completed in three weeks of April, 1867, his novel, *Tiger Lilies* (begun at Burwell's Bay in 1863, and continued in 1865), and in May took the story to New York to be published. It is a picture of the war, hastily drawn, and of course somewhat crude. It expresses strongly, however, the horror of war which had constantly grown in him during the progress of that struggle which he would not abandon until it was ended. He describes war as 'that strange, terrible flower of which the most wonderful specimen yet produced was grown by two wealthy planters of North America.' 'It is supposed by some,' he goes on (the passage is quoted in Dr. Ward's *Memorial*), 'that the seed of this American specimen (now dead) yet remains in the land ; but as for this author (who, with many friends, suffered from the unhealthy odors of the plant), he could find it in his heart to wish fervently that this seed, if there be verily any, might perish in the germ, utterly out of sight and life and memory, and out of the remote hope of resurrection, forever and ever, no matter in whose granary they are cherished !' The novel was published, but had little success. He returned to the South, and taught school for a year. In 1867 he was married to Miss Mary Day, of Macon. For five years following, he studied and practised law with his father.

During this time he had written but little in verse, yet some of that little was of exquisite quality. The first poems we have are those of 1865, 'The Dying Words of Stonewall Jackson' and 'The Tournament,' the second of which he used with some alterations in his 'Psalm of the West,' eleven years later. The lyric 'Night and Day' belongs to 1866, and in 1868 the 'Jacquerie' was planned and partly written. In 1868 he wrote also a lyric, 'Life and Song,' the last two lines of which have been often quoted in speaking of his life and of the poetry which was as yet hardly begun : —

> His song was only living aloud,
> His work, a singing with his hand.

There was little written in the following years, until 1874, except three dialect poems of Georgia life.

He could not remain devoted to the law, however. He felt more and more that his life was to be brief, and that he must do something in art, which is lasting.

'Were it not for some considerations which make such a proposition seem absurd in the highest degree,' he wrote to his wife early in 1873, 'I would think that I am shortly to die, and that my spirit hath been singing its swan-song before dissolution. All day my soul hath been cutting swiftly into the great space of the subtle, unspeakable deep, driven by wind after wind of heavenly melody.' He determined to devote himself for what was left of his life to music and literature. He tried New York, but finally settled in Baltimore, in December of this year, 1873, having obtained an engagement there as first flute in the Peabody Symphony Orchestra. He wrote to his father, who had protested against his purpose as unwise : 'My dear father, think how, for twenty years, through poverty, through pain, through weariness, through sickness, through the uncongenial atmosphere of a farcical college and of a bare army and then of an exacting business life, through all the discouragement of being wholly unacquainted with literary people and literary ways, — I say, think how, in spite of all these depressing circumstances, and of a thousand more which I could enumerate, these two figures of music and of poetry have steadily kept in my heart so that I could not banish them. Does it not seem to you as to me, that I begin to have the right to enroll myself among the devotees of these two sublime arts, after having followed them so long and so humbly, and through so much bitterness ? ' His father felt the force of this appeal, and generously helped Lanier, so far as he could, to carry out his ambitions.

At Baltimore he found what he had craved for, the opportunity to hear good music, and access to extensive libraries. In the comparative freedom and exhilaration of this new life were written the first poems really characteristic of his mature work, among them the beautiful tributes to Mrs. Lanier, ' My Springs,' ' In Absence,' ' Acknowledgment,' and ' Laus Mariae.' It was in the summer of 1874, in August, that he wrote his first poem which attracted atttention, ' Corn.' This poem opens with stanzas almost as beautiful as anything in Lanier's work, describing the full richness of summer in the South. As a whole, however, it is not entirely successful. The symphonic structure is not sustained to the end, and much of the last part of the poem is given to a description of the effect on Southern farmers of cotton speculation, and especially of borrowing money at ruinous rates to plant cotton instead of corn. That subject was quite in place in Lanier's dialect poems, ' Jones's Private Argyment,' and ' Thar 's more in the man than thar is in the land,' but here, in a poem of the quality of ' Corn,' it jars, and in both substance and expression is quite out of harmony with the rest of the poem. ' Corn,' though it is interesting historically as having won for Lanier his first recognition when it appeared in *Lippincott's Magazine* for February, 1875, and also for its attempt to express fitly in poetry the beauty of waving fields of our chief American grain, must, in final critical judgment, be accounted a failure. This is the less to be regretted because Lanier immediately after succeeded, with ' The Symphony,' in the chief things which he had failed to do in ' Corn.' In ' The Symphony,' published only four months later in the same magazine, he created a poem of real harmonic and symphonic structure throughout, and of far greater musical beauty than he had even attempted in ' Corn ;' and he achieved the amazing *tour de force* of making real poetry out of the money question. A little later, in a brief lyric, ' The Waving of the Corn,' he expresses the full beauty of the cornfield.

' The Symphony ' won him the friendship of Bayard Taylor, — a friendship which grew as the two men came to know each other better, and which is recorded in the letters that passed between them. His letters to another firm friend, Mr. Gibson Peacock, are also preserved, and are of great interest. He was devoted to a serious study of his two arts, and especially of the relations between them. Often he was compelled to interrupt his work either to go in search of health to Florida or Pennsylvania or the mountains of North Carolina, or to do hack writing for a mere living. But he persisted, with help and encouragement from his father and brother, from his friends, and most of all from his wife. To her he wrote: ' " Que mon nom soit flétri, que la France soit libre! " quoth Danton ; which is to say, interpreted by my environment : Let my name perish — the poetry is good poetry and the music is good music, and beauty dieth not, and the heart that needs it will find it.' He was chosen in 1876, at the instance of Bayard Taylor, to write the words of the Centennial Cantata, for which the music was composed by Dudley Buck. In this year he wrote also the beautiful ' Evening Song,' possibly his finest lyric; the poem ' Clover,' which ranks between ' Corn ' and ' The Symphony,' and has something of the qualities of both ; ' The Waving of the Corn,' just spoken of; and our finest Centennial poem (not forgetting Lowell's and Whitman's), the ' Psalm of the West.'

Meanwhile he was lecturing for schools and for private classes, writing descriptive articles in prose for *Lippincott's Magazine*, making a book on Florida for a railroad company (published by the Lippincotts in 1876), and cheerfully doing whatever he could to earn himself a living and win some leisure for original writing. In 1877 was published the first collection of his *Poems*, and this year was the one most productive of new pieces, though of brief ones. Such a condensed bit of lyric as ' The Stirrup-Cup,' however, is worth many a long poem. To this year belong also the ' Song of the Chattahoochee ' (one of his most popular lyrics, though perhaps not ultimately to be counted among the few of his very best), two of his best brief nature poems, ' Tampa Robins ' and ' From the Flats ' (the last is bound to haunt forever all true lovers of the hills), ' The Mocking-Bird,' ' The Bee,' ' Florida Sunday,' and the poems ' To Wagner ' and ' To Beethoven.'

His two best ballads, ' The Revenge of Hamish ' and ' How Love looked for Hell,' belong to 1878–79. The first seems to me unsurpassed in narrative technique. Objectivity can no farther go. It is a masterpiece of absolute detachment, yet of wonderful vividness. The second is also remarkable for the way in which it clothes abstractions with life, and makes vivid the vague idea that where Love comes, there Hell cannot be. These, each unique in its kind, and, belonging to the same year, his chief masterpiece in still another kind which is peculiarly his own, being a new creation, — ' The Marshes of Glynn,' — show the many possibilities of that talent which was not to reach its full development.

Bayard Taylor died in December, 1878, and Lanier wrote the poem ' To Bayard Taylor,' with its beautiful picture of the Elysium of the poets, its touches of Elizabethan phrasing, and, toward the end, its strong, condensed expression of the hard conditions and the struggle which were bearing heavily upon Lanier himself, but from which he was soon to escape into that open sun-lit land of the last two stanzas.

He had work still to do, however. Early in 1879 he was appointed Lecturer on English Literature in the Johns Hopkins University. This brought him the happy certainty of a fixed though small income. For his courses of 1879–80 and 1880–81 he prepared the lectures which, in revised form, now constitute his two most important prose volumes, *The Science of English Verse* and *The English Novel and its Development*. He made an engagement with the Scribners to complete a series of books for boys, of which four were published, two after his death: *The Boy's Froissart* (1878), *The Boy's King Arthur* (1880), *The Boy's Mabinogion* (1881), and *The Boy's Percy* (1882). In the winter of 1880–81 he was barely able to get through with twelve lectures at the University. The poem ' Sunrise ' was written with a fever temperature of 104, when, says Mrs. Lanier, ' the hand which first pencilled its lines had not strength to carry nourishment to the lips.' A last attempt to prolong his life was made by trying tent life in the mountains of North Carolina, but it was unsuccessful, and he died September 7, 1881.

Though younger by almost a generation than our chief elder poets, Lanier seems to be taking his rank almost without question among them. He did not complete his work. To his poet friend, Paul H. Hayne, he wrote: ' How I long to sing a thousand songs that oppress me, unsung, — is inexpressible. Yet the mere work that brings bread gives me no time.' When he died, his talent was growing. Unlike Poe, if he had lived he would probably have given us greater poems than he did. It is therefore hard to say what would have proved really characteristic of him had he completed any large mass of work. As it is, he has given us some beautiful and haunting lyrics, sometimes with touches of strange fancies like those in ' Night and Day ' and the ' Ballad of Trees and the Master ; ' he has written two of our finest ballads, both unique in kind; in the ' Psalm of the West ' he has written a poem of America that for range and beauty and historical completeness, and for the sweep of the whole from its superb opening up to just near the close, where it fails a little, deserves to stand beside or even above Lowell's ' Commemoration Ode ' and Whitman's ' Thou mother with thy equal brood.' And finally, there is one thing which, even in the small amount of his work, we may call distinctively characteristic, — the way of writing found in two poems so different in substance as ' The Symphony ' and ' The Marshes of Glynn.' ' Whatever turn I have for art,' he wrote to Paul H. Hayne, ' is purely musical, poetry being with me a mere tangent into which I shoot sometimes. . . . The very deepest of my life has been filled with music, which I have studied and cultivated far more than poetry.' Something of this music-passion has woven itself into his poetry. His theory that English verse has for its essential basis not accent, but strict musical quantity, is almost certainly a mistaken one. But the book he wrote to prove this mistaken theory is by far the most suggestive and inspiring that has ever dealt with the technique of verse. And in his own work he has written poetry more rich in music than we had before. He has learned all that there was to be learned from his predecessors, among them Swinburne, and then he has found for himself new melodies, and has taught something of them to the poets of a younger generation, — notably Bliss Carman and Richard Hovey.

INDEXES

INDEX OF POETS

INDEX OF FIRST LINES

INDEX OF TITLES